DATE DUE

THE TORTURE PAPERS

The Torture Papers consists of the so-called "torture memos" and reports that the U.S. government officials wrote to authorize and to document coercive interrogation and torture in Afghanistan, Guantánamo, and Abu Ghraib. This volume of documents presents for the first time a compilation of materials that prior to publication have existed only piecemeal in the public domain. The Bush Administration, concerned about the legality of harsh interrogation techniques, understood the desirability of establishing a legally viable argument to justify such procedures. The memos and reports in this volume document the systematic attempt of the U.S. government to authorize the way for torture techniques and coercive interrogation practices, forbidden under international law, with the concurrent express intent of evading liability in the aftermath of any discovery of these practices and policies.

Karen J. Greenberg is the Executive Director of the Center on Law and Security at the New York University School of Law, and editor of the *NYU Review of Law & Security*.

Joshua L. Dratel is President of the New York State Association of Criminal Defense Lawyers and serves on the Board of Directors of the National Association of Criminal Defense Lawyers and is lead defense counsel for David Hicks, an Australian detainee at Guantánamo.

The Torture Papers

THE ROAD TO ABU GHRAIB

Edited by

Karen J. Greenberg

Joshua L. Dratel

Introduction by Anthony Lewis

CAMBRIDGE
UNIVERSITY PRESS

Edited and compiled by
Karen J. Greenberg
Joshua L. Dratel, P.C.

With special thanks to the entire staff of The Center on
Law and Security

Any views expressed in the introductory matter in this volume are solely those
of the authors and do not reflect the views or opinions of any institution or
organization.

CAMBRIDGE UNIVERSITY PRESS
Cambridge, New York, Melbourne, Madrid, Cape Town, Singapore, São Paulo

Cambridge University Press
40 West 20th Street, New York, NY 10011-4211, USA

www.cambridge.org
Information on this title: www.cambridge.org/9780521853248

First published 2005

Printed in the United States of America

A catalog record for this publication is available from the British Library.

ISBN-13   978-0-521-85324-8 hardback
ISBN-10   0-521-85324-9 hardback

Contents

Reports

Contents

Acknowledgments

This volume could not have been produced without the dedicated work of many of our colleagues. In particular we would like to thank Kristin Henderson for her tireless and painstaking work helping to research, compile, and edit these documents. For his advice and information, we'd like to thank Major Michael D. Mori and for his expertise, Sam A. Schmidt. For their research, we'd like to thank Elizabeth Besobrasow and Steven Wright. We thank Andrew Peterson for his work on the index. Overall, we are indebted to the staff of the Center on Law and Security for supporting this volume in its early stages.

All of the above have helped bring this volume into being and we are therefore duly grateful.

Introduction

Anthony Lewis

The Torture Papers: The Road to Abu Ghraib includes the full texts of the legal memoranda that sought to argue away the rules against torture. They are an extraordinary paper trail to mortal and political disaster: to an episode that will soil the image of the United State in the eyes of the world for years to come. They also provide a painful insight into how the skills of the lawyer – skills that have done so much to protect Americans in this most legalized of countries – can be misused in the cause of evil.

We have the legal memoranda because committed reporters, from *The Washington Post* and others in the press, ferreted them out – until, finally, the government released official texts. Without the press, indeed, the whole torture episode might have remained hidden. The television program *Sixty Minutes* and Seymour Hersh, in *The New Yorker*, told the world what had gone on in Abu Ghraib and showed us the pictures. They relied on the unchallengeable findings of an inquiry by Major General Antonio M. Taguba into the conduct of a military police brigade in Iraq. The Taguba Report, too, is in *The Torture Papers*.

The mindset that produced the legal memos is easy enough to see. After the terrorist attacks of September 11, 2001, the Bush Administration reasoned that the United States was up against an enemy more insidious than any the country had faced. To defeat terrorism, it felt, we must have intelligence on the plans of al Qaeda and others.

The United States lacked what is called human intelligence: spies inside terrorist organizations. So officials focused on the hope of getting information by questioning captured terrorist suspects. They asked lawyers in the Justice Department and the Defense Department what methods could be used to extract information from suspects without violating the law.

Any lawyer acting for a business must be asked by its officials, from time to time, "Can we do this?" The lawyer understands that the company executives want her to say "Yes." She is expected to spell out how the company can do what it wants without getting into legal trouble. That was the implicit scenario here. Lawyers were asked how far interrogators could go in putting pressure on prisoners to talk without making themselves, the interrogators, liable for war crimes. Or if that was not the specific question put to the lawyers, they well understood that that was the issue. They responded with the advice that American interrogators could go very far – to the brink of killing prisoners – and not face legal consequences.

"Physical pain amounting to torture," Assistant Attorney General Jay S. Bybee advised the Counsel to the President, Alberto Gonzales, "must be equivalent in intensity to the pain accompanying serious physical injury such as organ failure, impairment of bodily function or even death."

That was Bybee's construction of the federal law against torture, to which the United States is a party. He adds that in the Justice Department's view, actions by interrogators "may be cruel, inhuman or degrading, but, still not produce pain and suffering of the requisite intensity."

Reading that advice, one has to imagine an interrogator making nice judgments about the suffering of his victim. In Argentina, during the tyranny of the generals, torturers in secret prisons sometimes had a doctor present at a torture session to judge when the prisoner was in danger of dying. Jacobo Timerman, a newspaper proprietor who was imprisoned by the regime, described how the doctor – after a torture session – asked his advice on a financial matter. It was as if the doctor were morally absent from reality.

The premise of the Bush Administration after September 11, 2001, was that the end, fighting terrorism, justified whatever means were chosen. It sought repeatedly to eliminate legal constraints on the means it adopted. Thus in November 2001, President Bush issued an order for trial by military tribunal of non-Americans charged with terrorist crimes. The order forbade the accused from going to any court, American or foreign. Keeping courts out was a major element in several programs.

The legal documents dealt with one large question in addition to the limits on interrogation techniques. That was the status of the hundreds of prisoners brought to the U.S. base at Guantánamo, Cuba, after the war in Afghanistan. Were they protected by the Geneva Convention, which the United States and almost all other countries have signed and which provides for the humane treatment of prisoners taken in conflicts? The Third Geneva Convention lays down rules for deciding whether a captive is a regular soldier, a spy or terrorist, or an innocent person picked up by chance. The issue is to be decided by a "competent tribunal."

In the 1991 Gulf War the American military held 1196 hearings before such tribunals. Most of them found the prisoner to be an innocent civilian. But this time the Bush administration legal memoranda found that the Guantánamo prisoners should not get the hearings required by the Third Geneva Convention.

The fourth memorandum in these volumes, from Deputy Assistant Attorney General John Yoo and another lawyer in the Justice Department's Office of Legal Counsel, Robert J. Delahunty, argued that the Geneva Convention dealt only with state parties, and al Qaeda was not a state. As for Taliban soldiers, it said that Afghanistan under the Taliban was a "failed state" to which the convention also did not apply. Although the Taliban had controlled almost all the country, the memo described it as a mere "militia or faction."

That memo went to White House Counsel Alberto Gonzales on January 9, 2002. Days later President Bush decided that the Third Geneva Convention did not apply to the prisoners at Guantánamo. All of them, he found, were "unlawful combatants" – a term not found in the convention. He made that finding without any hearings or any opportunity for the prisoners to contest the facts.

On January 26, Secretary of State Powell asked the President to reverse that decision, which he said would "reverse over a century of U.S. policy and practice....and undermine the protections of the law of war for our troops (Memo #8)". The State Department's Legal Adviser, William H. Taft IV, sent a memo (Memo #10) to White House Counsel Gonzales arguing that sticking to Geneva would show that the United States "bases its conduct on its international legal obligations and the rule of law, not just on its policy preferences."

Gonzales rejected the State Department view. In a memorandum (Memo #7) to the President he said, "the nature of the new war [on terrorism] places a high premium on ... the ability to quickly obtain information from captured terrorists and their sponsors in order to avoid further atrocities ..." He said this "new paradigm renders obsolete Geneva's strict limitations on questioning of enemy prisoners" and made other Geneva provisions "quaint."

The memorandum (Memo #4), submitted on Jan. 9, 2002, by John Yoo and Robert J. Delahunty of the Department of Justice, first raised the idea of overriding presidential power to order the use of torture. It said that "restricting the President's plenary power over military operations (including the treatment of prisoners)" would be "constitutionally dubious."

Seven months later Assistant Attorney General Jay S. Bybee hardened the "constitutionally dubious" argument into a flat assertion of presidential immunity from legal restraints on torture. In a memorandum to White House Counsel Gonzales, Bybee said that in a war like the one against terror, "the information gained from interrogations may prevent future attacks by foreign enemies. Any effort to apply [the criminal law against torture] in a manner that interferes with the President's direction of such core war matter as the detention and interrogation of enemy combatants thus would be unconstitutional."

The argument got further elaboration in a memorandum of March 6, 2003 (Memo #25), from an ad hoc group of government lawyers to Secretary of Defense Donald Rumsfeld, a memo also included in *The Torture Papers*. "Congress may no more regulate the President's ability to detain and interrogate enemy combatants," it argued, "than it may regulate his ability to direct troop movements on the battlefield." So presidential power overrode the International Convention Against Torture, to which the United States is a party, and the Congressional statute enforcing the convention.

Abu Ghraib became a focus of world attention when the photographs of humiliated prisoners were published. But there was also considerable disquiet about the prison at Guantánamo Bay. There were no incriminating photographs of Guantánamo, and everything about the prison was kept secret. When habeas corpus actions were brought in federal courts to challenge the detention of particular prisoners, the Bush Administration argued that the courts held no jurisdiction to hear the cases. (The Supreme Court eventually rejected that contention.)

But the very secrecy about Guantánamo produced criticism. A judge of Britain's highest court, Lord Steyn, called it a "legal black hole." When some British citizens who had been held there – after capture not in Afghanistan but in other countries – were sent home to Britain, they said they had been mistreated.

It also became clear that the American military and the Central Intelligence Agency were holding terrorist suspects at places other than Abu Ghraib and Guantánamo. Some were not listed with the Red Cross, which complained that it was unable to check on the condition of all American prisoners. And some died while under interrogation. One, an Iraqi general, Abed Hamed Mowhoush, was found in an autopsy to have died from "asphyxia due to smothering and chest compression."

What, then, did the legal memoranda on the treatment of prisoners do? A longtime national security advisor to President George H. W. Bush, Donald P. Gregg, wrote in *The New York Times* that the memoranda "cleared the way for the horrors that have been revealed in Iraq, Afghanistan and Guantánamo and make a mockery of the administration's assertions that a few misguided enlisted personnel perpetrated the vile abuse of prisoners. I can think of nothing that can more devastatingly undercut America's standing in the world or, more important, our view of ourselves, than those decisions."

Jacobo Timerman, the Argentine prisoner mentioned earlier in this introduction, was saved from likely death by pressure from the administration of President Jimmy Carter. He was released and went to Israel. I met him there years later, and we talked about interrogation of prisoners. He asked whether I would agree to torture a prisoner if he knew of a terrorist outrage that would shortly take place. After trying to avoid the question, I finally said, Yes, I would. "No!" he said. "You cannot start down that road."

The Supreme Court of Israel, with many painful examples of terror, agreed with Timerman's view when it considered the question of torture. It rejected the use of torture even when a suspect is thought to know the location of a "ticking bomb."

In an age when the ticking bomb may be a weapon of mass destruction, the question is not always easy to answer. But when officials are tempted to use torture, they should remember that suppositions of what a suspect knows are usually wrong. They should understand that statements extracted by torture have repeatedly been found to be useless. They should know, finally, that torture does terrible damage not only to the victim but to the torturer.

From Fear to Torture

Karen J. Greenberg

The word *torture*, long an outcast from the discourse of democracy, is now in frequent usage. Alongside the word, the practice of torture is now in place as well. The coercive techniques that have been discovered at Abu Ghraib and Guantánamo resulted from advice given by leading figures at the Department of Justice, the Department of Defense, and the White House. The policy came about as the result of a series of memos in which the Administration asked for – and was granted – the right to interrogate prisoners with techniques possibly outlawed by the Geneva Conventions and by American military and civil law. The authors of the memos then justified the interrogation techniques on the grounds that in these specific cases, the legal restrictions did not apply. The result is a carefully constructed anticipation of objections at the domestic and international levels and a legal justification based on considerations of failed states, non-state actors, and the national security agenda of the United States.

This volume contains the documentary record of the Bush Administration's path to the coercive interrogation of prisoners held on the suspicion of terrorist activity. Many of the documents included here were brought initially to public attention through the investigative work of reporters at *The Washington Post* and *Newsweek* as well as at the American Civil Liberties Union. Through the publication of these documents, we can now reconstruct the chronological, legal, and political story of how a traditionally banned form of interrogation became policy.

The assent to coercive interrogation techniques, defined under international law as torture, constitutes a landmark turn in American legal and political history. It did not happen without sustained debate on the part of Americans responsible for directing the course of their nation, individuals at the Pentagon, in the State Department, and in the Department of Justice. The memos do not overlook basic ethical and legal questions. From the start, the Administration is concerned about the legality of harsh interrogation techniques and the importance of establishing a legally viable argument for such procedures to be implemented. These memos argue, with increasing acknowledgment of the tenuous legal ground on which they stand, for the right to implement "Counter-Resistance Strategies." Most of the memos ask for approval without specifying the goal of such techniques. By October, 2002, the Commander of the U.S. Southern Command, James T. Hill, explains, "...despite our best efforts, some detainees have tenaciously resisted our current interrogation methods. Our respective staffs, the Office of the Secretary of Defense and Joint Task Force 170 have been trying to identify counter-resistant techniques that we can lawfully employ (Memo #16)." The result is the creation of three categories of torture and a final compendium of approved techniques taken from all three categories in light of the arguments outlined in the memos.

There are a number of moral and legal issues embedded in these documents. They include the matters of reciprocity, of human rights protocols, and of constitutionality. The concepts of rights and reciprocity are easy when it comes to the behavior of other nations, but it is in times of crisis and fear that such a principle is truly tested. In the wake of 9/11 and the stresses and strains of an undeclared war on Arab states and persons, the principle faltered at an early stage. The search for legal grounds for these strategies began with the argument that the Taliban and al Qaeda are not covered under the Geneva Conventions, the former on the grounds that Afghanistan was at the time a failed state, the latter because al Qaeda is a non-state actor. Therefore, the authors of these memos reasoned, the right of reciprocity for the United States would not be abrogated.

Despite raising numerous legal questions, there is much these memos overlook. Nowhere is the matter of precedent raised in terms of changes in the American treatment of prisoners; what kinds of across-the-board policies would the approval of such procedures launch? This lapse raises the further question, to what extent were these practices in place elsewhere within the American penal system, military or otherwise? Also missing is a discussion of the fact that these procedures were designed for use on detainees picked up in the Afghan theatre and yet they were applied, as the Reports included in this volume demonstrate, to alleged terrorists and to prisoners in Iraq. The justifications for this are hard to find. Also missing from these discussions is the matter of the effect of such procedures and policies upon those who implement them. As the American historian Arthur Schlesinger, Jr., recently suggested, "the abuse of captives brutalizes their captors."[1] Finally, there is but scant mention of such techniques. As Michael Dunlavey, an Army lawyer pointed out, while the techniques may work initially, over time, there is less proof of their efficacy.[2]

These concerns are but the beginning of the debate which must ultimately call into question not the Bush Administration but the American people. The use of coercive interrogation techniques was downplayed, not only by the military, but by the American press as well. The American public insisted in the early stages of the exposure of the memos and reports included in this volume that the practice could not possibly be systematic, reasoned, or intended. The general consensus was that Americans could not possibly be involved in such tactics. Which brings into focus yet another aspect of the decision to use torture; namely, what will be the spiritual cost, the overall damage to the character of the nation?

In the path to torture, there have been numerous individuals involved. They include: those who wrote the memos, those who ordered the torture, those who carried it out, and those in government and later in the public sector who refused to register the abuses as wrongdoing. Many have a distinctive history of academic accomplishment. John Yoo studied at Harvard (B.A.) and Yale (J.D.), taught at Stanford University,

---

[1] Arthur Schlesinger, Jr., "The Making of a Mess," *The New York Review of Books*, 42, September 23, 2004.
[2] October 11, 2002, Memo from Maj. Gen. Michael E. Dunlavey to Commander, U.S. Southern Command.

and now teaches at Boalt Hall at Berkeley. Alberto Gonzales attended Rice University and Harvard (J.D.). Donald Rumsfeld graduated from Princeton (A.B.). William J. Haynes II, earned his degrees from Davidson College (B.A.) and Harvard (J.D.). William H. Taft, IV, who advised against the policy of torture, attended Yale (B.A.) and Harvard (J.D.). Jack Goldsmith received his J.D. from Yale. Rumsfeld, Taft, Haynes, Timothy Flanigan and Jay S. Bybee worked in the administration of the first President Bush. Some of the main players in the torture narrative – for example, Bybee and John Ashcroft – have deeply religious beliefs. In addition to the authors and recipients of these memos, there remains the possibility that there is advice coming from numerous quarters that is not documented here. The confluence of prior associations, overlapping affiliations and other connections among the drafters of the torture memos remains for journalists and historians to discover over time.

Ultimately, what the reader is left with after reading these documents is a clear sense of the systematic decision to alter the use of methods of coercion and torture that lay outside of accepted and legal norms, a process that began early in 2002 and that was well defined by the end of that year, months before the invasion of Iraq. The considerations on torture included here relate exclusively therefore to Guantánamo. Not only did the lawyers and policy makers knowingly overstep legal doctrine, but they did so against the advice of individuals in their midst, notably Secretary of State Colin Powell and William H. Taft, Legal Advisor to the Secretary of State. Powell's memo, a virtual cry in the dark, warns that the policy will "undermine the protections of the law of war for our troops."[3] He warns also about the "negative international reaction"[4] that will follow and the possibility that the implementation of coercive interrogation practices will "undermine public support among critical allies, making military cooperation more difficult to sustain."[5] In regard to the war on terror, he foresees the possible deleterious effect upon anti-terrorist legal cooperation with Europe. Yet another voice of dissent comes many months later from Guantánamo Bay Staff Judge Advocate Diane E. Beaver, recommending "legal, medical, behavioral science and intelligence"[6] vetting of the recommended interrogation procedures.

The reports included in this volume show the use of these techniques in Abu Ghraib and against individuals picked up apparently outside of the Afghan theatre, leaving open the question of how and why these considerations were drafted for one context and utilized in the war on terror as well as in the war in Iraq. It remains for scholars and policy makers to explore the links between the initial policies that served Bagram Air Force Base and Guantánamo and the later polices in Afghanistan and against terror suspects picked up outside of the Afghan battlefield. It remains for lawyers and judges, military and civil, to recommend the remedies to address the legal license taken in accordance with these documents, remedies for lawyers, for government officials, for interrogators, and for agency policies as well. It remains for human rights activists, journalists, and others to discover the extent to which these procedures were utilized.

---

[3] January 26, 2001, Memo from Colin L. Powell to Counsel to the President and Assistant to the President for National Security Affairs.
[4] Ibid.
[5] Ibid.
[6] October 11, 2002, Memo from Diane E. Beaver to Commander, JTF 170.

With the documents before us, it is possible now to begin these explorations and to consider the record both as symptom of its time and as precedent to the future. Fear is an irrefutable catalyst. More than the law, more than treaties, it must stand the judgment of good men and women who flinch less from fear than from the loss of respect for one another. The constructive value of these memos and reports is to enable open-minded reflection and self-correction even in times such as these.

The Legal Narrative

Joshua L. Dratel

While the proverbial road to hell is paved with good intentions, the internal government memos collected in this publication demonstrate that the path to the purgatory that is Guantánamo Bay, or Abu Ghraib, has been paved with decidedly bad intentions. The policies that resulted in rampant abuse of detainees first in Afghanistan, then at Guantánamo Bay, and later in Iraq, were the product of three pernicious purposes designed to facilitate the unilateral and unfettered detention, interrogation, abuse, judgment, and punishment of prisoners: (1) the desire to place the detainees beyond the reach of any court or law; (2) the desire to abrogate the Geneva Convention with respect to the treatment of persons seized in the context of armed hostilities; and (3) the desire to absolve those implementing the policies of any liability for war crimes under U.S. and international law.

Indeed, any claim of good faith – that those who formulated the policies were merely misguided in their pursuit of security in the face of what is certainly a genuine terrorist threat – is belied by the policy makers' more than tacit acknowledgment of their unlawful purpose. Otherwise, why the need to find a location – Guantánamo Bay – purportedly outside the jurisdiction of the U.S. (or any other) courts? Why the need to ensure those participating that they could proceed free of concern that they could face prosecution for war crimes as a result of their adherence to the policy? Rarely, if ever, has such a guilty governmental conscience been so starkly illuminated in advance.

That, of course, begs the question: what was it that these officials, lawyers, and lay persons feared from the federal courts? An independent judiciary? A legitimate, legislated, established system of justice designed to promote fairness and accuracy? The Uniform Code of Military Justice, which governs courts-martial and authorizes military commissions? The message that these memoranda convey in response is unmistakable: these policy makers do not like our system of justice, with its checks and balances, and rights and limits, that they have been sworn to uphold. That antipathy for and distrust of our civilian and military justice systems is positively un-American.

However, that distaste for our justice system was not symmetrical, as the memos reveal how the legal analysis was contrived to give the policy architects and those who implemented it the benefit of the doubt on issues of intent and criminal responsibility while at the same time eagerly denying such accommodations to those at whom the policies were directed. Such piecemeal application of rights and law is directly contrary to our principles: equal application of the law, equal justice for all, and a refusal to discriminate based on status, including nationality or religion. A government cannot pick and choose what rights to afford itself, and what lesser privileges it confers on its captives, and still make any valid claim to fairness and due process.

The memoranda that comprise this volume follow a logical sequence: (1) find a location secure not only from attack and infiltration, but also, and perhaps more importantly in light of the December 28, 2001, memo that commences this trail, from intervention by the courts; (2) rescind the U.S.'s agreement to abide by the proscriptions of the Geneva Convention with respect to the treatment of persons captured during armed conflict; and (3) provide an interpretation of the law that protects policy makers and their instruments in the field from potential war crimes prosecution for their acts. The result, as is clear from the arrogant rectitude emanating from the memos, was unchecked power, and the abuse that inevitably followed.

The chronology of the memoranda also demonstrates the increasing rationalization and strained analysis as the objectives grew more aggressive and the position more indefensible – in effect, rationalizing progressively more serious conduct to defend the initial decisions and objectives, to the point where, by the time the first images of Abu Ghraib emerged in public, the government's slide into its moral morass, as reflected in the series of memos published in this volume, was akin to a criminal covering up a parking violation by incrementally more serious conduct culminating in murder.

The memos also reflect what might be termed the "corporatization" of government lawyering: a wholly result-oriented system in which policy makers start with an objective and work backward, in the process enlisting the aid of intelligent and well-credentialed lawyers who, for whatever reason – the attractions of power, careerism, ideology, or just plain bad judgment – all too willingly failed to act as a constitutional or moral compass that could brake their client's descent into unconscionable behavior constituting torture by any definition, legal or colloquial. That slavish dedication to a superior's imperatives does not serve the client well in the end and reduces the lawyer's function to that of a gold-plated rubber stamp.

Nor does any claim of a "new paradigm" provide any excuse, or even a viable explanation. The contention, set forth with great emphasis in these memoranda, that al Qaeda, as a fanatic, violent, and capable international organization, represented some unprecedented enemy justifying abandonment of our principles is simply not borne out by historical comparison. The Nazi party's dominance of the Third Reich is not distinguishable in practical terms from al Qaeda's influence on the Taliban government as described in these memos.

Al Qaeda's record of destruction, September 11th notwithstanding – and as a New Yorker who lived, and still lives, in the shadow of the Twin Towers, which cast a long shadow over lower Manhattan even in their absence, I am fully cognizant of the impact of that day – pales before the death machine assembled and operated by the Nazis. Yet we managed to eradicate Nazism as a significant threat without wholesale repudiation of the law of war, or a categorical departure from international norms, even though National Socialism, with its fascist cousins, was certainly a violent and dangerous international movement – even with a vibrant chapter here in the United States.

Indeed, like the Nazis' punctilious legalization of their "final solution," the memos reproduced here reveal a carefully orchestrated legal rationale, but one without valid legal or moral foundation. The threshold premise here, that Guantánamo Bay is outside the jurisdiction of the U.S. courts, was soundly rejected by the Supreme Court last June in *Rasul v. Bush*, and the successive conclusions built upon that premise will, like the corrupted dominoes they are, tumble in due course. There they will join the other legally instituted but forever discredited stains upon U.S. legal history: the internment of Japanese during World War II, the treatment of Native Americans, and slavery.

Review of the memoranda reveals that not all the players were villains, though. There were dissenters from this march toward ignominy. The Department of State pointed out the perils – to U.S. service personnel principally, who would likely be treated reciprocally if captured – of not applying the standards of the Geneva Convention, and the contradictory position of the United States with respect to the status of the Taliban as the existing government of Afghanistan. Military officers also manifested an implicit reticence, and even incredulity, in demanding explicit authority and direction before implementing the full range of "counter-resistance" techniques. Yet, unfortunately, the policy makers to whom they appealed were only too willing to oblige, and to ignore the cautions communicated by the State Department.

It would be remiss of those of us who have compiled these memoranda and reports to leave them as the record without offering some solutions. The most important change would be the recognition by the Executive that unilateral policy fails not only because it ignores the checks and balances of the other branches, but also because it creates policies distorted by only a single, subjective point of view. Even failing that voluntary reform, Congress must exercise its authority, through oversight and legislation, just as the courts have invoked their power of judicial review.

Lawyers and public officials need to be instructed, in school and on the job, to be cognizant of the real-life consequences of their policy choices. Government is not some academic political science competition, in which the prize goes to the student who can muster coherent doctrinal support, however flimsy, for the most outlandish proposition. Here, real people suffered real, serious, and lasting harm due to violations of whatever law applies – U.S., international, common, natural, moral, or religious – committed by our government, in our name.

As citizens, we surely enjoy rights, but just as surely responsibilities as well. We cannot look the other way while we implicitly authorize our elected officials to do the dirty work, and then, like Capt. Renault in *Casablanca*, be "shocked" that transgressions have occurred under our nose. The panic-laden fear generated by the events of September 11th cannot serve as a license – for our government in its policies, or for ourselves in our personal approach to grave problems – to suspend our constitutional heritage, our core values as a nation, or the behavioral standards that mark a civilized and humane society. That type of consistency in the face of danger, in the face of the unknown, defines courage and presents a road map for a future of which we can be proud.

Timeline

September 14, 2001: President Bush issues "Declaration of National Emergency by Reason of Certain Terrorist Attacks."

September 25, 2001: John Yoo, Deputy Assistant Attorney General, U.S. Department of Justice advises Timothy E. Flanigan, Deputy Council to the President, that the President has "broad constitutional power" in the matter of military force, military pre-emption and retaliatory measures against terrorists (persons, organization or States) and those who harbor them.

October 7, 2001:[1] *President Bush announces that on his orders, "the United States military has begun strikes against al Qaeda terrorist training camps and military installations of the Taliban regime in Afghanistan."*[2]

November 13, 2001: George W. Bush, *"Military Order of November 13, 2001," "Detention, Treatment and Trial of Certain Non-Citizens in the War Against Terrorism,"* authorizes the detention of alleged terrorists and subsequent trial by military commissions that, given the threat of terrorism, should not be subject to the same principles of law and rules of evidence recognized in US criminal courts.

December 28, 2001: Deputy Assistant Attorney General John C. Yoo and Deputy Assistant Attorney General Patrick F. Philbin advise William J. Haynes II, General Counsel, U.S. Department of Defense, that Federal Courts in the United States lack jurisdiction to hear habeus corpus petitions of prisoners held in Guantánamo Bay, Cuba. This opinion becomes the basis of the government's legal strategy of trying to prevent detainees from challenging their detention in U.S. courts.

January 9, 2002: Justice Department lawyer John C. Yoo, a U.C. Berkeley law professor, and Special Counsel Robert J. Delahunty advise William J. Haynes II, General Counsel, U.S. Department of Defense, that the Geneva Conventions do not protect members of the al Qaeda network or the Taliban militia.

January 16, 2002: The first suspected al Qaeda and Taliban prisoners arrive at Guantánamo Bay, Cuba.

January 19, 2002: Secretary of Defense Donald Rumsfeld informs the Chairman of the Joint Chiefs of Staff, Richard B. Myers, that al Qaeda and Taliban members are "not entitled to prisoners of war status" under the Geneva Conventions but should be treated "to the extent appropriate" in a manner consistent with the Geneva Conventions of 1949.

---

[1] *Italicized dates refer to events of note that took place, not to memos.*
[2] Presidential Address to the Nation, October 7, 2001. <www.whitehouse.gov/news/releases/2001/10/20011007-8>

January 22, 2002: Then–Assistant Attorney General Jay S. Bybee writes to White House Counsel Alberto R. Gonzales and Department of Defense General Counsel William J. Haynes II, arguing that the Geneva Conventions do not apply to "non-state actors" and are not entitled to prisoner of war status.

January 25, 2002: White House Counsel Alberto R. Gonzales, in a memo to President Bush, considers Secretary of State Colin Powell's objections "unpersuasive" on the grounds that determining that members of al Qaeda and the Taliban are not prisoners of war "holds open options for the future conflicts in which it may be more difficult to determine whether an enemy force as a whole meets the standard for POW status." This memo also refers to the President's decision that the Geneva Conventions, in the Treatment of the Prisoners of War, "do not apply with respect to the conflict with the Taliban," and "that al Qaeda and Taliban detainees are not prisoners of war" under the Geneva Conventions.

January 26, 2002: Secretary of State Colin Powell asks for reconsideration of the Administration's stance on al Qaeda and Taliban members as not entitled to POW status on the grounds that this determination should only be made on a case-by-case basis. He argues that this should be done in order not to jeopardize the United States in matters of reciprocity, international cooperation and legal vulnerability.

January 27, 2002: Defense Secretary Donald Rumsfeld visits Guantánamo Bay and says the prisoners there "will not be determined to be POWs." [3]

February 1, 2002: Attorney General John Ashcroft, in a memo to President Bush, argues that the Geneva Conventions do not apply to members of al Qaeda or the Taliban.

February 2, 2002: In a memo to White House Counsel Alberto Gonzales, State Department Legal Advisor William H. Taft IV argues that the Geneva Conventions *do* apply to the war in Afghanistan.

February 7, 2002: President Bush signs an order declaring, "I accept the legal conclusion of the Attorney General and the Department of Justice that I have the authority under the Constitution to suspend Geneva (Conventions) as between the United States and Afghanistan, but I decline to exercise that authority at this time." He then says that he is reserving the right to do so "in this or future conflicts."

February 7, 2002: In a memo to White House Counsel Alberto Gonzales, Assistant Attorney General in the Department of Justice's Office of Legal Counsel Jay S. Bybee writes that the Taliban do not deserve protection under Article 4 of the Third Geneva Convention because they do not meet legal conditions to be considered legal combatants.

February 26, 2002: DOJ Assistant Attorney General Jay S. Bybee concludes in a memo to General Counsel in the Department of Defense William J. Haynes III that information derived from military interrogations is admissible in Article III Courts, even without *Miranda* warnings. His memo raises the question of the relationship between coercive interrogation and Miranda rights.

August 1, 2002: Jay S. Bybee states in a memo to Alberto R. Gonzales that the text of the Torture Convention "prohibits only the most extreme acts by reserving criminal penalties solely for torture and declining to require such penalties for 'cruel, inhuman, or degrading treatment or punishment.'"

---

[3] "Rumsfeld Visits Camp X-Ray," CNN.com/Transcripts, January 27, 2002. <www.cnn.com/TRANSCRIPTS/0201/27/sun.09.html>

October 11, 2002: A series of memos are issued, considering acceptable counter-resistance techniques. These memos include:

- A memo from Commander Maj. Gen. Michael E. Dunlavey considering the "counter-resistance strategies." Dunlavey acknowledges the intelligence that has resulted, but expresses doubt about the effectiveness of such techniques over time.
- Cover letter from DOD Guantánamo Bay Staff Judge Advocate Diane E. Beaver, in which she recommends "that interrogators be properly trained in the use of the approved methods of interrogation," and that there be a legal review of interrogation techniques in Categories II and III. Her memo evaluates the interrogation techniques in Categories I, II, and III in terms of domestic and international law pertaining to interrogation and torture and recommends a more in-depth "legal, medical, behavioral science and intelligence review" of Categories II and III.
- Director of JTF 170 Guantánamo Bay Jerald Phifer's memo, which outlines Category I, II, and III techniques for counter-resistance strategies.

October 25, 2002: U.S. Southern Command Commander General James T. Hill sends a memo to Chairman of the Joint Chiefs of Staff Richard B. Myers, commenting upon the October 11 memos defining counter-resistance techniques and their legality. Hill is "uncertain whether all the techniques in the third category are legal under U.S. law, given the absence of judicial interpretation of the U.S. torture statute."

November 27, 2002: Department of Defense General Counsel William J. Haynes advises Secretary of Defense Donald Rumsfeld to apply only Category I and II techniques and "mild, non-injurious physical conduct" techniques from Category III during interrogations.

December 2, 2002: Secretary of Defense Rumsfeld approves the techniques outlined in William J. Haynes' November 27 memo.

January 15, 2003: In a memo to U.S. Southern Commander James T. Hill, Secretary of Defense Rumsfeld rescinds permission to use previously approved Category II and III techniques during Guantánamo interrogation and approves use of these techniques only on a case-by-case basis and with the approval of the Secretary of Defense. Rumsfeld also convenes a working group to assess legal policy and operational issues relating to detainees.

January 17, 2003: Memo from William J. Haynes designates Mary L. Walker, the General Counsel for the Department of the Air Force, to chair the Working Group assessing legal policy and operational issues relating to interrogation.

March 6, 2003: Working Group Report recommends taking the Geneva Conventions into account but determines that Taliban detainees do not qualify as prisoners of war and the Geneva Conventions do not apply to the other prisoners at Guantánamo, as they are non-state actors. The United States is, however, bound to the Torture Convention of 1994 (as long as it is in accord with U.S. constitutional Amendments 5, 8 and 14) which includes in the definition of torture the requirement of specific intent "to inflict severe mental pain or suffering" and in cases of mental pain, the damage must be prolonged. The report includes debate over 8th Amendment precedents on torture as well as standard defenses to criminal conduct.

March 19, 2003: President Bush announces that on his orders, "coalition forces have begun striking selected targets of military importance" in Iraq.[4]

---

[4] Presidential Address to the Nation, March 19, 2003. <www.whitehouse.gov/news/releases/2003/03/20030319-17>

April 4, 2003: The updated version of the March 6, 2003, Working Group Report argues that it may be necessary to interrogate detainees "in a manner beyond that which may be applied to a prisoner of war who is subject to the Geneva Conventions." In greater detail than the March 6 report, this report discusses the affirmative defenses for the use of torture and the legal technicalities that can be used to create a "good faith defense against prosecution." Includes a chart that lists the utility of various interrogation techniques, along with a system displaying their consistency with both U.S. domestic law and international norms.

April 16, 2003: In a memo to U.S. Southern Command Commander General James T. Hill, Secretary of State Rumsfeld provides a new list of approved interrogation techniques that include most Category I techniques and a limited number of Category II techniques. Some of the techniques listed require the specific approval of the Secretary of Defense, on the grounds that they may be perceived as in violation of the Geneva Conventions on prisoners of war.

March 19, 2004: Assistant Attorney General in the Office of Legal Counsel, Jack Goldsmith, justifies the forcible removal of persons who have not been accused of an offense from Iraq "for a brief but not indefinite period" for the purposes of interrogation. Goldsmith argues that Article 49 of the Fourth Geneva Convention prohibition on deportations does not apply to aliens in occupied territory and does not "forbid the removal from occupied territory . . . of 'protected persons' who are illegal aliens."

Missing Documents

These documents have not yet been declassified and/or are currently not obtainable.

1. Memorandum for Alberto R. Gonzales, Counsel to the President, from Patrick F. Philbin, Deputy Assistant Attorney General, Office of Legal Counsel, *Re: Legality of the Use of Military Commissions to Try Terrorists* (November 6, 2001).[1]
2. Memorandum for Alberto R. Gonzales, Counsel to the President, and William J. Haynes II, General Counsel, Department of Defense, from John C. Yoo, Deputy Assistant Attorney General, Office of Legal Counsel, and Robert J. Delahunty, Special Counsel, Office of Legal Counsel, *Re: Authority for Use of Military Force to Combat Terrorist Activities Within the Untied States* (October 17, 2001).[2]
3. *Information Paper, Subject: Background Information on Taliban Forces* (February 6, 2002), by Rear Admiral L.E. Jacoby, U.S. Navy, J-2.[3]
4. Memorandum for William J. Haynes II, General Counsel, Department of Defense, from Jay S. Bybee, Assistant Attorney General, Office of Legal Counsel, *Re: The President's Power as Commander in Chief to Transfer Captured Terrorists to the Control and Custody of Foreign Nations* (March 13, 2002).[4]

---

[1] This document is referred to in footnote 3 (p. 3) of the January 9, 2002, memo from John C. Yoo and Robert J. Delahunty.

[2] This document is referred to in footnote 104 (p. 29) of the January 22, 2002, memo from Jay S. Bybee. This document is ascribed a different date, October 23, 2001, in a subsequent document (the February 26, 2002, memo from Jay S. Bybee, at footnote 16, p. 21).

[3] This document is referred to in the text (at p. 2) of the February 7, 2002, memo from Jay S. Bybee. It is relevant because it was cited in that memo as a basis for concluding that the Taliban, as a whole, was not entitled to Prisoner of War status under the provisions of Geneva Convention III.

[4] This document is referred to at p. 38 of the August 1. 2002, memo from Jay S. Bybee.

Biographical Sketches

Ashcroft, John
Attorney General, U.S. Department of Justice
Ashcroft became U.S. Attorney General in January 2001. Prior to that, he served as Attorney General of Missouri for two terms and as Governor of Missouri from 1985 through 1993. He was elected to the U.S. Senate in 1994 and represented the state of Missouri there until the end of 2000.

Bybee, Jay S.
Assistant Attorney General, Office of Legal Counsel, U.S. Department of Justice
Bybee was appointed to the position of Assistant Attorney General by President George W. Bush in 2001. He joined the Department of Justice in 1984, where he worked in the Office of Legal Policy and the Appellate Staff of the Civil Division. From 1989 to 1991, he served in the White House as Associate Counsel to the President. From 1991 until his appointment in 2001, he taught law at Louisiana State University and the University of Nevada, Las Vegas.

Church Albert T. III, (Vice Admiral)
Director of the Navy Staff
Prior to serving as Director of the Navy Staff, Vice Admiral Church had two Director-level positions in the Navy. From July 1998 until March 2003, he served as both Director, Office of Budget in the Office of the Assistant Secretary of the Navy and Director, Fiscal Management Division, in the Office of the Chief of Naval Operations.

Delahunty, Robert J.
Associate Professor of Law, University of St. Thomas, Former Deputy General Counsel, White House Office of Homeland Security
Delahunty served as the Deputy General Counsel at the White House Office of Homeland Security from 2002 to 2003. He joined the U.S. Department of Justice in 1986, where he began working for the Office of Legal Counsel in 1989. He spent much of his legal career in the Office of Legal Counsel and in 1992, he was appointed Special Counsel in that department.

Dunlavey, Michael E. (Major General)
Former Operational Commander, Guantánamo Bay, Cuba
A career military man, Major General Dunlavey was made Commander of Terror Suspect Operations at Guantánamo Bay, Cuba, in 1997. Prior to that position, he served as Assistant Deputy Chief of Staff for Intelligence in the Office of the Deputy Chief of Staff for Intelligence.

Fay, George R. (Brigadier General)

Commanding General, U.S. Army Intelligence and Security Command (INSCOM)

A career military man, Brigadier General Fay became the INSCOM Acting Commander in July 2003. Prior to this position, he served as the Deputy Commanding General of INSCOM, a position he assumed in October 1999.

Flanigan, Timothy

Former Deputy White House Counsel

Flanigan is currently serving as the General Counsel for Corporate and International Law at Tyco, International. Prior to this, he was Deputy White House Counsel and a Deputy Assistant to President George W. Bush. Mr. Flanigan was a partner in the law firm White & Case and had previously served as Assistant Attorney General for the Department of Justice's Office of the Legal Counsel during the administration of the first President Bush. In 1985 and 1986, he served as a law clerk to Chief Justice Warren Burger of the United States Supreme Court.

Goldsmith, Jack Landman III

Former Assistant Attorney General, Office of Legal Counsel

Goldsmith is currently a Professor of Law at Harvard Law School. Until recently, he was an Assistant Attorney General in the Justice Department's Office of Legal Counsel for the Bush Administration. Previously, he taught law at the University of Chicago and the University of Virginia. He has written numerous books and articles in the field of international and foreign relations law.

Gonzales, Alberto R.

Assistant to the President and White House Counsel

Gonzales was appointed as Counsel to President George W. Bush in January 2001. Prior to his position in the White House, Gonzales served as a Justice of the Supreme Court of Texas, a position he was appointed to in 1999. He also served as Texas' Secretary of State from December 1997 to January 1999 and was the General Counsel to Governor Bush for three years prior to becoming Secretary of State.

Haynes William J. II

General Counsel, U.S. Department of Defense

Haynes was appointed to the position of General Counsel of the Department of Defense by President George Bush in May 2001. He serves as the chief legal officer of the Department of Defense and the legal advisor to the Secretary of Defense. In 1990, the President appointed him General Counsel of the Department of the Army, a position he held until 1993, when he joined the law firm Jenner & Block.

Hill, James T. (General)

Commander, U.S. Southern Command

General Hill was appointed the Commander of the U.S. Southern Command in October 2002. Since being commissioned by the infantry after his college graduation in 1968, General Hill has had numerous Commanding Military assignments. He also earned many medals and awards throughout his military career.

Jones, Anthony R. (Lieutenant General)

Deputy Commanding General/Chief of Staff U.S. Army Training and Doctrine Command, Fort Monroe, VA

A career military man, Lieutenant General Jones became the Deputy Commanding General and Chief of Staff for Headquarters, U.S. Army Training and Doctrine Command, in June 2003.

Mikolashek, Paul T. (Lieutenant General)

Commanding General, Third U.S. Army
A career military man, Lieutenant General Mikolashek became the Commanding General of the Third U.S. Army and U.S. Army Forces Central Command in June 2000. Prior to this position, he served as Commanding General for U.S. Army Southern European Task Force, a position he assumed in September 1998.

Philbin, Patrick F.

Deputy Assistant Attorney General, Office of Legal Counsel, U.S. Department of Justice
Philbin was appointed to the position of Deputy Assistant Attorney General in September 2001. Prior to joining the Justice Department, he was a partner in the Washington office of the law firm Kirkland & Ellis.

Powell, Colin L.

Secretary of State, U.S. Department of State
Powell was nominated to the position of Secretary of State by President Bush in December 2000 and was sworn in as Secretary in January 2001. Prior to becoming Secretary of State, Powell was the chairman of America's Promise – The Alliance for Youth. Prior to this position, he served as a professional soldier for 35 years. He was the Chairman of the Joint Chiefs of Staff in the Department of Defense from October 1989 to September 1993 and Assistant to the President for National Security Affairs from December 1987 to January 1989.

Rumsfeld, Donald F.

Secretary of Defense, U.S. Department of Defense
Rumsfeld was sworn in as Secretary of Defense for the second time in January 2001. He previously held this position from 1975 to1977, serving under President Ford. In addition, Rumsfeld served as White House Chief of Staff from 1974 to 1975, U.S. Ambassador to NATO from 1973 to 1974, and U.S. Congressman from 1962 to 1969. From 1977 to 2000, he worked in the private sector, during which time he was chief executive officer of two Fortune 500 companies.

Sanchez, Richardo S. (Lieutenant General)

Former Commander of Joint Task Force 7
A career military man, Lt. Gen. Sanchez was the commander of Combined Joint Task Force 7 and the senior military official in Iraq until July 2004. In July 2001, Lt. Gen. Sanchez became commanding general of V Corps' 1st Armored Division. He held that position for nearly two years before assuming command of the V Corps on June 14, 2003.

Schlesinger, James R.

Former U.S. Secretary of Defense
Schlesinger served as Secretary of Defense from 1973 to 1975. He currently is a Consultant to the U.S. Department of Defense, as well as a Commissioner on the U.S. Commission on National Security/21st Century/Hart-Rudman Commission and a member of the Homeland Security Advisory Council. Schlesinger's prior positions include Secretary of Energy (1977–79), Assistant to the President (1977), Director of the C.I.A. (1973), and Director of Strategic Studies (1967–69), and Senior Staff Member (1963–67), at the RAND Corporation.

Taft William H. IV

Legal Advisor, Office of the Legal Advisor, U.S. Department of State

Taft was appointed as the Legal Advisor to the Secretary of State in April 2001. Prior to this position, Taft was a litigation partner in the law firm Fried Franks, which he joined in 1992. From 1989 to 1992, he served as the U.S. Permanent Representative to NATO. He was the Deputy Secretary of Defense from January 1984 to April 1989 and Acting Secretary of Defense from January to March 1989. He also served as General Counsel for the Department of Defense from 1981 to 1984.

Taguba, Antonio M. (Major General)

U.S. Army Commander

A career military man, Major General Taguba is currently Deputy Assistant Secretary of Defense for readiness, training, and mobilization in the office of the Assistant Secretary of Defense for Reserve Affairs. Taguba was reassigned to this position, after serving as Deputy Commanding General, Third U.S. Army, U.S. Army Forces Central Command, and Coalition Forces Land Component Command. He previously was the Acting Director of the Army Staff, Headquarters, Department of the Army, The Pentagon.

Yoo, John C.

Professor of Law, Boalt Hall School of Law, University of California, Berkeley/Former Deputy Assistant Attorney General, Office of Legal Counsel, U.S. Department of Justice

Yoo served as Deputy Assistant Attorney General from 2001 to 2003. Prior to this position, he served as General Counsel of the U.S. Senate Judiciary Committee from 1995 to 1996. He has been a member of the Boalt faculty since 1993 and clerked for Justice Clarence Thomas on the U.S. Supreme Court.

Memoranda

U. S. Department of Justice

Office of the Legal Counsel

September 25, 2001

MEMORANDUM OPINION FOR TIMOTHY FLANIGAN,
  THE DEPUTY COUNSEL TO THE PRESIDENT

FROM: John C. Yoo
              Deputy Assistant Attorney General

THE PRESIDENT'S CONSTITUTIONAL AUTHORITY TO CONDUCT MILITARY OPERATIONS AGAINST TERRORISTS AND NATIONS SUPPORTING THEM

The President has broad constitutional power to take military action in response to the terrorist attacks on the United States on September 11, 2001. Congress has acknowledged this inherent executive power in both the War Powers Resolution and the Joint Resolution passed by Congress on September 14, 2001.

The President has constitutional power not only to retaliate against any person, organization, or State suspected of involvement in terrorist attacks on the United States, but also against foreign States suspected of harboring or supporting such organizations.

The President may deploy military force preemptively against terrorist organizations or the States that harbor or support them, whether or not they can be linked to the specific terrorist incidents of September 11.

September 25, 2001
MEMORANDUM OPINION FOR THE DEPUTY COUNSEL TO THE PRESIDENT

You have asked for our opinion as to the scope of the President's authority to take military action in response to the terrorist attacks on the United States on September 11, 2001. We conclude that the President has broad constitutional power to use military force. Congress has acknowledged this inherent executive power in both the War Powers Resolution, Pub. L. No. 93-148, 87 Stat. 555 (1973), *codified at* 50 U. S. C. §§ 1541–1548 (the "WPR"), and in the Joint Resolution passed by Congress on September 14, 2001, Pub. L. No. 107-40, 115 Stat. 224 (2001). Further, the President has the constitutional power not only to retaliate against any person, organization, or State suspected of involvement in terrorist attacks on the United States, but also against foreign States suspected of harboring or supporting such organizations. Finally, the President may deploy military force preemptively against terrorist organizations or the States that harbor or support them, whether or not they can be linked to the specific terrorist incidents of September 11.

Our analysis falls into four parts. First, we examine the Constitution's text and structure. We conclude that the Constitution vests the President with the plenary

authority, as Commander in Chief and the sole organ of the Nation in its foreign relations, to use military force abroad – especially in response to grave national emergencies created by sudden, unforeseen attacks on the people and territory of the United
States. Second, we confirm that conclusion by reviewing the executive and judicial
statements and decisions interpreting the Constitution and the President's powers under it. Third, we analyze the relevant practice of the United States, including recent
history, that supports the view that the President has the authority to deploy military
force in response to emergency conditions such as those created by the September 11,
2001, terrorist attacks. Finally, we discuss congressional enactments that, in our view,
acknowledge the President's plenary authority to use force to respond to the terrorist
attack on the United States.

   Our review establishes that all three branches of the Federal Government –
Congress, the Executive, and the Judiciary – agree that the President has broad authority to use military force abroad, including the ability to deter future attacks.

I

The President's constitutional power to defend the United States and the lives of its
people must be understood in light of the Founders' express intention to create a
federal government "cloathed with all the powers requisite to [the] complete execution
of its trust." The *Federalist* No. 23, at 122 (Alexander Hamilton) (Charles R. Kesler ed.,
1999). Foremost among the objectives committed to that trust by the Constitution is
the security of the Nation.[1] As Hamilton explained in arguing for the Constitution's
adoption, because "the circumstances which may affect the public safety are [not]
reducible within certain determinate limits,... it must be admitted, as a necessary
consequence that there can be no limitation of that authority which is to provide for the
defense and protection of the community in any matter essential to its efficiency." Id.[2]

   "It is 'obvious and unarguable' that no governmental interest is more compelling
than the security of the Nation." *Haig v. Agee*, 453 U.S. 280, 307 (1981) (citation omitted). Within the limits that the Constitution itself imposes, the scope and distribution
of the powers to protect national security must be construed to authorize the most

---

[1] "As Lincoln aptly said, '[is] it possible to lose the nation and yet preserve the Constitution?'"
Youngstown Sheet & Tube Co. v. Sawyer, 343 U.S. 579, 662 (1952) (Clark, J., concurring in judgment).
[2] *See also The Federalist No.* 34, at 175 (Alexander Hamilton) (Federal government is to possess "an
indefinite power of providing for emergencies as they might arise"); id. No. 41, at 224 (James Madi-
son) ("Security against foreign danger is one of the primitive objects of civil society.... The powers
requisite for attaining it must be effectually confided to the foederal councils."). Many Supreme Court
opinions echo Hamilton's argument that the Constitution presupposes the indefinite and unpredictable
nature of the "the circumstances which may affect the public safety," and that the federal government's
powers are correspondingly broad. *See, e.g., Dames & Moore v. Regan*, 453 U.S. 654, 662 (1981)
(noting that the President "exercis[es] the executive authority in a world that presents each day some
new challenge with which he must deal"); *Hamilton v. Regents*, 293 U.S. 245, 264 (1934) (federal
government's war powers are "well-nigh limitless" in extent); *Stewart v. Kahn*, 78 U.S. (11Wall.) 493,
506 (1870) ("The measures to be taken in carrying on war ... are not defined [in the Constitution]. The
decision of all such questions rests wholly in the discretion of those to whom the substantial powers
involved are confided by the Constitution."); *Miller v. United States*, 78 U.S. (11 Wall.) 268, 305 (1870)
("The Constitution confers upon Congress expressly power to declare war, grant letters of marque and
reprisal, and make rules respecting captures on land and water. Upon the exercise of these powers no
restrictions are imposed. Of course the power to declare war involves the power to prosecute it by all
means and in any manner in which war may be legitimately prosecuted.").

efficacious defense of the Nation and its interests in accordance "with the realistic purposes of the entire instrument." *Lichter v. United States*, 334 U.S. 742, 782 (1948). Nor is the authority to protect national security limited to actions necessary for "victories in the field." *Application of Yamashita*, 327 U.S. 1, 12 (1946). The authority over national security "carries with it the inherent power to guard against the immediate renewal of the conflict." Id.

We now turn to the more precise question of the President's inherent constitutional powers to use military force.

Constitutional Text. The text, structure and history of the Constitution establish that the Founders entrusted the President with the primary responsibility, and therefore the power, to use military force in situations of emergency. Article II, Section 2 states that the "President shall be Commander in Chief of the Army and Navy of the United States, and of the Militia of the several States, when called into the actual Service of the United States." U.S. Const. art. II, § 2, cl. 1. He is further vested with all of "the executive Power" and the duty to execute the laws. U.S. Const. art. II, § 1. These powers give the President broad constitutional authority to use military force in response to threats to the national security and foreign policy of the United States.[3] During the period leading up to the Constitution's ratification, the power to initiate hostilities and to control the escalation of conflict had been long understood to rest in the hands of the executive branch.[4]

By their terms, these provisions vest full control of the military forces of the United States in the President. The power of the President is at its zenith under the Constitution when the President is directing military operations of the armed forces, because the power of Commander in Chief is assigned solely to the President. It has long been the view of this Office that the Commander-in-Chief Clause is a substantive grant of authority to the President and that the scope of the President's authority to commit the armed forces to combat is very broad. See, e.g., Memorandum for Honorable Charles W. Colson, Special Counsel to the President, from William H. Rehnquist, Assistant Attorney General, Office of Legal Counsel, Re: *The President and the War Power: South Vietnam and the Cambodian Sanctuaries* (May 22, 1970) (the "Rehnquist Memo"). The President's complete discretion in exercising the Commander-in-Chief power has also been recognized by the courts. In the Prize Cases, 67 U.S. (2 Black) 635, 670 (1862), for example, the Court explained that, whether the President "in fulfilling his duties as Commander in Chief" had met with a situation justifying treating the southern States as belligerents and instituting a blockade, was a question "to be *decided by him*" and which the Court could not question, but

---

[3] See *Johnson v. Eisentrager*, 339 U.S. 763, 789 (1950) (President has authority to deploy United States armed forces "abroad or to any particular region"); Fleming v. Page, 50 U.S. (9 How.) 603, 615 (1850) ("As commander-in-chief, [the President] is authorized to direct the movements of the naval and military forces placed by law at his command, and to employ them in the manner he may deem most effectual"); *Loving v. United States*, 517 U.S. 748, 776 (1996) (Scalia, J., concurring in part and concurring in judgment) (The "inherent powers" of the Commander in Chief "are clearly extensive."); *Maul v. United States*, 274 U.S. 501, 515–16 (1927) (Brandeis & Holmes, JJ., concurring) (President "may direct any revenue cutter to cruise in any waters in order to perform any duty of the service"); *Massachusetts v. Laird*, 451 F.2d 26, 32 (1st Cir. 1971) (the President has "power as Commander-in-Chief to station forces abroad"); *Authority to Use United States Military Forces in Somalia*, 16 Op. O.L.C. 6 (1992).

[4] See John C. Yoo, *The Continuation of Politics by Other Means: The Original Understanding of War Powers*, 84 Cal. L. Rev. 167, 196–241 (1996).

must leave to "the political department of the Government to which this power was entrusted."[5]

Some commentators have read the constitutional text differently. They argue that the vesting of the power to declare war gives Congress the sole authority to decide whether to make war.[6] This view misreads the constitutional text and misunderstands the nature of a declaration of war. Declaring war is not tantamount to making war – indeed, the Constitutional Convention specifically amended the working draft of the Constitution that had given Congress the power to make war. An earlier draft of the Constitution had given to Congress the power to "make" war. When it took up this clause on August 17, 1787, the Convention voted to change the clause from "make" to "declare." 2 *The Records of the Federal Convention of 1787*, at 318–19 (Max Farrand ed., rev. ed. 1966) (1911). A supporter of the change argued that it would "leav[e] to the Executive the power to repel sudden attacks." Id. at 318. Further, other elements of the Constitution describe "engaging" in war, which demonstrates that the Framers understood making and engaging in war to be broader than simply "declaring" war. See U.S. Const. art. I, § 10, cl. 3 ("No State shall, without the Consent of Congress . . . engage in War, unless actually invaded, or in such imminent Danger as will not admit of delay."). A State constitution at the time of the ratification included provisions that

[5] See id. ("He must determine what degree of force the crisis demands."); *see also Eisentrager*, 339 U.S. at 789 ("Certainly it is not the function of the Judiciary to entertain private litigation – even by a citizen – which challenges the legality, the wisdom, or the propriety of the Commander-in-Chief in sending our armed forces abroad or to any particular region."); *Chicago & Southern Air Lines v. Waterman Steamship Corp.*, 333 U.S. 103, 111 (1948) ("The President, both as Commander-in-Chief and as the Nation's organ for foreign affairs, has available intelligence services whose reports are not and ought not to be published to the world. It would be intolerable that courts, without the relevant information, should review and perhaps nullify actions of the Executive taken on information properly held secret."); *Ramirez de Arellano v. Weinberger*, 745 F.2d 1500, 1561 (D.C. Cir. 1984) (Scalia, J., dissenting), vacated by 471 U.S. 1113 (1985); *Ex parte Vallandigham*, 28 F.Cas. 874, 922 (C.C.S.D. Ohio 1863) (No. 16,816) (in acting "under this power where there is no express legislative declaration, the president is guided solely by his own judgment and discretion"); *Hefleblower v. United States*, 21 Ct. Cl. 228, 238 (Ct. Cl. 1886) ("The responsibility of declaring what portions of the country were in insurrection and of declaring when the insurrection came to an end was accorded to the President; when he declared a portion of the country to be in insurrection the judiciary cannot try the issue and find the territory national; conversely, when the President declared the insurrection at an end in any portion of the country, the judiciary cannot try the issue and find the territory hostile."); cf. *United States v. Chemical Found., Inc.*, 272 U.S. 1, 12 (1926) ("It was peculiarly within the province of the Commander-in-Chief to know the facts and to determine what disposition should be made of enemy properties in order effectively to carry on the war.")

[6] See, e.g., Louis Fisher, *Presidential War Power* 185–206 (1995); John Hart Ely, *War and Responsibility*: *Constitutional Lessons of Vietnam and Its Aftermath* 3–5 (1993); Michael J. Glennon, *Constitutional Diplomacy* 80–84 (1990); Louis Henkin, *Constitutionalism, Democracy, and Foreign Affairs* 109 (1990); Harold Hongju Koh, *The National Security Constitution: Sharing Power After the Iran-Contra Affair* 158–61 (1990); Francis D. Wormuth & Edwin B. Firmage, *To Chain the Dog of War: The War Power of Congress in History and Law* (2d ed. 1989).

Other scholars, however, have argued that the President has the constitutional authority to initiate military hostilities without prior congressional authorization. See, e.g., Edward S. Corwin, *The President: Office and Powers* 1787–1984 (5th ed. 1984); Philip Bobbitt, *War Powers: An Essay on John Hart Ely's "War and Responsibility: Constitutional Lessons of Vietnam and Its Aftermath,"* 92 Mich. L. Rev. 1364 (1994); Robert H. Bork, *Erosion of the President's Power in Foreign Affairs*, 68 Wash. U. L. Q. 693 (1990); Henry P. Monaghan, *Presidential War-Making*, 50 B.U.L. Rev. 19 (1970); W. Michael Reisman, *Some Lessons from Iraq: International Law and Democratic Politics*, 16 Yale J. Int'l L. 203 (1991); Eugene V. Rostow, *"Once More unto the Breach:" The War Powers Resolution Revisited*, 21 Val. U.L. Rev. 1 (1986); John C. Yoo, *Kosovo, War Powers, and the Multilateral Future*, 148 U. Pa. L. Rev. 1673 (2000); Yoo, *supra* n.4.

prohibited the governor from "making" war without legislative approval, S.C. Const. art. XXVI (1776), *reprinted in* 6 *The Federal and State Constitutions* 3247 (Francis Newton Thorpe ed., 1909).[7] If the Framers had wanted to require congressional consent before the initiation of military hostilities, they knew how to write such provisions.

Finally, the Framing generation well understood that declarations of war were obsolete. Not all forms of hostilities rose to the level of a declared war: during the seventeenth and eighteenth centuries, Great Britain and colonial America waged numerous conflicts against other states without an official declaration of war.[8] As Alexander Hamilton observed during the ratification, "the ceremony of a formal denunciation of war has of late fallen into disuse." The Federalist No. 25, at 133 (Alexander Hamilton). Instead of serving as an authorization to begin hostilities, a declaration of war was only necessary to "perfect" a conflict under international law. A declaration served to fully transform the international legal relationship between two states from one of peace to one of war. See 1 William Blackstone, Commentaries *249–50. Given this context, it is clear that Congress's power to declare war does not constrain the President's independent and plenary constitutional authority over the use of military force.

Constitutional Structure. Our reading of the text is reinforced by analysis of the constitutional structure. First, it is clear that the Constitution secures all federal executive power in the President to ensure a unity in purpose and energy in action. "Decision, activity, secrecy, and dispatch will generally characterize the proceedings of one man in a much more eminent degree than the proceedings of any greater number." *The Federalist* No. 70, at 392 (Alexander Hamilton). The centralization of authority in the President alone is particularly crucial in matters of national defense, war, and foreign policy, where a unitary executive can evaluate threats, consider policy choices, and mobilize national resources with a speed and energy that is far superior to any other branch. As Hamilton noted, "Energy in the executive is a leading character in the definition of good government. It is essential to the protection of the community against foreign attacks." *Id.* at 391. This is no less true in war. "Of all the cares or concerns of government, the direction of war most peculiarly demands those qualities which distinguish the exercise of power by a single hand." *Id.* No. 74, at 415 (Alexander Hamilton).[9]

---

[7] A subsequent version made clear "that the governor and commander-in-chief shall have no power to commence war, or conclude peace, or enter into any final treaty" without legislative approval. S.C. Const. art. XXXIII (1778), reprinted in 6 The Federal and State Constitutions 3255 (Francis Newton Thorpe ed., 1909).

[8] Of the eight major wars fought by Great Britain prior to the ratification of the Constitution, war was declared only once before the start of hostilities. See Yoo, *supra* note 4, at 214–15. *See also* W. Taylor Reveley, III, *War Powers of the President and Congress: Who Holds the Arrows and Olive Branch?* 55 (1981) ("[U]ndeclared war was the norm in eighteenth-century European practice, a reality brought home to Americans when Britain's Seven Years' War with France began on this continent."); William Michael Treanor, *Fame, The Founding, and The Power to Declare War*, 82 Cornell L. Rev. 695, 709 (1997).

[9] James Iredell (later an Associate Justice of the Supreme Court) argued in the North Carolina Ratifying Convention that "[f]rom the nature of the thing, the command of armies ought to be delegated to one person only. The secrecy, despatch, and decision, which are necessary in military operations, can only be expected from one person." Debate in the North Carolina Ratifying Convention, in 4 Jonathan Elliott, *The Debates in the Several State Conventions on the Adoption of the Federal Constitution as Recommended by the General Convention at Philadelphia in 1787*, at 107 (2d ed. 1987). See also 3 Joseph Story, *Commentaries on the Constitution of the United States* § 1485 (1833) (in military

Second, the Constitution makes clear that the process used for conducting military hostilities is different from other government decisionmaking. In the area of domestic legislation, the Constitution creates a detailed, finely wrought procedure in which Congress plays the central role. In foreign affairs, however, the Constitution does not establish a mandatory, detailed, Congress-driven procedure for taking action. Rather, the Constitution vests the two branches with different powers – the President as Commander in Chief, Congress with control over funding and declaring war – without requiring that they follow a specific process in making war. By establishing this framework, the Framers expected that the process for warmaking would be far more flexible, and capable of quicker, more decisive action, than the legislative process. Thus, the President may use his Commander-in-Chief and executive powers to use military force to protect the Nation, subject to congressional appropriations and control over domestic legislation.

Third, the constitutional structure requires that any ambiguities in the allocation of a power that is executive in nature – such as the power to conduct military hostilities – must be resolved in favor of the executive branch. Article II, section 1 provides that "[t]he executive Power shall be vested in a President of the United States." U.S. Const. art. II, § 1. By contrast, Article I's Vesting Clause gives Congress only the powers "herein granted." Id. art. I, § 1. This difference in language indicates that Congress's legislative powers are limited to the list enumerated in Article I, section 8, while the President's powers include inherent executive powers that are unenumerated in the Constitution. To be sure, Article II lists specifically enumerated powers in addition to the Vesting Clause, and some have argued that this limits the "executive Power" granted in the Vesting Clause to the powers on that list. But the purpose of the enumeration of executive powers in Article II was not to define and cabin the grant in the Vesting Clause. Rather, the Framers unbundled some plenary powers that had traditionally been regarded as "executive," assigning elements of those powers to Congress in Article I, while expressly reserving other elements as enumerated executive powers in Article II. So, for example, the King's traditional power to declare war was given to Congress under Article I, while the Commander-in-Chief authority was expressly reserved to the President in Article II. Further, the Framers altered other plenary powers of the King, such as treaties and appointments, assigning the Senate a share in them in Article II itself.[10] Thus, the enumeration in Article II marks the points at which several traditional executive powers were diluted or reallocated. Any other, unenumerated executive powers, however, were conveyed to the President by the Vesting Clause.

There can be little doubt that the decision to deploy military force is "executive" in nature, and was traditionally so regarded. It calls for action and energy in execution, rather than the deliberate formulation of rules to govern the conduct of private

matters, "[u]nity of plan, promptitude, activity, and decision, are indispensable to success; and these can scarcely exist, except when single magistrate is entrusted exclusively with the power").

[10] Thus, Article II's enumeration of the Treaty and Appointments Clauses only dilutes the unitary nature of the executive branch in regard to the exercise of those powers, rather than transforming them into quasi-legislative functions. See *Constitutionality of Proposed Conditions to Senate Consent to the Interim Convention on Conservation of North Pacific Fur Seals*, 10 Op. O.L.C. 12, 17 (1986) ("Nothing in the text of the Constitution or the deliberations of the Framers suggests that the Senate's advice and consent role in the treaty-making process was intended to alter the fundamental constitutional balance between legislative authority and executive authority.").

individuals. Moreover, the Framers understood it to be an attribute of the executive. "The direction of war implies the direction of the common strength," wrote Alexander Hamilton, "and the power of directing and employing the common strength forms a usual and essential part in the definition of the executive authority." *The Federalist* No. 74, at 415 (Alexander Hamilton). As a result, to the extent that the constitutional text does not explicitly allocate the power to initiate military hostilities to a particular branch, the Vesting Clause provides that it remain among the President's unenumerated powers.

Fourth, depriving the President of the power to decide when to use military force would disrupt the basic constitutional framework of foreign relations. From the very beginnings of the Republic, the vesting of the executive, Commander-in-Chief, and treaty powers in the executive branch has been understood to grant the President plenary control over the conduct of foreign relations. As Secretary of State Thomas Jefferson observed during the first Washington Administration: "the constitution has divided the powers of government into three branches [and] has declared that the executive powers shall be vested in the president, submitting only special articles of it to a negative by the senate." Due to this structure, Jefferson continued, "the transaction of business with foreign nations is executive altogether; it belongs, then, to the head of that department, except as to such portions of it as are specially submitted to the senate. Exceptions are to be construed strictly." Thomas Jefferson, *Opinion on the Powers of the Senate* (1790), *reprinted in* 5 *The Writings of Thomas Jefferson*, at 161 (Paul L. Ford ed., 1895). In defending President Washington's authority to issue the Neutrality Proclamation, Alexander Hamilton came to the same interpretation of the President's foreign affairs powers. According to Hamilton, Article II "ought . . . to be considered as intended . . . to specify and regulate the principal articles implied in the definition of Executive Power; leaving the rest to flow from the general grant of that power." Alexander Hamilton, *Pacificus* No. 1 (1793), *reprinted in* 15 *The Papers of Alexander Hamilton*, at 33, 39 (Harold C. Syrett et al. eds., 1969). As future Chief Justice John Marshall famously declared a few years later, "The President is the sole organ of the nation in its external relations, and its sole representative with foreign nations. . . . The [executive] department . . . is entrusted with the whole foreign intercourse of the nation. . . ." 10 Annals of Cong. 613–14 (1800). Given the agreement of Jefferson, Hamilton, and Marshall, it has not been difficult for the executive branch consistently to assert the President's plenary authority in foreign affairs ever since.

In the relatively few occasions where it has addressed foreign affairs, the Supreme Court has agreed with the executive branch's consistent interpretation. Conducting foreign affairs and protecting the national security are, as the Supreme Court has observed, "'central' Presidential domains." *Harlow v. Fitzgerald*, 457 U.S. 800, 812 n.19 (1982). The President's constitutional primacy flows from both his unique position in the constitutional structure, and from the specific grants of authority in Article II that make the President both the Chief Executive of the Nation and the Commander in Chief. See *Nixon v. Fitzgerald*, 457 U.S. 731, 749–50 (1982). Due to the President's constitutionally superior position, the Supreme Court has consistently "recognized 'the generally accepted view that foreign policy [is] the province and responsibility of the Executive.'" Department of the *Navy v. Egan*, 484 U.S. 518, 529 (1988) (quoting *Haig v. Agee*, 453 U.S. at 293–94). "The Founders in their wisdom made [the President] not only the Commander-in-Chief but also the guiding organ in the conduct of our foreign affairs," possessing "vast powers in relation to the outside world." *Ludecke v.*

Watkins, 335 U.S. 160, 173 (1948). This foreign affairs power is exclusive: it is "the very delicate, plenary and exclusive power of the President as sole organ of the federal government in the field of international relations – a power which does not require as a basis for its exercise an act of Congress." *United States v. Curtiss-Wright Export Corp.*, 299 U.S. 304, 320 (1936).

Conducting military hostilities is a central tool for the exercise of the President's plenary control over the conduct of foreign policy. There can be no doubt that the use of force protects the Nation's security and helps it achieve its foreign policy goals. Construing the Constitution to grant such power to another branch could prevent the President from exercising his core constitutional responsibilities in foreign affairs. Even in the cases in which the Supreme Court has limited executive authority, it has also emphasized that we should not construe legislative prerogatives to prevent the executive branch "from accomplishing its constitutionally assigned functions." *Nixon v. Administrator of General Servs.*, 433 U.S. 425, 443 (1977).

II

Executive Branch Construction and Practice. The position we take here has long represented the view of the executive branch and of the Department of Justice. Attorney General (later Justice) Robert Jackson formulated the classic statement of the executive branch's understanding of the President's military powers in 1941:

> Article II, section 2, of the Constitution provides that the President "shall be Commander in Chief of the Army and Navy of the United States." By virtue of this constitutional office he has supreme command over the land and naval forces of the country and may order them to perform such military duties as, in his opinion, are necessary or appropriate for the defense of the United States. These powers exist in time of peace as well as in time of war.
>
>   . . . .
>
> Thus the President's responsibility as Commander in Chief embraces the authority to command and direct the armed forces in their immediate movements and operations designed to protect the security and effectuate the defense of the United States. . . . [T]his authority undoubtedly includes the power to dispose of troops and equipment in such manner and on such duties as best to promote the safety of the country.

Training of British Flying Students in the United States, 40 Op. Att'y Gen. 58, 61–62 (1941).[11] Other Attorneys General have defended similar accounts of the President constitutional powers and duties, particularly in times of unforeseen emergencies.

Attorney General William P. Barr, quoting the opinion of Attorney General Jackson just cited, advised the President in 1992 that "[y]ou have authority to commit troops overseas without specific prior Congressional approval 'on missions of good will or rescue, or for the purpose of protecting American lives or property or American

---

[11] At the time Attorney General Jackson delivered his opinion, the United States was a neutral, and thus his conclusions about the President's powers did not rest on any special considerations that might apply in time of war. Although he stated that he was "inclined to the opinion" that a statute (the Lend-Lease Act) authorized the decision under review, Jackson expressly based his conclusion on the President's constitutional authority. *Id.* at 61.

interests.'" *Authority to Use United States Military Forces in Somalia*, 16 Op. O.L.C. at 6 (citation omitted).

Attorney General (later Justice) Frank Murphy, though declining to define precisely the scope of the President's independent authority to act in emergencies or states of war, stated that:

> the Executive has powers not enumerated in the statutes – powers derived not from statutory grants but from the Constitution. It is universally recognized that the constitutional duties of the Executive carry with them the constitutional powers necessary for their proper performance. These constitutional powers have never been specifically defined, and in fact cannot be, since their extent and limitations are largely dependent upon conditions and circumstances.... The right to take specific action might not exist under one state of facts, while under another it might be the absolute duty of the Executive to take such action.

Request of the Senate for an Opinion as to the Powers of the President "In Emergency or State of War," 39 Op. Att'y Gen. 343, 347–48 (1939).

Attorney General Thomas Gregory opined in 1914 that "[i]n the preservation of the safety and integrity of the United States and the protection of its responsibilities and obligations as a sovereignty, [the President's] powers are broad." Censorship of Radio Stations, 30 Op. Att'y Gen. 291, 292 (1914).

Finally, in 1898, Acting Attorney General John K. Richards wrote:

> The preservation of our territorial integrity and the protection of our foreign interests is intrusted, in the first instance, to the President.... In the protection of these fundamental rights, which are based upon the Constitution and grow out of the jurisdiction of this nation over its own territory and its international rights and obligations as a distinct sovereignty, the President is not limited to the enforcement of specific acts of Congress. [The President] must preserve, protect, and defend those fundamental rights which flow from the Constitution itself and belong to the sovereignty it created.

Foreign Cables, 22 Op. Att'y Gen. 13, 25–26 (1898). Acting Attorney General Richards cited, among other judicial decisions, Cunningham v. Neagle, 135 U.S. 1, 64 (1890), in which the Supreme Court stated that the President's power to enforce the laws of the United States "include[s] the rights, duties and obligations growing out of the constitution itself, our international relations, and all the protection implied by the nature of the government under the constitution."

Opinions of the Office of Legal Counsel. Our Office has taken the position in recent Administrations, including those of Presidents Clinton, Bush, Reagan, Carter, and Nixon, that the President may unilaterally deploy military force in order to protect the national security and interests of the United States.

In 1995, we opined that the President "acting without specific statutory authorization, lawfully may introduce United States ground troops into Bosnia and Herzegovina ... to help the North Atlantic Treaty Organization ... ensure compliance with the recently negotiated peace agreement." *Proposed Deployment of United States Armed Forces in Bosnia and Herzegovina*, 19 Op. O.L.C. 327, 327 (1995) (the "Bosnia Opinion"). We interpreted the WPR to "lend[] support to the ... conclusion that the President has authority, without specific statutory authorization, to introduce troops into hostilities in a substantial range of circumstances." Id. at 335.

In *Deployment of United States Armed Forces into Haiti*, 18 Op. O.L.C. 173 (1994), we advised that the President had the authority unilaterally to deploy some 20,000 troops into Haiti. We relied in part on the structure of the WPR, which we argued "makes sense only if the President may introduce troops into hostilities or potential hostilities without prior authorization by the Congress." *Id.* at 175–76. We further argued that "in establishing and funding a military force that is capable of being projected anywhere around the globe, Congress has given the President, as Commander in Chief, considerable discretion in deciding how that force is to be deployed." *Id.* at 177. We also cited and relied upon the past practice of the executive branch in undertaking unilateral military interventions:

> In 1940, after the fall of Denmark to Germany, President Franklin Roosevelt ordered United States troops to occupy Greenland, a Danish possession in the North Atlantic of vital strategic interest to the United States.... Congress was not consulted or even directly informed.... Later, in 1941, the President ordered United States troops to occupy Iceland, an independent nation, pursuant to an agreement between himself and the Prime Minister of Iceland. The President relied upon his authority as Commander in Chief, and notified Congress only after the event.... More recently, in 1989, at the request of President Corazon Aquino, President Bush authorized military assistance to the Philippine government to suppress a coup attempt.

Id. at 178.

In *Authority to Use United States Military Forces in Somalia*, 16 Op. O.L.C. at 8, our Office advised that the President had the constitutional authority to deploy United States Armed Forces into Somalia in order to assist the United Nations in ensuring the safe delivery of relief to distressed areas of that country. We stated that "the President's role under our Constitution as Commander in Chief and Chief Executive vests him with the constitutional authority to order United States troops abroad to further national interests such as protecting the lives of Americans overseas." *Id.* at 8. Citing past practice (further discussed below), we pointed out that

> [f]rom the instructions of President Jefferson's Administration to Commodore Richard Dale in 1801 to 'chastise' Algiers and Tripoli if they continued to attack American shipping, to the present, Presidents have taken military initiatives abroad on the basis of their constitutional authority.... Against the background of this repeated past practice under many Presidents, this Department and this Office have concluded that the President has the power to commit United States troops abroad for the purpose of protecting important national interests.

Id. at 9 (citations omitted).

In *Overview of the War Powers Resolution*, 8 Op. O.L.C. 271, 275 (1984), we noted that "[t]he President's authority to deploy armed forces has been exercised in a broad range of circumstances [in] our history."

In *Presidential Power to Use the Armed Forces Abroad Without Statutory Authorization*, 4A Op. O.L.C. 185, 187 (1980), we stated that

> [o]ur history is replete with instances of presidential uses of military force abroad in the absence of prior congressional approval. This pattern of presidential initiative and congressional acquiescence may be said to reflect the implicit advantage held

by the executive over the legislature under our constitutional scheme in situations calling for immediate action. Thus, constitutional practice over two centuries, supported by the nature of the functions exercised and by the few legal benchmarks that exist, evidences the existence of broad constitutional power.

In light of that understanding, we advised that the President had independent constitutional authority unilaterally to order "(1) deployment abroad at some risk of engagement – for example, the current presence of the fleet in the Persian Gulf region; (2) a military expedition to rescue the hostages or to retaliate against Iran if the hostages are harmed; (3) an attempt to repel an assault that threatens our vital interests in that region." *Id.* at 185–86. See also *Presidential Powers Relating to the Situation in Iran*, 4A Op. O.L.C. 115, 121 (1979) ("It is well established that the President has the constitutional power as Chief Executive and Commander-in-Chief to protect the lives and property of Americans abroad. This understanding is reflected in judicial decisions... and recurring historic practice which goes back to the time of Jefferson.").

Finally, in the Rehnquist Memo at 8, we concluded that the President as Commander in Chief had the authority "to commit military forces of the United States to armed conflict... to protect the lives of American troops in the field."

Judicial Construction. Judicial decisions since the beginning of the Republic confirm the President's constitutional power and duty to repel military action against the United States through the use of force, and to take measures to deter the recurrence of an attack. As Justice Joseph Story said long ago, "[i]t may be fit and proper for the government, in the exercise of the high discretion confided to the executive, for great public purposes, to act on a sudden emergency, or to prevent an irreparable mischief, by summary measures, which are not found in the text of the laws." *The Apollon*, 22 U.S. (9 Wheat.) 362, 366–67 (1824). The Constitution entrusts the "power [to] the executive branch of the government to preserve order and insure the public safety in times of emergency, when other branches of the government are unable to function, or their functioning would itself threaten the public safety." *Duncan v. Kahanamoku*, 327 U.S. 304, 335 (1946) (Stone, C.J., concurring).

If the President is confronted with an unforeseen attack on the territory and people of the United States, or other immediate, dangerous threat to American interests and security, the courts have affirmed that it is his constitutional responsibility to respond to that threat with whatever means are necessary, including the use of military force abroad. *See, e.g., Prize Cases*, 67 U.S. at 635 ("If a war be made by invasion of a foreign nation, the President is not only authorized but bound to resist force by force... without waiting for any special legislative authority."); *Kahanamoku*, 327 U.S. at 336 (Stone, C.J., concurring) ("Executive has broad discretion in determining when the public emergency is such as to give rise to the necessity" for emergency measures); *United States v. Smith*, 27 F. Cas. 1192, 1230 (C.C.D.N.Y. 1806) (No. 16,342) (Paterson, Circuit Justice) (regardless of statutory authorization, it is "the duty... of the executive magistrate... to repel an invading foe")[12]; *Mitchell v. Laird*, 488 F.2d 611, 613 (D.C. Cir. 1973) ("there are some types of war which without Congressional approval, the President may begin to wage: for example, he may respond immediately without such

---

[12] Justice Paterson went on to remark that in those circumstances "it would I apprehend, be not only lawful for the president to resist such invasion, but also to carry hostilities into the enemy's own country." *Id.* at 1230.

approval to a belligerent attack")[13]; see also *Campbell v. Clinton*, 203 F.3d 19, 27 (D.C. Cir.) (Silberman, J. concurring) ("[T]he President has independent authority to repel aggressive acts by third parties even without specific statutory authorization."), *cert. denied*, 531 U.S. 815 (2000); id. at 40 (Tatel, J., concurring) ("[T]he President, as Commander in Chief, possesses emergency authority to use military force to defend the nation from attack without obtaining prior congressional approval."); Story, supra note 9, § 1485 ("[t]he command and application of the public force . . . to maintain peace, and to resist foreign invasion" are executive powers).

III

The historical practice of all three branches confirms the lessons of the constitutional text and structure. The normative role of historical practice in constitutional law, and especially with regard to separation of powers, is well settled.[14] Both the Supreme Court and the political branches have often recognized that governmental practice plays a highly significant role in establishing the contours of the constitutional separation of powers: "a systematic, unbroken, executive practice, long pursued to the knowledge of the Congress and never before questioned . . . may be treated as a gloss on 'executive Power' vested in the President by § 1 of Art. II." Youngstown Sheet & Tube Co., 343 U.S. at 610–11 (Frankfurter, J., concurring). Indeed, as the Court has observed, the role of practice in fixing the meaning of the separation of powers is implicit in the Constitution itself: "'the Constitution . . . contemplates that practice will integrate the dispersed powers into a workable government.'" *Mistretta v. United States*, 488 U.S. 361, 381 (1989) (citation omitted). In addition, governmental practice enjoys significant weight in constitutional analysis for practical reasons, on "the basis of a wise and quieting rule that, in determining . . . the existence of a power, weight shall be given to the usage itself – even when the validity of the practice is the subject of investigation." *United States v. Midwest Oil* Co., 236 U.S. 459, 473 (1915).

The role of practice is heightened in dealing with issues affecting foreign affairs and national security, where "the Court has been particularly willing to rely on the practical statesmanship of the political branches when considering constitutional questions." *Whether Uruguay Round Agreements Required Ratification as a Treaty*, 18 Op. O.L.C. 232, 234 (1994). "The persistence of these controversies (which trace back to the eighteenth century), and the nearly complete absence of judicial decisions resolving them, underscore the necessity of relying on congressional precedent to interpret

---

[13] The court further observed that "in a grave emergency [the President] may, without Congressional approval, take the initiative to wage war. . . . In such unusual situations necessity confers the requisite authority upon the President. Any other construction of the Constitution would make it self-destructive." Id. at 613–14. *Accord Massachusetts v. Laird*, 451 F.2d at 31 ("[t]he executive may without Congressional participation repel attack").

[14] As the Supreme Court has noted, "the decisions of the Court in th[e] area [of foreign affairs] have been rare, episodic, and afford little precedential value for subsequent cases." *Dames & Moore*, 453 U.S. at 661. In particular, the difficulty the courts experience in addressing "the broad range of vitally important day-to-day questions regularly decided by Congress or the Executive" with respect to foreign affairs and national security makes the judiciary "acutely aware of the necessity to rest [judicial] decision[s] on the narrowest possible ground capable of deciding the case." *Id.* at 660–61. Historical practice and the ongoing tradition of executive branch constitutional interpretation therefore play an especially important role in this area.

the relevant constitutional provisions." Id. at 236. Accordingly, we give considerable weight to the practice of the political branches in trying to determine the constitutional allocation of warmaking powers between them.

The historical record demonstrates that the power to initiate military hostilities, particularly in response to the threat of an armed attack, rests exclusively with the President. As the Supreme Court has observed, "[t]he United States frequently employs Armed Forces outside this country – over 200 times in our history – for the protection of American citizens or national security." *United States v. Verdugo-Urquidez*, 494 U.S. 259, 273 (1990). On at least 125 such occasions, the President acted without prior express authorization from Congress. See Bosnia Opinion, 19 Op. O.L.C. at 331. Such deployments, based on the President's constitutional authority alone, have occurred since the Administration of George Washington. See David P. Currie, *The Constitution in Congress: Substantive Issues in the First Congress, 1789–1791*, 61 U. Chi. L. Rev. 775, 816 (1994) ("[B]oth Secretary [of War] Knox and [President] Washington himself seemed to think that this [Commander in Chief] authority extended to offensive operations taken in retaliation for Indian atrocities.") (quoted in Bosnia Opinion, 19 Op. O.L.C. at 331 n.4. Perhaps the most significant deployment without specific statutory authorization took place at the time of the Korean War, when President Truman, without prior authorization from Congress, deployed United States troops in a war that lasted for over three years and caused over 142,000 American casualties. See Bosnia Opinion, 19 Op. O.L.C. at 331–32 n.5.

Recent deployments ordered solely on the basis of the President's constitutional authority have also been extremely large, representing a substantial commitment of the Nation's military personnel, diplomatic prestige, and financial resources. On at least one occasion, such a unilateral deployment has constituted full-scale war. On March 24, 1999, without any prior statutory authorization and in the absence of an attack on the United States, President Clinton ordered hostilities to be initiated against the Republic of Yugoslavia. The President informed Congress that, in the initial wave of air strikes, "United States and NATO forces have targeted the [Yugoslavian] government's integrated air defense system, military and security police command and control elements, and military and security police facilities and infrastructure.... I have taken these actions pursuant to my constitutional authority to conduct U.S. foreign relations and as Commander in Chief and Chief Executive." *Letter to Congressional leaders reporting on airstrikes against Serbian targets in the Federal Republic of Yugoslavia (Serbia and Montenegro)*, 1 Pub. Papers of William Jefferson Clinton 459, 459 (1999). Bombing attacks against targets in both Kosovo and Serbia ended on June 10, 1999, seventy-nine days after the war began. More than 30,000 United States military personnel participated in the operations; some 800 U.S. aircraft flew more than 20,000 sorties; more than 23,000 bombs and missiles were used. As part of the peace settlement, NATO deployed some 50,000 troops into Kosovo, 7,000 of them American.[15] In a News Briefing on June 10, 1999, Secretary of Defense William S.

---

[15] See *Campbell v. Clinton*, 203 F.3d at 40 (Tatel, J., concurring) (quoting testimony of Secretary of Defense Cohen that "'[w]e're certainly engaged in hostilities [in Yugoslavia], we're engaged in combat'"); Exec. Order No. 13119, 64 Fed. Reg. 18,797 (Apr. 16, 1999) (designating March 24, 1999, as "the date of the commencement of combatant activities" in Yugoslavia); John C. Yoo, *US Wars, US War Powers*, 1 Chi. J. Int'l L. 355 (2000).

Cohen summarized the effects of the campaign by saying,

> [t]hree months ago Yugoslavia was a heavily armed country with a significant air defense system. We reduced that defense system threat by destroying over 80 percent of Yugoslavia's modern aircraft fighters and strategic suface-to-air missiles. NATO destroyed a significant share of the infrastructure Yugoslavia used to support[] its military with, we reduced his capacity to make ammunition by two-thirds, and we eliminated all of its oil refining capacity and more than 40 percent of its military fuel supplies, Most important, we severely crippled the military forces in Kosovo by destroying more than 50 percent of the artillery and more than one-third of the armored vehicles.[16]

General Shelton of the Joint Chiefs of Staff reported that "about half of [Yugoslavia's] defense industry has either been damaged or destroyed. . . . [A]viation, 70 percent; armored vehicle production, 40 [percent]; petroleum refineries, 100 percent down; explosive production, about 50 percent; and 65 percent of his ammunition. . . . For the most part Belgrade is a city that's got about probably 70 percent without [electrical] power."[17] A report by General Ryan, Air Force Chief of Staff, on June 8, 1999, stated that

> Serbia's air force is essentially useless and its air defenses are dangerous but ineffective. Military armament production is destroyed. Military supply areas are under siege. Oil refinement has ceased and petroleum storage is systematically being destroyed. Electricity is sporadic, at best. Major transportation routes are cut. NATO aircraft are attacking with impunity throughout the country.[18]

Estimates near the time placed the number of Yugoslav military casualties at between five and ten thousand.[19] In recent decades, no President has unilaterally deployed so much force abroad.

   Other recent unilateral deployments have also been significant in military, foreign policy, and financial terms. Several such deployments occurred in the Balkans in the mid-1990s.[20] In December 1995, President Clinton ordered the deployment of 20,000 United States troops to Bosnia to implement a peace settlement. In February 1994, sixty United States warplanes conducted airstrikes against Yugoslav targets. In 1993, United States warplanes were sent to enforce a no-fly zone over Bosnia; in the same year, the President despatched United States troops to Macedonia as part of a United Nations peacekeeping operation.

   Major recent deployments have also taken place in Central America and in the Persian Gulf. In 1994, President Clinton ordered some 20,000 United States troops to be deployed into Haiti, again without prior statutory authorization from Congress, in reliance solely upon his Article II authority. *See Deployment of United States Armed Forces into Haiti, supra.* On August 8, 1990, in response to the Iraqi invasion of Kuwait and the consequent threat to Saudi Arabia, President Bush ordered the deployment

---

[16] *News Briefing, Office of the Assistant Secretary of Defense (Public Affairs),* June 10, 1999, available at http://www.defenselink.mil/news/Jun1999/t06101999_t0610asd.html (remarks of Sec. Cohen).
[17] *Id.* (remarks of Gen. Shelton).
[18] General Michael E. Ryan, *It may take time,* but it's inevitable, Air Force News (released June 8, 1999).
[19] See Nick Cook, *War of Extremes, in Jane's Defence Weekly* (July 7, 1999), *available* at http://www.janes.com/defense/news/kosovo/jdw990707_01_n.shtml.
[20] See Yoo, *supra* n.15, at 359.

of substantial forces into Saudi Arabia in Operation Desert Shield. The forces were equipped for combat and included two squadrons of F-15 aircraft and a brigade of the 82d Airborne Division; the deployment eventually grew to several hundred thousand. The President informed Congress that he had taken these actions "pursuant to my constitutional authority to conduct our foreign relations and as Commander in Chief." *Letter to Congressional Leaders*, 2 *Pub. Papers of George Bush* 1116 (1990). President Bush also deployed some 15,000 troops into Panama in December, 1990, for the purpose (among others) of protecting Americans living in Panama. See 2 Pub. Papers of George Bush 1722 (1989); see generally Abraham D. Sofaer, *The Legality of the United States Action in Panama*, 29 Colum. J. Transnat'l L. 281 (1991).

Further, when Congress has in fact authorized deployments of troops in hostilities, past Presidents have taken the position that such legislation, although welcome, was not constitutionally necessary. For example, in signing Pub. L. No. 102-01, 105 Stat. 3 (1991), authorizing the use of military force in Operation Desert Storm against Iraq, President Bush stated that "my request for congressional support did not, and my signing this resolution does not, constitute any change in the longstanding positions of the executive branch on either the President's constitutional authority to use the Armed Forces to defend vital U.S. interests or the constitutionality of the War Powers Resolution." *Statement on Signing the Resolution Authorizing the Use of Military Force Against Iraq*, 1 Pub. *Papers of George Bush* 40 (1991).[21] Similarly, President John F. Kennedy stated on September 13, 1962, that congressional authorization for a naval blockade of Cuba was unnecessary, maintaining that "I have full authority now to take such action." *Pub. Papers of John F. Kennedy* 674 (1962). And in a Report to the American People on October 22, 1962, President Kennedy asserted that he had ordered the blockade "under the authority entrusted to me by the Constitution *as endorsed* by the resolution of the Congress." *Id.* at 807 (emphasis added).[22] Thus, there is abundant precedent, much of it from recent Administrations, for the deployment of military force abroad, including the waging of war, on the basis of the President's sole constitutional authority.

Several recent precedents stand out as particularly relevant to the situation at hand, where the conflict is with terrorists. The first and most relevant precedent is also the most recent: the military actions that President William J. Clinton ordered on August 20, 1998, against terrorist sites in Afghanistan and Sudan. The second is the strike on Iraqi Intelligence Headquarters that President Clinton ordered on June 26, 1993. The third is President Ronald Reagan's action on April 14, 1986, ordering United States armed forces to attack selected targets at Tripoli and Benghazi, Libya.

---

[21] Further, in a press conference on January 9, 1991, President Bush was asked if he believed that he needed congressional authorization in order to begin offensive operations against Iraq. He answered, "I don't think I need it. I think Secretary Cheney expressed it very well the other day. There are different opinions on either side of this question, but Saddam Hussein should be under no question on this: I feel that I have the authority to fully implement the United Nations resolutions." *The President's News Conference on the Persian Gulf Crisis*, 1 Pub. *Papers of George Bush* 17, 20 (1991).

[22] An unsigned, unaddressed opinion in this Office's files, entitled *Blockade of Cuba* (Oct. 19, 1962), states that "the President, in the exercise of his constitutional power as Commander-in-Chief, can order a blockade without prior Congressional sanction and without a declaration of war by Congress." *Id.* at 9. Thus, the writers of the memorandum (presumably, either this Office or the State Department Legal Adviser's Office) determined that no Congressional authorization either existed or was necessary for the blockade ordered by President Kennedy.

(A) On August 20, 1998, President Clinton ordered the Armed Forces to strike at terrorist-related facilities in Afghanistan and Sudan "because of the threat they present to our national security." *Remarks in Martha's Vineyard, Massachusetts, on Military Action Against Terrorist Sites in Afghanistan and Sudan, 2 Pub. Papers of William J. Clinton* 1460 (1998). The President stated that the purpose of the operation was "to strike at the network of radical groups affiliated with and funded by Usama bin Ladin, perhaps the preeminent organizer and financier of international terrorism in the world today." Address to the Nation on Military Action Against Terrorist Sites in Afghanistan and Sudan, 2 Pub. Papers of William J. Clinton 1460 (1998). The strike was ordered in retaliation for the bombings of United States Embassies in Kenya and Tanzania, in which bin Laden's organization and groups affiliated with it were believed to have played a key role and which had caused the deaths of some 12 Americans and nearly 300 Kenyans and Tanzanians, and in order to deter later terrorist attacks of a similar kind against United States nationals and others. In his remarks at Martha's Vineyard, President Clinton justified the operation as follows:

> I ordered this action for four reasons: first, because we have convincing evidence these groups played the key role in the Embassy bombings in Kenya and Tanzania; second, because these groups have executed terrorist attacks against Americans in the past; third, because we have compelling information that they were planning additional terrorist attacks against our citizens and others with the inevitable collateral casualties we saw so tragically in Africa; and fourth, because they are seeking to acquire chemical weapons and other dangerous weapons.

Id. In his *Address* to the *Nation* on the same day, the President made clear that the strikes were aimed, not only at bin Laden's organization, but at other terrorist groups thought to be affiliated with it, and that the strikes were intended as retribution for other incidents caused by these groups, and not merely the then-recent bombings of the two United States embassies. Referring to the past acts of the interlinked terrorist groups, he stated:

> Their mission is murder and their history is bloody. In recent years, they killed American, Belgian, and Pakistani peacekeepers in Somalia. They plotted to assassinate the President of Egypt and the Pope. They planned to bomb six United States 747's over the Pacific. They bombed the Egyptian Embassy in Pakistan. They gunned down German tourists in Egypt.

Id. at 1460–61. Furthermore, in explaining why military action was necessary, the President noted that "law enforcement and diplomatic tools" to combat terrorism had proved insufficient, and that "when our very national security is challenged . . . we must take extraordinary steps to protect the safety of our citizens." *Id.* at 1461. Finally, the President made plain that the action of the two targeted countries in harboring terrorists justified the use of military force on their territory: "The United States does not take this action lightly. Afghanistan and Sudan have been warned for years to stop harboring and supporting these terrorist groups. But countries that persistently host terrorists have no right to be safe havens." *Id.*

The terrorist incidents of September 11, 2001, were surely far graver a threat to the national security of the United States than the 1998 attacks on our embassies (however appalling those events were). The President's power to respond militarily to the later attacks must be correspondingly broader. Nonetheless, President Clinton's action in 1998 illustrates some of the breadth of the President's power to act in the present circumstances.

First, President Clinton justified the targeting of particular groups on the basis of what he characterized as "convincing" evidence of their involvement in the embassy attacks. While that is not a standard of proof appropriate for a criminal trial, it is entirely appropriate for military and political decisionmaking. Second, the President targeted not merely one particular group or leader, but a network of affiliated groups. Moreover, he ordered the action, not only because of particular attacks on United States embassies, but because of a pattern of terrorist activity, aimed at both Americans and non-Americans, that had unfolded over several years. Third, the President explained that the military action was designed to deter future terrorist incidents, not only to punish past ones. Fourth, the President specifically justified military action on the territory of two foreign states because their governments had "harbor[ed]" and "support[ed]" terrorist groups for years, despite warnings from the United States.

(B) On June 26, 1993, President Clinton ordered a Tomahawk cruise missile strike on Iraqi Intelligence Service (the "IIS") headquarters in Baghdad. The IIS had planned an unsuccessful attempt to assassinate former President Bush in Kuwait in April, 1993. Two United States Navy surface ships launched a total of 23 missiles against the IIS center.

In a *Letter to Congressional Leaders on the Strike on Iraqi Intelligence Headquarters*, 1 *Pub. Papers of William J. Clinton* 940 (1993), the President referred to the failed assassination attempt and stated that "[t]he evidence of the Government of Iraq's violence and terrorism demonstrates that Iraq poses a continuing threat to United States nationals." He based his authority to order a strike against the Iraqi government's intelligence command center on "my constitutional authority with respect to the conduct of foreign relations and as Commander in Chief," as well as on the Nation's inherent right of self-defense. Id.

President Clinton's order was designed in part to deter and prevent future terrorist attacks on the United States – and most particularly future assassination attempts on former President Bush. Although the assassination attempt had been frustrated by the arrest of sixteen suspects before any harm was done, "nothing prevented Iraq from directing a second – possibly successful – attempt on Bush's life. Thus, the possibility of another assassination plot was 'hanging threateningly over [Bush's] head' and was therefore imminent. By attacking the Iraqi Intelligence Service, the United States hoped to prevent and deter future attempts to kill Bush."[23]

(C) On April 14, 1986, President Ronald Reagan, acting on his independent authority, ordered United States armed forces to engage in military action against the government of Colonel Gadhafi of Libya.[24] Thirty-two American aircraft attacked selected targets at Tripoli and Benghazi, Libya. Libyan officials reported thirty-seven people killed and an undetermined number injured. More than sixty tons of ordnance were used during the attack.

---

[23] Robert F. Teplitz, *Taking Assassination Attempts Seriously: Did the United States Violate International Law in Forcefully Responding to the Iraqi Plot to Kill George Bush?*, 28 Cornell Int'l L. J. 569, 609 (1995) (citation omitted).

[24] *See generally* Wallace F. Warriner, U.S.M.C., *The Unilateral Use of Coercion Under International Law: A Legal Analysis of the United States Raid on Libya on April 14, 1986*, 37 Naval L. Rev. 49 (1988); Teplitz, supra n.23, at 583–86.

For some time Libya had supported terrorist groups and organizations and indeed had itself ordered direct terrorist attacks on the United States.

> Under Gaddafi, Libya has declared its support of 'national liberation movements' and has allegedly financed and trained numerous terrorist groups and organizations, including Palestinian radicals, Lebanese leftists, Columbia's M-19 guerrillas, the Irish Republican Army, anti-Turkish Armenians, the Sandinistas in Nicaragua, Muslim rebels in the Philippines, and left-wing extremists in Europe and Japan.[25]

It had harbored a variety of terrorists, including Abu Nidal and the three surviving members of the Black September group that had killed eleven Israeli athletes at the 1972 Munich Olympic Games.[26] Libya's attacks on the United States included the murder of two United States diplomats in Khartoum (1973), the attempted assassination of Secretary of State Kissinger (1973), the burning of the United States Embassy in Tripoli (1979), the planned assassination of President Reagan, Secretary of State Haig, Secretary of Defense Weinberger, and Ambassador to Italy Robb (1981), and the hijacking of T.W.A. flight 847 (1985).[27] Libya had also been linked to terrorist events close to the time of the April, 1986, airstrike in which Americans and other had lost their lives. In January, 1986, American intelligence tied Libya to the December 27, 1985, bombings at the Rome and Vienna airports in which nineteen people, including 5 Americans, had died, and one hundred and twelve persons had been injured.

The particular event that triggered the President's military action had occurred on April 5, 1986, when a bomb exploded in the "Labelle," a Berlin discotheque frequented by U.S. military personnel. The blast killed three people (two Americans) and injured two hundred and thirty others (including seventy-nine Americans). Intelligence reports indicated that the bombing was planned and executed under the direct orders of the Government of Libya. The United States Ambassador to the United Nations stated that there was "direct, precise, and irrefutable evidence that Libya bears responsibility" for the bombing of the discotheque; that the "Labelle" incident was "only the latest in an ongoing pattern of attacks" by Libya against the United States and its allies; and that the United States had made "repeated and protracted efforts to deter Libya from its ongoing attacks," including "quiet diplomacy, public condemnation, economic sanctions, and demonstrations of military force." U.N. SCOR, 2674th mtg. at 16–17, U.N. Doc. S/PV.2674 (prov. ed. 1986).

Like the two unilateral Presidential actions discussed above, President Reagan's decision to use armed force in response to a terrorist attack on United States military personnel illustrates that the President has independent constitutional authority to use such force in the present circumstances.

IV

Our analysis to this point has surveyed the views and practice of the executive and judicial branches. In two enactments, the War Powers Resolution and the recent Joint Resolution, Congress has also addressed the scope of the President's independent constitutional authority. We think these two statutes demonstrate Congress's acceptance

[25] Teplitz, *supra* n.23, at 617 n.112.
[26] *See id.*
[27] *See id.* at n.113.

of the President's unilateral war powers in an emergency situation like that created by the September 11 incidents.

Furthermore, the President can be said to be acting at the apogee of his powers if he deploys military force in the present situation, for he is operating both under his own Article II authority and with the legislative support of Congress. Under the analysis outlined by Justice Jackson in *Youngstown Sheet & Tube Co., supra* (and later followed and interpreted by the Court in Dames & Moore, supra), the President's power in this case would be "at its maximum," 343 U.S. at 635 (Jackson, J., concurring), because the President would be acting pursuant to an express congressional authorization. He would thus be clothed with "all [authority] that he possesses in his own right plus all that Congress can delegate," id., in addition to his own broad powers in foreign affairs under Article II of the Constitution.

The War Powers Resolution. Section 2(c) of the WPR, reads as follows:

> The constitutional powers of the President as Commander-in-Chief to introduce United States Armed Forces into hostilities, or into situations where imminent involvement in hostilities is clearly indicated by the circumstances, are exercised only pursuant to (1) a declaration of war, (2) specific statutory authorization, or (3) *a national emergency created by attack upon the United States, its territories or possessions, or its armed forces*.

50 U.S.C. § 1541(c) (emphasis added).

The executive branch consistently "has taken the position from the very beginning that section 2(c) of the WPR does not constitute a legally binding definition of Presidential authority to deploy our armed forces." *Overview of the War Powers Resolution*, 8 Op. O.L.C. at 274.[28] Moreover, as our Office has noted, "even the defenders of the WPR concede that this declaration [in section 2(c)] – found in the 'Purpose and Policy' section of the WPR – either is incomplete or is not meant to be binding." *Deployment of United States Armed Forces into Haiti*, 18 Op. O.L.C. at 176; accord Bosnia Opinion, 19 Op. O.L.C. at 335 ("The executive branch has traditionally taken the position that the President's power to deploy armed forces into situations of actual or indicated hostilities is not restricted to the three categories specifically marked out by the Resolution."); *Presidential Powers Relating to the Situation in Iran*, 4A Op. O.L.C. at 121 ("[T]he Resolution's policy statement is not a comprehensive or binding formulation of the President's powers as Commander-in-Chief."). Nonetheless, section 2(c)(3) correctly identifies *one*, but by no means the only, Presidential authority to deploy military forces into hostilities.[29] In the present circumstances, the statute signifies Congress's recognition that the President's constitutional authority alone would enable him to take military measures to combat the organizations or

---

[28] Thus, the State Department took the view, in a letter of November 30, 1974, that section 2(c) was a "declaratory statement of policy." Further, in 1975, the Legal Adviser to the State Department listed six (non-exclusive) situations, not enumerated in section 2(c), in which the President had independent constitutional authority to deploy troops without either a declaration of war or specific statutory authorization. *See id.* at 274–75.

[29] We note that section 2(c) cannot itself qualify as a statutory authorization to act in national emergencies. It is rather a congressional acknowledgment of the President's *non*statutory, Article II-based powers. Section 8(d)(2) of the WPR, 50 U.S.C. § 1547, specifically provides that nothing in the WPR "shall be construed as granting any authority to the President . . . which authority he would not have had in the absence of this [joint resolution]."

groups responsible for the September 11 incidents, together with any governments that may have harbored or supported them.

Further, Congress's support for the President's power suggests no limits on the Executive's judgment whether to use military force in response to the national emergency created by those incidents. Section 2(c)(3) leaves undisturbed the President's constitutional authority to determine both when a "national emergency" arising out of an "attack against the United States" exists, and what types and levels of force are necessary or appropriate to respond to that emergency. Because the statute itself supplies no definition of these terms, their interpretation must depend on longstanding constitutional practices and understandings. As we have shown in Parts I–III of this memorandum, constitutional text, structure and practice demonstrate that the President is vested with the plenary power to use military force, especially in the case of a direct attack on the United States. Section 2(c)(3) recognizes the President's broad authority and discretion in this area.

Given the President's constitutional powers to respond to national emergencies caused by attacks on the United States, and given also that section 2(c)(3) of the WPR does not attempt to define those powers, we think that that provision must be construed simply as a recognition of, and support for, the President's pre-existing constitutional authority. Moreover, as we read the WPR, action taken by the President pursuant to the constitutional authority recognized in section 2(c)(3) cannot be subject to the substantive requirements of the WPR, particularly the interrelated reporting requirements in section 4 and the "cut off" provisions of section 5, 50 U.S.C. §§ 1543–1544.[30] Insofar as the Constitution vests the power in the President to take military action in the emergency circumstances described by section 2(c)(3), we do not think it can be restricted by Congress through, e.g., a requirement that the President either obtain congressional authorization for the action within a specific time frame, or else discontinue the action. Were this not so, the President could find himself unable to respond to an emergency that outlasted a statutory cut-off, merely because Congress had failed, for whatever reason, to enact authorizing legislation within that period.

To be sure, some interpreters of the WPR take a broader view of its scope. But on *any* reasonable interpretation of that statute, it must reflect an explicit understanding, shared by both the Executive and Congress, that the President may take *some* military actions – including involvement in hostilities – in response to emergencies caused by attacks on the United States. Thus, while there might be room for disagreement about the scope and duration of the President's emergency powers, there can be no reasonable doubt as to their existence.

The Joint Resolution of September 14, 2001. Whatever view one may take of the meaning of section 2(c)(3) of the WPR, we think it clear that Congress, in enacting the "Joint Resolution [t]o authorize the use of United States Armed Forces against those responsible for the recent attacks launched against the United States," Pub. L. No. 107–40, 115 Stat. 224 (2001), has confirmed that the President has broad

---

[30] True, the reporting requirement in section 4(a)(1) purports to apply to any case in which U.S. armed forces are introduced into hostilities "[i]n the absence of a declaration of war." 50 U.S.C. § 1543(a)(1). Further, the "cut off" provisions of section 5 are triggered by the report required by section 4(a)(1). Thus, the language of the WPR indicates an intent to reach action taken by the President pursuant to the authority recognized in section 2(c)(3), if no declaration of war has been issued. We think, however, that it would be beyond Congress's power to regulate the President's emergency authority in the manner prescribed by sections 4(a)(1) and 5.

constitutional authority to respond, by military means or otherwise, to the incidents of September 11.

First, the findings in the Joint Resolution include an express statement that "the President has authority under the Constitution to take action to deter and prevent acts of international terrorism against the United States." Id. This authority is in addition to the President's authority to respond to past acts of terrorism. In including this statement, Congress has provided its explicit agreement with the executive branch's consistent position, as articulated in Parts I–III of this memorandum, that the President has the plenary power to use force even before an attack upon the United States actually occurs, against targets and using methods of his own choosing.

Second, Congress also found that there is a "threat to the national security and foreign policy of the United States posed by the[] grave acts of violence" on September 11, and that "such acts continue to pose an unusual and extraordinary threat to the national security and foreign policy" of this country. Insofar as "the President's independent power to act depends upon the gravity of the situation confronting the nation," *Youngstown Sheet & Tube Co.*, 343 U.S. at 662 (Clark, J., concurring in judgment), these findings would support any presidential determination that the September 11 attacks justified the use of military force in response. Further, they would buttress any Presidential determination that the nation is in a state of emergency caused by those attacks. The Constitution confides in the President the authority, independent of any statute, to determine when a "national emergency" caused by an attack on the United States exists.[31] Nonetheless, congressional concurrence is welcome in making clear that the branches agree on seriousness of the terrorist threat currently facing the Nation and on the justifiability of a military response.

Third, it should be noted here that the Joint Resolution is somewhat narrower than the President's constitutional authority. The Joint Resolution's authorization to use force is limited only to those individuals, groups, or states that planned, authorized, committed, or aided the attacks, and those nations that harbored them. It does not, therefore, reach other terrorist individuals, groups, or states, which cannot be determined to have links to the September 11 attacks. Nonetheless, the President's broad constitutional power to use military force to defend the Nation, recognized by the Joint Resolution itself, would allow the President to take whatever actions he deems appropriate to pre-empt or respond to terrorist threats from new quarters.

Conclusion

In light of the text, plan, and history of the Constitution, its interpretation by both past Administrations and the courts, the longstanding practice of the executive branch, and the express affirmation of the President's constitutional authorities by Congress, we

---

[31] *See Prize Cases*, 67 U.S. at 670 (whether a state of belligerency justifying a blockade exists is to be decided by the President); see also *Sterling v. Constantin*, 287 U.S. 378, 399 (1932) ("By virtue of his duty to 'cause the laws to be faithfully executed', the Executive is appropriately vested with the discretion to determine whether an exigency requiring military aid for that purpose has arisen."); *Moyer v. Peabody*, 212 U.S. 78, 83 (1909) ("[T]he governor's declaration that a state of insurrection existed is conclusive of that fact."); *Campbell*, 203 F.3d at 26–27 (Silberman, J., concurring) (The Court in the Prize Cases "made clear that it would not dispute the President on measures necessary to repel foreign aggression"); cf. *Martin v. Mott*, 25 U.S. (12 Wheat.) 19, 30 (1827) (President had unreviewable discretion to determine when "emergency" existed under statute enabling him to call up militia).

think it beyond question that the President has the plenary constitutional power to take such military actions as he deems necessary and appropriate to respond to the terrorist attacks upon the United States on September 11, 2001. Force can be used both to retaliate for those attacks, and to prevent and deter future assaults on the Nation. Military actions need not be limited to those individuals, groups, or states that participated in the attacks on the World Trade Center and the Pentagon: the Constitution vests the President with the power to strike terrorist groups or organizations that cannot be demonstrably linked to the September 11 incidents, but that, nonetheless, pose a similar threat to the security of the United States and the lives of its people, whether at home or overseas.[32] In both the War Powers Resolution and the Joint Resolution, Congress has recognized the President's authority to use force in circumstances such as those created by the September 11 incidents. Neither statute, however, can place any limits on the President's determinations as to any terrorist threat, the amount of military force to be used in response, or the method, timing, and nature of the response. These decisions, under our Constitution, are for the President alone to make.

JOHN C. YOO
Deputy Assistant Attorney General
Office of Legal Counsel

---

[32] We of course understand that terrorist organizations and their state sponsors operate by secrecy and concealment, and that it is correspondingly difficult to establish, by the standards of criminal law or even lower legal standards, that particular individuals or groups have been or may be implicated in attacks on the United States. Moreover, even when evidence sufficient to establish involvement is available to the President, it may be impossible for him to disclose that evidence without compromising classified methods and sources, and so damaging the security of the United States. See, e.g., *Chicago & Southern Air Lines, Inc*, 333 U.S. at 111 ("The President . . . has available intelligence services whose reports are not and ought not to be published to the world."); see also Ruth Wedgwood, *Responding to Terrorism: The Strikes Against Bin Laden*, 24 Yale J. Int'l L. 559, 568–74 (1999) (analyzing difficulties of establishing and publicizing evidence of causation of terrorist incidents). But we do not think that the difficulty or impossibility of establishing proof to a criminal law standard (or of making evidence public) bars the President from taking such military measures as, in his best judgment, he thinks necessary or appropriate to defend the United States from terrorist attacks. In the exercise of his plenary power to use military force, the President's decisions are for him alone and are unreviewabl.

EXECUTIVE ORDERS

Federal Register: November 16, 2001
(Volume 66, Number 2)
Presidential Documents
Page 57831–57836

Military Order of November 13, 2001

Detention, Treatment, and Trial of Certain Non-Citizens in the War Against Terrorism

By the authority vested in me as President and as Commander in Chief of the Armed Forces of the United States by the Constitution and the laws of the United States of America, including the Authorization for Use of Military Force Joint Resolution (Public Law 107-40, 115 Stat. 224) and sections 821 and 836 of title 10, United States Code, it is hereby ordered as follows:

I. Findings

(a) International terrorists, including members of al Qaida, have carried out attacks on United States diplomatic and military personnel and facilities abroad and on citizens and property within the United States on a scale that has created a state of armed conflict that requires the use of the United States Armed Forces.

(b) In light of grave acts of terrorism and threats of terrorism, including the terrorist attacks on September 11, 2001, on the headquarters of the United States Department of Defense in the national capital region, on the World Trade Center in New York, and on civilian aircraft such as in Pennsylvania, I proclaimed a national emergency on September 14, 2001 (Proc. 7463, Declaration of National Emergency by Reason of Certain Terrorist Attacks).

(c) Individuals acting alone and in concert involved in international terrorism possess both the capability and the intention to undertake further terrorist attacks against the United States that, if not detected and prevented, will cause mass deaths, mass injuries, and massive destruction of property, and may place at risk the continuity of the operations of the United States Government.

(d) The ability of the United States to protect the United States and its citizens, and to help its allies and other cooperating nations protect their nations and their citizens, from such further terrorist attacks depends in significant part upon using the United States Armed Forces to identify terrorists and those who support them, to disrupt their activities, and to eliminate their ability to conduct or support such attacks.

(e) To protect the United States and its citizens, and for the effective conduct of military operations and prevention of terrorist attacks, it is necessary for individuals subject to this order pursuant to section 2 hereof to be detained, and, when tried, to be tried for violations of the laws of war and other applicable laws by military tribunals.

(f) Given the danger to the safety of the United States and the nature of international terrorism, and to the extent provided by and under this order, I find consistent with section 836 of title 10, United States Code, that it is not practicable to apply in military commissions under this order the principles of law and the rules of evidence generally recognized in the trial of criminal cases in the United States district courts.

(g) Having fully considered the magnitude of the potential deaths, injuries, and property destruction that would result from potential acts of terrorism against the United States, and the probability that such acts will occur, I have determined that an extraordinary emergency exists for national defense purposes, that this emergency constitutes an urgent and compelling government interest, and that issuance of this order is necessary to meet the emergency.

II. Definition and Policy

a. The term "individual subject to this order" shall mean any individual who is not a United States citizen with respect to whom I determine from time to time in writing that:

    (1) there is reason to believe that such individual, at the relevant times,

        i. is or was a member of the organization known as al Qaida;

        ii. has engaged in, aided or abetted, or conspired to commit, acts of international terrorism, or acts in preparation therefor, that have caused, threaten to cause, or have as their aim to cause, injury to or adverse effects on the United States, its citizens, national security, foreign policy, or economy; or

        iii. has knowingly harbored one or more individuals described in subparagraphs (i) or (ii) of subsection 2(a)(l) of this order; and

    (2) it is in the interest of the United States that such individual be subject to this order.

b. It is the policy of the United States that the Secretary of Defense shall take all necessary measures to ensure that any individual subject to this order is detained in accordance with section 3, and, if the individual is to be tried, that such individual is tried only in accordance with section 4.

c. It is further the policy of the United States that any individual subject to this order who is not already under the control of the Secretary of Defense but who is under the control of any other officer or agent of the United States or any State shall, upon delivery of a copy of such written determination to such officer or agent, forthwith be placed under the control of the Secretary of Defense.

III. Detention Authority of the Secretary of Defense

Any individual subject to this order shall be –

(a) detained at an appropriate location designated by the Secretary of Defense outside or within the United States;

(b) treated humanely, without any adverse distinction based on race, color, religion, gender, birth, wealth, or any similar criteria;

(c) afforded adequate food, drinking water, shelter, clothing, and medical treatment;

(d) allowed the free exercise of religion consistent with the requirements of such detention; and

(e) detained in accordance with such other conditions as the Secretary of Defense may prescribe.

IV. Authority of the Secretary of Defense Regarding Trials of Individuals Subject to this Order

a. Any individual subject to this order shall, when tried, be tried by military commission for any and all offenses triable by military commission that such individual is alleged to have committed, and may be punished in accordance with the penalties provided under applicable law, including life imprisonment or death.

b. As a military function and in light of the findings in section 1, including subsection (f) thereof, the Secretary of Defense shall issue such orders and regulations, including orders for the appointment of one or more military commissions, as may be necessary to carry out subsection (a) of this section.

c. Orders and regulations issued under subsection (b) of this section shall include, but not be limited to, rules for the conduct of the proceedings of military commissions, including pretrial, trial, and post-trial procedures, modes of proof, issuance of process, and qualifications of attorneys, which shall at a minimum provide for–

(1) military commissions to sit at any time and any place, consistent with such guidance regarding time and place as the Secretary of Defense may provide;

(2) a full and fair trial, with the military commission sitting as the triers of both fact and law;

(3) admission of such evidence as would, in the opinion of the presiding officer of the military commission (or instead, if any other member of the commission so requests at the time the presiding officer renders that opinion, the opinion of the commission rendered at that time by a majority of the commission), have probative value to a reasonable person;

(4) in a manner consistent with the protection of information classified or classifiable under Executive Order 12958 of April 17, 1995, as amended, or any successor Executive Order, protected by statute or rule from unauthorized disclosure, or otherwise protected by law, (A) the handling of, admission into evidence of, and access to materials and information, and (B) the conduct, closure of, and access to proceedings;

(5) conduct of the prosecution by one or more attorneys designated by the Secretary of Defense and conduct of the defense by attorneys for the individual subject to this order;

(6) conviction only upon the concurrence of two-thirds of the members of the commission present at the time of the vote, a majority being present;

(7) sentencing only upon the concurrence of two-thirds of the members of the commission present at the time of the vote, a majority being present; and

(8) submission of the record of the trial, including any conviction or sentence, for review and final decision by me or by the Secretary of Defense if so designated by me for that purpose.

V. Obligation of Other Agencies to Assist the Secretary of Defense

Departments, agencies, entities, and officers of the United States shall, to the maximum extent permitted by law, provide to the Secretary of Defense such assistance as he may request to implement this order.

VI. Additional Authorities of the Secretary of Defense

(a) As a military function and in light of the findings in section 1, the Secretary of Defense shall issue such orders and regulations as may be necessary to carry out any of the provisions of this order.

(b) The Secretary of Defense may perform any of his functions or duties, and may exercise any of the powers provided to him under this order (other than under section 4(c)(8) hereof) in accordance with section 113(d) of title 10, United States Code.

VII. Relationship to Other Law and Forums

a. Nothing in this order shall be construed to–
(1) authorize the disclosure of state secrets to any person not otherwise authorized to have access to them;
(2) limit the authority of the President as Commander in Chief of the Armed Forces or the power of the President to grant reprieves and pardons; or
(3) limit the lawful authority of the Secretary of Defense, any military commander, or any other officer or agent of the United States or of any State to detain or try any person who is not an individual subject to this order.

b. With respect to any individual subject to this order–
(1) military tribunals shall have exclusive jurisdiction with respect to offenses by the individual; and
(2) the individual shall not be privileged to seek any remedy or maintain any proceeding, directly or indirectly, or to have any such remedy or proceeding sought on the individual's behalf, in (i) any court of the United States, or any State thereof, (ii) any court of any foreign nation, or (iii) any international tribunal.

c. This order is not intended to and does not create any right, benefit, or privilege, substantive or procedural, enforceable at law or equity by any party, against the United States, its departments, agencies, or other entities, its officers or employees, or any other person.

d. For purposes of this order, the term "State" includes any State, district, territory, or possession of the United States.

e. I reserve the authority to direct the Secretary of Defense, at any time hereafter, to transfer to a governmental authority control of any individual subject to this order. Nothing in this order shall be construed to limit the authority of any such governmental authority to prosecute any individual for whom control is transferred.

VIII. Publication

This order shall be published in the Federal Register.
    GEORGE W. BUSH
    THE WHITE HOUSE,
    November 13, 2001.

U.S. Department of Justice

Office of Legal Counsel

Office of the Deputy Assistant Attorney General   *Washington, D.C. 20530*

December 28, 2001

MEMORANDUM FOR WILLIAM J. HAYNES, II
   GENERAL COUNSEL, DEPARTMENT OF DEFENSE

FROM: Patrick F. Philbin
               Deputy Assistant Attorney General

               John C. Yoo
               Deputy Assistant Attorney General

RE: *Possible Habeas Jurisdiction over Aliens Held in Guantanamo Bay, Cuba*

This memorandum addresses the question whether a federal district court would properly have jurisdiction to entertain a petition for a writ of habeas corpus filed on behalf of an alien detained at the U.S. naval base at Guantanamo Bay, Cuba ("GBC"). This question has arisen because of proposals to detain al Qaeda and Taliban members at GBC pending possible trial by military commission. If a federal district court were to take jurisdiction over a habeas petition, it could review the constitutionality of the detention and the use of a military commission, the application of certain treaty provisions, and perhaps even the legal status of al Qaeda and Taliban members.

We conclude that the great weight of legal authority indicates that a federal district court could not properly exercise habeas jurisdiction over an alien detained at GBC. Nonetheless, we cannot say with absolute certainty that any such petition would be dismissed for lack of jurisdiction. A detainee could make a non-frivolous argument that jurisdiction does exist over aliens detained at GBC, and we have found no decisions that clearly foreclose the existence of habeas jurisdiction there. On the other hand, it does not appear that any federal court has allowed a habeas petition to proceed from GBC, either. While we believe that the correct answer is that federal courts lack jurisdiction over habeas petitions filed by alien detainees held outside the sovereign territory of the United States, there remains some litigation risk that a district court might reach the opposite result.

I

The basis for denying jurisdiction to entertain a habeas petition filed by an alien held at GBC rests on *Johnson v. Eisentrager*, 339 U.S. 763 (1950). In that case, the Supreme Court held that federal courts did not have authority to entertain an application for habeas relief filed by an enemy alien who had been seized and held at all relevant times outside the territory of the United States. *See Id.* at 768–78. *Eisentrager* involved ... German ... aid the Japanese in China after Germany had surrendered in April 1945. They were seized, tried by military commission in Nanking, China and subsequently imprisoned in Germany. From there, they filed an application for habeas corpus in the District Court for the District of Columbia, naming as respondents the Secretary of Defense, Secretary of the Army, and the Joint Chiefs of Staff. *Id.* at 766–67. The Court concluded that the federal courts were without power to grant habeas relief because the plaintiffs were beyond the territorial sovereignty of the United States and outside the territorial jurisdiction of any U.S. court. As the Court explained:

> We have pointed out that the privilege of litigation has been extended to aliens, whether friendly or enemy, only because permitting their presence in the country implied protection. No such basis can be invoked here, for these prisoners at no relevant time were within any territory over which the United States is sovereign, and the scenes of their offense, their capture, their trial and their punishment were all beyond the territorial jurisdiction of any court of the United States.

Id. at 777–78.[1]

The Court seemed to acknowledge tacitly that the habeas application could fall within the literal terms of the federal statute defining the power of federal courts to grant habeas corpus relief. Then, as now, the statute did not expressly restrict the jurisdiction of courts to issue the writ solely to situations where a prisoner was held within the territorial jurisdiction of the court. Instead, the statute states simply that courts may grant the writ "within their respective jurisdictions." *See* 28 U.S.C. §2241 (1994) ("Writs of habeas corpus may be granted by the Supreme Court, any justice thereof, the district courts and any circuit judge within their respective jurisdictions."). It has been held sufficient for jurisdiction to grant the writ if a person with authority over the custody of the prisoner is within the jurisdiction of the court.[2] The Supreme Court assumed that, "while [the] prisoners are in immediate physical custody of an officer or officers not parties to the proceeding, respondents named in the petition have lawful authority to effect their release." 339 U.S. at 766–67. The Court, however, reasoned that the answer to the court's power did not lie in the statute. Rather, it explained that, for the question before it, "answers stem directly from fundamentals," and that they "cannot be found by casual reference to statutes or cases. 339 U.S. at 768. In analyzing those "fundamentals" the Court concluded that an alien held outside the United States cannot seek the writ of habeas corpus.

---

[1] *See also Johnson v. Eisentrager*, 339 U.S. 763, 763 (1950) ("We are cited to no instance where a court, in this or any other country where the writ is known, has issued it on behalf of an alien enemy who, at no relevant time and in no stage of his captivity, has been within its territorial jurisdiction.").

[2] *See* Wright, Miller & Cooper, *Federal Practice & Procedure: Jurisdiction 2d* §4268.1 (1988 & Supp. 2001). Courts have held that U.S. citizens held abroad, and therefore outside the territorial jurisdiction of any federal district court, are nevertheless entitled to seek habeas relief. *See Eraden v. 30th Judicial Circuit Court of Kentucky*, 410 U.S. 434, 495, 498 (1973) ("[N]othing more [is required] than that the court issuing the writ have jurisdiction over the custodian.... Where *American citizens* confirmed overseas (and thus outside the territory of any district court) have sought relief in habeas corpus, we have held, if only implicitly, that the petitioner's absence from the district does not present a jurisdictional obstacle to the consideration of the claim,") (emphasis added); *Kinnell v. Warner*, 356 F. Supp. 779, 780–81 (D. Haw. 1973) ("Petitioner, a member of the United States Navy, is now on the South China Seas aboard the aircraft carrier U.S.S. Enterprise... [but this] physical absence from the territorial jurisdiction of this district court does not per se bar this court's jurisdiction over his [habeas] petition."). As this memorandum explains, however, under *Eisentrager* different rules apply to enemy aliens held outside the United States.

The analysis from *Eisentrager* should apply to bar any habeas application filed by an alien held at GBC. In the critical passage that most nearly summarizes the Court's holding, the *Eisentrager* Court based its conclusion on the fact that the prisoners were seized, tried, and held in territory that was outside the sovereignty of the United States and outside the territorial jurisdiction of any court of the United States. We do not believe that the Court intended to establish a two-part test, distinguishing between "sovereign" territory and territorial "jurisdiction." Instead, we believe that the Court used the latter term interchangeably with the former to explain *why* an alien has no right to a writ of habeas corpus when held outside the sovereign territory of the United States. The same reasoning applies to GBC because it is outside the sovereign territory of the United States.

The United States holds GBC under a lease agreement with Cuba entered into in 1903. *See* Agreement Between the United States of America and the Republic of Cuba for the Lease to the United States of Lands in Cuba for Coaling and Naval Stations, Feb. 16–23, 1903, U.S.-Cuba, T.S. No. 418, 6 Bevans 1113 ("Lease Agreement").[3] That agreement expressly provides that "the United States recognizes the continuance of the ultimate sovereignty of the Republic of Cuba over the" lands and waters subject to the lease. *Id*. art. III. Although the agreement goes on to state that the United States "shall exercise complete jurisdiction and control over and within" the leased areas, it specifically reserves sovereignty to Cuba. *Id*.

The terms of the Lease Agreement are thus definitive on the question of sovereignty and should not be subject to question in the courts. The Supreme Court has acknowledged that "the determination of sovereignty over an area is for the legislative and executive departments" – that is, it is not a question on which the courts should second-guess the political branches. *Vermilya-Brown Co. v. Connell*, 335 U.S. 377, 380 (1948). Indeed, in *Vermilya-Brown* all nine members of the Supreme Court observed that the United States has no sovereignty over GBC. The issue in *Vermilya-Brown Co. v. Connell*, was whether the Fair Labor Standards Act ("FLSA") applied to a United States military base in Bermuda. Five members held that the FLSA applied to "foreign territory under lease for bases," *id*. at 390, while the four dissenters concluded that the FLSA applied only in "any Territory or possession of the United States," *id*. (Jackson, J., dissenting). All nine believed, however, that neither Bermuda nor GBC was subject to the sovereignty of the United States.

At the time when *Vermilya-Brown* was decided, the United States was operating military bases in Bermuda pursuant to a 99-year leasehold. That lease ended on September 1, 1995, when both bases were closed and the land returned to the Government of Bermuda. *See id*. at 378; *see also* www.virtualsources.com/Countries/Europe%20Countries/Bermuda.htm. Based on the terms of that leasehold, the majority noted the State Department's position that arrangements under which the [United States'] leased bases [of Bermuda] were acquired from Great Britain did not and were not intended to transfer sovereignty over the leased areas from Great Britain

---

[3] Further conditions were imposed in a subsequent agreement, among them a promise from the United States not to permit any commercial enterprise to operate on the base. *See* Lease of Certain Areas for Naval Coaling Stations, July 2, 1903, U.S.-Cuba, T.S. No. 426, 6 Bevans 1120. The Lease Agreement does not state a term for the lease, and it was continued by a subsequent agreement stating that it would continue "[u]ntil the two contracting parties agree in the modification or abrogation of the stipulations." Treaty between the United States and Cuba defining their relations, May 29, 1934, U.S.-Cuba, Article III, 48 Stat. 1682, 1683.

to the United States." 335 U.S. at 380. Accordingly, those five Justices concluded "that the leased area is under the sovereignty of Great Britain and that it is not territory of the United States in a political sense, that is, a part of its national domain." *Id.* at 380–81. Moreover, the majority specifically stated that the United States also has "a lease from the Republic of Cuba of an area at Guantanamo Bay for a coaling or naval station." and that "[t]he United States was granted by the Cuban lease substantially the same rights as it has in the Bermuda lease." *Id.* at 383 & n.5 (quoting 1903 US-Cuba agreement).

Similarly, the dissent contended that "Bermuda and like bases are not . . . our possessions." *Id.* at 392 (Jackson, J., dissenting). "Guantanamo Naval Base, . . . a leased base in Cuba . . . has been ruled by the Attorney General not to be a possession; it has not been listed by the State Department as among our 'non-self-governing territories,' and the Administrator of the very Act before us has not listed it among our possessions." *Id.* at 405 (Jackson, J., dissenting) (footnotes omitted). The disagreement in the case was not whether the United States exercised sovereignty over GBC – all agreed that the United States did not – but rather whether the FLSA applies extraterritorially to include U.S. military bases such as those in Bermuda and GBC. The *Eisentrager* analysis turns, of course, on whether the United States exercises sovereignty over a particular territory.

The *Vermilya-Brown* decision does not stand alone in concluding that the United States does not exercise sovereignty over GBC. More recently, in 1995, the Eleventh Circuit similarly relied on the terms of the Lease Agreement to conclude that GBC is not within the sovereign territory of the United States. See *Cuban American Bar Ass'n, Inc. v. Christopher*, 43 F.3d 1412, 1425 (11th Cir. 1995) ("The district court here erred in concluding that Guantanamo Bay was a 'United States territory.' We disagree that 'control and jurisdiction' is equivalent to sovereignty.") (citations omitted); *id.* (rejecting "the argument that our leased military bases abroad which continue under the sovereignty of foreign nations, hostile or friendly, are 'functional[ly] equivalent' to being land borders or ports of entry of the United States or otherwise within the United States") (alteration in original). And the District of Connecticut has likewise held that "sovereignty over the Guantanamo Bay does not rest with the United States." *Bird v. United States*, 923 F. Supp. 338, 343 (D. Conn. 1996). *See also id.* ("Because the 1903 Lease of Lands Agreement clearly establishes Cuba as the *de jure* sovereign over Guantanamo Bay, this Court need not speculate whether the United States is the *de facto* sovereign over the area.").

The position of GBC stands in sharp contrast to the status of the Philippine Islands in cases arising out of World War II. General Yamashita was tried in the Philippines by a U.S. military commission from October to December of 1945, and the Supreme Court chose to exercise habeas jurisdiction in reviewing the commission's decision. *See Applications of Yamashita*, 327 U.S. 1, 5 (1946). At that time, however, the Philippine Islands was an insular possession of the United States, and not a mere U.S. leasehold interest.' See *Eisentrager*, 339 U.S. at 780 ("By reason of our sovereignty at that time over these insular possessions, Yamashita stood much as did Quirin before American courts. Yamashita's offenses were committed on our territory, he was tried within the jurisdication of our *************** territory of the United States."). The United States exercised sovereignty over the Philippines until July 4, 1946, *see generally* 48 U.S.C. ch. 5 (1994), at which time the Philippines became an independent sovereign. The United States retained a military base there – and it was that condition which the

Vermilya-Brown Court compared to Bermuda and GBC. *See Vermilya-Brown*, 335 U.S. at 384 & n.7. The Court's treatment of the Philippines after July 4, 1946, thus affirms our conclusion that the United States interest in GBC today is markedly different, for *Eisentrager* purposes, than that in the Philippines prior to July 4, 1946.

GBC is also outside the "territorial jurisdiction of any court of the United States." *Eisentrager*, 339 U.S. 778. The territory of every federal district court is defined by statute. *See* 28 U.S.C. §§81–131 (1994); 48 U.S.C. §§1424, 1424b, 1821–1826 (1994). GBC is not included within the territory defined for any district. In contrast, other island bases that are considered territories or possessions of the United States are expressly defined within the jurisdiction of specific district courts, even if they are retained largely for military use. *See, e.g.*, 28 U.S.C. §91 (defining the District of Hawaii to include "the Midway Islands, Wake Island, Johnston Island, . . . Kingman Reef," and other islands).[4]

Finally, the executive branch has repeatedly taken the position under various statutes that GBC is neither part of the United States nor a possession or territory of the United States. For example, this Office has opined that GBC is not part of the "United States" for purposes of the Immigration and Naturalization Act. *See* Memorandum for the Associate Attorney General, from Larry L. Simms, Deputy Assistant Attorney General, Office of Legal Counsel, *Re: Status of Guantanamo Bay* (Oct. 27, 1981). Similarly, in 1929, the Attorney General opined that GBC was not a "possession" of the United States within the meaning of certain tariff acts. *See Customs Duties – Goods Brought into United States Naval Station at Guantanamo Bay, Cuba*, 35 Op. Att'y Gen. 536 (1929). GBC was "a mere governmental outpost beyond our borders" and "a place subject to the use, occupation and control of the United States," without being part of sovereign territory. *Id.* at 541, 540. Although neither of these opinions is directly on point here, because each addresses the status of GBC under a particular statutory definition, they demonstrate that the United States has consistently taken the position that GBC remains foreign territory, not subject to U.S. sovereignty.[5]

II

For the reasons outlined above, we believe that the rationale for holding that there is no jurisdiction to entertain a habeas petition from an alien held at GBC is very

---

[4] For your further information, we have attached a memorandum prepared by this office based on earlier research concerning potential habeas jurisdiction for detainees held at Midway, Wake and Tinian, which have also been considered as possible detention sites.

[5] We note that in one statute, Congress has expressly included GBC within a reference to U.S. territories or possessions. In extending the provisions of the Longshore and Harbor Workers' Compensation Act to military bases, section 1651(a) of title 42, United States Code, provides that the terms of that Act shall apply "upon any lands occupied or used by the United States for military or naval purposes in any Territory or possession outside the continental United States (including the United States Naval Operating Base, Guantanamo Bay, Cuba; and the Canal Zone)." *See also* 42 U.S.C. §1701(b)(1) (similar provision). By specifically including GBC within the term "Territory or possession" for purposes of extending a particular statutory scheme to military bases Congress in no way undermined the general proposition that GBC is not part of the sovereign territory of the United States. Part of the purpose of the provision was to extend the protection of the Longshore and Harbor Workers' Compensation Act even to bases in foreign nations, and the specific inclusion of GBC in one subsection of the provision cannot be understood as a general statement of the status of the base as a U.S. "possession."

strong and is the correct result under *Eisentrager*. Nevertheless, we caution that there is a potential ground for uncertainty arising from an arguable imprecision in the Supreme Court's language in *Eisentrager*. As noted above, in a critical passage the Court stated that habeas jurisdiction was not available because the aliens were not within "territory over which the United States is sovereign." 339 U.S. at 778. In the very same sentence, however, the Court also stated that habeas jurisdiction did not exist because the events and detention occurred outside "the territorial jurisdiction" of any federal court. *Id*. If an alien detainee is both outside the United States' sovereign territory and outside the territorial jurisdiction of a federal court, then it is clear that no habeas jurisdiction exists. We have explained above that we believe GBC meets those conditions. A non-frivolous argument might be constructed, however, that GBC, while not part of sovereign territory of the United States, *is* within the territorial jurisdiction of a federal court. In that scenario, the application of *Eisentrager*, might not be as clear. This is because "sovereignty" over territory and "jurisdiction" over territory could mean different things. A nation, for example, can retain its sovereignty over its territory, yet at the same time allow another nation to exercise limited jurisdiction within it.

It might be argued that the difference in language in *Eisentrager* must be given meaning which can only be done if there is a difference between "sovereignty" and "jurisdiction." A court could find that the U.S.-Cuba lease agreement lends itself rather well to this distinction, since it makes clear that the United States exercises "complete jurisdiction and control" over GBC, even though Cuba retains "sovereignty." Lease Agreement, 6 Bevans 1114, Although *Eisentrager* seems to permit aliens to bring habeas petitions only in areas within the sovereign control of the United States, which by the 1903 agreement does not extend to GBC, a court could find that *Eisentrager's* mention of territorial jurisdiction does not preclude habeas jurisdiction at GBC.

A district court also might find support in some cases, although (as explained below) we believe that these precedents are not good law. In *Haitian Centers Council, Inc. v. McNary*, 969 F.2d 1326 (2nd Cir. 1992), the Second Circuit stated that "Guantanamo Bay is a military installation that is subject to the *exclusive* control and jurisdiction of the United States." *Id*. at 1342. As a result of the United States' exclusive control, the court concluded that some constitutional rights applied to Haitian refugees held at GBC and that an interest group could file for a preliminary injunction in federal court in New York to vindicate those rights. The court also relied in part on the fact that certain U.S. criminal laws apparently applied to GBC under the definition of the United States' "special maritime and territorial jurisdiction" in section 7 of title 18, United States Code. *See id*. at 1342. That placed GBC, at least in some sense, under U.S. "jurisdiction." Similarly, in *Haitian Centers Council, Inc. v. Sale*, 823 F. Supp. 1028 (F.D.N.Y. 1993), the district court relied on *McNary* to hold that, because "Guantanamo Bay Naval Base . . . is under the complete control and jurisdiction of the United States government." aliens held there must be granted some constitutional protections. *Id*. at 1040.

For a number of reasons, however, we believe that a federal district court would not accept these arguments. First, the best reading of *Eisentrager* indicates that the Court was only permitting habeas jurisdiction within the sovereign territory of the United States, which does not include GBC. Second, no federal statutes include GBC within the territorial jurisdiction of any federal district court. The fact that the United

States can exercise some "jurisdiction" and "control" over the base is not the relevant factor for purposes of the analysis in *Eisentrager*. Presumably, the United States similarly exercised considerable "jurisdiction" and "control" over the Landsberg Prison, which was under the command of an American Army general at the time, where the applicants in *Eisentrager* were held. That, however, was not deemed relevant to the Court's analysis.

Third, the *McNary* and *Sale* cases cited earlier are not persuasive authority for extending habeas jurisdiction to GBC. To begin with, the cases did not address habeas jurisdiction at all and thus never squarely confronted the analysis in *Eisentrager*. Instead, *McNary*, for example, addressed whether the United States, in interdicting Haitian refugees and detaining them at GBC, had violated international treaties and agreements, statutes, and executive orders. In fact we have not found any case directly addressing habeas jurisdiction over an alien held at GBC. In addition, both *McNary* and *Sale* have been vacated. *McNary* was vacated as moot by the Supreme Court, *see* 509 U.S. 918 (1993), and *Sale* was subsequently vacated by Stipulated Order, *see Cuban American Bar Ass'n*, 43 F.3d at 1424. More importantly, the analysis in *Sale* has also been expressly rejected by the Eleventh Circuit. *See id*. at 1425 ("The district court here erred in [relying on *Sale* and] concluding that Guantanamo Bay was a 'United States territory,' We disagree that 'control and jurisdiction' is equivalent to sovereignty.") (citation omitted). Finally, to the extent the Second Circuit in *McNary* relied on the theory that GBC was within the "special maritime and territorial jurisdiction" of the United States under 18 U.S.C. §7, it is particularly weak authority for habeas jurisdiction here. Section 7 of title 18 defines places or circumstances where certain criminal laws of the United States shall apply to proscribe conduct. 18 U.S.C. §7 (1994). The mere fact that U.S. criminal law applies, however, does not bring a place within the territorial jurisdiction of a federal district court. As the Supreme Court explained in *Vermilya-Brown*, a nation may extend its statutes to regulate conduct "on areas under the control, though not within the territorial jurisdiction or sovereignty, of the nation enacting the legislation." 335 U.S. at 381. Laws are frequently applied extraterritorially to conduct occurring *outside* a nation's territorial jurisdiction, but the mere application of law in such a case does not alter the territorial jurisdiction of the courts or their power to grant the writ of habeas corpus. Indeed, the venue provision for cases arising under the special maritime and territorial jurisdiction of the United States expressly acknowledges this distinction. It sets out the venue for crimes that occur "out of the jurisdiction of any particular State or district." 18 U.S.C. §3238 (1994).

In addition, the Second Circuit has subsequently repudiated the cursory analysis in *McNary*, which essentially assumed that 18 U.S.C. §7 applied to GBC. Instead, the Second Circuit has held that the statute has no extraterritorial application. *See United States v. Gatlin*, 216 F. 3d 207, 214 (2nd Cir. 2000). After holding that §7 had no territorial application for the case before it, the *Gatlin* Court noted that "the United States base at Guantanamo Bay is technically outside the territorial boundaries of the United States" and declined to express a view on "whether our *dictum* in *McNary* was correct." *Id*. at 214 n.8.[6] *McNary's* reliance on 18 U.S.C.

---

[6] Although the Second Circuit has held that 18 U.S.C. §7 does not apply extraterritorially, we caution against relying too heavily on that rationale. This office has opined that GBC is within the special maritime and territorial jurisdiction of the United States under the provision. See *Installation of Slot*

§7 to demonstrate a form of "jurisdiction" over GBC is thus particularly unreliable authority here.

Fourth, and perhaps most importantly, a federal district court ought to be reluctant to extend habeas jurisdiction to GBC, when not clearly called for by statute, if doing so would interfere with matters solely within the discretion of the political branches of government. Detention and trial of al Qaeda and Taliban members is undertaken pursuant to the President's Commander-in-Chief and foreign affairs powers. Without a clear statement from Congress extending jurisdiction to GBC, a court should defer to the executive branch's activities and decisions prosecuting the war in Afghanistan.[7]

III

You have also asked us about the potential legal exposure if a detainee successfully convinces a federal district court to exercise habeas jurisdiction. There is little doubt that such a result could interfere with the operation of the system that has been developed to address the detainment and trial of enemy aliens. First, a habeas petition would allow a detainee to challenge the legality of his status and treatment under international treaties, such as the Geneva Conventions and the International Covenant on Civil and Political Rights. *See* 28 U.S.C. §2241(c)(4). Thus, a court could review, in part, the question whether and what international law norms may or may not apply to the conduct of the war in Afghanistan, both by the United States and its enemies. Second, a detainee could challenge the use of military commissions and the validity of any charges brought as violation of the laws of war under both international and domestic law. *See* 28 U.S.C. §2241(c)(3). Third, although the Supreme Court in *Ex parte Quirin*, 317 U.S. 1 (1942) foreclosed habeas review of the procedures used by military commissions, a petitioner could argue that subsequent developments in the law of habeas corpus require the federal courts to review the constitutionality of military commission procedures today. Fourth, a petitioner might even be able to question the constitutional authority of the President to use force in Afghanistan and the legality of Congress' statutory authorization in place of a declaration of war.

Finally, you have asked about the rights that an enemy alien habeas petitioner would enjoy as a litigant in federal court, assuming that the court has found jurisdiction to exist. We are aware of no basis on which a federal court would grant different litigant rights to a habeas petitioner simply because he is an enemy alien, other than to deny him habeas jurisdiction in the first place.

Machines on U.S. Naval Base, Guantanamo Bay, 6 Op. O.L.C. 236 (1982). We do not believe it is necessary to revisit that opinion here because, as outlined in text, whether or not GBC comes within 18 U.S.C. §7 is irrelevant for the question of habeas jurisdiction. In addition, we note that criminal prosecutions have been brought on the assumption that 18 U.S.C. §7 applies to GBC, although the issue does not appear to have been litigated *See, e.g., United States v. Lee*, 905 F.2d. G. 117, 117 & n.1 (1990).
[7] This point draws further support from the fact that, where Congress has intended to include GBC in any provision extending the reach of U.S. law, it has done so expressly. *See, e.g.*, 42 U.S.C. §1651(a)(2). Congress has shown that it will be express about extending U.S. law to GBC when it intends that result. Particularly where a judicial construction extending jurisdiction or the substantive reach of U.S. law would potentially interfere with the President's foreign affairs and Commander-in-Chief powers, such a clear statement should be required.

Conclusion

For the foregoing reasons, we conclude that a district court cannot properly entertain an application for a writ of habeas corpus by an enemy alien detained at Guantanamo Bay Naval Base, Cuba. Because the issue has not yet been definitively resolved by the courts, however, we caution that there is some possibility that a district court would entertain such an application.

Please let us know if we can be of any further assistance.

MEMO 4

U.S. Department of Justice

Office of Legal Counsel

Office of the Deputy Assistant Attorney General   *Washington, D.C. 20530*

January 9, 2002

MEMORANDUM FOR WILLIAM J. HAYNES II
  GENERAL COUNSEL, DEPARTMENT OF DEFENSE

FROM: John Yoo
             Deputy Assistant Attorney General

             Robert J. Delabunty
             Special Counsel

RE: *Application of Treaties and Laws to al Qaeda and Taliban Detainees*

You have asked for our Office's views concerning the effect of international treaties
and federal laws on the treatment of individuals detained by the U.S. Armed Forces
during the conflict in Afghanistan. In particular, you have asked whether the laws of
armed conflict apply to the conditions of detention and the procedures for trial of
members of al Qaeda and the Taliban militia. We conclude that these treaties do not
protect members of the al Qaeda organization, which as a non-State actor cannot be
a party to the international agreements governing war. We further conclude that these
treaties do not apply to the Taliban militia. This memorandum expresses no view as
to whether the President should decide, as a matter of policy, that the U.S. Armed
Forces should adhere to the standards of conduct in those treaties with respect to the
treatment of prisoners.

   We believe it most useful to structure the analysis of these questions by focusing
on the War Crimes Act, 18 U.S.C. § 2441 (Supp. III 1997) ("WCA"). The WCA directly
incorporates several provisions of international treaties governing the laws of war
into the federal criminal code. Part 1 of this memorandum describes the WCA and
the most relevant treaties that it incorporates: the four 1949 Geneva Conventions,
which generally regulate the treatment of non-combatants, such as prisoners of war
("POWs"), the injured and sick, and civilians.[1]

   Part II examines whether al Qaeda detainees can claim the protection of these
agreements. Al Qaeda is merely a violent political movement or organization and not
a nation-state. As a result, it is ineligible to be a signatory to any treaty. Because of

---

[1] The four Geneva Conventions for the Protection of Victims of War, dated August 12, 1949, were
ratified by the United States on July 14, 1955. These are the Convention for the Amelioration of the
Condition of the Wounded and Sick in Armed Forces in the Field, 6 U.S.T. 3115 ("Geneva Convention
I"); the Convention for the Amelioration of the Condition of Wounded, Sick and Shipwrecked Members of Armed Forces at Sea, 6 U.S.T. 3219 ("Geneva Convention II"); the Convention Relative to the
Treatment of Prisoners of War, 6 U.S.T. 3517 ("Geneva Convention III"); and the Convention Relative
to the Protection of Civilian Persons in Time of War, 6 U.S.T. 3317 ("Geneva Convention IV")

the novel nature of this conflict, moreover, we do not believe that al Qaeda would be included in non-international forms of armed conflict to which some provisions of the Geneva Conventions might apply. Therefore, neither the Geneva Conventions nor the WCA regulate the detention of al Qaeda prisoners captured during the Afghanistan conflict.

Part III discusses whether the same treaty provisions, as incorporated through the WCA, apply to the treatment of captured members of the Taliban militia. We believe that the Geneva Conventions do not apply for several reasons. First, the Taliban was not a government and Afghanistan was not – even prior to the beginning of the present conflict – a functioning State during the period in which they engaged in hostilities against the United States and its allies. Afghanistan's status as a failed state is ground alone to find that members of the Taliban militia are not entitled to enemy POW status under the Geneva Conventions. Further, it is clear that the President has the constitutional authority to suspend our treaties with Afghanistan pending the restoration of a legitimate government capable of performing Afghanistan's treaty obligations. Second, it appears from the public evidence that the Taliban militia may have been so intertwined with al Qaeda as to be functionally indistinguishable from it. To the extent that the Taliban militia was more akin to a non-governmental organization that used military force to pursue its religious and political ideology than a functioning government, its members would be on the same legal footing as al Qaeda.

In Part IV, we address the question whether any customary international law of armed conflict might apply to the al Qaeda or Taliban militia members detained during the course of the Afghanistan conflict. We conclude that customary international law, whatever its source and content, does not bind the President, or restrict the actions of the United States military, because it does not constitute federal law recognized under the Supremacy Clause of the Constitution. The President, however, has the constitutional authority as Commander-in-Chief to interpret and apply the customary or common laws of war in such a way that they would extend to the conduct of members of both al Qaeda and the Taliban, and also to the conduct of the U.S. Armed Forces towards members of those groups taken as prisoners in Afghanistan.

I. Background and Overview of the War Crimes Act and the Geneva Conventions

It is our understanding that your Department is considering two basic plans regarding the treatment of members of al Qaeda and the Taliban militia detained during the Afghanistan conflict. First, the Defense Department intends to make available a facility at the U.S. Navy base at Guantanamo Bay, Cuba, for the long-term detention of these individuals, who have come under our control either through capture by our military or transfer from our allies in Afghanistan. We have discussed in a separate memorandum the federal jurisdiction issues that might arise concerning Guantanamo Bay.[2] Second, your Department is developing procedures to implement the President's Military Order of November 13, 2001, which establishes military commissions for the

---

[2] *See* Memorandum for William J. Haynes II, General Counsel, Department of Defense, from Patrick F. Philbin, Deputy Assistant Attorney General, and John Yoo, Deputy Assistant Attorney General, *Re: Possible Habeas Jurisdiction over Aliens Held in Guantanamo Bay, Cuba* (Dec. 28, 2001).

trial of violations of the laws of war committed by non-U.S. citizens.[3] The question has arisen whether the Geneva Conventions, or other relevant international treaties or federal laws, regulate these proposed policies.

We believe that the WCA provides a useful starting point for our analysis of the application of the Geneva Conventions to the treatment of detainees captured in the Afghanistan theater of operations.[4] Section 2441 of Title 18 renders certain acts punishable as "war crimes." The statute's definition of that term incorporates, by reference, certain treaties or treaty provisions relating to the laws of war, including the Geneva Conventions.

A. Section 2441: An Overview

Section 2441 reads in full as follows:
War crimes

1. Offense. – Whoever, whether inside or outside the United States, commits a war crime, in any of the circumstances described in subsection (b), shall be fined under this title or imprisoned for life or any term of years, or both, and if death results to the victim, shall also be subject to the penalty of death.

2. Circumstances. – The circumstances referred to in subsection (a) are that the person committing such war crime or the victim of such war crime is a member of the Armed Forces of the United States or a national of the United States (as defined in section 101 of the Immigration and Nationality Act).

3. Definition. – As used in this section the term "war crime" means any conduct –

   (1) defined as a grave breach in any of the international conventions signed at Geneva 12 August 1949, or any protocol to such convention to which the United States is a party;

   (2) prohibited by Article 23, 25, 27, or 28 of the Annex to the Hague Convention IV, Respecting the Laws and Customs of War on Land, signed 18 October 1907;

   (3) which constitutes a violation of common Article 3 of the international conventions signed at Geneva, 12 August 1949, or any protocol to such convention to which the United States is a party and which deals with non-international armed conflict; or

   (4) of a person who, in relation to an armed conflict and contrary to the provisions of the Protocol on Prohibitions or Restrictions on the Use of Mines, Booby-Traps and Other Devices as amended at Geneva on 3 May 1996 (Protocol II as amended on 3 May 1996), when the United States is a party to such Protocol, wilfully kills or causes serious injury to civilians.

---

[3] *See generally* Memorandum for Alberto R. Gonzales, Counsel to the President, from Patrick F. Philbin, Deputy Assistant Attorney General, Office of Legal Counsel, *Re: Legality of the Use of Military Commissions to Try Terrorists* (Nov. 6, 2001).

[4] The rule of lenity requires that the WCA be read so as to ensure that prospective defendants have adequate notice of the nature of the acts that the statute condemns. *See, e.g., Castillo v. United States*, 530 U.S. 120, 131 (2000). In those cases in which the application of a treaty incorporated by the WCA is unclear, therefore, the rule of lenity requires that the interpretative issue be resolved in the defendant's favor.

18 U.S.C. § 2441.

Section 2441 lists four categories of war crimes. First, it criminalizes "grave breaches" of the Geneva Conventions, which are defined by treaty and will be discussed below. Second, it makes illegal conduct prohibited by articles 23, 25, 27 and 28 of the Annex to the Hague Convention IV. Third, it criminalizes violations of what is known as "common" Article 3, which is an identical provision common to all four of the Geneva Conventions. Fourth, it criminalizes conduct prohibited by certain other laws of war treaties, once the United States joins them. A House Report states that the original legislation "carries out the international obligations of the United States under the Geneva Conventions of 1949 to provide criminal penalties for certain war crimes." H.R. Rep. No. 104–698 at 1 (1996), *reprinted in* 1996 U.S.C.C.A.N. 2166. 2166. Each of those four conventions includes a clause relating to legislative implementation and to criminal punishment.[5]

In enacting section 2441, Congress also sought to fill certain perceived gaps in the coverage of federal criminal law. The main gaps were thought to be of two kinds: subject matter jurisdiction and personal jurisdiction. First, Congress found that "[t]here are major gaps in the prosecutability of individuals under federal criminal law for war crimes committed against Americans." H.R. Rep. No. 104–698 at 6, *reprinted in* 1996 U.S.C.C.A.N. at 2171. For example, "the simple killing of a[n American] prisoner of war" was not covered by any existing Federal statute. *Id.* at 5, *reprinted in* 1996 U.S.C.C.A.N. at 2170.[6] Second, Congress found that "[t]he ability to court martial members of our armed services who commit war crimes ends when they leave military service. [Section 244] would allow for prosecution even after discharge." *Id.* at 7, *reprinted in* 1996 U.S.C.C.A.N. at 2172.[7] Congress considered it important to fill this gap, not only in the interest of the victims of war crimes, but also of the accused. "The Americans prosecuted would have available all the procedural protections of the American justice system. These might be lacking if the United States extradited

---

[5] That common clause reads as follows:

> The [signatory Nations] undertake to enact any legislation necessary to provide effective penal sanctions for persons committing or ordering to be committed, any of the grave breaches of the present Convention. . . . Each [signatory nation] shall be under the obligation to search for persons alleged to have committed, or to have ordered to be committed, such grave breaches, and shall bring such persons, regardless of their nationality, before its own courts . . . It may also, if it prefers, . . . hand such persons over for trial to another [signatory nation], provided such [nation] has made out a *prima facie case*.

Geneva Convention I, Article 49; Geneva Convention II, art. 50; Geneva Convention III, Article 129; Geneva Convention IV, Article 146.

[6] In projecting our criminal law extraterritorially in order to protect victims who are United States nationals, Congress was apparently relying on the international law principle of passive personality. The passive personality principle "asserts that a state may apply law – particularly criminal law – to an act committed outside its territory by a person not its national where the victim of the act was its national" *United States v. Rezaq*, 134 F. 3d 1121, 1133 (D.C. Cir.), *cert. denied*, 525 U.S. 834 (1998). The principle marks recognition of the fact that "each nation has a legitimate interest that its nationals and permanent inhabitants not be maimed or disabled from self-support," or otherwise injured. *Lauritzen v. Larsen*, 345 U.S. 571, 586 (1953); *see also Hellenic Lines Ltd. v. Rhoditis*, 398 U.S. 306, 309 (1970).

[7] United States *ex rel. Toth v. Quaries,* 350 U.S. 11 (1955), the Supreme Court had held that a former serviceman could not constitutionally be tried before a court martial under the Uniform Code for Military Justice (the UCMJ) for crimes he was alleged to have committed while in the armed services.

the individuals to their victims' home countries for prosecution." *Id.*[8] Accordingly, Section 2441 criminalizes forms of conduct in which a U.S. national or a member of the Armed Forces may be either a victim or a perpetrator.

B. Grave Breaches of the Geneva Conventions

The Geneva Conventions were approved by a diplomatic conference on August 12, 1949, and remain the agreements to which more States have become parties than any other concerning the laws of war. Convention I deals with the treatment of wounded and sick in armed forces in the field; Convention II addresses treatment of the wounded, sick, and shipwrecked in armed forces at sea; Convention III regulates treatment of POWs; Convention IV addresses the treatment of citizens. While the Hague Convention IV establishes the rules of conduct against the enemy, the Geneva Conventions set the rules for the treatment of the victims of war.

The Geneva Conventions, like treaties generally, structure legal relationships between Nation States, not between Nation States and private, subnational groups or organizations.[9] All four Conventions share the same Article 2, known as "common Article 2." It states:

> In addition to the provisions which shall be implemented in peacetime, the present Convention shall apply to all cases of declared war or of any other armed conflict *which may arise between two or more of the High Contracting Parties*, even if the state of war is not recognized by one of them.

> The Convention shall also apply to all cases of partial or total occupation of the territory of a High Contracting Party, even if the said occupation meets with no armed resistance.

> Although one of the Powers in conflict may not be a party to the present Convention, the Powers who are parties thereto shall remain bound by it in their mutual relations. They shall furthermore be bound by the Convention in relation to the said Power, if the latter accepts and applies the provisions thereof.

> (Emphasis added).

As incorporated by § 2441 (c)(1), the four Geneva Conventions similarly define "grave breaches." Geneva Convention III on POWs defines a grave breach as:

> wilful killing, torture or inhuman treatment, including biological experiments, wilfully causing great suffering or serious injury to body or health, compelling a prisoner of war to serve in the forces of the hostile Power, or wilfully depriving a prisoner of war of the rights of fair and regular trial prescribed in this Convention.

---

[8] The principle of nationality in international law recognizes that (as Congress did here) a State may criminalize acts performed extraterritorially by its own nationals. *See, e.g., Skiriotes v. Florida*, 313 U.S. 69, 73 (1941); *Steele v. Bulova Watch Co.*, 344 U.S. 280, 282 (1952).

[9] *See Trans World Airlines, Inc. v. Franklin Mint Corp.*, 466 U.S. 243, 253 (1984) ("A treaty is in the nature of a contract between nations."); *The Head Money Cases*, 112, U.S. 580, 598 (1884) ("A treaty is primarily a compact between independent nations."); *United States ex rel. Saroop v. Garcia*, 109 F.3d 165, 167 (3d Cir. 1997) ("[T]reaties are agreements between nations."); *Vienna Convention on the Law of Treaties*, May 23, 1969, art. 2. § 1(a). 1155 U.N.T.S. 331, 333 ("[T]reaty' means an international agreement concluded between States in written form and governed by international law. . . .") (the "Vienna Convention"); *see generally Banco Naçional de Cuba v. Sabbatino*, 376 U.S. 398, 422 (1964) ("The traditional view of international law is that it establishes substantive principles for determining whether one country has wronged another.").

Geneva Convention III art. 130. As mentioned before, the Geneva Conventions require the High Contracting Parties to enact penal legislation to punish anyone who commits or orders a grave breach. *See. e.g., id.* art. 129. Further, each State party has the obligation to search for and bring to justice (either before its courts or by delivering a suspect to another State party) anyone who commits a grave breach. No State party is permitted to absolve itself or any other nation of liability for committing a grave breach.

Thus, the WCA does not criminalize all breaches of the Geneva Conventions. Failure to follow some of the regulations regarding the treatment of POWs, such as difficulty in meeting all of the conditions set forth for POW camp conditions, does not constitute a grave breach within the meaning of Geneva Convention III, art. 130. Only by causing great suffering or serious bodily injury to POWs, killing or torturing them, depriving them of access to a fair trial, or forcing them to serve in the Armed Forces, could the United States actually commit a grave breach. Similarly, unintentional, isolated collateral damage on civilian targets would not constitute a grave breach within the meaning of Geneva Convention IV, art. 147. Article 147 requires that for a grave breach to have occurred, destruction of property must have been done "wantonly" and without military justification, while the killing or injury of civilians must have been "wilful."

D. Common Article 3 of the Geneva Conventions

Section 2441 (c)(3) also defines as a war crime conduct that "constitutes a violation of common Article 3" of the Geneva Conventions. Article 3 is a unique provision that governs the conduct of signatories to the Conventions in a particular kind of conflict that is *not* one between High Contracting Parties to the Conventions. Thus, common Article 3 may require the United States, as a High Contracting Party, to follow certain rules even if other parties to the conflict are not parties to the Conventions. On the other hand, Article 3 requires state parties to follow only certain minimum standards of treatment toward prisoners, civilians, or the sick and wounded, rather than the Conventions as a whole.

Common Article 3 reads in relevant part as follows:

> In the case of armed conflict not of an international character occurring in the territory of one of the High Contracting Parties, each Party to the conflict shall be bound to apply, as a minimum, the following provisions:

> (1) Persons taking no active part in the hostilities, including members of armed forces who have laid down their arms and those placed *hors de combat* by sickness, wounds, detention, or any other cause, shall in all circumstances be treated humanely, without any adverse distinction founded on race, color, religion or faith, sex, birth or wealth, or any other similar criteria.

> To this end, the following acts are and shall remain prohibited at any time and in any place whatsoever with respect to the above-mentioned persons:

> (a) violence to life and person, in particular, murder of all kinds, mutilation, cruel treatment and torture;
> (b) taking of hostages;
> (c) outrages upon personal dignity, in particular, humiliating and degrading treatment;

(d) the passing of sentences and the carrying out of executions without previous judgment pronounced by a regularly constituted court, affording all the judicial guarantees which are recognized as indispensable by civilized peoples.

(2) The wounded and sick shall be collected and cared for. . . .

The application of the preceding provisions shall not affect the legal status of the Parties to the conflict.

Common Article 3 complements common Article 2. Article 2 applies to cases of declared war or of any other armed conflict that may arise between two or more of the High Contracting Parties, even if the state of war is not recognized by one of them.[10] Common Article 3, however, covers "armed conflict not of an international character" – a war that does not involve cross-border attacks – that occurs within the territory of one of the High Contracting Parties. There is substantial reason to think that this language refers specifically to a condition of civil war, or a large-scale armed conflict between a State and an armed movement within its own territory.

To begin with, Article 3's text strongly supports the interpretation that it applies to large-scale conflicts between a State and an insurgent group. First, the language at the end of Article 3 states that "[t]he application of the proceding provisions shall not affect the legal status of the Parties to the conflict." This provision was designed to ensure that a Party that observed Article 3 during a civil war would not be understood to have granted the "recognition of the insurgents as an adverse party." Frits Kalshoven, *Constraints on the Waging of War* 59 (1987). Second, Article 3 is in terms limited to "armed conflict . . . occurring *in the territory of one of the High Contracting Parties*" (emphasis added). This limitation makes perfect sense if the Article applies to civil wars, which are fought primarily or solely within the territory of a single state. The limitation makes little sense, however, as applied to a conflict between a State and a transnational terrorist group, which may operate from different territorial bases, some of which might be located in States that are parties to the Conventions and some of which might not be. In such a case, the Conventions would apply to a single armed conflict in some scenes of action but not in others – which seems inexplicable.

This interpretation is supported by commentators. One well-known commentary states that "a non-international armed conflict is distinct from an international armed conflict because of the legal status of the entities opposing each other the parties to the conflict are not sovereign States, but the government of a single State in conflict with one or more armed factions within its territory."[11] A legal scholar writing in the same year in which the Conventions were prepared stated that "a conflict not of an international character occurring in the territory of one of the High Contracting Parties . . . must normally mean a civil war."[12]

Analysis of the background to the adoption of the Geneva Conventions in 1949 confirms our understanding of common Article 3. It appears that the drafters of the Conventions had in mind only the two forms of armed conflict that were regarded as

---

[10] Article 2's reference to a state of war "not recognized" by a belligerent was apparently intended to refer to conflicts such as the 1937 war between China and Japan. Both sides denied that a state of war existed. *See* Joyce A. C. Gutteridge, *The Geneva Conventions of 1949*, 26 Brit. Y. B. Int'l L. 294, 298–99 (1949).

[11] Commentary as the Additional Protocols of 8 June 1977 to the Geneva Conventions of 12 August 1949, at ¶ 4339 (Yves Sandoz et al. eds., 1987).

[12] Gutteridge, *Supra* n.10, at 300.

matters of general *international* concern at the time: armed conflict between Nation States (subject to Article 2), and large-scale civil war within a Nation State (subject to Article 3). To understand the context in which the Geneva Conventions were drafted, it will be helpful to identify three distinct phases in the development of the laws of war.

First, the traditional law of war was based on a stark dichotomy between "belligerency" and "insurgency." The category of "belligerency" applied to armed conflicts between sovereign States (unless there was recognition of belligerency in a civil war), while the category of "insurgency" applied to armed violence breaking out within the territory of a sovereign State.[13] Correspondingly, international law treated the two classes of conflict in different ways. Inter-state wars were regulated by a body of international legal rules governing both the conduct of hostilities and the protection of noncombatants. By contrast, there were very few international rules governing civil unrest, for States preferred to regard internal strife as rebellion, mutiny and treason coming within the purview of national criminal law, which precluded any possible intrusion by other States.[14] This was a "clearly sovereignty-oriented" phase of international law.[15]

The second phase began as early as the Spanish Civil War (1936–39) and extended through the time of the drafting of the Geneva Conventions until relatively recently. During this period, State practice began to apply certain general principles of humanitarian law beyond the traditional field of State-to-State conflict to "those internal conflicts that constituted large-scale civil wars."[16] In addition to the Spanish Civil War, events in 1947 during the Civil War between the Communists and the Nationalist regime in China illustrated this new tendency.[17] Common Article 3, which was prepared during this second phase, was apparently addressed to armed conflicts akin to the Chinese and Spanish civil wars. As one commentator has described it, Article 3 was designed to restrain governments "in the handling of armed violence directed against them for the express purpose of secession or at securing a change in the government of a State," but even after the adoption of the Conventions it remained "uncertain whether [Article 3] applied to full-scale civil war."[18]

The third phase represents a more complete break than the second with the traditional "State-sovereignty-oriented approach" of international law. This approach gives central place to individual human rights. As a consequence, it blurs the distinction between international and internal armed conflicts, and even that between civil wars

---

[13] *See* Joseph H. Beale, Jr., *The Recognition of Cuban Belligerency*,9 Harv. L. Rev. 406, 406 n.1 (1896).

[14] *See The Prosecutor v. Dusko Tadic (Jurisdiction of the Tribunal).* (Appeals Chamber of the International Criminal Tribunal for the Former Yugoslavia 1995) (the "ICTY"), 105 I.L.R. 453, 504–05 (E. Lauterpacht and C. J. Greenwood eds., 1997).

[15] *Id.* at 505; *see also* Gerald Irving Draper, *Reflections of Law and Armed Conflicts* 107 (1998) ("Before 1949, in the absence of recognized belligerency accorded to the elements opposed to the government of a State, the law of war . . . had no application to internal armed conflicts. . . . International law had little or nothing to say as to how the armed rebellion was crushed by the government concerned, for such matters fell within the domestic jurisdiction of States. Such conflicts were often waged with great lack of restraint and cruelty. Such conduct was a domestic matter.").

[16] *Tadic*, 105 I.L.R. at 507. Indeed, the events of the Spanish Civil War, in which "both the republican Government [of Spain] and third States refused to recognize the [Nationalist] insurgents as belligerents." *id*. at 507, may be reflected in common Article 3's reference to "the legal status of the Parties to the conflict."

[17] *See Id.* at 508.

[18] *See* Draper, *Reflections on Law and Armed Conflicts, supra,* at 108.

and other forms of internal armed conflict. This approach is well illustrated by the ICTY's decision in *Tadic*, which appears to take the view that common Article 3 applies to non-international armed conflicts of *any* description, and is not limited to civil wars between a State and an insurgent group. In this conception, common Article 3 is not just a complement to common Article 2; rather, it is a catch-all that establishes standards for any and all armed conflicts not included in common Article 2.[19]

Nonetheless, despite this recent trend, we think that such an interpretation of common Article 3 fails to take into account, not only the language of the provision, but also its historical context. First, as we have described above, such a reading is inconsistent with the text of Article 3 itself, which applies only to "armed conflict not of an international character occurring in the territory of one of the High Contacting Parties." In conjunction with common Article 2, the text of Article 3 simply does not reach international conflicts where one of the parties is not a Nation State. If we were to read the Geneva Conventions as applying to all forms of armed conflict, we would expect the High Contracting Parties to have used broader language, which they easily could have done. To interpret common Article 3 by expanding its scope well beyond the meaning borne by the text is effectively to amend the Geneva Conventions without the approval of the State Parties to the agreements.

Second, as we have discussed, Article 3 was prepared during a period in which the traditional, State-centered view of international law was still dominant and was only just beginning to give way to a human-rights-based approach. Giving due weight to the State practice and doctrinal understanding of the time, it seems to us overwhelmingly likely that an armed conflict between a Nation State and a transnational terrorist

---

[19] An interpretation of common Article 3 that would apply it to all forms of non-international armed conflict accords better with some recent approaches to international humanitarian law. For example, the *Commentary on the Additional Protocols of 8 June 1977 to the Geneva Conventions of 12 August 1949, supra,* after first stating in the text that Article 3 applies when "the government of a single State [is] in conflict with one or more armed factions within its territory," thereafter suggests, in a footnote, that an armed conflict not of an international character "may also exist in which armed factions fight against each other without intervention by the armed forces of the established government." *Id.* ¶ 4339 at n. 2. A still broader interpretation appears to be supported by the language of the decision of the International Court of Justice (the "ICJ") in *Nicaragua v. United States* – which, it should be made clear, the United States refused to acknowledge by withdrawing from the compulsory jurisdiction of the ICJ:

> Article 3 which is common to all four Geneva Conventions of 12 August 1949 defines certain rules to be applied in *the armed conflicts of a non-international character*. There is no doubt that, in the event of international armed conflicts, these rules also constitute a minimum yardstick, in addition to the more elaborate rules which are also to apply to international conflicts; and they are rules which, in the Court's opinion, reflect what the Court in 1949 called "elementary considerations of humanity."

Military and Paramilitary Activities In and Against Nicaragua (Nicaragua v. United States), (International Court of Justice 1986), 76 I.L.R. 1, 448, ¶ 218 (E. Lauterpacht and C. J. Greenwood eds., 1988) (emphasis added). The ICJ's language is probably best read to suggest that all "armed conflicts" are either international or non-international, and that if they are non-international, they are governed by common Article 3. If that is the correct understanding of the quoted language, however, it should be noted that the result was merely stated as a conclusion, without taking account either of the precise language of Article 3 or of the background to its adoption. Moreover, while it was true that one of the conflicts to which the ICJ was addressing itself – "[t]he conflict between the *contras'* forces and those of the Government of Nicaragua" – "was an armed conflict which is "not of an international character,'" *id.* at 448, ¶ 219, that conflict was recognizably a civil war between a State and an insurgent group, not a conflict between or among violent factions in a territory in which the State had collapsed. Thus there is substantial reason to question the logic and scope of the ICJ's interpretation of common Article 3.

organization, or between a Nation State and a failed State harboring and supporting a transnational terrorist organization, could not have been within the contemplation of the drafters of common Article 3. These would have been simply unforeseen and, therefore, not provided for. Indeed, it seems to have been uncertain even a decade after the Conventions were signed whether common Article 3 applied to armed conflicts that were neither international in character nor civil wars but anti-colonialist wars of independence such as those in Algeria and Kenya. *See* Gerald Irving Draper, *The Red Cross Conventions* 15 (1957). Further, it is telling that in order to address this unforeseen circumstance, the State Parties to the Geneva Conventions did not attempt to distort the terms of common Article 3 to apply it to cases that did not fit within its terms. Instead, they drafted two new protocols (neither of which the United States has ratified) to adapt the Conventions to the conditions of contemporary hostilities.[20] Accordingly, common Article 3 is best understood not to apply to such armed conflicts.

Third, it appears that in enacting the WCA, Congress did not understand the scope of Article 3 to extend beyond civil wars to all other types of internal armed conflict. As discussed in our review of the legislative history, when extending the WCA to cover violations of common Article 3, the House apparently understood that it was codifying treaty provisions that "forbid atrocities occurring in both civil wars and wars between nations."[21] If Congress had embraced a much broader view of common Article 3, and hence of 18 U.S.C. § 2441, we would expect both the statutory text and the legislative history to have included some type of clear statement of congressional intent. The WCA regulates the manner in which the U.S. Armed Forces may conduct military operations against the enemy; as such, it potentially comes into conflict with the President's Commander-in-Chief power under Article II of the Constitution. As we have advised others earlier in this conflict, the Commander-in-Chief power gives the President the plenary authority in determining how best to deploy troops in the field.[22] Any congressional effort to restrict presidential authority by subjecting the conduct of the U.S. Armed Forces to a broad construction of the Geneva Convention, one that is not clearly borne by its text, would represent a possible infringement on presidential discretion to direct the military. We believe that the Congress must state explicitly its intention to take the constitutionally dubious step of restricting the President's plenary power over military operations (including the treatment of prisoners), and that unless Congress clearly demonstrates such an intent, the WCA must be read to avoid such constitutional problems.[23] As Congress has not signaled such a clear intention in this case, we conclude that common Article 3 should not be read to include all forms of non-international armed conflict.

---

[20] See, e.g., Protocol Additional to the Geneva Conventions of 12 August 1949, and Relating to the Protection of Victims of International Armed Conflicts (Protocol I), June 8, 1977, 1125 U.N.T.S. 4; Protocol Additional to the Geneva Conventions of 12 August 1949, and Relating to the Protection of Victims of Non-International Armed Conflicts (Protocol II), June 8 1977, 1125 U.N.T.S. 610.

[21] 143 Cong. Rec. H5865–66 (daily ed. July 28, 1997) (remarks of Rep. Jenkins).

[22] Memorandum for Timothy E. Flanigan, Deputy Counsel to the President, from John C. Yoo, Deputy Assistant Attorney General, Office of Legal Counsel, *Re: The President's Constitutional Authority to Conduct Military Operations Against Terrorists and Nations Supporting them* (Sept. 25, 2001).

[23] *Cf. Public Citizen v. Department of Justice*,491 U.S. 440, 466 (1989) (construing Federal Advisory Committee Act to avoid encroachment on presidential power); *Ashwander v. TVA*. 297 U.S. 288, 346–48 (1936) (Brandeis, J., concurring) (stating rule of avoidance); *Association of Am. Physicians & Surgeons, Inc. v. Clinton*, 997 F.2d 898, 906–11 (D.C. Cir. 1993) (same).

II. Application of WCA and Associated Treaties to al Qaeda

It is clear from the foregoing statements that members of the al Qaeda terrorist organization do not receive the protections of the laws of war. Therefore, neither their detention nor their trial by the U.S. Armed Forces is subject to the Geneva Conventions (or the WCA). Three reasons, examined in detail below, support this conclusion. First, al Qaeda's status as a non-State actor renders it ineligible to claim the protections of the Geneva Conventions. Second, the nature of the conflict precludes application of common Article 3 of the Geneva Conventions. Third, al Qaeda members fail to satisfy the eligibility requirements for treatment as POWs under Geneva Convention III.

Al Qaeda's status as a non-State actor renders it ineligible to claim the protections of the treaties specified by the WCA. Al Qaeda is not a State. It is a non-governmental terrorist organization composed of members from many nations, with ongoing operations in dozens of nations. Its members seem united in following a radical brand of Islam that seeks to attack Americans throughout the world. Non-governmental organizations cannot be parties to any of the international agreements here governing the laws of war. Al Qaeda is not eligible to sign the Geneva Conventions – and even if it were eligible, it has not done so. Common Article 2, which triggers the Geneva Convention provisions regulating detention conditions and procedures for trial of POWs, is limited only to cases of declared war or armed conflict "between two or more of the High Contracting Parties." Al Qaeda is not a High Contracting Party. As a result the U.S. military's treatment of al Qaeda members is not governed by the bulk of the Geneva Conventions, specifically those provisions concerning POWs. Conduct towards captured members of al Qaeda, therefore, also cannot constitute a violation of 18 U.S.C. § 2441(c)(1) or § 2441(c)(2).[24]

---

[24] Some difference in the language of the WCA might be thought to throw some doubt on the exact manner in which the statute incorporates these treaty norms. It might be argued, for example, with respect to the Hague Convention IV, that the WCA does not simply incorporate the terms of the treaty itself, with all of their limitations on application, but instead criminalizes the conduct described by that Convention. The argument starts from the fact that there is a textual difference in the way that the WCA references treaty provisions. Section 2441(c)(2) defines as a war crime conduct "prohibited" by the relevant sections of the Hague Convention IV. By contrast, § 2441 (c)(1) makes a war crime any conduct that constitutes a "grave breach" of the Geneva Conventions, and § 2441(c)(3) prohibits conduct "which constitutes a violation" of common Article 3 of the Geneva Convention. It might be argued that this difference indicates that § 2441(c)(2) does not *incorporate* the treaty into federal law; rather, it prohibits the conduct *described by* the treaty. Section 2441(c)(3) prohibits conduct "which constitutes a *violation* of common Article 3" (emphasis added), and that can only be conduct which is a treaty violation. Likewise, § 2441(c)(1) only criminalizes conduct that is a "grave breach" of the Geneva Conventions – which, again, must be a treaty violation. In other words, § 2441(c)(2) might be read to apply even when the Hague Convention IV, by its own terms, would not. On this interpretation, an act could violate § 2441(c)(2), whether or not the Hague Convention IV applied to the specific situation at issue.

   We do not think that this interpretation is tenable. To begin with, § 2441(c)(2) makes clear that to be a war crime, conduct must be *"prohibited,"* by the Hague Convention IV (emphasis added). Use of the word "prohibited," rather than phrases such as "referred to" or "described," indicates that the treaty must, by its own operation, proscribe the conduct at issue. If the Hague Convention IV does not itself apply to a certain conflict, then it cannot itself proscribe any conduct undertaken as part of that conflict. Thus, the most natural reading of the statutory language is that an individual must violate the Hague Convention IV in order to violate Section 2441(c)(2). Had Congress intended broadly to criminalize the types of conduct proscribed by the relevant Hague Convention IV provisions as such, rather than as treaty violations, it could have done so more clearly. Furthermore, the basic purpose of § 2441 was to implement, by appropriate legislation, the United States' treaty obligations. That purpose

Second, the nature of the conflict precludes application of common Article 3 of the Geneva Conventions. Al Qaeda is not covered by common Article 3, because the current conflict is not covered by the Geneva Conventions. As discussed in Part I, the text of Article 3, when read in harmony with common Article 2, shows that the Geneva Conventions were intended to cover either: a) traditional wars between Nation States (Article 2), or non-international civil wars (Article 3). Our conflict with al Qaeda does not fit into either category. The current conflict is not an international war between Nation States, but rather a conflict between a Nation State and a non-governmental organization. At the same time, the current conflict is not a civil war under Article 3, because it is a conflict of "an international character," rather than an internal armed conflict between parties contending for control over a government or territory. Therefore, the military's treatment of al Qaeda members captured in that conflict is not limited either by common Article 3 of the Geneva Conventions or 18 U.S.C. § 2441(c)(3), the provision of the WCA incorporating that article.[25]

Third, al Qaeda members fail to satisfy the eligibility requirements for treatment as POWs under Geneva Convention III. It might be argued that, even though it is not a State party to the Geneva Convention, al Qaeda could be covered by some protections in Geneva Convention III on the treatment of POWs. Article 4(A)(2) of the Geneva Convention III defines prisoners of war as including not only captured members of the armed forces of a High Contracting Party, but also irregular forces such as "[m]embers of other militias and members of other volunteer corps, including those of organized resistance movements." Geneva Convention III, art. 4. Article 4(A)(3) also includes as POWs "[m]embers of regular armed forces who profess allegiance to a government or an authority not recognized by the Detaining Power." *Id.* art. 4(A)(3). It might be claimed that the broad terms of these provisions could be stretched to cover al Qaeda.

This view would be mistaken. Article 4 does not expand the application of the Convention beyond the circumstances expressly addressed in common Articles 2 and 3. Unless there is a conflict subject to Article 2 or 3 (the Convention's jurisdictional provisions), Article 4 simply does not apply. As we have argued with respect to Article 3,

would be accomplished by criminalizing acts that were also violations of certain key provisions of the Annex to Hague Convention IV. It would not be served by criminalizing acts *of the kind* condemned by those provisions, whether or not they were treaty violations.

Nothing in the legislative history supports the opposite result. To the contrary, the legislative history suggests an entirely different explanation for the minor variations in language between §§ 2441(c)(1) and 2441(c)(2). As originally enacted, the WCA criminalized violations of the Geneva Conventions. See Pub. L. No. 104-192, § 2(a), 110 Stat. 2104, § 2401 (1996). In signing the original legislation, President Clinton urged that it be expanded to include other serious war crimes involving violation of the Hague Conventions IV and the Amended Protocol II. *See* 2 Pub. Papers of William J. Clinton 1323 (1996). The Expanded War Crimes Act of 1997, introduced as H.R. 1348 in the 105th Congress, was designed to meet these requests. Thus, § 2441(c)(2) was added as an amendment at a later time, and was not drafted at the same time and in the same process as § 2441(c)(1).

[25] This understanding is supported by the WCA's legislative history. When extending the WCA to cover violations of common Article 3, the House apparently understood that it was codifying treaty provisions that "forbid atrocities occurring in both civil wars and wars between nations." 143 Cong. Rec. H5865–66 (remarks of Rep. Jenkins). The Senate also understood that "[t]he inclusion of common Article 3 of the Geneva Conventions . . . expressly allows the United States to prosecute war crimes perpetrated in non-international conflicts, such as Bosnia and Rwanda." 143 Cong. Rec. S7544, S7589 (daily ed. July 16, 1997) (remarks of Sen. Leahy). In referring to Bosnia and Rwanda, both civil wars of a non-international character, Senator Leahy appears to have understood common Article 3 as covering only civil wars as well. Thus, Congress apparently believed that the WCA would apply only to traditional international wars between States, or purely internal civil wars.

and shall further argue with respect to Article 2, the conflict in Afghanistan does not fall within either Articles 2 or 3. As a result, Article 4 has no application. In other words, Article 4 cannot be read as an alternative, and far more expansive, statement of the application of the Convention. It merely specifies, where there is a conflict covered by the Convention, who must be accorded POW status.

Even if Article 4, however, were considered somehow to be jurisdictional as well as substantive, captured members of al Qaeda still would not receive the protections accorded to POWs. Article 4(A)(2), for example, further requires that the militia or volunteers fulfill the conditions first established by the Hague Convention IV of 1907 for those who would receive the protections of the laws of war. Hague Convention IV declares that the "laws, rights and duties of war" only apply to armies, militia, and volunteer corps when they fulfill four conditions: command by responsible individuals, wearing insignia, carrying arms openly, and obeying the laws of war. Hague Convention IV, Respecting the Laws and Customs of War on Land, Oct. 18, 1907, 36 Stat. 2277. Al Qaeda members have clearly demonstrated that they will not follow these basic requirements of lawful warfare. They have attacked purely civilian targets of no military value; they refused to wear uniform or insignia or carry arms openly, but instead hijacked civilian airliners, took hostages, and killed them; they have deliberately targeted and killed thousands of civilians; and they themselves do not obey the laws of war concerning the protection of the lives of civilians or the means of legitimate combat. Thus, Article 4(A)(3) is inapt because al Qaeda do not qualify as "regular armed forces," and its members do not quality for protection as lawful combatants under the laws of war.

III. Application of the Geneva Conventions to the Taliban Militia

Whether the Geneva Conventions apply to the detention and trial of members of the Taliban militia presents a more difficult legal question. Afghanistan has been a party to all four the Geneva Conventions since September 1956. Some might argue that this requires application of the Geneva Conventions to the present conflict with respect to the Taliban militia, which would then trigger the WCA. This argument depends, however, on the assumptions that during the period in which the Taliban militia was ascendant in Afghanistan, the Taliban was the *de facto* government of that nation, that Afghanistan continued to have the essential attributes of statehood, and that Afghanistan continued in good standing as a party to the treaties that its previous government had signed.

We think that all of these assumptions are disputable, and indeed false. The weight of informed opinion strongly supports the conclusion that, for the period in question, Afghanistan was a "failed State" whose territory had been largely overrun and held by violence by a militia or faction rather than by a government. Accordingly, Afghanistan was without the attributes of statehood necessary to continue as a party to the Geneva Conventions, and the Taliban militia like al Qaeda, is therefore not entitled to the protections of the Geneva Conventions. Furthermore, there appears to be substantial evidence that the Taliban was so dominated by al Qaeda and so complicit in its actions and purposes that the Taliban leadership cannot be distinguished from al Qaeda, and accordingly that the Taliban militia cannot stand on a higher footing under the Geneva Conventions.

A. Constitutional Authority

It is clear that, under the Constitution, the Executive has the plenary authority to determine that Afghanistan ceased at relevant times to be an operating State and therefore that members of the Taliban militia were and are not protected by the Geneva Conventions.[26] As an initial matter, Article II makes clear that the President is vested with all of the federal executive power, that he "shall be Commander-in-Chief," that he shall appoint, with the advice and consent of the Senate, and receive, ambassadors, and that he "shall have Power, by and with the Advice and Consent of the Senate, to make Treaties." U.S. Const. art II, § 2, cl. 2. Congress possesses its own specific foreign affairs powers, primarily those of declaring war, raising and funding the military, and regulating international commerce. While Article II, § 1 of the Constitution grants the President an undefined executive power, Article I, § 1 limits Congress to "[a]ll legislative Powers herein granted" in the rest of Article I.

From the very beginnings of the Republic, this constitutional arrangement has been understood to grant the President plenary control over the conduct of foreign relations. As Secretary of State Thomas Jefferson observed during the first Washington Administration: "The constitution has divided the powers of government into three branches [and] . . . has declared that 'the executive powers shall be vested in the President,' submitting only special articles of it to a negative by the Senate."[27] Due to this structure, Jefferson continued, "[t]he transaction of business with foreign nations is Executive altogether. It belongs then to the head of that department, *except* as to such portions of it as are specially submitted to the Senate. *Exceptions* are to be construed strictly."[28] In defending President Washington's authority to issue the Neutrality Proclamation. Alexander Hamilton came to the same interpretation of the President's foreign affairs powers. According to Hamilton, Article II "ought . . . to be considered as intended . . . to specify and regulate the principal articles implied in the definition of Executive Power, leaving the rest to flow from the general grant of that power."[29] As future Chief Justice John Marshall famously declared a few years later, "The President

---

[26] This is *not* to maintain that Afghanistan ceased to be a State party to the Geneva Conventions merely because it underwent a change of government in 1996, after the military successes of Taliban. The general rule of international law is that treaty relations survive a change of government. *See. e.g.*, 2 Marjorie M. Whiteman, *Digest of International Law* 771–73 (1963), J. L. Brierly, *The Law of Nations* 144–45 (6th ed. 1963); Eleanor C. McDowell, *Contemporary Practice of the United States Relating to International Law*, 71 Am. J. Int'l L. 337 (1977). However, although "[u]nder international law, a change in government alone generally does not alter a state's obligations to honor its treaty commitments . . . [a] different and more difficult question arises . . . when the state itself dissolves." Yoo, *supra* n.17, at 904. Furthermore, we are *not* suggesting that the United States' non recognition of the Taliban as the government of Afghanistan in and of itself deprived Afghanistan of party status under the Geneva Conventions. The general rule is that treaties may still be observed even as to State parties, the current governments of which have been unrecognized. *See New York Chinese TV Programs v. U.E. Enterprises*, 954 F.2d 847 (2d Cir.), *cert. denied*, 506 U.S. 827 (1992); *see also Restatement (Third) of the Foreign Relations Law of the United States* at § 202 emts. a, b; Egon Schwelb, *The Nuclear Test Ban Treaty and International Law*, 58 Am. J. Int'l L. 642, 655 (1964) (quoting statements of President Kennedy and Secretary of State Rusk that participation in a multilateral treaty does not affect recognition status).

[27] Thomas Jefferson, *Opinion on the Powers of the Senate Respecting Diplomatic Appointments* (1790), *reprinted in* 16 *The Papers of Thomas Jefferson* 378 (Julian P. Boyd ed., 1961).

[28] *Id.* at 379.

[29] Alexander Hamilton, Pacificus No. 1 (1793), *reprinted in* 15 *The Papers of Alexander Hamilton* 33, 39 (Harold C. Syrett et al. eds., 1969).

is the sole organ of the nation in its external relations, and its sole representative with foreign nations . . . The [executive] department . . . is entrusted with the whole foreign intercourse of the nation. . . ."[30] Given the agreement of Jefferson, Hamilton, and Marshall, it has not been difficult for the executive branch consistently to assert the President's plenary authority in foreign affairs ever since.

On the few occasions where it has addressed the question, the Supreme Court has lent its approval to the executive branch's broad powers in the field of foreign affairs. Responsibility for the conduct of foreign affairs and for protecting the national security are, as the Supreme Court has observed, "'central' Presidential domains."[31] The President's constitutional primacy flows from both his unique position in the constitutional structure, and from the specific grants of authority in Article II that make the President both the Chief Executive of the nation and the Commander-in-Chief.[32] Due to the President's constitutionally superior position, the Supreme Court has consistently "recognized 'the generally accepted view that foreign policy [is] the province and responsibility of the Executive."[33] This foreign affairs power is independent of Congress: it is "the very delicate, plenary and exclusive power of the President as sole organ of the federal government in the field of international relations – a power which does not require as a basis for its exercise an Act of Congress."[34]

Part of the President's plenary power over the conduct of the Nation's foreign relations is the interpretation of treaties and of international law. Interpretation of international law includes the determination whether a territory has the necessary political structure to qualify as a Nation State for purposes of treaty implementation. In *Clark v. Allen*, 331 U.S. 503 (1947), for example, the Supreme Court considered whether a 1923 treaty with Germany continued to exist after the defeat, occupation and partition of Germany by the victorious World War II Allies. The Court rejected the argument that the treaty "must be held to have failed to survive the [Second World War], since Germany, as a result of its defeat and the occupation by the Allies, has ceased to exist as an independent national or international community."[35] Instead, the Court held that "the question whether a state is in a position to perform its treaty obligations is essentially a political question. *Terlinden v. Ames*. 184 U.S. 270, 288 [(1902)]. We find no evidence that the political departments have considered the collapse and surrender of Germany as putting an end to such provisions of the treaty as survived the outbreak of the war or the obligations of either party in respect to them."[36]

Thus, *Clark* demonstrates the Supreme Court's sanction for the Executive's constitutional authority to decide the "political questions" whether Germany had ceased to exist as a Nation State and, if so, whether the 1923 treaty with Germany had become inoperative. Equally here, the executive branch should conclude that Afghanistan was not "in a position to perform its treaty obligations" because it lacked, at least throughout the Taliban's ascendancy, all the elements of statehood. If the Executive made such

[30] 10 Annals of Cong, 613–14 (1800).

[31] Harlow v. Fitzgerald, 457 U.S. 800, 812 n. 19 (1982).

[32] *Nixon v. Fitzgerald*, 457 U.S. 731, 749–50 (1982).

[33] *Department of the Navy v. Egan*, 484 U.S. 518, 529 (1988) (quoting *Haig v. Agee*, 453 U.S. 280, 293–94 (1981)).

[34] United States v. Curtiss-Wright Export Corp., 299 U.S. 304, 320 (1936).

[35] *Id.* at 514.

[36] *Id; see also id.* at 508–09 (President might have "formulated a national policy quite inconsistent with the enforcement" of the treaty).

a determination, the Geneva Conventions would be inoperative as to Afghanistan until it was in a position to perform its Convention duties. The federal courts would not review such political questions, but instead would defer to the decision of the Executive.

B. Status as a Failed State

There are ample grounds that demonstrate that Afghanistan was a failed State. Indeed, the findings of the State and Defense Departments, of foreign leaders, and of expert opinion overwhelmingly support such a conclusion.

International law recognizes many situations in which there may be a territory that has no "State." A variety of situations can answer to this description.[37] Of chief relevance here is the category of the "failed State." The case of Somalia in 1992 at the time of the United States intervention, provides a clear example of this category.

A "failed State" is generally characterized by the collapse or near-collapse of State authority. Such collapse is characterized by the inability of central authorities to maintain government institutions, ensure law and order or engage in normal dealings with other governments, and by the prevalence of violence that destabilizes civil society and the economy. The Executive can readily find that at the outset of this conflict, when the country was largely in the hands of the Taliban militia, there was no functioning central government in Afghanistan that was capable of providing the most basic services to the Afghan population, of suppressing endemic internal violence, or of maintaining normal relations with other governments. Afghanistan, consequently, was without the status of a State for purposes of treaty law, and the Taliban militia could not have qualified as the *de facto* government of Afghanistan. Rather, the Taliban militia would have had the status only of a violent faction or movement contending with other factions for control of that country.

We want to make clear that this Office does not have access to all of the facts related to the activities of the Taliban militia and al Qaeda in Afghanistan. Nonetheless, the available facts in the public record support our conclusion that Afghanistan was a failed state – including facts that pre-existed the military reversals suffered by the Taliban militia and the formation of the new transitional government pursuant to the Bonn agreement. Indeed, the departments best positioned to make such a determination appear to have reached that conclusion some time ago. Secretary of Defense Donald Rumsfeld, for example, declared at a November 2, 2001 press conference that the "Taliban is not a government. The government of Afghanistan does not exist today. The Taliban never was a government as such. It was a force in the country that is not substantially weakened – in many cases cloistered away from the people."[38]

---

[37] It is entirely possible in international law for a territory (even a populated one) to be without any State. In the *Western Sahara Case*. Advisory opinion, 1975 LCJ. 12 (Advisory Opinion May 22, 1975), the General Assembly requested the ICJ to decide the question whether the Western Sahara at the time of Spanish colonization was a territory belonging to no one. The question would have had no meaning unless there could be Stateless territory without a State. *See* D.J. Harris, *Cases and Materials on International Law* 113 (1991). The Transkei, a "homeland" created for the Xhosa people by the Republic of South Africa in 1976, was also a territory not internationally recognized as a State. *See id.* at 110–11.

[38] *Secretary Rumsfeld Media Availability on Route to Moscow* (Nov. 2, 2001), available at http://www.yale.edu./**************/sept.11/dod brief64.hern (visited Nov. 8, 2001).

The State Department has taken the same view. Near the start of the conflict, the Bureau of South Asian Affairs found that "[t]here is no functioning central government [in Afghanistan]. The country is divided among fighting factions. . . . The Taliban [is] a radical Islamic movement [that] occupies about 90% of the country."[39]

Prominent authorities and experts on Afghan affairs agree that Afghanistan was a failed State. As one leading scholar of international law has written, "[t]he most dramatic examples of the decline in state authority can be found in countries where government and civil order have virtually disappeared. Recent examples are Liberia, Somalia, and Afghanistan. The term 'failed states' has come to be used for these cases and others like them."[40] Lakhdar Brahimi, the United Nations mediator in Afghanistan and a former Algerian Foreign Minister, described Afghanistan under the Taliban as a "failed state which looks like an infected wound."[41] Tony Blair, the Prime Minister of Great Britain, on a visit to that country this month, declared that "Afghanistan has been a failed state for too long and the whole world has paid the price."[42]

Traditional legal analysis also makes clear that Afghanistan was a failed State during the period of the Taliban militia's existence. A State has failed when centralized governmental authority has almost completely collapsed, no central authorities are capable of maintaining government institutions or ensuring law and order, and violence has destabilized civil society and the economy.[43] A failed State will not

---

[39] *Background Note* (October, 2001), available at http://www.state.gov./***************5380 (visited Oct. 25, 2001), prepared by the Bureau of South Asian Affairs. *See also* Reuters AlertNet – Afghanistan, *Country Profiles* ("There are no state-constituted armed forces. It is not possible to show how ground forces' equipment has been divided among the different factions."), available at http://www.altertnet.org./**************/countryprofiles/152478?version***1 (visited Nov. 1, 2001).

[40] Oscar Schachter, *The Decline of the Nation-State and Its Implications for International Law*, 36 Colum. J. *************** L. 7, 18 (1997).

[41] Ahmed Rashid, Taliban: Militant Islam Oil & Fundamentalism in Central Asia 207 (2001).

[42] Philip Webster, *Blair's mission to Kabul*, in The Times of London (Jan. 8, 2002), 2002 WL 4171996.

[43] "States in which institutions and law and order have totally or partially collapsed under the pressure and amidst the confusion of erupting violence, yet which subsist as a short presence on the world map, are now commonly referred to as 'failed States' or ***************'" Daniel Thurer, *The failed State and International Law*, International Review of the Red Cross No. 836 (Dec. 31, 1999), available at http://www.icrc.org/eng/review (visited Oct. 22, 2001). Somewhat different tests have been used for determining whether a State has "failed." First, the most salient characteristic of a "failed State" seems to be the disappearance of a "central government." Yoram Dinstein, *The Thirteenth Waldemar A. Solf Lecture in International Law*, 166 Mil. L. Rev. 93, 103 (2000); *see also id.* ("All that remains is a multiplicity of groups of irregular combatants fighting each other."). Closely related to this test, but perhaps somewhat broader, is the definition of a "failed State" as "a situation where the government is unable to discharge basic governmental functions with respect to its populace and its territory. Consequently, laws are not made, cases are not decided, order is not preserved and societal cohesion deteriorates. Basic services such as medical care, education, infrastructure maintenance, tax collection and other functions and services rendered by central governing authorities cease to exist or exist only in limited areas." Ruth Gordon, *Growing Constitutions*, 1 U. Pa. J. Const. L. 528, 533–34 (1999). Professor Thurer distinguishes three elements (respectively, territorial, political and functional) said to characterize a "failed State": 1) failed States undergo an "implosion rather than an explosion of the structures of power and authority, the disintegration and destructuring of States rather than their dismemberment;" 2) they experience "the total or near total breakdown of structures guaranteeing law and order;" and 3) there are marked by "the absence of bodies capable, on the one hand, of representing the State at the international level and, on the other, of being influenced by the outside world." Thurer, *supra*.

satisfy some or all of the three traditional tests for "statehood" under international law:

1. Does the entity have a defined territory and population?
2. Are the territory/population under the control of its own government?
3. Does the entity engage in or have the capacity to engage in formal relations with other States?[44]

In another version of the traditional formulation, the State Department has identified four tests for "statehood":

i) Does the entity have effective control over a clearly defined territory and population?

ii) Is there an organized governmental administration of the territory?

iii) Does the entity have the capacity to act effectively to conduct foreign relations and to fulfill international obligations?

iv) Has the international community recognized the entity?[45]

Based on these factors, we conclude that Afghanistan under the Taliban militia was in a condition of "statelessness," and therefore was not a High Contracting Party to the Geneva Conventions for at least that period of time. The condition of having an organized governmental administration was plainly not met. Indeed, there are good reasons to doubt whether *any* of the conditions was met.

First, even before the outset of the conflict with the United States, the Taliban militia did not have effective control over a clearly defined territory and population. Even before the United States air strikes began, at least ten percent of the country, and the population within those areas, was governed by the Northern Alliance. A large part of the Afghan population in recent years has consisted of refugees: as of June, 2001, there were an estimated 2,000,000 Afghan refugees in Pakistan and as of December, 2000, an estimated 1,500,000 were in Iran.[46] These figures demonstrate that a significant segment of the Afghan population was never under the control of the Taliban militia. It is unclear how strong was the hold of the Taliban militia before the conflict, in light of the rapid military successes of the Northern Alliance in just a few weeks.

Indeed, the facts appear to show that Afghanistan appears to have been divided between different tribal and warring factions, rather than by any central state as such. As we have noted, the State Department has found that Afghanistan was not under the control of a central government, but was instead divided among different warlords and ethnic groups. The Taliban militia in essence represented only an ethnically Pashtun movement, a "tribal militia,"[47] that did not command the allegiance of other

---

[44] *See Restatement (Third) of the Foreign Relations Law of the United States*, at § 201; *see also* 1933 Montevideo Convention on Rights and Duties of States, art. I, 49 Stat. 3097, 28 Am. J. Int'l L. Supp. 75 (1934).

[45] Eleanor C. McDowell, Contemporary Practice of the United States Relating to International Law, 71 Am. J. Int'l L. 337 (1977).

[46] See CNN.com. In-Depth Specials, *War Against Terror*, available at http://www.cnn.com/SPECIALS/2001/trade.center/refugee.map.html (visited Nov. 1, 2001). Other estimates are lower but still extremely large numbers. *See e.g.*, Goodson, *supra*, at 149 (estimating 1.2 million Afghans living in Pakistan).

[47] Goodson, *supra*, at 115.

major ethnic groups in Afghanistan and that was apparently unable to suppress endemic violence in the country. As a prominent writer on the Taliban militia wrote well
before the current conflict began, "[e]ven if [the Taliban] were to conquer the north,
it would not bring stability, only continuing guerrilla war by the non-Pashtuns, but
this time from bases in Central Asia and Iran which would further destabilize the
region."[48]

Second, again even before the United States air strikes and the successes of
the Northern Alliance, an organized governmental administration did not exist in
Afghanistan. One expert on the Taliban concluded that the country had

> ceased to exist as a viable state and when a state fails civil society is destroyed. . . . The
> entire Afghan population has been displaced, not once but many times over. The
> physical destruction of Kabul has turned it into the Dresden of the late twenti-
> eth century. . . . There is no semblance of an infrastructure that can sustain society –
> even at the lowest common denominator of poverty. . . . The economy is a black hole
> that is sucking in its neighbours with illicit trade and the smuggling of drugs and
> weapons, undermining them in the process. . . . Complex relationships of power and
> authority built up over centuries have broken down completely. No single group
> or leader has the legitimacy to reunite the country. Rather than a national iden-
> tity or kinship-tribal-based identities, territorial-regional identities have become
> paramount. . . . [T]he Taliban refuse to define the Afghan state they want to consti-
> tute and rule over, largely because they have no idea what they want. The lack of
> a central authority, state organizations, a methodology for command and control
> and mechanisms which can reflect some level of popular participation . . . make it
> impossible for many Afghans to accept the Taliban or for the outside world to rec-
> ognize a Taliban government. . . . No warlord faction has ever felt itself responsible
> for the civilian population, but the Taliban are incapable of carrying out even the
> minimum of developmental work because they believe that Islam will take care of
> everyone.[49]

Another expert reached similar conclusions:

> Afghanistan today has become a violent society, bereft of political institutions that
> function correctly and an economy that functions at all. When this is coupled with
> the destruction of population and the physical infrastructure . . . , it becomes clear
> that Afghanistan is a country on the edge of collapse, or at least profound trans-
> formation. . . . With the Taliban, there are few meaningful governmental structures
> and little that actually functions.[50]

The State Department also came to such conclusions. In testimony early in October
2001 before the Senate Foreign Relations Committee's Subcommittee on Near East
and South Asian Affairs, Assistant Secretary of State for South Asian Affairs Christina
Rocca explained that:

> [t]wenty-two years of conflict have steadily devastated [Afghanistan], destroyed
> its physical and political infrastructure, shuttered its institutions, and wrecked
> its socio-economic fabric. . . . The Taliban have shown no desire to provide even
> the most rudimentary health, education, and other social services expected of any

---

[48] Rashid, *supra*, at 213.
[49] *Id.* at 207–08, 212–13.
[50] Goodson, *supra*, at 103–04; 115

government. Instead, they have chosen to devote their resources to waging war on the Afghan people, and exporting instability to their neighbors.[51]

Rather than performing normal government functions, the Taliban militia exhibited the characteristics of a criminal gang. The United Nations Security Council found that the Taliban militia extracted massive profits from illegal drug trafficking in Afghanistan and subsidized terrorism from those revenues.[52]

Third, the Taliban militia was unable to conduct normal foreign relations or to fulfill its international legal obligations. Indeed, the public record shows that the Taliban militia had become so subject to the domination and control of al Qaeda that it could not pursue independent policies with respect to the outside world.[53] Publicly known facts demonstrate that the Taliban was unwilling and perhaps unable to obey its international obligations and to conduct normal diplomatic relations. Thus, the Taliban has consistently refused to comply with United Nations Security Council Resolutions 1333 (2000) and 1267 (1999), which called on it to surrender Osama bin Laden to justice and to take other actions to abate terrorism based in Afghanistan.[54] Those resolutions also called on all States to deny permission for aircraft to take off or to land

[51] United States Department of State, International Information Programs, *Rocca Blames Taliban for Humanitarian Disaster in Afghanistan* (Oct. 10, 2001), available at http://www.usinfo.state.gov/regional./nea/sasia/afghan/text/1010roca.htm (visited Oct. 19, 2001).

[52] *See* U.N. Security Council Resolution 1333 (2000), available at http://www.yale.edu/lawweb/avalon/sept_11/unsecres_1333.htm (finding that "the Taliban benefits directly from the cultivation of illicit opium by imposing a tax on its production and indirectly benefits from the processing and trafficking of such opium, and these substantial resources strengthen the Taliban's capacity to harbor terrorists"). The United States Government has amassed substantial evidence that Taliban has condemned and profited from narco-trafficking, on a massive scale, with disastrous effects on neighboring countries. *See The Taliban, Terrorism, and Drug Trade*: Hearing Before the Subcomm. on Criminal Justice, Drug Policy and Human Resources of the House Comm. on Government Reform, 107th Cong. (2001) (testimony of William Bach, Director, Office of Asia, Africa, Europe, NIS Programs, Bureau of International Narcotics and Law Enforcement Affairs, Department of State; testimony of Asa Hutchinson, Administrator, Drug Enforcement Administration, U.S. Department of Justice). "The heroin explosion emanating from Afghanistan is now affecting the politics and economies of the entire region. It is crippling societies, distorting the economies of already fragile states and creating a new narco-elite which is at odds with the ever increasing poverty of the population." Rashid, *supra*, at 123; *see also* Goodson, *supra*, at 101–03; Peter Tomsen, *Untying the Afghan Knot*, 25 WTR Fletcher F. World Aff. 17, 18 (2001) ("Afghanistan is now the world's largest producer of opium"). Iran is estimated to have as many as three million drug addicts, largely as a result of Taliban's involvement in the drug trade. Rashid, *supra*, at 122, 203.

[53] *See e.g.* "2 U.S. Targets Bound by Fate," *The Washington Post* at A22 (Nov. 14, 2001) ("According to Thomas Gouttierre, an Afghan expert at the University of Nebraska and a former UN adviser, the so-called Afghan Arabs surrounding Bin Laden were much more educated and articulate than the often illiterate Taliban and succeeded in convincing them that they were at the head of a world-wide Islamic renaissance. 'Al Qaeda ended up hijacking a large part of the Taliban movement,' he said, noting that [Taliban supreme religious leader Mohammed] Omar and Bin Laden were 'very, very tight' by 1998."); "Bin Laden Paid Cash for Taliban," *The Washington Post* at A1 (Nov. 30, 2001) (reporting claims by former Taliban official of al Qaeda's corruption of Taliban officials).

[54] U.N. Security Council Resolution 1333 "strongly condemn[ed]" the Taliban for the "sheltering and training of terrorists and [the] planning of terrorist acts," and "deplor[ed] the fact that the Taliban continues to provide a safe haven to Osama Bin Laden and to allow him and others associated with him to operate a network of terrorist training camps from Taliban-controlled territory and to use Afghanistan as a base from which to sponsor international terrorist operations." U.N. Security Council Resolution 1214, ¶ 13 (1998) enjoined the Taliban to stop providing a sanctuary and training for terrorists. U.N. Security Council Resolution 1267, ¶ 2 (1999), stated that the Taliban's failure to comply with the Council's 1998 demand constituted a threat to the peace. *See* Sean D. Murphy, *Efforts to Obtain Custody of Osama Bin Laden*, 94 Am. J. Int'l L. 366 (2000).

if they were owned or operated by or for the Taliban, and to freeze funds and other resources owned or controlled by the Taliban. The Taliban also reportedly refused or was unable to extradite bin Laden at the request of Saudi Arabia in September, 1998, despite close relations between the Saudi government and itself. As a result, the Saudi government expelled the Afghan *charge d'affaires*.[55] The Taliban's continuing role in sheltering and supporting those believed to be responsible for the terrorist attacks of September 11, 2001 placed it in clear breach of international law, which required it to prevent the use of its territory as a launching pad for attacks against another Nation.[56]

Fourth, the Taliban militia was not recognized as the legitimate government of Afghanistan by the United States or by any member of the international community except Pakistan. Neither the United States nor the United Nations ever recognized that the Taliban militia were a government. The only two other States that had maintained diplomatic relations with it before the current conflict began (Saudi Arabia and the United Arab Emirates) soon severed them.[57] Even Pakistan had withdrawn its recognition before the end of hostilities between the United States and the Taliban forces. This *universal* refusal to recognize the Taliban militia as a government demonstrates that other nations and the United Nations concur in our judgment that the Taliban militia was no government and that Afghanistan had ceased to operate as a Nation State.

Based on the foregoing, we conclude that the evidence supports the conclusion that Afghanistan, when largely controlled by the Taliban, failed some, and perhaps all, of the ordinary tests of statehood. Nor do we think that the military successes of the United States and the Northern Alliance change that outcome. Afghanistan *was* stateless for the relevant period of the conflict, even if after the Bonn Agreement it becomes a State recognized by the United Nations, the United States, and most other nations.[58] If Afghanistan was in a condition of statelessness during the time of the

---

[55] See Yussef Bodansky, *Bin Laden: The Man Who Declared War on America* 301–02 (2001).

[56] See Robert F. Turner, *International Law and the Use of Force in Response to the World Trade Center and Pentagon Attacks*, available at http://jurist.law.pitt.edu/forumnew/34.htm (visited Oct. 25, 2001) ("If (as has been claimed by the US and UK governments) bin Laden masterminded the attacks on New York and Washington, Afghanistan is in breach of its state responsibility to take reasonable measures to prevent its territory from being used to launch attacks against other states. The United States and its allies thus have a legal right to violate Afghanistan's territorial integrity to destroy bin Laden and related terrorist targets. If the Taliban elects to join forces with bin Laden it, too, becomes a lawful target."); *see also* W. Michael Reisman, *International Legal Responses to Terrorism*, 22 Hous. J. Int'l L. 3, 40–42, 51–54 (1999).

[57] *See* "A Look at the Taliban," Sept. 30, 2001, available at http://www.usatoday.com/news/world/2001/thetaliban.htm (visited Oct. 19, 2001). Indeed, Pakistan had been the only country in the world that maintained an embassy in Kabul; the overwhelming majority of States and the United Nations recognized exiled President Burhamuddin Rabbani and his government as the country's legal authorities. *See* "Taliban tactics move to hostage ploy." Aug. 8, 2001, available at http://www.janes.com/regional_news/asia_pacific/news/jid/jid010808_1_n.shtml (visited Oct. 19, 2001).

[58] We do not think that the military successes of the United States and the Northern Alliance necessarily mean that Afghanistan's statehood was restored before the Bonn agreement, if only because the international community, including the United States, did not regard the Northern Alliance as constituting the government of Afghanistan. United Nations Security Council Resolution 1378, ¶, 1 (2001), available at http://www.yale.edu/lawweb/avalon/sept_11/unsecres_1378.htm (visited Nov. 19, 2001), expressed "strong support for the efforts of the Afghan people to establish a new and transitional administration leading to the formation of a government." (emphasis added); see also id. ¶ 3 (affirming that the United Nations should play a central role in supporting Afghan efforts to establish a "new and transitional administration leading to the formation of a new government"). The plain

conflict, the Taliban militia could not have been considered a government that was also a High Contracting Party to the Geneva Conventions.

The conclusion that members of the Taliban militia are not entitled to the protections accorded to POWs under the Geneva Conventions receives further support from other arguments. As we have already suggested, there is substantial evidence that the Taliban and al Qaeda were so closely intertwined that the Taliban cannot be regarded as an independent actor, and therefore cannot stand on a higher footing under the Geneva Conventions than al Qaeda. Mullah Mohammed Omar, the spiritual leader of the Taliban, appears to have been particularly susceptible to the more sophisticated leadership of al Qaeda, who "introduced him to the world of Islamic radicalism, global jihad and hatred of the United States," who exercised great religious and ideological influence over him, and who furnished him with personal favors such as a bombproof house in Kandahar.[59] In particular, Omar, who was born into poverty, and was virtually uneducated, seems to have worked closely with Osama bin Laden, who shared with Omar a vision of an international Islamic revolution.[60]

Al Qaeda also provided substantial material assistance to the Taliban militia. It made large sums available to Taliban leaders, and supplied them with "a steady stream of guerrilla fighters to assist the Taliban in their continuing battles with the Northern Alliance."[61] Because the Taliban was not equipped to maintain control over Afghanistan in the face of armed opposition from other factions, the Taliban became increasingly dependent on the money, weapons, recruits, and well-trained soldiers provided to it by al Qaeda. Al Qaeda in turn depended on the Taliban to provide it with bases for training camps and a refuge from the United States. Over the course of his dealings with it, bin Laden "pumped tens of millions of dollars into the Taliban, provided it with his most elite Arab fighting forces, and integrated his Qaeda network into key portfolios within the Taliban government.... [T]he two [movements] had long since melded together as one, through money, combat, and a shared radical interpretation of Islam."[62] Further, both because al Qaeda was capable of mustering more formidable military forces than the Taliban at any given point, and because failure to protect bin Laden would have cost the Taliban the support of radical Islamists, it may well have been impossible, for the Taliban to surrender bin Laden as directed by the United Nations, even if it had been willing to do.[63] In any event, by continuing to harbor bin Laden and al Qaeda and to assist them in material ways, the Taliban became complicit in its terrorist acts. Taking all these facts into account, together with other non-public information that may be available to the Executive, we think it fair to characterize the Taliban militia as functionally intertwined with al Qaeda, and therefore on the same footing as al Qaeda under the Geneva Conventions.

---

implication of this Resolution, which reflects the views of the United States, is that Afghanistan after Taliban did not have a government at that time.

[59] Murray Campbell, *Enigmatic Taliban cleric a poor leader*, The Globe and Mail, at A11 (Dec. 1, 2001).

[60] Indeed, there are press reports (which have also been denied) that a daughter of bin Laden married Omar, and a daughter of Omar married bin Laden.

[61] Michael Dobbs and Vernon Loeb, *supra* note 53.

[62] Michael Kranish and Indira A. R. Lakshmanan, *Partners in 'Jihad': Bin Laden Ties to Taliban: How Odd Alliances Marked Bin Laden's Path*, in *The Boston Globe* (Oct. 28, 2001), 2001 WL 3958881. This article contains especially detailed information about the close linkages between the two movements and their leaders.

[63] Peter McGrath and Gretel Kovach, *Bin Laden's Imprint: an expert on the radical leader says targeting the Saudi dissident won't eliminate his threat, in Newsweek* (Sept. 14, 2001), 2001 WL 24138958.

C. Implications Under the Geneva Conventions

Whether based on the view that Afghanistan was a failed State or on the view that Taliban was functionally indistinguishable from al Qaeda, the view that Afghanistan had ceased to be a party to the Geneva Conventions has two immediate ramifications. First, common Article 2 – and thus most of the substance of the Geneva Conventions – would not apply to the members of the Taliban militia, because that provision only applies to international wars between two State Parties to the Conventions. Second, even common Article 3's basic standards would not apply. This would be so, not only because the current conflict is not a non-international conflict subject to Article 3, but also because common Article 3 concerns only a non-international conflict that occurs "in the territory *of one of the High Contracting Parties*" (emphasis added). If Afghanistan was not a High Contracting Party during the time of the conflict, then a non-international conflict within its territory does not fall within the terms of Article 3.

We have considered the argument that, even if our conclusions held during the period when Afghanistan was largely under the Taliban's control (and thus in a condition of statelessness), they have ceased to hold in light of the Bonn Agreement. Afghanistan now has an internationally recognized government, and on that basis it might be argued that it has resumed its status as a High Contracting Party under the Geneva Conventions. It could then be argued that the protections of those Conventions – including the protections for prisoners of war – *now* clothe the Taliban militia, even if they did not during the Taliban's ascendancy.

This reasoning would be mistaken. First, even if Afghanistan now has a recognized government, it does not *necessarily* follow that its status as a party to the Conventions has been completely restored. Afghanistan still may not be in a position to fulfill its Convention responsibilities, and thus should not yet be accorded party status under the Conventions.[64] Thus, even though Germany had some form of government when the Supreme Court decided *Clark v. Allen* in 1947, the Court declared that whether Germany was "in a position to perform its treaty obligations"[65] was a political question, meaning that it remained open for the President to decide whether the treaty with Germany was in effect. We expect that the courts would properly recognize that it rests solely within the President's constitutional authority to determine whether Afghanistan has yet returned to the status of a state party to the Conventions.

Second, the jurisdictional provisions of the Conventions (common Articles 2 and 3) still remain inapplicable to the conflict between the United States and the Taliban militia. This is the case even assuming that, with the substantial cessation of that conflict, the status of Afghanistan as a party to the Conventions has been restored. Article 2 states that the Convention shall apply to all cases of declared war or other armed conflict between the High Contracting Parties. But there was no war or armed conflict between the United States and Afghanistan during the period before the Bonn Agreement if Afghanistan was stateless at that time. Not, of course, is there a state of war or armed conflict between the United States and Afghanistan *now*. Likewise,

---

[64] As one expert on Afghanistan has recently noted, "Afghanistan hasn't really had a credible central government since 1973, when the king was ousted.... They have been out of practice at seeing themselves as having a central authority of some kind." Kevin Whitelaw et al. *A Hunt in the Hills*, in *U.S. News & World Report* (Dec. 17, 2001), 2001 WL 30366330 (quoting Thomas Gouttierre of the University of Nebraska-Omaha.

[65] 331 U.S. at 514

Article 3 states that certain basic standards shall apply in the case of "an armed conflict not of an international character occurring in the territory of one of the High Contracting Parties." The most natural reading of this provision is that the conflict must have occurred in the territory of a State that was a High Contracting Party *at the time of the conflict.* So understood, Article 3 would not apply to the conflict with the Taliban.[66] Because the jurisdictional provisions remain inapplicable even if Afghanistan's status as a Convention party has been restored, Taliban prisoners remain outside the protections of the Conventions. As a result, they do not, for example, fall under the definition of "prisoners of war" in Geneva Convention III, art. 4.

Furthermore, even apart from the question whether Afghanistan was or remains a failed state, there are specific reasons why Geneva Convention III, relating to POWs, would not apply to captured Taliban militia. First, Article 4 of Geneva Convention III enumerates particular categories of persons who are entitled to POW status. In our judgment, Taliban captives do not fall within any of these categories, including that of Article 4(A)(3), "Members of regular armed forces who profess allegiance to a government or an authority not recognized by the Detaining Power." As we have discussed, the United Nations and almost all members of the world community, including the United States, refused to recognize the Taliban militia as the government of Afghanistan. Of the handful of States that did recognize it, all but Pakistan withdrew their recognition soon after the start of the conflict, and Pakistan later followed suit. Thus, the Taliban cannot even be considered "a government or authority" at all for purposes of this provision, since no other state in the world viewed the Taliban militia as qualifying as one. According the Taliban militia the status of the armed forces of a government, even when no other country in the world considered it as such, would be tantamount to allowing any political or violent movement to simply declare itself to be a government. Enjoyment of the rights and duties of a sovereign state should not be so easily accorded as by self-identification.

Second, even if a political group or movement could be considered to be "a government or authority" within the meaning of Article 4(A)(3), that group or movement would have to demonstrate that it considered itself bound by Geneva Convention III in order to be in a position to claim the Convention's benefits. Your Department, however, informs us that the Taliban militia failed to confirm its acceptance of the Geneva Conventions, did not fulfill its obligations, and it did not act consistently with the most fundamental obligations of the laws of war, such as the prohibition on using civilians to shield military forces.

Third, even if the Taliban considered themselves to be a party to Geneva Convention III, or even if they had stated publicly that they would comply with that Convention's provisions and in fact did so, Taliban captives would still have to meet other requirements of Article 4 to be entitled to POW status. For example, Article 4(A)(3) only covers "[m]embers of *regular armed forces*" (emphasis added). The Taliban militia, it seems, cannot be so characterized. To be sure, Article 4(A)(2) accords POW status to persons who are not in regular armed forces, *i.e.*, "[m]embers of other militias and members of other voluntary corps, including those of organized resistance movements." Nevertheless, Article 4 makes clear that these combatants are only afforded POW status if they meet certain conditions, including "that of being commanded by a person responsible for his subordinates," "that of having a fixed distinctive sign recognizable

---

[66] In addition, as we have noted, Article 3 is and was inapplicable because the conflict in Afghanistan is and was of an international character.

at a distance," and "that of conducting their operations in accordance with the laws and customs of war." Your Department advises us that the Taliban militia's command structure probably did not meet the first of these requirements; that the evidence strongly indicates that the requirement of a distinctive uniform was not met; and that the requirement of conducting operations in accordance with the law and customs of armed conflict was not met. Accordingly, we think that Taliban captives do not qualify for POW status either as members of regular armed forces or as combatants of other kinds covered by the Convention.[67]

D. Historical Application of the Geneva Conventions

We conclude by addressing a point of considerable significance. To say that the specific provisions of the Geneva and Hague Conventions do not apply in the current conflict with the Taliban militia *as a legal requirement* is by no means to say that the principles of the law of armed conflict cannot be applied *as a matter of U.S. Government policy*. The President as Commander-in-Chief can determine as a matter of his judgment for the efficient prosecution of the military campaign that the policy of the United States will be to enforce customary standards of the law of war against the Taliban and to punish any transgressions against those standards. Thus, for example, even though Geneva Convention III may not apply, the United States may deem it a violation of the laws and usages of war for Taliban troops to torture any American prisoners whom they may happen to seize. The U.S. military thus could prosecute Taliban militiamen for war crimes for engaging in such conduct.[68] A decision to apply the principles of the Geneva Conventions or of others laws of war as a matter of policy, not law, would be fully consistent with the past practice of the United States.

United States practice in post-1949 conflicts reveals several instances in which our military forces have applied the Geneva Conventions as a matter of policy, without acknowledging any legal obligation to do so. These cases include the wars in Korea and Vietnam and the interventions in Panama and Somalia.

Korea. The Korean War broke out on June 25, 1950, before any of the major State parties to the conflict (including the United States) had ratified the Geneva Conventions. Nonetheless, General Douglas MacArthur, the United Nations Commander in Korea, said that his forces would comply with the principles of the Geneva Conventions, including those relating to POWs. MacArthur stated: "My present instructions are to abide by the humanitarian principles of the 1949 Geneva Conventions, particularly common Article 3. In addition, I have directed the forces under my command to abide by the detailed provisions of the prisoner-of-war convention, since I have the means at my disposal to assure compliance with this convention by all concerned and have fully accredited the ICRC delegates accordingly."[69]

---

[67] We refrain from discussing more specific facts here due to the sensitive operational nature of such information.

[68] The President could, of course, also determine that it will be the policy of the United States to require its own troops to adhere to standards of conduct recognized under customary international law, and could prosecute offenders for violations. As explained above, the President is not *bound* to follow these standards by law, but may direct the armed forces to adhere to them as a matter of policy.

[69] Quoted in Joseph P. Bialke, United Nations Peace Operations: Applicable Norms and the Application of the Law of Armed Conflict, 50 A.F.L. Rev. 1, 63 n. 235 (2001).

VietNam. The United States through the State Department took the position that the Geneva Convention III "indisputably applies to the armed conflict in Viet Nam," and therefore that "American military personnel captured in the course of that armed conflict are entitled to be treated as prisoners of war."[70] We understand from the Defense Department that our military forces, as a matter of policy, decided at some point in the conflict to accord POW treatment (but not necessarily POW status) to Viet Cong members, despite the fact that they often did *not* meet the criteria for that status (set forth in Geneva Convention III, art. 4), *e.g.*, by not wearing uniforms or any other fixed distinctive signs visible at a distance.

Panama. The United States' intervention in Panama on December 20, 1989, came at the request and invitation of Panama's legitimately elected President, Guillermo Endara.[71] The United States had never recognized General Manuel Noriega, the commander of the Panamanian Defense Force, as Panama's legitimate ruler. Thus, in the view of the executive branch, the conflict was between the Government of Panama assisted by the United States on the one side and insurgent forces loyal to General Noriega on the other. It was not an international armed conflict between the United States and Panama, another State. Accordingly, it was not, in the executive's judgment, an international armed conflict governed by common Article 2 of the Geneva Conventions.[72] Nonetheless, we understand that, as a matter of policy, all persons captured or detained by the United States in the intervention – including civilians and members of paramilitary forces as well as members of the Panamanian Defense Force – were *treated* consistently with the Geneva Convention III, until their precise status

---

[70] *Entitlement of American Military Personnel Held by North Vietnam to Treatment as Prisoners of War Under the Geneva Convention of 1949 Relative to the Treatment of Prisoners of War*, July 13, 1966, reprinted in John Norton Moore, *Law and the Indo-China War* 635,639 (1972).

[71] *See United Sates v. Noriega*, 117 F.3d 1206, 1211 (11th Cir. 1997), *cert. denied*, 523 U.S. 1040 (1998).

[72] See Jan E. Aldykiewicz and Geoffrey S. Corn, *Authority to Court-Martial Non-U.S. Military Personnel for Serious Violations of International Humanitarian Law Committed During Internal Armed Conflict*, 167 Mil. I. Rev. 74, 77 n. 6 (2001). In *United States v. Noriega*, 808 F. Supp. 791, 794 (S.D. Fla. 1992), the district court held that the United States intervention to Panama in late 1989 was an international armed conflict under (common) Article 2 at the Geneva Convention III, and that General Noriega was entitled to POW status. To the extent that the holding assumed that the courts are free to determine whether a conflict is between the United States and another "State" regardless of the President's view whether the other party is a "State" or not, we disagree with it. By assuming the right to determine that the United States was engaged in an armed conflict with *Panama* – rather than with insurgent forces in rebellion against the recognized and legitimate Government of *Panama* – the district court impermissibly usurped the recognition power, a constitutional authority reserved to the President. The power to determine whether a foreign government is to be accorded recognition, and the related power to determine whether a condition of statelessness exists in a particular country, are exclusively executive. *See, e.g.*, *Baker v. Carr*, 369 U.S. 186, 212 (1962) (*[R]ecognition of foreign governments so strongly defies judicial treatment that without executive recognition a foreign state has been called 'a republic of whose existence we know nothing.' . . . Similarly, recognition of belligerency abroad is an executive responsibility. . . .') (citation omitted); *Kennett v. Chambers*, 55 U.S. (14 How.) 38, 50–51 (1852) ("[T]he question whether [the Republic of] Texas [while in rebellion against Mexico] had or had not at that time become an independent state, was a question for that department of our government exclusively which is charged with our foreign relations. And until the period when that department recognized it as an independent state, the judicial tribunals . . . were bound to consider . . . Texas as a part of the Mexican territory."); *Mingtai Fire & Marine Ins. Co. v. United Parcel Service*, 177 F.3d 1142, 1145 (9th Cir.) ("[T]he Supreme Court has repeatedly held that the Constitution commits to the Executive branch alone the authority to recognize and to withdraw recognition from, foreign regimes."), *cert. denied*, 528 U.S. 951 (1999).

under that Convention was determined. A 1990 letter to the Attorney General from the Legal Adviser to the State Department said that "[i]t should be emphasized that the decision to extend basic prisoner of war protections to such persons was based on strong policy considerations, and was not necessarily based on any conclusion that the United States was obligated to do so as a matter of law."[73]

Interventions in Somalia, Haiti and Bosnia. There was considerable factual uncertainty whether the United Nations Operation in Somalia in late 1992 and early 1993 rose to the level of an "armed conflict" that could be subject to common Article 3 of the Geneva Conventions particularly after the United Nations Task Force abandoned its previously neutral role and took military action against a Somali warlord, General Aideed. Similar questions have arisen in other peace operations, including those in Haiti and Bosnia. It appears that the U.S. military has decided, as a matter of policy, to conduct operations in such circumstances as if the Geneva Conventions applied, regardless of whether there is any legal requirement to do so. The U.S. Army Operational Law Handbook, after noting that "[i]n peace operations such as those in Somalia, Haiti, and Bosnia, the question frequently arises whether the [law of war] legally applies," states that it is "the position of the US, UN and NATO that their forces will apply the 'principles and spirit' of the [law of war] in these operations."[74]

E. Suspension of The Geneva Conventions as to Afghanistan

Even if Afghanistan under the Taliban were not deemed to have been a failed State, the President could still regard the Geneva Conventions as temporarily suspended during the current military action. As a constitutional matter, the President has the power to consider performance of some or all of the obligations of the United States under the Conventions suspended. Such a decision could be based on the finding that Afghanistan lacked the capacity to fulfill its treaty obligations or (if supported by the facts) on the finding that Afghanistan was in material breach of its obligations.

As the Nation's representative in foreign affairs, the President has a variety of constitutional powers with respect to treaties, including the powers to suspend them, withhold performance of them, contravene them or terminate them. The treaty power is fundamentally an executive power established in Article II of the Constitution and therefore power over treaty matters after advice and consent by the Senate are within the President's plenary authority. We have recently treated these questions in detail, and rely upon that advice here.[75]

The courts have often acknowledged the President's constitutional powers with respect to treaties. Thus, it has long been accepted that the President may determine whether a treaty has lapsed because a foreign State has gained or lost its independence,

---

[73] Letter for the Hon. Richard L. Thornburgh, Attorney General, from Abraham D. Sofaer, Legal Adviser, State Department at 2 (Jan, 31, 1990).

[74] *Quoted in* Bialke *supra*, at 56.

[75] *See* Memorandum for John Bellinger, III, Senior Associate Counsel and Legal Adviser to the National Security Council from John C. Yoo, Deputy Assistant Attorney General, Office of Legal Counsel, and Robert J. Delahunty, Special Counsel, Office of Legal Counsel, *Re: Authority of the President to Suspend Certain Provisions of the ABM Treaty* (Nov. 15, 2001); *see also* Memorandum for William Howard Taft, IV, Legal Adviser, Department of State, from John Yoo, Deputy Assistant Attorney General, Office of Legal Counsel, *Re: President's Constitutional Authority to Withdraw Treaties from the Senate* (Aug. 24, 2001).

or because it has undergone other changes in sovereignty.[76] Nonperformance of a particular treaty obligation may, in the President's judgment, justify withholding performance of one of the United States' treaty obligations, or contravening the treaty.[77] Further, the President may regard a treaty as suspended for several reasons. For example, he may determine that "the conditions essential to [the treaty's] continued effectiveness no longer pertain."[78] The President may also determine that a material breach of a treaty by a foreign government has rendered a treaty not merely voidable but void, as to that government.[79]

The President could justifiably exercise his constitutional authority over treaties by regarding the Geneva Conventions as suspended in relation to Afghanistan. The basis for such a determination would be a finding that under the Taliban militia, Afghanistan committed grave violations of international law and maintained close relationships with international terrorist organizations such as al Qaeda, which have attacked wholly civilian targets by surprise attack. As a result, Afghanistan under the Taliban could be held to have violated basic humanitarian duties under the Geneva Conventions and other norms of international law. Nonperformance of such basic duties could be taken to have demonstrated that Afghanistan could not be trusted to perform its commitments under the Conventions during the current conflict.[80] After the conflict, the President determine that relations under the Geneva Conventions with Afghanistan had been restored, once an Afghan government that was willing and able to execute the country's treaty obligations was securely established. Furthermore, if evidence of other material breaches of the Conventions by Afghanistan existed, that evidence could also furnish a basis for the President to decide to suspend performance of the United States' Convention obligations. A decision to regard the Geneva Conventions as suspended would not, of course, constitute a "denunciation" of the Conventions, for which procedures are prescribed in the Conventions.[81] The

[76] See Kennett, 55 U.S. at 47–48, 51; Terlinden 184 U.S. at 288; Saroop, 109 F.3d at 171 (collecting cases) Alexander Hamilton argued in 1793 that the revolution in France had triggered the power (indeed, the duty) of the President to determine whether the pre-existing treaty of alliance with the King of France remained in effect. The President's constitutional powers, he said, "include that of judging, to the case of a Revolution of Government in a foreign Country, whether the new rulers are competent organs of the National Will and ought to be recognised or not: And where a treaty antecedently exists between the States and such nation that right involves the power of giving operation or not to such treaty." Alexander Hamilton, *Pacificus* No. 1 (1793), *reprinted in* 15 *The Papers of Alexander Hamilton* 33, 41 (Harold C. Syrett et al. eds. 1969).
[77] See Taylor v. Morton, 23 F. Cas. 784, 787 (C.C.D. Mass. 1855) (No. 13,799) (Curtis, Circuit Justice), aff'd 67 U.S. (2 Black) 481 (1862).
[78] See International Load Line Convention, 40 Op. Att'y Gen. 119, 124 (1941). Changed conditions have provided a basis on which Presidents have suspended treaties in the past. For example, in 1939, President Franklin Roosevelt suspended the operation of the London Naval Treaty of 1936. "The war in Europe had caused several contracting parties to suspend the treaty, for the obvious reason that it was impossible to limit naval armaments. The notice of termination was therefore grounded on changed circumstances." David Gray Adler, *The Constitution and the Termination of Treaties*, 187 (1986).
[79] See, e.g. Charlton v. Kelly, 229 U.S. 447, 473 (1913); Escobedo v. United States, 623 F.2d 1098, 1106 (5th. Cir.), cert. denied, 449 U.S. 1036 (1980).
[80] It is possible for the President to suspend a multilateral treaty as to one but not all of the parties to the treaty. In 1986, the United States suspended the performance of its obligations under the Security Treaty (ANZUS Pact), T.I.A.S. 2493 3 U.S. T. 3420, entered into force April 29, 1952, as to New Zealand but not as to Australia. See Marian Nash (Leich), I *Cumulative Digest of United States Practice in International Law 1981–1988*, at 1279–81.
[81] See, e.g., Geneva Convention III, Article 142. The suspension of a treaty is distinct from the denunciation or termination of one. Suspension is generally a milder measure than termination, often being partial, temporary, or contingent upon circumstances that can be altered by the actions of the

President need not regard the Conventions as suspended in their entirety, but only in part.[82]

Although the United States has never, to our knowledge, suspended any provision of the Geneva Conventions, it is significant that on at least two occasions since 1949 – the Korean War and the Persian Gulf War – its practice has deviated from the clear requirements of Article 118 of Geneva Convention III. That Article prescribes the mandatory repatriation of POWs after the cessation of a covered conflict.[83] Although on both occasions the POWs themselves sought to avoid repatriation, Geneva Convention III provides that a POW may "in no circumstances renounce in part or in entirety" the right to repatriation. Moreover, the negotiating history of the Convention reveals that a proposal to make POW repatriation voluntary was considered and rejected, in large part on the ground that it would work to the detriment of the POWs.[84] Consequently, withholding of repatriation, even with the consent of the POWs, represented a deviation from the Convention's strict norms.

Korea. The Korean War broke out on June 25, 1950, before any of the major State parties to the conflict (including the United States) had ratified the Geneva Conventions. Nonetheless, the principle of repatriation of POWs had long been rooted in treaty and customary international law, including Article 20 of the Annex to Hague Convention IV, which states that "[a]fter the conclusion of peace, the repatriation of prisoners of war shall be carried out as quickly as possible."[85] Large numbers of Chinese and North Korean POWs held by the United Nations did not wish to be repatriated, however,

parties to the treaty. Moreover, at least in the United States, suspension of a treaty can be reversed by unilateral executive action, whereas termination, which annuls a treaty, and which is therefore more disruptive of international relationships, would require Senate consent to a new treaty in order to be undone. See Oliver J. Lassitzyn, *Treaties and Changed Circumstances (Rebus Sic Stantibus)*. 61 Am. J. Int'l L. 895, 916 (1967) ("It is difficult to see how a right of suspension would present greater dangers than a right of termination.").

[82] In general, the partial suspension of the provisions of a treaty (as distinct from both termination and complete suspension) is recognized as permissible under international law. Article 60 of the Vienna Convention explicitly permits the suspension of a treaty "in whole or in part." "[U]nder both treaty law and non-forcible reprisal law as a basis for responsive suspension it is clear that suspension may be only partial and need not suspend or terminate an agreement as a whole, in contrast, for example, with treaty withdrawal clauses." John Norton Moore, *Enhancing Compliance With International Law: A Neglected Remedy*, 39 Va. J. Int'l L. 881, 932 (1999). Although suspension of particular treaty provisions is recognized both in State practice and international law, we are not aware of any precedent for suspending a treaty as to *some*, but not *others*, of the persons otherwise protected by it. Thus, we can see no basis for suggesting that the President might suspend the Geneva Conventions as to the Taliban *leadership*, but not as to its rank and file members. However, the President could achieve the same outcome by suspending the Conventions, ordering the U.S. military to follow them purely as a matter of policy, and excepting the Taliban leadership from the coverage of this policy.

[83] Article 118 states in relevant part

> Prisoners of war shall be released and repatriated without delay after the cessation of active hostilities.

> In the absence of stipulations to the above effect in any agreement concluded between the Parties to the conflict with a view to the cessation of hostilities, or failing any such agreement, each of the Detaining Powers shall itself establish and excuse without delay a plan of repatriation in conformity the principle laid down in the forgoing paragraph.

[84] See Howard S. Levie, *The Korean Armistice Agreement and Its Aftermath*, 41 Naval L. Rev. 115, 125–27(1993).

[85] *See generally* 3 Charles Cheney Hyde, *International Law Chiefly as Interpreted and Applied by the United States*, ¶ 674 *at 1858–59 (2d ed. 1945).*

and special provisions for them (and for a small number of United Nations POWs in Communist hands) were made under the Armistice of July 27, 1953. "To supervise the repatriation, the armistice created a Neutral Nations Repatriation Commission, composed of representatives from Sweden, Switzerland, Poland, Czechoslovakia, and India. Within 60 days of signing the Armistice, prisoners who desired repatriation were to be directly repatriated in groups to the side to which they belonged at the time of their capture. Those prisoners not so repatriated were to be released to the Neutral Nations Repatriation Commission...for further disposition."[86] Altogether approximately 23,000 POWs refused repatriation. The majority (not quite 22,000) eventually went to Taiwan.[87]

The Persian Gulf War. At the cessation of hostilities in the Persian Gulf War, some 13,418 Iraqi POWs held by Allied forces were unwilling to be repatriated for fear of suffering punishment from their government for having surrendered. Notwithstanding the repatriation mandate of Geneva Convention III, the United States and its Allies executed an agreement with Iraq providing for only voluntary repatriation through a program administered by the International Committee of the Red Cross.[88]

F. Suspension Under International Law

Although the United States may determine either that Afghanistan was a failed State that could not be considered a party to the Geneva Conventions, or that the Geneva Conventions should otherwise be regarded as suspended under the present circumstances, there remains the distinct question whether such determinations would be valid as a matter of international law.[89] We emphasize that the resolution of that question, however, *has no bearing* on domestic constitutional issues, or on the application of the WCA. Rather, these issues are worth consideration as a means of justifying the actions of the United States in the world of international politics. While a close question, we believe that the better view is that, in certain circumstances, countries can suspend the Geneva Conventions consistently with international law.

International law has long recognized that the material breach of a treaty can be grounds for the party injured by the breach to terminate or withdraw from the treaty.[90] Under customary international law, the general rule is that breach of a multilateral treaty by a State Party justifies for suspension of that treaty with regard to that State. "A material breach of a multilateral treaty by one of the parties entitles...[a]

---

[86] *David M. Morriss, From War to Peace: A Study of Cease-Fire Agreements and the Evolving Role of the United Nations*, 36 Va. J. Int'l L. 801, 883 (1996).

[87] *Id* at 885.

[88] *See, id.* at 931 & n. 633.

[89] In general, of course, a decision by a State not to discharge its treaty obligations, even when effective as a matter of domestic law, does not necessarily relieve it of possible international liability for non-performance. *See generally Pigeon River Improvement, Slide & Boom Co. v. Charles W. Cox. Ltd.*, 291 U.S. 138, 160 (1934).

[90] *See Legal Consequences for States of the Continued Presence of South Africa in Namibia (South West Africa) Not-withstanding Security Council Resolution 276*, 1971 I.C.J. 16, 47 ¶ 98 (Advisory Opinion June 21, 1971) (holding it to be a "general principle of law that a right of termination on account of breach must be presumed to exist in respect of all treaties, except as regards provisions relating to the protection of the human person contained in treaties of a humanitarian character.... The silence of a treaty as to the existence of such a right cannot be interpreted as implying the exclusive of a right which has its source outside of the treaty, in general international law [.]").

party specially affected by the breach to invoke it as a ground for suspending the operation of the treaty in whole or in part in the relations between itself and the defaulting State."[91] Assuming that Afghanistan could have been found to be in material breach for having violated "a provision essential to the accomplishment of the object or purpose of the [Geneva Conventions]," suspension of the Conventions would have been justified.[92]

We note, however, that these general rules authorizing suspension "do not apply to provisions relating to the protection of the human person contained in treaties of a humanitarian character, in particular to provisions prohibiting any form of reprisals against persons protected by such treaties."[93] Although the United States is not a party to the Vienna Convention some lower courts have said that the Convention embodies the customary international law of treaties and the State Department has at various times taken the same view.[94] The Geneva Conventions must be regarded as "treaties of a humanitarian character," many of whose provisions relate to the protection of the human person."[95] Arguably, therefore, a determination of the United States that the Geneva Conventions were inoperative as to Afghanistan or a decision to regard them as suspended, might put the United States in breach of customary international law.

In addition, the Geneva Conventions could themselves be read to preclude suspension. Common Article 1 pledges the High Contracting Parties "to respect and to ensure respect for the present Convention *in all circumstances*" (emphasis added). Some commentators argue that this provision should be read to bar any State party from refusing to enforce their provisions, no matter the conduct of its adversaries. In other words, the duty of performance is absolute and does not depend upon reciprocal performance by other State parties.[96] Under this approach, the substantive terms of the Geneva Conventions could never be suspended, and thus any violation would always be illegal under international law.

This understanding of the Vienna and Geneva Conventions cannot be correct. There is no textual provision in the Geneva Conventions that clearly prohibits temporary suspension. The drafters included a provision that appears to preclude State parties from agreeing to absolve each other of violations.[97] They also included careful procedures for the termination of the agreements by individual State parties, including a provision that requires delay of a termination of a treaty, if that termination

---

[91] Vienna Convention on Treaties art. 60(2)(b).

[92] *Id*. art. 60(3).

[93] Id. art. 60(5). The Vienna Convention seems to prohibit or restrict the suspension of humanitarian treaties if the sole ground for suspension is material breach. It does not squarely address the case in which suspension is based, not on particular breaches by a party, but by the party's disappearance as a State or on its incapacity to perform its treaty obligations.

[94] *Fujitsu Ltd. v. Federal Express Corp.*, 247 F.3d 423, 433 (2d Cir.), *cert. denied*, 122 S. Ct. 206 (2001); Moore, *supra*, at 891–92 (quoting 1971 statement by Secretary of State William P. Rogers and 1986 testimony by Deputy Legal Adviser Mary V. Mochary).

[95] *See* Sir Ian Sinclair, *The Vienna Convention on the Law of Treaties* 191 (2d ed. 1984) (explaining intent and scope of reference to "humanitarian" treaties). Indeed, when the drafters of the Vienna Convention added paragraph 5 to Article 60, the Geneva Conventions were specifically mentioned as coming within it. *See* Harris, *supra* n.19, at 797.

[96] *See, e.g.*, Draper, *The Red Cross Conventions*, *supra*, at 8; *see also Military and Paramilitary Activities In and Against Nicaragua (Nicaragua v. United States)*, 76 I.L.R. at 448, ¶ 220.

[97] *See, e.g.*, Geneva Convention III, Article 131.

were to occur during a conflict, until the end of the conflict.[98] Yet, at the same time, the drafters of the Conventions did not address suspension at all, even though it has been a possible option since at least the eighteenth century.[99] Applying the canon of interpretation *expressio unius est exclusio alterius*, that the inclusion of one thing implies the exclusion of the other, we should presume that the State parties did not intend to preclude suspension. Indeed, if the drafters and ratifiers of the Geneva Conventions believed the treaties could not be suspended, while allowing for withdrawal and denunciation, they could have said so explicitly and easily in the text.

The text of the Conventions also makes it implausible to claim that *all* obligations imposed by the Geneva Conventions are absolute and that non-performance is *never* excusable. To begin with, the Conventions themselves distinguish "grave" breaches from others. They further provide that "[n]o High Contracting Party shall be allowed to absolve itself . . . . . of any liability incurred by itself . . . in respect of [grave] breaches."[100] If all of the obligations imposed by the Conventions were absolute and unqualified, it would serve its purpose to distinguish "grave" breaches from others, or to provide explicitly that no party could absolve itself from liability for grave breaches. Furthermore, although specific provisions of the Conventions rule out "reprisals" of particular kinds,[101] they do not rule out reprisals as such. Thus, Article 13 of Geneva Convention III, while defining certain misconduct with respect to prisoners of war as constituting a "serious breach" of the Convention, also states categorically that "[m]easures of reprisal *against prisoners of war* are prohibited." (emphasis added). Similarly, Article 60(5) of the Vienna Convention on Treaties states that the usual rules permitting treaty suspension in some instances "do not apply to provisions relating to the protection of the human person contained in treaties of a humanitarian character, in particular to provisions prohibiting any form of reprisals *against persons protected by such treaties*" (emphasis added). That provision seems to be an implicit prohibition only of a particular class of reprisals, not of all reprisals. Accordingly, it appears to be permissible, as a matter both of treaty law and of customary international law, to suspend performance of Geneva Convention obligations on a temporary basis. It also appears permissible to engage in reprisals in response to material breaches by an enemy, provided that the reprisals do not give rise to "grave" breaches or to reprisals against protected persons.

Finally, a blanket non-suspension rule makes little sense as a matter of international law and politics. If there were such a rule, international law would leave an injured party effectively remediless if its adversaries committed material breaches of the Geneva Conventions. Apart from its unfairness, that result would reward and

---

[98] *See, e.g., id.*, Article 142.

[99] *See Sinclair, supra*, at 192.

[100] Geneva Convention IV, art. 148.

[101] U.S. Army, *The Law of Land Warfare, Field Manual No. 27-10* (July 18, 1956), (the "FM 27-10"), defines "reprisals" as "acts of retaliation in the form of conduct which would otherwise be unlawful, resorted to by one belligerent against enemy personnel or property for acts of warfare committed by the other belligerent to violation of the law of war, for the purpose of enforcing future compliance with the recognized rules of civilized warfare. For example, the employment by a belligerent of a weapon the use of which is normally precluded by the law of war would constitute a lawful reprisal for intentional mistreatment of prisoners of war held by the enemy." *Id.*, ch. 8, ¶ 497(a). In general, international law disfavors and discourages reprisals. *See id.* ¶ 497(d). ("Reprisals are never adopted merely for revenge, but only as an unavoidable last resort to induce the enemy to desist from unlawful practices.") They are permitted, however, in certain specific circumstances.

encourage non-compliance with the Conventions. True, the Conventions appear to contemplate that enforcement will be promoted by voluntary action of the parties.[102] Furthermore, the Conventions provide for intervention by "the International Committee of the Red Cross or any other impartial humanitarian organization . . . subject to the consent of the Parties to the conflict concerned."[103] But the effectiveness of these provisions depends on the goodwill of the very party assumed to be committing material breaches, or on its sensitivity to international opinion. Likewise, the provision authorizing an impartial investigation of alleged violations also hinges on the willingness of a breaching party to permit the investigation and to abide by its result. Other conceivable remedies, such as the imposition of an embargo by the United Nations on the breaching party, may also be inefficacious in particular circumstances. If, for example, Afghanistan were bound by Geneva Convention III to provide certain treatment to United States prisoners of war but in fact materially breached such duties, a United Nations embargo might have little effect on its behavior. Finally, offenders undoubtedly face a risk of trial and punishment before national or international courts after the conflict is over. Yet that form of relief presupposes that the offenders will be subject to capture at the end of the conflict – which may well depend on whether or not they have been defeated. Reliance on post-conflict trials, as well as being uncertain, defers relief for the duration of the conflict. Without a power to suspend, therefore, parties to the Geneva Conventions would only be left with these meager tools to remedy widespread violation of the Conventions by others.

Thus, even if one were to believe that international law set out fixed and binding rules concerning the power of suspension, the United States could make convincing arguments under the Geneva Conventions itself, the Vienna Convention on Treaties, and customary international law in favor of suspending the Geneva Conventions as applied to the Taliban militia in the current war in Afghanistan.

IV. The Customary International Laws of War

So far, this memorandum has addressed the issue whether the Geneva Conventions and the WCA, apply to the detention and trial of al Qaeda and Taliban militia members taken prisoner in Afghanistan. Having concluded that these laws do not apply, we turn to your question concerning the effect, if any, of customary international law. Some may take the view that even if the Geneva Conventions, by their terms, do not govern the conflict in Afghanistan, the substance of these agreements has received such universal approval that it has risen to the status of customary international law. Regardless of its substance, however, customary international law cannot bind the executive branch under the Constitution because it is not federal law. This is a view that this Office has expressed before,[104] and is one consistent with the views of the federal courts,[105] and with executive branch arguments in the courts.[106] As a result,

---

[102] *See, e.g.,* the Geneva Convention III, Article 8; Geneva Convention IV, Article 9.

[103] Geneva Convention III. Article 9; Geneva Convention IV, Article 10.

[104] *See Authority of the Federal Bureau of Investigation to Override International Law in Extraterritorial Law Enforcement Activities,* 13 Op. O.L.C. 163 (1989).

[105] *See, e.g., United States v. Alvarez-Machain,* 504 U.S. 655 (1992)

[106] See, id. at 669–70, *Committee of United States Citizens Living in Nicaragua v. Reagan,* 859 F.2d 929, 935–36 (D. C. Cir. 1988); *Garcia-Mir v. Meese,* 788 F.2d 1446, 1453–55 (11th Cir.), *cert. denied,* 479 U.S. 889 (1986).

any customary international law of armed conflict in no way binds, as a legal matter, the President or the U.S. Armed Forces concerning the detention or trial of members of al Qaeda and the Taliban.

A. Is Customary International Law Federal Law?

Under the view promoted by many international law academics, any presidential violation of customary international law is presumptively unconstitutional.[107] These scholars argue that customary international law is federal law, and that the President's Article II duty under the Take Care Clause requires him to execute customary international law as well as statutes lawfully enacted under the Constitution. A President may not violate customary international law, therefore, just as he cannot violate a statute, unless he believes it to be unconstitutional. Relying upon cases such as *The Paquete Habana*, 175 U.S. 677, 700 (1900), in which the Supreme Court observed that "international law is part of our law," this position often claims that the federal judiciary has the authority to invalidate executive action that runs counter to customary international law.[108]

This view of customary international law is seriously mistaken. The constitutional text nowhere brackets presidential or federal power within the confines of international law. When the Supremacy Clause discusses the sources of federal law, it enumerates only this Constitution, and the Laws of the United States which shall be made in Pursuance thereof and all Treaties made, or which shall be made, under the Authority of the United States." U.S. Constitution VI International law is nowhere mentioned in the Constitution as an independent source of federal law or as a constraint on the political branches of government. Indeed, if it were, there would have been no need to grant to Congress the power to "define and punish . . . offenses against the Law of Nations."[109] It is also clear that the original understanding of the Framers was that Laws of the United States" did *not* include the law of nations, as international law was

---

[107] See, e.g., Michael J. Glennon, Raising the Paquete Habana: Is Violation of Customary International Law by the Executive Unconstitutional?, 80 NW. U. L. Rev. 321, 325 (1985); Louis Henkin, International Law As Law in the United States, 82 MICH L. REV. 1555, 1567 (1984); Jules Lobel, The Limits of Constitutional Power. Conflicts Between Foreign Policy and International Law, 71 VA. L. REV. 1071, 1179 (1985); see also Jonathan R. Charney, Agora: May the President Violate Customary International Law?, 80 AM J. INT'L L. 913 (1986).

[108] Recently, the status of customary international law within the federal legal systems has been the subject of sustained debate with legal academia. The legitimacy of incorporating customary international law as federal law has been subjected in these exchanges to crippling doubts. See Curtis A. Bradley & Jack L. Goldsmith, Customary International Law As Federal Common Law: A Critique of the Modern Position, 110 Harv. L. Rev. 815, 817 (1997), see also Phillip R. Trimble, A Revisionist View of Customary International Law, 33 UCLA L. Rev. 665, 672–673 (1986), Arthur M. Weisburd, The Executive Branch and International Law, 41 Vand. L. Rev. 1205, 1269 (1988). These claims have not gone unchallenged. Harold H. Koh. Is International Law Really State Law?, 111 Harv. L. Rev. 1824, 1827 (1998); Gerald L. Neuman, Sense and Nonsense About Customary International Law: A Response to Professors Bradley and Goldsmith, 66 Fordham L. Rev. 371, 371 (1997), Beth Stephens, The Law of Our Land: Customary International Law As Federal Law After Erie, 66 Fordham L. Rev. 393, 396–97 (1997). Bradley and Goldsmith have responded to their critics several times. See Curtis A. Bradley & Jack L. Goldsmith, Federal Courts and the incorporation of International Law, 111 Harv. L. Rev. 2260 (1998); Curtis A. Bradley & Jack L. Goldsmith, The Current Illegitimacy of International Human Rights Litigation, 66 Fordham L. Rev. 319, 330 (1997).

[109] U.S. Const art. 1, § 8

called in the late eighteenth century. In explaining the jurisdiction of the Article III courts to cases arising, "under the Constitution and the Laws of the United States," for the example, Alexander Hamilton did not include the law of nations as a source of jurisdiction.[110] Rather, Hamilton pointed out, claims involving the laws of nations would arise either in diversity cases or maritime cases,[111] which by definition do not involve "the Laws of the United States." Little evidence exists that those who attended the Philadelphia Convention in the summer of 1787 or the state ratifying conventions believed that federal law would have included customary international law, but rather that the law of nations was part of a general common law that was not true federal law.[112]

Indeed, allowing customary international law to rise to the level of federal law would create severe distortions in the structure of the Constitution. Incorporation of customary international law directly into federal law would bypass the delicate procedures, established by the Constitution for amending the Constitution or for enacting legislation.[113] Customary international law is not approved by two-thirds of Congress and three-quarters of the state legislatures, it has not been passed by both houses of Congress and signed by the President, nor is it made by the President with the advice and consent of two-thirds of the Senate. In other words, customary international law has not undergone the difficult hurdles that stand before enactment of constitutional amendments, statutes, or treaties. As such it can have no legal effect on the government or on American citizens because it is not law.[114] Even the inclusion of treaties in the Supremacy Clause does not render treaties automatically self-executing in federal court, not to mention self-executing against the executive branch.[115] If even treaties that have undergone presidential signature and senatorial advice and consent can have no binding legal effect in the United States, then it certainly must be the case that a source of rules that never undergoes any process established by our Constitution cannot be law.[116]

It is well accepted that the political branches have ample authority to override customary international law within their respective spheres of authority. This has been recognized by the Supreme Court since the earliest days of the Republic. In *The Schooner Exchange v. McFaddon*, for example, Chief Justice Marshall applied customary international law to the seizure of a French warship only because the

---

[110] *The Federalist No. 80*, at 447–49 (Alexander Hamilton) (Clinton Rossiter ed., 1999).

[111] *Id.* at 444–46.

[112] See, e.g., Stewart Jay, The Status of the Law of Nations in Early American Law, 42 Vand. L. Rev. 819, 830–37 (1989), Bradford R. Clark, Federal Common Law: A Structural Reinterpretation 144 U. Pa. L. Rev. 1245, 1306–12 (1996). Curtis A. Bradley & Jack L. Goldsmith, The Current Illegitimacy of International Human Rights Litigation, 66 Fordham L. Rev. 319, 333–36 (1997).

[113] *Cf. INS v. Chadha*, 462 U.S. 919 (1983) (invalidating legislative veto for failure to undergo bicameralism and presentment as required by Article I, Section 8 for all legislation).

[114] In fact, allowing customary international law to bear the force of federal law would create significant problems under the Appointments Clause and the non-delegation doctrine, as it would be law made completely outside the American legal system through a process of international practice, rather than either the legislative or officers of the United States authorized to do so.

[115] *See, e.g., Foster v. Neilson*, 27 U.S. (2 Pet) 253, 314 (1829).

[116] See John C. Yoo, Globalism and the Constitution: Treaties, Non-Self-Execution, and the Original Understanding, 99 Colum. L. Rev. 1955 (1999) (non-self-execution of treaties justified by the original understanding); John C. Yoo, Treaties and Public Lawmaking: A Textual and Structural Defense of Non-Self-Execution, 99 Colum. L. Rev. 2218 (1999) (demonstrating that constitutional text and structure require implementation of treaty obligations by federal statute).

United States government had not chosen a different rule.

> It seems then to the Court, to be a principle of public [international] law, that national ships of war, entering the port of a friendly power open for their reception, are to be considered as exempted by the consent of that power from its jurisdiction. Without doubt, the sovereign of the place is capable of destroying this implication. He may claim and exercise jurisdiction, either by employing force, or by subjecting such vessels to the ordinary tribunals.[117]

In *Brown v. United States*, 12 U.S. (8 Cranch) 110 (1814), Chief Justice Marshall again stated that customary international law "is a guide which the sovereign follows or abandons at his will. The rule, like other precepts of morality, of humanity, and even of wisdom, is addressed to the judgment of the sovereign; and although it cannot be disregarded by him without obloquy, yet it may be disregarded."[118] In twenty-first century words, overriding customary international law may prove to be a bad idea, or be subject to criticism, but there is no doubt that the government has the power to do it.

Indeed, proponents of the notion that customary international law is federal law can find little support in either history or Supreme Court case law. It is true that in some contexts mostly involving maritime, insurance, and commercial law, the federal courts in the nineteenth century looked to customary international law as a guide.[119] Upon closer examination of these cases, however, it is clear that customary international law had the status only of the general federal common law that was applied in federal diversity cases under *Swift v. Tyson*, 41 U.S. (16 Pet.)1 (1842). As such, it was not considered true federal law under the Supremacy Clause, it did not support Article III "arising under" jurisdiction; it did not pre-empt inconsistent state law; and it did not bind the executive branch. Indeed, even during this period the Supreme Court acknowledged that the laws of war did not qualify as true federal law and could not therefore serve as the basis for federal subject matter jurisdiction. In *New York Life Ins. Co. v. Hendren*, 92 U.S. 286, for example, the Supreme Court declared that it had no jurisdiction to review the general laws of war, as recognized by the law of nations applicable to this case, because such laws do not involve the constitution, laws, treaties, or executive proclamations of the United States."[120] The spurious nature of this type of law led the Supreme Court in the famous case of *Erie R.R. Co. v. Tompkins*, 304 U.S. 64, 78 (1938), to eliminate general federal common law.

Even the case most relied upon by proponents of customary international law's status as federal law, *The Paquete Habana*, itself acknowledge that customary international law is subject to override by the action of the political branches. *The Paquete Habana* involved the question whether U.S. armed vessels in wartime could capture certain fishing vessels belonging to enemy nationals and sell them as prize. In that case, the Court applied an international law rule, and did indeed say that "international law is part of our law."[121] But Justice Gray then continued, "*where there is no treaty and no controlling executive or legislative act or judicial decision*, resort must be

---

[117] 11 U.S. (7 Cranch) 116, 145–46 (1812) (emphasis added).
[118] *Id.* at 128.
[119] See, e.g., Oliver Am. Trading Co. v. Mexico, 264 U.S. 440, 442–43 (1924); Huntington v. Attrill, 146, U.S. 657, 683 (1892); New York Life Ins. Co. v. Hendren, 92 U.S. 286, 286–287 (1875).
[120] 92 U.S. 286, 286–87.
[121] *Id.* at 700.

had to the customs and usages of civilized nations." In other words, while it was willing to apply customary international law as general federal common law (this was the era of *Swift v. Tyson*), the Court also readily acknowledged that the political branches and even the federal judiciary could override it at any time. No Supreme Court decision in modern times has challenged that view.[122] Thus, under clear Supreme Court precedent, any presidential decision in the current conflict concerning the detention and trial of al Qaeda or Taliban militia prisoners would constitute a "controlling" executive act that would immediately and completely override any customary international law norms.

Constitutional text and Supreme Court decisions aside, allowing the federal courts to rely upon international law to restrict the President's discretion to conduct war would raise deep structural problems. First, if customary international law is indeed federal law, then it must receive all of the benefits of the Supremacy Clause. Therefore, customary international law would not only bind the President, but it also would pre-empt state law and even supersede inconsistent federal statutes and treaties that were enacted before the rule of customary international law came into being. This has never happened. Indeed, giving customary international law this power not only runs counter to the Supreme Court cases described above, but would have the effect of importing a body of law to restrain the three branches of American government that never underwent any approval by our democratic political process. If customary international law does not have these effects, as the constitutional text, practice and most sensible readings of the Constitution indicate, then it cannot be true federal law under the Supremacy Clause. As non-federal law, then, customary international law cannot bind the President or the executive branch, in any legally meaningful way, in its conduct of the war in Afghanistan.

Second, relying upon customary international law here would undermine the President's control over foreign relations and his Commander-in-Chief authority. As we have noted, the President under the Constitution is given plenary authority over the

---

[122] Two lines of cases are often cited for the proposition that the Supreme Court has found customary international law to be federal law. The first, which derives from Murray v. Schooner Charming Betsy, 6 U.S. (2 Cranch) 64 (1804). The "Charming Betsy" rule, as it is sometimes known, is a rule of construction that a statute should be construed when possible so as not to conflict with international law. This rule, however, does not apply international law of its own force, but instead can be seen as measure of judicial restraint that violating international law is a decision for the political branches to make, and that if they wish to do so, they should state clearly their intentions. The second, Banco Nacional de Cuba v. Sabbatino, 376 U.S. 398, applied the "act of state" doctrine, which generally precludes courts from examining the validity of the decisions of foreign governments taken on their own soil, as federal common law to a suit over expropriations by the Cuban government. As with Charming Betsy, however, the Court developed this rule as one of judicial self-restraint to preserve the flexibility of the political branches to decide how to conduct foreign policy.

Some supporters of customary international law as federal law rely on a third line of cases, beginning with Filártiga v. Peña-Irala, 630 F.2d 876 (2d Cir. 1980). In Filártiga, the Second Circuit read the federal Alien Tort Statute, 28 U.S.C. § 1350 (1994), to allow a tort suit in federal court against the former official of a foreign government for violating norms of international human rights law, namely torture. Incorporation of customary international law via the Alien Tort Statute, while accepted by several circuit courts, has never received the blessings of the Supreme Court and has been sharply criticized by some circuits, see, e.g., Tel-Oren v. Libyan Arab Republic, 726 F.2d 774, 808–10 (D.C. Cir. 1984) (Bork, J., concurring), cert. denied, 470 U.S. 1003 (1985), as well as by academics, see Curtis A. Bradley & Jack L. Goldsmith, The Current Illegitimacy of International Human Rights Litigation, 66 Fordharm L. rev. 319, 330 (1997).

conduct of the Nation's foreign relations and over the use of the military. Importing customary international law notions concerning armed conflict would represent a direct infringement on the President's discretion as the Commander-in-Chief and Chief Executive to determine how best to conduct the Nation's military affairs. Presidents and courts have agreed that the President enjoys the fullest discretion permitted by the Constitution in commanding troops in the field.[123] It is difficult to see what legal authority under our constitutional system would permit customary international law to restrict the exercise of the President's plenary power in this area, which is granted to him directly by the Constitution. Further, reading customary international law to be federal law would improperly inhibit the President's role as the representative of the Nation in its foreign affairs.[124] Customary law is not static; it evolves through a dynamic process of State custom and practice "States necessarily must have the authority to contravene international norms, however, for it is the process of changing state practice that allows customary international law to envolve."[125] As we observed in 1989, "[i]f the United States is to participate in the evolution of international law, the Executive must have the power to act inconsistently with international law where necessary."[126] The power to override or ignore customary international law, even the law applying to armed conflict, is "an integral part of the President's foreign affairs power."[127]

Third, if customary international law is truly federal law, it presumably must be enforceable by the federal courts. Allowing international law to interfere with the President's war power in this way, however, would expand the federal judiciary's authority into areas where it has little competence, where the Constitution does not textually call for its intervention, and where it risks defiance by the political branches. Indeed, treating customary international law as federal law would require the judiciary to intervene into the most deep political questions, those concerning war. This the federal courts have said they will not do, most notably during the Kosovo conflict.[128] Again, the practice of the branches demonstrates that they do not consider customary international law to be federal law. This position makes sense even at the level of democratic theory, because conceiving of international law as a restraint on warmaking would allow norms of questionable democratic origin to constrain actions validly taken under the U.S. Constitution by popularly accountable national representatives.

Based on these considerations of constitutional text, structure, and history, we conclude that any customary rules of international law that apply to armed conflicts

---

[123] *See* Memorandum for Timothy E. Flanigan, Deputy Counsel to the President, from John C. Yoo, Deputy Assistant Attorney General, Office of Legal Counsel, *Re: The President's Constitutional Authority to Conduct Military Operations Against Terrorists and Nations Supporting Them* (Sept. 25, 2001) (reviewing authorities).

[124] "When articulating principles of international law in its relations with other states, the Executive branch speaks not only as an interpreter of generally accepted and traditional rules, as would the courts, but also as an advocate of standards it believes desirable for the community of nations and protective of national concerns." Sabbatino, 376 U.S. at 432–33. See also Rappenecker v. United States, 509 F.Supp. 1024, 1029 (N.D. Cal. 1980) ("Under the doctrine of separation of powers, the making of those determinations [under international law] is entrusted to the President"); International Load line Convention, 40 Op. Att'y Gen. at 123–24 (President "speak[s] for the nation", in making determination under international law).

[125] 13 Op. O.L.C. at 170.

[126] *Id.*

[127] *Id.* at 171.

[128] *See, e.g., Campbell v. Clinton*, 203 F.3d 19, 40 (D.C. Cir.), *cert. denied*, 531 U.S. 815 (2000).

do not bind the President or the U.S. Armed Forces in their conduct of the war in Afghanistan.

B. Do the Customary Laws of War Apply to al Qaeda or the Taliban Militia?

Although customary international law does not bind the President, the President may still use his constitutional warmaking authority to subject members of al Qaeda or the Taliban militia to the laws of war. While this result may seem at first glance to be counter-intuitive, it is a product of the President's Commander-in-Chief and Chief Executive powers to prosecute the war effectively.

The President has the legal and constitutional authority to subject both al Qaeda and Taliban to the laws of war, and to try their members before military courts or commissions instituted under Title 10 of the United States Code, if he so chooses. Section 818 of title 10 provides in part that "[g]eneral courts-martial . . . have jurisdiction to try any person who by the law of war is subject to trial by a military tribunal and may adjudge any punishment permitted by the law of war" (except for capital punishment in certain cases). Section 821 allows for the trial of "offenders or offenses that by statute or by the law of war may be tried by military commissions, provost courts, or other military tribunals." We have described the jurisdiction and usage of military tribunals for you in a separate memorandum. We do not believe that these courts would lose jurisdiction to try members of al Qaeda or the Taliban militia for violations of the laws of war, even though we have concluded that the laws of war have no binding effect – *as federal law* – on the President.

This is so because the extension of the common laws of war to the present conflicts is, in essence, a *military* measure that the President can order as Commander-in-Chief. As the Supreme Court has recognized, "an important incident to the conduct of war is the adoption of measures by the military command not only to repel and defeat the enemy but to seize and subject to disciplinary measures those enemies who in their attempt to thwart or impede our military effort have violated the law of war."[129] In another case, the Court observed that "in the absence of attempts by Congress to limit the President's power, it appears that, as commander in Chief of the Army and Navy of the United States, he may, in time of war, establish and prescribe the jurisdiction and procedure of military commissions, and of tribunals in the nature of such commissions, in territory occupied by Armed Forces of the United States."[130] Thus, pursuant to his Commander-in-Chief authority, the President could impose the laws of war on members of al Qaeda and the Taliban militia as part of the measures necessary to prosecute the war successfully.

Moreover, the President's general authority over the conduct of foreign relations entails the specific power to express the views of the United States both on the content of international law generally and on the application of international law to specific facts. "When articulating principles of international law in its relations with other

---

[129] *See Ex parte Quirin*, 317 U.S. 1, 28–29 (1942); *cf. Hirota v. Mac Arthur*, 338 U.S. 197, 208 (1948) (Douglas, J. concurring) (Agreement with Allies to establish international tribunals to try accused war criminals who were enemy officials or armed service members was "a part of the prosecution of the war. It is a furtherance of the hostilities directed to a dilution of enemy power and involving contribution for wrongs done.")

[130] *Madsen v. Kinsela*, 343 U.S. 341, 348 (1952).

states, the Executive Branch speaks not only as an interpreter of generally accepted and traditional rules, as would the courts, but also as an advocate of standards it believes desirable for the community of nations and protective of national concerns."[131] Thus, the President can properly find the unprecedented conflict between the United States and transnational terrorist organizations a "war" for the purposes of the customary or common laws of war. Certainly, given the extent of hostilities both in the United States and Afghanistan since the September 11 attacks on the World Trade Center and the Pentagon, the scale of the military, diplomatic and financial commitments by the United States and its allies to counter the terrorist threats, and the expected duration of the conflict, it would be entirely reasonable for the President to find that a condition of "war" existed for purposes of triggering application of the common laws of war. He could also reasonably find that al Qaeda, the Taliban militia, and other related entities that are engaged in conflict with the United States were subject to the duties imposed by those laws. Even if members of these groups and organizations were considered to be merely "private" actors, they could nonetheless be held subject to the laws of war.[132]

In addition, Congress has delegated to the President sweeping authority with respect to the present conflict, and especially with regard to those organizations and individuals implicated in the terrorist attacks of September 11, 2001. In the wake of those incidents, congress enacted Pub. L. No. 107–40, 115 Stat. 224 (2001). Congress found that "On September 11, 2001 acts of treacherous violence were committed against the United States and its citizens *** render it both necessary and appropriate that the United States exercise its *** and to protect United States citizens both at home and abroad, and that such acts continue to pose an unusual and extraordinary threat to the national security and foreign policy of the United States." Section 2 of the statute authorized the President "to use all necessary and appropriate force against those nations, organizations, or persons he determines planned, authorized, committed or aided the terrorist attacks that occurred on September 11, 2001, or harbored such organizations or persons, in order to prevent any future acts of international terrorism against the United States by such nations, organizations or persons." Read together with the President's constitutional authorities as Commander-in-Chief and as interpreter of international law; this authorization allows the President to subject members of al Qaeda, the Taliban militia, and other affiliated groups to trial and punishment for violations of the common laws of war, if the President determines that it would further the conduct of military operations or contribute to the defense and security of the United States and its citizens.

C. May a U.S. Servicemember be Tried for Violations of the Laws of War?

You have also asked whether the laws of war, as incorporated, by reference in title 10 also apply to United States military personnel engaged in armed conflict with al Qaeda or with the Taliban militia. Even though the customary laws of war do not bind the President as federal law, the President may wish to extend some or all of

---

[131] *Sabbatino*, 376 U.S. at 432–33.
[132] *See Kadic v. Karadzic*, 70 F.3d 232, 243 (2d Cir.) ("The liability of private individuals for committing war crimes has been recognized since World War I and was confirmed at Nuremberg after World War II . . . and remains today an important aspect of international law."), *cert. denied*, 518 U.S. 1005 (1996).

such laws to the conduct of United States military operations in this conflict, or to the treatment of members of al Qaeda or the Taliban captured in the conflict. It is within his constitutional authority as Commander-in-Chief to do so. The common laws of war can be viewed as rules governing the conduct of military personnel in time of combat, and the President has undoubted authority to promulgate such rules and to provide for their enforcement.[133] The Army's Manual on the Law of Land Warfare, which represents the Army's interpretation of the customary international law governing armed conflict, can be expanded, altered, or overridden at any time by presidential act, as the Manual itself recognizes.[134] This makes clear that the source of authority for the application of the customary laws of war to the armed forces arises directly from the President *************** Chief power.

Moreover, the President has authority to limit or qualify the application of such rules. He could exempt, for example, certain operations from their coverage, or apply some but not all of the common laws of war to this conflict. This, too, is an aspect of the President's Commander-in-Chief authority. In narrowing the scope of the substantive prohibitions that apply in a particular conflict, the President may effectively determine the jurisdiction of military courts and commissions. He could thus preclude the trials of United States military personnel on specific charges of violations of the common laws of war.

Finally, a presidential determination concerning the application of the substantive prohibitions of the laws of war to the Afghanistan conflict would not preclude the normal system of military justice from applying to members of the U.S. Armed Services. Members of the Armed Services would still be subject to trial by courts martial for any violations of the Uniform Code of Military Justice (the "UCMJ") Indeed, if the President were to issue an order, listing certain common laws of war for the military to follow, failure to obey that order would constitute an offense under the UCMJ.[135] Thus, although the President is not constitutionally bound by the customary laws of war, he can still choose to require the U.S. Armed Forces to obey them through the UCMJ.

Thus, our view that the customary international laws of armed conflict do not bind the President does not, in any way, compel the conclusion that members of the U.S.

---

[133] The President has broad authority under the Commander-in-Chief Clause to take action to superintend the military that overlaps with Congress's power to create the armed forces and to make rules for their regulation. See Loving v. United States, 517 U.S. 748, 772 (1996) ("The President's duties as Commander-in-Chief . . . require him to take responsible and continuing action to superintend the military, including courts-martial."): United States v. Eliason, 41 U.S. (16 Pet.) 291, 301 (1842) ("The power of the executive to establish rules and regulations for the government of the army, is undoubted."). The executive branch has long asserted that the President has "the unquestioned power to establish rules for the government of the army" in the absence of legislation. Power of the President to Create a Militia Bureau in the War Department, 10 Op. Att'y Gen. 11, 14 (1861). Indeed, at an early date, Attorney General Wirt concluded that regulations issued by the President on his independent authority remained in force even after Congress repealed the statute giving them legislative sanction "in all cases where they do not conflict with positive legislation." Brevet Pay of General Macomb, 1 Op. Att'y Gen. 547, 549 (1822). These independent powers of the President as Commander-in-Chief have frequently been exercised in administering justice in cases involving members of the Armed forces: "([i]ndeed, until 1830, courts-martial were convened solely on [the President's] authority as Commander-in-Chief." Congressional Research Service, The Constitution of the United States of America: Analysis and Interpretation 479 (1987).

[134] FM 27–10, ch. 1, ¶ 7(c).

[135] 10 U.S.C. § 892 (2000).

Armed Forces who commit acts that might be considered war crimes would be free from military justice.

Conclusion

For the foregoing reasons, we conclude that neither the federal War Crimes Act nor the Geneva Conventions would apply to the detention conditions in Guantanamo Bay, Cuba, or to trial by military commission of al Qaeda or Taliban prisoners. We also conclude that customary international law has no binding legal effect on either the President or the military because it is not federal law, as recognized by the Constitution. Nonetheless, we also believe that the President as Commander-in-Chief, has the constitutional authority to impose the customary laws of war on both the al Qaeda and Taliban groups and the U.S. Armed Forces.

Please let us know if we can provide further assistance.

MEMO 5

Secretary of Defense

1000 Defense Pentagon

Washington, DC 20301-1000

Jan 19 2002

MEMORANDUM FOR CHAIRMAN OF THE JOINT CHIEFS OF STAFF

SUBJECT: Status of Taliban and Al Qaeda

(U) Transmit the following to the Combatant Commanders:

(U) The United States has determined that Al Qaeda and Taliban individuals under the control of the Department of Defense are not entitled to prisoner of war status for purposes of the Geneva Conventions of 1949.

(U) The Combatant Commanders shall, in detaining Al Qaeda and Taliban individuals under the control of the Department of Defense, treat them humanely and, to the extent appropriate and consistent with military necessity, in a manner consistent with the principles of the Geneva Conventions of 1949.

(U) The Combatant Commanders shall transmit this order to subordinate commanders, including Commander, Joint Task Force 160, for implementation.

(U) Keep me appropriately informed of the implementation of this order.

Classified by : SecDef
Reason: 1.5(d)
Declassify on: 01/19/12

DECLASSIFIED ON 4 FEB 2002
PER DOD GENERAL COUNCIL MEMO
Please Notify All Recipients to downgrade this Memorandum to Unclassified

U.S. Department of Justice

Office of Legal Counsel

Office of the Assistant Attorney General   *Washington, D.C. 20530*

January 22, 2002

Memorandum for Alberto R. Gonzales
Counsel to the President,
and William J. Haynes II
General Counsel of the Department of Defense

RE: *Application of Treaties and Laws to al Qaeda and Taliban Detainees*

You have asked for our Office's views concerning the effect of international treaties and federal laws on the treatment of individuals detained by the U.S. Armed Forces during the conflict in Afghanistan. In particular, you have asked whether certain treaties forming part of the laws of armed conflict apply to the conditions of detention and the procedures for trial of members of al Qaeda and the Taliban militia. We conclude that these treaties do not protect members of the al Qaeda organization, which as a non-State actor cannot be a party to the international agreements governing war. We further conclude that that President has sufficient grounds to find that these treaties do not protect members of the Taliban militia. This memorandum expresses no view as to whether the President should decide, as a matter of policy, that the U.S. Armed Forces should adhere to the standards of conduct in those treaties with respect to the treatment of prisoners.

We believe it most useful to structure the analysis of these questions by focusing on the War Crimes Act, 18 U.S.C. § 2441 (Supp. III 1997) ("WCA"). The WCA directly incorporates several provisions of international treaties governing the laws of war into the federal criminal code. Part I of this memorandum describes the WCA and the most relevant treaty that it incorporates: the Geneva Convention Relative to the Treatment of Prisoners of War ("Geneva III").[1]

Parts II and III of this memorandum discuss why other deviations from the text of Geneva III would not present either a violation of the treaty or of the WCA. Part II explains that al Qaeda detainees cannot claim the protections of Geneva III because the treaty does not apply to them. Al Qaeda is merely a violent political movement or organization and not a nation-State. As a result, it cannot be a state party to any treaty. Because of the novel nature of this conflict, moreover, a conflict with al Qaeda is not properly included in non-international forms of armed conflict to which some

---

[1] The four Geneva Conventions for the Protection of Victims of War, dated August 12, 1949, were ratified by the United States on July 14, 1955. These are the Convention for the Amelioration of the Condition of the Wounded and Sick in Armed Forces in the Field, 6 U.S.T. 3115 ("Geneva Convention I"); the Convention for the Amelioration of the Condition of Wounded, Sick and Shipwrecked Members of Armed Forces at Sea, 6 U.S.T. 3219 ("Geneva Convention II"); the Convention Relative to the Treatment of Prisoners of War, 6 U.S.T. 3517 ("Geneva Convention III"); and the Convention Relative to the Protection of Civilian Persons in Time of War, 6 U.S.T. 3317 ("Geneva Convention IV").

provisions of the Geneva Conventions might apply. Therefore, neither the Geneva Conventions nor the WCA regulate the detention of al Qaeda prisoners captured during the Afghanistan conflict.

Part III discusses why the President may decide that Geneva III, as a whole, does not protect members of the Taliban militia in the current situation. The President has the constitutional authority to temporarily suspend our treaty obligations to Afghanistan under the Geneva Conventions. Although he may exercise this aspect of the treaty power at his discretion, we outline several grounds upon which he could justify that action here. In particular, he may determine that Afghanistan was not a functioning State, and therefore that the Taliban militia was not a government, during the period in which the Taliban was engaged in hostilities against the United States and its allies. Afghanistan's status as a failed State is sufficient ground alone for the President to suspend Geneva III, and thus to deprive members of the Taliban militia of POW status. The President's constitutional power to suspend performance of our treaty obligations with respect to Afghanistan is not restricted by international law. It encompasses the power to suspend some treaties but not others, or some but not all obligations under a particular treaty. Should the President make such a determination, then Geneva III would not apply to Taliban prisoners and any failure to meet that treaty's requirements would not violate either our treaty obligations or the WCA.

Part IV examines justifications for any departures from Geneva III requirements should the President decline to suspend our treaty obligations toward Afghanistan. It explains that certain deviations from the text of Geneva III may be permissible, as a matter of domestic law, if they fall within certain justifications or legal exceptions, such as those for self-defense or infeasibility. Further, Part IV discusses the President's authority to find, even if Geneva III were to apply, that Taliban members do not qualify as POWs as defined by the treaty.

In Part V, we address the question whether, in the absence of any Geneva III obligations, customary international law requires, as a matter of federal law, that the President provide certain standards of treatment for al Qaeda or Taliban prisoners. We conclude that customary international law, as a matter of domestic law, does not bind the President or restrict the actions of the United States military, because it does not constitute either federal law made in pursuance of the Constitution or a treaty recognized under the Supremacy Clause.

I. Background and Overview of the War Crimes Act and the Geneva Conventions

It is our understanding that your Department is considering two basic plans regarding the treatment of members of al Qaeda and the Taliban militia detained during the Afghanistan conflict. First, the Defense Department intends to make available a facility at the U.S. Navy base at Guantanamo Bay, Cuba ("GTMO"), for the long-term detention of these individuals, who have come under our control either through capture by our military or transfer from our allies in Afghanistan. At the present moment, your Department has confined these individuals in temporary facilities, pending the construction of a more permanent camp at GTMO. While it is conceivable that some might argue that these facilities are not fully in keeping with the terms of Geneva III, we understand that they meet minimal humanitarian requirements consistent with the need to prevent violence and for force protection. We understand that GTMO authorities are providing these individuals with regular food and medical care, and that basic hygiene and sanitary standards are being maintained. You have further informed us that your plans for a longer-term facility at GTMO are still under development.[2]

Second, your Department is developing procedures to implement the President's Military Order of November 13, 2001, which establishes military commissions for the trial of violations of the laws of war committed by non-U.S. citizens.[3] The question has arisen whether Geneva III would restrict the proposed rules, or even require that only court-martial be used to try members of al Qaeda or the Taliban militia for war crimes.

We believe that the WCA provides a useful starting point for our analysis of the application of the Geneva Conventions to the treatment of detainees captured in the Afghanistan theater of operations.[4] Section 2441 of title 18 renders certain acts punishable as "war crimes." The statute's definition of that term incorporates, by reference, certain treaties or treaty provisions relating to the laws of war, including the Geneva Conventions.

A. Section 2441: An Overview

Section 2441 of Title 18 lists four categories of war crimes. First, it criminalizes "grave breaches" of the Geneva Conventions, which are defined by treaty and will be discussed below. Second, it makes illegal conduct prohibited by Articles 23, 25, 27 and 28 of the Annex to the Hague Convention IV Respecting the Laws and Customs of War on Land, Oct. 18, 1907, 36 Stat. 2277 ("Hague Convention IV"). Third, it criminalizes violations of what is known as "common Article 3," which is a provision common to all four of the Geneva Conventions. Fourth, it criminalizes conduct prohibited by certain other laws of war treaties, once the United States joins them. A House Report states that the original legislation "carries out the international obligations of the United States under the Geneva Conventions of 1949 to provide criminal penalties for certain war crimes." H.R. Rep. No. 104–698, at 1 (1996), *reprinted in* 1996 U.S.C.C.A.N. 2166, 2166. Each of those four conventions includes a clause relating to legislative implementation and to criminal punishment.[5]

---

[2] We have discussed in a separate memorandum the federal jurisdiction issues that might arise concerning Guantanamo Bay. *See* Memorandum for William J. Haynes, II, General Counsel, Department of Defense, from Patrick F. Philbin, Deputy Assistant Attorney General and John Yoo, Deputy Assistant Attorney General, Office of Legal Counsel, *Re: Possible Habeas Jurisdiction over Aliens Held in Guantanamo Bay, Cuba* (Dec. 28, 2001).

[3] *See generally* Memorandum for Alberto R. Gonzales, Counsel to the President, from Patrick F. Philbin, Deputy Assistant Attorney General, Office of Legal Counsel, *Re: Legality of the Use of Military Commissions to Try Terrorists* (Nov. 6, 2001).

[4] The rule of lenity requires that the WCA be read so as to ensure that prospective defendants have adequate notice of the nature of the acts that the statute condemns. *See, e.g., Castillo v. United States*, 530 U.S. 120, 131 (2000). In those cases in which the application of a treaty incorporated by the WCA is unclear, therefore, the rule of lenity requires that the interpretive issue be resolved in the defendant's favor.

[5] That common clause reads as follows:

> The [signatory Nations] undertake to enact any legislation necessary to provide effective penal sanctions for persons committing, or ordering to be committed, any of the grave breaches of the present Convention.... Each [signatory nation] shall be under the obligation to search for persons alleged to have committed, or to have ordered to be committed, such grave breaches, and shall bring such persons, regardless of their nationality, before its own courts.... It may also, if it prefers, ... hand such persons over for trial to another [signatory nation], provided such [nation] has made out a *prima facie* case.

Geneva Convention I, Article 49; Geneva Convention II, Article 50; Geneva Convention III, Article 129; Geneva Convention IV, Article 146.

In enacting section 2441, Congress sought to fill certain perceived gaps in the coverage of federal criminal law. The main gaps were thought to be of two kinds: subject matter jurisdiction and personal jurisdiction. First, Congress found that "[t]here are major gaps in the prosecutability of individuals under federal criminal law for war crimes committed against Americans."[6] For example, "the simple killing of a[n American] prisoner of war" was not covered by any existing Federal statute.[7] Second, Congress found that "[t]he ability to court martial members of our armed services who commit war crimes ends when they leave military service. [Section 2441] would allow for prosecution even after discharge."[8] Congress considered it important to fill this gap, not only in the interest of the victims of war crimes, but also of the accused. "The Americans prosecuted would have available all the procedural protections of the American justice system. These might be lacking if the United States extradited the individuals to their victims' home countries for prosecution."[9] Accordingly, section 2441 criminalizes forms of conduct in which a U.S. national or a member of the Armed Forces may be either a victim or a perpetrator.

B. Grave Breaches of the Geneva Conventions

The Geneva Conventions of 1949 remain the agreements to which more States have become parties than any other concerning the laws of war. Convention I deals with the treatment of the wounded and sick in armed forces in the field; Convention II addresses treatment of wounded, sick, and shipwrecked in armed forces at sea; Convention III regulates treatment of POWs; Convention IV addresses the treatment of citizens.

The Geneva Conventions, like treaties generally, structure legal relationships between nation-States, not between nation-States and private, transnational or subnational groups or organizations.[10] Article 2, which is common to all four Geneva Conventions, makes the application of the Conventions to relations between state parties clear. It states that: "the present Convention shall apply to all cases of declared

---

[6] H. R. Rep. No. 104-698, at 6, *reprinted in* 1996 U.S.C.C.A.N. at 2171.

[7] *Id*. at 5, *reprinted in* 1996 U.S.C.C.A.N. at 2170. In projecting our criminal law extraterritorially in order to protect victims who are United States nationals, Congress was apparently relying on the international law principle of passive personality. The passive personality principle "'asserts that a state may apply law – particularly criminal law – to an act commited outside its territory by a person not its national where the victim of the act was its national.'" *United States v. Rezaq*, 134 F.3d 1121, 1133 (D.C. Cir.), *cert. denied*, 525 U.S. 834 (1998). The principle marks recognition of the fact that "each nation has a legitimate interest that its national and permanent inhabitants not be maimed or disabled from self-support," or otherwise injured. *Lauritzen v. Larsen*, 345 U.S., 571, 586 (1953); *see also Hellenic Lines Ltd. v. Rhoditis*, 398 U.S. 306, 309 (1970).

[8] H.R. Rep. No. 104–698, at 7, *reprinted in* 1996 U.S.C.C.A.N. at 2172. In *United States ex rel. Toth v. Quarles*, 350 U.S. 11 (1955), the Supreme Court had held that a former serviceman could not constitutionally be tried before a court martial under the Uniform Code for Military Justice (the "UCMJ") for crimes he was alleged to have committed while in the armed services. The WCA cured this problem.

[9] H.R. Rep. No. 104–698, at 7, *reprinted in* 1996 U.S.C.C.A.N. at 2172. The principle of nationality in international law recognizes that (as Congress did here) a State may criminalize acts performed extraterritorially by its own nationals. *See, e.g., Skiriotes v. Florida*, 313 U.S. 69, 73 (1941); *Steele v. Bulova Watch Co.*, 344 U.S., 280, 282 (1952).

[10] *See Trans World Airlines, Inc. v. Franklin Mint Corp.*, 466 U.S. 243, 253 (1984) ("A treaty is in the nature of a contract between nations."); *The Head Money Cases*, 112 U.S. 580, 598 (1884) ("A treaty is primarily a compact between nations."); *United States ex rel.Saroop v. Gracia*, 109 F.3d 165, 167 (3d Cir. 1997) ("[T]reaties are agreements between nations.")

war or of any other armed conflict *which may arise between two or more of the High Contracting Parties*, even if the state of war is not recognized by one of them."[11] Similarly, it states that "[t]he Convention shall also apply to all cases of partial or total occupation of the territory of a High Contracting Party, even if the said occupation meets with no armed resistance."

As noted above, Section 2441(c)(I) criminalizes "grave breaches" of the Convention. Each of the four Geneva Conventions has a similar definition of "grave breaches." Geneva Convention III defines a grave breach as:

> wilful killing, torture or inhuman treatment, including biological experiments, wilfully causing great suffering or serious injury to body or health, compelling a prisoner of war to serve in the forces of the hostile Power, or wilfully depriving a prisoner of war of the rights of fair and regular trial prescribed in this Convention.

Geneva Convention III, Article 130. As mentioned before, the Geneva Conventions require the High Contracting Parties to enact penal legislation to punish anyone who commits or orders a grave breach. *See, e.g., id.* Article 129. Further, each State party has the obligation to search for and bring to justice (either before its courts or by delivering a suspect to another State party) anyone who commits a grave breach. No State party is permitted to absolve itself or any other nation of liability for committing a grave breach.

Given the specific definition of "grave breaches," it bears noting that not *all* breaches of the Geneva Conventions are criminalized under Section 2441. Failure to follow some of the regulations regarding the treatment of POWs, such as difficulty in meeting all of the conditions set forth for POW camp conditions, does not constitute a grave breach within the meaning of Geneva Convention III, Article 130. Only by causing great suffering or serious bodily injury to POWs, killing or torturing them, depriving them of access to a fair trial, or forcing them to serve in the Armed Forces, could the United States actually commit a grave breach.

C. *Common Article 3 of the Geneva Conventions*

Section 2441 (c)(3) also defines as a war crime conduct that "constitutes a violation of common Article 3" of the Geneva Conventions. Article 3 is a unique provision that governs the conduct of signatories to the Conventions in a particular kind of conflict that is *not* one between High Contracting Parties to the Conventions. Thus, common Article 3 may require the United States, as a High Contracting Party, to follow certain rules even if other parties to the conflict are not parties to the Conventions. On the other hand, Article 3 requires State parties to follow only certain minimum standards of treatment toward prisoners, civilians, or the sick and wounded – standards that are much less onerous and less detailed than those spelled out in the Conventions as a whole.[12]

---

[11] Geneva III Article 2 (emphasis added).

[12] Common Article 3 reads in relevant part as follows:

> In the case of armed conflict not of an international character occurring in the territory of one of the High Contracting Parties, each Party to the conflict shall be bound to apply, as a minimum, the following provisions:

> (1) Persons taking no active part in the hostilities, including members of armed forces who have laid down their arms and those placed *hors de combat* by sickness, wounds, detention, or any

Common Article 3 complements common Article 2. Article 2 applies to cases of declared war or of any other armed conflict that may arise between two or more of the High Contracting Parties, even if the state of war is not recognized by one of them.[13] Common Article 3, however, covers "armed conflict not of an international character" – a war that does not involve cross border attacks – that occur within the territory of one of the High Contracting Parties.

Common Article 3's text provides substantial reason to think that it refers specifically to a condition of civil war, or a large-scale armed conflict between a State and an armed movement within its own territory. First, the text of the provision refers specifically to an armed conflict that a) is not of an international character, and b) occurs in the territory of a state party to the Convention. It does not sweep in all armed conflicts, nor does it address a gap left by common Article 2 for international armed conflicts that involve non-State entities (such as an international terrorist organization) as parties to the conflict. Further, common Article 3 addresses only non-international conflicts that occur within the territory of a single state party, again, like a civil war. This provision would not reach an armed conflict in which one of the parties operated from multiple bases in several different states. Also, the language at the end of Article 3 states that "[t]he application of the preceding provisions shall not affect the legal status of the Parties to the conflict." This provision was designed to ensure that a state party that observed Article 3 during a civil war would not be understood to have granted the "recognition of the insurgents as an adverse party."[14]

This interpretation is supported by commentators. One well-known commentary states that "a non-international armed conflict is distinct from an international armed conflict because of the legal status of the entities opposing each other: the parties to the conflict are not sovereign States, but the government of a single State in conflict with one or more armed factions within its territory."[15] A legal scholar writing in the same year in which the Conventions were prepared stated that "a conflict not of

> other cause, shall in all circumstances be treated humanely, without any adverse distinction founded on race, color, religion or faith, sex, birth or wealth, or any other similar criteria.
>
> To this end, the following acts are and shall remain prohibited at any time and in any place whatsoever with respect to the above-mentioned persons:
>
> (a) violence to life and person, in particular, murder of all kinds, mutilation, cruel treatment and torture;
> (b) taking of hostages;
> (c) outrages upon personal dignity, in particular humiliating and degrading treatment;
> (d) the passing of sentences and the carrying out of executions without previous judgment pronounced by a regularly constituted court, affording all the judicial guarantees which are recognized as indispensable by civilized peoples.
>
> (2) The wounded and sick shall be collected and cared for. . . .
>
> The application of the preceding provisions shall not affect the legal status of the Parties to the conflict.

[13] Article 2's reference to a state of war "not recognized" by a belligerent was apparently intended to refer to conflicts such as the 1937 war between China and Japan. Both sides denied that a state of war existed. *See* Joyce A. C. Gutteridge, *The Geneva Conventions of 1949*, 26 Brit Y.B. Int'l L. 294, 298–99 (1949).

[14] Frits Kalshoven, *Constraints on the Waging of War 59* (1987).

[15] *Commentary on the Additional Protocols of 8 June 1977 to the Geneva Conventions of 12 August 1949*, at 1939 (Yves Sandoz et al. eds., 1987)

an international character occurring in the territory of one of the High Contracting Parties...must normally mean a civil war."[16]

Analysis of the background to the adoption of the Geneva Conventions in 1949 confirms our understanding of common Article 3. It appears that the drafters of the Conventions had in mind only the two forms of armed conflict that were regarded as matters of general *international* concern at the time: armed conflict between nation-States (subject to Article 2), and large-scale civil war within a nation-State (subject to Article 3). To understand the context in which the Geneva Conventions were drafted, it will be helpful to identify three distinct phases in the development of the laws of war.

First, the traditional laws of war were based on a stark dichotomy between "belligerency" and "insurgency." The category of "belligerency" applied to armed conflicts between sovereign States (unless there was recognition of belligerency in a civil war), while the category of "insurgency" applied to armed violence breaking out within the territory of a sovereign State.[17] International law treated the two classes of conflict in different ways. Inter-state wars were regulated by a body of international legal rules governing both the conduct of hostilities and the protection of non-combatants. By contrast, there were very few international rules governing armed conflict within a State, for States preferred to regard internal strife as rebellion, mutiny and treason coming within the purview of national criminal law, which precluded any possible intrusion by other States.[18] This was a "clearly sovereignty-oriented" phase of international law.[19]

The second phase began as early as the Spanish Civil War (1936–39) and extended through the time of the drafting of the Geneva Conventions until relatively recently. During this period, State practice began to apply certain general principles of humanitarian law beyond the traditional field of State-to-State conflict to "those internal conflicts that constituted large-scale civil wars."[20] In addition to the Spanish Civil War, events in 1947 during the civil war between the Communists and the Nationalist regime in China illustrated this new tendency.[21] Common Article 3, which was prepared during this second phase, was apparently addressed to armed conflicts akin to the Chinese and Spanish civil wars. As one commentator has described it, Article 3 was designed to restrain governments "in the handling of armed violence directed against them for the express purpose of secession or at securing a change in the government

---

[16] Gutteridge, *supra*, at 300.

[17] *See* Joseph H. Beale, Jr., *The Recognition of Cuban Belligerency*, 9 Harv. L. Rev. 406, 406 n.1 (1896).

[18] *See The Prosecutor v. Dusko Tadic (Jurisdiction of the Tribunal)* (Appeals Chamber of the International Criminal Tribunal for the Former Yugoslavia 1995) ("Tadic"), 105 I.L.R. 453, 504–05 (E. Lauterpacht & C.J. Greenwood eds., 1997).

[19] *id* at 505; *see also* Gerald Irving Draper, *Reflections on Law and Armed Conflicts* 107 (1998) ("Before 1949, in the absence of recognized belligerency accorded to the elements opposed to the government of a State, the law of war...had no application to internal armed conflicts.... International law had little or nothing to say as to how the armed rebellion was crushed by the government concerned, for such matters fell within the domestic jurisdiction of States. Such conflicts were often waged with great lack of restraint and cruelty. Such conduct was a domestic matter.").

[20] *Tadic*, 105 I.L.R. at 507. Indeed the events of the Spanish Civil War, in which "both the republican Government [of Spain] and third States refused to recognize the [Nationalist] insurgents as belligerents," *id.* at 507, may be reflected in common Article 3's reference to "the legal status of the Parties to the conflict."

[21] *See id.* at 508.

of a State," but even after the adoption of the Conventions it remained "uncertain whether [Article 3] applied to full-scale civil war."[22]

The third phase represents a more complete break than the second with the traditional "State-sovereignty-oriented approach" of international law. This approach gives central place to individual human rights. As a consequence, it blurs the distinction between international and internal armed conflicts. This approach is well illustrated by the decision of the International Criminal Tribunal for the Former Yugoslavia in *Prosecutor v. Tadic*, which appears to take the view that common Article 3 applies to all armed conflicts of *any* description other than those between state parties, and is not limited to internal conflicts between a State and an insurgent group. In this conception, common Article 3 is not just a complement to common Article 2; rather, it is a catch-all that establishes standards for any and all armed conflicts not included in common Article 2.[23]

Such an interpretation of common Article 3, however, ignores the text and the context in which it was ratified by the United States. If the state parties had intended the Conventions to apply to *all* forms of armed conflict, they could have used broader, clearer language. To interpret common Article 3 by expanding its scope well beyond the meaning borne by its text is effectively to amend the Geneva Conventions without the approval of the State parties to the agreements. Further, as we have discussed, Article 3 was ratified during a period in which the traditional, State-centered view of international law was still dominant and was only just beginning to give way to a human-rights-based approach. Giving due weight to the state practice and doctrinal understanding of the time, the idea of an armed conflict between a nation-State and a transnational terrorist organization (or between a nation-State and a failed State harboring and supporting a transnational terrorist organization) could not have been within the contemplation of the drafters of common Article 3. Conflicts of these kinds would have been unforeseen and were not provided for in the Conventions. Further, it is telling that in order to address this unforeseen circumstance, the State parties to the

---

[22] *See* Draper, *Reflections on Law and Armed Conflicts, supra*, at 108.

[23] Some international law authorities seem to suggest that common Article 3 is better read as applying to all forms of non-international armed conflict. The *Commentary on the Additional Protocols of 8 June 1977 to the Geneva Conventions of 12 August 1949, supra*, after first stating that Article 3 applies when "the government of a single State [is] in conflict with one or more armed factions within its territory," suggests, in a footnote, that an armed conflict not of an international character "may also exist in which armed factions fight against each other without intervention by the armed forces of the established government." *Id.* ¶ 4339 at n.2. A still broader interpretation appears to be supported by the language of the decision of the International Court of Justice (the "ICJ") in *Nicaragua v. United States* – which the United States refused to acknowledge by withdrawing from the compulsory jurisdiction of the ICJ. *Military and Paramilitary Activities In and Against Nicaragua (Nicaragua v. United States)*, (International Court of Justice 1986), 76 I.L.R. 1, 448, ¶ 218 (E. Lauterpacht & C.J. Greenwood eds., 1988). The ICJ's decision is probably best read to suggest that all "armed conflicts" are either international or non-international, and that if they are non-international, they are governed by common Article 3. If that is the correct understanding, however, the result was merely stated as a conclusion, without taking account either of the precise language of Article 3 or of the background to its adoption. Moreover, while it was true that one of the conflicts to which the ICJ was addressing itself – "[t]he conflict between the *contras*' forces and those of the Government of Nicaragua" – "was an armed conflict which is not of an international character,'" *id.* at 448, ¶ 219, that conflict was recognizably a civil war between a State and an insurgent group, not a conflict between or among violent factions in a territory in which the State had collapsed. Thus there is substantial reason to question the logic and scope of the ICJ's interpretation of common Article 3, which, in any event, is not binding as a matter of domestic law on the United States.

Geneva Conventions did not attempt to distort the terms of common Article 3 to apply it to cases that did not fit within its terms. Instead, they drafted two new protocols to adapt the Conventions to the conditions of contemporary hostilities.[24] The United States has not ratified these protocols, and hence cannot be held to the reading of the Geneva Conventions they promote. Thus, the WCA's prohibition on violations of common Article 3 would apply only to internal conflicts between a state party and an insurgent group, rather than to all forms of armed conflict not covered by common Article 2.

II. Application of WCA and Associated Treaties to al Qaeda

We conclude that Geneva III does not apply to the al Qaeda terrorist organization. Therefore, neither the detention nor trial of al Qaeda fighters is subject to Geneva III (or the WCA). Three reasons, examined in detail below, support this conclusion. First, al Qaeda is not a State and thus cannot receive the benefits of a State party to the Conventions. Second, al Qaeda members fail to satisfy the eligibility requirements for treatment as POWs under Geneva Convention III. Third, the nature of the conflict precludes application of common Article 3 of the Geneva Conventions.

Geneva III does not apply to a non-State actor such as the al Qaeda terrorist organization. Al Qaeda is not a State. It is a non-governmental terrorist organization composed of members from many nations, with ongoing operations in dozens of nations. Non-governmental organizations cannot be parties to any of the international agreements here governing the laws of war. Common Article 2, which triggers the Geneva Convention provisions regulating detention conditions and procedures for trial of POWs, is limited to cases of declared war or armed conflict "between two or more of the High Contracting Parties." Al Qaeda is not a High Contracting Party. As a result, the U.S. military's treatment of al Qaeda members is not governed by the bulk of the Geneva Conventions, specifically those provisions concerning POWs. Conduct towards captured members of al Qaeda, therefore, also cannot constitute a violation of 18 U.S.C. § 2441(c)(1).

Second, al Qaeda members fail to satisfy the eligibility requirements for treatment as POWs under Geneva Convention III. It might be argued that, even though it is not a State party to the Geneva Conventions, al Qaeda could be covered by some protections in Geneva Convention III. Article 4(A)(2) of Geneva III defines prisoners of war as including not only captured members of the armed forces of a High Contracting Party, but also irregular forces such as "[m]embers of other militias and members of other volunteer corps, including those of organized resistance movements." Article 4(A)(3) also includes as POWs "[m]embers of regular armed forces who profess allegiance to a government or an authority not recognized by the Detaining Power." *Id.* Article 4(A)(3). It might be claimed that the broad terms of these provisions could be stretched to cover al Qaeda.

This view would be mistaken. Article 4 does not expand the application of the Convention beyond the circumstances expressly addressed in common Articles 2 and 3. Unless there is a conflict subject to Article 2, Article 4 simply does not apply. If the

---

[24] Protocol Additional to the Geneva Conventions of 12 August 1949, and Relating to the Protection of Victims National Armed Conflicts (Protocol I), June 8, 1977, 1125 U.N.T.S. 4; Protocol Additional to the Geneva Conventions of 12 August 1949, and Relating to the Protection of Victims of Non-International Armed Conflicts Protocol II), June 8, 1977, 1125 U.N.T.S. 610.

conflict is one to which Article 3 applies, then Article 4 has no role because Article 3 does not trigger application of the rest of the provisions of Geneva III. Rather, Article 3 provides an alternative set of standards that requires only minimal humanitarian protections. As we have explained, the conflict with al Qaeda does not fall within Article 2. As a result, Article 4 has no application. In other words, Article 4 cannot be read as an alternative, and a far more expansive, statement of the application of the Convention. It merely specifies, where there is a conflict covered by Article 2 of the Convention, who must be accorded POW status.

Even if Article 4, however, were considered somehow to be jurisdictional as well as substantive, captured members of al Qaeda still would not receive the protections accorded to POWs. First, al Qaeda is not the "armed forces," volunteer forces, or militia of a state party that is a party to the conflict, as defined in Article 4(A)(1). Second, they cannot qualify as volunteer force, militia, or organized resistance force under Article 4(A)(2). That article requires that militia or volunteers fulfill four conditions: command by responsible individuals, wearing insignia, carrying arms openly, and obeying the laws of war. Al Qaeda members have clearly demonstrated that they will not follow these basic requirements of lawful warfare. They have attacked purely civilian targets of no military value; they refused to wear uniform or insignia or carry arms openly, but instead hijacked civilian airliners, took hostages, and killed them; and they themselves do not obey the laws of war concerning the protection of the lives of civilians or the means of legitimate combat. As these requirements also apply to any regular armed force under other treaties governing the laws of armed conflict,[25] al Qaeda members would not qualify under Article 4(A)(3) either, which provides POW status to captured individuals who are members of a "regular armed force" that professes allegiance to a government or authority not recognized by the detaining power. Members of al Qaeda, therefore, would not qualify for POW treatment under Article 4, even if it were somehow thought that they were participating in a conflict covered by common Article 2 or if Article 4 itself were thought to be jurisdictional in nature.

Third, the nature of the conflict precludes application of common Article 3 of the Geneva Conventions. As discussed in Part 1, the text of common Article 3, when read in harmony with common Article 2, shows that the Geneva Conventions were intended to cover either: a) traditional wars between state parties to the Conventions (Article 2), b) or non-international civil wars (Article 3). Our conflict with al Qaeda does not fit into either category. It is not an international war between nation-States because al Qaeda is not a State. Nor is this conflict a civil war under Article 3, because it *is* a conflict of "an international character." Al Qaeda operates in many countries and carried out a massive international attack on the United States on September 11, 2001. Therefore, the military's treatment of al Qaeda members is not limited either by common Article 3 or 18 U.S.C. § 2441(c)(3).

III. Application of the Geneva Conventions to the Taliban Militia

Whether the Geneva Conventions apply to the detention and trial of members of the Taliban militia presents a more difficult legal question. Afghanistan has been a party to all four Geneva Conventions since September 1956. Some might argue that this

---

[25] Hague Convention IV, Respecting the Laws and Customs of War on Land, Oct. 18, 1907, 36 Stat. 2277.

requires application of the Geneva Conventions to the present conflict with respect to the Taliban militia, which would then trigger the WCA. Nonetheless, we conclude that the President has more than ample grounds to find that our treaty obligations under Geneva III toward Afghanistan were suspended during the period of the conflict. Under Article II of the Constitution, the President has the unilateral power to suspend whole treaties or parts of them at his discretion. In this part, we describe the President's constitutional power and discuss the grounds upon which he can justify the exercise of that power.

There are several grounds under which the President could exercise that authority here. First, the weight of informed opinion indicates that, for the period in question, Afghanistan was a "failed State" whose territory had been largely held by a violent militia or faction rather than by a government. As a failed state, Afghanistan did not have an operating government nor was it capable of fulfilling its international obligations. Therefore, the United States could decide to partially suspend any obligations that the United States might have under Geneva III towards the Taliban militia. Second, there appears to be developing evidence that the Taliban leadership had become closely intertwined with, if not utterly dependent upon, al Qaeda. This would have rendered the Taliban more akin to a terrorist organization that used force not to administer a government, but for terrorist purposes. The President could decide that no treaty obligations were owed to such a force.

A. Constitutional Authority

Article II of the Constitution makes clear that the President is vested with all of the federal executive power, that he "shall be Commander-in-Chief," that he shall appoint, with the advice and consent of the Senate, and receive, ambassadors, and that he "shall have Power, by and with the Advice and Consent of the Senate, to make Treaties." U.S. Const. Article II, §2, cl. 2. Congress possesses its own specific foreign affairs powers, primarily those of declaring war, raising and funding the military, and regulating international commerce. While Article II, section I of the Constitution grants the President an undefined executive power, Article I, section I limits Congress to "all legislative Powers herein granted" in the rest of Article I.

From the very beginnings of the Republic, this constitutional arrangement has been understood to grant the President plenary control over the conduct of foreign relations. As Secretary of State Thomas Jefferson observed during the first Washington administration: "The constitution has divided the powers of government into three branches {and} ... has declared that 'the executive powers shall be vested in the President,' submitting only special articles of it to a negative by the Senate."[26] Due to this structure, Jefferson continued, "[t]he transaction of business with foreign nations is Executive altogether. It belongs then to the head of that department, *except* as to such portions of it as are specially submitted to the Senate. *Exceptions* are to be construed strictly."[27] In defending President Washington's authority to issue the Neutrality Proclamation, Alexander Hamilton came to the same interpretation of the President's foreign affairs powers. According to Hamilton, Article II "ought ... to be

---

[26] Thomas Jefferson, *Opinion on the Powers of the Senate Respecting Diplomatic Appointments* (1790), *reprinted in 6 The Papers of Thomas Jefferson* 378 (Julian P. Boyd ed., 1961).
[27] Id. at 379.

considered as intended . . . to specify and regulate the principal articles implied in the definition of Executive Power; leaving the rest to flow from the general grant of that power."[28] As future Chief Justice John Marshall famously declared a few years later, "The President is the sole organ of the nation in its external relations, and its sole representative with foreign nations . . . The [executive] department . . . is entrusted with the whole foreign intercourse of the nation . . ."[29]

On the few occasions where it has addressed the question, the Supreme Court has lent its approval to the executive branch's broad powers in the field of foreign affairs. Responsibility for the conduct of foreign affairs and for protecting the national security are, as the Supreme Court has observed, "central Presidential domains."[30] The President's constitutional primacy flows from both his unique position in the constitutional structure and from the specific grants of authority in Article II making the President the Chief Executive of the Nation and the Commander-in-Chief.[31] Due to the President's constitutionally superior position, the Supreme Court has consistently "recognized 'the generally accepted view that foreign policy [is] the province and responsibility of the Executive.'"[32] This foreign affairs power is independent of Congress: it is "the very delicate, plenary and exclusive power of the President as sole organ of the federal government in the field of international relations – a power which does not require as a basis for its exercise an Act of Congress."[33]

In light of these principles, any unenumerated executive power, especially one relating to foreign affairs, must be construed as within the control of the President. Although the Constitution does not specifically mention the power to suspend or terminate treaties, these authorities have been understood by the courts and long executive branch practice as belonging solely to the President. The treaty power is fundamentally an executive power established in Article II of the Constitution, and power over treaty matters post-ratification are within the President's plenary authority. As Alexander Hamilton declared during the controversy over the Neutrality Proclamation, "though treaties can only be made by the President and Senate, their activity may be continued or suspended by the President alone."[34] Commentators also have supported this view. According to the drafters of the *Restatement (Third) of the Foreign Relations Law of the United States*, the President has the power either "to suspend or terminate an [international] agreement in accordance with its terms," or "to make the determination that would justify the United States in terminating or suspending an agreement because of its violation by another party or because of supervening events, and to proceed to terminate or suspend the agreement on behalf of the United States."[35] Indeed, the President's power to terminate treaties, which has been accepted by practice and considered opinion of the three branches,[36] must include the lesser power of temporarily suspending them. We have

---

[28] Alexander Hamilton, *Pacificus* No. I (1793), *reprinted in* 15 *The Papers of Alexander Hamilton* 33, 39 (Harold C. Syrett et al. eds., 1969).

[29] 10 Annals of Cong. 613–14 (1800).

[30] *Harlow v. Fitzgerald*, 457 U.S. 800, 812 n. 19 (1982).

[31] *Nixon v. Fitzgerald*, 457 U.S. 731, 749–50 (1982).

[32] *Department of the Navy v. Egan*, 484 U.S. 518, 529 (1988) (quoting *Haig v. Agee*, 453 U.S. 280, 293–94 (1981)).

[33] *United States v. Curtiss-Wright Export Corp.*, 299 U.S. 304, 320 (1936).

[34] Hamilton, *Pacificus* No. l, *supra*, at 42.

[35] *Restatement (Third) of the Foreign Relations Law of the United States* § 339 (1987).

[36] *See, e.g.*, Memorandum for Alberto R. Gonzales, Counsel to the President, from: Jay S. Bybee, Assistant Attorney General, *Re: Authority of the President to Denounce the ABM Treaty (Dec. 14, 2001);*

discussed these questions in detail in recent opinions, and we follow their analysis here.[37]

The courts have often acknowledged the President's constitutional powers with respect to treaties. Thus, it has long been accepted that the President may determine whether a treaty has lapsed because a foreign State has gained or lost its independence, or because it has undergone other changes in sovereignty.[38] Non-performance of a particular treaty obligation may, in the President's judgment, justify a decision to suspend or terminate the treaty.[39] While Presidents have unrestricted discretion, as a matter of domestic law, in suspending treaties, they can base the exercise of this discretion on several grounds. For example, the President may determine that "the conditions essential to [the treaty's] continued effectiveness no longer pertain."[40] He can decide to suspend treaty obligations because of a fundamental change in circumstances, as the United States did in 1941 in response to hostilities in Europe.[41] The President may also determine that a material breach of a treaty by a foreign government has rendered a treaty not in effect as to that government.[42]

Exercising this constitutional authority, the President can decide to suspend temporarily our obligations under Geneva III toward Afghanistan. Other Presidents have partially suspended treaties, and have suspended the obligations of multilateral agreements with regard to one of the state parties.[43] The President could also determine that

Goldwater v. Carter, 617 F.2d 697, 706–07 (D.C. Cir.) (en banc), *vacated and remanded with instructions to dismiss*, 444 U.S. 996 (1979); Senate Comm. on Foreign Relations, 106th Cong., *Treaties and Other International Agreements: The Role of the United States Senate* 201 (Comm. Print 2001) (prepared by Congressional Research Service, Library of Congress) (footnotes omitted)

[37] *See* Memorandum for John Bellinger, III, Senior Associate Counsel and Legal Adviser to the National Security Council, from John C. Yoo, Deputy Assistant Attorney General and Robert J. Delahunty, Special Counsel, Office of Legal Counsel, *Re: Authority of the President to Suspend Certain Provisions of the ABM Treaty* (Nov. 15, 2001); *see also* Memorandum for William Howard Taft, IV, Legal Adviser, Department of State, from John Yoo, Deputy Assistant Attorney General, Office of Legal Counsel, *Re: President's Constitutional Authority to Withdraw Treaties from the Senate* (Aug. 24, 2001).

[38] *See Kennett v. Chambers*, 55 U.S. 38, 47–48, 51 (1852); *Terlinden v. Ames*, 184 U.S. 270, 288 (1902); *Saroop v. Garcia*, 109 F.3d 165, 171 (3d. Cir. 1997) (collecting cases). Alexander Hamilton argued in 1793 that the revolution in France had triggered the power (indeed, the duty) of the President to determine whether the pre-existing treaty of alliance with the King of France remained in effect. The President's constitutional powers, he said, "include that of judging, in the case of a Revolution of Government in a foreign Country, whether the new rulers are competent organs of the National Will and ought to be recognised or not: And where a treaty antecedently exists between the States and such nation that right involves the power of giving operation or not to such treaty."

Alexander Hamilton, *Pacificus* No. 1 (1793), *reprinted in* 15 *The Papers of Alexander Hamilton* 33, 41 (Harold C. Syrett et al. eds 1969).

[39] *See Taylor v. Morton*, 23 F. Cas. 784, 787 (C.C.D. Mass. 1855) (No. 13,799) (Curtis, Circuit Justice), *aff'd*. 67 U.S. (2 Black) 481 (1862).

[40] See International Load Line Convention, 40 Op. Att'y Gen. 119, 124 (1941). Changed conditions have provided a basis on which Presidents have suspended treaties in the past. For example, in 1939, President Franklin Roosevelt suspended the operation of the London Naval Treaty of 1936. "The war in Europe had caused several contracting parties to suspend the treaty, for the obvious reason that it was impossible to limit naval armaments. The notice of termination was therefore grounded on changed circumstances." David Gray Adler, *The Constitution and the Termination of Treaties* 187 (1986).

[41] *International Load Line Convention*, 40 Op. Att'y Gen. at 123.

[42] *See, e.g., Charlton v. Kelly*, 229 U.S. 447, 473 (1913); *Escobedo v. United States*, 623 F.2d 1098, 1106 (5th Cir.), *Cert.* denied, 449 U.S. 1036 (1980).

[43] In 1986, the United States suspended the performance of its obligations under the Security Treaty (ANZUS Pact), T.I.A.S. 2493, 3 U.S.T. 3420, *entered into force* April 29, 1952, as to New Zealand but not as to Australia. *See Marian Nash (Leich), I Cumulative Digest of United States Practice in International Law 1981–1988*, at 1279–81.

relations under the Geneva Conventions with Afghanistan should be restored once an Afghan government that is willing and able to execute the country's treaty obligations is securely established.[44] A decision to regard the Geneva Conventions as suspended would not constitute a "denunciation" of the Conventions, for which procedures are prescribed in the Conventions.[45] The President need not regard the Conventions as suspended in their entirety, but only in part.[46]

Among the grounds upon which a President may justify his power to suspend treaties is the collapse of a treaty partner, in other words, the development of a failed state that could not fulfill its international obligations and was not under the control of any government. This has been implicitly recognized by the Supreme Court. In *Clark v. Allen*, 331 U.S. 503 (1947), the Supreme Court considered whether a 1923 treaty with Germany continued to exist after the defeat, occupation and partition of Germany by the victorious World War II Allies. The Court rejected the argument that the treaty "must be held to have failed to survive the [Second World War], since Germany, as a result of its defeat and the occupation by the Allies, has ceased to exist as an independent national or international community."[47] Instead, the Court held that "the question whether a state is in a position to perform its treaty obligations is essentially a political question. *Terlinden v. Ames*, 184 U.S. 270, 288 [(1902)]. We find no evidence that the political departments have considered the collapse and surrender of Germany as putting an end to such provisions of the treaty as survived the outbreak of the war or the obligations of either party in respect to them."[48] In *Clark*, the Court also made clear that the President could consider whether Germany was able to perform its international obligations in deciding whether to suspend our treaty relationship with her.

Thus, suspension of the Geneva Conventions as to Afghanistan would not affect the United States' relationships under the Conventions with other state parties.

[44] On June 20, 1876, for example, President Grant informed Congress that he was suspending the extradition clause of the 1842 "Webster-Ashburton Treaty" with Great Britain, Convention as 10 Boundaries, Suppression of Slave Trade and Extradition, Aug. 9, 1842, U.S.-Gr. Brit., Art 10, 8 Stat. 572, 579. Grant advised Congress that the release of two fugitives whose extradition was sought by the United States amounted to the abrogation or annulment of the extradition clause, and that the executive branch in response would take no action to surrender fugitives sought by the British Government unless Congress signified that it do so. The clause remained suspended until it was reactivated by the British Government's resumed performance.

[45] *See, e.g.*, Geneva Convention III, art. 142. The suspension of a treaty is distinct from the denunciation or termination of one. Suspension is generally a milder measure than termination, often being partial, temporary, or contingent upon circumstances that can be altered by the actions of the parties to the treaty. Moreover, at least in the United States, suspension of a treaty can be reversed by unilateral executive action, whereas termination, which annuls a treaty, and which is therefore more disruptive of international relationships, would require Senate consent to a new treaty to be undone.

[46] In general, the partial suspension of the provisions of a treaty (as distinct from both termination and complete suspension) is recognized as permissible under international law. Article 60 of the Vienna Convention on treaties explicitly permits the suspension of a treaty "in whole or in part." "[U]nder both treaty law and non-forcible reprisal law as a basis for responsive suspension it is clear that suspension may be only partial and need not suspend or terminate an agreement as a whole, in contrast, for example, with treaty withdrawal clauses." John Norton Moore, *Enhancing Compliance With International Law: A Neglected Remedy*, 39 Va. J. Int'l L. 881, 932 (1999). It should be noted, however, that the United States is not a party to the Vienna Convention on treaties, although it has treated its rules as customary international law. This issue is explored in greater detail, *infra* Part III.C.

[47] 331 U.S. at 514.

[48] *Id.; see also id.* at 508–09 (President might have "formulated a national policy quite inconsistent with the enforcement" of the treaty).

Clark demonstrates the Supreme Court's sanction for the President's constitutional authority to decide the "political question" whether our treaty with Germany was suspended because Germany was not in a position to perform its international obligations. Equally here, the executive branch could conclude that Afghanistan was not "in a position to perform its treaty obligations" because it lacked, at least throughout the Taliban's ascendancy, a functioning central government and other essential attributes of statehood. Based on such facts, the President would have the ground to decide that the Nation's Geneva III obligations were suspended as to Afghanistan. The President could further decide that these obligations are suspended until Afghanistan became a functioning state that is in a position to perform its Convention duties. The federal courts would not review such political questions, but instead would defer to the decision of the President.

B. *Status as a Failed State*

There are ample grounds for the President to determine that Afghanistan was a failed State, and on that basis to suspend performance of our Geneva III obligations toward it.[49] Indeed, the findings of the State and Defense Departments, of foreign leaders, and of expert opinion support the conclusion that Afghanistan under the Taliban was without a functioning central government. The collapse of functioning political institutions in Afghanistan is a valid justification for the exercise of the President's authority to suspend our treaty obligations toward that country.

Such a determination would amount to finding that Afghanistan was a "failed state." A "failed State" is generally characterized by the collapse or near-collapse of State authority. Such a collapse is marked by the inability of central authorities to maintain government institutions, ensure law and order or engage in normal dealings with other governments, and by the prevalence of violence that destabilizes civil society and the economy.

An initial approach to the question whether Afghanistan was a failed State is to examine some of the traditional indicia of statehood.[50] A State has failed when centralized governmental authority has almost completely collapsed, no central authorities are capable of maintaining government institutions or ensuring law and order, and violence has destabilized civil society and the economy.[51] Borrowing from the

---

[49] We should not be understood to be saying that the President's basis for suspending the Geneva Conventions as to Afghanistan is merely the fact that Afghanistan underwent a change of government in 1996, after the military successes of Taliban. The general rule of international law is that treaty relations survive a change of government. *See, e.g.*, 2 Marjorie M. Whiteman, *Digest of International Law* 771–73 (1963); J.L. Brierly, *The Law of Nations* 144–45 (6th ed. 1963); Eleanor C. McDowell, *Contemporary Practice of the United States Relating to International Law*, 71 Am. J. Int'l L. 337 (1977). The general rule is that treaties may still be observed even as to State parties, the current governments of which have been unrecognized. *See New York Chinese TV Programs v. U.E. Enterprises*, 954 F.2d 847 (2d Cir. 1992); *see also Restatement (Third) of the Foreign Relations Law of the United States* § 202 emts. a, b (1987).

[50] It would be mistaken to argue that the concept of a failed State is not legal in nature, and thus cannot be taken into account in determining whether to suspend our Geneva III obligations toward Afghanistan. Legal scholars as well as political scientists have employed the concept for some time. Moreover, even if taken only as a category of political science, the term "failed State" encapsulates a description of structural conditions within a country such as Afghanistan that are directly relevant to considering whether that country has lapsed for *legal* purposes into a condition of statelessness.

[51] "States in which institutions and law and order have totally or partially collapsed under the pressure and amidst the confusion of erupting violence, yet which subsist as a ghostly presence on the world

Restatement (Third) of U.S. Foreign Relations Law, we may conclude that a state has "failed" if it cannot satisfy some or all of the three traditional tests for "statehood" under international law: i) whether the entity has a defined territory and population; ii) whether the territory/population is under the control of its own government; and iii) whether the entity engages in or has the capacity to engage in formal relations with other States.[52] The State Department has restated this formulation by elaborating a four-part test for statehood: i) whether the entity have effective control over a clearly defined territory and population; ii) whether an organized governmental administration of the territory exists; iii) whether the entity has the capacity to act effectively to conduct foreign relations and to fulfill international obligations; iv) whether the international community recognizes the entity.[53]

We want to make clear that this Office does not have access to all of the facts related to the activities of the Taliban militia and al Qaeda in Afghanistan. Nonetheless, the available facts in the public record would support the conclusion that Afghanistan was a failed State – including facts that pre-existed the military reversals suffered by the Taliban militia and the formation of the new transitional government pursuant to the Bonn Agreement. Indeed, there are good reasons to doubt whether *any* of the conditions were met.

First, even before the outset of the conflict with the United States, the Taliban militia did not have effective control over a clearly defined territory and population. It is unclear whether the Taliban militia ever fully controlled most of the territory of Afghanistan. At the time that the United States air strikes began, at least ten percent of the country, and the population within those areas, was governed by the Northern Alliance. Indeed, the facts suggest that Afghanistan was divided between different tribal and warning factions, rather than controlled by any central State. The Taliban militia in essence represented only an ethnically Pashtun movement, a "tribal

---

map, are now commonly referred to as 'failed States' or '*États sons gouvernmement*.'" Daniel Thurer, *The Failed State and International Law*, International Review of the Red Cross No. 836 (Dec. 31, 1999), available at http://www.icrc.org/eng/review (visited Jan. 10, 2002). Somewhat different tests have been used for determining whether a State has "failed." First, the most salient characteristic of a "failed State" seems to be the disappearance of a "central government." Yoram Dinstein, *The Thirteenth Woldemar A. Solf Lecture in International Law*, 166 Mil. L. Rev. 93, 103 (2000); *see also id.* ("All that remains is a multiplicity of groups of irregular combatants fighting each other."). Closely related to this test, but perhaps some what broader, is the definition of a "failed State" as "a situation where the government is unable to discharge basic governmental functions with respect to its populace and its territory. Consequently, laws are not made, cases are not decided, order is not preserved and societal cohesion deteriorates. Basic services such as medical care, education, infrastructure maintenance, tax collection and other functions and services rendered by central governing authorities cease to exist or exist only in limited areas." Ruth Gordon, *Growing Constitutions*, 1 U. Pa. J. Const. L. 528, 533–34 (1999). Professor Thurer distinguishes three elements (respectively, territorial, political and functional) said to characterize a "failed State": 1) failed States undergo an "implosion rather than an explosion of the structures of power and authority, the disintegration and destructuring of States rather than their dismemberment;" 2) they experience "the total or near total breakdown of structures guaranteeing law and order;" and 3) there are marked by "the absence of bodies capable, on the one hand, of repre-break senting the State at the international level and, on the other, of being influenced by the outside world."

[52] *See Restatement (Third) of the Foreign Relations Law of the United States* § 201; *see also* 1933 Montevideo Convention on Rights and Duties of States, art. I, 49 Stat. 3097, 28 Am. J. Int'l L. Supp. 75 (1934).

[53] Eleanor C. McDowell, *Contemporary Practice of the United States Relating to International Law*, 71 Am. J. Int'l L. 337 (1977).

militia,"[54] that did not command the allegiance of other major ethnic groups in Afghanistan and that was apparently unable to suppress endemic violence in the country. As a prominent writer on the Taliban militia wrote well before the current conflict began, "[e]ven if [the Taliban] were to conquer the north, it would not bring stability, only continuing guerrilla war by the non-Pashtuns, but this time from bases in Central Asia and Iran which would further destabilize the region."[55]

Second, again even before the United States air strikes and the successes of the Northern Alliance, an organized governmental administration did not exist in Afghanistan. One noted expert on the Taliban has concluded that the country had

> ceased to exist as a viable state.... The entire Afghan population has been displaced, not once but many times over. The physical destruction of Kabul has turned it into the Dresden of the late twentieth century.... There is no semblance of an infrastructure that can sustain society – even at the lowest common denominator of poverty.... The economy is a black hole that is sucking in its neighbors with illicit trade and the smuggling of drugs and weapons, undermining them in the process.... Complex relationships of power and authority built up over centuries have broken down completely. No single group or leader has the legitimacy to reunite the country. Rather than a national identity or kinship-tribal-based identities, territorial regional identities have become paramount....[T]he Taliban refuse to define the Afghan state they want to constitute and rule over, largely because they have no idea what they want. The lack of a central authority, state organizations, a methodology for command and control and mechanisms which can reflect some level of popular participation...make it impossible for many Afghans to accept the Taliban or for the outside world to recognize a Taliban government.... No warlord faction has ever felt itself responsible for the civilian population, but the Taliban are incapable of carrying out even the minimum of developmental work because they believe that Islam will take care of everyone.[56]

Another expert had reached similar conclusions before the outbreak of the conflict:

> Afghanistan today has become a violent society, bereft of political institutions that function correctly and an economy that functions at all. When this is coupled with the destruction of population and the physical infrastructure..., it becomes clear that Afghanistan is a country on the edge of collapse, or at least profound transformation.... With the Taliban, there are few meaningful governmental structures and little that actually functions.[57]

The State Department has come to similar conclusions. In a testimony early in October 2001 before the Senate Foreign Relations Committee's Subcommittee on Near East and South Asian Affairs, Assistant Secretary of State for South Asian Affairs Christina Rocca explained that:

> [t]wenty-two years of conflict have steadily devastated [Afghanistan], destroyed its physical and political infrastructure, shattered its institutions, and wrecked its socio-economic fabric.... The Taliban have shown no desire to provide even the most rudimentary health, education, and other social services expected of

---

[54] Larry P. Goodson, *Afghanistan's Endless War: State Failure, Regional Politics, and the Rise of the Taliban* 46, 115 (2001).

[55] Ahmed Rashid, *Taliban: Militant Islam, Oil & Fundamentalism in Central Asia* 213 (2001).

[56] *Id.* at 207–08, 212–13.

[57] Goodson, *supra*, at 103–04; 115.

any government. Instead, they have chosen to devote their resources to waging war on the Afghan people, and exporting instability to their neighbors.[58]

Rather than performing normal government functions, the Taliban militia exhibited the characteristics of a criminal gang. The United Nations Security Council found that the Taliban militia extracted massive profits from illegal drug trafficking in Afghanistan and subsidized terrorism from those revenues.[59]

Third, the Taliban militia was unable to conduct normal foreign relations or to fulfill its international legal obligations. Publicly known facts suggest that the Taliban was unable to obey its international obligations and to conduct normal diplomatic relations. Thus, the Taliban militia consistently refused to comply with United Nations Security Council Resolutions 1333 (2000) and 1267 (1999), which called on it to surrender Osama bin Laden to justice and to take other actions to abate terrorism based in Afghanistan.[60] Those resolutions also called on all States to deny permission for aircraft to take off or to land if they were owned or operated by or for the Taliban, and to freeze funds and other resources owned or controlled by the Taliban. Reportedly, the Taliban militia also may have been unable to extradite bin Laden at the request of Saudi Arabia in September, 1998, despite its close relations with the Saudi government. As a result, the Saudi government expelled the Afghan *charge d'affaires*.[61] The Taliban's continuing role in sheltering and supporting those believed to be responsible for the terrorist attacks of September 11, 2001, placed it in clear breach of international law, which required it to prevent the use of its territory as a launching pad for attacks against other nations.[62]

---

[58] United States Department of State, International Information Programs, *Rocca Blames Taliban for Humanitarian Disaster in Afghanistan* (Oct. 10, 2001), *available at* http://www.usinfo. state.gov/regional/nea/sasia/afghan/text2001/1010roca.htm (visited Jan. 10, 2001).

[59] *See* U.N. Security Council Resolution 1333 (2000), *available at* http://www.un.org/ *Docs/scres/2000/res 1333e.pdf* (finding that "the Taliban benefits directly from the cultivation of illicit opium by imposing a tax on its production and indirectly benefits from the processing and trafficking of such opium, and...these substantial resources strengthen the Taliban's capacity to harbor terrorists"). The United States Government has amassed substantial evidence that the Taliban has condoned and profited from narco-trafficking on a massive scale, with disastrous effects on neighboring countries. *See The Taliban, Terrorism, and Drug Trade: Hearing Before the Subcomm. on Criminal Justice, Drug Policy and Human Resources of the House Comm. on Government Reform*, 107th Cong. (2001) (testimony of William Bach, Director, Office of Asia, Africa, Europe, NIS Programs, Bureau of International Narcotics and Law Enforcement Affairs, Department of State; testimony of Asa Hutchinson, Administrator, Drug Enforcement Administration, U.S. Department of Justice).

[60] U.N. Security Council Resolution 1333 "strongly condemn[ed]" the Taliban for the "sheltering and training of terrorists and [the] planning of terrorist acts," and "deplor[ed]" the fact that the Taliban continues to provide a safe haven to Osama Bin Laden and to allow him and others associated with him to operate a network of terrorist training camps from Taliban-controlled territory and to use Afghanistan as a base from which to sponsor international terrorist operations." U.N. Security Council Resolution 1214, ¶ 13 (1998) enjoined the Taliban to stop providing a sanctuary and training for terrorists. U.N. Security Council Resolution 1267, ¶ 2 (1999), stated that the Taliban's failure to comply with the Council's 1998 demand constituted a threat to the peace. *See* Sean D. Murphy, *Efforts to Obtain Custody of Osama Bin Laden*, 94 Am. J. Int'l L. 366 (2000).

[61] *See* Yossef Bodansky, *Bin Laden: The Man Who Declared War on America* 301–02 (2001).

[62] *See* Robert F. Turner, *International Law and the Use of Force in Response to the World Trade Center and Pentagon Attacks, available at* http://jurist.law.pin.edu/forum/forumnew34.htm (visited Jan. 10, 2002) ("If (as has been claimed by the US and UK governments) bin Laden masterminded the attacks on New York and Washington, Afghanistan is in breach of its state responsibility to take reasonable measures to prevent its territory from being used to launch attacks against other states. The United

It has been suggested by government officials and independent press reports that the Taliban militia had become so subject to the domination and control of al Qaeda that it could not pursue independent policies with respect to the outside world.[63] Former Ambassador Robert Oakley described the relationship as "very close. The Taliban and bin Laden, particularly Mullah Omar, go way, way back . . . [Bin Laden] has helped the Taliban with material support since they began their movement in Afghanistan."[64] Richard Haass, Director of the State Department's Office of the Policy Planning Staff, has noted that the Taliban "have accepted substantial financial support from and proved themselves subservient to" al Qaeda.[65] Al Qaeda apparently supplied the Taliban regime with money, material, and personnel to help it gain the upper hand in its ongoing battles with the Northern Alliance.[66] Because al Qaeda was capable of mustering more formidable military forces than the Taliban at any given point, and because failure to protect bin Laden would have cost the Taliban the support of radical Islamists, it may well have been impossible for the Taliban to surrender bin Laden as directed by the United Nations, even if it had been willing to do so. While a policy decision to violate international law would not be grounds to deny statehood, if al Qaeda – a non-governmental terrorist organization – possessed such power within Afghanistan to prevent its alleged rulers from taking action against it as ordered by the U.N., this would indicate that the Taliban militia did not exercise sufficient governmental control within the territory to fulfill its international obligations.

The Taliban militia's failure to carry out its international obligations became even further apparent during the conflict itself. During the United States' campaign in Afghanistan, Secretary Rumsfeld noted that the Taliban "are using mosques for ammunition storage areas. They are using mosques for command and control and

States and its allies thus have a legal right to violate Afghanistan's territorial integrity to destroy bin Laden and related terrorist targets. If the Taliban elects to join forces with bin Laden, it, too, becomes a lawful target."); *see also* W. Michael Reisman, *International Legal Responses to Terrorism*, 22 Hous. J. Int'l L. 3, 40–42, 51–54 (1999).

[63] *See, e.g.*, Michael Dobbs & Vermon Loeb, *2 U.S. Targets Bound by Fate*, Wash. Post, Nov. 14, 2001 at A22 ("According to Thomas Gouttierre, an Afghan expert at the University of Nebraska and a former UN adviser, the so-called Afghan Arabs surrounding bin Laden were much more educated and articulate than the often illiterate Taliban and succeeded in convincing them that they were at the head of a worldwide Islamic renaissance. 'Al Qaeda ended up hijacking a large part of the Taliban movement,' he said, noting that [Taliban supreme religious leader Mohammed] Omar and bin Laden were 'very, very tight' by 1998."); Peter Baker, *Defector Says Bin Laden Had Cash, Taliban In His Pocket*, Wash. Post, Nov. 30, 2001 at A 1 (reporting claims by former Taliban official of al Qaeda's corruption of Taliban officials).

[64] *Online News Hour: The Taliban* (Sept. 15, 2001), *available at* http://www.pbs.org/newshour/bb/terrorism/july-dec01/taliban 9–15.html (visited Jan. 15, 2002).

[65] *The Bush Administration's Response to September 11th– and Beyond*, Remarks to the Council of Foreign. Relations (Oct. 15, 2001), *available at* http://www.yale.edu/lawweb/avalon/sept 11/haass 001.htm (visited Jan. 15, 2002).

[66] The so-called "55th Brigade," a military force consisting primarily of Arabs under Syrian and Saudi commanders, was based outside of Kabul and was trained, maintained and paid for by al Qaeda. It "provided crucial support to Taliban forces during offensives against the Northern Alliance over the past five years." Michael Jansen, *US focused initially on bin Laden Mercenaries*. The Irish Times on the Web (Oct. 30, 2001), *available at* http://www.ireland.coewspaper/world/2001/1030/wor6.htm (visited Jan. 15, 2001). According to some reports, these al Qaeda fighters were the most aggressive and ideologically committed forces available to the Taliban leadership, and were used to control other Taliban units. *See also* Michael Kranish & Indira A.R. Lakshmanan, *Partners in 'Jihad': Bin Laden Ties to Taliban*, Boston Globe, Oct. 28, 2001, at A 1. This article contains especially detailed information about the close linkages between the two movements and their leaders.

meeting places. They are putting tanks and artillery pieces in close proximity to hospitals, schools, and residential areas."[67] In a series of "Fact Sheets" issued during the campaign, the State Department described in detail many of the atrocities committed by the Taliban and al Qaeda before and during the United States' military operations. These included massacres of both prisoners and civilians. For example, the State Department reported that in August, 2000, the Taliban had "executed POWs in the streets of Herat as a lesson to the local population."[68] The State Department also reported on November 2, 2001, that "[t]he Taliban have put the Afghan civilian population in grave danger by deliberately hiding their soldiers and equipment in civilian areas, including in mosques."[69] According to the State Department, the Taliban "massacred hundreds of Afghan civilians, including women and children, in Yakaoloang, Mazar-l-Sharif, Bamiyan, Qezelabad, and other towns."[70] For example, the State Department noted, a report by the United Nations Secretary General regarding the July, 1999, massacre in the Shomaili Plains stated that "[t]he Taliban forces, who allegedly carried out these acts, essentially treated the civilian population with hostility and made no distinction between combatants and non-combatants."[71] All of this evidence goes to prove that the Taliban militia regularly refused to follow the laws of armed conflict, which, besides independently providing grounds for a presidential suspension of Geneva III, also demonstrate that Afghanistan had become a failed state and was under the control not of a government but of a violent terrorist group.

Fourth, the Taliban militia was not recognized as the legitimate government of Afghanistan by the United States or by any member of the international community except Pakistan. Neither the United States nor the United Nations ever recognized that the Taliban militia was a government. The only two other States that had maintained diplomatic relations with it before the current conflict began (Saudi Arabia and the United Arab Emirates) soon severed them.[72] Even Pakistan had withdrawn its recognition before the end of hostilities between the United States and the Taliban forces. This *universal* refusal to recognize the Taliban militia as a government demonstrates that other nations and the United Nations concurred in a judgment that the Taliban militia was no government and that Afghanistan had ceased to operate as a nation-State.

---

[67] *Transcript: Rumsfeld Says Taliban Functioning As Military Force Only. supra.*

[68] *Fact Sheet on Al Qaeda and Taliban Atrocities* (released Nov. 22, 2001 by Coalition Information Center), *available at* http://www.usinfo.state.gov/topical/pol/terror/01112301.htm (visited Jan. 15, 2002). The source cited for this particular report was the Defense Department.

[69] *Fact Sheet: Taliban Actions Imperil Afghan Civilians* (Nov. 2, 2001), *available at* http://wwww.usinfo.state.gov/topical/pol/terror/01110203.htm (visited Jan. 15, 2002). Further, the State Department publicized reports from *The Washington Post* that the Taliban was using entire villages as human shields to protect their stockpiles of ammunition and weapons, that they were relocating the police ministry in Kandahar to mosques, that they had taken over NGO relief organization buildings, and that they were discovered transporting tanks and mortar shells in the guise of humanitarian relief. *Fact Sheet: The Taliban's Betrayal of the Afghan People* (Nov. 6, 2001), *available at* http://www.usinfo.state.gov/topical/pol/terror/01110608.htm (visited Jan. 15, 2002).

[70] *Id.*

[71] *id.* (quoting report; no citation given).

[72] *See A Look at the Taliban*, USA Today, Sept. 30, 2001, *available at* http://www.usatoday.com/news/world/2001/the taliban.http (visited Jan. 10, 2002). Indeed, Pakistan had been the only country in the world that maintained an embassy in Kabul; the overwhelming majority of States and the United Nations recognized exiled President Burhanuddin Rabbani and his government as the country's legal authorities. *See Taliban tactics move to hostage play.* Aug. 8, 2001, available at http://www.janes.com/regional new/asia pacific/news/jid/ jid010808_1_n.shtml (visited Oct. 19, 2001).

Indeed, the cabinet departments of the U.S. Government best positioned to determine whether Afghanistan constituted a failed state appear to have reached that conclusion some time ago. Secretary of Defense Donald Rumsfeld, for example, declared at a November 2, 2001, press conference that the "Taliban is not a government. The government of Afghanistan does not exist today. The Taliban never was a government as such. It was a force in the country that is not substantially weakened – in many cases cloistered away from the people."[73] Secretary Rumsfeld has made substantially the same remarks on several other occasions. On October 29, 2001, he described the Taliban as "an illegitimate, un-elected group of terrorists."[74] And on November 4, 2001, he stated at a press conference with the Foreign Minister of Pakistan that "Taliban is not really functioning as a government as such. There is really not a government to speak of in Afghanistan today."[75] On November 11, 2001, the Secretary emphasized the extent to which Afghanistan had fallen under the control of al Qaeda: "for all practical purposes, the al Qaeda has taken over the country."[76] Secretary Rumsfeld's final statement indicates his belief that no real government functioned in Afghanistan, but rather that groups of armed, violent militants had come into control.

In the recent past, the State Department took the same view. Near the start of the conflict, the Bureau of South Asian Affairs found that "[t]here is no functioning central government [in Afghanistan]. The country is divided among fighting factions.... The Taliban [is] a radical Islamic movement [that] occupies about 90% of the country."[77] Undersecretary of State Paula J. Dobriansky said on October 29, 2001, that "young Afghans cannot remember a time when their country really worked. There was a time – a little over 20 years ago – when Afghanistan was a functioning state, a member of the world community.... Unfortunately it is now difficult to remember that functioning Afghanistan."[78] As recently as December 12, 2001, the State Department's Office of International Information Programs, drawing on Coalition Information Center materials and media reports, stated that *both* the Taliban and al Qaeda "are terrorist organizations," and characterized the Taliban's leader, Mullah Omar, as "a terrorist."[79]

Some international officials concur with the views of our Government. Lakhdar Brahimi, for example, the United Nations mediator in Afghanistan and a former Algerian Foreign Minister, described Afghanistan under the Taliban as a "failed state which looks like an infected wound."[80] Tony Blair, the Prime Minister of Great Britain, on a

---

[73] Secretary Rumsfeld Media Availability en Route to Moscow (Nov. 2, 2001), *available at* http://www.yale.edu/lawweb/avalon/sept II/dod brief64.htm (visited Jan. 15, 2002).

[74] *Rumsfeld Says Taliban to Blame for Casualties* (Oct. 29, 2001), *available at* http://www.usinfo.state.gov/topical/pol/terror/01102905.htm (visited Jan. 15, 2002).

[75] *Transcript: Rumsfeld Says Taliban Functioning As Military Force Only* (Nov. 4, 2001), *available at* http:www.usinfo.state.gov./topical/pol/terror/0110403.htm (visited Jan. 15, 2002).

[76] *Rumsfeld on Afghanistan Developments on "Fox News Sunday,"* (Nov. 12, 2001), available at http://www.usinfo.state.gov/topical/pol/terror/0111204.htm (visited Jan. 15, 2002).

[77] *Background Note* (October, 2001), available at http://www.state.gov/pa/bgn/index.cfm? docid=5380 (visited Jan. 10, 2002), prepared by the Bureau of South Asian Affairs. *See also* Reuters AlertNet – Afghanistan, *Country Profiles* ("There are no state-constituted armed forces. It is not possible to show how ground forces' equipment has been divided among the different factions."), *available at* http://www.alermet.org/thefacts/countryprofiles/152478?version-1 (visited Jan. 15, 2002).

[78] Paula J. Dobransky, *Afghanistan: Not Always a Baulefield* (Oct. 29, 2001), *available at* http://www.usinfo.state.gov/topical/pol/terror/01102908.htm (visited Jan. 15, 2002).

[79] *The End of the Taliban Reign of Terror in Afghanistan* (Dec. 12, 2001), *available at* http://www.usinfo.state.gov/topical/pol/terror/01121206.hnn (visited Jan. 15, 2002).

[80] Rashid, *supra*, at 207.

visit to that country this month, declared that "Afghanistan has been a failed state for too long and the whole world has paid the price."[81]

Based on the foregoing, it is apparent that the publicly-available evidence would support the conclusion that Afghanistan, when largely controlled by the Taliban militia, failed some, and perhaps all, of the ordinary tests of statehood. Nor do we think that the military successes of the United States and the Northern Alliance change that outcome. Afghanistan *was* effectively stateless for the relevant period of the conflict, even if after the Bonn Agreement it became a State recognized by the United Nations, the United States, and most other nations.[82] The President can readily find that at the outset of this conflict, when the country was largely in the hands of the Taliban militia, there was no functioning central government in Afghanistan that was capable of providing the most basic services to the Afghan population, of suppressing endemic internal violence, or of maintaining normal relations with other governments. In other words, the Taliban militia would not even qualify as the *de facto* government of Afghanistan. Rather, it would have the status only of a violent faction or movement contending with other factions for control of Afghanistan's territory, rather than the regular armed forces of an existing state. This would provide sufficient ground for the President to exercise his constitutional power to suspend our Geneva III obligations toward Afghanistan.

C. Suspension Under International Law

Although the President may determine that Afghanistan was a failed State as a matter of domestic law, there remains the distinct question whether suspension would be valid as a matter of international law.[83] We emphasize that the resolution of that question, however, *has no bearing* on domestic constitutional issues, or on the application of the WCA. Rather, these issues are worth consideration as a means of justifying the actions of the United States in the world of international politics. While a close question, we believe that the better view is that, in certain circumstances, countries can suspend the Geneva Conventions consistently with international law.

International law has long recognized that the material breach of a treaty can be grounds for the party injured by the breach to terminate or withdraw from the

---

[81] Philip Webster, *Blair's mission to Kabul*. The Times of London, Jan. 8, 2002, *available at* 2002 WL 4171996.

[82] We do not think that the military successes of the United States and the Northern Alliance necessarily meant that Afghanistan's statehood was restored before the Bonn agreement, if only because the international community, including the United States, did not regard the Northern Alliance as constituting the government of Afghanistan. United Nations Security Council Resolution 1378, ¶1 (2001), *available at* http://www.yale.edu/lawweb/avalon/sept11/unsecres1378.htm (visited Nov. 19, 2001), expressed "strong support for the efforts of the Afghan people to establish a new and transitional administration leading to the formation of a government" (emphasis added); *see also id.* ¶ 3 (affirming that the United Nations should play a central role in supporting Afghan efforts to establish a "new and transitional administration leading to the formation of a new government"). The plain implication of this Resolution, which reflects the views of the United States, is that Afghanistan after the Taliban did not have a government at that time.

[83] In general, of course, a decision by a State not to discharge its treaty obligations, even when effective as a matter of domestic law, does not necessarily relieve it of possible international liability for nonperformance. *See generally Pigeon River Improvement, Slide & Boom Co. v. Charles W. Cox, Ltd.*, 291 U.S. 138, 160 (1934).

treaty.[84] Under customary international law, the general rule is that breach of a multilateral treaty by a State party justifies the suspension of that treaty with regard to that State. "A material breach of a multilateral treaty by one of the parties entitles ... [a] party specially affected by the breach to invoke it as a ground for suspending the operation of the treaty in whole or in part in the relations between itself and the defaulting State."[85] If Afghanistan could be found in material breach for violating "a provision essential to the accomplishment of the object or purpose of the [Geneva Conventions]," suspension of the Conventions would have been justified.[86]

We note, however, that these general rules authorizing suspension "do not apply to provisions relating to the protection of the human person contained in treaties of a humanitarian character, in particular to provisions prohibiting any form of reprisals against persons protected by such treaties."[87] Although the United States is not a party to the Vienna Convention, some lower courts have said that the Convention embodies the customary international law of treaties, and the State Department has at various times taken the same view.[88] The Geneva Conventions must be regarded as "treaties of a humanitarian character," many of whose provisions "relat[e] to the protection of the human person."[89] Arguably, therefore, a decision by the United States to suspend Geneva III with regard to Afghanistan might put the United States in breach of customary international law.

In addition, the Geneva Conventions could themselves be read to preclude suspension. Common Article 1 pledges the High Contracting Parties "to respect and to ensure respect for the present Convention *in all circumstances*" (emphasis added). Some commentators argue that this provision should be read to bar any State party from refusing to enforce their provisions, no matter the conduct of its adversaries. In other words, the duty of performance is absolute and does not depend upon reciprocal performance by other State parties.[90] Under this approach, the substantive terms of the Geneva Conventions could never be suspended, and thus any violation would always be illegal under international law.

---

[84] See *Legal Consequences for States of the Continued Presence of South Africa in Namibia (South West Africa) Notwithstanding Security Council Resolution 276*, 1971 I.C.J. 16, 47, ¶ 98 (Advisory Opinion June 21, 1971) (holding it to be a "general principle of law that a right of termination on account of breach must be presumed to exist in respect of all treaties, except as regards provisions relating to the protection of the human person contained in treaties of a humanitarian character. ... The silence of a treaty as to the existence of such a right cannot be interpreted as implying the exclusion of a right which has its source outside of the treaty, in general international law[.]").

[85] Vienna Convention on Treaties, art. 60(2)(b).

[86] *Id.* art. 60(3).

[87] *Id.* art. 60(5). The Vienna Convention seems to prohibit or restrict the suspension of humanitarian treaties if the sole ground for suspension is material breach. It does not squarely address the case in which suspension is based, not on particular breaches by a party, but by the party's disappearance as a State or on its incapacity to perform its treaty obligations.

[88] *Fujitsu Ltd. v. Federal Express Corp.*, 247 F.3d 423, 433 (2d Cir.), *cert. denied*, 122 S. Ct. 206 (2001); Moore, *supra*, at 891–92 (quoting 1971 statement by Secretary of State William P. Rogers and 1986 testimony by Deputy Legal Adviser Mary V. Mochary).

[89] See Sir Ian Sinclair, *The Vienna Convention on the Law of Treaties* 191 (2d ed. 1984) (explaining intent and scope of reference to "humanitarian" treaties). Indeed, when the drafters of the Vienna Convention added paragraph 5 to Article 60, the Geneva Conventions were specifically mentioned as coming within it. *See* Harris, *supra*, at 797.

[90] *See, e.g.*, Draper, *The Red Cross Conventions, supra*, at 8; *see also Military and Paramilitary Activities In and Against Nicaragua (Nicaragua v. United States)*, 76 I.L.R. at 448, ¶ 220.

This understanding of the Vienna and Geneva Conventions cannot be correct. There is no textual provision in the Geneva Conventions that clearly prohibits temporary suspension. The drafters included a provision that precludes State parties from agreeing to absolve each other of violations.[91] They also included careful procedures for the termination of the agreements by individual State parties, including a provision that requires delay of a termination of a treaty, if that termination were to occur during a conflict, until the end of the conflict.[92] Yet, at the same time, the drafters of the Conventions did not address suspension at all, even though it has been a possible option since at least the eighteenth century.[93] Indeed, if the drafters and ratifiers of the Geneva Conventions believed the treaties could not be suspended, while allowing for withdrawal and denunciation, they could have said so explicitly and easily in the text.

A blanket non-suspension rule makes little sense as a matter of international law and politics. If there were such a rule, international law would leave an injured party effectively remediless if its adversaries committed material breaches of the Geneva Conventions. Apart from its unfairness, that result would reward and encourage non-compliance with the Conventions. True, the Conventions appear to contemplate that enforcement will be promoted by voluntary action of the parties.[94] Furthermore, the Conventions provide for intervention by "the International Committee of the Red Cross or any other impartial humanitarian organization . . . subject to the consent of the Parties to the conflict concerned."[95] But the effectiveness of these provisions depends on the goodwill of the very party assumed to be committing material breaches, or on its sensitivity to international opinion. Likewise, the provision authorizing an impartial investigation of alleged violations also hinges on the willingness of a breaching party to permit the investigation and to abide by its result. Other conceivable remedies, such as the imposition of an embargo by the United Nations on the breaching party, may also be inefficacious in particular circumstances. If, for example, Afghanistan were bound by Geneva Convention III to provide certain treatment to United States prisoners of war but in fact materially breached such duties, a United Nations embargo might have little effect on its behavior. Finally, offenders undoubtedly face a risk of trial and punishment before national or international courts after the conflict is over. Yet that form of relief presupposes that the offenders will be subject to capture at the end of the conflict – which may well depend on whether or not they have been defeated. Reliance on post-conflict trials, as well as being uncertain, defers relief for the duration of the conflict. Without a power to suspend, therefore, parties to the Geneva Conventions would only be left with these meager tools to remedy widespread violation of the Conventions by others.

Thus, even if one were to believe that international law set out fixed and binding rules concerning the power of suspension, the United States could make convincing arguments under the Geneva Conventions itself, the Vienna Convention on Treaties, and customary international law in favor of suspending the Geneva Conventions as applied to the Taliban militia in the current war in Afghanistan.

---

[91] *See, e.g.*, Geneva Convention III, art. 131.
[92] *See, e.g., id.*, art. 142.
[93] *See* Sinclair, *supra*, at 192.
[94] *See, e.g.*, the Geneva Convention III, art. 8; Geneva Convention IV, art. 9.
[95] Geneva Convention III, art. 9; Geneva Convention IV, art. 10.

D. Application of the Geneva Conventions As a Matter of Policy

We conclude this Part by addressing a matter of considerable significance for policymakers. To say that the President may suspend specific provisions of the Geneva Conventions *as a legal requirement* is by no means to say that the principles of the laws of armed conflict cannot be applied *as a matter of U.S. Government policy*. There are two aspects to such policy decisions, one involving the protections of the laws of armed conflict and the other involving liabilities under those laws.

First, the President may determine that for reasons of diplomacy or in order to encourage other States to comply with the principles of the Geneva Conventions or other laws of armed conflict, it serves the interests of the United States to *treat* al Qaeda or Taliban detainees (or some class of them) as if they were prisoners of war, even though they do not have any legal entitlement to that *status*. We express no opinion on the merits of such a policy decision.

Second, the President as Commander-in-Chief can determine as a matter of his judgment for the efficient prosecution of the military campaign that the policy of the United States will be to enforce customary standards of the law of war against the Taliban and to punish any transgressions against those standards. Thus, for example, even though Geneva Convention III does not apply as a matter of law, the United States may deem it a violation of the laws and usages of war for Taliban troops to torture any American prisoners whom they may happen to seize. The U.S. military thus could prosecute Taliban militiamen for war crimes for engaging in such conduct.[96]

A decision to apply the principles of the Geneva Conventions or of others laws of war as a matter of policy, not law, would be fully consistent with the past practice of the United States. United States practice in post-1949 conflicts reveals several instances in which our military forces have applied Geneva III as a matter of policy, without acknowledging any legal obligation to do so. These cases include the wars in Korea and Vietnam and the interventions in Panama and Somalia.

Korea. The Korean War broke out on June 25, 1950, before any of the major State parties to the conflict (including the United States) had ratified the Geneva Conventions. Nonetheless, General Douglas MacArthur, the United Nations Commander in Korea, declared that his forces would act consistently with the principles of the Geneva Conventions, including those relating to POWs. General MacArthur stated: "My present instructions are to abide by the humanitarian principles of the 1949 Geneva Conventions, particularly common Article 3. In addition, I have directed the forces under my command to abide by the detailed provisions of the prisoner-of-war convention, since I have the means at my disposal to assure compliance with this convention by all concerned and have fully accredited the ICRC delegates accordingly."[97]

It should be noted, however, that deciding to follow Geneva III as a matter of policy would allow the United States to deviate from certain provisions it did not believe were appropriate to the current conflict. In Korea, for example, the United States did not fulfill the requirement that it repatriate all POWs at the end of the conflict. Pursuant to the armistice agreement, thousands of Chinese and North Korean POWs who did

---

[96] The President could, of course, also determine that it will be the policy of the United States to require its own troops to adhere to standards of conduct recognized under customary international law, and could prosecute offenders for violations. As explained below, the President is not *bound* to follow these standards by law, but may direct the armed forces to adhere to them as a matter of policy.

[97] *Quoted* in Joseph P. Bialke, *United Nations Peace Operations: Applicable Norms and the Application of the Law of Armed Conflict*, 50 A.F.L. Rev. 1, 63 n. 235 (2001).

not wish to be repatriated were examined by an international commission, and many eventually ended up in Taiwan.[98]

VietNam. The United States through the State Department took the position that the Geneva Convention III "indisputably applies to the armed conflict in VietNam," and therefore that "American military personnel captured in the course of that armed conflict are entitled to be treated as prisoners of war."[99] We understand from the Defense Department that our military forces, as a matter of policy, decided at some point in the conflict to accord POW treatment (but not necessarily POW status) to Viet Cong members, despite the fact that they often did *not* meet the criteria for that status (set forth in Geneva Convention III, Article 4), e.g., by not wearing uniforms or any other fixed distinctive signs visible at a distance.

Panama. The United States' intervention in Panama on December 20, 1989, came at the request and invitation of Panama's legitimately elected President, Guillermo Endara.[100] The United States had never recognized General Manuel Noriega, the commander of the Panamanian Defense Force, as Panama's legitimate ruler. Thus, in the view of the executive branch, the conflict was between the Government of Panama assisted by the United States on the one side and insurgent forces loyal to General Noriega on the other. It was not an international armed conflict between the United States and Panama, another State. Accordingly, it was not, in the executive's judgment, an international armed conflict governed by common Article 2 of the Geneva Conventions.[101] Nonetheless, we understand that, as a matter of policy, all persons captured or detained by the United States in the intervention – including civilians and members of paramilitary forces as well as members of the Panamanian Defense

---

[98] David M. Morriss, *From War to Peace: A Study of Cease-Fire Agreements and the Evolving Role of the United Nations*, 36 Va. J. Int'l.L. 801, 883–85 (1996).

[99] *Entitlement of American Military Personnel Held by North Viet-Nam to Treatment as Prisoners of War Under the Geneva Convention of 1949 Relative to the Treatment of Prisoners of War, July 13, 1966, reprinted in* John Norton Moore, *Law and the Indo-China War* 635, 639 (1972).

[100] *See United States v. Noriego*, 117 F.3d 1206, 1211 (11th Cir. 1997).

[101] *See* Jan E. Aldykiewicz and Geoffrey S. Corn, *Authority to Court-Martial Non-U.S. Military Personnel for Serious Violations of International Humanitarian Law Committed During Internal Armed Conflict*, 167 Mil. L. Rev. 74, 77 n.6 (2001). In *United States v. Noriega*, 808 F. Supp. 791, 794 (S.D. Fla. 1992), the district court held that the United States' intervention in Panama in late 1989 was an international armed conflict under (common) Article 2 of the Geneva Convention III, and that General Noriega was entitled to POW status. To the extent that the holding assumed that the courts are free to determine whether a conflict is between the United States and another "State" regardless of the President's view whether the other party is a "State" or not, we disagree with it. By assuming the right to determine that the United States was engaged in an armed conflict with *Panama* – rather than with insurgent forces in rebellion against the recognized and legitimate Government of Panama – the district court impermissibly usurped the recognition power, a constitutional authority reserved to the President. The power to determine whether a foreign government is to be accorded recognition, and the related power to determine whether a condition of statelessness exists in a particular country, are exclusively executive. *See, e.g., Baker v. Carr*, 369 U.S. 186, 212 (1962) ("[R]ecognition of foreign governments so strongly defies judicial treatment that without executive recognition a foreign state has been called a republic of whose existence we know nothing.' . . . Similarly, recognition of belligerency abroad is an executive responsibility. . . .") (citation omitted); *Kennett v. Chambers*, 55 U.S. (14 How.) 38, 50–51 (1852) ("[T]he question whether [the Republic of] Texas [while in rebellion against Mexico] had or had not at that time become an independent state, was a question for that department of our government exclusively which is charged with our foreign relations. And until the period when that department recognized it as an independent state, the judicial tribunals . . . were bound to consider . . . Texas as a part of the Mexican territory."); *Mingtai Fire & Marine Ins. Co. v. United Parcel Service*, 177 F.3d 1142, 1145 (9th Cir.) ("[T]he Supreme Court has repeatedly held that the Constitution commits to the Executive branch alone the authority to recognize, and to withdraw recognition from foreign regimes."), *cert. denied*, 528 U.S. 951 (1999).

Force – were *treated* consistently with the Geneva Convention III, until their precise status under that Convention was determined. A 1990 letter to the Attorney General from the Legal Adviser to the State Department said that "[i]t should be emphasized that the decision to extend basic prisoner of war protections to such persons was based on strong policy considerations, and was not necessarily based on any conclusion that the United States was obligated to do so as a matter of law."[102]

Interventions in Somalia, Haiti and Bosnia. There was considerable factual uncertainty whether the United Nations Operation in Somalia in late 1992 and early 1993 rose to the level of an "armed conflict" that could be subject to common Article 3 of the Geneva Conventions, particularly after the United Nations Task Force abandoned its previously neutral role and took military action against a Somali warlord, General Aideed. Similar questions have arisen in other peace operations, including those in Haiti and Bosnia. It appears that the U.S. military has decided, as a matter of policy, to conduct operations in such circumstances as if the Geneva Conventions applied, regardless of whether there is any legal requirement to do so. The U.S. Army Operational Law Handbook, after noting that "[i]n peace operations, such as those in Somalia, Haiti and Bosnia, the question frequently arises whether the [laws of war] legally applies," states that it is "the position of the US, UN and NATO that their forces will apply the 'principles and spirit' of the [law of war] in these operations."[103]

It might be argued, however, that the United States has conceded that Geneva III applied, as a matter of law, in every conflict since World War II. The facts, as supplied by our research and by the Defense Department, demonstrate otherwise. Although the United States at times has declared in different wars that the United States would accord Geneva Convention III treatment to enemy prisoners, there are several examples where the United States clearly decided not to comply with Geneva III as a matter of law. Further, such a position confuses situations in which the United States said it would act *consistently* with the Geneva Conventions with those in which we admitted that enemy prisoners would receive POW status as a matter of law. Our conduct in Panama provides an important example. There, the United States never conceded that the forces of Manuel Noriega qualified as POWs under the Geneva Convention, but did provide for them as a policy matter as if they were POWs.

IV. Detention Conditions Under Geneva III

Even if the President decided not to suspend our Geneva III obligations toward Afghanistan, two reasons would justify some deviations from the requirements of Geneva III. This would be the case even if Taliban members legally were entitled to POW status. First, certain deviations concerning treatment can be justified on basic grounds of legal excuse concerning self-defense and feasibility. Second, the President could choose to find that none of the Taliban prisoners qualify as POWs under Article 4 of Geneva III, which generally defines the types of armed forces that may be considered POWs once captured. In the latter instance, Geneva III would apply and the Afghanistan conflict would fall within common Article 2's jurisdiction. The President, however, would be interpreting the treaty in light of the facts on the ground to find that the Taliban militia categorically failed the test for POWs within Geneva III's terms. We

---

[102] Letter for the Hon. Richard L. Thornburgh, Attorney General, from Abraham D. Sofaer, Legal Adviser, State Department at 2 (Jan. 31, 1990).
[103] *Quoted in* Bialke, *supra*, at 56.

should be clear that we have no information that the conditions of treatment for Taliban prisoners currently violate Geneva III standards, but it is possible that some may argue that our GTMO facilities do not fully comply with all of the treaty's provisions.

A. Justified Deviations from Geneva Convention Requirements

We should make clear that as we understand the facts, the detainees currently are being treated in a manner consistent with common Article 3 of Geneva III. This means that they are housed in basic humane conditions, are not being physically mistreated, and are receiving adequate medical care. They have not yet been tried or punished by any U.S. court system. As a result, the current detention conditions in GTMO do not violate common Article 3, nor do they present a grave breach of Geneva III as defined in Article 130. For purposes of domestic law, therefore, the GTMO conditions do not constitute a violation of the WCA, which criminalizes only violations of common Article 3 or grave breaches of the Conventions.

That said, some may very well argue that detention conditions currently depart from Geneva III requirements. Nonetheless, not all of these deviations from Geneva III would amount to an outright violation of the treaty's requirements. Instead, some departures from the text can be justified by some basic doctrines of legal excuse. We believe that some deviations would not amount to a treaty violation, because they would be justified by the need for force protection. Nations have the right to take reasonable steps for the protection of the armed forces guarding prisoners. At the national level, no treaty can override a nation's inherent right to self-defense. Indeed, the United Nations Charter recognizes this fundamental principle. Article 51 of the U.N. Charter provides that "[n]othing in the present Charter shall impair the inherent right of individual or collective self-defense if an armed attack occurs against a Member of the United Nations." As we have discussed in other opinions relating to the war on terrorism, the September 11 attacks on the Pentagon and the World Trade Center have triggered the United States' right to defend itself.[104] Our national right to self-defense must encompass the lesser included right to defend our own forces from prisoners who pose a threat to their lives and safety, just as the Nation has the authority to take measures in the field to protect the U.S. armed forces. Any Geneva III obligations, therefore, may be legally adjusted to take into account the needs of force protection.

The right to national self-defense is further augmented by the individual right to self-defense as a justification for modifications to Geneva III based on the need for force protection. Under domestic law, self-defense serves as a legal defense even to the taking of a human life. "[S]elf defense is ... embodied in our jurisprudence as a consideration totally eliminating any criminal taint.... It is difficult to the point of impossibility to imagine a right in any state to abolish self defense altogether...."[105] As the U.S. Court of Appeals for the District of Columbia Circuit has observed, "[m]ore

---

[104] Memorandum for Alberto R. Gonzales, Counsel to the President, from Patrick F. Philbin, Deputy Attorney General, Office of Legal Counsel, *Re: Legality of the Use of Military Commissions to Try Terrorists* at 22–33 (Nov. 6, 2001); Memorandum for Alberto R. Gonzales, Counsel to the President and William J. Haynes, II, General Counsel, Department of Defense, from John C. Yoo, Deputy Assistant Attorney General and Robert J. Delahunty, Special Counsel, Office of Legal Counsel, *Re: Authority for Use of Military Force to Combat Terrorist Activities Within the United States* at 2–3 (Oct. 17, 2001).

[105] *Griffin v. Mortin*, 785 F.2d 1172, 1186–87 & n.37 (4th Cir. 1986), *aff'd by an equally divided court*, 795 F.2d 22 (4th Cir. 1986) (en banc), *cert. denied*, 480 U.S. 919 (1987).

than two centuries ago, Blackstone, best known of the expositors of the English common law, taught that 'all homicide is malicious, and of course, amounts to murder,
unless... *excused* on the account of accident or self-preservation....' Self-defense, as
a doctrine legally exonerating the taking of human life, is as viable now as it was in
Blackstone's time...."[106] Both the Supreme Court and this Office have opined that
the use of force by law enforcement or the military is constitutional, even if it results
in the loss of life, if necessary to protect the lives and safety of officers or innocent
third parties.[107] Thus, as a matter of domestic law, the United States armed forces can
modify their Geneva III obligations to take into account the needs of military necessity
to protect their individual members.

Other deviations from Geneva III, which do not involve force protection, may still
be justified as a domestic legal matter on the ground that immediate compliance is
infeasible. Certain conditions, we have been informed, are only temporary until the
Defense Department can construct permanent facilities that will be in compliance
with Geneva. We believe that no treaty breach would exist under such circumstances.
The State Department has informed us that state practice under the Convention allows nations a period of reasonable time to satisfy their affirmative obligations for
treatment of POWs, particularly during the early stages of a conflict.[108] An analogy
can be drawn here to a similar legal doctrine in administrative law. For example, it is a
well-established principle that, where a statutory mandate fails to specify a particular
deadline for agency action, a federal agency's duty to comply with that mandate is lawfully discharged, as long as it is satisfied within a reasonable time. The Administrative
Procedure Act expressly provides that a "reviewing court shall... compel agency action unlawfully withheld or *unreasonably* delayed." 5 U.S.C. § 706 (emphasis added).
Courts have recognized accordingly that a federal agency has a reasonable time to
discharge its obligations.[109] Thus, "if an agency has no concrete deadline establishing
a date by which it must act,... a court must compel only action that is delayed unreasonably.... [W]hen an agency is required to act – either by organic statute or by the
APA – within an expeditious, prompt, or reasonable time, § 706 leaves in the courts
the discretion to decide whether agency delay is unreasonable."[110]

---

[106] *United States v. Peterson*, 483 F.2d 1222, 1228–29 (D.C. Cir.) (footnote omitted), *cert denied*, 414
U.S. 1007 (1973).

[107] *See Tennessee v. Garner*, 471 U.S. 1, 7, 11 (1985) (Fourth Amendment "seizure" caused by use
of force subject to reasonableness analysis); Memorandum to Files, from Robert Delahunty, Special
Counsel, Office of Legal Counsel, *Re: Use of Deadly Force Against Civil Aircraft Threatening to Attack
1996 Summer Olympic Games* (Aug. 19, 1996); *United States Assistance to Countries that Shoot Down
Civil Aircraft Involved in Drug Trafficking*, 18 Op. O.L.C. 148, 164 (1994) ("[A] USG officer or employee
may use deadly force against civil aircraft without violating [a criminal statute] if he or she reasonably
believes that the aircraft poses a threat of serious physical harm... to another person.").

[108] During the India-Pakistan conflicts between 1965 and 1971, prisoners were able to correspond with
their families, but there were "some difficulties in getting lists of all military prisoners" – "[e]specially
at the beginning of the conflict." Allan Rosas, *The Legal Status of Prisoners of War* at 186 (1976).
Similarly, during the 1967 War in the Middle East, Israeli authorities delayed access to Arab prisoners
on the grounds that "all facilities would be granted as soon as the prisoners were transferred to the
camp at Atlith... In the meantime, delegates had the opportunity to see some of the prisoners at
the transit camp at EI Quantara and Kusseima." *Id.* at 203 (citation omitted). Although Israel was
technically obliged under the Convention to provide access to Arab. POWs, immediate compliance
with that obligation was infeasible.

[109] *Sierra Club v. Thomas*, 828 F.2d 783, 794 (D. C. Cir. 1987).

[110] *Forest Guardians v. Babbitt*, 174 F.3d 1178, 1190 (10th Cir. 1999).

Here, Geneva III contains no strict deadlines for compliance. Indeed, it would be illogical to require immediate compliance, particularly if a nation were suddenly attacked and had no warning that POW facilities would be needed. Further, it might not be immediately practicable, given the conditions in the field where POWs would first be detained, to provide conditions that fully comply with Geneva III. Given that Geneva III has no mandated timetable, the armed forces have a reasonable time to satisfy their obligations of treatment with regard to POWs and are not guilty of breach when it is infeasible to achieve immediate compliance.

B. *Status of Taliban Prisoners Under Article 4*

Even if the President declines to suspend our obligations under Geneva III toward Afghanistan, it is possible that Taliban detainees still might not receive the legal status of POWs. Geneva III provides that once a conflict falls within common Article 2, combatants must fall within one of several categories in order to receive POW status. Article 4(A)(1)–(3) sets out the three categories relevant here: i) members of the armed forces of a party to the conflict, along with accompanying militia and volunteer forces; ii) members of militia or volunteer corps who are commanded by an individual responsible to his subordinates, who have a distinctive sign recognizable from a distance, who carry arms openly, and who obey the laws of war; and iii) members of regular armed forces who profess allegiance to a government or authority that is not recognized by the detaining power. Should "any doubt arise as to whether persons, having committed a belligerent act and having fallen into the hands of the enemy," Article 5 of Geneva III requires that these individuals "enjoy the protections of" the Convention until a tribunal has determined their status. As we understand it, as a matter of practice prisoners are presumed to have Article 4 POW status until a tribunal determines otherwise.

Although these provisions seem to contemplate a case-by-case determination of an individual detainee's status, the President could determine categorically that all Taliban prisoners fall outside Article 4. Under Article II of the Constitution, the President possesses the power to interpret treaties on behalf of the Nation.[111] He could interpret Geneva III, in light of the known facts concerning the operation of Taliban forces during the Afghanistan conflict, to find that all of the Taliban forces do not fall within the legal definition of prisoners of war as defined by Article 4. A presidential determination of this nature would eliminate any legal "doubt" as to the prisoners' status, as a matter of domestic law, and would therefore obviate the need for Article 5 tribunals.

We do not have, however, the facts available to advise your Department or the White House whether the President would have the grounds to apply the law to the facts in this categorical manner. Some of the facts which would be important to such a decision include: whether Taliban units followed a recognizable, hierarchical command-and-control structure, whether they wore distinctive uniforms, whether they operated in the open with their weapons visible, the tactics and strategies with which they conducted hostilities, and whether they obeyed the laws of war. If your

---

[111] Memorandum for John Bellinger, III, Senior Associate Counsel and Legal Adviser to the National Security Council, from John C. Yoo, Deputy Assistant Attorney General and Robert J. Delahunty, Special Counsel, Office of Legal Counsel, *Re: Authority of the President to Suspend Certain Provisions of the ABM Treaty* (Nov. 15, 2001).

Department were to conclude that the Afghanistan conflict demonstrated that the conduct of the Taliban militia had always violated these requirements, you would be justified in advising the President to determine that all Taliban prisoners are not POWs under Article 4.

It is important to recognize that if the President were to pursue this line of reasoning, the executive branch would have to find that the Afghanistan conflict qualifies as an international war between two state parties to the Conventions. Article 4 is not a jurisdictional provision, but is instead only applied once a conflict has fallen within the definition of an international conflict covered by common Article 2 of the Conventions. At this point in time, we cannot predict what consequences this acceptance of jurisdiction would have for future stages in the war on terrorism.

Nonetheless, if the President were to make such a determination, the WCA still would not impose any liability. As will be recalled, the WCA criminalizes either grave breaches of the Geneva Conventions or violations of common Article 3. If members of the Taliban militia do not qualify as POWs under Article 4, even though the conflict falls within common Article 2's jurisdictional provisions, then their treatment cannot constitute a grave breach under Geneva III. Article 130 of Geneva III states that a grave breach occurs only when certain acts are committed against "persons ... protected by the Convention." If the President were to find that Taliban prisoners did not constitute POWs under Article 4, they would no longer be persons protected by the Convention. Thus, their treatment could not give rise to a grave breach under Article 130, nor constitute a violation of the WCA.

Further, if the President were to find that all Taliban prisoners did not enjoy the status of POWs under Article 4, they would not be legally entitled to the standards of treatment in common Article 3. As the Afghanistan war is international in nature, involving as it does the use of force by state parties – the United States and Great Britain – which are outside of Afghanistan, common Article 3 by its very terms would not apply. Common Article 3, as we have explained earlier, does not serve as a catch-all provision that applies to all armed conflicts, but rather as a specific complement to common Article 2. Further, in reaching the Article 4 analysis, the United States would be accepting that Geneva Convention jurisdiction existed over the conflict pursuant to common Article 2. Common Article 3 by its text would not apply, and therefore any violation of its terms would not constitute a violation of the WCA.

V. Customary International Law

Thus far, this memorandum has addressed the issue whether the Geneva Conventions, and the WCA, apply to the detention and trial of al Qaeda and Taliban militia members taken prisoner in Afghanistan. Having concluded that these laws do not apply, we turn to the effect, if any, of customary international law. Some may take the view that even if the Geneva Conventions, by their terms, do not govern the treatment of al Qaeda and Taliban prisoners, the substance of these agreements has received such universal approval that it has risen to the status of customary international law. Customary international law, however cannot bind the executive branch under the Constitution because it is not federal law. This is a view that this Office has expressed before,[112] and

---

[112] See *Authority of the Federal Bureau of Investigation to Override International Law in Extraterritorial Law Enforcement Activities*, 13 Op. O.L.C. 163 (1989).

is one consistent with the views of the federal courts,[113] and with executive branch positions before the courts.[114] Although we are not currently aware whether any detention conditions currently would violate customary international law, it should be clear that customary international law would not bind the President.

A. *Is Customary International Law Federal Law?*

Under the view promoted by many international law academics, any presidential violation of customary international law is presumptively unconstitutional.[115] These scholars argue that customary international law is federal law, and that the President's Article II duty under the Take Care Claue requires him to execute customary international law as well as statutes lawfully enacted under the Constitution. A President may not violate customary international law, therefore, just as he cannot violate a statute, unless he believes it to be unconstitutional. Relying upon cases such as *The Paquete Habana*, 175 U.S. 677, 700 (1900), in which the Supreme Court observed that "international law is part of our law," this position often claims that the federal judiciary has the authority to invalidate executive action that runs counter to customary international law.[116]

This view of customary international law is seriously mistaken. The constitutional text nowhere brackets presidential or federal power within the confines of customary international law. When the Supremacy Clause discusses the sources of federal law, it enumerates only "this Constitution, and the Laws of the United States which shall be made in Pursuance there of; and all Treaties made, or which shall be made, under the Authority of the United States." U.S. Const. Article VI. Customary international law is nowhere mentioned in the Constitution as an independent source of federal law or as a constraint on the political branches of government. Indeed, if it were, there would have

[113] *See, e.g., United States v. Alvarez-Machain*, 504 U.S. 655 (1992).

[114] *See id.* at 669–70; *Committee of United States Citizens Living in Nicaragua v. Reagan*, 859 F.2d 929, 935–36 (D.C. Cir. 1988); Garcia-Mir v. Meese, 788 F.2d 1446, 1453–55 (11th Cir.), cert. denied. 479 U.S. 889 (1986).

[115] *See, e.g., Michael J. Glennon, Raising the Paquete Habana: Is Violation of Customary International Law by the Executive Unconstitutional?*, 80 Nw. U. L. Rev. 321, 325 (1985); Louis Henkin, *International Law As Law in the United States*, 82 Mich. L. Rev. 1555, 1567 (1984); Jules Lobel, *The Limits of Constitutional Power: Conflicts Between Foreign Policy and International Law*, 71 Va. L. Rev. 1071, 1179 (1985); *see also* Jonathan R. Charney, *Agora: May the President Violate Customary International Law?*, 80 Am. J. Int'l L. 913 (1986).

[116] Recently, the status of customary international law within the federal legal system has been the subject of sustained debate with legal academia. The legitimacy of incorporating customary international law as federal law has been subjected in these exchanges to crippling doubts. *See* Curtis A. Bradley & Jack L. Goldsmith, *Customary International Law As Federal Common Law: A Critique of the Modern Position*, 110 Harv. L. Rev. 815, 817 (1997); *see also* Phillip R. Trimble, *A Revisionist View of Customary International Law*, 33 UCLA L. Rev. 665, 672–673 (1986); Arthur M. Weisburd, *The Executive Branch and International Law*, 41 Vand. L. Rev. 1205, 1269 (1988). These claims have not gone unchallenged. *See* Harold H. Koh, *Is International Law Really State Law?*, III Harv. L. Rev. 1824, 1827 (1998); Gerald L. Neuman, *Sense and Nonsense About Customary International Law: A Response to Professors Bradley and Goldsmith*, 66 Fordham L. Rev. 371, 371 (1997); Beth Stephens, *The Law of Our Land: Customary International Law As Federal Law After Erie*, 66 Fordham L. Rev. 393, 396–97 (1997). Bradley and Goldsmith have responded to their critics several times. *See* Curtis A. Bradley & Jack L. Goldsmith, *Federal Courts and the Incorporation of International Law*, III Harv. L. Rev. 2260 (1998); Curtis A. Bradley & Jack L. Goldsmith, *The Current Illegitimacy of International Human Rights Litigation*, 66 Fordham L. Rev. 319,330 (1997).

been no need to grant to Congress the power to "define and punish . . . offenses against the Law of Nations."[117] It is also clear that the original understanding of the Framers was that "Laws of the United States" did *not* include the law of nations, as international law was called in the late eighteenth century. In explaining the jurisdiction of the Article III courts to cases arising "under the Constitution and the Laws of the United States," for example, Alexander Hamilton did not include the laws of nations as a source of jurisdiction.[118] Rather, Hamilton pointed out, claims involving the laws of nations would arise either in diversity cases or maritime cases,[119] which by definition do not involve "the Laws of the United States." Little evidence exists that those who attended the Philadelphia Convention in the summer of 1787 or the State ratifying conventions believed that federal law would have included customary international law, but rather that the laws of nations was part of a general common law that was not true federal law.[120]

Indeed, allowing customary international law to rise to the level of federal law would create severe distortions in the structure of the Constitution: Incorporation of customary international law directly into federal law would bypass the delicate procedures established by the Constitution for amending the Constitution or for enacting legislation.[121] Customary international law is not approved by two-thirds of Congress and three-quarters of the State legislatures, it has not been passed by both houses of Congress and signed by the President, nor is it made by the President with the advice and consent of two-thirds of the Senate. In other words, customary international law has not undergone the difficult hurdles that stand before enactment of constitutional amendments, statutes, or treaties. As such, it can have no legal effect on the government or on American citizens because it is not law.[122] Even the inclusion of treaties in the Supremacy Clause does not render treaties automatically self-executing in federal court, not to mention self-executing against the executive branch.[123] If even treaties that have undergone presidential signature and senatorial advice and consent can have no binding legal effect in the United States, then it certainly must be the case that a source of rules that never undergoes any process established by our Constitution cannot be law.

It is well accepted that the political branches have ample authority to override customary international law within their respective spheres of authority. This has been recognized by the Supreme Court since the earliest days of the Republic. In *The Schooner Exchange v. McFaddon*, for example, Chief Justice Marshall applied customary international law to the seizure of a French warship only because the

---

[117] U.S. Const. art. I, § 8, cl. 10.

[118] *The Federalist No. 80.* at 447–49 (Alexander Hamilton) (Clinton Rossiter ed., 1999).

[119] *Id.* at 444–46.

[120] *Id.*, e.g., Stewart Jay, *The Status of the Law of Nations in Early American Law*, 42 Vand. L. Rev. 819, 830–37 (1989); Bradford R. Clark, *Federal Common Law: A Structural Reinterpretation*, 144 U. Pa. L. Rev. 1245, 1306–12 (1996); Curtis A. Bradley & Jack L. Goldsmith, *The Current Illegitimacy of International Human Rights Litigation*, 66 Fordham L. Rev. 319, 333–36 (1997).

[121] *Cf. INS v. Chadha*, 462 U.S. 919 (1983) (invalidating legislative veto for failure to undergo bicameralism and presentment as required by Article I, Section 8 for all legislation).

[122] In fact, allowing customary international law to bear the force of federal law would create significant problems under the Appointments Clause and the non-delegation doctrine, as it would be law made completely outside the American legal system through a process of international practice, rather than either the legislature or officers of the United States authorized to do so.

[123] *See, e.g., Foster v. Neilson*, 27 U.S. (2 Pet.) 253, 314 (1829).

United States government had not chosen a different rule.

> It seems then to the Court, to be a principle of public [international] law, that national ships of war, entering the port of a friendly power open for their reception, are to be considered as exempted by the consent of that power from its jurisdiction. Without doubt, the sovereign of the place is capable of destroying this implication. He may claim and exercise jurisdiction, either by employing force, or by subjecting such vessels to the ordinary tribunals.[124]

In *Brown v. United States*, 12 U.S. (8 Cranch) 110 (1814), Chief Justice Marshall again stated that customary international law "is a guide which the sovereign follows or abandons at his will. The rule, like other precepts of morality, of humanity, and even of wisdom, is addressed to the judgment of the sovereign; and although it cannot be disregarded by him without obloquy, yet it may be disregarded."[125] In other words, overriding customary international law may prove to be a bad idea, or be subject to criticism, but there is no doubt that the government has the power to do it.

Indeed, proponents of the notion that customary international law is federal law can find little support in either history or Supreme Court case law. It is true that in some contexts, mostly involving maritime, insurance, and commercial law, the federal courts in the nineteenth century looked to customary international law as a guide.[126] Upon closer examination of these cases, however, it is clear that customary international law had the status only of the general federal common law that was applied in federal diversity cases under *Swift v. Tyson*, 41 U.S. (16 Pet.) 1 (1842). As such, it was not considered true federal law under the Supremacy Clause; it did not support Article III "arising under" jurisdiction; it did not preempt inconsistent state law; and it did not bind the executive branch. Indeed, even during this period, the Supreme Court acknowledged that the laws of war did not qualify as true federal law and could not therefore serve as the basis for federal subject matter jurisdiction. In *New York Life Ins. Co. v. Hendren*, 92 U.S. 286, for example, the Supreme Court declared that it had no jurisdiction to review "the general laws of war, as recognized by the law of nations applicable to this case," because such laws do not involve the Constitution, laws, treaties, or Executive proclamations of the United States.[127] The spurious nature of this type of law led the Supreme Court in the famous case of *Erie R.R. Co. v. Tompkins*, 304 U.S. 64, 78 (1938), to eliminate general federal common law.

Even the case most relied upon by proponents of customary international law's status as federal law, *The Paquete Habana*, itself acknowledges that customary international law is subject to override by the action of the political branches. *The Paquete Habana* involved the question whether U.S. armed vessels in wartime could capture certain fishing vessels belonging to enemy nationals and sell them as prize. In that case, the Court applied an international law rule, and did indeed say that "international law is part of our law."[128] But Justice Gray then continued, "*where there is no treaty and no controlling executive or legislative act or judicial decision*, resort must be had to the customs and usages of civilized nations." *Id.* (emphasis added). In other

---

[124] 11 U.S. (7 Cranch) 116, 145–46 (1812).

[125] *Id.* at 128.

[126] *See, e.g., Oliver Am. Trading Co. v. Mexico*, 264 U.S. 440, 442–43 (1924); *Huntington v. Attrill*, 146 U.S. 657, 683 (1892); *New York Life Ins. Co. v. Hendren*, 92 U.S. 286, 286–87 (1875).

[127] 92 U.S. 286, 286–87.

[128] 175 U.S. at 700.

words, while it was willing to apply customary international law as general federal common law (this was the era of *Swift v. Tyson*), the Court also readily acknowledged that the political branches and even the federal judiciary could override it at any time. No Supreme Court decision in modern times has challenged that view.[129] Thus, under clear Supreme Court precedent, any presidential decision in the current conflict concerning the detention and trial of al Qaeda or Taliban militia prisoners would constitute a "controlling" Executive act that would immediately and completely override any customary international law norms.

Constitutional text and Supreme Court decisions aside, allowing the federal courts to rely upon international law to restrict the President's discretion to conduct war would raise deep structural problems. First, if customary international law is indeed federal law, then it must receive all of the benefits of the Supremacy Clause. Therefore, customary international law would not only bind the President, but it also would preempt state law and even supersede inconsistent federal statutes and treaties that were enacted before the rule of customary international law came into being. This has never happened. Indeed, giving customary international law this power not only runs counter to the Supreme Court cases described above, but would have the effect of importing a body of law to restrain the three branches of American government that never underwent any approval by our democratic political process. If customary international law does not have these effects, as the constitutional text, practice and most sensible readings of the Constitution indicate, then it cannot be true federal law under the Supremacy Clause. As non-federal law, then, customary international law cannot bind the President or the executive branch, in any legally meaningful way, in its conduct of the war in Afghanistan.

Second, relying upon customary international law here would undermine the President's control over foreign relations and his Commander-in-Chief authority. As we have noted, the President under the Constitution is given plenary authority over the conduct of the Nation's foreign relations and over the use of the military. Importing customary international law nations concerning armed conflict would represent

---

[129] Two lines of cases are often cited for the proposition that the Supreme Court has found customary international law to be federal law. The first derives from *Murray v. Schooner Charming Betsy*, 6 U.S. (2 Cranch) 64 (1804). The *"Charming Betsy"* rule, as it is sometimes known, is a rule of construction that a statute should be construed when possible so as not to conflict with international law. This rule, however, does not apply international law of its own force, but instead can be seen as measure of judicial restraint: that violating international law is a decision for the political branches to make, and that if they wish to do so, they should state clearly their intentions. The second, *Banco Naçional de Cuba v. Sabbatino*, 376 U.S. 398, applied the "act of state" doctrine, which generally precludes courts from examining the validity of the decisions of foreign goverments taken on their own soil, as federal common law to a suit over expropriations by the Cuban government. As with *Charming Betsy*, however, the Court developed this rule as one of judicial self-restraint to preserve the flexibility of the political branches to decide how to conduct foreign policy.

Some supporters of customary international law as federal law rely on a third line of cases, beginning with *Filártiga v. Peña-Irala*, 630 F.2d 876 (2d Cir. 1980). In *Filártiga*, the Second Circuit read the federal Alien Tort Statute, 28 U.S.C. § 1350 (1994), to allow a tort suit in federal court against the former official of a foreign government for violating norms of international human rights law, namely torture. Incorporation of customary international law via the Alien Tort Statute, while accepted by several circuit courts, has never received the blessings of the Supreme Court and has been sharply criticized by some circuits, *see, e.g., Tel-Oren v. Libyan Arab Republic*, 726 F.2d 774, 808–10 (D.C. Cir. 1984) (Bork, J., concurring), *cert. denied*, 470 U.S. 1003 (1985), as well as by academics, see Curtis A. Bradley & Jack L. Goldsmith, *The Current Illegitimacy of International Human Rights Litigation*, 66 Fordham L. Rev. 319, 330 (1997).

a direct infringement on the President's discretion as the Commander-in-Chief and Chief Executive to determine how best to conduct the Nation's military affairs. Presidents and courts have agreed that the President enjoys the fullest discretion permitted by the Constitution in commanding troops in the field.[130] It is difficult to see what legal authority under our constitutional system would permit customary international law to restrict the exercise of the President's plenary power in this area, which is granted to him directly by the Constitution. Further, reading customary international law to be federal law would improperly inhibit the President's role as the representative of the Nation in its foreign affairs.[131] Customary law is not static; it evolves through a dynamic process of State custom and practice. "States necessarily must have the authority to contravene international norms, however, for it is the process of changing state practice that allows customary international law to evolve."[132] As we observed in 1989, "[i]f the United States is to participate in the evolution of international law, the Executive must have the power to act inconsistently with international law where necessary."[133] The power to override or ignore customary international law, even the law applying to armed conflict, is "an integral part of the President's foreign affairs power."[134]

Third, if customary international law is truly federal law, it presumably must be enforceable by the federal courts. Allowing international law to interfere with the President's war power in this way, however, would expand the federal judiciary's authority into areas where it has little competence, where the Constitution does not textually call for its intervention, and where it risks defiance by the political branches. Indeed, treating customary international law as federal law would require the judiciary to intervene into the most deep political questions, those concerning war. This the federal courts have said they will not do, most recently during the Kosovo conflict.[135] Again, the practice of the branches demonstrates that they do not consider customary international law to be federal law. This position makes sense even at the level of democratic theory, because conceiving of international law as a restraint on warmaking would allow norms of questionable democratic origin to constrain actions validly taken under the U.S. Constitution by popularly accountable national representatives.

Based on these considerations of constitutional text, structure, and history, we conclude that customary international law does not bind the President or the U.S. Armed Forces in their decisions concerning the detention conditions of al Qaeda and Taliban prisoners.

---

[130] *See* Memorandum for Timothy E. Flanigan, Deputy Counsel to the President, from John C. Yoo, Deputy Assistant Attorney General, Office of Legal Counsel, *Re: The President's Constitutional Authority to Conduct Military Operations Against Terrorists and Nations Supporting Them* (Sept. 25, 2001) (reviewing authorities).

[131] "When articulating principles of international law in its relations with other states, the Executive branch speaks not only as an interpreter of generally accepted and traditional rules, as would the courts, but also as an advocate of standards it believes desirable for the community of nations and protective of national concerns." *Sabbatino*, 376 U.S. at 432–33. *See also Rappenecker v. United States*, 509 F.Supp. 1024, 1029 (N.D. Cal. 1980) ("Under the doctrine of separation of powers, the making of those determinations [under international law] is entrusted to the President."); *International Load line Convention*, 40 Op. Att'y Gen. at 123–24 (President "speak[s] for the nation" in making determination under international law).

[132] 13 Op. O.L.C. at 170.

[133] *Id.*

[134] *Id.* at 171.

[135] *See. e.g., Campbell v. Clinton*, 203 F.3d 19, 40 (D.C. Cir.), *cert. denied*, 531 U.S. 815 (2000).

Conclusion

For the foregoing reasons, we conclude that neither the federal War Crimes Act nor the Geneva Conventions would apply to the detention conditions of al Qaeda prisoners. We also conclude that the President has the plenary constitutional power to suspend our treaty obligations toward Afghanistan during the period of the conflict. He may exercise that discretion on the basis that Afghanistan was a failed State. Even if he chose not to, he could interpret Geneva III to find that members of the Taliban militia failed to qualify as POWs under the terms of the treaty. We also conclude that customary international law has no binding legal effect on either the President or the military because it is not federal law, as recognized by the Constitution.

We should make clear that in reaching a decision to suspend our treaty obligations or to construe Geneva III to conclude that members of the Taliban militia are not POWs, the President need not make any specific finding. Rather, he need only authorize or approve policies that would be consistent with the understanding that al Qaeda and Taliban prisoners are not POWs under Geneva III.

Please let us know if we can provide further assistance.

Jay S. Bybee
Assistant Attorney General

January 25, 2002

MEMORANDUM FOR THE PRESIDENT

FROM: ALBERTO R. GONZALES

SUBJECT: DECISION RE APPLICATION OF THE GENEVA CONVENTION
             ON PRISONERS OF WAR TO THE CONFLICT WITH AL QAEDA
             AND THE TALIBAN

Purpose

On January 18, I advised you that the Department of Justice had issued a formal legal opinion concluding that the Geneva Convention III on the Treatment of Prisoners of War (GPW) does not apply to the conflict with al Qaeda. I also advised you that DOJ's opinion concludes that there are reasonable grounds for you to conclude that GPW does not apply with respect to the conflict with the Taliban. I understand that you decided that GPW does not apply and, accordingly, that al Qaeda and Taliban detainees are not prisoners of war under the GPW.

The Secretary of State has requested that you reconsider that decision. Specifically, he has asked that you conclude that GPW does apply to both al Qaeda and the Taliban. I understand, however, that he would agree that al Qaeda and Taliban fighters could be determined not to be prisoners of war (POWs) but only on a case-by-case basis following individual hearings before a military board.

This memorandum outlines the ramifications of your decision and the Secretary's request for reconsideration.

Legal Background

As an initial matter, I note that you have the constitutional authority to make the determination you made on January 18 that the GPW does not apply to al Qaeda and the Taliban. (Of course, you could nevertheless, as a matter of policy, decide to apply the principles of GPW to the conflict with al Qaeda and the Taliban.) The Office of Legal Counsel of the Department of Justice has opined that, as a matter of international and domestic law, GPW does not apply to the conflict with al Qaeda. OLC has further opined that you have the authority to determine that GPW does not apply to the Taliban. As I discussed with you, the grounds for such a determination may include:

- A determination that Afghanistan was a failed State because the Taliban did not exercise full control over the territory and people, was not recognized by the international community, and was not capable of fulfilling its international obligations (e.g., was in widespread material breach of its international obligations).

- A determination that the Taliban and its forces were, in fact, not a government, but a militant, terrorist-like group.

OLC's interpretation of this legal issue is definitive. The Attorney General is charged by statute with interpreting the law for the Executive Branch. This interpretive authority extends to both domestic and international law. He has, in turn, delegated this role to OLC, Nevertheless, you should be aware that the Legal Adviser to the Secretary of State has expressed a different view.

Ramifications of Determination that GPW Does Not Apply

The consequences of a decision to adhere to what I understood to be your earlier determination that the GPW does not apply to the Taliban include the following:

Positive:

- Preserves flexibility:
  - As you have said, the war against terrorism is a new kind of war. It is not the traditional clash between nations adhering to the laws of war that formed the backdrop for GPW. The nature of the new war places a high premium on other factors, such as the ability to quickly obtain information from captured terrorists and their sponsors in order to avoid further atrocities against American civilians, and the need to try terrorists for war crimes such as wantonly killing civilians. In my judgment, this new paradigm renders obsolete Geneva's strict limitations on questioning of enemy prisoners and renders quaint some of its provisions requiring that captured enemy be afforded such things as commissary privileges, scrip (i.e., advances of monthly pay), athletic uniforms, and scientific instruments.
  - Although some of these provisions do not apply to detainees who are not POWs, a determination that GPW does not apply to al Qaeda and the Taliban eliminates any argument regarding the need for case-by-case determinations of POW status. It also holds open options for the future conflicts in which it may be more difficult to determine whether an enemy force as a whole meets the standard for POW status.
  - By concluding that GPW does not apply to al Qaeda and the Taliban, we avoid foreclosing options for the future, particularly against nonstate actors.
- Substantially reduces the threat of domestic criminal prosecution under the War Crimes Act (18 U.S.C. 2441).
  - That statute, enacted in 1996, prohibits the commission of a "war crime" by or against a U.S. person, including U.S. officials. "War crime" for these purposes is defined to include any grave breach of GPW or any violation of common Article 3 thereof (such as "outrages against personal dignity"). Some of these provisions apply (if the GPW applies) regardless of whether the individual being detained qualifies as a POW. Punishments for violations of Section 2441 include the death penalty. A determination that the GPW is not applicable to the Taliban would mean that Section 2441 would not apply to actions taken with respect to the Taliban.
  - Adhering to your determination that GPW does not apply would guard effectively against misconstruction or misapplication of Section 2441 for several reasons.

○ First, some of the language of the GPW is undefined (it prohibits, for example, "outrages upon personal dignity" and "inhuman treatment"), and it is difficult to predict with confidence what actions might be deemed to constitute violations of the relevant provisions of GPW.

○ Second, it is difficult to predict the needs and circumstances that could arise in the course of the war on terrorism.

○ Third, it is difficult to predict the motives of prosecutors and independent counsels who may in the future decide to pursue unwarranted charges based on Section 2441. Your determination would create a reasonable basis in law that Section 2441 does not apply, which would provide a solid defense to any future prosecution.

Negative:

On the other hand, the following arguments would support reconsideration and reversal of your decision that the GPW does not apply to either al Qaeda or the Taliban:

■ Since the Geneva Conventions were concluded in 1949, the United States has never denied their applicability to either U.S. or opposing forces engaged in armed conflict, despite several opportunities to do so. During the last Bush Administration, the United States stated that it "has a policy of applying the Geneva Conventions of 1949 whenever armed hostilities occur with regular foreign armed forces, even if arguments could be made that the threshold standards for the applicability of the Conventions . . . are not met."

■ The United States could not invoke the GPW if enemy forces threatened to mistreat or mistreated U.S. or coalition forces captured during operations in Afghanistan, or if they denied Red Cross access or other POW privileges.

■ The War Crimes Act could not be used against the enemy, although other criminal statutes and the customary law of war would still be available.

■ Our position would likely provoke widespread condemnation among our allies and in some domestic quarters, even if we make clear that we will comply with the core humanitarian principles of the treaty as a matter of policy.

■ Concluding that the Geneva Convention does not apply may encourage other countries to look for technical "loopholes" in future conflicts to conclude that they are not bound by GPW either

■ Other countries may be less inclined to turn over terrorists or provide legal assistance to us if we do not recognize a legal obligation to comply with the GPW.

■ A determination that GPW does not apply to al Qaeda and the Taliban could undermine U.S. military culture which emphasizes maintaining the highest standards of conduct in combat, and could introduce an element of uncertainty in the status of adversaries.

Response to arguments for Applying GPW to the al Qaeda and the Taliban

On balance, I believe that the arguments for reconsideration and reversal are unpersuasive.

■ The argument that the U.S. has never determined that GPW did not apply is incorrect. In at least one case (Panama in 1989) the U.S. determined that GPW did not apply even though it determined for policy reasons to adhere to the convention. More importantly, as noted above, this is a new type of warfare – one not contemplated in 1949 when the GPW was framed – and requires a new approach in our actions toward captured terrorists. Indeed, as the statement quoted from the administration of President George Bush makes clear, the U.S. will apply GPW "whenever hostilities occur *with regular foreign armed forces.*" By its terms, therefore, the policy does not apply to a conflict with terrorists, or with irregular forces, like the Taliban, who are armed militants that oppressed and terrorized the people of Afghanistan.

- In response to the argument that we should decide to apply GPW to the Taliban in order to encourage other countries to treat captured U.S. military personnel in accordance with the GPW, it should be noted that your policy of providing humane treatment to enemy detainees gives us the credibility to insist on like treatment for our soldiers. Moreover, even if GPW is not applicable, we can still bring war crimes charges against anyone who mistreats U.S. personnel. Finally, I note that our adversaries in several recent conflicts have not been deterred by GPW in their mistreatment of captured U.S. personnel, and terrorists will not follow GPW rules in any event.
- The statement that other nations would criticize the U.S. because we have determined that GPW does not apply is undoubtedly true. It is even possible that some nations would point to that determination as a basis for failing to cooperate with us on specific matters in the war against terrorism. On the other hand, some international and domestic criticism is already likely to flow from your previous decision not to treat the detainees as POWs. And we can facilitate cooperation with other nations by reassuring them that we fully support GPW where it is applicable and by acknowledging that in this conflict the U.S. continues to respect other recognized standards.
- In the treatment of detainees, the U.S. will continue to be constrained by (i) its commitment to treat the detainees humanely and, to the extent appropriate and consistent with military necessity, in a manner consistent with the principles of GPW, (ii) its applicable treaty obligations, (iii) minimum standards of treatment universally recognized by the nations of the world, and (iv) applicable military regulations regarding the treatment of detainees.
- Similarly, the argument based on military culture fails to recognize that our military remain bound to apply the principles of GPW because that is what you have directed them to do.

MEMO 8

Washington, D.C. 20520

MEMORANDUM

TO: Counsel to the President
            Assistant to the President for National Security Affairs

FROM: Colin L. Powell

SUBJECT: Draft Decision Memorandum for the President on the Applicability of
            the Geneva Convention to the Conflict in Afghanistan

I appreciate the opportunity to comment on the draft memorandum. I am concerned that the draft does not squarely present to the President the options that
are available to him. Nor does it identify the significant pros and cons of each option. I hope that the final memorandum will make clear that the President's choice is
between

> Option 1: Determine that the Geneva Convention on the treatment of Prisoners of
> War (GPW) does not apply to the conflict on "failed State" or some other grounds.
> Announce this position publicly. Treat all detainees consistent with the principles
> of the GPW;

and

> Option 2: Determine that the Geneva Convention does apply to the conflict in
> Afghanistan, but that members of al Qaeda as a group and the Taliban individ-
> ually or as a group are not entitled to Prisoner of War status under the Convention.
> Announce this position publicly. Treat all detainees consistent with the principles
> of the GPW.

The final memorandum should first tell the President that both options have
the following advantages – that is there is no difference between them in these
respects:

- Both provide the same practical flexibility in how we treat detainees, including
  with respect to interrogation and length of the detention.
- Both provide flexibility to provide conditions of detention and trial that take into
  account constraints such as feasibility under the circumstances and necessary
  security requirements.
- Both allow us not to give the privileges and benefits of POW status to al Qaeda and
  Taliban.
- Neither option entails any significant risk of domestic prosecution against U.S.
  officials.

The memorandum should go on to identify the separate pros and cons of the two options as follows:

Option 1 – Geneva Convention does not apply to the conflict

Pros:

- This is an across-the-board approach that on its face provides maximum flexibility, removing any question of case-by-case determination for individuals.

Cons:

- It will reverse over a century of U.S. policy and practice in supporting the Geneva Conventions and undermine the protections of the law of war for our troops, both in this specific conflict and in general.
- It has a high cost in terms of negative international reaction, with immediate adverse consequences for our conduct of foreign policy.
- It will undermine public support among critical allies, making military cooperation more difficult to sustain.
- Europeans and others will likely have legal problems with extradition or other forms of cooperation in law enforcement, including bringing terrorists to justice.
- It may provoke some individual foreign prosecutors to investigate and prosecute our officials and troops.
- It will make us more vulnerable to domestic and international legal challenge and deprive us of important legal options:

  - It undermines the President's Military Order by removing an important legal basis for trying the detainees before Military Commissions.
  - We will be challenged in international fora (UN Commission on Human Rights, World Court, etc.).
  - The Geneva Conventions are a more flexible and suitable legal framework than other laws that would arguably apply (customary international human rights, human rights conventions). The GPW permits long-term detention without criminal charges. Even after the President determines hostilities have ended, detention continues if criminal investigations or proceedings are in process. The GPW also provides clear authority for transfer of detainees to third countries.
  - Determining GPW does not apply deprives us of a winning argument to oppose habeas corpus actions in U.S. courts.

Option 2 – Geneva Convention applies to the conflict

Pros:

- By providing a more defensible legal framework, it preserves our flexibility under both domestic and international law.
- It provides the strongest legal foundation for what we actually intend to do.
- It presents a positive international posture, preserves U.S. credibility and moral authority by taking the high ground, and puts us in a better position to demand and receive international support.

- It maintains POW status for U.S. forces, reinforces the importance of the Geneva Conventions, and generally supports the U.S. objective of ensuring its forces are accorded protection under the Convention.
- It reduces the incentives for international criminal investigations directed against U.S. officials and troops.

Cons:

- If, for some reason, a case-by-case review is used for Taliban, some may be determined to be entitled to POW status. This would not, however, affect their treatment as a practical matter.

I hope that you can restructure the memorandum along these lines, which it seems to me will give the President a much clearer understanding of the options available to him and their consequences. Quite aside from the need to identify options and their consequences more clearly, in its present form, the draft memorandum is inaccurate or incomplete in several respects. The most important factual errors are identified on the attachment.

Comments on the Memorandum of January 25, 2002

Purpose

(Second paragraph) The Secretary of State believes that al Qaeda terrorists as a group are not entitled to POW status and that Taliban fighters could be determined not to be POWs either as a group or on a case-by-case basis.

Legal Background

(First bullet) The Memorandum should note that any determination that Afghanistan is a failed State would be contrary to the official U.S. government position. The United States and the international community have consistently held Afghanistan to its treaty obligations and identified it as a party to the Geneva Conventions.

(Second paragraph) The Memorandum should note that the OLC interpretation does not preclude the President from reaching a different conclusion. It should also note that the OLC opinion is likely to be rejected by foreign governments and will not be respected in foreign courts or international tribunals which may assert jurisdiction over the subject matter. It should also note that OLC views are not definitive on the factual questions which are central to its legal conclusions.

Ramifications of Determination that GPW Does Not Apply

(Positive) The Memorandum identifies several positive consequences if the President determines the GPW does not apply. The Memorandum should note that these consequences would result equally if the President determines that the GPW does apply but that the detainees are not entitled to POW status.

(Negative. First bullet) The first sentence is correct as it stands. The second sentence is taken out of context and should be omitted. The U.S. position in Panama was that Common Article 3 of the Geneva Conventions did apply.

Response to Arguments for Applying GPW to the al Qaeda and the Taliban

(First bullet) The assertion in the first sentence is incorrect. The United States has never determined that the GPW did not apply to an armed conflict in which its forces have been engaged. With respect to the third sentence, while no one anticipated the precise situation that we face, the GPW was intended to cover all types of armed conflict and did not by its terms limit its application.

(Fourth bullet) The point is not clear. If we intend to conform our treatment of the detainees to universally recognized standards, we will be complying with the GPW.

MEMO 9

Office of the Attorney General
Washington, D.C. 20530

February 1, 2002

The President
The White House
Washington, DC

Dear Mr. President:

With your permission, I would like to comment on the National Security Council's discussion concerning the status of Taliban detainees. It is my understanding that the determination that al Qaeda and Taliban detainees are not prisoners of war remains firm. However, reconsideration is being given to whether the Geneva Convention III on prisoners of war applies to the conflict in Afghanistan.

There are two basic theories supporting the conclusion that Taliban combatants are not legally entitled to Geneva Convention protections as prisoners of war:

1. During relevant times of the combat, Afghanistan was a failed State. As such it was not a party to the treaty, and the treaty's protections do not apply;
2. During relevant times, Afghanistan *was* a party to the treaty, but Taliban combatants are not entitled to Geneva Convention III prisoner of war status because they acted as unlawful combatants.

If a *determination* is made that Afghanistan was a failed State (Option 1 above) and not a party to the treaty, various legal risks of liability, litigation, and criminal prosecution are minimized. This is a result of the Supreme Court's opinion in *Clark v. Allen* providing that when a President *determines* that a treaty does not apply, his determination is fully discretionary and will not be reviewed by the federal courts.

Thus, a Presidential determination against treaty applicability would provide the highest assurance that no court would subsequently entertain charges that American military officers, intelligence officials, or law enforcement officials violated Geneva Convention rules relating to field conduct, detention conduct or interrogation of detainees. The War Crimes Act of 1996 makes violation of parts of the Geneva Convention a crime in the United States.

In contrast, if a determination is made under Option 2 that the Geneva Convention applies but the Taliban are *interpreted* to be unlawful combatants not subject to the treaty's protections, *Clark v. Allen* does not accord American officials the same protection from legal consequences. In cases of Presidential *interpretation* of treaties which are confessed to apply, courts occasionally refuse to defer to Presidential interpretation. *Perkins v. Elg* is an example of such a case. If a court chose to review for itself the facts underlying a Presidential interpretation that detainees were unlawful combatants, it could involve substantial criminal liability for involved U.S. officials.

We expect substantial and ongoing legal challenges to follow the Presidential resolution of these issues. These challenges will be resolved more quickly and easily if they are foreclosed from judicial review under the *Clark* case by a Presidential determination that the Geneva Convention III on prisoners of war does not apply based on the failed state theory outlined as Option I above.

In sum, Option 1, a determination that the Geneva Convention does not apply, will provide the United States with the highest level of legal certainty available under American law.

It may be argued that adopting Option I would encourage other states to allege that U.S. forces are ineligible for Geneva Convention III protections in future conflicts. From my perspective, it would be far more difficult for a nation to argue falsely that America was a "failed State" than to argue falsely that American forces had, in some way, forfeited their right to protections by becoming unlawful combatants. In fact, the North Vietnamese did exactly that to justify mistreatment of our troops in Vietnam. Therefore, it is my view that Option 2, a determination that the Geneva Convention III applies to the conflict in Afghanistan and that Taliban combatants are not protected because they were unlawful, could well expose our personnel to a greater risk of being treated improperly in the event of detention by a foreign power.

Option 1 is a legal option. It does not foreclose policy and operational considerations regarding actual treatment of Taliban detainees. Option 2, as described above, is also a legal option, but its legal implications carry higher risk of liability, criminal prosecution, and judicially-imposed conditions of detainment – including mandated release of a detainee.

Clearly, considerations beyond the legal ones mentioned in this letter will shape and perhaps control ultimate decision making in the best interests of the United States of America.

Sincerely,
John Ashcroft
Attorney General

THE LEGAL ADVISER DEPARTMENT
OF STATE
WASHINGTON

February 2, 2002

MEMORANDUM

TO: Counsel to the President

FROM: William H. Taft, IV

SUBJECT: Comments on Your Paper on the Geneva Convention

The paper should make clear that the issue for decision by the President is whether the Geneva Conventions apply to the conflict in Afghanistan in which U.S. armed forces are engaged. The President should know that a decision that the Conventions do apply is consistent with the plain language of the Conventions and the unvaried practice of the United States in introducing its forces into conflict over fifty years. It is consistent with the advice of DOS lawyers and, as far as is known, the position of every other party to the Conventions. It is consistent with UN Security Council Resolution 1193 affirming that "All parties to the conflict (in Afghanistan) are bound to comply with their obligations under international humanitarian law and in particular the Geneva Conventions. . . ." It is not inconsistent with the DOJ opinion that the Conventions generally do not apply to our world-wide effort to combat terrorism and to bring al Qaeda members to justice.

From a policy standpoint, a decision that the Conventions apply provides the best legal basis for treating the al Qaeda and Taliban detainees in the way we intend to treat them. It demonstrates that the United States bases its conduct not just on its policy preferences but on its international legal obligations. Agreement by all lawyers that the War Crimes Act does not apply to our conduct means that the risk of prosecution under that statute is negligible. Any small benefit from reducing it further will be purchased at the expense of the men and women in our armed forces that we send into combat. A decision that the Conventions do not apply to the conflict in Afghanistan in which our armed forces are engaged deprives our troops there of any claim to the protection of the Convention in the event they are captured and weakens the protections accorded by the Conventions to our troops in future conflicts.

The structure of the paper suggesting a distinction between our conflict with al Qaeda and our conflict with the Taliban does not conform to the structure of the Conventions. The Conventions call for a decision whether they apply to the conflict in Afghanistan. If they do, their provisions are applicable to all persons involved in that conflict – al Qaeda, Taliban, Northern Alliance, U.S. troops, civilians, etc. If the Conventions do not apply to the conflict, no one involved in it will enjoy the benefit of their protections as a matter of law.

Status of Legal Discussions re
Application of Geneva Convention to
Taliban and al Qaeda

1. Legal Conclusion re War Crimes Act Liability

■ All lawyers involved in these discussions agree that the War Crimes Act does not
apply to any actions taken by U.S. officials with respect to al Qaeda or Taliban
detainees.

2. Applicability of GPW to Conflict With al Qaeda

■ DOJ lawyers have concluded as matter of law that our conflict with al Qaeda,
regardless of where it is carried out, is not covered by GPW. Lawyers from DOD,
WHC, and OVP support that legal conclusion.
  ■ DOJ, DOD, WHC, and OVP lawyers believe that this conclusion is desirable
  from a domestic law standpoint because it provides the best possible insulation
  from any misapplication of the War Crimes Act to the conflict with al Qaeda,
  whether in Afghanistan or elsewhere.
  ■ DOJ, DOD, WHC, and OVP lawyers further believe that this conclusion is
  appropriate for policy reasons because it emphasizes that the worldwide conflict
  with al Qaeda is a new sort of conflict, one not covered by GPW or some other
  traditional rules of warfare.
■ DOS lawyers believe that GPW applies to our treatment of al Qaeda members
captured in Afghanistan on the theory that GPW applies to the conflict in
Afghanistan, not to particular individuals or groups.
■ JCS lawyers do not object to DOJ's legal conclusion, provided that JCS' policy
concerns are addressed by statements that (1) the U.S. will treat all detainees as if the
convention applied; (2) emphasize the importance we attach to the convention; and
(3) emphasize our expectation that all other countries will treat our armed forces
consistent with the convention.

3. Applicability of GPW to Conflict With the Taliban

■ DOJ, WHC and OVP lawyers agree that the President has authority to determine to
suspend GPW as between the U.S. and Afghanistan based on a conclusion that
Afghanistan is a failed state.
■ DOS lawyers disagree with this conclusion and oppose such a determination.
■ JCS lawyers oppose the determination on policy grounds to the extent that those
policy considerations are not addressed as set forth in the last bullet of 1. above.
■ All relevant lawyers agree that (a) Taliban detainees are not POWs and (b) they do
not fit within the class of those entitled to any of the other (i.e., non-POW)
protections of GPW. Thus all relevant lawyers agree that Taliban detainees will not
benefit at all from GPW, whether or not GPW is suspended.

Status of Legal Discussions re
Application of Geneva Convention to
Taliban and al Qaeda

1. *Legal Conclusion re War Crimes Act Liability*

- All lawyers involved in these discussions agree that the War Crimes Act does not apply to any actions being taken by U.S. officials with respect to al Qaeda or Taliban detainees.

2. *Applicability of GPW to Conflict With al Qaeda*

- DOJ lawyers have concluded as matter of law that our conflict with al Qaeda, regardless of where it is carried out, is not covered by GPW. Lawyers from DOD, WHC, and OVP support that legal conclusion.
  - DOJ, DOD, WHC, and OVP lawyers believe that this conclusion is desirable from a domestic law standpoint because it provides the best possible insulation from any misapplication of the War Crimes Act to the conflict with al Qaeda, whether in Afghanistan or elsewhere.
  - DOJ, DOD, WHC, and OVP lawyers further believe that this conclusion is appropriate for policy reasons because it emphasizes that the worldwide conflict with al Qaeda is a new sort of conflict, one not covered by GPW or some other traditional rules of warfare.
- DOS lawyers believe that GPW applies to our treatment of al Qaeda members captured in Afghanistan on the theory that GPW applies to the conflict in Afghanistan, not to particular individuals or groups.
  - DOS lawyers believe this conclusion is desirable from a domestic and international law standpoint because it provides the best legal basis for our intended treatment of the detainees and strengthens the Geneva Convention protections of our forces in Afghanistan and other conflicts.
  - DOS lawyers further believe this conclusion is appropriate for policy reasons because it emphasizes that even in a new sort of conflict the United States bases its conduct on its international treaty obligations and the rule of law, not just on its policy preferences.
- JCS lawyers do not object to DOJ's (or DOS's) legal conclusion, provided that JCS' policy concerns are addressed by statements that (1) the U.S. will treat all detainees as if the convention applied; (2) emphasize the importance we attach to the convention; and (3) emphasize our expectation that all other countries will treat our armed forces consistent with the convention.

3. *Applicability of GPW to Conflict With the Taliban*

- DOJ, WHC and OVP lawyers agree that the President has authority to determine to suspend GPW as between the U.S. and Afghanistan based on a conclusion that Afghanistan is a failed state.
- DOS lawyers ~~disagree with this conclusion and oppose such a determination~~
- DOS lawyers do not agree that Afghanistan is failed State, that a failed State is relieved of its treaty obligations, or that the ***************
- JCS lawyers oppose the determination on policy grounds to the extent that those policy considerations are not addressed as set forth in the last bullet of 1. above.

■ DOJ lawyers believe that it is desirable to adhere to the President's determination of January 18 that GPW does not apply to our conflict with the Taliban in order to provide the best possible level of protection against misapplication of the War Crimes Act. OVP, DOD and WHC lawyers agree that the President's January 18 determination provides the best possible level of protection.

*[handwritten right margin: Omit.
1. unclear this ener]*

4. POW Status

■ The lawyers involved all agree that al Qaeda or Taliban soldiers are presumptively not POWs, consistent with the President's determination of January 18.

5. Further Screening

■ DOJ, WHC, and OVP lawyers believe ~~that the President has definitively determined~~ that al Qaeda and Taliban soldiers who come under U.S. control are not entitled to POW status. ~~They further believe that this determination is conclusive~~ and that no procedures are needed for further screening of any al Qaeda or Taliban detainees. ~~They also believe that non-POW status affords the flexibility to release or transfer~~ any prisoner determined not to be an appropriate candidate for detention, e.g., because he is a low level recruit who poses no continuing threat and who has no relevant information.

[handwritten right margin: The quest is being revised]

■ DOD, JCS and DOS lawyers believe that, in the unlikely event that "doubt should arise" as to whether a particular detainee does not qualify for POW status, we should be prepared to offer additional screening on a case-by-case basis, either *pursuant to* Article 5 of GPW (to the extent the convention applies) or *consistent with* Article 5 (to the extent it does not). [*The National security Advisor has advised the Canadian government that this is our policy.*]

[handwritten right margin: I confirm]

6. CIA Issues

[handwritten left margin: I. a does i relate the as be e the what liaison]

■ The lawyers involved all agree that the CIA is bound by the same legal restrictions as the U.S. military.

[handwritten symbol in right margin]

■ They further agree that the CIA enjoys the same high level of protection from liability under the War Crimes Act as the U.S. military.
■ CIA lawyers believe that, to the extent that GPW's protections do not apply as a matter of law but those protections are applied as a matter of policy, it is desirable to circumscribe that policy so as to limit its application to the CIA. The other lawyers involved did not disagree with or object to CIA's view.

Ⓐ [*indented bullets*]

■ *DOS lawyers believe this conclusion is desirable from a domestic and international law standpoint because it provides the best legal basis for our intended treatment of the detainees and strengthens the Geneva Convention protections of our forces in Afghanistan and other conflicts.*

■ *DOS lawyers further believe this conclusion is appropriate for policy reasons because it emphasizes that even in a new sort of conflict the United States bases its conduct on its international treaty obligations and the rule of law, not just to policy preferences.*

- All lawyers agree that ~~(a)~~ Taliban detainees are not POWs ~~and (b) they do not fit within the class of those entitled to any of the other (i.e. non-Pow) protections of GPW.~~ Thus all ~~relevant~~ lawyers agree that Taliban detainees will not benefit at all from GPW, whether or not GPW is suspended.
- DOJ lawyers believe that it is desirable to adhere to the President's determination of January 18 that GPW does not apply to our conflict with the Taliban in order to provide the best possible level of protection against misapplication of the War Crimes Act. OVP, DOD and WHC lawyers agree that the President's January 18 determination provides the best possible level of protection.

4. *POW Status*

- The lawyers involved all agree that al Qaeda or Taliban soldiers are presumptively not POWs, consistent with the President's determination of January 18.

5. *Further Screening*

- DOJ, WHC, and OVP lawyers believe ~~that the President has definitively determined~~ that al Qaeda and Taliban soldiers who come under U.S. control are not entitled to POW status. ~~They further believe that this determination is conclusive~~ and that no procedures are needed for further screening of any al Qaeda or Taliban detainees. They also believe that non-POW status affords the flexibility to release or transfer any prisoner determined not to be an appropriate candidate for detention, e.g., because he is a low-level recruit who poses no continuing threat and who has no relevant information.
- DOD, JCS and DOS lawyers believe that, in the unlikely event that "doubt should arise" as to whether a particular detainee does not qualify for POW status, we should be prepared to offer additional screening on a case-by-case basis, either *pursuant to* Article 5 of GPW (to the extent the Convention applies) or *consistent with* Article 5 (to the extent it does not). The National Security Advisor has advised the canadian government that this is our policy.

6. *CIA Issues*

- The lawyers involved all agree that the CIA is bound by the same legal restrictions as the U.S. military.
- They further agree that the CIA enjoys the same high level of protection from liability under the War Crimes Act as the U.S. military.
- CIA lawyers believe that, to the extent that GPW's protections do not apply as a matter of law but those protections are applied as a matter of policy, it is desirable to circumscribe that policy so as to limit its application to the CIA. The other lawyers involved did not disagree with or object to CIA's view.

The White House

Washington

February 7, 2002

MEMORANDUM FOR THE VICE PRESIDENT
  THE SECRETARY OF STATE
  THE SECRETARY OF DEFENSE
  THE ATTORNEY GENERAL
  CHIEF OF STAFF TO THE PRESIDENT
  DIRECTOR OF CENTRAL INTELLIGENCE
  ASSISTANT TO THE PRESIDENT FOR NATIONAL SECURITY AFFAIRS
  CHAIRMAN OF THE JOINT CHIEFS OF STAFF

SUBJECT: Humane Treatment of al Qaeda and Taliban Detainees

1. Our recent extensive discussions regarding the status of al Qaeda and Taliban detainees confirm that the application of the Geneva Convention Relative to the Treatment of Prisoners of War of August 12, 1949 (Geneva) to the conflict with al Qaeda and the Taliban involves complex legal questions. By its terms, Geneva applies to conflicts involving "High Contracting Parties," which can only be States. Moreover, it assumes the existence of "regular" armed forces fighting on behalf of States. However, the war against terrorism ushers in a new paradigm, one in which groups with broad, international reach commit horrific acts against innocent civilians, sometimes with the direct support of States. Our Nation recognizes that this new paradigm – ushered in not by us, but by terrorists – requires new thinking in the law of war, but thinking that should nevertheless be consistent with the principles of Geneva.

2. Pursuant to my authority as Commander-in-Chief and Chief Executive of the United States, and relying on the opinion of the Department of Justice dated January 22, 2002, and on the legal opinion rendered by the Attorney General in his letter of February 1, 2002, I hereby determine as follows:

   a. I accept the legal conclusion of the Department of Justice and determine that none of the provisions of Geneva apply to our conflict with al Qaeda in Afghanistan or elsewhere throughout the world because, among other reasons, al Qaeda is not a High Contracting Party to Geneva.

   b. I accept the legal conclusion of the Attorney General and the Department of Justice that I have the authority under the Constitution to suspend Geneva as between the United States and Afghanistan, but I decline to exercise that authority at this time. Accordingly, I determine that the provisions of Geneva will apply to our present conflict with the Taliban. I reserve the right to exercise this authority in this or future conflicts.

   c. I also accept the legal conclusion of the Department of Justice and determine that common Article 3 of Geneva does not apply to either al Qaeda or Taliban detainees, because, among other reasons, the relevant conflicts are international in scope and common Article 3 applies only to "armed conflict not of an international character."

   d. Based on the facts supplied by the Department of Defense and the recommendation of the Department of Justice, I determine that the Taliban detainees are unlawful combatants and, therefore, do not qualify as prisoners of war under Article 4 of Geneva. I note that, because Geneva does not apply to our conflict with al Qaeda, al Qaeda detainees also do not qualify as prisoners of war.

3. Of course, our values as a Nation, values that we share with many nations in the world, call for us to treat detainees humanely, including those who are not legally entitled to such treatment. Our Nation has been and will continue to be a strong supporter of Geneva and its principles. As a matter of policy, the United States Armed Forces shall continue to treat detainees humanely and, to the extent appropriate and consistent with military necessity, in a manner consistent with the principles of Geneva.

4. The United States will hold states, organizations, and individuals who gain control of United States personnel responsible for treating such personnel humanely and consistent with applicable law.

5. I hereby reaffirm the order previously issued by the Secretary of Defense to the United States Armed Forces requiring that the detainees be treated humanely and, to the extent appropriate and consistent with military necessity, in a manner consistent with the principles of Geneva.

6. I hereby direct the Secretary of State to communicate my determinations in an appropriate manner to our allies, and other countries and international organizations cooperating in the war against terrorism of global reach.

[Signed George Bush]

U.S. Department of Justice

Office of Legal Counsel

Office of the Assistant Attorney General   *Washington, D.C. 20530*

February 7, 2002

Memorandum for Alberto R. Gonzales
Counsel to the President

RE: *Status of Taliban Forces Under Article 4 of the Third Geneva Convention*
of 1949

You have asked for our Office's views concerning the status of members of the Taliban militia under Article 4 of the 1949 Geneva Convention (III) Relative to the Treatment of Prisoners of War ("GPW"). Assuming the accuracy of various facts provided to us by the Department of Defense ("DoD"), we conclude that the President has reasonable factual grounds to determine that no members of the Taliban militia are entitled to prisoner of war ("POW") status under GPW. First, we explain that the Taliban militia cannot meet the requirements of Article 4(A)(2), because it fails to satisfy at least three of the four conditions of lawful combat articulated in Article 1 of the Annex to the 1907 Hague Convention (IV) Respecting the Laws and Customs of War on Land ("Hague Convention"), which are expressly incorporated into Article 4(A)(2). Second, we note that neither Article 4(A)(1) nor Article 4(A)(3) apply to militia, and that the four conditions of lawful combat contained in the Hague Convention also govern Article 4(A)(1) and (3) determinations in any case. Finally, we explain why there is no need to convene a tribunal under Article 5 to determine the status of the Taliban detainees.

I

Article 4(A) of GPW defines the types of persons who, once they have fallen under the control of the enemy, are entitled to the legal status of POWs. The first three categories are the only ones relevant to the Taliban. Under Article 4(A)(1), individuals who are "members of the armed forces of a Party to the conflict," are entitled to POW status upon capture. Article 4(A)(3) includes as POWs members of "regular armed forces who profess allegiance to a government or an authority not recognized by the Detaining Power."

Article 4(A)(2) includes as POWs members of "other militias" and "volunteer corps," including "organized resistance movements" that belong to a Party to the conflict. In addition, members of militias and volunteer corps must "fulfill" four conditions: (a) "being commanded by a person responsible for his subordinates"; (b) "having a fixed distinctive sign recognizable at a distance"; (c) "carrying arms openly"; and (d) "conducting their operations in accordance with the laws and customs of war." Those four conditions reflect those required in the 1907 Hague Convention IV. *See Commentary to the Geneva Convention Relative to the Treatment of Prisoners of War* 49

(Red Cross 1952) ("Red Cross Commentary") ("during the 1949 Diplomatic Conference . . . there was unanimous agreement that the categories of persons to whom the Convention is applicable must be defined, in harmony with the Hague Regulations").

Should "any doubt arise as to whether persons, having committed a belligerent act and having fallen into the hands of the enemy," GPW Article 5 requires that these individuals "enjoy the protections of" the Convention until a tribunal has determined their status.

Thus, in deciding whether members of the Taliban militia qualify for POW status, the President must determine whether they fall within any of these three categories. Under Article II of the Constitution, the President possesses the power to interpret treaties on behalf of the Nation. Memorandum for John Bellinger, III, Senior Associate Counsel and Legal Adviser to the National Security Council, from John C. Yoo, Deputy Assistant Attorney General and Robert J. Delahunty, Special Counsel, Office of Legal Counsel, *Re: Authority of the President to Suspend Certain Provisions of the ABM Treaty* (Nov. 15, 2001). This includes, of course, the power to apply treaties to the facts of a given situation. Thus, the President may interpret GPW, in light of the known facts concerning the operation of Taliban forces during the Afghanistan conflict, to find that all of the Taliban forces do not fall within the legal definition of POW. A presidential determination of this nature would eliminate any legal "doubt" as to the prisoners' status, as a matter of domestic law, and would therefore obviate the need for Article 5 tribunals.

We believe that, based on the facts provided by the Department of Defense, see Rear Admiral L.E. Jacoby, U.S. Navy, J-2, *Information Paper, Subject: Background Information on Taliban Forces* (Feb. 6, 2002), the President has reasonable grounds to conclude that the Taliban, as a whole, is not legally entitled to POW status under Articles 4(A)(1) through (3).

II

As the Taliban have described themselves as a militia, rather than the armed forces of Afghanistan, we begin with GPW's requirements for militia and volunteer corps under Article 4(A)(2). Based on the facts presented to us by DoD, we believe that the President has the factual basis on which to conclude that the Taliban militia, as a group, fails to meet three of the four GPW requirements, and hence are not legally entitled to POW status.

First, there is no organized command structure whereby members of the Taliban militia report to a military commander who takes responsibility for the actions of his subordinates. The Taliban lacks a permanent, centralized communications infrastructure. Periodically, individuals declared themselves to be "commanders" and organized groups of armed men, but these "commanders" were more akin to feudal lords than military officers. According to DoD, the Taliban militia functioned more as many different armed groups that fought for their own tribal, local, or personal interests.

Moreover, when the armed groups organized, the core of the organization was often al Qaeda, a multinational terrorist organization, whose existence was not in any way accountable to or dependent upon the sovereign state of Afghanistan. We have previously concluded, as a matter of law, that al Qaeda members are not covered by GPW. See Memorandum for Alberto R. Gonzales, Counsel to the President and William

J. Haynes II, General Counsel of the Department of Defense, from Jay S. Bybee, Assistant Attorney General, Re: Applications of Treaties and Laws to al Qaeda and Taliban Detainees (Jan. 22, 2002). After October 7, when the United States armed forces began aerial bombing of al Qaeda and Taliban targets in Afghanistan, the distinction between Taliban and al Qaeda became even more blurred as al Qaeda assumed the lead in organizing the defense.

DoD's facts suggest that to the extent the Taliban militia was organized at all, it consisted of a loose array of individuals who had shifting loyalties among various Taliban and al Qaeda figures. According to DoD, the Taliban lacked the kind of organization characteristic of the military. The fact that at any given time during the conflict the Taliban were organized into some structured organization does not answer whether the Taliban leaders were responsible for their subordinates within the meaning of GPW. Armed men who can be recruited from other units, as DoD states, through defections and bribery are not subject to a commander who can discipline his troops and enforce the laws of war.

Second, there is no indication that the Taliban militia wore any distinctive uniform or other insignia that served as a "fixed distinctive sign recognizable at a distance." DoD has advised us that the Taliban wore the same clothes they wore to perform other daily functions, and hence they would have been indistinguishable from civilians. Some have alleged that members of the Taliban would wear black turbans, but apparently this was done by coincidence rather than design. Indeed, there is no indication that black turbans were systematically worn to serve as an identifying feature of the armed group.

Some of the Taliban militia carried a tribal flag. DoD has stated that there is no indication that any individual members of the Taliban wore a distinctive sign or insignia that would identify them if they were not carrying or otherwise immediately identified with a tribal flag. Moreover, DoD has not indicated that tribal flags marked only military, as opposed to civilian, groups.

Third, the Taliban militia carried arms openly. This fact, however, is of little significance because many people in Afghanistan carry arms openly. Although Taliban forces did not generally conceal their weapons, they also never attempted to distinguish themselves from other individuals through the arms they carried or the manner in which they carried them. Thus, the Taliban carried their arms openly, as GPW requires military groups to do, but this did not serve to distinguish the Taliban from the rest of the population. This fact reinforces the idea that the Taliban could neither be distinguished by their uniforms and insignia nor by the arms they carried from Afghani civilians.

Finally, there is no indication that the Taliban militia understood, considered themselves bound by, or indeed were even aware of, the Geneva Conventions or any other body of law. Indeed, it is fundamental that the Taliban followed their own version of Islamic law and regularly engaged in practices that flouted fundamental international legal principles. Taliban militia groups have made little attempt to distinguish between combatants and non-combatants when engaging in hostilities. They have killed for racial or religious purposes. Furthermore, DoD informs us of widespread reports of Taliban massacres of civilians, raping of women, pillaging of villages, and various other atrocities that plainly violate the laws of war.

Based on the above facts, apparently well known to all persons living in Afghanistan and joining the Taliban, we conclude that the President can find that the Taliban militia is categorically incapable of meeting the Hague conditions expressly spelled out in Article 4(A)(2) of GPW.

III

One might argue that the Taliban is not a "militia" under Article 4(A)(2), but instead constitutes the "armed forces" of Afghanistan. Neither Article 4(A)(1), which grants POW status to members of the armed forces of a state party, nor Article 4(A)(3), which grants POW status to the armed forces of an unrecognized power, defines the term "armed forces." Unlike the definition of militia in Article 4(A)(2), these two other categories contain no conditions that these groups must fulfill to achieve POW status. Moreover, because GPW does not expressly incorporate Article 4(A)(2)'s four conditions into either Article 4(A)(1) or (3), some might question whether members of regular armed forces need to meet the Hague conditions in order to qualify for POW status under GPW.

We conclude, however, that the four basic conditions that apply to militias must also apply, at a minimum, to members of armed forces who would be legally entitled to POW status. In other words, an individual cannot be a POW, even if a member of an armed force, unless forces also are: (a) "commanded by a person responsible for his subordinates"; (b) "hav[e] a fixed distinctive sign recognizable at a distance"; (c) "carry [] arms openly"; and (d) "conduct [] their operations in accordance with the laws and customs of war." Thus, if the President has the factual basis to determine that Taliban prisoners are not entitled to POW status under Article 4(A)(2) as members of a militia, he therefore has the grounds to also find that they are not entitled to POW status as members of an armed force under either Article 4(A)(1) or Article 4(A)(3).

Article 4(A)'s use of the phrase "armed force," we believe, incorporated by reference the four conditions for militia, which originally derived from the Hague Convention IV. There was no need to list the four Hague conditions in Article 4(A)(1) because it was well understood under preexisting international law that all armed forces were already required to meet those conditions. As would have been understood by the GPW's drafters, use of the term "armed forces" incorporated the four criteria, repeated in the definition of militia, that were first used in the Hague Convention IV.

The view that the definition of an armed force includes the four criteria outlined in Hague Convention IV and repeated in GPW is amply supported by commentators. As explained in a recently issued Department of the Army pamphlet, the four Hague conditions are "arguably part and parcel of the definition of a regular armed force. It is unreasonable to believe that a member of a regular armed force could conduct military operations in civilian clothing, while a member of the militia or resistance groups cannot. Should a member of the regular armed forces do so, it is likely that he would lose his claim to immunity and be charged as a spy or as an illegal combatant." Major Geoffrey S. Corn & Major Michael L. Smidt, *"To Be Or Not To Be, That Is The Question": Contemporary Military Operations and the Status of Captured Personnel*, Department of the Army Pamphlet 27-50-319, 1999-June. Army Law. 1, 14 n. 127 (1999). One scholar has similarly concluded that "[u]nder the Hague Convention, a person is a member of the armed forces of a state only if he satisfies the [four enumerated] criteria." Gregory M. Travalio, *Terrorism, International Law, and the Use of Military Force*, 18 Wis. Int'l LJ. 145, 184 n.140 (2000). *See also* Michael N. Schmitt, *Bellum Americanum: The U.S. View of Twenty-First Century War and Its Possible Implications*

For the Law of Armed Conflict, 19 Mich. J. Int'l L. 1051, 1078 (1998) ("[U]nder the Regulations annexed to Hague Convention IV, combatants were those who were members of the regular armed forces (or formal militia), were commanded by a person responsible for their conduct, wore a fixed distinctive emblem (or uniform), carried their weapons openly, and conducted operations in accordance with the law of war. The 1949 Geneva Convention on Prisoners of War extended this status to members of an organized resistance movement which otherwise complied with the Hague IV requirements.").

Further, it would be utterly illogical to read "armed forces" in Article 4(A)(1) and (3) as somehow relieving members of armed forces from the same POW requirements imposed on members of a militia. There is no evidence that any of the GPW's drafters or ratifiers believed that members of the regular armed forces ought to be governed by *lower standards* in their conduct of warfare than those applicable to militia and volunteer forces. Otherwise, a sovereign could evade the Hague requirements altogether simply by designating all combatants as members of the sovereign's regular armed forces. A sovereign, for example, could evade the status of spies as unlawful combatants simply by declaring all spies to be members of the regular armed forces, regardless of whether they wore uniforms or not. Further, it would make little sense to construe GPW to deny some members of militias or volunteer corps POW protection for failure to satisfy the Hague conditions (under Article 4(A)(2)), while conferring such status upon other members simply because they have become part of the regular armed forces of a party (under Article 4(A)(1)).

This interpretation of "armed force" in GPW finds direct support in the International Committee of the Red Cross, the non-governmental organization primarily responsible for, and most closely associated with, the drafting and successful completion of GPW. After the Conventions were established, the Committee started work on a Commentary on all of the Geneva Conventions. In its discussion of Article 4(A)(3) of GPW, the ICRC construed both Article 4(A)(1) and (3) to require all regular armed forces to satisfy the four Hague IV (and Article 4(A)(2)) conditions:

> [t]he expression "members of regular armed forces" denotes armed forces which differ from those referred to in subparagraph (1) of this paragraph in one respect only: the authority to which they profess allegiance is not recognized by the adversary as a Party to the conflict. These "regular armed forces" have all the material characteristics and all the attributes of armed forces in the sense of sub-paragraph (1): they wear uniform, they have an organized hierarchy and they know and respect the laws and customs of war. The delegates to the 1949 Diplomatic Conference were therefore fully justified in considering that there was no need to specify for such armed forces the requirements stated in subparagraph (2) (a), (b), (c) and (d).

Red Cross Commentary at 62–63 (emphasis added).

Numerous scholars have similarly interpreted GPW as applying the four conditions to Article 4(A)(1) and (3) as well as to Article 4(A)(2). As Professor Howard S. Levie, a leading expert on the laws of war and the Geneva Conventions in particular, has explained in his authoritative treatise:

> This enumeration [of the four conditions] does not appear in subparagraph 1, dealing with the regular armed forces. This does not mean that mere membership in the regular armed forces will automatically entitle an individual who is captured to prisoner-of-war status if his activities prior to and at the time of capture have

not met these requirements. The member of the regular armed forces wearing civilian clothes who is captured while in enemy territory engaged in an espionage or sabotage mission is entitled to no different treatment than that which would be received by a civilian captured under the same circumstances. Any other interpretation would be unrealistic as it would mean that the dangers inherent in serving as a spy or saboteur could be immunized merely by making the individual a member of the armed forces; and that members of the armed forces could act in a manner prohibited by other areas of the law of armed conflict and escape the penalties therefore, still being entitled to prisoner-of-war status.

Howard S. Levie, 59 International Law Studies: Prisoners of War in International Armed Conflict 36–37 (Naval War College 1977). Oxford Professor Ingrid Detter has similarly concluded that, under the 1949 Geneva Conventions,

> to be a combatant, a person would have to be:
>
> (a) commanded by a person responsible for his subordinates;
> (b) having a fixed distinctive sign recognizable at a distance;
> (c) carrying arms openly;
> (d) conducting their operations in accordance with the laws and customs of war.
>
> The same requirements as apply to irregular forces are presumably also valid for members of regular units. However, this is not clearly spelt out: there is no textual support for the idea that members of regular armed forces should wear uniform. On the other hand, there is ample evidence that this is a rule of law which has been applied to a number of situations to ascertain the status of a person. Any regular soldier who commits acts pertaining to belligerence in civilian clothes loses his privileges and is no longer a lawful combatant. 'Unlawful' combatants may thus be either members of the regular forces or members of resistance or guerilla movements who do not fulfil the conditions of lawful combatants.

Ingrid Detter, The Law of War 136–37 (Cambridge 2d ed. 2000). See also Christopher C. Burris, *The Prisoner of War Status of PLO Fedayeen*, 22 N.C. J. Int'l L. & Com. Reg. 943, 987 n.308 (1997) ("I am using Article 4A(2)'s four criteria because the armed forces of the Palestinian Authority, over 30,000 men under arms organized into roughly ten or more separate para military units, are more characteristic of militia units than the regular armed forces of a state. This is because these units are organized as police/security units, not exclusive combat units. See Graham Usher, Palestinian Authority, Israeli Rule, The Nation, Feb. 5, 1996, at 15, 16. Whether the Palestinian Authority's forces are considered militia or members of the armed forces, they still must fulfill Article 4A(2)'s four criteria.").[1]

---

[1] The only federal court we are aware of that has addressed this issue denied Article 4(A)(3) status to defendants because they could not satisfy the Hague conditions. In *United States v. Buck*, 690 F. Supp. 1291 (S.D.N.Y. 1988), the defendants claimed that they were entitled to POW status as military officers of the Republic of New Afrika, "a sovereign nation engaged in a war of liberation against the colonial forces of the United States government." *Id.* at 1293. That nation, it was contended, included "all people of African ancestry living in the United States." *Id.* at 1296. The court refused to extend POW status to the defendants. After determining that GPW did not apply at all due to the absence of an armed conflict as understood under Article 2, the court alternatively reasoned that the defendants could not satisfy any of the requirements of Article 4. *See id.* at 1298 (stating that, even if GPW applied, "it is entirely clear that these defendants would not fall within Article 4, upon which they initially relied"). The court first concluded that the defendants failed to meet the four Hague conditions expressly spelled out in Article 4(A)(2). The court then rejected POW status under Article 4(A)(3) "[f]or comparable reasons:"

Therefore, it is clear that the term "armed force" includes the four conditions first identified by Hague Convention IV and expressly applied by GPW to militia groups. In other words, in order to be entitled to POW status, a member of an armed force must (a) be "commanded by a person responsible for his subordinates"; (b) "hav[e] a fixed distinctive sign recognizable at a distance"; (c) "carry[] arms openly"; and (d) "conduct[] their operations in accordance with the laws and customs of war." We believe that the President, based on the facts supplied by DoD, has ample grounds upon which to find that members of the Taliban have failed to meet three of these four criteria, regardless of whether they are characterized as members of a "militia" or of an "armed force." The President, therefore, may determine that the Taliban, as a group, are not entitled to POW status under GPW.

IV

Under Article 5 of GPW, "[s]hould any doubt arise as to whether persons . . . belong to any of the categories enumerated in Article 4, such persons shall enjoy the protection of the present Convention until such time as their status has been determined by a competent tribunal." As we understand it, DoD in the past has presumed prisoners to be entitled to POW status until a tribunal determines otherwise. The presumption and tribunal requirement are triggered, however, only if there is "any doubt" as to a prisoner's Article 4 status.

Under Article II of the Constitution, the President possesses the power to interpret treaties on behalf of the Nation.[2] We conclude, in light of the facts submitted to us by the Department of Defense and as discussed in Parts II and III of this memorandum, that the President could reasonably interpret GPW in such a manner that none of the Taliban forces fall within the legal definition of POWs as defined by Article 4. A presidential determination of this nature would eliminate any legal "doubt" as to the prisoners' status, as a matter of domestic law, and would therefore obviate the need for Article 5 tribunals.

This approach is also consistent with the terms of Article 5. As the International Committee of the Red Cross has explained, the "competent tribunal" requirement of Article 5 applies "to cases of doubt as to whether persons having committed a belligerent act and having fallen into the hands of the enemy belong to any of the categories enumerated in Article 4." Red Cross Commentary at 77 Tribunals are thus designed to determine whether a particular set of facts falls within one of the Article 4

> Article 4(A)(2) requires that to qualify as prisoners of war, members of 'organized resistance movements' must fulfill the conditions of command by a person responsible for his subordinates; having a fixed distinctive sign recognizable at a distance; carrying arms openly; and conducting their operations in accordance with the laws and customs of war. The defendants at war and their associates cannot pretend to have fulfilled those conditions. For comparable reasons, Article 4(3)'s reference to members of 'regular armed forces who profess allegiance to a government or an authority not recognized by the Detaining Power', also relied upon by defendants, does not apply to the circumstances of this case.

Id. (emphasis added). The court reached this conclusion even though the Hague conditions are not explicitly spelled out in Article 4(A)(3) nothing in the court's discussion suggests that it would have construed Article 4(A)(1) any differently.

[2] *See* Memorandum for John Bellinger, III, Senior Associate Counsel and Legal Adviser to the National Security Council, from John C. Yoo, Deputy Assistant Attorney General and Robert J. Delahunty, Special Counsel, Office of Legal Counsel, *Re: Authority of the President to Suspend Certain Provisions of the ABM Treaty* (Nov. 15, 2001).

categories; they are not intended to be used to resolve the proper interpretation of those categories. The President, in other words, may use his constitutional power to interpret treaties and apply them to the facts, to make the determination that the Taliban are unlawful combatants. This would remove any "doubt" concerning whether members of the Taliban are entitled to POW status.

We therefore conclude that there is no need to establish tribunals to determine POW status under Article 5.

Please let us know if we can provide further assistance.

Jay S. Bybee
Assistant Attorney General

U.S. Department of Justice

Office of Legal Counsel

Office of the Assistant Attorney General   *Washington, D.C. 20530*

February 26, 2002

MEMORANDUM FOR WILLIAM J. HAYNES, II, GENERAL COUNSEL, DEPARTMENT OF DEFENSE

RE: *Potential Legal Constraints Applicable to Interrogations of Persons Captured by U.S. Armed Forces in Afghanistan*

You have asked a series of questions concerning legal constraints that may potentially apply to interrogation of persons captured in Afghanistan. Several of the issues you have raised relate to the applicability of the Supreme Court's decision in *Miranda v. Arizona*, 384 U.S. 436 (1966), to interrogations that may be conducted for various purposes (and by various personnel) ranging from obtaining intelligence for military operations and force protection to investigating crimes with a view to bringing subsequent prosecutions. As explained below, the Self-Incrimination Clause of the Fifth Amendment, as interpreted by the Supreme Court in *Miranda*, provides a trial right in a criminal prosecution before U.S. courts and governs the admissibility of statements made by the defendant in a custodial interrogation. The issue of the applicability of *Miranda* and restrictions it may place on conduct in interrogations, therefore, is best addressed in the context of the subsequent use that is made of statements obtained in custodial interrogation.

As we explain below, the Self-Incrimination Clause (and hence *Miranda*) does not apply in the context of a trial by military commission for violations of the laws of war. Accordingly, military commissions may admit statements made by a defendant in a custodial interrogation conducted without *Miranda* warnings. Therefore, to the extent that the only trial-related use of statements obtained in an interrogation will be before a military commission, there is no need to provide *Miranda* warnings.

As we understand it, the inquiry cannot end there because decisions have not yet been made concerning whether individuals being interrogated will be prosecuted and if so in what forum charges will be brought. The possibility still exists that some detainees may be prosecuted on criminal charges in Article III courts. Thus, you have asked how Article III courts may treat statements obtained in various scenarios without *Miranda* warnings and whether *Miranda* warnings should be given as a prudential matter to preserve the possibility of using statements in a criminal trial. Although unwarned statements made in the course of custodial interrogation by law enforcement officers are generally presumed to be compelled under *Miranda*, thereby rendering them inadmissible in criminal prosecutions before domestic courts, *Miranda* does not provide an iron-clad rule governing the voluntariness of all custodial statements. *Miranda* was designed to provide a constitutional rule of conduct to regulate the practices of law enforcement, and where its deterrent rationale does not apply, the Supreme Court has not extended it. Many of the interrogations in question here, which will be conducted for purposes of obtaining information for military operations and intelligence purposes, do not come within the rationale of *Miranda*. In addition, one of the specific exceptions to *Miranda* that the Supreme Court has crafted should extend, by a close analogy, to some of the interrogations contemplated here. We divide our discussion to address four categories of statements the United States may wish to admit into evidence in a subsequent criminal prosecution: (1) statements arising out of interrogation conducted by military and intelligence personnel to develop military operations and intelligence information; (2) statements obtained for criminal law enforcement purposes, whether by FBI interrogators or military personnel; (3) statements obtained in the course of a war crimes investigation by members of the criminal investigative services of one of the U.S. Armed Forces; and (4) statements obtained where the objectives of the questioning may be mixed, and the interrogation thus may not fall squarely into only one of the first three categories.

We conclude that the first category of statements is likely to be admissible in an Article III trial even if the statements are obtained without *Miranda* warnings. Statements from the second category are likely to be inadmissible if they arise from unwarned interrogation. There is a substantial risk that courts will apply *Miranda* to the third category as well. Finally, in the fourth category – where the objectives of the questioning may be mixed – results may be highly fact-dependent, but we believe that the subjective motivations of interrogators in pursuing particular questions should not alter the conclusion that an interrogation conducted for obtaining military and intelligence information should not require *Miranda* warnings.

We also explain that, even after statements are obtained in an unwarned custodial interrogation governed by *Miranda*, any subsequent, *Mirandized* confessions would be admissible in an Article III court, at least so long as any prior, unwarned interrogation did not involve coercion, or where there was an adequate break in events between any coercion and the subsequent, properly *Mirandized* interrogation.

Finally, in response to your other inquiries, we explain that the Sixth Amendment right to counsel does not apply prior to the initiation of adversary judicial criminal proceedings, and thus is not likely to apply to persons seized in Afghanistan and held overseas. In addition, the Citizens Protection Act, 28 U.S.C. § 530B (Supp. IV 1998), commonly known as the McDade Act – which places restrictions on government attorneys' conduct with respect to interrogations – does not apply to Defense Department lawyers.

I. The Self-Incrimination Clause Provides a Trial Right

As the Supreme Court has explained, the Self-Incrimination Clause of the Fifth Amendment, on which the *Miranda* decision is premised, is a "trial right of criminal defendants." *United States v. Verdugo-Urquidez*, 494 U.S. 259, 264 (1990). The clause provides that "[n]o person . . . shall be compelled *in any criminal case* to be a witness against himself." U.S. Const. Amend. V (emphasis added). "The Amendment has its roots in the Framers' belief that a system of justice in which the focus is on the extraction of proof of guilt from the defendant himself is often an adjunct to tyranny and may lead to the conviction of innocent persons. Thus, a violation of the constitutional guarantee occurs when one is 'compelled' by governmental coercion to bear witness against oneself in the criminal process." *Duckworth v. Eagan*, 492 U.S. 195, 209 (1989) (O'Connor, J., concurring).

The protection of the Self-Incrimination Clause is not limited, however, to statements compelled during the course of a court proceeding. Rather, it extends to prior statements subsequently introduced into evidence at a court proceeding. Beginning with *Bram v. United States*, 168 U.S. 532 (1897), the Supreme Court has held that the Clause bars the introduction in federal cases of involuntary confessions made during certain forms of custodial interrogation. *See also Withrow v. Williams*, 507 U.S. 680, 688 (1993). In *Miranda*, the Court held that the privilege against self-incrimination prohibits the admission into evidence of statements given by a suspect to the police during custodial interrogation unless a prior warning has been given advising the defendant of his rights. *See* 384 U.S. 436 (1966); *see also Illinois v. Perkins*, 496 U.S. 292, 296 (1990); *Duckworth*, 492 U.S. at 201 (in *Miranda*, "the Court established certain procedural safeguards that require police to advise criminal suspects of their rights under the Fifth and Fourteenth Amendments before commencing custodial interrogation"). The Court in *Miranda* "presumed that interrogation in certain custodial circumstances is inherently coercive and . . . that statements made under those circumstances are inadmissible unless the suspect is specifically informed of his *Miranda* rights and freely decides to forego those rights." *New York v. Quarles*, 467 U.S. 649, 654 (1984) (footnote omitted). In the years since first announcing the *Miranda* presumption, the Supreme Court has "frequently reaffirmed the central principle established by that case: if the police take a suspect into custody and then ask him questions without informing him of the rights enumerated [in *Miranda*], his responses cannot be introduced into evidence to establish his guilt." *Berkemer v. McCarthy*, 468 U.S. 420, 429 (1984).

It bears repeating that the *Miranda* presumption is premised on the "*trial right* of criminal defendants" provided by the Self-Incrimination Clause. *Verdugo-Urquidez*, 494 U.S. at 264 (emphasis added). The "sole concern" of that Clause, the Supreme Court has explained, is "insur[ing] that the testimony cannot lead to the infliction of criminal penalties on the witness." *Kastigar v. United States*, 406 U.S. 441, 453 (1972). Thus, "[a]lthough conduct by law enforcement officials prior to trial may ultimately impair that right, a constitutional violation occurs *only at trial*." *Verdugo-Urquidez*, 494 U.S. at 264 (emphasis added).[1] Thus, neither the Self-Incrimination Clause nor *Miranda* established a free-floating code of conduct regulating the manner in which agents of the federal government may conduct interrogations in any and all circumstances. In other words, neither the Self-Incrimination Clause nor *Miranda* prohibits an unwarned custodial interrogation as a constitutional violation *in itself*. Accordingly, it confuses analysis somewhat to speak in terms of an FBI or military interrogator "violating" *Miranda* or the Fifth Amendment simply by conducting an unwarned custodial interrogation. Whether or not *Miranda* applies to a given circumstance or requires warnings can only be assessed in view of the use the government makes of statements obtained in the interrogation. If the government never uses the statement in a criminal prosecution where the Self-Incrimination Clause applies, no question of a *Miranda* "violation" can ever arise. *See Quarles*, 467 U.S. at 686 (Marshall, J., dissenting) ("[T]he police are free to interrogate suspects without advising them of

---

[1] *See also Deshawn E. by Charlotte E. v. Safir*, 156 F.3d 340, 346 (2d Cir. 1998) ("Even if it can be shown that a statement was obtained by coercion, there can be no Fifth Amendment violation until that statement is introduced against the defendant in a criminal proceeding."); *United States v. Yunis*, 859 F.2d 953, 970 (D.C. Cir. 1988) (Mikva, J., concurring specially) ("[T]he focus of the Fifth Amendment protection continues to be the *use* of compelled, self-incriminatory evidence against the defendant at trial.").

their constitutional rights.... All the Fifth Amendment forbids is the introduction of coerced statements at trial.").

In addition, in addressing the scope of proper application of the *Miranda* warnings, it is critical to bear in mind that the Supreme Court has made clear – both in *Miranda* and in subsequent decisions – that the purpose of the *Miranda* rule is to provide a rule of conduct for law enforcement officers to prevent practices that might lead to defendants making involuntary statements. As the Court put it in *Miranda*, its goal was to set out "concrete constitutional guidelines for law enforcement agencies and courts to follow." 384 U.S. at 442. The Court has not treated *Miranda* as establishing an immutable rule that *any* statement made in any unwarned, custodial interrogation is necessarily involuntary under the Fifth Amendment and cannot be admitted at trial. Rather, in circumstances where the purpose of regulating the conduct of law enforcement officers would not be served, or is outweighed by other considerations, the Court has consistently declined to require that the *Miranda* procedures be followed in order for a custodial statement to be deemed admissible. For example, in *New York v. Quarles*, the Court held that when the police arrest a suspect under circumstances presenting an imminent danger to the public safety, they may, without informing him of his *Miranda* rights, ask questions necessary to elicit information that would neutralize the threat. The Court concluded that in such circumstances, the need to ensure public safety outweighed any benefit that might be gained from the ordinary rule of requiring *Miranda* warnings. 467 U.S. at 657. Similarly, in *Harris v. New York*, 401 U.S. 222 (1971), the Court sanctioned the use of statements obtained without *Miranda* warnings for purposes of impeaching a defendant upon cross-examination. Again, the Court explained that the goal of shaping the conduct of law enforcement officers did not require extending *Miranda* to exclude the use of unwarned statements for purposes of cross examination: "Assuming that the exclusionary rule has a deterrent effect on proscribed police conduct, sufficient deterrence flows when the evidence in question is made unavailable to the prosecution in its case in chief." *Id.* at 225.

As explained in more detail below, moreover, the Court's decisions limiting *Miranda* to circumstances where the purposes of *Miranda*'s judicially crafted code of conduct would be served have not been undermined by the recent pronouncement that *Miranda* states a constitutional requirement. *See Dickerson v. United States*, 530 U.S. 428 (2000). The *Dickerson* Court did not suggest that *Miranda* warnings are an absolute prerequisite for any custodial statement to be voluntary under the Fifth Amendment and that any statement obtained without the warnings is necessarily inadmissible. Rather, *Dickerson* expressly endorsed past decisions such as *Quarles* and *Harris* that made exceptions to the requirements of *Miranda* warnings and explained that they simply "illustrate the principle ... that no constitutional rule is immutable." *Id.* at 441.

II. Trials by Military Commissions

The Self-Incrimination Clause does not apply to trials by military commissions for violations of the laws of war. The Clause is limited by its terms to "any criminal case," U.S. Const., Amend. V, and the Supreme Court has long understood the rights guaranteed by the amendment to be limited to the scope they had at common law in criminal prosecutions at the time of the founding. *See, e.g., Ex parte Quirin*, 317 U.S. 1, 39–40 (1942); *Ex parte Wilson*, 114 U.S. 417, 423 (1885) ("The Fifth Amendment, declaring in what cases a grand jury should be necessary, . . . in effect, affirm[ed] the rule of the common law upon the same subject."). In *Quirin*, the Court concluded that a trial by military commission for violations of the laws of war was not a criminal prosecution that required a grand jury indictment at common law and thus expressly held that the Fifth Amendment's requirement of indictment by grand jury does not apply to military commissions. *See Quirin*, 317 U.S. at 40. *See also Application of Yamashita*, 327 U.S. 1 (1946). Under the same reasoning, the Self-Incrimination Clause also does not constrain the evidence that military commissions may receive. Trials by military commissions are not "criminal case[s]" within the terms of the Amendment. Rather, they are entirely creatures of the President's authority as Commander-in-Chief under Article II and are part and parcel of the conduct of a military campaign.[2] As a result, they are not constrained by the strictures placed on "criminal case[s]" by the Self-Incrimination Clause (or other provisions in the Bill of Rights). As the *Quirin* Court stated broadly (albeit in *dicta*), "the Fifth and Sixth Amendments did not restrict whatever authority was conferred by the Constitution to try offenses against the law of war by military commission." 317 U.S. at 45. *Cf. Miller v. United Slates*, 78 U.S. (11 Wall.) 268, 305 (1870) ("the war powers of the government . . . are not affected by the restrictions imposed by the Fifth and Sixth Amendments").

Accordingly, incriminating statements may be admitted in proceedings before military commissions even if the interrogating officers do not abide by the requirements of *Miranda*. *Cf. United States v. Bin Laden*, 132 F. Supp. 2d 168, 181, 182 n.10 (S.D.N.Y. 2001) (distinguishing, for purposes of application of the Fifth Amendment, "proceeding[s]" against " 'subject[s] of a foreign state at war with the United States'" and "operated pursuant to a temporary military commission specially constituted under the authority of the Joint Chiefs of Staff" from criminal trials before Article III courts (quoting *Johnson v. Eisentrager*, 339 U.S. 763, 769 n.2 (1950)); *Id.* at 189 ("*Miranda* only prevents an unwarned or involuntary statement from being used as evidence in a domestic criminal trial").[3]

Moreover, with respect to trials of foreign nationals conducted outside U.S. territory, our conclusion is additionally supported by the well-established fact that the Fifth Amendment does not confer rights upon aliens outside the sovereign territory of the United States. *See Verdugo-Urquidez*, 494 U.S. at 269 ("we have rejected the claim that aliens are entitled to Fifth Amendment rights outside the sovereign territory of the United States"); *Johnson v. Eisentrager*, 339 U.S. 763, 783 (1950) (finding "no authority whatever for holding that the Fifth Amendment confers rights upon all persons, whatever their nationality, wherever they are located and whatever their offenses"); *cf. United States v. Curtiss-Wright Export Corp.*, 299 U.S. 304, 318 (1936) ("Neither the Constitution nor the laws passed in pursuance of it have any force in foreign territory

---

[2] *See* Memorandum for Alberto R. Gonzales, Counsel to the President, from Patrick F. Philbin, Deputy Assistant Attorney General, Office of Legal Counsel, *Re: Legality of the Use of Military Commissions to Try Terrorists* (Nov. 6, 2001).

[3] *Cf. also* Telford Taylor, *Final Report to the Secretary of the Army on the Nuernberg War Crimes Trials Under Control Council Law No. 10*, at 59 (William S. Hein & Co., Inc. 1997) (1949) (although "interrogations . . . were carried out in a thoroughly humane fashion, and no objectionable means were used to elicit information from those who were questioned," "[t]hey were not carried out in the manner of 'pretrial interrogations' as known to American courts, and it would never have occurred to the interrogators, for example, to warn the individual being questioned that anything he said 'might be used against him.' ").

unless in respect of our own citizens. . . . "). Accordingly, U.S. military tribunals convened abroad are not required to grant aliens rights under the Self-Incrimination Clause.

III. Criminal Trials Before Article III Courts

Although the Self-Incrimination Clause of the Fifth Amendment does not confer rights upon aliens *outside* the sovereign territory of the United States, no issue of extraterritoriality would be involved if aliens were brought *into* the United States for trial in an Article III court. As the Supreme Court has explained, "[t]he privilege against self-incrimination guaranteed by the Fifth Amendment is a fundamental trial right of criminal defendants." *Verdugo-Urquidez*, 494 U.S. at 264. Any violation of the right would occur at the trial conducted here in the United States when statements made by the accused were offered into evidence.

The Supreme Court has never squarely held that the Self-Incrimination Clause applies in the criminal trial of an alien whose only connections to the United States consist of an attack on the country followed by his arrest overseas and transportation to the United States to stand trial. The United States, moreover, has recently argued in at least one case that the Self-Incrimination Clause does not apply in such a trial. *See Bin Laden*, 132 F. Supp. 2d at 181 & n.8.[4]

As a matter of original interpretation of the Fifth Amendment, there may be sound reasons for concluding that the Self-Incrimination Clause does not apply to a trial of an alien whose only connections to this country consist of the commission of a federal crime (perhaps taking place entirely abroad) and involuntary transportation to this country to stand trial. The Clause states: "nor shall any person . . . be compelled in any criminal case to be a witness against himself." U.S. Const. Amend. V. In extending this right to "any person," the Framers may have intended to encompass only a limited class of "person[s]" who could claim the protections of the Constitution. Some support for this interpretation can be found in the analysis the Supreme Court has applied in holding that the Fifth Amendment does not apply extraterritorially. In *Johnson v. Eisentrager*, the Court made clear that the terms of the amendment cannot be read literally to confer rights on "any person" – a reading that would include aliens overseas who had no connection whatsoever to the United States. As Justice Kennedy summarized in *Verdugo-Urquidez*, "the Constitution does not create, nor do general principles of law create, any juridical relation between our country and some undefined, limitless class of noncitizens who are beyond our territory." 494 U.S. at 275 (Kennedy, J., concurring). In describing the limitations on the class of "person[s]" to whom the Fifth Amendment extends, the Court explained that the alien "has been accorded a generous and ascending scale of rights as he increases his identity with our

---

[4] It appears that in other cases involving similar fact patterns the United States has not contested the application of the Fifth and Sixth Amendments. *See, e.g., Yunis*, 859 F.2d at 957 ("The parties have stipulated that Yunis, despite his alien status, can claim the protection of the Fifth Amendment to the American Constitution for interrogation that occurred outside the territory of the United States."). *Cf. also United States v. Yousef*, 925 F. Supp. 1063 (S.D.N.Y. 1996) (denying motion to suppress statement made on airplane from Pakistan to United States, because defendant had validly waived *Miranda* rights); *United States v. Noriega*, 746 F. Supp. 1506, 1529–32 (S.D. Fla. 1990) (rejecting motion to dismiss indictment on grounds that American invasion of Panama violated Due Process Clause, because alleged violations of rights involved only third parties and not Noriega himself).

society." *Eisentrager*, 339 U.S. at 770. Arguably, an alien whose only connection with the United States is an attack upon the country (or its citizens) followed by his arrest overseas and transportation to the United States to stand trial has not established any sort of connection with the country that warrants allowing him the protections of the Fifth Amendment.

Nevertheless, whatever the merits of such an interpretation as an original matter, we understand that your inquiry concerns the likely treatment of the Self-Incrimination Clause given the current state of the Supreme Court's jurisprudence. Approaching the question on that basis, we believe that the Supreme Court's analysis in prior decisions points to the conclusion that the Self-Incrimination Clause would likely be applied in a criminal trial of an alien in the United States even if the alien had no previous connection to this country. That is because the Court's decisions generally reflect a view that any criminal prosecution within the territorial boundaries of the United States is constrained by the requirements of the Fifth Amendment. Even in *Eisentrager*, for example, the Court's analysis centered repeatedly on the absence of the aliens in question from the territorial jurisdiction of the United States. *See* 339 U.S. at 769–78; *Id.* at 771 ("[I]n extending constitutional protections beyond the citizenry, the Court has been at pains to point out that it was the *alien's presence within the territorial jurisdiction* that gave the Judiciary power to act.") (emphasis added).

More importantly, in *Wong Wing v. United States*, 163 U.S. 228 (1896), the Court long ago concluded that the Fifth Amendment rights to grand jury indictment and due process applied to aliens subject to criminal punishment within the United States, *see id.* at 238. The Court's textual analysis of the Amendment focused on its broad terms guaranteeing that no "person" should be subject to certain treatments and concluded that it should have broad application covering all persons. Thus, the Court first noted that the Fourteenth Amendment's Due Process and Equal Protection Clauses, like the Fifth Amendment, speak in terms of rights guaranteed to "any person." *See id.* The Court explained that "[t]hese provisions are universal in their application to all persons within the territorial jurisdiction, without regard to any differences of race, of color, or nationality." *Id.* It concluded that "[a]pplying this reasoning to the Fifth and Sixth Amendments, it must be concluded that all persons within the territory of the United States are entitled to the protection guaranteed by those amendments." *Id.*

On its face, the analysis in *Wong Wing* was not limited to aliens who had established particular connections with this country. To the contrary, the Court framed its reasoning in terms applicable to aliens who had established no ties to the country because they had never effected a lawful entry into the United States. It thus contrasted Congress's power to "forbid aliens or classes of aliens from" entering the country with its power to subject "such aliens to infamous punishment at hard labor," which could be done only through "a judicial trial to establish the guilt of the accused." *Id.* at 237. Similarly, in one of the decisions marking the most restrictive view of the extraterritorial application of the Constitution – denying its application even to citizens abroad – the Court has stated in *dicta* that the constitutional guarantees in the Fifth and Sixth Amendments"apply only to citizens and others within the United States, *or who are brought there for trial for alleged offenses committed elsewhere."Ross v. McIntyre*, 140 U.S. 453, 464 (1891) (emphasis added). Taking a similar territorial approach, the Court has held that the Fifth Amendment's Due Process Clause applies to aliens even if their "presence in this country is unlawful, involuntary, or transitory." *Matthews v. Diaz*, 426 U.S. 67, 77 (1976).[5]

To be sure, in *Verdugo-Urquidez* the Court stated that *Wong Wing* addressed "resident aliens" and thus the decision cannot avail "an alien who has had no previous significant voluntary connection with the United States." 494 U.S. at 271. *See also id.* ("These cases, however [including *Wong Wing*], establish only that aliens receive constitutional protections when they have come within the territory of the United States and developed substantial connections with this country."). Despite that characterization, however, as noted above the analysis in *Wong Wing* did not distinguish between resident aliens and other aliens, and in subsequent cases since *Verdugo-Urquidez* the Court has described the decision in broader terms – terms consistent with the view that the Self-Incrimination Clause would apply to criminal trials of any aliens in the United States. *See Zadvydas v. Davis*, 121 S. Ct. 2491, 2501 (*Wong Wing* held that "all persons within the territory of the United States are entitled to the protection" of the Fifth Amendment, noting that decisions limiting application of constitutional rights to aliens "rested upon a basic territorial distinction"); *see also id.* at 2506 (Scalia, J., joined by Thomas, J., dissenting) (suggesting that *Wong Wing* draws no distinction between "aliens arrested and detained at the border" before entry and those already within the country).

The analysis in *Verdugo-Urquidez* itself, moreover, on balance tends to suggest that the present Court would be inclined to reach the same conclusion. *Verdugo-Urquidez* involved the application of the Fourth Amendment to searches and seizures conducted by U.S. law enforcement personnel on an alien's property outside the United States. In approaching that issue, the Court framed its entire analysis by first distinguishing the Fifth Amendment and explaining that the Fourth Amendment "operates in a different manner than the Fifth Amendment, which is not at issue in this case." 494 U.S. at 264. The Fifth Amendment, the Court emphasized, provides a "fundamental trial right," rather than directly regulating the conduct of police prior to trial. *Id.* In addition, the Court based its analysis largely on the particular terms of the Fourth Amendment, which limit the right it describes to "the people." *Id.* The Court emphasized that this limitation "contrasts with the words 'person' and 'accused' used in the Fifth and Sixth Amendments regulating procedure in criminal cases," thus suggesting that the procedure in criminal cases (within the United States) would be the same for all persons. *Id.* at 265–66. *See also id.* at 265 (the Fourth Amendment *"by contrast with the Fifth and Sixth Amendments*, extends its reach only to 'the people'") (emphasis added); *id.* at 269 (noting that the Fifth Amendment "speaks in the relatively universal term of 'person'"). Justice Kennedy, moreover, who provided the fifth vote for the majority, also wrote separately and noted that, where the "United States is prosecuting a foreign national in a court established under Article III, . . . all of the trial proceedings are governed

---

[5] It bears mention that in the immigration context the Court has developed a doctrine known as the "entry fiction" under which an alien who is detained at the border, even though physically present within the boundaries of the United States, is deemed legally not to have entered the United States. As a result, the alien does not possess constitutional protections that would attach upon entry. *See. e.g., Shaughnessy v. United States ex rel. Mezei*, 345 U.S. 206 (1953). It might be argued that an alien whose only presence in the country consists of his transportation here for trial similarly should be treated legally as lacking any presence sufficient to confer rights. Given the analysis outlined in text, we cannot predict that such an argument is likely to prevail. The one circuit court that has addressed the issue has rejected such an approach. *See United States v. Henry*, 604 F.2d 908, 914 (5th Cir. 1979).

by the Constitution." *Id.* at 278 (Kennedy, J., concurring). Given the Court's explicit acknowledgment of the textual differences between the Fourth Amendment and the Fifth Amendment, we think that *Verdugo-Urquidez* does not provide strong support for the claim that the Fifth Amendment does not apply to the trial in the United States of an alien who has no previous connections with this country.

Finally, it bears noting that the Court has consistently described the Self-Incrimination Clause as a fundamental trial right that is critical for protecting the integrity of the trial process. At times the Court has suggested that the Clause plays a critical role in ensuring the reliability of confessions and thus protects the truth-finding function of a trial. *See, e.g., Application of Gault*, 387 U.S. 1, 47 (1967) ("The privilege against self-incrimination is, of course, related to the question of the safeguards necessary to assure that admissions or confessions are reasonably trustworthy, that they are not the mere fruits of fear or coercion, but are reliable expressions of the truth."); *Molloy v. Hogan*, 378 U.S. 1, 7–8 (1964) ("[T]he American system of criminal prosecution is accusatorial, not inquisitorial, and . . . the Fifth Amendment privilege is its essential mainstay. Governments, state and federal, are thus constitutionally compelled to establish guilt by evidence independently and freely secured, and may not by coercion prove a charge against an accused out of his own mouth.") (citation omitted). At other points the Court has stressed that the privilege is critical "to preserving the integrity of a judicial system in which even the guilty are not to be convicted unless the prosecution 'shoulder the entire load.'" *Tehan v. United States ex rel. Shott*, 382 U.S. 406, 415 (1966); *see also id.* at 416 ("[T]he Fifth Amendment's privilege against self-incrimination is not an adjunct to the ascertainment of truth."). Under either rationale, the protection provided by the Clause is treated as critical for the integrity of the trial process itself. It thus seems likely that the Court would conclude that it applies in any criminal case, regardless of the status of the defendant as an alien.

Lower courts that have addressed the issue (albeit only in *dicta* in some cases), have concluded that the Self-Incrimination Clause does apply to trials of aliens, even if they have not established any connection with this country.[6]

The conclusion that the Self-Incrimination Clause will likely apply in any future trial, however, does not in itself answer the question how the decision in *Miranda* will apply. Under *Miranda*, evidence developed from custodial interrogation is not inflexibly presumed to be compelled, and thereby rendered inadmissible, simply because interrogators have neglected to provide the warnings outlined in *Miranda*. Not all custodial interrogation is subject to *Miranda*'s requirements. We address below four kinds of statements that the United States might wish to admit into evidence in an Article III trial: (1) statements arising out of interrogations intended to develop military operations and intelligence information; (2) statements obtained for criminal law enforcement purposes, whether by FBI interrogators or military personnel; (3) statements obtained in the course of a war crimes investigation by members of the criminal investigative services of one of the U.S. Armed Forces; and (4) statements

---

[6] *See United States v. Henry*, 604 F.2d 908, 914 (5th Cir. 1979) (stating in *dicta* that "an alien who is within the territorial jurisdiction of this country, whether it be at the border or in the interior . . . is entitled to those protections guaranteed by the Fifth Amendment in criminal proceedings which would include the *Miranda* warning") (citation omitted); *Jean v. Nelson*, 727 F.2d 957, 972–73 & n.22 (11th Cir. 1984) (*dicta*); *Bin Laden*, 132 F. Supp. 2d at 183 ("Fifth Amendment . . . protections seemingly apply with equal vigor to all defendants facing criminal prosecution at the hands of the United States, and without apparent regard to citizenship or community connection").

obtained in an interrogation that may have mixed objectives and does not fall purely into only one of the previous categories. We conclude that the first category of evidence is likely to be admissible in an Article III trial even if *Miranda* warnings are not given. The second category of evidence is likely to be inadmissible unless the interrogators comply with *Miranda*. There is a substantial risk that courts will apply *Miranda* to the third category as well. Finally, for interrogations in the fourth category, results will likely turn on a highly fact-dependent inquiry.

A. *Questioning by military and intelligence personnel for military operations and intelligence information*

We conclude that statements obtained in the course of interrogation by military and intelligence personnel for purposes of gathering intelligence and military operations information need not satisfy *Miranda* standards in order to be admitted at an Article III criminal trial. Our conclusion is based on two separate, independent grounds. First, although *Miranda* establishes a presumption that statements made during unwarned custodial interrogation are involuntary, and thus inadmissible at trial under the Self-Incrimination Clause, *Miranda* and its progeny make clear that this presumption of involuntariness is not immutable or universally applicable. In particular, the Court has treated *Miranda* as a rule designed to guide the conduct of officials in law enforcement agencies and has repeatedly limited the reach of *Miranda's* warning requirements based on the need for regulating the conduct of law enforcement officers. The fundamental objective of regulating that conduct has no application whatsoever in the context of interrogations of battlefield detainees for purposes of obtaining intelligence and military operations information. Under the reasoning that the Supreme Court has used to define the limits of *Miranda*, we conclude that interrogators engaged in such questioning need not give *Miranda* warnings to ensure that voluntary statements will be admissible in a later criminal trial. Second, we conclude that the established public-safety exception to *Miranda* should extend by analogy to interrogations of battlefield detainees for purposes of gathering intelligence and military operations information.

1. Miranda's *deterrence rationale does not apply*

As previously explained, the Supreme Court crafted the requirements of *Miranda* as a means for implementing the protections of the Self-Incrimination Clause. In *Miranda*, the Court held that, because the environment in a custodial police interrogation "contains inherently compelling pressures which work to undermine the individual's will to resist and to compel him to speak where he would not otherwise do so freely," 384 U.S. at 467, confessions made during the course of such custodial interrogation are presumptively involuntary and, unless certain warnings are given to defuse the coerciveness of the environment, must be excluded at trial under the Self-Incrimination Clause. *See generally Dickerson v. United States*, 530 U.S. 428 (2000). If *Miranda* stated an immutable presumption concerning the voluntariness of custodial statements, it might well mean that in *any* custodial interrogation – even an interrogation of a battlefield detainee undertaken to obtain information for military operations – *Miranda* warnings would have to be given for any statements to be admissible at a later trial. Interrogation in the custody of the armed forces after capture on the battlefield might be considered at least as inherently coercive a scenario as questioning in custody at a police station. And if *Miranda* provided an absolute rule concerning the voluntariness of statements in such a custodial interrogation, it might be read to mean that statements obtained in a military interrogation could not be used in a subsequent criminal trial if the requisite warnings had not been given.

The Supreme Court, however, has never taken such an approach to *Miranda*. To the contrary, the Court has emphasized that the presumption crafted in *Miranda* and the warnings outlined there were intended to establish guidelines for the conduct of law enforcement officers pursuing criminal investigations. Although the purpose of the guidelines was to ensure the voluntariness of any statements obtained from custodial interrogations, the standards of conduct were not intended to set down an inflexible rule for evaluating voluntariness under the Fifth Amendment. The focus of *Miranda*, in other words, is not establishing a universally applicable (and constitutionally mandated) standard for measuring the voluntariness of statements made in any custodial situation. Rather, it is designed to provide rules of conduct specifically for the guidance of U.S. law enforcement officials – or, as the Court put it, "concrete constitutional guidelines for law enforcement agencies and courts to follow." *Miranda*, 384 U.S. at 442.[7] *See also Dickerson*, 530 U.S. at 434–35 (quoting same language from *Miranda*). Thus, the Supreme Court has repeatedly emphasized that the requirements of *Miranda* are designed to regulate the conduct of custodial interrogations arising out of criminal law enforcement investigations. The *Miranda* Court focused its concern on "police" interrogation and practices, and in later cases the Court has emphasized that the rationale behind *Miranda* is providing a "deterrent effect on proscribed police conduct." *Harris*, 401 U.S. at 225. Similarly, in *Thompson v. Keohane*, 516 U.S. 99 (1995), the Court described *Miranda* in terms of the requirements it imposed on "law enforcement officers." *Id.* at 107. *See also Quarles*, 467 U.S. at 656 ("The *Miranda* decision was based in large part on this Court's view that the warnings which it required police to give to suspects in custody would reduce the likelihood that the suspects would fall victim to constitutionally impermissible practices of police interrogation. . . ."); *Rhode Island v. Innis*, 446 U.S. 291, 301 (1980) ("the *Miranda* safeguards were designed to vest a suspect in custody with an added measure of protection against coercive police practices"); *Fare v. Michael C.*, 442 U.S. 707, 718 (1979) ("*Miranda*'s holding has the virtue of informing police and prosecutors with specificity as to what they may do in conducting custodial interrogation. . . ."). When the Court has applied *Miranda* to interrogation by government officials other than law enforcement agents, it has done so based upon some finding of a nexus between the interrogation in question and criminal law enforcement. *See, e.g., Mathis v. United States*, 391 U.S. 1, 4 (1968) (applying *Miranda* to interview conducted by Internal Revenue Service agents with person in state custody largely upon basis that "tax investigations frequently lead to criminal prosecutions"); *Estelle v. Smith*, 451 U.S. 454, 466–69 (1981) (applying *Miranda* to court-ordered psychiatric examinations of criminal defendants); *United States v. Mata-Abundiz*, 717 F.2d 1277, 1279–80 (9th Cir. 1983) (applying *Miranda* to INS questioning of criminal suspect); *United States v. Gupta*, 183 F.3d 615, 617–18 (7th Cir. 1999) ("*Miranda* . . is a mismatch for the immigration process, at least at the

---

[7] To the extent the Court has referred to *Miranda* as providing "concrete constitutional guidelines" for *courts* to follow, it seems clear that what is meant is guidelines for courts to follow in their role of deterring improper conduct by law enforcement through exclusion of evidence.

outset.... Much more difficult is the question when ... the criminal investigation is far enough advanced [to trigger *Miranda*].”); *see also* 2 Wayne R. LaFave et al., Criminal Procedure § 6.10(c), at 622 (2d ed. 1999) (“[T]he courts have generally held that government agents not primarily charged with enforcement of the criminal law are under no obligation to comply with *Miranda*.”).

Where the rationale of shaping the conduct of law enforcement officers does not apply or is outweighed by other considerations, the Court has consistently concluded that *Miranda*’s requirements do not apply and that statements obtained during custodial interrogation without *Miranda* warnings may still be introduced into evidence consistent with the Fifth Amendment’s prohibition on compelled testimony. Thus, in *New York v. Quarles*, the Court concluded that where police need to obtain information critical for ensuring public safety, they need not provide *Miranda* warnings before initiating custodial questioning. 467 U.S. at 657–58. And in *Harris v. New York*, the Court concluded that *Miranda*’s purpose of providing a deterrent to regulate police conduct would be served sufficiently if un-*Mirandized* statements were excluded solely from the prosecution’s case in chief, but were permitted for impeachment purposes on cross-examination. *See Harris*, 401 U.S. at 225 (“Assuming that the exclusionary rule has a deterrent effect on proscribed police conduct, sufficient deterrence flows when the evidence in question is made unavailable to the prosecution in its case in chief.”). As the *Harris* Court explained, the benefits in terms of guiding conduct that would be derived from precluding the use of an unwarned statement upon cross-examination were too speculative and attenuated to outweigh the clear benefits that admitting the statements would provide in aiding “the jury in assessing [the defendant’s] credibility.” *Id*. The Court has thus demonstrated that the deterrent rationale behind *Miranda* limits the range of situations in which the case will be applied.

Similarly, drawing on the Supreme Court’s analysis in *Miranda* and its progeny, lower courts have identified other situations where *Miranda*’s goal of shaping police conduct has no application and where *Miranda*’s warning requirements therefore do not apply. For example, federal courts have repeatedly admitted unwarned custodial statements obtained by foreign police officers.[8,9] If *Miranda* provided an immutable

---

[8] *See, e.g., United States v. Nagelberg*, 434 F.2d 585, 587 n. 1 (2nd Cir. 1970) (“The *Miranda* rule has no application ... where the arrest and interrogation were by Canadian officers interested in Canadian narcotic and immigration offenses under their investigation. There is no showing that the statement was coerced or taken in violation of the laws of Canada. There is no claim of ‘rubbing pepper in the eyes,’ or other shocking conduct. The presence of an American officer should not destroy the usefulness of evidence legally obtained on the ground that methods of interrogation of another country, at least equally civilized, may vary from ours.”); *United States v. Chavarria*, 443 F.2d 904, 905 (9th Cir. 1971) (“so long as the trustworthiness of the confession satisfies legal standards, the fact that the defendant was not given *Miranda* warnings before questioning by foreign police will not, by itself, render his confession inadmissible”); *United States v. Heller*, 625 F.2d 594, 599 (5th Cir. 1980) (“statements obtained by foreign officers conducting interrogations in their own nations have been held admissible despite a failure to give *Miranda* warnings to the accused,” at least where the conduct does not “shock[] the conscience of the American court,” American officials did not “participate[] in the foreign search or interrogation,” and the foreign agents were not “acting as agents for their American counterparts”); *United States v. Covington*, 783 F.2d 1052, 1056 (9th Cir. 1985) (“the exclusionary rule is not applicable to interrogations performed by foreign police officers acting in their own country”); *United States v. Khan*, 993 F.2d 1368, 1376 n.7 (9th Cir. 1993) (“Statements given to police officers of a foreign country are not excludable because *Miranda* warnings are not given.”) (citation omitted).

[9] *See Neely v. Henkel*, 180 U.S. 109, 122–23 (1901) (“[T]he provisions of the Federal Constitution relating to the writ of habeas corpus, bills of attainder, ex post facto laws, trial by jury for crimes,

rule that an unwarned statement made in custodial interrogation is necessarily involuntary, such statements would be absolutely barred from use at trial under the Self-Incrimination Clause, regardless of whether they were obtained by foreign police or anyone else. Such statements are admitted into evidence, however, because the rationale behind *Miranda* – shaping police conduct – does not apply to foreign police. Foreign police, of course, are not subject to the requirements of the federal Constitution, and there is thus no basis for attempting to force them to comply with *Miranda*'s guidelines. Moreover, excluding statements obtained by foreign police without *Miranda* warnings would have no *practical* deterrent effect, because ensuring admissibility of evidence in U.S. courts is not a relevant incentive for police in another nation. As one court of appeals has explained,

> the United States Constitution cannot compel such specific, affirmative action by foreign sovereigns, so the policy of deterring so-called 'third degree' police tactics, which underlies the Miranda exclusionary rule, is inapposite to this case. Here the statements were not coerced, as revealed by testimony at the original trial which we have scrutinized. The evidence was therefore admissible.

Kilday v. United States, 481 F.2d 655 (5th Cir. 1973) (citations omitted).[10]

The Supreme Court's recent declaration that *Miranda* is a "constitutional decision," *Dickerson*, 530 U.S. at 438, does not alter the above analysis. It might be argued that after *Dickerson*, *Miranda* must be understood as a "constitutional rule" establishing a fixed test for determining whether statements are "compelled" for purposes of the Fifth Amendment. *Cf. id.* at 455–56 (Scalia, J., dissenting) (suggesting that this must be the implication of the Court's decision). That gloss on *Dickerson* might be used to cast doubt on the exceptions to *Miranda* noted above based on the theory that the exceptions are rooted in the mistaken idea that *Miranda* sets a prophylactic rule that is not constitutionally required. In *Quarles*, for example, the Court based its analysis in part on the statement that "[t]he prophylactic *Miranda* warnings therefore are 'not themselves rights protected by the Constitution but [are] instead measures to insure that the right against compulsory self-incrimination [is] protected.'" 467 U.S. at 654.[11]

and generally to the fundamental guaranties of life, liberty, and property embodied in that instrument . . . have no relation to crimes committed without the jurisdiction of the United States against the laws of a foreign country. . . . When an American citizen commits a crime in a foreign country he cannot complain if required to submit to such modes of trial and to such punishment as the laws of that country may prescribe for its own people.").

[10] Another court of appeals has similarly concluded that, "[w]hen the interrogation is by the authorities of a foreign jurisdiction, the exclusionary rule has little or no effect upon the conduct of foreign police." *Chavarria*, 443 F.2d at 905. Put simply, "applying the *Miranda* rule to foreign police officers will not affect their conduct, and therefore we decline to so extend the scope of that decision." *Commonwealth v. Wallace*, 248 N.E.2d 246, 248 (Mass. 1969). *See also United States v. Welch*, 455 F.2d 211, 212 (2d Cir. 1972) ("[S]ince the *Miranda* requirements were primarily designed to prevent United States police officers from relying upon improper interrogation techniques and as the requirements have little, if any, deterrent effect upon foreign police officers, the *Miranda* warnings should not serve as the *sine qua non* of admissibility."); *Yousef*, 925 F. Supp. at 1076 ("[T]he purpose of the rule that any statement taken in violation of *Miranda* is inadmissible is to prevent and deter United States law enforcement personnel from taking involuntary statements that are the result of unduly coercive custodial circumstances.").

[11] Similarly, at least some courts tied the exception for foreign police interrogations to the concept that *Miranda* is a "prophylactic" rule. One court, for example, explained that, because "[w]e have generally held that *prophylactic constitutional rules* designed to deter police misconduct do not apply to foreign police behavior," the "*Miranda* rules [have been held] inapplicable to Mexican police interrogations,"

Now that the Court has made clear that *Miranda* is a constitutional requirement in its own right, the argument would go, practical considerations such as deterrence cannot limit the application of *Miranda*'s rules.

That approach, however, distorts *Dickerson*. In establishing *Miranda* as a constitutional rule, *Dickerson* merely held that the body of law established by *Miranda* and its progeny set constitutional requirements determined by the Court that could not be disturbed by an act of Congress.[12] Nowhere did the *Dickerson* Court suggest that it was radically reforming the rationale behind *Miranda* and later cases to make *Miranda* an inflexible constitutional determination that *all* unwarned custodial statements are necessarily "compelled" testimony under the Fifth Amendment. Instead, the Court treated *Miranda*, as the language from the original decision itself suggests, as "constitutional guidelines for law enforcement agencies" crafted by the Court. 384 U.S. at 442. Because they were defined by the Court as constitutional requirements, Congress could not modify them, but in the Court's view, that did not mean that *courts* could not define limits on *Miranda* based on the same balancing of interests outlined in the cases above (and employed by courts in other constitutional contexts). In keeping with that understanding, the Court never cast doubt on the various limitations and exceptions to *Miranda* already embedded in the Court's jurisprudence. To the contrary, *Dickerson* explicitly embraced the Court's existing decisions. Addressing the decisions in *Quarles* and *Harris* specifically, the Court stated that they "illustrate the principle – not that *Miranda* is not a constitutional rule – but that no constitutional rule is immutable." 530 U.S. at 441. The Court concluded that "the sort of modifications represented by these cases are *as much a normal part of constitutional law* as the original decision," *id.* (emphasis added), and held that *Miranda "and its progeny in this Court"* continue to "govern the admissibility of statements made during custodial interrogation in both state and federal courts" *id.* at 432 (emphasis added). Thus, as one court of appeals has observed, "the *Dickerson* majority expressly incorporated existing decisions, like *Quarles*, into the 'constitutional' right to a *Miranda* warning it elucidated in *Dickerson*." *United States v. Talley*, 275 F.3d 560, 564–65 (6th Cir. 2001).

There is certainly nothing in *Dickerson* that expands *Miranda* to require warnings in all forms of custodial interrogation. In fact, the *Dickerson* Court repeatedly recognized that the core function of *Miranda* was to address "the advent of modern custodial *police* interrogation," which "brought with it an increased concern about confessions obtained by coercion." 530 U.S. at 434–35 (emphasis added). *See also id.* at 443 ("*Miranda* has become embedded in *routine police practice*") (emphasis added); *id.* (discussing the "impact of the *Miranda* rule on *legitimate law enforcement*") (emphasis added). Nowhere in the opinion did the Court indicate any inclination to depart from past practice and unhinge the scope of *Miranda* from the rationale of regulating U.S. law enforcement officers that has guided the Court in the past.

---

just as the "Fourth Amendment exclusionary rule does not apply to illegal searches conducted by Mexican authorities acting without substantial involvement by American officials." *United States v. Wolf*, 813 F.2d 970, 972 n.3 (9th Cir. 1987) (citations omitted, emphasis added).

[12] Two years after *Miranda* was decided, Congress enacted a provision now codified at 18 U.S.C. § 3501 (1994). By purporting to eliminate the warnings requirements of *Miranda* and restore voluntariness as the "touchstone of admissibility," section 3501 was intended to override *Miranda*. *Dickerson*, 530 U.S. at 436. *Dickerson* held that Congress could not override *Miranda*. *See id.* at 432 ("We hold that *Miranda*, being a constitutional decision of this Court, may not be in effect overruled by an Act of Congress[.]").

The same logic that has underpinned the exceptions to *Miranda* outlined above demonstrates that *Miranda* warnings have no application in interrogations conducted by military and intelligence officers for purposes of gathering intelligence and military operations information from a battlefield detainee. Nothing in the Court's explanation of *Miranda* and its progeny applies to, or even addresses, the interrogation of enemy prisoners in a military theater of operations for the purpose of obtaining military and intelligence information. Applying *Miranda*'s requirements in this context would do nothing to advance the goal that the Supreme Court has repeatedly treated as a guiding factor in determining the scope of *Miranda* – namely, regulating the conduct of law enforcement officials in criminal investigations. Indeed, where an interrogation is conducted for obtaining military operations and intelligence information, *Miranda*'s concerns for regulating questioning in the law enforcement context are irrelevant. The goal in such a scenario is not to carefully balance the rights of a criminal defendant under our constitutional system against the needs of law enforcement, but rather to ensure that our troops and intelligence officers can extract as much useful information as possible for protecting our troops and securing our military objectives. The Court's stated concerns for providing "constitutional guidelines for law enforcement agencies and courts," in other words, are a mismatch for this context. *Miranda*, 384 U.S. at 442.

The conclusion that the purposes of *Miranda* would not be served by applying the decision to interrogations conducted for military operations and intelligence information is bolstered by the fact that restrictions imposed by the Fourth, Fifth, and Sixth Amendments generally do not apply to the actions of our armed forces in an armed conflict. This Office recently opined that the Fourth Amendment does not apply to United States military actions, both within the United States and abroad, taken to combat terrorists in the wake of the September 11 attacks. *See* Memorandum for Alberto R. Gonzales, Counsel to the President & William J. Haynes, II, General Counsel, Department of Defense, from John C. Yoo, Deputy Assistant Attorney General & Robert J. Delahunty, Special Counsel, Office of Legal Counsel, *Re: Authority for Use of Military Force To Combat Terrorist Activities Within the United States* at 22–34 (Oct. 23, 2001). As we explained, in reversing a lower court decision to apply the Fourth Amendment extraterritorially to non-U.S. citizens, the Supreme Court pointed out the untenable consequences of applying the Fourth Amendment to United States military operations abroad. *See Verdugo-Urquidez*, 494 U.S. at 273–74. Such a rule would result in applying the Fourth Amendment "also to other foreign policy operations which might result in 'searches or seizures'" – a result that "would have significant and deleterious consequences for the United States in conducting activities beyond its boundaries." *Id.* at 273. The Court explained:

> The United States frequently employs Armed Forces outside this country – over 200 times in our history – for the protection of American citizens or national security. . . . Application of the Fourth Amendment to those circumstances could significantly disrupt the ability of the political branches to respond to foreign situations involving our national interest . . . [and] plunge [the political branches] into a sea of uncertainty as to what might be reasonable in the way of searches and seizures conducted abroad.

Id. at 273–74 (citations omitted). The Court further noted that in 1798 during the Quasi War with France, Congress authorized President Adams to order the seizure of French vessels on the high seas, and "it was never suggested that the Fourth Amendment restrained the authority of Congress or of United States agents to conduct operations such as this." *Id.* at 268. Thus, within the first decade after the Constitution's ratification, the Fourth Amendment was understood not to restrict military operations against the Nation's enemies.

Likewise, the Just Compensation Clause of the Fifth Amendment does not attach to actions taken as a matter of military necessity by United States Armed Forces in the field, even when those actions entail the destruction of property owned by United States citizens (and, indeed, even when the destruction occurs within the territory of the United States). The general rule is that "the government cannot be charged for injuries to, or destruction of, private property caused by military operations of armies in the field." *United States v. Pacific R.R.*, 120 U.S. 227, 239 (1887).

We believe that, as in the above cases, "significant and deleterious consequences," *Verdugo-Urquidez*, 494 U.S. at 273, would result from applying *Miranda* to the interrogation of a prisoner who was apparently a member of a transnational terrorist group, who was captured while engaged in military operations against the United States and its allies, and who was being questioned for the purpose of gathering intelligence of military value to the United States in the conflict. Interrogation of enemy prisoners is a practical necessity for waging war effectively. Prisoners are always interrogated for information concerning their unit, enemy troop positions and strength, and other information that may be relevant to military operations in the area, to force protection, and (particularly in this conflict) to broader national security and intelligence objectives. Such interrogation serves the specifically military and intelligence objectives of the armed forces in the field of combat and the interests of national security. It is not, and is not intended to be, a part of the law enforcement apparatus of the United States. Subjecting the conduct of all such interrogations to the standards outlined in *Miranda* based on the possibility that some statements from an interrogation might later be used in a criminal trial would make no sense.

To be sure, there is a distinction between applying the Fourth Amendment and other constitutional constraints to the conduct of military operations and "applying" *Miranda* to military interrogations. The Fourth Amendment, if applicable, would impose mandatory requirements on the conduct of the armed forces in the field. It would directly regulate the ways in which operations could be conducted and failures to comply would, in themselves, be violations of the Constitution, If *Miranda* applied, however, an unwarned custodial interrogation would not *in itself*, constitute any constitutional violation.[13] Thus, in one sense, "applying" *Miranda* would not *prohibit* the government from conducting interrogations as it chooses; rather, it would simply put the government to the choice of following *Miranda* or foregoing the use of any statements in later criminal trials.

But that distinction does not make a difference for the analysis here. The entire purpose behind *Miranda* as a constitutional rule is to put constraints on conduct. Where the rationale for developing those constraints does not apply, the correct result

---

[13] *See, e.g., Calif. Attorneys for Criminal Justice v. Butts*, 195 F.3d 1039, 1046–47 (9th Cir. 2000) ("a bare violation of *Miranda* is not enough to sustain a claim under § 1983," although "a failure to comply with *Miranda* can be viewed as an aggravation of other coercive tactics"); *Cooper v. Dupnik*, 963 F.2d 1220, 1243–44 (9th Cir. 1992) ("Our holding . . . does not create a Fifth Amendment cause of action under § 1983 for conduct that merely violates *Miranda* safeguards without also trespassing on the actual Constitutional right against self-incrimination that those safeguards are designed to protect.").

under *Miranda* and its progeny is that *Miranda* itself does not apply. And for many of the same reasons that it makes no sense to have the Fourth Amendment constrain the conduct of military operations, it also makes no sense to have the constitutionally based rules for interrogations in *Miranda* apply.

2. Statements obtained during interrogations undertaken to obtain military or intelligence information should be admissible under the public safety exception

Even if the broader rationale for rejecting the application of *Miranda* outlined above were not accepted, we believe that statements obtained in the course of interrogation for purposes of gathering intelligence and military operations information would be admissible at trial in an Article III court under an exception to *Miranda* closely analogous to, and based upon the same rationale as, the "'public safety' exception" announced by the Supreme Court in *New York v. Quarles*, 467 U.S. 649 (1984).

In *Quarles*, the police had chased a rape suspect – who was reportedly armed – into a supermarket, where they arrested him, frisked him, and discovered an empty shoulder holster. A police officer asked the suspect, "Where is the gun?" *Id.* at 674. The suspect, gesturing toward a stack of soap cartons, replied, "The gun is over there." *Id.* The Court held that "on these facts there is a 'public safety' exception to the requirement that *Miranda* warnings be given before a suspect's answers may be admitted into evidence, and that the availability of that exception does not depend upon the motivation of the individual officers involved." *Id.* at 655–56. The Court explained that in such a situation, the "need for answers to questions in a situation posing a threat to the public safety outweighs the need" for the "[p]rocedural safeguards" imposed by *Miranda*. *Id.* at 657. As the Court made clear in *Quarles*, the exception applies to "questions necessary to secure [police officers'] own safety or the safety of the public." *Id.* at 659. *See, e.g., United States v. DeSantis*, 870 F.2d 536, 539 (9th Cir. 1989) ("The 'public safety' exception . . . was intended to protect the police, as well as the public, from danger."); *United States v. Mobley*, 40 F.3d 688, 693 (4th Cir. 1994) (*Quarles* applies to "such circumstances posing an objective danger to the public or police"); *United States v. Khalil*, 214 F.3d 111,121 (2d Cir. 2000) (*Quarles* applies to statements about construction and stability of bombs seized during raid on defendant's apartment the night before).

We conclude that, where the interrogation of an enemy combatant captured in an area of military operations is at issue, the same reasoning applied in *Quarles* should apply to provide an exception from *Miranda* for questioning directed at eliciting information relevant to military operations and intelligence. If the police are permitted to bypass *Miranda* warnings in order to "secure their own safety or the safety of the public," 467 U.S. at 659, surely the exigencies of combat justify a similar exception for the interrogations contemplated here. As we understand it, interrogation of prisoners seized in battle is undertaken as a matter of course to determine information such as what units of the enemy forces are operating in the area, their position, strength, supply status, etc., as well as information of broader use for intelligence concerning enemy plans and capabilities for launching strikes against U.S. positions. In the context of an armed conflict, it seems readily apparent that *all* such information relates directly to the safety and protection of American troops, who are constantly exposed to the dangers of combat. In addition, in this conflict, given the demonstrated ability of the enemy to attack military and civilian targets around the globe, including within the United States (and given the repeated vows to continue such attacks), interrogations for intelligence and national security purposes may additionally develop information critical for thwarting further imminent loss of American lives far from the immediate scene of battle in Afghanistan. Thus, as in *Quarles*, the lives and safety of both the questioners and others will be directly at stake.

B. *Interrogations for criminal law enforcement purposes*

By contrast, we believe that statements obtained through interrogations conducted abroad for criminal law enforcement purposes – whether by FBI interrogators or military personnel – are unlikely to be admitted in an Article III criminal trial if *Miranda* requirements are not met.[14]

As outlined above, we believe that the Supreme Court would almost certainly conclude that the Self-Incrimination Clause applies to trials in Article III courts of aliens, even where an alien's only connection to this country is that he has been brought here to be tried. That in itself, however, does not automatically dictate that law enforcement officers interrogating aliens abroad to prepare for such prosecutions must be bound by the *Miranda* regime. There are sound arguments that the *Miranda* system of warnings, while a useful system for controlling the conduct of law enforcement officials operating in the United States, imposes an unwieldy burden in the vastly varying situations law enforcement officers must face while operating abroad. As some courts have noted, for example, when a suspect is in the custody of a foreign police force, some of the *Miranda* rights that are normally described to a suspect may not actually be available because they conflict with the law and procedures of the nation that has custody of the suspect. *See, e.g., Bin Laden*, 132 F. Supp. 2d at 188 ("foreign law may . . . ban all manner of defense counsel from even entering the foreign stationhouse, and such law necessarily trumps American procedure"); *United States v. Dopf*, 434 F.2d 205, 207(5th Cir. 1970) (*Miranda* satisfied where FBI agent told defendants held by Mexican officials that, because he had no jurisdiction in Mexico, "he could not furnish them with a lawyer in Mexico but [that he could] contact the American Consul on their behalf"). Even where, as here, the suspects are held by the United States government abroad, other factors may make the burdens of *Miranda* outweigh any benefits that *Miranda* may provide in deterring misconduct in run-of-the-mill prosecutions. In particular, it seems likely that when a battlefield detainee is being interrogated for military and intelligence information – a process that may extend over many days or weeks – the provision of *Miranda* warnings by *other* U.S. personnel who may wish to question the same detainee during the same time period for purposes of building a criminal case will make the detainee less likely to provide information vital to the objectives of military and intelligence questioning. In such a scenario, there is a sound argument that the disadvantages that will result from providing *Miranda* warnings (in terms of

---

[14] Whether an interrogation is conducted for criminal law enforcement purposes should not be evaluated based on the subjective motivations of the interrogators. Rather, it should be determined objectively based on the nature of the questions. If the questions are directed at eliciting information that is designed to build a case for a criminal prosecution, we believe that most courts would conclude that *Miranda*'s warning requirements apply.

lost information of military and intelligence value) outweigh any benefits to be gained from applying *Miranda* as a device for regulating police conduct.

It is difficult to predict with any accuracy how the Court would receive such arguments concerning why *Miranda* should not be extended here. Nevertheless, we believe that the weight of authority suggests that courts would require *Miranda* warnings in interrogations conducted by U.S. personnel abroad for law enforcement purposes. Several courts of appeal have already held that when U.S. law enforcement officers interrogate a suspect abroad or direct the questioning carried out by foreign police who are acting essentially as their agents, *Miranda* warnings must be given for any statements to be admissible at trial in the United States. *See Cranford v. Rodriguez*, 512 F.2d 860, 863 (10th Cir. 1975); *United States v. Heller*, 625 F.2d 594, 599 (5th Cir. 1980). Similarly, earlier this year the Southern District of New York concluded that in prosecutions stemming from the al Qaeda bombings of U.S. embassies in Africa, "*Miranda* must apply to *any* portion of an overseas interrogation that is, in *fact or form*, conducted by U.S. law enforcement." *Bin Laden*, 132 F. Supp. 2d at 187 (emphasis added). The court justified its holding by relying in large part on cases holding that "the lack of *Miranda* warnings will still lead to suppression if U.S. law enforcement themselves actively participated in the questioning, or if U.S. personnel, despite asking no questions directly, used the foreign officials as their interrogationl agents in order to circumvent the requirements of *Miranda*."*Id.* (citations omitted). The same principle could be applied to any interrogation conducted by U.S. personnel for law enforcement purposes – even if conducted by the military. Thus, we believe that there is a substantial risk that an Article III court would regard any attempt by military officers to engage in unwarned interrogation for the sole purpose of either developing criminal charges or facilitating a criminal prosecution as an attempt to "circumvent the requirements of *Miranda*."*Id.*

That said, it may not be necessary under these circumstances to apply the full panoply of warnings and rights that would ordinarily be required under *Miranda*. Under normal conditions, *Miranda* requires that a suspect be warned not only that he has a right to remain silent and that his statements will be used against him, but also that he has a right to have counsel present and to have counsel appointed if necessary. By contrast, courts have found that, at least where an individual is in the custody of officials of another country, whose practices may limit access to counsel, there may be practical limitations on the right to counsel. In other words, the right to counsel as it would be applied in the United States applies only "if the particular overseas context actually presents *no* obvious hurdle to the implementation of an accused's right to the assistance and presence of counsel." *Bin Laden*, 132 F. Supp. 2d at 188. Even then, only "due care" is required to avoid "foreclos[ing] an opportunity" to be represented by counsel "that in fact exists" – that is to say, only the opportunity to obtain counsel subject to the limits of applicable foreign law. *Id. See also Cranford*, 512 F.2d at 863 (FBI agents satisfied *Miranda* by advising suspect held abroad that he had right to consult U.S. Consul in Mexico rather than lawyer); *Dopf*, 434 F.2d at 206–7 (same).[15]

---

[15] In *Bin Laden*, which involved suspects in the custody of foreign officials, the court suggested that the following advice of rights could constitutionally be given to aliens interrogated by U.S. law enforcement officials:

> Under U.S. law, you have the right to talk to a lawyer to get advice before we ask you any questions and you can have a lawyer with you during questioning. Were we in the United States, if you could not afford a lawyer, one would be appointed for you, if you wished, before any questioning.

It is not clear whether analogous considerations would apply when the individual is in the custody of U.S. Armed Forces overseas. There may be strong arguments that providing a detainee appointed counsel while he is held by the armed forces is not a practical alternative (perhaps for reasons of security of the detention facility) and would unduly interfere with the military's own ongoing questioning of the subject for military and intelligence information. We could pursue further the extent to which modifications to the traditional *Miranda* warnings might be justified in this context if you so request.

C. Interrogations by investigative services of one of the U.S. Armed Forces investigating war crimes

We understand that members of the criminal investigative services of the individual branches of the U.S. Armed Forces may wish to interrogate persons in order to investigate the possible commission of war crimes for subsequent prosecution before military commissions. As noted in Part II of this memorandum, *Miranda* does not bar the admission of evidence in a proceeding before a military commission. We understand, however, that even if the armed forces begin interrogating an individual with a view to a military commission trial, the possibility remains that the individual will later be transferred to civilian custody for purposes of criminal prosecution before an Article III court in the United States. The question will then be whether *Miranda* bars any unwarned statements obtained by the military investigators.

Based on the analysis above, we believe that war crimes investigations by military personnel preparing for a possible trial by military commission are not the kind of law enforcement investigations that *Miranda* was intended to regulate. Although such investigations are, in some sense, "criminal" in nature, their primary purpose is the execution of the President's wartime power as Commander-in-Chief "to seize and subject to disciplinary measures those enemies who, in their attempt to thwart or impede our military effort, have violated the law of war," and not his authority as the nation's chief law enforcement officer. *Application of Yamashita*, 327 U.S. 1, 11 (1946).[16] After all, "[t]he trial and punishment of enemy combatants who have committed violations of the law of war is . . . a *part of the conduct of war* operating as a preventive measure

> Because you are not in our custody and we are not in the United States, we cannot ensure that you will be permitted access to a lawyer, or have one appointed for you, before or during any questioning.
>
> However, if you want a lawyer, we will ask the foreign authorities to permit access to a lawyer or to appoint one for you. If the foreign authorities agree, then you can talk to that lawyer to get advice before we ask you any questions and you can have that lawyer with you during questioning.
>
> If you want a lawyer, but the foreign authorities do not permit access at this time to a lawyer or will not now appoint one for you, then you still have the right not to speak to us at any time without a lawyer present.
>
> 132 F. Supp. 2d at 188 n. 16.

[16] This distinction is not a novel one. We recently opined that the Posse Comitatus Act, 18 U.S.C. § 1385 (1994), which generally prohibits the domestic use of the Armed Forces for law enforcement purposes absent constitutional or statutory authority to do so, does not forbid the use of military force for the military purpose of preventing and deterring terrorism within the United States. *See* Memorandum for Alberto R. Gonzales, Counsel to the President & William J. Haynes, II, General Counsel, Department of Defense, from John C. Yoo, Deputy Assistant Attorney General & Robert J. Delahunty, Special Counsel, Office of Legal Counsel, *Re: Authority for Use of Military Force To Combat Terrorist Activities Within the United States* at 15–20 (Oct. 23, 2001).

against such violations." *Id.* (emphasis added). *Miranda*'s guiding rationale based on regulating the conduct of law enforcement agencies does not properly apply in such a case. Thus, unwarned statements obtained by military investigators in that context should be admissible in a later trial in federal court.

Nevertheless, we caution that no courts have addressed this issue, the matter is not at all free from doubt, and there is a very substantial risk that a court would reach the opposite conclusion and decide that *Miranda*'s requirements do properly apply. A court could conclude that, while interrogations of battlefield detainees for intelligence and information related to operations are one matter (and outside the ambit of *Miranda*), a different matter is presented when there is a switch to any form of criminal investigation – even if the only intended objective at the time of the questioning is developing a case for a military commission trial. There is always the possibility that the investigation will lead to trial in an Article III court. Indeed, it might be argued that this possibility is enhanced here because the only person charged so far in relation to the attacks of September 11 has been charged in federal court (even though the attacks appear to involve several violations of the laws of war), and, in any event, some war crimes can also be prosecuted as violations of federal criminal law, *see* 18 U.S.C. § 2441 (Supp. III 1997).

Further support for applying *Miranda* to custodial interrogations by war crimes investigators might be drawn from Supreme Court decisions involving interrogation by government officials other than police officers. In *Mathis v. United States*, 391 U.S. 1 (1968), the Court extended the requirement of *Miranda* warnings to an interview conducted by an IRS agent with a person in custody on the ground that, even though the IRS had not yet begun any criminal investigation, "tax investigations frequently lead to criminal prosecutions," *id.* at 4. *See also id.* ("[A]s the investigating revenue agent was compelled to admit, there was always the possibility during his investigation that his work would end up in a criminal prosecution."); *cf. id.* at 7 (White, J., dissenting) (suggesting that the majority's statement may be "a hint that any in-custody questioning by an employee of the Government must be preceded by warnings if it is within the immensely broad area of investigations which 'frequently lead' to criminal inquiries"). Similarly, in *Estelle v. Smith*, 451 U.S. 454 (1981), the Court applied *Miranda* to statements made during a court-ordered psychiatric examination when the prosecution later attempted to use those statements against the defendant during the penalty phase of a criminal trial. The fact that the defendant "was questioned by a psychiatrist designated by the trial court to conduct a neutral competency examination, rather than by a police officer, government informant, or prosecuting attorney" was "immaterial." *Id.* at 467. Once the psychiatrist "went beyond simply reporting to the court on the issue of competence and testified for the prosecution at the penalty phase on the crucial issue of respondent's future dangerousness, *his role changed* and became essentially like that of an agent of the State recounting unwarned statements made in a postarrest custodial setting." *Id.* (emphasis added).[17] Thus, a court might

---

[17] *See also United States v. D.F.*, 63 F.3d 671, 682–83 (7th Cir. 1995) (Under *Mathis*, "it is not the particular job title that determines whether the government employee's questioning implicates the Fifth Amendment, but whether the prosecution of the defendant being questioned is among the purposes, definite or contingent, for which the information is elicited. . . . [A]lthough a government employee need not be a law enforcement official for his questioning to implicate the strictures of the Fifth Amendment, his questioning must be of a nature that reasonably contemplates the possibility of criminal prosecution.") (footnotes omitted); *Battie v. Estelle*, 655 F.2d 692, 699 (5th Cir. 1981) ("[T]he

exclude statements made during custodial interrogation by war crimes investigators unless the *Miranda* requirements are satisfied, on the grounds that such interrogation bears a similarly close nexus to law enforcement.

While we do not believe that this analysis would be correct, it undeniably presents a substantial risk. Accordingly, if a decision has not yet been made concerning where an individual will be prosecuted and if it is deemed essential to ensure that any statements obtained by military investigators may be used in a subsequent trial in an Article III court, we believe that it would be prudent to provide *Miranda* warnings.

D. Interrogations with Mixed or Dual Purposes

In some cases there may be claims that a given interrogation does not fall neatly into only one of the categories outlined above, or claims that the lines between categories have been blurred because there were different motives behind the questioning. It is possible, for example, that military interrogators primarily seeking information relevant to operations and intelligence may have some interest in determining whether a detainee was engaged in conduct chargeable as a crime or a war crime. As explained below, for the most part we believe that the subjective motives of the interrogator should not alter analysis, which should be guided instead by an objective assessment of the nature of the questioning.

First, and most importantly, under the reasoning outlined above, we have concluded that *Miranda* should not apply at all to military and intelligence officers' questioning conducted for obtaining military and intelligence information because officers acting in this capacity are not the intended objects of *Miranda*'s rules of conduct. Their subjective motivations in asking any particular questions should not alter this analysis. Nor should the analysis be affected even if it turns out after the fact that an objective assessment of certain particular questions demonstrates that the information sought was relevant solely to establishing the role of the detainee in a past criminal act. Such factors should not matter as long as overall, the primary objective of the questioning is military operations and intelligence information and the interrogators are in good faith pursuing their role in developing such information. Their particular motivations for asking certain questions or the exact nature of the information sought in particular questions should not serve as a basis for later claiming that *Miranda* warnings should have been supplied in such an interrogation.[18]

Second, we explained above that an extension of the public-safety exception should apply by analogy to interrogations for military and intelligence information, and the Supreme Court has directly addressed the question of dual motives behind questioning in the context of that exception. The Court made clear that the "availability of

---

particular office that the official who performs the custodial interrogation represents is inconsequential because *Miranda* was not concerned with the division of responsibility between the various state investigatory agencies but was concerned with official custodial interrogations of an accused and the use of statements obtained from an accused without an attorney in such circumstances to prove the State's case against the accused.").

[18] Of course, a different issue would be raised if it appeared that military and intelligence officers had taken it on themselves to develop a criminal investigation in order to exploit the absence of *Miranda* warnings in their interrogations or were merely acting as the proxies for law enforcement by asking questions at the direction of, for example, FBI agents. Determining where the line would be drawn requiring *Miranda* in such cases would likely depend on a highly fact-intensive inquiry into the particular circumstances.

[the public-safety] exception does not depend upon the motivation of the individual officers involved." 467 U.S. at 656. *See also id.* ("[T]he application of the exception which we recognize today should not be made to depend on *post hoc* findings at a suppression hearing concerning the subjective motivation of the arresting officer."). "Whatever the motivation" of those conducting the questioning, the Court concluded that the exception should apply if there were an objective basis for concluding that the questions were "reasonably prompted by a concern for the public safety." *Id.* In other words, where there is objectively "a situation posing a threat to the public safety," *id.* at 657, questions reasonably aimed at eliminating that threat can be asked without *Miranda* warnings. The Court thus drew a distinction between "questions necessary to secure [police officers'] own safety or the safety of the public and questions designed solely to elicit testimonial evidence from a suspect." *Id.* at 659.

We conclude that, to the extent the public-safety exception is extended by analogy to military and intelligence questioning, the same analysis of dual motives should apply. Thus, as long as there was an objectively reasonable basis to believe that the information sought by military and intelligence officers would reduce the dangers to the lives and safety of American military personnel, allied forces or others, we believe it would not matter if the questioners were also partially motivated by a law-enforcement concern.[19] Questions in the sort of interrogation we have described above seem reasonably related to the former purpose and are certainly not directed solely at the latter.

Finally, a similar dual motive analysis might be applied to argue that when law enforcement personnel – such as FBI agents – are questioning a detainee, it is only when they ask questions solely for law-enforcement purposes that *Miranda* is required. Where questions objectively can be said to be related to securing public safety, the *Quarles* exception should apply. Stated thus generally, we think this is a correct statement of the law, but we nevertheless caution, that it likely does not provide a very useful guide for conduct. As we understand the factual situation, detainees will likely be seized by the military and initially interrogated for operational and intelligence information. Much of this information will be most critical for securing safety within the theater and addressing military threats. The detainee may later be questioned by law enforcement personnel (and others acting at the direction of law enforcement). We think there is a substantial risk in this context that courts will view the change in personnel conducting the interrogations as a proxy for a change in the focus of the questioning and conclude that all such interrogations are for law enforcement purposes. Thus, even if some questions are reasonably related to "public safety" (as broadly conceived in this context), it may be more difficult to establish that the public-safety exception applies. In addition, to receive the benefit of the public-safety exception, it seems likely that law enforcement interrogators would have to ask

---

[19] The Court's holdings in "dual motive" cases under the Fourth Amendment also tend to support our conclusion in this context. As a general matter, the Fourth Amendment case law does not require that a search or seizure have only a single purpose so long as it is otherwise legitimate. Thus, the police may engage in (objectively justified) traffic stops even if their underlying motive may be to investigate other violations as to which no probable cause or even articulable suspicion exists. *See Whren v. United States*, 517 U.S. 806 (1996); *see also United States v. Villamonte-Marquez*, 462 U.S. 579, 584 n.3 (1983) (otherwise valid warrantless boarding of vessel by customs officials not invalidated by facts that state police officer accompanied customs officials and officers were following tip that vessel might be carrying marijuana).

questions related to public safety first before *Mirandizing* the detainee and proceeding with further questioning. We think it unlikely that a court would take the record of a broad-ranging interview, much of which was conducted plainly for the purpose of eliciting incriminating evidence, and parse out those questions and answers that are related to public safety to admit them into evidence. The Supreme Court's analysis in *Quarles* suggested that the exception was designed to permit officers to ask questions immediately as reasonably needed to address safety matters and then to *Mirandize* a suspect before further questioning. It seems likely that courts will attempt to adhere to that pattern. Because of these concerns, we think the most prudent approach would be to provide *Miranda* warnings at the outset when the interrogation is being conducted by law enforcement officers building a criminal case.[20]

IV. Subsequent Mirandizing *after failure to warn*

For purposes of determining whether *Miranda* warnings should be applied in the more doubtful scenarios considered above, it may be important to understand that if *Miranda* warnings are not given in an interview where it is later determined they were required, the result will *not* be that all statements subsequently made by the individual in later interviews will be inadmissible as "fruit of the poisonous tree." To the contrary, as a general matter, a subsequent, properly *Mirandized* statement may be used against an individual even if that individual has previously given an unwarned statement during questioning when *Miranda* warnings should have been provided.

The Supreme Court has held that a second, *Mirandized* statement is admissible so long as the earlier statement, although inadmissible itself under *Miranda*, was nevertheless voluntarily made. Where the first statement was involuntarily made; the second, *Mirandized* statement can still be admitted, but only where there has been an adequate break in events between the two statements to ensure that the later one is voluntary. In *Oregon v. Elstad*, 470 U.S. 298 (1985), the Court explained:

> [T]here is no warrant for presuming coercive effect [in a second, Mirandized confession] where the suspect's initial inculpatory statement, though technically in violation of Miranda, was voluntary. The relevant inquiry is whether, in fact, the second statement was also voluntarily made.... [A] suspect who has once responded to unwarned yet uncoercive questioning is not thereby disabled from waiving his rights and confessing after he has been given the requisite Miranda warnings.

Id. at 318. Thus, where the first statement was voluntary (even if unwarned), the Court refused to require the "break in the stream of events" that would have been required had the first statement been coerced. *Id.* at 310; *see also id.* at 318 (declining to require "a passage of time or break in events before a second, fully warned statement can be deemed voluntary"); *cf. Miranda*, 384 U.S. at 496 ("A different case would be presented if an accused [who had previously given an involuntary confession] were taken into

---

[20] Of course, there may be some specialized branches of law enforcement agencies (such as a counter-terrorism unit in the FBI) whose mission is instead to expose and thwart pending terrorist attacks. Their questioning, therefore, may be much more similar to questioning conducted for intelligence and national security objectives, and should be treated the same. Thus, an objective assessment of the type of information being sought in the questioning remains the critical touchstone for assessing the application of *Miranda*. We note simply that questioning by personnel traditionally associated with law enforcement will likely serve as a rough proxy for most courts in concluding that the questioning was for law-enforcement purposes.

custody by the second authority, removed both in time and place from his original surroundings, and then adequately advised of his rights and given an opportunity to exercise them.").

Elstad, moreover, has not been undermined by *Dickerson* and the determination that *Miranda* is a constitutional rule. Although the *Elstad* opinion relied in part on the view that *Miranda* was not a constitutional ruling, *see, e.g.*, 410 U.S. at 308, that rationale was not essential to its holding. As the Court noted, "[f]ailure to administer *Miranda* warnings creates a presumption of compulsion." *Elstad*, 470 U.S. at 307. Whether the presumption arises out of the Constitution or by judicial creation, it is that compulsion that triggers the Self-Incrimination Clause in the first place. Once warnings are given, however, the presumption of coercion evaporates. In the Court's words,

> a careful and thorough administration of Miranda warnings serves to cure the condition that rendered the unwarned statement inadmissible. The warning conveys the relevant information and thereafter the suspect's choice whether to exercise his privilege to remain silent should ordinarily be viewed as an 'act of free will.'

Id. at 310–11 (citation omitted). Indeed, to rule otherwise would

> effectively immunize a suspect who responds to pre-Miranda warning questions from the consequences of his subsequent informed waiver of the privilege of remaining silent. This immunity comes at a high cost to legitimate law enforcement activity, while adding little desirable protection to the individual's interest in not being compelled to testify against himself. When neither the initial nor the subsequent admission is coerced, little justification exists for permitting the highly probative evidence of a voluntary confession to be irretrievably lost to the factfinder.

Id. at 312 (citations omitted).

Nothing in this logic depends upon whether the presumption arose out of the Fifth Amendment itself or by judicial creation.[21] The touchstone of both the Self-Incrimination Clause and *Miranda* is compulsion, and as *Elstad* makes clear, there is no basis for presuming compulsion once an individual has been given *Miranda* warnings. Nothing in *Dickerson* alters that result. Rather, the *Dickerson* Court expressly noted that *Elstad* was consistent with its approach to treating *Miranda* as a constitutional decision and explained that *Elstad* "simply recognizes the fact that unreasonable searches under the Fourth Amendment are different from unwarned interrogation under the Fifth Amendment." 530 U.S. at 441. The Court thus made plain that the result in *Elstad* did not depend on the theory that *Miranda* was a "non-constitutional decision." *Id.* Instead, it rested on other differences between an unlawful search and unwarned interrogations, foremost among them being the fact (emphasized in *Elstad*) that, while an unlawful search may lead inexorably to the discovery of pieces of evidence such that they are the products of the unlawful act, in the context of

---

[21] *See also id.* at 308 ("[T]he absence of any coercion or improper tactics undercuts the twin rationales-trustworthiness and deterrence [of constitutional violations] – for a broader rule. Once warned, the suspect is free to exercise his own volition in deciding whether or not to make a statement to the authorities."); *id.* at 308–9 ("A living witness is not to be mechanically equated with the proffer of inanimate evidentiary objects illegally seized. . . . The living witness is an individual human personality whose attributes of will, perception, memory and *volition* interact to determine what testimony he will give.") (quotations omitted); *id.* at 314 ("A subsequent administration of *Miranda* warnings to a suspect who has given a voluntary but unwarned statement ordinarily should suffice to remove the conditions that precluded admission of the earlier statement.").

interviews with a suspect who has "attributes of will, perception, memory and *volition*,"*Elstad*, 470 U.S. at 309, there can be an intervening act of will when the suspect has been warned of his rights and yet consents to continue making statements to his interrogators.

The courts of appeals that have addressed the issue have agreed that the result in *Elstad* survives the decision in *Dickerson*. *See United States v. DeSumma*, 272 F.3d 176, 180 (3d Cir. 2001) ("We cannot agree with the defendant's reading of *Dickerson* because the Supreme Court appeared to anticipate and reject it. . . . We hold that the fruit of the poisonous tree doctrine does not apply to derivative evidence secured as a result of a voluntary statement obtained before *Miranda* warnings are issued."); *United States v. Orso*, 266 F.3d 1030, 1034 n.3 (9th Cir. 2001) ("The distinction was originally premised on the fact that a *Miranda* violation was not a violation of the Constitution, whereas a Fourth Amendment violation was. . . . Nonetheless, *Dickerson* seems to signal that the distinction set forth in *Elstad* continues unabated.").

VI. The Sixth Amendment Right to Counsel Does Not Apply Prior to the Initiation of Adversary Judicial Criminal Proceedings

The Sixth Amendment provides that "[i]n all criminal prosecutions, the accused shall enjoy the right . . . to have the Assistance of Counsel for his defence." U.S. Const. Amend. VI. Unless access to counsel must be provided in order to safeguard an independent constitutional right (such as the Fifth Amendment's protection against coerced confession), it is generally necessary that adversary proceedings be formally initiated before a particular phase of a prosecution can be said to "involve critical confrontations of the accused by the prosecution" such as to trigger application of the Sixth Amendment. *United States v. Wade*, 388 U.S. 218, 224 (1967). "'The Sixth Amendment right [to counsel] . . . does not attach until a prosecution is commenced, that is, at or after the initiation of adversary judicial criminal proceedings – whether by way of formal charge, preliminary hearing, indictment, information, or arraignment.'" *Texas v. Cobb*, 532 U.S. 162, 167–68 (2001) (quoting *McNeil v. Wisconsin*, 501 U.S. 171, 175 (1991)).

VII. The McDade Act Does Not Apply to Defense Department Interrogators

The McDade Act, 28 U.S.C. § 530B (Supp. IV 1998), reads as follows:
§ 530B. *Ethical standards for attorneys for the Government*

(a) An attorney for the Government shall be subject to State laws and rules, and local Federal court rules, governing attorneys in each State where such attorney engages in that attorney's duties, to the same extent and in the same manner as other attorneys in that State.
(b) The Attorney General shall make and amend rules of the Department of Justice to assure compliance with this section.
(c) As used in this section, the term "attorney for the Government" includes any attorney described in section 77.2(a) of part 77 of title 28 of the Code of Federal Regulations and also includes any independent counsel, or employee of such a counsel, appointed under Chapter 40.

Among the "State laws and rules" incorporated by this provision are likely to be state analogues to the American Bar Association's ("ABA") Model Rule of Professional

Conduct 4.2 (2001). Rule 4.2 reads as follows:

Rule 4.2 "Communication with Person Represented by Counsel"

In representing a client, a lawyer shall not communicate about the subject of the representation with a person the lawyer knows to be represented by another lawyer in the matter, unless the lawyer has the consent of the other lawyer or is authorized by law to do so.

Assuming that a state bar rule similar to Rule 4.2 is among the "State laws and rules" incorporated by section 530B, you have asked specifically whether lawyers on the Judge Advocate Generals' staffs in the Department of Defense are barred from questioning persons detained in Afghanistan or transferred to the custody of the Department of Defense who are represented by counsel. In particular, you have asked whether Defense Department lawyers could question John Walker (Lindh) without the consent of an attorney, Mr. James Brosnahan, claiming to represent him.[22]

Even assuming that a rule similar in substance to Rule 4.2 is incorporated by section 530B, it would not preclude questioning of Mr. Walker by military lawyers even without Mr. Brosnahan's consent for at least two reasons.[23]

First, section 530B does not apply to Department of Defense lawyers. Section 530B by its terms applies only to the conduct of an "attorney for the Government." And subsection 530B(c) expressly defines the term "attorney for the Government" to mean (in addition to an independent counsel and his employees under chapter 40) "any attorney described in section 77.2(a) of part 77 of title 28 of the Code of Federal Regulations." That regulation provides a definition of "government attorney" that largely limits the term to Department of Justice lawyers and does not include lawyers of the Department of Defense.[24] In addition, subsection 530B(b) directs the Attorney General to

---

[22] On December 4, 2001, Mr. James J. Brosnahan wrote to you, stating "I have been retained by the parents of John Walker Lindh to represent him in any matters that might arise." Letter for William J. Haynes, II, General Counsel, Department of Defense, from James J. Brosnahan, Morrison & Forester, LLP at 1 (Dec. 4, 2001). In that letter, Mr. Brosnahan also stated, "I would ask that no further interrogation of my client occur until I have the opportunity to speak with him. As an American citizen, he has the right to counsel and, under all applicable legal authorities, I ask for the right to speak with my client as soon as possible." *Id*.

[23] We note that Rule 4.2 applies only if Mr. Walker is in fact "represented by another lawyer in the matter." In his letter, Mr. Brosnahan stated that he was retained by Mr. Walker's parents to represent their son. We understand, however, that at the time the letter was written Mr. Brosnahan had never spoken with Mr. Walker. This case thus bears a striking resemblance to *Moran v. Burbine*, 475 U.S. 412 (1986). There, the suspect's sister had attempted to retain a lawyer to represent him, but the suspect waived his *Miranda* rights and confessed before learning of his sister's efforts. The Court found no violation of either *Miranda* or the Sixth Amendment. *See id.* at 425 ("Nor are we prepared to adopt a rule requiring that the police inform a suspect of an attorney's efforts to reach him."). The Court additionally noted "the Rhode Island Supreme Court's finding that, as a matter of state law, no attorney-client relationship existed between respondent and [the counsel obtained by his sister]." *Id.* at 429 n.3 (citing *State v. Burbine*, 451 A.2d 22, 29 (R.I. 1982)). *See also State v. Cline*, 405 A.2d 1192, 1199 (R.I. 1979) ("Generally, the relationship of attorney and client arises by reason of agreement between the parties.... Obviously, such a relationship could not exist between persons who had never met and who in all probability were unaware of each other's existence prior to the meeting in the Providence police station."); *cf. United States v. Weinstein*, 511 F.2d 622, 628 (2d Cir. 1975) ("[I]n a criminal proceeding any action taken by the court at the behest of a representative appointed without the defendant's knowledge or consent could not bind the fugitive defendant.... [T]he attorney moving on his behalf must at least have been authorized by the defendant to act as his counsel in the case.").

[24] *See* 28 C.F.R. § 77.2(a) (2001) ("The phrase *attorney for the government* means the Attorney General; the Deputy Attorney General; the Solicitor General; the Assistant Attorneys General for, and any attorney employed in, the Antitrust Division, Civil Division, Civil Rights Division, Criminal Division,

"make and amend rules of the Department of Justice to assure compliance with this section." That implementing mechanism – relying on rules for the Department of Justice – reinforces the conclusion that the provision applies solely to lawyers in that Department.

Second, Rule 4.2 would permit a covered Government attorney to communicate with a represented party even absent the party's counsel's consent if the Government attorney is "authorized by law to do so." We believe that an Executive Order by the President permitting Government attorneys to communicate with persons held by the armed forces in the current conflict – even if those persons are represented by counsel – would constitute, in the circumstances of this case, legal authorization within the meaning of such a rule. To assume otherwise would be to read a State ethics rule in a manner that significantly trammeled the President's authority as Commander-in-Chief to take necessary and appropriate measures to acquire information about enemy forces. Such a construction of state law should be avoided since state law cannot stand as an impermissible burden on the exercise of the President's constitutional authority with respect to military and foreign affairs. *See United States v. Pink*, 315 U.S. 203 (1942).

Finally, we note that even if the Government did in fact violate Rule 4.2 by having military lawyers interrogate represented persons (including Mr. Walker) without consent of counsel, it would not follow that the evidence obtained in that questioning would be inadmissible at trial. The Eleventh Circuit has held that neither section 530B nor the State ethics rules it incorporates requires the suppression in a federal proceeding of evidence obtained through a violation of such rules. "[A] state rule of professional conduct cannot provide an adequate basis for a federal court to suppress evidence that is otherwise admissible. Federal law, not state law, determines the admissibility of evidence in federal court." *United States v. Lowery*, 166 F.3d 1119, 1124 (11th Cir.), *cert. denied*, 528 U.S. 889 (1999). Moreover, the court held, section 530B did not require suppression of evidence obtained in violation of such State laws and rules: Congress did not "intend by that enactment to turn over to state supreme courts in every state – and state legislatures, too, assuming they can also enact codes of professional conduct for attorneys – the authority to decide that otherwise admissible evidence cannot be used in federal court." *Id.* at 1125; *accord Stern v. United States District Court for the District of Mass.*, 214 F.3d 4, 20 (1st Cir. 2000).

Please let us know if we can be of further assistance.

Jay S. Bybee
Assistant Attorney General

Environment and Natural Resources Division, and Tax Division; the Chief Counsel for the DEA and any attorney employed in that office; the General Counsel of the FBI and any attorney employed in that office or in the (Office of General Counsel) of the FBI; any attorney employed in, or head of, any other legal office in a Department of Justice agency, any United States Attorney; any Assistant United States Attorney; any Special Assistant to the Attorney General or Special Attorney duly appointed pursuant to 28 U.S.C. 515; any Special Assistant United States Attorney duly appointed pursuant to 28 U.S.C. 543 who is authorized to conduct criminal or civil law enforcement investigations or proceedings on behalf of the United States; and any other attorney employed by the Department of Justice who is authorized to conduct criminal or civil law enforcement proceedings on behalf of the United States. The phrase *attorney for the government* also includes any independent counsel, or employee of such counsel, appointed under chapter 40 of title 28, United States Code. The phrase *attorney for the government* does not include attorneys employed as investigators or other law enforcement agents by the Department of Justice who are not authorized to represent the United States in criminal or civil law enforcement litigation or to supervise such proceedings.").

U.S Department of Justice

Office of Legal Counsel

Office of the Assistant Attorney General   *Washington, D.C. 20530*

August 1, 2002

**Memorandum for Alberto R. Gonzales Counsel
to the President**

RE: *Standards of Conduct for Interrogation under 18 U.S.C. §§ 2340–2340A*

You have asked for our Office's views regarding the standards of conduct under the Convention Against Torture and Other Cruel, Inhuman and Degrading Treatment or Punishment as implemented by Sections 2340–2340A of title 18 of the United States Code. As we understand it, this question has arisen in the context of the conduct of interrogations outside of the United States. We conclude below that Section 2340A proscribes acts inflicting, and that are specifically intended to inflict, severe pain or suffering, whether mental or physical. Those acts must be of an extreme nature to rise to the level of torture within the meaning of Section 2340A and the Convention. We further conclude that certain acts may be cruel, inhuman, or degrading, but still not produce pain and suffering of the requisite intensity to fall within Section 2340A's proscription against torture. We conclude by examining possible defenses that would negate any claim that certain interrogation methods violate the statute.

In Part I, we examine the criminal statute's text and history. We conclude that for an act to constitute torture as defined in Section 2340, it must inflict pain that is difficult to endure. Physical pain amounting to torture must be equivalent in intensity to the pain accompanying serious physical injury, such as organ failure, impairment of bodily function, or even death. For purely mental pain or suffering to amount to torture under Section 2340, it must result in significant psychological harm of significant duration, e.g., lasting for months or even years. We conclude that the mental harm also must result from one of the predicate acts listed in the statute, namely: threats of imminent death; threats of infliction of the kind of pain that would amount to physical torture; infliction of such physical pain as a means of psychological torture; use of drugs or other procedures designed to deeply disrupt the senses, or fundamentally alter an individual's personality; or threatening to do any of these things to a third party. The legislative history simply reveals that Congress intended for the statute's definition to track the Convention's definition of torture and the reservations, understandings, and declarations that the United States submitted with its ratification. We conclude that the statute, taken as a whole, makes plain that it prohibits only extreme acts.

In Part II, we examine the text, ratification history, and negotiating history of the Torture Convention. We conclude that the treaty's text prohibits only the most extreme acts by reserving criminal penalties solely for torture and declining to require such penalties for "cruel, inhuman, or degrading treatment or punishment." This confirms our view that the criminal statute penalizes only the most egregious conduct. Executive branch interpretations and representations to the Senate at the time of ratification further confirm that the treaty was intended to reach only the most extreme conduct.

In Part III, we analyze the jurisprudence of the Torture Victims Protection Act, 28 U.S.C. § 1350 note (2000), which provides civil remedies for torture victims, to predict the standards that courts might follow in determining what actions reach the threshold of torture in the criminal context. We conclude from these cases that courts are likely to take a totality-of-the-circumstances approach, and will look to an entire course of conduct, to determine whether certain acts will violate Section 2340A. Moreover, these cases demonstrate that most often torture involves cruel and extreme physical pain. In Part IV, we examine international decisions regarding the use of sensory deprivation techniques. These cases make clear that while many of these techniques may amount to cruel, inhuman or degrading treatment, they do not produce pain or suffering of the necessary intensity to meet the definition of torture. From these decisions, we conclude that there is a wide range of such techniques that will not rise to the level of torture.

In Part V, we discuss whether Section 2340A may be unconstitutional if applied to interrogations undertaken of enemy combatants pursuant to the President's Commander-in-Chief powers. We find that in the circumstances of the current war against al Qaeda and its allies, prosecution under Section 2340A may be barred because enforcement of the statute would represent an unconstitutional infringement of the President's authority to conduct war. In Part VI, we discuss defenses to an allegation that an interrogation method might violate the statute. We conclude that, under the current circumstances, necessity or self-defense may justify interrogation methods that might violate Section 2340A.

I. 18 U.S.C. §§ 2340–2340A

Section 2340A makes it a criminal offense for any person "outside the United States [to] commit or attempt to commit torture."[1] Section 2340 defines the act of torture as an:

> act committed by a person acting under the color of law specifically intended to inflict severe physical or mental pain or suffering (other than pain or suffering incidental to lawful sanctions) upon another person within his custody or physical control.

---

[1] If convicted of torture, a defendant faces a fine or up to twenty years' imprisonment or both. If, however, the act resulted in the victim's death, a defendant may be sentenced to life imprisonment or to death. *See* 18 U.S.C.A. § 2340A(a). Whether death results from the act also affects the applicable statute of limitations. Where death does not result, the statute of limitations is eight years; if death results, there is no statute of limitations. *See* 18 U.S.C.A. § 3286(b) (West Supp. 2002); *id.* § 2332b(g)(5)(B) (West Supp. 2002). Section 2340A as originally enacted did not provide for the death penalty as a punishment. *See* Omnibus Crime Bill, Pub. L. No. 103–322, Title VI, Section 60020, 108 Stat. 1979 (1994) (amending section 2340A to provide for the death penalty); H. R. Conf. Rep. No. 103–711, at 388 (1994) (noting that the act added the death penalty as a penalty for torture).

Most recently, the USA Patriot Act, Pub. L. No. 107–56, 115 Stat. 272 (2001), amended section 2340A to expressly codify the offense of conspiracy to commit torture. Congress enacted this amendment as part of a broader effort to ensure that individuals engaged in the planning of terrorist activities could be prosecuted irrespective of where the activities took place. *See* H. R. Rep. No. 107–236, at 70 (2001) (discussing the addition of "conspiracy" as a separate offense for a variety of "Federal terrorism offense[s]").

18 U.S.C.A. § 2340(1); *see id.* § 2340A. Thus, to convict a defendant of torture, the prosecution must establish that: (1) the torture occurred outside the United States; (2) the defendant acted under the color of law; (3) the victim was within the defendant's custody or physical control; (4) the defendant specifically intended to cause severe physical or mental pain or suffering; and (5) that the act inflicted severe physical or mental pain or suffering. *See also* S. Exec. Rep. No. 101–30, at 6 (1990) ("For an act to be 'torture,' it must . . . cause severe pain and suffering, and be intended to cause severe pain and suffering."). You have asked us to address only the elements of specific intent and the infliction of severe pain or suffering. As such, we have not addressed the elements of "outside the United States," "color of law," and "custody or control."[2] At your request, we would be happy to address these elements in a separate memorandum.

A. *"Specifically Intended"*

To violate Section 2340A, the statute requires that severe pain and suffering must be inflicted with specific intent. *See* 18 U.S.C. § 2340(1). In order for a defendant to have acted with specific intent, he must expressly intend to achieve the forbidden act. *See United States v. Carter*, 530 U.S. 255, 269 (2000); Black's Law Dictionary at 814 (7th ed. 1999) (defining specific intent as "[t]he intent to accomplish the precise criminal act that one is later charged with"). For example, in *Ratzlaf v. United States*, 510 U.S. 135, 141 (1994), the statute at issue was construed to require that the defendant act with the "specific intent to commit the crime." (Internal quotation marks and citation omitted). As a result, the defendant had to act with the express "purpose to disobey the law" in order for the *mens rea* element to be satisfied. *Ibid.* (internal quotation marks and citation omitted)

Here, because Section 2340 requires that a defendant act with the specific intent to inflict severe pain, the infliction of such pain must be the defendant's precise objective. If the statute had required only general intent, it would be sufficient to establish guilt by showing that the defendant "possessed knowledge with respect to the *actus reus* of the crime." *Carter*, 530 U.S. at 268. If the defendant acted knowing that severe pain or suffering was reasonably likely to result from his actions, but no more, he would have acted only with general intent. *See id.* at 269; Black's Law Dictionary 813 (7th ed. 1999) (explaining that general intent "usu[ally] takes the form of recklessness (involving actual awareness of a risk and the culpable taking of that risk) or negligence (involving blameworthy inadvertence)"). The Supreme Court has used the following example to illustrate the difference between these two mental states:

> [A] person entered a bank and took money from a teller at gunpoint, but deliberately failed to make a quick getaway from the bank in the hope of being arrested so that

---

[2] We note, however, that 18 U.S.C. § 2340(3) supplies a definition of the term "United States." It defines it as "all areas under the jurisdiction of the United States including any of the places described in" 18 U.S.C. §§ 5 and 7, and in 49 U.S.C. § 46501(2). Section 5 provides that United States "includes all places and waters, continental or insular, subject to the jurisdiction of the United States." By including the definition set out in Section 7, the term "United States" as used in Section 2340(3) includes the "special maritime and territorial jurisdiction of the United States." Moreover, the incorporation by reference to Section 46501(2) extends the definition of the "United States" to "special aircraft jurisdiction of the United States."

he would be returned to prison and treated for alcoholism. Though this defendant knowingly engaged in the acts of using force and taking money (satisfying "general intent"), he did not intend permanently to deprive the bank of its possession of the money (failing to satisfy "specific intent").

Carter, 530 U.S. at 268 (citing 1 W. LaFave & A. Scott, Substantive Criminal Law §§ 3.5, at 315 (1986)).

As a theoretical matter, therefore, knowledge alone that a particular result is certain to occur does not constitute specific intent. As the Supreme Court explained in the context of murder, "the . . . common law of homicide distinguishes . . . between a person who knows that another person will be killed as a result of his conduct and a person who acts with the specific purpose of taking another's life[.]" *United States v. Bailey*, 444 U.S. 394, 405 (1980). "Put differently, the law distinguishes actions taken 'because of' a given end from actions taken in spite of their unintended but foreseen consequences." *Vacco v. Quill*, 521 U.S. 793, 802–03 (1997). Thus, even if the defendant knows that severe pain will result from his actions, if causing such harm is not his objective, he lacks the requisite specific intent even though the defendant did not act in good faith. Instead, a defendant is guilty of torture only if he acts with the express purpose of inflicting severe pain or suffering on a person within his custody or physical control. While as a theoretical matter such knowledge does not constitute specific intent, juries are permitted to infer from the factual circumstances that such intent is present. *See, e.g., United States v. Godwin*, 272 F.3d 659, 666 (4th Cir. 2001); *United States v. Karro*, 257 F.3d 112, 118 (2d Cir. 2001); *United States v. Wood*, 207 F.3d 1222, 1232 (10th Cir. 2000); *Henderson v. United States*, 202 F.2d 400, 403 (6th Cir. 1953). Therefore, when a defendant knows that his actions will produce the prohibited result, a jury will in all likelihood conclude that the defendant acted with specific intent.

Further, a showing that an individual acted with a good faith belief that his conduct would not produce the result that the law prohibits negates specific intent. *See, e.g., South Atl. Lmtd. Ptrshp. of Tenn. v. Reise*, 218 F.3d 518, 531 (4th Cir. 2002). Where a defendant acts in good faith, he acts with an honest belief that he has not engaged in the proscribed conduct. *See Cheek v. United States*, 498 U.S. 192, 202 (1991); *United States v. Mancuso*, 42 F.3d 836, 837 (4th Cir. 1994). For example, in the context of mail fraud, if an individual honestly believes that the material transmitted is truthful, he has not acted with the required intent to deceive or mislead. *See, e.g., United States v. Sayakhom*, 186 F.3d 928, 939–40 (9th Cir. 1999). A good faith belief need not be a reasonable one. *See Cheek*, 498 U.S. at 202.

Although a defendant theoretically could hold an unreasonable belief that his acts would not constitute the actions prohibited by the statute, even though they would as a certainty produce the prohibited effects, as a matter of practice in the federal criminal justice system it is highly unlikely that a jury would acquit in such a situation. Where a defendant holds an unreasonable belief, he will confront the problem of proving to the jury that he actually held that belief. As the Supreme Court noted in *Cheek*, "the more unreasonable the asserted beliefs or misunderstandings are, the more likely the jury . . . will find that the Government has carried its burden of proving" intent. *Id.* at 203–04. As we explained above, a jury will be permitted to infer that the defendant held the requisite specific intent. As a matter of proof, therefore, a good faith defense will prove more compelling when a reasonable basis exists for the defendant's belief.

B. "Severe Pain or Suffering"

The key statutory phrase in the definition of torture is the statement that acts amount to torture if they cause "severe physical or mental pain or suffering." In examining the meaning of a statute, its text must be the starting point. *See INS v. Phinpathya*, 464 U.S. 183, 189 (1984) ("This Court has noted on numerous occasions that in all cases involving statutory construction, our starting point must be the language employed by Congress,... and we assume that the legislative purpose is expressed by the ordinary meaning of the words used.") (internal quotations and citations omitted). Section 2340 makes plain that the infliction of pain or suffering per se, whether it is physical or mental, is insufficient to amount to torture. Instead, the text provides that pain or suffering must be "severe." The statute does not, however, define the term "severe." "In the absence of such a definition, we construe a statutory term in accordance with its ordinary or natural meaning." *FDIC v. Meyer*, 510 U.S. 471, 476 (1994). The dictionary defines "severe" as "[u]nsparing in exaction, punishment, or censure" or "[I]nflicting discomfort or pain hard to endure; sharp; afflictive; distressing; violent; extreme; as *severe* pain, anguish, torture." Webster's New International Dictionary 2295 (2d ed. 1935); *see* American Heritage Dictionary of the English Language 1653 (3d ed. 1992) ("extremely violent or grievous: *severe* pain") (emphasis in original); IX The Oxford English Dictionary 572 (1978) ("Of pain, suffering, loss, or the like: Grievous, extreme" and "of circumstances...: hard to sustain or endure"). Thus, the adjective "severe" conveys that the pain or suffering must be of such a high level of intensity that the pain is difficult for the subject to endure.

Congress' use of the phrase "severe pain" elsewhere in the United States Code can shed more light on its meaning. *See, e.g., West Va. Univ. Hosps., Inc. v. Casey*, 499 U.S. 83, 100 (1991) ("[W]e construe [a statutory term] to contain that permissible meaning which fits most logically and comfortably into the body of both previously and subsequently enacted law."). Significantly, the phrase "severe pain" appears in statutes defining an emergency medical condition for the purpose of providing health benefits. *See, e.g.,* 8 U.S.C. § 1369 (2000); 42 U.S.C § 1395w-22 (2000); *id.* § 1395x (2000); *id.* § 1395dd (2000); *id.* § 1396b (2000); *id.* § 1396u-2 (2000). These statutes define an emergency condition as one "manifesting itself by acute symptoms of sufficient severity (including *severe pain*) such that a prudent lay person, who possesses an average knowledge of health and medicine, could reasonably expect the absence of immediate medical attention to result in – placing the health of the individual... (i) in serious jeopardy, (ii) serious impairment to bodily functions, or (iii) serious dysfunction of any bodily organ or part." *Id.* § 1395w-22(d)(3)(B) (emphasis added). Although these statutes address a substantially different subject from Section 2340, they are nonetheless helpful for understanding what constitutes severe physical pain. They treat severe pain as an indicator of ailments that are likely to result in permanent and serious physical damage in the absence of immediate medical treatment. Such damage must rise to the level of death, organ failure, or the permanent impairment of a significant body function. These statutes suggest that "severe pain," as used in Section 2340, must rise to a similarly high level – the level that would ordinarily be associated with a sufficiently serious physical condition or injury such as death, organ failure, or serious impairment of body functions – in order to constitute torture.[3]

---

[3] One might argue that because the statute uses "or" rather than "and" in the phrase "pain or suffering" that "severe physical suffering" is a concept distinct from "severe physical pain." We believe the better

C. "Severe mental pain or suffering"

Section 2340 gives further guidance as to the meaning of "severe mental pain or suffering," as distinguished from severe physical pain and suffering. The statute defines "severe mental pain or suffering" as:

> the prolonged mental harm caused by or resulting from –
>
> (A) the intentional infliction or threatened infliction of severe physical pain or suffering;
>
> (B) the administration or application, or threatened administration or application, of mind-altering substances or other procedures calculated to disrupt profoundly the senses or the personality;
>
> (C) the threat of imminent death; or
>
> (D) the threat that another person will imminently be subjected to death, severe physical pain or suffering, or the administration or application of mind-altering substances or other procedures calculated to disrupt profoundly the senses or personality.

18 U.S.C. § 2340(2). In order to prove "severe mental pain or suffering," the statute requires proof of "prolonged mental harm" that was caused by or resulted from one of four enumerated acts. We consider each of these elements.

1. "Prolonged Mental Harm". As an initial matter, Section 2340(2) requires that the severe mental pain must be evidenced by "prolonged mental harm." To prolong is to "lengthen in time" or to "extend the duration of, to draw out." Webster's Third New International Dictionary 1815 (1988); Webster's New International Dictionary 1980 (2d ed. 1935). Accordingly, "prolong" adds a temporal dimension to the harm to the individual, namely, that the harm must be one that is endured over some period of time. Put another way, the acts giving rise to the harm must cause some lasting, though not necessarily permanent, damage. For example, the mental strain experienced by an individual during a lengthy and intense interrogation – such as one that state or local police might conduct upon a criminal suspect – would not violate Section 2340(2). On the other hand, the development of a mental disorder such as post-traumatic stress disorder, which can last months or even years, or even chronic depression, which also can last for a considerable period of time if untreated, might satisfy the prolonged

---

view of the statutory text is, however, that they are not distinct concepts. The statute does not define "severe mental pain" and "severe mental suffering" separately. Instead, it gives the phrase "severe mental pain or suffering" a single definition. Because "pain or suffering" is single concept for the purposes of "severe mental pain or suffering," it should likewise be read as a single concept for the purposes of severe physical pain or suffering. Moreover, dictionaries define the words "pain" and "suffering" in terms of each other. *Compare, e.g.,* Webster's Third New International Dictionary 2284 (1993) (defining suffering as "the endurance of . . . pain" or "a pain endured"); Webster's Third New International Dictionary 2284 (1986) (same); XVII The Oxford English Dictionary 125 (2d ed. 1989) (defining suffering as "the bearing or undergoing of pain"); *with, e.g.,* Random House Webster's Unabridged Dictionary 1394 (2d ed. 1999) (defining "pain" as "physical suffering"); The American Heritage Dictionary of the English Language 942 (College ed. 1976) (defining pain as "suffering or distress"). Further, even if we were to read the infliction of severe physical suffering as distinct from severe physical pain, it is difficult to conceive of such suffering that would not involve severe physical pain. Accordingly, we conclude that "pain or suffering" is a single concept within the definition of Section 2340.

harm requirement. *See* American Psychiatric Association, *Diagnostic and Statistical Manual of Mental Disorders* 426, 439–45 (4th ed. 1994) ("DSM-IV"). *See also* Craig Haney & Mona Lynch, *Regulating Prisons of the Future: A Psychological Analysis of Supermax and Solitary Confinement*, 23 N.Y.U. Rev. L. & Soc. Change 477, 509 (1997) (noting that post-traumatic stress disorder is frequently found in torture victims); *cf.* Sana Loue, *Immigration Law and Health* § 10:46 (2001) (recommending evaluating for post-traumatic stress disorder immigrant-client who has experienced torture).[4] By contrast to "severe pain," the phrase "prolonged mental harm" appears nowhere else in the U.S. Code nor does it appear in relevant medical literature or international human rights reports.

Not only must the mental harm be prolonged to amount to severe mental pain and suffering, but also it must be caused by or result from one of the acts listed in the statute. In the absence of a catch-all provision, the most natural reading of the predicate acts listed in Section 2340(2)(A)–(D) is that Congress intended it to be exhaustive. In other words, other acts not included within Section 2340(2)'s enumeration are not within the statutory prohibition. *See Leatherman v. Tarrant Country Narcotics Intelligence & Coordination Unit*, 507 U.S. 163, 168 (1993) ("*Expressio unius est exclusio alterius.*"); Norman Singer, 2A Sutherland on Statutory Construction § 47.23 (6th ed. 2000) ("[W]here a form of conduct, the manner of its performance and operation, and the persons and things to which it refers are designated, there is an inference that all omissions should be understood as exclusions.") (footnotes omitted). We conclude that torture within the meaning of the statute requires the specific intent to cause prolonged mental harm by one of the acts listed in Section 2340(2).

A defendant must specifically intend to cause prolonged mental harm for the defendant to have committed torture. It could be argued that a defendant needs to have specific intent only to commit the predicate acts that give rise to prolonged mental harm. Under that view, so long as the defendant specifically intended to, for example, threaten a victim with imminent death, he would have had sufficient *mens rea* for a conviction. According to this view, it would be further necessary for a conviction to show only that the victim factually suffered prolonged mental harm, rather than that the defendant intended to cause it. We believe that this approach is contrary to the text of the statute. The statute requires that the defendant specifically intend to inflict severe mental pain or suffering. Because the statute requires this mental state with respect to the infliction of severe mental pain, and because it expressly defines severe mental pain in terms of prolonged mental harm, that mental state must be present with respect to prolonged mental harm. To read the statute otherwise would read the phrase "the prolonged mental

---

[4] The DSM-IV explains that post-traumatic disorder ("PTSD") is brought on by exposure to traumatic events, such as serious physical injury or witnessing the deaths of others and during those events the individual felt "intense fear" or "horror." *Id.* at 424. Those suffering from this disorder reexperience the trauma through, *inter alia*, "recurrent and intrusive distressing recollections of the event," "recurrent distressing dreams of the event," or "intense psychological distress at exposure to internal or external cues that symbolize or resemble an aspect of the traumatic event." *Id.* at 428. Additionally, a person with PTSD "[p]ersistent[ly]" avoids stimuli associated with the trauma, including avoiding conversations about the trauma, places that stimulate recollections about the trauma; and they experience a numbing of general responsiveness, such as a "restricted range of affect (e.g., unable to have loving feelings)," and "the feeling of detachment or estrangement from others." *Ibid.* Finally, an individual with PTSD has "[p]ersistent symptoms of increased arousal," as evidenced by "irritability or outbursts of anger," "hypervigilance," "exaggerated startle response," and difficulty sleeping or concentrating. *Ibid.*

harm caused by or resulting from" out of the definition of "severe mental pain or suffering."

A defendant could negate a showing of specific intent to cause severe mental pain or suffering by showing that he had acted in good faith that his conduct would not amount to the acts prohibited by the statute. Thus, if a defendant has a good faith belief that his actions will not result in prolonged mental harm, he lacks the mental state necessary for his actions to constitute torture. A defendant could show that he acted in good faith by taking such steps as surveying professional literature, consulting with experts, or reviewing evidence gained from past experience. *See, e.g., Ratlzlaf*, 510 U.S. at 142 n.10 (noting that where the statute required that the defendant act with the specific intent to violate the law, the specific intent element "might be negated by, e.g., proof that defendant relied in good faith on advice of counsel.") (citations omitted). All of these steps would show that he has drawn on the relevant body of knowledge concerning the result proscribed that the statute, namely prolonged mental harm. Because the presence of good faith would negate the specific intent element of torture, it is a complete defense to such a charge. *See, e.g., United States v. Wall*, 130 F.3d 739, 746 (6th Cir. 1997); *United States v. Casperson*, 773 F.2d 216, 222–23 (8th Cir. 1985).

2. Harm Caused By Or Resulting From Predicate Acts. Section 2340(2) sets forth four basic categories of predicate acts. First in the list is the "intentional infliction or threatened infliction of severe physical pain or suffering." This might at first appear superfluous because the statute already provides that the infliction of severe physical pain or suffering can amount to torture. This provision, however, actually captures the infliction of physical pain or suffering when the defendant inflicts physical pain or suffering with general intent rather than the specific intent that is required where severe physical pain or suffering alone is the basis for the charge. Hence, this subsection reaches the infliction of severe physical pain or suffering when it is but the means of causing prolonged mental harm. Or put another way, a defendant has committed torture when he intentionally inflicts severe physical pain or suffering with the specific intent of causing prolonged mental harm. As for the acts themselves, acts that cause "severe physical pain or suffering" can satisfy this provision.

Additionally, the threat of inflicting such pain is a predicate act under the statute. A threat may be implicit or explicit. *See, e.g., United States v. Sachdev*, 279 F.3d 25, 29 (1st Cir. 2002). In criminal law, courts generally determine whether an individual's words or actions constitute a threat by examining whether a reasonable person in the same circumstances would conclude that a threat had been made. *See, e.g., Watts v. United States*, 394 U.S. 705, 708 (1969) (holding that whether a statement constituted a threat against the President's life had to be determined in light of all the surrounding circumstances); *Sachdev*, 279 F.3d at 29 ("a reasonable person in defendant's position would perceive there to be a threat, explicit, or implicit, of physical injury"); *United States v. Khorrami*, 895 F.2d 1186, 1190 (7th Cir. 1990) (to establish that a threat was made, the statement must be made "in a context or under such circumstances wherein a reasonable person would foresee that the statement would be interpreted by those to whom the maker communicates a statement as a serious expression of an intention to inflict bodily harm upon [another individual]") (citation and internal quotation marks omitted); *United States v. Peterson*, 483 F.2d 1222, 1230 (D.C. Cir. 1973) (perception of threat of imminent harm necessary to establish self-defense had to be "objectively reasonable in light of the surrounding circumstances"). Based on this common approach, we believe that the existence of a threat of severe pain or suffering should be assessed from the standpoint of a reasonable person in the same circumstances.

Second, Section 2340(2)(B) provides that prolonged mental harm, constituting torture, can be caused by "the administration or application or threatened administration or application, of mind-altering substances or other procedures calculated to disrupt profoundly the senses or the personality." The statute provides no further definition of what constitutes a mind-altering substance. The phrase "mind-altering substances" is found nowhere else in the U.S. Code nor is it found in dictionaries. It is, however, a commonly used synonym for drugs. *See, e.g., United States v. Kingsley*, 241 F.3d 828, 834 (6th Cir.) (referring to controlled substances as "mind-altering substance[s]") *cert. denied*, 122 S. Ct. 137 (2001); *Hogue v. Johnson*, 131 F.3d 466, 501 (5th Cir. 1997) (referring to drugs and alcohol as "mind-altering substance[s]"), *cert. denied*, 523 U.S. 1014 (1998). In addition, the phrase appears in a number of state statutes, and the context in which it appears confirms this understanding of the phrase. *See, e.g.,* Cal. Penal Code § 3500(c) (West Supp. 2000) ("Psychotropic drugs also include mind-altering . . . drugs. . . ."); Minn. Stat. Ann. § 260B.201(b) (West Supp. 2002) ("'chemical dependency treatment'" define as programs designed to "reduc[e] the risk of the use of alcohol, drugs, or other mind-altering substances").

This subparagraph, however, does not preclude any and all use of drugs. Instead, it prohibits the use of drugs that "disrupt profoundly the senses or the personality." To be sure, one could argue that this phrase applies only to "other procedures," not the application of mind-altering substances. We reject this interpretation because the terms of Section 2340(2) expressly indicate that the qualifying phrase applies to both "other procedures" *and* the "application of mind-altering substances." The word "other" modifies "procedures calculated to disrupt profoundly the senses." As an adjective, "other" indicates that the term or phrase it modifies is the remainder of several things. *See* Webster's Third New International Dictionary 1598 (1986) (defining "other" as "the one that remains of two or more") Webster's Ninth New Collegiate Dictionary 835 (1985) (defining "other" as "being the one (as of two or more) remaining or not included"). Or put another way, "other" signals that the words to which it attaches are of the same kind, type, or class as the more specific item previously listed. Moreover, where statutes couple words or phrases together, it "denotes an intention that they should be understood in the same general sense." Norman Singer, 2A Sutherland on Statutory Construction § 47:16 (6th ed. 2000); *see also Beecham v. United States*, 511 U.S. 368, 371 (1994) ("That several items in a list share an attribute counsels in favor of interpreting the other items as possessing that attribute as well."). Thus, the pairing of mind-altering substances with procedures calculated to disrupt profoundly the senses or personality and the use of "other" to modify "procedures" shows that the use of such substances must also cause a profound disruption of the senses or personality.

For drugs or procedures to rise to the level of "disrupt[ing] profoundly the senses or personality," they must produce an extreme effect. And by requiring that they be "calculated" to produce such an effect, the statute requires for liability the defendant has consciously designed the acts to produce such an effect.28 U.S.C. § 2340(2)(B). The word "disrupt" is defined as "to break asunder; to part forcibly; rend," imbuing the verb with a connotation of violence. Webster's New International Dictionary 753 (2d ed. 1935); *see* Webster's Third New International Dictionary 656 (1986) (defining disrupt as "to break apart: Rupture" or "destroy the unity or wholeness of"); IV

The Oxford English Dictionary 832 (1989) (defining disrupt as "[t]o break or burst asunder; to break in pieces; to separate forcibly"). Moreover, disruption of the senses or personality alone is insufficient to fall within the scope of this subsection; instead, that disruption must be profound. The word "profound" has a number of meanings, all of which convey a significant depth. Webster's New International Dictionary 1977 (2d ed. 1935) defines profound as: "Of very great depth; extending far below the surface or top; unfathomable[;] . . . [c]oming from, reaching to, or situated at a depth or more than ordinary depth; not superficial; deep-seated; chiefly with reference to the body; as a *profound* sigh, wound, or pain[;] . . . [c]haracterized by intensity, as of feeling or quality; deeply felt or realized; as, *profound* respect, fear, or melancholy; hence, encompassing; thoroughgoing; complete; as, *profound* sleep, silence, or ignorance." *See* Webster's Third New International Dictionary 1812 (1986) ("having very great depth: extending far below the surface . . . not superficial"). Random House Webster's Unabridged Dictionary 1545 (2d ed. 1999) also defines profound as "originating in or penetrating to the depths of one's being" or "pervasive or intense; thorough; complete" or "extending, situated, or originating far down, or far beneath the surface." By requiring that the procedures and the drugs create a *profound* disruption, the statute requires more than that the acts "forcibly separate" or "rend" the senses or personality. Those acts must penetrate to the core of an individual's ability to perceive the world around him, substantially interfering with his cognitive abilities, or fundamentally alter his personality.

The phrase "disrupt profoundly the senses or personality" is not used in mental health literature nor is it derived from elsewhere in U.S. law. Nonetheless, we think the following examples would constitute a profound disruption of the senses or personality. Such an effect might be seen in a drug-induced dementia. In such a state, the individual suffers from significant memory impairment, such as the inability to retain any new information or recall information about things previously of interest to the individual. *See* DSM-IV at 134.[5] This impairment is accompanied by one or more of the following: deterioration of language function, e.g., repeating sounds or words over and over again; impaired ability to execute simple motor activities, e.g., inability to dress or wave goodbye; "[in]ability to recognize [and identify] objects such as chairs or pencils" despite normal visual functioning; or "[d]isturbances in executive level functioning," i.e., serious impairment of abstract thinking. *Id.* at 134–35. Similarly, we think that the onset of "brief psychotic disorder" would satisfy this standard. *See id.* at 302–03. In this disorder, the individual suffers psychotic symptoms, including among other things, delusions, hallucinations, or even a catatonic state. This can last for one day or even one month. *See id.* We likewise think that the onset of obsessive-compulsive disorder behaviors would rise to this level. Obsessions are intrusive thoughts unrelated to reality. They are not simple worries, but are repeated doubts or even "aggressive or horrific impulses." *See id.* at 418. The DSM-IV further explains that compulsions include "repetitive behaviors (e.g., hand washing, ordering,

---

[5] Published by the American Psychiatric Association, and written as a collaboration of over a thousand psychiatrists, the DSM-IV is commonly used in U.S. courts as a source of information regarding mental health issues and is likely to be used in trial should charges be brought that allege this predicate act. *See, e.g., Atkins v. Virginia*, 122 S. Ct. 2242, 2245 n.3 (2002); *Kansas v. Crane*, 122 S. Ct. 867, 871 (2002); *Kansas v. Hendricks*, 521 U.S. 346, 359–60 (1997); *McClean v. Merrifield*, No. 00-CV-0120E(SC), 2002 WL 1477607 at *2 n.7 (W.D.N.Y. June 28, 2002); *Peeples v. Coastal Office Prods.*, 203 F. Supp. 2d. 432, 439 (D. Md. 2002); *Lassiegne v. Taco Bell Corp.*, 202 F. Supp. 2d 512, 519 (E.D. La. 2002).

checking)" and that "[b]y definition, [they] are either clearly excessive or are not connected in a realistic way with what they are designed to neutralize or prevent." *See id.* Such compulsions or obsessions must be "time-consuming." *See id.* at 419. Moreover, we think that pushing someone to the brink of suicide, particularly where the person comes from a culture with strong taboos against suicide, and it is evidenced by acts of self-mutilation, would be a sufficient disruption of the personality to constitute a "profound disruption." These examples, of course, are in no way intended to be exhaustive list. Instead, they are merely intended to illustrate the sort of mental health effects that we believe would accompany an action severe enough to amount to one that "disrupt[s] profoundly the senses or the personality."

The third predicate act listed in Section 2340(2) is threatening a prisoner with "imminent death." 18 U.S.C. § 2340(2)(C). The plain text makes clear that a threat of death alone is insufficient; the threat must indicate that death is "imminent." The "threat of imminent death" is found in the common law as an element of the defense of duress. *See Bailey*, 444 U.S. at 409. "[W]here Congress borrows terms of art in which are accumulated the legal tradition and meaning of centuries of practice, it presumably knows and adopts the cluster of ideas that were attached to each borrowed word in the body of learning from which it was taken and the meaning its use will convey to the judicial mind unless otherwise instructed. In such case, absence of contrary direction may be taken as satisfaction with widely accepted definitions, not as a departure from them." *Morissette v. United States*, 342 U.S. 246, 263 (1952). Common law cases and legislation generally define imminence as requiring that the threat be almost immediately forthcoming. 1 Wayne R. LaFave & Austin W. Scott, Jr., Substantive Criminal Law § 5.7, at 655 (1986). By contrast, threats referring vaguely to things that might happen in the future do not satisfy this immediacy requirement. *See United States v. Fiore*, 178 F.3d 917, 923 (7th Cir. 1999). Such a threat fails to satisfy this requirement not because it is too remote in time but because there is a lack of certainty that it will occur. Indeed, timing is an indicator of certainty that the harm *will* befall the defendant. Thus, a vague threat that someday the prisoner *might* be killed would not suffice. Instead, subjecting a prisoner to mock executions or playing Russian roulette with him would have sufficient immediacy to constitute a threat of imminent death. Additionally, as discussed earlier, we believe that the existence of a threat must be assessed from the perspective of a reasonable person in the same circumstances.

Fourth, if the official threatens to do anything previously described to a third party, or commits such an act against a third party, that threat or action can serve as the necessary predicate for prolonged mental harm. *See* 18 U.S.C. § 2340(2)(D). The statute does not require any relationship between the prisoner and the third party.

3. Legislative History. The legislative history of Sections 2340–2340A is scant. Neither the definition of torture nor these sections as a whole sparked any debate. Congress criminalized this conduct to fulfill U.S. obligations under the U.N. Convention Against Torture and Other Cruel, Inhuman or Degrading Treatment or Punishment ("CAT"), adopted Dec. 10, 1984, S. Treaty Doc. No. 100-20 (1988), 1465 U.N.T.S. 85 (entered into force June 26, 1987), which requires signatories to "ensure that all acts of torture are offenses under its criminal law." CAT Article 4. These sections appeared only in the Senate version of the Foreign Affairs Authorization Act, and the conference bill adopted them without amendment. *See* H. R. Conf. Rep. No. 103-482, at 229 (1994).

The only light that the legislative history sheds reinforces what is already obvious from the texts of Section 2340 and CAT: Congress intended Section 2340's definition of torture to track the definition set forth in CAT, as elucidated by the United States' reservations, understandings, and declarations submitted as part of its ratification. *See* S. Rep. No. 103-107, at 58 (1993) ("The definition of torture emanates directly from Article 1 of the Convention."); *id.* at 58–59 ("The definition for 'severe mental pain and suffering' incorporates the understanding made by the Senate concerning this term.").

4. *Summary.* Section 2340's definition of torture must be read as a sum of these component parts. *See Argentine Rep. v. Amerada Hess Shipping Corp.*, 488 U.S. 428, 434–35 (1989) (reading two provisions together to determine statute's meaning); *Bethesda Hosp. Ass'n v. Bowen*, 485 U.S. 399, 405 (1988) (looking to "the language and design of the statute as a whole" to ascertain a statute's meaning). Each component of the definition emphasizes that torture is not the mere infliction of pain or suffering on another, but is instead a step well removed. The victim must experience intense pain or suffering of the kind that is equivalent to the pain that would be associated with serious physical injury so severe that death, organ failure, or permanent damage resulting in a loss of significant body function will likely result. If that pain or suffering is psychological, that suffering must result from one of the acts set forth in the statute. In addition, these acts must cause long-term mental harm. Indeed, this view of the criminal act of torture is consistent with the term's common meaning. Torture is generally understood to involve "intense pain" or "excruciating pain," or put another way, "extreme anguish of body or mind." Black's Law Dictionary at 1498 (7th Ed. 1999); Random House Webster's Unabridged Dictionary 1999 (1999); Webster's New International Dictionary 2674 (2d ed. 1935). In short, reading the definition of torture as a whole, it is plain that the term encompasses only extreme acts.[6]

---

[6] Torture is a term also found in state law. Some states expressly proscribe "murder by torture." *See*, e.g., Idaho Code § 18-4001 (Michie 1997); N.C. Gen. Stat. Ann. § 14-17 (1999); *see also* Me. Rev. Stat. Ann. tit. 17-A, § 152-A (West Supp. 2001) (aggravated attempted murder is "[t]he attempted murder . . . accompanied by torture, sexual assault or other extreme cruelty inflicted upon the victim"). Other states have made torture an aggravating factor suppositing imposition of the death penalty. *See*, e.g., Ark. Code Ann. § 5-4-604(8)(B); Del. Code Ann. tit. 11, § 4209(e)(1)(*l*) (1995); Ga. Code Ann. § 17-10-30(b)(7) (1997);; 720 Ill. Comp. Stat. Ann. 5/9-1(b)(14) (West Supp. 2002); Mass. Ann. Laws ch. 279, § 69(a) (Law. Co-op. 1992); Mo. Ann. Stat. § 565.032(2)(7) (West 1999); Nev. Rev. Stat. Ann. 200-033(8) (Michie 2001); N.J. Stat. Ann. § 2C:11-3 (West Supp. 2002) (same); Tenn. Code Ann. § 39-13-204(i)(5) (Supp. 2001); *see also* Alaska Stat. § 12.55.125(a)(3) (2000) (term of 99 years' imprisonment mandatory where defendant subjected victim to "substantial physical torture"). *All of these laws support the conclusion that torture is generally an extreme act far beyond the infliction of pain or suffering alone.*

California law is illustrative on this point. The California Penal Code not only makes torture itself an offense, see Cal. Penal Code § 206 (West Supp. 2002), it also prohibits murder by torture, see Cal. Penal Code § 189 (West Supp. 2002), and provides that torture is an aggravating circumstance supporting the imposition of the death penalty, see Cal. Penal Code § 190.2 (West Supp. 2002). California's definitions of torture demonstrate that the term is reserved for especially cruel acts inflicting serious injury. Designed to "fill a gap in existing law dealing with extremely violent and callous criminal conduct[,]" *People v. Hale*, 88 Cal. Rptr. 2d 904, 913 (1999) (internal quotation marks and citation omitted), Section 206 defines the offense of torture as:

> [e]very person who, with the intent to cause *cruel* or *extreme* pain and suffering for the purpose of revenge, extortion, persuasion, or for any sadistic purpose, inflicts great bodily injury . . . upon the person of another, is guilty of torture. The crime of torture does not require any proof that the victim suffered pain.

II. U.N. Convention Against Torture and Other Cruel Inhuman or Degrading Treatment or Punishment

Because Congress enacted the criminal prohibition against torture to implement CAT, we also examine the treaty's text and history to develop a fuller understanding of the context of Sections 2340–2340A. As with the statute, we begin our analysis with the treaty's text. *See Eastern Airlines Inc. v. Floyd*, 499 U.S. 530, 534–35 (1991) ("When interpreting a treaty, we begin with the text of the treaty and the context in which the written words are used.) (quotation marks and citations omitted). CAT defines torture as:

> any act by which *severe* pain or suffering, whether physical or mental, is intentionally inflicted on a person for such purposes as obtaining from him or a third person information or a confession, punishing him for an act he or a third person has committed or is suspected of having committed, or intimidating or coercing him or a third person, or for any reason based on discrimination of any kind, when such pain or suffering is inflicted by or at the instigation of or with the consent or acquiescence of a public official or other person acting in an official capacity.

Article 1(1) (emphasis added). Unlike Section 2340, this definition includes a list of purposes for which such pain and suffering is inflicted. The prefatory phrase "such purposes as" makes clear that this list is, however, illustrative rather than exhaustive. Accordingly, severe pain or suffering need not be inflicted for those specific purposes to constitute torture; instead, the perpetrator must simply have a purpose of the same kind. More importantly, like Section 2340, the pain and suffering must be severe to reach the threshold of torture. Thus, the text of CAT reinforces our reading of Section 2340 that torture must be an extreme act.[7]

(Emphasis added). With respect to sections 190.2 and 189, neither of which are statutorily defined, California courts have recognized that torture generally means an "[a]ct or process of inflicting severe pain, esp[ecially] as a punishment to extort confession, or in revenge. . . . Implicit in that definition is the requirement of an intent to cause pain and suffering in addition to death." *People v. Barrera*, 18 Cal. Rptr. 2d 395, 399 (Ct. App. 1993) (quotation marks and citation omitted). Further, "'murder by torture was and is considered among the most reprehensible types of murder because of the calculated nature of the acts causing death." *Id.* at 403 (quoting *People v. Wiley*, 133 Cal. Rptr. 135, 138 (1976) (in bank)). The definition of murder by torture special circumstance, proscribed under Cal. Penal Code § 190.2, likewise shows an attempt to reach the most heinous acts imposing pain beyond that which a victim suffers through death alone. To establish murder by torture special circumstance, the "intent to kill, intent to torture, and infliction of an extremely painful act upon a living victim" must be present. *People v. Bemore*, 94 Cal. Rptr. 2d 840, 861 (2000). The intent to torture is characterized by a "'sadistic intent to cause the victim to suffer pain in addition to the pain of death.'" *Id.* at 862 (quoting *People v. Davenport*, 221 Cal. Rptr. 794, 875 (1985)). Like the Torture Victims Protection Act and the Convention Against Torture, discussed *infra* at Parts II and III, each of these California prohibitions against torture require an evil intent – such as cruelty, revenge or even sadism. Section 2340 does not require this additional intent, but as discussed *supra* pp. 2–3, requires that the individual specifically intended to cause severe pain or suffering. Furthermore, unlike Section 2340, neither section 189 nor section 206 appear to require proof of actual pain to establish torture.

[7] To be sure, the text of the treaty requires that an individual act "intentionally." This language might be read to require only general intent for violations of the Torture Convention. We believe, however, that the better interpretation is that the use of the phrase "intentionally" also created a specific intent-type standard. In that event, the Bush administration's understanding represents only an explanation of how the United States intended to implement the vague language of the Torture Convention. If, however, the Convention established a general intent standard, then the Bush understanding represents a modification of the obligation undertaken by the United States.

CAT also distinguishes between torture and other acts of cruel, inhuman, or degrading treatment or punishment.[8] Article 16 of CAT requires state parties to "undertake to prevent ... other acts of cruel, inhuman or degrading treatment or punishment *which do not amount to torture* as defined in Article 1." (Emphasis added). CAT thus establishes a category of acts that are not to be committed and that states must endeavor to prevent, but that states need not criminalize, leaving those acts without the stigma of criminal penalties. CAT reserves criminal penalties and the stigma attached to those penalties for torture alone. In so doing, CAT makes clear that torture is at the farthest end of impermissible actions, and that it is distinct and separate from the lower level of "cruel, inhuman, or degrading treatment or punishment." This approach is in keeping with CAT's predecessor, the U.N. Declaration on the Protection from Torture. That declaration defines torture as "an aggravated and deliberate form of cruel, inhuman or degrading treatment or punishment." Declaration on Protection from Torture, UN Res. 3452, Art. 1(2) (Dec. 9, 1975).

A. *Ratification History*

Executive branch interpretation of CAT further supports our conclusion that the treaty, and thus Section 2340A, prohibits only the most extreme forms of physical or mental harm. As we have previously noted, the "division of treaty-making responsibility between the Senate and the President is essentially the reverse of the division of lawmaking authority, with the President being the draftsman of the treaty and the Senate holding the authority to grant or deny approval." *Relevance of Senate Ratification History to Treaty Interpretation*, 11 Op. O.L.C. 28, 31 (Apr. 9, 1987) ("Sofaer Memorandum"). Treaties are negotiated by the President in his capacity as the "sole organ of the federal government in the field of international relations." *United States v. Curtiss-Wright Export Corp.*, 299 U.S. 304, 320 (1936). Moreover, the President is responsible for the day-to-day interpretation of a treaty and retains the power to unilaterally terminate a treaty. *See Goldwater v. Carter*, 617 F.2d 697, 707–08 (D.C. Cir.) (en banc) *vacated and remanded with instructions to dismiss on other grounds*, 444 U.S.

---

[8] Common Article 3 of Geneva Convention on prisoners of war, Convention Relative to the Treatment of Prisoners of War, 6 U.S.T. 3517 ("Geneva Convention III") contains somewhat similar language. Article 3(1)(a) prohibits "violence to life and person, in particular murder of all kinds, mutilation, *cruel treatment and torture.*" (Emphasis added). Article 3(1)(c) additionally prohibits "outrages upon personal dignity, in particular, humiliating and degrading treatment." Subsection (c) must forbid more conduct than that already covered in subsection (a) otherwise subsection (c) would be superfluous. Common Article 3 does not, however, define either of the phrases "outrages upon personal dignity" or "humiliating and degrading treatment." International criminal tribunals, such as those respecting Rwanda and former Yugoslavia have used common Article 3 to try individuals for committing inhuman acts lacking any military necessity whatsoever. Based on our review of the case law, however, these tribunals have not yet articulated the full scope of conduct prohibited by common Article 3. Memorandum for John C. Yoo, Deputy Assistant Attorney General, Office of Legal Counsel, from James C. Ho, Attorney-Advisor, Office of Legal Counsel, *Re: Possible Interpretations of Common Article 3 of the 1949 Geneva Convention Relative to the Treatment of Prisoners of War* (Feb. 1, 2002).

We note that Section 2340A and CAT protect any individual from torture. By contrast, the standards of conduct established by common Article 3 of Convention III, do not apply to "an armed conflict between a nation-state and a transnational terrorist organization." Memorandum for Alberto R. Gonzales, Counsel to the President and William J. Haynes, II, General Counsel, Department of Defense, from Jay S. Bybee, Assistant Attorney General, Office of Legal Counsel, *Re: Application of Treaties and Laws to al Qaeda and Taliban Detainees* at 8 (Jan. 22, 2002).

996 (1979). The Executive's interpretation is to be accorded the greatest weight in ascertaining a treaty's intent and meaning. *See, e.g., United States v. Stuart*, 489 U.S. 353, 369 (1989) ("'the meaning attributed to treaty provisions by the Government agencies charged with their negotiation and enforcement is entitled to great weight'") (quoting *Sumitomo Shoji America, Inc. v. Avagliano*, 457 U.S. 176, 184–85 (1982)); *Kolovrat v. Oregon*, 366 U.S. 187, 194 (1961) ("While courts interpret treaties for themselves, the meaning given them by the department of government particularly charged with their negotiation and enforcement is given great weight."); *Charlton v. Kelly*, 229 U.S. 447, 468 (1913) ("A construction of a treaty by the political departments of the government, while not conclusive upon a court . . . , is nevertheless of much weight.").

A review of the Executive branch's interpretation and understanding of CAT reveals that Congress codified the view that torture included only the most extreme forms of physical or mental harm. When it submitted the Convention to the Senate, the Reagan administration took the position that CAT reached only the most heinous acts. The Reagan administration included the following understanding:

> The United States understands that, in order to constitute torture, an act must be a deliberate and calculated act of an extremely cruel and inhuman nature, specifically intended to inflict excruciating and agonizing physical or mental pain or suffering.

S. Treaty Doc. No. 100–20, at 4–5. Focusing on the treaty's requirement of "severity," the Reagan administration concluded, "The extreme nature of torture is further emphasized in [this] requirement." S. Treaty Doc. No. 100–20, at 3 (1988); S. Exec. Rep. 101–30, at 13 (1990). The Reagan administration also determined that CAT's definition of torture fell in line with "United States and international usage, [where it] is usually reserved for extreme deliberate and unusually cruel practices, for example, sustained systematic beatings, application of electric currents to sensitive parts of the body and tying up or hanging in positions that cause extreme pain." S. Exec. Rep. No. 101–30, at 14 (1990). In interpreting CAT's definition of torture as reaching only such extreme acts, the Reagan administration underscored the distinction between torture and other cruel, inhuman, or degrading treatment or punishment. In particular, the administration declared that Article 1's definition of torture ought to be construed in light of Article 16. *See* S. Treaty Doc. No. 100–20, at 3. Based on this distinction, the administration concluded that: "'Torture' is thus to be distinguished from lesser forms of cruel, inhuman, or degrading treatment or punishment, which are to be deplored and prevented, but are not so universally and categorically condemned as to warrant the severe legal consequences that the Convention provides in case of torture." S. Treaty Doc. 100–20, at 3. Moreover, this distinction was "adopted in order to emphasize that torture is at the extreme end of cruel, inhuman and degrading treatment or punishment." S. Treaty Doc. No. 100–20, at 3. Given the extreme nature of torture, the administration concluded that "rough treatment as generally falls into the category of 'police brutality,' while deplorable, does not amount to 'torture.'" S. Treaty Doc. No. 100–20, at 4.

Although the Reagan administration relied on CAT's distinction between torture and "cruel, inhuman, or degrading treatment or punishment," it viewed the phrase "cruel, inhuman, or degrading treatment or punishment" as vague and lacking in a universally accepted meaning. Of even greater concern to the Reagan administration was that because of its vagueness this phrase could be construed to bar acts not prohibited by the U.S. Constitution. The administration pointed to *Case of X v. Federal Republic of Germany* as the basis for this concern. In that case, the European Court of Human Rights determined that the prison officials' refusal to recognize a prisoner's sex change might constitute degrading treatment. *See* S. Treaty Doc. No. 100–20, at 15 (citing European Commission on Human Rights, *Dec. on Adm.*, Dec. 15, 1977, *Case of X v. Federal Republic of Germany* (No. 6694/74), 11 Dec. & Rep. 16)). As a result of this concern, the Administration added the following understanding:

> The United States understands the term, 'cruel, inhuman or degrading treatment or punishment,' as used in Article 16 of the Convention, to mean the cruel, unusual, and inhumane treatment or punishment prohibited by the Fifth, Eighth and/or Fourteenth Amendments to the Constitution of the United States."

S. Treaty Doc. No. 100–20, at 15–16. Treatment or punishment must therefore rise to the level of action that U.S. courts have found to be in violation of the U.S. Constitution in order to constitute cruel, inhuman, or degrading treatment or punishment. That which fails to rise to this level must fail, *a fortiori*, to constitute torture under Section 2340.[9]

The Senate did not give its advice and consent to the Convention until the first Bush administration. Although using less vigorous rhetoric, the Bush administration joined the Reagan administration in interpreting torture as only reaching extreme acts. To ensure that the Convention's reach remained limited, the Bush administration submitted the following understanding:

> The United States understands that, in order to constitute torture, an act must be specifically intended to inflict severe physical or mental pain or suffering and that mental pain or suffering refers to prolonged mental pain caused by or resulting from (1) the intentional infliction or threatened infliction of severe physical pain or suffering; (2) administration or application, or threatened administration or application, of mind altering substances or other procedures calculated to disrupt profoundly the senses or the personality; (3) the threat of imminent death; or (4) the threat that another person will imminently be subjected to death, severe physical pain or suffering, or the administration or application of mind-altering substances or other procedures calculated to disrupt profoundly the senses or personality.

---

[9] The vagueness of "cruel, inhuman and degrading treatment" enables the term to have a far-ranging reach. Article 3 of the European Convention on Human Rights similarly prohibits such treatment. The European Court of Human Rights has construed this phrase broadly, even assessing whether such treatment has occurred from the subjective standpoint of the victim. *See* Memorandum from James C. Ho, Attorney-Advisor to John C. Yoo, Deputy Assistant Attorney General, *Re: Possible Interpretations of Common Article 3 of the 1949 Geneva Convention Relative to the Treatment of Prisoners of War* (Feb. 1, 2002) (finding that European Court of Human Right's construction of inhuman or degrading treatment "is broad enough to arguably forbid even standard U.S. law enforcement interrogation techniques, which endeavor to breakdown a detainee's 'moral resistance' to answering questions.").

Moreover, despite the Reagan and Bush administrations' efforts to limit the reach of the cruel, inhuman and degrading treatment language, it appears to still have a rather limitless reach. *See id.* (describing how the Eighth Amendment ban on "cruel and unusual punishment" has been used by courts to, *inter alia*, "engage in detailed regulation of prison conductions, including the exact size cells, exercise, and recreational activities, quality of food, access to cable television, Internet, and law libraries.")

S. Exec. Rep. No. 101–30, at 36. This understanding accomplished two things. First, it ensured that the term "intentionally" would be understood as requiring specific intent. Second, it added form and substance to the otherwise amorphous concept of *mental* pain or suffering. In so doing, this understanding ensured that mental torture would rise to a severity seen in the context of physical torture. The Senate ratified CAT with this understanding, and as is obvious from the text, Congress codified this understanding almost verbatim in the criminal statute.

To be sure, it might be thought significant that the Bush administration's language differs from the Reagan administration understanding. The Bush administration said that it had altered the CAT understanding in response to criticism that the Reagan administration's original formulation had raised the bar for the level of pain necessary for the act or acts to constitute torture. *See* Convention Against Torture: Hearing Before the Senate Comm. On Foreign Relations, 101st Cong. 9–10 (1990) ("1990 Hearing") (prepared statement of Hon. Abraham D. Sofaer, Legal Adviser, Department of State). While it is true that there are rhetorical differences between the understandings, both administrations consistently emphasize the extraordinary or extreme acts required to constitute torture. As we have seen, the Bush understanding as codified in Section 2340 reaches only extreme acts. The Reagan understanding, like the Bush understanding, ensured that "intentionally" would be understood as a specific intent requirement. Though the Reagan administration required that the "act be deliberate and calculated" *and* that it be inflicted with specific intent, in operation there is little difference between requiring specific intent alone and requiring that the act be deliberate and calculated. The Reagan understanding's also made express what is obvious from the plain text of CAT: torture is an extreme form of cruel and inhuman treatment. The Reagan administration's understanding that the pain be "excruciating and agonizing" is in substance not different from the Bush administration's proposal that the pain must be severe.

The Bush understanding simply took a rather abstract concept – excruciating and agonizing mental pain – and gave it a more concrete form. Executive branch representations made to the Senate support our view that there was little difference between these two understandings and that the further definition of mental pain or suffering merely sought to remove the vagueness created by concept of "agonizing and excruciating" mental pain. *See* 1990 Hearing, at 10 (prepared statement of Hon. Abraham D. Sofaer, Legal Adviser, Department of State) ("no higher standard was intended" by the Reagan administration understanding than was present in the Convention or the Bush understanding); *id.* at 13–14 (statement of Mark Richard, Deputy Assistant Attorney General, Criminal Division, Department of Justice) ("In an effort to overcome this unacceptable element of vagueness [in the term "mental pain"], we have proposed an understanding which defines severe mental pain constituting torture with sufficient specificity . . . to protect innocent persons and meet constitutional due process requirements.") Accordingly, we believe that the two definitions submitted by the Reagan and Bush administrations had the same purpose in terms of articulating a legal standard, namely, ensuring that the prohibition against torture reaches only the most extreme acts. Ultimately, whether the Reagan standard would have been even higher is a purely academic question because the Bush understanding clearly established a very high standard.

Executive branch representations made to the Senate confirm that the Bush administration maintained the view that torture encompassed only the most extreme acts. Although the ratification record, i.e., testimony, hearings, and the like, is generally not accorded great weight in interpreting treaties, authoritative statements made by representatives of the Executive Branch are accorded the most interpretive value. *See* Sofaer Memorandum, at 35–36. Hence, the testimony of the executive branch witnesses defining torture, in addition to the reservations, understandings and declarations that were submitted to the Senate by the Executive branch, should carry the highest interpretive value of any of the statements in the ratification record. At the Senate hearing on CAT, Mark Richard, Deputy Assistant Attorney General, Criminal Division, Department of Justice, offered extensive testimony as to the meaning of torture. Echoing the analysis submitted by the Reagan administration, he testified that "[t]orture is understood to be that barbaric cruelty which lies at the top of the pyramid of human rights misconduct." 1990 Hearing, at 16 (prepared statement of Mark Richard). He further explained, "As applied to physical torture, there appears to be some degree of consensus that the concept involves conduct, the mere mention of which sends chills down one's spine[.]" *Id.* Richard gave the following examples of conduct satisfying this standard: "the needle under the fingernail, the application of electrical shock to the genital area, the piercing of eyeballs, etc." *Id.* In short, repeating virtually verbatim the terms used in the Reagan understanding, Richard explained that under the Bush administration's submissions with the treaty "the essence of torture" is treatment that inflicts "excruciating and agonizing physical pain." *Id.* (emphasis added).

As to mental torture, Richard testified that "no international consensus had emerged [as to] what degree of mental suffering is required to constitute torture[,]" but that it was nonetheless clear that severe mental pain or suffering "does not encompass the normal legal compulsions which are properly a part of the criminal justice system[:] interrogation, incarceration, prosecution, compelled testimony against a friend, etc, – notwithstanding the fact that they may have the incidental effect of producing mental strain." *Id.* at 17. According to Richard, CAT was intended to "condemn as torture intentional acts such as those designed to damage and destroy the human personality." *Id.* at 14. This description of mental suffering emphasizes the requirement that any mental harm be of significant duration and lends further support for our conclusion that mind-altering substances must have a profoundly disruptive effect to serve as a predicate act.

Apart from statements from Executive branch officials, the rest of a ratification record is of little weight in interpreting a treaty. *See generally* Sofaer Memorandum. Nonetheless, the Senate understanding of the definition of torture largely echoes the administrations' views. The Senate Foreign Relations Committee Report on CAT opined: "[f]or an act to be 'torture' it must be an *extreme* form of cruel and inhuman treatment, cause *severe* pain and suffering and be *intended to cause severe* pain and suffering." S. Exec. Rep. No. 101–30, at 6 (emphasis added). Moreover, like both the Reagan and Bush administrations, the Senate drew upon the distinction between torture and cruel, inhuman or degrading treatment or punishment in reaching its view that torture was extreme.[10] Finally, the Senate concurred

---

[10] Hearing testimony, though the least weighty evidence of meaning of all of the ratification record, is not to the contrary. Other examples of torture mentioned in testimony similarly reflect acts resulting in intense pain: the "gouging out of childrens' [sic] eyes, the torture death by molten rubber, the use of electric shocks," cigarette burns, hanging by hands or feet. 1990 Hearing at 45 (Statement of Winston

with the administrations' concern that "cruel, inhuman, or degrading treatment or punishment" could be construed to establish a new standard above and beyond that which the Constitution mandates and supported the inclusion of the reservation establishing the Constitution as the baseline for determining whether conduct amounted to cruel, inhuman, degrading treatment or punishment. *See* 136 Cong. Rec. 36,192 (1990); S. Exec. Rep. 101–30, at 39.

B. *Negotiating History*

CAT's negotiating history also indicates that its definition of torture supports our reading of Section 2340. The state parties endeavored to craft a definition of torture that reflected the term's gravity. During the negotiations, state parties offered various formulations of the definition of torture to the working group, which then proposed a definition based on those formulations. Almost all of these suggested definitions illustrate the consensus that torture is an extreme act designed to cause agonizing pain. For example, the United States proposed that torture be defined as "includ[ing] any act by which extremely severe pain or suffering . . . is deliberately and maliciously inflicted on a person." J. Herman Burgers & Hans Danelius, *The United Nations Convention Against Torture: A Handbook on the Convention Against Torture and Other Cruel Inhuman and Degrading Treatment or Punishment* 41 (1988) ("CAT Handbook"). The United Kingdom suggested an even more restrictive definition, i.e., that torture be defined as the "*systematic and intentional* infliction of *extreme* pain or suffering rather than *intentional* infliction of *severe* pain or suffering." *Id.* at 45 (emphasis in original). Ultimately, in choosing the phrase "severe pain," the parties concluded that this phrase "sufficient[ly] . . . convey[ed] the idea that only acts of a certain gravity shall . . . constitute torture." *Id.* at 117.

In crafting such a definition, the state parties also were acutely aware of the distinction they drew between torture and cruel, inhuman, or degrading treatment or punishment. The state parties considered and rejected a proposal that would have defined torture merely as cruel, inhuman or degrading treatment or punishment. *See id.* at 42. Mirroring the Declaration on Protection From Torture, which expressly defined torture as an "aggravated and deliberate form of cruel, inhuman or degrading treatment or punishment," some state parties proposed that in addition to the definition of torture set out in paragraph 2 of Article 1, a paragraph defining torture as "an aggravated and deliberate form of cruel, inhuman or degrading treatment or punishment" should be included. *See id.* at 41; *see also* S. Treaty Doc. No. 100–20, at 2 (the U.N. Declaration on Protection from Torture (1975) served as "a point of departure for the drafting of [CAT]"). In the end, the parties concluded that the addition of such a paragraph was superfluous because Article 16 "impl[ies] that torture is the gravest form of such treatment or punishment." *CAT Handbook* at 80; *see* S. Exec. Rep. No. 101–30, at 13 ("The negotiating history indicates that [the phrase 'which do not amount to torture'] was adopted in order to emphasize that torture is at the extreme end of cruel, inhuman and degrading treatment or punishment and that Article 1 should be construed with this in mind.").

Nagan, Chairman, Board of Directors, Amnesty International USA); *id.* at 79 (Statement of David Weissbrodt, Professor of Law, University of Minnesota, on behalf of the Center for Victims of Torture, the Minnesota Lawyers International Human Rights Committee).

Additionally, the parties could not reach a consensus about the meaning of "cruel, inhuman, or degrading treatment or punishment." *See CAT Handbook* at 47. Without a consensus, the parties viewed the term as simply "'too vague to be included in a convention which was to form the basis for criminal legislation in the Contracting States.'" *Id.* This view evinced by the parties reaffirms the interpretation of CAT as purposely reserving criminal penalties for torture alone.

CAT's negotiating history offers more than just support for the view that pain or suffering must be extreme to amount to torture. First, the negotiating history suggests that the harm sustained from the acts of torture need not be permanent. In fact, "the United States considered that it might be useful to develop the negotiating history which indicates that although conduct resulting in permanent impairment of physical or mental faculties is indicative of torture, it is not an essential element of the offence." *Id.* at 44. Second, the state parties to CAT rejected a proposal to include in CAT's definition of torture the use of truth drugs, where no physical harm or mental suffering was apparent. This rejection at least suggests that such drugs were not viewed as amounting to torture per se. *See id.* at 42.

C. Summary

The text of CAT confirms our conclusion that Section 2340A was intended to proscribe only the most egregious conduct. CAT not only defines torture as involving severe pain and suffering, but also it makes clear that such pain and suffering is at the extreme end of the spectrum of acts by reserving criminal penalties solely for torture. Executive interpretations confirm our view that the treaty (and hence the statute) prohibits only the worst forms of cruel, inhuman, or degrading treatment or punishment. The ratification history further substantiates this interpretation. Even the negotiating history displays a recognition that torture is a step far-removed from other cruel, inhuman or degrading treatment or punishment. In sum, CAT's text, ratification history and negotiating history all confirm that Section 2340A reaches only the most heinous acts.

III. U.S. Judicial Interpretation

There are no reported cases of prosecutions under Section 2340A. *See* Beth Stephens, *Corporate Liability: Enforcing Human Rights Through Domestic Litigation*, 24 Hastings Int'l & Comp. L. Rev. 401, 408 & n.29 (2001); Beth Van Schaack, *In Defense of Civil Redress: The Domestic Enforcement of Human Rights Norms in the Context of the Proposed Hague Judgments Convention*, 42 Harv. Int'l L. J. 141, 148–49 (2001); Curtis A. Bradley, *Universal Jurisdiction and U.S. Law*, 2001 U. Chi. Legal F. 323, 327–28. Nonetheless, we are not without guidance as to how United States courts would approach the question of what conduct constitutes torture. Civil suits filed under the Torture Victims Protection Act ("TVPA"), 28 U.S.C. § 1350 note (2000), which supplies a tort remedy for victims of torture, provide insight into what acts U.S. courts would conclude constitute torture under the criminal statute.

The TVPA contains a definition similar in some key respects to the one set forth in Section 2340. Moreover, as with Section 2340, Congress intended for the TVPA's definition of torture to follow closely the definition found in CAT. *See Xuncax v. Gramajo*, 886 F. Supp. 162, 176 n.12 (D. Mass 1995) (noting that the definition of torture in the TVPA tracks the definitions in Section 2340 and CAT).[11] The TVPA defines torture as:

(1)... any act, directed against an individual in the offender's custody or physical control, by which severe pain or suffering (other than pain or suffering arising only from or inherent in, or incidental to, lawful sanctions), whether physical or mental, is intentionally inflicted on that individual for such purposes as obtaining from that individual or a third person information or a confession, punishing that individual for an act that individual or a third person has committed or is suspected of having committed, intimidating or coercing that individual or a third person, or for any reason based on discrimination of any kind; and

(2) mental pain or suffering refers to prolonged mental harm caused by or resulting from –

(A) the intentional infliction or threatened infliction of severe physical pain or suffering;
(B) the administration or application, or threatened administration or application, of mind altering substances or other procedures calculated to disrupt profoundly the senses or the personality;
(C) the threat of imminent death; or
(D) the threat that another individual will imminently be subjected to death, severe physical pain or suffering, or the administration or application of mind altering substances or other procedures calculated to disrupt profoundly the senses or personality.

28 U.S.C. § 1350 note § 3(b). This definition differs from Section 2340's definition in two respects. First, the TVPA definition contains an illustrative list of purposes for which such pain may have been inflicted. See id. Second, the TVPA includes the phrase "arising only from or inherent in, or incidental to lawful sanctions"; by contrast, Section 2340 refers only to pain or suffering "incidental to lawful sanctions." Id. Because the purpose of our analysis here is to ascertain acts that would cross the threshold of producing "severe physical or mental pain or suffering," the list of illustrative purposes for which it is inflicted, generally would not affect this analysis.[12] Similarly, to the extent that the absence of the phrase "arising only from or inherent in" from Section 2340 might affect the question of whether pain or suffering was part of lawful sanctions and thus not torture, the circumstances with which we are concerned here are solely that of interrogations, not the imposition of punishment subsequent to judgment. These differences between the TVPA and Section 2340 are therefore not sufficiently significant to undermine the usefulness of TVPA cases here.[13]

---

[11] See also 137 Cong. Rec. 34,785 (statement of Rep. Mazzoli) ("Torture is defined in accordance with the definition contained in [CAT]"); see also Torture Victims Portection Act: Hearing and Markup on H.R. 1417 Before the Subcomm. On Human Rights and International Organizations of the House Comm. on Foreign Affairs, 100th Cong. 38 (1988) (Prepared Statement of the Association of the Bar of the City of New York, Committee on International Human Rights) ("This language essentially tracks the definition of 'torture' adopted in the Torture Convention.").

[12] This list of purposes is illustrative only. Nevertheless, demonstrating that a defendant harbored any of these purposes "may prove valuable in assisting in the establishment of intent at trial." Matthew Lippman, *The Development and Drafting of the United Nations Convention Against Torture and Other Cruel Inhuman or Degrading Treatment or Punishment*, 17 B.C. Int'l & Comp. L. Rev. 275, 314 (1994).

[13] The TVPA also requires that an individual act "intentionally." As we noted with respect to the text of CAT, see *supra* n. 7, this language might be construed as requiring general intent. It is not clear

In suits brought under the TVPA, courts have not engaged in any lengthy analysis of what acts constitute torture. In part, this is due to the nature of the acts alleged. Almost all of the cases involve physical torture, some of which is of an especially cruel and even sadistic nature. Nonetheless, courts appear to look at the entire course of conduct rather than any one act, making it somewhat akin to a totality-of-the-circumstances analysis. Because of this approach, it is difficult to take a specific act out of context and conclude that the act in isolation would constitute torture. Certain acts do, however, consistently reappear in these cases or are of such a barbaric nature, that it is likely a court would find that allegations of such treatment would constitute torture: (1) severe beatings using instruments such as iron barks, truncheons, and clubs; (2) threats of imminent death, such as mock executions; (3) threats of removing extremities; (4) burning, especially burning with cigarettes; (5) electric shocks to genitalia or threats to do so; (6) rape or sexual assault, or injury to an individual's sexual organs, or threatening to do any of these sorts of acts; and (7) forcing the prisoner to watch the torture of others. Given the highly contextual nature of whether a set of acts constitutes torture, we have set forth in the attached appendix the circumstances in which courts have determined that the plaintiff has suffered torture, which include the cases from which these seven acts are drawn. While we cannot say with certainty that acts falling short of these seven would *not* constitute torture under Section 2340, we believe that interrogation techniques would have to be similar to these in their extreme nature and in the type of harm caused to violate the law.

Despite the limited analysis engaged in by courts, a recent district court opinion provides some assistance in predicting how future courts might address this issue. In *Mehinovic v. Vuckovic*, 198 F. Supp. 2d 1322, (N.D. Ga. 2002), the plaintiffs, Bosnian Muslims, sued a Bosnian Serb, Nikola Vuckovic, for, among other things, torture and cruel and inhumane treatment. The court described in vivid detail the treatment the plaintiffs endured. Specifically, the plaintiffs experienced the following:

Vuckovic repeatedly beat Kemal Mehinovic with a variety of blunt objects and boots, intentionally delivering blows to areas he knew to already be badly injured, including Mehinovic's genitals. *Id.* at 1333–34. On some occasions he was tied up and hung against windows during beatings. *Id.* Mehinovic, was subjected to the game of "Russian roulette" *See id.* Vuckovic, along with other guards, also forced Mehinovic to run in a circle while the guards swung wooden planks at him. *Id.*

Like Mehinovic, Muhamed Bicic was beaten repeatedly with blunt objects, to the point of loss of consciousness. *See Id* at 1335. He witnessed the severe beatings of other prisoners, including his own brother. "On one occasion, Vuckovic ordered Bicic to get on all fours while another soldier stood or rode on his back and beat him with a baton – a game the soldiers called 'horse.'" *Id.* Bicic, like Mehinovic, was subjected to the game of Russian roulette. Additionally, Vuckovic and the other guards forcibly extracted a number of Bicic's teeth. *Id.* at 1336.

Safet Hadzialijagic was subjected to daily beatings with "metal pipes, bats, sticks, and weapons." *Id.* at 1337. He was also subjected to Russian roulette *See id.* at 1336–37.

Hadzialijagic also frequently saw other prisoners being beaten or heard their screams as they were beaten. Like Bicic, he was subjected to the teeth extraction

---

that this is so. We need not resolve that question, however, because we review the TVPA cases solely to address the acts that would satisfy the threshold of inflicting "severe physical or mental pain or suffering."

incident. On one occasion, Vuckovic rode Hadzialijagic like a horse, simultaneously hitting him in the head and body with a knife handle. During this time, other soldiers kicked and hit him. He fell down during this episode and was forced to get up and continue carrying Vuckovic. *See id.* "Vuckovic and the other soldiers [then] tied Hadzialijagic with a rope, hung him upside down, and beat him. When they noticed that Hadzialijagic was losing consciousness, they dunked his head in a bowl used as a toilet." *Id.* Vuckovic then forced Hadzialijagic to lick the blood off of Vuckovic's boots and kicked Hadzialijagic as he tried to do so. Vuckovic then used his knife to carve a semi-circle in Hadzialijagic's forehead. Hadzialijagic went into cardiac arrest just after this incident and was saved by one of the other plaintiffs. *See id.*

Hasan Subasic was brutally beaten and witnessed the beatings of other prisoners, including the beating and death of one of his fellow prisoners and the beating of Hadzialijagic in which he was tied upside down and beaten. *See id.* at 1338–39. *Id.* at 1338. Subasic also was subjected to the teeth pulling incident. Vuckovic personally beat Subasic two times, punching him and kicking him with his military boots. In one of these beatings, "Subasic had been forced into a kneeling position when Vuckovic kicked him in the stomach." *Id.*

The district court concluded that the plaintiffs suffered both physical and mental torture at the hands of Vuckovic.[14] With respect to physical torture, the court broadly outlined with respect to each plaintiff the acts in which Vuckovic had been at least complicit and that it found rose to the level of torture. Regarding Mehinovic, the court determined that Vuckovic's beatings of Mehinovic in which he kicked and delivered other blows to Mehinovic's face, genitals, and others body parts, constituted torture. The court noted that these beatings left Mehinovic disfigured, may have broken ribs, almost caused Mehinovic to lose consciousness, and rendered him unable to eat for a period of time. As to Bicic, the court found that Bicic had suffered severe physical pain and suffering as a result of Vuckovic's repeated beatings of him in which Vuckovic used various instruments to inflict blows, the "horse" game, and the teeth pulling incident. *See id.* at 1346. In finding that Vuckovic inflicted severe physical pain on Hadzialijagic, the court unsurprisingly focused on the beating in which Vuckovic tied Hadzialijagic upside down and beat him. *See id.* The court pointed out that in this incident, Vuckovic almost killed Hadzialijagic. *See id.* The court further concluded that Subasic experienced severe physical pain and thus was tortured based on the beating in which Vuckovic kicked Subasic in the stomach. *See id.*

The court also found that the plaintiffs had suffered severe mental pain. In reaching this conclusion, the court relied on the plaintiffs' testimony that they feared they would be killed during beatings by Vuckovic or during the "game" of Russian roulette. Although the court did not specify the predicate acts that caused the prolonged mental

---

[14] The court also found that a number of acts perpetrated against the plaintiffs constituted cruel, inhuman, or degrading treatment but not torture. In its analysis, the court appeared to fold into cruel, inhuman, or degrading treatment two distinct categories. First, cruel, inhuman, or degrading treatment includes acts that "do not rise to the level of 'torture.'" *Id.* at 1348. Second, cruel, inhuman, or degrading treatment includes acts that "do not have the same purposes as 'torture.'" *Id.* By including this latter set of treatment as cruel, inhuman or degrading, the court appeared to take the view that acts that would otherwise constitute torture fall outside that definition because of the absence of the particular purposes listed in the TVPA and the treaty. Regardless of the relevance of this concept to the TVPA or CAT, the purposes listed in the TVPA are not an element of torture for purposes of sections 2340–2340A.

harm, it is plain that both the threat of severe physical pain and the threat of imminent death were present and persistent. The court also found that the plaintiffs established the existence of prolonged mental harm as each plaintiff *"continues* to suffer long-term psychological harm as a result of [their] ordeals." *Id.* (emphasis added). In concluding that the plaintiffs had demonstrated the necessary "prolonged mental harm," the court's description of that harm as ongoing and "long-term" confirms that, to satisfy the prolonged mental harm requirement, the harm must be of a substantial duration.

The court did not, however, delve into the nature of psychological harm in reaching its conclusion. Nonetheless, the symptoms that the plaintiffs suffered and continue to suffer are worth noting as illustrative of what might in future cases be held to constitute mental harm. Mehinovic had "anxiety, flashbacks, and nightmares and has difficulty sleeping." *Id.* at 1334. Similarly, Bicic, "suffers from anxiety, sleeps very little, and has frequent nightmares" and experiences frustration at not being able to work due to the physical and mental pain he suffers. *Id.* at 1336. Hadzialijagic experienced nightmares, at times required medication to help him sleep, suffered from depression, and had become reclusive as a result of his ordeal. *See id.* at 1337–38. Subasic, like the others, had nightmares and flashbacks, but also suffered from nervousness, irritability, and experienced difficulty trusting people. The combined effect of these symptoms impaired Subasic's ability to work. *See id.* at 1340. Each of these plaintiffs suffered from mental harm that destroyed his ability to function normally, on a daily basis, and would continue to do so into the future.

In general, several guiding principles can be drawn from this case. First, this case illustrates that a single incident can constitute torture. The above recitation of the case's facts shows that Subasic was clearly subjected to torture in a number of instances, e.g., the teeth pulling incident, which the court finds to constitute torture in discussing Bicic. The court nevertheless found that the beating in which Vuckovic delivered a blow to Subasic's stomach while he was on his knees sufficed to establish that Subasic had been tortured. Indeed, the court stated that this incident "caus[ed] Subasic to suffer severe pain." *Id.* at 1346. The court's focus on this incident, despite the obvious context of a course of torturous conduct, suggests that a course of conduct is unnecessary to establish that an individual engaged in torture. It bears noting, however, that there are no decisions that have found an example of torture on facts that show the action was isolated, rather than part of a systematic course of conduct. Moreover, we believe that had this been an isolated instance, the court's conclusion that this act constituted torture would have been in error, because this single blow does not reach the requisite level of severity.

Second, the case demonstrates that courts may be willing to find that a wide range of physical pain can rise to the necessary level of "severe pain or suffering." At one end of the spectrum is what the court calls the "nightmarish beating" in which Vuckovic hung Hadzialijagic upside down and beat him, culminating in Hadzialijagic going into cardiac arrest and narrowly escaping death. *Id.* It takes little analysis or insight to conclude that this incident constitutes torture. At the other end of the spectrum, is the court's determination that a beating in which "Vuckovic hit plaintiff Subasic and kicked him in the stomach with his military boots while Subasic was forced into a kneeling position[]" constituted torture. *Id.* To be sure, this beating caused Subasic substantial pain. But that pain pales in comparison to the other acts described in this case. Again, to the extent the opinion can be read to endorse the view that this single act and the attendant pain, considered in isolation, rose to the level of "severe pain or suffering," we would disagree with such a view based on our interpretation of the criminal statute.

The district court did not attempt to delineate the meaning of torture. It engaged in no statutory analysis. Instead, the court merely recited the definition and described the acts that it concluded constituted torture. This approach is representative of the approach most often taken in TVPA cases. The adoption of such an approach suggests that torture generally is of such an extreme nature – namely, the nature of acts are so shocking and obviously incredibly painful – that courts will more likely examine the totality of the circumstances, rather than engage in a careful parsing of the statute. A broad view of this case, and of the TVPA cases more generally, shows that only acts of an extreme nature have been redressed under the TVPA's civil remedy for torture. We note, however, that *Mehinovic* presents, with the exception of the single blow to Subasic, facts that are well over the line of what constitutes torture. While there are cases that fall far short of torture, see *infra* app., there are no cases that analyze what the lowest boundary of what constitutes torture. Nonetheless, while this case and the other TVPA cases generally do not approach that boundary, they are in keeping with the general notion that the term "torture" is reserved for acts of the most extreme nature.

IV. International Decisions

International decisions can prove of some value in assessing what conduct might rise to the level of severe mental pain or suffering. Although decisions by foreign or international bodies are in no way binding authority upon the United States, they provide guidance about how other nations will likely react to our interpretation of the CAT and Section 2340. As this Part will discuss, other Western nations have generally used a high standard in determining whether interrogation techniques violate the international prohibition on torture. In fact, these decisions have found various aggressive interrogation methods to, at worst, constitute cruel, inhuman, and degrading treatment, but not torture. These decisions only reinforce our view that there is a clear distinction between the two standards and that only extreme conduct, resulting in pain that is of an intensity often accompanying serious physical injury, will violate the latter.

A. European Court of Human Rights

An analogue to CAT's provisions can be found in the European Convention on Human Rights and Fundamental Freedoms (the "European Convention"). This convention prohibits torture, though it offers no definition of it. It also prohibits cruel, inhuman, or degrading treatment or punishment. By barring both types of acts, the European Convention implicitly distinguishes between them and further suggests that torture is a grave act beyond cruel, inhuman, or degrading treatment or punishment. Thus, while neither the European Convention nor the European Court of Human Rights decisions interpreting that convention would be authority for the interpretation of Sections 2340–2340A, the European Convention decisions concerning torture nonetheless provide a useful barometer of the international view of what actions amount to torture.

The leading European Court of Human Rights case explicating the differences between torture and cruel, inhuman, or degrading treatment or punishment is *Ireland v. the United Kingdom* (1978).[15] In that case, the European Court of Human Rights examined interrogation techniques somewhat more sophisticated than the rather rudimentary and frequently obviously cruel acts described in the TVPA cases. Careful attention to this case is worthwhile not just because it examines methods not used in the TVPA cases, but also because the Reagan administration relied on this case in reaching the conclusion that the term torture is reserved in international usage for "extreme, deliberate, and unusually cruel practices." S. Treaty Doc. 100–20, at 4.

The methods at issue in *Ireland* were:

(1) Wall Standing. The prisoner stands spreadeagle against the wall, with fingers high above his head, and feet back so that he is standing on his toes such that his all of his weight falls on his fingers.
(2) Hooding. A black or navy hood is placed over the prisoner's head and kept there except during the interrogation.
(3) Subjection to Noise. Pending interrogation, the prisoner is kept in a room with a loud and continuous hissing noise.
(4) Sleep Deprivation. Prisoners are deprived of sleep pending interrogation.
(5) Deprivation of Food and Drink. Prisoners receive a reduced diet during detention and pending interrogation.

The European Court of Human Rights concluded that these techniques used in combination, and applied for hours at a time, were inhuman and degrading but did not amount to torture. In analyzing whether these methods constituted torture, the court treated them as part of a single program. *See Ireland.* ¶ 104. The court found that this program caused "if not actual bodily injury, at least intense physical and mental suffering to the person subjected thereto and also led to acute psychiatric disturbances during the interrogation." *Id.* ¶ 167. Thus, this program "fell into the category of inhuman treatment[.]" *Id.* The court further found that "[t]he techniques were also degrading since they were such as to arouse in their victims feeling of fear, anguish and inferiority capable of humiliating and debasing them and

---

[15] According to one commentator, the Inter-American Court of Human Rights has also followed this decision. *See* Julie Lantrip, *Torture and Cruel, Inhuman and Degrading Treatment in the Jurisprudence of the Inter-American Court of Human Rights*, 5 ILSA J. Int'l & Comp. L. 551, 560–61 (1999). The Inter-American Convention to Prevent and Punish Torture, however, defines torture much differently than it is defined in CAT or U.S. law. *See* Inter-American Convention to Prevent and Punish Torture, opened for signature Dec. 9, 1985, art. 2, OAS T.S. No. 67 (entered into force Feb. 28, 1987 but the United States has never signed or ratified it). It defines torture as "any act intentionally performed whereby physical or mental pain or suffering is inflicted on a person for purposes of criminal investigation, as a means of intimidation, as personal punishment, as a preventive measure, as a penalty or for any other purpose. Torture shall also be understood to be the use of methods upon a person intended to obliterate the personality of the victim or to diminish his physical or mental capacities, even if they do not cause physical pain or mental anguish." Article 2. While the Inter-American Convention to Prevent and Punish Torture does not require signatories to criminalize cruel, inhuman, or degrading treatment or punishment, the textual differences in the definition of torture are so great that it would be difficult to draw from that jurisprudence anything more than the general trend of its agreement with the *Ireland* decision.

possible [sic] breaking their physical or moral resistance." *Id.* Yet, the court ultimately concluded:

> Although the five techniques, as applied in combination, undoubtedly amounted to inhuman and degrading treatment, although their object was the extraction of confession, the naming of others and/or information and although they were used systematically, they did not occasion suffering of the particular *intensity* and *cruelty* implied by the word torture . . .

Id. (emphasis added). Thus, even though the court had concluded that the techniques produce "intense physical and mental suffering" and "acute psychiatric disturbances," they were not sufficient intensity or cruelty to amount to torture.

The court reached this conclusion based on the distinction the European Convention drew between torture and cruel, inhuman, or degrading treatment or punishment. The court reasoned that by expressly distinguishing between these two categories of treatment, the European Convention sought to "attach a special stigma to deliberate inhuman treatment causing very serious and cruel suffering." *Id.* ¶ 167. According to the court, "this distinction derives principally from a difference in the intensity of the suffering inflicted." *Id.* The court further noted that this distinction paralleled the one drawn in the U.N. Declaration on the Protection From Torture, which specifically defines torture as "'an aggravated and deliberate form of cruel, inhuman or degrading treatment or punishment.'" *Id.* (quoting U.N. Declaration on the Protection From Torture).

The court relied on this same "intensity/cruelty" distinction to conclude that some physical maltreatment fails to amount to torture. For example, four detainees were severely beaten and forced to stand spreadeagle up against a wall. *See id.* ¶ 110. Other detainees were forced to stand spreadeagle while an interrogator kicked them "continuously on the inside of the legs." *Id.* ¶ 111. Those detainees were beaten, some receiving injuries that were "substantial" and, others received "massive" injuries. *See id.* Another detainee was "subjected to . . . 'comparatively trivial' beatings" that resulted in a perforation of the detainee's eardrum and some "minor bruising." *Id.* ¶ 115. The court concluded that none of these situations "attain[ed] the particular level [of severity] inherent in the notion of torture." *Id.* ¶ 174.

B. Israeli Supreme Court

The European Court of Human Rights is not the only other court to consider whether such a program of interrogation techniques was permissible. In *Public Committee Against Torture in Israel v. Israel*, 38 I.L.M. 1471 (1999), the Supreme Court of Israel reviewed a challenge brought against the General Security Service ("GSS") for its use of five techniques. At issue in *Public Committee Against Torture In Israel* were: (1) shaking, (2) the Shabach, (3) the Frog Crouch, (4) excessive tightening of handcuffs, and (5) sleep deprivation. "Shaking" is "the forceful shaking of the suspect's upper torso, back and forth, repeatedly, in a manner which causes the neck and head to dangle and vacillate rapidly." *Id.* ¶ 9. The "Shabach" is actually a combination of methods wherein the detainee

> is seated on a small and low chair, whose seat is tilted forward, towards the ground. One hand is tied behind the suspect, and placed inside the gap between the chair's seat and back support. His second hand is tied behind the chair, against its back

support. The suspect's head is covered by an opaque sack, falling down to his shoulders. Powerfully loud music is played in the room.

Id. ¶ 10.

The "frog crouch" consists of "consecutive, periodical crouches on the tips of one's toes, each lasting for five minute intervals." *Id.* ¶ 11. The excessive tightening of handcuffs simply referred to the use handcuffs that were too small for the suspects' wrists. *See id.* ¶ 12. Sleep deprivation occurred when the Shabach was used during "intense non-stop interrogations."[16] *Id.* ¶ 13.

While the Israeli Supreme Court concluded that these acts amounted to cruel, and inhuman treatment, the court did not expressly find that they amounted to torture. To be sure, such a conclusion was unnecessary because even if the acts amounted only to cruel and inhuman treatment the GSS lacked authority to use the five methods. Nonetheless, the decision is still best read as indicating that the acts at issue did not constitute torture. The court's descriptions of and conclusions about each method indicate that the court viewed them as merely cruel, inhuman or degrading but not of the sufficient severity to reach the threshold of torture. While its descriptions discuss necessity, dignity, degradation, and pain, the court carefully avoided describing any of these acts as having the severity of pain or suffering indicative of torture. *See id.* at ¶ ¶ 24–29. Indeed, in assessing the *Shabach* as a whole, the court even relied upon the European Court of Human Right's *Ireland* decision for support and it did not evince disagreement with that decision's conclusion that the acts considered therein did not constitute torture. *See id.* ¶ 30.

Moreover, the Israeli Supreme Court concluded that in certain circumstances GSS officers could assert a necessity defense.[17] CAT, however, expressly provides that "[n]o exceptional circumstance whatsoever, whether a state of war or a threat of war, internal political instability or any other public emergency may be invoked as a justification of torture." Article 2(2). Had the court been of the view that the GSS methods constituted torture, the Court could not permit this affirmative defense under CAT. Accordingly, the court's decision is best read as concluding that these methods amounted to cruel and inhuman treatment, but not torture.

In sum, both the European Court on Human Rights and the Israeli Supreme Court have recognized a wide array of acts that constitute cruel, inhuman, or degrading treatment or punishment, but do not amount to torture. Thus, they appear to permit, under international law, an aggressive interpretation as to what amounts to torture, leaving that label to be applied only where extreme circumstances exist.

---

[16] The court did, however, distinguish between this sleep deprivation and that which occurred as part of routine interrogation, noting that some degree of interference with the suspect's regular sleep habits was to be expected. *Public Committee Against Torture in Israel* ¶ 23.

[17] In permitting a necessity defense, the court drew upon the ticking time bomb hypothesis proffered by the GSS as a basis for asserting a necessity defense. In that hypothesis, the GSS has arrested a suspect, who holds information about the location of a bomb and the time at which it is set to explode. The suspect is the only source of this information, and without that information the bomb will surely explode, killing many people. Under those circumstances, the court agreed that the necessity defense's requirement of imminence, which the court construed as the "imminent nature of the act rather than that of danger," would be satisfied. *Id.* ¶ 34. It further agreed "that in appropriate circumstances" this defense would be available to GSS investigators. *Id.* ¶ 35.

V. *The President's Commander-in-Chief Power*

Even if an interrogation method arguably were to violate Section 2340A, the statute would be unconstitutional if it impermissibly encroached on the President's constitutional power to conduct a military campaign. As Commander-in-Chief, the President has the constitutional authority to order interrogations of enemy combatants to gain intelligence information concerning the military plans of the enemy. The demands of the Commander-in-Chief power are especially pronounced in the middle of a war in which the nation has already suffered a direct attack. In such a case, the information gained from interrogations may prevent future attacks by foreign enemies. Any effort to apply Section 2340A in a manner that interferes with the President's direction of such core war matters as the detention and interrogation of enemy combatants thus would be unconstitutional.

A. *The War with Al Qaeda*

At the outset, we should make clear the nature of the threat presently posed to the nation. While your request for legal advice is not specifically limited to the current circumstances, we think it is useful to discuss this question in the context of the current war against the al Qaeda terrorist network. The situation in which these issues arise is unprecedented in recent American history. Four coordinated terrorist attacks, using hijacked commercial airliners as guided missiles, took place in rapid succession on the morning of September 11, 2001. These attacks were aimed at critical government buildings in the Nation's capital and landmark buildings in its financial center. These events reach a different scale of destructiveness than earlier terrorist episodes, such as the destruction of the Murrah Building in Oklahoma City in 1994. They caused thousands of deaths. Air traffic and communications within the United States were disrupted; national stock exchanges were shut for several days; and damage from the attack has been estimated to run into the tens of billions of dollars. Moreover, these attacks are part of a violent campaign against the United States that is believed to include an unsuccessful attempt to destroy an airliner in December 2001; a suicide bombing attack in Yemen on the *U.S.S. Cole* in 2000; the bombings of the United States Embassies in Kenya and in Tanzania in 1998; a truck bomb attack on a U.S. military housing complex in Saudi Arabia in 1996; an unsuccessful attempt to destroy the World Trade Center in 1993; and the ambush of U.S. servicemen in Somalia in 1993. The United States and its overseas personnel and installations have been attacked as a result of Osama Bin Laden's call for a "jihad against the U.S. government, because the U.S. government is unjust, criminal and tyrannical."[18]

In response, the Government has engaged in a broad effort at home and abroad to counter terrorism. Pursuant to his authorities as Commander-in-Chief, the President in October, 2001, ordered the Armed Forces to attack al Qaeda personnel and assets in Afghanistan, and the Taliban militia that harbored them. That military campaign appears to be nearing its close with the retreat of al Qaeda and Taliban forces from their strongholds and the installation of a friendly provisional government in Afghanistan. Congress has provided its support for the use of forces against those linked to the

---

[18] *See Osama Bin Laden v. The U.S.: Edicts and Statements*, CNN Interview with Osama bin Laden, March 1997, *available at* http://www.pbs.org/wgbh/pages/frontline/shows/binladen/who/edicts.html.

September 11 attacks, and has recognized the President's constitutional power to use force to prevent and deter future attacks both within and outside the United States. S. J. Res. 23, Pub. L. No. 107–40, 115 Stat. 224 (2001). We have reviewed the President's constitutional power to use force abroad in response to the September 11 attacks in a separate memorandum. *See* Memorandum for Timothy E. Flanigan, Deputy Counsel to the President, from John C. Yoo, Deputy Assistant Attorney General, Office of Legal Counsel, *Re: The President's Constitutional Authority to Conduct Military Operations Against Terrorists and Nations Supporting Them* (Sept. 25, 2001) ("September 11 War Powers Memorandum"). We have also discussed the President's constitutional authority to deploy the armed forces domestically to protect against foreign terrorist attack in a separate memorandum. *See* Memorandum for Alberto R. Gonzales, Counsel to the President and William J. Haynes, II, General Counsel, Department of Defense, from John C. Yoo, Deputy Assistant Attorney General and Robert J. Delahunty, Special Counsel, Office of Legal Counsel, *Re: Authority for Use of Military Force to Combat Terrorist Activities Within the United States* at 2–3 (Oct. 17, 2001). The Justice Department and the FBI have launched a sweeping investigation in response to the September 11 attacks, and last fall Congress enacted legislation to expand the Justice Department's powers of surveillance against terrorists. *See* The USA Patriot Act, Pub. L. No. 107–56, 115 Stat. 272 (Oct. 26, 2001). This spring, the President proposed the creation of a new cabinet department for homeland security to implement a coordinated domestic program against terrorism.

Despite these efforts, numerous upper echelon leaders of al Qaeda and the Taliban, with access to active terrorist cells and other resources, remain at large. It has been reported that the al Qaeda fighters are already drawing on a fresh flow of cash to rebuild their forces. *See* Paul Haven, *U.S.: al-Qaida Trying to Regroup*, Associated Press, Mar. 20, 2002. As the Director of the Central Intelligence Agency has recently testified before Congress, "al Qaeda and other terrorist groups will continue to plan to attack this country and its interests abroad. Their modus operandi is to have multiple attack plans in the works simultaneously, and to have al Qaeda cells in place to conduct them." Testimony of George J. Tenet, Director of Central Intelligence, Before the Senate Armed Services Committee at 2 (Mar. 19, 2002). Nor is the threat contained to Afghanistan. "Operations against US targets could be launched by al Qaeda cells already in place in major cities in Europe and the Middle East. al Qaeda can also exploit its presence or connections to other groups in such countries as Somalia, Yemen, Indonesia, and the Philippines." *Id.* at 3. It appears that al Qaeda continues to enjoy information and resources that allow it to organize and direct active hostile forces against this country, both domestically and abroad.

Al Qaeda continues to plan further attacks, such as destroying American civilian airliners and killing American troops, which have fortunately been prevented. It is clear that bin Laden and his organization have conducted several violent attacks on the United States and its nationals, and that they seek to continue to do so. Thus, the capture and interrogation of such individuals is clearly imperative to our national security and defense. Interrogation of captured al Qaeda operatives may provide information concerning the nature of al Qaeda plans and the identities of its personnel, which may prove invaluable in preventing further direct attacks on the United States and its citizens. Given the massive destruction and loss of life caused by the September 11 attacks, it is reasonable to believe that information gained from al Qaeda personnel could prevent attacks of a similar (if not greater) magnitude from occurring in the United States. The case of Jose Padilla, a.k.a. Abdullah Al Mujahir, illustrates the importance of such information. Padilla allegedly had journeyed to Afghanistan and Pakistan, met with senior al Qaeda leaders, and hatched a plot to construct and detonate a radioactive dispersal device in the United States. After allegedly receiving training in wiring explosives and with a substantial amount of currency in his position, Padilla attempted in May, 2002, to enter the United States to further his scheme. Interrogation of captured al Qaeda operatives allegedly allowed U.S. intelligence and law enforcement agencies to track Padilla and to detain him upon his entry into the United States.

B. *Interpretation to Avoid Constitutional Problems*

As the Supreme Court has recognized, and as we will explain further below, the President enjoys complete discretion in the exercise of his Commander-in-Chief authority and in conducting operations against hostile forces. Because both "[t]he executive power and the command of the military and naval forces is vested in the President," the Supreme Court has unanimously stated that it is *"the President alone* who is constitutionally invested with the *entire charge of hostile operations." Hamilton v. Dillin*, 88 U.S. (21 Wall.) 73, 87 (1874) (emphasis added). That authority is at its height in the middle of a war.

In light of the President's complete authority over the conduct of war, without a clear statement otherwise, we will not read a criminal statute as infringing on the President's ultimate authority in these areas. We have long recognized, and the Supreme Court has established a canon of statutory construction that statutes are to be construed in a manner that avoids constitutional difficulties so long as a reasonable alternative construction is available. *See, e.g., Edward J. DeBartolo Corp. v. Florida Gulf Coast Bldg. & Constr. Trades Council*, 485 U.S. 568, 575 (1988) (citing *NLRB v. Catholic Bishop of Chicago*, 440 U.S. 490, 499–501, 504 (1979)) ("[W]here an otherwise acceptable construction of a statute would raise serious constitutional problems, [courts] will construe [a] statute to avoid such problems unless such construction is plainly contrary to the intent of Congress."). This canon of construction applies especially where an act of Congress could be read to encroach upon powers constitutionally committed to a coordinate branch of government. *See, e.g., Franklin v. Massachusetts*, 505 U.S. 788, 800–1 (1992) (citation omitted) ("Out of respect for the separation of powers and the unique constitutional position of the President, we find that textual silence is not enough to subject the President to the provisions of the [Administrative Procedure Act]. We would require an express statement by Congress before assuming it intended the President's performance of his statutory duties to be reviewed for abuse of discretion."); *Public Citizen v. United States Dep't of Justice*, 491 U.S. 440, 465–67 (1989) (construing Federal Advisory Committee Act not to apply to advice given by American Bar Association to the President on judicial nominations, to avoid potential constitutional question regarding encroachment on Presidential power to appoint judges).

In the area of foreign affairs, and war powers in particular, the avoidance canon has special force. *See, e.g., Dep't of Navy v. Egan*, 484 U.S. 518, 530 (1988) ("unless Congress specifically has provided otherwise, courts traditionally have been reluctant to intrude upon the authority of the Executive in military and national security affairs."); *Japan Whaling Ass'n v. American Cetacean Soc'y*, 478 U.S. 221, 232–33 (1986) (construing federal statutes to avoid curtailment of traditional presidential prerogatives in foreign affairs). We do not lightly assume that Congress has acted to interfere with the President's constitutionally superior position as Chief Executive and Commander-in-Chief in the area of military operations. *See Egan*, 484 U.S. at 529 (quoting *Haig v. Agee*, 453 U.S. 280, 293–94 (1981)). *See also Agee*, 453 U.S. at 291 (deference to Executive Branch is "especially" appropriate "in the area...of...national security").

In order to respect the President's inherent constitutional authority to manage a military campaign against al Qaeda and its allies, Section 2340A must be construed as not applying to interrogations undertaken pursuant to his Commander-in-Chief authority. As our Office has consistently held during this Administration and previous Administrations, Congress lacks authority under Article I to set the terms and conditions under which the President may exercise his authority as Commander-in-Chief to control the conduct of operations during a war. *See, e.g.*, Memorandum for Daniel J. Bryant, Assistant Attorney General, Office of Legislative Affairs, from Patrick F. Philbin, Deputy Assistant Attorney General, Office of Legal Counsel, *Re: Swift Justice Authorization Act* (Apr. 8, 2002); Memorandum for Timothy E. Flanigan, Deputy Counsel to the President, from John C. Yoo, Deputy Assistant Attorney General, Office of Legal Counsel, *Re: The President's Constitutional Authority to Conduct Military Operations Against Terrorists and Nations Supporting Them* (Sep. 25, 2001) ("Flanigan Memorandum"); Memorandum for Andrew Fois, Assistant Attorney General, Office of Legislative Affairs, from Richard L. Shiffrin, Deputy Assistant Attorney General, Office of Legal Counsel, *Re: Defense Authorization Act* (Sep. 15, 1995). As we discuss below, the President's power to detain and interrogate enemy combatants arises out of his constitutional authority as Commander-in-Chief. A construction of Section 2340A that applied the provision to regulate the President's authority as Commander-in-Chief to determine the interrogation and treatment of enemy combatants would raise serious constitutional questions. Congress may no more regulate the President's ability to detain and interrogate enemy combatants than it may regulate his ability to direct troop movements on the battlefield. Accordingly, we would construe Section 2340A to avoid this constitutional difficulty, and conclude that it does not apply to the President's detention and interrogation of enemy combatants pursuant to his Commander-in-Chief authority.

This approach is consistent with previous decisions of our Office involving the application of federal criminal law. For example, we have previously construed the congressional contempt statute not to apply to executive branch officials who refuse to comply with congressional subpoenas because of an assertion of executive privilege. In a published 1984 opinion, we concluded that

> if executive officials were subject to prosecution for criminal contempt whenever they carried out the President's claim of executive privilege, it would significantly burden and immeasurably impair the President's ability to fulfill his constitutional duties. Therefore, the separation of powers principles that underlie the doctrine of executive privilege also would preclude an application of the contempt of Congress statute to punish officials for aiding the President in asserting his constitutional privilege.

Prosecution for Contempt of Congress of an Executive Branch Official Who Has As-
serted A Claim of Executive Privilege, 8 Op. O.L.C. 101, 134 (May 30, 1984). Likewise,
we believe that, if executive officials were subject to prosecution for conducting interrogations when they were carrying out the President's Commander-in-Chief powers,
"it would significantly burden and immeasurably impair the President's ability to fulfill his constitutional duties." These constitutional principles preclude an application
of Section 2340A to punish officials for aiding the President in exercising his exclusive
constitutional authorities. *Id.*

C. The Commander-in-Chief Power

It could be argued that Congress enacted 18 U.S.C. § 2340A with full knowledge and
consideration of the President's Commander-in-Chief power, and that Congress intended to restrict his discretion in the interrogation of enemy combatants. Even were
we to accept this argument, however, we conclude that the Department of Justice could
not enforce Section 2340A against federal officials acting pursuant to the President's
constitutional authority to wage a military campaign.

Indeed, in a different context, we have concluded that both courts and prosecutors
should reject prosecutions that apply federal criminal laws to activity that is authorized pursuant to one of the President's constitutional powers. This Office, for example,
has previously concluded that Congress could not constitutionally extend the congressional contempt statute to executive branch officials who refuse to comply with
congressional subpoenas because of an assertion of executive privilege. We opined
that "courts ... would surely conclude that a criminal prosecution for the exercise of
a presumptively valid, constitutionally based privilege is not consistent with the Constitution." 8 Op. O.L.C. at 141. Further, we concluded that the Department of Justice
could not bring a criminal prosecution against a defendant who had acted pursuant to
an exercise of the President's constitutional power. "The President, through a United
States Attorney, need not, indeed may not, prosecute criminally a subordinate for asserting on his behalf a claim of executive privilege. Nor could the Legislative Branch or
the courts require or implement the prosecution of such an individual." *Id.* Although
Congress may define federal crimes that the President, through the Take Care Clause,
should prosecute, Congress cannot compel the President to prosecute outcomes
taken pursuant to the President's own constitutional authority. If Congress could
do so, it could control the President's authority through the manipulation of federal
criminal law.

We have even greater concerns with respect to prosecutions arising out of the exercise of the President's express authority as Commander-in-Chief than we do with
prosecutions arising out of the assertion of executive privilege. In a series of opinions examining various legal questions arising after September 11, we have explained
the scope of the President's Commander-in-Chief power.[19] We briefly summarize the
findings of those opinions here. The President's constitutional power to protect the
security of the United States and the lives and safety of its people must be understood
in light of the Founders' intention to create a federal government "clothed with all

---

[19] *See, e.g.*, September 11 War Powers Memorandum; Memorandum for Alberto R. Gonzales, Counsel
to the President, from Patrick F. Philbin, Deputy Assistant Attorney General, Office of Legal Counsel,
Re: Legality of the Use of Military Commissions to Try Terrorists (Nov. 6, 2001).

the powers requisite to the complete execution of its trust." *The Federalist* No. 23, at 147 (Alexander Hamilton) (Jacob E. Cooke ed. 1961). Foremost among the objectives committed to that trust by the Constitution is the security of the nation. As Hamilton explained in arguing for the Constitution's adoption, because "the circumstances which may affect the public safety" are not "reducible within certain determinate limits,"

> it must be admitted, as a necessary consequence, that there can be no limitation of that authority, which is to provide for the defence and protection of the community, in any matter essential to its efficacy.

Id. at 147–48. Within the limits that the Constitution itself imposes, the scope and distribution of the powers to protect national security must be construed to authorize the most efficacious defense of the nation and its interests in accordance "with the realistic purposes of the entire instrument." *Lichter v. United States*, 334 U.S. 742, 782 (1948).

The text, structure and history of the Constitution establish that the Founders entrusted the President with the primary responsibility, and therefore the power, to ensure the security of the United States in situations of grave and unforeseen emergencies. The decision to deploy military force in the defense of United States interests is expressly placed under Presidential authority by the Vesting Clause, U.S. Const. Art. I, § 1, cl. 1, and by the Commander-in-Chief Clause, *id.*, § 2, cl. 1.[20] This Office has long understood the Commander-in-Chief Clause in particular as an affirmative grant of authority to the President. *See, e.g.*, Memorandum for Charles W. Colson, Special Counsel to the President, from William H. Rehnquist, Assistant Attorney General, Office of Legal Counsel, *Re: The President and the War Power: South Vietnam and the Cambodian Sanctuaries* (May 22, 1970) ("Rehnquist Memorandum"). The Framers understood the Clause as investing the President with the fullest range of power understood at the time of the ratification of the Constitution as belonging to the military commander. In addition, the structure of the Constitution demonstrates that any power traditionally understood as pertaining to the executive – which includes the conduct of warfare and the defense of the nation – unless expressly assigned in the Constitution to Congress, is vested in the President. Article II, Section 1 makes this clear by stating that the "executive Power shall be vested in a President of the United States of America." That sweeping grant vests in the President an unenumerated "executive power" and contrasts with the specific enumeration of the powers – those "herein" – granted to Congress in Article I. The implications of constitutional

---

[20] *See Johnson v. Eisentrager*, 339 U.S. 763, 789 (1950) (President has authority to deploy United States armed forces "abroad or to any particular region"); *Fleming v. Page*, 50 U.S. (9 How.) 603, 614–15 (1850) ("As Commander-in-Chief, [the President] is authorized to direct the movements of the naval and military forces placed by law at his command, and to employ them in the manner he may deem most effectual") *Loving v. United States*, 517 U.S. 748, 776 (1996) (Scalia, J., concurring in part and concurring in judgment) (The "inherent powers" of the Commander-in-Chief "are clearly extensive."); *Maul v. United States*, 274 U.S. 501, 515–16 (1927) (Brandeis & Holmes, JJ., concurring) (President "may direct any revenue cutter to cruise in any waters in order to perform any duty of the service"); *Commonwealth of Massachusetts v. Laird*, 451 F.2d 26, 32 (1st Cir. 1971) (the President has "power as Commander-in-Chief to station forces abroad"); *Ex parte Vallandigham*, 28 F.Cas. 874, 922 (C.C.S.D. Ohio 1863) (No. 16,816) (in acting "under this power where there is no express legislative declaration, the president is guided solely by his own judgment and discretion"); *Authority to Use United States Military Forces in Somalia*, 16 Op. O.L.C. 6, 6 (Dec. 4, 1992) (Barr, Attorney General).

text and structure are confirmed by the practical consideration that national security decisions require the unity in purpose and energy in action that characterize the Presidency rather than Congress.[21]

As the Supreme Court has recognized, the Commander-in-Chief power and the President's obligation to protect the nation imply the ancillary powers necessary to their successful exercise. "The first of the enumerated powers of the President is that he shall be Commander-in-Chief of the Army and Navy of the United States. And, of course, the grant of war power includes all that is necessary and proper for carrying those powers into execution." *Johnson v. Eisentrager*, 339 U.S. 763, 788 (1950). In wartime, it is for the President alone to decide what methods to use to best prevail against the enemy. *See, e.g.*, Rehnquist Memorandum; Flanigan Memorandum at 3. The President's complete discretion in exercising the Commander-in-Chief power has been recognized by the courts. In the *Prize Cases*, 67 U.S. (2 Black) 635, 670 (1862), for example, the Court explained that whether the President "in fulfilling his duties as Commander-in-Chief" had appropriately responded to the rebellion of the southern states was a question "to be *decided by him*" and which the Court could not question, but must leave to "the political department of the Government to which this power was entrusted."

One of the core functions of the Commander-in-Chief is that of capturing, detaining, and interrogating members of the enemy. *See, e.g.*, Memorandum for William J. Haynes, II, General Counsel, Department of Defense, from Jay S. Bybee, Assistant Attorney General, Office of Legal Counsel, *Re: The President's Power as Commander in Chief to Transfer Captured Terrorists to the Control and Custody of Foreign Nations* at 3 (March 13, 2002) ("the Commander-in-Chief Clause constitutes an independent grant of substantive authority to engage in the detention and transfer of prisoners captured in armed conflicts"). It is well settled that the President may seize and detain enemy combatants, at least for the duration of the conflict, and the laws of war make clear that prisoners may be interrogated for information concerning the enemy, its strength, and its plans.[22] Numerous Presidents have ordered the capture, detention,

---

[21] Judicial decisions since the beginning of the Republic confirm the President's constitutional power and duty to repel military action against the United States and to take measures to prevent the recurrence of an attack. As Justice Joseph Story said long ago, "[i]t may be fit and proper for the government, in the exercise of the high discretion confided to the executive, for great public purposes, to act on a sudden emergency, or to prevent an irreparable mischief, by summary measures, which are not found in the text of the laws." *The Apollon*, 22 U.S. (9 Wheat.) 362, 366–67 (1824). If the President is confronted with an unforeseen attack on the territory and people of the United States, or other immediate, dangerous threat to American interests and security, it is his constitutional responsibility to respond to that threat with whatever means are necessary. *See, e.g.*, *The Prize Cases*, 67 U.S. (2 Black) 635, 668 (1862) ("If a war be made by invasion of a foreign nation, the President is not only authorized but bound to resist force by force . . . without waiting for any special legislative authority."); *United States v. Smith*, 27 F. Cas. 1192, 1229–30 (C.C.D.N.Y. 1806) (No. 16,342) (Paterson, Circuit Justice) (regardless of statutory authorization, it is "the duty . . . of the executive magistrate . . . to repel an invading foe"); *see also* 3 Story, *Commentaries* § 1485 ("[t]he command and application of the public force . . . to maintain peace, and to resist foreign invasion" are executive powers).

[22] The practice of capturing and detaining enemy combatants is as old as war itself. *See* Allan Rosas, The Legal Status of Prisoners of War 44–45 (1976). In modern conflicts, the practice of detaining enemy combatants and hostile civilians generally has been designed to balance the humanitarian purpose of sparing lives with the military necessity of defeating the enemy on the battlefield. *Id.* at 59–80. While Article 17 of the Geneva Convention Relative to the Treatment of Prisoners of War, Aug. 12, 1949, 6 U.S.T. 3517, places restrictions on interrogation of enemy combatants, members of al Qaeda and the Taliban militia are not legally entitled to the status of prisoners of war as defined in

and questioning of enemy combatants during virtually every major conflict in the Nation's history, including recent conflicts such as the Gulf, Vietnam, and Korean wars. Recognizing this authority, Congress has never attempted to restrict or interfere with the President's authority on this score. *Id.*

Any effort by Congress to regulate the interrogation of battlefield combatants would violate the Constitution's sole vesting of the Commander-in-Chief authority in the President. There can be little doubt that intelligence operations, such as the detention and interrogation of enemy combatants and leaders, are both necessary and proper for the effective conduct of a military campaign. Indeed, such operations may be of more importance in a war with an international terrorist organization than one with the conventional armed forces of a nation-state, due to the former's emphasis on secret operations and surprise attacks against civilians. It may be the case that only successful interrogations can provide the information necessary to prevent the success of covert terrorist attacks upon the United States and its citizens. Congress can no more interfere with the President's conduct of the interrogation of enemy combatants than it can dictate strategic or tactical decisions on the battlefield. Just as statutes that order the President to conduct warfare in a certain manner or for specific goals would be unconstitutional, so too are laws that seek to prevent the President from gaining the intelligence he believes necessary to prevent attacks upon the United States.

VI. Defenses

In the foregoing parts of this memorandum, we have demonstrated that the ban on torture in Section 2340A is limited to only the most extreme forms of physical and mental harm. We have also demonstrated that Section 2340A, as applied to interrogations of enemy combatants ordered by the President pursuant to his Commander-in-Chief power would be unconstitutional. Even if an interrogation method, however, might arguably cross the line drawn in Section 2340, and application of the statute was not held to be an unconstitutional infringement of the President's Commander-in-Chief authority, we believe that under the current circumstances certain justification defenses might be available that would potentially eliminate criminal liability. Standard criminal law defenses of necessity and self-defense could justify interrogation methods needed to elicit information to prevent a direct and imminent threat to the United States and its citizens.

A. Necessity

We believe that a defense of necessity could be raised, under the current circumstances, to an allegation of a Section 2340A violation. Often referred to as the "choice of evils" defense, necessity has been defined as follows:

> Conduct that the actor believes to be necessary to avoid a harm or evil to himself or to another is justifiable, provided that:
>
> (a) the harm or evil sought to be avoided by such conduct is greater than that sought to be prevented by the law defining the offense charged; and

the Convention. *See* Memorandum for Alberto R. Gonzales, Counsel to the President and William J. Haynes, II, General Counsel, Department of Defense, from Jay S. Bybee, Assistant Attorney General, Office of Legal Counsel, *Re: Application of Treaties and Laws to al Qaeda and Taliban Detainees* (Jan. 22, 2002).

(b) neither the Code nor other law defining the offense provides exceptions or defenses dealing with the specific situation involved; and

(c) a legislative purpose to exclude the justification claimed does not otherwise plainly appear.

Model Penal Code § 3.02. *See also* Wayne R. LaFave & Austin W. Scott, 1 Substantive Criminal Law § 5.4 at 627 (1986 & 2002 supp.) ("LaFave & Scott"). Although there is no federal statute that generally establishes necessity or other justifications as defenses to federal criminal laws, the Supreme Court has recognized the defense. *See United States v. Bailey*, 444 U.S. 394, 410 (1980) (relying on LaFave & Scott and Model Penal Code definitions of necessity defense).

The necessity defense may prove especially relevant in the current circumstances. As it has been described in the case law and literature, the purpose behind necessity is one of public policy. According to LaFave and Scott, "[t]he law ought to promote the achievement of higher values at the expense of lesser values, and sometimes the greater good for society will be accomplished by violating the literal language of the criminal law." LaFave & Scott, at 629. In particular, the necessity defense can justify the intentional killing of one person to save two others because "it is better that two lives be saved and one lost than that two be lost and one saved." *Id.* Or, put in the language of a choice of evils, "the evil involved in violating the terms of the criminal law (. . . even taking another's life) may be less than that which would result from literal compliance with the law (. . . two lives lost)." *Id.*

Additional elements of the necessity defense are worth noting here. First, the defense is not limited to certain types of harms. Therefore, the harm inflicted by necessity may include intentional homicide, so long as the harm avoided is greater (i.e., preventing more deaths). *Id.* at 634. Second, it must actually be the defendant's intention to avoid the greater harm; intending to commit murder and then learning only later that the death had the fortuitous result of saving other lives will not support a necessity defense. *Id.* at 635. Third, if the defendant reasonably believed that the lesser harm was necessary, even if, unknown to him, it was not, he may still avail himself of the defense. As LaFave and Scott explain, "if A kills B reasonably believing it to be necessary to save C and D, he is not guilty of murder even though, unknown to A, C and D could have been rescued without the necessity of killing B." *Id.* Fourth, it is for the court, and not the defendant to judge whether the harm avoided outweighed the harm done. *Id.* at 636. Fifth, the defendant cannot rely upon the necessity defense if a third alternative is open and known to him that will cause less harm.

It appears to us that under the current circumstances the necessity defense could be successfully maintained in response to an allegation of a Section 2340A violation. On September 11, 2001, al Qaeda launched a surprise covert attack on civilian targets in the United States that led to the deaths of thousands and losses in billions of dollars. According to public and governmental reports, al Qaeda has other sleeper cells within the United States that may be planning similar attacks. Indeed, al Qaeda plans apparently include efforts to develop and deploy chemical, biological and nuclear weapons of mass destruction. Under these circumstances, a detainee may possess information that could enable the United States to prevent attacks that potentially could equal or surpass the September 11 attacks in their magnitude. Clearly, any harm that might occur during an interrogation would pale to insignificance compared to the harm avoided by preventing such an attack, which could take hundreds or thousands of lives.

Under this calculus, two factors will help indicate when the necessity defense could appropriately be invoked. First, the more certain that government officials are that a particular individual has information needed to prevent an attack, the more necessary interrogation will be. Second, the more likely it appears to be that a terrorist attack is likely to occur, and the greater the amount of damage expected from such an attack, the more that an interrogation to get information would become necessary. Of course, the strength of the necessity defense depends on the circumstances that prevail, and the knowledge of the government actors involved, when the interrogation is conducted. While every interrogation that might violate Section 2340A does not trigger a necessity defense, we can say that certain circumstances could support such a defense.

Legal authorities identify an important exception to the necessity defense. The defense is available "only in situations wherein the legislature has not itself, in its criminal statute, made a determination of values." *Id.* at 629. Thus, if Congress explicitly has made clear that violation of a statute cannot be outweighed by the harm avoided, courts cannot recognize the necessity defense. LaFave and Israel provide as an example an abortion statute that made clear that abortions even to save the life of the mother would still be a crime; in such cases the necessity defense would be unavailable. *Id.* at 630. Here, however, Congress has not explicitly made a determination of values vis-à-vis torture. In fact, Congress explicitly removed efforts to remove torture from the weighing of values permitted by the necessity defense.[23]

B. Self-Defense

Even if a court were to find that a violation of Section 2340A was not justified by necessity, a defendant could still appropriately raise a claim of self-defense. The right to self-defense, even when it involves deadly force, is deeply embedded in our law, both as to individuals and as to the nation as a whole. As the Court of Appeals for the D.C. Circuit has explained:

> More than two centuries ago, Blackstone, best known of the expositors of the English common law, taught that "all homicide is malicious, and of course amounts to murder, unless... excused on the account of accident or self-preservation..." Self-defense, as a doctrine legally exonerating the taking of human life, is as viable now as it was in Blackstone's time.

---

[23] In the CAT, torture is defined as the intentional infliction of severe pain or suffering "for such purpose as obtaining from him or a third person information or a confession." CAT Article 1.1. One could argue that such a definition represented an attempt to to indicate that the good of of obtaining information – no matter what the circumstances – could not justify an act of torture. In other words, necessity would not be a defense. In enacting Section 2340, however, Congress removed the purpose element in the definition of torture, evidencing an intention to remove any fixing of values by statute. By leaving Section 2340 silent as to the harm done by torture in comparison to other harms, Congress allowed the necessity defense to apply when appropriate.

Further, the CAT contains an additional provision that "no exceptional circumstances whatsoever, whether a state of war or a threat of war, internal political instability or any other public emergency, may be invoked as a justification of torture." CAT Article 2.2. Aware of this provision of the treaty, and of the definition of the necessity defense that allows the legislature to provide for an exception to the defense, see Model Penal Code § 3.02(b), Congress did not incorporate CAT Article 2.2 into Section 2340. Given that Congress omitted CAT's effort to bar a necessity or wartime defense, we read Section 2340 as permitting the defense.

United States v. Peterson, 483 F.2d 1222, 1228–29 (D.C. Cir. 1973). Self-defense is a common-law defense to federal criminal law offenses, and nothing in the text, structure or history of Section 2340A precludes its application to a charge of torture. In the absence of any textual provision to the contrary, we assume self-defense can be an appropriate defense to an allegation of torture.

The doctrine of self-defense permits the use of force to prevent harm to another person. As LaFave and Scott explain, "one is justified in using reasonable force in defense of another person, even a stranger, when he reasonably believes that the other is in immediate danger of unlawful bodily harm from his adversary and that the use of such force is necessary to avoid this danger." *Id.* at 663–64. Ultimately, even deadly force is permissible, but "only when the attack of the adversary upon the other person reasonably appears to the defender to be a deadly attack." *Id.* at 664. As with our discussion of necessity, we will review the significant elements of this defense.[24] According to LaFave and Scott, the elements of the defense of others are the same as those that apply to individual self-defense.

First, self-defense requires that the use of force be *necessary* to avoid the danger of unlawful bodily harm. *Id.* at 649. A defender may justifiably use deadly force if he reasonably believes that the other person is about to inflict unlawful death or serious bodily harm upon another, and that it is necessary to use such force to prevent it. *Id.* at 652. Looked at from the opposite perspective, the defender may not use force when the force would be as equally effective at a later time and the defender suffers no harm or risk by waiting. *See* Paul H. Robinson, 2 Criminal Law Defenses § 131(c) at 77 (1984). If, however, other options permit the defender to retreat safely from a confrontation without having to resort to deadly force, the use of force may not be necessary in the first place. La Fave and Scott at 659–60.

Second, self-defense requires that the defendant's belief in the necessity of using force be reasonable. If a defendant honestly but unreasonably believed force was necessary, he will not be able to make out a successful claim of self-defense. *Id.* at 654. Conversely, if a defendant reasonably believed an attack was to occur, but the facts subsequently showed no attack was threatened, he may still raise self-defense. As LaFave and Scott explain, "one may be justified in shooting to death an adversary who, having threatened to kill him, reaches for his pocket as if for a gun, though it later appears that he had no gun and that he was only reaching for his handkerchief." *Id.* Some authorities, such as the Model Penal Code, even eliminate the reasonability element, and require only that the defender honestly believed – regardless of its unreasonableness – that the use of force was necessary.

Third, many legal authorities include the requirement that a defender must reasonably believe that the unlawful violence is "imminent" before he can use force in his defense. It would be a mistake, however, to equate imminence necessarily with timing – that an attack is immediately about to occur. Rather, as the Model Penal Code explains, what is essential is that, the defensive *response* must be "immediately necessary." Model Penal Code § 3.04(1). Indeed, imminence may be merely another way of expressing the requirement of necessity. Robinson at 78. LaFave and Scott, for

---

[24] Early cases had suggested that in order to be eligible for defense of another, one should have some personal relationship with the one in need of protection. That view has been discarded. LaFave & Scott at 664.

example, believe that the imminence requirement makes sense as part of a necessity defense because if an attack is not immediately upon the defender, the defender has other options available to avoid the attack that do not involve the use of force. LaFave and Scott at 656. If, however, the fact of the attack becomes certain and no other options remain, the use of force may be justified. To use a well-known hypothetical, if A were to kidnap and confine B, and then tell B he would kill B one week later, B would be justified in using force in self-defense, even if the opportunity arose before the week had passed. *Id.* at 656; *see also* Robinson at § 131(c)(1) at 78. In this hypothetical situation, while the attack itself is not imminent, B's use of force becomes immediately necessary whenever he has an opportunity to save himself from A.

Fourth, the amount of force should be proportional to the threat. As LaFave and Scott explain, "the amount of force which [the defender] may justifiably use must be reasonably related to the threatened harm which he seeks to avoid." LaFave and Scott at 651. Thus, one may not use deadly force in response to a threat that does not rise to death or serious bodily harm. If such harm may result, however, deadly force is appropriate. As the Model Penal Code § 3.04(2)(b) states, "[the] use of deadly force is not justifiable . . . unless the actor believes that such force is necessary to protect himself against death, serious bodily injury, kidnapping or sexual intercourse compelled by force or threat."

Under the current circumstances, we believe that a defendant accused of violating Section 2340A could have, in certain circumstances, grounds to properly claim the defense of another. The threat of an impending terrorist attack threatens the lives of hundreds if not thousands of American citizens. Whether such a defense will be upheld depends on the specific context within which the interrogation decision is made. If an attack appears increasingly likely, but our intelligence services and armed forces cannot prevent it without the information from the interrogation of a specific individual, then the more likely it will appear that the conduct in question will be seen as necessary. If intelligence and other information support the conclusion that an attack is increasingly certain, then the necessity for the interrogation will be reasonable. The increasing certainty of an attack will also satisfy the imminence requirement. Finally, the fact that previous al Qaeda attacks have had as their aim the deaths of American citizens, and that evidence of other plots have had a similar goal in mind, would justify proportionality of interrogation methods designed to elicit information to prevent such deaths.

To be sure, this situation is different from the usual self-defense justification, and, indeed, it overlaps with elements of the necessity defense. Self-defense as usually discussed involves using force against an individual who is about to conduct the attack. In the current circumstances, however, an enemy combatant in detention does not himself present a threat of harm. He is not actually carrying out the attack; rather, he has participated in the planning and preparation for the attack, or merely has knowledge of the attack through his membership in the terrorist organization. Nonetheless, leading scholarly commentators believe that interrogation of such individuals using methods that might violate Section 2340A would be justified under the doctrine of self-defense, because the combatant by aiding and promoting the terrorist plot "has culpably caused the situation where someone might get hurt. If hurting him is the only means to prevent the death or injury of others put at risk by his actions, such torture should be permissible, and on the same basis that self-defense is permissible."

Michael S. Moore, *Torture and the Balance of Evils*, 23 Israel L. Rev. 280, 323 (1989) (symposium on Israel's Landau Commission Report).[25] Thus, some commentators believe that by helping to create the threat of loss of life, terrorists become culpable for the threat even though they do not actually carry out the attack itself. They may be hurt in an interrogation because they are part of the mechanism that has set the attack in motion, *id.* at 323, just as is someone who feeds ammunition or targeting information to an attacker. Under the present circumstances, therefore, even though a detained enemy combatant may not be the exact attacker – he is not planting the bomb, or piloting a hijacked plane to kill civilians – he still may be harmed in self-defense if he has knowledge of future attacks because he has assisted in their planning and execution.

Further, we believe that a claim by an individual of the defense of another would be further supported by the fact that, in this case, the nation itself is under attack and has the right to self-defense. This fact can bolster and support an individual claim of self-defense in a prosecution, according to the teaching of the Supreme Court in *In re Neagle*, 135 U.S. 1 (1890). In that case, the State of California arrested and held deputy U.S. Marshal Neagle for shooting and killing the assailant of Supreme Court Justice Field. In granting the writ of habeas corpus for Neagle's release, the Supreme Court did not rely alone upon the marshal's right to defend another or his right to self-defense. Rather, the Court found that Neagle, as an agent of the United States and of the executive branch, was justified in the killing because, in protecting Justice Field, he was acting pursuant to the executive branch's inherent constitutional authority to protect the United States government. *Id.* at 67 ("We cannot doubt the power of the president to take measures for the protection of a judge of one of the courts of the United States who, while in the discharge of the duties of his office, is threatened with a personal attack which may probably result in his death."). That authority derives, according to the Court, from the President's power under Article II to take care that the laws are faithfully executed. In other words, Neagle as a federal officer not only could raise self-defense or defense of another, but also could defend his actions on the ground that he was implementing the Executive Branch's authority to protect the United States government.

If the right to defend the national government can be raised as a defense in an individual prosecution, as *Neagle* suggests, then a government defendant, acting in his official capacity, should be able to argue that any conduct that arguably violated Section 2340A was undertaken pursuant to more than just individual self-defense or defense of another. In addition, the defendant could claim that he was fulfilling the Executive Branch's authority to protect the federal government, and the nation, from attack. The September 11 attacks have already triggered that authority, as recognized both under domestic and international law. Following the example of *In re Neagle*, we conclude that a government defendant may also argue that his conduct of an interrogation, if properly authorized, is justified on the basis of protecting the nation from attack.

---

[25] Moore distinguishes that case from one in which a person has information that could stop a terrorist attack, but who does not take a hand in the terrorist activity itself, such as an innocent person who learns of the attack from her spouse. Moore, 23 Israel L. Rev. at 324. Such individuals, Moore finds, would not be subject to the use of force in self-defense, although they might be under the doctrine of necessity.

There can be little doubt that the nation's right to self-defense has been triggered under our law. The Constitution announces that one of its purposes is "to provide for the common defense." U.S. Const., Preamble. Article I, § 8 declares that Congress is to exercise its powers to "provide for the common Defence." *See also* 2 Pub. Papers of Ronald Reagan 920, 921 (1988–89) (right of self-defense recognized by Article 51 of the U.N. Charter). The President has a particular responsibility and power to take steps to defend the nation and its people. *In re Neagle*, 135 U.S. at 64. *See also* U.S. Const., Article IV. § 4 ("The United States shall . . . protect [each of the States] against Invasion"). As Commander-in-Chief and Chief Executive, he may use the armed forces to protect the nation and its people. *See, e.g., United States v. Verdugo-Urquidez*, 494 U.S. 259, 273 (1990). And he may employ secret agents to aid in his work as Commander-in-Chief. *Totten v. United States*, 92 U.S. 105, 106 (1876). As the Supreme Court observed in *The Prize Cases*, 67 U.S. (2 Black) 635 (1862), in response to an armed attack on the United States "the President is not only authorized but bound to resist force by force . . . without waiting for any special legislative authority." *Id.* at 668. The September 11 events were a direct attack on the United States, and as we have explained above, the President has authorized the use of military force with the support of Congress.[26]

As we have made clear in other opinions involving the war against al Qaeda, the nation's right to self-defense has been triggered by the events of September 11. If a government defendant were to harm an enemy combatant during an interrogation in a manner that might arguably violate Section 2340A, he would be doing so in order to prevent further attacks on the United States by the al Qaeda terrorist network. In that case, we believe that he could argue that his actions were justified by the executive branch's constitutional authority to protect the nation from attack. This national and international version of the right to self-defense could supplement and bolster the government defendant's individual right.

Conclusion

For the foregoing reasons, we conclude that torture as defined in and proscribed by Sections 2340–2340A, covers only extreme acts. Severe pain is generally of the kind difficult for the victim to endure. Where the pain is physical, it must be of an

---

[26] While the President's constitutional determination alone is sufficient to justify the nation's resort to self-defense, it also bears noting that the right to self-defense is further recognized under international law. Article 51 of the U.N. Charter declares that "[n]othing in the present Charter shall impair the inherent right of individual or collective self-defense if an armed attack occurs against a Member of the United Nations until the Security Council has taken the measures necessary to maintain international peace and security." The attacks of September 11, 2001 clearly constitute an armed attack against the United States, and indeed were the latest in a long history of al Qaeda sponsored attacks against the United States. This conclusion was acknowledged by the United Nations Security Council on September 28, 2001, when it unanimously adopted Resolution 1373 explicitly "reaffirming the inherent right of individual and collective self-defence as recognized by the charter of the United Nations." This right of self-defense is a right to effective self-defense. In other words, the victim state has the right to use force against the aggressor who has initiated an "armed attack" until the threat has abated. The United States, through its military and intelligence personnel, has a right recognized by Article 51 to continue using force until such time as the threat posed by al Qaeda and other terrorist groups connected to the September 11th attacks is completely ended" Other treaties reaffirm the right of the United States to use force in its self-defense. See, e.g., Inter-American Treaty of Reciprocal Assistance, art. 3, Sept. 2, 1947, T.I.A.S. No. 1838, 21 U.N.T.S. 77 (Rio Treaty); North Atlantic Treaty, art. 5, Apr. 4, 1949, 63 Stat 2241, 34 U.N.T.S. 243.

intensity akin to that which accompanies serious physical injury such as death or organ failure. Severe mental pain requires suffering not just at the moment of infliction but it also requires lasting psychological harm, such as seen in mental disorders like post-traumatic stress disorder. Additionally, such severe mental pain can arise only from the predicate acts listed in Section 2340. Because the acts inflicting torture are extreme, there is significant range of acts that though they might constitute cruel, inhuman, or degrading treatment or punishment fail to rise to the level of torture.

Further, we conclude that under the circumstances of the current war against al Qaeda and its allies, application of Section 2340A to interrogations undertaken pursuant to the President's Commander-in-Chief powers may be unconstitutional. Finally, even if an interrogation method might violate Section 2340A, necessity or self-defense could provide justifications that would eliminate any criminal liability.

Please let us know if we can be of further assistance.

Jay S. Bybee
Assistant Attorney General

APPENDIX

Cases in which U.S. courts have concluded the defendant tortured the plaintiff:

- Plaintiff was beaten and shot by government troops while protesting the destruction of her property. *See Wiwa v. Royal Dutch Petroleum*, 2002 WL 319887 at *7 (S.D.N.Y. Feb. 28, 2002).
- Plaintiff was removed from ship, interrogated, and held incommunicado for months. Representatives of the defendant threatened her with death if she attempted to move from quarters where she was held. She was forcibly separated from her husband and unable to learn of his welfare or whereabouts. *See Simpson v. Socialist People's Libyan Arab Jamahiriya*, 180 F. Supp. 2d 78, 88 (D.D.C. 2001) (Rule 12(b)(6) motion).
- Plaintiff was held captive for five days in a small cell that had no lights, no window, no water, and no toilet. During the remainder of his captivity, he was frequently denied food and water and given only limited access to the toilet. He was held at gunpoint, with his captors threatening to kill him if he did not confess to espionage. His captors threatened to cut off his fingers, pull out his fingernails, and shock his testicles. *See Daliberti v. Republic of Iraq*, 146 F. Supp. 2d 19, 22–23, 25 (D.D.C. 2001) (default judgment).
- Plaintiff was imprisoned for 205 days. He was confined in a car park that had been converted into a prison. His cell had no water or toilet and had only a steel cot for a bed. He was convicted of illegal entry into Iraq and transferred to another facility, where he was placed in a cell infested with vermin. He shared a single toilet with 200 other prisoners. While imprisoned he had a heart attack but was denied adequate medical attention and medication. *See Daliberti v. Republic of Iraq*, 146 F. Supp. 2d 19, 22–23 (D.D.C. 2001) (default judgment).
- Plaintiff was imprisoned for 126 days. At one point, a guard attempted to execute him, but another guard intervened. A truck transporting the plaintiff ran over a pedestrian at full speed without stopping. He heard other prisoners being

beaten and he feared being beaten. He had serious medical conditions that were not promptly or adequately treated. He was not given sufficient food or water. *See Daliberti v. Republic of Iraq*, 146 F. Supp. 2d 19, 22–23 (D.D.C. 2001) (default judgment).

- Allegations that guards beat, clubbed, and kicked the plaintiff and that the plaintiff was interrogated and subjected to physical and verbal abuse sufficiently stated a claim for torture so as to survive Rule 12(b)(6) motion. *See Price v. Socialist People's Libyan Arab Jamahiriya*, 110 F. Supp. 2d 10 (D.D.C. 2000).

- Plaintiffs alleged that they were blindfolded, interrogated and subjected to physical, mental, and verbal abuse while they were held captive. Furthermore, one plaintiff was held eleven days without food, water, or bed. Another plaintiff was held for four days without food, water, or a bed, and was also stripped naked, blindfolded, and threatened with electrocution of his testicles. The other two remaining plaintiffs alleged that they were not provided adequate or proper medical care for conditions that were life threatening. The court concluded that these allegations sufficiently stated a claim for torture and denied defendants Rule 12(b)(6) motion. *See Daliberti v. Republic v. Iraq*, 97 F. Supp. 2d 38, 45 (D.D.C. 2000) (finding that these allegations were "more than enough to meet the definition of torture in the [TVPA]").

- Plaintiff's kidnappers pistol-whipped him until he lost consciousness. They then stripped him and gave him only a robe to wear and left him bleeding, dizzy, and in severe pain. He was then imprisoned for 1,908 days. During his imprisonment, his captors sought to force a confession from him by playing Russian roulette with him and threatening him with castration. He was randomly beaten and forced to watch the beatings of others. Additionally, he was confined in a rodent and scorpion infested cell. He was bound in chains almost the entire time of his confinement. One night during the winter, his captors chained him to an upper floor balcony, leaving him exposed to the elements. Consequently, he developed frostbite on his hands and feet. He was also subjected to a surgical procedure for an unidentified abdominal problem. *See Cicippio v. Islamic Republic of Iran*, 18 F. Supp. 2d 62 (D.D.C. 1998).

- Plaintiff was kidnapped at gunpoint. He was beaten for several days after his kidnapping. He was subjected to daily torture and threats of death. He was kept in solitary confinement for two years. During that time, he was blindfolded and chained to the wall in a six-foot by six-foot room infested with rodents. He was shackled in a stooped position for 44 months and he developed eye infections as a result of the blindfolds. Additionally, his captors did the following: forced him to kneel on spikes, administered electric shocks to his hands; battered his feet with iron bars and struck him in the kidneys with a rifle; struck him on the side of his head with a hand grenade, breaking his nose and jaw; placed boiling tea kettles on his shoulders; and they laced his food with arsenic. *See Cicippio v. Islamic Republic of Iran*, 18 F. Supp. 2d 62 (D.D.C. 1998).

- Plaintiff was pistol-whipped, bound and gagged, held captive in darkness or blindfold for 18 months. He was kept chained at either his ankles or wrists, wearing nothing but his undershorts and a t-shirt. As for his meals, his captors gave him pita bread and dry cheese for breakfast, rice with dehydrated soup for lunch, and a piece of bread for dinner. Sometimes the guards would spit into his food. He was regularly beaten and incessantly interrogated; he overheard the deaths and beatings of other prisoners. *See Cicippio v. Islamic Republic of Iran*, 18 F. Supp. 2d 62, (D.D.C. 1998).

- Plaintiff spent eight years in solitary or near solitary confinement. He was threatened with death, blindfolded and beaten while handcuffed and fettered. He was denied sleep and repeatedly threatened him with death. At one point, while he was shackled to a cot, the guards placed a towel over his nose and mouth and then poured water down his nostrils. They did this for six hours. During this incident, the guards threatened him with death and electric shock. Afterwards, they left him shackled to his cot for six days. For the next seven months, he was imprisoned in a hot, unlit cell that measured 2.5 square meters. During this seven-month period, he was shackled to his cot – at first by all his limbs and later by one hand or one foot. He remained shackled in this manner except for the briefest moments, such as when his captors permitted him to use the bathroom. The handcuffs cut into his flesh. *See Hilao v. Estate of Marcos*, 103 F.3d 789, 790 (9th Cir. 1996). The court did not, however, appear to consider the solitary confinement per se to constitute torture. *See id.* at 795 (stating that to the extent that [the plaintiff's] years in solitary confinement do not constitute torture, they clearly meet the definition of prolonged arbitrary detention.").

- High-ranking military officers interrogated the plaintiff and subjected him to mock executions. He was also threatened with death. *See Hilao v. Estate of Marcos*, 103 F.3d 789, 795 (9th Cir. 1996).

- Plaintiff, a nun, received anonymous threats warning her to leave Guatemala. Later, two men with a gun kidnapped her. They blindfolded her and locked her in an unlit room for hours. The guards interrogated her and regardless of the answers she gave to their questions, they burned her with cigarettes. The guards then showed her surveillance photographs of herself. They blindfolded her again, stripped her, and raped her repeatedly. *See Xuncax v. Gramajo*, 886 F. Supp. 162, 176 (1995).

- Plaintiffs were beaten with truncheons, boots, and guns and threatened with death. Nightsticks were used to beat their backs, kidneys, and the soles of their feet. The soldiers pulled and squeezed their testicles. When they fainted from the pain, the soldiers revived them by singeing their nose hair with a cigarette lighter. They were interrogated as they were beaten with iron barks, rifle butts, helmets, and fists. One plaintiff was placed in the "djak" position, i.e., with hands and feet bound and suspended from a pole. Medical treatment was withheld for one week and then was sporadic and inadequate. *See Paul v. Avril*, 901 F. Supp. 330, 332 (S.D. Fla. 1994).

- Alien subjected to sustained beatings for the month following his first arrest. After his second arrest, suffered severe beatings and was burned with cigarettes over the course of an eight-day period. *Al-Saher v. INS*, 268 F.3d 1143, 1147 (9th Cir. 2001) (deportation case).

- Decedent was attacked with knifes and sticks, and repeatedly hit in the head with the butt of a gun as he remained trapped in his truck by his attackers. The attackers then doused the vehicle with gasoline. Although he managed to get out of the truck, he nonetheless burned to death. *Tachiona v. Mugabe*, No. 00 Civ. 6666VMJCF, 2002 WL 1424598 at *1 (S.D.N.Y. July 1, 2002).

- Decedent was attacked by spear, stick, and stone wielding supporters of defendant. He was carried off by the attackers and "was found dead the next day, naked and lying in the middle of the road[.]" From the physical injuries, it was determined that he had been severely beaten. According to his death certificate, he died from "massive brain injury from trauma; assault; and laceration of the right lung." *Tachiona v. Mugabe*, No. 00 Civ. 6666VMJCF, 2002 WL 1424598 at *2 (S.D.N.Y. July 1, 2002).

- Decedent was abducted, along with five others. He and the others were severely beaten and he was forced to drink diesel oil. He was then summarily executed. *Tachiona v. Mugabe*, No. 00 Civ. 6666VMJCF, 2002 WL 1424598 at *4(S.D.N.Y. July 1, 2002).

- Forced sterilization constitutes torture. *Bi Zhu Lin v. Ashcroft*, 183 F. Supp. 2d 551 (D. Conn. 2002) (noting determination by immigration judge that such conduct constitutes torture).

There are two cases in which U.S. courts have rejected torture claims on the ground that the alleged conduct did not rise to the level of torture. In *Faulder v. Johnson*, 99 F. Supp. 2d 774 (S.D. Tex. 1999), the district court rejected a death row inmate's claim that psychological trauma resulting from repeated stays of his execution and his 22-year-wait for that execution was torture under CAT. The court rejected this contention because of the United States' express death penalty reservation to CAT. *See id.* In *Eastman Kodak v. Kavlin*, 978 F. Supp. 1078, 1093 (S.D. Fla. 1997), the plaintiff was held for eight days in a filthy cell with drug dealers and an AIDS patient. He received no food, no blanket and no protection from other inmates. Prisoners murdered one another in front of the plaintiff. *Id.* The court flatly rejected the plaintiff's claim that this constituted torture.

U.S. Department of Justice

Office of Legal Counsel

Office of the Deputy Assistant Attorney General   *Washington, D.C. 20530*

August 1, 2002

The Honorable Alberto R. Gonzales
Counsel to the President
The White House
Washington, D.C.

Dear Judge Gonzales:

You have requested the views of our Office concerning the legality, under international law, of interrogation methods to be used during the current war on terrorism. More specifically, you have asked whether interrogation methods used on captured al Qaeda operatives, which do not violate the prohibition on torture found in 18 U.S.C. § 2340–2340A, would either: a) violate our obligations under the Torture Convention,[1] or b) create the basis for a prosecution under the Rome Statute establishing the International Criminal Court (ICC).[2] We believe that interrogation methods that comply with § 2340 would not violate our international obligations under the Torture Convention, because of a specific understanding attached by the United States to its instrument of ratification. We also conclude that actions taken as part of the interrogation of al Qaeda operatives cannot fall within the jurisdiction of the ICC, although it would be impossible to control the actions of a rogue prosecutor or judge. This letter summarizes our views; a memorandum opinion will follow that will more fully explain our reasoning.

I

Section 2340A makes it a criminal offense for any person "outside the United States [to] commit or attempt to commit torture."[3] The act of torture is defined as an:

---

[1] Convention Against Torture and Other Cruel, Inhuman or Degrading Treatment or Punishment, adopted Dec. 10, 1984, S. Treaty Doc. No. 100-20 (1988), 1465 U.N.T.S. 85 (entered into force June 26, 1987).

[2] U.N. Doc. A/CONF.183/9 (1998), reprinted in 37 I.L.M. 999 (1998) [hereinafter ICC Statute].

[3] If convicted of torture, a defendant faces a fine or up to twenty years' imprisonment or both. If, however, the act resulted in the victim's death, a defendant may be sentenced to life imprisonment or to death. *See* 18 U.S.C.A. § 2340A(a). Whether death results from the act also affects the applicable statute of limitations. Where death does not result, the statute of limitations is eight years; if death results, there is no statute of limitations. *See* 18 U.S.C.A. § 3286(b) (West Supp. 2002); *id.* § 2332b(g)(5)(B) (West Supp. 2002). Section 2340A as originally enacted did not provide for the death penalty as a punishment. *See* Omnibus Crime Bill, Pub. L. No. 103-322, Title VI, Section 60020, 108 Stat. 1979 (1994) (amending section 2340A to provide for the death penalty); H. R. Conf. Rep. No. 103-711, at 388 (1994) (noting that the act added the death penalty as a penalty for torture).

Most recently, the USA Patriot Act, Pub. L. No. 107-56, 115 Stat. 272 (2001), amended section 2340A to expressly codify the offense of conspiracy to commit torture. Congress enacted this amendment

act committed by a person acting under the color of law specifically intended to inflict severe physical or mental pain or suffering (other than pain or suffering incidental to lawful sanctions) upon another person within his custody or physical control.

18 U.S.C.A. § 2340(1); *see id.* § 2340A. Thus, to convict a defendant of torture, the prosecution must establish that: (1) the torture occurred outside the United States; (2) the defendant acted under the color of law; (3) the victim was within the defendant's custody or physical control; (4) the defendant specifically intended to cause severe physical or mental pain or suffering; and (5) that the act inflicted severe physical or mental pain or suffering. *See also* S. Exec. Rep. No. 101-30, at 6 (1990) ("For an act to be 'torture,' it must . . . cause severe pain and suffering, and be intended to cause severe pain and suffering."). As we have explained elsewhere, in order to violate the statute a defendant must have specific intention to inflict severe pain or suffering – in other words, "the infliction of such pain must be the defendant's precise objective." See Memorandum for Alberto R. Gonzales, Counsel to the President, from: Jay S. Bybee, Assistant Attorney General, Office of Legal Counsel, *Re: Standards of Conduct for Interrogation under under 18 U.S.C. §§ 2340–2340A* at 3 (August 1, 2002).

> Section 2340 further defines "severe mental pain or suffering" as:
> the prolonged mental harm caused by or resulting from –
>
> (A) the intentional infliction or threatened infliction of severe physical pain or suffering;
> (B) the administration or application, or threatened administration or application, of mind-altering substances or other procedures calculated to disrupt profoundly the senses or the personality;
> (C) the threat of imminent death; or
> (D) the threat that another person will imminently be subjected to death, severe physical pain or suffering, or the administration or application of mind-altering substances or other procedures calculated to disrupt profoundly the senses or personality.

18 U.S.C. § 2340(2). As we have explained, in order to inflict severe mental or suffering,a defendant both must commit one of the four predicate acts, such as threatening imminent death, and intend to cause "prolonged mental harm."

II

You have asked whether interrogation methods used on al Qaeda operatives that comply with 18 U.S.C. §§ 2340–2340A nevertheless could violate the United States' obligations under the Torture Convention. The Torture Convention defines torture as:

> any act by which severe pain or suffering, whether physical or mental, is intentionally inflicted on a person for such purposes as obtaining from him or a third person information or a confession, punishing him for an act he or a third person has committed or is suspected of having committed, or intimidating or coercing

as part of a broader effort to ensure that individuals engaged in the planning of terrorist activities could be prosecuted irrespective of where the activities took place. *See* H. R. Rep. No. 107-236, at 70 (2001) (discussing the addition of "conspiracy" as a separate offense for a variety of "Federal terrorism offense[s]").

him or a third person, or for any reason based on discrimination of any kind, when such pain or suffering is inflicted by or at the instigation of or with the consent or acquiescence of a public official or other person acting in an official capacity.

Article 1(1) (emphasis added).

Despite the apparent differences in language between the Convention and § 2340, international law clearly could not hold the United States to an obligation different than that expressed in § 2340. When it acceded to the Convention, the United States attached to its instrument of ratification a clear understanding that defined torture in the exact terms used by § 2340. The first Bush administration submitted the following understanding of the treaty:

> The United States understands that, in order to constitute torture, an act must be specifically intended to inflict severe physical or mental pain or suffering and that mental pain or suffering refers to prolonged mental pain caused by or resulting from (1) the intentional infliction or threatened infliction of severe physical pain or suffering; (2) administration or application, or threatened administration or application, of mind altering substances or other procedures calculated to disrupt profoundly the senses or the personality; (3) the threat of imminent death; or (4) the threat that another person will imminently be subjected to death, severe physical pain or suffering, or the administration or application of mind-altering substances or other procedures calculated to disrupt profoundly the senses or personality.

S. Exec. Rep. No. 101-30, at 36. The Senate approved the Convention based on this understanding, and the United States included the understanding in its instrument of ratification.[4]

This understanding accomplished two things. First, it made crystal clear that the intent requirement for torture was specific intent. By its terms, the Torture Convention might be read to require only general intent although we believe the better argument is that that the Convention's use of the phrase "intentionally inflicted" also created a specific intent-type standard. Second, it added form and substance to the otherwise amorphous concept of *mental* pain or suffering. In so doing, this understanding ensured that mental torture would rise to a severity comparable to that required in the context of physical torture.

It is one of the core principles of international law that in treaty relations a nation is not bound without its consent. Under international law, a reservation made when ratifying a treaty validly alters or modifies the treaty obligation, subject to certain conditions that will be discussed below. Vienna Convention on the Law of Treaties, May 23, 1969, 1155 U.N.T.S. 331 (entered into force Jan. 27, 1980); 1 Restatement of the Law (Third) of the Foreign Relations Law of the one nation, Germany appears to have commented on the United States' reservations, and even Germany did not oppose any U.S. reservation outright.

Thus, we conclude that the Bush administration's understanding created a valid and effective reservation to the Torture Convention. Even if it were otherwise, there is no international court to review the conduct of the United States under the Convention. In an additional reservation, the United States refused to accept the jurisdiction of the ICJ (which, in any event, could hear only a case brought by another state, not

---

[4] *See* http://www.un.org/Depts/Treaty/final/ts2/newfiles/part_boo/iv_boo/iv_9.html.

by an individual) to adjudicate cases under the Convention. Although the Convention creates a Committee to monitor compliance, it can only conduct studies and has no enforcement powers.

III

You have also asked whether interrogations of al Qaeda operatives could be subject to criminal investigation and prosecution by the ICC. We believe that the ICC cannot take action based on such interrogations.

First, as noted earlier, one of the most established principles of international law is that a state cannot be bound by treaties to which it has not consented. Although President Clinton signed the Rome Statute, the United States has withdrawn its signature from the agreement before submitting it to the Senate for advice and consent – effectively terminating it. The United States, therefore, cannot be bound by the provisions of the ICC Treaty nor can U.S. nationals be subject to ICC prosecution. We acknowledge, however, that the binding nature of the ICC treaty on non-parties is a complicated issue and do not attempt to definitively answer it here.

Second, even if the ICC could in some way act upon the United States and its citizens, interrogation of an al Qaeda operative could not constitute a crime under the Rome Statute. Even if certain interrogation methods being contemplated amounted to torture (and we have no facts that indicate that they would), the Rome Statute makes torture a crime subject to the ICC's jurisdiction in only two contexts. Under Article 7 of the Rome Statute, torture may fall under the ICC's jurisdiction as a crime against humanity if it is committed as "part of a widespread and systematic attack directed against any civilian population." Here, however, the interrogation of al Qaeda operatives is not occurring as part of such an attack. The United States' campaign against al Qaeda is an attack on a non-state terrorist organization, not a civilian population. If anything, the interrogations are taking place to elicit information that could prevent attacks on civilian populations.

Under Article 8 of the Rome statute, torture can fall within the ICC's jurisdiction as a war crime. In order to constitute a war crime, torture must be committed against "persons or property protected under the provisions of the relevant Geneva Conventions." Rome Statute, Art. 8. On February 27, 2002, the President determined that neither members of the al Qaeda terrorist network nor Taliban soldiers were entitled to the legal status of prisoners of war under the Convention Relative to the Treatment of Prisoners of War, 6 U.S.T. 3517 ("GPW"). As we have explained elsewhere, members of al Qaeda cannot receive the protections accorded to POWs under GPW because al Qaeda is a non-state terrorist organization that has not signed the Conventions. Memorandum for Alberto R. Gonzales, Counsel to the President and William J. Haynes, II, General Counsel, Department of Defense, from Jay S. Bybee, Assistant Attorney General, Office of Legal Counsel, *Re: Application of Treaties and Laws to al Qaeda and Taliban Detainees* at 8 (Jan. 22, 2002). The President has appropriately determined that al Qaeda members are not POWs under the GPW, but rather are illegal combatants, who are not entitled to the protections of any of the Geneva Conventions. Interrogation of al Qaeda members, therefore, cannot constitute a war crime because Article 8 of the Rome Statute applies only to those protected by the Geneva Conventions.

We cannot guarantee, however, that the ICC would decline to investigate and prosecute interrogations of al Qaeda members. By the terms of the Rome Statute, the ICC is not checked by any other international body, not to mention any democratically-elected or accountable one. Indeed, recent events indicate that some nations even believe that the ICC is not subject to the authority of the United Nations Security Council. It is possible that an ICC official would ignore the clear limitations imposed by the Rome Statute, or at least disagree with the President's interpretation of GPW. Of course, the problem of the "rogue prosecutor" is not limited to questions about the interrogation of al Qaeda operatives, but is a potential risk for any number of actions that have been undertaken during the Afghanistan campaign, such as the collateral loss of civilian life in the bombing of legitimate military targets. Our Office can only provide the best reading of international law on the merits. We cannot predict the political actions of international institutions.

Please let us know if we can be of further assistance.

Sincerely,
John C. Yoo
Deputy Assistant Attorney General

UNCLASSIFIED

~~SECRET/NOFORN~~

DEPARTMENT OF DEFENSE
UNITED STATES SOUTHERN COMMAND
OFFICE OF THE COMMANDER
3511 NW 91ST AVENUE
MIAMI, FL 33172-1217

SCCDR   25 October 2002

MEMORANDUM FOR Chairman of the Joint Chiefs of Staff, Washington, DC 20318-9999

SUBJECT: Counter-Resistance Techniques

1. The activities of Joint Task Force 170 have yielded critical intelligence support for forces in combat, combatant commanders, and other intelligence/law enforcement entities prosecuting the War on Terrorism. However, despite our best efforts, some detainees have tenaciously resisted our current interrogation methods. Our respective staff, the Office of the Secretary of Defense, and Joint Task Force 170 have been trying to identify counter-resistant techniques that we can lawfully employ.

2. I am forwarding Joint Task Force 170's proposed counter-resistance techniques. I believe the first two categories of techniques are legal and humane. I am uncertain whether all the techniques in the third category are legal under US law, given the absence of judicial interpretation of the US torture statute. I am particularly troubled by the use of implied or expressed threats of death of the detainee or his family. However, I desire to have as many options as possible at my disposal and therefore request that Department of Defense and Department of Justice lawyers review the third category of techniques.

3. As part of any review of Joint Task Force 170's proposed strategy, I welcome any suggested interrogation methods that others may propose. I believe we should provide our interrogators with as many legally permissible tools as possible.

4. Although I am cognizant of the important policy ramifications of some of these proposed techniques, I firmly believe that we must quickly provide Joint Task Force 170 counter-resistance techniques to maximize the value of our intelligence collection mission.

Encls   James T. Hill

                                   General, US Army

Commander

1. JTF 170 CDR Memo
   dtd 11 October, 2002
2. JTF 170 SJA Memo
   dtd 11 October, 2002
3. JTF 170 J-2 Memo
   dtd 11 October, 2002

Declassify Under the Authority of Executive Order 12958
by Executive Secretary, Office of the Secretary of Defense
By William P. Marriott, CAPT, UNSN
June 21, 2004

~~SECRET/NOFORN~~

DEPARTMENT OF DEFENSE
JOINT TASK FORCE 170
GUANTANAMO BAY, CUBA
APO AE 09860

JTF 170-CG   11 October 2002

MEMORANDUM FOR Commander, United States Southern Command, 3511 NW
91st Avenue, Miami, Florida 33172-1217

SUBJECT: Counter-Resistance Strategies

1. Request that you approve the interrogation techniques delineated in the enclosed Counter-Resistance Strategies memorandum. I have reviewed this memorandum and the legal review provided to me by the JTF-170 Staff Judge Advocate and concur with the legal analysis provided.

2. I am fully aware of the techniques currently employed to gain valuable intelligence in support of the Global War on Terrorism. Although these techniques have resulted in significant exploitable intelligence, the same methods have become less effective over time. I believe the methods and techniques delineated in the accompanying J-2 memorandum will enhance our efforts to extract additional information. Based on the analysis provided by the JTF-170 SJA, I have concluded that these techniques do not violate U.S. or international laws.

3. My point of contact for this issue is LTC Jerald Phifer at DSN 660-3476.

2 Encls   MICHAEL E. DUNLAVEY
1. JTF 170-J2 Memo,   Major General, USA
   11 Oct 02   Commanding
2. JTF 170-SJA Memo,
   11 Oct 02

DEPARTMENT OF DEFENSE
JOINT TASK FORCE 170
GUANTANAMO BAY, CUBA
APO AE 09860

JTF 170-SJA   11 October 2002

MEMORANDUM FOR Commander, Joint Task Force 170

SUBJ: Legal Review of Aggressive Interrogation Techniques

1. I have reviewed the memorandum on Counter-Resistance Strategies, dated 11 Oct 02, and agree that the proposed strategies do not violate applicable federal law. Attached is a more detailed legal analysis that addresses the proposal.

2. I recommend that interrogators be properly trained in the use of the approved methods of interrogation, and that interrogations involving category II and III methods undergo a legal review prior to their commencement.

3. This matter is forwarded to you for your recommendation and action.

2 Encls   DIANE E. BEAVER
1. JTF 170-J2 Memo,   LTC, USA
    11 Oct 02   Staff Judge Advocate
2. JTF 170-SJA Memo,
    11 Oct 02

SECRET/NOFORN

DEPARTMENT OF DEFENSE
JOINT TASK FORCE 170
GUANTANAMO BAY, CUBA
APO AE 09860

JTF-J2   11 October 2002

MEMORANDUM FOR Commander, Joint Task Force 170

SUBJECT: Request for approval of Counter-Resistance Strategies

1. (U) PROBLEM: The current guidelines for interrogation procedures at GTMO limit the ability of interrogators to counter advanced resistance.

2. (U) Request approval for use of the following interrogation plan.

   a. Category I techniques. During the initial category of interrogation the detainee should be provided a chair and the environment should be generally comfortable. The format of the interrogation is the direct approach. The use of rewards like cookies or cigarettes may be helpful. If the detainee is determined by the interrogator to be uncooperative, the interrogator may use the following techniques.

   (1) Yelling at the detainee (not directly in his ear or to the level that it would cause physical pain or hearing problems)

   (2) Techniques of deception:

   (a) Multiple interrogator techniques.

   (b) Interrogator identity. The interviewer may identify himself as a citizen of a foreign nation or as an interrogator from a country with a reputation for harsh treatment of detainees.

   b. Category II techniques. With the permission of the OIC, Interrogation Section, the interrogator may use the following techniques.

   (1) The use of stress positions (like standing), for a maximum of four hours.

   (2) The use of falsified documents or reports.

   (3) Use of the isolation facility for up to 30 days. Request must be made to through the OIC, Interrogation Section, to the Director, Joint Interrogation Group (JIG). Extensions beyond the initial 30 days must be approved by the Commanding General For selected detainees, the OIC, Interrogation Section, will approve all contacts with the detainee, to include medical visits of a non-emergent nature.

   (4) Interrogating the detainee in an environment other than the standard interrogation booth

   (5) Deprivation of light and auditory stimuli

227

(6) The detainee may also have a hood placed over his head during transportation and questioning. The hood should not restrict breathing in any way and the detainee should be under direct observation when hooded.

(7) The use of 20 hour interrogations

(8) Removal of all comfort items (including religious items)

(9) Switching the detainee from hot rations to MREs

(10) Removal of clothing

(11) Forced grooming (shaving of facial hair etc...)

(12) Using detainees individual phobias (such as fear of dogs) to induce stress.

c. Category III techniques. Techniques in this category may be used only by submitting a request through the Director, JIG, for approval by the Commanding General with appropriate legal review and information to Commander, USSOUTHCOM. These techniques are required for a very small percentage of the most uncooperative detainees (less than 3%). The following techniques and other aversive techniques, such as those used in U.S. military interrogation resistance training or by other U.S. government agencies, may be utilized in a carefully coordinated manner to help interrogate exceptionally resistant detainees. Any of these techniques that require more than light grabbing, poking, or pushing, will be administered only by individuals specifically trained in their safe application.

(1) The use of scenarios designed to convince the detainee that death or severely painful consequences are imminent for him and/or his family.

(2) Exposure to cold weather or water (with appropriate medical monitoring).

(3) Use of a wet towel and dripping water to induce the misperception of suffocation.

(4) Use of mild, non-injurious physical contact such as grabbing, poking in the chest with the finger, and light pushing.

3. (U) The POC for this memorandum is the undersigned at 3476.

JERALD PHIFER
LTC, USA
Director, J2

SECRET/NOFORN

DEPARTMENT OF DEFENSE
JOINT TASK FORCE 170
GUANTANAMO BAY, CUBA
APO AE 09860

JTF 170-SJA   11 October 2002

MEMORANDUM FOR Commander, Joint Task Force 170

SUBJECT: Legal Brief on Proposed Counter-Resistance Strategies

1. (U) ISSUE: To ensure the security of the United States and its Allies, more aggressive interrogation techniques than the ones presently used, such as the methods proposed in the attached recommendation, may be required in order to obtain information from detainees that are resisting interrogation efforts and are suspected of having significant information essential to national security. This legal brief references the recommendations outlined in the JTF-170-J2 memorandum, dated 11 October 2002.

2. (U) FACTS: The detainees currently held at Guantanamo Bay, (GTMO), are not protected by the Geneva Conventions (GC). Nonetheless, DoD interrogators trained to apply the Geneva Conventions have been using commonly approved methods of interrogation such as rapport building through the direct approach, rewards, the multiple interrogator approach, and the use of deception. However, because detainees have been able to communicate among themselves and debrief each other about their respective interrogations, their interrogation resistance strategies have become more sophisticated. Compounding this problem is the fact that there is no established clear policy for interrogation limits and operations at GTMO, and many interrogators have felt in the past that they could not do anything that could be considered "controversial" in accordance with President Bush's 7 February 2002 directive, the detainees are not Enemy Prisoners of War (EPW). They must be treated humanely and, subject to military necessity, in accordance with the principles of GC.

3. (U) DISCUSSION: The Office of the Secretary of Defense (OSD) has not adopted specific guidelines regarding interrogation techniques for detainee operations at GTMO. While the procedures outlined in, Army FM 34–52 Intelligence Interrogation (28 September 1992), are utilized, they are constrained by, and conform to the GC and applicable international law, and therefore are not binding. Since the detainees are not EPWs, the Geneva Conventions limitations that ordinarily would govern captured enemy personnel interrogations are not binding on U.S. personnel conducting detainee interrogations at GTMO. Consequently, in the absence of specific binding guidance, and in accordance with the President's directive to treat the detainees humanely, we must look to applicable international and domestic law in order to determine the legality of the more aggressive interrogation techniques recommended in the J2 proposal.

a. (U) International Law: Although no international body of law directly applies, the more notable international treaties and relevant law are listed below.

(1) (U) In November of 1994, the United States ratified The Convention Against Torture and Other Cruel, Inhumane or Degrading Treatment or Punishment. However, the United States took a reservation to Article 16, which defined cruel, inhumane and degrading treatment or punishment, by instead deferring to the current standard articulated in the 8th Amendment to the United States Constitution. Therefore, the United States is only prohibited from committing those acts that would otherwise be prohibited under the United States Constitutional Amendment against cruel and unusual punishment. The United States ratified the treaty with the understanding that the convention would not be self-executing, that is, that it would not create a private cause of action in U.S. Courts. This convention is the principal U.N. treaty regarding torture and other cruel, inhumane, or degrading treatment.

(2) (U) The International Covenant on Civil and Political Rights (ICCPR), ratified by the United States in 1992, prohibits inhumane treatment in Article 7, and arbitrary arrest and detention in Article 9. The United States ratified it on the condition that it would not be self-executing, and it took a reservation to Article 7 that we would only be bound to the extent that the United States Constitution prohibits cruel and unusual punishment.

(3) (U) The American Convention on Human Rights forbids inhumane treatment, arbitrary imprisonment, and requires the state to promptly inform detainees of the charges against them, to review their practical confinement and to conduct a trial within a reasonable time. The United States signed the convention on 1 June 1977, but never ratified it.

(4) (U) The Rome Statute established the International Criminal Court and criminalized inhumane treatment, unlawful deportation, and imprisonment. The United States not only failed to ratify the Rome Statute, but also later withdrew from it.

(5) (U) The United Nations' Universal Declaration of Human Rights, prohibits inhumane or degrading punishment, arbitrary arrest, detention, or exile. Although international declarations may provide evidence of customary international law (which is considered binding on all nations even without a treaty), they are not enforceable by themselves.

(6) (U) There is some European case law stemming from the European Court of Human Rights on the issue of torture. The Court ruled on allegations of torture and other forms of inhumane treatment by the British in the Northern Ireland conflict. The British authorities developed practices of interrogation such as forcing detainees to stand for long hours, placing black hoods over their heads, holding the detainees prior to interrogation in a room with continuing loud notice, and depriving them of sleep, food, and water. The European Court concluded that these acts did not rise to the level of torture as defined in the Convention Against Torture, because torture was defined as an aggravated form of cruel, inhuman, or degrading treatment or punishment. However, the Court did find that these techniques constituted cruel, inhumane, and degrading treatment. Nonetheless, and as previously mentioned, not only is the

United States not a part of the European Human Rights Court, but as previously stated, it only ratified the definition of cruel, inhuman, and degrading treatment consistent with the U.S. Constitution. See also *Mehjnovic v. Vuckovic*, 198 F. Supp. 2d 1322 (N.D. Geor. 2002); *Committee Against Torture v. Israel*, Supreme Court of Israel, 6 Sep 99, 7 BHRC 31; *Ireland v. UK* (1978), 2 EHRR 25.

b. (U) Domestic Law. Although the detainee interrogations are not occurring in the continental United States, U.S. personnel conducting said interrogations are still bound by applicable Federal Law, specifically, the Eighth Amendment of the United States Constitution, 18 U.S.C. §2340, and for military interrogators, the Uniform Code of Military Justice (UCMJ).

(1) (U) The Eighth Amendment of the United States Constitution provides that excessive bail shall not be required, nor excessive fines imposed, nor cruel and unusual punishment inflicted. There is a lack of Eighth Amendment case law relating in the context of interrogations, as most of the Eighth Amendment litigation in federal court involves either the death penalty, or 42 U.S.C. §1983 actions from inmates based on prison conditions. The Eighth Amendment applies as to whether or not torture or inhumane treatment has occurred under the federal torture statute.[1]

(a) (U) A principal case in the confinement context that is instructive regarding Eighth Amendment analysis (which is relevant because the United States adopted the Convention Against Torture, Cruel, Inhumane and Degrading Treatment, it did so deferring to the Eighth Amendment of the United States Constitution) and conditions of confinement if a U.S. court were to examine the issue is *Hudson v. McMillian* 503 U.S. 1 (1992). The issue in *Hudson* stemmed from a 42 U.S.C. §1983 action alleging that a prison inmate suffered minor bruises, facial swelling, loosened teeth, and a cracked dental plate resulting from a beating by prison guards while he was cuffed and shackled. In this case the Court held that there was no governmental interest in beating an inmate in such a manner. The Court further ruled that the use of excessive physical force against a prisoner might constitute an unusual punishment, even though the inmate does not suffer serious injury.

(b) (U) In *Hudson* the Court relied on *Whitley v. Albers* 475 U.S. 312 (1986), as the seminal case that establishes whether a constitutional violation has occurred. The Court stated that the extent of the injury suffered by an inmate is only one of the factors to be considered, but that there is no significant injury requirement in order to establish an Eighth Amendment violation, and that the absence of serious injury is relevant to, but does not end, the Eighth Amendment inquiry. The Court based its decision on the "... settled rule that the unnecessary and wanton infliction of pain ... constitutes cruel and unusual punishment forbidden by the Eighth Amendment." *Whitley* at 319, *quoting Ingraham v. Wright*, 430 U.S. 651, 670 (1977). The *Hudson* Court then held that in the excessive force or conditions of confinement context, the Eighth Amendment violation test delineated by the Supreme Court in *Hudson* is that when prison officials maliciously and sadistically use force to cause harm, contemporary standards of decency are always violated, whether or not significant injury is evident. The extent of

---

[1] Notwithstanding the argument that U.S. personnel are bound by the Constitution, the detainees confined at GTMO have no jurisdictional standing to bring. Section 1983 action alleging an Eighth Amendment violation in U.S. Federal Court.

injury suffered by an inmate is one factor that may suggest whether the use of force could plausibly have been thought necessary in a particular situation, but the question of whether the measure taken inflicted unnecessary and wanton pain and suffering, ultimately turns on whether force was applied in a good faith effort to maintain or restore discipline, or maliciously and sadistically for the *very* (emphasis added) purpose of causing harm. If so, the Eighth Amendment claim will prevail.

(c) (U) At the District Court level, the typical conditions-of-confinement claims involve a disturbance of the inmate's physical comfort, such as sleep deprivation or loud noise. The Eighth Circuit ruled in *Singh v. Holcomb*, 1992 U.S. App. LEXIS 24790, that an allegation by an inmate that he was constantly deprived of sleep which resulted in emotional distress, loss of memory, headaches, and poor concentration, did not show either the extreme deprivation level, or the officials' culpable state of mind required to fulfill the objective component of an Eighth Amendment conditions-of-confinement claim.

(d) (U) In another sleep deprivation case alleging an Eighth Amendment violation, the Eighth Circuit established a totality of the circumstances test, and stated that if a particular condition of detention is reasonably related to a legitimate governmental objective, it does not, without more, amount to punishment. In *Ferguson v. Cape Girardeau County*, 88 F3d 647 (8th Cir. 1996), the complainant was confined to a 5–1/2 by 5–1/2 foot cell without a toilet or sink, and was forced to sleep on a mat on the floor under bright lights that were on twenty-four hours a day. His Eighth Amendment claim was not successful because he was able to sleep at some point, and because he was kept under those conditions due to a concern for his health, as well as the perceived danger that he presented. This totality of the circumstances test has also been adopted by the Ninth Circuit. In *Green v. CSO Strack*, 1995 U.S. App. LEXIS 14451, the Court held that threats of bodily injury are insufficient to state a claim under the Eighth Amendment, and that sleep deprivation did not rise to a constitutional violation where the prisoner failed to present evidence that he either lost sleep or was otherwise harmed.

(e) (U) Ultimately, an Eighth Amendment analysis is based primarily on whether the government had a good faith legitimate governmental interest, and did not act maliciously and sadistically for the very purpose of causing harm.

(2) (U) The torture statute (18 U.S.C. §2340) is the United States' codification of the signed and ratified provisions of the Convention Against Torture and Other Cruel, Inhuman or Degrading Treatment or Punishment, and pursuant to subsection 2340B, does not create any substantive or procedural rights enforceable by law by any party in any civil proceeding.

(a) (U) The statute provides that "whoever outside the United States commits or attempts to commit torture shall be fined under this title or imprisoned not more than 20 years, or both, and if death results to any person from conduct prohibited by this subsection, shall be punished by death or imprisoned for any term of years or for life."

(b) (U) Torture is defined as "an act committed by a person acting under color of law *specifically intended* (emphasis added) to inflict severe physical or mental pain or suffering (other than pain or suffering incident to lawful sanctions) upon another person within his custody or physical control." The statute defines "severe mental pain or suffering" as "the *prolonged mental harm caused by or resulting* (emphasis added) from the intentional infliction or threatened infliction of severe physical pain or suffering; or the administration or application, or threatened administration or application, of mind-altering substances or other procedures calculated to disrupt profoundly the senses of the personality; or the threat of imminent death; or the threat that another person will imminently be subjected to death, severe physical pain or suffering, or the administration or application of mind-altering substances or other procedures calculated to disrupt profoundly the senses or personality."

(c) (U) Case law in the context of the federal torture statute and interrogations is also lacking, as the majority of the case law involving torture relates to either the illegality of brutal tactics used by the police to obtain confessions (in which the Court simply states that these confessions will be deemed as involuntary for the purposes of admissibility and due process, but does not actually address torture or the Eighth Amendment), or the Alien Torts Claim Act, in which federal courts have defined that certain uses of force (such as kidnapping, beating and raping of a nun with the consent or acquiescence of a public official. See *Ortiz v. Gramajo* 886 F. Supp. 162 (D. Mass. 1995)) constituted torture. However, no case law on point within the context of 18 USC 2340.

(3) (U) Finally, U.S. military personnel are subject to the Uniform Code of Military Justice. The punitive articles that could potentially be violated depending on the circumstances and results of an interrogation are: Article 93 (cruelty and maltreatment), Article 118 (murder), Article 119 (manslaughter), Article 124 (maiming), Article 128 (assault), Article 134 (communicating a threat, and negligent homicide), and the inchoate offenses of attempt (Article 80), conspiracy (Article 81), accessory after the fact (Article 78), and solicitation (Article 82). Article 128 is the article most likely to be violated because a simple assault can be consummated by an unlawful demonstration of violence which creates in the mind of another a reasonable apprehension of receiving immediate bodily harm, and a specific intent to actually inflict bodily harm is not required.

4. (U) ANALYSIS: The counter-resistance techniques proposed in the JTF-170-J2 memorandum are lawful because they do not violate the Eighth Amendment to the United States Constitution or the federal torture statute as explained below. An international law analysis is not required for the current proposal because the Geneva Conventions do not apply to these detainees since they are not EPWs.

(a) (U) Based on the Supreme Court framework utilized to assess whether a public official has violated the Eight Amendment, so long as the force used could plausibly have been thought necessary in a particular situation to achieve a legitimate governmental objective, and it was applied in a good faith effort and not maliciously or sadistically for the very purpose of causing harm, the proposed techniques are likely to pass constitutional muster. The federal torture statute will not be violated so long as any of the proposed strategies are not specifically intended to cause severe physical pain or suffering or prolonged mental harm. Assuming that severe physical pain is not inflicted, absent any evidence that any of these strategies will in fact cause prolonged and long lasting mental harm, the proposed methods will not violate the statute.

(b) (U) Regarding the Uniform Code of Military Justice, the proposal to grab, poke in the chest, push lightly, and place a wet towel or hood over the detainee's head would constitute a per se violation of Article 128 (Assault). Threatening a detainee with death may also constitute a violation of Article 128, or also Article 134 (communicating a threat). It would be advisable to have permission or immunity in advance from the convening authority, for military members utilizing these methods.

(c) (U) Specifically, with regard to Category I techniques, the use of mild and fear related approaches such as yelling at the detainee is not illegal because in order to communicate a threat, there must also exist an intent to injure. Yelling at the detainee is legal so long as the yelling is not done with the intent to cause severe physical damage or prolonged mental harm. Techniques of deception such as multiple interrogator techniques, and deception regarding interrogator identity are all permissible methods of interrogation, since there is no legal requirement to be truthful while conducting an interrogation.

(d) (U) With regard to Category II methods, the use of stress positions such as the proposed standing for four hours, the use of isolation for up to thirty days, and interrogating the detainee in an environment other than the standard interrogation booth are all legally permissible so long as no severe physical pain is inflicted and prolonged mental harm intended, and because there is a legitimate governmental objective in obtaining the information necessary that the high value detainees on which these methods would be utilized possess, for the protection of the national security of the United States, its citizens, and allies. Furthermore, these methods would not be utilized for the "very malicious and sadistic purpose of causing harm," and absent medical evidence to the contrary, there is no evidence that prolonged mental harm would result from the use of these strategies. The use of falsified documents is legally permissible because interrogators may use deception to achieve their purpose.

(e) (U) The deprivation of light and auditory stimuli, the placement of a hood over the detainee's head during transportation and questioning, and the use of 20 hour interrogations are all legally permissible so long as there is an important governmental objective, and it is not done for the purpose of causing harm or with the intent to cause prolonged mental suffering. There is no legal requirement that detainees must receive four hours of sleep per night, but if a U.S. Court ever had to rule on this procedure, in order to pass Eighth Amendment scrutiny, and as a cautionary measure, they should receive some amount of sleep so that no severe physical or mental harm will result. Removal of comfort items is permissible because there is no legal requirement to provide comfort items. The requirement is to provide adequate food, water, shelter, and medical care. The issue of removing published religious items or materials would be relevant if these were United States citizens with a First Amendment right. Such is not the case with the detainees. Forced grooming and removal of clothing are not illegal, so long as it is not done to punish or cause harm, as there is a legitimate governmental objective to obtain information, maintain health standards in the camp and protect both the detainees and the guards. There is no illegality in removing hot meals because there is no specific requirement to provide hot meals, only adequate food. The use of the detainee's phobias is equally permissible.

(f) (U) With respect to the Category III advanced counter-resistance strategies, the use of scenarios designed to convince the detainee that death or severely painful consequences are imminent is not illegal for the same aforementioned reasons that there is a compelling governmental interest and it is not done intentionally to cause prolonged harm. However, caution should be utilized with this technique because the torture statute specifically mentions making death threats as an example of inflicting mental pain and suffering. Exposure to cold weather or water is permissible with appropriate medical monitoring. The use of a wet towel to induce the misperception of suffocation would also be permissible if not done with the specific intent to cause prolonged mental harm, and absent medical evidence that it would. Caution should be exercised with this method, as foreign courts have already advised about the potential mental harm that this method may cause. The use of physical contact with the detainee, such as pushing and poking will technically constitute an assault under Article 128, UCMJ.

5. (U) RECOMMENDATION: I recommend that the proposed methods of interrogation be approved, and that the interrogators be properly trained in the use of the approved methods of interrogation. Since the law requires examination of all facts under a totality of circumstances test, I further recommend that all proposed interrogations involving category II and III methods must undergo a legal, medical, behavioral science, and intelligence review prior to their commencement.

6. (U) POC: Captain Michael Borders, $x3536$.

Declassify Under the Authority of Executive Order 12958
By Executive Secretary, Office of the Secretary of Defense
By William P. Marriott, CAPT, USN
June 21, 2004

DIANE E. BEAVER
LTC, USA
Staff Judge Advocate

UNCLASSIFIED

UNCLASSIFIED

GENERAL COUNSEL OF THE DEPARTMENT OF DEFENSE
1600 DEFENSE PENTAGON
WASHINGTON, D. C. 20301-1600
~~GENERAL COUNSEL~~

2002 DEC -2 AM 11: 03

ACTION MEMO

OFFICE OF THE
SECRETARY OF DEFENSE

November 27, 2002 (1:00 PM)

DEPSEC_____

FOR: SECRETARY OF DEFENSE

FROM: William J. Haynes II, General Counsel ~~(signature)~~

SUBJECT: Counter-Resistance Techniques

- The Commander of USSOUTHCOM has forwarded a request by the Commander of Joint Task Force 170 (now JTF GTMO) for approval of counter-resistance techniques to aid in the interrogation of detainees at Guantanamo Bay (Tab A).

- The request contains three categories of counter-resistance techniques, with the first category the least aggressive and the third category the most aggressive (Tab B).

- I have discussed this with the Deputy, Doug Feith and General Myers. I believe that all join in my recommendation that, as a matter of policy, you authorize the Commander of USSOUTHCOM to employ, in his discretion, only Categories I and II and the fourth technique listed in Category III ("Use of mild, non-injurious physical contact such as grabbing, poking in the chest with the finger, and light pushing").

- While all Category III techniques may be legally available, we believe that, as a matter of policy, a blanket approval of Category III techniques is not warranted at this time. Our Armed Forces are trained to a standard of interrogation that reflects a tradition of restraint.

RECOMMENDATION: That SECDEF approve the USSOUTHCOM Commander's use of those counter-resistance techniques listed in Categories I and II and the fourth technique listed in Category III during the interrogation of detainees at Guantanamo Bay.

SECDEF DECISION

Approved _~~(signature)~~_ Disapproved _____ Other _____

Attachments
As stated

However, I stand for 8-10 hours
A day. Why is standing limited to 4 hours?

cc: CJCS, USD(P)

D.R DEC 0 2 2002

Page 1 of 2
X04030-02

UNCLASSIFIED

MEMO 21

GENERAL COUNSEL OF THE
DEPARTMENT OF DEFENSE
1000 DEFENSE PENTAGON
WASHINGTON, D. C. 20301-1000

OFFICE OF THE SECRETARY OF DEFENSE   November 27, 2002 (1:00 PM)

DEPSEC_____

ACTION MEMO

FOR: SECRETARY OF DEFENSE

FROM: William J. Haynes II, General Counsel

SUBJECT: Counter-Resistance Techniques

- The Commander of USSOUTHCOM has forwarded a request by the Commander of Joint Task Force 170 (now JTF GTMO) for approval of counter-resistance techniques to aid in the interrogation of detainees at Guantanamo Bay (Tab A).

- The request contains three categories of counter-resistance techniques, with the first category the least aggressive and the third category the most aggressive (Tab B).

- I have discussed this with the Deputy, Doug Feith and General Myers. I believe that all join in my recommendation that, as a matter of policy, you authorize the Commander of USSOUTHCOM to employ, in his discretion, only Categories I and II and the fourth technique listed in Category III ("Use of mild, non-injurious physical contact such as grabbing, poking in the chest with the finger, and light pushing").

- While all Category III techniques may be legally available, we believe that, as a matter of policy, a blanket approval of Category III techniques is not warranted at this time. Our Armed Forces are trained to a standard of interrogation that reflects a tradition of restraint.

RECOMMENDATION: That SECDEF approve the USSOUTHCOM Commander's use of those counter-resistance techniques listed in Categories I and II and the fourth technique listed in Category III during the interrogation of detainees at Guantanamo Bay.

SECDEF DECISION

Approved *signed by Donald Rumsfeld* Disapproved_____ Other_____
handwritten note: However, I stand for 8–10 hours a day. Why is standing limited to 4 hours? D. R.
Attachments
As stated

cc: CJCS, USD(P)

MEMO 22

SECRETARY OF DEFENSE

1000 DEFENSE PENTAGON

WASHINGTON, DC 20301-1000

JAN 15 2003

MEMORANDUM FOR THE GENERAL COUNSEL OF THE DEPARTMENT
OF DEFENSE

SUBJECT: Detainee Interrogations (U)

(U) Establish a working group within the Department of Defense to assess the legal, policy, and operational issues relating to the interrogations of detainees held by the U.S. Armed Forces in the war on terrorism.

(U) The working group should consist of experts from your Office, the Office of the Under Secretary of Defense for Policy, the Military Departments, and the Joint Staff. The working group should address and make recommendations as warranted on the following issues:

- (U) Legal considerations raised by interrogation of detainees held by U.S. Armed Forces.
- (U) Policy considerations with respect to the choice of interrogation techniques, including:
  - (U) contribution to intelligence collection
  - (U) effect on treatment of captured US military personnel
  - (U) effect on detainee prosecutions
  - (U) historical role of US armed forces in conducting interrogations
- (U) Recommendations for employment of particular interrogation techniques by DoD interrogators.

(U) You should report your assessment and recommendations to me within 15 days.

Classified by: Secretary Rumsfeld
Reason: 1.5(c)
Declassify on: 10 years

Declassify Under the Authority of Executive Order 12958
By Executive Secretary, Office of the Secretary of Defense
By William P. Marriott, CAPT, USN
June 21, 2004

~~SECRET/NOFORN~~

SECRETARY OF DEFENSE

1000 DEFENSE PENTAGON

WASHINGTON, DC 20301-1000

JAN 15 2003

MEMORANDUM FOR COMMANDER USSOUTHCOM

SUBJECT: Counter-Resistance Techniques (U)

(U) My December 2, 2002, approval of the use of all Category II techniques and one Category III technique during interrogations at Guantanamo is hereby rescinded. Should you determine that particular techniques in either of these categories are warranted in an individual case, you should forward that request to me. Such a request should include a thorough justification for the employment of those techniques and a detailed plan for the use of such techniques.

(U) In all interrogations, you should continue the humane treatment of detainees, regardless of the type of interrogation technique employed.

(U) Attached is a memo to the General Counsel setting in motion a study to be completed within 15 days. After my review, I will provide further guidance.

Classified by: Secretary Rumsfeld
Reason: 1.5(c)
Declassify on: 10 years

Declassify Under the Authority of Executive Order 12958
By Executive Secretary, Office of the Secretary of Defense
By William P. Marriott, CAPT, USN
June 21, 2004

[Signed Donald Rumsfeld]

~~SECRET/NOFORN~~

MEMO 24

GENERAL COUNSEL OF THE DEPARTMENT OF DEFENSE
1600 DEFENSE PENTAGON
WASHINGTON, D.C. 20301-1600

JAN 17 2003

MEMORANDUM FOR THE GENERAL COUNSEL OF THE DEPARTMENT
OF THE AIR FORCE

SUBJECT: Working Group to Assess Legal, Policy, and Operational Issues
Relating to Interrogation of Detainees Held by the U.S. Armed Forces
in the War on Terrorism (U)

(U) You are hereby designated as the Chair of an intradepartmental working group
and my executive agent to prepare an assessment and recommendations for me that
are responsive to the attached memorandum of the Secretary of Defense, "Detainee
Interrogations," dated January 15, 2003. In carrying out these responsibilities, you
should call upon the resources of the offices of those indicated as recipients of copies
of this memorandum, including requesting their participation, or that of members of
their staffs, in this working group.

(U) Please provide me with periodic updates as available. I expect your effort to address and provide recommendations, as warranted, pertaining to the issues set out
in the Secretary's memorandum. Your analysis should take into account the various
potential geographic locations where U.S. Armed Forces may hold detainees.

(U) You should provide your assessment and recommendations to me by January 29,
2003. I appreciate your willingness to assume this important responsibility.

William J. Haynes II

Attachment:
As stated.
cc:

Under Secretary of Defense (Policy)
Acting Assistant Secretary of Defense (SO/LIC)
General Counsel of the Department of the Army
General Counsel of the Department of the Navy
Director of the Joint Staff
Director, Defense Intelligence Agency
Counsel for the Commandant of the Marine Corps
The Judge Advocate General of the Army
The Judge Advocate General of the Navy
The Judge Advocate General of the Air Force
Staff Judge Advocate for the Commandant of the Marine Corps

UNCLASSIFIED WHEN SEPARATED FROM ATTACHMENT

Working Group Report on
Detainee Interrogations in the Global War on Terrorism:
Assessment of Legal, Historical, Policy, and Operational Considerations

6 March 2003

Classified by: Secretary Rumsfeld
Reason: 1.5(C)
Declassify on: 10 years

II. International Law

(U) The following discussion addresses the requirements of international law, as it pertains to the Armed Forces of the United States, as interpreted by the United States. As will be apparent in other sections of this analysis, other nations and international bodies may take a more restrictive view, which may affect our policy analysis and thus is considered elsewhere.

A. The Geneva Conventions

(U) The laws of war contain obligations relevant to the issue of interrogation techniques and methods. It should be noted, however, that it is the position of the U.S. Government that none of the provisions of the Geneva Convention Relative to the Treatment of Prisoners of War of August 12, 1949 (Third Geneva Convention) apply to al Qaeda detainees because, *inter alia*, al Qaeda is not a High Contracting Party to the Convention.[1] As to the Taliban, the U.S. position is that the provisions of Geneva apply to our present conflict with the Taliban, but that Taliban detainees do not qualify as prisoners of war under Article A of the Geneva Convention.[2] The Department of Justice has opined that the Geneva Convention Relative to the Protection of Civilian Personnel in time of War (Fourth Geneva Convention) does not apply to unlawful combatants.

B. The 1994 Convention Against Torture

(U) The United States' primary obligation concerning torture and related practices derives from the Convention Against Torture and Other Cruel, Inhuman, or Degrading Treatment or Punishment (commonly referred to as "the Torture Convention"). The United States ratified the Convention in 1994, but did so with a variety of Reservations and Understandings.

[Footnotes 1 and 2 have been blocked out on the original document – Ed.]

(U) Article 1 of the Convention defines the term "torture" for purpose of the treaty.[3] The United States conditioned its ratification of the treaty on an understanding that:

> ... in order to constitute torture, an act must be specifically intended to inflict severe physical or mental pain or suffering and that mental pain or suffering refers to prolonged mental harm caused by or resulting from (1) the intentional infliction or threatened infliction of severe physical pain or suffering; (2) the administration or application, or threatened administration or application, of mind altering substances or other procedures calculated to disrupt profoundly the senses or the personality; (3) the threat of imminent death; or (4) the threat that another person will imminently be subjected to death, severe physical pain or suffering, or the administration or application of mind altering substances or other procedures calculated to disrupt profoundly the senses or personality.[4]

(U) Article 2 of the Convention requires the Parties to "take effective legislative, administrative, judicial and other measures to prevent acts of torture in any territory under its jurisdiction". The U.S. Government believed existing state and federal criminal law was adequate to fulfill this obligation, and did not enact implementing legislation. Article 2 also provides that acts of torture cannot be justified on the grounds of exigent circumstances, such as a state of war or public emergency, or on orders from a superior officer or public authority.[5] The United States did not have an Understanding or Reservation relating to this provision.

(U) Article 3 of the Convention contains an obligation not to expel, return, or extradite a person to another state where there are "substantial grounds" for believing that the person would be in danger of being subjected to torture. The U.S. understanding relating to this article is that it only applies "if it is more likely than not" that the person would be tortured.

(U) Under Article 5, the Parties are obligated to establish jurisdiction over acts of torture when committed in any territory under its jurisdiction or on board a ship or aircraft registered in that state, or by its nationals wherever committed. The "special maritime and territorial jurisdiction of the United States" under 18. U.S.C. § 7 satisfies the U.S. obligation to establish jurisdiction over torture committed in territory under U.S. jurisdiction or on board a U.S. registered ship or aircraft. However, the additional requirement of Article 5 concerning jurisdiction over acts of torture by U.S. nationals "wherever committed" needed legislative implementation. Chapter 113C of Title 18 of the U.S. Code provides federal criminal jurisdiction over an extraterritorial act or attempted act of torture if the offender is a U.S. national. The statute

---

[3] (U) Article 1 provides: "For the purposes of this Convention, the term 'torture' means any act by which severe pain or suffering, whether physical or mental, is intentionally inflicted on a person for such purposes as obtaining from him or a third person information or a confession, punishing him for an act he or a third person has committed or is suspected of having committed, or intimidating or coercing him or a third person, or for any reason based on discrimination of any kind, when such pain or suffering is inflicted by or at the instigation of or with the consent or acquiescence of a public official acting in an official capacity. It does not include pain or suffering arising only from, inherent in or incidental to lawful sanctions."

[4] (U) 18 U.S.C. § 2340 tracks this language. For a further discussion of the U.S. understandings and reservations, see the Initial Report of the U.S. to the U.N. Committee Against Torture, dated October 15, 1999.

[5] (U) But see discussion to the contrary at the Domestic Law section on the necessity defense.

defines "torture" consistent with the U.S. Understanding on Article 1 of the Torture Convention.

(U) The United States is obligated under Article 10 of the Convention to ensure that law enforcement and military personnel involved in interrogations are educated and informed regarding the prohibition against torture. Under Article 11, systematic reviews of interrogation rules, methods, and practices are also required.

(U) In addition to torture, the Convention prohibits cruel, inhuman and degrading treatment or punishment within territories under a Party's jurisdiction (Article 16). Primarily because the meaning of the term "degrading treatment" was vague and ambiguous, the United States imposed a Reservation on this article to the effect that it considers itself **************** that such treatment or punishment means the cruel, unusual and inhumane treatment or punishment prohibited by the Fifth, Eighth, and Fourteenth Amendments to the U.S. Constitution (see discussion *infra*, in the Domestic Law section).

(U) In sum, the obligations under the Torture Convention apply to the interrogation of unlawful combatant detainees, but the Torture Convention prohibits torture only as defined in the U.S. Understanding, and prohibits "cruel, inhuman, and degrading treatment and punishment" only to the extent of the U.S. Reservation relating to the U.S. Constitution.

(U) An additional treaty to which the United States is a party is the International Covenant on Political and Civil Rights, ratified by the United States in 1992, Article 7 of this treaty provides that "No one shall be subjected to torture or to cruel, inhuman or degrading treatment or punishment." The United States' ratification of the Covenant was subject to a Reservation that "the United States considers itself bound by Article 7 only to the extent that cruel, inhuman, or degrading treatment or punishment means the cruel and unusual treatment or punishment prohibited by the Fifth, Eighth, and/or Fourteenth Amendments to the Constitution of the United States." Under this treaty, a "Human Rights Committee" may, with the consent of the Party in question, consider allegations that such Party is not fulfilling its obligations under the Covenant. The United States has maintained consistently that the Covenant does not apply outside the United States or its special maritime and territorial jurisdiction, and that it does not apply to operations of the military during an international armed conflict.

C. Customary International Law

(U) The Department of Justice has concluded that customary international law cannot bind the Executive Branch under the Constitution, because it is not federal law.[6] In particular, the Department of Justice has opined that "under clear Supreme Court precedent, any presidential decision in the current conflict concerning the detention and trial of al Qaeda or Taliban militia prisoners would constitute a "controlling" Executive act that would immediately and completely override any customary international law".[7]

---

[6] (U) Memorandum dated January 22, 2002, *Re: Application of Treaties and Laws to al Qaeda and Taliban Detainees* at 32.

[7] (U) Memorandum dated January 22, 2002, *Re: Application of Treaties and Laws to al Qaeda and Taliban Detainees* at 35.

III. Domestic Law

A. Federal Criminal Law

1. Torture Statute

(U) 18 U.S.C. § 2340 defines as torture any *"act committed by a person acting under the color of law specifically intended to inflict severe physical or mental pain ..."* The intent required is the intent to inflict severe physical or mental pain. 18 U.S.C. § 2340A requires that the offense occur "outside the United States". Jurisdiction over the offense extends to any national of the United States or any alleged offender present in the United States, and could, therefore, reach military members, civilian employees of the United States, or contractor employees.[8] The "United States" is defined to include all areas under the jurisdiction of the United States, including the special maritime and territorial jurisdiction (SMTJ) of the United States. SMTJ is a statutory creation[9] that extends the criminal jurisdiction of the United States for designated crimes to defined areas.[10] The effect is to grant federal court criminal jurisdiction for the specifically identified crimes.

(U) Guantanamo Bay Naval Station (GTMO) is included within the definition of the special maritime and territorial jurisdiction of the United States, and accordingly, is within the United States for purposes of § 2340, Thus, the Torture Statute does not apply to the conduct of U.S. personnel at GTMO. That GTMO is within the SMTJ of the United States is manifested by the prosecution of civilian dependents and employees living in GTMO in Federal District Courts based on SMTJ jurisdiction and Department of Justice opinion[11] and the clear intention of Congress as reflected in the 2001 amendment to the SMTJ. The USA Patriot Act (2001) amended § 7 to add subsection 9, which provides:

> "With respect to offenses committed by or against a national of the United States as that term is used in section 101 of the Immigration and Nationality Act –
>
> (A) the premises of United States diplomatic, consular, military or other United States Government missions or entities in foreign States, including the buildings, parts of buildings, and land appurtenant or ancillary thereto or used for purposes of maintaining those missions or entities, irrespective of ownership; and

---

[8] (U) Section 2340A provides, *"Whoever outside* the United States commits or attempts to commit torture shall be fined or imprisoned..." (emphasis added).

[9] (U) 18 USC § 7, "Special maritime and territorial jurisdiction of the United States" includes any lands under the exclusive or concurrent jurisdiction of the United States.

[10] (U) Several paragraphs of 18 USC § 7 are relevant to the issue at hand. Paragraph 7(3) provides: [SMTJ includes:] "Any lands reserved or acquired for the use of the United States, and under the exclusive or concurrent jurisdiction thereof, or any place..." Paragraph 7(7) provides: [SMTJ includes:] "Any place outside the jurisdiction of any nation to an offense by or against a national of the United States." Similarly, paragraphs 7(1) and 7(5) extend SMTJ jurisdiction to, "the high seas, any other waters within the admiralty and maritime jurisdiction of the United States and out of the jurisdiction of any particular state, and any vessel belonging in whole or in part to the United States..." and to "any aircraft belonging in whole or in part to the United States... while such aircraft is in flight over the high seas, or over any other waters within the admiralty and maritime jurisdiction of the United States and out of the jurisdiction of any particular State".

[11] (U) 6 Op.OLC 236 (1982). The issue was the status of GTMO for purposes of a statute banning slot-machines on "any land where the United States government exercises exclusive or concurrent jurisdiction".

(B) residences in foreign States and the land appurtenant or ancillary thereto, ir-respective of ownership, used for purposes of those missions or entities or used by United States personnel assigned to those missions or entities.

Nothing in this paragraph shall be deemed to supersede any treaty or inter-national agreement with which this paragraph conflicts. This paragraph does not apply with respect to an offense committed by a person described in section 3261(a) of this title.

(U) Any person who commits an enumerated offense in a location that is considered within the special maritime and territorial jurisdiction is subject to the jurisdiction of the United States.

(U) For the purposes of this discussion, it is assumed that an interrogation done for official purposes in under "color of law" and that detainees are in DOD's custody or control.

(U) Although Section 2340 does not apply to interrogations at GTMO, it would apply to U.S. operations outside U.S. jurisdiction, such as Afghanistan. The following analysis is relevant to such activities.

(U) To convict a defendant of torture, the prosecution must establish that (1) the torture occurred outside the United States; (2) the defendant acted under color of law; (3) the victim was within the defendant's custody or physical control; (4) the defendant specifically intended to cause severe physical or mental pain or suffering; and (5) that the act inflicted severe physical or mental pain or suffering. See also S. Exec. Rep. No. 101-30, at 6 (1990). ("For an act to be 'torture,' it must . . . cause severe pain and suffering, and be intended to cause severe pain and suffering.")

a. "Specifically Intended"

(U) To violate Section 2340A, the statute requires that severe pain and suffering must be inflicted with specific intent. See 18 U.S.C. § 2340(1). In order for a defendant to have acted with specific intent, he must have expressly intended to achieve the forbid-den act. See United States v. Carter, 530 U.S. 255, 269 (2000); Black's Law Dictionary at 814 (7th ed. 1999) (defining specific intent as "[t]he intent to accomplish the precise criminal act that one is later charged with"). For example, in Ratzlaf v. United States, 510 U.S. 135, 141 (1994), the statute at issue was construed to require that the de-fendant act with the "specific intent to commit the crime". (Internal quotation marks and citation omitted). As a result, the defendant had to act with the express "purpose to disobey the law" in order for the mens rea element to be satisfied. Ibid. (Internal quotation marks and citation omitted.)

(U) Here because Section 2340 requires that a defendant act with the specific in-tent to inflict severe pain the infliction of such pain must be the defendant's precise objective. If the statute had required only general intent, it would be sufficient to es-tablish guilt by showing that the defendant "possessed knowledge with respect to the actus reus, of the crime" Carter, 530 U.S. at 268. If the defendant acted knowing that severe pain or suffering was reasonably likely to result from his actions, but no more, he would have acted only with general intent. See id at 269; Black's Law Dictionary: 813 (7th ed. 1999) (explaining that general intent "usu[ally] takes the form of reck-lessness (involving actual awareness of a risk and the culpable taking of that risk) or negligence (involving blameworthy inadvertence)"). The Supreme Court has used the following example to illustrate the difference between these two mental states:

[A] person entered a bank and took money from a teller at gunpoint, but deliberately failed to make a quick getaway from the bank in the hope of being arrested so that he would be returned to prison and treated for alcoholism. Though this defendant knowingly engaged in the acts of using force and taking money (satisfying "general intent"), he did not intend permanently to deprive the bank of its possession of the money (failing to satisfy "specific intent").

Carter, 530 U.S. at 268 (citing 1 W. Lafave & A. Scott, Substantive Criminal Law § 3.5, at 315 (1986).

(U) As a theoretical matter, therefore, knowledge alone that a particular result is certain to occur does not constitute specific intent. As the Supreme Court explained in the context of murder, "the ... common law of homicide distinguishes ... between a person who knows that another person will be killed as a result of his conduct and a person who acts with the specific purpose of taking another's life[.]" *United States v. Bailey*, 444 U.S. 394, 405 (1980). "Put differently, the law distinguishes actions taken "because of a given end from actions taken 'in spite' of their unintended but foreseen consequences." *Vacco v. Quill*, 521 U.S. 793, 802–03 (1997). Thus, even if the defendant knows that severe pain will result from his actions, if causing such harm is not his objective, he lacks the requisite specific intent even though the defendant did not act in good faith. Instead, a defendant is guilty of torture only if he acts with the express purpose of inflicting severe pain or suffering on a person within his custody or physical control. While as a theoretical matter such knowledge does not constitute specific intent, juries are permitted to infer from the factual circumstances that such intent is present. *See, e.g., United States v. Godwin*, 272 F.3d 659, 666 (4th Cir. 2001); *United States v. Karro*, 257 F.3d 112, 118 (2d Cir. 2001); *United States v. Wood*, 207 F.3d 1222, 1232 (10th Cir. 2000); *Henderson v. United States*, 202 F.2d 400, 403 (6th Cir.1953). Therefore, when a defendant knows that his actions will produce the prohibited result, a jury will in all likelihood conclude that the defendant acted with specific intent.

(U) Further, a showing that an individual acted with a good faith belief that his conduct would not produce the result that the law prohibits negates specific intent. *See, e.g., South Atl. Ltd. Ptrshp. of Tenn. v. Reise*, 218 F.3d 518, 531 (4th Cir. 2002). Where a defendant acts in good faith, he acts with an honest belief that he has not engaged in the prescribed conduct. *See Cheek v. United States*, 498 U.S. 192, 202 (1991); *United States v. Mancuso*, 42 F.3d 836, 837 (4th Cir. 1994). For example, in the context of mail fraud, if an individual honestly believes that the material transmitted is truthful, he has not acted with the required intent to deceive or mislead. *See, e.g., United States v. Sayakhom*, 186 F.3d 928, 939–40 (9th Cir. 1999). A good faith belief need not be a reasonable one. *See Cheek*, 498 U.S. at 202.

(U) Although a defendant theoretically could hold an unreasonable belief that his acts would not constitute the actions prohibited by the statute, even though they would as a certainty produce the prohibited effects, as a matter of practice in the federal criminal justice system, it is highly unlikely that a jury would acquit in such a situation. Where a defendant holds an unreasonable belief, he will confront the problem of proving to the jury that he actually held that belief. As the Supreme Court noted in *Cheek*, "the more unreasonable the asserted beliefs or misunderstandings are, the more likely the jury ... will find that the Government has carried its burden of providing knowledge". *Id* at 203–04. As explained above, a jury will be permitted to infer that the defendant held the requisite specific intent. As a matter of proof, therefore, a good faith defense will prove more compelling when a reasonable basis exists for the defendant's belief.

b. "Severe Pain or Suffering"

(U) The key statutory phrase in the definition of torture is the statement that acts amount to torture if they cause "severe physical or mental pain or suffering". In examining the meaning of a statute, its text must be the starting point. *See INS v. Phinpathya*, 464 U.S. 183, 189 (1984) ("This Court has noted on numerous occasions that in all cases involving statutory construction, our starting point must be the language employed by Congress . . . and we assume that the legislative purpose is expressed by the ordinary meaning of the words used.") (internal quotations and citations omitted). Section 2340 makes plain that the infliction of pain or suffering per se, whether it is physical or mental, is insufficient to amount to torture. Instead, the text provides that pain or suffering must be "severe." The statute does not, however, define the term "severe". "In the absence of such a definition, we construe a statutory term in accordance with its ordinary or natural meaning." *FDIC v. Meyer*, 510 U.S. 471, 476 (1994). The dictionary defines "severe" as "[u]nsparing in exaction, punishment, or censure" or "[i]nflicting discomfort or pain hard to endure; sharp; afflictive; distressing; violent; extreme; as *severe* pain, anguish, torture". Webster's New International Dictionary 2295 (2d ed. 1935); *see* American Heritage Dictionary of the English Language 1653 (3d ed. 1992) ("extremely violent or grievous: *severe* pain") (emphasis in original); IX The Oxford English Diction "4TY 572 (1978) ("Of pain, suffering, loss, or the like: Grievous, extreme" and "of circumstances . . . hard to sustain or endure"). Thus, the adjective "severe" conveys that the pain or suffering must be of such a high level of intensity that the pain is difficult for the subject to endure.

c. "Severe mental pain or suffering"

(U) Section 2340 gives further guidance as to the meaning of "severe mental pain or suffering," as distinguished from severe physical pain and suffering. The statute defines "severe mental pain or suffering" as:

the prolonged mental harm caused by or resulting from –

(a) the intentional infliction or threatened infliction of severe physical pain or suffering.

(b) the administration or application, or threatened administration or application, of mind-altering substances or other procedures calculated to disrupt profoundly the senses or the personality.

(c) the threat of imminent death; or

(d) the threat that another person will imminently be subjected to death, severe physical pain or suffering, or the administration or application of mind-altering substances or other procedures calculated to disrupt profoundly the senses or personality.

18 U.S.C. § 2340(2). In order to prove "severe mental pain or suffering", the statute requires proof of "prolonged mental harm" that was caused by or resulted from one of four enumerated acts. We consider each of these elements.

i. "Prolonged Mental Harm"

(U) As an initial matter, Section 2340(2) requires that the severe mental pain must be evidenced by "prolonged mental harm". To prolong is to "lengthen in time" or to "extend the duration of, to draw out". Webster's Third New International Dictionary 1815 (1988); Webster's New International Dictionary 1980 (2d ed. 1935). Accordingly, "prolong" adds a temporal dimension to the harm to the individual, namely, that the harm must be one that is endured over some period of time. Put another way, the acts giving rise to the harm must cause some lasting, though not necessarily permanent, damage. For example, the mental strain experienced by an individual during a lengthy and intense interrogation, such as one that state or local police might conduct upon a criminal suspect, would not violate Section 2340(2). On the other hand, the development of a mental disorder such as post-traumatic stress disorder, which can last months or even years, or even chronic depression, which also can last for a considerable period of time if untreated, might satisfy the prolonged harm requirement. *See* American Psychiatric Association, *Diagnostic and Statistical Manual of Mental Disorders* 426, 439–45 (4th ed. 1994) ("DSM-IV"). *See also* Craig Haney & Mona Lynch, *Regulating Prisons of the Future: A Psychological Analysis of Supermax and Solitary Confinement,* 23 N.Y.U. Rev. L. & Soc. Change 477, 509 (1997) (noting that post-traumatic stress disorder is frequently found in torture victims); *cf* Sana Loue, *Immigration Law and Health* § 10:46 (2001) (recommending evaluating for post-traumatic stress disorder immigrant-client who has experienced torture).[12] By contrast to "severe pain" the phrase "prolonged mental harm" appears nowhere else in the U.S. Code nor does it appear in relevant medical literature or international human rights reports.

(U) Not only must the mental harm be prolonged to amount to severe mental pain and suffering, but also it must be caused by or result from one of the acts listed in the statute. In the absence of a catch-all provision, the most natural reading of the predicate acts listed in Section 2340(2)(A)(D) is that Congress intended the list to be exhaustive. In other words, other acts not included within Section 2340(2)'s enumeration are not within the statutory prohibition. *See Leatherman v. Tarrant County Narcotics Intelligence & Coordination Unit*, 507 U.S. 163, 168 (1993) ("*Expressio unius est exclusio alterius*"); Norman Singer, 2A Sutherland on Statutory Construction § 47.23 (6th ed. 2000) ("[W]here a form of conduct the manner of its performance and operation, and the persons and things to which it refers are designated, there is an inference that all omissions should be understood as exclusions.") (footnotes omitted). We conclude that torture within the meaning of the statute requires the specific intent to cause prolonged mental harm by one of the acts listed in Section 2340(2).

---

[12] The DSM-IV explains that post-traumatic disorder ("PTSD") is brought on by exposure to traumatic events, such as serious physical injury or witnessing the deaths of others and during those events the individual felt "intense fear" or "horror" *Id.* at 424. Those suffering from this disorder re-experience the trauma through, *inter alia*, "recurrent and intrusive distressing recollections of the event," "recurrent distressing dreams of the event," or intense psychological distress at exposures to internal or external cues that symbolize or resemble an aspect of the traumatic event." *Id,* at 428. Additionally, a person with PTSD "[p]ersistent[ly]" avoids stimuli associated with the trauma, including avoiding conversations about the trauma, places that stimulate recollections about the trauma, and they experience a numbing of general responsiveness, such as a "restricted range of affect (e.g., unable to have loving feelings)", and "the feeling of detachment of estrangement from others." *Ibid.* Finally, an individual with PTSD has "[p]ersistent symptoms of increased arousal," as evidenced by "irritability or outbursts of anger", "hypervigilance," "exaggerated startle response," and difficulty sleeping or concentrating. *Ibid.*

(U) A defendant must specifically intend to cause prolonged mental harm for the defendant to have committed torture. It could be argued that a defendant needs to have specific intent only to commit the predicate acts that give rise to prolonged mental harm. Under that view, so long as the defendant specifically intended to, for example, threaten a victim with imminent death, he would have had sufficient *mens rea* for a conviction. According to this view, it would be further necessary for a conviction to show only that the victim factually suffered prolonged mental harm, rather than that the defendant intended to cause it. We believe that this approach is contrary to the text of the statute. The statute requires that the defendant specifically intend to inflict severe mental pain or suffering. Because the statute requires this mental state with respect to the infliction of severe mental pain and because it expressly defines severe mental pain in terms of prolonged mental harm, that mental state must be present with respect to prolonged mental harm. To read the statute otherwise would read the phrase "prolonged mental harm caused by or resulting from" out of the definition of "severe mental pain or suffering".

(U) A defendant could negate a showing of specific intent to cause severe mental pain or suffering by showing that he had acted in good faith that his conduct would not amount to the acts prohibited by the statute. Thus, if a defendant has a good faith belief that his actions will not result in prolonged mental harm, he lacks the mental state necessary for his actions to constitute torture. A defendant could show that he acted in good faith by taking such steps as surveying professional literature, consulting with experts, or reviewing evidence gained from past experience. *See, e.g., Ratlzlaf*, 510 *U.S.* at 142 n.10 (noting that where the statute required that the defendant act with the specific intent to violate the law, the specific intent element "might be negated by, e.g., proof that defendant relied in good faith on advice of counsel.") (citations omitted). All of these steps would show that he has drawn on the relevant body of knowledge concerning the result proscribed by the statute, namely prolonged mental harm. Because the presence of good faith would negate the specific intent element of torture, good faith may be a complete defense to such a charge. *See, e.g., United States v. Wall*, 130 F.3d 739, 746 (6th Cir. 1997); *United States v. Casperson*, 773 F.2d 216, 222–23 (8th Cir. 1985).

ii. Harm Caused By Or Resulting From Predicate Acts

(U) Section 2340(2) sets forth four basic categories of predicate acts. The first category is the "intentional infliction or threatened infliction of severe physical pain or suffering". This might at first appear superfluous because the statute already provides that the infliction of severe physical pain or suffering can amount to torture. This provision, however, actually captures the infliction of physical pain or suffering when the defendant inflicts physical pain or suffering with general intent rather than the specific intent that is required where severe physical pain or suffering alone is the basis for the charge. Hence, this subsection reaches the infliction of severe physical pain or suffering when it is only the means of causing prolonged mental harm. Or put another way, a defendant has committed torture when he intentionally inflicts severe physical pain or suffering with the specific intent of causing prolonged mental harm. As for the acts themselves, acts that cause "severe physical pain or suffering" can satisfy this provision.

(U) Additionally, the threat of inflicting such pain is a predicate act under the statute. A threat may be implicit or explicit. *See, e.g., United States v. Sachdev*, 279 F.3d 25, 29 (1st Cir. 2002). In criminal law, courts generally determine whether an individual's words or actions constitute a threat by examining whether a reasonable person in the same circumstances would conclude that a threat had been made. *See, e.g., Watts v. United States*, 394 *U.S.* 70S, 708 (1969) (holding that whether a statement constituted a threat against the president's life had to be determined in light of all the surrounding circumstances); *Sachdev*, 279 F.3d at 29 ("a reasonable person in defendant's position would perceive there to be a threat, explicit or implicit, of physical injury"); *United States v. Khorrami*, 895 F.2d 1186, 1190 (7th Cir. 1990) (to establish that a threat was made, the statement must be made "in a context or under such circumstances wherein a reasonable person would foresee that the statement would be interpreted by those to whom the maker communicates a statement as a serious expression of an intention to inflict bodily harm upon [another individual]") (citation and internal quotation marks omitted); *United States v. Peterson*, 483 F.2d 1222, 1230 (D.C. Cir. 1973) (perception of threat of imminent harm necessary to establish self-defense had to be "objectively reasonable in light of the surrounding circumstances"). Based on this common approach, we believe that the existence of a threat of severe pain or suffering should be assessed from the standpoint of a reasonable person in the same circumstances.

(U) Second, Section 2340(2)(B) provides that prolonged mental harm, constituting torture, can be caused by "the administration or application or threatened administration or application of mind-altering substances or other procedures calculated to disrupt profoundly the senses or the personality". The statute provides no further definition of what constitutes a mind-altering substance. The phrase "mind-altering substances" is found nowhere else in the U.S. Code, nor is it found in dictionaries. It is, however, a commonly use synonym for drugs. *See, e.g., United States v. Kingsley*, 241 F.3d 828, 834 (6th Cir.) (referring to controlled substances as "mind-altering substance[s]") *cert. denied*, 122 S. Ct. 137 (2001); *Hogue v. Johnson*, 131 F.3rd 466, 501 (5th Cir. 1997) (referring to drugs and alcohol as "mind-altering substance[s]"), *cert. denied*, 523 U.S. 1014 (1998). In addition, the phrase appears in a number of state statutes, and the context in which it appears confirms this understanding of the phrase. *See, e.g.,* Cal. Penal Code § 3500 (c) (West Supp. 2000) ("Psychotropic drugs also include mind-altering...drugs..."); Minn. Stat. Ann. § 260B.201(b) (West Supp. 2002) ("'chemical dependency treatment'" define as programs designed to "reduc[e] the risk of the use of alcohol, drugs, or other mind-altering substances").

(U) This subparagraph, section 2340(2)(B), however, does not preclude any and all use of drugs. Instead, it prohibits the use of drugs that "disrupt profoundly the senses or the personality". To be sure, one could argue that this phrase applies only to "other procedures", not the application of mind-altering substances. We reject this interpretation because the terms of Section 2340(2) expressly indicate that the qualifying phrase applies to both "other procedures" *and* the "application of mind-altering substances". The word "other" modifies "procedures calculated to disrupt profoundly the senses". As an adjective, "other" indicates that the term or phrase it modifies is the remainder of several things. *See* Webster's Third New International Dictionary 1598 (1986) (defining "other" as "being the one (as of two or more) remaining or not included"). Or put another way, "other" signals that the words to which it attaches are of the same kind, type, or class as the more specific item previously listed. Moreover, where a statute couple words or phrases together, it "denotes an intention that they should be understood in the same general sense." Norman Singer, 2A Sutherland on Statutory Construction § 47:16 (6th ed. 2000); *see also Beecham v. United States*, 511 U.S. 368, 371 (1994) ("That several items in a list share an attribute counsels in favor of interpreting the other items as possessing that attribute as well."). Thus, the pairing of mind-altering substances with procedures calculated to disrupt profoundly the sense or personality and the use of "other" to modify "procedures" shows that the use of such substances must also cause a profound disruption of the senses or personality.

(U) For drugs or procedures to rise to the level of "disrupt[ing] profoundly the sense or personality", they must produce an extreme effect. And by requiring that they be "calculated" to produce such an effect, the statute requires that the defendant has consciously designed the acts to produce such an effect, 28 U.S.C. § 2340(2)(B). The word "disrupt" is defined as "to break asunder; to part forcibly; rend," imbuing the verb with a connotation of violence. Webster's New International Dictionary 753 (2d ed. 1935); *see* Webster's Third New International Dictionary 656 (1986) (defining disrupt as "to break apart: Rupture" or "destroy the unity or wholeness of"); IV the Oxford English Dictionary 832 (1989) (defining disrupt as "[t]o break or burst asunder, to break in pieces; to separate forcibly"). Moreover, disruption of the senses or personality alone is insufficient to fall within the scope of this subsection; instead, that disruption must be profound. The word "profound" has a number of meanings, all of which convey a significant depth. Webster's New International Dictionary 1977 (2d ed. 1935 defines profound as: "Of very great depth; extending far below the surface or top; unfathomable [;] . . . [c]oming from, reaching to, or situated at a depth or more than ordinary depth; not superficial; deep-seated; chiefly with reference to the body; as a *profound* sigh, wounded, or pain[;] . . . [c]haracterized by intensity, as of feeling or quality; deeply felt or realized; as, *profound* respect, fear, or melancholy; hence, encompassing; thoroughgoing; complete; as, *profound* sleep, silence, or ignorance." *See* Webster's Third New International Dictionary 1812 (1986) ("having very great depth: extending far below the surface . . . not superficial"). Random House Webster's Unabridged Dictionary 1545 (2d ed. 1999) also defines profound as "originating in or penetrating to the depths of one's being" or "pervasive or intense; thorough; complete" or "extending, situated, or originating far down, or far beneath the surface." By requiring that the procedures and the drugs create a *profound* disruption, the statute requires more than the acts "forcbility separate" or "rend" the senses or personality. Those acts must penetrate to the core of an individual's ability to perceive the world around him, substantially interfering with his cognitive abilities, or fundamentally alter his personality.

(U) The phrase "disrupt profoundly the senses or personality" is not used in mental health literature nor is it derived from elsewhere in U.S. law. Nonetheless, we think the following examples would constitute a profound disruption of the senses or personality. Such an effect might be seen in a drug-induced dementia. In such a state, the individual suffers from significant memory impairment, such as the inability to retain any new information or recall information about things previously of interest to the individual. *See* DSM-IV at 134.[13] This impairment is accompanied by one or more of the following: deterioration of language function, e.g., repeating sounds or words over and over again; impaired ability to execute simple motor activities, e.g.,

---

[13] (U) Published by the American Psychiatric Association, and written as a collaboration of over a thousand psychiatrists, the DSM-IV is commonly used in U.S. courts as a source of information regarding mental health issues and is likely to be used in trial should charges be brought that allege this predicate act. *See, e.g., Atkins v. Virginia*, 122 S. Ct. 2242, 2245 n. 3 (2002); *Kansas v. Crane*, 122 S. Ct. 867, 871 (2002); *Kansas v. Hendricks*, 521 U.S. 346, 359–60 (1997); *McClean v. Merifield*, No. 00-CV-0120E(SC). 2002 WL 1477607 at *2 n. 7 (W. D. N Y. June 28, 2002); *Peeples v. Coastal Office Prods.*, 203 F. Supp 2d 432, 439 (D. Md 2002); *Lassigne v. Taco Bell Corp.*, 202 P. Supp 2d 512, 519 (E.D. La. 2002).

inability to dress or wave goodbye; "[in]ability to recognize [and identify] objects such as chairs or pencils" despite normal visual functioning; or "[d]isturbances in executive level functioning", i.e., serious impairment of abstract thinking. *Id.* At 134–35. Similarly, we think that the onset of "brief psychotic disorder" would satisfy this standard. *See id.* at 302–03. In this disorder, the individual suffers psychotic symptoms, including among other things, delusions, hallucinations, or even a catatonic state. This can last for one day or even one month. *See id.* We likewise think that the onset of obsessive-compulsive disorder behaviors would rise to this level. Obsessions are intrusive thoughts unrelated to reality. They are not simple worries, but are repeated doubts or even "aggressive or horrific impulses." *See id.* at 418. The DSM-IV further explains that compulsions include "repetitive behaviors (e.g. hand washing, ordering, checking)" and that "[b]y definition, [they] are either clearly excessive or are not connected in a realistic way with what they are designed to neutralize or prevent". *See id.* Such compulsions or obsessions must be "time-consuming". *See id* at 419. Moreover, we think that pushing someone to the brink of suicide (which could be evidenced by acts of self-mutilation), would be a sufficient disruption of the personality to constitute a "profound disruption". These examples, of course, are in no way intended to be an exhaustive list. Instead, they are merely intended to illustrate the sort of mental health effects that we believe would accompany an action severe enough to amount to one that "disrupt[s] profoundly the sense or the personality".

(U) The third predicate act listed in Section 2340(2) is threatening an individual with "imminent death". 18 U.S.C. § 2340(2)(C). The plain text makes clear that a threat of death alone is insufficient, the threat must indicate that death is "imminent". The "threat of imminent death" is found in the common law as an element of the defense of *duress, See Bailey*, 444 U.S. at 409. "[W]here Congress borrows terms of art in which are accumulated the legal tradition and meaning of centuries of practice, it presumably knows and adopts the cluster of ideas that were attached to each borrowed word in the body of learning from which it was taken and the meaning its use will convey to the judicial mind unless otherwise instructed. In such case, absence of contrary direction may be taken as satisfaction with widely accepted definitions, not as a departure from them." *Morissette v. United States*, 342 U.S. 246, 263 (1952). Common law cases and legislation generally define "imminence" as requiring that the threat be almost immediately forthcoming. 1 Wayne R. LaFave & Austin W. Scott, Jr., Substantive Criminal Law § 5.7, at 655 (1986). By contrast, threats referring vaguely to things that might happen in the future do not satisfy this immediacy requirement. *See United States v. Fiore*, 178 F. 3rd 917, 923 (7th Cir. 1999). Such a threat fails to satisfy this requirement not because it is too remote in time but because there is a lack of certainty that it will occur. Indeed, timing is an indicator of certainty that the harm will befall the defendant. Thus, a vague threat that someday the prisoner *might* be killed would not suffice. Instead, subjecting a prisoner to mock executions or playing Russian roulette with him would have sufficient immediacy to constitute a threat of imminent death. Additionally, as discussed earlier, we believe that the existence of a threat must be assessed from the perspective of a reasonable person in the same circumstances.

(U) Fourth, if the official threatens to do anything previously described to a third party, or commits such an act against a third party, that threat or action can serve as the necessary predicate for prolonged mental harm. *See* 18 U.S.C. § 2340(2)(D). The statute does not require any relationship between the prisoner and the third party.

2. Other Federal Crimes that Could Relate to Interrogation Techniques

(U) Through the SMTJ, the following federal crimes are generally applicable to actions by military or civilian personnel; murder (18 U.S.C. § 1111), manslaughter (18 U.S.C. § 1112), assault (18 U.S.C. § 113), maiming (18 U.S.C. § 114), kidnapping (18 U.S.C. § 1201). These, as well as war crimes (18 U.S.C. § 2441)[14] and conspiracy (18 U.S.C. § 371), are discussed below.

a. Assaults within maritime and territorial jurisdiction, 18 U.S.C. § 113

(U) 18 U.S.C. § 113 proscribes assault within the special maritime and territorial jurisdiction. Although section 113 does not define assault, courts have construed the term "assault" in accordance with that term's common law meaning. *See, e.g., United States v. Estrada-Fernandez*, 150 F.3d 491, 494 n.1 (5th Cir. 1998); *United States v. Juvenile-Male*, 930 F.2d 727, 728 (9th Cir. 1991). At common law an assault is an attempted battery or an act that puts another person in reasonable apprehension of bodily harm. *See e.g., United States v. Bayes*, 210 F.3d 64, 68 (1st Cir. 2000). Section 113 reaches more than simple assault, sweeping within its ambit acts that would at common law constitute battery.

(U) 18 U.S.C. § 113 proscribes several specific forms of assault. Certain variations require specific intent, to wit: assault with intent to commit murder (imprisonment for not more than twenty years); assault with intent to commit any felony (except murder and certain sexual abuse offenses) (fine and/or imprisonment for not more than ten years); assault with a dangerous weapon, with intent to do bodily harm, and without just cause or excuse (fine and/imprisonment for not more than ten years, or both); Other defined crimes require only general intent, to wit: assault by striking, beating, or wounding (fine and/or imprisonment for not more than six months); simple assault (fine and/or imprisonment for not more than six months), or if the victim of the assault is an individual who has not attained the age of 16 years (fine and/or imprisonment for not more than 1 year); assault resulting in serious bodily injury (fine and/or imprisonment for not more than ten years); assault resulting in substantial bodily injury to an individual who has not attained the age of 16 years (fine and/or imprisonment for not more than 5 years). "Substantial bodily injury" means bodily injury which involves (a) a temporary but substantial disfigurement; or (b) a temporary but substantial loss or impairment of the function of any bodily member, organ, or mental faculty "Serious bodily injury" means bodily injury which involves (a) a substantial risk of death; (b) extreme physical pain; (c) protracted and obvious disfigurement; or (d) protracted loss or impairment of the function of a bodily member, organ, or mental faculty. "Bodily injury" means (a) a cut, abrasion, bruise, burn, or disfigurement; (b) physical pain; (c) illness; (d) impairment of the function of a bodily member, organ, or mental faculty, or (e) any other injury to the body, no matter how temporary.

---

[14] (U) 18 U.S.C. § 2441 criminalizes the commission of war crimes by U.S. nationals and members of the U.S. Armed Forces. Subsection (c) defines war crimes as (1) grave breaches of any of the Geneva Conventions; (2) conduct prohibited by the Hague Convention IV, Respecting the Law and Customs of War on Land, signed 18 October 1907; or (3) conduct that constitutes a violation of common Article 3 of the Geneva Conventions. The Department of Justice has opined that this statute does not apply to conduct toward al Qaeda or Taliban operatives because the President has determined that they are not entitled to the protections of Geneva and the Hague Regulations.

b. Maiming 18 U.S.C. § 114

(U) Whoever with the intent to torture (as defined in section 2340), maims, or disfigures, cuts, bites, or slits the nose, ear, or lip, or cuts out or disables the tongue, or puts out or destroys an eye, or cuts off or disables a limb or any member of another person; or whoever, and with like intent, throws or pours upon another person, any scalding water, corrosive acid, or caustic substance shall be fined and/or imprisoned not more than twenty years. This is a specific intent crime.

c. Murder, 18 U.S.C. § 1111

(U) Murder is the unlawful killing of a human being with malice aforethought. Every murder perpetrated by poison, lying in wait, or any other kind of wilful, deliberate, malicious, and premeditated killing; or committed in the perpetration of, or attempt to perpetrate, any arson, escape, murder, kidnapping, treason, espionage, sabotage, aggravated sexual abuse or sexual abuse, burglary, or robbery, or perpetrated from a premeditated design unlawfully and maliciously to effect the death of any human being other than him who is killed, is murder in the first degree. Any other murder is murder in the second degree. If within the SMTJ, whoever is guilty of murder in the first degree shall be punished by death or by imprisonment for life, whoever is guilty of murder in the second degree, shall be imprisoned for any term of years or for life. Murder is a specific intent crime.

d. Manslaughter, 18 U.S.C. § 1112

(U) Manslaughter is the unlawful killing of a human being without malice. It is of two kinds: (a) voluntary, upon a sudden quarrel or heat of passion and (b) involuntary, in the commission of an unlawful act not amounting to a felony, or in the commission in an unlawful manner, or without due caution and circumspection, of a lawful act which might produce death.

(U) If within the SMTJ whoever is guilty of voluntary manslaughter, shall be fined and/or imprisoned not more than ten years; whoever is guilty of involuntary manslaughter, shall be fined and/or imprisoned not more than six years. Manslaughter is a general intent crime. A death resulting from the exceptional interrogation techniques may subject the interrogator to a charge of manslaughter, most likely of the involuntary sort.

e. Interstate Stalking, 18 U.S.C. § 2261A

(U) 18 U.S.C. § 2261A provides that "[w]hoever . . . travels . . . within the special maritime and territorial jurisdiction of the United States . . . with the intent to kill, injure, harass, or intimidate another person, and in the course of or as a result of, such travel places that person in reasonable fear of the death of, or serious bodily injury of that person." Thus there are three elements to a violation of 2261A: (1) defendant traveled in interstate commerce; (2) he did so with the intent to injury, harass, intimidate another person; (3) the person he intended to harass or injure was reasonably placed in fear of death or serious bodily injury as a result of that travel. *See United States v. Al-Zubaidy*, 283 F.3d 804, 808 (6th Cir. 2002).

(U) The travel itself must have been undertaken with the specific intent to harass or intimidate another. Or put another way, at the time of the travel itself, the defendant must have engaged in that travel for the precise purpose of harassing another person.

See Al-Zubaidy, 283 F.3d at 809 (the defendant "must have intended to harass or injure [the victim] at the time he crossed the state line").

(U) The third element is not fulfilled by the mere act of travel itself. *See United States v. Crawford*, No. 00-CR-59-B-S, 2001 WL 185140 (D. Me. Jan. 26, 2001) ("A plain reading of the statute makes clear that the statute requires the actor to place the victim in reasonable fear, rather than, as Defendant would have it, that his travel place the victim in reasonable fear.").

(U) It is unlikely that this statute's purpose is aimed at interrogations.

f. Conspiracy, 18 U.S.C. § 2 and 18 U.S.C. § 371[15]

(U) Conspiracy to commit crime is a separate offense from crime that is the object of the conspiracy.[16] Therefore, where someone is charged with conspiracy, a conviction cannot be sustained unless the Government establishes beyond a reasonable doubt that the defendant had the specific intent to violate the substantive statute.[17]

(U) As the Supreme Court most recently stated, "the essence of a conspiracy is 'an agreement to commit an unlawful act." *United States v. Jimenez Recio*, –S.Ct, 2003 WL 139612 at – (Jan 12, 2003) (quoting *Ianelli v. United States*, 420 U.S. 770, 777 (1975). Moreover, "[t]hat agreement is a 'distinct evil,' which 'may exist and be punished whether or not the substantive crime ensues", *Id* at (quoting *Salinas v. United States*, 522 U.S. 52. 65 (1997).

3. Legal doctrines under the Federal Criminal Law that could render specific conduct, otherwise criminal, not unlawful

(U) Generally, the following discussion identifies legal doctrines and defenses applicable to the interrogation of unlawful combatants, and the decision process related to them. In practice, their efficacy as to any person or circumstance will be fact-dependent.

a. Commander-in-Chief Authority

(U) As the Supreme Court has recognized, and as we will explain further below, the President enjoys complete discretion in the exercise of his Commander-in-Chief authority including in conducting operations against hostile forces. Because both "[t]he executive power and the command of the military and naval forces is vested in the President," the Supreme Court has unanimously stated that it is *the President alone*

---

[15] (U) 18 U.S.C. § 2 Principals
(a) Whoever Commits an offense against the United States or aids, abets, counsels, commands, induces or procures its commission, is punishable as a principal.
(b) Whoever wilfully causes an act to be done which if directly performed by him or another would be an offense against the United States, is punishable as a principal.
18 U.S.C. § 371. Conspiracy to commit offense or to defend United States
If two or more persons conspire either to commit any offense against the United States, or to defraud the United States, or any agency thereof in any manner or for any purpose, and one or more of such persons do any act to effect the object of the conspiracy, each shall be fined under this title or imprisoned not more than five years, or both.
If, however, the offense, the commission of which is the object of the conspiracy, is a misdemeanor only, the punishment for such conspiracy shall not exceed the maximum punishment provided for such misdemeanor
[16] (U) *United States v. Rabinowich*, 238 US 78, 59, 35 S.Ct 682, L Bd 1211 (1915).
[17] (U) *United States v. Cangiano*, 491 F.2d 906 (2nd Cir. 1974), cert denied 419 U.S. 904 (1974).

who is constitutionally invested with the *entire charge of hostile operations.*" *Hamilton v. Dillin*, 88 U.S. (21 Wall.) 73, 87 (1874) (emphasis added).

(U) In light of the President's complete authority over the conduct of war without a clear statement otherwise, criminal statutes are not read as infringing on the President's ultimate authority in these areas. The Supreme Court has established a canon of statutory construction that statutes are to be construed in a manner that avoids constitutional difficulties so long as a reasonable alternative construction is available. *See, e.g., Edward J. DeBartolo Corp. v. Florida Gulf Coast Bldg. & Constr. Trades Council*, 485 U.S. 568, 575 (1988) (citing *NLRB v. Catholic Bishop of Chicago*, 440 U.S. 490, 499–501, 504 (1979)) ("[W]here an otherwise acceptable construction of a statute would raise serious constitutional problems, [courts] will construe [a] statute to avoid such problems unless such construction is plainly contrary to the intent of Congress.") This canon of construction applies especially where an act of Congress could be read to encroach upon powers constitutionally committed to a coordinate branch of government. *See, e.g., Franklin v. Massachusetts*, 505 U.S. 788, 800–1 (1992) (citation omitted) ("Out of respect for the separation of powers and the unique constitutional position of the President, we find that textual silence is not enough to subject the President to the provisions of the [Administrative Procedure Act]. We would require an express statement by Congress before assuming it intended the President's performance of his statutory duties to be reviewed for abuse of discretion."); *Public Citizen V. United States Dep't of Justice*, 491 U.S. 440, 465–67 (1989) (construing Federal Advisory Committee Act not to apply to advice given by American Bar Association to the President on judicial nominations, to avoid potential constitutional question regarding encroachment on Presidential power to appoint judges).

(U) In the area of foreign affairs, and war powers in particular, the avoidance canon has special force. *See, e.g., Dept of Navy v. Egan*, 484 U.S. 518, 530 (1988) ("unless Congress specifically has provided otherwise, courts traditionally have been reluctant to intrude upon the authority of the Executive in military and national security affairs); *Japan Whaling Ass'n v. American Cetacean Socy*, 478 U.S. 221, 232-33 (1986) (construing federal statutes to avoid curtailment of traditional presidential prerogatives in foreign affairs). It should not be lightly assumed that Congress has acted to interfere with the President's constitutionally superior position as Chief Executive and Commander-in-Chief in the area of military operations. *See Egan*, 484 U.S. at 529 (quoting *Haig v. Agee* 1453 U.S. 280, 293–94 (1981). *See also Agee*, 453 U.S. at 291 (deference to Executive Branch is "especially" appropriate "in the area of national security").

(U) In order to respect the President's inherent constitutional authority to manage a military campaign, 18 U.S.C. §2340A (the prohibition against torture) must be construed as inapplicable to interrogations undertaken pursuant to his Commander-in-Chief authority. Congress lacks authority under Article 1 to set the terms and conditions under which the President may exercise his authority as Commander-in-Chief to control the conduct of operations during a war. The President's power to detain and interrogate enemy combatants arises out of his constitutional authority as Commander-in-Chief. A construction of Section 2340A that applied the provision to regulate the President's authority as Commander-in-Chief to determine the interrogation and treatment of enemy combatants would raise serious constitutional questions. Congress may no more regulate the President's ability to detain and interrogate enemy combatants than it may regulate his ability to direct troop movements on the battlefield. Accordingly, we would construe Section 2340A to avoid this constitutional difficulty, and conclude that it does not apply to the President's detention and interrogation of enemy combatants pursuant to his Commander-in-Chief authority.

(U) This approach is consistent with previous decisions of the DOJ involving the application of federal criminal law. For example, DOJ has previously construed the congressional contempt statute as inapplicable to executive branch officials who refuse to comply with congressional subpoenas because of an assertion of executive privilege. In a 1984 opinion. DOJ concluded that

> if executive officials were subject to prosecution for criminal contempt whenever they carried out the President's claim of executive privilege, it would significantly burden and immeasurably impair the President's ability to fulfill his constitutional duties. Therefore, the separation of powers principles that underlie the doctrine of executive privilege also would preclude an application of the contempt of Congress statute to punish officials for aiding the President in asserting his constitutional privilege.

Prosecution for Contempt of Congress of an Executive Branch Official Who Has Asserted A Claim of Executive Privilege. 8:Op O.L.C. 101, 134 (May 30, 1984). Likewise, if executive officials were subject to prosecution for conducting interrogations when they were carrying out the President's Commander-in-Chief powers, "it would significantly burden and immeasurably impair the President's ability to fulfill his constitutional duties." These constitutional principles preclude an application of Section 2340A to punish officials for aiding the President in exercising his exclusive constitutional authorities. *Id.*

(U) It could be argued that Congress enacted 18 U.S.C. § 2340A with full knowledge and consideration of the President's Commander-in-Chief power, and that Congress intended to restrict his discretion; however, the Department of Justice could not enforce Section 2340A against federal officials acting pursuant to the President's constitutional authority to wage a military campaign. Indeed, in a different contact, DOJ has concluded that both courts and prosecutors should reject prosecutions that apply federal criminal laws to activity that is authorized pursuant to one of the President's constitutional powers. DOJ, for example, has previously concluded that Congress could not constitutionally extend the congressional contempt statute to executive branch officials who refuse to comply with congressional subpoenas because of an assertion of executive privilege. They opined that "courts . . . would surely conclude that a criminal prosecution for the exercise of a presumptively valid, constitutionally based privilege is not consistent with the Constitution." 8 Op. O.L.C. at 141. Further, DOJ concluded that it could not bring a criminal prosecution against a defendant who had acted pursuant to an exercise of the President's constitutional power. "The President, through a United States Attorney, need not, indeed may not, prosecute criminally a subordinate for asserting on his behalf a claim of executive privilege. Nor could the Legislative Branch or the courts require or implement the prosecution of such an individual." *Id.* Although Congress may define federal crimes that the President, through the Take Care Clause, should prosecute, Congress cannot compel the President to prosecute outcomes taken pursuant to the President's own constitutional authority. If Congress could do so, it could control the President's authority through the manipulation of federal criminal law.

(U) There are even greater concerns with respect to prosecutions arising out of the exercise of the President's express authority as Commander-in-Chief than with prosecutions arising out of the assertion of executive privilege. In a series of opinions examining various legal questions arising after September 11, 2001, DOJ explained the scope of the President's Commander-in-Chief power. We briefly summarize the findings of those opinions here. The President's constitutional power to protect the security of the United States and the lives and safety of its people must be understood in light of the Founders' intention to create a federal government "clothed with all the powers requisite to the complete execution of its trust." *The Federalist* No. 23, at 147 (Alexander Hamilton) (Jacob E. Cooke ed. 1961). Foremost among the objectives committed to that trust by the Constitution is the security of the nation. As Hamilton explained in arguing for the Constitution's adoption, because "the circumstances which may affect the public safety" are not reducible within certain determinate limits,

> it must be admitted, as necessary consequence, that there can be no limitation of that authority, which is to provide for the defense and protection of the community, in any matter essential to its efficacy.

Id. at 147–48. Within the limits that the Constitution itself imposes, the scope and distribution of the powers to protect national security must be construed to authorize the most efficacious defense of the nation and its interests in accordance "with the realistic purpose of the entire instrument." *Lichter v. United States*, 334 U.S. 742, 782 (1948).

(U) The text, structure, and history of the Constitution establish that the Founders entrusted the President with the primary responsibility, and therefore the power to ensure the security of United States in situations of grave and unforeseen emergencies. The decision to deploy military force in the defense of United States interests is expressly placed under Presidential Authority by the Vesting Clause, U.S. Const. Art. I, § 1. cl. 1, and by the Commander-in-Chief Clause, *id.* § 2, cl. 1.[18] DOJ has long understood the Commander-in-Chief Clause in particular as an affirmative grant of authority to the President. The Framers understood the Clause as investing the President with the fullest range of power understood at the time of the ratification of the Constitution as belonging to the military commander. In addition, the Structure of the Constitution demonstrates that any power traditionally understood as pertaining to the executive which includes the conduct of warfare and the defense of the nation unless expressly assigned in the Constitution to Congress, is vested in the President.

---

[18] (U) *See Johnson v. Eisentrager*, 339 U.S. 763, 789 (1950) (President has authority to deploy United States armed forces "abroad or to any particular region"); *Fleming v. Page*, 50 U.S. (9 How) 603, 614–15 (1950) ("As Commander-in-Chief, [the President] is authorized to direct the movements of the naval and military forces placed by law at his command, and to employ them in the manner he may deem most effectual) *Loving v. United States*, 517 U.S. 748, 776 (1996) (Scalia, J., concurring in part and concurring in judgment) (The inherent powers of the Commander-in-Chief "are clearly extensive."); *Maul v. United States*, 274 U.S. 501, 515–16 (1927) (Brandeis & Holmes. J., concurring) (President "may direct any revenue letter to cruise in any water in order to perform any duty of the service"); *Commonwealth Massachusetts v. Laird*, 451 F.2d 26, 32 (1st Cir. 1971) (the President has "power as Commander-in-Chief to station forces abroad"); *Ex parte Vallandigham*, 28 F.Cas. 874, 922 (C.C.S.D. Ohio (1863) (No. 16,816) (in acting "under this power where there is no express legislative declaration, the President is guided solely by his own judgment land discretion"); *Authority to Use United States Military Forces in Somalia*, 16 Op. O.L.C. 6,6 *(Dec. 4, 1992) (Barr, Attorney General)*.

Article II, Section 1 makes this clear by stating that the "executive Power shall be vested in a President of the United States of America." That sweeping grant vests in the President an unenumerated "executive power" and contrasts with the specific enumeration of the powers those "herein" granted to Congress in Article I. The implications of constitutional text and structure are confirmed by the practical consideration that national security decisions require the unity in purpose and energy in action that characterize the Presidency rather than Congress.[19]

(U) As the Supreme Court has recognized, the Commander-in-Chief power and the President's obligation to protect the nation imply the ancillary powers necessary to their successful exercise. "The first of the enumerated powers of the President is that he shall be Commander-in-Chief of the Army and Navy of the United States. And of course, the grant of war power includes all that is necessary and proper for carrying those powers into execution." *Johnson v. Eisentrager*, 339 U.S. 763, 788 (1950). In wartime, it is for the President alone to decide what methods to use to best prevail against the enemy. The President's complete discretion in exercising the Commander-in-Chief power has been recognized by the courts. In the *Prize Cases*, 67 U.S. (2 Black) 635, 670 (1862), for example, the Court explained that whether the President, "in fulfilling his duties as Commander-in-Chief", had appropriately responded to the rebellion of the southern states was a question "to be *decided by him*" and which the Court could not question, but must leave to "the political department of the Government to which this power was entrusted".

(U) One of the core functions of the Commander-in-Chief is that of capturing, detaining, and interrogating members of the enemy. It is well settled that the President may seize and detain enemy combatants, at least for the duration of the conflict, and the laws of war make clear that prisoners-may be interrogated for information concerning the enemy, its strength, and its plans. Numerous Presidents have ordered the capture, detention, and questioning of enemy combatants during virtually every major conflict in the Nation's history, including recent conflicts in Korea, Vietnam, and the Persian Gulf. Recognizing this authority, Congress has never attempted to restrict or interfere with the President's authority on this score.

(U) Any effort by Congress to regulate the interrogation of unlawful combatants would violate the Constitution's sole vesting of the Commander-in-Chief authority in the President. There can be little doubt that intelligence operations, such as the detention and interrogation of enemy combatants and leaders, are both necessary and

---

[19] (U) Judicial decisions since the beginning of the Republic confirm the President's constitutional power and duty to repel military action against the United States and to take measures to prevent the recurrence of an attack. As Justice Joseph Story said long ago, "[I]t may be fit and proper for the government, in the exercise of the high discretion confided to the executive, for great public purposes, to act on a sudden emergency, or to prevent an irreparable mischief, by summary measures, which are not found in the text of the laws." *The Apollon*, 22 U.S. (9 Wheat) 362, 366–67 (1824). If the President is confronted with an unforeseen attack on the territory and people of the United States, or other immediate dangerous threat to American interests and security, it is his constitutional responsibility to respond to that threat with whatever means are necessary. *See e.g., The Prize Cases*, 67 U.S. (2 Black) 635, 668 (1862) ("If a war be made by invasion or a foreign nation, the President is not only authorised but bound to resist force by force . . . without waiting for any special legislative authority."); *United States v. Smith*, 27 F.Cas; 1192, 1229–30 (C.C.D.N.Y, 1-06) (No. 16,342) (Paterson, Circuit Justice) (regardless of statutory authorization. It is "the duty . . . of the executive magistrate . . . to repel an invading foe") *see also* 3 Story, *commentaries* § 1485 ("[t]he command and application of the public force . . . to maintain peace, and to resist foreign invasion" are executive powers).

proper for the effective conduct of a military campaign. Indeed, such operations may be of more importance in a war with an international terrorist organization than one with the conventional armed forces of a nation-state, due to the former's emphasis on secret operations and surprise attacks against civilians. It may be the case that only successful interrogations can provide the information necessary to prevent the success of covert terrorist attacks upon the United States and its citizens. Congress can no more interfere with the President's conduct of the interrogation of enemy combatants than it can dictate strategy or tactical decisions on the battlefield. Just as statutes that order the President to conduct warfare in a certain manner or for specific goals would be unconstitutional, so too are laws that seek to prevent the President from gaining the intelligence he believes necessary to prevent attacks upon the United States.

(U) As this authority is inherent in the President, exercise of it by subordinates would be best if it can be shown to have been derived from the President's authority through Presidential directive or other writing.[20]

b. Necessity

(U) The defense of necessity could be raised, under the current circumstances, to an allegation of a violation of a criminal statute. Often referred to as the "choice of evils" defense, necessity has been defined as follows:

> Conduct that the actor believes to be necessary to avoid a harm or evil to himself or to another is justifiable, provided that:
> (a) the harm or evil sought to be avoided by such conduct is greater than that sought to be prevented by the law defining the offense charged; and
> (b) neither the Code nor other law defining the offense provides exceptions or defenses dealing with the specific situation involved; and
> (c) a legislative purpose to exclude the justification claimed does not otherwise plainly appear.

Model Penal Code § 3.02. *See also* Wayne R. LaFave & Austin W. Scott, 1 Substantive Criminal Law § 5.4 at 627 (1986 & 2002 supp.) ("LaFave & Scott"). Although there is no federal statute that generally establishes necessity or other justifications as defenses to federal criminal laws, the Supreme Court has recognized the defense. *See United States v. Bailey*, 444 U.S. 394, 410 (1980) (relying on LaFave & Scott and Model Penal Code definitions of necessity defense).

(U) The necessity defense may prove especially relevant in the current circumstances. As it has been described in the case law and literature, the purpose behind necessity is one of public policy. According to LaFave & Scott, "the law ought to promote the achievement of higher values at the expense of lesser values, and sometimes the greater good for society will be accomplished by violating the literal language of the criminal law." LaFave & Scott, at 629. In particular, the necessity defense can justify the intentional killing of one person to save two others because "it is better that two lives be saved and one lost than that two be lost and one saved." *Id.* Or, put in the language of a choice of evils, "the evil involved in violating the terms of the criminal law (. . . even taking another's life) may be less than that which would result from literal compliance with the law (. . . two lives lost)". *Id.*

---

[20] (U) We note that this view is consistent with that of the Department of Justice.

(U) Additional elements of the necessity defense are worth noting here. First, the defense is not limited to certain types of harms. Therefore, the harm inflicted by necessity may include intentional homicide, so long as the harm avoided is greater (i.e., preventing more deaths) *Id.* at 634. Second, it must actually be the defendant's intention to avoid the greater harm; intending to commit murder and then learning only later that the death had the fortuitous result of saving other lives will not support a necessity defense. *Id.* at 635. Third, if the defendant reasonably believes that the lesser harm as necessary, even if, unknown to him, it was not, he may still avail himself of the defense. As LaFave and Scott explain, "if A kills B reasonably believing it to be necessary to save C and D, he is not guilty of murder even though, unknown to A, C and D could have been rescued without the necessity of killing B." *Id.* Fourth, it is for the court, and not the defendant to judge whether the harm avoided outweighed the harm done. *Id.* at 636. Fifth, the defendant cannot rely upon the necessity defense if a third alternative that will cause less harm is open and known to him.

(U) Legal authorities identify an important exception to the necessity defense. The defense is available "only in situations wherein the legislature has not itself, in its criminal statute, made a determination of values." *Id* at 629. Thus, if Congress explicitly has made clear that violation of a statute cannot be outweighed by the harm avoided, courts cannot recognize the necessity defense. LaFave and Israel provide as an example an abortion statute that made clear that abortions even to save the life of the mother would still be a crime; in such cases the necessity defense would be unavailable. *Id.* at 630. Here, however, Congress has not explicitly made a determination of values vis-a-vis torture. In fact, Congress explicitly removed efforts to remove torture from the weighing of values permitted by the necessity defense.[21]

c. Self-Defense

(U) Even if a court were to find that necessity did not justify the violation of a criminal statute, a defendant could still appropriately raise a claim of self-defense. The right to self-defense, even when it involves deadly force, is deeply embedded in our law, both as to individuals and as to the nation as a whole. As the Court of Appeals for the D.C. Circuit has explained:

> More than two centuries ago, Blackstone, best known of the expositors of the English common law taught that "all homicide is malicious, and of course amounts to murder, unless . . . excused on the account of accident or self-preservation".

---

[21] In the CAT, torture is defined as the intentional infliction of severe pain or suffering "for such purposes as obtaining from him or a third person information or a confession." CAT Article 1.1. One could argue that such a definition represented an attempt to indicate that the good of obtaining information-no matter what the circumstances – could not justify an act of torture. In other words, necessity would not be a defense. In enacting Section 2340, however, Congress removed the purpose element in the definition of torture, evidencing an intention to remove any fixing of values by statute. By leaving Section 2340 silent as to the harm done by torture in comparison to other hands, Congress allowed the necessity defense to apply when appropriate.

Further, the CAT contains an additional provision that "no exceptional circumstances whatsoever, whether a state of war or a threat of war, internal political instability or any other public emergency, may be invoked as a justification of torture." CAT Article 22. Aware of this provision of the treaty and of the definition of the necessity defense that allows the legislature to provide *for* an exception to the defense, See Model Penal Code § 3,02(b). Congress did not incorporate CAT Article 2.2 into Section 2–4. Given that Congress omitted CAT's effort to bar a necessity or wartime defense, Section 2340 could be read as permitting the defense.

> Self-defense, as a doctrine legally exonerating the taking of human life, is as viable now as it was in Blackstone's time.

United States v. Peterson, 483 F.2d 1222, 1228–29 (D.C. Cir. 1973). Self-defense is a common-law defense to federal criminal law offenses, and nothing in the text, structure or history of Section 2340A precludes its application to a charge of torture. In the absence of any textual provision to the contrary, we assume self-defense can be an appropriate defense to an allegation of torture.

(U) The doctrine of self-defense permits the use of force to prevent harm to another person. As LaFave and Scott explain, one is justified in using reasonable force in defense of another person, even a stranger, when he reasonably believes that the other is in immediate danger of unlawful bodily harm from his adversary and that the use of such force is necessary to avoid this danger." *Id.* at 663–64. Ultimately, even deadly force is permissible, but "only when the attack of the adversary upon the other, person reasonably appears to the defender to be a deadly attack." *Id.* at 664. As with our discussion of necessity, we will review the significant elements of this defense.[22] According to LaFave and Scott, the elements of the defense of others are the same as those that apply to individual self-defense.

(U) First, self-defense requires that the use of force be *necessary* to avoid the danger of unlawful bodily harm. *Id.* at 649. A defender may justifiably use deadly force if he reasonably believes that the other person is about to inflict unlawful death or serious bodily harm upon another, and that it is necessary to use such force to prevent it. *Id.* at 652. Looked at from the opposite perspective, the defender may not use force when the force would be as equally effective at a later time and the defender suffers no harm or risk by waiting. *See* Paul H. Robinson, 2 Criminal Law Defenses § 131(c) at 77 (1984). If, however, other options permit the defender to retreat safely from confrontation without having to resort to deadly force, the use of force may not be necessary in the first place. LaFave and Scott, at 659–60.

(U) Second, self-defense requires that the defendant's belief in the necessity of using force be reasonable. If a defendant honestly but unreasonably believed force was necessary, he will not be able to make out a successful claim of self-defense. *Id.* at 654, Conversely, if a defendant reasonably believed an attack was to occur, but the facts subsequently showed no attack was threatened, he may still raise self-defense. As LaFave and Scott explain, "one may be justified in shooting to death an adversary who, having threatened to kill him, reaches for his pocket as if for a gun, though it later appears that he had no gun and that he was only reaching for his handkerchief." *Id.* Some authorities such as the Model Penal Code, even eliminate the reasonability element, and require only that the defender honestly believed regardless of its reasonableness – that the use of force was necessary.

(U) Third, many legal authorities include the requirement that a defender must reasonably believe that the unlawful violence is "imminent" before he can use force in his defense. It would be a mistake, however, to equate imminence necessarily with timing – that an attack is immediately about to occur. Rather, as the Model Penal Code explains, what is essential is that the defensive *response*/must be "immediately necessary." Model Penal Code § 3.04(1). Indeed, imminence must be merely another

---

[22] (U) Early cases had suggested that in order to be eligible for defense of another, one should have some personal relationship with the one in need of protection. That view has been discarded. LaFave & Scott at 664.

way of expressing the requirement of necessity. Robinson at 78. LaFave and Scott, for example, believe that the imminence requirement makes sense as part of a necessity defense because if an attack is not immediately upon the defender, the defender may have other options available to avoid the attack that do not involve the use of force. LaFave and Scott at 656. If, however, the fact of the attack becomes certain and no other options remain the use of force may be justified. To use a well-known hypothesis, if A were to kidnap and confine B, and then tell B he would kill B one week later, B would be justified in using force in self-defense, even if the opportunity arose before the week had passed. *Id.* at 656; *see also* Robinson at § 131(c)(1) at 78. In this hypothetical, while the attack itself is not imminent, B's use of force becomes immediately necessary whenever he has an opportunity to save himself from A.

(U) Fourth, the amount of force should be proportional to the threat. As LaFave and Scott explain, "the amount of force which [the defender] may justifiably use must be reasonably related to the threatened harm which he seeks to avoid." LaFave and Scott at 651. Thus, one may not use deadly force in response to a threat that does not rise to death or serious bodily harm. If such harm may result however, deadly force is appropriate.

(U) A claim by an individual of the defense of another would be further supported by the fact that in this case, the nation itself is under attack and has the right to self-defense. This fact can bolster and support an individual claim of self-defense in a prosecution, according to the Supreme Court in *In re Neagle*, 135 U.S. 1 (1890). In that case, the State of California arrested and held deputy U.S. Marshal Neagle for shooting and killing the assailant of Supreme Court Justice Field. In granting the writ of habeas corpus for Neagle's release, the Supreme Court did not rely alone upon the marshal's right to defend another or his right to self-defense. Rather, the Court found that Neagle, as an agent of the United States and of the executive branch, was justified in the killing because in protecting Justice Field, he was acting pursuant to the executive branch's inherent constitutional authority to protect the United States government. *Id.* at 67 ("We cannot doubt the power of the President to take measures for the protection of a judge of one of the courts of the United States who, while in the discharge of the duties of his office, is threatened with a personal attack which may probably result in his death. That authority derives, according to the Court, from the President's power under Article II to take care that the laws are faithfully executed. In other words, Neagle as a federal officer not only could raise self-defense or defense of another, but also could defend his actions on the ground that he was implementing the Executive Branch's authority to protect the United States government.

(U) If the right to defend the national government can be raised as a defense in an individual prosecution as *Neagle* suggests, then a government defendant, acting in his official capacity, should be able to argue that any conduct that arguably violated a criminal prohibition was undertaken pursuant to more than just individual self-defense or defense of another. In addition, the defendant could claim that he was fulfilling the Executive Branch's authority to protect the federal government, and the nation, from attack. The September 11 attacks have already triggered that authority, as recognized both under domestic and international law. Following the example of *In re Neagle*, we conclude that a government defendant may also argue that his conduct of an interrogation properly authorized, is justified on the basis of protecting the nation from attack.

(U) There can be little doubt that the nation's right to self-defense has been triggered under our law. The Constitution announces that one of its purposes is "to provide for the common defense." U.S. Const., Preamble. Article I, § 8 declares that Congress is to exercise its powers to "provide for the common defense". *See also* 2 Pub. Papers of Ronald Reagan 920, 921 1988–89) (right to self-defense recognized by Article 51 of the U.N. Charter). The President has particular responsibility and power to take steps to defend the nation and its people. *In re Neagle*, 135 U.S. at 64. *See also* U.S. Const., art. IV, § 4 ("The United States shall . . . protect [each of the States] against Invasion"). As Commander-in-Chief and Chief Executive, he may use the Armed Forces to protect the nation and its people. *See, e.g., United States v. Verdugo-Urquidez*, 494 U.S. 259, 273 (1990). And he may employ secret agents to aid in his work as Commander-in-Chief. *Totten v. United States*. 92 U.S. 105, 106 (1876). As the Supreme Court observed in *The Prize Cases*, 67 U.S. (2 Black) 635 (1862), in response to an armed attack on the United States "the President is not only authorized but bound to resist force by force . . . without waiting for any special legislative authority." *Id.* at 668. The September 11 events were a direct attack on the United States, and as we have explained above, the President has authorized the use of military force with the support of Congress.[24]

(U) As DOJ has made clear in opinions involving the war on al Qaeda, the nation's right to self-defense has been triggered by the events of September 11. If a government defendant were to harm an enemy combatant during an interrogation in a manner that might arguably violate criminal prohibition, he would be doing so in order to prevent further attacks on the United States by the al Qaeda terrorist network. In that case, DOJ believes that he could argue that the executive branch's constitutional authority to protect the nations from attack justified his actions. This national and international version of the right to self-defense could supplement and bolster the government defendant's individual right.

d. Law Enforcement Actions

(U) Use of force in military law enforcement is authorized for (1) self-defense and defense of others against a hostile person when in imminent danger of death or serious bodily harm *by the hostile person*; (2) to prevent the actual theft or sabotage of assets vital to national security; (3) to prevent the actual theft or sabotage of resources

---

[24] (U) While the President's constitutional determination alone is sufficient to justify the nation's resort to self-defense it also bears noting that the right to self-defense is further recognized under international law. Article 51 of the U.N. charter declares that "[n]othing in the present Charter shall impair the inherent right of individual or collective self-defense if an armed attack occurs against a Member of the United Nations until the Security Council has taken the measures necessary to maintain international peace and security". The attacks of September 11, 2001, clearly constitute an armed attack against the United States, and indeed were the latest in a long history of al Qaeda sponsored attacks against the United States. This conclusion was acknowledged by the United Nations Security Council on September 29, 2001, when it unanimously adopted Resolution 1373 explicitly "raffirming the inherent right of individual and collective defense as recognized by the charter of the United Nations. This right of self-defense is a right to effective self-defense. In other words, the victim state has the right to use force against the aggressor who has initiated an "armed attack" until the threat has abated. The United States, through its military and intelligence personnel, has a right recognized by Article 51 to continue using force until such time as the threat posed by al Qaeda and other terrorist groups connected to the September 11 attack is completely ended." Other treaties re affirm the right of the United States to use force in its self-defense. See, e.g., Inter-American Treaty of Reciprocal Assistance, art. 3, Sept. 2, 1947, T.I.A.S. No. 1838, 21 U.N.T.S. 77 (Rio Treaty); North Atlantic Treaty. art. 5, Apr. 4, 1949, 3 Stat. 2241, 34 U.N.T.S. 243.

that are inherently dangerous to others; (4) to prevent the commission of a serious crime that involves imminent danger of death or serious bodily harm; (5) to prevent the destruction of vital public utilities or similar critical infrastructure; (6) for apprehension; and (7) to prevent escape (DODD 5210.56, 1 Nov 2001). These justifications contemplate the use of force against a person who has committed, is committing, or is about to commit, a serious offense. This recognized concept that force used for such purposes is not unlawful could be argued to apply, at least by analogy, to the use of force against a detainee to extract intelligence to prevent a serious and imminent terrorist incident. However, we are unaware of any authority for the proposition. For an analogous discussion pertaining to the pending commission of a serious crime, see the "necessity" and "self-defense" discussions, *supra*.

e. Superior Orders

(U) Under both international law and U.S. law, an order to commit an obviously criminal act, such as the wanton killing of a noncombatant or the torture of a prisoner, is an *unlawful* order and will not relieve a subordinate of his responsibility to comply with the law of armed conflict.[25] Only if the individual did not know of the unlawfulness of an order, and he could not reasonably be expected under the circumstances to recognize the order as unlawful, will the defense of obedience of a superior order protect a subordinate from the consequences of violation of the law of armed conflict.[26]

(U) Under international law, the fact that a war crime is committed pursuant to the orders of a military or civilian superior does not by itself relieve the subordinate committing it from criminal responsibility under international law.[27] It may, however, be considered in mitigation of punishment.[28]

(U) For instance, the Charter of the International Military Tribunal at Nuremberg, art. 8, stated:

> The fact that the Defendant acted pursuant to order of his Government or of a superior shall not free him from responsibility, but may be considered in mitigation of punishment if the Tribunal determines that justice so requires.[29]

(U) Similarly, the Statute for the International Tribunal for Yugoslavia, and the Statute for the International Criminal Tribunal for Rwanda provide (in Articles 7(4) & 6(4), respectively) provide:

> The fact that an accused person acted pursuant to an order of a Government or of a superior shall not relieve him of criminal responsibility, but may be considered in anticipation of punishment if the Tribunal determines that justice so requires.

---

[25] (U) *See Section* 6.1.4, Annotated Supplement to the Commander's Handbook on the Law of Naval Operations (NWP 1–14M 1997)

[26] *Id.*

[27] Conversely, the International Criminal Court reflects the traditional view. Article 33 of the Rome Statute, recognises the defense of superior orders: "1. The fact that a crime within the jurisdiction of the Court has been committed by a person pursuant to an order of a Government or of a superior, whether military or civilian, shall not relieve that person of criminal responsibility unless: (a) The person was under a legal obligation to obey orders of the Government or superior in question: (b) The person did not know that the order was unlawful; and (c) The order was not manifestly unlawful. 2. For the purposes of this article, orders to commit genocide or crimes against humanity are manifestly unlawful."

[28] *Id.* at § 6.2.5.5.1

[29] *See* U.S. Naval War College, International Law Documents, at 1944–45, 255 (1946).

(U) As to the general attitude taken by military tribunals toward the plea of superior orders, the following statement is representative:

> It cannot be questioned that acts done in time of war under the military authority of an enemy cannot involve any criminal liability on the part of officers or soldiers if the acts are not prohibited by the conventional or customary rules of war. Implicit obedience to orders of superior officers is almost indispensable to every military system. But this implies obedience to lawful orders only. If the act done pursuant to a superior's orders be murder, the production of the order will not make it any less so. It may mitigate but it cannot justify the crime. We are of the view, however, that if the illegality of the order was not known to the inferior, and he could not reasonably have been expected to know of its illegality, no wrongful intent necessary to the commission of a crime exists and the interior [sic] will be protected. But the general rule is the members of the armed forces are bound to obey only the lawful orders of their commanding officers and they cannot escape criminal liability by obeying a command which violates international law and outrages fundamental concepts of justice.

The Hostage Case (*United States v. Wilhelm List et al.*), 11 TWC 1236.

(U) The International Military Tribunal at Nuremberg declared in its judgment that the test of responsibility for superior orders "is not the existence of the order, but whether moral choice was in fact possible."[30]

(U) Domestically, the UCMJ discusses the defense of superior order in The Manual Courts-Martial, which provides in R.C.M. 916(d), MCM 2002:

> It is a defense to any offense that the accused was acting pursuant to orders unless the accused knew the orders to be unlawful or a person of ordinary sense and understanding would have known the orders to be unlawful. An act performed pursuant to a lawful order is justified. An act performed pursuant to an unlawful order is excused unless the accused knew it to be unlawful or a person or ordinary sense and understanding would have known the orders to be unlawful.

Inference of lawfulness. An order requiring the performance of a military duty or act may be inferred to be lawful and it is disobeyed at the peril of the subordinate.[31]

(U) In sum, the defense of superior orders will generally be available for U.S. Armed Forces personnel engaged in exceptional interrogations except where the conduct goes so far as to be patently unlawful.

4. Lack of DOJ Representation for DOD Personnel Charged with a Criminal Offense

(U) DOJ representation of a defendant is generally not available in federal criminal proceedings, even when the defendant's actions occur within the scope of federal employment.[32]

---

[30] (U) 1 Trial of Major War Criminals before the International Military Tribunal, Nuremberg 14 November 1945–1 October 1946, at 224 (1947), *excerpted in* U.S. Naval War College, International Law Documents, 1946–1947, at 260 (1948).

[31] (U) This inference does not apply to a patently illegal order, such as one that directs the commission of a crime. (Article 90, UCMJ).

[32] (U) 28 CFR § 50.15 (a)(4)

B. Federal Civil Statutes

1. 28 U.S.C. § 1350

(U) 28 U.S.C. § 1350 extends the jurisdiction of the U.S. District Courts to *"any civil action by an alien for a tort only, committed in violation of the law of nations or a treaty of the United States".*[33] Section 1350 is a vehicle by which victims of torture and other human rights violations by their native government and its agents have sought judicial remedy for the wrongs they've suffered. However, all the decided cases we have found involve foreign nationals suing in U.S. District Courts for conduct by foreign actors/governments.[34] The District Court for the District of Columbia has determined that section 1350 actions, by the GTMO detainees, against the United States or its agents acting within the scope of employment fail. This is because (1) the United States has not waived sovereign immunity to such suits like those brought by the detainees, and (2) the *Eisentrager* doctrine barring habeas access also precludes other potential avenues of jurisdiction.[35] This of course leaves interrogators vulnerable in their individual capacity for conduct a court might find tortuous. Assuming a court would take jurisdiction over the matter and grant standing to the detainee[36], it is possible that this statute would provide an avenue of relief for actions of the United States or its agents found to violate customary international law. The application of international law, specifically that which might be considered custom, is discussed *supra* in Section IV at "International Considerations that May Affect Policy Determinations".

2. Torture Victims Protection Act (TVPA)

(U) In 1992, President Bush signed into law the Torture Victims Protection Act of 1991.[37] Appended to the U.S. Code as a note to section 1350, the TVPA specifically creates a cause of action for individuals (or their successors) who have been subjected to torture or extra-judicial killing by "an individual who, under actual or apparent authority, or color of law, *of any foreign nation* – (1) subjects an individual to torture shall, in a civil action, be liable for damages to that individual; or (2) subjects an individual to extra-judicial killing shall, in a civil action, be liable for damages.... " (emphasis added)[38] It thus appears that the TVPA does not apply to the conduct of U.S. agents acting under the color of law.

---

[33] (U) 28 U.S.C. § 1350, the Alien Tort Claim Act (ATCA).

[34] (U) See, for example, *Abebe-Jira v. Negewo*, No. 93–9133, United States Court of Appeals, Eleventh Circuit, Jan 10, 1996. In this case the 11th Circuit concluded, "the Alien Tort Claims Act establishes a federal forum where courts may fashion domestic common law remedies to give effect to violations of customary international law."

[35] (U) *Al Odah v. United States*, (D.D.C., 2002)

[36] (U) *Filartiga v. Pena-Irala* 630 F.2d 876 (2nd Cir. 1980) 885, note 18, "conduct of the type alleged here [torture] would be actionable under 42 U.S.C. § 1983, or undoubtedly the Constitution, if performed by a government official."

[37] (U) Pub L. No. 102–256, 106 Stat 73, 28 U.S.C. § 1350 (note).

[38] (U) The definition of torture used in PL 102–256 is: "any act, directed against an individual in the offender's custody or physical control, by which severe pain or suffering (other than pain or suffering arising only from or inherent to, or incidental to lawful sanctions) whether physical or mental, is intentionally inflicted on that individual for such purposes as obtaining from that individual or a third person information or a confession, punishing that individual for an act that individual or a third person has committed or is suspected of having committed, intimidating or coercing that individual or a

C. Applicability of the United States Constitution

1. Applicability of the Constitution to Aliens Outside the United States

(U) Nonresident enemy aliens do not enjoy constitutional rights outside the sovereign territory of the United States.[39] The courts have held that unlawful combatants do not gain constitutional rights upon transfer to GTMO as unlawful combatants merely because the U.S. exercises extensive dominion and control over GTMO.[40] Moreover, because the courts have rejected the concept of "de facto sovereignty," constitutional rights apply to aliens only on sovereign U.S. territory. (See discussion under "Jurisdiction of Federal Courts", *infra*.)

(U) Although U.S. constitutional rights do not apply to aliens at GTMO, the U.S. criminal laws do apply to acts committed there by virtue of GTMO's status as within the special maritime and territorial jurisdiction.

2. The Constitution Defining U.S. Obligations Under International Law

(U) In the course of taking reservations to the Convention Against Torture and Other Cruel, and Inhuman or Degrading Treatment or Punishment, the United States determined that the Convention's prohibitions against cruel, inhuman or degrading treatment or punishment applied only to the extent that such conduct was prohibited by the Fifth, Eighth and Fourteenth Amendments to our Constitution.[41] Consequently, analysis of these amendments is significant in determining the extent to which the United States is bound by the Convention. It should be clear, however, that aliens held at GTMO do not have constitutional rights under the Fifth Amendment's Due Process clause or the Eighth Amendment. See, *Johnson v. Eisenberger*, 339 U.S. 763 (1950) and *Verdugo-Urquidez*, 494 U.S. 259 (1990).

a. Eighth Amendment

(U) "An examination of the history of the Amendment and the decisions of this [Supreme] Court construing the proscription against cruel and unusual punishment confirms that it was designed to protect those convicted of crimes."[42] The import of this looking is that, assuming a detainee could establish standing to challenge his treatment, the claim would not lie under the Eighth Amendment. Accordingly, it does not appear detainees could successfully pursue a claim regarding their pre-conviction treatment under the Eighth Amendment.

---

third person, or for any reason based on discrimination of any kind." This is similar, but broader, than the definition in the Torture Statute. The definition of mental pain and suffering is the same as in the Torture Statute.

[39] (U) *Eisentrager* at 764.

[40] (U) *Al Odah v. United States*, (D.D.C., 2002).

[41] (U) Articles of ratification, 21 Oct. 1994: "I. The Senate's advice and consent is subject to the following reservation (1) That the United States considers itself bound by the obligation under Article 16 to prevent 'cruel, inhuman, or degrading treatment or punishment, only insofar as the term cruel, inhuman, or degrading treatment or punishment' means the cruel, unusual and inhumane treatment or punishment prohibited by the Fifth, Eighth, and/or Fourteenth Amendments in the Constitution of the United States." Available at the UN documents site http://193.194.138.190/html/***3/treaty12_asp.htm.

[42] (U) *Ingraham v. Wright*, 430 U.S. 651, 664 (1977). In *Ingraham*, a case about corporal punishment in a public junior high school, the Court analyzed the claim under the Amendment's Due Process clause concluding that the conduct did not violate the Fourteenth Amendment, even though it involved up to 10 whacks with a wooden paddle.

(U) The standards of the Eighth Amendment are relevant, however, due to the U.S. Reservation to the Torture Convention's definition of cruel, inhuman, and degrading treatment. Under "cruel and unusual punishment" jurisprudence, there are two lines of analysis: (1) conditions of confinement, and (2) excessive force. As a general matter, the excessive forces analysis applies to the official use of physical force, often in situations in which an inmate has attacked another inmate or a guard whereas the conditions of confinement analysis applies to such things as administrative segregation. Under the excessive force analysis, "a prisoner alleging excessive force must demonstrate that the defendant acted 'maliciously and sadistically to cause harm.'" *Porter v. Nussle*, 534 U.S. 516, 528 (2002) (quoting *Hudson v. McMillan*, 503 U.S. I, at 7). Excessive force requires the unnecessary and wanton infliction of pain. *Whitney v. Albers*, 475 U.S. 312, 319 (1986).

(U) A condition of confinement is not, "cruel and unusual" unless it (1) is "sufficiently serious" to implicate constitutional protection, *Id.* at 347, and (2) reflects "deliberate indifference" to the prisoner's health or safety, *Farmer v. Brennan* 511 U.S. 825, 834 (1994). The first element is objective, and inquires whether the challenged condition is cruel and unusual. The second, so-called "subjective" element requires examination of the actor's intent and inquires whether the challenged condition is imposed as punishment. *Wilson v. Seiter*, 501 U.S. 294, 300 (1991) ("The source of the intent requirement is not the predilections of this Court, but the Eighth Amendment itself, which bans only cruel and unusual *punishment*. If the pain inflicted is not formally meted out *as punishment* by the statute or sentencing judge, some mental element must be attributed to the inflicting officer before it can qualify.").

(U) The Supreme Court has noted that "[n]o static 'test' can exist by which courts determine whether conditions of confinement are cruel and unusual, for the Eighth Amendment must draw its meaning from the evolving standards of decency that mark the progress of a maturing society." *Rhodes*, 452 U.S. at 146 (citation omitted). *See also Estelle v. Gamble*, 429 U.S. 97, 102 (1976) (stating that the Eighth Amendment embodies "broad and idealistic concepts of dignity, civilized standards, humanity, and decency") Nevertheless, certain guidelines emerge from the Supreme Court's jurisprudence.

(U) The Court has established that "only those deprivations denying 'the minimal civilized measures of life's necessities' sufficiently grave to form the basis of an Eighth Amendment violation." Wilson, 501 U.S. at 298, *quoting Rhodes*, 452 U.S. at 347. It is not enough for a prisoner to show that he has been subjected to conditions that are merely restrictive and even harsh" as such conditions are simply "part of the penalty that criminal offenders pay for their offenses against society." *Rhodes*, 452 U.S. at 347. See also Wilson at 399 ("the Constitution does not mandate comfortable prisons"). Rather, a prisoner must show that he has suffered a "serious deprivation of basic human needs," *id.* at 347, such as "essential food, medical care, or sanitation," *Id.* at 348, *See also Wilson*, 501 U.S. at 304 (requiring "the deprivation of a single, identifiable human need such as food, warmth, or exercise"). "The Amendment: also imposes [the duty on officials to] provide humane conditions of confinement; prison officials must ensure that inmates receive adequate food, clothing, shelter, and medical care, and must take reasonable measures to guarantee the safety of the inmates." *Farmer*, 511 U.S. at 832 (citations omitted). The Court has also articulated an alternative test inquiring whether an inmate was exposed to "a substantial risk or serious harm." *Id* at 837. *See also DeSpain v. Uphoff*, 264 F.3d 965, 971 (10th Cir. 2001) ("In order to satisfy the [objective] requirement, the inmate must show that he is incarcerated under conditions posing a substantial risk of serious harm.")

(U) The various conditions of confinement are not to be assessed under a totality of the circumstances approach. In *Wilson v. Seiter*, 501 U.S. 294 (1991), The Supreme Court expressly rejected the contention that "each condition must be considered as part of the overall conditions challenged." *Id.* at 304 (internal quotation marks and citation omitted). Instead, the Court concluded that "Some conditions of confinement may establish an Eighth Amendment violation 'in combination' when each would not do so alone, but only when they have a mutually enforcing effect that produces the deprivation of a single identifiable human need such as food, warmth, or exercise, for example, a low cell temperature at night combined with a failure to issue blankets." *Id.* at 304. As the Court further explained, "Nothing so amorphous as 'overall conditions' can rise to the level of cruel and unusual punishment when no specific deprivation of a single human need exists" *Id.* at 305.

(U) To demonstrate deliberate indifference, a prisoner must demonstrate "that the official was subjectively aware of that risk". *Former v. Brennon* 511 U.S. 125 (1994) As the Supreme Court further explained:

> We hold ... that a prison official cannot be found liable under the Eighth Amendment for denying any inmate humane conditions of confinement unless the official knows of and regards an excessive risk to inmate health or safety; the official must both be aware of facts from which the inference can be drawn that a substantial risk of serious harm exists and he must also draw the inference.

Farmer v. Brennan 511 U.S. 825, 837 (1994). This standard requires greater culpability than mere negligence. *See Farmer v. Brennan*, 511 U.S. 825, 837 (1994); *Wilson v. Seiter*, 501 U.S. 294, 302 (1991) ("mere negligence would satisfy neither [the *Whitley* standard of malicious and sadistic infliction] nor the more lenient deliberate indifference standard") (internal quotation marks omitted).

(U) The second line of cases considers the use of force against prisoners. The situation often arises in cases addressing the use of force while quelling prison disturbances. In cases involving the excessive use of force the central question is whether the force was applied with good intentions in an attempt to restore order or maliciously and sadistically with the purpose of causing harm.[43] Malicious and sadistic use of force always violates contemporary standards of decency and would constitute cruel and unusual punishment.[44] The courts apply a subjective test when examining intent of the official. In determining whether a correctional officer has used excessive force in violation of the Eighth Amendment, courts look to several factors including: (1) "the need for the application of force"; (2) "the relationship between the need and the amount of force that was used"; (3) "the extent of injury inflicted"; (4) "the extent of the threat to the safety of staff and inmates, as reasonably perceived by responsible officials on the basis of the facts known to them"; and (5) "any efforts made to temper the severity of a forceful response."[45] Great deference is given to the prison official in the carrying out of his duties.[46]

---

[43] (U) *Whitley v. Albers*, 475 U.S. (1986)
[44] (U) *Hudson v. McMillan*, 503 U.S. 1, 9 (1992)
[45] (U) *Whitley* at 321.
[46] (U) *Whitley v. Albers*, 475 U.S. (1986).

(U) One of the Supreme Court's most recent opinions on conditions of confinement – *Hope v. Pelzer*, 122 S.Ct.2508: (2002) – illustrates the Court's focus on the necessity of the actions undertaken in response to a disturbance in determining the officer's subjective state of mind.[47] In *Hope*, following an "exchange of vulgar remarks" between the inmate Hope and an officer, the two got into a "wrestling match". *Id* at 2512. Additional officers intervened and restrained Hope. See *id.* These officers then took Hope back to prison. Once there, they required him to take off his shirt and then attached him to the hitching post, where he remained in the sun for the next seven hours. See *Id*, at 2512–13. During this time, Hope received no bathroom breaks. He was given water only once or twice and at least one guard taunted him about being thirsty. See *id.* at 2513. The Supreme Court concluded that the facts Hope alleged stated an "obvious" Eighth Amendment violation. *Id* at 2514. The obviousness of this violation stemmed from the utter lack of necessity for the actions the guards undertook. The Court emphasized that "any safety concerns" arising from the scuffle between Hope and the officer "had long since abated by the time [Hope] was attached to the hitching post" and that there was a "clear lack of an emergency situation". *Id.* As a result, the Court found that "[t]his punitive treatment amount[ed] to [the] gratuitous infliction of 'wanton and unnecessary' pain that our precedent clearly prohibits." *Id.* at 2515. Thus, the necessity of the governmental action bears upon both the conditions of confinement analysis as well as the excessive force analysis.

(U) The government interest here is of the highest magnitude. The typical prison case, the protection of other inmates or officers, the protection of the inmate alleged to have suffered the cruel and unusual punishment, or even the maintenance of order in the prison provide valid government interests for various deprivations. *See e.g., Anderson v. Nasser*, 438 F.2d 183, 193 (5th Cir. 1971) ("protect[ing] inmates from self-inflicted injury, protect[ing] the general prison population and personnel from violate acts on his part, prevent[ing] escape" are all legitimate penological interests that would permit the imposition of solitary confinement); *McMahon v. Beard*, 583 F.2d 172, 175 (5th Cir. 1978) (prevention if inmate suicide is a legitimate interest). If the protection of one person or even prison administration can be deemed to be valid governmental interests in such cases frequently permitted deprivations, it follows *a fortiori* that the interest of the United States here – obtaining intelligence vital to the protection of untold thousands of American citizens – can be no less valid. To be sure, no court has encountered the precise circumstances hereunder Eighth Amendment jurisprudence. Nonetheless, it can be forcefully argued that there can be no more compelling government interest than that which is presented here. *See Hope v. Pelzer*, 122 S. Ct. 2508 (2002) ("The unnecessary and wanton infliction of pain constitutes cruel and unusual punishment forbidden by the Eighth Amendment. We have said that among unnecessary and wanton inflictions of pain are those that are totally without penological justification.")

---

[47] (U) Although the officers' actions in Hope were undertaken in response to a scuffle between an inmate and a guard, the case is more properly thought of a "conditions of confinement" case rather than an "excessive force" case. By examining the officers' actions through the "deliberate indifference standard" the Court analyzed it as a "conditions of confinement" case. The deliberate indifference standard is inapplicable to claims of excessive force.

b. Fifth Amendment and Fourteenth Amendment[48]

(U) "It is now the settled doctrine . . . that the Due Process Clause embodies a system of rights based on moral principles so deeply embedded in the traditions and feelings of our people as to be deemed fundamental to a civilized society as conceived by our whole history. Due Process is that which comports with the deepest notions of what is fair and right and just."[49] Due process is violated if a practice or rule "offends some principle of justice so rooted in the traditions and conscience of our people as to be ranked as fundamental".[50]

(U) Standing by itself, the phrase "due process" would seem to refer solely and simply to procedure, to process in court, and therefore to be so limited that "due process of law" would be what the legislative branch enacted it to be. But that is not the interpretation which has been placed on the term. "It is manifest that it was not left to the legislative power to enact any process which might be devised. The article is a restraint on the legislative as well as on the executive and judicial powers of the government, and cannot be so construed as to leave Congress free to make any process 'due process of law' by its mere will."[51] With this viewpoint, the Supreme Court has carved out a role for the courts to judge the legislative and executive acts for their effect on the rights of the peoples.

(U) All persons within the territory of the United States are entitled to the protections of due process, including corporations, aliens, and presumptively citizens seeking readmission to the United States. It is effective in the District of Columbia and in territories which are part of the United States, but does not apply of its own force to unincorporated territories. But, it does not reach enemy alien belligerents engaged in hostilities against the United States and/or tried by military tribunals outside the territorial jurisdiction of the United States.[52] The *Eisentrager* doctrine works to prevent access by enemy belligerents, captured and held abroad, to U.S. courts. Further, in *United States v. Verdugo-Urquidez*, 494 U.S. 259 (1990), the Supreme Court held that aliens outside the United States did not have Fourth Amendment rights against the U.S. government. Indeed, in that case, the Court observed that extension of constitutional rights to aliens outside of the United States would interfere with the military operations against the nation's enemies.

(U) Even if a Court were to find mistakenly that unlawful combatants at GTMO did have constitutional rights, it is unlikely that due process would pose any standards beyond those required by the Eighth Amendment. In 1972 the Supreme Court held that "[f]ederal courts sit not to supervise prisons but to enforce the constitutional rights of all persons, which include prisoners . . . "[53] The Supreme Court's review of state criminal justice systems under the due process clause has never been subject to precise statement of metes? and bounds. In each case the Court asks whether the challenged practice or policy violates "a fundamental principle of liberty and

[48] (U) Because the Due Process considerations under the Fifth and Fourteenth amendments are the same for our purposes, this analysis considers them together.
[49] (U) *Solesbee v. Balkcom*, 339 U.S. 9, 16 (1950) (Justice Frankfurter dissenting).
[50] (U) *Snyder v. Massachusetts*, 291 U.S. 97, 105 (1934).
[51] (U) *Marray's Lessee v. Hoboken Land and Improvement Co.* 59 U.S. (18 How) 272, 276 (1856).
[52] (U) *Johnson v. Eisentrager*, 339 U.S. 763 (1950); *In re Yamashita*, 327 U.S. 1 (1946). Justices Rutledge and Murphy in the latter case argued that the due process clause applies to every human being, including enemy belligerents.
[53] (U) *Cruz v. Belo*; 405 U.S. 319, 321 (1972)

justice which inheres in the very idea of a free government and is the inalienable right of a citizen of such government".[54] The Court has generally treated challenges to prison conditions as a whole under the cruel and unusual punishments clause of the Eighth Amendment, rather than the Fifth Amendment's Due Process Clause, and challenges to particular incidents and practices under the due process clause as well as under more specific provisions, such as the First Amendment speech and religion clauses.[55]

(U) On the other hand, some conduct is so egregious that there is no justification. In *Rochin v. California*, the Supreme Court found that the State's actions in unlawfully entering the defendant's room, grappling with him to prevent him from swallowing the evidence, and then transporting him to the hospital to have his stomach pumped "shocked the conscience." The Court said of the police methods "they are methods too close to the rack and the screw to permit of constitutional differentiation".[61] Even though *Rochin* is about evidence seizure, the rationale for judicial intervention is the infringement of the process. Explaining the importance of due process the Court said "involuntary verbal confessions . . . are inadmissible under the Due Process Clause even [if true] . . . Coerced confessions offend the community's sense of fair play and decency. So here, to sanction the brutal conduct . . . would be to afford brutality the cloak of law. Nothing would be more calculated to discredit law and thereby to brutalize the temper of a society."[62] Only interrogation techniques that "shock the conscience" would not be analyzed under the standard due process balancing test.

(U) The Fifth Amendment standards are also relevant due to the U.S. Reservations to the Torture Convention's definition of cruel, inhuman, and degrading treatment.

(U) Under the Fifth Amendment right to Due Process, substantive due process protects an individual from "the exercise of power without any reasonable justification in the service of any legitimate governmental objective." *County of Sacramento v. Lewis*, 523 U.S. 833, 846 (1998). Under substantive due process "only the most egregious official conduct can be said to be arbitrary in the constitutional sense." *Id* at 846 (internal quotation marks omitted). That conduct must "shock the conscience." *See generally id; Rochin v. California*, 342 U.S. 165 (1952).[63] By contrast to deprivations in

---

[54] (U) *Twining v. New Jersey*, 211 U.S. 78, 106 (1908)

[55] (U) By way of example, the courts have recognized several rights of prisoners. Prisoners have a right to be free of racial segregation in prisons, except for the necessities of prison security and discipline. *Lee v. Washington*, 390 U.S. 333 (1968). They have the right to petition for redress of grievances, which includes access to the courts for purposes of presenting their complaints, *Ex parte Hull*, 312 U.S. 546 (1941); *White v. Ragen*, 324 U.S. 760 (1945). Prisoners must have reasonable access to a law library or to persons trained in the law. *Younger v. Gilmore*, 404 U.S. 15 (1971); *Bounds v. Smith*, 430 U.S. 817 (1978) and to bring actions in federal courts to recover for damages wrongfully done them by prison administrators, *Haines v. Kerner*, 404 U.S. 519 (1972); *Preiser v. Rodriguez*, 411 U.S. 475 (1973). And they have a right, circumscribed by legitimate prison administration considerations, to fair and regular treatment during their incarceration.

[61] (U) *Rochin v. California*, 342 U.S. 165, 172 (1952).

[62] (U) Id. at 174.

[63] (U) In the seminal case of *Rochin v California*, 342 U.S. 165 (1952), the police had some information that the defendant was selling drugs. Three officers went to and entered the defendant's home without a warrant and forced open the door to defendant's bedroom. Upon opening the door, the officers saw two pills and asked the defendant about them. The defendant promptly put them in his mouth. The officers "jumped upon him and attempted to extract the capsules." 342 U.S. at 166. The police tried to pull the pills out of his mouth but despite considerable struggle the defendant swallowed

procedural due process, which can occur so long as the government affords adequate processes, government actions that "shock the conscience" are prohibited irrespective of the procedures the government may employ in undertaking those actions. *See generally Rochin v. California*, 342 U.S. 164 (1952).

(U) To shock the conscience, the conduct at issue must involve more than mere negligence. *See County of Sacramento*, 523 U.S. at 849. *See also Daniel v. Williams*, 474 U.S. 327 (1986) ("Historically, this guarantee of due process has been applied to deliberate decisions of government officials to deprive a person of life, liberty, or property.") (collecting cases). Instead, "[I]t is ... behavior on the other end of the culpability spectrum that would most probably support a substantive due process claim: conduct intended to injure in some way unjustifiable by any government interest is the sort of official action most likely to rise to the conscience-shocking level." *Id.* In some circumstances, however, recklessness or gross negligence may suffice. *See id.* The requisite level of culpability is ultimately "not subject to mechanical application in unfamiliar territory." *Id.* at 850. As the Court explained: "Deliberate indifference that shocks in one environment may not be so patently egregious in another and our concern with preserving the constitutional proportions of substantive due process demands an exact analysis of circumstances before any abuse of power is condemned as conscience shocking." *Id.* Nonetheless, the Court opined that as a general matter such a standard would be appropriate where there is a real possibility for actual deliberation as opposed to those circumstances, such as responding to a prison riot, where quick decision must be made and a heightened level of culpability is thus more appropriate. *See id.* at 851–52.

(U) This standard appears to be an evolving one as the Court's most recent opinion regarding this standard emphasized that the conscience shocked was the "contemporary conscience." *County of Sacramento*, 523 U.S. at 847 n.8 (emphasis added). The court explained that while a judgment of what shocks the conscience "may be informed by a history of liberty protection, it necessarily reflects a traditional understanding of executive behavior, of contemporary practice, and of the standards of blame generally applied to them." *Id.* Despite the evolving nature of the standard, the standard is objective rather than subjective. The *Rochin* Court cautioned that although "the gloss has ... has not been fixed" as to what substantive due process is, judges "may not drawn on "their" merely personal and private notions and disregard the limits that bind judges in their judicial function ... [T]hese limits are derived from considerations that are fused in the whole nature of our judicial process." *Id.* At 170. *United States v. Lovasco*, 431 U.S. 783 (1973) (reaffirming that the test is objective rather than subjective). As the Court explained, the conduct issue must "do more than offend some fastidious squeamishness or private sentimentalism' in order to violate due process. *Rochin*, 342 U.S. 165, 172.

(U) The Supreme Court also clarified in *Ingraham v. Wright*, 430 U.S. 651 (1977), that under substantive due process, "[t]there is, of course, a *de minimis* level of imposition with which the Constitution is not concerned." *Id.* at 674. And as Fourth Circuit

---

them. The police then took the defendant to a hospital where a doctor forced an ermetic solution into the defendant's stomach by sticking a tube down his throat and into his stomach, which caused the defendant to vomit up the pills. The pills did in fact contain morphine. *See id.* The Court found that the actions of the police officers "shocked the conscience" and therefore violated Rochin's due process rights. *Id* at 170.

has noted, it is a "principle... inherent in the Eighth and the Fourteenth Amendments" that "[n]ot... every malevolent touch by a prison guard gives rise to a federal cause of action". *See Johnson v. Glick*, 481 F.2d at 1033 ("Not every push or shove, even if it may later seem unnecessary in the peace of a judge's chambers, violates a prisoner's constitutional rights")." *Riley v. Dorton*, 115 F.3d 1159, 1167 (4th Cir. 1997) (quoting *Hudson*, 503 U.S. at 9). Instead, the [shock-the-conscience]... inquiry.... [is] whether the force applied caused injury so severe, and was so inspired by malice or sadism... that it amounted to a brutal and inhumane abuse of official power literally shocking to the conscience." *Webb v. McCullough*, 828 F.2d 1151, 1158 (6th Cir. 1987). Examples of physical brutality that "shock the conscience" include: rape of plaintiff by uniformed officer, see *Jones v. Wellham*, 104 F.3d 620 (4th Cir. 1997); police officer struck plaintiff in retaliation for photographing police officer, see *Shillinford v. Holmes*, 634 F.2d 263 (5th Cir. 1981); police officer shot a fleeing suspect's legs without any probable cause other than the suspect's running and failing to stop, see *Aldridge v. Mullins* 377 F.Supp. 850 (M.D. Term. 1972) aff'd, 474 1189 (6th Cir. 1973). Moreover, beating or sufficiently threatening someone during the course of an interrogation can constitute conscience shocking behavior. See *Gray v. Spillman*, 925 F.2d 90, 91 (4th Cir. 1991) (plaintiff was beaten and threatened with further beating if he did not confess). By contrast, for example, actions such as verbal insults and an angry slap of "medium force" did not constitute behavior that "shocked the conscience." See *Riley v. Dorton*, 115 F.3d 1159, 1168 n.4 (4th Cir. 1997) (finding claims that such behavior shocked the conscience "meritless"). We note, however, that courts have distinguished between the use of force in interrogations and the use of force in the prison or arrest settings. The Fifth Circuit has held that "the use of physical violence against a person who is in the presence of the police for custodial interrogation, who poses no threat to others, and who does not otherwise initiate action which would indicate to a reasonably prudent police officer that the use of force is justified, is a constitutional violation." *Ware v. Reed*, 709 F.2d 345, 351 (5th Cir. 1983).

(U) Physical brutality is not the only conduct that may meet the shock-the-conscience standard. In *Cooper v. Dupnik*, 963 F.2d 1220 (9th Cir. 1992) (en banc), the Ninth Circuit held that certain psychologically-coercive interrogation techniques could constitute a violation of substantive due process. The interrogators techniques were "designed to instill stress, hopelessness, and fear, and to break [the suspect's] resistance." *Id.* at 1229. The officers planned to ignore any request for a lawyer and to ignore the suspect's right to remain silent, with the express purpose that any statements he might offer would help keep him from testifying in his own defense. *See id.* at 1249. It was this express purpose that the court found to be the "aggravating factor" leading in its conclusion that the conduct of the police "shocked the conscience." *Id.* at 1249. The court reasoned that while "it is a legitimate purpose of police investigation to gather evidence and muster information that will surround a guilty defendant and make it difficult if not impossible for him to escape justice [,]" when the methods chosen to gather evidence and information are deliberately unlawful and flout the Constitution, the legitimacy is lost." *Id.* at 1250. In *Wilkins v. May*, 872 F.2d 190 (7th Cir. 1989), the Seventh Circuit found that severe mental distress inflicted on a suspect could be a basis for a substantive due process claim. *See id.* at 195. *See also Rhrodes v. Robinson*, 612 P.2d 766, 771 (3d Cir. 1979) (claim of emotional harm could be the basis of a substantive due process claim). The *Wilkins* court found that under certain circumstances interrogating a suspect with gun at his head could violate those rights.

See 872 F.2d at 195. Whether it would rise to the level of violation depended upon whether the plaintiff was able to show "misconduct that a reasonable person would find so beyond the norm of proper police procedure as to shock the conscience, and that it is, calculated to induce not merely momentary fear or anxiety, but severe mental suffering, in the plaintiff." *Id.* On the other hand, we note that merely deceiving the suspect does not shock the conscience, see, e.g., *United States v. Byran*, 145 F.3d 405 (1st Cir. 1998) (assuring defendant he was not in danger of prosecution did not shock the conscience) nor does the use of sympathy or friends as intermediaries, see, e.g., *United States v. Sintob*, 901 F.2d 799, 809 (9th Cir. 1990).

D. Jurisdiction of Federal Courts

1. Jurisdiction to Consider Constitutional Claims

(U) The federal habeas statute provides that courts may only grant the writ "within their respective jurisdictions". This has been interpreted to limit a court's subject matter jurisdiction over habeas cases to those in which a custodian lies within the jurisdiction. For U.S. citizens, habeas jurisdiction lies regardless of where the detention occurs. The habeas action must be brought in the district in which a custodian resides or, if all custodians are outside the United States, in the District of Columbia. For aliens, there is no habeas jurisdiction outside the sovereign territory of the United States.[64]

(U) As construed by the courts, habeas jurisdiction is coterminous with the reach of constitutional rights, although that result is a matter of statutory construction. Congress has the power to extend habeas jurisdiction beyond the reach of constitutional rights but may not place greater restrictions on it.

(U) In *Johnson v. Eisentrager*, the Supreme Court ruled that enemy aliens, captured on the field of battle abroad by the U.S. Armed Forces, tried abroad for war crimes, and incarcerated abroad do not have access to the U.S. courts[65] over a habeas petition filed by German nationals seized by U.S. soldiers in China. *Eisentrager* considered habeas corpus petitions by German soldiers captured during WWII in China supporting the Japanese, convicted by Military Commission sitting in China, and incarcerated in Germany and concluded that United States courts lacked jurisdiction.[66]

[64] (U) *Johnson v. Eisentrager*, 339 U.S. 763 (1950).

[65] (U) *Johnson v. Eisentrager*, 339 U.S. 763, 777 (1950)"We are here confronted with a decision whose basic premise is that these prisoners are entitled, as a constitutional right, to sue in some court of the United States for a writ of habeas corpus. To support that assumption we must hold that a prisoner of our military authorities is constitutionally entitled to the writ, even though he (a) is an enemy alien; (b) has never been or resided in the United States; (c) was captured outside of our territory and there held in military custody as a prisoner of war; (d) was tried and convicted by a Military Commission sitting outside the United States; (e) for offenses against laws of war committed outside the United States; (f) and is at all times imprisoned outside the United States." With those words, the Supreme Court held that: "a non-resident enemy alien has no access to our courts in wartime." Currently, the D.C. Circuit is considering the appeal of several detainees at GTMO in which action the District Court denied their writ of habeas corpus challenging their detention. *Al Odah et. al. v. United States*, Nos. 02-5251,02-5284, and 02-5288 (D.C. Circ. 2002).

[66] For a fuller discussion of Habeas Corpus law as it applies to Naval Base, Guantánamo Bay, *see* memorandum, LCDR F. Greg Bowman of 29 Jan 02, subj: CRIMINAL JURISDICTION AND ITS EFFECTS OF AVAILABILITY OF THE WRIT OF HABEAS CORPUS AT U.S. NAVAL BASE GUANTANAMO BAY, CUBA (on file).

(U) Recently, unlawful combatants detained at Guantanamo Bay, Cuba (GTMO) have sought review in U.S. district court through the writ of habeas corpus, 28 U.S.C. § 2241.[67]

(U) Two courts have examined, and rejected, petitioners' claims that U.S. exclusive jurisdiction over GTMO results in a form of "de facto sovereignty" and, therefore, vests habeas jurisdiction in the federal courts.

2. Other Bases for Federal Jurisdiction

(U) In addition, one group of GTMO detainees has challenged conditions of confinement through the Alien Tort Claims Act (ATCA) and the Administrative Procedures Act (APA). The courts have declined to exercise jurisdiction on those theories in each case to date.[68] Petitioners in *Al Odah* attempted to circumvent the territorial limitations of habeas by bringing their action under the APA and ATCA. The district court found that, although petitioners did not seek release from custody, their suit challenging conditions of confinement was, nonetheless, required to be brought under habeas.

(U) The court also held, in the alternative, that it lacked jurisdiction even if petitioners were not barred by the exclusive nature of habeas actions. The ATCA provides the "district courts shall have original jurisdiction of any civil action by an alien for a tort only, committed in violation of the law of nations or treaty of the United States." 18 U.S.C. § 1350. The ATCA, although it provides federal jurisdiction over private suits, does not waive sovereign immunity for a suit against the United States. The courts have held that the APA's waiver of sovereign immunity for nonmonetary damages can theoretically be used to maintain an ATCA action against the United States. The *Al Odah* Court, however, found that the APA's exemption for "military authority exercised in the field in time of war or in occupied territory" precluded the ATCA.

3. The Military Extraterritorial Jurisdiction Act

(U) The Military Extraterritorial Jurisdiction Act (MEJA), 18 U.S.C. § 3261 *et seq*, extends Federal criminal jurisdiction for serious Federal offenses committed outside the United States to civilian persons accompanying the Armed Forces (e.g., civilian employees and contractor employees), and to members of the Armed Forces who committed a criminal act while subject in the UCMJ but who are no longer are subject to the UCMJ or who committed the offense with a defendant not subject in the UCMJ. The standard is that if the conduct by the individual would "constitute an offense punishable by imprisonment for more than one year *if the conduct had been engaged in within the special maritime and territorial jurisdiction of the United States.*" (emphasis added). In the absence of implementing regulations, the practical effect of MEJA is uncertain; however, MEJA remains Federal law.

E. The Uniform Code of Military Justice

(U) The Uniform Code of Military Justice (UCMJ) applies to United States Forces on active duty, at all times and in all places throughout the world. Members of the

---

[67] (U) *Coalition of Clergy v. Bush*, 189 F. Supp. 2d 1036 (CD. Cal.), affirmed in part and vacuted in part, 310 F.3d 1153 (9th Cir. 2002); *Rasul v. Bush*, 215 F.2d 55 (D.D.C. 2002).

[68] (U) The ACTA and APA theories, rejected in the District Court for D.C., are awaiting review in the D.C. Circuit at this time in the *Rasul* and *Al Odah* cases.

Reserve component and retired regular officers can, under certain circumstances, also be subject to the UCMJ, as can civilians accompanying the Armed Forces in time of war under certain-circumstances.[69]

1. Offenses

(U) A member of UCMJ provisions potentially apply to service members involved in the interrogation and supervision of the interrogation of detainees, Most significant are the following.[70]

a. Cruelty, Oppression or Maltreatment, Art 93

(U) The elements of the offense are that the alleged victim was subject to the orders of the accused and that the accused was cruel toward, oppressed, or maltreated the victim. The cruelty, etc. need not be physical. Subject to the orders of, includes persons, subject to the UCMJ or not, who are by some reason of some duty are required to obey the lawful orders of the accused, even if not in the direct chain of command of the accused. "Cruel", "oppressed", and "maltreated" refer to unwarranted, harmful, abusive, rough or other unjustifiable treatment that, under all the circumstances, results in physical or mental pain or suffering and is unwarranted, unjustified and unnecessary for any lawful purpose. It is measured by an objective standard. MCM IV-25; MJB, Section 3-17-1.

b. Reckless Endangerment, Art 134

(U) The elements of the offense are that the accused engaged in wrongful conduct that was reckless or wanton and that the conduct was likely to produce death or grievous bodily harm. "[L]ikely to produce" means the natural or probable consequences of particular conduct. "[G]rievous bodily harm" includes injuries comparable to fractured or dislocated bones, serious damage to internal organs. MCM IV-119; MJB, Section 3-100A-1.

c. Assault, Art 128

(U) This article encompasses the following offenses:

(U) Simple assault – The elements are that the accused attempted or offered to do bodily harm to an individual and that such attempt or offer was done with unlawful force and violence. An act of force or violence is unlawful if done without legal justification or excuse and without the consent of the victim. The use of threatening words accompanied by a menacing act or gesture may constitute an assault. MCM IV-81; MJB, Section 3-54-1.

(U) Assault Consummated by a battery – An assault resulting in actual infliction of bodily harm is a battery. Bodily harm means any physical injury to or offensive touching however slight. MCM IV-83; MJB, Section 3-54-1A

(U) Aggravated (use of a dangerous weapon, means or force) – In addition to the elements of an assault, this offense requires that the means or force attempted or offered was used in a manner likely to produce death or grievous bodily harm. Any

---

[69] (U) Article 2 UCMJ; Rules for Courts-Martial, Rule 202, and Discussion.

[70] (U) The following are extracted from the Department of the Army Pamphlet 27-9, Military Judges' Benchbook (MJB), which summarizes the requirements of the Manual For Courts-Martial (MCM) and case law applicable to trials by courts martial.

object, regardless of its normal use, could become a means likely to inflict grievous bodily harm depending on the manner in which it is actually used. MCM IV-84; MJB, Section 3-54-8

(U) There are multiple instances in which authority and context permit touching by police officers, prison guards, training NCOs, etc. – that would not be lawful under other circumstances. A central issue would be how clearly the limits of authority were defined and whether under the circumstances the individual exceeded the scope of that authority.

d. Involuntary Manslaughter, Art 119

(U) The elements of this offense are that acts or omissions constituting culpable negligence resulted in an unlawful killing. Culpable negligence contemplates a level of heedlessness in circumstances in which, when viewed in the light of human experience, might foreseeably result in death. MCM IV-64. Failure to assiduously follow protocols providing for the health and safety of detainees during interrogations of detainees could amount to such culpable negligence. MJB, Section 3-44-2.

e. Unpremeditated Murder, Art 118

(U) The relevant elements of the offense are that the person is dead, his death resulted from the act or failure to act of the accused, that the killing was unlawful, without legal justification, and at that time the accused had the intent to inflict great bodily harm upon the person. MCM IV-118, MJB, Section 3-43-2.

f. Disobedience of Orders, Art 92

(U) This offense is committed when the accused, having a duty to do so, fails to obey lawful orders or regulations. MCM IV-23; MJB, Section 3-16. The duty to obey may extend to treaties and statutes as well as regulations. The Convention against Torture and the general case law regarding cruel and unusual punishment may be relevant here as it is for Article 93. *See generally, Wilson v. Seiter*, 501 U.S. 294 (1991).

g. Dereliction of Duty, Art 92

(U) A dereliction occurs when an individual knew or should have known of certain prescribed duties and either willfully or through neglect was derelict in the performance of those duties. MCM IV-24; MJB, Section 3-16-4. Customs of the service as well as statutes and treaties that have become the law of the land may create duties for purposes of this article.

h. Maiming, Art 124

(U) The elements of this offense are that the accused intentionally inflicted an injury on a person, and whether intended or not, that the injury seriously disfigured the person's body, destroyed or disabled an organ or member, or seriously diminished the person's physical vigor. MCM IV-77; MJB, Section 3-50-1.

2. Affirmative Defenses under the UCMJ (R.C.M. 916)

(U) In order for any use of force to be lawful, it must either be justified under the circumstances or an accepted affirmative defense is present to excuse the otherwise unlawful conduct. No case law was found that defines at what point force or violence becomes either lawful or unlawful during war. Each case is by its nature, dependent upon the factual circumstances surrounding the incident.

(U) Applying accepted rules for the law of armed conflict, the use of force is only authorized when there is a military purpose and the force used is no greater than necessary to achieve the objective. The existence of war does not in and of itself justify all forms of assault. For instance, in *United States v. Calley*, 22 U.S.C.M.A. 534, 48 C.M.R. 19 (1973), the court recognized that "while it is lawful to kill an enemy in the heat and exercise of war, to kill such an enemy after he has laid down his arms ... is murder." Further, the fact that the law of war has been violated pursuant to an order of a superior authority, whether military or civil, does not deprive the act in question of its character of a war crime, nor does it constitute a defense in the trial of an accused individual, unless he did not know and could not reasonably have been expected to know that the act ordered was unlawful. In all cases where the order is held not to constitute a defense to an allegation of war crime, the fact that the individual was acting pursuant to orders may be considered in mitigation of punishment. The thrust of these holdings is that even in war, limits to the use and extent of force apply.

a. Self-Defense

(U) For the right of self-defense to exist, the accused must have had a reasonable apprehension that death or grievous bodily harm was about to be inflicted on himself. The test is whether, under the same facts and circumstances, an ordinary prudent adult person faced with the same situation would have believed that there were grounds to fear immediate death or serious bodily harm (an objective test) and the person must have actually believed that the amount of force used was required to protect against death or serious bodily harm (a subjective test). Grievous bodily harm means serious bodily injury. It does not mean minor injuries such as a black eye or a bloody nose, but does mean fractured or dislocated bones, deep cuts, torn members of the body, serious damage to internal organs, or other serious bodily injuries. MJB, Section 5-2. (See also the discussion of "Self-Defense" under the discussion of Federal law, *supra.*)

b. Defense of Another

(U) For this defense, the accused must have had a reasonable belief that harm was about to be inflicted and that the accused actually believed that force was necessary to protect that person. The accused must actually believe that the amount of force used was necessary to protect against the degree of harm threatened, MJB, Section 5-3-1.

c. Accident

(U) This defense arises when an accused is doing a lawful act in a lawful manner, free of any negligence, and unforeseeable or unintentional death or bodily harm occurs. MJB, Section 5-4.

d. Mistake of Fact

(U) If ignorance or mistake of a fact concerns an element of an offense involving specific intent, the ignorance or mistake need only exist in the mind of the accused, i.e., if the circumstances of an event were as the accused believed, there would be no offense. For crimes not involving specific intent, the ignorance or mistake must be both honest (actual) and reasonable. The majority of the crimes discussed above do not require specific intent. For instance, in the case of violations of general orders, knowledge is presumed. Most of the "mistakes" would likely be mistakes of law in that the accused would not believe that the conduct was unlawful. While mistakes of law are generally not a defense, unawareness of a law may be a defense to show the absence of a criminal state of mind when actual knowledge is not necessary to establish the offense. MJB, Section 5-11.

e. Coercion or duress

(U) It is a defense to any offense except killing an innocent person that the accused's participation in the offense was caused by a reasonable apprehension that the accused or another innocent person would be immediately killed or would immediately suffer serious bodily injury if the accused did not commit the act. This apprehension must reasonably continue throughout the commission of the act. If the accused has any reasonable opportunity to avoid committing the act without subjecting the accused or another innocent person to the harm threatened, this defense shall not apply. R.C.M. 916(h), MOB, Section 5-5.

(U) To establish a duress defense it must be shown that an accused's participation in the offence was caused by a reasonable apprehension that the accused or another innocent person would be immediately killed or would immediately suffer serious bodily harm if the accused did not commit the act. The apprehension must reasonably continue throughout the commission of the act. If the accused has any reasonable opportunity to avoid committing the act without subjecting the accused or another innocent person to the harm threatened, this defense shall not apply. The Court of Appeals stated in *United States v. Fleming*, 23 C.M.R. 7 (1957), that the defense of duress is available to an accused only if his commission of the crime charged resulted from reasonable fear of imminent death or grievous bodily harm to himself or his family. The risk of injury must continue throughout the criminal venture.

f. Obedience to Orders (MJB, Sections 5-8-1 and 5-8-2)

(U) The viability of obedience to orders as a defense turns on the directives and policy of the service member's Chain of Command. For example, when the interrogator at the direction of the command employs the use of physical force as an interrogation method, he/she would certainly raise the defense of obedience to orders. The question then becomes one of degree. While this may be a successful defense to simple assaults or batteries, it would unlikely be as successful to more serious charges such as manslaughter, and maiming. Within the middle of the spectrum lay those offenses for which the effectiveness of this defense becomes less clear. Those offenses would include conduct unbecoming an officer, reckless endangerment, cruelty, and negligent homicide.

(U) Obedience to orders provides a viable defense only to the extent that the accused acted under orders, and did not know (nor would a person of ordinary sense have known), the orders were unlawful. Thus, the viability of this defense is keyed to the accused's (or a reasonable person's) knowledge of the lawfulness of the order. Common sense suggests that the more aggressive and physical the technique authorized (ordered) by the command, the more unlikely the reasonable belief that the order to employ such methods is lawful.

(U) In order for any use of force to be lawful, it must either (i) be justified under the circumstances or (ii) an accepted affirmative defense is present to excuse the otherwise unlawful conduct. No case law was found that defines at what point force or violence becomes either lawful or unlawful during war. Each case is by its nature, dependent upon the factual circumstances surrounding the incident.

(U) Applying accepted rules for the law of armed conflict, the use of force is only authorized when there is a military purpose and the force used is no greater than necessary to achieve the objective. The existence of war does not in and of itself justify all forms of assault. For instance, in *US v. Calley*, the court recognized that "while it is lawful to kill an enemy 'in the heat and exercise of war, to kill such an enemy after he has laid down his arms ... is murder.' Further, the fact that the law of war has been violated pursuant to an order of a superior authority, whether military or civil, does not deprive the act in question of its character of a war crime, nor does it constitute a defense in the trial of an accused individual, unless he did not know and could not reasonably have been expected to know that the act ordered was unlawful. In all cases where the order is held not to constitute a defense to an allegation of war crime, the fact that the individual was acting pursuant to orders may be considered in mitigation of punishment." The thrust of these holdings is that even in war, limits to the use and extent of force apply.

g. Necessity

(U) Another common law affirmative defense is one of necessity. This defense is recognized by a number of states and is applicable when: 1) the harm must be committed under the pressure of physical or natural force, rather than human force; 2) the harm sought to be avoided is greater than (or at least equal to) that harm sought to be prevented by the law defining the offense charged; 3) the actor reasonably believes at the moment that his act is necessary and is designed to avoid the greater harm; 4) the actor must be without fault in bringing about the situation; and 5) the harm threatened must be imminent, leaving no alternative by which to avoid the greater harm.

(U) However, military courts have treated the necessity defense with disfavor, and in fact, some have refused to accept necessity as a permissible defense (the MCM does not list necessity as an affirmative defense under RCM 916). "The problem with the necessity defense is that it involves a weighing of evil inflicted against evil avoided and is, thereby, difficult to legislate." The courts also have been reluctant to embrace the defense due to a "fear that private moral codes will be substituted for legislative determination, resulting in a necessity exception that swallows the rule of law." *United State v. Rankins*, 34 MJ 326 (CMA 1992).

(U) The effect of these cases is that the MCM recognizes that an accused may commit an illegal act in order to avoid the serious injury or death of the accused or an innocent person. However, military law limits this defense only when there is an imminent and confirming harm that requires immediate action to prevent. Once the immediacy is gone, the defense will no longer apply. Ostensibly, the use of force to acquire information from an unlawful combatant, absent immediate and compelling circumstances, will not meet the elements established by the MCM and case law, (But see the necessity defense in the discussion of Federal *law, supra.*)

3. Legal doctrines could render specific conduct, otherwise criminal, *not* Unlawful

See discussion of Commander-in-Chief Authority, *supra.*

IV. Considerations Affecting Policy

A. Historical Role of U.S. Armed Forces

1. Background

(U) The basic principles of interrogation doctrine, procedures, and techniques applicable to Army intelligence interrogations from June 1945 through May 1987 were contained in field manual (FM) 30-15, Examination of Personnel and Documents. FM 30-15 set forth Army doctrine pertaining to the basic principles of intelligence interrogation and established the procedures and techniques applicable to Army intelligence interrogations of non-U.S. personnel. The other Services report that they too apply the provisions of this Field Manual.

2. Interrogation Historical Overview.

(U) FM 30-15 stated that the principles and techniques of interrogation discussed within the manual are to be used within the constraints established by humanitarian international law and the Uniform Code of Military Justice ("UCMJ"). The fundamental principle underlying Army doctrine concerning intelligence interrogations between 1945 and the issuance of current doctrine in 1987 (FM 34-52), is that the commander may utilize all available resources and lawful means in the accomplishment of his mission and for the protection and security of his unit. However, a strong caveat to this principle noted, "treaty commitments and policy of the United States, international agreements, international law, and the UCMJ require the conduct of military to conform with the law of war." FM 30-15 also recognized that Army intelligence interrogations must conform to the "specific prohibitions, limitations, and restrictions established by the Geneva Conventions of 12 August 1949 for the handling and treatment of personnel captured or detained by military forces" (citing FM 27-10, The Law of Land Warfare).

(U) FM 30-15 also stated that "violations of the customary and treaty law applicable to the conduct of war normally constitute a concurrent violation of the Uniform Code of Military Justice and will be prosecuted under that code." The manual advised Army personnel that it was "the direct responsibility of the Commander to insure that the law of war is respected in the conduct of warfare by forces in his command." Thus, the intelligence interrogation techniques outlined in FM 30-15 were based upon conduct sanctioned under international law and domestic U.S. law and as constrained within the UCMJ.

(U) Historically, the intelligence staff officer (G2/S2) was the primary Army staff officer responsible for all intelligence functions within the command structure. This responsibility included interrogation of enemy prisoners of war (EPW), civilian internees, and other captured or detained persons. In conducting interrogations, the intelligence staff officer was responsible for insuring that these activities were executed in accordance with international and domestic U.S. law, United States Government policy, and the applicable regulations and field manuals regarding the treatment and handling of EPWs, civilian internees, and other captured or detained persons. In the maintenance of interrogation collection, the intelligence staff officer was required to provide guidance and training to interrogators assign collection, requirements, promulgate regulations, directives, and field manuals regarding intelligence interrogation, and insure that interrogators were trained in international and domestic U.S. law and the applicable Army publications.

(U) FM 30-15 stated that intelligence interrogations are an act involving the questioning and examination of a source in order to obtain the maximum amount of usable information. Interrogations are of many types, such as the interview, a debriefing, and an elicitation. However, the FM made clear that the principles of objective, initiative, accuracy, prohibitions against the use of force, and security apply to all types of interrogations. The manual indicated that the goal is to collect usable and reliable information, in a lawful manner, promptly, while meeting the intelligence requirements of the command.

(U) FM 30-15 emphasized a prohibition on the use of force during interrogations. This prohibition included the actual use of force, mental torture, threats, and exposure to inhumane treatment of any kind. Interrogation doctrine, procedures, and techniques concering the use of force are based upon prohibitions in international and domestic U.S. law. FM 30-15 stated that experience revealed that the use of force was unnecessary in gaining cooperation and was a poor interrogation technique, given that its use produced unreliable information, damaged future interrogations, and induced those being interrogated to offer information viewed as expected in order to prevent the use of force. However FM 30-15 stated that the prohibition on the use of force, mental or physical must not be confused with the use of psychological tools and deception techniques designed to induce a source into providing intelligence information.

(U) The Center for Military History has been requested to conduct a search of government databases, to include the Investigative Records Repository, for documentation concerning the historical participation of the U.S. Armed Forces in interrogations and any archival materials related to interrogation techniques. As of the writing of this analysis, no reply has been received.

3. Current Doctrine

(U) In May 1987, the basic principles of current doctrine, procedures, and techniques applicable to Army intelligence interrogations were promulgated in Field Manual (FM) 34-52, Intelligence Interrogation, FM 34-52 provides general guidance for commanders, staff officers, and other personnel in the use of interrogation elements in Army intelligence units. It also outlines procedures for handling sources of interrogations, the exploitation and processing of documents, and the reporting of intelligence gained through interrogation. Finally, FM 34-52 covers directing and supervising Interrogation operations, conflict scenarios, and their impact on interrogation operations to include peacetime interrogation operations.

(U) Army interrogation doctrine today, and since 1945, places particular emphasis on the humane handling of captured personnel. Interrogators receive specific instruction by Army judge Advocates on the requirements of international and domestic US law, to include constraints established by the Uniform Code of Military Justice (e.g., assault, cruelty and communicating a threat).

(U) FM 34-52 adopted the principles and framework for conducting intelligence interrogations as stated in FM 30-15. FM 34-52 maintained the established Army doctrine that intelligence interrogations involved the art of questioning and examining a source in order to obtain the maximum amount of usable information. FM 34-52 also reiterated Army doctrine that the principles of objective, initiative, accuracy, prohibition on use of force, and security apply to all types of interrogations. The goal of intelligence interrogations under current doctrine is the same, the collection of usable and reliable information promptly and in a lawful manner, while meeting the intelligence requirements of the command.

(U) FM 34-52 and the curriculum at U.S. Army Intelligence Center, Fort Huachuca, continue to emphasize a prohibition on the use of force. As stated in its predecessor, FM 34-52 defines the use of force to include actual force, mental torture, threats, and exposure to inhumane treatment of any kind. The underlying basis for this prohibition is the proscriptions contained in international and domestic U.S. law. Current Army intelligence interrogation doctrine continues to view the use of force as unnecessary to gain the cooperation of captured personnel. Army interrogation experts view the use of force as an inferior technique that yields information of questionable quality. The primary concerns in addition to the effect on information quality, are the adverse effect on future interrogations and the behavioral change on those being interrogated (offering particular information to avoid the use of force). However, the Army's doctrinal prohibition on the use of force does not proscribe legitimate psychological tools and deception techniques.

(U) FM 34-52 outlines procedures and approach techniques for conducting Army interrogations. While the approach techniques are varied, there are three common purposes: establish and maintain control over the source and the interrogation, establish and maintain rapport between the interrogator and the source, and manipulate the source's emotions and weaknesses to gain willing cooperation. Approved techniques include: Direct Incentive; Emotional (Love & Hate); Increased Fear Up (Harsh & Mild); Decreased Fear Down; Pride and Ego (Up & Down); Futility Technique; We Know All; Establish Your Identity, Repetition; File and Dossier, and Mutt and Jeff (Friend & Foe). These techniques are discussed at greater length in Section V. *infra.*

B. Presidential and Secretary of Defense Directives

(U) The President's Military Order that addresses the detention, treatment, and trial of certain non-citizens in the war against terrorism,[71] provides, *inter alia*, that any

[The rest of this document has not been released. – Ed.]

---

[71] (U) *Military Order – Detention, Treatment and Trial of Certain Non-Citizens in the War Against Terrorism, President of the United States, November 13, 2001.*

UNCLASSIFIED

~~SECRET/NOFORN~~

Working Group Report
on
Detainee Interrogations in the Global War on Terrorism:
Assessment of Legal, Historical, Policy, and Operational Considerations

April 4, 2003

Classified by: Secretary Rumsfeld
Reason: 1.5(C)
Declassify on: 10 years

Declassify Under the Authority of Executive Order 12958
By Executive Secretary, Office of the Secretary of Defense
William P. Marriott, CAPT, USN
June 21, 2004

DETAINEE INTERROGATIONS IN THE GLOBAL WAR ON TERRORISM:
Assessment of Legal, Historical, Policy and Operational Considerations

I. Introduction

(S/NF) (U) On January 15, 2003, the Secretary of Defense (SECDEF), directed the General Counsel of the Department of Defense (DOD GC) to establish a working group within the Department of Defense (DOD) to assess the legal, policy, and operational issues relating to the interrogations of detainees held by the United States Armed Forces in the war on terrorism. Attachment 1.

(S/NF) (U) On January 16, 2003, the DOD GC asked the General Counsel of the Department of the Air Force to convene this working group, comprising representatives of the following entities: the Office of the Undersecretary of Defense (Policy), the Defense Intelligence Agency, the General Counsels of the Air Force, Army, and Navy and Counsel to the Commandant of the Marine Corps, the Judge Advocates General of the Air Force, Army, Navy, and Marines, and the Joint Staff Legal Counsel and J5. Attachment 2. The following assessment is the result of the collaborative efforts of those organizations, after consideration of diverse views, and was informed by a Department of Justice opinion.

(S/NF) (U) In preparing this assessment, it was understood that military members, civilian employees of the United States, and contractor employees currently participate in interrogations of detainees. Further, those who participate in the decision processes comprise military personnel and civilians.

(U) Our review is limited to the legal and policy considerations applicable to interrogation techniques applied to unlawful combatants in the Global War on Terrorism interrogated outside the sovereign territory of the United States by DOD personnel in DOD interrogation facilities. Interrogations can be broadly divided into two categories: strategic and tactical. This document addresses only strategic interrogations that are those conducted: (i) at a fixed location created for that purpose; (ii) by a task force or higher level component and (iii) other than in direct and immediate support of on going military operations. All tactical interrogations, including battlefield interrogations, remain governed by existing doctrine and procedures and are not directly affected by this review.

(U) In considering interrogation techniques for possible application to unlawful combatants in the "strategic" category, it became apparent that those techniques could be divided into three types: (i) routine (those that have been ordinarily used by interrogators for routine interrogations), (ii) techniques comparable to the first type but not formally recognized, and (iii) more aggressive counter-resistance techniques than would be used in routine interrogations. The third type would only be appropriate when presented with a resistant detainee who there is good reason to believe possesses critical intelligence.

Many of the techniques of the second and third types have been requested for approval by USSOUTHCOM and USCENTCOM. The working group's conclusions regarding these three types of techniques, including recommendations for appropriate safeguards, are presented at the end of this report.

(U) This assessment comes in the context of a major threat to the security of the United States by terrorist forces who have demonstrated a ruthless disregard for even minimal standards of civilized behavior, with a focused intent to inflict maximum casualties on the United States and its people, including its civilian population. In this context, intelligence regarding their capabilities and intentions is of vital interest to the United States and its friends and allies. Effective interrogations of those unlawful combatants who are under the control of the United States have proven to be and will remain a critical source of this information necessary to national security.

(C) (U) Pursuant to the Confidential Presidential Determination, dated February 7, 2002 (Humane Treatment of al Qaeda and Taliban Detainees), the President determined that members of al Qaeda and the Taliban are unlawful combatants and therefore are not entitled to the protections of the Geneva Conventions as prisoners of war or otherwise. However, as a matter of policy, the President has directed U.S. Armed Forces to treat al Qaeda and Taliban detainees "humanely" and "to the extent appropriate and consistent with military necessity, in a manner consistent with the principles" of the Geneva Conventions. Due to the unique nature of the war on terrorism in which the enemy covertly attacks innocent civilian populations without warning, and further due to the critical nature of the information believed to be known by certain of the al Qaeda and Taliban detainees regarding future terrorist attacks, it may be appropriate for the appropriate approval authority to authorize as a military necessity the interrogation of such unlawful combatants in a manner beyond that which may be applied to a prisoner of war who is subject to the protections of the Geneva Conventions.

(U) In considering this issue, it became apparent that any recommendations and decisions must take into account the international and domestic law, past practices and pronouncements of the United States, DOD policy considerations, practical interrogation considerations, the views of other nations, and the potential impacts on the United States, its Armed Forces generally, individual interrogators, and those responsible for authorizing and directing specific interrogation techniques.

(U) We were asked specifically to recommend techniques that comply with all applicable law and are believed consistent with policy considerations not only of the United States but which may be unique to DOD. Accordingly, we undertook that analysis and conducted a technique-specific review that has produced a summary chart (Attachment 3) for use in identifying the recommended techniques.

II. *International Law*

(U) The following discussion addresses the requirements of international law, as it pertains to the Armed Forces of the United States, as interpreted by the United States. As will be apparent in other sections of this analysis, other nations and international bodies may take a more restrictive view, which may affect our policy analysis. These views are addressed in the "Considerations Affecting Policy" section below.

A. *The Geneva Conventions*

(U) The laws of war contain obligations relevant to the issue of interrogation techniques and methods. It should be noted, however, that it is the position of the U.S. Government that none of the provisions of the Geneva Convention Relative to the Treatment of Prisoners of War of August 12, 1949 (Third Geneva Convention) apply to al Qaeda detainees because, *inter alia*, al Qaeda is not a High Contracting Party to the Convention.[1] As to the Taliban, the U.S. position is that the provisions of Geneva apply to our present conflict with the Taliban, but that Taliban detainees do not qualify as prisoners of war under Article 4 of the Geneva Convention.[2] The Department of Justice has advised that the Geneva Convention Relative to the Protection of Civilian Personnel in time of War (Fourth Geneva Convention) does not apply to unlawful combatants.

B. *The 1994 Convention Against Torture*

(U) The United States' primary obligation concerning torture and related practices derives from the Convention Against Torture and Other Cruel, Inhuman, or Degrading Treatment or Punishment (commonly referred to as "the Torture Convention"). The United States ratified the Convention in 1994, but did so with a variety of Reservations and Understandings.

(U) Article 1 of the Convention defines the term "torture" for purpose of the treaty.[3] The United States conditioned its ratification of the treaty on an understanding that:

> . . . in order to constitute torture, an act must be specifically intended to inflict severe physical or mental pain or suffering and that mental pain or suffering refers

---

[1] (U) The President determined that "none of the provisions of Geneva apply to our conflict with al Qaeda in Afghanistan or elsewhere throughout the world because, among other reasons, al Qaeda is not a High Contracting Party to Geneva." Confidential Presidential Determination, subject: Humane Treatment of al Qaeda and Taliban Detainees, dated Feb. 7, 2002.

[2] (U) The President determined that "the Taliban detainees are unlawful combatants and, therefore, do not qualify as prisoners of war under Article 4 of Geneva." *Id.*

[3] (U) Article 1 provides: "For the purposes of this Convention, the term 'torture' means any act by which severe pain or suffering, whether physical or mental, is intentionally inflicted on a person for such purposes as obtaining from him or a third person information or a confession, punishing him for an act he or a third person has committed or is suspected of having committed, or intimidating or coercing him or a third person, or for any reason based on discrimination of any kind, when such pain or suffering is inflicted by or at the instigation of or with the consent or acquiescence of a public official acting in an official capacity. It does not include pain or suffering arising only from, inherent in or incidental to lawful sanctions."

to prolonged mental harm caused by or resulting from (1) the intentional infliction or threatened infliction of severe physical pain or suffering; (2) the administration or application, or threatened administration or application, of mind altering substances or other procedures calculated to disrupt profoundly the senses or the personality; (3) the threat of imminent death; or (4) the threat that another person will imminently be subjected to death, severe physical pain or suffering, or the administration or application of mind-altering substances or other procedures calculated to disrupt profoundly the senses or personality.[4]

(U) Article 2 of the Convention requires the Parties to "take effective legislative, administrative, judicial and other measures to prevent acts of torture in any territory under its jurisdiction." The U.S. Government believed existing state and federal criminal law was adequate to fulfill this obligation, and did not enact implementing legislation. Article 2 also provides that acts of torture cannot be justified on the grounds of exigent circumstances, such as a state of war or public emergency, or on orders from a superior officer or public authority.[5] The United States did not have an Understanding or Reservation relating to this provision (however the U.S. issued a Declaration stating that Article 2 is not self-executing).

(U) Article 3 of the Convention contains an obligation not to expel, return, or extradite a person to another state where there are "substantial grounds" for believing that the person would be in danger of being subjected to torture. The U. S. understanding relating to this article is that it only applies "if it is more likely than not" that the person would be tortured.

(U) Under Article 5, the Parties are obligated to establish jurisdiction over acts of torture when committed in any territory under its jurisdiction or on board a ship or aircraft registered in that state, or by its nationals wherever committed. The U.S. has criminal jurisdiction over territories under U.S. jurisdiction and onboard U.S. registered ships and aircraft by virtue of the special maritime and territorial jurisdiction of the United States (the "SMTJ") established under 18 U.S.C. §7. Acts that would constitute torture are likely to be criminal acts under the SMTJ as discussed in Section III.A.2 below. Accordingly, the U.S. has satisfied its obligation to establish jurisdiction over such acts in territories under U.S. jurisdiction or on board a U.S. registered ship or aircraft. However, the additional requirement of Article 5 concerning jurisdiction over acts of torture by U.S. nationals "wherever committed" needed legislative implementation. Chapter 113C of Title 18 of the U.S. Code provides federal criminal jurisdiction over an extraterritorial act or attempted act of torture if the offender is a U.S. national. The statute defines "torture" consistent with the U.S. Understanding on Article 1 of the Torture Convention.

(U) The United States is obligated under Article 10 of the Convention to ensure that law enforcement and military personnel involved in interrogations are educated and informed regarding the prohibition against torture. Under Article 11, systematic reviews of interrogation rules, methods, and practices are also required.

(U) In addition to torture, the Convention prohibits cruel, inhuman and degrading treatment or punishment within territories under a Party's jurisdiction (Article 16):

---

[4] (U) 18 U.S.C. §2340 tracks this language. For a further discussion of the U.S. understandings and reservations, see the Initial Report of the U.S. to the U.N. Committee Against Torture, dated October 15, 1999.

[5] (U) See discussion in the Domestic Law section on the necessity defense.

Primarily because the meaning of the term "cruel, inhuman and degrading treatment or punishment" was vague and ambiguous, the United States imposed a Reservation on this article to the effect that it is bound only to the extent that such treatment or punishment means the cruel, unusual and inhumane treatment or punishment prohibited by the Fifth, Eighth, and Fourteenth Amendments to the U.S. Constitution (see discussion *infra*, in the Domestic Law section).

(U) In sum, the obligations under the Torture Convention apply to the interrogation of unlawful combatant detainees, but the Torture Convention prohibits torture only as defined in the U.S. Understanding, and prohibits "cruel, inhuman, and degrading treatment and punishment" only to the extent of the U.S. Reservation relating to the U.S. Constitution.

(U) An additional treaty to which the United States is a party is the International Covenant on Political and Civil Rights, ratified by the United States in 1992. Article 7 of this treaty provides that "No one shall be subjected to torture or to cruel, inhuman or degrading treatment or punishment." The United States' ratification of the Covenant was subject to a Reservation that "the United States considers itself bound by Article 7 only to the extent that cruel, inhuman, or degrading treatment or punishment means the cruel and unusual treatment or punishment prohibited by the Fifth, Eighth, and/or Fourteenth Amendments to the Constitution of the United States." Under this treaty, a "Human Rights Committee" may, with the consent of the Party in question, consider allegations that such Party is not fulfilling its obligations under the Covenant. The United States has maintained consistently that the Covenant does not apply outside the United States or its special maritime and territorial jurisdiction, and that it does not apply to operations of the military during an international armed conflict.

C. Customary International Law

(U) The Department of Justice has concluded that customary international law cannot bind the Executive Branch under the Constitution because it is not federal law.[6] In particular, the Department of Justice has opined that "under clear Supreme Court precedent, any presidential decision in the current conflict concerning the detention and trial of al Qaeda or Taliban militia prisoners would constitute a "controlling" Executive act that would immediately and completely override any customary international law."[7]

III. Domestic Law

A. Federal Criminal Law

1. Torture Statute

(U) 18 U.S.C. § 2340 defines as torture any *"act committed by a person acting under the color of law specifically intended to inflict severe physical or mental pain. . . ."* The intent required is the intent to inflict severe physical or mental pain. 18 U.S.C. § 2340A requires that the offense occur "outside the United States." Jurisdiction over the

---

[6] (U) Memorandum dated January 22, 2002, *Re: Application of Treaties and Laws to al Qaeda and Taliban Detainees* at 32.

[7] (U) Memorandum dated January 22, 2002, *Re: Application of Treaties and Laws to al Qaeda and Taliban Detainees* at 35.

offense extends to any national of the United States or any alleged offender present in the United States, and could, therefore, reach military members, civilian employees of the United States, or contractor employees.[8] The "United States" is defined to include all areas under the jurisdiction of the United States, including the special maritime and territorial jurisdiction (SMTJ) of the United States. SMTJ is a statutory creation[9] that extends the criminal jurisdiction of the United States for designated crimes to defined areas.[10] The effect is to grant federal court criminal jurisdiction for the specifically identified crimes.

(U) The USA Patriot Act (2001) amended the definition of the SMTJ to add subsection 9, which provides:

"With respect to offenses committed by or against a national of the United States as that term is used in section 101 of the Immigration and Nationality Act –

(a) the premises of United States diplomatic, consular, military or other United States Government missions or entities in foreign States, including the buildings, parts of buildings, and land appurtenant or ancillary thereto or used for purposes of maintaining those missions or entities, irrespective of ownership; and

(b) residences in foreign States and the land appurtenant or ancillary thereto, irrespective of ownership, used for purposes of those missions or entities or used by United States personnel assigned to those missions or entities.

Nothing in this paragraph shall be deemed to supersede any treaty or international agreement with which this paragraph conflicts. This paragraph does not apply with respect to an offense committed by a person described in section 3261(a) of this title.

(U) By its terms, the plain language of new subsection 9 includes Guantanamo Bay Naval Station (GTMO) within the definition of the SMTJ, and accordingly makes GTMO within the United States for purposes of § 2340. As such, the Torture Statute does not apply to the conduct of U.S. personnel at GTMO. Prior to passage of the Patriot Act in 2001, GTMO was still considered within the SMTJ as manifested by (i) the prosecution of civilian dependents and employees living in GTMO in Federal District Courts based on SMTJ jurisdiction, and (ii) a Department of Justice opinion[11] to that effect.

---

[8] (U) Section 2340A provides, *"Whoever outside* the United States commits or attempts to commit torture shall be fined or imprisoned . . ." (emphasis added).

[9] (U) 18 USC § 7, "Special maritime and territorial jurisdiction of the United States" includes any lands under the exclusive or concurrent jurisdiction of the United States.

[10] (U) Several paragraphs of 18 USC § 7 are relevant to the issue at hand. Paragraph 7(3) provides: [SMTJ includes:]" Any lands reserved or acquired for the use of the United States, and under the exclusive or concurrent jurisdiction thereof, or any place. . . ." Paragraph 7(7) provides: [SMTJ includes:] "Any place outside the jurisdiction of any nation to an offense by or against a national of the United States." Similarly, paragraphs 7(1) and 7(5) extend SMTJ jurisdiction to, "the high seas, any other waters within the admiralty and maritime jurisdiction of the United States and out of the jurisdiction of any particular state, and any vessel belonging in whole or in part to the United States. . ." and to "any aircraft belonging in whole or in part to the United States . . . while such aircraft is in flight over the high seas, or over any other waters within the admiralty and maritime jurisdiction of the United States and out of the jurisdiction of any particular State."

[11] (U) 6 Op. OLC 236 (1982). The issue was the status of GTMO for purposes of a statute banning slot-machines on "any land where the United States government exercises exclusive or concurrent jurisdiction."

(U) Any person who commits an enumerated offense in a location that is considered within the special maritime and territorial jurisdiction is subject to the jurisdiction of the United States.

(U) For the purposes of this discussion, it is assumed that an interrogation done for official purposes is under "color of law" and that detainees are in DOD's custody or control.

(U) Although Section 2340 does not apply to interrogations at GTMO, it could apply to U.S. operations outside U.S. jurisdiction, depending on the facts and circumstances of each case involved. The following analysis is relevant to such activities.

(U) To convict a defendant of torture, the prosecution must establish that: (1) the torture occurred outside the United States; (2) the defendant acted under color of law; (3) the victim was within the defendant's custody or physical control; (4) the defendant specifically intended to cause severe physical or mental pain or suffering; and (5) that the act inflicted severe physical or mental pain or suffering. *See also* S. Exec. Rep. No. 101-30, at 6 (1990). ("For an act to be 'torture,' it must... cause severe pain and suffering, and be intended to cause severe pain and suffering.")

a. "Specifically Intended"

(U) To violate Section 2340A, the statute requires that severe pain and suffering must be inflicted with specific intent. *See* 18 U.S.C. § 2340(1). In order for a defendant to have acted with specific intent, he must have expressly intended to achieve the forbidden act. *See United States v. Carter*, 530 U.S. 255, 269 (2000); Black's Law Dictionary at 814 (7th ed. 1999) (defining specific intent as "[t]he intent to accomplish the precise criminal act that one is later charged with"). For example, in *Ratzlaf v. United States*, 510 U.S. 135, 141 (1994), the statute at issue was construed to require that the defendant act with the "specific intent to commit the crime." (Internal quotation marks and citation omitted). As a result, the defendant had to act with the express "purpose to disobey the law" in order for the *mens rea* element to be satisfied. *Ibid.* (Internal quotation marks and citation omitted.)

(U) Here, because Section 2340 requires that a defendant act with the specific intent to inflict severe pain, the infliction of such pain must be the defendant's precise objective. If the statute had required only general intent, it would be sufficient to establish guilt by showing that the defendant "possessed knowledge with respect to the *actus reus* of the crime." *Carter*, 530 U.S. at 268. If the defendant acted knowing that severe pain or suffering was reasonably likely to result from his actions, but no more, he would have acted only with general intent. *See id* at 269; Black's Law Dictionary: 813 (7th ed. 1999) (explaining that general intent "usu[ally] takes the form of recklessness (involving actual awareness of a risk and the culpable taking of that risk) or negligence (involving blameworthy inadvertence)"). The Supreme Court has used the following example to illustrate the difference between these two mental states:

> [A] person entered a bank and took money from a teller at gunpoint, but deliberately failed to make a quick getaway from the bank in the hope of being arrested so that he would be returned to prison and treated for alcoholism. Though this defendant knowingly engaged in the acts of using force and taking money (satisfying "general intent"), he did not intend permanently to deprive the bank of its possession of the money (failing to satisfy "specific intent").

Carter, 530 U.S. at 268 (citing 1 W. Lafave & A. Scott, Substantive Criminal Law § 3.5, at 315 (1986).

(U) As a theoretical matter, therefore, knowledge alone that a particular result is certain to occur does not constitute specific intent. As the Supreme Court explained in the context of murder, "the ... common law of homicide distinguishes ... between a person who knows that another person will be killed as a result of his conduct and a person who acts with the specific purpose of taking another's life[.]" *United States v. Bailey*, 444 U.S. 394, 405 (1980). "Put differently, the law distinguishes actions taken 'because of' a given end from actions taken 'in spite' of their unintended but foreseen consequences." *Vacco v. Quill*, 521 U.S. 793, 802–03 (1997). Thus, even if the defendant knows that severe pain will result from his actions, if causing such harm is not his objective, he lacks the requisite specific intent even though the defendant did not act in good faith. Instead, a defendant is guilty of torture only if he acts with the express purpose of inflicting severe pain or suffering on a person within his custody or physical control. While as a theoretical matter such knowledge does not constitute specific intent, juries are permitted to infer from the factual circumstances that such intent is present. *See, e.g., United States v. Godwin*, 272 F.3d 659, 666 (4th Cir. 2001); *United States v. Karro*, 257 F.3d 112, 118 (2d Cir. 2001); *United States v. Wood*, 207 F.3d 1222, 1232 (10th Cir. 2000); *Henderson v. United States*, 202 F.2d 400, 403 (6th Cir.1953). Therefore, when a defendant knows that his actions will produce the prohibited result, a jury will in all likelihood conclude that the defendant acted with specific intent.

(U) Further, a showing that an individual acted with a good faith belief that his conduct would not produce the result that the law prohibits negates specific intent. *See, e.g., South Atl. Lmtd. Ptrshp. of Tenn v. Reise*, 218 F.3d 518, 531 (4th Cir. 2002). Where a defendant acts in good faith, he acts with an honest belief that he has not engaged in the proscribed conduct. *See Cheek v. United States*, 498 U.S. 192, 202 (1991); *United States v. Mancuso*, 42 F.3d 836, 837 (4th Cir. 1994). For example, in the context of mail fraud, if an individual honestly believes that the material transmitted is truthful, he has not acted with the required intent to deceive or mislead. *See, e.g., United States v. Sayakhom*, 186 F.3d 928, 939–40 (9th Cir. 1999). A good faith belief need not be a reasonable one. *See Cheek*, 498 U.S. at 202.

(U) Although a defendant theoretically could hold an unreasonable belief that his acts would not constitute the actions prohibited by the statute, even though they would as a certainty produce the prohibited effects, as a matter of practice in the federal criminal justice system, it is highly unlikely that a jury would acquit in such a situation. Where a defendant holds an unreasonable belief, he will confront the problem of proving to the jury that he actually held that belief. As the Supreme Court noted in *Cheek*, "the more unreasonable the asserted beliefs or misunderstandings are, the more likely the jury ... will find that the Government has carried its burden of proving knowledge." *Id* at 203–04. As explained above, a jury will be permitted to infer that the defendant held the requisite specific intent. As a matter of proof, therefore, a good faith defense will prove more compelling when a reasonable basis exists for the defendant's belief.

b. "Severe Pain or Suffering"

(U) The key statutory phrase in the definition of torture is the statement that acts amount to torture if they cause "severe physical or mental pain or suffering." In examining the meaning of a statute, its text must be the starting point. *See INS v.*

Phinpathya, 464 U.S. 183, 189 (1984) ("This Court has noted on numerous occasions that in all cases involving statutory construction, our starting point must be the language employed by Congress ... and we assume that the legislative purpose is expressed by the ordinary meaning of the words used.") (internal quotations and citations omitted). Section 2340 makes plain that the infliction of pain or suffering per se, whether it is physical or mental, is insufficient to amount to torture. Instead, the text provides that pain or suffering must be "severe." The statute does not, however, define the term "severe." "In the absence of such a definition, we construe a statutory term in accordance with its ordinary or natural meaning." *FDIC v. Meyer*, 510 U.S. 471, 476 (1994). The dictionary defines "severe" as "[u]nsparing in exaction, punishment, or censure" or "[i]nflicting discomfort or pain hard to endure; sharp; afflictive; distressing; violent; extreme; as *severe* pain, anguish, torture." Webster's New International Dictionary 2295 (2d ed. 1935); *see* American Heritage Dictionary of the English Language 1653 (3d ed. 1992) ("extremely violent or grievous: *severe* pain") (emphasis in original); IX The Oxford English Dictionary" 572 (1978) ("Of pain, suffering, loss, or the like: Grievous, extreme" and "of circumstances ... hard to sustain or endure"). Thus, the adjective "severe" conveys that the pain or suffering must be of such a high level of intensity that the pain is difficult for the subject to endure.

c. "Severe mental pain or suffering"

(U) Section 2340 gives further guidance as to the meaning of "severe mental pain or suffering," as distinguished from severe physical pain and suffering. The statute defines "severe mental pain or suffering" as:

> the prolonged mental harm caused by or resulting from –

> (a) the intentional infliction or threatened infliction of severe physical pain or suffering;

> (b) the administration or application, or threatened administration or application, of mind-altering substances or other procedures calculated to disrupt profoundly the senses or the personality;

> (c) the threat of imminent death; or

> (d) the threat that another person will imminently be subjected to death, severe physical pain or suffering, or the administration or application of mind-altering substances or other procedures calculated to disrupt profoundly the senses or personality.

18 U.S.C. § 2340(2). In order to prove "severe mental pain or suffering," the statute requires proof of "prolonged mental harm" that was caused by or resulted from one of four enumerated acts. We consider each of these elements.

i. *"Prolonged Mental Harm"*

(U) As an initial matter, Section 2340(2) requires that the severe mental pain must be evidenced by "prolonged mental harm." To prolong is to "lengthen in time" or to "extend the duration of, to draw out." Webster's Third New International Dictionary 1815 (1988); Webster's New International Dictionary 1980 (2d ed. 1935). Accordingly, "prolong" adds a temporal dimension to the harm to the individual, namely, that the harm must be one that is endured over some period of time. Put another way, the

acts giving rise to the harm must cause some lasting, though not necessarily permanent, damage. For example, the mental strain experienced by an individual during a
lengthy and intense interrogation, such as one that state or local police might conduct
upon a criminal suspect, would not violate Section 2340(2). On the other hand, the
development of a mental disorder such as post-traumatic stress disorder, which can
last months or even years, or even chronic depression, which also can last for a considerable period of time if untreated, might satisfy the prolonged harm requirement.
See American Psychiatric Association, *Diagnostic and Statistical Manual of Mental Disorders* 426, 439–45 (4th ed. 1994) ("DSM-IV"). *See also* Craig Haney & Mona Lynch,
*Regulating Prisons of the Future: A Psychological Analysis of Supermax and Solitary
Confinement*, 23 N.Y.U. Rev. L. & Soc. Change 477, 509 (1997) (noting that post-
traumatic stress disorder is frequently found in torture victims); *cf* Sana Loue, *Immigration Law and Health* § 10:46 (2001) (recommending evaluating for post-traumatic
stress disorder immigrant-client who has experienced torture).[12] By contrast to
"severe pain" the phrase "prolonged mental harm" appears nowhere else in the U.S.
Code nor does it appear in relevant medical literature or international human rights
reports.

(U) Not only must the mental harm be prolonged to amount to severe mental pain
and suffering, but also it must be caused by or result from one of the acts listed in the
statute. In the absence of a catchall provision, the most natural reading of the predicate
acts listed in Section 2340(2)(A)(D) is that Congress intended the list to be exhaustive.
In other words, other acts not included within Section 2340(2)'s enumeration are not
within the statutory prohibition. *See Leatherman v. Tarrant County Narcotics Intelligence & Coordination Unit*, 507 U.S. 163, 168 (1993) ("*Expressio unius est exclusio
alterius*"); Norman Singer, 2A Sutherland on Statutory Construction § 47.23 (6th ed.
2000) ("[W]here a form of conduct the manner of its performance and operation, and
the persons and things to which it refers are designated, there is an inference that
all omissions should be understood as exclusions.") (footnotes omitted). We conclude
that torture within the meaning of the statute requires the specific intent to cause
prolonged mental harm by one of the acts listed in Section 2340(2).

(U) A defendant must specifically intend to cause prolonged mental harm for the
defendant to have committed torture. It could be argued that a defendant needs to have
specific intent only to commit the predicate acts that give rise to prolonged mental
harm. Under that view, so long as the defendant specifically intended to, for example,
threaten a victim with imminent death, he would have had sufficient *mens rea* for a
conviction. According to this view, it would be further necessary for a conviction to

---

[12] The DSM-IV explains that post-traumatic disorder ("PTSD") is brought on by exposure to traumatic events, such as serious physical injury or witnessing the deaths of others and during those
events the individual felt "intense fear" or "horror." *Id* at 424. Those suffering from this disorder re-
experience the trauma through, *inter alia*, "recurrent and intrusive distressing recollections of the
event", "recurrent distressing dreams of the event", or "intense psychological distress at exposure to
internal or external cues that symbolize or resemble an aspect of the traumatic event." *Id.* at 428. Additionally, a person with PTSD "[p]ersistent[ly]" avoids stimuli associated with the trauma, including
avoiding conversations about the trauma, places that stimulate recollections about the trauma, and
they experience a numbing of general responsiveness, such as a "restricted range of affect (e,g., unable
to have loving feelings)", and "the feeling of detachment or estrangement from others." *Ibid.* Finally,
an individual with PTSD has "[p]ersistent symptoms of increased arousal," as evidenced by "irritability or outbursts of anger," "hypervigilance," "exaggerated startle response," and difficulty sleeping or
concentrating. *Ibid.*

show only that the victim factually suffered prolonged mental harm, rather than that the defendant intended to cause it. We believe that this approach is contrary to the text of the statute. The statute requires that the defendant specifically intend to inflict severe mental pain or suffering. Because the statute requires this mental state with respect to the infliction of severe mental pain and because it expressly defines severe mental pain in terms of prolonged mental harm, that mental state must be present with respect to prolonged mental harm. To read the statute otherwise would read the phrase "prolonged mental harm caused by or resulting from" out of the definition of "severe mental pain or suffering."

(U) A defendant could negate a showing of specific intent to cause severe mental pain or suffering by showing that he had acted in good faith that his conduct would not amount to the acts prohibited by the statute. Thus, if a defendant has a good faith belief that his actions will not result in prolonged mental harm, he lacks the mental state necessary for his actions to constitute torture. A defendant could show that he acted in good faith by taking such steps as surveying professional literature, consulting with experts, or reviewing evidence gained from past experience. *See, e.g., Ratzlaf*, 510 U.S. at 142 n.10 (noting that where the statute required that the defendant act with the specific intent to violate the law, the specific intent element "might be negated by, e.g., proof that defendant relied in good faith on advice of counsel.") (citations omitted). All of these steps would show that he has drawn on the relevant body of knowledge concerning the result proscribed by the statute, namely prolonged mental harm. Because the presence of good faith would negate the specific intent element of torture, good faith may be a complete defense to such a charge. *See, e.g., United States* v. *Wall*, 130 F.3d 739, 746 (6th Cir. 1997); *United States* v. *Casperson*, 773 F.2d 216, 222–23 (8th Cir. 1985).

ii. Harm Caused By Or Resulting From Predicate Acts

(U) Section 2340(2) sets forth four basic categories of predicate acts. The first category is the "intentional infliction or threatened infliction of severe physical pain or suffering." This might at first appear superfluous because the statute already provides that the infliction of severe physical pain or suffering can amount to torture. This provision, however, actually captures the infliction of physical pain or suffering when the defendant inflicts physical pain or suffering with general intent rather than the specific intent that is required where severe physical pain or suffering alone is the basis for the charge. Hence, this subsection reaches the infliction of severe physical pain or suffering when it is only the means of causing prolonged mental harm. Or put another way, a defendant has committed torture when he intentionally inflicts severe physical pain or suffering with the specific intent of causing prolonged mental harm. As for the acts themselves, acts that cause "severe physical pain or suffering" can satisfy this provision.

(U) Additionally, the threat of inflicting such pain is a predicate act under the statute. A threat may be implicit or explicit. *See, e.g., United States* v. *Sachdev*, 279 F.3d 25, 29 (1st Cir. 2002). In criminal law, courts generally determine whether an individual's words or actions constitute a threat by examining whether a reasonable person in the same circumstances would conclude that a threat had been made. *See, e.g., Watts* v. *United States*, 394 U.S. 70S, 708 (1969) (holding that whether a statement constituted a threat against the President's life had to be determined in light of all the surrounding circumstances); *Sachdev*, 279 F.3d at 29 ("a reasonable person in defendant's position would perceive there to be a threat, explicit or implicit, of physical injury"); *United States v. Khorrami*, 895 F.2d 1186, 1190 (7th Cir. 1990) (to establish that a threat was made, the statement must be made "in a context or under such circumstances wherein a reasonable person would foresee that the statement would be interpreted by those to whom the maker communicates a statement as a serious expression of an intention to inflict bodily harm upon [another individual]") (citation and internal quotation marks omitted); *United States v. Peterson*, 483 F.2d 1222, 1230 (D.C. Cir. 1973) (perception of threat of imminent harm necessary to establish self-defense had to be "objectively reasonable in light of the surrounding circumstances"). Based on this common approach, we believe that the existence of a threat of severe pain or suffering should be assessed from the standpoint of a reasonable person in the same circumstances.

(U) Second, Section 2340(2)(B) provides that prolonged mental harm, constituting torture, can be caused by "the administration or application or threatened administration or application of mind-altering substances or other procedures calculated to disrupt profoundly the senses or the personality." The statute provides no further definition of what constitutes a mind-altering substance. The phrase "mind-altering substances" is found nowhere else in the U.S. Code, nor is it found in dictionaries. It is however, a commonly use synonym for drugs. *See, e.g., United States v. Kingsley*, 241 F.3d 828, 834 (6th Cir.) (referring to controlled substances as "mind-altering substance[s]") *cert. denied*, 122 S. Ct. 137 (2001); *Hogue v. Johnson*, 131 F.3rd 466, 501 (5th Cir. 1997) (referring to drugs and alcohol as "mind-altering substance[s]"), *cert denied*, 523 U.S. 1014 (1998). In addition, the phrase appears in a number of state statutes, and the context in which it appears confirms this understanding of the phrase. *See, e.g.,* Cal. Penal Code § 3500 (c) (West Supp. 2000) ("Psychotropic drugs also include mind-altering... drugs ... "); Minn. Stat. Ann. § 260B.201(b) (West Supp. 2002) ("'chemical dependency treatment'" define as programs designed to "reduc[e] the risk of the use of alcohol, drugs, or other mind-altering substances").

(U) This subparagraph, section 2340(2)(B), however, does not preclude any and all use of drugs. Instead, it prohibits the use of drugs that "disrupt profoundly the senses or the personality." To be sure, one could argue that this phrase applies only to "other procedures," not the application of mind-altering substances. We reject this interpretation because the terms of Section 2340(2) expressly indicate that the qualifying phrase applies to both "other procedures" *and* the "application of mind-altering substances." The word "other" modifies "procedures calculated to disrupt profoundly the senses." As an adjective, "other" indicates that the term or phase it modifies is the remainder of several things. *See* Webster's Third New International Dictionary 1598 (1986) (defining "other" as "being the one (as of two or more) remaining or not included"). Or put another way, "other" signals that the words to which it attaches are of the same kind, type, or class as the more specific item previously listed. Moreover, where a statute couple words or phrases together, it "denotes an intention that they should be understood in the same general sense." Norman Singer, 2A Sutherland on Statutory Construction § 47:16 (6th ed. 2000); *see also Beecham v. United States*, 511 U.S. 368, 371 (1994) ("That several items in a list share an attribute counsels in favor of interpreting the other items as possessing that attribute as well."). Thus, the pairing of mind-altering substances with procedures calculated to disrupt profoundly the sense or personality and the use of "other" to modify "procedures" shows that the use of such substances must also cause a profound disruption of the senses or personality.

(U) For drugs or procedures to rise to the level of "disrupt[ing] profoundly the sense or personality," they must produce an extreme effect. And by requiring that they be "calculated" to produce such an effect, the statute requires that the defendant has consciously designed the acts to produce such an effect. 28 U.S.C. § 2340(2)(B). The word "disrupt" is defined as "to break asunder; to part forcibly; rend," imbuing the verb with a connotation of violence. Webster's New International Dictionary 753 (2d ed. 1935); *see* Webster's Third New International Dictionary 656 (1986) (defining disrupt as "to break apart: Rupture" or "destroy the unity or wholeness of"); IV the Oxford English Dictionary 832 (1989) (defining disrupt as "[t]o break or burst asunder; to break in pieces; to separate forcibly"). Moreover, disruption of the senses or personality alone is insufficient to fall within the scope of this subsection; instead, that disruption must be profound. The word "profound" has a number of meanings, all of which convey a significant depth. Webster's New International Dictionary 1977 (2d ed. 1935 defines profound as: "Of very great depth; extending far below the surface or top; unfathomable [;] ... [c]oming from, reaching to, or situated at a depth or more than ordinary depth; not superficial; deep-seated; chiefly with reference to the body; as a *profound* sigh, wounded, or pain[;] ... [c]haracterized by intensity, as of feeling or quality; deeply felt or realized; as, *profound* respect, fear, or melancholy; hence, encompassing; thoroughgoing; complete; as, *profound* sleep, silence, or ignorance." *See* Webster's Third New International Dictionary 1812 (1986) ("having very great depth: extending far below the surface ... not superficial"). Random House Webster's Unabridged Dictionary 1545 (2d ed. 1999) also defines profound as "originating in or penetrating to the depths of one's being" or "pervasive or intense; thorough; complete" or "extending, situated, or originating far down, or far beneath the surface." By requiring that the procedures and the drugs create a *profound* disruption, the statute requires more than the acts "forcibility separate" or "rend" the senses or personality. Those acts must penetrate to the core of an individual's ability to perceive the world around him, substantially interfering with his cognitive abilities, or fundamentally alter his personality.

(U) The phrase "disrupt profoundly the senses or personality" is not used in mental health literature nor is it derived from elsewhere in U.S. law. Nonetheless, we think the following examples would constitute a profound disruption of the senses or personality. Such an effect might be seen in a drug-induced dementia. In such a state, the individual suffers from significant memory impairment, such as the inability to retain any new information or recall information about things previously of interest to the individual. *See* DSM-IV at 134.[13] This impairment is accompanied by one or more of the following: deterioration of language function, e.g., repeating sounds or words over and over again; impaired ability to execute simple motor activities, e.g., inability to dress or wave goodbye; "[in]ability to recognize [and identify] objects such as chairs or pencils" despite normal visual functioning; or "[d]isturbances

---

[13] (U) Published by the American Psychiatric Association, and written as a collaboration of over a thousand psychiatrists, the DSM-IV is commonly used in U.S. courts as a source of information regarding mental health issues and is likely to be used in trial should charges be brought that allege this predicate act. *See, e.g., Atkins v. Virginia*, 122 S. Ct. 2242, 2245 n. 3 (2002); *Kansas v. Crane*, 122 S. Ct. 867, 871 (2002); *Kansas v. Hendricks*, 521 U.S. 346, 359–60 (1997); *McClean v. Merrifield*, No. 00-CV-0120E(SC), 2002 WL 1477607 at *2 n. 7 (W.D.N.Y. June 28, 2002); *Peeples v. Coastal Office Prods.*, 203 F. Supp 2d 432, 439 (D. Md 2002); *Lassiegne v. Taco Bell Corp.*, 202 F. Supp 2d 512, 519 (E.D. La. 2002).

in executive level functioning", i.e., serious impairment of abstract thinking. *Id.* At 134–35. Similarly, we think that the onset of "brief psychotic disorder" would satisfy this standard. *See id.* at 302–03. In this disorder, the individual suffers psychotic symptoms, including among other things, delusions, hallucinations, or even a catatonic state. This can last for one day or even one month. *See id.* We likewise think that the onset of obsessive-compulsive disorder behaviors would rise to this level. Obsessions are intrusive thoughts unrelated to reality. They are not simple worries, but are repeated doubts or even "aggressive or horrific impulses." *See id.* at 418. The DSM-IV further explains that compulsions include "repetitive behaviors (e.g., hand washing, ordering, checking)" and that "[b]y definition, [they] are either clearly excessive or are not connected in a realistic way with what they are designed to neutralize or prevent." *See id.* Such compulsions or obsessions must be "time-consuming." *See id* at 419. Moreover, we think that pushing someone to the brink of suicide (which could be evidenced by acts of self-mutilation), would be a sufficient disruption of the personality to constitute a "profound disruption." These examples, of course, are in no way intended to be an exhaustive list. Instead, they are merely intended to illustrate the sort of mental health effects that we believe would accompany an action severe enough to amount to one that "disrupt[s] profoundly the sense or the personality."

(U) The third predicate act listed in Section 2340(2) is threatening an individual with "imminent death." 18 U.S.C. § 2340(2)(C). The plain text makes clear that a threat of death alone is insufficient; the threat must indicate that death is "imminent." The "threat of imminent death" is found in the common law as an element of the defense of duress. *See Bailey*, 444 U.S. at 409. "[W]here Congress borrows terms of art in which are accumulated the legal tradition and meaning of centuries of practice, it presumably knows and adopts the cluster of ideas that were attached to each borrowed word in the body of learning from which it was taken and the meaning its use will convey to the judicial mind unless otherwise instructed. In such case, absence of contrary direction may be taken as satisfaction with widely accepted definitions, not as a departure from them." *Morissette v. United States*, 342 U.S. 246, 263 (1952). Common law cases and legislation generally define "imminence" as requiring that the threat be almost immediately forthcoming. 1 Wayne R. LaFave & Austin W. Scott, Jr., Substantive Criminal Law § 5.7, at 655 (1986). By contrast, threats referring vaguely to things that might happen in the future do not satisfy this immediacy requirement. *See United States v. Fiore*, 178 F. 3rd 917, 923 (7th Cir. 1999). Such a threat fails to satisfy this requirement not because it is too remote in time but because there is a lack of certainty that it will occur. Indeed, timing is an indicator of certainty that the harm will befall the defendant. Thus, a vague threat that someday the prisoner *might* be killed would not suffice. Instead, subjecting a prisoner to mock executions or playing Russian roulette with him would have sufficient immediacy to constitute a threat of imminent death. Additionally, as discussed earlier, we believe that the existence of a threat must be assessed from the perspective of a reasonable person in the same circumstances.

(U) Fourth, if the official threatens to do anything previously described to a third party, or commits such an act against a third party, that threat or action can serve as the necessary predicate for prolonged mental harm. *See* 18 U.S.C. § 2340(2)(D). The statute does not require any relationship between the prisoner and the third party.

2. Other Federal Crimes that Could Relate to Interrogation Techniques

(U) The following are federal crimes in the special maritime and territorial jurisdiction of the United States: murder (18 U.S.C. § 1111), manslaughter (18 U.S.C. § 1112), assault (18 U.S.C. § 113), maiming (18 U.S.C. § 114), kidnapping (18 U.S.C. § 1201). These, as well as war crimes (18 U.S.C. § 2441)[14] and conspiracy (18 U.S.C. § 371), are discussed below.

a. Assaults within maritime and territorial jurisdiction, 18 U.S.C. § 113

(U) 18 U.S.C. § 113 proscribes assault within the special maritime and territorial jurisdiction. Although section 113 does not define assault, courts have construed the term "assault" in accordance with that term's common law meaning. *See, e.g., United States v. Estrada-Fernandez*, 150 F.3d 491, 494 n.1 (5th Cir. 1998); *United States v. Juvenile-Male*, 930 F.2d 727, 728 (9th Cir. 1991). In common law an assault is an attempted battery or an act that puts another person in reasonable apprehension of bodily harm. *See e.g., United States v. Bayes*, 210 F.3d 64, 68 (1st Cir. 2000). Section 113 reaches more than simple assault, sweeping within its ambit acts that would in common law constitute battery.

(U) 18 U.S.C. § 113 proscribes several specific forms of assault. Certain variations require specific intent, to wit: simple assault (fine and/or imprisonment for not more than six months); assault with intent to commit murder (imprisonment for not more than twenty years); assault with intent to commit any felony (except murder and certain sexual abuse offenses) (fine and/or imprisonment for not more than ten years); assault with a dangerous weapon, with intent to do bodily harm, and without just cause or excuse (fine and/imprisonment for not more than ten years, or both). Other defined crimes require only general intent, to wit: assault by striking, beating, or wounding (fine and/or imprisonment for not more than six months); assault where the victim is an individual who has not attained the age of 16 years (fine and/or imprisonment for not more than 1 year); assault resulting in serious bodily injury (fine and/or imprisonment for not more than ten years); assault resulting in substantial bodily injury to an individual who has not attained the age of 16 years (fine and/or imprisonment for not more than 5 years). "Substantial bodily injury" means bodily injury which involves (a) a temporary but substantial disfigurement; or (b) a temporary but substantial loss or impairment of the function of any bodily member, organ, or mental faculty. "Serious bodily injury" means bodily injury which involves (a) a substantial risk of death; (b) extreme physical pain; (c) protracted and obvious disfigurement; or (d) protracted loss or impairment of the function of a bodily member, organ, or mental faculty. "Bodily injury" means (a) a cut, abrasion, bruise, burn, or disfigurement; (b) physical pain; (c) illness; (d) impairment of the function of a bodily member, organ, or mental faculty; or (e) any other injury to the body, no matter how temporary.

---

[14] (U) 18 U.S.C. § 2441 criminalizes the commission of war crimes by U.S. nationals and members of the U.S. Armed Forces. Subsection (c) defines war crimes as (1) grave breaches of any of the Geneva Conventions; (2) conduct prohibited by the Hague Convention IV, Respecting the Law and Customs of War on Land, signed 18 October 1907; or (3) conduct that constitutes a violation of common Article 3 of the Geneva Conventions. The Department of Justice has opined that this statute does not apply to conduct toward al Qaeda or Taliban operatives because the President has determined that they are not entitled to the protections of Geneva and the Hague Regulations.

b. Maiming, 18 U.S.C. § 114

(U) Whoever with the intent to torture (as defined in section 2340), maims, or disfigures, cuts, bites, or slits the nose, ear, or lip, or cuts out or disables the tongue, or puts out or destroys an eye, or cuts off or disables a limb or any member of another person; or whoever, and with like intent, throws or pours upon another person, any scalding water, corrosive acid, or caustic substance shall be fined and/or imprisoned not more than twenty years. This is a specific intent crime.

c. Murder, 18 U.S.C. § 1111

(U) Murder is the unlawful killing of a human being with malice aforethought. Every murder perpetrated by poison, lying in wait, or any other kind of wilful, deliberate, malicious, and premeditated killing; or committed in the perpetration of, or attempt to perpetrate, any arson, escape, murder, kidnapping, treason, espionage, sabotage, aggravated sexual abuse or sexual abuse, burglary, or robbery; or perpetrated from a premeditated design unlawfully and maliciously to effect the death of any human being other than him who is killed; is murder in the first degree. Any other murder is murder in the second degree. If within the SMTJ, whoever is guilty of murder in the first degree shall be punished by death or by imprisonment for life; whoever is guilty of murder in the second degree, shall be imprisoned for any term of years or for life. Murder is a specific intent crime.

d. Manslaughter, 18 U.S.C. § 1112

(U) Manslaughter is the unlawful killing of a human being without malice. It is of two kinds: (a) voluntary, upon a sudden quarrel or heat of passion and (b) involuntary, in the commission of an unlawful act not amounting to a felony, or in the commission in an unlawful manner, or without due caution and circumspection, of a lawful act which might produce death.

(U) If within the SMTJ whoever is guilty of voluntary manslaughter, shall be fined and/or imprisoned not more than ten years; whoever is guilty of involuntary manslaughter, shall be fined and/or imprisoned not more than six years. Manslaughter is a general intent crime. A death resulting from the exceptional interrogation techniques may subject the interrogator to a charge of manslaughter, most likely of the involuntary sort.

e. Interstate Stalking, 18 U.S.C. § 2261A

(U) 18 U.S.C. § 2261 A provides that "[w]hoever ... travels ... within the special maritime and territorial jurisdiction of the United States ... with the intent to kill, injure, harass, or intimidate another person, and in the course of or as a result of, such travel places that person in reasonable fear of the death of, or serious bodily injury of that person." Thus there are three elements to a violation of 2261A: (1) defendant traveled in interstate commerce; (2) he did so with the intent to injure, harass, intimidate another person; (3) the person he intended to harass or injure was reasonably placed in fear of death or serious bodily injury as a result of that travel. *See United States v. Al-Zubaidy*, 283 F.3d 804, 808 (6th Cir. 2002).

(U) The travel itself must have been undertaken with the specific intent to harass or intimidate another. Or put another way, at the time of the travel itself, the defendant must have engaged in that travel for the precise purpose of harassing another person.

See Al-Zubaidy, 283 F.3d at 809 (the defendant "must have intended to harass or injure [the victim] at the time he crossed the state line").

(U) The third element is not fulfilled by the mere act of travel itself. *See United States v. Crawford*, No. 00-CR-59-B-S, 2001 WL 185140 (D. Me. Jan. 26, 2001) ("A plain reading of the statute makes clear that the statute requires the actor to place the victim in reasonable fear, rather than, as Defendant would have it, that his travel place the victim in reasonable fear.").

f. Conspiracy, 18 U.S.C. § 2 and 18 U.S.C. § 371[15]

(U) Conspiracy to commit crime is a separate offense from crime that is the object of the conspiracy.[16] Therefore, where someone is charged with conspiracy, a conviction cannot be sustained unless the Government establishes beyond a reasonable doubt that the defendant had the specific intent to violate the substantive statute.[17]

(U) As the Supreme Court most recently stated, "the essence of a conspiracy is 'an agreement to commit an unlawful act.'" *United States v. Jimenez Recio*, –S.Ct.-, 2003 WL 139612 at *– (Jan. 12, 2003) (quoting *Iannelli v. United States*, 420 U.S. 770, 777 (1975). Moreover, "[t]hat agreement is a 'distinct evil,' which 'may exist and be punished whether or not the substantive crime ensues.", Id at * (quoting *Salinas v. United States*, 522 U.S. 52. 65 (1997).

3. Legal doctrines under the Federal Criminal Law that could render specific conduct, otherwise criminal, *not* unlawful

(U) Generally, the following discussion identifies legal doctrines and defenses applicable to the interrogation of unlawful combatants, and the decision process related to them. In practice, their efficacy as to any person or circumstance will be fact-dependent.

a. Commander-in-Chief Authority

(U) As the Supreme Court has recognized, and as we will explain further below, the President enjoys complete discretion in the exercise of his Commander-in-Chief authority including in conducting operations against hostile forces. Because both "[t]he executive power and the command of the military and naval forces is vested in the President," the Supreme Court has unanimously stated that it is *the President alone* who is constitutionally invested with the *entire charge of hostile operations.*" *Hamilton v. Dillin*, 88 U.S. (21 Wall.) 73, 87 (1874) (emphasis added).

---

[15] (U) 18 U.S.C. § 2. Principals
    (a) Whoever commits an offense against the United States or aids, abets, counsels, commands, induces or procures its commission, is punishable as a principal.
    (b) Whoever wilfully causes an act to be done which if directly performed by him or another would be an offense against the United States, is punishable as a principal.
    18 U.S.C. § 371. Conspiracy to commit offense or to defraud United States
    If two or more persons conspire either to commit any offense against the United States, or to defraud the United States, or any agency thereof in any manner or for any purpose, and one or more of such persons do any act to effect the object of the conspiracy, each shall be fined under this title or imprisoned not more than five years, or both.
    If, however, the offense, the commission of which is the object of the conspiracy, is a misdemeanor only, the punishment for such conspiracy shall not exceed the maximum punishment provided for such misdemeanor.
[16] (U) *United States v Rabinowich*, 238 US 78, 59, 35 S.Ct 682, L Ed 1211 (1915).
[17] (U) *United States v. Cangiano*, 492 F.2d 906 (2nd Cir. 1974), cert denied 419 U.S. 904 (1974).

(U) In light of the President's complete authority over the conduct of war, without a clear statement otherwise, criminal statutes are not read as infringing on the President's ultimate authority in these areas. The Supreme Court has established a canon of statutory construction that statutes are to be construed in a manner that avoids constitutional difficulties so long as a reasonable alternative construction is available. *See, e.g., Edward J. DeBartolo Corp. v. Florida Gulf Coast Bldg. & Constr. Trades Council*, 485 U.S. 568, 575 (1988) (citing *NLRB v. Catholic Bishop of Chicago*, 440 U.S. 490, 499–501, 504 (1979)) ("[W]here an otherwise acceptable construction of a statute would raise serious constitutional problems, [courts] will construe [a] statute to avoid such problems unless such construction is plainly contrary to the intent of Congress.") This canon of construction applies especially where an act of Congress could be read to encroach upon powers constitutionally committed to a coordinate branch of government. *See, e.g., Franklin v. Massachusetts*, 505 U.S. 788, 800–1 (1992) (citation omitted) ("Out of respect for the separation of powers and the unique constitutional position of the President, we find that textual silence is not enough to subject the President to the provisions of the [Administrative Procedure Act]. We would require an express statement by Congress before assuming it intended the President's performance of his statutory duties to be reviewed for abuse of discretion."); *Public Citizen V. United States Dep't of Justice*, 491 U.S. 440, 465–67 (1989) (construing Federal Advisory Committee Act not to apply to advice given by American Bar Association to the President on judicial nominations, to avoid potential constitutional question regarding encroachment on Presidential power to appoint judges).

(U) In the area of foreign affairs, and war powers in particular, the avoidance canon has special force. *See, e.g., Dept of Navy v. Egan*, 484 U.S. 518, 530 (1988) ("unless Congress specifically has provided otherwise, courts traditionally have been reluctant to intrude upon the authority of the Executive in military and national security affairs."); *Japan Whaling Ass'n v. American Cetacean Socy*, 478 U.S. 221, 232–33 (1986) (construing federal statutes to avoid curtailment of traditional presidential prerogatives in foreign affairs). It should not be lightly assumed that Congress has acted to interfere with the President's constitutionally superior position as Chief Executive and Commander-in-Chief in the area of military operations. *See Egan*, 484 U.S. at 529 (quoting *Haig v. Agee*, 1453 U.S. 280, 293–94 (1981). *See also Agee*, 453 U.S. at 291 (deference to Executive Branch is "especially" appropriate "in the area of national security").

(U) In order to respect the President's inherent constitutional authority to manage a military campaign, 18 U.S.C. § 2340A (the prohibition against torture) as well as any other potentially applicable statute must be construed as inapplicable to interrogations undertaken pursuant to his Commander-in-Chief authority. Congress lacks authority under Article 1 to set the terms and conditions under which the President may exercise his authority as Commander-in-Chief to control the conduct of operations during a war. The President's power to detain and interrogate enemy combatants arises out of his constitutional authority as Commander-in-Chief. A construction of Section 2340A that applied the provision to regulate the President's authority as Commander-in-Chief to determine the interrogation and treatment of enemy combatants would raise serious constitutional questions. Congress may no more regulate the President's ability to detain and interrogate enemy combatants than it may regulate his ability to direct troop movements on the battlefield. Accordingly, we would construe Section 2340A to avoid this constitutional difficulty, and conclude that it does not apply to the President's detention and interrogation of enemy combatants pursuant to his Commander-in-Chief authority.

(U) This approach is consistent with previous decisions of the DOJ involving the application of federal criminal law. For example, DOJ has previously construed the congressional contempt statute as inapplicable to executive branch officials who refuse to comply with congressional subpoenas because of an assertion of executive privilege. In a 1984 opinion, DOJ concluded that

> if executive officials were subject to prosecution for criminal contempt whenever they carried out the President's claim of executive privilege, it would significantly burden and immeasurably impair the President's ability to fulfill his constitutional duties. Therefore, the separation of powers principles that underlie the doctrine of executive privilege also would preclude an application of the contempt of Congress statute to punish officials for aiding the President in asserting his constitutional privilege.

Prosecution for Contempt of Congress of an Executive Branch Official Who Has Asserted A Claim of Executive Privilege, 8 Op. O.L.C. 101, 134 (May 30, 1984). Likewise, if executive officials were subject to prosecution for conducting interrogations when they were carrying out the President's Commander-in-Chief powers, "it would significantly burden and immeasurably impair the President's ability to fulfill his constitutional duties." These constitutional principles preclude an application of Section 2340A to punish officials for aiding the President in exercising his exclusive constitutional authorities. *Id.*

(U) It could be argued that Congress enacted 18 U.S.C. § 2340A with full knowledge and consideration of the President's Commander-in-Chief power, and that Congress intended to restrict his discretion; however, the Department of Justice could not enforce Section 2340A against federal officials acting pursuant to the President's constitutional authority to wage a military campaign. Indeed, in a different context, DOJ has concluded that both courts and prosecutors should reject prosecutions that apply federal criminal laws to activity that is authorized pursuant to one of the President's constitutional powers. DOJ, for example, has previously concluded that Congress could not constitutionally extend the congressional contempt statute to executive branch officials who refuse to comply with congressional subpoenas because of an assertion of executive privilege. They opined that "courts . . . would surely conclude that a criminal prosecution for the exercise of a presumptively valid, constitutionally based privilege is not consistent with the Constitution." 8 Op. O.L.C. at 141. Further, DOJ concluded that it could not bring a criminal prosecution against a defendant who had acted pursuant to an exercise of the President's constitutional power. "The President, through a United States Attorney, need not, indeed may not, prosecute criminally a subordinate for asserting on his behalf a claim of executive privilege. Nor could the Legislative Branch or the courts require or implement the prosecution of such an individual." *Id.* Although Congress may define federal crimes that the President, through the Take Care Clause, should prosecute, Congress cannot compel the President to prosecute outcomes taken pursuant to the President's own constitutional authority. If Congress could do so, it could control the President's authority through the manipulation of federal criminal law.

(U) There are even greater concerns with respect to prosecutions arising out of the exercise of the President's express authority as Commander-in-Chief than with prosecutions arising out of the assertion of executive privilege. In a series of opinions examining various legal questions arising after September 11, 2001, DOJ explained the scope of the President's Commander-in-Chief power. We briefly summarize the findings of those opinions here. The President's constitutional power to protect the security of the United States and the lives and safety of its people must be understood in light of the Founders' intention to create a federal government "clothed with all the powers requisite to the complete execution of its trust." *The Federalist* No. 23, at 147 (Alexander Hamilton) (Jacob E. Cooke ed. 1961). Foremost among the objectives committed to that trust by the Constitution is the security of the nation. As Hamilton explained in arguing for the Constitution's adoption, because "the circumstances which may affect the public safety" are not reducible within certain determinate limits,

> it must be admitted, as necessary consequence, that there can be no limitation of that authority, which is to provide for the defense and protection of the community, in any matter essential to its efficacy.

Id. at 147–48. Within the limits that the Constitution itself imposes, the scope and distribution of the powers to protect national security must be construed to authorize the most efficacious defense of the nation and its interests in accordance "with the realistic purposes of the entire instrument." *Lichter v. United States*, 334 U.S. 742, 782 (1948).

(U) The text, structure, and history of the Constitution establish that the Founders entrusted the President with the primary responsibility, and therefore the power, to ensure the security of United States in situations of grave and unforeseen emergencies. The decision to deploy military force in the defense of United States interests is expressly placed under Presidential Authority by the Vesting Clause, U.S. Const. Art. I, § 1, cl. 1, and by the Commander-in-Chief Clause, *id.*, § 2, cl. 1.[18] DOJ has long understood the Commander-in-Chief Clause in particular as an affirmative grant of authority to the President. The Framers understood the Clause as investing the President with the fullest range of power understood at the time of the ratification of the Constitution as belonging to the military commander. In addition, the Structure of the Constitution demonstrates that any power traditionally understood as pertaining to the executive which includes the conduct of warfare and the defense of the nation unless expressly assigned in the Constitution to Congress, is vested in the President. Article II, Section 1 makes this clear by stating that the "executive Power shall be

---

[18] (U) *See Johnson v. Eisentrager*, 339 U.S. 763, 789 (1950) (President has authority to deploy United States armed forces "abroad or to any particular region"); *Fleming v. Page*, 50 U.S. (9 How) 603, 614–15 (1950) ("As Commander-in-Chief, [the President] is authorized to direct the movements of the naval and military forces placed by law at his command, and to employ them in the manner he may deem most effectual") *Loving v. United States*, 517 U.S. 748, 776 (1996) (Scalia, J., concurring in part and concurring in judgment) (The inherent powers of the Commander-in-Chief "are clearly extensive."); *Maul v. United States*, 274 U.S. 501, 515–16 (1927) (Brandeis & Holmes, JJ., concurring) (President "may direct any revenue cutter to cruise in any water in order to perform any duty of the service"); *Commonwealth Massachusetts v. Laird*, 451 F.2d 26, 32 (1st Cir. 1971) (the President has "power as Commander-in-Chief to station forces abroad"); *Ex parte Vallandigham*, 28 F.Cas. 874, 922 (C.C.S.D. Ohio (1863) (No. 16,816) (in acting "under this power where there is no express legislative declaration, the President is guided solely by his own judgment land discretion"); *Authority to Use United States Military Forces in Somalia, 16 Op. O.L.C. 6,6 (Dec. 4,1992) (Barr, Attorney General)*

vested in a President of the United States of America." That sweeping grant vests in the President an unenumerated "executive power" and contrasts with the specific enumeration of the powers-those "herein" granted to Congress in Article 1. The implications of constitutional text and structure are confirmed by the practical consideration that national security decisions require the unity in purpose and energy in action that characterize the Presidency rather than Congress.[19]

(U) As the Supreme Court has recognized, the Commander-in-Chief power and the President's obligation to protect the nation imply the ancillary powers necessary to their successful exercise. "The first of the enumerated powers of the President is that he shall be Commander-in-Chief of the Army and Navy of the United States. And of course, the grant of war power includes all that is necessary and proper for carrying those powers into execution." *Johnson v. Eisentrager*, 339 U.S. 763, 788 (1950). In wartime, it is for the President alone to decide what methods to use to best prevail against the enemy. The President's complete discretion in exercising the Commander-in-Chief power has been recognized by the courts. In the *Prize Cases*, 67 U.S. (2 Black) 635, 670 (1862), for example, the Court explained that whether the President, "in fulfilling his duties as Commander in Chief", had appropriately responded to the rebellion of the southern states was a question "to be *decided by him*" and which the Court could not question, but must leave to "the political department of the Government to which this power was entrusted."

(U) One of the core functions of the Commander-in-Chief is that of capturing, detaining, and interrogating members of the enemy. It is well settled that the President may seize and detain enemy combatants, at least for the duration of the conflict, and the laws of war make clear that prisoners may be interrogated for information concerning the enemy, its strength, and its plans. Numerous Presidents have ordered the capture, detention, and questioning of enemy combatants during virtually every major conflict in the Nation's history, including recent conflicts in Korea, Vietnam, and the Persian Gulf. Recognizing this authority, Congress has never attempted to restrict or interfere with the President's authority on this score.

(U) Any effort by Congress to regulate the interrogation of unlawful combatants would violate the Constitution's sole vesting of the Commander-in-Chief authority in the President. There can be little doubt that intelligence operations, such as the detention and interrogation of enemy combatants and leaders, are both necessary and proper for the effective conduct of a military campaign. Indeed, such operations

---

[19] (U) Judicial decisions since the beginning of the Republic confirm the President's constitutional power and duty to repel military action against the United States and to take measures to prevent the recurrence of an attack. As Justice Joseph Story said long ago, "[I]t may be fit and proper for the government, in the exercise of the high discretion confided to the executive, for great public purposes, to act on a sudden emergency, or to prevent an irreparable mischief, by summary measures, which are not found in the text of the laws." *The Apollon*, 22 U.S. (9 Wheat) 362, 366–67 (1824). If the President is confronted with an unforeseen attack on the territory and people of the United States, or other immediate dangerous threat to American interests and security, it is his constitutional responsibility to respond to that threat with whatever means are necessary. *See e.g., The Prize Cases*, 67 U.S. (2 Black) 635, 668 (1862) ("If a war be made by invasion or a foreign nation, the President is not only authorized but bound to resist force by force ... without waiting for any special legislative authority."); *United States v. Smith*, 27 F. Cas; 1192,1229–30 (C.C.D.N.Y, 1.$$06) (No. 16,342) (Paterson, Circuit Justice) (regardless of statutory authorization. it is "the duty ... of the executive magistrate ... to repel an invading foe") *see also* 3 Story, *Commentaries* § 1485 ("[t]he command and application of the public force ... to maintain peace, and to resist foreign invasion" are executive powers).

may be of more importance in a war with an international terrorist organization than one with the conventional armed forces of a nation-state, due to the former's emphasis on secret operations and surprise attacks against civilians. It may be the case that only successful interrogations can provide the information necessary to prevent the success of covert terrorist attacks upon the United States and its citizens. Congress can no more interfere with the President's conduct of the interrogation of enemy combatants than it can dictate strategy or tactical decisions on the battlefield. Just as statutes that order the President to conduct warfare in a certain manner or for specific goals would be unconstitutional, so too are laws that seek to prevent the President from gaining the intelligence he believes necessary to prevent attacks upon the United States.

(U) As this authority is inherent in the President, it would be appropriate within the context of the war on terrorism for this authority to be stated expressly in a Presidential directive or other writing.[20]

b. Necessity

(U) The defense of necessity could be raised, under the current circumstances, to an allegation of a violation of a criminal statute. Often referred to as the "choice of evils" defense, necessity has been defined as follows:

Conduct that the actor believes to be necessary to avoid a harm or evil to himself or to another is justifiable, provided that:

(a) the harm or evil sought to be avoided by such conduct is greater than that sought to be prevented by the law defining the offense charged; and
(b) neither the Code nor other law defining the offense provides exceptions or defenses dealing with the specific situation involved; and
(c) a legislative purpose to exclude the justification claimed does not otherwise plainly appear.

Model Penal Code § 3.02. *See also* Wayne R. LaFave & Austin W. Scott, 1 Substantive Criminal Law § 5.4 at 627 (1986 & 2002 supp.) ("LaFave & Scott"). Although there is no federal statute that generally establishes necessity or other justifications as defenses to federal criminal laws, the Supreme Court has recognized the defense. *See United States v. Bailey*, 444 U.S. 394, 410 (1980) (relying on LaFave & Scott and Model Penal Code definitions of necessity defense).

(U) The necessity defense may prove especially relevant in the current circumstances. As it has been described in the case law and literature, the purpose behind necessity is one of public policy. According to LaFave & Scott, "the law ought to promote the achievement of higher values at the expense of lesser values, and sometimes the greater good for society will be accomplished by violating the literal language of the criminal law." LaFave & Scott, at 629. In particular, the necessity defense can justify the intentional killing of one person to save two others because "it is better that two lives be saved and one lost than that two be lost and one saved." *Id.* Or, put in the language of a choice of evils, "the evil involved in violating the terms of the criminal law (. . . even taking another's life) may be less than that which would result from literal compliance with the law (. . . two lives lost)." *Id.*

---

[20] (U) Although application of the Commander-in-Chief authority does not require a specific written directive, as an evidentiary matter a written Presidential directive or other document would serve to memorialize the authority.

(U) Additional elements of the necessity defense are worth noting here. First, the defense is not limited to certain types of harms. Therefore, the harm inflicted by necessity may include intentional homicide, so long as the harm avoided is greater (i.e., preventing more deaths) *Id.* at 634. Second, it must actually be the defendant's intention to avoid the greater harm; intending to commit murder and then learning only later that the death had the fortuitous result of saving other lives will not support a necessity defense. *Id.* at 635. Third, if the defendant reasonably believes that the lesser harm as necessary, even if, unknown to him, it was not, he may still avail himself of the defense. As LaFave and Scott explain, "if A kills B reasonably believing it to be necessary to save C and D, he is not guilty of murder even though, unknown to A, C and D could have been rescued without the necessity of killing B." *Id.* Fourth, it is for the court, and not the defendant to judge whether the harm avoided outweighed the harm done. *Id.* at 636. Fifth, the defendant cannot rely upon the necessity defense if a third alternative that will cause less harm is open and known to him.

(U) Although not every interrogation that could violate the provisions of Section 2340A or other potentially applicable statutes would trigger a necessity defense, it appears that under the current circumstances there may be support for such defense. On September 11, 2001, al Qaeda launched a surprise covert attack on civilian targets in the United States that led to the deaths of thousands and financial losses in billions of dollars. According to public and governmental reports, al Qaeda has other sleeper cells within the United States that may be planning similar attacks. Indeed, al Qaeda's plans apparently include efforts to develop and deploy chemical, biological, and nuclear weapons of mass destruction. Under these circumstances, a detainee may possess information that could enable the United States to prevent attacks that potentially could equal or surpass the September 11 attacks in their magnitude. Clearly, any harm that might occur during an interrogation would pale to insignificance compared to the harm avoided by preventing such an attack, which could take hundreds or thousands of lives.

(U) Under this rationale, two factors will help indicate when the necessity defense could appropriately be invoked. First, the more certain that government officials are that a particular individual has information needed to prevent an attack, the more necessary interrogation will be. Second, the more likely it appears that a terrorist attack is likely to occur, and the greater the amount of damage expected from such an attack, the more that an interrogation to get information would become necessary. Of course, the strength of the necessity defense depends on the circumstances that prevail, and the knowledge of the government actors involved, when the interrogation is conducted. While every interrogation that might violate Section 2340A or other potentially applicable statutes does not trigger a necessity defense, we can say that certain circumstances could support such a defense.

(U) Legal authorities identify an important exception to the necessity defense. The defense is available "only in situations wherein the legislature has not itself, in its criminal statute, made a determination of values." *Id.* at 629. Thus, if Congress explicitly has made clear that violation of a statute cannot be outweighed by the harm avoided, courts cannot recognize the necessity defense. LaFave and Israel provide as an example an abortion statute that made clear that abortions even to save the life of the mother would still be a crime; in such cases the necessity defense would be unavailable. *Id.* at 630. Here, however, Congress has not explicitly made a determination of values vis-a-vis torture. In fact, Congress explicitly removed efforts to remove torture from the weighing of values permitted by the necessity defense.[21]

c. Self-Defense

(U) Even if a court were to find that necessity did not justify the violation of a criminal statute, a defendant could still appropriately raise a claim of self-defense. The right to self-defense, even when it involves deadly force, is deeply embedded in our law, both as to individuals and as to the nation as a whole. As the Court of Appeals for the D.C. Circuit has explained:

> More than two centuries ago, Blackstone, best known of the expositors of the English common law taught that "all homicide is malicious, and of course amounts to murder, unless... excused on the account of accident or self-preservation." Self-defense, as a doctrine legally exonerating the taking of human life, is as viable now as it was in Blackstone's time.

United States v. Peterson, 483 F.2d 1222, 1228–29 (D.C. Cir. 1973). Self-defense is a common-law defense to federal criminal law offenses, and nothing in the text, structure or history of Section 2340A precludes its application to a charge of torture. In the absence of any textual provision to the contrary, we assume self-defense can be an... appropriate defense to an allegation of torture.

(U) The doctrine of self-defense permits the use of force to prevent harm to another person. As LaFave and Scott explain, one is justified in using reasonable force in defense of another person, even a stranger, when he reasonably believes that the other is in immediate danger of unlawful bodily harm from his adversary and that the use of such force is necessary to avoid this danger." *Id.* at 663–64. Ultimately, even deadly force is permissible, but "only when the attack of the adversary upon the other, person reasonably appears to the defender to be a deadly attack." *Id.* at 664. As with our discussion of necessity, we will review the significant elements of this defense.[22] According to LaFave and Scott, the elements of the defense of others are the same as those that apply to individual self-defense.

---

[21] In the CAT, torture is defined as the intentional infliction of severe pain or suffering "for such purposes as obtaining from him or a third person information or a confession." CAT Article 1.1. One could argue that such a definition represented an attempt to indicate that the good of obtaining information no matter what the circumstances – could not justify an act of torture. In other words, necessity would not be a defense. In enacting Section 2340, however, Congress removed the purpose element in the definition of torture, evidencing an intention to remove any fixing of values by statute. By leaving Section 2340 silent as to the harm done by torture in comparison to other harms, Congress allowed the necessity defense to apply when appropriate.

Further, the CAT contains an additional provision that "no exceptional circumstances whatsoever, whether a state of war or a threat of war, internal political instability or any other public emergency, may be invoked as a justification of torture," CAT Article 2.2. Aware of this provision of the treaty and of the definition of the necessity defense that allows the legislature to provide *for* an exception to the defense, See Model Penal Code § 3,02(b), Congress did not incorporate CAT article 2.2 into Section 2–4. Given that Congress omitted CATs effort to bar a necessity or wartime defense, Section 2340 could be read as permitting the defense.

[22] (U) Early cases had suggested that in order to be eligible for defense of another, one should have some personal relationship with the one in need of protection. That view has been discarded. LaFave & Scott at 664.

(U) First, self-defense requires that the use of force be *necessary* to avoid the danger of unlawful bodily harm. *Id.* at 649. A defender may justifiably use deadly force if he reasonably believes that the other person is about to inflict unlawful death or serious bodily harm upon another, and that it is necessary to use such force to prevent it. *Id.* at 652. Looked at from the opposite perspective, the defender may not use force when the force would be as equally effective at a later time and the defender suffers no harm or risk by waiting. *See* Paul H. Robinson, 2 Criminal Law Defenses § 131 (c) at 77 (1984). If, however, other options permit the defender to retreat safely from confrontation without having to resort to deadly force, the use of force may not be necessary in the first place. LaFave and Scott, at 659–60.

(U) Second, self-defense requires that the defendant's belief in the necessity of using force be reasonable. If a defendant honestly but unreasonably believed force was necessary, he will not be able to make out a successful claim of self-defense. *Id.* at 654. Conversely, if a defendant reasonably believed an attack was to occur, but the facts subsequently showed no attack was threatened, he may still raise self-defense. As LaFave and Scott explain, "one may be justified in shooting to death an adversary who, having threatened to kill him, reaches for his pocket as if for a gun, though it later appears that he had no gun and that he was only reaching for his handkerchief." *Id.* Some authorities such as the Model Penal Code, even eliminate the reasonability element, and require only that the defender honestly believed regardless of its reasonableness – that the use of force was necessary.

(U) Third, many legal authorities include the requirement that a defender must reasonably believe that the unlawful violence is "imminent" before he can use force in his defense. It would be a mistake, however, to equate imminence necessarily with timing – that an attack is immediately about to occur. Rather, as the Model Penal Code explains, what is essential is that the defensive *response* must be "immediately necessary." Model Penal Code § 3.04(1). Indeed, imminence must be merely another way of expressing the requirement of necessity. Robinson at 78. LaFave and Scott, for example, believe that the imminence requirement makes sense as part of a necessity defense because if an attack is not immediately upon the defender, the defender may have other options available to avoid the attack that do not involve the use of force. LaFave and Scott at 656. If, however, the fact of the attack becomes certain and no other options remain the use of force may be justified. To use a well-known hypothesis, if A were to kidnap and confine B, and then tell B he would kill B one week later, B would be justified in using force in self-defense, even if the opportunity arose before the week had passed. *Id.* at 656; *see also* Robinson at § 131(c)(1) at 78. In this hypothesis, while the attack itself is not imminent, B's use of force becomes immediately necessary whenever he has an opportunity to save himself from A.

(U) Fourth, the amount of force should be proportional to the threat. As LaFave and Scott explain, "the amount of force which [the defender] may justifiably use must be reasonably related to the threatened harm which he seeks to avoid." LaFave and Scott at 651. Thus, one may not use deadly force in response to a threat that does not rise to death or serious bodily harm. If such harm may result however, deadly force is appropriate.

As the Model Penal Code § 3.04(2)(b) states, "[t]he use of deadly force is not justifiable unless the actor believes that such force is necessary to protect himself against death, serious bodily injury, kidnapping or sexual intercourse compelled by force or threat."

(S/NF) (U) Under the current circumstances, a defendant accused of violating the criminal prohibitions described above could have, in certain circumstances, grounds to properly claim the defense of another. The threat of an impending terrorist attack threatens the lives of hundreds if not thousands of American citizens. Whether such a defense will be upheld depends on the specific context within which the interrogation decision is made. If an attack appears increasingly likely, but our intelligence services and Armed Forces cannot prevent it without the information from the interrogation of a specific individual, then the more likely it will appear that the conduct in question will be seen as necessary. If intelligence and other information support the conclusion that attack is increasingly certain, then the necessity for the interrogation will be reasonable. The increasing certainty of an attack will also satisfy the imminence requirement. Finally, the fact that previous al Qaeda attacks have had as their aim the deaths of American citizens, and that evidence of other plots have had a similar goal in mind, would justify proportionality of interrogation methods designed to elicit information to prevent them.

(S/NF) (U) To be sure, this situation is different from the usual self-defense justification, and indeed, it overlaps with elements of the necessity defense. Self-defense as usually discussed involves using force against an individual who is about to conduct the attack. In the current circumstances, however, an enemy combatant in detention does not himself present a threat of harm. He is not actually carrying out the attack, rather he has participated in the planning and preparation for the attack, or merely has knowledge of the attack through his membership in the terrorist organization. Nonetheless, leading scholarly commentators believe that interrogation of such individuals using methods that might violate Section 2340A would be justified under the doctrine of self-defense, because the combatant by aiding and promoting the terrorist plot "has culpably caused the situation where someone might get hurt. If hurting him is the only means to prevent the death or injury of others put at risk by his actions, such torture should be permissible, and on the same basis that self-defense is permissible." Michael S. Moore, *Torture and the Balance of Evils*, 23 Israel L. Rev. 280, 323 (1989) (symposium on Israel's Landau Commission Report).[23] *See* also Alan M. Dershowitz, *Is It Necessary to Apply "Physical Pressure" to Terrorists – and to Lie About It?*, 23 Israel L. Rev. 192, 199–200 (1989). Thus, some commentators believe that by helping to create the threat of loss of life, terrorists become culpable for the threat even though they do not actually carry out the attack itself. If necessary, they may be hurt in an interrogation because they are part of the mechanism that has set the attack in motion, just as is someone who feeds ammunition or targeting information to an attacker. *Moore*, at 323.

(U) A claim by an individual of the defense of another would be further supported by the fact that in this case, the nation itself is under attack and has the right to self-defense. This fact can bolster and support an individual claim of self-defense in a prosecution, according to the Supreme Court in *In re Neagle*, 135 U.S. 1 (1890). In that case, the State of California arrested and held deputy U.S. Marshal Neagle for

---

[23] (U) Moore distinguishes that case from one in which a person has information that could stop a terrorist attack, but who does not take a hand in the terrorist activity itself, such as an innocent person who learns of the attack from her spouse. Moore, 23 Israel L. Rev. at 324. Such individuals, Moore finds, would not be subject to the use of force in self-defense, although they might under the doctrine of necessity.

shooting and killing the assailant of Supreme Court Justice Field. In granting the writ of habeas corpus for Neagle's release, the Supreme Court did not rely alone upon the marshal's right to defend another or his right to self-defense. Rather, the Court found the Neagle, as an agent of the United States and of the executive branch, was justified in the killing because in protecting Justice Field, he was acting pursuant to the executive branch's inherent constitutional authority to protect the United States government. *Id.* at 67 ("We cannot doubt the power of the President to take measures for the protection of a judge of one of the courts of the United States who, while in the discharge of the duties of his office, is threatened with a personal attack which may probably result in his death.") That authority derives, according to the Court, from the President's power under Article II to take care that the laws are faithfully executed. In other words, Neagle as a federal officer not only could raise self-defense or defense of another, but also could defend his actions on the ground that he was implementing the Executive Branch's authority to protect the United States government.

(U) If the right to defend the national government can be raised as a defense in an individual prosecution as *Neagle* suggests, then a government defendant, acting in his official capacity, should be able to argue that any conduct that arguably violated a criminal prohibition was undertaken pursuant to more than just individual self-defense or defense of another. In addition, the defendant could claim that he was fulfilling the Executive Branch's authority to protect the federal government, and the nation, from attack. The September 11 attacks have already triggered that authority, as recognized both under domestic and international law. Following the example of *In re Neagle*, we conclude that a government defendant may also argue that his conduct of an interrogation properly authorized, is justified on the basis of protecting the nation from attack.

(U) There can be little doubt that the nation's right to self-defense has been triggered under our law. The Constitution announces that one of its purposes is "to provide for the common defense." U.S. Const., Preamble. Article I, § 8 declares that Congress is to exercise its powers to "provide for the common defense." *See also* 2 Pub. Papers of Ronald Reagan 920, 921 1988–89) (right to self-defense recognized by Article 51 of the U.N. Charter). The President has particular responsibility and power to take steps to defend the nation and its people. *In re Neagle*, 135 U.S at 64. *See also* U.S. Const., art. IV, § 4 ("The United States shall . . . protect [each of the States] against Invasion"). As Commander-in-Chief and Chief Executive, he may use the Armed Forces to protect the nation and its people. *See, e.g., United States v. Verdugo-Urquidez*, 494 U.S. 259, 273 (1990). And he may employ secret agents to aid in his work as Commander-in-Chief. *Totten v. United States*, 92 U.S. 105, 106 (1876). As the Supreme Court observed in *The Prize Cases*, 67 U.S. (2 Black) 635 (1862), in response to an armed attack on the United States "the President is not only authorized but bound to resist force by force . . . without waiting for any special legislative authority." *Id.* at 668. The September 11 events were a direct attack on the United States, and as we have explained above, the President has authorized the use of military force with the support of Congress.[24]

---

[24] (U) While the President's constitutional determination alone is sufficient to justify the nation's resort to self-defense, it also bears noting that the right to self-defense is further recognized under international law. Article 51 of the U.N. Charter declares that "[n]othing in the present Charter shall impair the inherent right of individual or collective self-defense if an armed attack occurs against a Member of the United Nations until the Security Council has taken the measures necessary to maintain international peace and security." The attacks of September 11, 2001, clearly constitute an armed

(U) As DOJ has made clear in opinions involving the war on al Qaeda, the nation's right to self-defense has been triggered by the events of September 11. If a government defendant were to harm an enemy combatant during an interrogation in a manner that might arguably violate criminal prohibition, he would be doing so in order to prevent further attacks on the United States by the al Qaeda terrorist network. In that case, DOJ believes that he could argue that the executive branch's constitutional authority to protect the nation from attack justified his actions. This national and international version of the right to self-defense could supplement and bolster the government defendant's individual right.

d. Military Law Enforcement Actions

(U) Use of force in military law enforcement is authorized for (1) self-defense and defense of others against a hostile person when in imminent danger of death or serious bodily harm *by the hostile person*; (2) to prevent the actual theft or sabotage of assets vital to national security; (3) to prevent the actual theft or sabotage of resources that are inherently dangerous to others; (4) to prevent the commission of a serious crime that involves imminent danger of death or serious bodily harm; (5) to prevent the destruction of vital public utilities or similar critical infrastructure; (6) for apprehension; and (7) to prevent escape. (DODD 5210.56, 1 Nov 2001). These justifications contemplate the use of force against a person who has committed, is committing, or is about to commit, a serious offense. Although we are not aware of any authority that applies these concepts in the interrogation context, the justified use of force in military law enforcement may provide useful comparisons to the use of force against a detainee to extract intelligence for the specific purpose of preventing a serious and imminent terrorist incident.

e. Superior Orders

(U) Under both international law and U.S. law, an order to commit an obviously criminal act, such as the wanton killing of a non-combatant or the torture of a prisoner, is an *unlawful* order and will not relieve a subordinate of his responsibility to comply with the law of armed conflict.[25] Only if the individual did not know of the unlawfulness of an order, and he could not reasonably be expected under the circumstances to recognize the order as unlawful, will the defense of obedience of a superior order protect a subordinate from the consequences of violation of the law of armed conflict.[26]

---

attack against the United States, and indeed were the latest in a long history of al Qaeda sponsored attacks against the United States. This conclusion was acknowledged by the United Nations Security Council on September 29, 2001, when it unanimously adopted Resolution 1373 explicitly "reaffirming the inherent right of individual and collective defense as recognized by the charter of the United Nations. This right of self-defense is a right to effective self-defense. In other words, the victim state has the right to use force against the aggressor who has initiated an "armed attack" until the threat has abated. The United States, through its military and intelligence personnel, has a right recognized by Article 51 to continue using force until such time as the threat posed by al Qaeda and other terrorist groups connected to the September 11 attack is completely ended." Other treaties re-affirm the right of the United States to use force in its self-defense. See, e.g., Inter-American Treaty of Reciprocal Assistance, art. 3, Sept. 2, 1947, T.I.A.S. No. 1838, 21 U.N.T.S. 77 (Rio Treaty); North Atlantic Treaty, art. 5, Apr. 4, 1949, 3 Stat. 2241, 34 U.N.T.S. 243.

[25] (U) *See* Section 6.1.4, Annotated Supplement to the Commander's Handbook on the Law of Naval Operations (NWP 1-14M 1997).
[26] *Id.*

(U) Under international law, the fact that a war crime is committed pursuant to the orders of a military or civilian superior does not by itself relieve the subordinate committing it from criminal responsibility under international law.[27] It may, however, be considered in mitigation of punishment.[28]

(U) For instance, the Charter of the International Military Tribunal at Nuremberg, Article 8, stated:

> The fact that the Defendant acted pursuant to order of his Government or of a superior shall not free him from responsibility, but may be considered in mitigation of punishment if the Tribunal determines that justice so requires.[29]

(U) Similarly, the Statute for the International Tribunal for Yugoslavia, and the Statute for the International Criminal Tribunal for Rwanda (in Articles 7(4) & 6(4), respectively) provide:

> The fact that an accused person acted pursuant to an order of a Government or of a superior shall not relieve him of criminal responsibility, but may be considered in anticipation of punishment if the Tribunal determines that justice so requires.

(U) As to the general attitude taken by military tribunals toward the plea of superior orders, the following statement is representative:

> It cannot be questioned that acts done in time of war under the military authority of an enemy cannot involve any criminal liability on the part of officers or soldiers if the acts are not prohibited by the conventional or customary rules of war. Implicit obedience to orders of superior officers is almost indispensable to every military system. But this implies obedience to lawful orders only. If the act done pursuant to a superior's orders be murder, the production of the order will not make it any less so. It may mitigate but it cannot justify the crime. We are of the view, however, that if the illegality of the order was not known to the inferior, and he could not reasonably have been expected to know of its illegality, no wrongful intent necessary to the commission of a crime exists and the interior [*sic*] will be protected. But the general rule is the members of the armed forces are bound to obey only the lawful orders of their commanding officers and they cannot escape criminal liability by obeying a command which violates international law and outrages fundamental concepts of justice.

The Hostage Case (United States v. Wilhelm List et al.), 11 TWC 1236.

(U) The International Military Tribunal at Nuremberg declared in its judgment that the test of responsibility for superior orders "is not the existence of the order, but whether moral choice was in fact possible."[30]

---

[27] The International Criminal Court also takes this view. Article 33 of the Rome Statute, recognizes that: "1. The fact that a crime within the jurisdiction of the Court has been committed by a person pursuant to an order of a Government or of a superior, whether military or civilian, shall not relieve that person of criminal responsibility unless: (a) The person was under a legal obligation to obey orders of the Government or superior in question; (b) The person did not know that the order was unlawful; and (c) The order was not manifestly unlawful. 2. For the purposes of this article, orders to commit genocide or crimes against humanity are manifestly unlawful."

[28] *Id.*, at § 6.2.5.5.1.

[29] *See* U.S. Naval War College, International Law Documents, at 1944–45, 255 (1946).

[30] (U) 1 Trial of Major War Criminals before the International Military Tribunal, Nuremberg 14 November 1945–1 October 1946, at 224 (1947), *excerpted in* U.S. Naval War College, International Law Documents, 1946–1947, at 260 (1948).

(U) Domestically, the UCMJ discusses the defense of superior order in The Manual Courts-Martial, which provides in R.C.M. 916(d), MCM 2002:

> It is a defense to any offense that the accused was acting pursuant to orders unless the accused knew the orders to be unlawful or a person of ordinary sense and understanding would have known the orders to be unlawful. An act performed pursuant to a lawful order is justified. An act performed pursuant to an unlawful order is excused unless the accused knew it to be unlawful or a person of ordinary sense and understanding would have known the orders to be unlawful.

Inference of lawfulness. An order requiring the performance of a military duty or act may be inferred to be lawful and it is disobeyed at the peril of the subordinate.[31]

(U) In sum, the defense of superior orders will generally be available for U.S. Armed Forces personnel engaged in exceptional interrogations except where the conduct goes so far as to be patently unlawful.

4. Lack of DOJ Representation for DOD Personnel Charged with a Criminal Offense

(U) DOJ representation of a defendant is generally not available in federal criminal proceedings, even when the defendant's actions occur within the scope of federal employment.[32]

B. Federal Civil Statutes

1. 28 U.S.C. § 1350

(U) 28 U.S.C. § 1350 extends the jurisdiction of the U.S. District Courts to *"any civil action by an alien for a tort only, committed in violation of the law of nations or a treaty of the United States."*[33] Section 1350 is a vehicle by which victims of torture and other human rights violations by their native government and its agents have sought judicial remedy for the wrongs they've suffered. However, all the decided cases we have found involve foreign nationals suing in U.S. District Courts for conduct by foreign actors/governments.[34] The District Court for the District of Columbia has determined that Section 1350 actions, by the GTMO detainees, against the United States or its agents acting within the scope of employment fail. This is because (1) the United States has not waived sovereign immunity to such suits like those brought by the detainees, and (2) the *Eisentrager* doctrine barring habeas access also precludes other potential avenues of jurisdiction.[35] This of course leaves interrogators vulnerable in their individual capacity for conduct a court might find to constitute torture. Assuming a court would take jurisdiction over the matter and grant standing to the detainee[36], it

---

[31] (U) This inference does not apply to a patently illegal order, such as one that directs the commission of a crime. (Article 90, UCMJ).

[32] (U) 28 CFR § 50.15 (a)(4).

[33] (U) 28 U.S.C. § 1350, the Alien Tort Claim Act (ATCA).

[34] (U) See, for example, *Abebe-Jira v. Negewo*, No. 93-9133, United States Court of Appeals, Eleventh Circuit, Jan 10, 1996. In this case the 11th Circuit concluded, "the Alien Tort Claims Act establishes a federal forum where courts may fashion domestic common law remedies to give effect to violations of customary international law."

[35] (U) *Al Odah v. United States*, (D.D.C., 2002)

[36] (U) *Filartiga v. Pena-Irala*, 630 F.2d 876 (2nd Cir. 1980) 885, note 18, "conduct of the type alleged here [torture] would be actionable under 42 U.S.C. § 1983, or undoubtedly the Constitution, if performed by a government official."

is possible that this statute would provide an avenue of relief for actions of the United States or its agents found to violate customary international law. The Department of Justice has argued that Section 1350 does not provide a cause of action and is merely jurisdictional in nature. The Department of Justice is currently studying whether to participate in the ongoing Section 1350 litigation.

2. Torture Victims Protection Act (TVPA)

(U) In 1992, President Bush signed into law the Torture Victims Protection Act of 1991.[37] Appended to the U.S. Code as a note to section 1350, the TVPA specifically creates a cause of action for individuals (or their successors) who have been subjected to torture or extra-judicial killing by "an individual who, under actual or apparent authority, or color of law, *of any foreign nation* – (1) subjects an individual to torture shall, in a civil action, be liable for damages to that individual; or (2) subjects an individual to extra-judicial killing shall, in a civil action, be liable for damages. ..." (emphasis added)[38] Thus, the TVPA does not apply to the conduct of U.S. agents acting under the color of law.

C. Applicability of the United States Constitution

1. Applicability of the Constitution to Aliens Outside the United States

(U) Non-resident enemy aliens do not enjoy constitutional rights outside the sovereign territory of the United States.[39] The courts have held that unlawful combatants do not gain constitutional rights upon transfer to GTMO as unlawful combatants merely because the U.S. exercises extensive dominion and control over GTMO.[40] Moreover, because the courts have rejected the concept of "de facto sovereignty," constitutional rights apply to aliens only on sovereign U.S. territory. (See discussion under "Jurisdiction of Federal Courts", *infra*.)

(U) Although U.S. constitutional rights do not apply to aliens at GTMO, the U.S. criminal laws do apply to acts committed there by virtue of GTMO's status as within the special maritime and territorial jurisdiction.

2. The Constitution Defining U.S. Obligations Under International Law

(U) In the course of taking reservations to the Convention Against Torture and Other Cruel, and Inhuman or Degrading Treatment or Punishment, the United States determined that the Convention's prohibitions against cruel, inhuman or degrading treatment or punishment applied only to the extent that such conduct was prohibited by

[37] (U) Pub. L. No. 102-256, 106 Stat. 73, 28 U.S.C § 1350 (note).
[38] (U) The definition of torture used in PL 102-256 is: "any act, directed against an individual in the offender's custody or physical control, by which severe pain or suffering (other than pain or suffering arising only from or inherent in, or incidental to lawful sanctions) whether physical or mental, is intentionally inflicted on that individual for such purpose as obtaining from that individual or a third person information or a confession, punishing that individual for an act that individual or a third person has committed or is suspected of having committed, intimidating or coercing that individual or a third person, or for any reason based on discrimination of any kind." This definition is substantially similar (with no meaningful difference) to the definition in the Torture Statute. The definition of mental pain and suffering is the same as in the Torture Statute.
[39] (U) *Eisentrager* at 764.
[40] (U) *Al Odah v. United States*, (D.D.C., 2002).

the Fifth, Eighth and Fourteenth Amendments to our Constitution.[41] Consequently, analysis of these amendments is significant in determining the extent to which the United States is bound by the Convention. It should be clear however, that aliens held at GTMO do not have constitutional rights under the Fifth Amendment's Due Process clause or the Eighth Amendment. *See Johnson v. Eisentrager*, 339 U.S. 763 (1950); *U.S. v. Verdugo-Urquidez*, 494 U.S. 259 (1990).

a. Eighth Amendment

(U) "An examination of the history of the Amendment and the decisions of this [Supreme] Court construing the proscription against cruel and unusual punishment confirms that it was designed to protect those convicted of crimes."[42] The import of this holding is that, assuming a court would mistakenly hold that it had jurisdiction to hear a detainee's claim, the claim would not lie under the Eighth Amendment. Accordingly, detainees could not pursue a claim regarding their pre-conviction treatment under the Eight Amendment.

(U) The standards of the Eighth Amendment are relevant, however, due to the U.S. Reservation to the Torture Convention's definition of cruel, inhuman, and degrading treatment. Under "cruel and unusual punishment" jurisprudence, there are two lines of analysis that are relevant to the conduct of interrogations: (1) conditions of confinement, and (2) excessive force. As a general matter, the excessive force analysis applies to the official use of physical force, often in situations in which an inmate has attacked another inmate or a guard whereas the conditions of confinement analysis applies to such things as administrative segregation. Under the excessive force analysis, "a prisoner alleging excessive force must demonstrate that the defendant acted 'maliciously and sadistically'" for the very purpose of causing harm. *Porter v. Nussle*, 534 U.S. 516, 528 (2002) (quoting *Hudson v. McMillan*, 503 U.S.1. at 7). Excessive force requires the unnecessary and wanton infliction of pain. *Whitney v. Albers*, 475 U.S. 312, 319 (1986).

(U) A condition of confinement is not "cruel and unusual" unless it (1) is "sufficiently serious" to implicate constitutional protection, *id.* at 347, and (2) reflects "deliberate indifference" to the prisoner's health or safety, *Farmer v. Brennan* 511 U.S. 825, 834 (1994). The first element is objective, and inquires whether the challenged condition is cruel and unusual. The second, so-called "subjective" element requires examination of the actor's intent and inquires whether the challenged condition is imposed as punishment. *Wilson v. Seiter*, 501 U.S. 294, 300 (1991) ("The source of the intent requirement is not the predilections of this Court, but the Eighth Amendment itself, which bans only cruel and unusual *punishment*. If the pain inflicted is not formally meted out *as punishment* by the statute or sentencing judge, some mental element must be attributed to the inflicting officer before it can qualify.").

---

[41] (U) Articles of ratification, 21 Oct 1994: "1. The Senate's advice and consent is subject to the following reservations: (1) That the United States considers itself bound by the obligation under Article 16 to prevent 'cruel, inhuman, or degrading treatment or punishment', only insofar as the term 'cruel, inhuman, or degrading treatment or punishment' means the cruel, unusual and inhumane treatment or punishment prohibited by the Fifth, Eighth, and/or Fourteenth Amendments to the Constitution of the United States." Available at the UN documents site: http://193.194.138.190/html/menu3/treaty12_asp.htm.

[42] (U) *Ingraham v. Wright*, 430 U.S. 651, 664 (1977). In *Ingraham*, a case about corporal punishment in a public junior high school, the Court analyzed the claim under the Fourteenth amendment's Due Process clause, concluding that the conduct did not violate the Fourteenth amendment, even though it involved up to 10 whacks with a wooden paddle.

(U) The Supreme Court has noted that "[n]o static 'test' can exist by which courts determine whether conditions of confinement are cruel and unusual, for the Eighth Amendment must draw its meaning from the evolving standards of decency that mark the progress of a maturing society." *Rhodes*, 452 U.S. at 146 (citation omitted). *See also Estelle v. Gamble*, 429 U.S. 97, 102 (1976) (stating that the Eighth Amendment embodies "broad and idealistic concepts of dignity, civilized standards, humanity, and decency"). Nevertheless, certain guidelines emerge from the Supreme Court's jurisprudence.

(U) The Court has established that "only those deprivations denying 'the minimal civilized measures of life's necessities' sufficiently grave to form the basis of an Eighth Amendment violation." *Wilson*, 501 U.S. at 298, *quoting Rhodes*, 452 U.S. at 347. It is not enough *for* a prisoner to show that he has been subjected to conditions that are merely "restrictive and even harsh," as such conditions are simply "part of the penalty that criminal offenders pay *for* their offenses against society." *Rhodes*, 452 U.S. at 347. *See also Wilson* at 349 ("the Constitution does not mandate comfortable prisons"). Rather, a prisoner must show that he has suffered a "serious deprivation of basic human needs," *id.* at 347, such as "essential food, medical care, or sanitation," *Id.* at 348. *See also Wilson*, 501 U.S. at 304 (requiring "the deprivation of a single, identifiable human need such as food, warmth, or exercise"). "The Amendment also imposes [the duty on officials to] provide humane conditions of confinement; prison officials must ensure that inmates receive adequate food, clothing, shelter, and medical care, and must take reasonable measures to guarantee the safety of the inmates." *Farmer*, 511 U.S. at 832 (citations omitted). The Court has also articulated an alternative test inquiring whether an inmate was exposed to "a substantial risk or serious harm." *Id.* at 837. *See also DeSpain v. Uphoff*, 264 F.3d 965, 971 (10th Cir. 2001) ("In order to satisfy the [objective] requirement, the inmate must show that he is incarcerated under conditions posing a substantial risk of serious harm.").

(U) The various conditions of confinement are not to be assessed under a totality of the circumstances approach. In *Wilson v. Seiter*, 501 U.S. 294 (1991), the Supreme Court expressly rejected the contention that "each condition must be considered as part of the overall conditions challenged." *Id.* at 304 (internal quotation marks and citation omitted). Instead the Court concluded that "Some conditions of confinement may establish an Eighth Amendment violation 'in combination' when each would not do so alone, but only when they have a mutually enforcing effect that produces the deprivation of a single identifiable human need such as food, warmth, or exercise – for example, a low cell temperature at night combined with a failure to issue blankets." *Id.* at 304. As the Court further explained, "Nothing so amorphous as 'overall conditions' can rise to the level of cruel and unusual punishment when no specific deprivation of a single human need exists." *Id.* at 305.

(U) To demonstrate deliberate indifference, a prisoner must demonstrate "that the official was subjectively aware of that risk." *Farmer v. Brennan* 511 U.S. 125 (1994). As the Supreme Court further explained:

> We hold . . . that a prison official cannot be found liable under the Eighth Amendment for denying any inmate humane conditions of confinement unless the official knows of and regards an excessive risk to inmate health or safety, the official must both be aware of facts from which the inference can be drawn that a substantial risk of serious harm exists and he must also draw the inference.

Farmer v. Brennan 511 U.S. 825, 837 (1994). This standard requires greater culpability than mere negligence. *See Farmer v. Brennan*, 511 U.S. 825, 837 (1994); *Wilson v. Seiter*, 501 U.S. 294, 302 (1991) ("mere negligence would satisfy neither [the *Whitley* standard of malicious and sadistic infliction] nor the more lenient deliberate indifference standard") (internal quotation marks omitted).

(U) The second line of cases considers the use of force against prisoners. The situation often arises in cases addressing the use of force while quelling prison disturbances. In cases involving the excessive use of force the central question is whether the force was applied in good faith in an attempt to maintain or restore discipline or maliciously and sadistically with the very purpose of causing harm.[43] Malicious and sadistic use of force always violates contemporary standards of decency and would constitute cruel and unusual punishment.[44] The courts apply a subjective test when examining intent of the official. In determining whether a correctional officer has used excessive force in violation of the Eighth Amendment, courts look to several factors including: (1) "the need for the application of force"; (2) "the relationship between the need and the amount of force that was used"; (3) "the extent of injury inflicted"; (4) "the extent of the threat to the safety of staff and inmates, as reasonably perceived by responsible officials on the basis of the facts known to them"; and (5) "any efforts made to temper the severity of a forceful response."[45] Great deference is given to the prison official in the carrying out of his duties.[46]

(U) One of the Supreme Court's most recent opinions on conditions of confinement – *Hope v. Pelzer*, 122 S.Ct. 2508 (2002) – illustrates the Court's focus on the necessity of the actions undertaken in response to a disturbance in determining the officer's subjective state of mind.[47] In *Hope*, following an "exchange of vulgar remarks" between the inmate Hope and an officer, the two got into a "wrestling match." *Id.* at 2512. Additional officers intervened and restrained Hope. *See id.* These officers then took Hope back to prison. Once there, they required him to take off his shirt and then attached him to the hitching post; where the remained in the sun for the next seven hours. *See id.* at 2512–13. During this time, Hope received no bathroom breaks. He was given water only once or twice and at least one guard taunted him about being thirsty. *See id.* at 2513. The Supreme Court concluded that the facts Hope alleged stated an "obvious" Eighth Amendment violation. *Id* at 2514. The obviousness of this violation stemmed from the utter lack of necessity for the actions the guards undertook. The Court emphasized that "any safety concerns" arising from the scuffle between Hope and the officer "had long since abated by the time [Hope] was attached to the hitching post" and that there was a "clear lack of an emergency situation." *Id.* As a result, the Court found that "[t]his punitive treatment amount[ed] to [the] gratuitous infliction of 'wanton and unnecessary' pain that our precedent clearly prohibits." *Id.* at 2515.

---

[43] (U) Actions taken in "good-faith . . . to maintain or restore discipline" do not constitute excessive force. *Whitley v. Albers*, 475 U.S. 312, 320–21 (1986)

[44] (U) *Hudson v. McMillian*, 503 U.S. 1, 9 (1992)

[45] (U) *Whitley* at 321.

[46] (U) *Whitley v. Albers*, 475 U.S. (1986).

[47] (U) Although the officers' actions in Hope were undertaken in response to a scuffle between an inmate and a guard, the case is more properly thought of as a "conditions of confinement" case rather than an "excessive force" case. By examining the officers' actions through the "deliberate indifference standard" the Court analyzed it as a "conditions of confinement" case. The deliberate indifference standard is inapplicable to claims of excessive force.

Thus, the necessity of the governmental action bears upon both the conditions of confinement analysis as well as the excessive force analysis.

(U) In determining whether the government's actions are "wanton and unnecessary," consideration must be given to the government's legitimate interests. In the context of the war on terrorism and the collection of intelligence from detainees regarding future attacks, the legitimate government interest is of the highest magnitude. In the typical conditions of confinement case, the protection of other inmates or officers, the protection of the inmate alleged to have suffered the cruel and unusual punishment, or even the maintenance of order in the prison, provide valid government interests for various deprivations. *See, e.g., Anderson v. Nosser,* 438 F.2d 183, 193 (5th Cir. 1971) ("protect[ing] inmates from self-inflicted injury, protect[ing] the general prison population and personnel from violate acts on his part, [and] prevent[ing] escape" are all legitimate penological interests that would permit the imposition of solitary confinement); *McMahon v. Beard,* 583 F.2d 172, 175 (5th Cir. 1978) (prevention of inmate suicide is a legitimate interest). As with excessive force, no court has encountered the precise circumstances here under conditions of confinement jurisprudence. Nonetheless, there can be no more compelling government interest than that which is presented here and, depending upon the precise factual circumstances of an interrogation, e.g., where there is credible information that the detainee had information that could avert a threat, deprivations that may be caused would not be wanton or unnecessary.

b. Fifth Amendment and Fourteenth Amendment[48]

(U) All persons within the territory of the United States are entitled to the protections of Due Process as provided by the Fifth and Fourteenth Amendments, including corporations, aliens, and presumptively citizens seeking readmission to the United States. However, the Due Process Clause does not apply to enemy alien belligerents engaged in hostilities against the United States and/or tried by military tribunals outside the territorial jurisdiction of the United States.[49] The *Eisentrager* doctrine works to prevent access by enemy belligerents, captured and held abroad, to U.S. courts. Further, in *United States v. Verdugo-Urquidez,* 494 U.S. 259 (1990), the Supreme Court held that aliens outside the United States did not have Fourth Amendment rights against the U.S. government. Indeed, in that case, the Court observed that extension of constitutional rights to aliens outside of the United States would interfere with the military operations against the nation's enemies.

(U) In the detainee context, the standards of the Due Process Clauses are relevant due to the U.S. Reservation to the Torture Convention's definition of cruel, inhuman, and degrading treatment, which the United States has defined to mean conduct prohibited under the Due Process Clause of the Fifth and Fourteenth Amendments (in addition to the standards under the Eighth Amendment discussed above). The Due Process jurisprudence is divided into two distinct categories – procedural due process and substantive due process. Procedural due process is manifest in issues pertaining to the provision of adequate administrative and/or judicial process, including notice and an opportunity to be heard. Substantive due process involves questions of force being

---

[48] (U) Because the Due Process considerations under the Fifth and Fourteenth amendments are the same for our purposes, this analysis considers them together.

[49] (U) *Johnson v. Eisentrager,* 339 U.S. 763 (1950); *In re Yamashita,* 327 U.S. 1 (1946).

excessive in light of the government interest being addressed. In the detainee context, the limits of substantive due process define the scope of permissible interrogation techniques that may be applied to unlawful combatants held outside the United States.

(U) Under the Fifth Amendment right to Due Process, substantive due process protects an individual from "the exercise of power without any reasonable justification in the service of any legitimate governmental objective." *County of Sacramento v. Lewis*, 523 U.S. 833, 846 (1998). Under substantive due process "only the most egregious official conduct can be said to be arbitrary in the constitutional sense." *Id* at 846 (internal quotation marks omitted). That conduct must "shock the conscience." *See generally id; Rochin v. California*, 342 U.S. 165 (1952).[50] By contrast to deprivations in procedural due process, which cannot occur so long as the government affords adequate processes, government actions that "shock the conscience" are prohibited irrespective of the procedures the government may employ in undertaking those actions. *See generally Rochin v. California*, 342 U.S. 164 (1952).

(U) To shock the conscience, the conduct at issue must involve more than mere negligence by the government official. *See County of Sacramento*, 523 U.S. at 849. *See also Daniel v. Williams*, 474 U.S. 327 (1986) ("Historically, this guarantee of due process has been applied to *deliberate* decisions of government officials to deprive a person of life, liberty, or property.") (collecting cases). Instead, "[I]t is . . . behavior on the other end of the culpability spectrum that would most probably support a substantive due process claim: conduct intended to injure in some way unjustifiable by any government interest is the sort of official action most likely to rise to the conscience-shocking level." *See County of Sacramento*, 523 U.S. at 849. In some circumstances, however, recklessness or gross negligence may suffice. *See id.* The requisite level of culpability is ultimately "not . . . subject to mechanical application in unfamiliar territory." *Id.* at 850. As the Court explained: "Deliberate indifference that shocks in one environment may not be so patently egregious in another, and our concern with preserving the constitutional proportions of substantive due process demands an exact analysis of circumstances before any abuse of power is condemned as conscience shocking." *Id.* As a general matter, deliberate indifference would be an appropriate standard where there is a real possibility for actual deliberation. In other circumstances, however, where quick decisions must be made (such as responding to a prison riot), a heightened level of culpability is more appropriate. *See id.* at 851–52.

(U) The shock-the-conscience standard appears to be an evolving one as the Court's most recent opinion regarding this standard emphasized that the conscience shocked was the "*contemporary* conscience." *Id.* at 847 n.8 (emphasis added). The court explained that while a judgment of what shocks the conscience "may be informed by a history of liberty protection, it necessarily reflects a traditional understanding of

---

[50] (U) In the seminal case of *Rochin v California*, 342 U.S. 165 (1952), the police had some information that the defendant was selling drugs. Three officers went to and entered the defendant's home without a warrant and forced open the door to defendant's bedroom. Upon opening the door, the officers saw two pills and asked the defendant about them. The defendant promptly put them in his mouth. The officers "jumped upon him and attempted to extract the capsules." *Id.* at 166. The police tried to pull the pills out of his mouth but despite considerable struggle the defendant swallowed them. The police then took the defendant to a hospital where a doctor forced an ermetic solution into the defendant's stomach by sticking a tube down his throat and into his stomach, which cause the defendant to vomit up the pills. The pills did in fact contain morphine. *See id.* The Court found that the actions of the police officers "shocked the conscience" and therefore violated Rochin's due process rights. *Id* at 170.

executive behavior, of contemporary practice, and of the standards of blame generally applied to them." *Id.* Despite the evolving nature of the standard, the standard is objective rather than subjective. The Supreme Court has cautioned that although "the gloss has ... has not been fixed" as to what substantive due process is, judges "may not drawn on [their] merely personal and private notions and disregard the limits that bind judges in their judicial function ... [T]hese limits are derived from considerations that are fused in the whole nature of our judicial process." *Rochin*, 342 U.S. at 170. *See also, United States v. Lovasco*, 431 U.S. 783 (1973) (reaffirming that the test is objective rather than subjective). As the Court further explained, the conduct at issue must "do more than offend some fastidious squeamishness or private sentimentalism' in order to violate due process. *Rochin*, 342 U.S. at 172.

(U) The Supreme Court also clarified in *Ingraham v. Wright*, 430 U.S. 651 (1977), that under substantive due process, "[t]there is, of course, a *de minimis* level of imposition with which the Constitution is not concerned." *Id.* at 674. And as Fourth Circuit has noted, it is a "principle ... inherent in the Eighth [Amendment] and [substantive due process" that "[n]ot ... every malevolent touch by a prison guard gives rise to a federal cause of action. *See Johnson v. Glick*, 481 F.2d at 1033 ("Not every push or shove, even if it may later seem unnecessary in the peace of a judge's chambers, violates a prisoner's constitutional rights")." *Riley v. Dorton*, 115 F.3d 1159, 1167 (4th Cir. 1997) (quoting *Hudson*, 503 U.S. at 9). Instead, "the [shock-the-conscience] ... inquiry. ... [is] whether the force applied caused injury so severe, and was so disproportionate to the need presented and so inspired by malice or sadism ... that it amounted to a brutal and inhumane abuse of official power literally shocking to the conscience." *Webb v. McCullough*, 828 F.2d 1151, 1158 (6th Cir. 1987). Examples of physical brutality that "shock the conscience" include: the rape of a plaintiff by uniformed officer, see *Jones v. Wellham*, 104 F.3d 620 (4th Cir. 1997); a police officer striking a plaintiff in retaliation for the plaintiff photographing the police officer, see *Shillinford v. Holmes*, 634 F.2d 263 (5th Cir. 1981); police officer shot a fleeing suspect's legs without any probable cause other than the suspect's running and failing to stop, see *Aldridge v. Mullins*, 377 F. Supp. 850 (M.D. Tenn. 1972) *aff'd*, 474 1189 (6th Cir. 1973). Moreover, beating or sufficiently threatening someone during the course of an interrogation can constitute conscience-shocking behavior. See *Gray v. Spillman*, 925 F.2d 90, 91 (4th Cir. 1991) (plaintiff was beaten and threatened with further beating if he did not confess). By contrast, for example, actions such as verbal insults and an angry slap of "medium force" did not constitute behavior that "shocked the conscience." *See Riley v. Dorton*, 115 F.3d 1159, 1168 n.4 (4th Cir. 1997) (finding claims that such behavior shocked the conscience "meritless").

(U) Physical brutality is not the only conduct that may meet the shock-the-conscience standard. In *Cooper v. Dupnik*, 963 F.2d 1220 (9th Cir. 1992) (en banc), the Ninth circuit held that certain psychologically-coercive interrogation techniques could constitute a violation of substantive due process. The interrogators techniques were "designed to instill stress, hopelessness, and fear, and to break [the suspect's] resistance." *Id.* at 1229. The officers planned to ignore any request for a lawyer and to ignore the suspect's right to remain silent, with the express purpose that any statements he might offer would help keep him from testifying in his own defense. *See id.* at 1249. It was this express purpose that the court found to be the "aggravating factor" that lead it to conclude that the conduct of the police "shocked the conscience." *Id.* at 1249. The court reasoned that while "it is a legitimate purpose of police investigation to gather evidence and muster information that will surround a guilty defendant and make it difficult if not impossible for him to escape justice[,]" "when the methods chosen to gather evidence and information are deliberately unlawful and flout the Constitution, the legitimacy is lost." *Id.* at 1250. In *Wilkins v. May*, 872 F.2d 190 (7th Cir. 1989), the Seventh Circuit found that severe mental distress inflicted on a suspect could be a basis for a substantive due process claim. *See id.* at 195. *See also Rhodes v. Robinson*, 612 F.2d 766, 771 (3d Cir. 1979) (claim of emotional harm could be the basis of a substantive due process claim). The *Wilkins* court found that under certain circumstances interrogating a suspect with a gun at his head could violate those rights. *See* 872 F.2d at 195. Whether it would rise to the level of violation depended upon whether the plaintiff was able to show "misconduct that a reasonable person would find so beyond the norm of proper police procedure as to shock the conscience, and that it is calculated to induce not merely momentary fear or anxiety, but severe mental suffering, in the plaintiff." *Id.* On the other hand, we note that merely deceiving the suspect does not shock the conscience, see, e.g., *United States v. Byram*, 145 F.3d 405 (1st Cir. 1998) (assuring defendant he was not in danger of prosecution did not shock the conscience) nor does the use of sympathy or friends as intermediaries, see, e.g., *United States v. Simtob*, 901 F.2d 799, 809 (9th Cir. 1990).

(U) Although substantive due process jurisprudence is not necessarily uniform in all applications, several principles emerge. First, whether conduct is conscience-shocking turns in part on whether it is without any justification, i.e., it is "inspired by malice or sadism." *Webb*, 828 F.2d at 1158. Although unlawful combatants may not pose a threat to others in the classic sense seen in substantive due process cases, the detainees here may be able to prevent great physical injury to countless others through their knowledge of future attacks. By contrast, if the interrogation methods were undertaken solely to produce severe mental suffering, they might shock the conscience. Second, the official must have acted with more than mere negligence. Because, generally speaking, there will be time for deliberation as to the methods of interrogation that will be employed, it is likely that the culpability requirement here is deliberate indifference. *See County of Sacramento*, 523 U.S. at 851–52. Thus, an official must know of a serious risk to the health or safety of a detainee and he must act in conscious disregard for that risk in order to violate due process standards. Third, this standard permits some physical contact. Employing a shove or slap as part of an interrogation would not run afoul of this standard. Fourth, the detainee must sustain some sort of injury as a result of the conduct, e.g., physical injury or severe mental distress, in order for the constraints of substantive due process to be applicable.

D. Jurisdiction of Federal Courts

1. Jurisdiction to Consider Constitutional Claims

(U) The federal habeas statute provides that courts may only grant the writ "within their respective jurisdictions." This has been interpreted to limit a court's subject matter jurisdiction over habeas cases to those in which a custodian lies within the jurisdiction. For U.S. citizens, habeas jurisdiction lies regardless of where the detention occurs. The habeas action must be brought in the district in which a custodian resides or, if all custodians are outside the United States, in the District of Columbia.

For aliens, there is no habeas jurisdiction outside the sovereign territory of the United States.[51]

(U) As construed by the courts, habeas jurisdiction is coterminous with the reach of constitutional rights, although that result is a matter of statutory construction. Congress has the power to extend habeas jurisdiction beyond the reach of constitutional rights but may not place greater restrictions on it.

(U) In *Johnson v. Eisentrager*, the Supreme Court ruled that enemy aliens, captured on the field of battle abroad by the U.S. Armed Forces, tried abroad for war crimes, and incarcerated abroad do not have access to the U.S. courts[52] over a habeas petition filed by German nationals seized by U.S. soldiers in China. *Eisentrager* considered habeas corpus petitions by German soldiers captured during WWII in China supporting the Japanese, convicted by Military Commission sitting in China, and incarcerated in Germany and concluded that United States courts lacked jurisdiction.[53]

(U) Recently, unlawful combatants detained at Guantanamo Bay, Cuba (GTMO) have sought review in U.S. district court through the writ of habeas corpus, 28 U.S.C. § 2241.[54]

(U) Two courts have examined, and rejected, petitioners' claims that U.S. exclusive jurisdiction over GTMO results in a form of "de facto sovereignty" and, therefore, vests habeas jurisdiction in the federal courts.

2. Other Bases for Federal Jurisdiction

(U) In addition, one group of GTMO detainees has challenged conditions of confinement through the Alien Tort Claims Act (ATCA) and the Administrative Procedures Act (APA). The courts have declined to exercise jurisdiction on those theories in each case to date. Petitioners in *Al Odah* attempted to circumvent the territorial limitations of habeas by bringing their action under the APA and ATCA, however the U.S. Court of Appeals for the District of Columbia held that the courts did not have jurisdiction with respect to the petitioners' claims under any theory, finding that their status as aliens unconnected to the United States makes them beyond the jurisdiction of the federal courts. *See Odah v. United States*, 321 F.3rd 1134 (DC Cir. 2003).[55]

(U) The court also held, in the alternative, that it lacked jurisdiction even if petitioners were not barred by the exclusive nature of habeas actions. The ATCA provides

---

[51] (U) *Johnson v. Eisentrager*, 339 U.S. 763 (1950).

[52] (U) *Johnson v. Eisentrager*, 339 U.S. 763, 777 (1950). "We are here confronted with a decision whose basic premise is that these prisoners are entitled, as a constitutional right, to sue in some court of the United States for a writ of habeas corpus. To support that assumption we must hold that a prisoner of our military authorities is constitutionally entitled to the writ, even though he (a) is an enemy alien; (b) has never been or resided in the United States; (c) was captured outside of our territory and there held in military custody as a prisoner of war; (d) was tried and convicted by a Military Commission sitting outside the United States; (e) for offenses against laws of war committed outside the United States; (f) and is at all times imprisoned outside the United States." With those words, the Supreme Court held that: "a non-resident enemy alien has no access to our courts in wartime."

[53] (U) For a fuller discussion of Habeas Corpus law as it applies to Naval Base, Guantanamo Bay, *see* memorandum, LCDR F. Greg Bowman of 29 Jan 02, subj: CRIMINAL JURISDICTION AND ITS EFFECTS OF AVAILABILITY OF THE WRIT OF HABEAS CORPUS AT U.S. NAVAL BASE, GUANTANAMO BAY, CUBA (on file).

[54] (U) *Coalition of Clergy v. Bush*, 189 F. Supp. 2d 1036 (C.D. Cal.), affirmed in part and vacated in part, 310 F.3d 1153 (9th Cir. 2002); *Rasul v. Bush*, 215 F.2d 55 (D.D.C. 2002).

[55] (U) The concurring opinion in *Odah* argued that, in addition to not providing a means of jurisdiction, the ACTA also did not provide an independent cause of action.

the "district courts shall have original jurisdiction of any civil action by an alien for a tort only, committed in violation of the law of nations or a treaty of the United States." 18 U.S.C. § 1350. The ATCA, although it provides federal jurisdiction over private suits, does not waive sovereign immunity for a suit against the United States. The courts have held that the APA's waiver of sovereign immunity for non-monetary damages can theoretically be used to maintain an ATCA action against the United States. The *Al Odah* Court, however, found that the APA's exemption for "military authority exercised in the field in time of war or in occupied territory" precluded the ATCA.

3. The Military Extraterritorial Jurisdiction Act

(U) The Military Extraterritorial Jurisdiction Act (MEJA), 18 U.S.C. § 3261 *et seq*, extends Federal criminal jurisdiction for serious Federal offenses committed outside the United States to civilian persons accompanying the Armed Forces (e.g., civilian employees and contractor employees), and to members of the Armed Forces who committed a criminal act while subject to the UCMJ but who are no longer subject to the UCMJ or who committed the offense with a defendant not subject to the UCMJ. The standard is that if the conduct by the individual would "constitute an offense punishable by imprisonment for more than one year *if the conduct had been engaged in within the special maritime and territorial jurisdiction of the United States.*" (emphasis added).

E. The Uniform Code of Military Justice

(U) The Uniform Code of Military Justice (UCMJ) applies to United States Forces on active duty, at all times and in all places throughout the world. Members of the Reserve component and retired regular officers can, under certain circumstances, also be subject to the UCMJ, as can civilians accompanying the Armed Forces in time of war under certain circumstances.[56]

1. Offenses

(U) A number of UCMJ provisions potentially apply to service members involved in the interrogation and supervision of the interrogation of detainees. Most significant are the following:[57]

a. Cruelty, Oppression or Maltreatment, Art 93

(U) The elements of the offense are that the alleged victim was subject to the orders of the accused and that the accused was cruel toward, oppressed, or maltreated the victim. The cruelty, etc. need not be physical. Subject to the orders of, includes persons, subject to the UCMJ or not, who are by some reason of some duty required to obey the lawful orders of the accused, even if not in the direct chain of command of the accused. "Cruel," "oppressed," and "maltreated" refer to unwarranted, harmful, abusive, rough or other unjustifiable treatment that, under all the circumstances, results in physical or mental pain or suffering and is unwarranted, unjustified and

---

[56] (U) Article 2 UCMJ; Rules for Courts-Martial, Rule 202, and Discussion.

[57] (U) The following are extracted from the Department of the Army Pamphlet 27-9, Military Judges' Benchbook (MJB), which summarizes the requirements of the Manual For Courts-Martial (MCM) and case law applicable to trials by courts martial.

unnecessary for any lawful purpose. It is measured by an objective standard. MCM IV-25; MJB, Section 3-17-1.

b. Reckless Endangerment, Art 134

(U) The elements of the offense are that the accused engaged in wrongful conduct that was reckless or wanton and that the conduct was likely to produce death or grievous bodily harm. "[L]ikely to produce" means the natural or probable consequences of particular conduct. "[G]rievous bodily harm" includes injuries comparable to fractured or dislocated bones, serious damage to internal organs. MCM IV-119; MJB, Section 3-100A-1.

c. Assault, Art 128

(U) This article encompasses the following offenses:

(U) Simple assault – The elements are that the accused attempted or offered to do bodily harm to an individual and that such attempt or offer was done with unlawful force and violence. An act of force or violence is unlawful if done without legal justification or excuse and without the consent of the victim. The use of threatening words accompanied by a menacing act or gesture may constitute an assault. MCM IV-81; MJB, Section 3-54-1.

(U) Assault consummated by a battery – An assault resulting in actual infliction of bodily harm is a battery. Bodily harm means any physical injury to or offensive touching, however slight. MCM IV-83; MJB, Section 3-54-1A

(U) Aggravated assault (use of a dangerous weapon, means or force) – In addition to the elements of an assault, this offense requires that the means or force attempted or offered was used in a manner likely to produce death or grievous bodily harm. Any object, regardless of its normal use, could become a means likely to inflict grievous bodily harm depending on the manner in which it is actually used. MCM IV-84; MJB, Section 3-54-8

(U) There are multiple instances in which authority and context permit touching – by police officers, prison guards, training NCOs, etc. – that would not be lawful under other circumstances. A central issue would be how clearly the limits of authority were defined and whether under the circumstances the individual exceeded the scope of that authority.

d. Involuntary Manslaughter, Art 119

(U) The elements of this offense are that acts or omissions constituting culpable negligence resulted in an unlawful killing. Culpable negligence contemplates a level of heedlessness in circumstances in which, when viewed in the light of human experience, might foreseeably result in death. MCM IV-64. Failure to develop and follow reasonable protocols providing for the health and safety of detainees during interrogations of detainees could amount to such culpable negligence. MJB, Section 3-44-2.

e. Unpremeditated Murder, Art 118

(U) The relevant elements of the offense are that the person is dead, his death resulted from the act or failure to act of the accused, that the killing was unlawful, without legal justification, and at that time the accused had the intent to inflict great bodily harm upon the person. MCM IV-118, MJB, Section 3-43-2.

f. Disobedience of Orders, Art 92

(U) This offense is committed when the accused, having a duty to do so, fails to obey lawful orders or regulations. MCM IV-23; MJB, Section 3-16. The duty to obey may extend to treaties and statutes as well as regulations. The Convention against Torture and the general case law regarding cruel and unusual punishment may be relevant here as it is for Article 93. *See generally, Wilson v. Seiter*, 501 U.S. 294 (1991).

g. Dereliction of Duty, Art 92

(U) A dereliction occurs when an individual knew or should have known of certain prescribed duties and either willfully or through neglect was derelict in the performance of those duties, MCM IV-24; MJB, Section 3-16-4. Customs of the service as well as statutes and treaties that have become the law of the land may create duties for purposes of this Article.

h. Maiming, Art 124

(U) The elements of this offense are that the accused intentionally inflicted an injury on a person, and whether intended or not, that the injury seriously disfigured the person's body, destroyed or disabled an organ or member, or seriously diminished the person's physical vigor. MCM IV-77; MJB, Section 3-50-1.

2. Affirmative Defenses under the UCMJ (R.C.M. 916)

(U) In order for any use of force to be lawful, it must either be justified under the circumstances or an accepted affirmative defense is present to excuse the otherwise unlawful conduct. No case law was found that defines at what point force or violence becomes either lawful or unlawful during war. Each case is by its nature, dependent upon the factual circumstances surrounding the incident.

(U) Applying accepted rules for the law of armed conflict, the use of force is only authorized when there is a military purpose and the force used is no greater than necessary to achieve the objective. The existence of war does not in and of itself justify all forms of assault. For instance, in *United States v. Calley*, 22 U.S.C.M.A. 534, 48 C.M.R.19 (1973), the court recognized that "while it is lawful to kill an enemy in the heat and exercise of war, to kill such an enemy after he has laid down his arms . . . is murder." Further, the fact that the law of war has been violated pursuant to an order of a superior authority, whether military or civil, does not deprive the act in question of its character of a war crime, nor does it constitute a defense in the trial of an accused individual, unless he did not know and could not reasonably have been expected to know that the act ordered was unlawful. In all cases where the order is held not to constitute a defense to an allegation of war crime, the fact that the individual was acting pursuant to orders may be considered in mitigation of punishment. The thrust of these holdings is that even in war, limits to the use and extent of force apply.

a. Self-Defense

(U) For the right of self-defense to exist, the accused must have had a reasonable apprehension that death or grievous bodily harm was about to be inflicted on himself. The test is whether, under the same facts and circumstances, an ordinary prudent adult person faced with the same situation would have believed that there were grounds to fear immediate death or serious bodily harm (an objective test) and the person must have actually believed that the amount of force used was required to protect against death or serious bodily harm (a subjective test). Grievous bodily harm means serious bodily injury. It does not mean minor injuries such as a black eye or a bloody nose, but does mean fractured or dislocated bones, deep cuts, torn members of the body, serious damage to internal organs, or other serious bodily injuries. MJB, Section 5-2. (See also the discussion of "Self-Defense" under the discussion of Federal law, *supra*.)

b. Defense of Another

(U) For this defense, the accused must have had a reasonable belief that harm was about to be inflicted and that the accused actually believed that force was necessary to protect that person. The accused must actually believe that the amount of force used was necessary to protect against the degree of harm threatened. MJB, Section 5-3-1.

c. Accident

(U) This defense arises when an accused is doing a lawful act in a lawful manner, free of any negligence, and unforeseeable or unintentional death or bodily harm occurs. MJB, Section 5-4.

d. Mistake of Fact

(U) If ignorance or mistake of a fact concerns an element of an offense involving specific intent, the ignorance or mistake need only exist in the mind of the accused, i.e., if the circumstances of an event were as the accused believed, there would be no offense. For crimes not involving specific intent, the ignorance or mistake must be both honest (actual) and reasonable. The majority of the crimes discussed above do not require specific intent. For instance, in the case of violations of general orders, knowledge is presumed. Most of the "mistakes" would likely be mistakes of law in that the accused would not believe that the conduct was unlawful. While mistakes of law are generally not a defense, unawareness of a law may be a defense to show the absence of a criminal state of mind when actual knowledge is not necessary to establish the offense. MJB, Section 5-11.

e. Coercion or duress

(U) It is a defense to any offense except killing an innocent person that the accused's participation in the offense was caused by a reasonable apprehension that the accused or another innocent person would be immediately killed or would immediately suffer serious bodily injury if the accused did not commit the act. This apprehension must reasonably continue throughout the commission of the act. If the accused has any reasonable opportunity to avoid committing the act without subjecting the accused or another innocent person to the harm threatened, this defense shall not apply. R.C.M. 916(h), MJB, Section 5-5.

(U) To establish a duress defense it must be shown that an accused's participation in the offense was caused by a reasonable apprehension that the accused or another innocent person would be immediately killed or would immediately suffer serious bodily harm if the accused did not commit the act. The apprehension must reasonably continue throughout the commission of the act. If the accused has any reasonable opportunity to avoid committing the act without subjecting the accused or another innocent person to the harm threatened, this defense shall not apply. The Court of Appeals stated in *United States v. Fleming*, 23 C.M.R. 7 (1957), that the defense of duress is available to an accused only if his commission of the crime charged resulted from reasonable fear of imminent death or grievous bodily harm to himself or his family. The risk of injury must continue throughout the criminal venture.

f. Obedience to Orders (MJB, Sections 5-8-1 and 5-8-2)

(U) The viability of obedience to orders as a defense turns on the directives and policy of the service member's Chain of Command. For example, when the interrogator at the direction of the command employs the use of physical force as an interrogation method, he/she would certainly raise the defense of obedience to orders. The question then becomes one of degree. While this may be a successful defense to simple assaults or batteries, it would unlikely be as successful to more serious charges such as maiming and manslaughter. Within the middle of the spectrum lay those offenses for which the effectiveness of this defense becomes less clear. Those offenses would include conduct unbecoming an officer, reckless endangerment, cruelty, and negligent homicide.

(U) Obedience to orders provides a viable defense only to the extent that the accused acted under orders, and did not know (nor would a person of ordinary sense have known), the orders were unlawful. Thus, the viability of this defense is keyed to the accused's (or a reasonable person's) knowledge of the lawfulness of the order. Common sense suggests that the more aggressive and physical the technique authorized (ordered) by the command, the more unlikely the reasonable belief that the order to employ such methods is lawful.

(U) In order for any use of force to be lawful, it must either (i) be justified under the circumstances or (ii) an accepted affirmative defense is present to excuse the otherwise unlawful conduct. No case law was found that defines at what point force or violence becomes either lawful or unlawful during war. Each case is by its nature, dependent upon the factual circumstances surrounding the incident.

(U) Applying accepted rules for the law of armed conflict, the use of force is only authorized when there is a military purpose and the force used is no greater than necessary to achieve the objective. The existence of war does not in and of itself justify all forms of assault. For instance, in *US v. Calley*, the court recognized that "while it is lawful to kill an enemy "in the heat and exercise of war, to kill such an enemy after he has laid down his arms . . . is murder." Further, the fact that the law of war has been violated pursuant to an order of a superior authority, whether military or civil, does not deprive the act in question of its character of a war crime, nor does it constitute a defense in the trial of an accused individual, unless he did not know and could not reasonably have been expected to know that the act ordered was unlawful. In all cases where the order is held not to constitute a defense to an allegation of war crime, the fact that the individual was acting pursuant to orders may be considered in mitigation of punishment." The thrust of these holdings is that even in war, limits to the use and extent of force apply.

g. Necessity

(U) Another common law affirmative defense is one of necessity. This defense is recognized by a number of states and is applicable when: 1) the harm must be committed under the pressure of physical or natural force, rather than human force; 2) the harm sought to be avoided is greater than (or at least equal to) that harm sought to be prevented by the law defining the offense charged; 3) the actor reasonably believes at the moment that his act is necessary and is designed to avoid the greater harm; 4) the actor must be without fault in bringing about the situation; and 5) the harm threatened must be imminent, leaving no alternative by which to avoid the greater harm.

(U) However, military courts have treated the necessity defense with disfavor, and in fact, some have refused to accept necessity as a permissible defense (the MCM does not list necessity as an affirmative defense under RCM 916). "The problem with the necessity defense is that it involves a weighing of evil inflicted against evil avoided and is, thereby, difficult to legislate." The courts also have been reluctant to embrace the defense due to a "fear that private moral codes will be substituted for legislative determination, resulting in a necessity exception that swallows the rule of law." *United States v. Rankins*, 34 MJ 326 (CMA 1992).

(U) The effect of these cases is that the MCM recognizes that an accused may commit an illegal act in order to avoid the serious injury or death of the accused or an innocent person. However, military law limits this defense only when there is an imminent and continuing harm that requires immediate action to prevent. Once the immediacy is gone, the defense will no longer apply. Ostensibly, the use of force to acquire information from an unlawful combatant, absent immediate and compelling circumstances, will not meet the elements established by the MCM and case law. (But see the necessity defense in the discussion of Federal law, *supra.*)

3. Legal doctrines could render specific conduct, otherwise criminal, *not* unlawful

See discussion of Commander-in-Chief Authority, *supra.*

IV. Considerations Affecting Policy

A. Historical Role of U.S. Armed Forces

1. Background

(U) The basic principles of interrogation doctrine, procedures, and techniques applicable to Army intelligence interrogations from June 1945 through May 1987 were contained in Field Manual (FM) 30-15, Examination of Personnel and Documents. FM 30-15 set forth Army doctrine pertaining to the basic principles of intelligence interrogations and established the procedures and techniques applicable to Army intelligence interrogations of non-U.S. personnel. The other Services report that they too apply the provisions of this Field Manual.

2. Interrogation Historical Overview

(U) FM 30-15 stated that the principles and techniques of interrogation discussed within the manual are to be used within the constraints established by humanitarian international law and the Uniform Code of Military Justice ("UCMJ"). The fundamental principle underlying Army doctrine concerning intelligence interrogations between 1945 and the issuance of current doctrine in 1987 (FM 34-52), is that the commander may utilize all available resources and lawful means in the accomplishment of his mission and for the protection and security of his unit. However, a strong caveat to this principle noted, "treaty commitments and policy of the United States, international agreements, international law, and the UCMJ require the conduct of military to conform with the law of war." FM 30-15 also recognized that Army intelligence interrogations must conform to the "specific prohibitions, limitations, and restrictions established by the Geneva Conventions of 12 August 1949 for the handling and treatment of personnel captured or detained by military forces" (citing FM 27-10, The Law of Land Warfare).

(U) FM 30-15 also stated that "violations of the customary and treaty law applicable to the conduct of war normally constitute a concurrent violation of the Uniform Code of Military Justice and will be prosecuted under that code." The manual advised Army personnel that it was "the direct responsibility of the Commander to insure that the law of war is respected in the conduct of warfare by forces in his command." Thus, the intelligence interrogation techniques outlined in FM 30-15 were based upon conduct sanctioned under international law and domestic U.S. law and as constrained within the UCMJ.

(U) Historically, the intelligence staff officer (G2/S2) was the primary Army staff officer responsible for all intelligence functions within the command structure. This responsibility included interrogation of enemy prisoners of war (EPW), civilian internees, and other captured or detained persons. In conducting interrogations, the intelligence staff officer was responsible for insuring that these activities were executed in accordance with international and domestic U.S. law, United States Government policy, and the applicable regulations and field manuals regarding the treatment and handling of EPWs, civilian internees, and other captured or detained persons. In the maintenance of interrogation collection, the intelligence staff officer was required to provide guidance and training to interrogators, assign collection requirements, promulgate regulations, directives, and field manuals regarding intelligence interrogation, and insure that interrogators were trained in international and domestic U.S. law and the applicable Army publications.

(U) FM 30-15 stated that intelligence interrogations are an art involving the questioning and examination of a source in order to obtain the maximum amount of usable information. Interrogations are of many types, such as the interview, a debriefing, and an elicitation. However, the FM made clear that the principles of objective, initiative, accuracy, prohibitions against the use of force, and security apply to all types of interrogations. The manual indicated that the goal is to collect usable and reliable information, in a lawful manner, promptly, while meeting the intelligence requirements of the command.

(U) FM 30-15 emphasized a prohibition on the use of force during interrogations. This prohibition included the actual use of force, mental torture, threats, and exposure to inhumane treatment of any kind. Interrogation doctrine, procedures, and techniques concerning the use of force are based upon prohibitions in international and domestic U.S. law. FM 30-15 stated that experience revealed that the use of force was unnecessary to gain cooperation and was a poor interrogation technique, given that its use produced unreliable information, damaged future interrogations, and induced those being interrogated to offer information viewed as expected in order to prevent the use of force. However, FM 30-15 stated that the prohibition on the use of force, mental or physical, must not be confused with the use of psychological tools and deception techniques designed to induce a source into providing intelligence information.

(U) The Center for Military History has been requested to conduct a search of government databases, to include the Investigative Records Repository, for documentation concerning the historical participation of the U.S. Armed Forces in interrogations and any archival materials related to interrogation techniques. As of the writing of this analysis, no reply has been received.

3. Current Doctrine

(U) In May 1987, the basic principles of current doctrine, procedures, and techniques applicable to Army intelligence interrogations were promulgated in Field Manual (FM) 34-52, Intelligence Interrogation. FM 34-52 provides general guidance for commanders, staff officers, and other personnel in the use of interrogation elements in Army intelligence units. It also outlines procedures for handling sources of interrogations, the exploitation and processing of documents, and the reporting of intelligence gained through interrogation. Finally, FM 34-52 covers directing and supervising interrogation operations, conflict scenarios, and their impact on interrogation operations, to include peacetime interrogation operations.

(U) Army interrogation doctrine today, and since 1945, places particular emphasis on the humane handling of captured personnel. Interrogators receive specific instruction by Army Judge Advocates on the requirements of international and domestic US law, to include constraints established by the Uniform Code of Military Justice (e.g. assault, cruelty and maltreatment, and communicating a threat).

(U) FM 34-52 adopted the principles and framework for conducting intelligence interrogations as stated in FM 30-15. FM 34-52 maintained the established Army doctrine that intelligence interrogations involved the art of questioning and examining a source in order to obtain the maximum amount of useable information. FM 34-52 also reiterated Army doctrine that the principles of objective, initiative, accuracy, prohibition on the use of force, and security apply to all types of interrogations. The goal of intelligence interrogation under current doctrine is the same, the collection of usable and reliable information promptly and in a lawful manner, while meeting the intelligence requirements of the command.

(U) FM 34-52 and the curriculum at U.S. Army Intelligence Center, Fort Huachuca, continue to emphasize a prohibition on the use of force. As stated in its predecessor, FM 34-52 defines the use of force to include actual force, mental torture, threats, and exposure to inhumane treatment of any kind. The underlying basis for this prohibition is the proscriptions contained in international and domestic U.S. law. Current Army intelligence interrogation doctrine continues to view the use of force as unnecessary to gain the cooperation of captured personnel. Army interrogation experts view the use of force as an inferior technique that yields information of questionable quality. The primary concerns, in addition to the effect on information quality, are the adverse effect on future interrogations and the behavioral change on those being interrogated (offering particular information to avoid the use of force). However, the Army's doctrinal prohibition on the use of force does not proscribe legitimate psychological tools and deception techniques.

(U) FM 34-52 outlines procedures and approach techniques for conducting Army interrogations. While the approach techniques are varied, there are three common purposes: establish and maintain control over the source and the interrogation, establish and maintain rapport between the interrogator and the source, and manipulate the source's emotions and weaknesses to gain willing cooperation. Approved techniques include: Direct, Incentive; Emotional (Love & Hate); Increased Fear Up (Harsh & Mild); Decreased Fear Down; Pride and Ego (Up & Down); Futility Technique; We Know All; Establish Your Identity; Repetition; File and Dossier; and Mutt and Jeff (Friend & Foe). These techniques are discussed at greater length in Section V, *infra*.

B. Presidential and Secretary of Defense Directives

(U) The President's Military Order that addresses the detention, treatment, and trial of certain non-citizens in the war against terrorism,[58] provides, *inter alia*, that any individual subject to the order be "treated humanely, without any adverse distinction based on race, color, religion, gender, birth, wealth, or any similar criteria; afforded adequate food, drinking water, shelter, clothing, and medical treatment; and allowed the free exercise of religion consistent with the requirements of the detention."

(S/NF) (U) A Department of Defense memorandum[59] to the Chairman of the Joint Chiefs of Staff, with instructions to forward it to the Combatant Commanders, stated that "the United States has determined that al Qaeda and Taliban individuals under the control of the Department of Defense are not entitled to prisoner of war status for the purposes of the Geneva Conventions of 1949." The memorandum further directed that "[t]he Combatant Commanders shall in detaining al Qaeda and Taliban individuals under the control of the Department of Defense treat them humanely and, to the extent appropriate and consistent with military necessity, in a manner consistent with the principles of the Geneva Conventions of 1949."

(S/NF) (U) The President has directed that "[a]s a matter of policy, the United States Armed Forces shall continue to treat detainees humanely and, to the extent appropriate and consistent with military necessity, in a manner consistent with the principles of Geneva."[60]

C. DOD-Specific Policy Considerations

(U) (The information in this section was derived from guidance provided by the Office of the Assistant Secretary of Defense (Special Operations and Low-Intensity Conflict)).

(S/NF) (U) The first priority of any detainee interrogation is to obtain intelligence on imminent or planned terrorist attacks against the United States and its citizens or interests. A clearly related priority is to obtain intelligence to enable the United States to conduct the ongoing war on terrorism effectively. Detainee interrogations have proven instrumental to United States efforts to uncover terrorist cells and thwart planned attacks.

(S/NF) (U) The Secretary of the Army (DoD lead for criminal investigations) will continue to assess, concurrently, the value of information on detainee activities for prosecution considerations. See *War Crimes and Related Investigations Within the US Central Command Area of Operations*, Secretary of Defense, January 19, 2002.

[58] (U) *Military Order – Detention, Treatment, and Trial of Certain Non-Citizens in the War Against Terrorism*, President of the United States, November 13, 2001.
[59] (U) Department of Defense Memorandum – Status of Taliban and al Qaeda, Secretary of Defense, January 19, 2002.
[60] (U) White House Memorandum – Humane Treatment of al Qaeda and Taliban Detainees, President of the United States, February 7, 2002.

(S/NF) (U) In the event of a request to shift the priority of interrogations from intelligence gathering to prosecution considerations, the following factors, among others, should be considered before such a request is approved:

- the nature of the impending threat to national security and to individuals;
- the imminence of the threat;
- the ability of the detainee to provide useful information to eliminate the threat; and
- potential benefit derived from an effective interrogation compared to the potential benefit from a better opportunity for effective prosecution.

(S/NF) (U) For routine interrogations, standard U.S. Armed Forces doctrine will be utilized.

(S/NF) (U) For interrogations involving exceptional techniques[61] approved by the Secretary of Defense, standard doctrine may be used as well as the specifically authorized exceptional techniques. However, such interrogations may be applied only in limited, designated settings approved by SECDEF or his designee, staffed by personnel specifically trained in their use and subject to a command/decision authority at a level specifically designated by the SECDEF for this purpose.

(S/NF) (U) Choice of interrogation techniques involves a risk benefit analysis in each case, bounded by the limits of DOD policy and U.S. law. When assessing whether to use exceptional interrogations techniques, consideration should be given to the possible adverse effects on U.S. Armed Forces culture and self-image, which at times in the past may have suffered due to perceived law of war violations. DOD policy, reflected in the DOD Law of War Program implemented in 1979 and in subsequent directives, greatly restored the culture and self-image of U.S. Armed Forces by establishing high benchmarks of compliance with the principles and spirit of the law of war, and thereby humane treatment of all persons in U.S. Armed Forces' custody.[62] In addition consideration should be given to whether implementation of such exceptional techniques is likely to result in adverse effects on DOD personnel who become POWs, including possible perceptions by other nations that the United States is lowering standards related to the treatment of prisoners, generally.

(S/NF) (U) All interrogation techniques should be implemented deliberately following a documented strategy designed to gain the willing cooperation of the detainee using the least intrusive interrogation techniques and methods.

(S/NF) (U) All interrogations involving exceptional methods approved by the appropriate authority must be applied in the context of a comprehensive plan for their use, singly or in combination with other techniques. At a minimum, the plan should include:

- appropriate approval authority;
- supervisory requirements to insure appropriate application of methods;

---

[61] (U) In this context, an "exceptional" technique is one that is more aggressive than routine techniques and is designated an exceptional technique by the SECDEF, requiring special procedures and levels of approval for use.

[62] *See* DODD 5100.77 DoD Law of War Program, para 5.3.1 (9 Dec 98, canceling DODD 5100.77 of 10 Jul 79); DODD 2310.1 DoD Program for EPOW and Other Detainees, para 3.1 (18 Aug 94); CJCSI 5819.01B Implementation of the DoD LOW Program, para 4a (25 Mar 02).

- specifics on the application of technique(s) including appropriate duration, intervals between applications and events that would require termination of the technique; and
- requirements for the presence or availability (as appropriate) of qualified medical personnel.

(S/NF) (U) Implementation of approved exceptional techniques must be approved at the command authority level specified for the particular method.

D. Potential Effects on Prosecutions

(S/NF) (U) Although the primary purpose of detainee interrogations is obtaining intelligence on imminent or planned terrorist attacks against the United States and its citizens or interests, the United States may later decide to prosecute detainees. This section will discuss whether evidence obtained in interrogations will be admissible in either military commissions or U.S. court proceedings.

(S/NF) (U) The stated objective of detainee interrogations is to obtain information of intelligence value. Information obtained as a result of interrogations may later be used in criminal prosecutions. Depending on the techniques employed, the admissibility of any information may depend on the forum considering the evidence. In addition, the admissibility of an admission or confession necessarily will be fact-specific, in that the exact techniques used with a specific detainee will determine whether the information will be admissible. Although the goal of intelligence interrogation is to produce a willingly cooperative and compliant subject, a successful interrogation nevertheless may produce a statement that might be argued to be involuntary for purposes of criminal proceedings.

(U) Prosecution by the United States is possible in a military commission, court-martial, or in an Article III court.

(S/NF) (U) The standard of admissibility for military commissions is simply whether the evidence has probative value to a reasonable person. *(Military Commissions Order No 1, para 6(D)(1))*. Although this is a fairly low threshold, many of the techniques may place a burden on the prosecution's ability to convince commission members that the evidence meets even that lower standard. As the interrogation methods increase in intensity, the likelihood that the information will be deemed coerced and involuntary and thus held inadmissible increases. Although voluntariness of the confession is not a specific threshold question on admissibility, it can reasonably be expected that the defense will raise voluntariness, challenging the probative value of the information and hence, its admissibility. If the statement is admitted, voluntariness will undoubtedly be a factor considered by the members in determining the weight to be given the information.

(S/NF) (U) Any trials taking place in either U.S. federal courts or by courts-martial will be conducted pursuant to statutory and constitutional standards and limitations. To be admissible, statements made during interrogation must be determined to be voluntary. *Schneckloth v. Bustamonte*, 412 U.S. 218 (1973). The judge must first determine whether the statements were the product of free will, i.e., the defendant's will was not overborne by the interrogators. *Mincey v. Arizona*, 437 U.S. 385 (1978) (the defendant's will was simply overborne and due process of law requires that statements obtained as these were cannot be used in any way against the defendant at his trial). This issue can also be raised before the trier of fact. If the actions taken to secure a statement constitute torture, the statement would be inadmissible. *Brown v. Mississippi*, 297 U.S. 278 (1936) (confessions procured by means "revolting to the sense of justice" could not be used to secure a conviction). It should be noted that conduct does not need to rise to the level of "torture" or "cruel, inhuman and degrading treatment or punishment" for it to cause a statement to be considered involuntary, and therefore inadmissible. As such, the more aggressive the interrogation technique used, the greater the likelihood it could adversely affect the admissibility of any acquired statements or confessions.

(U) Mechanism for Challenge. The defense can be expected to challenge detainee statements through a motion to suppress the detainee statement or to challenge the entire proceeding through a motion to dismiss for egregious prosecutorial misconduct.

(S/NF) (U) Other Considerations. One of the Department of Defense's stated objectives is to use the detainees' statements in support of ongoing and future prosecutions. The method of obtaining these statements and its effect on voluntariness may also affect the usability of these statements against other accused in any criminal forum. Statements produced where the will of the detainee has been overborne will in all likelihood be viewed as inherently suspect and of questionable value.

(S/NF) (U) Consideration must be given to the public's reaction to methods of interrogation that may affect the military commission process. The more coercive the method, the greater the likelihood that the method will be met with significant domestic and international resistance. This in turn may lower international and domestic acceptance of the military commission process as a whole. In addition, the military commission will be faced with balancing the stated objective of open proceedings with the need not to publicize interrogation techniques. Consequently, having these techniques become public or substantially closing the proceedings in order to protect the techniques from disclosure could be counterproductive and could undermine confidence in the outcome. Finally, the timing of the prosecutions must be considered. Revelation of the techniques presumably will reduce their effectiveness against current and future detainees.

E. International Considerations That May Affect Policy Determinations

(U) This section provides a discussion of international law that, although not binding on the United States, could be cited to by other countries to support the proposition that the interrogation techniques used by the U.S. contravene international legal standards. The purpose of providing this international law discussion is to inform the Department of Defense's policy considerations when deciding if, when and how to employ the interrogation techniques against unlawful combatants held outside the United States.

1. Geneva Conventions

(S/NF) (U) To the extent that other nation states do not concede the U.S. position that the Geneva Conventions do not apply to the detainees, there are several provisions of the Third Geneva Convention that may be relevant considerations regarding interrogation techniques.[63] Article 13 requires that POWs must at all times be treated humanely,

---

[63] (U) Geneva Convention Relative to the Treatment of Prisoners of War, opened for signature Aug. 12, 1949, 6 U.S.T. 3316, 75 U.N.T.S. 135.

and that any unlawful act or omission by the detaining power that causes death or seriously endangers the health of a POW will be regarded as a serious breach of the Convention. In addition, POWs must be protected against acts of violence or intimidation. Under Article 14 of the Convention, POWs are entitled to respect for their person and their honor. Article 17 prohibits physical or mental torture and any other form of coercion of POWs in order to secure information. POWs who refuse to answer may not be threatened, insulted, or exposed to unpleasant or disadvantageous treatment. Article 130 provides that torture or inhuman treatment, or willfully causing great suffering or serious injury to body or health of a POW are considered "grave breaches" of the Convention. Article 129 of the Convention requires Parties to search for, extradite or prosecute those persons alleged to have committed, or have ordered to be committed, grave breaches.

(S/NF) (U) These articles of the Third Geneva Convention may provide an opportunity for other States Parties to allege that they consider the United States to be in violation of the Convention through its treatment of detainees. To the extent any such treatment could be considered by them to be torture or inhuman treatment, such acts could be considered "grave breaches" and punishable as war crimes.

(S/NF) (U) In addition, even if they argue that the Taliban and al Qaeda detainees are not entitled to POW status, they may consider that the guarantees contained in Article 75 of the First Additional Protocol to the Geneva Conventions are measures by which the United States' actions could be evaluated. See, *infra*, this Section, paragraph 3. Additional arguments may be made by other nations that the protections of the Geneva Conventions are comprehensive and apply to unlawful combatants.[64]

2. Convention Against Torture

(S/NF) (U) Article 7 of the Torture Convention requires that a State Party either extradite or prosecute a person found within its territory who has been alleged to have committed acts of torture.[65] As discussed, *supra*, the United States implemented this provision in Chapter 113C of Title 18, United States Code, which provides for federal

---

[64] (U) For example, other countries may argue as follows: The central theme of the Geneva Conventions is humanity. With regard to persons affected by armed conflict, Pictet's *Commentary* states: "In short, all the particular cases we have just been considering confirm a general principle which is embodied in all four Geneva Conventions of 1949. Every person in enemy hands must have some status under international law, he is either a prisoner of war, and as such covered by the Third Convention, a civilian covered by the Fourth Convention, or again, a member of the medical personnel of the armed forces who is covered by the First Convention. There is no intermediate status; nobody in enemy hands can be outside the law." Pictet, Commentary to the Fourth Geneva Convention Relative to the Protection of Civilian Persons in Time of War (GC IV), Article 4, Paragraph 4, ICRC, Geneva, 1958. Other nations may disagree with the U.S. government view that GC IV is not applicable to those individuals detained in the war on terrorism and argue that GC IV protects those persons who have engaged in hostile or belligerent conduct but who are not entitled to treatment as prisoners of war. GC IV, Article 4; *see generally* Army Field Manual 27–10, *The Laws of Land Warfare* (1956), paragraphs 246–248. In fact, Pictet's *Commentary* on Article 4, paragraph 4 of GC IV states: "if, for some reason, prisoner of war status – to take one example – were denied to them [persons who find themselves in the hands of a party to the conflict], they would become protected persons under the present Convention." Further GC IV, Article 32 specifically prohibits the torture, corporal punishment, or physical suffering of protected persons. Accordingly, the United States may face the argument from other nations that the President may not place these detainees in an intermediate status, outside the law, and then arguably subject them to torture.
[65] (U) Convention Against Torture and Other Cruel, Inhuman or Degrading Treatment or Punishment, entered into force for the United States on Nov. 20, 1994, 1465 U.N.T.S. 85.

criminal jurisdiction over an extraterritorial act or attempted act of torture, if the alleged offender is present in the United States, regardless of the nationality of the victim or the alleged offender. All States Parties to the Convention are required to establish this same jurisdiction in their countries. Accordingly, governments could potentially assert jurisdiction over U.S. personnel found in their territory, and attempt to prosecute them for conduct they consider to be violations of the Torture Convention.

3. Customary International Law/Views of Other Nations

(U) "Customary international law results from a general and consistent practice of states followed by them from a sense of legal obligation."[66]

(U) The United States' primary obligation concerning torture and other related practices derives from the Convention Against Torture and Other Cruel, Inhuman, and Degrading Treatment and Punishment. Although not consistent with U.S. views, some international commentators maintain that various human rights conventions and declarations (including the Geneva Conventions) represent "customary international law" binding on the United States.[67]

(U) Although not binding on the United States, the following international human rights instruments may inform the views of other nations as they assess the actions of the United States relative to detainees.

(U) One of the first major international declarations on human rights protections was the 1948 Universal Declaration of Human Rights (adopted Dec. 10, 1948, G.A. Res. 217A (III), U.N. Doc. A/810). This Declaration, which is not itself binding or enforceable against the United States, states at Article 5 that "no one shall be subjected to torture or to cruel, inhuman or degrading treatment or punishment." Although there is a specific definition for "torture" in the subsequent 1994 Convention Against Torture, there is no commonly accepted definition in the international community of the terms "cruel, inhuman, and degrading punishment or treatment."

(U) The American Convention on Human Rights[68] was signed by the United States in 1977 but the United States never ratified it. It states in Article 5 that "no one shall be subjected to torture or to cruel, inhuman or degrading punishment or treatment," and that "all persons deprived of their liberty shall be treated with respect for the inherent dignity of the human person."

(U) In 1975, the U. N. General Assembly adopted the Declaration on Protection of All Persons from Being Subjected to Torture and other Cruel, Inhumane or Degrading Punishment (G.A. Res 34/52, U.N. Doc. A/10034). As with previous U. N. declarations, the Declaration itself is not binding on nations. This Declaration provides (Article 2) that the proscribed activities are "an offense to human dignity and shall be condemned as a denial of the purposes of the Charter of the United Nations and as a violation of the human rights and fundamental freedoms proclaimed in the Universal Declaration of Human Rights."

(U) Article 75 of the First Additional Protocol to the Geneva Conventions, to which the U.S. is not a party, prohibits physical and mental torture, outrages upon personal dignity (in particular humiliating and degrading treatment), or threats to commit any of the foregoing against detainees "who do not benefit from more favorable treatment

---

[66] (U) The Restatement (Third) of the Foreign Relations Law of the U.S, § 102(2).
[67] (U) See, e.g., McDougal, Lasswell, and Chen, Human Rights and World Public Order (1980).
[68] (U) 1144 U.N.T.S. 123 (Nov. 22, 1969).

under the [Geneva] Conventions."[69] (The First Additional Protocol does not define any of these terms.) According to International Committee of the Red Cross (ICRC) Commentaries, where the status of a prisoner of war or of a protected person is denied to an individual, the protection of Article 75 must be provided to them at a minimum.[70]

(U) The Geneva Convention Relative to the Protection of Civilian Persons in Time of War provides, *inter alia*, that persons protected by the Civilians Convention are those who, at a given moment and in any manner whatsoever, find themselves in the hands of a Party to the conflict that is a country of which they are not nationals.[71] Such persons are at all times to be treated humanely and protected against all acts of violence or threats thereof. The Department of Justice has determined that this Convention applies only to civilians but does not apply to unlawful combatants.[72]

4. International Criminal Court

(S/NF) (U) The Rome Statute of the International Criminal Court (ICC),[73] which the U. S. has made clear it opposes and to which it has no intention of becoming a party, contains provisions prohibiting the infliction of severe physical or mental pain or suffering (including for such purposes as obtaining information). These violations are considered by the signatories to be war crimes of torture and of inhuman treatment (Article 8) and crimes against humanity (Article 7). The affected persons must be protected under one or more of the Geneva Conventions in order for the prohibition to be applicable. Other governments could take a position contrary to the U.S. position on this point. For those State Parties to the ICC that take the position that the ICC grants universal jurisdiction to detain individuals suspected of committing prohibited acts, if these countries obtain control over U.S. personnel, they may view it as within their jurisdiction to surrender such personnel to the ICC. In an effort to preclude this possibility, the United States is currently negotiating "Article 98" agreements with as many countries as possible to provide for protection of U.S. personnel from surrender to the ICC.[74]

(S/NF) (U) States with whom the United States has not concluded Article 98 agreements, and that perceive certain interrogation techniques to constitute torture or inhuman treatment, may attempt to use the Rome Statute to prosecute individuals found

---

[69] (U) Protocol Additional to the Geneva Convention of 12 August 1949, and relating to the Protection of Victims of International Armed Conflict (Protocol I), June 8, 1977, 1125 U.N.T.S. 3.

[70] (U) Commentary on the Additional Protocols of 8 June 1977 to the Geneva Conventions of 12 August 1949, ICRC, at 863–65 (1987).

[71] (U) Geneva Convention Relative to the Protection of Civilian Persons in Time of War, opened for signature Aug. 12, 1949, 6 U.S.T. 3365, 75 U.N.T.S 287, see Articles 4 and 27.

[72] (U) Other nations, which, unlike the United States, have accepted Article 75, may argue that since the Taliban and al Qaeda detainees are not entitled to POW status under the Geneva Conventions, Article 75 should be applicable as customary international law, notwithstanding their status as unlawful combatants.

[73] (U) Rome Statute of the International Criminal Court, July 17, 1998, U.N. Doc. A/CONF. 183/9 (1998).

[74] (U) Parties to the Rome Statute are obligated to surrender individuals at the request of the ICC for prosecution, unless such surrender would be inconsistent with the requested state's obligations "under an international agreement pursuant to which the consent of the sending state is required to surrender a person of that state to the ICC." (Rome Statute, Article 98 (2)). While the U.S. is not a party to the Rome Statute, Article 98 agreements would provide an exception to an ICC party's general obligation to surrender persons.

in their territory responsible for such interrogations.[75] In such cases, the U.S. Government will reject as illegitimate any attempt by the ICC, or a state on its behalf, to assert the jurisdiction of the Rome Statute over U.S. nationals without the prior express consent of the United States.

V. Techniques

(U) The purpose of all interviews and interrogations is to get the most information from a detainee with the least intrusive method, always applied in a humane and lawful manner with sufficient oversight by trained investigators or interrogators.

Operating instructions must be developed based on command policies to insure uniform, careful, and safe application of any interrogations of detainees.

(S/NF) (U) Interrogations must always be planned, deliberate actions that take into account numerous, often interlocking factors such as a detainee's current and past performance in both detention and interrogation, a detainee's emotional and physical strengths and weaknesses, an assessment of possible approaches that may work on a certain detainee in an effort to gain the trust of the detainee, strengths and weaknesses of interrogators, and augmentation by other personnel for a certain detainee based on other factors.

(S/NF) (U) Interrogation approaches are designed to manipulate the detainee's emotions and weaknesses to gain his willing cooperation. Interrogation operations are never conducted in a vacuum; they are conducted in close cooperation with the units detaining the individuals. The policies established by the detaining units that pertain to searching, silencing, and segregating also play a role in the interrogation of a detainee. Detainee interrogation involves developing a plan tailored to an individual and approved by senior interrogators. Strict adherence to policies/standard operating procedures governing the administration of interrogation techniques and oversight is essential.

(S/NF) (U) Listed below are interrogation techniques all believed to be effective but with varying degrees of utility. Techniques 1–19, 22–26 and 30, applied singly, are purely verbal and/or involve no physical contact that could produce pain or harm and no threat of pain or harm. It is important that interrogators be provided reasonable latitude to vary techniques depending on the detainee's culture, strengths, weaknesses, environment, extent of training in resistance techniques as well as the urgency of obtaining information that the detainee is known to have. Each of the techniques requested or suggested for possible use for detainees by USSOUTHCOM and USCENTCOM is included. Some descriptions include certain limiting parameters; these have been judged appropriate by senior interrogators as to effectiveness.

(S/NF) (U) *While techniques are considered individually within this analysis, it must be understood that in practice, techniques are usually used in combination; the cumulative effect of all techniques to be employed* must *be considered before any decisions are made regarding approval for particular situations.* The title of a particular technique is not always fully descriptive of a particular technique. With respect to the employment of any techniques involving physical contact, stress or that could produce physical

---

[75] (U) Article 25(3) of the Rome Statute provides individual criminal responsibility for a person who, *inter alia*, "orders, solicits, or induces" or otherwise facilitates through aiding, abetting, or assisting in the commission of a crime.

pain or harm, a detailed explanation of that technique must be provided to the decision authority prior to any decision.

Note: Techniques 1–17 are further explained in Field Manual 34–52.

1. (S/NF) (U) **Direct:** Asking straightforward questions.

2. (S/NF) (U) **Incentive/Removal of Incentive:** Providing a reward or removing a privilege, above and beyond those that are required by the Geneva Convention, from detainees, (Privileges above and beyond POW-required privileges).

3. (S/NF) (U) **Emotional Love:** Playing on the love a detainee has for an individual or group.

4. (S/NF) (U) **Emotional Hate:** Playing on the hatred a detainee has for an individual or group.

5. (S/NF) (U) **Fear Up Harsh:** Significantly increasing the fear level in a detainee.

6. (S/NF) (U) **Fear Up Mild:** Moderately increasing the fear level in a detainee.

7. (S/NF) (U) **Reduced Fear:** Reducing the fear level in a detainee.

8. (S/NF) (U) **Pride and Ego Up:** Boosting the ego of a detainee.

9. (S/NF) (U) **Pride and Ego Down:** Attacking or insulting the ego of a detainee, not beyond the limits that would apply to a POW.

10. (S/NF) (U) **Futility:** Invoking the feeling of futility of a detainee.

11. (S/NF) (U) **We Know All:** Convincing the detainee that the interrogator knows the answer to questions he asks the detainee.

12. (S/NF) (U) **Establish Your Identity:** Convincing the detainee that the interrogator has mistaken the detainee for someone else.

13. (S/NF) (U) **Repetition Approach:** Continuously repeating the same question to the detainee within interrogation periods of normal duration.

14. (S/NF) (U) **File and Dossier:** Convincing detainee that the interrogator has a damning and inaccurate file, which must be fixed.

15. (S/NF) (U) **Mutt and Jeff:** A team consisting of a friendly and harsh interrogator. The harsh interrogator might employ the Pride and Ego Down technique.

16. (S/NF) (U) **Rapid Fire:** Questioning in rapid succession without allowing detainee to answer.

17. (S/NF) (U) **Silence:** Staring at the detainee to encourage discomfort.

18. (S/NF) (U) **Change of Scenery Up:** Removing the detainee from the standard interrogation setting (generally to a location more pleasant, but no worse).

19. (S/NF) (U) **Change of Scenery Down:** Removing the detainee from the standard interrogation setting and placing him in a setting that may be less comfortable; would not constitute a substantial change in environmental quality.

20. (S/NF) (U) **Hooding:** This technique is questioning the detainee with a blindfold in place. For interrogation purposes, the blindfold is not on other than during interrogation.

21. (S/NF) (U) **Mild Physical Contact:** Lightly touching a detainee or lightly poking the detainee in a completely non-injurious manner. This also includes

softly grabbing of shoulders to get the detainee's attention or to comfort the detainee.

22. (S/NF) (U) **Dietary Manipulation:** Changing the diet of a detainee; no intended deprivation of food or water; no adverse medical or cultural effect and without intent to deprive subject of food or water, e.g., hot rations to MREs.

23. (S/NF) (U) **Environmental Manipulation:** Altering the environment to create moderate discomfort (e.g., adjusting temperature or introducing an unpleasant smell). Conditions would not be such that they would injure the detainee. Detainee would be accompanied by interrogator at all times.

24. (S/NF) (U) **Sleep Adjustment:** Adjusting the sleeping times of the detainee (e.g., reversing sleep cycles from night to day.) This technique is NOT sleep deprivation.

25. (S/NF) (U) **False Flag:** Convincing the detainee that individuals from a country other than the United States are interrogating him.

26. (S/NF) (U) **Threat of Transfer:** Threatening to transfer the subject to a third country that subject is likely to fear would subject him to torture or death. (The threat would not be acted upon nor would the threat include any information beyond the naming of the receiving country.)

(U) The following list includes additional techniques that are considered effective by interrogators, some of which have been requested by USCENTCOM and USSOUTHCOM. They are more aggressive counter-resistance techniques that may be appropriate for detainees who are extremely resistant to the above techniques, and who the interrogators strongly believe have vital information. All of the following techniques indicate the need for technique-specialized training and written procedures to insure the safety of all persons, along with appropriate, specified levels of approval and notification for each technique.

27. (S/NF) (U) **Isolation:** Isolating the detainee from other detainees while still complying with basic standards of treatment.

28. (S/NF) (U) **Use of Prolonged Interrogations:** The continued use of a series of approaches that extend over a long period of time (e.g., 20 hours per day per interrogation).

29. (S/NF) (U) **Forced Grooming:** Forcing a detainee to shave hair or beard. (Force applied with intention to avoid injury. Would not use force that would cause serious injury.)

30. (S/NF) (U) **Prolonged Standing:** Lengthy standing in a "normal" position (non-stress). This has been successful, but should never make the detainee exhausted to the point of weakness or collapse. Not enforced by physical restraints. Not to exceed four hours in a 24-hour period.

31. (S/NF) (U) **Sleep Deprivation:** Keeping the detainee awake for an extended period of time. (Allowing individual to rest briefly and then awakening him, repeatedly.) Not to exceed four days in succession.

32. (S/NF) (U) **Physical Training:** Requiring detainees to exercise (perform ordinary physical exercises actions) (e.g., running, jumping jacks); not to exceed 15 minutes in a two-hour period; not more than two cycles, per 24-hour periods) Assists in generating compliance and fatiguing the detainees. No enforced compliance.

33. (S/NF) (U) **Face slap/Stomach slap:** A quick glancing slap to the fleshy part of the cheek or stomach. These techniques are used strictly as shock measures and

do not cause pain or injury. They are only effective if used once or twice together. After the second time on a detainee, it will lose the shock effect. Limited to two slaps per application; no more than two applications per interrogation.

34. ~~(S/NF)~~ (U) **Removal of Clothing:** Potential removal of all clothing; removal to be done by military police if not agreed to by the subject. Creating a feeling of helplessness and dependence. This technique must be monitored to ensure the environmental conditions are such that this technique does not injure the detainee.

35. ~~(S/NF)~~ (U) **Increasing Anxiety by Use of Aversions:** Introducing factors that of themselves create anxiety but do not create terror or mental trauma (e.g., simple presence of dog without directly threatening action). This technique requires the commander to develop specific and detailed safeguards to insure the detainee's safety.

VI. Evaluation of Useful Techniques

~~(S/NF)~~ (U) The working group considered each of the techniques enumerated in Section V, *supra*, in light of the legal, historical, policy and operational considerations discussed in this paper. In the course of that examination it became apparent that any decision whether to authorize a technique is essentially a risk benefit analysis that generally takes into account the expected utility of the technique, the likelihood that any technique will be in violation of domestic or international law, and various policy considerations. Generally, the legal analysis that was applied is that understood to comport with the views of the Department of Justice. Although the United States, as a practical matter, may be the arbiter of international law in deciding its application to our national activities, the views of other nations are relevant in considering their reactions, potential effects on our captured personnel in future conflicts, and possible liability to prosecution in other countries and international forums for interrogators, supervisors and commanders involved in interrogation processes and decisions.

~~(S/NF)~~ (U) The Conclusions section of this analysis, *infra*, summarizes salient conclusions that were applied to our analysis of individual techniques. As it suggests, the lawfulness and the effectiveness of individual techniques will, in practice, depend on the specific facts. The lawfulness will depend in significant part on procedural protections that demonstrate a legitimate purpose and that there was no *intent* to inflict significant mental or physical pain – and, in fact, avoid that. Because of this, the assessment of each technique presumed that the safeguards and procedures described in the "DOD-Specific Policy Considerations" section of this paper would be in place. The importance of this is underscored by the fact that, in practice, techniques are usually applied in combination, and as the legal analysis of this paper indicates, the significance and effect on an individual detainee of the specific combination of techniques employed, and their manner of application will determine the lawfulness of any particular interrogation.

~~(S/NF)~~ (U) In addition, the lawfulness of the application of any particular technique, or combination of techniques, may depend on the practical necessity for imposition of the more exceptional techniques. As the analysis explains, legal justification for action that could otherwise be unlawful (e.g., relying upon national necessity and self-defense) depends in large part on whether the specific circumstances would justify the imposition of more aggressive techniques. Interrogation of an individual known to have facts essential to prevent an immediate threat of catastrophic harm to large populations may support use of "exceptional" techniques, particularly when milder techniques have been unavailing. But this is a determination that will always be case-specific. Consequently, use of each technique should be a decision level appropriate to the gravity of the particular case (both for the nation and for the detainee).

(S/NF) (U) The chart at Attachment 3 reflects the result of the risk/benefit assessment for each technique considered, "scored" for each technique, relevant considerations and given an overall recommendation. In addition, it notes specific techniques that, based on this evaluation, should be considered "exceptional techniques" (marked with an "E") subject to particular limitations described in the "DOD-Specific Policy Considerations" section (generally, not routinely available to interrogators, use limited to specifically designated locations and specifically trained interrogators, special safeguards, and appropriately senior employment decision levels specified). For each "exceptional" technique, a recommendation for employment decision level is indicated as well.

VII. Conclusions Relevant to Interrogation of Unlawful Combatants Under DOD Control Outside the United States

(S/NF) (U) As a result of the foregoing analysis of legal, policy, historical, and operational considerations, the following general conclusions can be drawn relevant to interrogation of unlawful combatants captured in the war on terrorism under DOD control outside the United States:

(S/NF) (U) Under the Third Geneva Convention, U.S. forces are required to treat captured personnel as POWs until an official determination is made as to their status. Once a determination has been made that captured personnel are unlawful combatants, as is currently the case with captured Taliban and al Qaeda operatives, they do not have a right to the protections of the Third Geneva Convention.

(U) Customary international law does not provide legally-enforceable restrictions on the interrogation of unlawful combatants under DOD control outside the United States.

(U) The United States Constitution does not protect those individuals who are not United States citizens and who are outside the sovereign territory of the United States.

(S/NF) (U) Under the Torture Convention, no person may be subjected to torture. Torture is defined as an act specifically *intended* to inflict severe physical or mental pain or suffering and that mental pain or suffering refers to *prolonged* mental harm caused by or resulting from (1) the *intentional* infliction or *threatened infliction of severe physical pain or suffering*; (2) the administration or application, or threatened application, of mind altering substances or other procedures *calculated* to disrupt profoundly the senses or personality; (3) the threat of imminent death; or (4) the threat that another person will *imminently* be subjected to death, severe physical pain or suffering, or the administration or application, or threatened application, of mind-altering substances or other procedures calculated to disrupt profoundly the senses or personality.

(S/NF) (U) Under the Torture Convention, no person may be subjected to cruel, inhuman or degrading treatment. The United States has defined its obligations under the Torture Convention as conduct prohibited by the Fifth, Eighth, and Fourteenth

Amendments to the Constitution of the United States. These terms, as defined by U.S. courts, could be understood to mean: to inflict pain or harm without a legitimate purpose; to inflict pain or injury for malicious or sadistic reasons; to deny the minimal civilized measures of life's necessities and such denial reflects a deliberate indifference to health and safety; and to apply force and cause injury so severe and so disproportionate to the legitimate government interest being served that it amounts to a brutal and inhumane abuse of official power literally shocking the conscience.

(U) For actions outside the United States and the special maritime and territorial jurisdiction of the United States, 18 U.S.C. § 2340 applies. For actions occurring within the United States and the special maritime and territorial jurisdiction of the United States, various Federal statutes would apply.

(S/NF) (U) The President has directed, pursuant to his Military Order dated November 13, 2001, that the U.S. Armed Forces treat detainees humanely and that the detainees be afforded adequate food, drinking water, shelter, clothing and medical treatment.

(S/NF) (U) Pursuant to the Confidential Presidential Determination, dated February 7, 2002, the U.S. Armed Forces are to treat detainees in a manner consistent with the *principles* of Geneva, to the extent *appropriate* and consistent with *military necessity*.

(U) Under Article 10 of the Torture Convention, the United States is obligated to ensure that law enforcement and military personnel involved in interrogations are educated and informed regarding the prohibition against torture, and under Article 11, systematic reviews of interrogation rules, methods, and practices are also required.

(U) Members of the U.S. Armed Forces are, at all times and all places, subject to prosecution under the UCMJ for, among other offenses, acts which constitute assault, assault consummated by a battery, assault with the intent to inflict grievous bodily harm, manslaughter, unpremeditated murder, and maltreatment of those subject to their orders. Under certain circumstances, civilians accompanying the Armed Forces may be subject to the UCMJ.

(U) Civilian employees and employees of DOD contractors may be subject to prosecution under the Federal Criminal Code for, among other offenses, acts which constitute assault (in various degrees), maiming, manslaughter, and murder.

(S/NF) (U) Defenses relating to Commander-in-Chief authority, necessity and self-defense or defense of others may be available to individuals whose actions would otherwise constitute these crimes, and the extent of availability of those defenses will be fact-specific. Certain relevant offenses require specific intent to inflict particular degrees of harm or pain, which could be refuted by evidence to the contrary (e.g., procedural safeguards). Where the Commander-in-Chief authority is being relied upon, a Presidential written directive would serve to memorialize this authority.

(S/NF) (U) The lawfulness and appropriateness of the use of many of the interrogation techniques we examined can only be determined by reference to specific details of their application, such as appropriateness and safety for the particular detainee, adequacy of supervision, specifics of the application including their duration, intervals between applications, combination with other techniques, and safeguards to avoid harm (including termination criteria and the presence or availability of qualified medical personnel.) (We have recommended appropriate guidance and protections.)

(S/NF) (U) Other nations, including major partner nations, may consider use of techniques more aggressive than those appropriate for POWs violative of international law or their own domestic law, potentially making U.S. personnel involved in the use of such techniques subject to prosecution for perceived human rights violations in other nations or to being surrendered to international fora, such as the ICC; this has the potential to impact future operations and overseas travel of such personnel.

(S/NF) (U) Some nations may assert that the U.S. use of techniques more aggressive than those appropriate for POWs justifies similar treatment for captured U.S. personnel.

(S/NF) (U) Should information regarding the use of more aggressive interrogation techniques than have been used traditionally by U.S. forces become public, it is likely to be exaggerated or distorted in the U.S. and international media accounts, and may produce an adverse effect on support for the war on terrorism.

(S/NF) (U) The more aggressive the interrogation technique used, the greater the likelihood that it will affect adversely the admissibility of any acquired statements or confessions in prosecutions against the person interrogated, including in military commissions (to a lesser extent than in other U.S. courts).

(S/NF) (U) Carefully drawn procedures intended to prevent unlawful levels of pain or harm not only serve to avoid unlawful results but should provide evidence helpful to demonstrate that the specific intent required for certain offenses did not exist.

(S/NF) (U) General use of exceptional techniques (generally, having substantially greater risk than those currently, routinely used by U.S. Armed Forces interrogators), even though lawful, may create uncertainty among interrogators regarding the appropriate limits of interrogations. They should therefore be employed with careful procedures and only when fully justified.

(S/NF) (U) Participation by U.S. military personnel in interrogations which use techniques that are more aggressive than those appropriate for POWs would constitute a significant departure from traditional U.S. military norms and could have an adverse impact on the cultural self-image of U.S. military forces.[76]

(S/NF) (U) The use of exceptional interrogation techniques should be limited to specified strategic interrogation facilities; when there is a good basis to believe that the detainee possesses critical intelligence; when the detainee is medically and operationally evaluated as suitable (considering all techniques in combination); when interrogators are specifically trained for the technique(s); a specific interrogation plan (including reasonable safeguards, limits on duration, intervals between applications, termination criteria and the presence or availability of qualified medical personnel); when there is appropriate supervision; and, after obtaining appropriate specified senior approval level for use with any specific detainee (after considering the foregoing and receiving legal advice).

VIII. Recommendations

(U) We recommend:

(S/NF) (U) 1. The working group recommends that techniques 1–26 on the attached chart be approved for use with unlawful combatants outside the United States, subject

---

[76] Those techniques considered in this review that raise this concern are relatively few in number and generally indicated by yellow or red (or green with a significant footnote) under major partner views in Attachment 3.

to the general limitations set forth in this Legal and Policy Analysis; and that techniques 27–35 be approved for use with unlawful combatants outside the United States subject to the general limitations as well as the specific limitations regarding "exceptional" techniques as follows: conducted at strategic interrogation facilities; where there is a good basis to believe that the detainee possesses critical intelligence; the detainee is medically and operationally evaluated as suitable (considering all techniques to be used in combination); interrogators are specifically trained for the technique(s); a specific interrogation plan (including reasonable safeguards, limits on duration, intervals between applications, termination criteria and the presence or availability of qualified medical personnel) is developed; appropriate supervision is provided; and, appropriate specified senior level approval is given for use with any specific detainee (after considering the foregoing and receiving legal advice).

(S/NF) (U) 2. SECDEF approve the strategic interrogation facilities that are authorized to use the "exceptional techniques" (such facilities at this time include Guantanamo, Cuba; additional strategic interrogation facilities will be approved on a case-by-case basis).

(S/NF) (U) 3. As the Commander-in-Chief authority is vested in the President, we recommend that any exercise of that authority by DOD personnel be confirmed in writing through Presidential directive or other document.

(S/NF) (U) 4. That DOD policy directives and implementing guidance be amended as necessary to reflect the determinations in paragraph one and subsequent determinations concerning additional possible techniques.

(S/NF) (U) 5. That commanders and supervisors, and their legal advisers, involved with the decisions related to employment of "exceptional techniques" receive specialized training regarding the legal and policy considerations relevant to interrogations that make use of such techniques.

(S/NF) (U) 6. That OASD (PA) prepare a press plan to anticipate and address potential public inquiries and misunderstandings regarding appropriate interrogation techniques.

(S/NF) (U) 7. That a procedure be established for requesting approval of additional interrogation techniques similar to that for requesting "supplementals" for ROEs; the process should require the requestor to describe the technique in detail, justify its utility, describe the potential effects on subjects, known hazards and proposed safeguards, provide a legal analysis, and recommend an appropriate decision level regarding use on specific subjects. This procedure should ensure that SECDEF is the approval authority for the addition of any technique that could be considered equivalent in degree to any of the "exceptional techniques" addressed in this report (in the chart numbers 27–35, labeled with an "E"), and that he establish the specific decision level required for application of such techniques.

(S/NF) (U) 8. DOD establish specific understandings with other agencies using DOD detailed interrogators regarding the permissible scope of the DOD interrogator's activities.

Classified by: Secretary Rumsfeld
Reason: 1.5(C)
Declassify on: 10 years

UNCLASSIFIED
War on Terrorism
Detainee Interrogation Working Group
Summary of Analysis and Recommendations
Pertaining to Unlawful Combatants Outside of the U.S.[1]

Legend:
- ● Red
- ○ Yellow
- ◍ Green

Proposed Interrogation Techniques[2] (see attached description/limitations)	Utility: Contribution to Intelligence Collection (Useful)	Law IAW U.S. Interpretation		
		Torture Convention [Torture]	Torture Convention [Cruel, Inhuman Degrading]	U.S. Domestic Law
1. Direct	High	◍	◍	◍
2. Incentive or Removal	High	◍	◍	◍
3. Emotional Love	High	◍	◍	◍
4. Emotional Hate	High	◍	◍	◍
5. Fear Up Harsh	High	◍	◍	◍
6. Fear Up Mild	High	◍	◍	◍
7. Reduced Fear	High	◍	◍	◍
8. Pride and ego up	High	◍	◍	◍
9. Pride and ego down	High	◍	◍	◍
10. Futility	High	◍	◍	◍
11. We Know All	High	◍	◍	◍
12. Establish Your Identity	High	◍	◍	◍

Note: Green denotes no significant constraint on use raised by the respective area of consideration listed at top of each column, assuming adequate procedural safeguards. Yellow Indicates area of consideration does not preclude use but there are problematic aspects that cannot be eliminated by procedural safeguards (see footnote). Red Indicates major issue in area of consideration that cannot be eliminated.

UNCLASSIFIED

Figure 1.1.

UNCLASSIFIED

War on Terrorism
Detainee Interrogation Working Group
Summary of Analysis and Recommendations
Pertaining to Unlawful Combatants Outside of the U.S.[1]

Legend: ● Red ○ Yellow ▨ Green

Proposed Interrogation Techniques[2] (see attached description/limitations)	Policy							Recommendation
	Consistency with Historical U.S. Forces Interrogation Role	Consistency with Prior U.S. Public Statements	Consistency with Major Partner Nation Views	Effect on Captured U.S. Forces	Potential Adverse Effect for Participants/Supervisors/COC	Potential Effect on Detainee Prosecutions	Other	Re Unlawful Combatants
1. Direct	Green	Green	Green	Green	Green	Green	Yellow	Green
2. Incentive or Removal	Green	Green	Yellow (3)	Green	Green	Red (4)	Yellow	Green
3. Emotional Love	Green	Green	Green	Green	Green	Green	Yellow	Green
4. Emotional Hate	Green	Green	Green	Green	Green	Green	Yellow	Green
5. Fear Up Harsh	Green	Green	Green	Green	Green	Green	Yellow	Green
6. Fear Up Mild	Green	Green	Green	Green	Green	Green	Yellow	Green
7. Reduced Fear	Green	Green	Green	Green	Green	Green	Yellow	Green
8. Pride and ego up	Green	Green	Green	Green	Green	Green	Yellow	Green
9. Pride and ego down	Green	Green	Yellow (5)	Green	Green	Green	Yellow	Green
10. Futility	Green	Green	Green	Green	Green	Green	Yellow	Green
11. We Know All	Green	Green	Green	Green	Green	Green	Yellow	Green
12. Establish Your Identity	Green	Green	Green	Green	Green	Green	Yellow	Green

Note: Green denotes no significant constraint on use raised by the respective area of consideration listed at top of each column, assuming adequate procedural safeguards. Yellow indicates area of consideration does not preclude use but there are problematic aspects that cannot be eliminated by procedural safeguards (see footnote). Red indicates major issue in area of consideration that cannot be eliminated.

UNCLASSIFIED

UNCLASSIFIED

Legend:
- ● Red
- ○ Yellow
- ◉ Green

Proposed Interrogation Techniques [2] (see attached description/limitations)	Utility — Contribution to Intelligence Collection (Useful)	Law IAW U.S. Interpretation — Torture Convention [Torture]	Law IAW U.S. Interpretation — Torture Convention [Cruel, Inhuman Degrading]	U.S. Domestic Law
13. Repetition Approach	Low		◉	◉
14. File and Dossier	High	◉	◉	◉
15. Mutt and Jeff	High	◉	◉	◉
16. Rapid Fire	High	◉	◉	◉
17. Silence	Medium	◉	◉	◉
18. Change of Scenery Up	High	◉	◉	◉
19. Change of Scenery Down	High	◉	◉	◉
20. Hooding	High	◉	◉	◉
21. Mild Physical Contact	High	◉	◉	◉
22. Dietary Manipulation	High	◉	◉	◉
23. Environmental manipulation	High	◉	◉	◉
24. Sleep Adjustment	High	●	◉	◉
25. False Flag	High	●	●	◉

Note: Green denotes no significant constraint on use raised by the respective area of consideration listed at top of each column, assuming adequate procedural safeguards. Yellow indicates area of consideration does not preclude use but there are problematic aspects that cannot be eliminated by procedural safeguards (see footnote). Red indicates major issue in area of consideration that cannot be eliminated.

UNCLASSIFIED

Figure 1.2.

Legend:
- ● Red
- ○ Yellow
- ◍ Green

Proposed Interrogation Techniques 2 (see attached description/limitations)	Policy							Recommendation
	Consistency with Historical U.S. Forces Interrogation Role	Consistency with Prior U.S. Public Statements	Consistency with Major Partner Nation Views	Effect on Captured U.S. Forces	Potential Adverse Effect for Participants/Supervisors/COC	Potential Effect on Detainee Prosecutions	Other	Re Unlawful Combatants
13. Repetition Approach	Green	Green	Green	Green	Green	Green	Yellow	Green
14. File and Dossier	Green	Green	Green	Green	Green	Green	Yellow	Green
15. Mutt and Jeff	Green	Green	Yellow [6]	Green	Green	Green	Yellow	Green
16. Rapid Fire	Green	Green	Green	Green	Green	Green	Yellow	Green
17. Silence	Green	Green	Green	Green	Green	Green	Yellow	Green
18. Change of Scenery Up	Green	Green	Green	Green	Green	Green	Yellow	Green
19. Change of Scenery Down	Green	Green	Green	Green	Green	Green	Yellow	Green
20. Hooding	Green	Green	Green	Green	Green	Green	Yellow	Green
21. Mild Physical Contact	Green	Green	Green	Green [7]	Green	Green	Yellow	Green
22. Dietary Manipulation	Green	Green	Green	Green	Green	Green	Yellow	Green
23. Environmental Manipulation	Green	Green	Green [8]	Green	Green	Green	Yellow	Green
24. Sleep Adjustment	Green	Green	Green	Green	Green	Green [9]	Yellow	Green
25. False Flag	Green	Green	Green	Green	Green	Green	Yellow	Green

Note: Green denotes no significant constraint on use raised by the respective area of consideration listed at top of each column, assuming adequate procedural safeguards. Yellow indicates area of consideration does not preclude use but there are problematic aspects that cannot be eliminated by procedural safeguards (see footnote). Red indicates major issue in area of consideration that cannot be eliminated.

Legend: ● Red ○ Yellow ◍ Green

Proposed Interrogation Techniques [see attached description/limitations]	Utility — Contribution to Intelligence Collection (Useful)	Law IAW U.S. Interpretation		U.S. Domestic Law
		Torture Convention [Torture]	Torture Convention [Cruel, Inhuman, Degrading]	
26. Threaten to transfer to a 3rd country	Medium	◍ Green	◍ Green	◍ Green
27. Isolation	High	◍ Green [11]	◍ Green [12]	◍ Green [13]
28. Use of Prolonged interrogations	High [17]	◍ Green	◍ Green	◍ Green
29. Forced Grooming	High	◍ Green	◍ Green [19]	○ Yellow [20]
30. Prolonged Standing	High	◍ Green	◍ Green	◍ Green
31. Sleep Deprivation	High	◍ Green	◍ Green	◍ Green
32. Physical Training	High	◍ Green	◍ Green	◍ Green
33. Face or Stomach Slap	High	◍ Green	◍ Green	◍ Green
34. Removal of Clothing	High	◍ Green	○ Yellow [34]	○ Yellow [35]
35. Increasing Anxiety by Use of Aversions	High	◍ Green	○ Yellow [38]	○ Yellow [39]

Note: Green denotes no significant constraint on use raised by the respective area of consideration listed at top of each column, assuming adequate procedural safeguards. Yellow indicates area of consideration does not preclude use but there are problematic aspects that cannot be eliminated by procedural safeguards (see footnote). Red indicates major issue in area of consideration that cannot be eliminated.

UNCLASSIFIED

Figure 1.3.

Legend:
- ● Red
- ○ Yellow
- ◍ Green

Proposed Interrogation Techniques 2 (see attached description/limitations)	Policy							Recommendation
	Consistency with Historical U.S. Forces Interrogation Role	Consistency with Prior U.S. Public Statements	Consistency with Major Partner Nation Views	Effect on Captured U.S. Forces	Potential Adverse Effect for Participants/Supervisors/COC	Potential Effect on Detainee Prosecutions	Other	Re Unlawful Combatants
26. Threaten to transfer to a 3rd country	Green	Green	Green	Green	Green	Green (10)	Yellow	Green
27. Isolation	Green (14)	Green	Yellow (15)	Green	Green	Red (16)	Yellow	Green — E (Cbt.C)
28. Use of Prolonged Interrogations	Green	Green	Green	Green	Green	Green (18)	Yellow	Green — E (GO/FO)
29. Forced Grooming	Yellow (21)	Green	Yellow (22)	Green	Green	Yellow	Yellow	Green — E (GO/FO)
30. Prolonged Standing	Green	Green	Green	Green	Green	Red (23)	Yellow	Green — E (GO/FO)
31. Sleep Deprivation	Green	Green	Yellow (24)	Yellow	Yellow	Green (25)	Green (26)	Green — E (Cbt.C)
32. Physical Training	Green	Green	Green	Green	Green	Green (27)	Yellow	Green — E (GO/FO)
33. Face or Stomach Slap	Yellow (28)	Green	Green (29)	Yellow (30)	Yellow (31)	Green (32)	Green (33)	Green — E (GO/FO)
34. Removal of Clothing	Green	Green	Yellow	Green (36)	Green	Yellow	Yellow (37)	Yellow — E (Cbt.C)
35. Increasing Anxiety by Use of Aversions	Green	Green	Yellow	Green (40)	Green	Yellow (41)	Yellow	Yellow — E (Cbt.C)

Note: Green denotes no significant constraint on use raised by the respective area of consideration listed at top of each column, assuming adequate procedural safeguards. Yellow indicates area of consideration does not preclude use but there are problematic aspects that cannot be eliminated by procedural safeguards (see footnote). Red indicates major issue in area of consideration that cannot be eliminated.

UNCLASSIFIED

General Comments on Techniques Chart

"E" denotes recommendation that technique be considered "exceptional" and subject to the following limitations: (i) limited to use only at strategic interrogation facilities; (ii) there is a good basis to believe that the detainee possesses critical intelligence; (iii) the detainee is medically and operationally evaluated as suitable (considering all techniques to be used in combination); (iv) interrogators are specifically trained for the technique(s); (v) a specific interrogation plan (including reasonable safeguards, limits on duration, intervals between applications, termination criteria and the presence or availability of qualified medical personnel) has been developed; (vi) there is appropriate supervision; and, (vii) there is appropriate specified senior approval for use with any specific detainee (after considering the foregoing and receiving legal advice).

"(Cbt.C)" denotes recommendation that approval level for use of technique for a specific detainee be no lower than the Combatant Commander.

"(GO/FO)" denotes recommendation that approval level for use of technique for a specific detainee be no lower than a General Officer or Flag Officer.

The title of a particular technique is not always fully descriptive of a particular technique. With respect to the employment of any techniques involving physical contact or stress or that could produce physical pain or harm, a detailed explanation of that technique must be provided to the decision authority prior to any decision.

Recommendation: The working group recommends that techniques 1–26 be approved for use with unlawful combatants outside the U.S. subject to the general limitations set forth in the Legal and Policy Analysis; and that techniques 27–35 be approved for use with unlawful combatants outside the U.S. subject to the general limitations as well as the specific limitations regarding "exceptional" techniques set forth above and in the Legal and Policy Analysis. If additional techniques are requested for use in the future, sufficient information regarding the technique must be provided to the appropriate command authority so that a legal/policy analysis can be conducted and recommendations for use made.

Note: Green denotes no significant constraint on use raised by the respective area of consideration listed at the top of each column, assuming adequate procedural safeguards. Yellow indicates area of consideration does not preclude use but there are problematic aspects that cannot be eliminated by procedural safeguards (see footnote). Red indicates major issue in area of consideration that cannot be eliminated.

Footnotes

1. These recommendations assume that procedures and safeguards substantially similar to those set forth in the "Policy" Section of the Legal and Policy Analysis are followed. **The analysis relates to each individual technique; use of techniques in combination could significantly affect the legality and wisdom of their application.**

2. Techniques 1–19, 22–26, 30 and 35, applied singly, are purely verbal and/or involve no physical contact that could produce pain or harm; no threat of pain or harm.

3. *As a matter of policy, for countries that assert that POW protections should apply to detainees*: Other nations may consider that provision and retention of religious

items (e.g., the Koran) are protected under international law (see, Geneva III, Article 34).

4. May affect admissibility of statements provided based on voluntariness consideration (lesser issue for military commissions).

5. *For countries that assert that POW protections apply to detainees*: Article 17 of Geneva III provides. "Prisoners of war who refuse to answer may not be threatened, insulted, or exposed to any unpleasant or disadvantageous treatment of any kind."

6. *As a matter of policy, for countries that assert that POW protections should apply to detainees*: Would be inconsistent with Geneva III, Article 13 which provides that POWs must be protected against acts of intimidation.

7. *As a matter of policy, for countries that assert that POW protections should apply to detainees*: Possible that other nations would disregard "mild" aspect and use as justification for abuse of U.S. POWs.

8. International case law suggests that technique might in some circumstances be viewed by other countries as inhumane.

9. May affect admissibility of statements provided based on voluntariness consideration (lesser issue for military commissions).

10. May significantly affect admissibility of statements provided based on voluntariness consideration (lesser issue for military commissions).

11. The use of isolation as an interrogation technique requires detailed implementation instructions, including specific guidelines regarding the length of isolation, medical and psychological review, and approval for extensions of the length of isolation by the appropriate level in the chain of command.

12. To avoid implementation that could transgress, the use of isolation as an interrogation technique requires detailed implementation instructions, including specific guidelines regarding the length of isolation, medical and psychological review, and approval for extensions of the length of isolation by the appropriate level in the chain of command.

13. To avoid implementation that could transgress, the use of isolation as an interrogation technique requires detailed implementation instructions, including specific guidelines regarding the length of isolation, medical and psychological review, and approval for extensions of the length of isolation by the appropriate level in the chain of command.

14. Not known to have been generally used for interrogation purposes for longer than 30 days.

15. *As a matter of policy, for countries that assert that POW protections should apply to detainees*: Would be inconsistent with the requirements of Geneva III, Article 13 which provides that POWs must be protected against acts of intimidation; Article 14 which provides that POWs are entitled to respect for their person; Article 34 which prohibits coercion (see commentary to paragraph 4), and Article 126 which ensures access and basic standards of treatment.

16. May affect admissibility of statements provided based on voluntariness consideration (lesser issue for military commissions).

17. Utility is "high" for the first four to five days, "medium" for the following four to six days, and "low" thereafter.

18. May significantly affect admissibility of statements provided based on voluntariness consideration (lesser issue for military commissions).

19. Where there are religious or cultural sensitivities, this technique could raise issue of "degrading" if not applied in accordance with general limitations.

20. At practical level, may raise issues whether excessive force was used.

21. This technique has not been used historically by U.S. forces. As such, no color code was assigned.

22. This technique could be viewed by major partner nations as degrading in some circumstances.

23. May affect admissibility of statements provided based on voluntariness consideration (lesser issue for military commissions).

24. As a matter of policy, for consideration of other nations' views, the Committee against Torture, established under Article 17 of the Convention Against Torture (CAT), has interpreted "sleep deprivation for prolonged periods" to be a violation of both Article 16 of the CAT as cruel, inhuman, or degrading treatment as well as constituting torture under Article 1 of the CAT. Concluding Observations of the Committee against Torture, U.N. Doc. A/52/44, paragraphs 253–260. See also, Judgment on the Interrogation Methods Applied by the GSS, Nos HC 5100/94, HC 4054/95, HC 5188/96, HC 7563/97, HC 7628/97, HC 1043/99 (Sup Ct of Israel, sitting as the High Court of Justice, Sep 6, 1999). Finally, the European Court of Human Rights (ECHR) has held that sleep deprivation, in conjunction with four other problematic techniques (wall standing, hooding, subjection to noise, and deprivation of food and drink), did constitute "inhuman and degrading treatment". Ireland v. United Kingdom, 25 Eur. Ct. H.R. (Ser. A) (1978).

25. May significantly affect admissibility of statements provided based on voluntariness consideration (lesser issue for military commissions).

26. Knowledge of this technique may have a significant adverse effect on public opinion.

27. May affect admissibility of statements provided based on voluntariness consideration (lesser issue for military commissions).

28. Technique used historically until the Vietnam war, however not officially sanctioned.

29. As a matter of policy, for consideration of other nations' views, the Committee against Torture has generally denounced the use of "moderate physical pressure" as a permissible interrogation technique. See also, Tyrer v. United Kingdom, 26 Eur. Ct. H.R. (Ser. A) (1978) (spanking of student with three lashes of a birch rod violated European Convention on Human Rights). See also, Article 5 of the American Convention on Human Rights prohibits not only "torture" and "cruel, inhuman or degrading punishment or treatment" but it also provides that: "Every person has the right to have his physical, mental, and moral integrity respected."

30. As a matter of policy, other nations could interpret this as condoning assault on the detainee and encourage the use against U.S. POWs.

31. Potential to be subject to charge of assault in international jurisdictions.

32. May significantly affect admissibility of statements provided based on voluntariness consideration (lesser issue for military commissions).

33. Knowledge of this technique may have significant adverse effect on public opinion.

34. Depending on application of technique, could be construed as degrading.

35. At practical level, may raise issues whether excessive force was used as force may be required to remove clothing.

36. Other nations may use as excuse to apply to U.S. POWs.

37. Knowledge of this technique may have a significant adverse effect on public opinion.

38. Legal exposure would be dependant on specific technique employed. Depending on technique used and subject response, potential exists that technique could be viewed as violating Fifth/Eighth/Fourteenth Amendment standards, and therefore violate U.S. interpretation of Torture Convention.

38. Legal exposure would be dependant on specific technique employed. Depending on technique used and subject response, potential exists that technique could be viewed as violating Fifth/Eighth/Fourteenth Amendment standards, and therefore violate U.S. interpretation of Torture Convention.

40. Could provide basis for other nations to justify use of more aggravated mental techniques on U.S. POWs.

41. May significantly affect admissibility of statements provided based on voluntariness consideration (lesser issue for military commissions).

Description of Interrogation Techniques

1. **Direct:** Asking straightforward questions.

2. **Incentive/Removal of Incentive:** Providing a reward or removing a privilege, above and beyond those that are required by the Geneva Convention, from detainees.

3. **Emotional Love:** Playing on the love a detainee has for an individual or group.

4. **Emotional Hate:** Playing on the hatred a detainee has for an individual or group.

5. **Fear Up Harsh:** Significantly increasing the fear level in a detainee.

6. **Fear Up Mild:** Moderately increasing the fear level in a detainee.

7. **Reduced Fear:** Reducing the fear level in a detainee.

8. **Pride and Ego Up:** Boosting the ego of a detainee.

9. **Pride and Ego Down:** Attacking or insulting the ego of a detainee, not beyond the limits that would apply to a POW.

10. **Futility:** Invoking the feeling of futility of a detainee.

11. **We Know All:** Convincing the detainee that the interrogator knows the answer to questions he asks the detainee.

12. **Establish Your Identity:** Convincing the detainee that the interrogator has mistaken the detainee for someone else.

13. **Repetition Approach:** Continuously repeating the same question to the detainee within interrogation periods of normal duration.

14. **File and Dossier:** Convincing detainee that the interrogator has a damning and inaccurate file, which must be fixed.

15. **Mutt and Jeff:** A team consisting of a friendly and harsh interrogator. The harsh interrogator might employ the Pride and Ego Down technique.

16. **Rapid Fire:** Questioning in rapid succession without allowing detainee to answer.

17. **Silence:** Staring at the detainee to encourage discomfort.

18. **Change of Scenery Up:** Removing the detainee from the standard interrogation setting (generally to a location more pleasant, but no worse).

19. **Change of Scenery Down:** Removing the detainee from the standard interrogation setting and placing him in a setting that may be less comfortable; would not constitute a substantial change in environmental quality.

20. **Hooding:** This technique is questioning the detainee with a blindfold in place. For interrogation purposes, the blindfold is not on other than during interrogation.

21. **Mild Physical Contact:** Lightly touching a detainee or lightly poking the detainee in a completely non-injurious manner. This also includes softly grabbing of shoulders to get the detainee's attention or to comfort the detainee.

22. **Dietary Manipulation:** Changing the diet of a detainee; no intended deprivation of food or water; no adverse medical or cultural effect and without intent to deprive subject of food or water, e.g., hot rations to MREs.

23. **Environmental Manipulation:** Altering the environment to create moderate discomfort (e.g., adjusting temperature or introducing an unpleasant smell). Conditions would not be such that they would injure the detainee. Detainee would be accompanied by interrogator at all times.

24. **Sleep Adjustment:** Adjusting the sleeping times of the detainee (e.g., reversing sleep cycles from night to day.) This technique is NOT sleep deprivation.

25. **False Flag:** Convincing the detainee that individuals from a country other than the United States are interrogating him.

26. **Threat of Transfer:** Threatening to transfer the subject to a third country that subject is likely to fear would subject him to torture or death. (The threat would not be acted upon, nor would the threat include any information beyond the naming of the receiving country.)

27. **Isolation:** Isolating the detainee from other detainees while still complying with basic standards of treatment.

28. **Use of Prolonged Interrogations:** The continued use of a series of approaches that extend over a long period of time (e.g., 20 hours per day per interrogation).

29. **Forced Grooming:** Forcing a detainee to shave hair or beard. (Force applied with intention to avoid injury. Would not use force that would cause serious injury.)

30. **Prolonged Standing:** Lengthy standing in a "normal" position (non-stress). This has been successful, but should never make the detainee exhausted to the point of weakness or collapse. Not enforced by physical restraints. Not to exceed four hours in a 24-hour period.

31. **Sleep Deprivation:** Keeping the detainee awake for an extended period of time. (Allowing individual to rest briefly and then awakening him, repeatedly.) Not to exceed four days in succession.

32. **Physical Training:** Requiring detainees to exercise (perform ordinary physical exercises actions) (e.g., running, jumping jacks); not to exceed 15 minutes in a two-hour period; not more than two cycles per 24-hour period. Assists in generating compliance and fatiguing the detainees. No enforced compliance.

33. **Face slap/Stomach slap:** A quick glancing slap to the fleshy part of the cheek or stomach. These techniques are used strictly as shock measures and do not cause pain or injury. They are only effective if used once or twice together. After the second time on a detainee, it will lose the shock effect. Limited to two slaps per application; no more than two applications per interrogation.

34. **Removal of Clothing:** Potential removal of all clothing; removal to be done by military police if not agreed to by the subject. Creating a feeling of helplessness and

dependence. This technique must be monitored to ensure the environmental conditions are such that this technique does not injure the detainee.

35. **Increasing Anxiety by Use of Aversions:** Introducing factors that of themselves create anxiety but do not create terror or mental trauma (e.g., simple presence of dog without directly threatening action). This technique requires the commander to develop specific and detailed safeguards to insure detainee's safety.

UNCLASSIFIED
SECRET/NOFORN
UNCLASSIFIED WHEN SEPARATED FROM ATTACHMENT

~~SECRET/NOFORN~~

THE SECRETARY OF DEFENSE
1000 DEFENSE PENTAGON
WASHINGTON, DC 20301-1000
APR 16 2003

MEMORANDUM FOR THE COMMANDER, US SOUTHERN COMMAND

SUBJECT: Counter-Resistance Techniques in the War on Terrorism (S)

~~(S/NF)~~ (U) I have considered the report of the Working Group that I directed be established on January 15, 2003.

~~(S/NF)~~ (U) I approve the use of specified counter-resistance techniques, subject to the following:

(U) a. The techniques I authorize are those lettered A-X, set out at Tab A.

(U) b. These techniques must be used with all the safeguards described at Tab B.

~~(S)~~ (U) c. Use of these techniques is limited to interrogations of unlawful combatants held at Guantanamo Bay, Cuba.

~~(S)~~ (U) d. Prior to the use of these techniques, the Chairman of the Working Group on Detainee Interrogations in the Global War on Terrorism must brief you and your staff.

~~(S/NF)~~ (U) I reiterate that US Armed Forces shall continue to treat detainees humanely and, to the extent appropriate and consistent with military necessity, in a manner consistent with the principles of the Geneva Conventions. In addition, if you intend to use techniques B, I, O, or X, you must specifically determine that military necessity requires its use and notify me in advance.

~~(S/NF)~~ (U) If, in your view, you require additional interrogation techniques for a particular detainee, you should provide me, via the Chairman of the Joint Chiefs of Staff, a written request describing the proposed technique, recommended safeguards, and the rationale for applying it with an identified detainee.

~~(S/NF)~~ (U) Nothing in this memorandum in any way restricts your existing authority to maintain good order and discipline among detainees.

Attachments: [Signed Donald Rumsfeld]
As stated

Declassified Under Authority of Executive Order 12958
By Executive Secretary, Office of the Secretary of Defense
William P. Marriott, CAPT, USN
June 18, 2004

Classified By: Secretary of Defense
Reason: 1.5(a)
Declassify On: 2 April 2013

~~SECRET/NOFORN~~

NOT RELEASABLE TO
FOREIGN NATIONALS

TAB A

INTERROGATION TECHNIQUES

(S/NF) (U) The use of techniques A – X is subject to the general safeguards as provided below as well as specific implementation guidelines to be provided by the appropriate authority. Specific implementation guidance with respect to techniques A – Q is provided in Army Field Manual 34–52. Further implementation guidance with respect to techniques R – X will need to be developed by the appropriate authority.

(S/NF) (U) Of the techniques set forth below, the policy aspects of certain techniques should be considered to the extent those policy aspects reflect the views of other major U.S. partner nations. Where applicable, the description of the technique is annotated to include a summary of the policy issues that should be considered before application of the technique.

A. (S/NF) (U) Direct: Asking straightforward questions.

B. (S/NF) (U) Incentive/Removal of Incentive: Providing a reward or removing a privilege, above and beyond those that are required by the Geneva Convention, from detainees. [Caution: Other nations that believe that detainees are entitled to POW protections may consider that provision and retention of religious items (e.g., the Koran) are protected under international law (see, Geneva III, Article 34). Although the provisions of the Geneva Convention are not applicable to the interrogation of unlawful combatants, consideration should be given to these views prior to application of the technique.]

C. (S/NF) (U) Emotional Love: Playing on the love a detainee has for an individual or group.

D. (S/NF) (U) Emotional Hate: Playing on the hatred a detainee has for an individual or group.

E. (S/NF) (U) Fear Up Harsh: Significantly increasing the fear level in a detainee.

F. (S/NF) (U) Fear Up Mild: Moderately increasing the fear level in a detainee.

G. (S/NF) (U) Reduced Fear: Reducing the fear level in a detainee.

H. (S/NF) (U) Pride and Ego Up: Boosting the ego of a detainee.

Classified By:Secretary of Defense
Reason:1.5(a)
Declassify On:2 April 2013

NOT RELEASABLE TO
FOREIGN NATIONALS

I. (S/NF) (U) Pride and Ego Down: Attacking or insulting the ego of a detainee, not beyond the limits that would apply to a POW. [Caution: Article 17 of Geneva III provides, "Prisoners of war who refuse to answer may not be threatened, insulted, or exposed to any unpleasant or disadvantageous treatment of any kind." Other nations that believe that detainees are entitled to POW protections may consider this technique inconsistent with the provisions of Geneva. Although the provisions of Geneva are not applicable to the interrogation of unlawful combatants, consideration should be given to these views prior to application of the technique.]

J. (S/NF) (U) Futility: Invoking the feeling of futility of a detainee.

K. (S/NF) (U) We Know All: Convincing the detainee that the interrogator knows the answer to questions he asks the detainee.

L. (S/NF) (U) Establish Your Identity: Convincing the detainee that the interrogator has mistaken the detainee for someone else.

M. (S/NF) (U) Repetition Approach: Continuously repeating the same question to the detainee within interrogation periods of normal duration.

N. (S/NF) (U) File and Dossier: Convincing detainee that the interrogator has a damning and inaccurate file, which must be fixed.

O. (S/NF) (U) Mutt and Jeff: A team consisting of a friendly and harsh interrogator. The harsh interrogator might employ the Pride and Ego Down technique. [Caution: Other nations that believe that POW protections apply to detainees may view this technique as inconsistent with Geneva III, Article 13 which provides that POWs must be protected against acts of intimidation. Although the provisions of Geneva are not applicable to the interrogation of unlawful combatants, consideration should be given to these views prior to application of the technique.]

P. (S/NF) (U) Rapid Fire: Questioning in rapid succession without allowing detainee to answer.

Q. (S/NF) (U) Silence: Staring at the detainee to encourage discomfort.

R. (S/NF) (U) Change of Scenery Up: Removing the detainee from the standard interrogation setting (generally to a location more pleasant, but no worse).

S. (S/NF) (U) Change of Scenery Down: Removing the detainee from the standard interrogation setting and placing him in a setting that may be less comfortable; would not constitute a substantial change in environmental quality.

T. (S/NF) (U) Dietary Manipulation: Changing the diet of a detainee; no intended deprivation of food or water; no adverse medical or cultural effect and without intent to deprive subject of food or water, e.g., hot rations to MREs.

U. (S/NF) (U) Environmental Manipulation: Altering the environment to create moderate discomfort (e.g., adjusting temperature or introducing an unpleasant smell). Conditions would not be such that they would injure the detainee. Detainee would be accompanied by interrogator at all times. [Caution: Based on court cases in other countries, some nations may view application of this technique in certain circumstances to be inhumane. Consideration of these views should be given prior to use of this technique.]

V. (S/NF) (U) Sleep Adjustment: Adjusting the sleeping times of the detainee (e.g., reversing sleep cycles from night to day.) This technique is NOT sleep deprivation.

W. (S/NF) (U) False Flag: Convincing the detainee that individuals from a country other than the United States are interrogating him.

X. (S/NF) (U) Isolation: Isolating the detainee from other detainees while still complying with basic standards of treatment. [Caution: The use of isolation as an interrogation technique requires detailed implementation instructions, including specific guidelines regarding the length of isolation, medical and psychological review, and approval for extensions of the length of isolation by the appropriate level in the chain of command. This technique is not known to have been generally used for interrogation purposes for longer than 30 days. Those nations that believe detainees are subject to POW protections may view use of this technique as inconsistent with the requirements of Geneva III, Article 13 which provides that POWs must be protected against acts of intimidation; Article 14 which provides that POWs are entitled to respect for their person; Article 34 which prohibits coercion and Article 126 which ensures access and basic standards of treatment. Although the provisions of Geneva are not applicable to the interrogation of unlawful combatants, consideration should be given to these views prior to application of the technique.]

TAB B

GENERAL SAFEGUARDS

(S/NF) (U) Application of these interrogation techniques is subject to the following general safeguards: (i) limited to use only at strategic interrogation facilities; (ii) there is a good basis to believe that the detainee possesses critical intelligence; (iii) the detainee is medically and operationally evaluated as suitable (considering all techniques to be used in combination); (iv) interrogators are specifically trained for the technique(s); (v) a specific interrogation plan (including reasonable safeguards, limits on duration, intervals between applications, termination criteria and the presence or availability of qualified medical personnel) has been developed; (vi) there is appropriate supervision; and, (vii) there is appropriate specified senior approval for use with any specific detainee (after considering the foregoing and receiving legal advice).

(U)The purpose of all interviews and interrogations is to get the most information from a detainee with the least intrusive method, always applied in a humane and lawful manner with sufficient oversight by trained investigators or interrogators. Operating Instructions must be developed based on command policies to insure uniform, careful, and safe application of any interrogations of detainees.

(S/NF) (U) Interrogations must always be planned, deliberate actions that take into account numerous, often interlocking factors such as a detainee's current and past performance in both detention and interrogation, a detainee's emotional and physical strengths and weaknesses, an assessment of possible approaches that may work on a certain detainee in an effort to gain the trust of the detainee, strengths and weaknesses of interrogators, and augmentation by other personnel for a certain detainee based on other factors.

(U) Interrogation approaches are designed to manipulate the detainee's emotions and weaknesses to gain his willing cooperation. Interrogation operations are never conducted in a vacuum: they are conducted in close cooperation with the units detaining the individuals. The policies established by the detaining units that pertain to searching, silencing, and segregating also play a role in the interrogation of a detainee. Detainee interrogation involves developing a plan tailored to an individual and approved by senior interrogators. Strict adherence to policies/standard operating procedures governing the administration of interrogation techniques and oversight is essential.

Classified By: Secretary of Defense
Reason:1.5(a)
Declassify On: 2 April 2013

(S/NF) (U) It is important that interrogators be provided reasonable latitude to vary techniques depending on the detainee's culture, strengths, weaknesses, environment, extent of training in resistance techniques as well as the urgency of obtaining information that the detainee is known to have.

(S/NF) (U) While techniques are considered individually within this analysis, it must be understood that in practice, techniques are usually used in combination; the cumulative effect of all techniques to be employed must be considered before any decisions are made regarding approval for particular situations. The title of a particular technique is not always fully descriptive of a particular technique. With respect to the employment of any techniques involving physical contact, stress or that could produce physical pain or harm, a detailed explanation of that technique must be provided to the decision authority prior to any decision.

U.S. Department of Justice

Office of Legal Counsel

Office of the Assistant Attorney General   *Washington, D.C. 20530*

March 19, 2004

MEMORANDUM

TO: William H. Taft, IV
                General Counsel
                Department of State

                William J. Haynes, II
                General Counsel
                Department of Defense

                John Bellinger
                Legal Adviser for National Security

                Scott Muller
                General Counsel
                Central Intelligence Agency

FROM: Jack Goldsmith
                Assistant Attorney General
                Office of Legal Counsel

Gentleman:

Attached is a draft of an opinion, requested by Judge Gonzales, concerning the meaning of Article 49 of the Fourth Geneva Convention as it applies in occupied Iraq. I would appreciate any comments you may have at your earliest convenience. As always, it is important that you keep this draft opinion a very close hold. Thanks.

Attachment

cc: David Leitch

U.S. Department of Justice

Office of Legal Counsel

Office of the Assistant Attorney General   *Washington, D.C. 20530*

DRAFT 3/19/04

**MEMORANDUM FOR ALBERTO R. GONZALES,
    COUNSEL TO THE PRESIDENT**

RE: *Permissibility of Relocating Certain "Protected Persons" from
               Occupied Iraq*

Article 49 of the 1949 Geneva Convention (IV) Relative to the Protection of Civilian Persons in Time of War, Aug. 12, 1949, 6 U.S.T. 3516, 75 U.N.T.S. 287 ("GC" or "Convention") prohibits "[i]ndividual or mass forcible transfers, as well as deportations of protected persons from occupied territory to the territory of the Occupying Power or to that of any other country, occupied or not, ... regardless of their motive."[1] This opinion elaborates on interim guidance provided in October 2003 concerning the permissibility under GC of relocating certain "protected persons" detained in occupied Iraq to places outside that country.[2] We now conclude that the United States may,

---

[1] The entirety of article 49 is as follows:

   Individual or mass forcible transfers, as well as deportations of protected persons from occupied territory to the territory of the Occupying Power or to that of any other country, occupied or not, are prohibited, regardless of their motive.

   Nevertheless, the Occupying Power may undertake total or partial evacuation of a given area if the security of the population or imperative military reasons so demand. Such evacuations may not involve the displacement of protected persons outside the bounds of the occupied territory except when for material reasons it is impossible to avoid such displacement. Perons thus evacuated shall be transferred back to their homes as soon as hostilities in the area in question have ceased.

   The Occupying Power undertaking such transfers or evacuations shall ensure, to the greatest practicable extent, that proper accommodation is provided to receive the protected persons, that the removals are effected in satisfactory conditions of hygiene, health, safety and nutrition that members of the same family are not separated.

   The Protecting Power shall be informed of any transfers and evacuations as soon as they have taken place.

   The Occupying Power shall not detain protected persons in an area particularly exposed to the dangers of war unless the security of the population or imperative military reasons so demand.

   The Occupying Power shall not deport or transfer parts of its own civilian population into the territory it occupies.

[2] While GC confers certain protections on "the whole of the populations of the countries in conflict," GC, art. 13; *see also id.* Part II (Title) ("General Protections of Populations against Certain Consequences of War"). it limits most of its protections to a narrower class of "protected persons," *id.* art. 4. *See generally* Memorandum for Alberto R. Gonzales, Counsel to the President, *Re: "Protected Persons" in Occupied Iraq* (Mar. 18, 2004). Among GC's provisions whose benefits are generally restricted to "protected persons" are those included in Part III, including Article 49. *See* Part III (Tide) ("Status and Treatment of Protected Persons"). *See also* Jean S. Pictct, *Commentary on the Geneva Convention Relative to the Protection of Civilian Persons in Time of War* 278 (1958) (stating that article 49 "prohibits the

consistent with article 49, (1) remove "protected persons" who are illegal aliens from Iraq pursuant to local immigration law; and (2) relocate "protected persons" (whether illegal aliens or not) from Iraq to another country to facilitate interrogation, for a brief but not indefinite period, so long as adjudicative proceedings have not been initiated against them.

I. *Removal of "Protected Persons" Who Are Illegal Alliens*

We first consider whether removing a "protected person" who is an illegal alien from occupied territory constitutes a "deportation" or "forcible transfer" within the meaning of article 49(1)'s prohibition. We consider each term in turn.

We begin with "deportation." Under United States law, this term denotes the removal of an alien. *See, e.g.,* 8 U.S.C. 1227(a)(1)(B) ("Any alien who is present in the United States in violation of this chapter or any other law of the United States is deportable."). *Black's Law Dictionary* of 1951, two years after GC, confirms the point. It defines the term "[i]n American Law" as "[t]he removal or sending back of an alien to the country from which he came."[3] If this American law meaning of "deportation" were the meaning of the word in article 49, then that article would apply to the removal of "protected persons" who are illegal aliens from occupied territory.

But article 49(1) – or at least the core of it – represents a codification of the customary international law of armed conflict as it stood at the time the Convention was drafted. *See, e.g.,* Alfred M. De Zayas, *International Law and Mass Population Transfers*, 16 Harv. Int'l L. J. 207, 210 (1975) (asserting that article 49(1) "merely codif[ies] the prohibition of deportations of civilians from occupied territories which in fact already existed in the laws and customs of war"). And in that body of law, "deportation" is a term of art with a quite different meaning that appears to be derived from Roman law. *Black's Law Dictionary* carefully contrasts the American law meaning of "deportation" with its meaning under Roman law: "A perpetual banishment, depriving the banished of his rights *as a citizen." Black's Law Dictonary 526* (4th ed. 1951) (emphasis added); *see also id.* at 525 ("Deportatio. Lat. In the civil law. A kind of banishment, where a condemned person was sent or carried away to some foreign country, usually to an island. . . *and thus taken out of the number of Roman citizens.")* (emphasis added). Under this Roman law definition, a prohibition on deportation would not apply to the removal of illegal aliens. As shown below, the term "deportation" in the international law of armed conflict possessed this Roman meaning in the nineteenth century, through World Wars I and II, and at the time of GC's drafting.

As early as 1863, Article 23 of the Lieber Code stated that "[p]rivate *citizens* are no longer murdered, enslaved, or *carried off to distant parts."* F. Lieber, "Instructions for the Government of Armies of the United States in the Field," art. 23 (1863) (emphases

---

forcible transfer or deportation from occupied territory *of protected persons")* (emphasis added); *id.* at 283 ("describing the meaning given them ["deportations" and "transfers"] in [article 49] paragraph 1, i.e., the compulsory movement of *protected persons* from occupied territory") (emphasis added).

[3] Black's Law Dictionary 526 (4th ed. 1951). Even in domestic Anglo-American law of that time, however, "deportation" was not strictly limited to the removal of aliens. *See, e.g., Co-Operative Comm. on Japanese Canadians v. Attorney-General for Canada*, 13 I.L.R. 23, 27 (Privy Council 1946)(sustaining deportation under Canadian war-related legislation of British and Candian nationals, "deportation" is "not a word that is misused when applied to persons not aliens").

added).[4] While this provision does not itself use the term "deportation," it is widely recognized as a principal progenitor of the customary prohibition on deportations during wartime codified in article 49. *See, e.g.,* Jean-Marie Henckaerts, *Deportation and Transfer of Civilians in Time of War*, 26 Vand. J. Trans. L. 469, 482-83 (1993) (citing article 23 of the Lieber Code as support for the conclusion that article 49 embodied customary international law); Natsu Taylor Saito, *Justice Held Hostage: U.S. Disregard for International Law in the World War II Internment of Japanese Peruvians – A Case Study*, 40 B.C.L. Rev. 275, 305-06 (1998) (stating that "the United States had condemned the *deportation* of civilians in Lieber's Code") (emphasis added). Significantly, the Lieber Code's prohibition of carrying off *citizens* to distant parts reflects the Roman meaning of "deportation" described above.

Article 23 of the Lieber Code reflected the state of the customary laws of war during the Civil War, and from that time through World War I. Despite this rule, Germany deported 160,000 Belgians from the Belgian "Government General" and the Zone d'étape to Germany, during World War I. Germany's action was widely condemned as a violation of customary international law. *See, e.g.,* Myres S. McDougal and Florentino P. Felciano, *Law and Minimum World Public Order* 806 (1961); John H.E. Fried, *Transfer of Civilian Manpower From Occupied Territory*, 40 Am. J. Int'l L. 303, 308-11 (1946). For example, the United States State Department protested during the War that the deportation of Belgians violated "humane principles of international practice." *The Krupp Case*, 9 Trials of War Criminals Before the Nuermberg Military Tribunals 1, 1429-30 (1946-49). And after the War ended, the Responsibilities Commission of the 1919 Paris Peace Conference condemned "[d]eportation of civilians" as a violation of the laws and customs of war. *See Commission on the Responsibility of the Authors of the War and on Enforcement of Penalties: Report Presented to the Preliminary Peace Conference*, 14 Am. J. Int'l L. 95, 114 (1920). While the condemnation, as sometimes articulated, was directed at the deportation of *inhabitants* of occupied territory, *see* International Law 345-46 (Hersh Lauterpacht ed., 6th ed. 1944) (stating, in light of "civilized world['s]" reaction to First World War deportation of Belgians and Germans, that "there is no right to deport *inhabitants* to the country of the occupant") (emphasis edded), nothing in the historical record suggests that this term was intended or understood to include illegal aliens, that the condemnation extended to the removal of such persons pursuant to local law, or that the customary law of war had evolved so significantly beyond the Lieber Code's prohibition.

Furthermore, article 49 was written against the background of World War II, and it is the particular atrocities of that war that most directly inform the text. In World War II, Nazi-occupied countries were treated as "vast reservoirs of manpower," and deportations of civilians for purposes of forced labor and slave labor "assumed staggering proportions."[5] The Nazis also employed mass deportations to resettle from

[4] Issued for the Union Army during the Civil War, the Lieber Code "was the first instance in western history in which the government of a sovereign nation established formal guidelines for its army's conduct toward its enemies." Richard Hartigan, *Lieber's Code and the Law of War* 1-2 (1983). It "has had a major influence on the drafting of . . . such treaties as . . . the Geneva Conventions and, of course, on the formation of customary law." Theodor Meron, *Human Rights and Humanitarian Norms as Customary Law* 49n. 131 (1989), and remains "a benchmark for the conduct of an army toward an enemy army and population." Hartigan, *supra*, at 1.

[5] *See* Myres S. McDougal and Florentino P. Felciano, *Law and Minimum World Public Order* 806 (1961). On June 30, 1943, the German Commissioner-General of Manpower declared that the number of

areas conquered or annexed by Germany indigenous non-German populations, such as "over 100,000 French who were expelled from Alsace-Lorraine into Vichy France and over one million Poles who were deported from the western parts of occupied Poland (*Warthegau*) into the so-called Government-General of Poland." Alfred De Zayas, *The Right to One's Homeland, Ethnic Cleansing, and the International Criminal Tribunal for the Former Yugoslavia*, 6 Crim. L.F. 257, 264 (1995). These roundly and universally condemned atrocities explicitly informed the drafting of Article 49. *See, e.g.*, 2A *Final Record*, at 664 (summarizing statement of the Chairman, which "noted that the Committee was unanimous in its condemnation of the abominable practice of deportation.... He suggested that deportations should, in the same way as the taking of hostages, be solemnly prohibited in the Preamble"); Jean S. Pictet, *Commentary on the Geneva Convention Relative to the Protection of Civilian Persons in Time of War* 278 (1958) ("There is doubtless no need to give an account here of the painful recollections called forth by the 'deportations' of the Second World War, for they are still present in everyone's memory.... The thought of the physical and mental suffering endured by these 'displaced persons', among whom there were a great many women, children, old people and sick, can only lead to thankfulness for the prohibition embodied in this paragraph, which is intended to forbid such hateful practices for all time.").

Here, again, however, there is no evidence that the outrage of the world extended to the removal of *illegal aliens* from occupied territory in accordance with local immigration law, and indeed there is no evidence that international law has ever disapproved of such removals. *Cf.* Awn Shawhat Al-Khasawneh, Special Rapporteur, *The Realization of Economic, Social and Cultural Rights: The human rights dimension of population transfer, including the implantation of settlers*, Progress report prepared for the Economic and Social Council, United Nations Commission on Human Rights, E/CN.4/Sub.2/1994/18, *available at* http://www.unhcr.ch/Huridocda/Huridoca.nsf/0/e74eOcf. ¶ 51 (*citing* Guy Goodwin-Gill, *International Law and the Movement of Persons Between States* 262 (1978)) ("Among the grounds upon which the expulsion of aliens on an individual basis is justified in State practice are: entry in breach of law [and] breach of conditions of admission."). The ICRC's account illustrates the point. In summarizing the war-time events that were uppermost in the minds of the drafters as they framed article 49(1), the ICRC Commentary lamented, in particular, "that millions of human beings were torn *from their homes*, separated from their families and deported *from their country*, usually under inhumane conditions." Pictet, *supra*, at 278 (emphases added). And in discussing pre-Convention customary law (including the Nuremberg Trials), the ICRC Commentary remarks that a "great many ... decisions" by the Nuremberg "and other courts" have "stated that the deportation of *inhabitants* of occupied territory is contrary to the laws and customs of war." Pictet, *supra*, at 279 n.3 (emphasis added).[6]

---

foreign workers, including prisoners of war, engaged in the German war economy reached 12,100,000. *See id.; see also* John H.E. Fried, *Transfer of Civilian Manpower From Occupied Territory*, 40 Am. J. Int'l L. 303, 312-13 (1946); 1 Trial of the Major War Criminals Before the International Military Tribunal 244 (New York: *AMS* Press, 1971).

[6] Again, we do not understand the word "inhabitants" to include illegal aliens. During Nuremberg trials that addressed the crime of "deporting civilians," the terms "citizens" and "inhabitants" were used somewhat loosely and interchangeably. For example, in the trial of Field Marshal Erhard Milch, the indictment defined the crime of deportation to involve "citizens," the prosecutor described the crime to involve "people who had been uprooted from their homes in occupied territories," the three-Judge

Accordingly, we conclude that the word "deportations" in article 49 bears the term-of-art meaning that it bore in Roman times and in international law from the Lieber Code through World Wars I and II and right up to the drafting of GC: removal of a person from a country where he has a legal right to be. *Cf., e.g., Community for Creative Non-Violence v. Reid*, 490 U.S. 730, 739-40 (1989) (invoking the "well established" principle that "[w]here Congress uses terms that have accumulated settled meaning under ... the common law, a court must infer, unless the statute otherwise dictates, that Congress means to incorporate the established meaning of these terms"); *Air France v. Saks*, 470 U.S. 392, 399 (1985) (applying similar principles to treaty interpretation). Indeed, "deportation" continues to retain the same term-of-art meaning in the law of international armed conflict today. *See* Rome Statute of the International Criminal Court, July 17, 1998, U.N. Doc. A/CONF.183/9, reprinted in 37 I.L.M. 999 (1998) article 7(2)(d) (defining the "crime against humanity" of "deportation or forcible transfer of population" as "forced displacement of the persons concerned by expulsion or other coercive acts *from the area in which they are lawfully present*, without grounds permitted under international law") (emphasis added); *Prosecutor v. Krnojelac*, Case No.: IT-97-25, Appeals Chamber Judgement, 17 Sept. 2003, Separate Opinion of Judge Schomburg ¶15 ("[T]he actus reus of deportation is forcibly removing or uprooting individuals from the territory and the environment *in which they are lawfully present*.") (emphasis added); *Prosecutor v. Blaskic*, Case No. IT-95-14, Trial Chamber Judgement, 3 Mar. 2000, ¶234 ("The deportation or forcible transfer of civilians means forced displacement of the persons concerned by expulsion or other coercive acts from the area *in which they are lawfully present*, without grounds permitted under international law.") (emphasis added; internal quotation marks omitted). For all these reasons, it follows that article 49's prohibition on "deportations" does not bar the removal of "protected persons" who are illegal aliens from occupied territory pursuant to local immigration law.

Article 49 prohibits "forcible *transfers*" in addition to "deportations." We conclude that what has been said about the latter largely applies to the former. Passages from the ICRC Commentary and the negotiating record illustrate that the words "transfers" and "deportations" were used loosely and, at times, interchangeably to capture the atrocities practiced by the Nazis and the Japanese in occupied territories. *See* 4 Pictet, *Commentary* at 278 ("There is doubtless no need to give an account here of the painful recollections called forth by the '*deportations*' of the Second World War. It will suffice to mention that millions of human beings were torn from their homes, separated from their families and *deported* from their country, usually under inhumane conditions. These mass *transfers* took place for the greatest possible variety of reasons....") (emphases added); 2A *Final Record*, at 664 (summarizing statement of Mr. Slamet (Netherlands) that "[i]n Indonesia, during the last war, numbers of women

---

Tribunal convicted the defendant for the crime as charged, Judge Musmanno's concurring opinion described the crime as extending to the occupied territory's "inhabitants," and the concurring opinion of Judge Phillips described it as extending to the "population" of occupied territory. *United States v. Milch*, 2 Trials of War Criminals Before the Nuremberg Military Tribunals 353, 691-93, 790, 879, 866 (1946-1949). We have found no evidence that any of these formulations were intended or understood to reflect an extension of the customary prohibition of deportations to reach illegal aliens. *See also The RuSHA Case*, A Trial of War Criminals Before the Nuremberg Military Tribunals 1, 610 (1949) (defendants charged with "[e]vacuating enemy *populations from their native lands*") (emphases added).

and children had been *transferred* to unhealthy climates and forced to build roads, and had died as a result") (emphasis added); *id.* at 664 (summarizing statement of Mr. Clattenburg (U.S.), which "quoted the case of part of the population of the little island of Wake who had been *transferred* to Japan") (emphasis added); *id.* at 664 (summarizing statement of the Chairman, which "noted that the Committee was unanimous in its condemnation of the abominable practice of *deportation*.... He suggested that *deportations* should, in the same way as the taking of hostages, be solemnly prohibited in the Preamble.") (emphasis added).

Furthermore, at least when used in connection with "deportations" as a term of art in the international law of armed conflict, "transfers" also appears to connote the relocation of an individual from an area where he is lawfully present. *See, e.g.*, Rome Statute of the International Criminal Court, July 17, 1998, U.N. Doc. A/CONF.183/9, reprinted in 37 I.L.M. 999 (1998) article 7(2)(d) (defining "deportation or *forcible transfer* of population" as "forced displacement of the persons concerned by expulsion or other coercive acts *from the area in which they are lawfully present*, without grounds permitted under international law") (emphases added); *Prosecutor v. Blaskic*, ¶234 ("The deportation or *forcible transfer* of civilians means forced displacement of the persons concerned by expulsion or other coercive acts from the area *in which they are lawfully present*, without grounds permitted under international law.") (emphasis added; internal quotation marks omitted).

Consistent with GC's negotiating record and this more general term-of-art usage, many sources speak of article 49(1) – and implicitly acknowledge its limitation to those lawfully present in occupied territory – without making any distinction between "forcible transfers" and "deportations." *See, e.g.*, S.C. Res. 694 (1991) (Under GC, article 49. "Israel, the occupying power, must refrain from deporting any *Palestinian* civilian from the occupied territories" (emphasis added)); *Kasawari v. Minister of Defence*, HC 456/85, 39(3) Piskei Din 401, digested in 16 Israel Y.B. Hum. Rts. 330, 334 (1986) ("[w]hatever the interpretation of Article 49 may be, it is not applicable to the expulsion of a person who enters an area illegally after the commencement of its belligerent occupation."); Kurt Rene Radley, *The Palestinian Refugees: The Right to Return in International Law*, 72 Am. J. Int'l L. 586, 598 (1978) ("Article 49 forbids the forced and permanent removal of persons from territory *to which they are native*.") (emphasis added); Jean-Marie Henckaerts, *Mass Expulsion in Modern International Law and Practice* 144 ("Article 49 comes into play whenever people are forcibly moved *from their ordinary residences*.") (emphasis added); *see also* Raymund T. Yingling and Robert W. Ginnane, *The Geneva Convention of 1949*, 46 Am. J. Int'l L. 393, 419 (1952) (article 49(1) serves the purpose of preventing a belligerent occupier from "buttress[ing] its home economy and war industry with the forced labor of *the inhabitants* of territory which it has occupied") (emphasis added).

We conclude, accordingly, that article 49(1)'s prohibition on "forcible transfers," like its prohibition on "deportations," does not extend to the removal, pursuant to local immigration law, of "protected persons" who are illegal aliens.

This conclusion comports with common sense. It would be surprising if the Convention were a welcome mat to occupied territory, granting all who enter in violation of local law an instant and (during occupation) irrevocable right to stay. *Cf. Affo v. Commander Israel Defence Force in the West Bank*, 83 I.L.M. 139, 153 (Isr. 1988) ("[O]ne should not view the content of Article 49 as anything but a reference to those arbitrary deportations of groups of nationals as were carried out during World War II for purposes of subjugation, extermination and for similarly cruel reasons. [One should reject an interpretation entailing that] a murderer who escaped to the occupied territory would have a safe haven, which would preclude his transfer to the authorized jurisdiction."). It is also consistent with the general presumption under customary international law, as reflected in Article 43 of the Regulations Respecting the Laws and Customs of War on Land, annexed to Convention (IV) Respecting the Laws and Customs of War on Land, Oct. 18, 1907, art. 42(1), 36 Stat. 2277, I Bevans 631 ("Hague Regulations"), that an occupying power should maintain and enforce the domestic laws of the country occupied.[7] Article 43 of the Hague Regulations provides: "The authority of the legitimate power having actually passed into the hands of the occupant, the latter shall take all steps in his power to re-establish and insure, as far as possible, public order and safety, while respecting, unless absolutely prevented, the laws in force in the country." The exigencies of "public order and safety" will not often "absolutely prevent[]" enforcement of local immigration laws. To the contrary, enforcement of such laws will usually prove essential to maintaining the security of the occupied territory. And while the occupying power may be "absolutely prevented" from enforcing local law by a requirement of the Geneva Conventions, *see* Memorandum for Alberto R. Gonzales, Counsel to the President, and William J. Haynes II, General Counsel of the Department of Defense, from Jay S. Bybee, Assistant Attorney General, *Re: Authority of the President Under Domestic and International Law To Make Fundamental Institutional Changes to the Government of Iraq* 15 (Apr. 14, 2003) ("*Fundamental Institutional Changes Memorandum*"), reading GC to require a suspension of local immigration law would put great and unjustifiable strain on the duty of the occupying power to "insure . . . public order and safety."[8]

[7] Although GC incorporates by reference the Hague Regulations when applied to relations between "Powers who are bound by" the IV Hague Convention, *see* article 154, Iraq is not a party to the Hague, Convention, and therefore cannot be considered bound by that Convention as a matter of treaty law. The United States is likewise under no treaty-based obligation to apply the Hague Regulations to the occupation of Iraq because Iraq is not a "Contracting Power" under the IV Hague Regulations. *See* Hague Convention art, 2, 36 Stat. 2290 ("The provisions contained in the Regulations referred to in Article 1, as well as in the present convention, do not apply except between Contracting Powers, and then only if all the belligerents are parties to the Convention."); Memorandum for Alberto R. Gonzales, Counsel to the President, and William J. Haynes II, General Counsel of the Department of Defense, from Jay S. Bybee, Assistant Attorney General, *Re: Authority of the President Under Domestic and International Law To Make Fundamental Institutional Changes to the Government of Iraq* 10 (Apr. 14, 2003) (stating that "the Hague Regulations do not expressly govern the U.S. conflict with Iraq"). The Hague Regulations are, however, generally taken to be declaratory of customary international law, and the United States may choose to comply with them on that basis. *See generally id.* at 10; *see also United States v. Yousef*, 327 F.3d 56, 92 (2d Cir. 2003) ("Principles of customary international law reflect the practices and customs of States in the international arena that are applied in a consistent fashion and that are generally recognized by what used to be called 'civilized states.'") For present purposes, however, the point is that GC should, as a general matter, be read to be consistent with the principles reflected in the Hague Regulations, whether or not those Regulations apply in a particular case.

[8] It is true that one might reverse the point and argue that the power to change local immigration law under article 43 of the Hague Regulations amounts to a power to eviscerate article 49's prohibition on "deportations" and "forcible transfers." And indeed the custom and practice of occupying powers have at times included "extensive changes" to the laws of an occupied territory, *Fundamental Institutional Changes Memorandum* at II. But this power does not amount to a power to eviscerate article 49, because those changes may only be imposed in accordance with certain "enumerated purposes," such as the occupying power's need to maintain order and security, *id.* at 13, or in order to protect rights guaranteed by the Convention, *id.* at 15. It follows that an occupying power could not, for example, change local immigration law to render all citizens of the occupied territory illegal aliens.

Of course, even the broadest reading of article 49 would not work a complete suspension of local immigration law in Iraq. Rather, it would only suspend the provisions for deportation. Violators of Iraqi immigration law, however, are subject not only to deportation but also to imprisonment. *See* Iraqi Law No. 118 of 1978, article 24; *see also id.*, article 25. Under customary international law as reflected in article 43 of the Hague Regulations, then, the occupying power may be obliged to enforce Iraqi immigration law at least to the extent of imprisoning its transgressors. This requirement would flow not only from the obligation to "respect, unless absolutely prevented, the laws in force in the country," but also from the more general obligation to maintain "public order and safety" – which, whatever else it entails, would presumably include the arrest of law-breakers, *See* Iraqi Law No. 118 of 1978, article 25 ("The Director General [of Nationality] is vested with the penal authority under the Criminal Procedure Law which empowers him to detain the [illegal alien] in custody until he is deported or expelled from the territory of the Republic of Iraq."). The Convention itself makes this requirement explicit: "The penal laws of the occupied territory shall remain in force, with the exception that they may be repealed or suspended by the Occupying Power in cases where they constitute a threat to its security or an obstacle to the application of the present Convention." GC, art. 64. Under the broadest reading of the prohibitions in article 49(1), then, an occupier might be required to imprison illegal aliens, but forbidden from taking the milder step of escorting them to the border instead. It is doubtful that article 49's drafters intended such an implausible result.

In sum, historical context as well as common sense demonstrates that the terms "deportations" and "forcible transfers" in article 49 are terms of art that do not apply to the removal of "protected persons" in occupied territory who are present there in violation of current local law. We conclude, therefore, that the United States would not violate article 49(1) by removing "protected persons" who are illegal aliens from Iraq pursuant to local immigration law."[9]

II. *Temporary Transnational Relocation of "Protected Persons" to Facilitate Interrogation*

We next consider whether GC permits the United States to relocate "protected persons" (whether illegal aliens or not) from Iraq to another country temporarily, to facilitate interrogation. Because GC makes special provision for "protected persons" who have been "accused of offenses," we consider such persons first. We then consider "protected persons" who have not been so accused.

A. *"Protected Persons" Who Have Been Accused of an Offense*

GC specifically provides that "[p]rotected persons accused of offences shall be detained in the occupied country, and if convicted they shall serve their sentences therein." GC, art. 76(1). This provision is unambiguous: "protected persons" who have been "accused of offenses" may not be removed from occupied territory either for pretrial detention or for postconviction imprisonment.

We need not attempt to ascertain the precise meaning of "accused" in this context, for the following can be said with some confidence. Once adjudicative proceedings

---

[9] We recommend that if the choice is made to pursue this course, careful records should be maintained confirming the illegal status of each alien who is removed under current domestic law.

have been initiated against a person, that person has been "accused" within the meaning of Article 76. The initiation of such proceedings may take any form. *Cf. Brewer v. Williams*, 430 U.S. 386 (1977) (noting that certain criminal procedure protections are triggered by initiation of judicial proceedings, "whether by way of formal charge, preliminary hearing, indictment, information, or arraignment"), *quoting Kirby v. Illinois*, 406 U.S. 682 (1972). On the other hand, mere suspicion of an offense would not constitute an accusation, nor would an interrogation based upon such suspicion. *Cf.* Wayne R. LaFave *et al.*, 3 Criminal Procedure, §11.2(b) (1999) ("[The Supreme] Court [has] reaffirmed … that a person does not become an accused for Sixth Amendment purposes simply because he has been detained by the government with the intention of filing charges against him"), *citing United States v. Gouveia*, 467 U.S. 180 (1984). Thus, if an occupying power merely detains a "protected person" for questioning – even if that person is strongly suspected of committing an offense – that person is not yet "accused" for purposes of article 76.[10]

In short, once adjudicative proceedings have been initiated against a "protected person," the person is "accused of an offense" for purposes of article 76, and may not be detained outside of occupied Iraq. But until that time, article 76 does not apply.

B. *"Protected Persons" Who Have Not Been Accused of an Offense*

Finally, we consider whether Article 49(1)'s prohibition of "forcible transfers" and "deportations" bars the United States from temporarily relocating (and detaining) a "protected person" who has not been "accused of an offense" to a location outside of Iraq to facilitate interrogation.

It might be thought that the juxtaposition of the words "deportations" and "transfers" in article 49 reflects a dichotomy between permanent relocations, on the one hand, and temporary relocations, on the other. The word "deportation" does clearly connote permanence. *See Black's Law Dictionary* 526 (4th ed. 1951) (defining "deportation" in Roman law, as "[a] perpetual banishment"); *see also supra* Part I (concluding the meaning of "deportation" as a term of art in the international law of armed conflict flows from its meaning in Roman law). And the word "transfer," by contrast, does not necessarily have that same connotation. *See* XI Oxford English Dictionary 257 (1933) ("conveyance or removal from one place, person, etc. to another"). Were article 49 read in this manner, it would prohibit the United States from temporarily relocating a "protected person" from Iraq to facilitate interrogation.

---

[10] Iraqi law appears to draw a similar distinction, treating someone as a "suspect" during an investigation and as an "accused" once he has been charged in an indictment or summoned or named in a criminal arrest warrant. *See, e.g.,* Statute of the Iraqi Special Tribunal, art. 18(b)-(d) (Dec. 10, 2003) (available at http://www.cpa.iraq.org/human_rights/Statute.htm) (using the term "suspect" to describe person under investigation and "accused" to describe someone charged in an indictment); Iraqi Law on Criminal Proceedings (Law Number 23 of 1971) ¶¶54, 56 (available at https://www.jagcnet.army.mil/JAGCNETInternet/Homepages/AC/CLAMO-Public.nsf/0/85256alc006sc77385256d34006030dc/Body/M2/Iraqi%2520Criminal%2520Procedure%2520Code%2 520English.pdf?OpenElement) (referring to a complaint made against a "suspect" and questioning of "suspects" by examining magistrate during course of initial investigation): *id.* ¶¶87,93 (providing for issuance of a summons to, or an arrest warrant for, an "accused"); *id.* ¶105 (referring to person subject to arrest warrant, or who may be arrested by someone who witnessed him committing an offense, as an "accused").

While this dichotomy has some surface appeal, we ultimately reject it. The phrase "forcible transfers" and the word "deportations," when used as terms of art in the international law of armed conflict, *see supra* Part I, and especially when used in connection with each other, both convey a sense of *uprooting* from one's home. *See, e.g.*, Pictet, *supra*, at 278 (emphasis added) (recalling the "deportations" and "mass transfers" that had occurred during World War II, where "millions of human beings were *torn from their homes*, separated from their families and deported from their country, usually under inhumane conditions") (emphasis added); *United States v. Milch*, 2 Trials of War Criminals Before the Nuremberg Military Tribunals 353, 790 (1946-1949) (prosecutor's description of the crime of "deportation" as involving "people who had been *uprooted from their homes* in occupied territory") (emphasis added); *Prosecutor v. Krnojelac*, Case No.: IT-97-25, Appeals Chamber Judgement, 17 Sept. 2003. Separate Opinion of Judge Schomburg ¶15 ("[T]he actus reus of deportation is forcibly removing or *uprooting* individuals from the territory and the environment in which they are lawfully present.") (emphasis added). The concept of uprooting from one's home clearly suggests *resettlement*, and while it may include not only permanent, but also extended or at least indefinite resettlement, it cannot reasonably be expanded to encompass mere temporary absence, for a brief and definite period, from one's still-established home. *Cf. Kurt Rene Radley, The Palestinian Refugess: The Right to Return in International Law*, 72 Am. J. Int'l L. 586, 598 (1978) ("Article 49 forbids the forced and *permanent* removal of persons from territory to which they are native," (emphasis added)); 2A *Final Record*, at 664 (summarizing statement of Mr. Slamet (Netherlands) that "[i]n Indonesia, during the last war, numbers of women and children had been transferred to unhealthy climates and forced to build roads, and had died as a result"); *id.* at 664 (summarizing statement of Mr, Clattenburg (U.S.), which "quoted the case of part of the population of the little island of Wake who had been transferred to Japan"); GC Art. 49(2) (carving out an exception to Article 49(1)'s prohibition of forcible transfers or deportations to allow evacuations, including transnational evacuations, required to protect the security of the population or by imperative military reasons, provided that "[p]ersons thus evacuated shall be transferred back to their homes as soon as hostilities in the area in question have ceased").[11]

This reading is confirmed by the Convention's structure. As we explain below, if the word "transfer" were read to embrace all temporary relocations, however brief, it would create a prohibition inconsistent with a duty imposed by another provision of the Convention, cause a different paragraph of article 49 to create an implausible

---

[11] For purposes of resolving the questions presented, we need not resolve the precise differences between "deportations" and "forcible transfers under article 49. We presume that these concepts do not overlap entirely. *See Air France v. Saks*, 470 U.S. 392, 397-98 (1985) (where drafters use different terms in the same treaty, they are ordinarily presumed "to mean something different"). One possible distinction is that "deportation," unlike "transfer," perhaps technically entails not only uprooting and resettlement from an area where one is lawfully present but also denationalization or extinguishment of any rights in one's home country. *See Black's Law Dictionary* 526 (4th ed. 1951) (defining "deportation") ("A perpetual banishment, depriving the banished of his rights as a citizen."); *id.* at 525 ("Deportation Lat. In the civil law. A kind of banishment, where a condemned person was sent or carried away to some foreign country, usually to an island ... *and thus taken out the number of Roman citizens.*") (emphasis added); *cf.* 2A Final Record at 621 (observation of Mr. Castberg (Norway) regarding the plight of "ex-German Jews denationalized by the German Government who found themselves in territories subsequently occupied by the German Army"). While we need not embrace this distinction for purposes of this opinion, we note that it is fully consistent with our analysis and conclusions.

result, and render two other provisions of GC entirely superfluous. These structural considerations confirm that article 49 uses the term "transfers," consistent with its connotations when used as a term of art in connection with "deportations" in the law of armed conflict, to refer to relocations involving uprooting and resettlement for a permanent, extended, or at least indefinite duration.

First, we consider article 49's relationship with article 24. Article 24 provides: "The Parties to the conflict shall facilitate the reception of ... children [who are under 15, who are orphaned or separated from their families as a result of the war] in a neutral country for the duration of the conflict with the consent of the Protecting Power." This provision appears in Part II of GC and therefore "cover[s] the whole of the populations of the countries in conflict," GC, article 13, including all individuals in occupied territory, *see* Pictet, *supra*, at 118-19, whether "protected persons" or not. At first glance, article 24's *duty* to relocate certain children – including those who are "protected persons" – to a neutral country might appear to be flatly inconsistent with article 49(1)'s categorical *prohibition* of "forcible transfers" and "deportations" of "protected persons." The relationship between articles 24 and 49(1) is easily understood, however, once it is recognized that the crux of article 49(1) is a prohibition on forcibly *uprooting people from their homes*. The children provided for in article 24 are precisely those who have been orphaned or separated from their homes already, by the war. Thus, relocating such children (even without their consent) does not implicate the central concerns of article 49(1).

Second, article 49(6) provides: "The Occupying Power shall not *deport or transfer* parts of its own civilian population into the territory it occupies." (Emphasis added). As the ICRC commentary explains, this provision was "intended to prevent a practice adopted during the Second World War by certain Powers, which transferred portions of their own population to occupied territory for political or racial reasons or in order, as they claimed, to colonize those territories. Such transfers worsened the economic situation of the native population and endangered their separate existence as a race." Pictet, *supra*, at 283. This practice was often closely related to practices at which article 49(1) was directed – resettling the citizens of occupied countries out of occupied territory. As the International Military Tribunal concluded during the Nuremberg trial, the Nazis had undertaken a "gigantic program" that included three "interwoven and interrelated" aims: "to evacuate and resettle large areas of the conquered territories; to Germanize masses of the population of the conquered territories; and to utilize other masses of the population as slave labor within the Reich." *The RuSHA Case*, 4 Trials of War Criminals Before the Nuremberg Military Tribunals 1, 125 (1949); *see also id.* at 610 (defendants charged with "[e]vacuating enemy populations from their native lands and resettling so-called 'ethnic Germans' (*Volksdeutsche*) on such lands").

Not only do articles 49(1) and 49(6) address related wartime practice, they both do so by prohibiting certain *transfers* and *deportations*. There is a strong presumption that the same words will bear the same meaning throughout the same treaty. *Cf. e.g., Air France v. Saks*, 470 U.S. 392, 398 (1985). This presumption is particularly strong when, as here, the words appear multiple times within the same article.

If "transfer" is understood throughout article 49 to entail – consistent with technical usage – permanent, extended, or at least indefinite resettlement, then the scope of article 49(6)'s prohibition closely corresponds to its intended purpose. By contrast, if "transfer" is understood throughout article 49 to mean any relocation, however brief, then article 49(6) would have a much broader scope and would prohibit an occupying power from placing any members of its civilian population in the occupied country even temporarily. While such a prohibition arguably might not extend to civilian adjuncts to the military occupation administration, it probably would at least extend to various employees of private contractors and non-governmental organizations, *Cf.* GC III, article 4(A)(4) (including as potential prisoners of war "[p]ersons who accompany the armed forces without actually being members thereof, such as civilian members of military aircraft crews, war correspondents, supply contractors, members of labour units or of services responsible for the welfare of the armed forces, provided that they have received authorization from the armed forces which they accompany"). Such a result is far removed from article 49(6)'s intended purpose and would work to the manifest disadvantage of the inhabitants of occupied territory. For these reasons, it seems very implausible that article 49(6)'s prohibition of deportations and transfers *into* occupied territory should be construed so expansively. *See Zicherman v. Korean Air Lines*, 516 U.S. 217, 221-222 (1996) (choosing from among different possible definitions of a treaty term the definition that avoided implausible results). It follows, therefore, that article 49(1)'s prohibition of forcible transfers and deportations *out of* occupied territory likewise should not be construed to extend to temporary transnational relocations of brief but not indefinite duration.[12]

Third, if article 49(1) banned all relocations out of occupied territory, no matter how brief, two different provisions of GC would be superfluous. Article 51 of GC, which makes provision for compelling the labor of "protected persons," provides: "The work shall be carried out only in occupied territory where the persons whose services have been requisitioned are." If article 49 forbade all relocations from occupied territory to another country, this portion of article 51 would be entirely superfluous. But "[t]his phrase, like all the other words of the treaty, is to be given a meaning, if reasonably possible, and rules of construction may not be resorted to render it meaningless or inoperative." *Factor v. Laubenheimer*, 290 U.S. 276, 303-04 (1933). By contrast, if article 49(1) does not forbid brief transnational relocations, article 51 serves an important, independent purpose. While extended or indefinite relocations for purposes of forced labor might constitute "forcible transfers" and thus be prohibited under article 49(1) as well as article 51, at least some instances of briefly bringing an accused "protected person" across a border to engage in forced labor – on a daily basis, for example – would not fall within the scope of the prohibition of article 49 but would be barred by article 51.

Even more relevant to the issue at hand, article 76 of the Convention provides: "Protected persons accused of offences shall be detained in the occupied country, and if convicted they shall serve their sentences therein." If article 49(1) forbade all relocations, however temporary, from occupied territory to another country, then this portion of article 76 too would be entirely superfluous. It follows, therefore, that briefly relocating accused "protected persons" outside of occupied territory for pre-trial

---

[12] We note one significant textual difference between articles 49(1) and 49(6). While the former provision bars only *forcible* transfers (as well as deportations), the latter does not so limit the transfers that it prohibits. We do not read the absence of "forcible" from the latter provision to eliminate connotations of uprooting and resettlement, but rather to indicate that (unlike article 49(1)) article 49(6) prohibits voluntary as well as coercive resettlement. This interpretation is fully consistent with one of the principal purposes of article 49(6). as indicated by the ICRC Commentary quoted in the text – preventing an occupying power from colonizing occupied territory with its own civilian population. Colonization, of course, can be voluntary as well as forcible, but either way it entails uprooting and resettlement.

detention and interrogation – though forbidden by article 76 – falls outside the scope of the prohibition of article 49(1). But if briefly relocating an accused "protected person" to a foreign country for detention and interrogation (though forbidden by article 76) is beyond the scope of article 49, then the otherwise indistinguishable act of briefly relocating a "protected person" who is *not* accused to a foreign country for detention and interrogation (which is *not* forbidden by article 76) must also fall outside the scope of article 49's prohibition.[13]

It might, at first, appear surprising that a different result obtains for accused persons than for those who are not (or are not yet) accused. But special procedural protections often attach to individuals, including suspected offenders, only after they are accused. *See, e.g.,* U.S. Const. amend. VI ("[i]n all criminal prosecutions, the *accused* shall enjoy" various procedural protections) emphasis added); *United States v. Ash*, 413 U.S. 300, 320-21 (1973) (Stewart, J., concurring in judgment) ("[the initiation of] adversary judicial proceedings ... marks the commencement of the 'criminal prosecutions' to which alone the explicit guarantees of the Sixth Amendment [of the U.S. Constitution] are applicable"). "It is only at that time "that the government has committed itself to prosecute, and only then that the adverse positions of government and defendant have solidified. It is then that a defendant finds himself faced with the prosecutorial forces of organized society, and immersed in the intricacies of substantive and procedural criminal law.'" *United States v. Gouveia*, 467 U.S. 180, 189 (1984) (quoting *Kirby v. Illinois*, 406 U.S. 682, 689 (1972)). And in this context, the distinction between those who are and are not accused makes eminent sense: only after a person is accused must he be allowed to prepare his defense, and for this he may require access to resources that are available to him only in his native country.

Thus technical usage suggests, and GC's structure confirms, that Article 49(1)'s prohibition of "deportations" and "forcible transfers" does not extend to all transnational relocations. And, for the reasons we have explained, we conclude that it is permissible to relocate "protected persons" who have not been accused of an offense from Iraq to another country, for a brief but not indefinite period, for purposes of interrogation.[14]

---

[13] We note that the ICRC Commentary appears to take the position that the portions of articles 51 and 76 discussed in the text are, in fact, superfluous: "[t]he provision [of article 76] under which any sentence of imprisonment must be served in the occupied territory itself is based on the fundamental principle forbidding deportations laid down in Article 49." Pictet, *supra* al 363; *see also id.* at 279 (asserting without analysis that Article 49(1)'s prohibition is "strengthened by other Articles in the cases in which its observance appeared to be least certain" and citing, *inter alia*, Articles 51(2) and 76(1)). We do not find this reasoning persuasive. Article 49 may well lay down a fundamental principle, but the scope of this principle must be ascertained by traditional rules of treaty interpretation, including the rule that each provision of a treaty "is to be given a meaning, if reasonably possible, and rules of construction may not be resorted to render it meaningless or inoperative." *Factor*, 290 U.S. at 303-304.

[14] While we conclude that GC does not prohibit temporary relocations of "protected persons" from occupied territory for a brief but not indefinite period, neither technical usage nor the Convention provides clear or precise guidance regarding exactly how long a "protected person" may be held outside occupied territory without running afoul of Article 49. Furthermore, violations of Article 49 may constitute "[g]rave breaches" of the Convention, art 147, and thus "war crimes" under federal criminal law, 18 U.S.C. §2441. For these reasons, we recommend that any contemplated relocations of "protected persons" from Iraq to facilitate interrogation be carefully evaluated for compliance with Article 49 on a case-by-case basis. We will provide additional guidance as necessary to facilitate such evaluations.

Furthermore, although we have previously indicated that only those who "find themselves ... in the hands of a Party to the conflict or Occupying Power" in "occupied territory" or the "territory of a

III. *Conclusion*

Article 49 does not forbid the removal from occupied territory, pursuant to local immigration law, of "protected persons" who are illegal aliens. Nor does it preclude the temporary relocation of "protected persons" (whether illegal aliens or not) who have not been accused of an offense from occupied Iraq to another country, for a brief but not indefinite period, to facilitate interrogation.

Please let us know if we can provide further assistance.

Jack I. Goldsmith III
Assistant Attorney General

party to the conflict" receive the benefits of "protected person" status, *Protected Persons Memorandum* at 5-6, this does not mean that a "protected person" who is captured in occupied territory and then temporarily relocated by the occupying power to a different location thereby forfeits the benefits of "protected person" status. On the contrary, we believe he would ordinarily retain these benefits. *Cf.* Art. 49(2) (providing that, in some circumstances, protected persons may be evacuated outside of occupied territory, but that such persons must be transferred back to their homes as soon as possible).

Reports

The ICRC Report

Report of the International Committee of the Red Cross (ICRC) on the Treatment by the Coalition Forces of Prisoners of War and Other Protected Persons by the Geneva Conventions in Iraq During Arrest, Internment and Interrogation

February 2004

TABLE OF CONTENTS

EXECUTIVE SUMMARY

In its "Report on the Treatment by the Coalition Forces of Prisoners of War and other protected persons in Iraq", the International Committee of the Red Cross (ICRC) draws the attention of the Coalition Forces (hereafter called "the CF") to a number of serious violations of International Humanitarian Law. These violations have been documented and sometimes observed while visiting prisoners of war, civilian internees and other protected persons by the Geneva Conventions (hereafter called persons deprived of their liberty when their status is not specifically mentioned) in Iraq between March and November 2003. During its visits to places of internment of the CF, the ICRC collected allegations during private interviews with persons deprived of their liberty relating to the treatment by the CF of protected persons during their capture, arrest, transfer, internment and interrogation.

The main violations, which are described in the ICRC report and presented confidentially to the CF, include:

- Brutality against protected persons upon capture and initial custody, sometimes causing death or serious injury
- Absence of notification of arrest of persons deprived of their liberty to their families causing distress among persons deprived of their liberty and their families
- Physical or psychological coercion during interrogation to secure information
- Prolonged solitary confinement in cells devoid of daylight
- Excessive and disproportionate use of force against persons deprived of their liberty resulting in death or injury during their period of internment

Serious problems of conduct by the CF affecting persons deprived of their liberty are also presented in the report:

- Seizure and confiscation of private belongings of persons deprived of their liberty
- Exposure of persons deprived of their liberty to dangerous tasks
- Holding persons deprived of their liberty in dangerous places where they are not protected from shelling

According to allegations collected by ICRC delegates during private interviews with persons deprived of their liberty, ill-treatment during capture was frequent. While certain circumstances might require defensive precautions and the use of force on the part of battle group units, the ICRC collected allegations of ill-treatment following capture which took place in Baghdad, Basrah, Ramadi and Tikrit, indicating a consistent pattern with respect to times and places of brutal behavior during arrest. The repetition of such behavior by CF appeared to go beyond the reasonable, legitimate and proportional use of force required to apprehend suspects or restrain persons resisting arrest or capture, and seemed to reflect a usual modus operandi by certain CF battle group units.

According to the allegations collected by the ICRC, ill-treatment during interrogation was not systematic, except with regard to persons arrested in connection with suspected security offences or deemed to have an "intelligence" value in. In these cases, persons deprived of their liberty under supervision of the Military Intelligence were at high risk of being subjected to a variety of harsh treatments ranging from insults, threats and humiliations to both physical and psychological coercion, which in some cases was tantamount to torture, in order to force cooperation with their interrogators.

The ICRC also started to document what appeared to be widespread abuse of power and ill-treatment by the Iraqi police which is under the responsibility of the Occupying Powers, including threats to hand over persons in their custody to the CF so as to extort money from them, effective hand over of such persons to the custody of the CF on allegedly fake accusations, or invoking CF orders or instructions to mistreat persons deprived of their liberty during interrogation.

In the case of the "High Value Detainees" held in Baghdad International Airport, their continued internment, several months after their arrest, in strict solitary confinement in cells devoid of sunlight for nearly 23 hours a day constituted a serious violation of the Third and Fourth Geneva Conventions.

The ICRC was also concerned about the excessive and disproportionate use of force by some detaining authorities against persons deprived of their liberty involved during their internment during periods of unrest or escape attempts that caused death and serious injuries. The use of firearms against persons deprived of their liberty in circumstances where methods without using firearms could have yielded the same result could amount to a serious violation of International Humanitarian Law. The ICRC reviewed a number of incidents of shootings of persons deprived of their liberty with live bullets, which have resulted in deaths or injuries during periods of unrest related to conditions of internment or escape attempts. Investigations initiated by the CF into these incidents concluded that the use of firearms against persons deprived of their liberty was legitimate. However, non-lethal measures could have been used to obtain the same results and quell the demonstrations or neutralize persons deprived of their liberty trying to escape.

Since the beginning of the conflict, the ICRC has regularly brought its concerns to the attention of the CF. The observations in the present report are consistent with those made earlier on several occasions orally and in writing to the CF throughout 2003. In spite of some improvements in the material conditions of internment, allegations of ill-treatment perpetrated by members of the CF against persons deprived of their liberty continued to be collected by the ICRC and thus suggested that the use of ill-treatment against persons deprived of their liberty went beyond exceptional cases and might be considered as a practice tolerated by the CF.

The ICRC report does not aim to be exhaustive with regard to breaches of International Humanitarian Law by the CF in Iraq. Rather, illustrates priority areas that warrant attention and corrective action on the part of CF, in compliance with their International Humanitarian Law obligations.

Consequently the ICRC asks the authorities of the CF in Iraq:

- to respect at all times the human dignity, physical integrity and cultural sensitivity of the persons deprived of their liberty held under their control
- to set up a system of notifications of arrest to ensure quick and accurate transmission of information to the families of persons deprived of their liberty
- to prevent all forms of ill-treatment, moral or physical coercion of persons deprived of their liberty in relation to interrogation

- to set up an internment regime which ensures the respect of the psychological integrity and human dignity of the persons deprived of their liberty
- to ensure that all persons deprived of their liberty are allowed sufficient time every day outside in the sunlight, and that they are allowed to move and exercise in the outside yard
- to define and apply regulations and sanctions compatible with International Humanitarian Law and to ensure that persons deprived of their liberty are fully informed upon arrival about such regulations and sanctions to thoroughly investigate violations of International Humanitarian Law in order to determine responsibilities and prosecute those found responsible for violations of International Humanitarian Law
- to ensure that battle group units arresting individuals and staff in charge of internment facilities receive adequate training enabling them to operate in a proper manner and fulfill their responsibilities as arresting authority without resorting to ill-treatment or making excessive use of force.

INTRODUCTION

1. The International Committee of the Red Cross (ICRC) is mandated by the High Contracting Parties to the Geneva Conventions to monitor the full application of and respect for the Third and Fourth Geneva Conventions regarding the treatment of persons deprived of their liberty. The ICRC reminds the High Contracting Parties concerned, usually in a confidential way, of their humanitarian obligations under all four Geneva Conventions, in particular the Third and Fourth Geneva Conventions as far as the treatment of persons deprived of their liberty is concerned and under Protocol 1 of 1977 additional to the Geneva Conventions, confirmed and reaffirmed rules of customary law and universally acknowledged principles of humanity.

The information contained in this report is based on allegations collected by the ICRC in private interviews with persons deprived of their liberty during its visits to places of internment of the Coalition Forces (CF) between March and November 2003. The allegations have been thoroughly revised in order to present this report as factually as possible. The report is also based on other accounts given either by fellow persons deprived of their liberty inside internment facilities or by family members. During this period, the ICRC conducted some 29 visits in 14 internment facilities in the central and southern parts of the country. The testimonies were collected in Camp Cropper (Core Holding Area, Military Intelligence section, "High Value Detainees" section): Al-Salihlyye, Tasferat and Al-Russafa prisons; Abu Ghraib Correctional Facility (including Camp Vigilant and the "Military Intelligence" section); Umm Qasr and Camp Bucca, as well as several temporary internment places such as Tallil Trans-shipment Place, Camp Condor, Amarah Camp and the Field Hospital in Shaibah.

The ICRC conditions for visits to persons deprived of their liberty in internment facilities are common for all countries where the organization operates. They can be expressed as follows:

- The ICRC must have access to all persons deprived of their liberty who come within its mandate in their place of internment

- The ICRC must be able to talk freely and in private with the persons deprived of their liberty of its choice and to register their identity
- The ICRC must be authorized to repeat its visits to the persons deprived of their liberty
- The ICRC must be notified of arrests, transfers and releases by the detaining authorities

Each visit to persons deprived of their liberty is carried out in accordance with ICRC's working procedures expressed as follows:

- At the beginning of each visit, the ICRC delegates speak with the detaining authorities to present the ICRC's mandate and the purpose of the visit as well as to obtain general information on internment conditions, total of interned population and movements of persons deprived of their liberty (release, arrest, transfer, death, hospitalization).
- The ICRC delegates, accompanied by the detaining authorities tour the internment premises.
- The ICRC delegates hold private interviews with persons of their choice who are deprived of their liberty, with no time limit in a place freely chosen and if necessary register them.
- At the end of each visit, the delegates hold a final talk with the detaining authorities to inform them about the ICRC's findings and recommendations.

2. The aim of the report is to present information collected by the ICRC concerning the treatment of prisoners of war by the CF, civilian internees and other protected persons deprived of their liberty during the process of arrest, transfer, internment and interrogation.

3. The main places of internment where mistreatment allegedly took place included battle group unit stations; the military intelligence sections of Camp Cropper and Abu Ghraib Correctional Facility; Al-Baghdadi, Heat Base and Habbania Camp in Ramadi governorate; Tikrit holding area (former Saddam Hussein Islamic School); a former train station in Al-Khaim, near the Syrian border, turned into a military base; the Ministry of Defense and Presidential Palace in Baghdad, the former *mukhabarat* office in Basrah, as well as several Iraqi police stations in Baghdad.

4. In most cases, the allegations of ill-treatment referred to acts that occurred prior to the internment of persons deprived of their liberty in regular internment facilities, while they were in the custody of arresting authorities or military and civilian intelligence personnel. When persons deprived of their liberty were transferred to regular internment facilities, such as those administered by the military police, where the behavior of guards was strictly supervised, ill-treatment of the type described in this report usually ceased. In these places, violations of provisions of International Humanitarian Law relating to the treatment of persons deprived of their liberty were a result of the generally poor standard of internment conditions (long-term internment in unsuitable temporary facilities) or of the use of what appeared to be excessive force to quell unrest or to prevent attempted escapes.

1. TREATMENT DURING ARREST

5. Protected persons interviewed by ICRC delegates have described a fairly consistent pattern with respect to times and places of brutality by members of the CF arresting them.

6. Arrests as described in these allegations tended to follow a pattern. Arresting authorities entered houses usually after dark, breaking down doors, waking up residents roughly, yelling orders, forcing family members into one room under military guard while searching the rest of the house and further breaking doors, cabinets and other property. They arrested suspects, tying their hands in the back with flexi-cuffs, hooding them, and taking them away. Sometimes they arrested all adult males present in a house, including elderly, handicapped or sick people. Treatment often included pushing people around, insulting, taking aim with rifles, punching and kicking and striking with rifles. Individuals were often led away in whatever they happened to be wearing at the time of arrest – sometimes in pyjamas or underwear – and were denied the opportunity to gather a few essential belongings, such as clothing, hygiene items, medicine or eyeglasses. Those who surrendered with a suitcase often had their belongings confiscated. In many cases personal belongings were seized during the arrest, with no receipt being issued (*see section 6, below*).

7. Certain CF military intelligence officers told the ICRC that in their estimate between 70% and 90% of the persons deprived of their liberty in Iraq had been arrested by mistake. They also attributed the brutality of some arrests to the lack of proper supervision of battle group units.

8. *In accordance with provisions of International Humanitarian Law which oblige the CF to treat prisoners of war and other protected persons humanely and to protect them against acts of violence, threats thereof, intimidation and insults (Articles 13, 14, 17, 87, Third Geneva Convention; Articles 5, 27, 31, 32, 33 Fourth Geneva Convention), the ICRC asks the authorities of the CF to respect at all times the human dignity, physical integrity and cultural sensitivity of the persons deprived of their liberty held under their control. The ICRC also asks the authorities of the CF to ensure that battle group units arresting individuals receive adequate training enabling them to operate in a proper manner and fulfill their responsibilities without resorting to brutality or using excessive force.*

1.1 Notification to families and information for arrestees

9. In almost all instances documented by the ICRC, arresting authorities provided no information about who they were, where their base was located, nor did they explain the cause of arrest. Similarly, they rarely informed the arrestee or his family where he was being taken and for how long, resulting in the de facto "disappearance" of the arrestee for weeks or even months until contact was finally made.

10. When arrests were made in the streets, along the roads, or at checkpoints, families were not informed about what had happened to the arrestees until they managed to trace them or received news about them through persons who had been deprived of their liberty but were later released, visiting family members of fellow persons deprived of their liberty, or ICRC Red Cross Messages. In the absence of a system

to notify the families of the whereabouts of their arrested relatives, many were left without news for months, often fearing that their relatives unaccounted for were dead.

11. Nine months into the present conflict, there is still no satisfactorily functioning system of notification to the families of captured or arrested persons, even though hundreds of arrests continue to be carried out every week. While the main places of internment (Camp Bucca and Abu Ghraib) are part of a centralized notification system through the National Information Bureau (and their data are forwarded electronically to the ICRC on a regular basis), other places of internment such as Mossul or Tikrit are not. Notifications from those places therefore depend solely on capture or internment cards as stipulated by the Third and Fourth Geneva Conventions.

Since March 2003 capture cards have often been filled out carelessly, resulting in unnecessary delays of several weeks or months before families were notified, and sometimes resulting in no notification at all. It is the responsibility of the detaining authority to see to it that each capture or internment card is carefully filled out so that the ICRC is in a position to effectively deliver them to families. The current system of General Information Centers (GIC), set up under the responsibility of the Humanitarian Assistance Coordination Centers (HACC), while an improvement, remains inadequate, as families outside the main towns do not have access to them, lists made available are not complete and often outdated and do not reflect the frequent transfers from one place of internment to another. In the absence of a better alternative, the ICRC's delivery of accurate capture cards remains the most reliable, prompt and effective system to notify the families, provided cards are property filled out.

The ICRC has raised this issue repeatedly with the detaining authorities since March 2003, including at the highest level of the CF in August 2003. Despite some improvement, hundreds of families have had to wait anxiously for weeks and sometimes months before learning of the whereabouts of their arrested family members. Many families travel for weeks throughout the country from one place of internment to another in search of their relatives and often come to learn about their whereabouts informally (through released detainees) or when the person deprived of his liberty is released and returns home.

12. Similarly, transfers, cases of sickness at the time of arrest, deaths, escapes or repatriations continue to be notified only insufficiently or are not notified at all by the CF to the families in spite of their obligation to do so under International Humanitarian Law.

13. *In accordance with the provisions of both the Third Geneva Convention (Articles 70, 122, 123) and the Fourth Geneva Convention (Articles 106, 136, 137, 138, 140), the ICRC reminds the CF of their treaty-based obligation to notify promptly the families of all prisoners of war and other protected persons captured or arrested by them. Within one week, prisoners of war and civilian internees must be allowed to fill out capture or internment cards mentioning at the very least their capture/arrest, address (current place of detention/internment) and state of health. These cards must be forwarded as rapidly as possible and may not be delayed in any manner. As long as there is no centralized system of notifications of arrest set up by CF, it is of paramount importance that these capture cards be filled out properly, so as to allow the ICRC to transmit them rapidly to the concerned families.*

14. *The same obligation of notification to families of captured or arrested persons applies to transfers, cases of sickness, deaths, escapes and repatriation and identification of the dead of the adverse party. All these events must be notified to the ICRC with the full details of the persons concerned, so as to allow the ICRC to inform the concerned families (Articles 120, 121, 122, 123 Third Geneva Convention; Articles 129, 130, 136, 137, 140 Fourth Geneva Convention).*

2. TREATMENT DURING TRANSFER AND INITIAL CUSTODY

15. The ICRC collected several allegations indicating that following arrest persons deprived of their liberty were ill-treated, sometimes during transfer from their place of arrest to their initial internment facility. This ill-treatment would normally stop by the time the persons reached a regular internment facility, such as Camp Cropper, Camp Bucca or Abu Ghraib. The ICRC also collected one allegation of death resulting from harsh conditions of interment and ill-treatment during initial custody.

16. One allegation collected by the ICRC concerned the arrest of nine men by the CF in a hotel in Basrah on 13 September 2003. Following their arrest, the nine men were made to kneel, face and hands against the ground, as if in a prayer position. The soldiers stamped on the back of the neck of those raising their head. They confiscated their money without issuing a receipt. The suspects were taken to Al-Hakimiya, a former office previously used by the *mukhabarat* in Basrah and then beaten severely by CF personnel. One of the arrestees died following the ill-treatment **INTENTIONALLY DELETED** (aged 28, married, father of two children). Prior to his death, his co-arrestees heard him screaming and asking for assistance.

The issued "International Death Certificate" mentioned "Cardio-respiratory arrest – asphyxia" as the condition directly leading to the death. As to the cause of that condition, it mentioned "Unknown" and "Refer to the coroner". The certificate did not bear any other mention, An eyewitness' description of the body given to the ICRC mentioned a broken nose, several broken ribs and skin lesions on the face consistent with beatings. The father of the victim was informed of his death on 18 September, and was invited to identify the body of his son. On 3 October, the commander of the CF in Basrah presented to him his condolences and informed him that an investigation had been launched and that those responsible would be punished. Two other persons deprived of their liberty were hospitalised with severe injuries. Similarly, a week later, an ICRC medical doctor examined them in the hospital and observed large haematomas with dried scabs on the abdomen, buttocks, sides, thigh, wrists, nose and forehead consistent with their accounts of beatings received.

17. During a visit of the ICRC in Camp Bucca on 22 September 2003, a 61-year old person deprived of his liberty alleged that he had been tied, hooded and forced to sit on the hot surface of what he surmised to be the engine of a vehicle, which had caused severe burns to his buttocks. The victim had lost consciousness. The ICRC observed large crusted lesions consistent with his allegation.

18. The ICRC examined another person deprived of his liberty in the "High Value Detainees" section in October 2003 who had been subjected to a similar treatment. He had been hooded, handcuffed in the back, and made to lie face down, on a hot

surface during transportation. This had caused severe skin burns that required three months hospitalization. At the time of the interview he had been recently discharged from hospital. He had to undergo several skin grafts, the amputation of his right index finger, and suffered the permanent loss of the use of his left fifth finger secondary to burn-induced skin retraction. He also suffered extensive burns over the abdomen, anterior aspects of the lower extremities, the palm of his right hand and the sole of his left foot. The ICRC recommended to the CF that the case be investigated to determine the cause and circumstances of the injuries and the authority responsible for the ill-treatment. At the time of writing the results of the report were still pending.

19. During transportation following arrest, persons deprived of their liberty were almost always hooded and tightly restrained with flexi-cuffs. There were occasionally haematoma and linear marks compatible with repeated whipping or beating. He had wrist marks compatible with tight flexi-cuffs. The ICRC also collected allegations of deaths as a result of harsh internment conditions, ill-treatment, lack of medical attention, or the combination thereof, notably in Tikrit holding area formerly known as the Saddam Hussein Islamic School.

22. Some CF military intelligence officers told the ICRC that the widespread ill-treatment of persons deprived of their liberty during arrest, initial internment and "tlactical questioning" was due to a lack of military police on the ground to supervise and control the behavior and activities of the battle groups units, and the lack of experience of intelligence officers in charge of the "tactical questioning".

23. *In accordance with the provision of International Humanitarian Law which obliges the CF to treat prisoners of war and other protected persons humanely and to protect them against acts of violence, threats thereof, intimidation and insults (Articles 13, 14, 17, 87, Third Geneva Convention; Articles 5, 27, 31, 32, 33 Fourth Geneva Convention), the ICRC asks the authorities of the CF to respect at all times the human dignity, physical integrity and cultural sensitivity of the persons deprived of their liberty held in Iraq under their control.*

The ICRC also asks the authorities of the CF to ensure that battle group units transferring and/or holding individuals receive adequate training enabling them to operate in a proper manner and meet their responsibilities without resorting to brutality or using excessive force.

3. TREATMENT DURING INTERROGATION

24. Arrests were usually followed by temporary internment at battle group level or at initial interrogation facilities managed by military intelligence personnel, but accessible to other intelligence personnal (especially in the case of security detainees). The ill-treatment by the CF personnel during interrogation was not systematic, except with regard to persons arrested in connection with suspected security offences or deemed to have an "intelligence" value. In these cases, persons deprived of their liberty supervised by the military intelligence were subjected to a variety of ill-treatments ranging from insults and humiliation to both physical and psychological coercion that in some cases might amount to torture in order to force them to cooperate with their interrogators. In certain cases, such as in Abu Ghraib military intelligence section, methods of

physical and psychological coercion used by the interrogators appeared to be part of the standard operating procedures by military intelligence personnel to obtain confessions and extract information. Several military intelligence officers confirmed to the ICRC that it was part of the military intelligence process to hold a person deprived of his liberty naked in a completely dark and empty call for a prolonged period to use inhumane and degrading treatment, including physical and psychological coercion, against persons deprived of their liberty to secure their cooperation.

3.1 Methods of Ill-treatment

25. The methods of ill-treatment most frequently alleged during interrogation included.

- Hooding, used to prevent people from seeing and to disorient them, and also to prevent them from breathing freely. One or sometimes two bags, sometimes with an elastic blindfold over the eyes which, when slipped down, further impeded proper breathing. Hooding was sometimes used in conjunction with beatings thus increasing anxiety as to when blows would come. The practice of hooding also allowed the interrogators to remain anonymous and thus to act with impunity. Hooding could last for periods from a few hours to up to two to four consecutive days, during which hoods were lifted only for drinking, eating or going to the toilets;
- Handcuffing with flexi-cuffs, which were sometimes made so tight and used for such extended periods that they caused skin lesions and long-term after-effects on the hands (nerve damage), as observed by the ICRC;
- Beatings with hard objects (including pistols and rifles), slapping, punching, kicking with knees or feet on various parts of the body (legs, sides, lower back, groin);
- Pressing the face into the ground with boots;
- Threats (of ill-treatment, reprisals against family members, imminent execution or transfer to Guantanamo):
- Being stripped naked for several days while held in solitary confinement in an empty and completely dark cell that included a latrine.
- Being held in solitary confinement combined with threats (to intern the individual indefinitely, to arrest other family members, to transfer the individual to Guantanamo), insufficient sleep, food or water deprivation, minimal access to showers (twice a week), denial of access to open air and prohibition of contacts with other persons deprived of their liberty;
- Being paraded naked outside cells in front of other persons deprived of their liberty, and guards, sometimes hooded or with women's underwear over the head;
- Acts of humiliation such as being made to stand naked against the wall of the cell with arms raised or with women's underwear over the head for prolonged periods – while being laughed at by guards, including female guards, and sometimes photographed in this position;
- Being attached repeatedly over several days, for several hours each time, with handcuffs to the bars of their cell door in humiliating (i.e. naked or in underwear) and/or uncomfortable position causing physical pain;
- Exposure while hooded to loud noise or music, prolonged exposure while hooded to the sun over several hours, including during the hottest time of the day

when temperatures could reach 50 degrees Celsius (122 degrees Fahrenheit) or higher;

• Being forced to remain for prolonged periods in stress positions such as squatting or standing with or without the arms lifted.

26. These methods of physical and psychological coercion were used by the military intelligence in a systematic way to gain confessions and extract information or other forms of cooperation from persons who had been arrested in connection with suspected security offences or deemed to have an "intelligence value".

3.2 Military Intelligence section, "Abu Ghraib Correctional Facility"

27. In mid-October 2003, the ICRC visited persons deprived of their liberty undergoing interrogation by military intelligence officers in Unit 1A, the "isolation section" of Abu Ghraib Correctional Facility. Most of these persons deprived of their liberty had been arrested in early October. During the visit, ICRC delegates directly witnessed and documented a variety of methods used to secure the cooperation of the persons deprived of their liberty with their interrogators. In particular they witnessed the practice of keeping persons deprived of their liberty completely naked in totally empty concrete cells and in total darkness, allegedly for several consecutive days. Upon witnessing such cases, the ICRC interrupted its visits and requested an explanation from the authorities. The military intelligence officer in charge of the interrogation explained that this practice was "part of the process". The process appeared to be a give-and-take policy whereby persons deprived of their liberty were "drip-fed" with new items (clothing, bedding, hygiene articles, lit cell, etc.) in exchange for their "cooperation". The ICRC also visited other persons deprived of their liberty held in total darkness, others in dimly lit cells who had been allowed to dress following periods during which they had been held naked. Several had been given women's underwear to wear under their jumpsuit (men's underwear was not distributed), which they felt to be humiliating.

The ICRC documented other forms of ill-treatment, usually combined with those described above, including threats, insults, verbal violence, sleep deprivation caused by the playing of loud music or constant light in cells devoid of windows, tight handcuffing with flexi-cuffs causing lesions and wounds around the wrists. Punishment included being made to walk in the corridors handcuffed and naked, or with women's underwear on the head, or being handcuffed either dressed or naked to the iron bars or the cell door. Some persons deprived of their liberty presented physical marks and psychological symptoms, which were compatible with these allegations. The ICRC medical delegate examined persons deprived of their liberty presenting signs of concentration difficulties, memory problems, verbal expression difficulties, incoherent speech, acute anxiety reactions, abnormal behaviour and suicidal tendencies. These symptoms appeared to have been caused by the methods and duration of interrogation. One person held in isolation that the ICRC examined, was unresponsive to verbal and painful stimuli. His heart rate was 120 beats per minute and his respiratory rate 18 per minute. He was diagnosed as suffering from somatoform (mental) disorder, specifically a conversion disorder, most likely due to the ill-treatment he was subjected to during interrogation.

According to the allegations collected by the ICRC, detaining authorities also continued to keep persons deprived of their liberty during the period of interrogation, uninformed of the reason for their arrest. They were often questioned without knowing what they were accused of. They were not allowed to ask questions and were not provided with an opportunity to seek clarification about the reason for their arrest. Their treatment tended to vary according to their degree of cooperation with their interrogators: those who cooperated were accorded preferential treatment such as being allowed contacts with other persons deprived of their liberty, being allowed to phone their families, being given clothes, bedding equipment, food, water or cigarettes, being allowed access to showers, being held in a lit cell, etc.

3.3 Umm Qasr (JFIT) and Camp Bucca (JIF/ICE)

28. Since the establishment of Umm Qasr camp and its successor, Camp Bucca, persons deprived of their liberty undergoing interrogation, whether they had been arrested by British, Danish, Dutch or Italian armed forces were segregated from other internees in a separate section of the camp designed for investigation. This section was initially operated by the British Armed Forces who called it Joint Field Intelligence Team (JFIT). On 7 April, its administration was handed over to the US Armed Forces, which renamed it Joint Interrogation Facility/Interrogation Control Element (JIF/ICE). On 25 September 2003 its administration was handed back to the British Armed Forces.

29. The CF intelligence personnel interrogated persons deprived of their liberty of concern to them in this section. They were either accused of attacks against the CF or deemed to have an "intelligence value". They could be held there from a few days to several weeks, until their interrogation was completed. During a visit in September 2003, the ICRC interviewed in that section several persons deprived of their liberty that had been held there for periods from three to four weeks.

30. Initially, inmates were routinely treated by their guards with general contempt, with petty violence such as having orders screamed at them and being cursed, kicked, struck with rifle butts, roughed up or pushed around. They were reportedly handcuffed in the back and hooded for the duration of the interrogation and were prohibited from talking to each other or to the guards. Hooding appeared to be motivated by security concerns as well as to be part of standard intimidation techniques used by military intelligence personnel to frighten inmates into cooperating. This was combined with deliberately maintaining uncertainty about what would happen to the inmates, and a generally hostile attitude on the part of the guards. Conditions of internment improved according to the degree of cooperation of the persons deprived of his liberty. Interrogated persons deprived of their liberty were held in two separate sections. Those under initial investigation were reportedly not allowed to talk to each other (purportedly to avoid exchange of information and "versions of events" between them). They were not allowed to stand up or walk out of the tent but they had access to water with which to wash themselves. Once they had cooperated with their interrogators, they were transferred to the "privileged" tent where the above mentioned restrictions were lifted.

31. Persons deprived of their liberty undergoing interrogation by the CF were allegedly subjected to frequent cursing, insults and threats, both physical and verbal,

such as having rifles aimed at them in a general way or directly against the temple, the back of the head, or the stomach, and threatened with transfer to Guantanamo, death or indefinite internment. Besides mentioning the general climate of intimidation maintained as one of the methods used to pressure persons deprived of their liberty to cooperate with their interrogators, none of those interviewed by the ICRC in Umm Qasr and Camp Bucca spoke of physical ill-treatment during interrogation. All allegations of ill-treatment referred to the phase of arrest, initial internment (at collecting points, holding areas) and "tactical questioning" by military intelligence officers attached to battle group units, prior to transfer to Camp Bucca.

3.4 Previous actions taken by the ICRC in 2003 on the issue of treatment

32. On 1 April, the ICRC informed orally the political advisor of the commander of British Armed Forces at the CF Central Command in Doha about methods of ill-treatment used by military intelligence personnel to interrogate persons deprived of their liberty in the internment camp of Umm Qasr. This intervention had the immediate effect to stop the systematic use of hoods and flexi-cuffs in the interrogation section of Umm Qasr. Brutal treatment of persons deprived of their liberty also allegedly ceased when the 800th MP Brigade took over the guarding of that section in Umm Qasr. UK Forces handed over Umm Qasr holding area to the 800th MP Brigade on 09.04.03. The 800th MP Brigade then built Camp Bucca two kilometers away.

33. In May 2003, the ICRC sent to the CF a memorandum based on over 200 allegations of ill-treatment of prisoners of war during capture and interrogation at collecting points, battle group stations and temporary holding areas. The allegations were consistent with marks on bodies observed by the medical delegate. The memorandum was

INTENTIONALLY DELETED

handed over to US Central Command in Doha, Sate of Qatar. Subsequently, one improvement consisted in the removal of wristbands with the remark "terrorist" given to foreign detainees.

34. In early July, the ICRC sent the CF a working paper detailing approximately 50 allegations of ill-treatment in the military intelligence section of Camp Cropper at Baghdad International Airport. They included a combination of petty and deliberate acts of violence aimed at securing the cooperation of the persons deprived of their liberty with their interrogators: threats (to intern individuals indefinitely, to arrest other family members, to transfer individuals to Guantanamo) against persons deprived of their liberty or against members of their families (in particular wives and daughters); hooding: tight handcuffing; use of stress positions (kneeling, squatting, standing with arms raised over the head) for three or four hours; taking aim at individuals with rifles, striking them with rifle butts, slaps, punches, prolonged exposure to the sun, and isolation in dark cells. ICRC delegates witnessed marks on the bodies of several persons deprived of their liberty consistent with their allegations. In one illustrative case, a person deprived of his liberty arrested at home by the CF on suspicion of involvement in an attack against the CF, was allegedly beaten during interrogation in a location in the vicinity of Camp Cropper. He alleged that he had been hooded and cuffed with flexi-cuffs, threatened to be tortured and killed, urinated on, kicked in the head, lower back and groin, force-fed a baseball which was tied into the mouth

using a scarf and deprived of sleep for four consecutive days, interrogators would allegedly take turns ill-treating him. When he said he would complain to the ICRC he was allegedly beaten more. An ICRC medical examination revealed haematoma in the lower back, blood in urine, sensory loss in the right hand due to tight handcuffing with flexi-cuffs, and a broken rib.

Shortly after that intervention was sent, the military intelligence internment section was closed and persons deprived of their liberty were transferred to what became the "High Value Detainees" section of the airport, a regular internment facility under the command of the 115th Military Police Battalion. From this time onwards, the ICRC observed that the ill-treatment of this category of persons deprived of their liberty by military intelligence declined significantly and even stopped, while their interrogation continued through to the end of the year 2003.

3.5 Allegations of ill-treatment by Iraqi police

35. The ICRC has also collected a growing body of allegations relating to widespread abuse of power and ill-treatment of persons in the custody of Iraqi police. This included the extensive practice of threatening to handover these persons to the CF for internment, or claiming to act under the CF instructions, in order to abuse their power and extort money from persons taken in custody. Allegations collected by the ICRC indicated that numerous people had been handed over to the CF on the basis of unfounded accusations (of hostility against the CF, or belonging to opposition forces) because they were unable or unwilling, to pay bribes to the police. Alleged ill-treatment during arrest and transportation included hooding, tight handcuffing, verbal abuse, beating with fists and rifle butts, and kicking. During interrogation, the detaining authorities allegedly whipped persons deprived of their liberty with cables on the back, kicked them in the lower parts of the body, including in the testicles, handcuffed and left them hanging from the iron bars of the cell windows or doors in painful positions for several hours at a time, and burned them with cigarettes (signs on bodies witnessed by ICRC delegates). Several persons deprived of their liberty alleged that they had been made to sign a statement that they had not been allowed to read. These allegations concerned several police stations in Baghdad including Al-Qana, Al-Jiran Al-Kubra in al-Amariyya, Al-Hurriyyeh in Al-Doura, Al-Salhiyye in Salhiyye, and Al-Baiah. Many persons deprived of their liberty drew parallels between police practices under the occupation with those of the former regime.

36. In early June 2003, for instance, a group of persons deprived of their liberty was taken to the former police academy after they had been arrested. There, they were allegedly hooded and cuffed and made to stand against a wall while a policeman placed his pistol against their heads and pulled the trigger in a mock execution (the pistol was in fact unloaded); they were also allegedly forced to sit on chairs where they were hit on the legs, the soles of their feet and on their sides with sticks. They also allegedly had water poured on their legs and had electrical shocks administered to them with stripped tips of electric wires. The mother of one of the persons deprived of liberty was reportedly brought in and the policemen threatened to mistreat her. Another person deprived of his liberty was threatened with having his wife brought in and raped. They were made to fingerprint their alleged confessions of guilt, which resulted in their transfer to the CF to be interned pending trial.

37. *The ICRC reminds the authorities of the CF that prisoners of war and other protected persons in the custody of occupying forces must be humanely treated at all times; they must not be subjected to cruel or degrading treatment; and must be protected against all acts of violence (Articles 13, 14, Third Geneva Convention; Article 27, Fourth Geneva Convention). Torture and other forms of physical and psychological coercion against prisoners of war and other interned persons for the purpose of extracting confession or information is prohibited in all cases and under all circumstances without exception (Articles 17 and 87, Third Geneva Convention; Articles 5, 31 and 32, Fourth Geneva Convention). Confessions extracted under coercion or torture can never be used as evidence of guilt (Articles 99, Third Geneva Convention, Article 31, Fourth Geneva Convention). Such violations of International Humanitarian Law should be thoroughly investigated in order to determine responsibilities and prosecute those found responsible (Article 129, Third Geneva Convention and Article 146, Fourth Geneva Convention).*

4. TREATMENT IN REGULAR INTERNMENT FACILITIES

4.1 General conditions of treatment

38. The ICRC assessed the treatment of persons deprived of their liberty in regular internment facilities by the CF personnel as respectful, with a few individual exceptions due to individual personalities or occasional loss of control on the part of the guards. Abusive behavior by guards, when reported to their officers, was usually quickly reprimanded and disciplined by superiors.

39. The ICRC often noted a serious communication gap between detention personnel and persons deprived of their liberty, primarily due to the language barrier, which resulted in frequent misunderstandings. This was compounded by a widespread attitude of contempt on the part of guards, in reaction to which persons deprived of their liberty, which often complained of being treated like inferiors, adopted a similar attitude.

40. The ICRC occasionally observed persons deprived of their liberty being slapped, roughed up, pushed around or pushed to the ground either because of poor communication (a failure to understand or a misunderstanding of orders given in English was construed by guards as resistance or disobedience), a disrespectful attitude on the part of guards, a reluctance by persons deprived of their liberty to comply with orders, or a loss of temper by guards.

41. Disciplinary measures included being taken out of the compound, handcuffed and made to stand, sit, squat or lie down in the sand under the sun for up to three or four hours, depending on the breach of discipline (disrespectful behavior towards guards, communication between persons deprived of their liberty transferring from one compound to another, disobeying orders); temporary suspension of cigarette distribution, and temporary segregation in disciplinary confinement sections of the detention facilities.

42. Despite the fact that reductions in the availability of water or food rations or, more commonly, cigarettes were occasionally observed, the prohibition on collective punishment provided for under International Humanitarian Law (Articles 26.6, 87.3, Third Geneva Convention and Article 33, Fourth Geneva Convention) appeared to be generally respected by the detaining authorities.

4.2 "High Value Detainees" section, Baghdad International Airport

43. Since June 2003, over a hundred "high value detainees" have been held for nearly 23 hours a day in strict solitary confinement in small concrete cells devoid of daylight. This regime of complete isolation strictly prohibited any contact with other persons deprived of their liberty, guards, family members (except through Red Cross Messages) and the rest of the outside world. Even spouses and members of the same family were subject to this regime. Persons deprived of their liberty whose "investigation" was nearing completion were reportedly allowed to exercise together outside their cells for twenty minutes twice a day or go to the showers or toilets together. The other persons deprived of their liberty still under interrogation reportedly continued to be interned in total "segregation" (i.e., they were allowed to exercise outside their cells for twenty minutes twice a day and to go to the showers or toilets but always alone and without any contact with others). Most had been subjected to this regime for the past five months. Attempts to contact other persons deprived of their liberty or simply to exchange glances or greetings were reportedly sanctioned by reprimand or temporary deprivation of time outside their cells. Since August 2003, the detainees have been provided with the Koran. They have been allowed to receive books of a non-political nature, but no newspapers or magazines on current affairs. The internment regime appeared to be motivated by a combination of security concerns (isolation of the persons deprived of their liberty from the outside world) and the collection of intelligence. All had been undergoing interrogation since their internment, in spite of the fact that none had been charged with criminal offence.

On 30 October 2003, the ICRC wrote to the Detaining Authorities recommending that this policy be discontinued and replaced by a regime of internment consistent with the CF's obligations under the Geneva Conventions.

44. *The internment of persons in solitary confinement for months at a time in cells devoid of daylight for nearly 23 hours a day is more severe than the forms of internment provided for in the Third and Fourth Geneva Conventions (investigation of criminal offences or disciplinary punishment). It cannot be used as a regular, ordinary mode of holding of prisoners of war or civilian internees. The ICRC reminds the authorities of the Coalition Forces in Iraq that internment of this kind contravenes Articles 21, 25, 89, 90, 95, 103 of the Third Geneva Convention and Articles 27, 41, 42, 78, 82, 118, 125 of the Fourth Geneva Convention. The ICRC recommends to the authorities of the CF that they set up an internment regime which ensures respect for the psychological integrity and human dignity of the persons deprived of their liberty and that they make sure that all persons deprived of their liberty are allowed sufficient time every day outside in the sunlight and the opportunity to move about and exercise in the outside yard.*

5. EXCESSIVE AND DISPROPORTIONATE USE OF FORCE AGAINST PERSONS DEPRIVED OF THEIR LIBERTY BY THE DETAINING AUTHORITIES

45. Since March 2003, the ICRC recorded, and in some cases, witnessed, a number of incidents in which guards shot at persons deprived of their liberty with live

ammunition, in the context either of unrest relating to internment conditions or of escape attempts by individuals:

Camp Cropper, 24 May 2003: In the context of a hunger strike, unrest broke out in the camp prior to ICRC visit. One person deprived of his liberty suffered a gunshot wound.

Camp Cropper, 9 June 2003: Six persons deprived of their liberty were injured by live ammunition after a guard opened fire on the group in an attempt to quell a demonstration.

Camp Cropper, 12 June 2003: Two, or possibly three, persons deprived of their liberty were shot at when they attempted to escape through the barbed wire fence. One of them, Akheel Abd Al-Hussein from Baghdad, was wounded and later died after being taken to the hospital. The other person deprived of his liberty was recaptured and received treatment for gunshot wounds.

Abu Ghraib, 13 June 2003: When unrest flared up, guards from three watchtowers opened fire at the demonstrators, injuring seven persons deprived of their liberty and killing another, Alaa Jasim Hassan. The authorities investigated the matter and concluded that the "shooting was justified as the "three tower [guards] determined that the lives of the interior guards were threatened".

Abu Ghraib, late June 2003: During unrest, one person deprived of his liberty was injured by live ammunition when a guard opened fire.

Abu Ghraib, 24 November 2003: During a riot four detainees were killed by US MP guards. The killing took place after unrest erupted in one of the compounds (no 4). The detainees claimed to be unhappy with the situation of detention. Specifically, lack of food, clothing, but more importantly the lack of judicial guarantees and, especially important during the time of Eid al-Fitr, lack of family visits or lack of contacts all together. The detainees alleged to have gathered near the gate whereupon the guards panicked and started shooting. Initially, non-lethal ammunition was used which was subsequently replaced by live ammunition.

The report handed over by the CF to the ICRC states that detainees were trying to force open the gate. It further states that several verbal warnings were given and non-lethal ammunition fired at the crowd, After 25 minutes deadly force was applied resulting in the death of four detainees.

INTENTIONALLY DELETED

The narrative report furnished by the CF does not address the reason for the riot in any way and does not give any recommendations as to how a similar incident could be avoided. It does not question the use of lethal force during such an incident.

Camp Bucca, 16–22 April 2003: ICRC delegates witnessed a shooting incident, which caused the death of one person deprived of his liberty and injury of another. A first shot was fired on the ground by a soldier located outside the compound in a bid to rescue one of the guards, allegedly being threatened by a prisoner of war armed with a stick, the second shot injured a prisoner of war in the left forearm, and the third shot killed another prisoner of war.

Camp Bucca, 22 September 2003: Following unrest in a section of the camp, one person deprived of his liberty, allegedly throwing stones, was fired upon by a guard in a watchtower. He suffered a gunshot wound to the upper part of the chest, the bullet passed through the chest and exited from the back. The investigation undertaken by the CF concluded that "the compound guards correctly utilized the rules of engagement and that numerous non-lethal rounds were dispersed to no avail." The person deprived of his liberty "was the victim of a justifiable shooting". An ICRC delegate and an interpreter witnessed most of the events. At no point did the persons deprived of their liberty, and the victim shot at, appear to pose a serious threat to the life or security of the guards who could have responded to the situation with less brutal measures. The shooting showed a clear disregard for human life and security of the persons deprived of their liberty.

46. These incidents were investigated summarily by the CF. They concluded in all cases that a legitimate use of firearms had been made against persons deprived of their liberty, who, except perhaps in Abu Ghraib on 13 June 2003, were unarmed and did not appear to pose any serious threat to anyone's life justifying the use of firearms. In all cases, less extreme measures could have been used to quell the demonstrations or neutralize persons deprived of their liberty trying to escape.

47. In connection with the 22 September 2003 incident, the ICRC wrote on 23 October to the Commander of the 800th MP Brigade and recommended the adoption of crowd control measures consistent with the rules and principles of the Third and Fourth Geneva Conventions and other applicable international norms relating to the use of force or firearms by law-enforcement personnel.

48. Since May 2003, the ICRC repeatedly recommended to the CF to use non-lethal methods to deal with demonstrations, riots or escape attempts. In Camp Cropper, its recommendations were heeded. After the initial deplorable incidents no further shooting of persons deprived of their liberty has occurred since November 2003. In mid-July, the ICRC witnessed a demonstration in that camp, in spite of some violence by the persons deprived of their liberty, the problem was efficiently dealt with by the camp commander without any excessive use of force. He called in anti-riot military policemen, refrained from any act that might have provoked further anger from the persons deprived of their liberty, waited patiently for the emotions to calm down and then sought to establish dialogue with the persons deprived of their liberty through their section representatives. The unrest was quieted down without any violence.

49. *The ICRC reminds the authorities of the CF that the use of firearms against persons deprived of their liberty, especially against those who are escaping or attempting to escape is an extreme measure which should not be disproportionate to the legitimate objective to be achieved (to apprehend the individual) and shall always be preceded by warning appropriate to the circumstances (Article 42 Third Geneva Convention).*

The CF detaining personnel should be provided with adequate training to deal with incidents in their internment facilities. Firearms should not be used except when a suspected offender offers armed resistance or otherwise jeopardizes the lives of others and only when less extreme measures are not sufficient to restrain or apprehend him (Article 3 of the Code of Conduct for Law Enforcement Officials and Article 9 of the Basic Principles on the Use of Force and Firearms by Law Enforcement Officials).

In every instance in which a firearm is discharged, a report should be made promptly to the competent authorities. All deaths or serious injuries of a person deprived of his liberty caused or suspected to have been caused by a sentry should be immediately followed by a proper inquiry by the Detaining Power which should ensure the prosecution of any person(s) found responsible (Article 121, Third Geneva Convention; Article 131, Fourth Geneva Convention).

6. SEIZURE AND CONFISCATION OF PRIVATE BELONGINGS OF PERSONS DEPRIVED OF THEIR LIBERTY

50. The ICRC collected numerous allegations of seizure and confiscation of private property (money, cars and other valuables) by the CF in the context of arrests. In only a few cases were receipts issued to the arrested person or his family, detailing the items confiscated. This was perceived by persons deprived of their liberty as outright theft or pillage. The following examples will serve to illustrate the allegations:

- **INTENTIONALLY DELETED**
  alleged that the CF took US$22,000 in cash and his personal luggage during his arrest;
- **INTENTIONALLY DELETED**
  claimed that large amounts of money and personal effects were confiscated by the CF when he was arrested at his home on 27–28 May 2003. The items confiscated allegedly included 71,450,000 Iraqi dinars, 14,000 US dollars, two wedding rings, a video camera, a watch, real-estate property documents, his wife's residential documents, his father's will, his private diaries, as well as most of the family private documents and personal identity and other papers;
- **INTENTIONALLY DELETED**
  claimed that his car was confiscated when he was arrested by the CF in Basrah on 16 July 2003.
- **INTENTIONALLY DELETED**
  claimed that CF confiscated two million Iraqi dinars when arrested at his home on 21 August 2003;
- **INTENTIONALLY DELETED**
  claimed that his money and two cars were confiscated when he was arrested by the CF on 11 August 2003.

51. In Camp Cropper, Camp Bucca and Abu Ghraib, a system was gradually put in place whereby personal belongings in the possession of persons deprived of their liberty at the time of their arrival in these facilities which they could not keep with them (money, other valuables, spare clothing, identity papers) were registered and kept until their release. In these cases, a receipt was usually issued to the person deprived of his liberty and his belongings were returned when he was released. However, this system took no account of the property seized during arrest.

52. In response to property loss or damage caused to property by the CF during raids and also to complaints regarding pension or salaries, the CF established a compensation system open to everyone, including internees and the general public Complaints could be filed at General Information Centers (GIC), set up under the responsibility of the Humanitarian Assistance Coordination Centers (HACC).

Supporting evidence, which is problematic given that arresting authorities rarely issue receipts, should back claims. The ICRC is not yet able to assess the efficiency of this compensation system although it has had the possibility to visit one of the GICs. There are nine GICs in the city of Baghdad and one in the city of Mosul, there are however none in the other parts of the country therefore depriving a large number of persons of the possibility to file complaints

53. *In accordance with international legal provisions, the ICRC reminds the authorities of the CF that pillage is prohibited by international Humanitarian Law (Article 33, Fourth Geneva Convention), that private property may not be confiscated (Article 46.2, 1907 Hague Convention No IV), and that an army of occupation can only take possession of cash, funds, and realizable securities which are strictly the property of the State. (Article 53, 1907 Hague Convention No IV).*

In addition, persons deprived of their liberty shall be permitted to retain articles of personal use. Valuables may not be taken from them except in accordance with an established procedure and receipts must be issued. (Article 18. 68.2, Third Geneva Convention and Article 97, Fourth Geneva Convention).

7. EXPOSURE OF INTERNEES/DETAINEES TO DANGEROUS TASKS

54. On 3 September 2003 in Camp Bucca, three persons deprived of their liberty were severely injured by the explosion of what apparently was a cluster bomb:

INTENTIONALLY DELETED
(bilateral below-knee amputation)

INTENTIONALLY DELETED
(bilateral above-knee amputation)

INTENTIONALLY DELETED
(left above-knee amputation)

They were part of a group of 10 persons deprived of their liberty involved in voluntary work to clear rubbish along the barbed-wire fence of the camp. They were transferred to the British Field Military Hospital where they received appropriate medical treatment. Their injuries required limb amputations.

55. On 23 October 2003, the ICRC wrote to the officer commanding the 800th MP Brigade to request an investigation into the incident. The ICRC encouraged the CF not to engage persons deprived of their liberty in dangerous labour.

56. *The ICRC recommends to the authorities of the CF that all three victims be properly compensated as provided for by both Third and Fourth Geneva Conventions (Article 68, Third Geneva Convention and Article 95, Fourth Geneva Convention).*

8. PROTECTION OF PERSONS DEPRIVED OF THEIR LIBERTY AGAINST SHELLING

57. Since its reopening by the CF, Abu Ghraib prison has been the target of frequent night shelling by mortars and other weapons, which resulted, on several occasions, in persons deprived of their liberty being killed or injured. During the month of July, the Commander of the facility reported at least 25 such attacks. On 16 August, three mortar rounds landed in the prison compound, killing at least five and injuring 67 persons deprived of their liberty. Subsequent attacks caused further deaths and injuries. An ICRC team visited Abu Ghraib on 17 August and noticed the lack of protective measures: while the CF personnel were living in concrete buildings, all persons deprived of their liberty were sheltered under tents in compounds which had no bunkers or any other protection, rendering them totally vulnerable to shelling.

Persons deprived of their liberty alleged that they had not been advised on what to do to protect themselves in the event of shelling. They were dismayed and felt that the authorities "did not care". After these attacks, security was improved around the prison compound to reduce the risk of further attacks. However, steps taken to ensure the protection of persons deprived of their liberty remained insufficient. The inmates were allowed to fill and place sandbags around the perimeter of each tent. By late October, sandbags had not been placed around all tents and those sandbags that were in place did not offer adequate protection from shelling or projectile explosions.

58. *In accordance with International Humanitarian Law provisions, the ICRC reminds the authorities of the CF that the detaining power must not set up places of internment in areas particularly exposed to the dangers of war (Article 23.1, Third Geneva Convention and Article 83, Fourth Geneva Convention). In all places of internment exposed to air raids and other hazards of war, shelters adequate in number and structure to ensure the necessary protection must be made available. In the event of an alarm, the internees must be free to enter such shelters as quickly as possible (Article 23.2, Third Geneva Convention and Article 88, Fourth Geneva Convention). When a place of internment is found to be unsafe, persons deprived of their liberty should be transferred to other places of internment, offering adequate security and living conditions in accordance with the Third and Fourth Geneva Conventions.*

CONCLUSION

59. This ICRC report documents serious violations of International Humanitarian Law relating to the conditions of treatment of the persons deprived of their liberty held by the CF in Iraq. In particular, it establishes that persons deprived of their liberty face the risk of being subjected to a process of physical and psychological coercion, in some cases tantamount to torture, in the early stages of the internment process.

60. Once the interrogation process is over, the conditions of treatment for the persons deprived of their liberty generally improve, except in the "High Value Detainee" section at Baghdad International Airport where persons deprived of their liberty have been held for nearly 23 hours a day in strict solitary confinement in small concrete cells

devoid of daylight, an internment regime which does not comply with provisions of the Third and Fourth Geneva Conventions.

61. During internment, persons deprived of their liberty also risk being victims of disproportionate and excessive use of force on the part of detaining authorities attempting to restore order in the event of unrest or to prevent escapes.

62. Another serious violation of International Humanitarian Law described in the report is the CF's inability or lack of will to set up a system of notifications of arrests for the families of persons deprived of liberty in Iraq. This violation of provisions of International Humanitarian Law causes immense distress among persons deprived of their liberty and their families, the latter fearing that their relatives unaccounted for are dead. The uncaring behaviour of the CF and their inability to quickly provide accurate information on persons deprived of their liberty for the families concerned also seriously affects the image of the Occupying Powers amongst the Iraqi population.

63. In addition to recommendations highlighted in the report relating to conditions of internment, information given to persons deprived of their liberty upon arrest, and the need to investigate violations of International Humanitarian Law and to prosecute those found responsible, the ICRC wishes particularly to remind the CF of their duty:

- to respect at all times the human dignity, physical integrity and cultural sensitivity of persons deprived of their liberty held under their control;
- to set up a system of notifications of arrests to ensure that the families of persons deprived of their liberty are quickly and accurately informed;
- to prevent all forms of ill-treatment and moral or physical coercion of persons deprived of their liberty in connection with interrogations;
- to instruct the arresting and detaining authorities that causing serious bodily injury or serious harm to the health of protected persons is prohibited under the Third and Fourth Geneva Conventions
- to set up an internment regime that ensures respect for the psychological integrity and human dignity of the persons deprived of their liberty
- to ensure that battle group units arresting individuals and staff in charge of internment facilities receive adequate training enabling them to operate in a proper manner and fulfill their responsibilities without resorting to ill-treatment or using excessive force.

The practices described in this report are prohibited under International Humanitarian Law. They warrant serious attention by the CF. In particular, the CF should review their policies and practices, take corrective action and improve the treatment of prisoners of war and other protected persons under their authority. This report is part of the bilateral and confidential dialogue undertaken by the ICRC with the CF. In the future, the ICRC will continue its bilateral and confidential dialogue with the CF in accordance with provisions of International Humanitarian Law, on the basis of its monitoring of the conditions of arrest, interrogation and internment of persons deprived of their liberty held by the CF.

The Taguba Report

Article 15-6 Investigation of the 800th Military Police Brigade

March 2004

TABLE OF CONTENTS

REFERENCES

1. Geneva Convention Relative to the Treatment of Prisoners of War, 12 August 1949
2. Geneva Convention for the Amelioration of the Condition of the Wounded and Sick in the Armed Forces in the Field, 12 August 1949
3. Geneva Convention for the Amelioration of the Condition of the Wounded, Sick and Ship-wrecked Members of Armed Forces at Sea, 12 August 1949
4. Geneva Convention Protocol Relative to the Status of Refugees, 1967
5. Geneva Convention Relative to the Status of Refugees, 1951
6. Geneva Convention for the Protection of War Victims, 12 August 1949
7. Geneva Convention Relative to the Protection of Civilian Persons in Time of War, 12 August 1949
8. DOD Directive 5100.69, "DOD Program for Prisoners of War and other Detainees," 27 December 1972
9. DOD Directive 5100.77 "DOD Law of War Program," 10 July 1979
10. STANAG No. 2044, Procedures for Dealing with Prisoners of War (PW) (Edition 5), 28 June 1994
11. STANAG No. 2033, Interrogation of Prisoners of War (PW) (Edition 6), 6 December 1994
12. AR 190-8, Enemy Prisoners of War, Retained Personnel, Civilian Internees, and Other Detainees, 1 October 1997
13. AR 190-47, The Army Corrections System, 15 August 1996
14. AR 190-14, Carrying of Firearms and Use of Force for Law Enforcement and Security Duties, 12 March 1993
15. AR 195-5, Evidence Procedures, 28 August 1992
16. AR 190-11, Physical Security of Arms, Ammunition and Explosives, 12 February 1998
17. AR 190-12, Military Police Working Dogs, 30 September 1993
18. AR 190-13, The Army Physical Security Program, 30 September 1993
19. AR 380-67, Personnel Security Program, 9 September 1988
20. AR 380-5, Department of the Army Information Security, 31 September 2000
21. AR 670-1, Wear and Appearance of Army Uniforms and Insignia, 5 September 2003
22. AR 190-40, Serious Incident Report, 30 November 1993
23. AR 15-6, Procedures for Investigating Officers and Boards of Officers, 11 May 1988
24. AR 27-10, Military Justice, 6 September 2002
25. AR 635-200, Enlisted Personnel, 1 November 2000
26. AR 600-8-24, Officer Transfers and Discharges, 29 June 2002
27. AR 500-5, Army Mobilization, 6 July 1996
28. AR 600-20, Army Command Policy, 13 May 2002
29. AR 623-105, Officer Evaluation Reports, 1 April 1998
30. AR 175-9, Contractors Accompanying the Force, 29 October 1999
31. FM 3-19.40, Military Police Internment/Resettlement Operations, 1 August 2001
32. FM 3-19.1, Military Police Operations, 22 March 2001
33. FM 3-19.4, Military Police Leaders' Handbook, 4 March 2002
34. FM 3-05.30, Psychological Operations, 19 June 2000
35. FM 33-1-1, Psychological Operations Techniques and Procedures, 5 May 1994
36. FM 34-52, Intelligence Interrogation, 28 September 1992
37. FM 19-15, Civil Disturbances, 25 November 1985
38. FM 3-0, Operations, 14 June 2001
39. FM 101-5, Staff Organizations and Functions, 23 May 1984
40. FM 3-19.30, Physical Security, 8 January 2001
41. FM 3-21.5, Drill and Ceremonies, 7 July 2003

42. ARTEP 19-546-30 MTP, Mission Training Plan for Military Police Battalion (IR)
43. ARTEP 19-667-30 MTP, Mission Training Plan for Military Police Guard Company
44. ARTEP 19-647-30 MTP, Mission Training Plan for Military Police Escort Guard Company
45. STP 19-95B1-SM, Soldier's Manual, MOS 95B, Military Police, Skill Level 1, 6 August 2002
46. STP 19-95C14-SM-TG, Soldier's Manual and Trainer's Guide for MOS 95C Internment/Resettlement Specialist, Skill Levels 1/2/3/4, 26 March 1999
47. STP 19-95C1-SM MOS 95C, Corrections Specialist, Skill Level 1, Soldier's Manual, 30 September 2003
48. STP 19-95C24-SM-TG MOS 95C, Corrections Specialist, Skill Levels 2/3/4, Soldier's Manual and Trainer's Guide, 30 September 2003
49. Assessment of DOD Counter-Terrorism Interrogation and Detention Operations in Iraq, (MG Geoffrey D. Miller, Commander JTF-GTMO, Guantanamo Bay, Cuba), 9 September 2003
50. Assessment of Detention and Corrections Operations in Iraq, (MG Donald J. Ryder, Provost Marshal General), 6 November 2003
51. CJTF-7 FRAGO #1108, Subject: *includes*- para 3.C.8 & 3.C.8.A.1, Assignment of 205 MI BDE CDR Responsibilities for the Baghdad Central Confinement Facility (BCCF), 19 November 2003
52. CJTF-7 FRAGO #749, Subject: Intelligence and Evidence-Led Detention Operations Relating to Detainees, 24 August 2003
53. 800th MP BDE FRAGO # 89, Subject: Rules of Engagement, 26 December 2003
54. CG CJTF-7 Memo: CJTF-7 Interrogation and Counter-Resistance Policy, 12 October 2003
55. CG CJTF-7 Memo: Dignity and Respect While Conducting Operations, 13 December 2003
56. Uniform Code of Military Justice and Manual for Courts Martial, 2002 Edition

BACKGROUND

1. (U) On 19 January 2004, Lieutenant General (LTG) Ricardo S. Sanchez, Commander, Combined Joint Task Force Seven (CJTF-7) requested that the Commander, US Central Command, appoint an Investigating Officer (IO) in the grade of Major General (MG) or above to investigate the conduct of operations within the 800th Military Police (MP) Brigade. LTG Sanchez requested an investigation of detention and internment operations by the Brigade from 1 November 2003 to the present. LTG Sanchez cited recent reports of detainee abuse, escapes from confinement facilities, and accountability lapses, which indicated systemic problems within the brigade and suggested a lack of clear standards, proficiency, and leadership. LTG Sanchez requested a comprehensive and all-encompassing inquiry to make findings and recommendations concerning the fitness and performance of the 800th MP Brigade. (ANNEX 2)

2. (U) On 24 January 2003, the Chief of Staff of US Central Command (CENTCOM), MG R. Steven Whitcomb, on behalf of the CENTCOM Commander, directed that the Commander, Coalition Forces Land Component Command (CFLCC), LTG David D. McKiernan, conduct an investigation into the 800th MP Brigade's detention and internment operations from 1 November 2003 to present. CENTCOM directed that the investigation should inquire into all facts and circumstances surrounding recent reports of suspected detainee abuse in Iraq. It also directed that the investigation inquire into detainee escapes and accountability lapses as reported by CJTF-7, and to gain a more comprehensive and all-encompassing inquiry into the fitness and performance of the 800th MP Brigade. (ANNEX 3)

3. (U) On 31 January 2004, the Commander, CFLCC, appointed MG Antonio M. Taguba, Deputy Commanding General Support, CFLCC, to conduct this investigation. MG Taguba was directed to conduct an informal investigation under AR 15-6 into the 800th MP Brigade's detention and internment operations. Specifically, MG Taguba was tasked to:

a. (U) Inquire into all the facts and circumstances surrounding recent allegations of detainee abuse, specifically allegations of maltreatment at the Abu Ghraib Prison (Baghdad Central Confinement Facility (BCCF));

b. (U) Inquire into detainee escapes and accountability lapses as reported by CJTF-7, specifically allegations concerning these events at the Abu Ghraib Prison;

c. (U) Investigate the training, standards, employment, command policies, internal procedures, and command climate in the 800th MP Brigade, as appropriate;

d. (U) Make specific findings of fact concerning all aspects of the investigation, and make any recommendations for corrective action, as appropriate. (ANNEX 4)

4. (U) LTG Sanchez's request to investigate the 800th MP Brigade followed the initiation of a criminal investigation by the US Army Criminal Investigation Command (USACIDC) into specific allegations of detainee abuse committed by members of the 372nd MP Company, 320th MP Battalion in Iraq. These units are part of the 800th MP Brigade. The Brigade is an Iraq Theater asset, TACON to CJTF-7, but OPCON to CFLCC at the time this investigation was initiated. In addition, CJTF-7 had several reports of detainee escapes from US/Coalition Confinement Facilities in Iraq over the past several months. These include Camp Bucca, Camp Ashraf, Abu Ghraib, and the High Value Detainee (HVD) Complex/Camp Cropper. The 800th MP Brigade operated these facilities. In addition, four Soldiers from the 320th MP Battalion had been formally charged under the Uniform Code of Military Justice (UCMJ) with detainee abuse in May 2003 at the Theater Internment Facility (TIF) at Camp Bucca, Iraq. (ANNEXES 5-18, 34 and 35)

5. (U) I began assembling my investigation team prior to the actual appointment by the CFLCC Commander. I assembled subject matter experts from the CFLCC Provost Marshal (PM) and the CFLCC Staff Judge Advocate (SJA). I selected COL Kinard J. La Fate, CFLCC Provost Marshal to be my Deputy for this investigation. I also contacted the Provost Marshal General of the Army, MG Donald J. Ryder, to enlist the support of MP subject matter experts in the areas of detention and internment operations. (ANNEXES 4 and 19)

6. (U) The Investigating Team also reviewed the Assessment of DoD Counter-Terrorism Interrogation and Detention Operations in Iraq conducted by MG Geoffrey D. Miller, Commander, Joint Task Force Guantanamo (JTF-GTMO). From 31 August to 9 September 2003, MG Miller led a team of personnel experienced in strategic interrogation to HQ, CJTF-7 and the Iraqi Survey Group (ISG) to review current Iraqi Theater ability to rapidly exploit internees for actionable intelligence. MG Miller's team focused on three areas: intelligence integration, synchronization, and fusion; interrogation operations; and detention operations. MG Miller's team used JTF-GTMO procedures and interrogation authorities as baselines. (ANNEX 20)

7. (U) The Investigating Team began its inquiry with an in depth analysis of the Report on Detention and Corrections in Iraq, dated 5 November 2003, conducted by MG Ryder and a team of military police, legal, medical, and automation experts. The CJTF-7 Commander, LTG Sanchez, had previously requested a team of subject matter experts to assess, and make specific recommendations concerning detention and corrections operations. From 13 October to 6 November 2003, MG Ryder personally led this assessment/assistance team in Iraq. (ANNEX 19)

ASSESSMENT OF DoD COUNTER-TERRORISM INTERROGATION AND DETENTION OPERATIONS IN IRAQ (MG MILLER'S ASSESSMENT)

1. (S/NF) The principal focus of MG Miller's team was on the strategic interrogation of detainees/internees in Iraq. Among its conclusions in its Executive Summary were that CJTF-7 did not have authorities and procedures in place to affect a unified strategy to detain, interrogate, and report information from detainees/internees in Iraq. The Executive Summary also stated that detention operations must act as an enabler for interrogation. (ANNEX 20)

2. (S/NF) With respect to interrogation, MG Miller's Team recommended that CJTF-7 dedicate and train a detention guard force subordinate to the Joint Interrogation Debriefing Center (JIDC) Commander that "sets the conditions for the successful interrogation and exploitation of internees/detainees." Regarding Detention Operations, MG Miller's team stated that the function of Detention Operations is to provide a safe, secure, and humane environment that supports the expeditious collection of intelligence. However, it also stated "it is essential that the guard force be actively engaged in setting the conditions for successful exploitation of the internees." (ANNEX 20)

3. (S/NF) MG Miller's team also concluded that Joint Strategic Interrogation Operations (within CJTF-7) are hampered by lack of active control of the internees within the detention environment. The Miller Team also stated that establishment of the Theater Joint Interrogation and Detention Center (JIDC) at Abu Ghraib (BCCF) will consolidate both detention and strategic interrogation operations and result in synergy between MP and MI resources and an integrated, synchronized, and focused strategic interrogation effort. (ANNEX 20)

4. (S/NF) MG Miller's team also observed that the application of emerging strategic interrogation strategies and techniques contain new approaches and operational art. The Miller Team also concluded that a legal review and recommendations on internee interrogation operations by a dedicated Command Judge Advocate is required to maximize interrogation effectiveness. (ANNEX 20)

IO COMMENTS ON MG MILLER'S ASSESSMENT

1. (S/NF) MG Miller's team recognized that they were using JTF-GTMO operational procedures and interrogation authorities as baselines for its observations and recommendations. There is a strong argument that the intelligence value of detainees held

at JTF-Guantanamo (GTMO) is different than that of the detainees/internees held at Abu Ghraib (BCCF) and other detention facilities in Iraq. Currently, there are a large number of Iraqi criminals held at Abu Ghraib (BCCF). These are not believed to be international terrorists or members of al Qaeda, Anser Al Islam, Taliban, and other international terrorist organizations. (ANNEX 20)

2. (S/NF) The recommendations of MG Miller's team that the "guard force" be actively engaged in setting the conditions for successful exploitation of the internees would appear to be in conflict with the recommendations of MG Ryder's Team and AR 190-8 that military police "do not participate in military intelligence supervised interrogation sessions." The Ryder Report concluded that the OEF template whereby military police actively set the favorable conditions for subsequent interviews runs counter to the smooth operation of a detention facility. (ANNEX 20)

REPORT ON DETENTION AND CORRECTIONS
IN IRAQ (MG RYDER'S REPORT)

1. (U) MG Ryder and his assessment team conducted a comprehensive review of the entire detainee and corrections system in Iraq and provided recommendations addressing each of the following areas as requested by the Commander CJTF-7:

a. (U) Detainee and corrections system management
b. (U) Detainee management, including detainee movement, segregation, and accountability
c. (U) Means of command and control of the detention and corrections system
d. (U) Integration of military detention and corrections with the Coalition Provisional Authority (CPA) and adequacy of plans for transition to an Iraqi-run corrections system
e. (U) Detainee medical care and health management
f. (U) Detention facilities that meet required health, hygiene, and sanitation standards
g. (U) Court integration and docket management for criminal detainees
h. (U) Detainee legal processing
i. (U) Detainee databases and records, including integration with law enforcement and court databases (ANNEX 19)

2. (U) Many of the findings and recommendations of MG Ryder's team are beyond the scope of this investigation. However, several important findings are clearly relevant to this inquiry and are summarized below (emphasis is added in certain areas):

A. (U) Detainee Management (including movement, segregation, and accountability)

1. (U) There is a wide variance in standards and approaches at the various detention facilities. Several Division/Brigade collection points and US monitored Iraqi prisons had flawed or insufficiently detailed use of force and other standing operating

procedures or policies (e.g. weapons in the facility, improper restraint techniques, detainee management, etc.) Though, there were no military police units purposely applying inappropriate confinement practices. (ANNEX 19)

2. (U) Currently, due to lack of adequate Iraqi facilities, Iraqi criminals (generally Iraqi-on-Iraqi crimes) are detained with security internees (generally Iraqi-on-Coalition offenses) and EPWs in the same facilities, though segregated in different cells/compounds. (ANNEX 19)

3. (U) The management of multiple disparate groups of detained people in a single location by members of the same unit invites confusion about handling, processing, and treatment, and typically facilitates the transfer of information between different categories of detainees. (ANNEX 19)

4. (U) The 800th MP (I/R) units did not receive Internment/Resettlement (I/R) and corrections specific training during their mobilization period. Corrections training is only on the METL of two MP (I/R) Confinement Battalions throughout the Army, one currently serving in Afghanistan, and elements of the other are at Camp Arifjan, Kuwait. MP units supporting JTF-GTMO received ten days of training in detention facility operations, to include two days of unarmed self-defense, training in interpersonal communication skills, forced cell moves, and correctional officer safety. (ANNEX 19)

B. (U) **Means of Command and Control of the Detention and Corrections System**

1. (U) The 800th MP Brigade was originally task organized with eight MP(I/R) Battalions consisting of both MP Guard and Combat Support companies. Due to force rotation plans, the 800th redeployed two Battalion HHCs in December 2003, the 115th MP Battalion and the 324th MP Battalion. In December 2003, the 400th MP Battalion was relieved of its mission and redeployed in January 2004. The 724th MP Battalion redeployed on 11 February 2004 and the remainder is scheduled to redeploy in March and April 2004. They are the 310th MP Battalion, 320th MP Battalion, 530th MP Battalion, and 744th MP Battalion. The units that remain are generally understrength, as Reserve Component units do not have an individual personnel replacement system to mitigate medical losses or the departure of individual Soldiers that have reached 24 months of Federal active duty in a five-year period. (ANNEX 19)

2. (U) The 800th MP Brigade (I/R) is currently a CFLCC asset, TACON to CJTF-7 to conduct Internment/Resettlement (I/R) operations in Iraq. All detention operations are conducted in the CJTF-7 AO; Camps Ganci, Vigilant, Bucca, TSP Whitford, and a separate High Value Detention (HVD) site. (ANNEX 19)

3. (U) The 800th MP Brigade has experienced challenges adapting its task organizational structure, training, and equipment resources from a unit designed to conduct standard EPW operations in the COMMZ (Kuwait). Further, the doctrinally trained MP soldier-to-detainee population ratio and facility layout templates are predicated on

a compliant, self-disciplining EPW population, and not criminals or high-risk security internees. (ANNEX 19)

4. (U) EPWs and Civilian Internees should receive the full protection of the Geneva Conventions, unless the denial of these protections is due to specifically articulated military necessity (e.g., no visitation to preclude the direction of insurgency operations). (ANNEX 19 and 24)

5. (U) AR 190-8, *Enemy Prisoners of War, Retained Personnel, Civilian Internees, and other Detainees*, FM 3-19.40, *Military Police Internment and Resettlement Operations*, and FM 34-52, *Intelligence Interrogations*, require military police to provide an area for intelligence collection efforts within EPW facilities. Military Police, though adept at passive collection of intelligence within a facility, do not participate in Military Intelligence supervised interrogation sessions. Recent intelligence collection in support of Operation Enduring Freedom posited a template whereby military police actively set favorable conditions for subsequent interviews. Such actions generally run counter to the smooth operation of a detention facility, attempting to maintain its population in a compliant and docile state. **The 800th MP Brigade has not been directed to change its facility procedures to set the conditions for MI interrogations, nor participate in those interrogations.** (ANNEX 19 and 21-23)

6. MG Ryder's Report also made the following, inter alia, near-term and mid-term recommendations regarding the command and control of detainees:

a. (U) Align the release process for security internees with DoD Policy. The process of screening security internees should include intelligence findings, interrogation results, and current threat assessment.

b. (U) Determine the scope of intelligence collection that will occur at Camp Vigilant. Refurbish the Northeast Compound to separate the screening operation from the Iraqi run Baghdad Central Correctional Facility. **Establish procedures that define the role of military police soldiers securing the compound, clearly separating the actions of the guards from those of the military intelligence personnel.**

c. (U) **Consolidate all Security Internee Operations, except the MEK security mission, under a single Military Police Brigade Headquarters for OIF 2.**

d. (U) **Insist that all units identified to rotate into the Iraqi Theater of Operations (ITO) to conduct internment and confinement operations in support of OIF 2 be organic to CJTF-7.** (ANNEX 19)

IO COMMENTS REGARDING MG RYDER'S REPORT

1. (U) The objective of MG Ryder's Team was to observe detention and prison operations, identify potential systemic and human rights issues, and provide near-term, mid-term, and long-term recommendations to improve CJTF-7 operations and transition of the Iraqi prison system from US military control/oversight to the Coalition Provisional Authority and eventually to the Iraqi Government. The Findings and Recommendations of MG Ryder's Team are thorough and precise and should be implemented immediately. (ANNEX 19)

2. (U) Unfortunately, many of the systemic problems that surfaced during MG Ryder's Team's assessment are the very same issues that are the subject of this investigation. In fact, many of the abuses suffered by detainees occurred during, or near to, the time of that assessment. As will be pointed out in detail in subsequent portions of this report, I disagree with the conclusion of MG Ryder's Team in one critical aspect, that being its conclusion that the 800th MP Brigade had not been asked to change its facility procedures to set the conditions for MI interviews. **While clearly the 800th MP Brigade and its commanders were not tasked to set conditions for detainees for subsequent MI interrogations, it is obvious from a review of comprehensive CID interviews of suspects and witnesses that this was done at lower levels.** (ANNEX 19)

3. (U) I concur fully with MG Ryder's conclusion regarding the effect of AR 190-8. Military Police, though adept at passive collection of intelligence within a facility, should not participate in Military Intelligence supervised interrogation sessions. Moreover, Military Police should not be involved with setting **"favorable conditions"** for subsequent interviews. These actions, as will be outlined in this investigation, clearly run counter to the smooth operation of a detention facility. (ANNEX 19)

PRELIMINARY INVESTIGATIVE ACTIONS

1. (U) Following our review of MG Ryder's Report and MG Miller's Report, my investigation team immediately began an in depth review of all available documents regarding the 800th MP Brigade. We reviewed in detail the voluminous CID investigation regarding alleged detainee abuses at detention facilities in Iraq, particularly the Abu Ghraib (BCCF) Detention Facility. We analyzed approximately fifty witness statements from military police and military intelligence personnel, potential suspects, and detainees. We reviewed numerous photos and videos of actual detainee abuse taken by detention facility personnel, which are now in the custody and control of the US Army Criminal Investigation Command and the CJTF-7 prosecution team. The photos and videos are not contained in this investigation. We obtained copies of the 800th MP Brigade roster, rating chain, and assorted internal investigations and disciplinary actions involving that command for the past several months. (**ALL ANNEXES Reviewed by Investigation Team**)

2. (U) In addition to military police and legal officers from the CFLCC PMO and SJA Offices we also obtained the services of two individuals who are experts in military police detention practices and training. These were LTC Timothy Weathersbee, Commander, 705th MP Battalion, United States Disciplinary Barracks, Fort Leavenworth, and SFC Edward Baldwin, Senior Corrections Advisor, US Army Military Police School, Fort Leonard Wood. I also requested and received the services of Col (Dr) Henry Nelson, a trained US Air Force psychiatrist assigned to assist my investigation team. (ANNEX 4)

3. (U) In addition to MG Ryder's and MG Miller's Reports, the team reviewed numerous reference materials including the 12 October 2003 CJTF-7 Interrogation and Counter-Resistance Policy, the AR 15-6 Investigation on Riot and Shootings at Abu Ghraib on 24 November 2003, the 205th MI Brigade's Interrogation Rules of Engagement

(IROE), facility staff logs/journals and numerous records of AR 15-6 investigations and Serious Incident Reports (SIRs) on detainee escapes/shootings and disciplinary matters from the 800th MP Brigade. (ANNEXES 5-20, 37, 93, and 94)

4. (U) On 2 February 2004, I took my team to Baghdad for a one-day inspection of the Abu Ghraib Prison (BCCF) and the High Value Detainee (HVD) Complex in order to become familiar with those facilities. We also met with COL Jerry Mocello, Commander, 3rd MP Criminal Investigation Group (CID), COL Dave Quantock, Commander, 16th MP Brigade, COL Dave Phillips, Commander, 89th MP Brigade, and COL Ed Sannwaldt, CJTF-7 Provost Marshal. On 7 February 2004, the team visited the Camp Bucca Detention Facility to familiarize itself with the facility and operating structure. In addition, on 6 and 7 February 2004, at Camp Doha, Kuwait, we conducted extensive training sessions on approved detention practices. We continued our preparation by reviewing the ongoing CID investigation and were briefed by the Special Agent in Charge, CW2 Paul Arthur. We refreshed ourselves on the applicable reference materials within each team member's area of expertise, and practiced investigative techniques. I met with the team on numerous occasions to finalize appropriate witness lists, review existing witness statements, arrange logistics, and collect potential evidence. We also coordinated with CJTF-7 to arrange witness attendance, force protection measures, and general logistics for the team's move to Baghdad on 8 February 2004. (ANNEXES 4 and 25)

5. (U) At the same time, due to the Transfer of Authority on 1 February 2004 between III Corps and V Corps, and the upcoming demobilization of the 800th MP Brigade Command, I directed that several critical witnesses who were preparing to leave the theater remain at Camp Arifjan, Kuwait until they could be interviewed (ANNEX 29). My team deployed to Baghdad on 8 February 2004 and conducted a series of interviews with a variety of witnesses (ANNEX 30). We returned to Camp Doha, Kuwait on 13 February 2004. On 14 and 15 February we interviewed a number of witnesses from the 800th MP Brigade. On 17 February we returned to Camp Bucca, Iraq to complete interviews of witnesses at that location. From 18 February thru 28 February we collected documents, compiled references, did follow-up interviews, and completed a detailed analysis of the volumes of materials accumulated throughout our investigation. On 29 February we finalized our executive summary and out-briefing slides. On 9 March we submitted the AR 15-6 written report with findings and recommendations to the CFLCC Deputy SJA, LTC Mark Johnson, for a legal sufficiency review. The out-brief to the appointing authority, LTG McKiernan, took place on 3 March 2004. (ANNEXES 26 and 45-91)

FINDINGS AND RECOMMENDATIONS

(Part One)

(U) The investigation should inquire into all of the facts and circumstances surrounding recent allegations of detainee abuse, specifically, allegations of maltreatment at the Abu Ghraib Prison (Baghdad Central Confinement Facility).

1. (U) The US Army Criminal Investigation Command (CID), led by COL Jerry Mocello, and a team of highly trained professional agents have done a superb job of investigating several complex and extremely disturbing incidents of detainee abuse at the Abu Ghraib Prison. They conducted over 50 interviews of witnesses, potential criminal suspects, and detainees. They also uncovered numerous photos and videos portraying in graphic detail detainee abuse by Military Police personnel on numerous occasions from October to December 2003. Several potential suspects rendered full and complete confessions regarding their personal involvement and the involvement of fellow soldiers in this abuse. Several potential suspects invoked their rights under Article 31 of the Uniform Code of Military Justice (UCMJ) and the Fifth Amendment of the U.S. Constitution. (ANNEX 25)

2. (U) In addition to a comprehensive and exhaustive review of all of these statements and documentary evidence, we also interviewed numerous officers, NCOs, and junior enlisted soldiers in the 800th MP Brigade, as well as members of the 205th Military Intelligence Brigade working at the prison. We did not believe it was necessary to re-interview all the numerous witnesses who had previously provided comprehensive statements to CID, and I have adopted those statements for the purposes of this investigation. (ANNEXES 26, 34, 35, and 45-91)

REGARDING PART ONE OF THE INVESTIGATION, I MAKE THE FOLLOWING SPECIFIC FINDINGS OF FACT:

1. (U) That Forward Operating Base (FOB) Abu Ghraib (BCCF) provides security of both criminal and security detainees at the Baghdad Central Correctional Facility, facilitates the conducting of interrogations for CJTF-7, supports other CPA operations at the prison, and enhances the force protection/quality of life of Soldiers assigned in order to ensure the success of ongoing operations to secure a free Iraq. (ANNEX 31)

2. (U) That the Commander, 205th Military Intelligence Brigade, was designated by CJTF-7 as the Commander of FOB Abu Ghraib (BCCF) effective 19 November 2003. That the 205th MI Brigade conducts operational and strategic interrogations for CJTF-7. That from 19 November 2003 until Transfer of Authority (TOA) on 6 February 2004, COL Thomas M. Pappas was the Commander of the 205th MI Brigade and the Commander of FOB Abu Ghraib (BCCF). (ANNEX 31)

3. (U) That the 320th Military Police Battalion of the 800th MP Brigade is responsible for the Guard Force at Camp Ganci, Camp Vigilant, & Cellblock 1 of FOB Abu Ghraib (BCCF). That from February 2003 to until he was suspended from his duties on 17 January 2004, LTC Jerry Phillabaum served as the Battalion Commander of the 320th MP Battalion. That from December 2002 until he was suspended from his duties, on 17 January 2004, CPT Donald Reese served as the Company Commander of the 372nd MP Company, which was in charge of guarding detainees at FOB Abu Ghraib. I further find that both the 320th MP Battalion and the 372nd MP Company were located within the confines of FOB Abu Ghraib. (ANNEXES 32 and 45)

4. (U) That from July of 2003 to the present, BG Janis L. Karpinski was the Commander of the 800th MP Brigade. (ANNEX 45)

5. (S) That between October and December 2003, at the Abu Ghraib Confinement Facility (BCCF), numerous incidents of sadistic, blatant, and wanton criminal abuses were inflicted on several detainees. This systemic and illegal abuse of detainees was intentionally perpetrated by several members of the military police guard force (372nd Military Police Company, 320th Military Police Battalion, 800th MP Brigade), in Tier (section) 1-A of the Abu Ghraib Prison (BCCF). The allegations of abuse were substantiated by detailed witness statements (ANNEX 26) and the discovery of extremely graphic photographic evidence. Due to the extremely sensitive nature of these photographs and videos, the ongoing CID investigation, and the potential for the criminal prosecution of several suspects, the photographic evidence is not included in the body of my investigation. The pictures and videos are available from the Criminal Investigative Command and the CTJF-7 prosecution team. In addition to the aforementioned crimes, there were also abuses committed by members of the 325th MI Battalion, 205th MI Brigade, and Joint Interrogation and Debriefing Center (JIDC). Specifically, on 24 November 2003, SPC Luciana Spencer, 205th MI Brigade, sought to degrade a detainee by having him strip and returned to cell naked. (ANNEXES 26 and 53)

6. (S) I find that the intentional abuse of detainees by military police personnel included the following acts:

a. (S) Punching, slapping, and kicking detainees; jumping on their naked feet;
b. (S) Videotaping and photographing naked male and female detainees;
c. (S) Forcibly arranging detainees in various sexually explicit positions for photographing;
d. (S) Forcing detainees to remove their clothing and keeping them naked for several days at a time;
e. (S) Forcing naked male detainees to wear women's underwear;
f. (S) Forcing groups of male detainees to masturbate themselves while being photographed and videotaped;
g. (S) Arranging naked male detainees in a pile and then jumping on them;
h. (S) Positioning a naked detainee on a MRE Box, with a sandbag on his head, and attaching wires to his fingers, toes, and penis to simulate electric torture;
i. (S) Writing "I am a Rapest" (sic) on the leg of a detainee alleged to have forcibly raped a 15-year old fellow detainee, and then photographing him naked;
j. (S) Placing a dog chain or strap around a naked detainee's neck and having a female soldier pose for a picture;
k. (S) A male MP guard having sex with a female detainee;
l. (S) Using military working dogs (without muzzles) to intimidate and frighten detainees, and in at least one case biting and severely injuring a detainee;
m. (S) Taking photographs of dead Iraqi detainees. (ANNEXES 25 and 26)

7. (U) These findings are amply supported by written confessions provided by several of the suspects, written statements provided by detainees, and witness statements. In reaching my findings, I have carefully considered the pre-existing statements of the following witnesses and suspects (ANNEX 26):

a. (U) SPC Jeremy Sivits, 372nd MP Company – **Suspect**
b. (U) SPC Sabrina Harman, 372nd MP Company – **Suspect**

c. (U) SGT Javal S. Davis, 372nd MP Company – **Suspect**

d. (U) PFC Lynndie R. England, 372nd MP Company – **Suspect**

e. (U) Adel Nakhla, Civilian Translator, Titan Corp., Assigned to the 205th MI Brigade – **Suspect**

f. (U) SPC Joseph M. Darby, 372nd MP Company

g. (U) SGT Neil A. Wallin, 109th Area Support Medical Battalion

h. (U) SGT Samuel Jefferson Provance, 302nd MI Battalion

i. (U) Torin S. Nelson, Contractor, Titan Corp., Assigned to the 205th MI Brigade

j. (U) CPL Matthew Scott Bolanger, 372nd MP Company

k. (U) SPC Mathew C. Wisdom, 372nd MP Company

l. (U) SSG Reuben R. Layton, Medic, 109th Medical Detachment

m. (U) SPC John V. Polak, 229th MP Company

8. (U) In addition, several detainees also described the following acts of abuse, which under the circumstances, I find credible based on the clarity of their statements and supporting evidence provided by other witnesses (**ANNEX 26**):

a. (U) Breaking chemical lights and pouring the phosphoric liquid on detainees;

b. (U) Threatening detainees with a charged 9mm pistol;

c. (U) Pouring cold water on naked detainees;

d. (U) Beating detainees with a broom handle and a chair;

e. (U) Threatening male detainees with rape;

f. (U) Allowing a military police guard to stitch the wound of a detainee who was injured after being slammed against the wall in his cell;

g. (U) Sodomizing a detainee with a chemical light and perhaps a broom stick.

h. (U) Using military working dogs to frighten and intimidate detainees with threats of attack, and in one instance actually biting a detainee.

9. (U) I have carefully considered the statements provided by the following detainees, which under the circumstances I find credible based on the clarity of their statements and supporting evidence provided by other witnesses:

a. (U) Amjed Isail Waleed, Detainee # 151365

b. (U) Hiadar Saber Abed Miktub-Aboodi, Detainee # 13077

c. (U) Huessin Mohssein Al-Zayiadi, Detainee # 19446

d. (U) Kasim Mehaddi Hilas, Detainee # 151108

e. (U) Mohanded Juma Juma (sic), Detainee # 152307

f. (U) Mustafa Jassim Mustafa, Detainee # 150542

g. (U) Shalan Said Alsharoni, Detainee, # 150422

h. (U) Abd Alwhab Youss, Detainee # 150425

i. (U) Asad Hamza Hanfosh, Detainee # 152529

j. (U) Nori Samir Gunbar Al-Yasseri, Detainee # 7787

k. (U) Thaar Salman Dawod, Detainee # 150427

l. (U) Ameen Sa'eed Al-Sheikh, Detainee # 151362

m. (U) Abdou Hussain Saad Faleh, Detainee # 18470 (**ANNEX 26**)

10. (U) I find that contrary to the provision of AR 190-8, and the findings found in MG Ryder's Report, Military Intelligence (MI) interrogators and Other US Government

Agency's (OGA) interrogators actively requested that MP guards set physical and mental conditions for favorable interrogation of witnesses. Contrary to the findings of MG Ryder's Report, I find that personnel assigned to the 372nd MP Company, 800th MP Brigade were directed to change facility procedures to "set the conditions" for MI interrogations. I find no direct evidence that MP personnel actually participated in those MI interrogations. (ANNEXES 19, 21, 25, and 26).

11. (U) I reach this finding based on the actual proven abuse that I find was inflicted on detainees and by the following witness statements. (ANNEXES 25 and 26):

a. (U) **SPC Sabrina Harman**, 372nd MP Company, stated in her sworn statement regarding the incident where a detainee was placed on a box with wires attached to his fingers, toes, and penis, "that her job was to keep detainees awake." She stated that MI was talking to CPL Grainer. She stated: **"MI wanted to get them to talk. It is Grainer and Frederick's job to do things for MI and OGA to get these people to talk."**

b. (U) <u>SGT Javal S. Davis,</u> 372nd MP Company, stated in his sworn statement as follows: **"I witnessed prisoners in the MI hold section, wing 1A being made to do various things that I would question morally. In Wing 1A we were told that they had different rules and different SOP for treatment. I never saw a set of rules or SOP for that section just word of mouth. The Soldier in charge of 1A was Corporal Granier. He stated that the Agents and MI Soldiers would ask him to do things, but nothing was ever in writing he would complain (sic)."** When asked why the rules in 1A/1B were different than the rest of the wings, SGT Davis stated: **"The rest of the wings are regular prisoners and 1A/B are Military Intelligence (MI) holds."** When asked why he did not inform his chain of command about this abuse, SGT Davis stated: **"Because I assumed that if they were doing things out of the ordinary or outside the guidelines, someone would have said something. Also the wing belongs to MI and it appeared MI personnel approved of the abuse."** SGT Davis also stated that he had heard MI insinuate to the guards to abuse the inmates. When asked what MI said he stated: **"Loosen this guy up for us." "Make sure he has a bad night." "Make sure he gets the treatment."** He claimed these comments were made to CPL Granier and SSG Frederick. Finally, SGT Davis stated that (sic): **"the MI staffs to my understanding have been giving Granier compliments on the way he has been handling the MI holds. Example being statements like, "Good job, they're breaking down real fast. They answer every question. They're giving out good information, Finally, and Keep up the good work. Stuff like that."**

c. (U) <u>SPC Jason Kennel,</u> 372nd MP Company, was asked if he were present when any detainees were abused. He stated: **"I saw them nude, but MI would tell us to take away their mattresses, sheets, and clothes."** He could not recall who in MI had instructed him to do this, but commented that, "if they wanted me to do that they needed to give me paperwork." He was later informed that "we could not do anything to embarrass the prisoners."

d. (U) <u>Mr. Adel L. Nakhla</u>, a US civilian contract translator was questioned about several detainees accused of rape. He observed (sic): **"They (detainees) were all naked, a bunch of people from MI, the MP were there that night and the inmates were** ordered by SGT Granier and SGT Frederick ordered the guys while questioning them to admit what they did. They made them do strange exercises by sliding on their stomach, jump up and down, throw water on them and made them some wet, called them all kinds of names such as "gays" do they like to make love to guys, then they handcuffed their hands together and their legs with shackles and started to stack them on top of each other by insuring that the bottom guys penis will touch the guy on tops butt."

e. (U) <u>SPC Neil A Wallin</u>, 109th Area Support Medical Battalion, a medic testified that: "Cell 1A was used to house high priority detainees and cell 1B was used to house the high risk or trouble making detainees. During my tour at the prison I observed that when the male detainees were first brought to the facility, some of them were made to wear female underwear, which I think was to somehow break them down."

12. (U) I find that prior to its deployment to Iraq for Operation Iraqi Freedom, the 320th MP Battalion and the 372nd MP Company had received no training in detention/internee operations. I also find that very little instruction or training was provided to MP personnel on the applicable rules of the Geneva Convention Relative to the Treatment of Prisoners of War, FM 27-10, AR 190-8, or FM 3-19.40. Moreover, I find that few, if any, copies of the Geneva Conventions were ever made available to MP personnel or detainees. (ANNEXES 21-24, 33, and multiple witness statements)

13. (U) Another obvious example of the Brigade Leadership not communicating with its Soldiers or ensuring their tactical proficiency concerns the incident of detainee abuse that occurred at Camp Bucca, Iraq, on May 12, 2003. Soldiers from the 223rd MP Company reported to the 800th MP Brigade Command at Camp Bucca, that four Military Police Soldiers from the 320th MP Battalion had abused a number of detainees during inprocessing at Camp Bucca. An extensive CID investigation determined that four soldiers from the 320th MP Battalion had kicked and beaten these detainees following a transport mission from Talil Air Base. (ANNEXES 34 and 35)

14. (U) Formal charges under the UCMJ were preferred against these Soldiers and an Article-32 Investigation conducted by LTC Gentry. He recommended a general court martial for the four accused, which BG Karpinski supported. Despite this documented abuse, there is no evidence that BG Karpinski ever attempted to remind 800th MP Soldiers of the requirements of the Geneva Conventions regarding detainee treatment or took any steps to ensure that such abuse was not repeated. Nor is there any evidence that LTC(P) Phillabaum, the commander of the Soldiers involved in the Camp Bucca abuse incident, took any initiative to ensure his Soldiers were properly trained regarding detainee treatment. (ANNEXES 35 and 62)

RECOMMENDATIONS AS TO PART ONE OF THE INVESTIGATION:

1. (U) Immediately deploy to the Iraq Theater an integrated multi discipline Mobile Training Team (MTT) comprising of subject matter experts in internment/resettlement operations, international and operational law, information technology, facility

management, interrogation and intelligence gathering techniques, chaplains, Arab cultural awareness, and medical practices as it pertains to I/R activities. This team needs to oversee and conduct comprehensive training in all aspects of detainee and confinement operations.

2. (U) That all military police and military intelligence personnel involved in any aspect of detainee operations or interrogation operations in CJTF-7, and subordinate units, be immediately provided with training by an international/operational law attorney on the specific provisions of The Law of Land Warfare FM 27-10, specifically the Geneva Convention Relative to the Treatment of Prisoners of War, Enemy Prisoners of War, Retained Personnel, Civilian Internees, and Other Detainees, and AR 190-8.

3. (U) **That a single commander in CJTF-7 be responsible for overall detainee operations throughout the Iraq Theater of Operations.** I also recommend that the Provost Marshal General of the Army assign a minimum of two (2) subject matter experts, one officer and one NCO, to assist CJTF-7 in coordinating detainee operations.

4. (U) That detention facility commanders and interrogation facility commanders ensure that appropriate copies of the Geneva Convention Relative to the Treatment of Prisoners of War and notice of protections be made available in both English and the detainees' language and be prominently displayed in all detention facilities. Detainees with questions regarding their treatment should be given the full opportunity to read the Convention.

5. (U) That each detention facility commander and interrogation facility commander publish a complete and comprehensive set of Standing Operating Procedures (SOPs) regarding treatment of detainees, and that all personnel be required to read the SOPs and sign a document indicating that they have read and understand the SOPs.

6. (U) That in accordance with the recommendations of MG Ryder's Assessment Report, and my findings and recommendations in this investigation, all units in the Iraq Theater of Operations conducting internment/confinement/detainment operations in support of Operation Iraqi Freedom be OPCON for all purposes, to include action under the UCMJ, to CJTF-7.

7. (U) Appoint the C3, CJTF as the staff proponent for detainee operations in the Iraq Joint Operations Area (JOA). (MG Tom Miller, C3, CJTF-7, has been appointed by COMCJTF-7).

8. (U) That an inquiry UP AR 381-10, Procedure 15 be conducted to determine the extent of culpability of Military Intelligence personnel, assigned to the 205th MI Brigade and the Joint Interrogation and Debriefing Center (JIDC) regarding abuse of detainees at Abu Ghraib (BCCF).

9. (U) That it is critical that the proponent for detainee operations is assigned a dedicated Senior Judge Advocate, with specialized training and knowledge of international and operational law, to assist and advise on matters of detainee operations.

FINDINGS AND RECOMMENDATIONS

(Part Two)

(U) The Investigation inquire into detainee escapes and accountability lapses as reported by CJTF-7, specifically allegations concerning these events at the Abu Ghraib Prison:

REGARDING PART TWO OF THE INVESTIGATION, I MAKE THE FOLLOWING SPECIFIC FINDINGS OF FACT:

1. The 800th MP Brigade was responsible for theater-wide Internment and Resettlement (I/R) operations. (**ANNEXES 45 and 95**)

2. (U) The 320th MP Battalion, 800th MP Brigade was tasked with detainee operations at the Abu Ghraib Prison Complex during the time period covered in this investigation. (**ANNEXES 41, 45, and 59**)

3. (U) The 310th MP Battalion, 800th MP Brigade was tasked with detainee operations and Forward Operating Base (FOB) Operations at the Camp Bucca Detention Facility until TOA on 26 February 2004. (**ANNEXES 41 and 52**)

4. (U) The 744th MP Battalion, 800th MP Brigade was tasked with detainee operations and FOB Operations at the HVD Detention Facility until TOA on 4 March 2004. (**ANNEXES 41 and 55**)

5. (U) The 530th MP Battalion, 800th MP Brigade was tasked with detainee operations and FOB Operations at the MEK holding facility until TOA on 15 March 2004. (**ANNEXES 41 and 97**)

6. (U) Detainee operations include accountability, care, and well being of Enemy Prisoners of War, Retained Person, Civilian Detainees, and Other Detainees, as well as Iraqi criminal prisoners. (**ANNEX 22**)

7. (U) The accountability for detainees is doctrinally an MP task IAW FM 3-19.40. (**ANNEX 22**)

8. (U) There is a general lack of knowledge, implementation, and emphasis of basic legal, regulatory, doctrinal, and command requirements within the 800th MP Brigade and its subordinate units. (**Multiple witness statements in ANNEXES 45-91**).

9. (U) The handling of detainees and criminal prisoners after in-processing was inconsistent from detention facility to detention facility, compound to compound, encampment to encampment, and even shift to shift throughout the 800th MP Brigade AOR. (**ANNEX 37**)

10. (U) Camp Bucca, operated by the 310th MP Battalion, had a "Criminal Detainee In-Processing SOP" and a "Training Outline" for transferring and releasing detainees, which appears to have been followed. (**ANNEXES 38 and 52**)

11. (U) Incoming and outgoing detainees are being documented in the National Detainee Reporting System (NDRS) and Biometric Automated Toolset System (BATS) as required by regulation at all detention facilities. However, it is underutilized and often does not give a "real time" accurate picture of the detainee population due to untimely updating. (ANNEX 56)

12. (U) There was a severe lapse in the accountability of detainees at the Abu Ghraib Prison Complex. The 320th MP Battalion used a self-created "change sheet" to document the transfer of a detainee from one location to another. For proper accountability, it is imperative that these change sheets be processed and the detainee manifest be updated within 24 hours of movement. At Abu Ghraib, this process would often take as long as four days to complete. This lag-time resulted in inaccurate detainee Internment Serial Number (ISN) counts, gross differences in the detainee manifest and the actual occupants of an individual compound, and significant confusion of the MP Soldiers. The 320th MP Battalion S-1, CPT Theresa Delbalso, and the S-3, MAJ David DiNenna, explained that this breakdown was due to the lack of manpower to process change sheets in a timely manner. (ANNEXES 39 and 98)

13. (U) The 320th Battalion TACSOP requires detainee accountability at least four times daily at Abu Ghraib. However, a detailed review of their operational journals revealed that these accounts were often not done or not documented by the unit. Additionally, there is no indication that accounting errors or the loss of a detainee in the accounting process triggered any immediate corrective action by the Battalion TOC. (ANNEX 44)

14. (U) There is a lack of standardization in the way the 320th MP Battalion conducted physical counts of their detainees. Each compound within a given encampment did their headcounts differently. Some compounds had detainees line up in lines of 10, some had them sit in rows, and some moved all the detainees to one end of the compound and counted them as they passed to the other end of the compound. (ANNEX 98)

15. (U) FM 3-19.40 outlines the need for two roll calls (100% ISN band checks) per day. The 320th MP Battalion did this check only two times per week. Due to the lack of real-time updates to the system, these checks were regularly inaccurate. (ANNEXES 22 and 98)

16. (U) The 800th MP Brigade and subordinate units adopted non-doctrinal terms such as "band checks," "roll-ups," and "call-ups," which contributed to the lapses in accountability and confusion at the soldier level. (ANNEXES 63, 88, and 98)

17. (U) Operational journals at the various compounds and the 320th Battalion TOC contained numerous unprofessional entries and flippant comments, which highlighted the lack of discipline within the unit. There was no indication that the journals were ever reviewed by anyone in their chain of command. (ANNEX 37)

18. (U) Accountability SOPs were not fully developed and standing TACSOPs were widely ignored. Any SOPs that did exist were not trained on, and were never distributed

to the lowest level. Most procedures were shelved at the unit TOC, rather than at the subordinate units and guards mount sites. (**ANNEXES 44, 67, 71, and 85**)

19. (U) Accountability and facility operations SOPs lacked specificity, implementation measures, and a system of checks and balances to ensure compliance. (**ANNEXES 76 and 82**)

20. (U) Basic Army Doctrine was not widely referenced or utilized to develop the accountability practices throughout the 800th MP Brigade's subordinate units. Daily processing, accountability, and detainee care appears to have been made up as the operations developed with reliance on, and guidance from, junior members of the unit who had civilian corrections experience. (**ANNEX 21**)

21. (U) Soldiers were poorly prepared and untrained to conduct I/R operations prior to deployment, at the mobilization site, upon arrival in theater, and throughout their mission. (**ANNEXES 62, 63, and 69**)

22. (U) The documentation provided to this investigation identified 27 escapes or attempted escapes from the detention facilities throughout the 800th MP Brigade's AOR. Based on my assessment and detailed analysis of the substandard accountability process maintained by the 800th MP Brigade, it is highly likely that there were several more unreported cases of escape that were probably "written off" as administrative errors or otherwise undocumented. 1LT Lewis Raeder, Platoon Leader, 372nd MP Company, reported knowing about at least two additional escapes (one from a work detail and one from a window) from Abu Ghraib (BCCF) that were not documented. LTC Dennis McGlone, Commander, 744th MP Battalion, detailed the escape of one detainee at the High Value Detainee Facility who went to the latrine and then outran the guards and escaped. Lastly, BG Janis Karpinski, Commander, 800th MP Brigade, stated that there were more than 32 escapes from her holding facilities, which does not match the number derived from the investigation materials. (**ANNEXES 5-10, 45, 55, and 71**)

23. (U) The Abu Ghraib and Camp Bucca detention facilities are significantly over their intended maximum capacity while the guard force is undermanned and under resourced. This imbalance has contributed to the poor living conditions, escapes, and accountability lapses at the various facilities. The overcrowding of the facilities also limits the ability to identify and segregate leaders in the detainee population who may be organizing escapes and riots within the facility. (**ANNEXES 6, 22, and 92**)

24. (U) The screening, processing, and release of detainees who should not be in custody takes too long and contributes to the overcrowding and unrest in the detention facilities. There are currently three separate release mechanisms in the theater-wide internment operations. First, the apprehending unit can release a detainee if there is a determination that their continued detention is not warranted. Secondly, a criminal detainee can be released after it has been determined that the detainee has no intelligence value, and that their release would not be detrimental to society. BG Karpinski had signature authority to release detainees in this second category. Lastly, detainees accused of committing "Crimes Against the Coalition," who are held throughout the separate facilities in the CJTF-7 AOR, can be released upon a determination that

they are of no intelligence value and no longer pose a significant threat to Coalition Forces. The release process for this category of detainee is a screening by the local US Forces Magistrate Cell and a review by a Detainee Release Board consisting of BG Karpinski, COL Marc Warren, SJA, CJTF-7, and MG Barbara Fast, C-2, CJTF-7. MG Fast is the "Detainee Release Authority" for detainees being held for committing crimes against the coalition. According to BG Karpinski, this category of detainee makes up more than 60% of the total detainee population, and is the fastest growing category. However, MG Fast, according to BG Karpinski, routinely denied the board's recommendations to release detainees in this category who were no longer deemed a threat and clearly met the requirements for release. According to BG Karpinski, the extremely slow and ineffective release process has significantly contributed to the overcrowding of the facilities. (**ANNEXES 40, 45, and 46**)

25. (U) After Action Reviews (AARs) are not routinely being conducted after an escape or other serious incident. No lessons learned seem to have been disseminated to subordinate units to enable corrective action at the lowest level. The Investigation Team requested copies of AARs, and none were provided. (**Multiple Witness Statements**)

26. (U) Lessons learned (i.e. Findings and Recommendations from various 15-6 Investigations concerning escapes and accountability lapses) were rubber stamped as approved and ordered implemented by BG Karpinski. There is no evidence that the majority of her orders directing the implementation of substantive changes were ever acted upon. Additionally, there was no follow-up by the command to verify the corrective actions were taken. Had the findings and recommendations contained within their own investigations been analyzed and actually implemented by BG Karpinski, many of the subsequent escapes, accountability lapses, and cases of abuse may have been prevented. (**ANNEXES 5-10**)

27. (U) The perimeter lighting around Abu Ghraib and the detention facility at Camp Bucca is inadequate and needs to be improved to illuminate dark areas that have routinely become avenues of escape. (**ANNEX 6**)

28. (U) Neither the camp rules nor the provisions of the Geneva Conventions are posted in English or in the language of the detainees at any of the detention facilities in the 800th MP Brigade's AOR, even after several investigations had annotated the lack of this critical requirement. (**Multiple Witness Statements and the Personal Observations of the Investigation Team**)

29. (U) The Iraqi guards at Abu Ghraib BCCF) demonstrate questionable work ethics and loyalties, and are a potentially dangerous contingent within the Hard-Site. These guards have furnished the Iraqi criminal inmates with contraband, weapons, and information. Additionally, they have facilitated the escape of at least one detainee. (**ANNEX 8 and 26-SPC Polak's Statement**)

30. (U) In general, US civilian contract personnel (Titan Corporation, CACI, etc. . .), third country nationals, and local contractors do not appear to be properly supervised within the detention facility at Abu Ghraib. During our on-site inspection, they wandered about with too much unsupervised free access in the detainee area. Having civilians in various outfits (civilian and DCUs) in and about the detainee area

causes confusion and may have contributed to the difficulties in the accountability process and with detecting escapes. (**ANNEX 51, Multiple Witness Statements, and the Personal Observations of the Investigation Team**)

31. (U) SGM Marc Emerson, Operations SGM, 320th MP Battalion, contended that the Detainee Rules of Engagement (DROE) and the general principles of the Geneva Convention were briefed at every guard mount and shift change on Abu Ghraib. However, none of our witnesses, nor our personal observations, support his contention. I find that SGM Emerson was not a credible witness. (**ANNEXES 45, 80, and the Personal Observations of the Investigation Team**)

32. (U) Several interviewees insisted that the MP and MI Soldiers at Abu Ghraib (BCCF) received regular training on the basics of detainee operations; however, they have been unable to produce any verifying documentation, sign-in rosters, or soldiers who can recall the content of this training. (**ANNEXES 59, 80, and the Absence of any Training Records**)

33. (S/NF) The various detention facilities operated by the 800th MP Brigade have routinely held persons brought to them by Other Government Agencies (OGAs) without accounting for them, knowing their identities, or even the reason for their detention. The Joint Interrogation and Debriefing Center (JIDC) at Abu Ghraib called these detainees "ghost detainees." On at least one occasion, the 320th MP Battalion at Abu Ghraib held a handful of "ghost detainees" (6–8) for OGAs that they moved around within the facility to hide them from a visiting International Committee of the Red Cross (ICRC) survey team. This maneuver was deceptive, contrary to Army Doctrine, and in violation of international law. (**ANNEX 53**)

34. (U) The following riots, escapes, and shootings have been documented and reported to this Investigation Team. Although there is no data from other missions of similar size and duration to compare the number of escapes with, the most significant factors derived from these reports are twofold. First, investigations and SIRs lacked critical data needed to evaluate the details of each incident. Second, each investigation seems to have pointed to the same types of deficiencies; however, little to nothing was done to correct the problems and to implement the recommendations as was ordered by BG Karpinski, nor was there any command emphasis to ensure these deficiencies were corrected:

a. (U) **4 June 03- This escape was mentioned in the 15–6 Investigation covering the 13 June 03 escape, recapture, and shootings of detainees at Camp Vigilant (320th MP Battalion).** However, no investigation or additional information was provided as requested by this investigation team. (**ANNEX 7**)

b. (U) **9 June 03- Riot and shootings of five detainees at Camp Cropper. (115th MP Battalion)** Several detainees allegedly rioted after a detainee was subdued by MPs of the 115th MP Battalion after striking a guard in compound B of Camp Cropper. A 15-6 investigation by 1LT Magowan (115th MP Battalion, Platoon Leader) concluded that a detainee had acted up and hit an MP. After being subdued, one of the MPs took off his DCU top and flexed his muscles to the detainees, which further escalated the riot. The MPs were overwhelmed and the guards fired lethal rounds to protect the life of the compound MPs, whereby five detainees were wounded. Contributing factors were poor communications, no clear chain of command, facility-obstructed views of posted guards, the QRF did not have non-lethal equipment, and the SOP was inadequate and outdated. (ANNEX 5)

c. (U) 12 June 03- Escape and recapture of detainee #8399, escape and shooting of detainee # 7166, and attempted escape of an unidentified detainee from Camp Cropper Holding Area (115th MP Battalion). Several detainees allegedly made their escape in the nighttime hours prior to 0300. A 15–6 investigation by CPT Wendlandt (115th MP Battalion, S-2) concluded that the detainees allegedly escaped by crawling under the wire at a location with inadequate lighting. One detainee was stopped prior to escape. An MP of the 115th MP Battalion search team recaptured detainee # 8399, and detainee # 7166 was shot and killed by a soldier during the recapture process. Contributing factors were overcrowding, poor lighting, and the nature of the hardened criminal detainees at that location. It is of particular note that the command was informed at least 24 hours in advance of the upcoming escape attempt and started doing amplified announcements in Arabic stating the camp rules. The investigation pointed out that rules and guidelines were not posted in the camps in the detainees' native languages. (ANNEX 6)

d. (U) 13 June 03- Escape and recapture of detainee # 8968 and the shooting of eight detainees at Abu Ghraib (BCCF) (320th MP Battalion). Several detainees allegedly attempted to escape at about 1400 hours from the Camp Vigilant Compound, Abu Ghraib (BCCF). A 15-6 investigation by CPT Wyks (400th MP Battalion, S-1) concluded that the detainee allegedly escaped by sliding under the wire while the tower guard was turned in the other direction. This detainee was subsequently apprehended by the QRF. At about 1600 the same day, 30–40 detainees rioted and pelted three interior MP guards with rocks. One guard was injured and the tower guards fired lethal rounds at the rioters injuring seven and killing one detainee. (ANNEX 7)

e. (U) 05 November 03- Escape of detainees # 9877 and # 10739 from Abu Ghraib (320th MP Battalion). Several detainees allegedly escaped at 0345 from the Hard-Site, Abu Ghraib (BCCF). An SIR was initiated by SPC Warner (320th MP Battalion, S-3 RTO). The SIR indicated that two criminal prisoners escaped through their cell window in tier 3A of the Hard-Site. No information on findings, contributing factors, or corrective action has been provided to this investigation team. (ANNEX 11)

f. (U) 07 November 03- Escape of detainee # 14239 from Abu Ghraib (320th MP Battalion). A detainee allegedly escaped at 1330 from Compound 2 of the Ganci Encampment, Abu Ghraib (BCCF). An SIR was initiated by SSG Hydro (320th MP Battalion, S-3 Asst. NCOIC). The SIR indicated that a detainee escaped from the North end of the compound and was discovered missing during distribution of the noon meal, but there is no method of escape listed in the SIR. No information on findings, contributing factors, or corrective action has been provided to this investigation team. (ANNEX 12)

g. (U) 08 November 03- Escape of detainees # 115089, # 151623, # 151624, # 116734, # 116735, and # 116738 from Abu Ghraib (320th MP Battalion). Several detainees allegedly escaped at 2022 from Compound 8 of the Ganci encampment, Abu Ghraib. An SIR was initiated by MAJ DiNenna (320th MP Battalion, S-3). The SIR indicated that five–six prisoners escaped from the North end of the compound, but there is no method of escape listed in the SIR. No information on findings, contributing factors, or corrective action has been provided to this investigation team. (ANNEX 13)

h. (U) **24 November 03- Riot and shooting of 12 detainees # 150216, #150894, #153096, 153165, #153169, #116361, #153399, #20257, #150348, #152616, #116146, and #152156 at Abu Ghraib (320th MP Battalion).** Several detainees allegedly began to riot at about 1300 in all of the compounds at the Ganci encampment. This resulted in the shooting deaths of three detainees, nine wounded detainees, and nine injured US Soldiers. A 15–6 investigation by COL Bruce Falcone (220th MP Brigade, Deputy Commander) concluded that the detainees rioted in protest of their living conditions, that the riot turned violent, the use of non-lethal force was ineffective, and, after the 320th MP Battalion CDR executed "Golden Spike," the emergency containment plan, the use of deadly force was authorized. Contributing factors were lack of comprehensive training of guards, poor or non-existent SOPs, no formal guard-mount conducted prior to shift, no rehearsals or ongoing training, the mix of less than lethal rounds with lethal rounds in weapons, no AARs being conducted after incidents, ROE not posted and not understood, overcrowding, uniforms not standardized, and poor communication between the command and soldiers. (ANNEX 8)

i. (U) **24 November 03- Shooting of detainee at Abu Ghraib (320th MP Battalion).** A detainee allegedly had a pistol in his cell and around 1830 an extraction team shot him with less than lethal and lethal rounds in the process of recovering the weapon. A 15–6 investigation by COL Bruce Falcone (220th Brigade, Deputy Commander) concluded that one of the detainees in tier 1A of the Hard Site had gotten a pistol and a couple of knives from an Iraqi Guard working in the encampment. Immediately upon receipt of this information, an ad-hoc extraction team consisting of MP and MI personnel conducted what they called a routine cell search, which resulted in the shooting of an MP and the detainee. Contributing factors were a corrupt Iraqi Guard, inadequate SOPs, the Detention ROE in place at the time was ineffective due to the numerous levels of authorization needed for use of lethal force, poorly trained MPs, unclear lanes of responsibility, and ambiguous relationship between the MI and MP assets. (ANNEX 8)

j. (U) **13 December 03- Shooting by non-lethal means into crowd at Abu Ghraib (320th MP Battalion).** Several detainees allegedly got into a detainee-on-detainee fight around 1030 in Compound 8 of the Ganci encampment, Abu Ghraib. An SIR was initiated by SSG Matash (320th MP Battalion, S-3 Section). The SIR indicated that there was a fight in the compound and the MPs used a non-lethal crowd-dispersing round to break up the fight, which was successful. No information on findings, contributing factors, or corrective action has been provided to this investigation team. (ANNEX 14)

k. (U) **13 December 03- Shooting by non-lethal means into crowd at Abu Ghraib (320th MP Battalion).** Several detainees allegedly got into a detainee-on-detainee fight around 1120 in Compound 2 of the Ganci encampment, Abu Ghraib. An SIR was initiated by SSG Matash (320th MP Battalion, S-3 Section). The SIR indicated that there was a fight in the compound and the MPs used two non-lethal shots to disperse the crowd, which was successful. No information on findings, contributing factors, or corrective action has been provided to this investigation team. (ANNEX 15)

l. (U) **13 December 03- Shooting by non-lethal means into crowd at Abu Ghraib (320th MP Battalion).** Approximately 30–40 detainees allegedly got into a detainee-on-detainee fight around 1642 in Compound 3 of the Ganci encampment, Abu Ghraib (BCCF). An SIR was initiated by SSG Matash (320th MP Battalion, S-3 Section). The SIR indicates that there was a fight in the compound and the MPs used a non-lethal crowd-dispersing round to break up the fight, which was successful. No information on findings, contributing factors, or corrective action has been provided to this investigation team. (ANNEX 16)

m. (U) **17 December 03- Shooting by non-lethal means of detainee from Abu Ghraib (320th MP Battalion).** Several detainees allegedly assaulted an MP at 1459 inside the Ganci Encampment, Abu Ghraib (BCCF). An SIR was initiated by SSG Matash (320th MP BRIGADE, S-3 Section). The SIR indicated that three detainees assaulted an MP, which resulted in the use of a non-lethal shot that calmed the situation. No information on findings, contributing factors, or corrective action has been provided to this investigation team. (ANNEX 17)

n. (U) **07 January 04- Escape of detainee #115032 from Camp Bucca (310th MP Battalion).** A detainee allegedly escaped between the hours of 0445 and 0640 from Compound 12, of Camp Bucca. Investigation by CPT Kaires (310th MP Battalion S-3) and CPT Holsombeck (724th MP Battalion S-3) concluded that the detainee escaped through an undetected weakness in the wire. Contributing factors were inexperienced guards, lapses in accountability, complacency, lack of leadership presence, poor visibility, and lack of clear and concise communication between the guards and the leadership. (ANNEX 9)

o. (U) **12 January 04- Escape of Detainees #115314 and #109950 as well as the escape and recapture of five unknown detainees at the Camp Bucca Detention Facility (310th MP Battalion).** Several detainees allegedly escaped around 0300 from Compound 12, of Camp Bucca. An AR 15-6 Investigation by LTC Leigh Coulter (800th MP Brigade, OIC Camp Arifjan Detachment) concluded that three of the detainees escaped through the front holding cell during conditions of limited visibility due to fog. One of the detainees was noticed, shot with a non-lethal round, and returned to his holding compound. That same night, four detainees exited through the wire on the South side of the camp and were seen and apprehended by the QRF. Contributing factors were the lack of a coordinated effort for emplacement of MPs during implementation of the fog plan, overcrowding, and poor communications. (ANNEX 10)

p. (U) **14 January 04- Escape of detainee #12436 and missing Iraqi guard from Hard-Site, Abu Ghraib (320th MP Battalion).** A detainee allegedly escaped at 1335 from the Hard Site at Abu Ghraib (BCCF). An SIR was initiated by SSG Hydro (320th MP Battalion, S-3 Asst. NCOIC). The SIR indicates that an Iraqi guard assisted a detainee to escape by signing him out on a work detail and disappearing with him. At the time of the second SIR, neither missing person had been located. No information on findings, contributing factors, or corrective action has been provided to this investigation team. (ANNEX 99)

q. (U) **26 January 04- Escape of detainees #s 115236, 116272, and 151933 from Camp Bucca (310th MP Battalion).** Several detainees allegedly escaped between the hours of 0440 and 0700 during a period of intense fog. Investigation by CPT Kaires (310th MP Battalion S-3) concluded that the detainees crawled under a fence when visibility was only 10–15 meters due to fog. Contributing factors were the limited visibility (darkness under foggy conditions), lack of proper accountability reporting, inadequate number of guards, commencement of detainee feeding during low visibility operations, and poorly rested MPs. (ANNEX 18)

35. (U) As I have previously indicated, this investigation determined that there was virtually a complete lack of detailed SOPs at any of the detention facilities. Moreover, despite the fact that there were numerous reported escapes at detention facilities throughout Iraq (in excess of 35), AR 15-6 Investigations following these escapes were simply forgotten or ignored by the Brigade Commander with no dissemination to other facilities. After-Action Reports and Lessons Learned, if done at all, remained at individual facilities and were not shared among other commanders or soldiers throughout the Brigade. The Command never issued standard TTPs for handling escape incidents. (ANNEXES 5-10, **Multiple Witness Statements, and the Personal Observations of the Investigation Team**)

RECOMMENDATIONS REGARDING PART TWO OF THE INVESTIGATION:

1. (U) ANNEX 100 of this investigation contains a detailed and referenced series of recommendations for improving the detainee accountability practices throughout the OIF area of operations.

2. (U) Accountability practices throughout any particular detention facility must be standardized and in accordance with applicable regulations and international law.

3. (U) The NDRS and BATS accounting systems must be expanded and used to their fullest extent to facilitate real time updating when detainees are moved and or transferred from one location to another.

4. (U) "Change sheets," or their doctrinal equivalent must be immediately processed and updated into the system to ensure accurate accountability. The detainee roll call or ISN counts must match the manifest provided to the compound guards to ensure proper accountability of detainees.

5. (U) Develop, staff, and implement comprehensive and detailed SOPs utilizing the lessons learned from this investigation as well as any previous findings, recommendations, and reports.

6. (U) SOPs must be written, disseminated, trained on, and understood at the lowest level.

7. (U) Iraqi criminal prisoners must be held in separate facilities from any other category of detainee.

8. (U) All of the compounds should be wired into the master manifest whereby MP Soldiers can account for their detainees in real time and without waiting for their change sheets to be processed. This would also have the change sheet serve as a way to check up on the accuracy of the manifest as updated by each compound. The BATS and NDRS system can be utilized for this function.

9. (U) Accountability lapses, escapes, and disturbances within the detainment facilities must be immediately reported through both the operational and administrative Chain of Command via a Serious Incident Report (SIR). The SIRs must then be tracked and followed by daily SITREPs until the situation is resolved.

10. (U) Detention Rules of Engagement (DROE), Interrogation Rules of Engagement (IROE), and the principles of the Geneva Conventions need to be briefed at every shift change and guard mount.

11. (U) AARs must be conducted after serious incidents at any given facility. The observations and corrective actions that develop from the AARs must be analyzed by the respective MP Battalion S-3 section, developed into a plan of action, shared with the other facilities, and implemented as a matter of policy.

12. (U) There must be significant structural improvements at each of the detention facilities. The needed changes include significant enhancement of perimeter lighting, additional chain link fencing, staking down of all concertina wire, hard site development, and expansion of Abu Ghraib (BCCF).

13. (U) The Geneva Conventions and the facility rules must be prominently displayed in English and the language of the detainees at each compound and encampment at every detention facility IAW AR 190-8.

14. (U) Further restrict US civilians and other contractors' access throughout the facility. Contractors and civilians must be in an authorized and easily identifiable uniform to be more easily distinguished from the masses of detainees in civilian clothes.

15. (U) Facilities must have a stop movement/transfer period of at least one hour prior to every 100% detainee roll call and ISN counts to ensure accurate accountability.

16. (U) The method for doing head counts of detainees within a given compound must be standardized.

17. (U) Those military units conducting I/R operations must know of, train on, and constantly reference the applicable Army Doctrine and CJTF command policies. The references provided in this report cover nearly every deficiency I have enumerated. Although they do not, and cannot, make up for leadership shortfalls, all soldiers, at all levels, can use them to maintain standardized operating procedures and efficient accountability practices.

FINDINGS AND RECOMMENDATIONS

(Part Three)

(U) Investigate the training, standards, employment, command policies, internal procedures, and command climate in the 800th MP Brigade, as appropriate:

Pursuant to Part Three of the Investigation, select members of the Investigation team (Primarily COL La Fate and I) personally interviewed the following witnesses:

1. (U) BG Janis Karpinski, Commander, 800th MP Brigade
2. (U) COL Thomas Pappas, Commander, 205th MI Brigade
3. (U) COL Ralph Sabatino, CFLCC Judge Advocate, CPA Ministry of Justice (Interviewed by COL Richard Gordon, CFLCC SJA)
4. (U) LTC Gary W. Maddocks, S-5 and Executive Officer, 800th MP Brigade
5. (U) LTC James O'Hare, Command Judge Advocate, 800th MP Brigade
6. (U) LTC Robert P. Walters Jr., Commander, 165th MI Battalion (Tactical Exploitation)
7. (U) LTC James D. Edwards, Commander, 202nd MI Battalion
8. (U) LTC Vincent Montera, Commander, 310th MP Battalion
9. (U) LTC Steve Jordan, former Director, Joint Interrogation and Debriefing Center/LNO to the 205th MI Brigade
10. (U) LTC Leigh A. Coulter, Commander, 724th MP Battalion and OIC Arifjan Detachment, 800th MP Brigade
11. (U) LTC Dennis McGlone, Commander, 744th MP Battalion
12. (U) MAJ David Hinzman, S-1, 800th MP Brigade
13. (U) MAJ William D. Proietto, Deputy CJA, 800th MP Brigade
14. (U) MAJ Stacy L. Garrity, S-1 (FWD), 800th MP Brigade
15. (U) MAJ David W. DiNenna, S-3, 320th MP Battalion
16. (U) MAJ Michael Sheridan, XO, 320th MP Battalion
17. (U) MAJ Anthony Cavallaro, S-3, 800th MP Brigade
18. (U) CPT Marc C. Hale, Commander, 670th MP Company
19. (U) CPT Donald Reese, Commander, 372nd MP Company
20. (U) CPT Darren Hampton, Assistant S-3, 320th MP Battalion
21. (U) CPT John Kaires, S-3, 310th MP Battalion
22. (U) CPT Ed Diamantis, S-2, 800th MP Brigade
23. (U) CPT Marc C. Hale, Commander, 670th MP Company
24. (U) CPT Donald Reese, Commander, 372nd MP Company
25. (U) CPT James G. Jones, Commander, 229th MP Company
26. (U) CPT Michael Anthony Mastrangelo, Jr., Commander, 310th MP Company
27. (U) CPT Lawrence Bush, IG, 800th MP Brigade
28. (U) 1LT Lewis C. Raeder, Platoon Leader, 372nd MP Company
29. (U) 1LT Elvis Mabry, Aide-de-camp to Brigade Commander, 800th MP Brigade
30. (U) 1LT Warren E. Ford, II, Commander, HHC 320th MP Battalion

31. (U) 2LT David O. Sutton, Platoon Leader, 229th MP Company
32. (U) CW2 Edward J. Rivas, 205th MI Brigade
33. (U) CSM Joseph P. Arrington, Command Sergeant Major, 320th MP Battalion
34. (U) SGM Pascual Cartagena, Acting Command Sergeant Major, 800th MP Brigade
35. (U) CSM Timothy L. Woodcock, Command Sergeant Major, 310th MP Battalion
36. (U) 1SG Dawn J. Rippelmeyer, First Sergeant, 977th MP Company
37. (U) SGM Mark Emerson, Operations SGM, 320th MP Battalion
38. (U) MSG Brian G. Lipinski, First Sergeant, 372nd MP Company
39. (U) MSG Andrew J. Lombardo, Operations Sergeant, 310th MP Battalion
40. (U) SFC Daryl J. Plude, Platoon Sergeant, 229th MP Company
41. (U) SFC Shannon K. Snider, Platoon SGT, 372nd MP Company
42. (U) SFC Keith A. Comer, 372nd MP Company
43. (U) SSG Robert Elliot, Squad Leader, 372nd MP Company
44. (U) SSG Santos A. Cardona, Army Dog Handler, 42nd MP Detachment, 16th MP Brigade
45. (U) SGT Michael Smith, Army Dog Handler, 523rd MP Detachment, 937th Engineer Group
46. (U) MA1 William J. Kimbro, USN Dog Handler, NAS Signal and Canine Unit
47. (U) Mr. Steve Stephanowicz, US civilian Contract Interrogator, CACI, 205th MI Brigade
48. (U) Mr. John Israel, US civilian Contract Interpreter, Titan Corporation, 205th MI Brigade (ANNEXES 45-91)

REGARDING PART THREE OF THE INVESTIGATION, I MAKE THE FOLLOWING SPECIFIC FINDINGS OF FACT:

1. (U) I find that BG Janis Karpinski took command of the 800th MP Brigade on 30 June 2003 from BG Paul Hill. BG Karpinski has remained in command since that date. The 800th MP Brigade comprises eight MP battalions in the Iraqi TOR: 115th MP Battalion, 310th MP Battalion, 320th MP Battalion, 324th MP Battalion, 400th MP Battalion, 530th MP Battalion, 724th MP Battalion, and 744th MP Battalion. (ANNEXES 41 and 45)

2. (U) Prior to BG Karpinski taking command, members of the 800th MP Brigade believed they would be allowed to go home when all the detainees were released from the Camp Bucca Theater Internment Facility following the cessation of major ground combat on 1 May 2003. At one point, approximately 7,000 to 8,000 detainees were held at Camp Bucca. Through Article-5 Tribunals and a screening process, several thousand detainees were released. Many in the command believed they would go home when the detainees were released. In late May-early June 2003 the 800th MP Brigade was given a new mission to manage the Iraqi penal system and several detention centers. This new mission meant Soldiers would not redeploy to CONUS when anticipated. Morale suffered, and over the next few months there did not appear to have been any attempt by the Command to mitigate this morale problem. (ANNEXES 45 and 96)

3. (U) There is abundant evidence in the statements of numerous witnesses that soldiers throughout the 800th MP Brigade were not proficient in their basic MOS skills, particularly regarding internment/resettlement operations. Moreover, there is no evidence that the command, although aware of these deficiencies, attempted to correct them in any systemic manner other than ad hoc training by individuals with civilian corrections experience. (**Multiple Witness Statements and the Personal Observations of the Investigation Team**)

4. (U) I find that the 800th MP Brigade was not adequately trained for a mission that included operating a prison or penal institution at Abu Ghraib Prison Complex. As the Ryder Assessment found, I also concur that units of the 800th MP Brigade did not receive corrections-specific training during their mobilization period. MP units did not receive pinpoint assignments prior to mobilization and during the post mobilization training, and thus could not train for specific missions. The training that was accomplished at the mobilization sites were developed and implemented at the company level with little or no direction or supervision at the Battalion and Brigade levels, and consisted primarily of common tasks and law enforcement training. However, I found no evidence that the Command, although aware of this deficiency, ever requested specific corrections training from the Commandant of the Military Police School, the US Army Confinement Facility at Mannheim, Germany, the Provost Marshal General of the Army, or the US Army Disciplinary Barracks at Fort Leavenworth, Kansas. (**ANNEXES 19 and 76**)

5. (U) I find that without adequate training for a civilian internee detention mission, Brigade personnel relied heavily on individuals within the Brigade who had civilian corrections experience, including many who worked as prison guards or corrections officials in their civilian jobs. Almost every witness we interviewed had no familiarity with the provisions of AR 190-8 or FM 3-19.40. It does not appear that a Mission Essential Task List (METL) based on in-theater missions was ever developed nor was a training plan implemented throughout the Brigade. (**ANNEXES 21, 22, 67, and 81**)

6. (U) I also find, as did MG Ryder's Team, that the 800th MP Brigade as a whole, was understrength for the mission for which it was tasked. Army Doctrine dictates that an I/R Brigade can be organized with between 7 and 21 battalions, and that the average battalion size element should be able to handle approximately 4,000 detainees at a time. This investigation indicates that BG Karpinski and her staff did a poor job allocating resources throughout the Iraq JOA. Abu Ghraib (BCCF) normally housed between 6,000 and 7,000 detainees, yet it was operated by only one battalion. In contrast, the HVD Facility maintains only about 100 detainees, and is also run by an entire battalion. (**ANNEXES 19, 22, and 96**)

7. (U) Reserve Component units do not have an individual replacement system to mitigate medical or other losses. Over time, the 800th MP Brigade clearly suffered from personnel shortages through release from active duty (REFRAD) actions, medical evacuation, and demobilization. In addition to being severely undermanned, the quality of life for soldiers assigned to Abu Ghraib (BCCF) was extremely poor. There was no DFAC, PX, barbershop, or MWR facilities. There were numerous mortar attacks, random rifle and RPG attacks, and a serious threat to soldiers and detainees in

the facility. The prison complex was also severely overcrowded and the Brigade lacked adequate resources and personnel to resolve serious logistical problems. Finally, because of past associations and familiarity of soldiers within the Brigade, it appears that friendship often took precedence over appropriate leader and subordinate relationships. (ANNEX 101, **Multiple Witness Statements, and the Personal Observations of the Investigation Team**)

8. (U) With respect to the 800th MP Brigade mission at Abu Ghraib (BCCF), I find that there was clear friction and lack of effective communication between the Commander, 205th MI Brigade, who controlled FOB Abu Ghraib (BCCF) after 19 November 2003, and the Commander, 800th MP Brigade, who controlled detainee operations inside the FOB. There was no clear delineation of responsibility between commands, little coordination at the command level, and no integration of the two functions. Coordination occurred at the lowest possible levels with little oversight by commanders. (ANNEXES 31, 45, and 46)

9. (U) I find that this ambiguous command relationship was exacerbated by a CJTF-7 Fragmentary Order (FRAGO) 1108 issued on 19 November 2003. Paragraph 3.C.8, Assignment of 205th MI Brigade Commander's Responsibilities for the Baghdad Central Confinement Facility, states as follows:

> 3.C.8. A. (U) 205 MI BRIGADE.
>
> 3.C.8. A. 1. (U) EFFECTIVE IMMEDIATELY COMMANDER 205 MI BRIGADE ASSUMES RESPONSIBILITY FOR THE BAGHDAD CONFINEMENT FACILITY (BCCF) AND IS APPOINTED THE FOB COMMANDER. UNITS CURRENTLY AT ABU GHRAIB (BCCF) ARE TACON TO 205 MI BRIGADE FOR "SECURITY OF DETAINEES AND FOB PROTECTION."

Although not supported by BG Karpinski, FRAGO 1108 made all of the MP units at Abu Ghraib TACON to the Commander, 205th MI Brigade. This effectively made an MI Officer, rather than an MP Officer, responsible for the MP units conducting detainee operations at that facility. This is not doctrinally sound due to the different missions and agendas assigned to each of these respective specialties. (ANNEX 31)

10. (U) Joint Publication 0-2, Unified Action Armed Forces (UNAAF), 10 July 2001 defines Tactical Control (TACON) as the detailed direction and control of movements or maneuvers within the operational area necessary to accomplish assigned missions or tasks. (ANNEX 42)

> "TACON is the command authority over assigned or attached forces or commands or military capability made available for tasking that is limited to the detailed direction and control of movements or maneuvers within the operational area necessary to accomplish assigned missions or tasks. TACON is inherent in OPCON and may be delegated to and exercised by commanders at any echelon at or below the level of combatant commander."

11. (U) Based on all the facts and circumstances in this investigation, I find that there was little, if any, recognition of this TACON Order by the 800th MP Brigade or the 205th MI Brigade. Further, there was no evidence if the Commander, 205th MI Brigade clearly informed the Commander, 800th MP Brigade, and specifically the Commander,

320th MP Battalion assigned at Abu Ghraib (BCCF), on the specific requirements of this TACON relationship. (ANNEXES 45 and 46)

12. (U) It is clear from a comprehensive review of witness statements and personal interviews that the 320th MP Battalion and 800th MP Brigade continued to function as if they were responsible for the security, health and welfare, and overall security of detainees within Abu Ghraib (BCCF) prison. Both BG Karpinski and COL Pappas clearly behaved as if this were still the case. (ANNEXES 45 and 46)

13. (U) With respect to the 320th MP Battalion, I find that the Battalion Commander, LTC (P) Jerry Phillabaum, was an extremely ineffective commander and leader. Numerous witnesses confirm that the Battalion S-3, MAJ David W. DiNenna, basically ran the battalion on a day-to-day basis. At one point, BG Karpinski sent LTC (P) Phillabaum to Camp Arifjan, Kuwait for approximately two weeks, apparently to give him some relief from the pressure he was experiencing as the 320th Battalion Commander. This movement to Camp Arifjan immediately followed a briefing provided by LTC (P) Phillabaum to the CJTF-7 Commander, LTG Sanchez, near the end of October 2003. BG Karpinski placed LTC Ronald Chew, Commander of the 115th MP Battalion, in charge of the 320th MP Battalion for a period of approximately two weeks. LTC Chew was also in command of the 115th MP Battalion assigned to Camp Cropper, BIAP, Iraq. I could find no orders, either suspending or relieving LTC (P) Phillabaum from command, nor any orders placing LTC Chew in command of the 320th. In addition, there was no indication this removal and search for a replacement was communicated to the Commander CJTF-7, the Commander 377th TSC, or to Soldiers in the 320th MP Battalion. Temporarily removing one commander and replacing him with another serving Battalion Commander without an order and without notifying superior or subordinate commands is without precedent in my military career. LTC (P) Phillabaum was also reprimanded for lapses in accountability that resulted in several escapes. The 320th MP Battalion was stigmatized as a unit due to previous detainee abuse which occurred in May 2003 at the Bucca Theater Internment Facility (TIF), while under the command of LTC (P) Phillabaum. Despite his proven deficiencies as both a commander and leader, BG Karpinski allowed LTC (P) Phillabaum to remain in command of her most troubled battalion guarding, by far, the largest number of detainees in the 800th MP Brigade. LTC (P) Phillabaum was suspended from his duties by LTG Sanchez, CJTF-7 Commander on 17 January 2004. (ANNEXES 43, 45, and 61)

14. (U) During the course of this investigation I conducted a lengthy interview with BG Karpinski that lasted over four hours, and is included verbatim in the investigation Annexes. BG Karpinski was extremely emotional during much of her testimony. What I found particularly disturbing in her testimony was her complete unwillingness to either understand or accept that many of the problems inherent in the 800th MP Brigade were caused or exacerbated by poor leadership and the refusal of her command to both establish and enforce basic standards and principles among its soldiers. (ANNEX 45 and the Personal Observations of the Interview Team)

15. (U) BG Karpinski alleged that she received no help from the Civil Affairs Command, specifically, no assistance from either BG John Kern or COL Tim Regan. She blames much of the abuse that occurred in Abu Ghraib (BCCF) on MI personnel and

stated that MI personnel had given the MPs "ideas" that led to detainee abuse. In addition, she blamed the 372nd Company Platoon Sergeant, SFC Snider, the Company Commander, CPT Reese, and the First Sergeant, MSG Lipinski, for the abuse. She argued that problems in Abu Ghraib were the fault of COL Pappas and LTC Jordan because COL Pappas was in charge of FOB Abu Ghraib. (ANNEX 45)

16. (U) BG Karpinski also implied during her testimony that the criminal abuses that occurred at Abu Ghraib (BCCF) might have been caused by the ultimate disposition of the detainee abuse cases that originally occurred at Camp Bucca in May 2003. She stated that "about the same time those incidents were taking place out of Baghdad Central, the decisions were made to give the guilty people at Bucca plea bargains. So, the system communicated to the soldiers, the worst that's gonna happen is, you're gonna go home." I think it important to point out that almost every witness testified that the serious criminal abuse of detainees at Abu Ghraib (BCCF) occurred in late October and early November 2003. The photographs and statements clearly support that the abuses occurred during this time period. The Bucca cases were set for trial in January 2004 and were not finally disposed of until 29 December 2003. There is entirely no evidence that the decision of numerous MP personnel to intentionally abuse detainees at Abu Ghraib (BCCF) was influenced in any respect by the Camp Bucca cases. (ANNEXES 25, 26, and 45)

17. (U) Numerous witnesses stated that the 800th MP Brigade S-1, MAJ Hinzman and S-4, MAJ Green, were essentially dysfunctional, but that despite numerous complaints, these officers were not replaced. This had a detrimental effect on the Brigade Staff's effectiveness and morale. Moreover, the Brigade Command Judge Advocate, LTC James O'Hare, appears to lack initiative and was unwilling to accept responsibility for any of his actions. LTC Gary Maddocks, the Brigade XO did not properly supervise the Brigade staff by failing to lay out staff priorities, take overt corrective action when needed, and supervise their daily functions. (ANNEXES 45, 47, 48, 62, and 67)

18. (U) In addition to poor morale and staff inefficiencies, I find that the 800th MP Brigade did not articulate or enforce clear and basic Soldier and Army standards. I specifically found these examples of unenforced standards:

a. There was no clear uniform standard for any MP Soldiers assigned detention duties. Despite the fact that hundreds of former Iraqi soldiers and officers were detainees, MP personnel were allowed to wear civilian clothes in the FOB after duty hours while carrying weapons. (ANNEXES 51 and 74)

b. Some soldiers wrote poems and other sayings on their helmets and soft caps. (ANNEXES 51 and 74)

c. In addition, numerous officers and senior NCOs have been reprimanded/disciplined for misconduct during this period. Those disciplined include; (ANNEXES 43 and 102)

    1). (U) BG Janis Karpinski, Commander, 800th MP Brigade

       • Memorandum of Admonishment by LTG Sanchez, Commander, CJTF-7, on 17 January 2004.

2). (U) LTC (P) Jerry Phillabaum, Commander, 320th MP Battalion
- GOMOR from BG Karpinski, Commander 800th MP Brigade, on 10 November 2003, for lack of leadership and for failing to take corrective security measures as ordered by the Brigade Commander; filed locally
- Suspended by BG Karpinski, Commander 800th MP Brigade, 17 January 2004; Pending Relief for Cause, for dereliction of duty

3). (U) LTC Dale Burtyk, Commander, 400th MP Battalion
- GOMOR from BG Karpinski, Commander 800th MP Brigade, on 20 August 2003, for failure to properly train his soldiers. (Soldier had negligent discharge of M-16 while exiting his vehicle, round went into fuel tank); filed locally.

4). (U) MAJ David DiNenna, S-3, 320th MP Battalion
- GOMOR from LTG McKiernan, Commander CFLCC, on 25 May 2003, for dereliction of duty for failing to report a violation of CENTCOM General Order #1 by a subordinate Field Grade Officer and Senior Noncommissioned Officer, which he personally observed; returned to soldier unfiled.
- GOMOR from BG Karpinski, Commander 800th MP Brigade, on 10 November 03, for failing to take corrective security measures as ordered by the Brigade Commander; filed locally.

5). (U) MAJ Stacy Garrity, Finance Officer, 800th MP Brigade
- GOMOR from LTG McKiernan, Commander CFLCC, on 25 May 2003, for violation of CENTCOM General Order #1, consuming alcohol with an NCO; filed locally.

6). (U) CPT Leo Merck, Commander, 870th MP Company
- Court-Martial Charges Preferred, for Conduct Unbecoming an Officer and Unauthorized Use of Government Computer in that he was alleged to have taken nude pictures of his female soldiers without their knowledge; Trial date to be announced.

7). (U) CPT Damaris Morales, Commander, 770th MP Company
- GOMOR from BG Karpinski, Commander 800th MP Brigade, on 20 August 2003, for failing to properly train his soldiers (Soldier had negligent discharge of M-16 while exiting his vehicle, round went into fuel tank); filed locally.

8). (U) CSM Roy Clement, Command Sergeant Major, 800th MP Brigade
- GOMOR and Relief for Cause from BG Janis Karpinski, Commander 800th MP Brigade, for fraternization and dereliction of duty for fraternizing with junior enlisted soldiers within his unit; GOMOR officially filed and he was removed from the CSM list.

9). (U) CSM Edward Stotts, Command Sergeant Major, 400th MP Battalion
- GOMOR from BG Karpinski, Commander 800th MP Brigade, on 20 August 2003, for failing to properly train his soldiers (Soldier had negligent discharge of M-16 while exiting his vehicle, round went into fuel tank); filed locally

10). (U) 1SG Carlos Villanueva, First Sergeant, 770th MP Company
- GOMOR from BG Karpinski, Commander 800th MP Brigade, on 20 August 2003, for failing to properly train his soldiers (Soldier had negligent

discharge of M-16 while exiting his vehicle, round went into fuel tank); filed locally.

11). (U) MSG David Maffett, NBC NCO, 800th MP Brigade,

   • GOMOR from LTG McKiernan, Commander CFLCC, on 25 May 2003, for violation of CENTCOM General Order #1, consuming alcohol; filed locally.

12). (U) SGM Marc Emerson, Operations SGM, 320th MP Battalion,

   • Two GO Letters of Concern and a verbal reprimand from BG Karpinski, Commander 800th MP Brigade, for failing to adhere to the guidance/directives given to him by BG Karpinski; filed locally.

d. (U) Saluting of officers was sporadic and not enforced. LTC Robert P. Walters, Jr., Commander of the 165th Military Intelligence Battalion (Tactical Exploitation), testified that the saluting policy was enforced by COL Pappas for all MI personnel, and that BG Karpinski approached COL Pappas to reverse the saluting policy back to a no-saluting policy as previously existed. (**ANNEX 53**)

19. (U) I find that individual soldiers within the 800th MP Brigade and the 320th Battalion stationed throughout Iraq had very little contact during their tour of duty with either LTC (P) Phillabaum or BG Karpinski. BG Karpinski claimed, during her testimony, that she paid regular visits to the various detention facilities where her soldiers were stationed. However, the detailed calendar provided by her Aide-de-Camp, 1LT Mabry, does not support her contention. Moreover, numerous witnesses stated that they rarely saw BG Karpinski or LTC (P) Phillabaum. (**Multiple Witness Statements**)

20. (U) In addition I find that psychological factors, such as the difference in culture, the soldiers' quality of life, the real presence of mortal danger over an extended time period, and the failure of commanders to recognize these pressures contributed to the perversive atmosphere that existed at Abu Ghraib (BCCF) Detention Facility and throughout the 800th MP Brigade. (**ANNEX 1**).

21. As I have documented in other parts of this investigation, I find that there was no clear emphasis by BG Karpinski to ensure that the 800th MP Brigade Staff, Commanders, and Soldiers were trained to standard in detainee operations and proficiency or that serious accountability lapses that occurred over a significant period of time, particularly at Abu Ghraib (BCCF), were corrected. AR 15-6 Investigations regarding detainee escapes were not acted upon, followed up with corrective action, or disseminated to subordinate commanders or soldiers. Brigade and unit SOPs for dealing with detainees if they existed at all, were not read or understood by MP Soldiers assigned the difficult mission of detainee operations. Following the abuse of several detainees at Camp Bucca in May 2003, I could find no evidence that BG Karpinski ever directed corrective training for her soldiers or ensured that MP Soldiers throughout Iraq clearly understood the requirements of the Geneva Conventions relating to the treatment of detainees. (**Multiple Witness Statements and the Personal Observations of the Investigation Team**)

22. On 17 January 2004 BG Karpinski was formally admonished in writing by LTG Sanchez regarding the serious deficiencies in her Brigade. LTG Sanchez found that the performance of the 800th MP Brigade had not met the standards set by the Army

or by CJTF-7. He found that incidents in the preceding six months had occurred that reflected a lack of clear standards, proficiency and leadership within the Brigade. LTG Sanchez also cited the recent detainee abuse at Abu Ghraib (BCCF) as the most recent example of a poor leadership climate that "permeates the Brigade." I totally concur with LTG Sanchez' opinion regarding the performance of BG Karpinski and the 800th MP Brigade. (**ANNEX 102 and the Personal Observations of the Investigating Officer**)

RECOMMENDATIONS AS TO PART THREE OF THE INVESTIGATION:

1. (U) That **BG Janis L. Karpinski, Commander, 800th MP Brigade** be Relieved from Command and given a General Officer Memorandum of Reprimand for the following acts which have been previously referred to in the aforementioned findings:

- Failing to ensure that MP Soldiers at theater-level detention facilities throughout Iraq had appropriate SOPs for dealing with detainees and that Commanders and Soldiers had read, understood, and would adhere to these SOPs.
- Failing to ensure that MP Soldiers in the 800th MP Brigade knew, understood, and adhered to the protections accorded to detainees in the Geneva Convention Relative to the Treatment of Prisoners of War.
- Making material misrepresentations to the Investigation Team as to the frequency of her visits to her subordinate commands.
- Failing to obey an order from the CFLCC Commander, LTG McKiernan, regarding the withholding of disciplinary authority for Officer and Senior Noncommissioned Officer misconduct.
- Failing to take appropriate action regarding the ineffectiveness of a subordinate Commander, LTC (P) Jerry Phillabaum.
- Failing to take appropriate action regarding the ineffectiveness of numerous members of her Brigade Staff including her XO, S-1, S-3, and S-4.
- Failing to properly ensure the results and recommendations of the AARs and numerous 15-6 Investigation reports on escapes and shootings (over a period of several months) were properly disseminated to, and understood by, subordinate commanders.
- Failing to ensure and enforce basic soldier standards throughout her command.
- Failing to establish a Brigade METL.
- Failing to establish basic proficiency in assigned tasks for soldiers throughout the 800th MP Brigade.
- Failing to ensure that numerous and reported accountability lapses at detention facilities throughout Iraq were corrected.

2. (U) That **COL Thomas M. Pappas, Commander, 205th MI Brigade**, be given a General Officer Memorandum of Reprimand and Investigated UP Procedure 15, AR 381-10, US Army Intelligence Activities for the following acts which have been previously referred to in the aforementioned findings:

- Failing to ensure that soldiers under his direct command were properly trained in and followed the IROE.

- Failing to ensure that soldiers under his direct command knew, understood, and followed the protections afforded to detainees in the Geneva Convention Relative to the Treatment of Prisoners of War.
- Failing to properly supervise his soldiers working and "visiting" Tier 1 of the Hard-Site at Abu Ghraib (BCCF).

3. (U) That **LTC (P) Jerry L. Phillabaum, Commander, 320th MP Battalion,** be Relieved from Command, be given a General Officer Memorandum of Reprimand, and be removed from the Colonel/O-6 Promotion List for the following acts which have been previously referred to in the aforementioned findings:

- Failing to properly ensure the results, recommendations, and AARs from numerous reports on escapes and shootings over a period of several months were properly disseminated to, and understood by, subordinates.
- Failing to implement the appropriate recommendations from various 15-6 Investigations as specifically directed by BG Karpinski.
- Failing to ensure that soldiers under his direct command were properly trained in Internment and Resettlement Operations.
- Failing to ensure that soldiers under his direct command knew and understood the protections afforded to detainees in the Geneva Convention Relative to the Treatment of Prisoners of War.
- Failing to properly supervise his soldiers working and "visiting" Tier 1 of the Hard-Site at Abu Ghraib (BCCF).
- Failing to properly establish and enforce basic soldier standards, proficiency, and accountability.
- Failure to conduct an appropriate Mission Analysis and to task organize to accomplish his mission.

4. (U) **That LTC Steven L. Jordan, Former Director, Joint Interrogation and Debriefing Center and Liaison Officer to 205th Military Intelligence Brigade,** be relieved from duty and be given a General Officer Memorandum of Reprimand for the following acts which have been previously referred to in the aforementioned findings:

- Making material misrepresentations to the Investigating Team, including his leadership roll at Abu Ghraib (BCCF).
- Failing to ensure that soldiers under his direct control were properly trained in and followed the IROE.
- Failing to ensure that soldiers under his direct control knew, understood, and followed the protections afforded to detainees in the Geneva Convention Relative to the Treatment of Prisoners of War.
- Failing to properly supervise soldiers under his direct authority working and "visiting" Tier 1 of the Hard-Site at Abu Ghraib (BCCF).

5. (U) That **MAJ David W. DiNenna, Sr., S-3, 320th MP Battalion,** be relieved from his position as the Battalion S-3 and be given a General Officer Memorandum of Reprimand for the following acts which have been previously referred to in the aforementioned findings:

- Received a GOMOR from LTG McKiernan, Commander CFLCC, on 25 May 2003, for dereliction of duty for failing to report a violation of CENTCOM General Order #1 by a subordinate Field Grade Officer and Senior Non-commissioned Officer, which he personally observed; GOMOR was returned to the soldier and not filed.
- Failing to take corrective action and implement recommendations from various 15-6 investigations even after receiving a GOMOR from BG Karpinski, Commander 800th MP Brigade, on 10 November 03, for failing to take corrective security measures as ordered; GOMOR was filed locally.
- Failing to take appropriate action and report an incident of detainee abuse, whereby he personally witnessed a soldier throw a detainee from the back of a truck.

6. (U) That **CPT Donald J. Reese, Commander, 372nd MP Company,** be relieved from Command and be given a General Officer Memorandum of Reprimand for the following acts which have been previously referred to in the aforementioned findings:

- Failing to ensure that soldiers under his direct command knew and understood the protections afforded to detainees in the Geneva Convention Relative to the Treatment of Prisoners of War.
- Failing to properly supervise his soldiers working and "visiting" Tier 1 of the Hard-Site at Abu Ghraib (BCCF).
- Failing to properly establish and enforce basic soldier standards, proficiency, and accountability.
- Failing to ensure that soldiers under his direct command were properly trained in Internment and Resettlement Operations.

7. (U) That **1LT Lewis C. Raeder, Platoon Leader, 372nd MP Company,** be relieved from his duties as Platoon Leader and be given a General Officer Memorandum of Reprimand for the following acts which have been previously referred to in the aforementioned findings:

- Failing to ensure that soldiers under his direct command knew and understood the protections afforded to detainees in the Geneva Convention Relative to the Treatment of Prisoners of War.
- Failing to properly supervise his soldiers working and "visiting" Tier 1 of the Hard-Site at Abu Ghraib (BCCF).
- Failing to properly establish and enforce basic soldier standards, proficiency, and accountability.
- Failing to ensure that soldiers under his direct command were properly trained in Internment and Resettlement Operations.

8. (U) That **SGM Marc Emerson, Operations SGM, 320th MP Battalion,** be relieved from his duties and given a General Officer Memorandum of Reprimand for the following acts which have been previously referred to in the aforementioned findings:

- Making a material misrepresentation to the Investigation Team stating that he had "never" been admonished or reprimanded by BG Karpinski, when in fact he had been admonished for failing to obey an order from BG Karpinski to "stay out of the towers" at the holding facility.

- Making a material misrepresentation to the Investigation Team stating that he had attended every shift change/guard-mount conducted at the 320th MP Battalion, and that he personally briefed his soldiers on the proper treatment of detainees, when in fact numerous statements contradict this assertion.
- Failing to ensure that soldiers in the 320th MP Battalion knew and understood the protections afforded to detainees in the Geneva Convention Relative to the Treatment of Prisoners of War.
- Failing to properly supervise his soldiers working and "visiting" Tier 1 of the Hard-Site at Abu Ghraib (BCCF).
- Failing to properly establish and enforce basic soldier standards, proficiency, and accountability.
- Failing to ensure that his Soldiers were properly trained in Internment and Resettlement Operations.

9. (U) That **1SG Brian G. Lipinski, First Sergeant, 372nd MP Company,** be relieved from his duties as First Sergeant of the 372nd MP Company and given a General Officer Memorandum of Reprimand for the following acts which have been previously referred to in the aforementioned findings:

- Failing to ensure that soldiers in the 372nd MP Company knew and understood the protections afforded to detainees in the Geneva Convention Relative to the Treatment of Prisoners of War.
- Failing to properly supervise his soldiers working and "visiting" Tier 1 of the Hard-Site at Abu Ghraib (BCCF).
- Failing to properly establish and enforce basic soldier standards, proficiency, and accountability.
- Failing to ensure that his soldiers were properly trained in Internment and Resettlement Operations.

10. (U) That **SFC Shannon K. Snider, Platoon Sergeant, 372nd MP Company,** be Relieved from his duties, receive a General Officer Memorandum of Reprimand, and receive action under the Uniform Code of Military Justice for the following acts which have been previously referred to in the aforementioned findings:

- Failing to ensure that soldiers in his platoon knew and understood the protections afforded to detainees in the Geneva Convention Relative to the Treatment of Prisoners of War.
- Failing to properly supervise his soldiers working and "visiting" Tier 1 of the Hard-Site at Abu Ghraib (BCCF).
- Failing to properly establish and enforce basic soldier standards, proficiency, and accountability.
- Failing to ensure that his soldiers were properly trained in Internment and Resettlement Operations.
- Failing to report a soldier, who under his direct control, abused detainees by stomping on their bare hands and feet in his presence.

11. (U) That **Mr. Steven Stephanowicz, Contract US Civilian Interrogator, CACI, 205th Military Intelligence Brigade,** be given an Official Reprimand to be placed in his

employment file, termination of employment, and generation of a derogatory report to revoke his security clearance for the following acts which have been previously referred to in the aforementioned findings:

- Made a false statement to the investigation team regarding the locations of his interrogations, the activities during his interrogations, and his knowledge of abuses.
- Allowed and/or instructed MPs, who were not trained in interrogation techniques, to facilitate interrogations by "setting conditions" which were neither authorized and in accordance with applicable regulations/policy. He clearly knew his instructions equated to physical abuse.

12. (U) **That Mr. John Israel, Contract US Civilian Interpreter, CACI, 205th Military Intelligence Brigade**, be given an Official Reprimand to be placed in his employment file and have his security clearance reviewed by competent authority for the following acts or concerns which have been previously referred to in the aforementioned findings:

- Denied ever having seen interrogation processes in violation of the IROE, which is contrary to several witness statements.
- Did not have a security clearance.

13. (U) I find that there is sufficient credible information to warrant an Inquiry UP Procedure 15, AR 381-10, US Army Intelligence Activities, be conducted to determine the extent of culpability of MI personnel, assigned to the 205th MI Brigade and the Joint Interrogation and Debriefing Center (JIDC) at Abu Ghraib (BCCF). Specifically, I suspect that **COL Thomas M. Pappas, LTC Steve L. Jordan, Mr. Steven Stephanowicz,** and **Mr. John Israel** were either directly or indirectly responsible for the abuses at Abu Ghraib (BCCF) and strongly recommend immediate disciplinary action as described in the preceding paragraphs as well as the initiation of a Procedure 15 Inquiry to determine the full extent of their culpability. (**ANNEX 36**)

OTHER FINDINGS/OBSERVATIONS

1. (U) Due to the nature and scope of this investigation, I acquired the assistance of Col (Dr.) Henry Nelson, a USAF Psychiatrist, to analyze the investigation materials from a psychological perspective. He determined that there was evidence that the horrific abuses suffered by the detainees at Abu Ghraib (BCCF) were wanton acts of select soldiers in an unsupervised and dangerous setting. There was a complex interplay of many psychological factors and command insufficiencies. A more detailed analysis is contained in **ANNEX 1** of this investigation.

2. (U) During the course of this investigation I conducted a lengthy interview with BG Karpinski that lasted over four hours, and is included verbatim in the investigation Annexes. BG Karpinski was extremely emotional during much of her testimony. What I found particularly disturbing in her testimony was her complete unwillingness to either understand or accept that many of the problems inherent in the 800th MP Brigade were caused or exacerbated by poor leadership and the refusal of her

command to both establish and enforce basic standards and principles among its soldiers. (ANNEX 45)

3. (U) Throughout the investigation, we observed many individual soldiers and some subordinate units under the 800th MP Brigade that overcame significant obstacles, persevered in extremely poor conditions, and upheld the Army Values. We discovered numerous examples of soldiers and sailors taking the initiative in the absence of leadership and accomplishing their assigned tasks.

a. (U) The 744th MP Battalion, commanded by LTC Dennis McGlone, efficiently operated the HVD Detention Facility at Camp Cropper and met mission requirements with little to no guidance from the 800th MP Brigade. The unit was disciplined, proficient, and appeared to understand their basic tasks.

b. (U) The 530th MP Battalion, commanded by LTC Stephen J. Novotny, effectively maintained the MEK Detention Facility at Camp Ashraf. His soldiers were proficient in their individual tasks and adapted well to this highly unique and non-doctrinal operation.

c. (U) The 165th MI Battalion excelled in providing perimeter security and force protection at Abu Ghraib (BCCF). LTC Robert P. Walters, Jr., demanded standards be enforced and worked endlessly to improve discipline throughout the FOB.

4. (U) The individual soldiers and sailors that we observed and believe should be favorably noted include:

a. (U) Master-at-Arms First Class William J. Kimbro, US Navy Dog Handler, knew his duties and refused to participate in improper interrogations despite significant pressure from the MI personnel at Abu Ghraib.

b. (U) SPC Joseph M. Darby, 372nd MP Company discovered evidence of abuse and turned it over to military law enforcement.

c. (U) 1LT David O. Sutton, 229th MP Company, took immediate action and stopped an abuse, then reported the incident to the chain of command.

CONCLUSION

1. (U) Several US Army Soldiers have committed egregious acts and grave breaches of international law at Abu Ghraib/BCCF and Camp Bucca, Iraq. Furthermore, key senior leaders in both the 800th MP Brigade and the 205th MI Brigade failed to comply with established regulations, policies, and command directives in preventing detainee abuses at Abu Ghraib (BCCF) and at Camp Bucca during the period August 2003 to February 2004.

2. (U) Approval and implementation of the recommendations of this AR 15-6 Investigation and those highlighted in previous assessments are essential to establish the conditions with the resources and personnel required to prevent future occurrences of detainee abuse.

ANNEXES

1. Psychological Assessment
2. Request for investigation from CJTF-7 to CENTCOM
3. Directive to CFLCC from CENTCOM directing investigation
4. Appointment Memo from CFLCC CDR to MG Taguba
5. 15-6 Investigation 9 June 2003
6. 15-6 Investigation 12 June 2003
7. 15-6 Investigation 13 June 2003
8. 15-6 Investigation 24 November 2003
9. 15-6 Investigation 7 January 2004
10. 15-6 Investigation 12 January 2004
11. SIR 5 November 2003
12. SIR 7 November 2003
13. SIR 8 November 2003
14. SIR 13 December 2003
15. SIR 13 December 2003
16. SIR 13 December 2003
17. SIR 17 December 2003
18. Commander's Inquiry 26 January 2004
19. MG Ryder's Report, 6 November 2003
20. MG Miller's Report, 9 September 2003
21. AR 190-8, Enemy Prisoners of War, Retained Personnel, Civilian Internees, and Other Detainees, 1 October 1997
22. FM 3-19.40, Military Police Internment/Resettlement Operations, 1 August 2001
23. FM 34-52, Intelligence Interrogation, 28 September 1992
24. Fourth Geneva Convention, 12 August 1949
25. CID Report on criminal abuses at Abu Ghraib, 28 January 2004
26. CID Interviews, 10–25 January 2004
27. 800th MP Brigade Roster, 29 January 2004
28. 205th MI Brigade's IROE, Undated
29. TOA Order (800th MP Brigade) and letter holding witnesses
30. Investigation Team's witness list
31. FRAGO #1108
32. Letters suspending several key leaders in the 800th MP Brigade and Rating Chain with suspensions annotated
33. FM 27-10, Military Justice, 6 September 2002
34. CID Report on abuse of detainees at Camp Bucca, 8 June 2003
35. Article 32 Findings on abuse of detainees at Camp Bucca, 26 August 2003
36. AR 381-10, 1 July 1984
37. Excerpts from log books, 320th MP Battalion
38. 310th MP Battalion's Inprocessing SOP
39. 320th MP Battalion's "Change Sheet"
40. Joint Interrogation and Debriefing Center's (JIDC) Slides, Undated
41. Order of Battle Slides, 12 January 2004
42. Joint Publication 0–2, Unified Actions Armed Forces, 10 July 2001

43. General Officer Memorandums of Reprimand
44. 800th MP Battalion's TACSOP
45. BG Janis Karpinski, Commander, 800th MP Brigade
46. COL Thomas Pappas, Commander, 205th MI Brigade
47. COL Ralph Sabatino, CFLCC Judge Advocate, CPA Ministry of Justice
48. LTC Gary W. Maddocks, S-5 and Executive Officer, 800th MP Brigade
49. LTC James O'Hare, Command Judge Advocate, 800th MP Brigade
50. LTC Robert P. Walters Jr., Commander, 165th MI Battalion (Tactical exploitation)
51. LTC James D. Edwards, Commander, 202nd MI Battalion
52. LTC Vincent Montera, Commander 310th MP Battalion
53. LTC Steve Jordan, former Director, Joint Interrogation and Debriefing Center/ LNO to the 205th MI Brigade
54. LTC Leigh A. Coulter, Commander 724th MP Battalion and OIC Arifjan Detachment, 800th MP Brigade
55. LTC Dennis McGlone, Commander, 744th MP Battalion
56. MAJ David Hinzman, S-1, 800th MP Brigade
57. MAJ William D. Proietto, Deputy CJA, 800th MP Brigade
58. MAJ Stacy L. Garrity, S-1 (FWD), 800th MP Brigade
59. MAJ David W. DiNenna, S-3, 320th MP Battalion
60. MAJ Michael Sheridan, XO, 320th MP Battalion
61. MAJ Anthony Cavallaro, S-3, 800th MP Brigade
62. CPT Marc C. Hale, Commander, 670th MP Company
63. CPT Donald Reese, Commander, 372nd MP Company
64. CPT Darren Hampton, Assistant S-3, 320th MP Battalion
65. CPT John Kaires, S-3, 310th MP Battalion
66. CPT Ed Diamantis, S-2, 800th MP Brigade
67. LTC Jerry L. Phillabaum, Commander, 320th MP Battalion
68. CPT James G. Jones, Commander, 229th MP Company
69. CPT Michael A. Mastrangelo, Jr., Commander, 310th MP Company
70. CPT Lawrence Bush, IG, 800th MP Brigade
71. 1LT Lewis C. Raeder, Platoon Leader, 372nd MP Company
72. 1LT Elvis Mabry, Aide-de-Camp to Brigade Commander, 800th MP Brigade
73. 1LT Warren E. Ford, II, Commander, HHC 320th MP Battalion
74. 2LT David O. Sutton, Platoon Leader, 229th MP Company
75. CW2 Edward J. Rivas, 205th MI Brigade
76. CSM Joseph P. Arrison, Command Sergeant Major, 320th MP Battalion
77. SGM Pascual Cartagena, Command Sergeant Major, 800th MP Brigade
78. CSM Timothy L. Woodcock, Command Sergeant Major, 310th MP Battalion
79. 1SG Dawn J. Rippelmeyer, First Sergeant, 977th MP Company
80. SGM Mark Emerson, Operations SGM, 320th MP Battalion
81. MSG Brian G. Lipinski, First Sergeant, 372nd MP Company
82. MSG Andrew J. Lombardo, Operations Sergeant, 310th MP Battalion
83. SFC Daryl J. Plude, Platoon Sergeant, 229th MP Company
84. SFC Shannon K. Snider, Platoon SGT, 372nd MP Company
85. SFC Keith A. Comer, 372nd MP Company
86. SSG Robert Elliot, Squad Leader, 372nd MP Company

87. SSG Santos A. Cardona, Army Dog Handler
88. SGT Michael Smith, Army Dog Handler
89. MA1 William J. Kimbro, USN Dog Handler
90. Mr. Steve Stephanowicz, US civilian contract Interrogator, CACI, 205th MI Brigade
91. Mr. John Israel, US civilian contract Interpreter, Titan Corporation, 205th MI Brigade
92. FM 3-19.1, Military Police Operations, 22 March 2001
93. CJTF-7 IROE and DROE, Undated
94. CJTF-7 Interrogation and Counter Resistance Policy, 12 October 2003
95. 800th MP Brigade Mobilization Orders
96. Sample Detainee Status Report, 13 March 2004
97. 530th MP Battalion Mission Brief, 11 February 2004
98. Memorandum for Record, CPT Ed Ray, Chief of Military Justice, CFLCC, 9 March 2004
99. SIR 14 January 2004
100. Accountability Plan Recommendations, 9 March 2004
101. 2LT Michael R. Osterhout, S-2, 320th MP Battalion
102. Memorandum of Admonishment from LTG Sanchez to BG Karpinski, 17 January 2004
103. Various SIRs from the 800th MP Brigade/320th MP Battalion
104. 205th MI Brigade SITREP to MG Miller, 12 December 2003
105. SGT William A. Cathcart, 372nd MP Company
106. 1LT Michael A. Drayton, Commander, 870th MP Company

AR 15-6 Investigation – Allegations
of Detainee Abuse at Abu Ghraib

PSYCHOLOGICAL ASSESSMENT

Certain factors can interact and contribute to horrific outcomes, such as the Iraqi detainee abuse at the end of 2003 at Abu Ghraib (also known as the Baghdad Central Correctional Facility [BCCF]). This is clearly an example of aberrant behavior.

First, Soldiers were immersed in the Islamic culture, a culture that many were encountering for a first time. Clearly there are major differences in worship and beliefs, and there is the association of Muslims with terrorism. All these causes exaggerate differences and create misperceptions that can lead to fear or devaluation of a people. Second, quality of life at Abu Ghraib was poor, and lacking most amenities present in other camps in Iraq. The population at BCCF was disparate, consisting of hardened Iraqi criminals watched by corrupt Iraqi prison guards, as well as the varying types of detainees: males, females, juveniles, criminals, terrorists, and mentally ill. BCCF is a closed environment, an environment that would wear on its occupants (MPs, MI personnel, and detainees) over a prolonged period of time. Third, all present at Abu Ghraib were truly in personal danger. Daily mortar attacks from without and sporadic prisoner riots from within led to several deaths and numerous injuries of both Soldiers and detainees alike.

Fourth, command factors were a key player at the BCCF. There was not only a lack of interaction but also friction between the MP and MI command elements. A lack of proper training and supervision was present. There was a failure to respond to recommendations of corrective actions contained in several AARs, 15-6s, and even the recommendations highlighted in MGs Miller and Ryder assessment reports. Leaders were unwilling to accept responsibility. Discipline, when taken, was lenient, leading to the realization that the BDE or BN chains of command would essentially do nothing, thus contributing to a mentality that "I can get away with this."

Specifically, there were several commanders and NCOs who were ineffective leaders. Take, for instance, BG Karpinski, Cdr 800th MP BDE. On the bases of her four-hour interview and our examination of the interviews and sworn statements of others, we concluded that she was unable to delegate taskings and did many taskings on her own. Though with good intentions, she lessened or dismissed punishments recommended by her staff. She was painfully aware of several problems in the 800th MP BDE, including personnel, logistics, administration, and supplies, but she was not capable of demanding solutions from her chain of command. She felt herself a victim, and she propagated a negativity that permeated throughout the BDE.

Given this atmosphere of danger, promiscuity, and negativity, the worst human qualities and behaviors came to the fore and a perversive dominance came to prevail, especially at Abu Ghraib. Inadequate and immoral men and women desiring dominance may be drawn to fields such as corrections and interrogation, where they can be in absolute control over others. CPL Grainer had a civilian prison job. SSG Frederick was also in corrections. Through our investigation, we identified them as ringleaders of the abuse; but note carefully that they collaborated with other MP Soldiers and several unknown MI personnel, to include Soldiers as well as their U.S. civilian contract interrogators and interpreters. Witnesses report pairs of civilian interrogators and interpreters carrying out detainee abuse, as well as an interpreter raping a male juvenile detainee. In fact, the MI unit seemed to be operating in a conspiracy of silence. Still, it is important to remember that dominance in and of itself is not improper. In fact, interrogators knowingly dominate their subjects, and sometimes even intimidate, in order to obtain intelligence. But clearly the behavior at BCCF crossed the line. The sadistic and psychopathic behavior was appalling and shocking.

In CPI Grainer and SSG Frederick's area of responsibility at tier 1A/1B of the Hard-Site, it was commonplace for detainees to be abused. MP dog handlers cooperated with MI interrogators under the MPs' watch to use dogs to frighten, intimidate, and even bite detainees. ILT Raeder, a platoon leader and acting company commander of 372nd MP Company, was openly hostile and allowed his guards to carry illegal weapons. MP dog handler SGT Smith was disrespectful and racist (he said, "After working at the prison for so long, the dogs came not to like Iraqi detainees. They didn't like the Iraqi culture, smell, sound, skin tone, hair color, or anything about them."). Detainee abuse was common knowledge among the enlisted Soldiers at Abu Ghraib. Abuse with sexual themes (see below) occurred and was witnessed, condoned, and photographed, but never reported. Even officers witnessed abuse on several occasions or had knowledge of abuse at the BCCF.

As mentioned earlier, everyday life was extremely stressful. And several MP and MI Soldiers were especially indifferent and vindictive against detainees involved in any violence toward Coalition Forces or who exhibited deviant behavior. On 23 August 03, an MI Soldier kicked and beat a passive, cuffed detainee who was suspected of mortaring BCCF; this incident was witnessed by officers and NCOs alike. On 28-29 October 03, CPI. Grainer and SSG Frederick received three detainees involved in rape of a male juvenile. MI Soldiers instructed them to "rough them up." CPL Grainer and SSG Frederick shackled the three together, lying on the floor, simulating gay sex. On 8 November 03, MP guards brought seven hooded detainees to the Hard-Site who had rioted in Camp Ganci earlier that day. They were stripped, told to get on their hands and knees, and placed face forward in a pyramid. Other Soldiers stopped by to view. PFC England said, "We would joke around, everyone would laugh at the things we had them do." On 24 November 03, a detainee shot a MP guard (who was unhurt) with a pistol smuggled in to him by the Iraqi prison guards. He sustained lethal shotgun rounds to his legs. Then later, after returning from the hospital, CPL Grainer beat him severely, including direct blows to his leg wounds.

Clearly some detainees at Abu Ghraib were totally humiliated and degraded. This is a classic example of the legal formula that "predisposition + opportunity = criminal behavior." Predisposition included the psychological factors of negativity, anger, hatred, and desire to dominate and humiliate. And, with an unsupervised workplace in which no threat of appropriate punishment would be forthcoming, there was opportunity. Moreover, competent authority needs to expedite the detainee release process so that detainees without intelligence value will be rapidly released. And we can learn from the program in place at Dover Air Force Base, where the remains of servicemen are received. Psychiatrists or psychologists are always present, and General Officers have the opportunity to observe the entire process of personnel conducting mortuary affairs operations, and how they cope with conditions of their workplace.

Finally, we must be ever ready to prevent the recurrence of such inhumane behavior to the best of our ability. But when such behavior occurs, the guilty must face swift, decisive, and appropriate justice. While justice is being served, an investigation team needs to analyze the organization and needs to deal with it accordingly. It seems incomprehensible that such misdeeds could happen in a facility, even in a prison complex as notorious as Abu Ghraib. But they did.

But BCCF would be a troublesome arena today even for a well trained MP or MI unit conducting detainee and interrogation operations. Compare and contrast the differences between the detention missions of the Soldiers of Desert Storm and Operation Iraqi Freedom. The Desert Storm Soldiers dealt with male enemy prisoners in a war that lasted a matter of hours. At war's end, they released and repatriated the prisoners. In OIF-2, the war is ongoing with no end in sight, and the detainees are in fixed and exposed camp facilities. These detainees are male and female, young and old; they may be innocent, may have high intelligence value, or may be terrorists or criminals. No matter who they are, if they are at Abu Ghraib, they are remanded in deplorable, dangerous living conditions, as are the Soldiers. Every day, the Soldiers must deal with extremely frustrated and hostile detainees who are in total limbo concerning their fate and release; the Soldiers must always be on their guard. And, depending if they are MP or MI Soldiers, they are pressured to either prevent escape or obtain intelligence rapidly. Thus, BCCF has both depressive and anxiety-laden elements that would grind down even the most motivated Soldier and lead to anger and possibly loss of control.

This new "psychological battlefield" requires a new support system for today's MP guard and MI specialist. Of course they must receive all prerequisite training and be knowledgeable on international law and information technology. But they should receive respite away from these detention camps periodically. Physicians and chaplains are needed for the body and spirit, but mental health providers are needed for the mind. A psychiatrist or psychologist should be on the lookout for significant anger/depressive/anxiety symptoms, and he/she would also provide education and support to prevent Soldiers from any negative conditioning that could impair job performance. Our Soldiers deserve no less.

Assessment by:
COL Henry Nelson
USAF Psychiatrist
Member, AR 15-6 Investigation Team – 800th MP Brigade

MG Miller's Report

**ASSESSMENT OF DoD COUNTERTERRORISM INTERROGATION
AND DETENTION OPERATIONS IN IRAQ (U)**

1. **(S/NF) Introduction** – From 31 August to 9 September 2003, MG Geoffrey Miller, US Army, Commander, Joint Task Force Guantanamo (JTF-GTMO) led a team of personnel experienced in strategic interrogation (Annex A) to HQ, CJTF-7, Baghdad, to conduct assistance visits to CJTF-7, TF-20, and the Iraqi Survey Group (ISG) to discuss current theater ability to rapidly exploit internees for actionable intelligence. The team focused on three areas: intelligence integration, synchronization, and fusion; interrogation operations, and detention operations. The team used JTF-GTMO operational procedures and interrogation authorities as baselines.

2. **(S/NF) Executive Summary** – The dynamic operational environment in Iraq requires an equally dynamic intelligence apparatus. To improve velocity and operational effectiveness of counterterrorism interrogation, attention in three major mission areas is needed. The team observed that the Task Force did not have authorities and procedures in place to affect a unified strategy to detain, interrogate, and report information from detainees/internees in Iraq. Additionally, the corps commander's information needs required an in-theater analysis capability integrated throughout the interrogation operations structure to allow for better and faster reach-back to other worldwide intelligence databases. Last, the detention operations function must act as an enabler for interrogation.

(S/NF) The command has initiated a system to drive the rapid exploitation of internees to answer CJTF-7, theater, and national level counter terrorism requirements. This is the first stage toward the rapid exploitation of detainees. Receipt of additional resources currently in staffing will produce a dramatic improvement in the speed of delivering actionable intelligence and leveraging the effectiveness of the interrogation efforts. Our assessment is, given the implementation of the attached recommendations, a significant improvement in actionable intelligence will be realized within thirty days.

3. **(S/NF) Functions:** Integration – Synchronization – Fusion (Point of contact (POC) is MR D****************)

   a. **(U) Integration** – Defined as: to organize HUMINT collection and analytical resources under a coordinating authority that can rapidly task, direct, conduct analysis, and action intelligence gained from interrogations.

   (S/NF) Observation – HUMINT collection and analysis is being performed by several autonomous entities in the theater, resulting in duplication of effort and imperfect information flow.

(S/NF) Recommendation – Establish a robust coordinating authority to direct and coordinate all HUMINT collection and analysis in Iraq. Supplement this authority with a collection management operation focused to support the needs of the Global War on Terrorism (GWOT), the Theater Commander and CJTF-7 Commanders' intelligence and targeting objectives. Additional resources are required for the CJTF-7 CJ2X to sustain this effort.

(S/NF) Observation – HUMINT collection priorities were not clearly defined, leading to ambiguous collection efforts. There are a large number of collection priorities that require a clear prioritization as to which requirements support the commander's critical information requirements.

(S/NF) Recommendation/Action In-progress – CJTF-7 CJ2X has established a clear method of prioritization for collection requirements. Requirements are now being combined into areas of focus to drive interrogation tasking and operations.

b. **(U) Synchronization** – Defined as: to establish a defined process and procedure to integrate the prioritization and tasking of all interrogation assets. (POC is MR J***************)

(S/NF) Observation – No written guidance specifically addressing interrogation policies and authorities was disseminated to units.

(S/NF) Recommendation/ Action In-progress – CJTF-7 is drafting approval documents containing the authorities, policies and practices to outline requirements to process, interrogate, and exploit security internees.

(S/NF) Observation – DoD assets and other autonomous entities are active in the theater collecting information and conducting analysis under independent chains of command. Information sharing is not fully integrated. The various organizations are generally unaware of each other's capabilities, interests, and mutual information needs. They also lack protocols for coordinating access to internees, and for sharing the information collected and analysis performed.

(S/NF) Recommendation – CJTF-7 is establishing a HUMINT Collection and Targeting meeting that provides a weekly forum for system information sharing, internee access, and tasking protocols to fully leverage the participation of all entities active in the theater (to include Special Operations Forces (SOF), the Criminal Investigative Task Force, Central Intelligence Agency, and the Iraqi Survey Group) to support the CJTF-7 commander's intelligence and targeting objectives.

c. **(U) Fusion** – Fusion is defined as assuring that all required resources and actions to support internee operations are properly integrated, supervised, executed and assessed to support the commander's intent. (POC is ***************)

(S/NF) Observation – The resiliency and global reach of GWOT targets requires much closer cooperation between the strategic analytical community and the collectors and analysts in the field. Military intelligence analysts at the CJTF-7 ACE, CJ2X, and in the field are closely focused on the tactical mission and are generally unaware of the assets and capabilities of the broader national intelligence community and the existence of dedicated CT analytical centers, such as DIA's Joint Intelligence Task Force Combating Terrorism (JITF-CT) and the CIA's Counterterrorism Center (CTC).

(S/NF) Recommendation – Expedite the exchange of Counterterrorism information and analysis between collectors in the field and the national intelligence community by integrating the Interrogator Tiger Teams with analysts at the CJTF-7 CJ2X and national intelligence community through JITF-CT. Energize the analysis-collection feedback loop of the intelligence cycle with robust, timely, GWOT oriented, collection management planning and execution.

4. (U) **Interrogation** – Setting the conditions to exploit internees to respond to questions that answer theater commanders' critical questions. (POC is ***************)

(S/NF) Summary – Tactical interrogation operations differ greatly from strategic interrogation operations. The interrogators within CJTF-7 have been accomplishing the tactical mission, at a high rate of professionalism and effectiveness since the beginning of the war. As the CJTF transitions to a new phase of operations, the category of internees to interrogate and analytical backstopping required necessitates transition to strategic interrogation operations. The interrogation mission is hindered by an absence of analytical resources and reach-back data systems. The detention operation does not yet set conditions for successful interrogations. Interrogations are conducted without a clear strategy for implementing a long-term approach strategy and clearly defined interrogation policies and authorities. To achieve rapid exploitation of internees it is necessary to integrate detention operations, interrogation operations and collection management under one command authority.

(S/NF) Observation – There is minimal analytical support to the interrogation mission. Interrogators continue to use tactical interrogation methods in a transitioning strategic environment.

(S/NF) Recommendation – Establish and train Interrogation Tiger Teams comprised of one interrogator and one analyst, both with SCI access. CJTF-7 has established an initial cadre of integrated Interrogation Tiger Teams from current assets and scheduled deploying interrogators and analysts to attend strategic interrogator and analyst training at Tiger Team University, USAICS, and Fort Huachuca in October 03.

(S/NF) Observation – CJFT-7s two interrogation facilities operate with their own independent collection focus without an integrated coordinating element. Coordination between facilities is conducted informally and inconsistently.

(S/NF) Recommendation – Consolidate the interrogation mission at one Joint Interrogation Debriefing Center (JIDC)/strategic interrogation facility under CJTF-7 command. This action has been initiated.

(S/NF) Observation – Detention operations do not enable the interrogation mission.

(S/NF) Recommendation – Dedicate and train a detention guard force subordinate to the JIDC Commander that sets the conditions for the successful interrogation and exploitation of internees/detainees. This action is now in progress.

(S/NF) Observation – The lack of awareness of available analytical databases by interrogators and analysts limits the ability to conduct effective integrated interrogation operations.

(S/NF) Recommendation – Train analysts to incorporate databases including DIMS, CT-link, web-safe, CIA Source, Harmony, and Coliseum in interrogation planning and execution. This training is provided at Tiger Team University and can be leveraged with a sustained theater training program.

(S/NF) Observation – Analysts at JIDC (Joint Interrogation Debriefing Center) interrogation operations section have limited access to automated intelligence systems that would allow the analyst to reach back to national level resources. The primary collection facilities (Abu Gharib) requires at a minimum 2 JWICS terminal to meet full operational capability.

(S/NF) Recommendation – Provide the necessary systems and bandwidth to enable direct analytical support to interrogation operations. See paragraph 6 (Information Technology).

(S/NF) Observation – There is no Behavioral Science Consultation Team (BSCT) to support interrogation operations. These teams comprised of operational behavioral psychologists and psychiatrists are essential in developing integrated interrogation strategies and assessing interrogation intelligence production.

(S/NF) Recommendation – Provide 1 BSCT to support interrogation operations.

(S/NF) Observation – The system procedures to rapidly transfer/return fully exploited internee intelligence sources back to the internee general population or recommend their release require assessment and streamlining.

(S/NF) Recommendation – Assess and refine transfer criteria to support continued rapid exploitation of high value internees and the release of fully exploited or low value internees in a more timely manner.

(S/NF) Observation – Task Force 20 (TF-20) lacks adequate number of trained interrogator-analyst Tiger Teams for mission requirements.

(S/NF) Recommendation: That CJTF-7 provide TF-20 Tiger Team support.

(S/NF) Observation – The application of emerging strategic interrogation strategies and techniques contain new approaches and operational art. Legal review and recommendations of internee interrogation operations by a dedicated command staff judge advocate is required to maximize interrogation effectiveness.

(S/NF) Recommendation – Dedicate a judge advocate(s) to advise commanders and interrogation leadership on requirements to operate within approved interrogation authorities, responsible for the detention and intelligence missions. This action is in progress.

5. **(U) Detention Operations** (POC is) **************

(U) Functions – Provide a safe, secure and humane environment that supports the expeditious collection of intelligence.

(S/NF) Summary – The importance of the rapid collection and dissemination of intelligence is vital for success and must be emphasized in the conduct of detention operations. It is essential that the guard force be actively engaged in setting the conditions for successful exploitation of the internees. Joint strategic interrogation operations are hampered by lack of active control of the internees within the detention environment. The pending establishment of the theater joint interrogation detention center at Abu Gharib will consolidate both detention and strategic interrogation operations and result in synergy between MP and MI resources and an integrated, synchronized and focused strategic interrogation effort.

(S/NF) Observation – Minimal operational procedures and guidance were available for internee in-processing, collection and integration of intelligence, security procedures, internee discipline standards and procedures for reacting to emergencies situations in the detention facilities.

(S/NF) Recommendation – Develop a comprehensive set of detention physical security SOPs. Conduct training for detention center leadership and staff on the implementation of these procedures. JTF-GTMO SOPs for physical security and detention operations were provided to CJTF-7 staff.

(S/NF) Observation – Some of the detention facility guard force interviewed were unable to apply their standing orders and Rules of Engagement procedures to hypothetical situations – e.g. escaping internees.

(S/NF) Recommendations – Scenario-based training for the current operational and future theater operational environment is recommended to ensure standing procedures (e.g. Rules of Engagement) are known and their application thoroughly understood by the detention leadership and staff.

(S/NF) Observation – Detention operations must be structured to ensure detention environment focuses the internee's confidence and attention on their interrogators. The MP detention staff should be an integrated element supporting the interrogation functions and received orientation training to support interrogation operations.

(S/NF) Recommendation – Assign, train, and sustain interrogator and detention staff team building focused on improving the collection of intelligence. MP detention staff training programs utilized by JTF-GTMO were provided to CJTF-7 for consideration and baseline implementation.

Observation – Disciplinary procedures for internees are arbitrary or not clearly defined

(S/NF) Recommendation/Action In-progress – The unit is updating its operating procedures for implementing disciplinary measures related to detainee operations.

(S/NF) Observation – Males, females and juveniles are detained in the same camp in close proximity to each other. Full utilization of a classification system that is sensitive to group dynamics is not currently in place.

(S/NF) Recommendation/Action In-progress – Procedures to segregate males, females, and juvenile internees in the detention facility to prevent unauthorized contact are being refined.

(S/NF) Observation- Some detainees who had infectious medical conditions were detained in the general internee population. This mingling of internees could result in possible contamination of other detainees and soldier detention staff. Detainees suffering from apparent mental illness were segregated in a holding pen that was normally used for disciplinary purposes.

(S/NF) Recommendation – Special needs sections of the detention facility should be developed for internees with contagious medical conditions and internees who exhibit mental illness.

6. **(U) Information Technology (IT) (POC is ***************)**

(U) Functions – IT focus is streamlined information gathering resulting in rapid intelligence analysis and exploitation.

(S/NF) Observation- Current information management systems do not support rapid, integrated exploitation of intelligence community databases.

(S/NF) Recommendation – Create a robust automated knowledge center, incorporating information and documents currently located in diverse data stores to allow for sharing of all information on internees. (See Annex B for specific IT comments.)

7. **(U) Conclusion** – Actions to improve the Task Force's ability to conduct counterterrorist strategic interrogations were being developed at the time of this report's drafting. Provision of resources is crucial to success. Expeditious fill of two leadership billets – one as Chief of the HUMINT Operations Center (HOC) and the other as Chief, HUMINT Analysis Center (HAC), CJTF-7, is essential to enable successful joint, integrated interrogation operations. Concurrently, assignment of expert analysts is required to form Tiger Teams and populate the HAC.

GEOFFREY D. MILLER
Major General, U.S. Army

ANNEX A: ASSESSMENT TEAM MEMBERS

Team Leader

| MG Geoffrey Miller, USA | JTF-GTMO | Commander |

Synchronization Team

MR ***************	DIA	Former JTF-GTMO Joint Interrogation Group Dir.
MR ***************	DIA/DHS	Former JTF-GTMO Interrogation Control Ele.Chief
MR ***************	CIA	Former JTF-GTMO CTC Chief
CDR *************** USNR	JITF-CT	Former JTF-GTMO Analysis Chief
LTC *************** USA	JATF SOUTH	Former JTF-GTMO Staff Judge Advocate
CPT *************** USA	JTF-GTMO	Information Technology Chief
MR ***************	CITF	Former JTF-GTMO Crim. Invest. Task Force Chief

Interrogation Operations Team

LtCol *************** USAF	DIA/DHS	Former JTF-GTMO Interrogation Control Ele Chief
CW3 *************** USA	470th MI BDE	Former GTMO Saudi Team Chief
CW3 *************** USA	JTF-GTMO	Central Asia Team Chief
SSGT *************** USA	JTF-GTMO	Central Asia Team Analyst
MSG *************** USA	JTF-GTMO	Saudi Team Noncommissioned Officer-in-Charge
SSG *************** USA	JTF-GTMO	Saudi Team Analyst
SSG *************** USA	JTF-GTMO	Special Projects Interrogator
SSG *************** USA	JTF-GTMO	Special Projects Analyst

Detention Operations Team

| CSM *************** USA | JTF-GTMO | Camp Delta Superintendent |
| CPT *************** USA | JTF-GTMO | Camp Delta Company Commander |

ANNEX B: INFORMATION TECHNOLOGY SOLUTIONS

The goal of a theater-wide intelligence information technology initiative is *fused intelligence* which will allow for a faster interrogation cycle, faster exchange of information, minimize manual processes, eliminate redundancy, manpower savings, rapid data mining, focused interrogation plan, and an automated collection plan.

ISSUES

– There isn't sufficient bandwidth or connectivity available to support current interrogation operations and consolidated internee database for near-real time information sharing

   ○ Some locations have SIPR connectivity but it is slow and unreliable. Some locations do not have enough SIPR drops to support the mission and personnel.

– There are diverse data stores to include MS Excel spreadsheets, MS Access databases. MS Word documents that are not shared by the various internee camps

   ○ There isn't a theater level network that reaches out to all the units for the purpose of sharing folder, files, and documents, with the exception of email. Email is not an effective way of sharing information for the purpose of conducting data mining and intelligence exploitation.

– There are no standardized information gathering and reporting methods that will allow for tracking of information collected from internees from the time of capture and through the intelligence requirements management and interrogation process.

   ○ There isn't a comprehensive collection management and dissemination system in place.

– There isn't an effective method to link internees to other internees or associates, organizations, locations, and facilities or to associate documents to internees to allow analysis to quickly search all information pertaining to an internee.

OPTIONS

– Implement a theater level network that supports folder, file, and document sharing.

   ○ Ensure bandwidth is adequate to support the network traffic and all the users.
   ○ Ensure that all units have access to the network with adequate number of workstations to support the mission, especially for those units that capture and/or initially process internees and those units that conduct analysis and interrogations.

– Develop a database that incorporates the various data stores, from the time of capture and through the intelligence analysis and interrogation process.

   ○ The web-based Joint Detainee Information Management System (JDIMS) developed for and currently utilized by JTF Guantanamo, with some tailoring and modifications, will be adequate to meet this need of a consolidated internee database. The database also contains a collection management and dissemination module that manages all requirements and reporting on internees. It also contains an online reports writing feature, which allows the analysts and interrogators to create reports and immediately share information.

○ The Detention Information Management System (DIMS) also developed for and utilized by JTF Guantanamo to capture initial detainee information as well as operational data gathered by the military police, will allow for input of internee information from the time of capture and throughout their stay at the detention facilities when not being interrogated

○ A Joint Detainee Information Management System-Iraq will share data with JTF Guantanamo detainee database and make it available to the intelligence community. By sharing detainee information, the intelligence community will benefit from a web-based single source of detainee information readily available to them via the SIPR network.

○ A similar system should be implemented in Afghanistan for the detainee operations conducted there.

The goal of a worldwide-integrated detainee database is to address the needs of detainee interrogation operations and to share information regardless of location. It is the tool to bridge intelligence and technology in order to achieve information dominance and efficient operational control over the detainee/internee population and allow for near-real time data mining, information visualization, and intelligence exploitation to combat the Global War on Terrorism.

HEADQUARTERS
COMBINED JOINT TASK FORCE SEVEN
BAGHDAD IRAQ
APO AE 09335

REPLY TO
ATTENTION OF

CJTF7 – CG   12 OCT 2003

MEMORANDUM FOR

C2, Combined Joint Task Force Seven, Baghdad, Iraq 09335
C3, Combined Joint Task Force Seven, Baghdad, Iraq 09335
Commander, 205th Military Intelligence Brigade, Baghdad, Iraq 09335

SUBJECT: CJTF-7 Interrogation and Counter-Resistance Policy

1. (S//NF) This memorandum establishes the interrogation and counter-resistance policy for security internees under the control of CJTF-7. Security internees are civilians who are detained pursuant to Articles 5 and 78 of the Geneva Convention Relative to the Protection of Civilian Persons in Time of War of August 12. 1949 (hereinafter. Geneva Convention).

2. (Sf I approve the use of specified interrogation and counter-resistance approaches A as described in Enclosure 1. relating to security internees, subject to the following:

a. (S//NF) Use of these approaches is limited to interrogations of security internees under the control of CJTF-7.

b. (S//NF) These approaches must be used in combination with the safeguards described in Enclosure 2.

c. (S//NF) Segregation of security internees will be required in many instances to ensure the success of interrogations and to prevent the sharing of interrogation methods among internees. Segregation may also be necessary to protect sources from other detainees or otherwise provide for their security. Additionally, the Geneva Convention provides that security internees under definite suspicion of activity hostile to the security of Coalition forces shall, where absolute military necessity requires, be regarded as having forfeited rights of communication. Accordingly, these security internees may be segregated. I must approve segregation in all cases where such segregation will exceed 30 days in duration, whether consecutive nonconsecuitive. Submit written requests with supporting rationale tome through the CJTF-7 C2. A legal review from the CJTF-7 SJA must accompany each request

d. (S//NF) In employing each of the authorized approaches, the interrogator must maintain control of the interrogation: The interrogator should appear to be the one who controls all aspects of the interrogation to include the lighting, heating and configuration of the interrogation room, as well as the food, clothing and shelter given to the security internee.

3. (S//NF) Requests for use of approaches not listed in Enclosure 1 will be submitted to me through CJTF-7 C2, and will include a description of the proposcd approach and recommended safeguards. A legal review from the CJTF-7 SJA will accompany each request

4. (S//NF) Nothing in this policy limits existing authority for maintenance of good order and discipline among persons under Coalition control.

5. (S//NF) This policy supersedes the CJTF – 7 Interrogation and Counter-Resistance Policy signed on 14 September 2003.

6. (S//NF) POC is MAJ Daniel Kazmier, DNVT 558-0709, DSN 318 822-1050.

2 Encls   RICARIDO S. SANCHEZ
1. Interrogation Approaches (SI)   Lieutenant General, USA
2. General Safeguards   Commanding

CF: Commander, US Central Command

INTERROGATION APPROACHES (Security Internees)

(S//NF) Use of the following approaches is subject to the application of the general safeguards provided in enclosure (2). Specific implementation guidance with respect to approaches A-Q is provided in U.S. Army Field Manual 34-52. Brigade Commanders may provide additional implementation guidance.

A. (S//NF) Direct: Asking straightforward questions. The most effective of all approaches, it is the most simple and efficient approach to utilize.

B. (S//NF) Incentive/Removal of Incentive: Providing a reward or removing a privilege, above and beyond those required by the Geneva Convention. Possible incentives may include favorite food items, changes in environmental quality, or other traditional or regional comforts not required by the Geneva Convention.

C. (S//NF) Emotional Love: flaying on the love a security internee has for an individual or group. May involve an incentive, such as allowing communication with the individual or group.

D. (S/.NF) Emotional Hate: Playing on the genuine hatred or desire for revenge a security internee has for an individual or group.

E. (S//NF) Fear Up Harsh: Significantly increasing the fear level in a security internee.

F. (S//NF) Fear Up Mild: Moderately increasing the fear level in a security internee.

G. (S/INF) Reduced Fear: Reducing the fear level in a security internee or calming him by convincing him that he will be properly and humanely treated.

H. (S//NF) Pride and Ego Up: Flattering or boosting the ego of a security internee.

I. (S//NF) Pride and Ego Down: Attacking or insulting the pride or ego of a security internee.

J. (S//NF) Futility: Invoking the feeling in a security internee that it is useless to resist by playing on the doubts that already exist In his mind.

K. (S//NF) We Know All: Convincing the security internee that the interrogator already knows the answers to questions being asked.

L. (S//NF) Establish Your Identity: Convincing the security internee that the interrogator has mistaken the security internee for someone else. The security internee is encouraged to "clear his name."

M. (S//NF) Repetition: Continuously repeating the same question to the security internee during an interrogation to encourage full and candid answers to questions.

N. (S//NF) File and Dossier: Convincing security internee that the interrogator has a voluminous, damning and inaccurate file, which must be corrected by the security internee.

O. (S//NF) Muti and Jeff: An interrogation team consisting of a friendly and a harsh interrogator. This approach is designed to cause the security internee to have a feeling of hostility toward one interrogator and a feeling of gratitude toward the other.

P. (S//NF) Rapid Fire: Questioning in rapid succession without allowing security internee to answer questions fully.

Q. (S//NF) Silence: Stating at the security internee to encourage discomfort.

GENERAL SAFEGUARDS

(S//NF) Application of these interrogation approaches is subject to the following general safeguards:

(i) limited to use by trained interrogation personnel; (ii) there is a reasonable basis to believe that the security internee possesses information of intelligence value: (iii) the security internee is medically evaluated as a suitable candidate for interrogation (considering all approaches to be used in combination): (iv) interrogators are specifically trained for the approaches; (v) a specific interrogation plan, including reasonable safeguards, limits on duration, intervals between applications, termination criteria and the presence or availability of qualified medical personnel has been developed: and (vi) there is appropriate supervision.

(U) The purpose of all interviews and interrogations is to get the most information from a security internee with the least intrusive method, applied in a humane and lawful manner with sufficient oversight by trained investigators or interrogators. Interrogators and supervisory personnel will ensure uniform, careful, and safe conduct of interrogations.

(S//NF) Interrogations must always be planned, deliberate actions that take into account factors such as a security internee's current and past performance in both detention and interrogation; a security internee's emotional and physical strengths and weaknesses; assessment of approaches and individual techniques that may be effective; strengths and weaknesses of interrogators; and factors which may necessitate the augmentation of personnel.

(S//NP) Interrogation approaches are designed to manipulate the security internee's emotions and weaknesses to gain his willing cooperation. Interrogation operations are never conducted in a vacuum: they are conducted in close cooperation with the detaining units. Detention regulations and policies established by detaining units should be harmonized to ensure consistency with the interrogation policies of the intelligence collection unit. Such consistency will help to maximize the credibility of the interrogation team and the effectiveness of the interrogation. Strict adherence to such regulations, policies and standard operating procedures is essential.

(S//NF) Interrogators must appear to completely control the interrogation environment. It is important that interrogators be provided reasonable latitude to vary approaches depending on the security internee's cultural background, strengths, weaknesses, environment, extent of resistance training, as well as the urgency with which information believed in the possession of the security internee must be obtained.

(S//NF) Interrogators must ensure the safety of security internees, and approaches must in no way endanger them. Interrogators will ensure that security internees are allowed adequate sleep; and that diets provide adequate food and water and cause no adverse medical or cultural effects. Where segregation is necessary, security internees must be monitored for adverse medical or psychological reactions. Should military working dogs be present during interrogations, they will be muzzled and under control of a handler at all times to ensure safety.

(S//NF) While approaches are considered individually within this analysis, it must be understood that in practice, approaches are usually used in combination. The title of a particular approach is not always fully descriptive of a particular approach. The cumulative effect of all approaches to be employed must be considered before any decision is made regarding approval of a particular interrogation plan.

DEPARTMENT OF THE ARMY
JOINT INTERROGATION AND DEBRIEFING CENTER
ABU GHRAIB, IRAQ APO AE 09335

REPLY TO
ATTENTION OF

AETV-MI   30 November 03

MEMORANDUM THRU Commander, CJTF-7, ATTN: C2 (AETV-CJ2), BG(P) Fast, Victory
Base, Iraq, APO AE 09342

Commander, CJTF-7, ATTN: Staff Judge Advocate (AETV-JA), COL Warren, Victory Base,
Iraq, APO AE 09342

FOR Commander, CJTF-7, LTG Sanchez, Victory Base, Iraq, APO AE 09342

SUBJECT: Request for Exception to CJTF-7 Interrogation and Counter Resistance Policy

1. Request exception to the CJTF-7 Interrogation and Counter Resistance Policy to authorize the
Joint Interrogation and Debriefing Center (JDIC) interrogator to be authorized to use the Fear up
Harsh and isolation approaches during interrogations with the following detainee.

   a. Name: J█████ █ K█████

   b. ISN: 151363

   c. Date request employment of approach: As soon as possible.

      d. Circumstances of capture: Detainee is a Syrian male, █ years of age, captured in an
attempted IED attack in Baghdad, IZ. Detainee is an admitted foreign fighter who came to
commit Jihad against Coalition Forces in Iraq. He was captured with ███ ███ ███ ███
and ████████ while attempting to set up an IED.

      e. Assessment of detainee: Detainee is at the point where he is resigned to the hope that
Allah will see him through this episode in his life, therefore he feels no need to speak with
interrogators. Detainee will not answer open ended questions, has a smug attitude and is running
counter approaches on interrogators. Detainee needs to be put in a position where he will feel
that the only option to get out of jail is to speak with interrogators.

      f. Potential information: Detainee can provide information related to safe houses,
facilitators, financing, recruitment and operations of foreign fighter smuggling into Iraq.
Detainee can also potentially provide names and target information of local facilitators in Ar-
Ramadi. Detainee can also confirm information provided from others captured with him.

      g. Limitations of approach: Detainee will be interrogated in the Camp Vigilant Steel site.
Detainee argues that Allah is the only one that can decide his fate. Interrogators will establish

SECRET//NOFORN

AETV-MI
SUBJECT: Request for Exception to CJTF-7 Interrogation and Counter Resistance Policy

control of detainee by allowing detainee to take this stance then implement a Fear up harsh approach. Interrogators will reinforce the fact that we have attempted to help him time and time again and that they are now putting it in Allah's hands. Interrogators will at a maximum throw tables, chairs, invade his personal space and continuously yell at the detainee. Interrogators will not physically touch or harm the detainee, will take all necessary precautions that all thrown objects are clear of the detainee and will not coerce the detainee in any way. If the detainee has not broken yet, interrogators will move into the segregation phase of the approach. Interrogators will coordinate with Military Police guards in the segregation area prior to initiation of this phase. For the segregation phase of the approach the MPs will put an empty sandbag onto the prisoners head before moving him out of Vigilant B. This measure will be for force protection purposes and transporting the detainee to the segregation area by HMMWV. MPs will be transporting the detainee with the interrogators present. During transportation, the Fear up Harsh approach will be continued, highlighting the Allah factor. Interrogators will take all necessary precautions in conjunction with the MPs to ensure detainee's safety during transport. Upon arrival at site, MP guards will take him into custody. MP working dogs will be present and barking during this phase. Detainee will be strip searched by guards with the empty sandbag over his head for the safety of himself, prison guards, interrogators and other prisoners. Interrogators will wait outside the room while detainee is strip searched. Interrogators will watch from a distance while detainee is placed in the segregation cell. Detainee will be put on the adjusted sleep schedule (attached) for 72 hours. Interrogations will be conducted continuously during this 72 hour period. The approaches which will be used during this phase will include, fear up harsh, pride and ego down, silence and loud music. Stress positions will also be used in accordance with CJTF-7 IROE in order to intensify the approach.

2. The approval for this approach is essential due to the information this detainee possesses. It will greatly enhance and expedite the collection effort in support of CJTF-7 Intelligence requirements and could potentially save countless lives of American soldiers in the future.

3. POC for this action is CPT Fitch, 205th MI Bde SJA at DNVT 302-559-4031 or via SIPR at c5cm205misja@205mi.c5.army.smil.mil or CPT Wood, JIDC Interrogation OIC, at DNVT 302-559-1764 or via SIPR at Carolyn.wood@us.army.smil.mil.

                    THOMAS M. PAPPAS
                    COL, MI
                    Commanding

Exception to the CJTF-7 Interrogation and Counter Resistance Policy is granted/not granted.

AETV-MI
SUBJECT: Request for Exception to CJTF-7 Interrogation and Counter Resistance Policy

RICARDO S. SANCHEZ
LTG, USA
Commanding

RI PLY 9
ATTENTION OF

CJTF7-CG

19 January 2004

MEMORANDUM FOR Commander, United States Central Command

SUBJECT: Request for Investigating Officer

1. I request that you appoint an investigating officer, in the grade of Major General or above, to investigate the conduct of operations within the 800th Military Police Brigade. The Brigade is a theater asset, assigned to CFLCC, but TACON to CJTF-7.

2. Specifically, I request an investigation of the detention and internment operations conducted by the brigade from 1 November 2003 to the present. Recent reports of detainee abuse, escapes, and accountability lapses indicate systemic problems within the brigade and suggest a lack of clear standards, proficiency, and leadership. Several investigations, including a USACIDC investigation, into various aspects of the Brigade's operations are on-going. The purpose of this request is to gain a more comprehensive and all-encompassing inquiry, conducted by a senior leader from outside of CJTF-7, to make findings and recommendations concerning the fitness and performance of the 800th MP Brigade.

3. The CJTF-7 point of contact for this request is COL Marc Warren, DSN 318-836-1122.

RICARDO S. SANCHEZ
Lieutenant General, USA
Commanding

CF:
LTG McKiernan

DATE: 28 JAN 04

FROM: SAC, ABU GRHUYEB PRISON COMPLEX (CID)
TO: DIRECTOR, USACRC, USACIDC, FORT BELVOIR, VA
      CDR, HQUSACIDC //CIOP-ZA//
      CDR, 10TH MP BN (CID)(ABN)(FWD)//OPS//
      CDR, 3D MP GROUP (CID)//OPS//
      SJA, 4ID
      LNO CID, CJTF-7 (FOR FURTHER DISTRIBUTION)
      CDR, 800TH MP BDE
      CDR, 320TH MP BN
      CDR, 205TH MI BDE

SUBJECT: CID REPORT - 7TH STATUS/SSI - 0003-04-CID
83130-6C/5C2B/5Y2B/5Y2D/5Y2E/5X1/5M3/5X5/5X7

DRAFTER: PIERON, TYLER M.
RELEASER: ARTHUR, PAUL D.

UNCLASSIFIED - FOR OFFICIAL USE ONLY

Sworn Statements

File Number : 0013-04-CID609-
Location   : Kuwait BO, 3D MP GRP (CID)
Date   : 26 Jan 2004   Time: 1211
Statement Of: WALLIN, NEIL ALLEN
SSN   : ██████████   Grade/Status: E5/SGT
Org/Address : B CO, 109TH AREA SUPPORT MEDICAL BATTALION (ASMB),
              VERMILLION, SD 57069

I, NEIL A. WALLIN, WANT TO MAKE THE FOLLOWING STATEMENT UNDER OATH:
I was assigned as a medic at the Abu Ghruyeb, Prison, in
Baghdad, Iraq from Aug 03 to Dec 03. During that time I
observed a couple incidents that occurred in the Hard Cell area
of Camp Vigilant, Iraq. Camp Vigilant was one of four areas
within the prison and it contained the Hard Cell area where
priority prisoners where detained. Also the Hard Cells were
used to house any person(s) who were considered to be high risk,
either to themselves or others. Cell 1A was used to house high
priority detainee's and cell 1B was used to house the high risk
or trouble making detainee's. During my tour at the prison
I observed that when the male detainee's were first brought
to the facility, some of them were made to wear female
underwear, which I think was was to somehow break them down.
This practiced was not continued after their integration
to the prison. Sometime in Oct 03, I was asked to to evaluate a
detainee we called "one of the three stooges" or "one of the
three wise men". I do not know his real name. This detainee,
who was in cell 1A, had a 2 1/2 inch laceration on his chin,
which ran along his jaw bone and required about 13 stitches. At
the time I evaluated the detainee, I observed blood on the wall
near a metal weld, which I believed to be the place where the
detainee received his injury. I do not know how he was injured
or if it was done by himself or another. Later during my tour I
also observed SGT ██████ slap the face of a detainee we called
"Jihad Jerry" or "Gus". I believe his name was H██████. This
detainee, who was in cell 1B, had taken several swings at SGT
██████ and was often times placed in restraints. This detainee
was being evaluated because he refused to eat or drink and had
to sustained by intravenous means. I do not think that SGT
██████ struck the detainee out of anger but rather to show the
detainee that his assaults upon the corrections personal would
not be allowed to go unpunished. Also this detainee had made
verbal threats on several occasions that he would kill members
of the prison staff. There was also another incident where I
observed a video tape of a detainee we called "Shitboy". This
detainee was known for inserting various objects into his
rectum. This detainee was also known for consuming and throwing
his feces and urine. The video tape contained a segment where
this detainee was seen in four point restraints chained to a
door. The detainee was seen banging his head against the wall,
about five or six times, very hard.
Q: SA JONES
A: SGT WALLIN
Q: Do you know of any other instances where detainee's have been
assaulted, abused or degraded?
A: No.
Q: Have you observed or have heard anything pertaining to the
abuse or degradation of any of the detainee's?
A: No.
Q: Do you have anything to add to this statement?
A: No.///End of Statement///

472

For use of this form, see AR 190-45; The proponent agency of the Deputy Chief of Staff for Personnel.

LOCATION	DATE	TIME	FILE NUMBER
Abu Ghraib, Baghdad Iraq	27 Jan 04	1717	

LAST NAME, FIRST NAME, MIDDLE NAME	SOCIAL SECURITY NUMBER	GRADE/STATUS
SMITH, Michael Joseph		SGT

ORGANIZATION OR ADDRESS
320 MP BN , deployed with duty at Abu Ghraib, Iraq

I, Michael J. Smith, want to make the following statement under oath:

Q. Explain the incident with your dog when SSG ASHTON asked you to be present?
A. We were in one of the tiers at the hard site that was not being used, for controlled aggression training, when SSG ASHTON approached me about using my dog for an interview. It just so happened that I saw COL PAPPAS in the parking lot right after he asked about using my dog for the interview and he had stated that it was allowed. So myself and SGT CARDONA took our dogs over to the interrogation house they have. SSG KLESOWITCH briefed me on how he wanted the dog used. He wanted me to have the dog go and bark by the door, so I told him I would conduct a building search and the dog would sniff the door and sense there was someone there and then the dog would start barking. So at that point I took my dog over to the room where the detainee was and he did sniff under door and started barking. I took my dog out of the area. A little while later they came back to us and asked this time for us to bring both dogs over to the site of the interrogation. They explained the detainee would be sitting by the door and the door open. We had both of our dogs at a 45-degree to him and they proceeded to bark. Prior to us bringing the dogs over to the room this time they said that we could not take the dogs into the room without a muzzle. When we got to the room the detainee was sitting in the doorway, with his feet in the doorway and the door was open. My dog and SGT CARDONA's dog were both barking at the detainee and we never got closer then 18 inches. Neither dog had a muzzle on.
Q. Did you ever see a written permission slip that a dog could be used for this interview?
A. No.
Q. Did you know at this time that a written memo was needed to use the dogs?
A. I did not know you needed a memo, COL PAPPAS had not told me anything about a memo when I had talked with him.
Q. Did it appear the detainee was afraid of the dogs?
A. I could not tell, because all of my concentration was on controlling my dog.
Q. Was your dog barking and growling at the detainee?
A. Yes.
Q. Did anyone ever ask you to muzzle your dog?
A. No.
Q. Were there any other events when you used your dog during an interview of a detainee?
A. Yes.
Q. Explain that incident?
A. SGT CARDONA and I were at the hard site doing patrol. SSG FREDERICK asked us if we could come by with the dogs because they SSG FREDERICK wanted to question a detainee about a window. We waited out side while they pulled the detainee outside into the hallway. Someone said OK, bring them in, when went in. I was the first one in, the detainee was lying down flat on the floor and he was nude. As I entered the room the detainee rose to his feet, took a 90-degree turn and went against the wall. I took a 45 degree angle on the inside of the building and SGT CARDONA was at the other 45 angle with an exit, CPL GRANER was directly in front of him, telling him to get down, get down. The man went to his knees for a couple of seconds and then MJS

MJS

Page 1 of 2

473

Got up and went at CPL GRANER. The prisoner kicked GRANER one time in the chin. I peeled my dog off and CARDONA peeled his dog off at first. Since the prisoner was attacking an MP, he allowed his dog to go in and bite the detainee. CARDONA then called his dog off the detainee and pulled the dog back. GRANER then told the man again to get down, and the prisoner continues to be combative and went back at GRANER. CARDONA let his dog go again on the detainee and the dog bit the detainee again. CARDONA called the dog off and by that point there was 5 to 6 MP's who took the prison to the floor and cuffed him.

Q. Was the detainee combative when you first walked into the area?
A. Not when he was lying on the ground. Once he saw the dogs he was not combative he was just not listening.
Q. Do you know if the detainee understood English?
A. No.
Q. Did the detainee show any emotion that you can recall?
A. He showed fear.
Q. Was the detainee crying?
A. I do not recall.
Q. Why do you think the detainee charged at GRANER?
A. I have no idea.
Q. Do you recall how many MP's were present when you first got there?
A. No.
Q. Were you present when they gave the detainee medical attention?
A. Yes.
Q. DO you know who stitched up his wounds?
A. No.
Q. DO you know if anyone took any pictures during this event?
A. Yes.
Q. Who took the pictures?
A. I do not know, but I have seen the pictures. SGT CARDONA needed the pictures for his documentation.
Q. Do you have anything to add to this statement?
A. No.///End of Statement/// *MJS*

AFFIDAVIT

I, _Michael J. Smith_ HAVE READ OR HAVE HAD READ TO ME THIS STATEMENT WHICH BEGINS ON PAGE 1 AND ENDS ON PAGE _2_. I FULLY UNDERSTAND THE CONTENTS OF THE ENTIRE STATEMENT MADE BY ME. THE STATEMENT IS TRUE. I HAVE INITIALED ALL CORRECTIONS AND HAVE INITIALED THE BOTTOM OF EACH PAGE CONTAINING THE STATEMENT. I HAVE MADE THIS STATEMENT FREELY WITHOUT HOPE OF BENEFIT OR REWARD, WITHOUT THREAT OR PUNISHMENT, AND WITHOUT COERCION, UNLAWFUL INFLUENCE, OR UNLAWFUL INDUCEMENT.

(Signature of Person Making Statement)

WITNESSES:

_____
ORGANIZATION OR ADDRESS

_____
ORGANIZATION OR ADDRESS

_____

_____

SUBSCRIBED AND SWORN BEFORE ME, A PERSON BY LAW TO ADMINISTER OATHS, THIS _27th_ DAY OF _Jan 04_
AT _Abu Gharib Prison, Iraq_____

_____
(Signature of Person Administering Oath)

__Warren D. Worth_____
(Name of Person Administering Oath)

__Article 136, UCMJ_____
(Authority to Administer Oath)

INITIALS OF PERSON MAKING STATEMENT
MJS

PAGES 2 OF 2 PAGES

DA Form 2823 (AUTOMATED)

474

| LOCATION
Abu Ghraib, Iraq, APO AE 09335 | DATE
22 Jul 04 | Time
1204 | FILE NUMBER |
| LAST NAME, FIRST NAME, MIDDLE NAME
STEFANOWICZ, Steven Anthony | SOCIAL SECURITY NUMBER | | GRADE/STATUS
CIV |

ORGANIZATION OR ADDRESS
CACI, Abu Ghraib Correctional Facility, Abu Ghraib, Iraq, APO AE 09335

I Steven A. STEFANOWICZ, want to make the following Statement under oath:
Incident with hearing unusual sounds coming from the Segregation Hole in isolation wing alpha, around or about 20 DEC 03. After the conclusion of an interrogation that included SGT Mike Eckroth, Steve Stefanowicz and John Israel (terp) in the stairwell of Segragation. The detainee was returned into MP custody of SGT Cathcart and SSG Elliot. After the detainee was received by the two MP's, the interrogation team walked ahead of the MP's and detainee. The detainee was being placed into the Segregation Hole according to the approved interrogation plan and the sound of the detainee falling or possibly being struck was heard. The interrogation team looked back and the MP's were coming out of the facility and closed the door. Both SGT Eckroth and I looked at each other and asked what was the sound as we walked up the steps to the MP office area. Both of us (SGT Eckroth and Steve Stefanowicz) felt very uncomfortable with what we had heard and when the two MP's returned to the MP office area, located on the second deck, in between section alpha and bravo, we confronted the MP's. The reaction of SGT Cathcart was that he was agitated with the comment or suggestion. SGT Cathcart did reply to our questioning, but I can't recall the exact words of his statement, other than he was not happy. Explanation of an approved interrogation plan. When an interrogation plan outside the approved Interrogation Rules of Engagement (IROE) is requested by an interrogator, the plan must be reviewed and approved by Col Tom Papus and the Jag Officer. However, in some circumstance, this approval must go up to the office of General Sanchez for direct approval. In response to questions by the investigator and the special treatment of a detainee. The following is a description of the process of an ongoing interrogation. A detainee that I am actively interrogating was placed on an approved Sleep Meal Management Program. This program, has very specific and detailed rules required for implementation. In terms of what I have used recently over a 25 day period of time to interrogate the detainee. In this case, the detainee is provided with 4 hours of sleep per 24 hour period. The configuration of this sleep//wake program can be divided in any configuration and needs to be written out in detail for each day and approved through the appropriate chain of command, OIC, COL Papus and Jag. In this example, the final approving authority was COL Tom Papus. To elaborate on a typical 72 hour program recently used, the sleep/meal management portion cannot continue more that 72 consecutive hours. At which point, a 12 hour uninterrupted sleep session is mandatory before the program can continue. During a typical SMMS program, the MP's are responsible for administering the written program provided by the interrogator. A copy of the detailed, written program that they receive and keep on record in the office, during the duration of the session. In all cases, the NCO managing the alpha wing or responsible for the section are verbally briefed about the program, the details of the program, the detainee and intelligence value of the detainee (background). In addition, the MP's are advised that during the awake time period of an approved SMMS program, the MP's are allowed to do what is necessary to keep the detainee awake in the allotted period of time as long it adheres to approved rules of engagement and S^AS

| EXHIBIT | INITIALS OF PERSON MAKING STATEMENT
SAS | PAGE 1 OF 2 PAGES |

DA FORM 2823, JUL 72   U.S. Government Printing Office: 1993 – 342-027/80494

proper treatment of the detainee. For example, this current detainee does not like to conform to proper grooming standards. So, I've referred to the MP's to give the detainee his special treatment. This is to include, showering of the detainee (not excessively) daily if necessary, having the detainee brush his teeth and the maintaining of short hair and no facial hair. Hence, the MP's are not directed when and how this is to be administered, but that it can be used to keep the detainee awake when the detainee is more prone to sleep.

Q. Have you ever had an incident where one of your detainees was bruised or complained of being assaulted by any of the guards?

A. No.

Q. Have you ever verbally requested one of the guards to assault one of your detainees?

A. No.

Q. Have you seen or heard any other type of suspicious incidents that would indicate abuse of the prisoners besides what you have listed in the above statement?

A. No.

Q. Do you know of any type of pictures that show abuse of detainees?

A. No.

Q. Do you have anything else to add to this statement concerning the matters under investigation?

A. No.

//End of Statement//

AFFIDAVIT

I, Steven A. STEFANOWICZ, HAVE READ OR HAD READ TO ME THIS STATEMENT, WHICH BEGINS ON PAGE 1, AND ENDS ON PAGE 2. I FULLY UNDERSTAND THE CONTENTS OF THE ENTIRE STATEMENT MADE BY ME. THE STATEMENT IS TRUE. I HAVE INITIALED ALL CORRECTIONS AND HAVE INITIALED THE BOTTOM OF EACH PAGE CONTAINING THE STATEMENT. I HAVE MADE THIS STATEMENT FREELY WITHOUT HOPE OR BENEFIT OR REWARD, WITHOUT THREAT OF PUNISHMENT, AND WITHOUT COERCION, UNLAWFUL INFULENCE, OR UNLAWFUL INDUCEMENT.

(Signature of Person Making Statement)

WITNESSES

Subscribed and sworn to before me, a person authorized by Law to administer oaths, this 22nd day of January, 2004 at Abu Ghraib, Iraq, APO AE 09335.

(Signature of Person Administering Oath)

SA NEAL C. GRUHN

ORGANIZATION OR ADDRESS

10TH Military Police Battalion (CID)

Baghdad, Iraq, APO AE 09335

(Typed Name of Person Administering Oath)

Article 136, UCMJ or 5 USC 903

ORGANIZATION OR ADDRESS

(Authority to Administer Oaths)

INITIALS OF PERSON MAKING STATEMENT

U.S. Government Printing Office: 1993 – 342-027/80494

476

SWORN STATEMENT

For use of this form, see AR 190-45; the proponent agency is ODCSOPS

PRIVACY ACT STATEMENT

AUTHORITY: Title 10 USC Section 301; Title 5 USC Section 2951; E.O. 9397 dated November 22, 1943 *(SSN).*

PRINCIPAL PURPOSE: To provide commanders and law enforcement officials with means by which information may be accurately

ROUTINE USES: Your social security number is used as an additional/alternate means of identification to facilitate filing and retrieval.

DISCLOSURE: Disclosure of your social security number is voluntary.

1. LOCATION Abu Ghraib Prison, Abu Ghraib, Iraq	2. DATE *(YYYYMMDD)* 2004/01/21	3. TIME 1449	4. FILE NUMBER

5. LAST NAME, FIRST NAME, MIDDLE NAME SPENCER, LUCIANA NMN	6. SSN ▮▮▮▮▮▮	7. GRADE/STATUS SPC

8. ORGANIZATION OR ADDRESS
66TH MILITARY INTELLIGENCE GROUP, WURZBURG, GM APO AE 09244 (DEPLOYED TO ABU GHRAIB PRISON)

9.

I, LUCIANA SPENCER , WANT TO MAKE THE FOLLOWING STATEMENT UNDER OATH:

When I began working the night shift I discussed with the MP's what their SOP was for detainee treatment. They informed me that they had no SOP. I informed them of my IROE and made clear to them what i was and wasn't allowed to do or see. I made clear to them that their prison was their prison and they can handle buisness how they see fit, however i follow different rules and i asked them to respect the fact that i have to follow those rules. I am good friends with the MP's that work at this detention facility and they trust me. I also am very specific with those MP's as to what level of knowledge i want to have concerning this detention facility. I didn't see any acts of torture or mistreatment. The MP's did prepare prisoners prior to interrogations by haveing them do physical exercises and yelling at them. The interrogators would verbally discuss, with a MP, a detainee and his cooperativeness and various methods to deal with a detainee such as physical exercise at random hours of the night and yelling. I was aware that some MP's were taking pictures of detainees and had them on their computers. I have seen detainees naked. When a detainee threw his feces, the MP's had him take a cold shower then roll in the dirt outside then stand until he was dry then they showered him in cold water again. When the detainee was naked he was laughed at and yelled at. I have seen an MP slap a detainee. When a detainee was doing physical exercises as punishment then refused to continue after given a rest a MP encouraged him to continue.

Q. What does IROE?
A. Interrogation Rule of Engagement.
Q. What shift did you work on?
A. When I first got here I worked day shift for the first week. After that we moved to night shift.
Q. How much time did you spend in the Isolation area during the night shift?
A. It depended on how many detainees we had in the isolation area. On average it would be two hours. Some nights longer depended on the interview.
Q. Where did the interrogations occur?
A. In the showers, stair well, or property room.
Q. Was there any MP's present during the interrogations?
A. No.
Q. Were the detainees clothed ot unclothed during the interrogations?
A. During all mine they were.
Q. Is removing the clothing of the detainee a MI interrogation tactic?
A. I used it on one interrogation and my Team Leader did not approve of it. She thought it shoul dhave been more specified. Statements were taken and it was brought up to CPT WOODS and LTC JORDAN.
Q. What was the outcome of?
A. I was moved out of the Tiger Team and placed in Operations.
Q. What is a Tiger Team?
A. It is an interrogator and an analysist.
Q. Who were the MP's that worked on the night shift?
A. SSG FREDERICK, SGT GRANER and AMBUHL. These are the ones that I saw mostly working.
Q. Who was the MP that struck the detainee?
A. GRANER.
Q. Who else was present when this occurred?
A. Two other detainees, CPT BRINSON might have been there, I can not remember who else was there. I am really unsure if CPT BRINSON was even there.
Q. How many times did GRANER strike the detainee?
A. Just once with a open hand.
Q. Who was the detainee?

10. EXHIBIT	11. INITIALS OF PERSON MAKING STATEMENT LS.	PAGE 1 OF 4 PAGES

ADDITIONAL PAGES MUST CONTAIN THE HEADING "STATEMENT _____ TAKEN AT _____ DATED _____

THE BOTTOM OF EACH ADDITIONAL PAGE MUST BEAR THE INITIALS OF THE PERSON MAKING THE STATEMENT, AND PAGE NUMBER MUST BE BE INDICATED.

DA FORM 2823, DEC 1998   DA FORM 2823, JUL 72, IS OBSOLETE   USAPA V1.00

477

A. He had a beard and dark hair. I did not know his name or NDRS #.

Q. Did you see GRANER strike, push to the floor, punch, kick or slap any other detainee?

A. No.

Q. Did you see GRANER posing detainees in sexual positions at any time?

A. No.

Q. Did you see GRANER engaged in sexual intercourse with detainees in the isolation area?

A. No.

Q. Did you see GRANER engaged in sexual intercourse with anyone else in the isolation area?

A. No.

Q. Was there anyone in the isolation area that was not authorized?

A. No.

Q. What time did you shift start in the isolation area?

A. It started about 2200 to 0800.

Q. Were pictures taken of the detainees in the isolation area?

A. Yes, I believe so. I never saw anyone, but there were cameras in the area. I know they took pictures of me in the area.

Q. Did you ever see FREDERICK strike, kick, punch, push to the floor, and/or slap detainees?

A. No.

Q. Were you present at any time when detainees were beaten?

A. Other than the one slap, No.

Q. Did you punch, slap, kick, push to the floor, and/or jump on detainees?

A. No.

Q. Did you see anyone else punch, slap, kick, push to the floor, and/or jump on detainees?

A. Just the slap and then they are transporting detainees.

Q. What was the uniform for your team in the isolation area?

A. We would were DCU's without nametags.

Q. Did you observe pictures of the detainees in sexual positions?

A. I saw a screen sayer for a computer that was up in the isolation area. The screen save had detainees naked in a pyramid.

Q. Do you know who took the picture?

A. No.

Q. Do you know whose computer it was?

A. No.

Q. Do you know who the detainees were?

A. No. All you saw was Asses.

Q. Did you see other soldiers who were not MP's in the isolation area after hours?

A. Just other MI soldiers.

Q. Were you involved in any abuse of the detainees?

A. No.

Q. Were you present for any of the abuse against the detainee?

A. Only the slap.

Initials 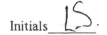 Page 2 of 4 Pages

Q Did you report it to anyone?

A. No.

Q. Why did you not report it?

A. I did not think it was abusive.

Q. Do you recall when it occurred?

A. That was after I was working in operations, some time in Dec 03, before CPT BRISNSON left. I know it was on a Sunday as I watched football after I left. I think it was a Carolina game against possibly Green Bay.

Q. Did anyone else show you photo's of the detainees in the hard site?

A. No.

Q. Has anyone discussed this case with you other than this office?

A. Yes, I was talking to SSG FREDERICK and he told me there was an investigation into detainee abuse.

Q. Do you wish to add anything else to your statement?

A. No.///END OF STATEMENT///

Initials LS.   Page 3 of 4   Pages

STATEMENT OF _Luciana Spencer_ TAKEN AT _Abu Ghraib_ DATED _21 Jan 04_

9. STATEMENT *(Continued)*

```
File Number   : 0003-04-CID149-83130
Location      : Baghdad Correctional Facility, Baghdad, Iraq
Date          : 21 Jan 04 SP
Time          : 1520 SP
Statement of  : Samuel Jefferson PROVANCE
Grade/Status  : E5/RA
SSN           : ███████████
Org/Address   : A 302ⁿᵈ MI BN
```

I **Samuel Jefferson PROVANCE**, WANT TO MAKE THE FOLLOWING STATEMENT UNDER OATH:
Around the middle to the end of October I was talking to a female from the Nevada
National Guard MP unit that was stationed here. She was very skinny, she was
white, but very tanned, she had black and gray hair, and she was old, I don't
remember her rank, but she was made the unit armorer during this time. She told
me that they were the first unit here, and they were the ones who started setting
this place up. She was the oldest female among that unit. She was telling me
about writing these journals that talked about all of her experiences here in
Iraq and the wrongdoings she witnessed (and their cover up). In those journals
she said there were killings, torture, you name it she said it. She was
referring to all of the things that had been done here. She told me that the
commander and the first sergeant hated her because she would voice opposition to
them about the treatment of the people. She also told me that she mailed the
journals home (to a friend or to herself) before they could be found so that the
commander could not take them from her.

In late October SPC SCHLEGEL said that the MP's told her that these two detainees
had raped a 14-year-old boy, so the MP's were handcuffing the detainees in
contorted positions to each other and making it look like the two detainees were
having sex with each other. I SPC SCHLEGEL told me that the detainees may have
been naked at the time. She also said that the MP's made the detainees in
isolation take their clothes off and wear women's underwear.

Around the end of October I was just discussing with SPC Hannah SCHLEGEL about
how there were some bad things going on, as far as the prisoners are getting
treated. She said yeah and she told me about a detainee who had gotten his eye
busted open. SPC SCHLEGEL said that she asked the MP how his eye got busted, and
the MP replied that he fell down.

When I returned from leave in the middle of December I was eating at the chow
hall at Camp Victory, when I overheard SPC ██████████ and three other people
talking about what's going on at Abu Gharib. He was telling them about the
things that the MP's were doing to the detainees. He said that he was invited to
join in on these things, so he did. The MP's were using the detainees as
practice dummies, like they would show each other how to knock someone out by
knocking the detainee out. They did this while another detainee would watch,
when the other detainee would start to get scared, the MP's would calm him down,

EXHIBIT ____   INITIALS OF PERSON MAKING STATEMENT SP   PAGE 1 OF 3 PAGES and then hit him in some other way. He was also saying that the MP's were telling him how to hit the detainees so that you didn't leave a mark, and telling him what instruments to use so that they didn't leave marks.

After I came back from leave in the beginning of December I was talking to SPC ▓▓▓▓▓▓, and she was telling me how the guards would bring the dogs down to the cells and use them to scare the detainees. She told me that she thought it was funny because after they would take the dogs away, one MP would bark like a dog, and they would all watch as the detainees would run from him because they thought there was a dog in the room.

When the people from my unit came up here to fill slots and act as guards, they were taken on a tour of the isolation area, when they were down there the MP's would tell them that they could do whatever they wanted to the detainees. I was told that all they ended up doing is yelling at the detainees and make them do PT. SGT BROWN told me that he was worried about his soldiers being exposed to that kind of behavior, and being encouraged to do so. SPC DELGADO, SPC HEIDENRICH, SPC GRIFFIN, SPC PAZDERSKI, SPC CAUDILL, and SPC KERSEY were all present for that. SPC KERSEY and SPC CAUDILL are not on the guard force; they are still doing analysis.

Q: SA Ryan D. BOSTAIN.
A: SGT Samuel J. PROVANCE.
Q: Do you know anybody specifically who was abusing the detainees?
A: Everything I know is what I've heard, all of these things take place down in isolation or in the booth.
Q: Do you know if anybody has taken any unauthorized photographs?
A: I know SPC ▓▓▓▓▓▓ had photos of the facility, but not of the detainees. I'm sure they were for sentimental value. Those photos were on the common drive, and I was told by my chain of command to delete the photos, so I did.
Q: Did SPC ▓▓▓▓▓▓ ever tell you if she was involved with the abuse of the detainees?
A: Just being there for the dog incident. She seemed really apathetic every time I said anything about it. She thought it was really funny to see the detainees run back into their cells from the dogs.
Q: Do you have anything else you wish to add to this statement?
A: Every time I said something about how I was worried about the treatment of the detainees, they would either say, thy are the enemy and if I was out there they would kill me, so they didn't care. I'm glad that something is finally being done, it's kind of shameful what's been going on.
Q: Do you have anything else you wish to add to this statement?
A. No.///**END OF STATEMENT**///JP

STATEMENT OF: **Samuel Jefferson PROVANCE**; TAKEN AT: ___1520___ ; DATED: January 21, 2004 CONTINUED:

AFFIDAVIT

I, **Samuel Jefferson PROVANCE** HAVE READ OR HAVE HAD READ TO ME THIS STATEMENT WHICH BEGINS ON PAGE 1 AND ENDS ON PAGE 3. I FULLY UNDERSTAND THE CONTENTS OF THE ENTIRE STATEMENT MADE BY ME. THE STATEMENT IS TRUE. I HAVE INITIALED ALL CORRECTIONS AND HAVE INITIALED THE BOTTOM OF EACH PAGE CONTAINING THE STATEMENT. I HAVE MADE THIS STATEMENT FREELY WITHOUT HOPE OF BENEFIT OR REWARD, WITHOUT THREAT OF PUNISHMENT, AND WITHOUT COERCION, UNLAWFUL INFLUENCE, OR UNLAWFUL INDUCEMENT.

---------_(Signature)_-----------
(Signature of Person Making Statement)

        Subscribed and sworn to before me, a person authorized by law to administer oath, this January 21, 2004, at Baghdad, Iraq.

----------_(Signature)_----------
(Signature of Person Administering Oath)

SPECIAL AGENT RYAN D. BOSTAIN, 6117
323RD MILITARY POLICE DETACHMENT (CID)(DSE)

(Typed Name of Person Administering Oath)

ARTICLE 136 UCMJ

(Authority to Administer Oath)

WITNESS:

EXHIBIT ___   INITIALS OF PERSON MAKING STATEMENT _SP_   PAGE _3_ OF _3_ PAGES

TRANSLATION OF SWORN STATEMENT PROVIDED BY A▮▮▮ ▮▮ W▮▮▮▮▮
Detainee # 151365, 1430/21 JAN 04:

"I am the person named above. I entered Abu Ghraib prison on 10 Jul 2003, that was after they brought me from Baghdadi area. They put me in the tent area and then they brought me to Hard Site. The first day they put me in a dark room and started hitting me in the head and stomach and legs.

They made me raise my hands and sit on my knees. I was like that for four hours. Then the Interrogator came and he was looking at me while they were beating me. Then I stayed in this room for 5 days, naked with no clothes. They then took me to another cell on the upper floor. On 15 Oct 2003 they replaced the Army with the Iraqi Police and after that time they started punishing me in all sorts of ways. And the first punishment was bringing me to Room #1, and they put handcuffs on my hand and they cuffed me high for 7 or 8 hours. And that caused a rupture to my right hand and I had a cut that was bleeding and had pus coming from it. They kept me this way on 24, 25 and 26 October. And in the following days, they also put a bag over my head, and of course, this whole time I was without clothes and without anything to sleep on. And one day in November, they started different type of punishment, where an American Police came in my room and put the bag over my head and cuffed my hands and he took me out of the room into the hallway. He started beating me, him, and 5 other American Police. I could see their feet, only, from under the bag. A couple of those police they were female because I heard their voices and I saw two of the police that were hitting me before they put the bag over my head. One of them was wearing glasses. I couldn't read his name because he put tape over his name. Some of the things they did was make me sit down like a dog, and they would hold the string from the bag and they made me bark like a dog and they were laughing at me. And that policeman was a tan color, because he hit my head to the wall. When he did that, the bag came off my head and one of the police was telling me to crawl in Arabic, so I crawled on my stomach and the police were spitting on me when I was crawling and hitting me on my back, my head and my feet. It kept going on until their shift ended at 4 o'clock in the morning. The same thing would happen in the following days.

And I remember also one of the police hit me on my ear, before the usual beating, cuffing, bagging, dog position and crawling until 6 people gathered. And one of them was an Iraqi translator named ▮▮▮▮, he is a tan color, he has a mustache. Then the police started beating me on my kidneys and then they hit me on my right ear and it started bleeding and I lost conciousness. Then the Iraqi translator picked me up and told me "You are going to sleep". The when I went into the room, I woke up again. I was unconscious for about two minutes. The policeman dragged me into the room where he washed my ear and they called the doctor. The Iraqi doctor came and told me he couldn't take me to the clinic, so he fixed me in the hallway. When I woke up, I saw 6 of the American Police.

A few days before they hit me on my ear, the American police, the guy who wears glasses, he put red woman's underwear over my head. And then he tied me to the window

484

that is in the cell with my hands behind my back until I lost consciousness. And also when I was in Room #1 they told me to lay down on my stomach and they were jumping from the bed onto my back and my legs. And the other two were spitting on me and calling me names, and they held my hands and legs. After the guy with the glasses got tired, two of the American soldiers brought me to the ground and tied my hands to the door while laying down on my stomach. One of the police was pissing on me and laughing on me. He then released my hands and I want and washed, and then the soldier came back into the room, and the soldier and his friend told me in a loud voice to lie down, so I did that. And then the policeman was opening my legs, with a bag over my head, and he sat down between my legs on his knees and I was looking at him from under the bag and they wanted to do me because I saw him and he was opening his pants, so I started screaming loudly and the other police starting hitting me with his feet on my neck and he put his feet on my head so I couldn't scream. Then they left and the guy with the glasses comes back with another person and he took me out of the room and they put me inside the dark room again and they started beating me with the broom that was there. And then they put the loudspeaker inside the room and they closed the door and he was yelling in the microphone. Then they broke the glowing finger and spread it on me until I was glowing and they were laughing. They took me to the room and they signaled me to get on to the floor. And one of the police he put a part of his stick that he always carries inside my ass and I felt it going inside me about 2 centimeters, approximately. And I started screaming, and he pulled it out and he washed it with water inside the room. And the two American girls that were there when they were beating me, they were hitting me with a ball made of sponge on my dick. And when I was tied up in my room, one of the girls, with blonde hair, she is white, she was playing with my dick. I saw inside this facility a lot of punishment just like what they did to me and more. And they were taking pictures of me during all these instances."

TRANSLATED BY:

signature

Mr. Johnson ISHO
Translator, Category II
Titan Corporation
Assigned to:

    Prisoner Interview/Interrogation Team (PIT)(CID)(FWD)
    10TH Military Police Battalion (CID)(ABN)(FWD)
    3rd Military Police Group (CID), USACIDC
    Abu Ghraib Prison Complex (ABPC)
    Abu Ghraib, Iraq APO AE 09335

VERIFIED BY:

signature

Mr. Abdelilah ALAZADI
Translator, Category II
Titan Corporation

SWORN STATEMENT

For use of this form, see AR 190-45: The proponent agency of the Deputy Chief of Staff for Personnel.

LOCATION	DATE	TIME	FILE NUMBER
Abu Ghraib, Baghdad Iraq	21 Jan 04 ᵀˢᴺ	11:44 TsN	

LAST NAME, FIRST NAME, MIDDLE NAME	SOCIAL SECURITY NUMBER	GRADE/STATUS
NELSON, Torin, Steed	▮▮▮▮	Contractor

ORGANIZATION OR ADDRESS
, deployed with duty at Abu Ghraib, Iraq

I, Torin S Nelson, want to make the following statement under oath:

As far as some of the things we talked about yesterday. The people I suggest you look at is ▮▮ J▮▮▮▮, ▮▮ D▮▮▮▮, these two gentlemen, I have looked at their files. I sat next to an interrogation that J▮▮▮▮▮ was doing one day, where he was breaking a tables and chairs in the room with the detainee. MR D▮▮▮▮ has a reputation for breaking the tables in the room.. Look into file 155215, K▮▮▮▮▮▮ A▮▮▮▮▮▮▮ He is my detainee now. One of the first times I interviewed him at the beginning of Jan 04, he showed me a large bruise to his left forearm that was about six to eight inches long, and he stated he got it from being grabbed and being thrown around. He had a bump on his forehead over his left eye that he related he received that from being thrown into a wall. He said that the interrogator grabbed him and threw him down. He is evasive and deceptive, but when he is talking about how people have treated him, I tend to believe it based on the stuff that I have heard and seen. Evidently the people who talking to him before I was working him were very hard on him. ▮▮ J▮▮▮▮ was the person working him before. M▮▮▮▮ M▮▮▮▮ I think his number is155800. I would look at the interrogation on 12 Jan 04, of this detainee, and talk to the interpreter of that helped interview him. He should be able to give you more information. I am working his brother at the time. His story is very forth coming and very cooperative. Talk to SPC SCHLAGEL was working another detainee who is the brother of my detainee; this person related to SPC SCHALGELS detainee, I think the number is 155794, as well about this incident. Pull up the fill on this detainee M▮▮▮▮ After the first interview, ▮▮ J▮▮▮▮ says to put this guy in isolation because he is not being forthright in his information. ▮ is a young interrogator, he is very excited and motivated, and he believes everyone here should be broken. Ali Darwiche, and interpreter he might have info. Simon has seen a lot of stuff that goes on. Simon is an interpreter with Titan as well. He has stated that he has witnessed some of the interrogators being ruff. I do not know if it was abuse. There is another incident SPC LUCIANA SPENCER was involved in where one of her detainees, she wanted to degrade him; she stripped him naked and made him walk back. She was moved into Bn Ops, and taken out of the interrogation role. LTC JORDAN would know more about that. I would really look at the files for the detainees of D▮▮▮▮ and J▮▮▮▮▮. A▮▮▮▮▮▮▮▮ was the detainee that was allegedly taken and thrown out of the vehicle handcuffed. I believe the incident was witness by Ali Darwiche. He is on leave in the states and is getting married. You would have to go through Titan to get his info. A▮▮▮▮▮▮▮ was sitting in the vehicle sandbagged, the interrogator who I think might have been D▮▮▮▮ or J▮▮▮▮, grabbed him and threw him out of the vehicle to the ground, the interrogator then yells at him for falling on the ground, and then started dragging or pulling the detainee by the cuffs. This information came from Ali Darwiche. We were doing an interview and he provided this information out side of what he was interpreting.

Q. Do you have anything to add to this statement?

A. No.///End of Statement/// TsN

TsN

Not Used TSN

I, ___Torin S. Nelson___ HAVE READ OR HAVE HAD READ TO ME THIS STATEMENT WHICH BEGINS ON PAGE 1 AND ENDS ON PAGE _2_. I FULLY UNDERSTAND THE CONTENTS OF THE ENTIRE STATEMENT MADE BY ME. THE STATEMENT IS TRUE. I HAVE INITIALED ALL CORRECTIONS AND HAVE INITIALED THE BOTTOM OF EACH PAGE CONTAINING THE STATEMENT. I HAVE MADE THIS STATEMENT FREELY WITHOUT HOPE OF BENEFIT OR REWARD, WITHOUT THREAT OR PUNISHMENT, AND WITHOUT COERCION, UNLAWFUL INFLUENCE, OR UNLAWFUL INDUCEMENT.

(Signature of Person Making Statement)

WITNESSES:

_____

ORGANIZATION OR ADDRESS

_____

ORGANIZATION OR ADDRESS

_____

_____

SUBSCRIBED AND SWORN BEFORE ME, A PERSON BY LAW TO ADMINISTER OATHS, THIS _21st_ DAY OF __Jan 04

AT _Abu Gharib Prison, Iraq_____

(Signature of Person Administering Oath)

___Warren D. Worth_____
(Name of Person Administering Oath)

UCMJ, ART.JCL 136
(Authority to Administer Oath)

INITIALS OF PERSON MAKING STATEMENT
T SN

PAGES 2 OF 2 PAGES

DA Form 2823 (AUTOMATED)

LOCATION	DATE	Time	FILE NUMBER
Rusafa II Prison Compound, Baghdad	20 Jan 04	1520	0003-04-CID149-83130

LAST NAME, FIRST NAME, MIDDLE NAME	SOCIAL SECURITY NUMBER	GRADE/STATUS
A███████ H███ ███ ███ ███	ISN #13077	CIV/DETAINEE

ORGANIZATION OR ADDRESS
Rusafa II Prison Compound, Baghdad, Iraq

I, H███ ███ ███ A███████ want to make the following Statement under oath:

When first I went to the hard site, the Americans soldiers took me, there were two soldiers, a translator named Abu Hamed. We stood in the hallway before the hard site and they started taking off our clothes one after another. After they took off my clothes the American soldier removed who was wearing glasses, night guard, and I saw an American female soldier which they call her Ms. Maya, in front of me they told me to stroke my penis in front of her. And then they covered my head again, and as I was doing whatever they asked me to do, they removed the bag off my head, and I saw my friend, he was the one in front of me on the floor. And then they told me to sit on the floor facing the wall. They brought another prisoner on my back and he was also naked. Then they ordered me to bend onto my knees and hands on the ground. And then they placed three others on our backs, naked. And after that they order me to sleep on my stomach and they ordered the other guy to sleep on top of me in the same position and the same way to all of us. And there were six of us. They were laughing, taking pictures, and they were stepping on our hands with their feet. And they started taking one after another and they wrote on our bodies in English. I don't know what they wrote, but they were taking pictures after that. Then, after that they forced us to walk like dogs on our hands and knees. And we had to bark like a dog and if we didn't do that, they start hitting us hard on our face and chest with no mercy. After that, they took us to our cells, took the mattresses out and dropped water on the floor and they made us sleep on our stomachs on the floor with the bags on our head and they took pictures of everything. Mr. Joyner shows up in the morning and give us our mattresses, blankets and food, but the second guy who wears the glasses was the opposite; he takes the mattresses, tie our hands, hit us and don't give us food. All that lasted for 10 days and the translator Abu Hamed was there. I only saw him when I arrived, but after that I knew he was there because I heard his voice during all of that. ///End of Statement////

EXHIBIT	INITIALS OF PERSON MAKING STATEMENT	
		PAGE 1 OF 2 PAGES

ADDITIONAL PAGES MUST CONTAIN THE HEADING "STATEMENT OF___TAKEN AT___DATED___CONTINUED." THE BOTTOM OF EACH ADDITIONAL PAGE MUST BEAR THE INITIALS OF THE PERSON MAKING THE STATEMENT AND BE INITIALED AS "PAGE___OF___PAGES." WHEN ADDITIONAL PAGES ARE UTILIZED, THE BACK OF PAGE 1 WILL BE LINED OUT AND THE STATEMENT WILL BE CONCLUDED ON THE REVERSE SIDE OF ANOTHER COPY OF THIS FORM.

DA FORM 2823, JUL 72   U.S. Government Printing Office: 1993– 342-027/80494

////NOT USED////

Translated By:

Lauriene I. Dice (signature)

Lauriene H. DICE
Interpreter, Category II
Titan Corporation Inc.
Camp Doha, Kuwait

Verified By:

Jahron Isho (signature)

Johnson ISHO
Interpreter, Category II
Titan Corporation Inc.
Camp Doha, Kuwait

Prisoner Interview/Interrogation Team (PIT)(CID)(FWD)
Baghdad Correctional Facility
Abu Ghraib, IZ APO AE 09335

489

SWORN STATEMENT

For use of this form, see AR 190-45; the proponent agency is Office of The Deputy Chief of Staff for Personnel.

LOCATION ABU GHURAYB CID	DATE 20 JAN	TIME 0945	FILE NUMBER

LAST NAME, FIRST NAME, MIDDLE NAME
LANGIANESE, SETH A

SOCIAL SECURITY NUMBER ▮▮▮▮▮

GRADE/STATUS E-4 SPC ACTIVE DUTY

ORGANIZATION OR ADDRESS
323 MI, JIDC, AG

I, SETH ANTHONY LANGIANESE , WANT TO MAKE THE FOLLOWING STATEMENT UNDER OATH:

I was at the internet cafe, it was in December or January I am not sure when. I was with SPC Porter and we were just checking our Emails, ect. When Porter started looking at Pictures an MP had down loaded from her camera, some were of the detainees on there knees - it looked like Ganci. Prisoners, she had taken some from the sky above AG, and she had some pics of her by a water buffalo...... I cannot remember what computer they were downloaded on and I am positive they won't still be there. The pictures were of the prisoners (looked like a whole camp) of the prisoners on their knees, hands behind their heads - possibly why their camp was being searched - possibly 2-3 pics

Q. Describe the MP you saw?
A. A female, by a water buffalo - that's about all I remember

Q. Do you know who this MP female is?
A. No, an MP

Q. Do you have anything to add to this statement?
A. No /// END OF STATEMENT ///

EXHIBIT	INITIALS OF PERSON MAKING STATEMENT	PAGE 1 OF 2 PAGES

ADDITIONAL PAGES MUST CONTAIN THE HEADING "STATEMENT OF ___ TAKEN AT ___ DATED ___ CONTINUED." THE BOTTOM OF EACH ADDITIONAL PAGE MUST BEAR THE INITIALS OF THE PERSON MAKING THE STATEMENT AND BE INITIALED AS "PAGE ___ OF ___ PAGES." WHEN ADDITIONAL PAGES ARE UTILIZED, THE BACK OF PAGE 1 WILL BE LINED OUT, AND THE STATEMENT WILL BE CONCLUDED ON THE REVERSE SIDE OF ANOTHER COPY OF THIS FORM.

DA FORM 2823
1 JUL 72

SUPERSEDES DA FORM 2823, 1 JAN 68, WHICH WILL BE USED.

STATEMENT OF _SPC LANGIANE_ TAKEN AT _Abu G,_ DATED _20 Jan 04_ CONTINUED:

FILE NUMBER:

STATEMENT (Continued)

Not Used

AFFIDAVIT

I, _SETH ANTHONY Langance_, HAVE READ OR HAVE HAD READ TO ME THIS STATEMENT WHICH BEGINS ON PAGE 1 AND ENDS ON PAGE 2. I FULLY UNDERSTAND THE CONTENTS OF THE ENTIRE STATEMENT MADE BY ME. THE STATEMENT IS TRUE. I HAVE INITIALED ALL CORRECTIONS AND HAVE INITIALED THE BOTTOM OF EACH PAGE CONTAINING THE STATEMENT. I HAVE MADE THIS STATEMENT FREELY WITHOUT HOPE OF BENEFIT OR REWARD, WITHOUT THREAT OF PUNISHMENT, AND WITHOUT COERCION, UNLAWFUL INFLUENCE, OR UNLAWFUL INDUCEMENT.

(Signature of Person Making Statement)

WITNESSES:

Subscribed and sworn to before me, a person authorized by law to administer oaths, this _20_ day of _JAN_, 20 _04_ at _____

_____
ORGANIZATION OR ADDRESS

_W~ D._
(Signature of Person Administering Oath)

SA Warren D. Worth
(Typed Name of Person Administering Oath)

_____
ORGANIZATION OR ADDRESS

Article 136, UCMJ
(Authority To Administer Oaths)

INITIALS OF PERSON MAKING STATEMENT

PAGE _2_ OF _2_ PAGES

491

SWORN STATEMENT

For use of this form, see AR 190-45: The proponent agency of the Deputy Chief of Staff for Personnel.

LOCATION	DATE	TIME CP	FILE NUMBER
Abu Ghraib, Baghdad Iraq	CP 20 Jan 04	1025	

LAST NAME, FIRST NAME, MIDDLE NAME	SOCIAL SECURITY NUMBER	GRADE/STATUS
Porter, Canyon Elijah	▓▓▓▓▓▓▓	E4

ORGANIZATION OR ADDRESS
JIDC , deployed with duty at Abu Ghraib, Iraq

I, SPC Canyon Porter , want to make the following statement under oath:

At some point in the last two weeks to a month, I witnessed some pictures of detainees being stored on a computer at the internet cafe. At 1100 I left the FAC at the JIDC building to take my lunch/internet break. As usual, I stop by the internet cafe to check my email and on this occasion I also sent some pictures from my digital camera. I went to the folder I thought my pictures were stored in and came across 5-10 pictures that weren't mine, but I recognized as photos of the Vigilant and Ganci camps. Several of the photos were of detainees, some praying. At the time I didn't think to check the clarity of the pictures, and I'm unsure if the detainees could be identified.

Two of the pictures were of a female soldier, age 18-25, PFC-SPC, though I cannot recall her name. She had red hair and seemed to be of medium build. I assume that it was her photos, though they could have been taken by a friend. I am not certain that these pictures were sent via email, but that is almost always the case, as there would be no other reason to save them on a computer. I sent off my emails and then went to lunch with a couple friends whom I don't recall at this time. As we were sitting to eat, the soldier in the pictures stood up at the table in front of me. As she put her gear on, I recognized her as the female from the pictures and pointed her out to my friends. I have not seen her since, but I would recognize her or her name if I did. At the time I thought it was incredibly stupid to do what she had done, but did not consider it terribly wrong as the photos did not appear to be demeaning. This is the first time I have brought this matter to anyone's attention, with the exception of my friends that day. end of statement CP

CP

Page 1 of 2 CP

492

FILE NUMBER:

STATEMENT OF SPC Porter TAKEN AT Abu Ghrayb DATED 20 JAN 04 CONTINUED:

STATEMENT (Continued)

Not used CP

AFFIDAVIT

I, SPC Conyon E Porter , HAVE READ OR HAVE HAD READ TO ME THIS STATEMENT WHICH BEGINS ON PAGE 1 AND ENDS ON PAGE 2. I FULLY UNDERSTAND THE CONTENTS OF THE ENTIRE STATEMENT MADE BY ME: THE STATEMENT IS TRUE. I HAVE INITIALED ALL CORRECTIONS AND HAVE INITIALED THE BOTTOM OF EACH PAGE CONTAINING THE STATEMENT. I HAVE MADE THIS STATEMENT FREELY WITHOUT HOPE OF BENEFIT OR REWARD, WITHOUT THREAT OF PUNISHMENT, AND WITHOUT COERCION, UNLAWFUL INFLUENCE, OR UNLAWFUL INDUCEMENT.

(Signature of Person Making Statement)

WITNESSES

Subscribed and sworn to before me, a person authorized by law to administer oaths, this 20 day of JAN , 20 04 at

ORGANIZATION OR ADDRESS

(Signature of Person Administering Oath)

SA Warren D. Worm
(Typed Name of Person Administering Oath)

ORGANIZATION OR ADDRESS

ARTICLE 136 UCMJ 2
(Authority To Administer Oaths)

INITIALS OF PERSON MAKING STATEMENT

PAGE 2 OF 2 PAGES

493

Statements on 19 Jan 2004

For use of this form, see AR 190-45: The proponent agency of the Deputy Chief of Staff for Personnel.

LOCATION Abu Ghraib, Baghdad Iraq	DATE 19 Jan 04	TIME 1108	FILE NUMBER

LAST NAME, FIRST NAME, MIDDLE NAME KENNER, Jason A.	SOCIAL SECURITY NUMBER	GRADE/STATUS SPC, Ad Res.

ORGANIZATION OR ADDRESS
372nd MP Co, Cumberland, MD, deployed with duty at Abu Ghraib, Iraq

I, Jason A. Kenner _____ want to make the following statement under oath:

Q. Have you ever been present when any detainees were abused?

A. I saw them nude, but MI would tell us to take away their mattress, sheets, and clothes.

Q. Who at MI instructed you to do this?

A. I do not really remember their names. I told them if they wanted me to do that they needed to give me paperwork. A few times prior to requiring paper work I did take away mattresses and sheets. JAK

Q. Is paperwork required in order to take away clothes, mattresses and sheets?

A. Before I left on leave it had started to be required.

Q. Did you ever take any thing away from a detainee that MI told you to without paperwork?

A. A few times before the paperwork stuff started. I don't believe anyone told me specifically that I could not do that; it is I just know not to do that. At one point we were informed that we could not do anything to embarrass the prisoners. As it was explained to me, if it would embarrass me, do not do it.

Q. What shift do you work on?

A. Day shift.

Q. Would you ever come to work and find prisoners that were handcuffed, nude, or both?

A. Yes.

Q. Would you give them their clothes back?

A. It would depend on if I were briefed if I could give them the clothes back.

Q. Did you ever work on the same tier as CPL GARNER and SSG FREDERICK?

A. A few times I did relieve GARNER, and a few times when I was a runner, SSG FREDERICK would be in the office at the same time.

Q. Did you ever find that GRANER had taken something from a prisoner he should not have?

A. No.

Q. Have you ever seen any pictures that were taken of detainees?

A. No.

Q. Is there any events at the prison you feel CID should know about?

A. No.

Q. Do you have anything to add to this statement?

A. No///End of Statement/// JAK

JAK

PAGE 1 OF 2

Not Used

AFFIDAVIT

I, __Jason A. KENNER__ HAVE READ OR HAVE HAD READ TO ME THIS STATEMENT WHICH BEGINS ON PAGE 1 AND ENDS ON PAGE _2_. I FULLY UNDERSTAND THE CONTENTS OF THE ENTIRE STATEMENT MADE BY ME. THE STATEMENT IS TRUE. I HAVE INITIALED ALL CORRECTIONS AND HAVE INITIALED THE BOTTOM OF EACH PAGE CONTAINING THE STATEMENT. I HAVE MADE THIS STATEMENT FREELY WITHOUT HOPE OF BENEFIT OR REWARD, WITHOUT THREAT OR PUNISHMENT, AND WITHOUT COERCION, UNLAWFUL INFLUENCE, OR UNLAWFUL INDUCEMENT.

_____
(Signature of Person Making Statement)

WITNESSES:

SUBSCRIBED AND SWORN BEFORE ME, A PERSON BY LAW TO ADMINISTER OATHS, THIS/ 9 16th DAY OF __Jan 04
AT _Abu Gharib Prison, Iraq_____

_____
ORGANIZATION OR ADDRESS

_____
(Signature of Person Administering Oath)

_____
ORGANIZATION OR ADDRESS

___Warren D. Worth_____
(Name of Person Administering Oath)

_____

_Article 136, UCMJ_____
(Authority to Administer Oath)

_____

INITIALS OF PERSON MAKING STATEMENT

PAGES 2 OF PAGES

DA Form 2823 (AUTOMATED)

Statements on 18 Jan 2004

SWORN STATEMENT
For use of this form, see AR 190-45: The proponent agency of the Deputy Chief of Staff for Personnel.

LOCATION	DATE	TIME	FILE NUMBER
Abu Ghraib, Baghdad Iraq	18 Jan 04 ᵃᵈᵉˡ	15:10 pm ᵃᵈᵉˡ	

LAST NAME, FIRST NAME, MIDDLE NAME	SOCIAL SECURITY NUMBER	GRADE/STATUS
NAKHLA, Adel L.	▮▮▮▮▮	CIV

ORGANIZATION OR ADDRESS
Titan Corporation, Abu Ghraib Correctional Facility, Abu Ghraib, Iraq 99335

I, _Adel Nakhla_ want to make the following statement under oath:

Q. Are you making this statement on your own free will?
A. Yes.
Q. Have you been advised that you do not have to answer or questions or say anything?
A. Yes.
Q. Are you able to leave at this time if you decide to terminate this interview?
A. Yes.
Q. Has anyone threatened you in anyway?
A. No.
Q. Are you currently taking any medications that would impede your ability to answer these questions?
A. No.
Q. On 14 Jan 04. when you gave CID a sworn statement, was that a truthful statement?
A. I did not say the part of how I held the detainees foot that was on the floor so he would not run away.
Q. Why did you hold the foot down of the detainee?
A. So he would not run away and he would answer the question. I held it with my hand. Not in any powerful way.
Q. Did anyone ask you to hold the foot of the detainee?
A. No.
Q. Did anyone force you to hold the foot of the detainee?
A. No. I thought I was helping the MP's to get to the truth.
Q. How many interrogations have you been a part of since arriving at Abu Ghraib?
A. Maybe between 80 and 100 interviews.
Q. What agencies do you assist in the interviews?
A. MI and MP's, and some OGA.
Q. Have many times have you seen MI, MP, or OGA interrogate three detainees at the same time, handcuffed and nude. on the floor?
A. One time.
Q. Are you aware of the guidelines that are allowed by MI, MP and OGA when they are interviewing a detainee?
A. We were briefed on the guidelines. CPT WOOD briefed us back in November sometime.
Q. Was this briefing prior to the incident mentioned above?
A. After this incident.
Q. Do you think that what the MPs and the MI were doing to the three detainees was a correct form of interrogation?
A. No. I think they took matters into their own hands.
Q. Why was it not the correct form of interrogations?
A. Well first of all they wanted to interview the detainees they should have let MI talk to them. I do not think

MPs are qualified here to do these interviews.

Q. So you realize this was an unauthorized interrogation?

A. Yes. I did not know if it was authorized or not.

Q. Did any of the men the detainees in this incident speak English?

A. No.

Q. Were you the only translator at this incident?

A. Yes. I even apologized to the detainees after this was down. I told them I thought what had happened was very degrading.

Q. What specifically did you tell the detainees to do?

A. Don't try to run away. stop right there, are you gay, do you like what is happening to you, are you all gays, you must like that position. These were some of the questions or things that I told them.

Q. Did you realize at the time that you were saying these things to the detainees that it was wrong to tell them these things the soldiers wanted you to say?

A. I do realize it was wrong at that time to say these things.

Q. Why was it was wrong to say these thing to the detainees?

A. Because it was degrading to them.

Q. Why did you translate these things anyway?

A. I thought that was what I was required to do as a translator.

Q. Did you ever receive any briefing how detainees would be treated?

A. No.

Q. Were you ever told who you could report detainee abuse to?

A. No. The only thing that is logical is to report it to your boss or to the unit.

Q. Do you feel what you said to these detainees was wrong?

A. Yes.

Q. Did you ever translate for GRANER or FREDERICK on any other occasion when they abused the detainees?

A. Just when they would shake them. Nothing that was significant.

Q. Have you ever hit or assaulted any detainee?

A. I just held his foot, and I shook them by grabbing their clothes.

Q. Was there ever a time when you were in a cell with a detainee alone?
A. I do not recall ever being alone in a cell with any detainee. I always have a guard present when I am in the cell.
Q. Have you ever been in a cell alone and the detainee was nude?
A. No not alone. Only when they were being questioned by MI or someone and I was translating.
Q. Did you ever engage in sexual intercourse with a male detainee?
A. No.
Q. Were you ever present when photographs of detainees were taken?
A. When they took the picture of the detainee that busted his chin, I was present for that.
R. Who took this picture?
A. GRANER.
Q. Why did GRANER take the picture?
A. I do not know. Maybe to prove he was injured.
Q. How did this detainee get injured?
A. GRANER pushed the detainee against the wall.
Q. Did you witness this act?
A. No. I was upstairs at the time.
Q. Who else was there?
A. I think Megan AMBUHL was in the office up stairs; maybe FREDERICK or he came after.
Q. Why did GRANER push this detainee into the wall?
A. I do not know. GRANER did not say why he did it.
Q. Who stitched the detainee's chin up?
A. The medics and GRANER helped sew up the wound.
Q. Did you ever witness GRANER or FREDERICK assault any other detainees?
A. To the extent of injury no, but they would shake the detainee around. Especially when they detainee was a high-ranking officer or political value.
Q. Did you ever take any pictures of the detainees?
A. No.
Q. Do you have a personal computer here?
A. No.
Q. Have you ever seen any other MP's conduct interviews of the detainees?
A. I have seen AMBUHL shake some of the detainees.
Q. Do you have anything to add to this statement?
A. No.///End of Statement///

INITIALS OF PERSON MAKING STATEMENT

TRANSLATION OF STATEMENT PROVIDED BY H████ ████ ██ A██
████████ Detainee # 19446, 1242/18 JAN 04:

"I was in the solitary confinement, me and my friends. We were treated badly. They took our clothes off, even the underwear and they beat us very hard, and they put a hood over my head. And when I told them I am sick they laughed at me and beat me. And one of them brought my friend and told him "stand here" and they brought me and had me kneel in front of my friend. They told my friend to masturbate and told me to masturbate also, while they were taking pictures. After that they brought my friends, H████ A████ N███, A████ H████, M████ and I, and they put us 2 on the bottom, 2 on top of them, and 2 on top of those and one on top. They took pictures of us and we were naked. After the end of the beating, they took us to our separate cells and they opened the water in the cell and told us to lay face down in the water and we stayed like that until the morning, in the water, naked, without clothes. Then one of the other shift gave us clothes, but the second shift took the clothes away at night and handcuffed us to the beds.

The number of the guards was 4. Two of them male, and one of them had a chain tattoo on his arm and wearing eyeglasses. The other one had a tattoo on his back like a dragon. The female wearing eyeglasses was short and had short hair. The second female hair was yellow and she was medium height.

Q: IEM
A: H████ █████ ███ A████████
Q: How did you feel when the guards were treating you this way?
A: I was trying to kill myself but I didn't have any way of doing it.
Q: Did the guards force you to crawl on your hands and knees on the ground?
A: Yes. They forced us to do this thing.
Q: What were the guards doing while you were crawling on your hands and knees?
A: They were sitting on our backs like riding animals.
Q: When you were on each other, what were the guards doing?
A: They were taking pictures and writing on our asses.
Q: How many times did the guards treat you this way?
A: The first time, when I just go in, and the second day they put us in the water and handcuffed us.
Q: Did you see the guards treat the other inmates this way?
A: I didn't see, but I heard screams and shouts in another area."

TRANSLATION OF STATEMENT PROVIDED BY H███ ████ ██ A██
███████ Detainee # 19446, 1242/18 JAN 04 (Continued):

TRANSLATED BY: VERIFIED BY:

Mr. Abdelilah ALAZADI   Mr. Johnson ISHO
Translator, Category II   Translator, Category II
Titan Corporation   Titan Corporation
Assigned to:
    Prisoner Interview/Interrogation Team (PIT)(CID)(FWD)
    10TH Military Police Battalion (CID)(ABN)(FWD)
    3rd Military Police Group (CID), USACIDC
    Abu Ghraib Prison Complex (ABPC)
    Abu Ghraib, Iraq APO AE 09335

TRANSLATION OF STATEMENT PROVIDED BY K███ █████████ H███, Detainee
151108, 1300/18 JAN 04:

"In the name of God, I swear to God that everything I witnessed everything I am talking about, I am not saying this to gain any material thing, and I was not pressured to do this by any forces. First, I am going to talk only about what happened to me in Abu Ghraib Jail. I will not talk about what happened when I was in jail before, because they did not ask me about that, but it was very bad.

1. They stripped me of all my clothes, even my underwear. They gave me woman's underwear, that was rose color with flowers in it and they put the bag over my face. One of them whispered in my ear, "today I am going to fuck you", and he said this in Arabic. Whoever was with me experienced the same thing. That's what the American soldiers did, and they had a translator with them, named Abu Hamid and a female soldier, who's skin was olive colored and this was on October 3 or 4, 2003 around 3 or 4 in the afternoon. When they took me to the cell, the translator Abu Hamid came with an American soldier and his rank was sergeant (I believe). And he called told me "faggot" because I was wearing the woman's underwear, and my answer was "no". Then he told me "why are you wearing this underwear", then I told them "because you make me wear it". The transfer from Camp B to the Isolation was full of beatings, but the bags were over our heads, so we couldn't see their faces. And they forced me to wear this underwear all the time, for 51 days. And most of the days I was wearing nothing else.

2. I faced more harsh punishment from Grainer. He cuffed my hands with irons behind my back to the metal of the window, to the point my feet were off the ground and I was hanging there, for about 5 hours just because I asked about the time, because I wanted to pray. And then they took all my clothes and he took the female underwear and he put it over my head. After he released me from the window, he tied me to my bed until before dawn. He took me to the shower room. After he took me to the shower room, he brought me to my room again. He prohibited me from eating food that night, even though I was fasting that day. Grainer and the other two soldiers were taking pictures of every thing they did to me. I don't know if they took a picture of me because they beat me so bad I lost consciousness after an hour or so.

3. They didn't give us food for a whole day and a night, while we were fasting for Ramadan. And the food was only one package of emergency food.

Now I am talking about what I saw:

1. They brought three prisoners completely naked and they tied them together with cuffs and they stuck one to another. I saw the American soldiers hitting them with a football and they were taking pictures. I saw Grainer punching one of the prisoners right in his face very hard when he refused to take off his underwear and I heard them begging for help. And also the American soldiers told to do like homosexuals (fucking). And there was one of the American soldiers they called Sergeant (black skin) there was 7 to 8 soldiers there also. Also female soldiers were taking pictures and that was in the first day

503

of Ramadan. And they repeated the same thing the second day of Ramadan. And they were ordering them to crawl while they were cuffed together naked.

2. I saw ▮▮▮▮▮▮▮▮▮▮▮▮▮ fucking a kid, his age would be about 15 – 18 years. The kid was hurting very bad and they covered all the doors with sheets. Then when I heard the screaming I climbed the door because on top it wasn't covered and I saw ▮▮▮ ▮▮▮, who was wearing the military uniform putting his dick in the little kid's ass. I couldn't see the face of the kid because his face wasn't in front of the door. And the female soldier was taking pictures. ▮▮▮▮▮▮▮ I think he is ▮▮▮▮ because of his accent, and he was not skinny or short, and he acted like a homosexual (gay). And that was in cell #23 as best as I remember.

3. In the cell that is almost under it, on the North side, and I was right across from it on the other side. They put the sheets again on the doors. Grainer and his helper they cuffed one prisoner in Room #1, named A▮▮▮, he was Iraqi citizen. They tied him to the bed and they were inserted the phosphoric light in his ass and he was yelling for God's help. A▮▮▮ used to get hit and punished a lot because I heard him screaming and they prohibited us from standing near the door when they do that. That was Ramadan, around 12 midnight approximately when I saw them putting the stick in his ass. The female soldier was taking pictures.

4. I saw more than once men standing on a water bucket that was upside down and they were totally naked. And carrying chairs over their heads standing under the fan of the hallway behind the wooden partition and also in the shower.

Not one night for all the time I was there passed without me seeing, hearing or feeling what was happening to me

And I am repeating the oath / I swear on Allah almighty on the truth of what I said. Allah is my witness."

TRANSLATED BY: VERIFIED BY:

Johnson Isho (signature)   (signature)

Mr. Johnson ISHO   Mr. Abdelilah ALAZADI
Translator, Category II   Translator, Category II
Titan Corporation   Titan Corporation
Assigned to:
    Prisoner Interview/Interrogation Team (PIT)(CID)(FWD)
    10TH Military Police Battalion (CID)(ABN)(FWD)
    3rd Military Police Group (CID), USACIDC
    Abu Ghraib Prison Complex (ABPC)
    Abu Ghraib, Iraq APO AE 09335

TRANSLATION OF STATEMENT PROVIDED BY M███████ J███ Detainee
152307, 1200/18 JAN 04:

"I am going to start from the first day I went into A1. They stripped me from my clothes and all the stuff that they gave me and I spent 6 days in that situation. And then they gave me a blanket only. 3 days after that, they gave me a mattress, and after a short period of time, approximately at 2 at night, the door opened and Grainer was there. He cuffed my hands behind my back and he cuffed my feet and he took me to the shower room. When they finished interrogating me, the female interrogator left. And then Grainer and another man, who looked like Grainer but doesn't have glasses, and has a thin mustache, and he was young and tall, came into the room. They threw pepper on my face and the beating started. This went on for a half hour. And then he started beating me with the chair until the chair was broken. After that they started choking me. At that time I thought I was going to die, but it's a miracle I lived. And then they started beating me again. They concentrated on beating me in my heart until they got tired from beating me. They took a little break and then they started kicking me very hard with their feet until I passed out.

In the second scene at the night shift, I saw a new guard that wears glasses and has a red face. He charged his pistol and pointed it at a lot of the prisoners to threaten them with it. I saw things no one would see, they are amazing. They come in the morning shift with two prisoners and they were father and son. They were both naked. They put them in front of each other and they counted 1, 2, 3, and then removed the bags from their heads. When the son saw his father naked he was crying. He was crying because of seeing his father. And then at night, Grainer used to throw the food into the toilet and said "go take it and eat it". And I saw also in Room #5 they brought the dogs. Grainer brought the dogs and they bit him in the right and left leg. He was from Iran and they started beating him up in the main hallway of the prison."

TRANSLATED BY: VERIFIED BY:

Mr. Johnson ISHO   Mr. Abdelilah ALAZADI
Translator, Category II   Translator, Category II
Titan Corporation   Titan Corporation
Assigned to.
         Prisoner Interview/Interrogation Team (PIT)(CID)(FWD)
         10TH Military Police Battalion (CID)(ABN)(FWD)
   .   3rd Military Police Group (CID), USACIDC
         Abu Ghraib Prison Complex (ABPC)
         Abu Ghraib, Iraq APO AE 09335

TRANSLATION OF STATEMENT PROVIDED BY M███ ███ M██████,
Detainee # 150542, 1140/18 JAN 04:

"Before Ramadan, Grainer started covering all the rooms with bed sheets. Then I heard screams coming from Room #1, at that time I was in Room #50 and it's right below me so I looked into the room. I saw A███ in Room #1, who was naked and Grainer was putting the phosphoric light up his ass. A████ was screaming for help. There was another tall white man who was with Grainer, he was helping him. There was also a white female soldier, short, she was taking pictures of A███. A███ is now in cell #50."

TRANSLATED BY:

Johnson Isho signature

Mr. Johnson ISHO
Translator, Category II
Titan Corporation
Assigned to:

VERIFIED BY:

Abdelilah Alazadi signature

Mr. Abdelilah ALAZADI
Translator, Category II
Titan Corporation

Prisoner Interview/Interrogation Team (PIT)(CID)(FWD)
10TH Military Police Battalion (CID)(ABN)(FWD)
3rd Military Police Group (CID), USACIDC
Abu Ghraib Prison Complex (ABPC)
Abu Ghraib, Iraq APO AE 09335

Statements on 17 Jan 2004

"One of those days the guards tortured the prisoners. Those guards are Grainer, Davis and another man. First they tortured the man whose name is Amjid Iraqi. They stripped him of his clothes and beat him until he passed out and they cursed him and when they took off of his head I saw blood running from his head. They took him to solitary confinement and they were beating him every night.

The evening shift was sad for the prisoners. They brought three prisoners handcuffed to each other and they pushed the first one on top of the others to look like they are gay and when they refused, Grainer beat them up until they put them on top of each other and they took pictures of them. And after that they beat up an Iraqi whose name is A███ whom they ordered to stand on a food carton and they were pouring water on him and it was the coldest of times. When they torture him they took gloves and they beat his dick and testicles with the gloves and they handcuffed him to the cell door for half a day without food or water. After that they brought young Iraqi prisoners and Grainer tortured them by pouring water on them from the second floor until one of them started crying and screaming and started saying "my heart". They brought the doctors to treat him and they thought he was going to die. After they brought six people and they beat them up until they dropped on the floor and one of them his nose was cut and the blood was running from his nose and he was screaming but no one was responding and all this beating from Grainer and Davis and another man, whom I don't know the name. The Doctor came to stitch the nose and the Grainer asked the doctor to learn how to stitch and it's true, the guard learned how to stitch. He took the string and the needle and he sat down to finish the stitching until the operation succeeded. And then the other man came to take pictures of the injured person who was laying on the ground. And after that they beat up the rest of the group until they fall to the ground. Every time one of them fell on the ground they drag them up to stand on his feet. Grainer beat up a man whose name is A███ S████ and he was beating him until he gotten almost crazy. And he was telling him go up to the second floor as he was naked. And they opened the prisoners cells to see him running naked. And after they put him in his cell for four days they were pouring water on him and he couldn't sleep. Before that he was in cell number 4. They hanged him and he was screaming but no one helped him.

There was a translator named A██ A██ the ████████ He was helping Grainer and Davis and others whom I don't know, like they were watching a live movie of three young guys being put up by A██ A██ on top of each other. And everyone was taking pictures of this whole thing with cameras. This is what I saw and what I remember to be true."

TRANSLATION OF STATEMENT PROVIDED BY S███████ A███████
Detainee # 150422, 1630/17 JAN 04: (CONTINUED)

TRANSLATED BY: VERIFIED BY:

Mr. Abdelilah ALAZADI   Mr. Johnson ISHO
Translator, Category II   Translator, Category II
Titan Corporation   Titan Corporation
Assigned to:
    Prisoner Interview/Interrogation Team (PIT)(CID)(FWD)
    10TH Military Police Battalion (CID)(ABN)(FWD)
    3rd Military Police Group (CID), USACIDC
    Abu Ghraib Prison Complex (ABPC)
    Abu Ghraib, Iraq APO AE 09335

TRANSLATION OF STATEMENT PROVIDED BY A█████ Y████ Detainee #
150425, 1445/17 JAN 04:

"One day while in the prison the guard came and found a broken toothbrush, and they
said that I was going to attack the American Police; I said that the toothbrush wasn't
mine. They said we are taking away your clothes and mattress for 6 days and we are not
going to beat you. But the next day the guard came and cuffed me to the cell door for 2
hours, after that they took me to a closed room and more than five guards poured cold
water on me, and forced me to put my head in someone's urine that was already in that
room. After that they beat me with a broom and stepped on my head with their feet while
it was still in the urine. They pressed my ass with a broom and spit on it. Also a female
soldier, whom I don't know the name was standing on my legs. They used a loudspeaker
to shout at me for 3 hours, it was cold. But to tell the truth in daytime Joiner gave me my
clothes and at night Grainer took them away. The truth is they gave me my clothes after 3
days, they didn't finish the 6 days and thank you."

TRANSLATED BY: VERIFIED BY:

Mr. Abdelilah ALAZADI   Mr. Johnson ISHO
Translator, Category II   Translator, Category II
Titan Corporation   Titan Corporation
Assigned to:
        Prisoner Interview/Interrogation Team (PIT)(CID)(FWD)
        10TH Military Police Battalion (CID)(ABN)(FWD)
        3rd Military Police Group (CID), USACIDC
        Abu Ghraib Prison Complex (ABPC)
        Abu Ghraib, Iraq APO AE 09335

510

"Two days before Ramadan Grainer the guard came with the other guards, they brought two prisoners and they made them take off all their clothes down to naked by the two guards Grainer and Davis and then they were beating them a lot. One of the prisoners was bleeding from a cut he got over his eye. Then they called the doctor who came and fixed him. After that they stated beating him again.

They removed all my clothes down to naked for seven days and they were bringing a group of people to watch me naked.

They brought a prisoner with a civil case, his name is S███ He was brought by Grainer the guard and Davis and there was a third guard, I don't know his name. They beat him a lot then they removed all his clothing then they put wire up his ass and they started taking pictures of him.

Grainer used to hang the prisoners by hand to the doors and windows in a way that was very painful for several hours and we heard them screaming.

One day Grainer and Davis brought 6 generals and they stripped them down to naked. They started torturing them and taking pictures and they were enjoying that. When the doctor came to fix the injured person, Grainer took the needle from the doctor and started stitching the cut on the injured person.

A few days before Ramadan, Grainer and Davis, and another person that came with them used beat up a man named "A█████" who was in room number one. They were beating his very hard with a stick and Grainer was pissing on him and beating him for about a week until they injured his eye and the doctor came.

Grainer and Davis, and a third man, used to beat up a prisoner who was from ████ and strip him all night. We heard him screaming all night.

Every time a new prisoner came Grainer and Davis stripped them, beat them and took pictures. I remember one prisoner named "W█████".

Important Point:
All the guards excluding Grainer and Davis are very good with the prisoners and the prisoners like them and respect them and are very happy with them. They give a good image of the United States and they prove by their good treatment the big difference between the Baath Party and the United States."

TRANSLATION OF STATEMENT PROVIDED BY M█████ █████ M███████
Detainee # 150542, 1610/17 JAN 04: (Continued)

TRANSLATED BY: VERIFIED BY:

Mr. Johnson ISHO   Mr. Abdelilah ALAZADI
Translator, Category II   Translator, Category II
Titan Corporation   Titan Corporation
Assigned to:
    Prisoner Interview/Interrogation Team (PIT)(CID)(FWD)
    10TH Military Police Battalion (CID)(ABN)(FWD)
    3rd Military Police Group (CID), USACIDC
    Abu Ghraib Prison Complex (ABPC)
    Abu Ghraib, Iraq APO AE 09335

TRANSLATION OF VERBAL STATEMENT PROVIDED BY A ███ ███ H███████. Detainee # 152529, 1605/17 JAN 04:

"One the date of November 5, 2003, when the US forces transferred to Isolation, when they took me out of the car, an American soldier hit me with his hand on my face. And then they stripped me naked and they took me under the water and then he made me crawl the hallway until I was bleeding from my chest to my knees and my hands. And after that he put me back into the cell and an hour later he took me out from the cell the second time to the shower room under cold water and them he made me get up on a box, naked, and he hit me on my manhood. I don't know with what, then I fell down on the ground. He made me crawl on the ground. And then he tied my hands in my cell naked until morning time until Joyner showed up and released my hands and took me back to my room and gave me my clothes back. About two days later my interrogation came up, when it was done a white soldier wearing glasses picked me from the room I was in. He grabbed my head and hit it against the wall and then tied my hand to the bed until noon the next day and then two days later the same soldier and he took all my clothes and my mattress and he didn't give me anything so I can sleep on except my jump suit for 3 days. Then Joyner came and gave me a blanket and my clothes a second time."

TRANSLATED BY: VERIFIED BY:

Mr. Johnson ISHO   Mr. Abdelilah ALAZADI
Translator, Category II   Translator, Category II
Titan Corporation   Titan Corporation
Assigned to:

    Prisoner Interview/Interrogation Team (PIT)(CID)(FWD)
    10TH Military Police Battalion (CID)(ABN)(FWD)
    3rd Military Police Group (CID), USACIDC
    Abu Ghraib Prison Complex (ABPC)
    Abu Ghraib, Iraq APO AE 09335

SWORN STATEMENT

For use of this form, see AR 190-45: The proponent agency of the Deputy Chief of Staff for Personnel.

LOCATION	DATE MSB	TIME	FILE NUMBER
Abu Ghraib, Baghdad Iraq	17 Jan 04	1950 MSB	

LAST NAME, FIRST NAME, MIDDLE NAME	SOCIAL SECURITY NUMBER	GRADE/STATUS
BOLINGER, Matthew Scott	███████	CPL/E4

ORGANIZATION OR ADDRESS
372nd MP Co, Cumberland, MD, deployed with duty at Abu Ghraib, Iraq

1, Matthew Scott Bolinger MSB __ want to make the following statement under oath:

Maybe around the middle part of November 04, I was going to CPL GRANER's room with SPC ENGLAND, because she had to get something out of GRANER's room. SPC ENGLAND was under restriction from seeing GRANER for an inappropriate relationship. After we enter the room, we saw then ███████████, now ███████████, who was playing a video game in the room, and GRANER was also there. GRANER told me to check this out and that is when he pulled a CD out from under his mattress in a CD case. GRANER put the CD in the computer and then walk away to help ENGLAND find whatever it was she was looking for. As GRANER got up to walk away, the video popped up, it did not having any sound to it. There was a female bent over, kind of leaning over, she was in the prison, and ██████ was behind her. At one point the camera popped up and that is when I saw the person behind the girl and recognize that it was ██████ who was having sex with her. Then the camera moved to her face and I could really only see her eyes, and then it went back to showing both of them. I could not really see ██████ penetrating her, but his pants were around his ankles, and I could tell that he had no underwear at least that I could see. The underwear could have been with the pants around his ankles. The girl was completely nude. I got to see about 20 to 25 seconds of this video, and then GRANER quickly shut it off. GRANER was just moving very quick to get that video off the screen.

██

Q. Why do you think that ██████████ and her were having sex?
A. Mostly from the motion of the girl's body. She would bounce, as his mid section would hit her. I have seen other people having sex before in videos and it looked like that.
Q. Do you know whom the girl was?
A. No.
Q. How do you know it was in the prison?
A. Cause you could see the corner of the jail cell through out the video.
Q. Do you know who was holding the camera?
A. I have no idea.
Q. What kind of pants did ██████████ have on?
A. DCU.
Q. How far away did it appear the camera was from them when they were having sex?
A. It looked like it was really close. That is why you could only see a little at a time. They filled up the frame of the camera.
Q. Have you ever seen any other videos or images of the prison or detainees?
A. Just the ones of the females acting like they are urinating in the jail cells. I think it was in tier one in the back left hand side where the urinals in the floor are. The pictures were of both ██████████ and ██████████ they had their hands across their knees and their DCU pants around their ankles and they were acting like they were pissing in the toilets.
Q. Do you have anything to add to this statement?
A. No///END OF STATEMENT/// MSB

MSB

Page 1 of 2

514

Not Used

MSB

I, ___Matthew Scott Bolin___ HAVE READ OR HAVE HAD READ TO ME THIS STATEMENT WHICH BEGINS ON PAGE 1 AND ENDS ON PAGE _2_. I FULLY UNDERSTAND THE CONTENTS OF THE ENTIRE STATEMENT MADE BY ME. THE STATEMENT IS TRUE. I HAVE INITIALED ALL CORRECTIONS AND HAVE INITIALED THE BOTTOM OF EACH PAGE CONTAINING THE STATEMENT. I HAVE MADE THIS STATEMENT FREELY WITHOUT HOPE OF BENEFIT OR REWARD, WITHOUT THREAT OR PUNISHMENT, AND WITHOUT COERCION, UNLAWFUL INFLUENCE, OR UNLAWFUL INDUCEMENT.

(Signature of Person Making Statement)

WITNESSES:

_____

ORGANIZATION OR ADDRESS

_____

ORGANIZATION OR ADDRESS

_____

_____

SUBSCRIBED AND SWORN BEFORE ME, A PERSON BY LAW TO ADMINISTER OATHS, THIS __17th__ DAY OF __Jan 04

AT _Abu Gharib Prison, Iraq_____

(Signature of Person Administering Oath)

___Warren D. Worth_____
(Name of Person Administering Oath)

ART 136 (UCMJ)
(Authority to Administer Oath)

INITIALS OF PERSON MAKING STATEMENT
MSB

PAGES   2   OF   2   PAGES

DA Form 2823 (AUTOMATED)

LOCATION	DATE	TIME	FILE NUMBER
Baghdad Correctional Facility	17 JAN 04	1731	0003-04-CID149-83130

LAST NAME, FIRST NAME, MIDDLE NAME	SOCIAL SECURITY NUMBER	GRADE/STATUS
A███████ N███ █	ISN #7787	CIV/INTERNEE

ORGANIZATION OR ADDRESS
Prison 2A, Baghdad Correction Facility, Abu Ghraib, APO AE 09335

I, N█████ █ A███████ want to make the following Statement under oath:

One day in Ramadan, I don't know the exact date; we were involved in a fight in Compound 2, so they transferred us to the hardsite. As soon as we arrived, they put sandbags over our heads and they kept beating us and called us bad names. After they removed the sandbags they stripped us naked as a newborn baby. Then they ordered us to hold our penises and stroke it and this was only during the night. They started to take photographs as if it was a porn movie. And they treated us like animals not humans. They kept doing this for a long time. No one showed us mercy. Nothing but cursing and beating. Then they started to write words on our buttocks, which we didn't know what it means. After that they left us for the next two days naked with no clothes, with no mattresses, as if we were dogs. And every single night this military guy comes over and beat us and handcuffed us until the end of his shift at 0400. This was for three days and he didn't serve us dinner except for bread and tea. If we had chicken, he would throw it away. The first night when they stripped us naked they made us get on our hands and knees and they started to pile us one on top of the other. They started to take pictures from the front and from the back. And if anyone want to know the details of this, take the negative from the night guard and you will find everything I said was true. The next day the day shift gave us clothes and when the night shift started, the same guard who tortured us the night before came and took the clothes and left us naked and handcuffed to the bed. At the end of his shift he uncuffed us and then he punch us in the stomach and hit us on the head and face. Then he goes home. I kept thinking what is he going to do to us the next night, this white man with the white glasses. When I see him I'm scared to death. Again, watch the pictures in his belongings. He and the two short female soldiers and the black soldier during this dark night. When we were naked he ordered us to stroke, acting like we're masturbating and when we start to do that he would bring another inmate and sit him down on his knees in front of the penis and take photos which looked like this inmate was putting the penis in his mouth. Before that, I felt that someone was playing with my penis with a pen. After this they make H█████ stand in front of me and they forced me to slap him on the face, but I refused cause he is my friend. After this they asked H████ to hit me, so he punched my stomach. I asked him to do that, so they don't beat him like they had beaten me when I refused to hit H████ N█ S███ H████ M█████ S█ H███ H███ H███ A███ S██, those are the names of the people who were there at this night which we felt like 1000 nights.

Q: IEM
A: N███ █████ A████████
Q: How many soldiers were there that night?
A: 3 men and 2 women.
Q: Do you know the names of the soldiers?
A: I don't know the soldiers names, but I know what one of them looks like and this was their supervisor. The reason why I know him because I saw him every single night I spent there.
Q: What did the supervisor look like?
A: He's white, muscular, wearing clear medical glasses. He had a blu tattoo on one of his shoulders. I don't know which shoulder and I don't know what tattoo it resembled. And he works every night from 4 pm to 4 am. ///End of Statement///

EXHIBIT	INITIALS OF PERSON MAKING STATEMENT	
		PAGE 1 OF 2 PAGES

Translated By:

[signature]

Gawdat HUSSEIN
Interpreter, Category II
Titan Corporation Inc.
Camp Doha, Kuwait
Date: 17 Jan 04

AFFIDAVIT

I, N███████ A███████ HAVE READ OR HAD READ TO ME THIS STATEMENT, WHICH BEGINS ON PAGE 1, AND ENDS ON PAGE 2. I FULLY UNDERSTAND THE CONTENTS OF THE ENTIRE STATEMENT MADE BY ME. THE STATEMENT IS TRUE. I HAVE INITIALED ALL CORRECTIONS AND HAVE INITIALED THE BOTTOM OF EACH PAGE CONTAINING THE STATEMENT. I HAVE MADE THIS STATEMENT FREELY WITHOUT HOPE OR BENEFIT OR REWARD, WITHOUT THREAT OF PUNISHMENT, AND WITHOUT COERCION, UNLAWFUL INFULENCE, OR UNLAWFUL INDUCEMENT.

Original signed
(Signature of Person Making Statement)

WITNESSES

Gawdat Hussein

Subscribed and sworn to before me, a person authorized by Law to administer oaths, this 14th day of January, 2004 at Prisoner Interrogation Team (PIT)(CID)(FWD), Baghdad Correctional Facility, Abu Ghraib, 09335

ORGANIZATION OR ADDRESS

(Signature of Person Administering Oath)

SA MANORA IEM

(Typed Name of Person Administering Oath)

Article 136, UCMJ or 5 USC 303

(Authority to Administer Oaths)

INITIALS OF PERSON MAKING STATEMENT

PAGE 2 OF 2 PAGES

LOCATION Abu Ghraib, Iraq, APO AE 09335	DATE 17 Jan 04	Time 1404	FILE NUMBER
LAST NAME, FIRST NAME, MIDDLE NAME JOYNER, Hydrue S.	SOCIAL SECURITY NUMBER ▮▮▮▮		GRADE/STATUS E5/Reserves

ORGANIZATION OR ADDRESS
372nd Military Police Company, Abu Ghraib Correctional Facility, Abu Ghraib, Iraq, APO AE 09335

I, Hydrue S. JOYNER, want to make the following Statement under oath:

I am assigned to the 372nd Military Police Company, currently assigned to the Abu Ghraib Correctional Facility located in Abu Ghraib, Iraq. I work at the hard site in the 1A Military Intelligence (M.I.) tier during the day shift; which is from 0400 to 1600 hours. On January 16th 2004 on or about 1400 hours I was interviewed by Agent PIERON about a situation of suspected prisoner abuse by Military Police personnel. As I stated in my interview I never personally witnessed any abuse by Military Police personnel. I was next asked to view digital pictures and video for identification of suspected Military Police personnel that may have been involved and any inmates that I may be able to identify. After viewing the digital pictures and video I did make positive identification on the following Military personnel, SSG FREDERICK; CPL GRANER; SPC ENGLAND; SPC HARMAN; and SPC SIVITS. I was also able to recognize the following inmates from the same digital pictures and video, inmate #20092 who was nicknamed "Gus" this inmate was released from the prison approximately two months ago, and two inmates who were suspected of committing rape; whose names I do not recall but their inmate numbers are ▮▮▮▮ and ▮▮▮▮

Q: SA BOBECK
A: SGT JOYNER
Q: Did you ever see "Gus" having to crawl around like a dog?
A: No that didn't happen on my shift..
Q: Prior to this incident, did you ever hear of any rumors that abuse was occurring during the night shift?
A: I heard rumors, I thought it was prisoners making that up and I didn't think anyone would be that stupid.
Q: Do you know the inmate who had "rapest" written on him?
A: No.
Q: Do you of any other inmates who may have been abused by the night shift?
A: Maybe "trigger".
Q: How did you feel when you saw the pictures on the CD?
A: It made me want to throw-up, I couldn't believe what I was seeing.
Q: Do you know who any of the Military Intelligence personnel were in the pictures?
A: No.
Q: Have you ever been directed by the Military Intelligence personnel or any other government agency to "soften-up" a prisoner prior to the interrogation?
A: Yes, I would have them do physical training to tire them out.
Q: Do you know Steve (NFI)?
A: Yes, he would come in and interview prisoners and sometimes ask me show a prisoner "special attention".
Q: What did "special attention" mean to you?
A: Basically it meant to give the prisoner physical training or to making sure they were awake.

EXHIBIT	INITIALS OF PERSON MAKING STATEMENT HJ	PAGE 1 OF 2 PAGES

ADDITIONAL PAGES MUST CONTAIN THE HEADING "STATEMENT OF___TAKEN AT___DATED___CONTINUED."
THE BOTTOM OF EACH ADDITIONAL PAGE MUST BEAR THE INITIALS OF THE PERSON MAKING THE STATEMENT AND BE INITIALED AS "PAGE___OF___PAGES." WHEN ADDITIONAL PAGES ARE UTILIZED, THE BACK OF PAGE 1 WILL BE LINED OUT AND THE STATEMENT WILL BE CONCLUDED ON THE REVERSE SIDE OF ANOTHER COPY OF THIS FORM.

DA FORM 2823, JUL 72

U.S. Government Printing Office: 1993 – 342-027/80494

Q: Can you describe what the Military Intelligence personnel looked like?
A: I did not know any of their names and they did not use their names. They were all males, but none of them had any scars or tattoos or any distinctive mark that I could identify.
Q: Do you know anyone who still has any pictures of the abuse?
A: No.
Q: Do you have anything else to add to this statement?
A: No.////END OF STATEMENT/// HJ

AFFIDAVIT

I, Hydrue S. JOYNER, HAVE READ OR HAD READ TO ME THIS STATEMENT, WHICH BEGINS ON PAGE 1, AND ENDS ON PAGE 2. I FULLY UNDERSTAND THE CONTENTS OF THE ENTIRE STATEMENT MADE BY ME. THE STATEMENT IS TRUE. I HAVE INITIALED ALL CORRECTIONS AND HAVE INITIALED THE BOTTOM OF EACH PAGE CONTAINING THE STATEMENT. I HAVE MADE THIS STATEMENT FREELY WITHOUT HOPE OR BENEFIT OR REWARD, WITHOUT THREAT OF PUNISHMENT, AND WITHOUT COERCION, UNLAWFUL INFULENCE, OR UNLAWFUL INDUCEMENT.

(Signature of Person Making Statement)

WITNESSES

Subscribed and sworn to before me, a person authorized by Law to administer oaths, this 17th day of January, 2004 at Abu Ghraib, Iraq, APO AE 09335.

(Signature of Person Administering Oath)

ORGANIZATION OR ADDRESS
12TH Military Police Detachment (CID)
Baghdad International Airport (BIAP), Iraq, APO AE 09335

SA Scott E. BOBECK

(Typed Name of Person Administering Oath)
Article 136, UCMJ or 5 USC 903

ORGANIZATION OR ADDRESS

(Authority to Administer Oaths)

INITIALS OF PERSON MAKING STATEMENT HJ

PAGE 2 OF 2 PAGES

TRANSLATION OF STATEMENT PROVIDED BY T████ D████, Detainee # 150427, 1440/17 JAN 04:

"I went to the Solitary Confinement on the Sep/10/2003. I was there for 67 days of suffering and little to eat and the torture I saw myself. When I asked the guard Joyner about the time and he cuffed my hand to the door then when his duty ended the second guard came, his name is Grainer. he released my hand from the door and he cuffed my hand in the back. Then I told him I did not do anything to get punished this way so when I said that he hit me hard on my chest and he cuffed me to the window of the room about 5 hours and did not give me any food that day and I stayed without food for 24 hours. I saw lots of people getting naked for a few days getting punished in the first days of Ramadan. They came with two boys naked and they were cuffed together face to face and Grainer was beating them and a group of guards were watching and taking pictures from top and bottom and there was three female soldiers laughing at the prisoners. The prisoners, two of them, were young. I don't know their names."

TRANSLATED BY: VERIFIED BY:

Mr. Johnson ISHO   Mr. Abdelilah ALAZADI
Translator, Category II   Translator, Category II
Titan Corporation   Titan Corporation
Assigned to:
    Prisoner Interview/Interrogation Team (PIT)(CID)(FWD)
    10TH Military Police Battalion (CID)(ABN)(FWD)
    3rd Military Police Group (CID), USACIDC
    Abu Ghraib Prison Complex (ABPC)
    Abu Ghraib, Iraq APO AE 09335

Statements on 16 Jan 2004

LOCATION	DATE	Time	FILE NUMBER
TIRE 1A, Baghdad Correctional Facility	16 Jan 04	1722	0003-04-CID149-83130

LAST NAME, FIRST NAME, MIDDLE NAME	SOCIAL SECURITY NUMBER	GRADE/STATUS
A███ A███	NDRS #151362	CIV/DETAINEE

ORGANIZATION OR ADDRESS
Baghdad Correctional Facility, Abu Ghraib, Iraq APO AE 09335

I, A███ A███ want to make the following Statement under oath:

I am A███ A███. I was arrested on the 7 Oct 2003. They brought me over to Abu Ghraib Prison they put me in a tent for one night. During this night the guards every one or two hours and threaten me with torture and punishment. The second day they transferred me to the hard site. Before I got in, a soldier put a sand bag over my head. I didn't see anything after that. They took me inside the building and started to scream at me. The stripped me naked, they asked me, "Do you pray to Allah?" I said, "Yes." They said, "Fuck you" and "Fuck him." One of them said, "You are not getting out of here health, you are getting out of here handicap." And he said to me, "Are you married?" I said, "Yes." They said, "If your wife saw you like this, she will be disappointed." One of them said, "But if I saw her now, she would not be disappointed now because I would rape her." Then one of them took me to the shower, removed the sand bag, and I saw him; a black man, he told me to take a shower and he said he would come inside and rape me and I was very scared. Then they put the sand bag over my head and took me to cell #5. And for the next five days I didn't sleep because they use to come to my cell, asking me to stand up for hours and hours. And they slammed the outer door, which made a loud scary noise inside the cell. And this black soldier took me once more to the showers, stood there staring at my body. And he threaten he was going to rape me again. After that, they started to interrogate me. I lied to them so they threaten me with hard punishment. Then other interrogators came over and told me, "If you tell the truth, we will let you go as soon as possible before Ramadan," so I confessed and said the truth. Four days after that, they took me to the camp and I didn't see those interrogators anymore. New interrogators came and re-interrogated me. After I told them the truth they accused me of being lying to them. After 18 days in the camp, they sent me to the hard site. I asked the interrogators why? They said they did not know. Two days before Ied (End of Ramadan), an interrogator came to me with a women and an interpreter. He said I'm one step away from being in prison forever. He started the interrogation with this statement and end it with this statement. The first day of Ied, the incident of "Firing" happened. I got shot with several bullets in my body and got transferred to the hospital. And there, the interrogator "Steve" came to me and threaten me with the hardest torture when I go back to the prison. I said to him, "I'm sorry about what happened." He said to me, "Don't be sorry now, because you will be sorry later." After several days he came back and said to me, "If I put you under torture, do you think this would be fair?" I said to him, "Why?" He said he needed more information from me. I told him, "I already told you everything I know." He said, "We'll see when you come back to the prison." After 17 or 18 days, I was released from the hospital, went back to Abu Ghraib, he took me somewhere and the guard put a pistol to my head. He said, "I wish I can kill you right now." I spend the night at this place and next morning they took me to the hard site. They received me there with screaming, shoving, pushing and pulling. They forced me to walk from the main gate to my cell. Otherwise they would beat my broken leg. I was in a very bad shape. When I went to the cell, they took my crutches and I didn't see it since. Inside the cell, they asked me to strip naked; they didn't give me blanket or clothes or anything. Every hour or two, soldiers came, threatening me they were going to kill me and torture me and I'm going to be in prison forever and they might transfer me to Guantanamo Bay. One of them came and told me that he failed to shoot me the first time, but he will make sure he will succeed next time. And he said to me they were going to throw a pistol or a knife in my cell, then

EXHIBIT	INITIALS OF PERSON MAKING STATEMENT	
		PAGE 1 OF 3 PAGES

ADDITIONAL PAGES MUST CONTAIN THE HEADING "STATEMENT OF___TAKEN AT___DATED___CONTINUED."
THE BOTTOM OF EACH ADDITIONAL PAGE MUST BEAR THE INITIALS OF THE PERSON MAKING THE STATEMENT AND BE INITIALED AS "PAGE___OF___PAGES." WHEN ADDITIONAL PAGES ARE UTILIZED, THE BACK OF PAGE 1 WILL BE LINED OUT AND THE STATEMENT WILL BE CONCLUDED ON THE REVERSE SIDE OF ANOTHER COPY OF THIS FORM.

DA FORM 2823, JUL 72

U.S. Government Printing Office: 1993 – 342-027/80494

ADDENDUM TO RESUME OF SERVICE CAREER

Colonel JANIS LEIGH KARPINSKI, Military Intelligence (USAR)

<u>CURRENT OCCUPATION</u> Self employed as a Corporate Consultant for Executive Training Programs and Corporate Improvement Programs, Hilton Head Island, South Carolina

NATURE, SCOPE AND EXTENT OF RESPONSIBILITIES

Design, develop and implement executive training programs, management training programs, and corporate improvement strategies, with worldwide application. Contract proposals may encompass the scope of work, may include training objectives, realistic executive training experiences, improvement strategies, or business diversification plans. Training may include conducting appropriately stressful executive training, designed specifically to expose personnel to typically demanding executive situations and decision-making opportunities. The work involves travel to domestic and international locations.

4

shoot me. Sometime they said, "We will make you wish to die and it will not happen." The night guard came over, his name is GRANER, open the cell door, came in with a number of soldiers. They forced me to eat pork and they put liquor in my mouth. They put this substance on my nose and forehead and it was very hot. The guards started to hit me on my broken leg several times with a solid plastic stick. He told me he got shot in his leg and he showed me the scare and he would retaliate from me for this. They stripped me naked. One of them told me he would rape me. He drew a picture of a woman to my back and makes me stand in shameful position holding my buttocks. Someone else asked me, "Do you believe in anything?" I said to him, "I believe in Allah." So he said, "But I believe in torture and I will torture you." When I go home to my country, I will ask whoever comes after me to torture you. Then they handcuffed me and hung me to the bed. They ordered me to curse Islam and because they started to hit my broken leg, I cursed my religion. They ordered me to thank Jesus that I'm alive. And I did what they ordered me. This is against my belief. They left me hang from the bed and after a little while I lost consciousness. When I woke up, I found myself still hang between the bed and the floor. Until now, I lost feeling in three fingers in my right hand. I sat on the bed, one of them stood by the door and pee'd on me. And he said, "GRANER, your prisoner pee'd on himself." And then GRANER came and laughed. After several hours GRANER came and uncuffed me, then I slept. In the morning until now, people I don't know come over and humiliate me and threaten that they will torture me. The second night, GRANER came hand hung me to the cell door. I told him, "I have a broken shoulder, I'm afraid it will break again, cause the doctor told me 'don't put your arms behind your back.'" He said, "I don't care." Then he hung me to the door for more than eight hours. I was screaming from pain the whole night. GRANER and others use to come and ask me, "does it hurt." I said, "Yes." They said, "Good." And they smack me on the back of the head. After that, a soldier came and uncuffed me. My right shoulder and my wrist was in bad shape and great pain. (When I was hung to the door, I lost consciousness several times) Then I slept. In the morning I told the doctor that I think my shoulder is broken because I can't my hand. I feel sever pain. He checked my shoulder and told me, "I will bring another doctor to see you tomorrow." The next day, the other doctor checked my shoulder and said to me, he's taking me to the hospital the next day for X-rays. And the next day he took me to the hospital and X-rayed my shoulder and the doctor told me, "Your shoulder is not broke, but your shoulder is badly hurt." Then they took me back to the hard site. Every time I leave and come back. I have to crawl back to my cell because I can't walk. The next day, other soldiers came at night and took photos of me while I'm naked. They humiliated me and made of me and threaten me. After that, the interrogators came over and identify the person who gave me the pistols between some pictures. And this guy wasn't in the pictures. When I told them that, they said they will torture me and they will come every single night to ask me the same question accompanied with soldiers having weapons and they point a weapon to my head and threaten that they will kill me; sometime with dogs and they hang me to the door allowing the dogs to try to bite me. This happened for a full week or more.

Q: IEM
A: A███████ A█████
Q: Have you ever seen GRANER beating a prisoner?
A: No.
Q: Have you ever seen GRANER/any guards pile naked prisoners over each other?
A: No.
Q: Have you ever seen GRANER/any guards taking photographs of prisoners?
A: No.
Q: Have you ever seen GRANER/any guards taking photographs during punishment time?
A: No.
Q: Have you ever seen GRANER/any soldiers taking photographs while beating prisoners?

INITIALS OF PERSON MAKING STATEMENT	PAGE 2 OF 3 PAGES

STATEMENT OF Hiadar Saber Abed Miktub AL-ABOODI TAKEN AT BAGHDAD CORRECTIONAL FACILITY, IRAQ DATED 20 JAN 04 CONTINUED

Q: Have you ever seen any soldier positioning naked prisoners on top of each other?
A: No.
Q: Have you ever seen any guard/American soldier position naked prisoners in sexual positions?
A: No. ////End of Statement///

Translated By:

Gawdat HUSSEIN
Interpreter, Category II
Titan Corporation Inc
Camp Doha, Kuwait

Prisoner Interview/Interrogation Team (PIT)(CID)(FWD)
Baghdad Correctional Facility
Abu Ghraib, IZ APO AE 09335

AFFIDAVIT

I, H███████████A███████████ HAVE READ OR HAD READ TO ME THIS STATEMENT, WHICH BEGINS ON PAGE 1,
AND ENDS ON PAGE 3. I FULLY UNDERSTAND THE CONTENTS OF THE ENTIRE STATEMENT MADE BY ME. THE STATEMENT IS TRUE.
I HAVE INITIALED ALL CORRECTIONS AND HAVE INITIALED THE BOTTOM OF EACH PAGE CONTAINING THE STATEMENT. I HAVE MADE
THIS STATEMENT FREELY WITHOUT HOPE OR BENEFIT OR REWARD, WITHOUT THREAT OF PUNISHMENT, AND WITHOUT COERCION,
UNLAWFUL INFULENCE. OR UNLAWFUL INDUCEMENT.

_____
(Signature of Person Making Statement)

WITNESSES

Gawdat Hussein

Subscribed and sworn to before me, a person authorized by Law to
administer oaths, this 20 day of January, 2003 at Baghdad Correctional
Facility, Abu Ghraib, IZ APO AE 09335

ORGANIZATION OR ADDRESS

_____
(Signature of Person Administering Oath)
SA MANORA IEM

(Typed Name of Person Administering Oath)
Article 136, UCMJ or 5 USC 303
(Authority to Administer Oaths)

INITIALS OF PERSON MAKING STATEMENT

PAGE 3 OF 3 PAGES

U.S. Government Printing Office: 1993 – 342-027/80494

525

"On the third day, after five o'clock, Mr. Grainer came and took me to Room #37, which is the shower room, and he started punishing me. Then he brought a box of food and he made me stand on it with no clothing, except a blanket. Then a tall black soldier came and put electrical wires on my fingers and toes and on my penis, and I had a bag over my head. Then he was saying "which switch is on for electricity." And he came with a loudspeaker and he was shouting near my ear and then he brought the camera and he took some pictures of me, which I knew because of the flash of the camera. And he took the hood off and he was describing some poses he wanted me to do, and the I was tired and I fell down. And then Mr. Grainer came and made me stand up on the stairs and made me carry a box of food. I was so tired and I dropped it. He started screaming at me in English. He made me lift a white chair high in the air. Then the chair came down and then Mr. Joyner took the hood off my head and took me to my room. And I slept after that for about an hour and then I woke up at the headcount time. I couldn't go to sleep after that because I was very scared."

TRANSLATED BY:

Mr. Abdelilah ALAZADI
Translator, Category II
Titan Corporation
Assigned to:

VERIFIED BY:

Mr. Johnson ISHO
Translator, Category II
Titan Corporation

Prisoner Interview/Interrogation Team (PIT)(CID)(FWD)
10TH Military Police Battalion (CID)(ABN)(FWD)
3rd Military Police Group (CID), USACIDC
Abu Ghraib Prison Complex (ABPC)
Abu Ghraib, Iraq APO AE 09335

For use of this form, see AR 190-45: The proponent agency of the Deputy Chief of Staff for Personnel.

LOCATION Abu Ghraib, Baghdad Iraq	DATE 16 SH 15 Jan 04	TIME 1227 SH	FILE NUMBER
LAST NAME, FIRST NAME, MIDDLE NAME HARMAN, Sabrina D	SOCIAL SECURITY NUMBER ███████		GRADE/STATUS SPC, Ad Res.
ORGANIZATION OR ADDRESS 372nd MP Co, Cumberland, MD, deployed with duty at Abu Ghraib, Iraq			

I, Sabrina D Harman want to make the following statement under oath:

Q. Were you truthful in your first statement to CID?

A. No.

Q What did not tell the truth about?

A. Writing rapist on the guy's leg.

Q. Was there anything else that you did not tell CID about?

A. Just stuff I did not remember.

Q. Did you take any of the photographs of the detainee's home during R&R leave?

A. Yes.

Q. Where are the photographs now?

A. In my apartment The photographs are by the computer. They are on a CD rom. The CD is located in the CD rack, on the right hand side of the computer. I think it is blue or green case, all of the rest of them are red. It may have the word picture wrote on the outside of it.

Q. Did you show theses photographs to anyone while home?

A. Kelly, my roommate.

Q. Whose apartment are these photographs in?

A. Mine. I pay the rent for the apartment.

Q. Will you give Army CID consent to retrieve the photographs from the apartment?

A. Yes.

Q. Did you email or show anyone else the photographs?

A. No.

Q. Do you have any more copies of the photographs here or anywhere else?

A. No.

Q. Who else has copies of these photographs?

A. FREDERICK, GRANER, M█████, Ops 4th Platoon, 372nd; DARBY, L█████, and R█████ there are ██████████████; I am not sure which one has them.

Q. Who else might have copies of these photographs?

A. I know that people from MI have them because they were swapping pictures.

Q. Who was swapping pictures?

A. FREDERICK and I think GRANER as well. I do not know what type of pictures they were swapping.

Q. Did you ever talk to anyone else while home about the photographs?

A. Just the girl from CNN. We were at a club called Cobalt in DC. Somehow we got introduced and I told her was I worked. She told me were she worked. She gave me her business card, and we went our separate ways.

Q. DO you have her business card still?

A. Probably not, but Kelly might know her.

Q. Did you tell her the substance of the photographs?

A. I am sure I did, but I do not remember what I said. SH

SH

Q. DO you have anything to add to this statement?

A. No.///End of Statement//// S.H

AFFIDAVIT

I, Sabrina D. HARMAN _____ HAVE READ OR HAVE HAD READ TO ME THIS STATEMENT WHICH BEGINS ON PAGE 1 AND ENDS ON PAGE __2__. I FULLY UNDERSTAND THE CONTENTS OF THE ENTIRE STATEMENT MADE BY ME. THE STATEMENT IS TRUE. I HAVE INITIALED ALL CORRECTIONS AND HAVE INITIALED THE BOTTOM OF EACH PAGE CONTAINING THE STATEMENT. I HAVE MADE THIS STATEMENT FREELY WITHOUT HOPE OF BENEFIT OR REWARD, WITHOUT THREAT OR PUNISHMENT, AND WITHOUT COERCION, UNLAWFUL INFLUENCE, OR UNLAWFUL INDUCEMENT.

S. Harm

(Signature of Person Making Statement)

WITNESSES:

SUBSCRIBED AND SWORN BEFORE ME, A PERSON BY LAW TO ADMINISTER OATHS, THIS __16th__ DAY OF __Jan 04__

AT _Abu Gharib Prison, Iraq_____

_____

ORGANIZATION OR ADDRESS

(Signature of Person Administering Oath)

_____

ORGANIZATION OR ADDRESS

___Warren D. Worth_____

(Name of Person Administering Oath)

_____

___Article 136, UCMJ_____

(Authority to Administer Oath)

INITIALS OF PERSON MAKING STATEMENT   SH

| PAGES | 2 | OF | 2 | PAGES |

<u>**ARTICLE 15-6 INVESTIGATION INTERVIEW**</u>

2

3 **At Camp Doha, Kuwait, on 15 February 2004:**

4 **MAJOR GENERAL ANTONIO M. TAGUBA, U.S. Army, CFLCC Deputy Commanding**

5 **General deposing.**

6 **MASTER SERGEANT JOHN E. DAVIS, U.S. Army, CFLCC-SJA, Senior Court**

7 **Reporter, has been detailed reporter for this interview and has been**

8 **previously sworn.**

9 **BRIGADIER GENERAL JANIS L. KARPINSKI, U.S. Army, was sworn, and**

10 **interviewed as follows:**

So let me ask you again. So the

9   responsibility for the actions of those soldiers, that were charged

10 by CID for mistreating those detainees should fall on the MI as

11 opposed to the MPs?

12   A.   The responsibility? No sir. I saw some of the pictures.

13 The--I think the MI gave the MPs the ideas. And I think----

14   Q.   So there's some complicity to that?

15   A.   Yes sir.

16   Q.   You're suggesting that there is?

17   A.   ----And I think that it became sport. And--and even saying

18 this makes me feel sick to my stomach, but, they were enjoying what

19 they were doing and the MPs who saw this opportunity-- seized the

20 opportunity. I don't know if they shared the ideas with the MIs or

21 whatever they did, but there was definitely agreement, and-- then

22 some of the procedures they were following, they just elaborated on.

23 And-- and I would imagine and I don't know this to be fact, but would

134

imagine it went something like this-- in the DFAC or when they were

sitting around the Internet Café. "Oh yeah, you should see what we

do to the prisoners sometime." "Can I come over and watch?" "Oh

yeah. How about Thursday." And because we had a clerk over there

who was thoroughly enjoying all of this sport, and the pictures

anyway, and she was the girlfriend of the guy who was one of the

kingpins in this. We had a guy from the maintenance who must have

been one of the invited participants and-- these are bad people.

That was the first time I knew that they would do such a thing as to

bring a dog handler in there to use for interrogation. I had never

heard of such a thing and I certainly didn't authorize it. And if I

had heard about it, I would have stopped it. I don't believe we've

ever had a dog in the hard facility.

Q. Speaking of dogs. Did you know that between the Army and

the Navy dog handlers that they were not placed in their one command

and control that they operated separately?

A. That was at the direction of-- I don't want to put anybody

on the hook, but I believe it was CFLCC. It's a-- it's a CENTCOM

asset.

Q. But, somebody requested for them.

A. We did. But there were already two dogs there. The MI

either brought them from Anaconda or-- and they said they were

strictly for their operation.

135

1 Q. Certainly, somebody requested for them. At least the three

2 Navy dogs. That they would be placed under one command and control

3 and be utilized properly without proper authority for employment.

4 A. Yes, sir.

5 Q. Did you check on them?

6 A. No sir, I didn't.

7 Q. Okay. Alright. Given the circumstances then, do you

8 believe that perhaps proper supervision at night since these events

9 happened between the periods of 2200 and 0400 and who would you place

10 that supervision responsibility to?

11 A. There is a and-- and it is precisely the reason that

12 Sergeant Snyder is relieved from-- or suspended from his position

13 right now. Because he was responsible. He was the Sergeant of the

14 Guard, the NCOIC, whatever term they were using. He was all of those

15 things. And a platoon sergeant.

16 Q. Did you know what the Platoon Leader or the Company

17 Commander were doing?

18 A. I do not. And I talked to the Captain Reese myself. And

19 he said randomly he or the First Sergeant, or both of them would go

20 through all of the facilities.

21 Q. During night or day?

22 A. Nighttime, daytime, afternoon, lunchtime, feeding time.

136

532

1   Q.   Would you be surprised to hear that Captain Reese's

2   priorities was not detain-- detention operations, it was improving

3   the facilities seventy percent of the time?

4   A.   I would be surprised to hear that, yes sir, because that's

5   not what he told me.

6   Q.   Alright.

7   A.   And I don't-- what would he be improving? The LSA?

8   Q.   I was just conveying to you what he put on his statement

9   and he conveyed to me.

10   A.   Because the contract there was for Iraqi contractor work to

11   do the facility work, it was not for----

12   Q.   That was what he conveyed and umm--as far as he was

13   concerned, his chain of command knew of his priorities. Thereby

14   depended and over-relied on personnel who had correctional facilities

15   experience. Did he tell you that?

16   A.   He did not.

17   Q.   Okay.

18   A.   Him and the First Sergeant both talked about how they were

19   fully involved in the operation. He didn't say anything about

20   seventy percent of his time doing facilities management.

21   Q.   He put that on the Sworn Statement. And that's exactly

22   what he intimated in the----

137

1   A.   Well, he's had enough time to figure out what the best

2   avenue approach is, I guess.

3   Q.   Well, let me put it this way. Knowing that the importance

4   of that particular facility, how often did you talk to the company

5   commanders?

6   A.   I--

7   Q.   Did you senior rate all the company commanders?

8   A.   I did. Uh-- I saw all the company commanders. I-- I would

9   tell you that the-- unfortunately, that the largest gap of time uh--

10   between seeing a company commander and between seeing a company

11   commander and seeing him again was more than six weeks with Captain

12   Merck.

13   Q.   Would it surprise for you to know that there's at least one

14   Company, the 320th as we speak today, or then at that time, that was

15   assigned to that Battalion, 320th, and up until I believe two weeks

16   ago was being utilized as a filler company?

17   A.   [Pause] Would it surprise me to know that?

18   Q.   That they were not employing him in his capability as a

19   cohesive company with his capability, but yet he's being used as the-

20   -you fill here, you fill there. So, basically,----

21   A.   his company was spread out.

22   Q.   Right. And he doesn't have a function.

138

534

1   A.   He-- if he's being used as filler, I mean, he's doing an MP

2   mission.

3   Q.   He's doing an MP mission that----

4   A.   The Company Commander doesn't have a----

5   Q.   ----the Company Commander is not responsible for any

6   specific mission because his Company was being utilized as a filler

7   company. Individual----

8   A.   I would tell you----

9   Q.   ----fillers, not as a platoon, not as a squad, it was fill

10   this and fill that.

11   A.   I will tell you, sir. It doesn't surprise me. Uh--I

12   didn't know about it, but like I said, I saw all those company

13   commanders out there whenever I visited----

14   Q.   Sure, but nobody ever mentioned any problems of how things

15   are being----

16   A.   No, because the personnel numbers were so serious and Major

17   Sheridan was really making the best effort to get those internal

18   taskings reduced. And it took a whole MP Company just to do the

19   taskings. It got better when we got-- when the 82nd put a Company on

20   the same compound.

21   Q.   How many Companies did the 320th have?

22   A.   Umm--

23   Q.   Six, seven, eight?

139

535

1   A.   No, no. The 372nd, the 670th, the 186th, and some of them

2   were guard companies and some of them were combat support.

3   Q.   You had the 229th. 229th MP Company's also there. It's an I

4   and R Company.

5   A.   Some of them come up-- some of them came up because we were

6   getting ready to--some of the other companies to leave.

7   Q.   General Karpinski, what would you recommend for corrections

8   of detainee abuses?

9   A.   Sir, I--I actually started to make some of the-- I think--

10   I started to implement for the rotational forces coming in. I called

11   the Battalion Commanders that were coming in behind the rotational

12   brigades when I could get in touch with them at their mob station. I

13   told them that they needed to, ya know, get the people involved, to

14   give briefings to their soldiers before they deployed over here about

15   the potential for detainee abuse. The indicators--the processes or

16   procedures to head off infractions, to continue to reinforce it.

17   Umm--and I think that soldiers need to be reminded. I-- I-- at the--

18   at the guard mount, at shift change, on duty. You take an example of

19   an MP company like the 320th MP Company, which is out at Abu Ghraib.

20   They were down at Talil, they're a combat support company, but their

21   First Sergeant and the Company Commander were very much involved in

22   the Company and the operations. Talked to soldiers all the time,

23   gathered them in small groups. The First Sergeant was fully engaged.

                                    140

1   Q.   Is that Captain Masterangelo?

2   A.   It is.

3   Q.   Would it surprise you that he was the one who is saying it
4   is not utilized as a Company up there today? That he is being used a
5   filler Company.

6   A.   He's not being used as a filler Company, sir.

7   Q.   How do you know that?

8   A.   Well, I know what they're doing. They were the-- they
9   were-- they're not doing a combat support MP mission, because that's
10   how they-- they weren't deployed to do that mission. They-- couple
11   of the teams, the driving teams were tasked to the TOC to do my PSD.
12   My two vehicles were from the 320th MP Company. He had some MP units
13   that were doing the escort missions down to CPA or down to Bucca if
14   we were transporting prisoners. He would-- so he's got a variety of
15   missions, but they're not filler personnel. He may have used some of
16   his MPs to do some of the force protection towers. But there isn't a
17   Company that's doing only force protection. I wish I had the luxury,
18   I'm sure the battalions do too.

19   Q.   His comment to me was, when I asked him, "What specifically
20   is your mission set?" And-- then he mentioned something about I have
21   compounds boom, boom, boom, boom. I don't recall those compounds,
22   and I said, "So you're directly responsible for those compounds
23   then?" He said, "No, that's relegated to Headquarters and

141

1 Headquarters Company 220th MP Battalion. So what is your extent of

2 your responsibility?" I said, "I just provide personnel." So in

3 essence----

4   A.   Well that's not what his support form said, and that's not

5 how he was rated, and that was never my impression when we walked to

6 the different compounds that were under his control.

7   Q.   Well, the support form-- the support form doesn't really,

8 and you mentioned that that everybody should have-- could have

9 mistaken your support form for that of command philosophy?

10 Basically----

11   A.   Sir, I never focused on that.----

12   Q.   Well, I'm just making a comment to the comment you made.

13   A.   Yes, sir. But----

14   Q.   ----And so, basically, the Company Commander is given a

15 mission and the Company Commander felt that he's got a capability to

16 provide. And the Company Commander felt that he's not-- his

17 capability's not being utilized. Cause I asked him directly, "What

18 is your mission?" And his response to me was, "I'm a filler Company,

19 sir." Today, I said, "How long has it been going on?" He says,

20 "From the time I arrived until last week."

21   A.   Well, that's not true. He was down at Talil, they didn't

22 have a vigorous mission down at Talil, they went out and did the same

142

thing. They did law enforcement, patrols, down to the prisons in
Najaf.

Q.   Do you know what the 229th MP Company's mission is?

A.   They're responsible for the URF and for the compounds at
Ganci.

Q.   So, basically they're being utilized as a guard company?

A.   They are. All of our MP units are being utilized as an
escort guard or guard company for this confinement mission.

Q.   Would it surprise you that Captain Jones trained himself
and nobody ever validated him prior to deployment?

A.   That does not surprise me.

Q.   Did you know that he had prior experience as an MP, prior
to taking command of that Company from the Virginia Army National
Guard?

A.   I did not.

Q.   Did you know that he had to provide support to the canine
unit, both Army and Navy, but he does not have command and control of
those canine units?

A.   That's with the HHC or with the Headquarters of the 320th?

Q.   Somehow, somebody's yet to find a house where those dogs
were. That's what I mean. It's knowing what each of those Companies
do, because it's their capability that you want to utilize. Okay,
what other recommendations would you make?

143

1   A.   I think that the-- the span of control covering the whole

2   country of Iraq is too big without the additional assets, either

3   aviation assets, or transportation assets, engineer. General

4   Wodjakowski did tell me several times that they did not do a good job

5   of supporting us. We were running 15 civilian jails and 5 internment

6   facilities, and he said, "You're running three internment facilities,

7   how hard can that be?" He didn't know what we were doing.

8   Q.   How often did-- you had the SUAs. I guess in the separate

9   unit updates provided it depicted at least number of detain--

10   detention centers you were-- you were operating; number of Iraqi

11   prisons that you were overseeing or providing training for; number of

12   other things that you were missioned for; number of detainees that

13   were accounted for, based on the last report; and personnel situation

14   and your operational revenues to accomplish that mission. Umm--when

15   those were posted, to include your maintenance capabilities, what was

16   the-- what was the percentage-- what would you-- what would you

17   consider as your C rating would be?

18   A.   Overall?

19   Q.   Overall.

20   A.   C-3 at best.

21   Q.   And that was amplified, you mentioned repeatedly to the

22   Battalion, to the CJTF-7?

144

1   A.   It was. I-- I said to-- now when Colonel--General West

2   came in, he wasn't there originally, I don't remember who his

3   predecessor was who was the 4. But General West was-- and-- and

4   General Davis who was the Engineer Commander at the time, both of

5   them gave me tremendous support, but it was after we had found

6   another way, another mechanism to do it.

7   Q.   Sure. Which was network with your fellow general officers.

8   A.   General.

9   Q.   Networking with your fellow general officers, you know.

10 Was that helpful to you?

11   A.   They-- General West was very helpful. General Davis was

12 very helpful. The CA guy who is General Kern, and said several times

13 "I don't know anything about detention operations, but, ya know, tell

14 me what else is going on." We couldn't get CA support. We could not

15 get CA support. I spent time with General little bit of time with

16 General Hahn and uh--and really the only time General Sanchez or even

17 General Wodjakowski spent any time or showed any interest in anything

18 I was doing was when there was a problem.

19   Q.   You--previously you appeared very critical of General

20 Sanchez or General Wodjakowski for their lack of concern or lack of

21 support on behalf of your mission and on behalf of your soldiers.

22 Would you kind of draw conclusions as to why that is? Your

23 perception why that is?

                                145

1   A.   I think that General Sanchez is [pause] I think that his

2   ego will not allow him to accept a Reserve Brigade, a Reserve General

3   Officer and certainly not a female succeeding in a combat

4   environment. And I think he looked at the 800th MP Brigade as the

5   opportunity to find a scapegoat for anything that his active

6   component MI Brigade or his active component MP Brigade was failing

7   at. And if I was not capable, why didn't he tell me? Why didn't

8   somebody tell me sit down and let me give you some suggestions

9   because when DEPSECDEF Wolfowitz came into the theater, the first

10   time he came out to Baghdad Central he stayed an extra hour and

11   forty-five minutes because he was so proud of me and what the MPs

12   were doing. And he told General Sanchez that, and one night when he

13   got behind schedule on another visit, he asked specifically if he

14   could see General Karpinski before he left because he wanted to hear

15   how the prisons were coming. And on the headphones in the

16   helicopter, General Sanchez and General Fast, who was briefing him,

17   he said, "Am I going to have an opportunity to see General Karpinski?

18   Because she always does a good job for me." And I thought at that

19   time, this is not a good thing. It is never good to be more popular

20   than your boss. If I was not doing my job, I wasn't aware of it.

21   And I'm sorry, but I took care of those soldiers, I took care of

22   those detainees. We provided support beyond what anybody expected to

23   the CPA to keep Ambassador Bremer out of trouble. Because when Major

146

542

1   Pifrim and Colonel Spain were trying to push all the jails off on us

2   in a briefing to General Sanchez, Major Pifrim said, "Well we don't

3   care if they're eating or not, sir, that's the Iraqi's

4   responsibility." And he corrected them. And we made sure that they

5   were eating and that they did have water. They didn't. Because in

6   spite of what General Sanchez was telling them, they were doing the

7   easy thing. And I think General Sanchez has no use for Reserve

8   component or National Guard soldiers. And he has little use, would

9   not see it as time well spent, mentoring me. How dare I succeed as a

10 female, as a Reservist, as an MP, in his combat environment? How

11 dare I. And I became determined to show him that I would.

12   Q.   Who would you pin the responsibility on the actions of

13 those individuals at Abu Ghraib?

14   A.   The MPs that were involved. That's who I'd pin it on and

15 I'd pin it on Snyder, the Platoon Sergeant, and the First Sergeant,

16 Captain Reese.

17   Q.   You wouldn't pin it on anybody else but them?

18   A.   I would--it was Colonel Phillabaum's domain but it was

19 Colonel Pappas' FOB. And he was the one who established the

20 limitation for those cell blocks. He was the one, and Colonel Jordan

21 was the one, whether he's here to say it or not, he was the one who

22 set the rules. Major Sheridan limited them and influenced them to

23 the extent he could by taking the MPs out of unhealthy and

147

1   inappropriate settings. But they were still the guards in those cell

2   blocks. And they were still the ones who did those things that they

3   did to those detainees.

4   Q.   Do you think proper training, supervision, and effective

5   leadership, not just for that Battalion, but throughout the entire

6   Brigade would have sufficed, could have prevented it?

7   A.   No sir, no sir. Because it's not typical.

8   Q.   Given the fact that that same Battalion was involved in the

9   Bucca incident back in May?

10   A.   Sir, I talked to-- was a different Company-- no that's not

11 an excuse, I talked to Phillabaum and I talked to Dinenna, and I

12 talked to them----

13   Q.   It's your Brigade.----

14   A.   Yes sir, yes sir. ----I talked to them the next day when I

15 found out about it, when I was out there. I talked to all the

16 Company Commanders and the First Sergeants. And-- and they asked

17 good questions. And they raised the issues again about fair and

18 decent treatment and when were they going to see magistrates, and

19 when were they going to be able to give answers, and how can you say

20 dignity and respect and then not give them anything that they're--

21 even the basics that they're entitled to: clean clothes, decent

22 food, bed or a mat to sleep on. These are bad people and people who

23 were led by bad people in that situation. But, once again, it was a

148

544

1   good MP, a good soldier who turned them in. I talked to Phillabaum

2   about the consistency in these events. And that isn't something you

3   would put in an attribute column when you say, what did I do right or

4   what did I do wrong in this situation. "Did you exploit the

5   opportunity?" I asked him. "Did you exploit the opportunity to talk

6   to soldiers if they were assigned to the Battalion and tell them,

7   'This is what happened at Bucca and this is not tolerated here.'?"

8   And, no he didn't. Did he use the lessons learned? No he didn't.

9   Did he know how to do it? I don't even know if he did.

10   Q.   You think possibly a command policy memo from you or

11 General Hill would have stipulated lessons learned at Bucca that it

12 not be repeated?

13   A.   I think that would have been extremely helpful. The other-

14 - the other----

15   Q.   But none of those memos fell out and you didn't follow up

16 on that memo?

17   A.   No sir. And when the incident down at Bucca was resolved,

18 we spent months working on it and-- and I don't wanna say me, because

19 I don't wanna-- I can't take credit for the hard work that was done.

20 The 32, the CID investigations, the supervision of them at Bag-- at--

21 down at Arifjan. I think it was the first time they were effectively

22 supervised when Colonel Coulter got them under control. But the

23 system failed us. And it was because the tenure had changed. And at

149

1   about the same time when those incidents were taking place out of

2   Baghdad Central, the decisions were made to give the guilty people at

3   Bucca plea bargains. So, the system communicated to the soldiers,

4   the worst that's gonna happen is, you're gonna go home.

5   Q.   Where would you place them if they were not going to be

6   remanded to go home?

7   A.   It was supposed to go to a court martial, and it didn't.

8   And suggestion by a Company Commander out there at Baghdad Central,

9   was that-- in front of everybody else, was that "Ma'am, everybody

10 knows the reason it didn't go to a court martial was because they

11 were protecting that Lieutenant Colonel who took a prisoner out to

12 the clearing barrel and cleared his weapon into the clearing barrel

13 right next to his head. And they wanted to be able to forgive him."

14 So that was the change in attitude. And I said,----

15   Q.   Do you think that was associated in that?

16   A.   Yes, sir. He said it there in front of a group of people

17 and nobody turned around like they were shocked by this revelation.

18 So I knew that that was what was permeating. What I told them during

19 that meeting was, "Look, let me tell you something, the UCMJ system

20 in my opinion is fair and impartial. And people who make decisions

21 to go to court martials or take other actions, do so with extensive

22 advice and study and everything else, whether you believe that or

23 not, okay." This took seven months to complete. But, let's talk

150

1 about results, okay? There were four cases. One that was considered

2 a relatively weak case, was plea bargained out, and the individual

3 signed a statement saying that this was planned, it was orchestrated,

4 and there was definitely collusion or whatever that word is that they

5 use.

6   Q.   But did you know that the events actually happened since

7 you were not there?

8   A.   Alright, well, I only know it from the Article 32 from

9 reviewing that case and then for recommending it go to court martial.

10 But I do know the results and I know why they--they gave that plea

11 bargain, or the plea package to the first individual. And that

12 individual signed statements saying this was planned, it was by

13 design, Master Sergeant Girman orchestrated the plan. She told us

14 exactly what to do, etc. etc. So, she gets an other than honorable

15 and goes home, yes. And she understands her responsibility to come

16 back in case it goes to a court martial. I said, "Do you realize

17 that if we went to a court martial on any one of those cases, any of

18 them if there were four or ten or twelve whatever the original number

19 was, the were all going to be tried individually because that's your

20 right under UCMJ. And do you realize that if we went to a court

21 martial and the board said or the panel said, "Not guilty," those

22 individuals come back as MPs and maybe back to the same unit or the

23 same battalion. And is that a factor, considering your options?

151

1   Absolutely. And I got a lot of stares that time, because there's

2   another side to the story there, there's another perspective.

3   Q.   I don't think unless they get a bar to re-enlistment that

4   they'll ever make it back to wear the uniform.

5   A.   Well, they won't now because they are permanently barred

6   from coming back in. They are reduced. They are-- all of their

7   benefits and privileges from this deployment are suspended. So, we

8   get what we want from that action. And rather than take the risk-- I

9   mean, I-- I didn't like it at first, but I understood it, after

10 conversation with Captain Ray and Colonel Johnson. But, I wanted to

11 make sure that the leadership element out there at Baghdad Central

12 understood it because that seemed to be their concern that these guys

13 knew that all they would get would be a trip home.

14   Q.   Well, put in that perspective, then General Karpinski, when

15 everything is put before the courts, and I have no reason why you

16 will not be placed before the military court system, and the

17 revelations of all these inhumane treatment of detainees. You think

18 for one moment that those MPs that were accused of those allegations

19 were not made complicit of those-- the unit that they served under,

20 the battalion that they served under, the brigade that they served

21 under, that they will reveal all sorts of things that will put your

22 entire command under the microscope.

23   A.   Absolutely.

                          152

1   Q.   The fact of the matter is that that will be the second

2   incident to which the 800th MP Brigade would be associated with

3   potentially war crimes?

4   A.   Yes, sir.

5   Q.   How would you deal with that?

6   A.   The same way I've dealt with other situations in this

7   Theater of Operation. Tell the truth. And we were spread throughout

8   the theater of Iraq with a mission and the MPs have countless

9   examples of how well they performed and how professional they were

10   and are. And do you get, out of 3,400 people; do you get some bad

11   MPs? Yes. And do some of them have a history of this in their

12   civilian job? Yes. And does their civilian employer have a

13   responsibility to report these infractions to the military? No. Now

14   were there mistakes made? Yes. And are we taking actions to make

15   sure that they don't occur again? Yes. Can we guarantee they won't?

16   No. Because we've never forged this road before.

17   Q.   Nobody has.

18   A.   Yes, sir. So we have to rely on values and those people

19   have none, at least if the pictures tell the story. I don't care

20   what their specialty is; it's just more offensive because they're

21   MPs. What they did was vulgar and abusive. And I hope it-- it never

22   reaches the media's attention. I can't-- I can't-- I didn't get a

23   vote. Nobody said, "Okay, you're taking over command of the 800th MP

153

1   Brigade now, and what happened before doesn't count." Because it

2   does. And-- and all I can hope to do, is to make it better. Not on

3   the run, not on the fly, but with conscientious-- conscientious

4   effort and-- and leadership. I am a good leader. And taking all of

5   this out of context, and using this example of what the 800th MP

6   Brigade is capable of doing, is what is typical, I say, of what

7   Sanchez is all about. I told my soldiers this morning when they were

8   leaving, "You go home with your heads held high, because you did

9   everything and more that was asked of you, expected of you, and you

10 did it better than anybody else. You're all heroes to me, so no

11 matter what is said, nobody can take it away from you." And I

12 believe it, and I want those 19- and 20- and 35-year old soldiers to

13 believe it, because it's true. And Sanchez doesn't give a flip about

14 a soldier. And I never said that before. And he cares less about a

15 Reservist and a Guardsman.

16   Q.   You think in your heart that that's true.

17   A.   Yes, yes, sir I do.

18   Q.   Did you spread any of these thoughts with any of your

19 civilians?

20   A.   Never. Because what I said to them was, "General Sanchez

21 has an enormous job. He was a division commander before." I used

22 all the right expressions.

23   Q.   Do you shift all this blame?

                            154

550

1   A.   No I'm not. I'm not shifting all of anything. I'm taking

2   responsibility, but the situation accurately is a shared

3   responsibility. And they failed us and trying to cover their

4   failures it's going to cost the 800th MP Brigade or me? Okay.

5   Because it'll give me an opportunity to tell the truth. I know what

6   they were doing and we kept finding a way to succeed. So they'd give

7   us some more. When I took the-- when I briefed General Sanchez on

8   the condition of the civilian jails and why the progress was so slow.

9   He turns on me, and he says, "What's wrong with you Karpinski, you

10   were briefing me just a month ago or five weeks ago that, you know,

11   they were going to be on track and we were going to have capacity for

12   3,100 by now." And I said, "Sir, because the construction is not

13   taking place. And I've been to every one of the facilities and I see

14   no evidence of appropriate expenditure of funds; millions of

15   dollars." I said, "I'm not a contractor, but I know what $25,000

16   worth of work should look like, and I know what $2 million worth of

17   work should look like. And there's no evidence of it anywhere."

18   "And what have you done?" "I went to the finance office at CPA. I

19   looked for the IG's office at CPA. I looked for the GAO office at

20   CPA. I talked to finance officer at Arifjan at the 377th. I talked

21   to Colonel Warren. I talked to General Wodjakowski." "Well what

22   happened to the money?" I said, "I don't know, sir. It was a cash

23   operation and I suspect that the two subject matter experts borrowed

155

1 some of it permanently." "Are you suggesting that they

2 misappropriated funds?" "Yes sir, I am. If the evidence of the

3 construction of the facilities is-- is what I have to go by, because

4 there is no GAO and there's no IG at CPA. And they wouldn't show me

5 the contracts that they let for all these places. But I do know that

6 the only place where construction is taking place is at Abu Ghraib,

7 because my MPs are there. They're not the contracting officer

8 representatives." And he turned to his SJA and said, "Since this has

9 been dumped in my lap, tell me the next step I take." He never came

10 back and asked for information. He never came back and asked for the

11 information I had, or the evidence I had accumulated. Nobody ever

12 came back to me and said this is what took place. As a matter of

13 fact, Colonel Warren said to me, "You want to steer clear of the

14 issue." I'm not blaming General Sanchez or General Wodjakowski. I

15 just want them to take responsibility for what they didn't do. And I

16 don't ever expect a person like General Sanchez to change his

17 personality or his way of thinking or his way of succeeding or

18 anything else. I have only ever asked for a fair chance. And, no

19 sir, he did not give it me or anybody in the 800th MP Brigade.

20   Q.   Fair enough. Do you have any closing comments you want to

21 make?

22   A.   No, sir.

23   Q.   Thank you General Karpinski.

156

552

1   Witness was warned and excused.

2   [Session completed at 2035 15 February 2004.]

Brigadier General JANIS LEIGH KARPINSKI, Military Intelligence (USAR)

Commander
800ᵗʰ Military Police Brigade
Uniondale, New York 11553-1002
since May 2003

YEARS OF COMMISSION SERVICE Over 25 years

CURRENT OCCUPATION Self employed as a Corporate Consultant for Executive Training Programs and Corporate Improvement Programs, Hilton Head Island, South Carolina

MILITARY SCHOOLS ATTENDED
Military Police Officer Basic and Advanced Courses
Military Intelligence Officer Advanced Course
United States Army Command and General Staff College
United States Army War College

EDUCATIONAL DEGREES
Kean College of New Jersey - BA Degree - English/Secondary Education
Embry Riddle Aeronautical University - MAA Degree - Aviation Management
United States Army War College - MSS Degree - Strategic Studies

FOREIGN LANGUAGE None recorded

PROMOTIONS	DATES OF APPOINTMENT	
Rank	Component	Date
2LT	AUS	5 Apr 77
1LT	AUS	24 Apr 79
CPT	AUS	12 Mar 81
MAJ	USAR	4 Apr 89
LTC	USAR	3 Apr 96
COL	USAR	30 Mar 01
BG	USAR	28 Jun 03

MAJOR DUTY ASSIGNMENTS

FROM   TO

USAR - Not on Active Duty
Apr 77   Apr 77   Control Group

Active Duty
Apr 77   Oct 77   Student, Women Officer Orientation and Military Police Officer Basic Courses, Fort McClellan, Alabama
Oct 77   Nov 77   Student, Airborne Course, Fort Benning, Georgia
Nov 77   Jun 78   Platoon Leader, 21st Military Police Company, Fort Bragg, North Carolina

554

Brigadier General JANIS LEIGH KARPINSKI, Military Intelligence (USAR)

Active Duty (continued)

Jun	78	Dec	78	Traffic Officer, 503rd Military Police Battalion, Fort Bragg, North Carolina
Jan	79	Apr	80	Intelligence Officer, 46th Support Group, Fort Bragg, North Carolina
May	80	Dec	80	Assistant S2 Officer, 7th Special Forces Group, Fort Bragg, North Carolina
Jan	81	Feb	82	S2 Officer, 7th Special Forces Group, Fort Bragg, North Carolina
Feb	82	Aug	82	Student, Military Police Officer Advanced Course, Fort McClellan, Alabama
Sep	82	Jan	83	Operations/Anti-Terrorism Officer, United States Army Europe, Office of the Provost Marshal, Mannheim, Germany
Feb	83	Mar	85	Operations Officer, European Command Executive Agency, 42nd Military Police Group, Mannheim, Germany
Apr	85	Sep	85	Assistant Adjutant, 42nd Military Police Group, Mannheim, Germany
Sep	85	Nov	85	Operations Officer, Provost Marshall, Fort McPherson, Georgia
Dec	85	Mar	87	Commander, Company B, Fort McPherson, Georgia (Sep 86-Feb 87, non-rated)

USAR - Not on Active Duty

Mar	87	Aug	88	Executive Officer, 273rd Military Intelligence Company, Dobbins Air Force Base, Marietta, Georgia
Aug	88	Sep	88	Special Projects Officer, 337th Operations and Analysis Detachment, East Point, Georgia
Sep	88	Aug	90	Military Intelligence Targeting Officer, Third United States Army, Fort Gillem, Georgia (Sep-Dec 88, Dec 89-Aug 90, non-rated)

Active Duty

Aug	90	Sep	90	Operations and Targeting Officer (Desert Shield), Third United States Army, Army Component Central Command, Deployed, Riyadh, Kingdom of Saudi Arabia (non-rated)
Sep	90	Jan	92	Commander, Military Basic Training Team (Desert Storm), Abu Dhabi, United Arab Emirates, United States Army John Fitzgerald Kennedy Special Warfare Center and School, Fort Bragg, North Carolina (Sep 91-Jan 92, non-rated)
Jan	03	May	03	Chief of Staff, 81st Regional Support Command, Birmingham, Alabama
May	03	Present		Commander, 800th Military Police Brigade, Deployed, Baghdad, Iraq Operation Iraqi Freedom and Operation Enduring Freedom

USAR - Not on Active Duty

Jan	92	May	93	Intelligence Officer, Third United States Army, Fort Gillem, Georgia (non-rated)
May	93	Dec	96	Control Group
Dec	96	Dec	98	Commander, 160th Military Police Battalion, Tallahassee, Florida (Mar-Apr 98, non-rated)
Jan	99	Nov	00	Director of Operations, 641st Area Support Group, Saint Petersburg, Florida
Nov	00	Apr	02	Chief of Staff, Readiness Command, Fort Jackson, South Carolina
May	02	Sep	02	Commander, 641st Area Support Group, Saint Petersburg, Florida

2

Brigadier General LEIGH KARPINSKI, Military Intelligence (USAR)

<u>USAR - Not on Active Duty (continued)</u>

Sep 02   Jan   03   Chief of Staff, 81st Regional Support Command, Birmingham, Alabama

<u>SUMMARY OF JOINT EXPERIENCE</u> Operation Iraqi Freedom and Operation Enduring Freedom

<u>US DECORATIONS AND BADGES</u>
Bronze Star Medal
Meritorious Service Medal (with Oak Leaf Cluster)
Army Commendation Medal (with 2 Oak Leaf Clusters)
Senior Parachutist Badge

As of 01 January 2004

3

The Association of the Bar of the City of New York
Committee on International Human Rights
Committee on Military Affairs and Justice's Report

Human Rights Standards Applicable to the United States'
Interrogation of Detainees

April, 2004

EXECUTIVE SUMMARY / INTRODUCTION

This Report is a joint effort of the Association of the Bar of the City of New York's Committees on International Human Rights and Military Affairs and Justice, undertaken to consider allegations – reported in the press and by human rights and humanitarian organizations conducting their own investigations – that individuals detained by the United States at its military and intelligence facilities in connection with the initial War in Afghanistan and the subsequent ongoing conflict in Afghanistan, are being subjected to interrogation techniques that constitute torture or cruel, inhuman or degrading treatment.[1] We note at the outset, however, that although this project was initially motivated by allegations regarding the treatment of detainees from the War in Afghanistan, the international law and human rights standards discussed herein – with the exception of Geneva Convention protections applicable only to situations of international armed conflict – apply broadly and with equal force to the treatment of detainees captured in other situations, including detainees picked up in other countries in connection with the broader "War on Terror."[2] In this Report, we will examine the international legal standards governing United States military and civil authorities in interrogating detainees and propose ways of assuring that those standards are enforced.

THE ALLEGED INTERROGATION PRACTICES

These allegations first surfaced in December 2002, when the U.S. military announced that it had begun a criminal investigation into the death of a 22 year-old Afghan farmer and part-time taxi driver who had died of "blunt force injuries to lower extremities complicating coronary artery disease" while in U.S. custody at Bagram Air Force Base in Afghanistan.[3] Since then, details about interrogation techniques allegedly employed at U.S. detention facilities – most of which are off-limits to outsiders and some of which are in undisclosed locations – have come from government officials speaking on the condition that they would not be identified and from the few prisoners who have been released. Some examples of "stress and duress" interrogation "techniques" reportedly being practiced by U.S. Department of Defense ("DOD") and Central

---

[1] For purposes of this Report, the term "War in Afghanistan" refers to the period of international armed conflict in Afghanistan – from October 2001 to June 2002, when the Taliban was the governing force in Afghanistan, and the phrase "ongoing conflict in Afghanistan" refers to the period after June 18, 2002 when Hamid Karzai was elected as Afghanistan's transitional head of state, and the U.S. and other international parties were operating in Afghanistan at the invitation of this new Afghanistan government. This distinction becomes important in discussing the protections afforded to detainees by the Geneva Conventions. *See* Section II of this Report.

[2] An assessment of the parameters and legal implications of the "War on Terror," a term coined by the Administration, is beyond the scope of this Report.

[3] Carlotta Gall, *U.S. Military Investigating Death of Afghan In Custody*, N.Y. Times, Mar. 4, 2003, at A14. According to the *New York Times*, another Afghan man died of a pulmonary embolism or a blood clot in the lung while in U.S. custody at Bagram on December 3, 2002. Both men died within days of arriving at Bagram. Human Rights Watch has criticized the U.S. government for failing, one year after the first two deaths at Bagram – which were classified as homicides, to release the results of its investigation. *See* Press Releases & Documents, Voice of America, Rights Group Criticizes U.S. Military for Treatment of Afghan Detainees (Dec. 1, 2003) (printed at 2003 WL 66801402).

Intelligence Agency ("CIA") personnel at U.S. detention facilities include: forcing detainees to stand or kneel for hours in black hoods or spray-painted goggles, 24-hour bombardment with lights, "false-flag" operations meant to deceive a captive about his whereabouts, withholding painkillers from wounded detainees, confining detainees in tiny rooms, binding in painful positions, subjecting detainees to loud noises, and sleep deprivation.[4] In addition, the U.S. is reportedly "rendering" suspects to the custody of foreign intelligence services in countries where the practice of torture and cruel, inhuman or degrading treatment during interrogation is well-documented.[5]

THE ADMINISTRATION'S RESPONSES

The Association and others have written to U.S. government officials to ask whether there is any factual basis for these allegations and whether steps are being taken to ensure that detainees are interrogated in accordance with U.S. law and international standards prohibiting torture and "cruel, inhuman or degrading" treatment falling short of torture ("CID").[6]

In response to inquiries from Human Rights Watch, U.S. Department of Defense General Counsel William J. Haynes has stated that: "United States policy condemns and prohibits torture" and that, when "questioning enemy combatants, U.S. personnel are required to follow this policy and applicable laws prohibiting torture."[7] CIA General Counsel Scott W. Muller, citing to the need to protect intelligence sources and methods, has responded to our inquiries by stating only that "in its various activities around the world the CIA remains subject to the requirements of U.S. law" and that

[4] See, e.g., Dana Priest & Barton Gellman, U.S. Decries Abuse but Defends Interrogations; "Stress and Duress" Tactics used on Terrorism Suspects Held in Secret Overseas Facilities, WASH. POST, Dec. 26, 2002, at A01; Eric Lichtblau & Adam Liptak, Questioning to Be Legal, Humane and Aggressive, The White House Says Now, N.Y. Times, Mar. 4, 2003, at A13; Jess Bravin & Gary Fields, How do U.S. Interrogators Make A Captured Terrorist Talk, Wall St. J., Mar 4, 2003, at Bl; Tania Branigan, Ex-Prisoners Allege Rights Abuses By U.S. Military, Wash. Post, Aug. 19, 2003, at A02. While standards and conditions of confinement – addressed by many of the international legal instruments examined in this Report – would be included in any exhaustive inquiry into the treatment of detainees at U.S. detention centers, in this Report we are focusing more narrowly on the legality of interrogation methods.
[5] Captives have reportedly been "rendered" by the U.S. to Jordan, Egypt, Morocco, Saudi Arabia and Syria, in secret and without resort to legal process. See, e.g., Peter Finn, Al Qaeda Recruiter Reportedly Tortured; Ex-Inmate in Syria Cites Others' Accounts, Wash. Post, Jan. 31, 2003, at A14; Dana Priest and Barton Gellman, U.S. Decries Abuse but Defends Interrogations; "Stress and Duress" Tactics used on Terrorism Suspects Held in Secret Overseas Facilities, Wash. Post, Dec. 26, 2002, at A01; Rajiv Chandrasekaran & Peter Finn, U.S. Behind Secret Transfer of Terror Suspects, Wash. Post. Mar. 11, 2002, at A01.
[6] See, e.g., Letter from Kenneth Roth, Executive Director, Human Rights Watch to President George W. Bush (Dec. 26, 2002) (available at http://www.hrw.org/press/2002/12/us1227.htm); Letter from Human Rights Groups to President George W. Bush (Jan. 31, 2003); Letter from Ernest Duff, The National Consortium of Torture Treatment Programs to President George W. Bush (Feb. 5, 2003); Letter from Sen. Patrick Leahy to Condoleezza Rice (June 2, 2002); Letter from ABCNY Committees on Military Affairs and Justice and International Human Rights to Scott W. Muller, General Counsel, CIA (June 4, 2003); Letter from Sen. Patrick J. Leahy to William J. Haynes, II, General Counsel, DOD (Sept. 9, 2003).
[7] See Letter from William J. Haynes II, General Counsel, DOD, to Kenneth Roth, Executive Director, Human Rights Watch (Apr. 2, 2003). The Administration's use of the terms "enemy combatants" and "unlawful combatants" to detain persons indefinitely without administrative or judicial proceedings is novel.

allegations of unlawful behavior are reported by the CIA to the Department of Justice and are subject to investigation.[8]

In response to an inquiry made by U.S. Senator Patrick J. Leahy regarding U.S. policy, Haynes stated that U.S. policy entails "conducting interrogations in a manner that is consistent with the Convention Against Torture and Other Cruel, Inhuman, or Degrading Treatment or Punishment ("CAT"), as ratified by the U.S. in 1994, and with the Federal anti-torture statute, 18 U.S.C. §§ 2340–2340A, which Congress enacted to fulfill U.S. obligations under the CAT."[9] Haynes also stated that U.S. policy is "to treat all detainees and conduct all interrogations, wherever they may occur, in a manner consistent with" the U.S. obligation, pursuant to Article 16 of CAT, namely, "to prevent other acts of cruel, inhuman, or degrading treatment or punishment which do not amount to torture" insofar as such treatment is "prohibited by the Fifth, Eighth, and/or Fourteenth Amendments."[10] Haynes assured Senator Leahy "that credible allegations of illegal conduct by U.S. personnel will be investigated and, as appropriate, reported to proper authorities."[11] Furthermore, Haynes stated that the U.S. does not "expel, return (*'refouler'*) or extradite individuals to other countries where the U.S. believes it is 'more likely than not' that they will be tortured," that "United States policy is to obtain specific assurances from the receiving country that it will not torture the individual being transferred to that country," and that "the United States would take steps to investigate credible allegations of torture and take appropriate action if there were reason to believe that those assurances were not being honored."[12]

Both Haynes and Muller have declined, however, to give details concerning the specific interrogation methods used by U.S. personnel at U.S. military and CIA detention facilities.

LEGAL STANDARDS PROHIBITING TORTURE AND CRUEL, INHUMAN OR DEGRADING TREATMENT

Although we are not in a position to investigate the factual basis for the allegations of torture and cruel, inhuman or degrading interrogation practices at U.S. detention facilities that have been made, we can describe the legal principles which should guide our military and intelligence personnel in their conduct. Accordingly, in this Report

---

[8] *See* Letter from Scott W. Muller, General Counsel, CIA to Miles P. Fischer and Scott Horton, chair of the Committee on Military Affairs and Justice and then-chair of the Committee on International Human Rights, respectively (June 23, 2003). A CIA senior official has informally indicated that the agency complies with applicable law in reliance on the advice of its legal staff. However, we have been unable to confirm what legal advice has been given by CIA counsel or what means have been used to assure compliance with that advice.

[9] *See* Letter from William J. Haynes II, General Counsel, DOD, to Sen. Patrick J. Leahy (June 25, 2003). At the November 20–21, 2003, Annual Review of the Field of National Security Law conference of the American Bar Association's Standing Committee on National Security Law, Muller stated publicly in response to a question by a member of the Committee on Military Affairs and Justice that Haynes' June 25, 2003 letter to Sen. Leahy articulates the policy position of "the entire U.S. government." Copies of the correspondence cited in fn. 6–9 are attached to this Report as Appendix A.

[10] *Id.*

[11] *Id.*

[12] *Id.*

we examine the international and U.S. law standards against which the interrogation practices used on detainees should be assessed. We also address the question of whether there are any circumstances posed by the post-September 11 world in which abrogation of our country's obligations to prevent and punish torture and cruel, inhuman or degrading treatment should be permitted in the interrogation of terrorist suspects.

The Convention Against Torture

First and foremost, the U.S. obligation to prohibit and prevent the torture and cruel, inhuman or degrading treatment of detainees in its custody is set forth in the Convention Against Torture And Other Cruel, Inhuman, or Degrading Treatment ("CAT"), to which the U.S. is a party.[13] When the U.S. ratified CAT in 1994, it did so subject to a reservation providing that the U.S. would prevent "cruel, inhuman or degrading treatment" insofar as such treatment is prohibited under the Fifth, Eighth, and/or Fourteenth Amendments.[14] Thus, the U.S. is obligated to prevent not only torture, but also conduct considered cruel, inhuman or degrading under international law if such conduct is also prohibited by the Fifth, Eighth and Fourteenth Amendments. In interpreting U.S. obligations, we look to the U.N. Committee Against Torture's interpretations of CAT as well as U.S. case law decided in the immigration and asylum law context, under the Alien Tort Claims and Torture Victim Protection Acts and concerning the treatment of detainees and prisoners under the Fifth, Eighth and/or Fourteenth Amendments. We also examine the procedural mechanisms available under U.S. law to punish violations of CAT – including prosecution under federal criminal law (18 U.S.C. §§ 2340–2340A) and the Uniform Code of Military Justice ("UCMJ").

Other International Legal Standards which Bind the United States

While there is a dearth of U.S. case law applying CAT's prohibition against torture and cruel, inhuman or degrading treatment in the interrogation context, there is a wealth of international law sources which offer guidance in interpreting CAT. Some of these international legal standards are, without question, binding on the U.S., such as: the International Covenant on Civil and Political Rights (the "ICCPR"),[15] the law of *jus cogens* and customary international law. Another international legal instrument which has been ratified by the U.S. and is relevant to the interrogation practices being examined by this Report is the Inter-American Declaration on the Rights and Duties of Man.[16] Other sources, such as the European Convention

---

[13] Convention Against Torture and Other Cruel, Inhuman or Degrading Treatment or Punishment, *opened for signature* Feb. 4, 1985, G.A. Res. 46, U.N. GAOR 39th Sess., Supp. No. 51, at 197, U.N. Doc. A/RES/39/708 (1984), *reprinted in* 23 I.L.M. 1027 (1984) ("CAT").
[14] 136 Cong. Rec. S17486-01, 1990 WL 168442.
[15] G.A. Res. 2200A (XXI), U.N. GAOR, 21st Sess., Supp. No. 16, at 52, U.N. Doc. A/6316.
[16] O.A.S. RES. XXX, OEA/Ser. L.V./II. 82 Doc. Rev. 1, at 17.

for the Protection of Human Rights and Fundamental Freedoms,[17] also provide guidance.

The applicability of the Geneva Conventions to the detainees from the War in Afghanistan, however, presents a more contentious issue. The Administration's official position is that the Geneva Conventions do not apply to Al Qaeda detainees, and that neither the Taliban nor Al Qaeda detainees are entitled to prisoner of war ("POW") status thereunder. Nevertheless, the Administration has stated that it is treating such individuals "humanely and, to the extent appropriate and consistent with military necessity, in a manner consistent with the principles of the Third Geneva Convention of 1949," and that the detainees "will not be subjected to physical or mental abuse or cruel treatment."[18] The Administration has never explained how it determines what interrogation techniques are "appropriate" or "consistent with military necessity," or how it squares that determination with U.S. obligations under human rights and customary international law. For POW and civilian detainees who meet the relevant criteria of Geneva Convention (III) Relative to the Treatment of Prisoners of War ("Geneva III") and Geneva Convention (IV) Relative to the Protection of Civilian Persons in Time of War ("Geneva IV"), respectively, all coercion is prohibited.[19] Moreover, any detainee whose POW status is in doubt is entitled to a hearing and determination by a competent tribunal and, pending such determination, any such detainee must be treated as a POW. Concern for the safety of U.S. forces weighs in favor of extending POW status liberally. At a minimum, all detainees – regardless of POW or civilian status – are entitled to humane treatment and prompt hearings under human rights and customary international law, including the protections of Article 3 common to all four Geneva Conventions ("Common Article 3") and Article 75 of the Protocol Additional to the Geneva Conventions of 12 August 1949 and Related to the Protection of Victims of International Armed Conflicts ("Additional Protocol I").[20] We urge the U.S. to promptly establish proper screening procedures for all detainees, whether or not they served with forces that met the specific criteria of Geneva III.

Legal Standards which the United States Should Look to for Guidance

Other relevant sources of law, such as the seminal 1999 Israeli Supreme Court decision on interrogation methods employed by the Israeli General Security Service, *Judgment*

---

[17] 213 U.N.T.S. 221.

[18] *See White House Fact Sheet: Status of Detainees at Guantanamo* (Feb. 7, 2002) (*available at* http://www.whitehouse.gov/news/releases/2002/02/print/20020207-13.html).

[19] Geneva Convention (III) Relative to the Treatment of Prisoners of War, 6 U.S.T. 3316, 1949 U.S.T. LEXIS 483 ("Geneva III"); Geneva Convention (IV) Relative to the Protection of Civilian Persons in Time of War, 6 U.S.T. 3516, 1949 U.S.T. LEXIS 434 ("Geneva IV").

[20] Additional Protocol I, *reprinted in* 16 I.L.M. 1391. While neither the United States nor Afghanistan is a signatory to Additional Protocol I, it is generally acknowledged that certain provisions are binding as a matter of customary international law. And although the terms of Common Article 3 specifically limit its scope to internal conflicts, it is considered by customary international law to have broader scope.

Concerning The Legality Of The General Security Service's Interrogation Methods,[21] and decisions of the European Court of Human Rights, although not legally binding on the U.S., also offer useful guidance in our interpretation of CAT. These foreign decisions indicate that the "War on Terror" is not unprecedented. As the Israeli and Northern Ireland experiences demonstrate, the U.S. is not the only country to have faced terrorism within its borders, despite the unique tragedy of September 11 and the potential threat of weapons of mass destruction that could expand the loss of life by orders of magnitude. We can and should learn from the experience of other countries whose courts have grappled with the need to permit effective interrogation while at the same time upholding the standards of human rights and the rule of law.

Standards in the Time of Terror

There is an inherent tension between the need to obtain potentially life-saving information through interrogation of terrorist suspects and the legal requirement of upholding the standards set forth in CAT. We grappled with the question of whether there are any circumstances under which torture or cruel, inhuman or degrading treatment would be permissible in a post-September 11 world. While we acknowledge the real danger posed to the United States by al Qaeda and other terrorist organizations, we concluded that there are no such exceptions to CAT's absolute prohibition of torture.

Condoning torture under any circumstances erodes one of the most basic principles of international law and human rights and contradicts our values as a democratic state. Permitting the abuse of detainees in U.S. custody, perhaps under so-called "torture warrants," not only harms the detainees themselves; it compromises the moral framework of our interrogators and damages our society as a whole. If U.S. personnel are allowed to engage in brutal interrogation methods which denigrate the dignity and humanity of detainees, we sanction conduct which we as a nation (along with the international community) has clearly determined is wrong and immoral. Accordingly, we unanimously condemn the torture of detainees under any circumstances. We note that U.S. constitutional jurisprudence on "cruel, inhuman or degrading" treatment, which has been made relevant to CAT by the U.S. reservation, is an extremely important source of guidance on this subject. On the other hand, much of this jurisprudence evolved in the context of domestic criminal justice administration, and how these precedents would be applied in a case arising out of the interrogation and detention covered by this Report is, in the absence of more definitive authority, a matter of some speculation.

RECOMMENDATIONS

We applaud the statements in William Haynes' June 25, 2003 letter to Senator Leahy affirming the policy of the U.S. regarding its commitment to CAT. To make that policy

---

[21] 38 I.L.M. 1471 (Sept. 6, 1999).

meaningful, we make the following recommendations:

1. <u>Training and Education</u>. All law enforcement personnel, civilian or military, medical personnel, public officials and other persons who may be involved in the custody, interrogation or treatment of anyone under any form of detention or imprisonment should be informed and educated regarding the prohibition against torture and cruel, inhuman or degrading treatment, as applied in practice. This requires, as provided in Article 11 of CAT, that the U.S. keep under systematic review interrogation rules, instructions, methods and practices as well as arrangements for the custody and treatment of such detainees.[22] Above all, commanders should not condone non-compliance nor permit an environment in which troops are encouraged to provide lip service to compliance but yet think that non-compliance is acceptable.

Given that CIA personnel are not generally subject to the UCMJ, possibly not even when accompanying the armed forces in the field, special procedures should be available to provide reasonable assurance that compliance with CAT is being taught and maintained by intelligence agencies. That assurance might best be provided by the applicable committees of the Congress exercising oversight responsibility in conjunction with the inspectors general of the applicable agencies.

2. <u>Prompt Investigation of Violations</u>. As required by Article 12 of CAT, the U.S. must ensure that allegations of abusive conduct are taken seriously and are fully and impartially investigated.[23] Thus, any individual who alleges that he or she has been subjected to torture must be provided with a meaningful opportunity to complain to, and to have his/her case promptly and impartially examined by, competent authorities. Steps must be taken to ensure that the complainant and witnesses are protected against all ill-treatment and intimidation.

3. <u>Expand the Scope and Reach of Section 2340</u>. Consistent with its obligation under Article 4 of CAT to ensure that all acts of torture are offenses under its criminal law[24] – and since 18 U.S.C. § 2340 does not, by its terms, apply to acts constituting torture committed in extraterritorial detention centers under U.S. jurisdiction – the U.S. must expand the geographic reach of Section 2340 so that the prescriptions of CAT are applicable at all U.S. detention centers.

4. <u>Fully Utilize the UCMJ</u>. The U.S. must more fully utilize the procedures and protections available under the UCMJ to prosecute all violations of CAT by the armed forces or others subject to the UCMJ.

5. <u>Independent Investigation of Human Rights Compliance in Other Countries</u>. As provided by Article 3 of CAT, the U.S. must not "render" detainees to other countries where there are substantial grounds for belief that the detainees would be in danger of being subjected to torture.[25] In determining whether there are "substantial grounds

---

[22] CAT, Art. 11.
[23] *Id.*, Art. 12.
[24] *Id.*, Art. 4.
[25] *Id.*, Art. 3.

for belief" that a detainee would be in danger of torture if rendered to another country, U.S. authorities must take into account all the relevant considerations concerning that country, including independently investigating whether there exists a consistent pattern of gross, flagrant or mass violations of human rights in the country.[26]

6. Grant POW Status to Detainees Whose Status is in Doubt and Possibly as a Matter of Policy. The U.S. should adhere to Geneva III's requirement that any detainee whose POW status is in "doubt" is entitled to POW status – and, therefore, cannot be subjected to coercive treatment – until a "competent tribunal," which must be convened promptly, determines otherwise.[27] We urge the U.S. to consider the policy grounds for extending POW treatment to regular force combatants, whether or not legally required to do so, as it has done in prior conflicts.

7. Prompt Screening and Hearings for All Detainees. In keeping with the spirit of the Geneva Conventions and human rights law, we urge the U.S. to provide proper screening procedures and hearings to all detainees.[28]

We now turn to a more detailed discussion of the international standards applicable to interrogation procedures.

THE CONVENTION AGAINST TORTURE

The U.N. Convention Against Torture and Other Cruel, Inhuman or Degrading Treatment or Punishment ("CAT") is the primary source of international law relevant to the treatment of detainees.[29] CAT has been ratified by the U.S., and its prohibitions against torture and cruel, inhuman or degrading treatment or punishment have been implemented in our domestic law.

Specifically, U.S. law implements CAT's prohibition against torture in the immigration and asylum contexts, under the Alien Tort Claims and Torture Victim Protection Acts, by criminal statute and under the UCMJ. Under CAT, the U.S. is also obligated to prevent "cruel, inhuman or degrading treatment or punishment" as defined in international law; however, by express reservation, the U.S. interprets this obligation in keeping with standards of treatment required by the Fifth, Eighth and Fourteenth Amendments. Accordingly, under CAT, American military and intelligence personnel involved in the interrogation of detainees may not torture those detainees, nor may

---

[26] For example, a lawsuit was recently filed by the Center for Constitutional Rights on behalf of Maher Arar, a Syrian-born Canadian citizen alleging that U.S. authorities deported him to Jordan in September 2002, where he was driven across the border and handed over to Syrian authorities. The Arar Complaint alleges that, although the U.S. Department of State's 2003 Country Reports designated Syria as a government that practices systemic torture, U.S. officials allegedly relied on assurances from the Syrian government that Arar would not be tortured. Arar has alleged that he was tortured repeatedly in a Syrian prison for 10 months, often with cables and electrical cords. *See* Complaint in *Maher Arar v. John Ashcroft, et al. (available at* http://www.ccr-ny.org/v2/legal/September_11th/docs/ArarComplaint.pdf).
[27] Geneva III, Art. 5.
[28] We note that the Department of Defense has recently circulated for comment administrative review procedures for enemy combatants at Guantanamo Bay Naval Base. *See* http://www.defenselink.mil/news/ Mar2004/ d20040303ar.pdf. While welcoming such a review process, we do not consider it to meet the requirement for status determination under the Geneva Conventions.
[29] *Supra* note 13.

they subject them to cruel, inhuman or degrading treatment that is, or would be, forbidden under the Fifth, Eighth and/or Fourteenth Amendments.

CAT'S DEFINITIONS OF – AND PROHIBITIONS AGAINST – TORTURE AND CRUEL, INHUMAN OR DEGRADING TREATMENT

CAT defines and prohibits torture, as defined, and cruel, inhuman or degrading treatment or punishment in general terms. In addition, it also sets out steps ratifying countries must take to prevent, investigate, and criminalize acts of torture;[30] prohibits the extradition or other rendering (also known as *"refoulement"*) of a person to a country that would likely subject such person to torture;[31] creates a Committee to oversee the implementation of CAT by ratifying countries; and sets forth procedures for inquiries, individual communications, and inter-State complaints.

CAT's preamble acknowledges that torture and other cruel, inhuman or degrading treatment or punishment are already prohibited under Article 5 of the Universal Declaration of Human Rights and Article 7 of the ICCPR. Thus, rather than simply mirroring the prohibitions from these instruments, Article 1 of CAT provides additional guidance to states parties in preventing and punishing torture by setting forth an explicit definition of torture:

> ... torture means any act by which severe pain or suffering, whether physical or mental, is intentionally inflicted on a person for such purposes as obtaining from him or a third person information or a confession, punishing him for an act he or a third person has committed or is suspected of having committed, or intimidating or coercing him or a third person, or for any reason based on discrimination of any kind, when such pain or suffering is inflicted by or at the instigation of or with the consent or acquiescence of a public official or other person acting in an official capacity. It does not include pain or suffering arising only from, inherent in or incidental to lawful sanctions.

This definition makes it clear that the result of torture need not be physical pain or suffering, but can also be mental. In addition, torture is defined to include such conduct undertaken for the purpose of obtaining information. Finally, the prohibition is not directed at private citizens, acting independently of government; it applies rather to acts committed by government officials and agents, or persons acting with official consent or acquiescence.

CAT's prohibition of torture is absolute. An order from a superior officer or a public authority may not be invoked as a justification of torture. Specifically, Article 2(2) provides: "No exceptional circumstances whatsoever, whether a state of war or a threat or war, internal political instability or any other public emergency, may be invoked as a justification of torture."

---

[30] *Id*. Article 4.1 states: "Each State Party shall ensure that all acts of torture are offences under its criminal law. The same shall apply to an attempt to commit torture and to an act by any person which constitutes complicity or participation in torture."

[31] *Id*. Article 3.1 states: "No State Party shall expel, return (*'refouler'*) or extradite a person to another State where there are substantial grounds for believing that he would be in danger of being subjected to torture."

Although CAT does not provide a definition of CID punishment or treatment, Article 16 requires ratifying countries to prevent "other acts of cruel, inhuman or degrading treatment or punishment which do not amount to torture...." This language suggests that cruel, inhuman or degrading treatment is on a continuum with torture.

CAT requires each signatory state to prevent the commission of the prohibited acts within any territory under the state's jurisdiction. Specifically, each ratifying country must ensure that any official who may be involved in the interrogation of anyone under any form of detention or imprisonment is informed of and educated about the prohibitions against torture and cruel, inhuman or degrading treatment. CAT also requires each ratifying country to ensure that allegations of torture and CID treatment are fully and impartially investigated. *See* CAT Articles 12 and 16(1).

CAT'S PROHIBITION AGAINST TORTURE AND CID TREATMENT AS INTERPRETED BY THE U.N. COMMITTEE AGAINST TORTURE

The U.N. Committee Against Torture, created by CAT, is charged with monitoring implementation of the treaty by ratifying countries through the determination of individual complaints, considering country reports submitted under CAT, and resolving inter-State disputes. Given the importance of international standards in interpreting U.S. domestic law[32] as well as the recent *Lawrence v. Texas* decision, in which the U.S. Supreme Court expressly looked to foreign and international law for guidance,[33] U.N. Committee decisions are relevant to the assessment of whether the actions of U.S. personnel involved in the interrogation of detainees constitute torture or cruel; inhuman or degrading treatment.

The U.N. Committee has concluded that the following acts[34] constitute torture under CAT:

- daily beatings and detaining someone in a small, uncomfortable space for two weeks;[35]
- forcing someone to sleep on the floor of a cell while handcuffed following interrogation;[36]
- in severe cases, sleep deprivation;[37] and
- the threat of torture.[38]

---

[32] *See Murray v. The Charming Betsy*, 6 U.S. (2 Cranch) 64, 118 (1804) (a statute "ought never to be construed to violate the law of nations, if any other possible construction remains"). *See also United States v. P.L.O.*, 695 F. Supp. 1456, 1468 (S.D.N.Y. 1988) (noting "the lengths to which our courts have sometimes gone in construing domestic statutes so as to avoid conflict with international agreements...").

[33] *Lawrence v. Texas*, 539 U.S. 558 (2003).

[34] This list is by no means comprehensive. Practices were selected for inclusion here because of their similarity to the practices allegedly used by U.S. agents with respect to detainees held in connection with the War in Afghanistan and the ongoing conflict in Afghanistan. The findings and concluding observations of the Committee Against Torture are available at http://www.unhchr.ch/tbs/doc.nsf.

[35] *Case of A. (name withheld) v. The Netherlands*, Committee Against Torture, Comm. No. 91/1997 (1998), U.N. Doc. No. CAT/C/21/D/91/1997.

[36] *See* Inquiry under Article 20: Committee Against Torture, Findings concerning Peru (2001), U.N. Doc. No. A/56/44, at para. 35.

[37] Concluding Observations concerning Republic of Korea (1996), U.N. Doc. No. A/52/44, at para. 56.

[38] Concluding Observations concerning New Zealand (1993), U.N. Doc. No. A/48/44, at para. 148.

Furthermore, the U.N. Committee has recommended that the use of a blindfold during questioning be expressly prohibited.[39] More generally, the U.N. Committee has expressed concern that States have defined torture too narrowly, covering only "systematic blows or other violent acts."[40] The U.N. Committee has also expressed concern whether the penal law of one State was too narrow in defining torture because it failed to prohibit "certain aspects of torture, such as psychological pressure, threats and intimidation."[41]

The U.N. Committee has found that the following acts amount to cruel, inhuman or degrading treatment or punishment under CAT:

- depriving someone of food and/or water;[42]
- in some cases, binding someone in a restraint chair;[43]
- the use by prison authorities of instruments of physical restraint that may cause unnecessary pain and humiliation;[44] and
- long periods of detention (two weeks or more) in detention cells that are substandard (this conduct may amount to torture if the period of detention is extremely long).[45]

The U.N. Committee has found that the following acts may amount to torture when used in combination with other forms of CID:

- being restrained in very painful conditions;
- being hooded;
- the sounding of loud music for prolonged periods;
- sleep deprivation for prolonged periods;
- violent shaking; and
- using cold air to chill.[46]

In sum, the U.N. Committee Against Torture has indicated that the classification of treatment as CID or torture is often a matter of severity, intensity, and the totality of the circumstances. Combining several forms of cruel, inhuman or degrading treatment will frequently amount to torture, and ratifying countries are required under CAT to refrain from all such practices, whether they reach the level of severity to be considered torture or not. Thus, according to U.N. Committee jurisprudence, alleged interrogation practices such as forcing detainees to stand or kneel for hours in black hoods or spray-painted goggles, 24-hour bombardment with lights, binding detainees

---

[39] *See* Inquiry Under Article 20: Committee Against Torture, Findings concerning Turkey (1993), U.N. Doc. No. A/48/44/Add. 1, at para. 48.

[40] Concluding Observations concerning Azerbaijan (2003), U.N. Doc. No. CAT/C/CR/30/1, at para. 5(b).

[41] Concluding Observations concerning Germany (1993), U.N. Doc. No. A/48/44, at para. 167.

[42] *Id.; see also* Concluding Observations concerning New Zealand (1998), U.N. Doc. No. A/53/44, at para. 175.

[43] Concluding Observations concerning the United States (2000), U.N. Doc. No. A/55/44, at para. 179(e).

[44] Concluding Observations concerning Australia (2000), U.N. Doc. No. A/56/44, at para. 52(b).

[45] *Supra* note 36.

[46] These techniques were found by the Committee to constitute "breaches of Article 16 and also constitute torture as defined in Article 1 of the Convention. This conclusion is particularly evident where such methods of interrogation are used in combination, which appears to be the standard case." Concluding Observations concerning Israel (1997), U.N. Doc. No. A/52/44, at para. 257.

in painful positions, withholding painkillers from wounded detainees, and subjecting detainees to loud noises and sleep deprivation, at a minimum, constitute cruel, inhuman or degrading treatment and may, depending on the circumstances, rise to the level of torture. U.N. Committee decisions critical of blindfolding, psychological pressure and threats and intimidation strongly suggest that "false-flag" operations meant to deceive detainees about their whereabouts and "stress and duress" interrogation techniques are also prohibited.

U.S. LAW IMPLEMENTING CAT'S PROHIBITIONS AGAINST TORTURE AND CRUEL, INHUMAN OR DEGRADING TREATMENT OR PUNISHMENT

The Senate adopted a resolution of advice and consent to U.S. ratification of CAT, subject to the declaration that it be deemed non-self-executing, on October 27, 1990.[47] The U.S. ratified CAT in October 1994, and CAT entered into force with respect to the United States on 20 November 1994.[48] The implementation in U.S. immigration, extradition, criminal and civil tort law of CAT's prohibition against torture, as well as the express application of U.S. constitutional standards to CAT's prohibition against CID treatment, indicates that many of the interrogation practices allegedly being used by the U.S. against detainees may be prohibited under international and U.S. law.

U.S. Understandings and Reservations in Ratifying CAT

The United States conditioned its ratification of CAT upon certain understandings related to CAT's definition of torture in Article 1. In one such understanding, the U.S. specified that mental pain or suffering within the meaning of "torture" refers to prolonged mental harm caused by or resulting from: (1) the intentional infliction or threatened infliction of severe physical pain or suffering; (2) the administration or application, or threatened administration or application, of mind-altering substances or other procedures calculated to disrupt profoundly the senses or the personality; (3) the threat of imminent death; or (4) the threat that another person will imminently be subjected to death, severe physical pain or suffering, or the administration or application of mind-altering substances or other procedures calculated to disrupt profoundly the senses or the personality.[49] Another U.S. understanding pertains to

---

[47] See 136 CONG. REC. 36,198 (daily ed. Oct. 27, 1990). The instrument of ratification included the declaration that "the provisions of Articles 1 through 16 of [CAT] are not self-executing." See United Nations Treaty Collection: Declarations and Reservations, (available at http://www.unhchr.ch/html/menu3/b/treaty 12_asp.htm).

In the case of a self-executing treaty, "no domestic legislation is required to give [it] the force of law in the United States."*Trans World Airlines, Inc. v. Franklin Mint Corp.*, 466 U.S. 243, 252 (1984). By contrast, a non-self-executing treaty is one that "must be implemented by legislation before it gives rise to a private cause of action." *Mannington Mills, Inc. v. Congoleum Corp.*, 595 F.2d 1287, 1298 (3d Cir. 1979).

[48] See Ratification Status for CAT, United States of America (available at www.unhchr.ch). The U.S. has not opted out of the inquiry procedure under Article 20. It has entered a declaration accepting the interstate complaint procedure set up by Article 21. The U.S. has not, however, accepted the competence of the Committee under Article 22 to receive and consider complaints on behalf of individuals subject to its jurisdiction who claim to be victims of a violation of CAT.

[49] See 136 CONG. REC. S17486-01 (daily ed. Oct. 27, 1990).

defects in criminal procedure: non-compliance with applicable legal procedural standards (such as Miranda warnings) does not per se constitute "torture."[50]

When ratifying CAT, the United States also took the following reservation: "the United States considers itself bound by the obligation under Article 16 to prevent 'cruel, inhuman or degrading treatment or punishment,' only insofar as the term 'cruel, inhuman or degrading treatment or punishment' means the cruel, unusual and inhumane treatment or punishment prohibited by the Fifth, Eighth, and Fourteenth Amendments to the Constitution of the United States."[51]

The Implementation of CAT's Prohibition against Torture in U.S. Legislation, Regulation and Case Law

CAT's prohibition of official acts amounting to torture has been implemented in the United States through legislation, regulations and case law pertaining to, *inter alia*, (1) immigration, (2) claims of torture in removal and extradition proceedings, (3) criminal sanctions for torture, and (4) tort claims alleging torture. Through the application of these implementing laws and regulations, U.S. courts have interpreted CAT's substantive provisions in a variety of contexts.[52]

U.S. Immigration Law and Torture
As previously noted, all countries that ratify CAT are obligated to ensure that detainees are not deported or extradited to countries where they are likely to be tortured. In 1998, the United States enacted the Foreign Affairs Reform and Restructuring Act of 1998, § 2242, Pub. L. No. 105–277, Div. G, 112 Stat. 2681, 2681–822 (Oct. 21, 1998) (the "FARR Act"), implementing this obligation. In 1999, the Immigration and Naturalization Service ("INS") promulgated regulations effectuating the FARR Act in the immigration and asylum context, providing aliens in exclusion, deportation or removal proceedings with grounds to seek withholding of removal based on CAT. *See* 8 C.F.R. § 208.18 (2004), *et seq.* These regulations incorporate CAT's definition of torture verbatim, with the following qualification: "Torture is an extreme form of cruel and inhuman treatment and does not include lesser forms of cruel, inhuman or degrading treatment or punishment that do not amount to torture." *See* 8 C.F.R. § 208.18(a)(2) (2004). These regulations further define mental pain or suffering consistently with the U.S. understandings to CAT, and exclude from the definition of torture acts which result in "unanticipated or unintended severity of pain and suffering." *See* 8 C.F.R. § 208.18(a)(5) (2004).

A number of federal court cases and Board of Immigration Appeals ("BIA") decisions address torture claims in the immigration context. The BIA has held that the following abuses of detainees and prisoners, for example, amount to torture:

---

[50] *See* 136 Cong. Rec. 36192, 36198 (daily ed. Oct. 27, 1990).

[51] Under international law, reservations are invalid if they violate the "object and purpose" of the treaty. *See* Vienna Convention on the Law of Treaties, *opened for signature* May 23, 1969, 1155 U.N.T.S. 331, at Art. 19(c). This Report assumes that the U.S. reservation with respect to Article 16 of CAT is valid.

[52] Because the focus of this Report is on what laws apply to agents of the United States government in detention centers located outside of United States territory, this discussion does not examine state or federal penal or civil rights statutes that would also apply to interrogation occurring on American soil.

"'suspension for long periods in contorted positions, burning with cigarettes, sleep deprivation, and . . . severe and repeated beatings with cables or other instruments on the back and on the soles of the feet,' . . . beatings about the ears, resulting in partial or complete deafness, and punching in the eyes, leading to partial or complete blindness." *Matter of G-A-*, 23 I & N Dec. 366, 370 (BIA 2002) (internal citations omitted).[53] Furthermore, persons seeking asylum or withholding of removal have successfully challenged deportation under Sections 208 and 241(b)(3) of the Immigration & Nationality Act ("INA") when they have a well-founded fear of future persecution. Although "persecution" is not defined in the INA, it is understood to encompass treatment falling short of torture.

U.S. Extradition of Fugitives Who Face Threat of Torture

In the extradition context, torture claims are governed by regulations enacted by the Department of State under the FARR Act. Under these regulations, individuals sought for extradition may present a claim that they are likely to be tortured if surrendered to the requesting state. These claims are considered by the U.S. Secretary of State, who is responsible for implementing CAT's obligation not to extradite an individual to a State where he or she is in danger of being subject to torture. Specifically, section 95 of 22 C.F.R. (2004) provides, in relevant part, that the Secretary of State must consider whether a person facing extradition from the U.S. "is more likely than not" to be tortured in the State requesting extradition, and that appropriate policy and legal offices must review and analyze the information relevant to the torture allegation. The extradition regulations, and the decisions interpreting them,[54] demonstrate that U.S. administrative bodies and courts view CAT's prohibition against extradition to torture as binding on the U.S. even when the extraditable individual is accused of wrongdoing.

U.S. Implementation of CAT's Criminal Law Requirements

18 U.S.C. §§ 2340 and 2340A were enacted to fulfill CAT's requirement that each ratifying country criminalize all acts of torture, including attempts to commit torture and complicity in torture.[55] Section 2340 defines torture as:

> an act committed by a person acting under the color of law specifically intended to inflict severe physical or mental pain or suffering (other than pain or suffering incidental to lawful sanctions) upon another person within his custody or physical control . . .

---

[53] This had also been the position of the Ninth Circuit. *See Al-Saher v. INS*, 268 F.3d 1143 (9th Cir. 2001) (holding that severe beatings and cigarette burns sustained over periods of days, weeks and months constitutes torture). More recently, however, the Ninth Circuit has held that neither serious persecution (*e.g.*, threats, unjust charges, fines, illegal searches and seizures) nor verbal abuse alone amount to torture. *See Gui v. INS*, 280 F.3d 1217 (9th Cir. 2002); *Quant v. Ashcroft*, 2003 U.S. App. LEXIS 6616 (9th Cir. 2003).

[54] *See, e.g., Cornejo-Barreto v. Seifert*, 218 F.3d 1004, 1016–17 (9th Cir. 2000) (individuals certified as extraditable by the Secretary of State who fear torture may petition for judicial review of the Secretary's decision using CAT standards protecting against *non-refoulement*); *Mu-Xing Wang v. Ashcroft*, 320 F.3d 130 (2d Cir. 2003) (following *Cornejo-Barreto's* holding that habeas review is available for CAT claims, but in the context of removal); *Ogbudimkpa v. Ashcroft*, 342 F.3d 207 (3d Cir. 2003) (same).

[55] The Senate Committee on the Judiciary acknowledged the relationship of 18 U.S.C. § 2340 to CAT and the Torture Victim Protection Act in a 2002 report. *See* S. REP. NO. 107-44 (2002), at 10-11.

"Severe mental pain or suffering" is also defined, using the same wording as the U.S. understandings concerning Article 1 of CAT set forth in Section I(C)(1) above. *See* 18 U.S.C. § 2340. As discussed further below, however, this statute applies only to U.S. nationals (or others present in the U.S.) who have committed or attempted or conspired to commit acts of torture "outside of the United States."[56]

U.S. Case Law Interpretations of Torture in Tort Claims

Two U.S. statutes provide for civil suits against those who commit acts of torture abroad. The Alien Tort Claims Act of 1789 ("ATCA"), 28 U.S.C. § 1350, states that "[t]he district courts shall have original jurisdiction of any civil action by an alien for a tort only, committed in violation of the law of nations or a treaty of the United States." The Torture Victim Protection Act of 1991 ("TVPA"), 28 U.S.C. § 1350, provides that:

> an individual who, under actual or apparent authority, or color of law, of any foreign nation – (1) subjects an individual to torture shall, in a civil action, be liable for damages to that individual; or (2) subjects an individual to extrajudicial killing shall, in a civil action, be liable for damages to the individual's legal representative, or to any person who may be a claimant in an action for wrongful death.[57]

The TVPA extends a civil remedy to U.S. citizen torture victims, while the ATCA provides a remedy for aliens only.

U.S. courts applying the ATCA and TVPA have found that the following acts constitute torture: subjecting detainees to interrogation sessions lasting 14 hours *(Xuncax v. Gramajo*, 886 F. Supp. 162, 170 (D. Mass 1995)); beating with hands *(Tachiona v. Mugabe*, 234 F. Supp. 2d 401, 420–423 (S.D.N.Y. 2002); *Cabiri v. Assasie-Gyimah*, 921 F. Supp. 1189, 1191, 1196 (S.D.N.Y. 1996); *Abebe-Jira v. Negewo*, 72 F.3d 844, 845 (11th Cir. 1996)); threatening with death *(Abebe-Jira v. Negewo*, 72 F.3d 844, 845 (11th Cir. 1996)); and using techniques to exacerbate pain or injury *(Abebe-Jira v. Negewo*, 72 F.3d 844, 845-6 (11th Cir. 1996)).

Conclusion: CAT's Prohibition against Torture as Implemented in U.S. Legislation and Regulation

U.S. domestic laws prohibiting, or providing a cause of action to victims of, torture are consistent with the standards of CAT. However, these U.S. statutes and regulations are limited to specific contexts – such as, refugee claims, extradition of foreign fugitives, criminalizing acts of torture committed outside the U.S. by U.S. officials, and providing compensation to victims of torture committed by aliens. Accordingly, the U.S. has yet to fulfill its obligation, under CAT, to enact laws which adequately prevent

---

[56] A restrictive interpretation of the scope of the statute is found in the U.S. Dept. of Justice, Criminal Resource Manual 20 (Oct. 1997), which provides: "Section 2340A of Title 18, United States Code, prohibits torture committed by public officials under color of law against persons within the public official's custody or control.... The statute applies only to acts of torture committed outside the United States. There is Federal extraterritorial jurisdiction over such acts whenever the perpetrator is a national of the United States or the alleged offender is found within the United States, irrespective of the nationality of the victim or the alleged offender."

[57] *See* S. REP. NO. 102–249 (1991) (stating that the TVPA would "carry out the intent of the Convention Against Torture and Other Cruel, Inhuman or Degrading Treatment or Punishment, which was ratified by the U.S. Senate on October 27, 1990").

U.S. officials and individuals acting with their consent from subjecting any detainee to torture and which punish such conduct wherever it occurs.

CAT's Prohibition against "Cruel, Inhuman or Degrading Treatment," as Interpreted by United States Law

As previously noted, the U.S.'s reservation to Article 16 of CAT provides that the United States considers itself bound by Article 16 only insofar as CID treatment is understood to mean "the cruel, unusual and inhumane treatment or punishment prohibited by the Fifth, Eighth and Fourteenth Amendments."

The Senate Foreign Relations Committee report states that this reservation is the outgrowth of concern that "degrading treatment or punishment . . . has been interpreted as potentially including treatment that would probably not be prohibited by the U.S. Constitution" and cites, as an example of what the United States would not find "degrading" under the U.S. Constitution, a holding by the European Commission of Human Rights that the refusal of authorities to give formal recognition to an individual's change of sex might constitute degrading treatment.[58] This explanation suggests that the reservation was intended to prevent the importation of foreign social values or mores into U.S. law, rather than any view that international norms of CID treatment are out of step with U.S. law.

In assessing interrogation conduct under Article 16 of CAT, the U.S. should look to international standards defining cruel, inhuman or degrading treatment. If such conduct is prohibited under international law, the U.S. is bound to prevent such conduct unless it would not be prohibited under the Fifth, Eighth and Fourteenth Amendments. The Committees take note that much of the case law under the three Amendments arises in the context of domestic criminal justice proceedings. How this jurisprudence would be applied in a case relating to the detention and interrogation of foreign combatants is not completely clear. For instance, on the one hand some of the special protections provided in the American criminal justice system with respect to interrogations would be of doubtful applicability, particularly considering an asserted state interest in national security. On the other, the absence of a legitimate state interest in punishment might mandate a higher standard of treatment of detainees generally.

Fifth and Fourteenth Amendment Standards

The Constitution's guarantee of due process forbids compulsion to testify, at least for domestic law enforcement purposes, by fear of hurt, torture or exhaustion. See *Adamson v. California*, 332 U.S. 46 (1947) (armed Texas Rangers on several successive nights took defendant from county jail into the woods, whipped him, asked him each time about a confession, interrogated him from approximately 11 p.m. to 3 a.m. and warned him not to speak to anyone about the nightly trips); *Brown v. Mississippi*, 297 U.S. 278 (1936) (confessions obtained by mock executions and whippings); *Ashcraft v. Tennessee*, 322 U.S. 143, 154 (1944) (defendant was taken into custody by police officers and for 36 hours thereafter was held incommunicado, without sleep or rest,

---

[58] *See* Report of the Committee on Foreign Relations, Convention Against Torture and Other Cruel, Inhuman, or Degrading Treatment or Punishment, S. EXEC. REP. NO. 30, 101st Cong., 2d Sess. 25 (1990) (statement of Mr. Pell) (citing *Case of X. v. Federal Republic of Germany* (No. 6694/74)).

and interrogated without respite by relays of officers, experienced investigators, and highly trained lawyers); *see also Ashcraft v. Tennessee*, 327 U.S. 274 (1946). However, the presence of unlawful police coercion motivated by "immediate necessity to find the victim and save his life" to extract a confession has been found by one appeals court to be insufficient to exclude a subsequent confession.[59]

Due process also prohibits actions taken under color of law that are "so brutal and offensive to human dignity" that they "shock the conscience."[60] The Supreme Court has given content to the phrase "shocks the conscience" by reference to the spectrum of fault standards in tort law. Intentional infliction of injury unjustifiable by any government interest is the sort of official action which could rise to the conscience-shocking level.[61] All applicable sources of law are consistent in prohibiting such extreme conduct.

Eighth Amendment Standards

The Eighth Amendment prohibits "cruel and unusual punishments."[62] In the context of law enforcement, U.S. courts have long held that the norms articulated under the Cruel and Unusual Punishment Clause establish a minimum level of protection, applicable even to pretrial detainees.[63]

While the Supreme Court initially interpreted the Eighth Amendment as prohibiting only barbaric or torturous punishments, this interpretation was early broadened in two respects: (i) to prevent disproportionate punishments (*Weems v. United States*, 217 U.S. 349 (1910)) and (ii) to address non-physical forms of cruel and unusual punishment (*e.g., Trop v. Dulles*, 356 U.S. 86 (1958) (in case involving denationalization as a punishment for desertion from the United States Army, the Court noted that "evolving standards of decency that mark the progress of a maturing society" should inform interpretation of the Eighth Amendment)). In 1947, the Supreme Court recognized that wanton or unnecessary infliction of pain also constitutes cruel and unusual punishment. *Louisiana ex rel. Francis v. Resweber*, 329 U.S. 459, 463 (1947).

In cases brought by prisoners under the Eighth Amendment alleging that excessive force was used against them by government officials, courts consider both the objective component (whether the wrongdoing was "harmful enough" to implicate the Eighth Amendment) and the subjective component (whether the officials acted with a sufficiently culpable state of mind) of the challenged conduct. *Hudson v. McMillian*, 503 U.S. 1, 8 (1992). In order to establish that the objective component of an

---

[59] *Leon v. Wainwright*, 734 F.2d 770 n.5 (11th Cir. 1984) (kidnapping conviction confirmed based on a confession obtained following a prior coerced confession).

[60] *Rochin v. California*, 342 U.S. 165, 172 (1952).

[61] *County of Sacramento v. Lewis*, 523 U.S. 833, 848–49 (1998).

[62] The UCMJ, discussed below, provides that no "cruel or unusual punishment" may be adjudged by any court-martial or inflicted upon any person subject to the UCMJ (10 U.S.C.S. §855). In general, military courts have applied the Supreme Court's interpretation of the Eighth Amendment to claims raised under this provision. *See, e.g., United States v. Avila*, 53 M.J. 99, 2000 CAAF LEXIS 569 (C.A.A.F. 2000). Thus, under the UCMJ, POWs and persons who under the law of war are subject to trial for military offences by a military tribunal are not to be punished in a cruel or unusual manner, within the meaning of the Eighth Amendment.

[63] *City of Revere v. Massachusetts Gen. Hosp.*, 463 U.S. 239, 244 (1983). *See also County of Sacramento v. Lewis*, 523 U.S. 833, 849–50 (1998) (citation omitted) ("We held in *City of Revere v. Massachusetts Gen. Hospital* that 'the due process rights of a [pretrial detainee] are at least as great as the Eighth Amendment protections available to a convicted prisoner'").

Eighth Amendment violation is satisfied, a prisoner need not prove he has sustained significant injury. However, the extent of injury suffered is one factor that may suggest "whether the use of force could plausibly have been thought necessary" in a particular situation, "or instead evinced such wantonness with respect to the unjustified infliction of harm as is tantamount to a knowing willingness that it occur."[64] The subjective component involves, in the context of force used by prison officials, "whether force was applied in a good-faith effort to maintain or restore discipline, or maliciously and sadistically for the very purpose of causing harm."[65]

ENFORCEMENT OF CAT UNDER U.S. LAW

18 U.S.C. §§ 2340–2340B

As stated above, the United States' attempt to comply with its obligation under CAT to criminalize torture is codified in 18 U.S.C. § 2340A. Section 2340A criminalizes conduct by a U.S. national or a foreign national present in the U.S. who, acting under color of law, commits or attempts to commit torture outside the United States. The statute is exclusively criminal and may not be construed as creating any right enforceable in a civil proceeding. *See* 18 U.S.C. § 2340B. Section 2340A generally applies to acts committed by U.S. nationals overseas (everywhere *except* "all areas under the jurisdiction of the United States, including any of the places described in sections 5 and 7 of this title and Section 46501(2) of Title 49.") When the Section was enacted the reach of the cross-referenced provisions, notably 18 U.S.C. § 7, was uncertain.[66] However, Section 7 was broadened in the USA PATRIOT Act to clarify jurisdiction over crimes committed against U.S. citizens on U.S. property abroad by extending U.S. criminal jurisdiction over certain crimes committed at its foreign diplomatic, military and other facilities, and by cross-reference excluded those places from the reach of Section 2340A. The resulting drastic limitation of jurisdiction under 18 U.S.C. § 2340A appears unintended. We recommend that Congress amend Section 2340A to assure that it applies to U.S. government premises abroad without prejudice to the expansion of U.S. criminal jurisdiction under other statutes.

The U.S. did not enact a specific criminal statute outlawing torture within the United States, out of deference to federal-state relations and because it determined that existing federal and state criminal law was sufficient to cover any domestic act that would qualify as torture under CAT.[67] It is submitted that the inapplicability of state law to U.S. facilities abroad and the lack of other federal criminal law comparable

---

[64] *Hudson v. McMillian*, 503 U.S. 1, 7 (1992) (quoting *Whitley v. Albers*, 475 U.S. 312, 321 (1986)).

[65] *Whitley v. Albers*, 475 U.S. 312, 320–21 (1986) (quoting *Johnson v. Glick*, 481 F.2d 1028, 1033 (2d Cir. 1973)).

[66] *Compare U.S. v. Gatlin*, 216 F.3d 207 (2d Cir 2000) *with U.S. v. Corey*, 232 F.3d 1166 (9th Cir 2000). However, the question was substantially mooted for most purposes by the passage of the Military Extraterritorial Jurisdiction Act of 2000, Pub. L. 106–503, 112 Stat. 2488, which subjects persons accompanying the armed forces abroad to U.S. civilian criminal jurisdiction, even if outside the "special maritime and territorial jurisdiction."

[67] *See* U.S. Dept. of State, Initial Report of the United States of America to the U.N. Committee against Torture, U.N. Doc. CAT/C/28/Add.5 (1999), at para. 178.

to Section 2340A leaves a serious vacuum in carrying out the obligations of the U.S. under CAT.

Unfortunately the U.S. has never enforced 18 U.S.C. § 2340A, and has thereby fallen far short of its obligations under international law and its professed ideals. The United States has failed to utilize 18 U.S.C. § 2340A to prosecute either U.S. agents suspected of committing torture outside the jurisdiction of the U.S. or foreign torturers living within the United States. Indeed, Amnesty International reported in 2002 that in the eight years following the enactment of 18 U.S.C. § 2340 and § 2340A, not a single case had been brought under that section.[68]

Uniform Code of Military Justice

The UCMJ may be used to prosecute in courts-martial certain acts of ill-treatment carried out, whether within the United States or overseas, by American military personnel and possibly certain civilians accompanying such personnel. This federal statute is essentially a complete set of criminal laws that includes both crimes that are normally part of a criminal code as well as uniquely military and wartime offenses.

As a jurisdictional matter, the UCMJ applies worldwide (10 U.S.C. § 805), and persons subject to the UCMJ include any U.S. service member (10 U.S.C. § 802) as well as certain civilians "[i]n time of war . . . serving with or accompanying an armed force in the field" (10 U.S.C. § 802(a)(10)) and POWs (10 U.S.C. § 802(a)(9)).[69] Because courts-martial have jurisdiction to try "any person who by the law of war is subject to trial by a military tribunal" for any offense against the laws of war (10 U.S.C. § 818), the UCMJ would seem to apply also to "unlawful combatants" deemed by the Administration not to qualify for POW status under Geneva III.

The broad statutory application of the UCMJ to civilians associated in various ways with the armed forces has been judicially limited in deference to the requirements of Article III, Section II, of the Constitution and the Fifth and Sixth Amendments protecting the right to trial by jury. As so limited, the UCMJ does not apply to civilians who have no military status in peacetime, even if they are accompanying United States forces overseas as employees or dependents. Although courts' interpretations of the terms "serving", "accompanying" and "in the field" suggest a broad application, the "time of war" requirement is construed narrowly when applied to civilians.[70] As

---

[68] *Amnesty International Report Charges U.S. is "Safe Haven" for Torturers Fleeing Justice; Eight Years On, U.S. Has Failed to Prosecute Single Individual for Torture*, Amnesty International Press Release (2002) (*available at* http://www.amnestyusa.org/news/2002/usa04102002.html). *See also* William J. Aceves United States of America: A Safe Haven For Torturers (Amnesty International USA Publications 2002), at 50.

[69] The UCMJ does not define the POW. Thus it is uncertain whether POW in the UCMJ has the same meaning as in Geneva III

[70] *United States v. Averette*, 19 U.S.C.M.A. 363, 365–66, 41 C.M.R. 363, 365–66 (1970) (the phrase "in time of war" is limited to "a war formally declared by Congress"; even though the Vietnam conflict "qualified as a war as that word is generally used and understood[,] . . . such a recognition should not serve as a shortcut for a formal declaration of war, at least in the sensitive area of subjecting civilians to military jurisdiction"). *Cf. United States v. Anderson*, 17 U.S.C.M.A. 588, 589, 38 C.M.R. 386, 387 (1968) (United States' involvement in Vietnam conflict "constitutes a 'time of war' . . . within the meaning of" Article 43(a) of the UCMJ, which provides that there is no statute of limitations over certain offenses committed "in time of war").

recently as 1998, the Court of Appeals for the Armed Forces[71] analyzed the propriety of the application of the UCMJ to civilians and stated:

> As a matter of constitutional law, the Supreme Court has held that Congress may not extend court-martial jurisdiction to cover civilians who have no military status in peacetime, even if they are accompanying United States forces overseas as employees or dependents.

Willenbring v. Neurauter, 48 M.J. 152, 157, 1998 CAAF LEXIS 43 (C.A.A.F. 1998). The line of cases in this area generally focuses on the application of the UCMJ to civilian contractors and civilian dependents of service members. *See, e.g., Robb v. United States*, 456 F.2d 768 (Ct. Cl. 1972) (civilian engineer employed by U.S. Navy in Vietnam was not subject to UCMJ); *Reid v. Covert*, 354 U.S. 1 (1957) (no jurisdiction over civilian dependents of service members stationed overseas in peacetime for capital offenses). No cases directly address whether CIA operatives conducting para military operations with the regular armed forces or interrogations within a military base are considered civilians for purposes of UCMJ application. In *Reid v. Covert*, the Supreme Court stated, "[e]ven if it were possible, we need not attempt here to precisely define the boundary between 'civilians' and members of the 'land and naval Forces.' We recognize that there might be circumstances where a person could be 'in' the armed services... even though he had not formally been inducted into the military or did not wear a uniform." *See* 354 U.S. at 22.[72] In any event, where a CIA operative is a detached service member who has not been formally discharged from military service (as is often the case in practice), the UCMJ would generally apply to such person in time of war or peace.

The UCMJ provides the strongest substantive basis for potential prosecution of torture or CID treatment in federal criminal law, specifically outlawing cruel or unusual punishment, torture under 18 U.S.C. § 2340 and a variety of related offenses. Article 55 of the UCMJ provides that:

> Punishment by flogging, or by branding, marking, or tattooing on the body, or any other cruel or unusual punishment, may not be adjudged by any court-martial or inflicted upon any person subject to this chapter. The use of irons, single or double, except for the purpose of safe custody, is prohibited.

10 U.S.C. § 855.[73] Article 55 is unique in its specific definition of "cruel *or* unusual punishment" as an offense.[74] While most military courts have followed the Supreme Court's analytical framework of protections under the Eighth Amendment as they

---

[71] The Court of Appeals for the Armed Forces (formerly the Court of Military Appeals) is a civilian Article I court hearing appeals from the intermediate appellate courts for each of the Army, Navy (and Marines) and Air Force, subject to possible appeal to the United States Supreme Court.

[72] As previously noted, the Military Extraterritorial Jurisdiction Act of 2000, *see supra* note 66, eliminated any gap in jurisdiction resulting from *Reid v. Covert* by conferring jurisdiction on federal courts over civilians accompanying the armed forces abroad.

[73] The protections of Article 55 apply to "any person subject to" the UCMJ. And as stated previously, the UCMJ would seem to apply to unlawful combatants under 10 U.S.C. § 818.

[74] The Articles of War preceding the UCMJ prohibited "cruel and unusual punishment," but the phrase was changed to "cruel *or* unusual punishment" in Article 55 (emphasis added). *See* Articles of War 41, Manual for Courts-Martial, U.S. Army, 1929 at 212, and 1949 at 284. The legislative history of Article 55 provides no rationale why the word "and" was changed to "or." *United States v. White*, 54 M.J. 469, 2001 CAAF LEXIS 497 (C.A.A.F. 2001).

pertain to cruel and unusual punishment,[75] several military courts have found that Article 55 provides greater protections than those given under the Eighth Amendment.[76] It is notable that Article 55 applies at least the equivalent of the protection afforded by the Eighth Amendment even if the victim is not otherwise entitled to constitutional rights (*e.g.*, a non-citizen apprehended and detained outside the U.S. and arguably not entitled to such rights).[77]

Moreover, the UCMJ effectively provides a basis for the prosecution of military personnel in courts-martial for the offense of torture in violation of 18 U.S.C. § 2340. Article 134 of the UCMJ (10 U.S.C. § 934) provides:

> Though not specifically mentioned in this chapter, all disorders and neglects to the prejudice of good order and discipline in the armed forces, all conduct of a nature to bring discredit upon the armed forces, and crimes and offenses not capital, of which persons subject to this chapter may be guilty, shall be taken cognizance of by a general, special, or summary court-martial, according to the nature and degree of the offense, and shall be punished at the discretion of that court.

Article 134 makes punishable acts in three categories of offenses not specifically covered in any other article of the UCMJ: Clause 1 offenses involving disorders and neglect to the prejudice of good order and discipline; Clause 2 offenses involving conduct of a nature to bring discredit upon the armed forces; and Clause 3 offenses entailing non-capital crimes or offenses that violate Federal law.

In order to successfully charge an individual under Clauses 1 and 2 of this Article, the government must show: (i) that the accused did or failed to do certain acts; and (ii) that, under the circumstances, the accused's conduct was to the prejudice of good order and discipline in the armed forces or was of a nature to bring discredit upon the armed forces.[78] Under Clause 1, the acts must be directly prejudicial to good order and discipline, rather than remotely so. Under Clause 2, discredit is interpreted to mean "injure the reputation of," and encompasses conduct that brings the service "into disrepute or which tends to lower it in public esteem."[79] With respect to Clause 3 offenses, as a general rule, any offense created by Federal statute may be prosecuted as an Article 134 offense. *United States v. Perkins*, 47 C.M.R. 259 (Ct. of Mil. Rev. 1973).[80]

---

[75] *See United States v. Kinsch*, 54 M.J. 641, 2000 CCA LEXIS 237 (A.C.C.A. 2000). *See also* Section I(C)(3)(b) of this Report for a fuller discussion of the Eighth Amendment prohibition of cruel and unusual treatment and punishment.

[76] *See United States v. Wappler*, 2 C.M.A. 393, 9 C.M.R. 23, 1953 CMA LEXIS 897 (C.M.A. 1953); *White*, 54 M.J. at 473; *United States v. Avila*, 53 M.J. 99, 2000 CAAF LEXIS 569 (C.A.A.F. 2000).

[77] Compare the federal criminal civil rights statutes, 18 U.S.C. §§ 241 and 242, and the civil statute 42 U.S.C. § 1983, all of which apply only where the victim is entitled to constitutional rights.

[78] Manual for Courts-Martial, United States, (1995 edition) (the "Manual"), Paragraph 60.b (1–2). The Manual is issued by the President as a regulation under the authority granted by Congress under Article 3 of the UCMJ.

[79] Manual, Paragraph 60.c (3).

[80] According to the Manual, however, the doctrine of preemption "prohibits application of Article 134 to conduct covered by Articles 80 through 132. For example, larceny is covered in Article 121, and if an element of that offense is lacking – for example, intent – there can be no larceny or larceny type offense, either under Article 121 or, because of preemption, under Article 134." Manual, Paragraph 60.c (5)(a). In effect, Article 134 may not be employed to salvage a charge where the charge could not be sustained under the substantive offense provisions of the UCMJ or Federal statute. Accordingly,

Thus, a service member whose conduct is alleged to violate 18 U.S.C. § 2340, the federal enactment of CAT, could be prosecuted under Article 134 of the UCMJ, as a Clause 3 violation. Moreover, multiple counts alleging Article 134 violations also could be brought in such a situation, as such conduct could be construed as prejudicial to good order and discipline and/or of a nature to bring discredit upon the armed forces. *Perkins*, 47 C.M.R. at 263–264.

Finally, criminal charges for torture or CID conduct could be brought under a variety of other provisions[81] including "cruelty."[82] The last of these offenses is generally intended to be applied to mistreatment of U.S. service members by their superiors, but by its terms it is not so limited and has been applied to intentional mistreatment of detainees.[83] And in instances where specific orders are in place regarding the treatment of detainees, as is recommended in this Report, failure to obey such orders is punishable under 10 U.S.C. § 892. A number of service members in Iraq are or have been investigated or tried for assaulting detainees, under the assault provision of the UCMJ (Article 128), and in at least one case the alleged assault occurred in the context of an interrogation.[84]

The UCMJ is thus the substantively most extensive body of federal criminal law relating to the interrogation of detainees by U.S. military personnel and, in time of

conduct which violated Article 55 discussed above or any other substantive provision of the UCMJ could not be charged under Article 134. These remain alternative, not cumulative provisions.

[81] For example, murder (10 U.S.C. § 918), manslaughter (10 U.S.C. § 919), dereliction of duty (10 U.S.C. § 892).

For purposes of this Report, we assume that U.S. military interrogations of detainees are conducted for intelligence gathering purposes and not with an investigatory intent to elicit incriminating responses in anticipation of criminal prosecution. However, should the focus of the interrogation shift from an intelligence to a law enforcement nature, Miranda warnings under Article 31 of the UCMJ (10 U.S.C. § 831) would be required. The failure to give such warnings is a criminal offense under Article 98 of the UCMJ (10 U.S.C. § 898).

[82] *See* Article 93 of the UCMJ (10 U.S.C. § 893). Two Marines face charges for assault, cruelty and dereliction of duty involving the treatment and death of an Iraqi prisoner. *See* Associated Press Newswires, *Two Marines Face Trial After Iraqi Dies*, Apr. 14, 2004; Tony Perry, *Iraqi Prisoner Died After Marine Grabbed His Throat, Officials Say*, L.A. TIMES, Oct. 22, 2003, at B06. It is not believed that the incident involved interrogation, but it is notable that such alleged offenses involved Marine infantry reservists who had not been trained in the treatment of prisoners (apart from one with relevant peacetime background) and are reported to have been given only a brief orientation before being assigned to this duty. As advocated elsewhere in this Report, proper training of U.S. military and intelligence personnel is essential to achieve compliance with the U.S.'s obligations under CAT.

[83] Article 93 prohibits a person subject to the jurisdiction of the UCMJ from committing acts of "cruelty toward, or oppression or maltreatment of, any person subject to his orders." The phrase "any person subject to his orders" in Article 93 is defined as: "not only those persons under the direct or immediate command of the accused but extends to all persons, subject to the...[UCMJ] or not, who by reason of some duty are required to obey the lawful orders of the accused, regardless whether the accused is in the direct chain of command over the person." Manual for Courts-Martial, United States, (1995 edition), Part IV, P 17c(1).

[84] An officer in Iraq was charged under Article 28 (10 U.S.C. § 928) for firing his pistol near an Iraqi detainee's head in the course of an interrogation in order to elicit details about a planned ambush or assassination. Thomas E. Ricks, *Army Accuses Officer In Iraq Of Firing Pistol Near Prisoner*, Wash. Post, Oct. 30, 2003, at A14. The officer faced a possible court-martial and up to eight years imprisonment. Following a UCMJ Article 32 hearing (which is akin to a grand jury or preliminary hearing), the division's commanding general ordered that the officer be fined and allowed to retire. *See U.S. Officer Fined for Harsh Interrogation Tactics* (Dec. 13, 2003) (*available at* http://www.cnn.com/2003/US/12/12/sprj.nirq.west.ruling).

war, its reach could possibly extend to civilians such as CIA agents accompanying such personnel. It prohibits such persons from subjecting detainees to torture and "cruel or unusual punishment" within or without the United States and regardless of the applicability of constitutional rights.

SUMMARY

CAT's prohibition against torture is absolute. By ratifying CAT, the United States has accepted that the prohibition of torture is non-derogable. Moreover, by implementing prohibitions against torture in immigration, extradition, criminal and civil tort law contexts, the U.S. has given CAT's prohibition against torture the force of U.S. law. Furthermore, by stipulating that CAT's prohibition on CID treatment or punishment means the cruel and unusual treatment or punishment prohibited by the U.S. Constitution, the U.S. has made relevant the case law providing that detainees cannot be subjected to interrogation techniques: that force them to answer law enforcement questions by "fear of hurt, torture or exhaustion," *Adamson v. California, supra*; that are "brutal and offensive to human dignity," *Rochin v. California, supra*; that fall below the "evolving standards of decency that mark the progress of a maturing society," *Trop v. Dulles, supra*; or which deliberately inflict force or pain (in the context of resotring prison order or safety), *Hudson v. McMillian, supra*. However, U.S. enforcement of CAT in our domestic criminal law – particularly with respect to acts of torture or CID treatment by U.S. civilians or by U.S. officials in extra-territorial areas under U.S. jurisdiction – has been incomplete. We urge the U.S. to fill in the gaps in preventing and punishing torture and CID treatment left by 18 U.S.C. § 2340A and to fully utilize the UCMJ to fulfill its obligations under CAT.

THE GENEVA CONVENTIONS

The four Geneva Conventions of 1949 are the core of the international law of armed conflict applicable to the treatment of detainees, albeit not the complete body of applicable law. The applicability of the Geneva Conventions to persons captured by the United States in connection with the War in Afghanistan and the ongoing conflict in Afghanistan, however, is highly controversial. The most hotly contested issue is whether those al Qaeda and Taliban detainees who were captured before the creation of the Karzai government are entitled to POW status under Geneva Convention III Relative to the Treatment of Prisoners of War ("Geneva III"). This issue is of particular significance because Geneva III flatly prohibits "any form of coercion" of POWs in interrogation – the most protective standard of treatment found in international law. Likewise, Geneva Convention IV Relative to the Protection of Civilian Persons in Time of War ("Geneva IV") protects "civilian" detainees who qualify as "protected persons" from "coercion."[85] We also should note that the issues regarding Geneva III and Geneva IV are affected by whether the person was detained either before or after the Karzai government was established. Before the Karzai government, the U.S. was engaged in an international armed conflict with Afghanistan, which

---

[85] *See* Section II(C) for a discussion of who qualifies as a "protected person" under Geneva IV.

was governed by the Taliban (albeit the U.S. did not recognize that government). After the establishment of the Karzai government, the conflict in Afghanistan became an internal one – as the U.S. and other international organizations were present in Afghanistan with the consent of the Karzai government to assist in maintaining order. Geneva III and Geneva IV apply only in situations of international armed conflict and, therefore, ceased to apply once the Afghan conflict became an internal one. *See* Geneva IV, Art. 6.

In this section, we will examine the Administration's position that al Qaeda and Taliban detainees are not POWs under Geneva III and some critiques of the Administration's position. We submit that, regardless of whether a detainee enjoys status as a POW or civilian protected person under the Geneva Conventions, the Conventions nevertheless are relevant to the interrogation of detainees in the following respects:

First, the requirements of humane treatment embodied in Common Article 3 of the Geneva Conventions and Article 75 of Additional Protocol I protect all detainees captured in situations of international or internal armed conflict, regardless of "legal" status.[86] Of course, all detainees – including those captured outside of Afghan territory or in connection with the "War on Terror" – are entitled to the protection provided by human rights law, including CAT, the ICCPR and customary international law.

Second, notwithstanding its position on the POW status of Taliban and al Qaeda detainees, the Administration has undertaken that it will treat all detainees in a manner consistent with the principles of Geneva III. Accordingly, the interrogation techniques

---

[86] "Common Article 3" provides that detainees "shall in all circumstances be treated humanely" and prohibits the following acts "at any time and in any place whatsoever": "violence to life and person, in particular murder of all kinds, mutilation, cruel treatment and torture;" and "outrages upon personal dignity, in particular, humiliating or degrading treatment." Common Article 3 also provides that the "wounded and sick shall be collected and cared for."

Although neither the United States nor Afghanistan is a party to Additional Protocol I, it is generally acknowledged that relevant sections of Protocol I constitute either binding customary international law or good practice, in particular, the minimum safeguards guaranteed by Article 75(2). *See* Michael J. Matheson, *Remarks on the United States Position on the Relation of Customary International Law to the 1977 Protocols Additional to the 1949 Geneva Conventions, reprinted in The Sixth Annual American Red Cross-Washington College of Law Conference on International Humanitarian Law: A Workshop on Customary International Law and the 1977 Protocols Additional to the 1949 Geneva Conventions*, 2 Am. U. J. Int'l L. & Pol'y 415, 425–6 (1987).

Article 75 provides that "persons who are in the power of a Party to the conflict and who do not benefit from more favourable treatment under the Conventions" "shall be treated humanely in all circumstances" and that each state Party "shall respect the person, honour, convictions and religious practices of all such persons." Paragraph 2 of Article 75 prohibits, "at any time and in any place whatsoever, whether committed by civilian or military agents": "violence to the life, health, or physical or mental well-being of persons, in particular . . . torture of all kinds, whether physical or mental," "corporal punishment," and "mutilation"; "outrages upon personal dignity, in particular, humiliating and degrading treatment . . . and any form of indecent assault"; and "threats to commit any of the foregoing acts."

The U.S. rejection of Additional Protocol I was explained in a presidential note to the Senate in the following terms: "Protocol I. . . . would grant combatant status to irregular forces even if they do not satisfy the traditional requirements to distinguish themselves from the civilian population and otherwise comply with the laws of war. This would endanger civilians among whom terrorists and other irregulars attempt to conceal themselves. These problems are so fundamental in character that they cannot be remedied through reservations. . . ." *See* 1977 U.S.T. LEXIS 465.

reportedly being used on detainees at Bagram and other U.S. detention facilities should be considered in light of the text and spirit of the Geneva Conventions.

Third, if there is doubt as to whether a detainee meets Geneva III criteria for POW status, that detainee is entitled to interim POW status until a "competent tribunal" determines his or her legal status. Because the U.S. government has not convened "competent tribunals" to determine the status of any detainees, all detainees for whom POW status is in doubt are entitled to interim POW status.[87]

Finally, even accepting the interpretation that the Third and Fourth Geneva Conventions contain gaps leaving certain detainees captured in the War in Afghanistan (*i.e.*, citizens of co-belligerents and neutrals) without POW or "protected person" civilian status, the Geneva Conventions are supplemented by human rights law and customary international legal norms which have the force of law in the United States. For example, even where a detainee may not be entitled to a hearing under Geneva III, he is entitled to a hearing to determine the justification for his detention under Article 9 of the ICCPR. Many detainees may not be combatants at all and may be simply innocent bystanders mistakenly detained or wrongfully turned over to the U.S. military by the Northern Alliance.[88] They deserve prompt hearings in which they are given an opportunity to establish their non-combatant status.

APPLICATION OF THE GENEVA CONVENTIONS TO THE AFGHAN CONFLICT GENERALLY

Both the U.S. and Afghanistan are parties to the Geneva Conventions. Article 2 common to all four Conventions provides that the Conventions "apply to all cases of declared war or of any other armed conflict" between two or more parties to the Conventions so long as a state of war is recognized by a party to the conflict. The Conventions also apply to all cases of partial or total occupation of the territory of a signatory, even if the occupation meets with no armed resistance. *See* Geneva Conventions, Article 2. Signatories to the Conventions are bound by its terms regardless of whether an additional party to the conflict is a signatory. *Id.* The Administration's position is that the Geneva Conventions apply to the War in Afghanistan.[89]

---

[87] *See* Geneva III, Art. 5; *see also* U.S. Dept. of Army, Field Manual 27–10, "Law of Land Warfare", Art. 71 (1956); U.S. Dept. of Army, REGULATION 190–8 Military Police, "Enemy Prisoners of War, Retained Personnel, Civilian Internees and Other Detainees," § 1–5 (a)(2) (1997).

[88] *See. e.g.*, Dep't of Defense, Secretary Rumsfeld Media Availability en route to Camp X-Ray (Jan. 27, 2002) (*available at* http://www.defenselink.mil/news/Jan2002/t01282002_t0127sd2.html) ("Sometimes when you capture a big, large group there will be someone who just happened to be in there that didn't belong in there.") (remarks of Respondent, Secretary of Defense Donald H. Rumsfeld); Carlotta Gall, *Freed Afghan, 15, Recalls a Year at Guantánamo*, N.Y. Times, Feb. 11, 2004, at A03 (quoting released teenager claiming to have been captured by non-U.S. forces and handed over to the Americans while looking for a job); Jan McGirk, *Pakistani Writes of His U.S. Ordeal*, Boston Globe, Nov. 17, 2002, at A30 ("Pakistan intelligence sources said Northern Alliance commanders could receive $5,000 for each Taliban prisoner and $20,000 for a[n] [al] Qaeda fighter. As a result, bounty hunters rounded up any men who came near the battlegrounds and forced them to confess.").

[89] *See, e.g.*, Sean D. Murphy, *Contemporary Practice of the United States Relating to International Law*, 96 AM. J. INT'L L. 461, 476–77 (2002).

GENEVA III

Relevant Legal Standards

Under Geneva III, combatants are entitled to POW status if they are members of the armed forces (other than medical personnel and chaplains). The specific requirements for combatant/POW status are set forth in Article 4 of Geneva III[90] and Articles 43 and 44 of Additional Protocol I.[91]

If there is any doubt as to whether captured persons meet Article 4's criteria for POW status, such persons are entitled to interim POW status until a "competent tribunal" determines their legal status.[92]

---

[90] Article 4-A of Geneva III provides, in part:

> Prisoners of war, in the sense of the present Convention, are persons belonging to one of the following categories, who have fallen into the power of the enemy:
>
> Members of the armed forces of a Party to the conflict as well as members of militias or volunteer corps forming part of such armed forces.
>
> Members of other militias and members of other volunteer corps, including those of organized resistance movements, belonging to a Party to the conflict and operating in or outside their own territory, even if this territory is occupied, provided that such militias or volunteer corps, including such organized resistance movements, fulfill the following conditions:
> > (a) of being commanded by a person responsible for his subordinates;
> > (b) that of having a fixed distinctive sign recognizable at a distance;
> > (c) that of carrying arms openly;
> > (d) that of conducting their operations in accordance with the laws and customs of war.
> Members of regular armed forces who profess allegiance to a government or an authority not recognized by the Detaining Power. . . .

[91] Article 43 of Additional Protocol I provides: "The armed forces of a Party to a conflict consist of all organized armed forces, groups and units which are under a command responsible to that Party for the conduct or its subordinates, even if that Party is represented by a government or an authority not recognized by an adverse Party. Such armed forces shall be subject to an internal disciplinary system which, inter alia, shall enforce compliance with the rules of international law applicable in armed conflict."

[92] *See* Geneva III, Art. 5; *see also*, U.S. Dept. of Army, Field Manual 27–10, "Law of Land Warfare", Art. 71 (1956); U.S. Dept. of Army, REGULATION 190–8 Military Police, "Enemy Prisoners of War, Retained Personnel, Civilian Internees and Other Detainees," § 1–5 (a)(2) (1997). Under U.S. military regulations, a "competent tribunal" pursuant to Article 5 of Geneva III consists of three commissioned officers. The regulations also require that persons whose status is to be determined be advised of their rights; be permitted to attend all open sessions, call witnesses and question witnesses called by the tribunal; be permitted (but not compelled) to testify or otherwise address the tribunal; and be provided with an interpreter. The regulations provide for the tribunal's determination of a detainee's status in closed session by a majority vote and require a preponderance of the evidence to support the tribunal's finding. *See* Erin Chlopak, *Dealing with the Detainees at Guantánamo Bay: Humanitarian and Human Rights Obligations Under the Geneva Conventions*, HUM RTS. BR. (Spring 2002), at 6, 8.

It should be noted that the "competent tribunal" outlined in ARMY REG. 190-8, § 1–6 is a quick, administrative process that is highly dependent upon the availability of witnesses during ongoing combat and support operations. Unsworn statements may be presented as evidence, and a record of the proceedings is developed. Although the tribunal may or may not include military lawyers such as members of the Staff Judge Advocate General ("JAG"), JAG lawyers will subsequently review the record. The record may also be the basis for any further proceedings for war crimes or for any other penalty.

Fundamentally, the tribunal determines only status and does not adjudicate liability. Tribunals are required under Geneva III only when status of the detainee is in doubt. When, for example, 10,000 uniformed members of a regular enemy infantry division surrender as a body, there is no need for a tribunal. When, however, non-uniformed, but possibly military, personnel mix with refugees, that is a classic situation for such tribunals.

Geneva III mandates that POWs be treated humanely at all times. This includes freedom from physical and mental torture, acts of violence, intimidation and insult, and exposure to public humiliation.[93] Pursuant to Article 14, POWs also "are entitled in all circumstances to respect for their persons and their honour. ... [and] shall retain the full civil capacity which they enjoyed at the time of their capture."

With respect to interrogation, in particular, Article 17 of Geneva III provides: "No physical or mental torture, nor any other form of coercion, may be inflicted on prisoners of war to secure from them information of any kind whatever. Prisoners of war who refuse to answer may not be threatened, insulted, or exposed to any unpleasant or disadvantageous treatment of any kind." Under Article 17, POWs are only obligated to provide their name, rank, date of birth, and army, personal or serial identification number or equivalent information. Geneva III does not, however, prohibit non-coercive interrogation of POWs. POWs may be interrogated, but they are not obliged to respond to such interrogation, nor may they be threatened, coerced into responding or punished for failing to respond. The Geneva Conventions also do not "preclude classic plea bargaining" – *i.e.*, the offer of leniency or other incentives in return for cooperation.[94]

Thus, to the extent detainees from the War in Afghanistan are considered POWs or to the extent their POW status is in "doubt" pending the determination of status by a competent tribunal, interrogation tactics which rise to the level of "coercion" are prohibited by Geneva III.

The United States' Position

In sharp contrast with past conflicts (such as Vietnam and Korea) in which it was U.S. policy to presume that military prisoners were entitled to POW status regardless of the possible non-qualification of their forces under Geneva III, from the very outset of the War in Afghanistan, United States officials labeled captured al Qaeda and Taliban prisoners "unlawful combatants," and stated that the Geneva Conventions were, therefore, entirely inapplicable to their treatment.[95] The United States reasoned that al Qaeda was not entitled to the protections of the Geneva Conventions because: (1) Geneva III could not apply to members of a non-State organization, such as al Qaeda, (2) the conflict was not an internal conflict such that al Qaeda members could benefit from the protection of Common Article 3, and (3) in any event, al Qaeda members failed to meet the requirements set forth in Article 4(A)(2) of Geneva III.[96]

---

[93] Specifically, Article 13 of Geneva III provides:

> Prisoners of war must at all times be humanely treated. Any unlawful act or omission by the Detaining Power causing death or seriously endangering the health of a prisoner of war in its custody is prohibited, and will be regarded as a serious breach of the present Convention. In particular, no prisoner of war may be subjected to physical mutilation or to medical or scientific experiments of any kind which are not justified by the medical, dental or hospital treatment of the prisoner concerned and carried out in his interest.
> Likewise, prisoners of war must at all times be protected, particularly against acts of violence or intimidation and against insults and public curiosity.

[94] Manooher Mofidi and Amy E. Eckert, *"Unlawful Combatants" or "Prisoners of War": The Law and Politics of Labels*, 36 CORNELL INT'L L.J. 59, 89 (2003).

[95] Murphy, *supra* note 89, at 476–77.

[96] *Id.*

The United States argued further that, since Afghanistan was not a functioning state during the conflict and the Taliban was not recognized as a legitimate government, Geneva III could not apply to the Taliban.[97]

After vigorous criticism was leveled against these arguments, Secretary of State Colin Powell requested that the Administration reconsider its position.[98] On February 7, 2002, in response to Powell's comments, the Administration partially reversed its initial position. Although the Administration continues to argue that the Geneva Conventions are inapplicable to al Qaeda captives, President Bush announced that Geneva III was applicable to the Taliban because both the U.S. and Afghanistan were signatories to the Convention and the parties had been involved in an armed conflict. However, President Bush further argued that because the Taliban had violated the laws of war and associated closely with al Qaeda, "[u]nder the terms of the Geneva Convention ... the Taliban detainees do not qualify as POWs."[99] The decision in *United States v. Lindh*, 212 F. Supp. 2d 541 (E.D. Va. 2002), which specifically addresses the issue of whether the Taliban are entitled to POW status under Geneva III, sheds further light on the U.S. position.[100]

---

[97] *Id.*

[98] Powell asked that the Administration recognize that the Geneva Conventions apply to the conflict between the U.S. and Taliban regime and that the Administration convene a "competent tribunal" to determine the status of the prisoners pursuant to Article 5 of Geneva III. *See* Katharine Q. Seelye, *A Nation Challenged: The Prisoners; Powell Asks Bush to Review Stand on War Captives*, N.Y. TIMES, Jan. 27, 2002, at A01; William Safire, Editorial, *Colin Powell Dissents*, N.Y. Times, Jan. 28, 2002, at A15.

[99] *See supra* note 18.

U.S. Secretary of Defense Donald Rumsfeld, responding to a request for clarification, referred to Article 4(a)(2) of Geneva III to explain why the Taliban could not qualify for POW status: "The Taliban [like al Qaeda] also did not wear uniforms, they did not have insignia, they did not carry their weapons openly, and they were tied tightly at the waist to al Qaeda. They behaved like them, they worked with them, they functioned with them, they cooperated with respect to communications, they cooperated with respect to supplies and ammunition." Secretary of Defense Donald H. Rumsfeld, Remarks on Ferry from Air Terminal to Main Base, Guantánamo Bay, Cuba (Jan. 27, 2002) (transcript *available at* http://www.defenselink.mil/transcripts/2002/t01282002_t0127sd2.html).

[100] Applying the four-part test from Article 4(a)(2) of Geneva III to the determination, the *Lindh* court found that the Taliban had an insufficient internal system of military command or discipline, that the "Taliban typically wore no distinctive sign that could be recognized by opposing combatants," and that the "Taliban regularly targeted civilian populations in clear contravention of the laws and customs of war." *Lindh*, 212 F. Supp. 2d at 558. Implicitly the *Lindh* Court held that the four conditions listed in Geneva III, Article 4(a)(2) also apply to "regular armed forces." *Id.* at 557. In concluding that the Taliban were not regular armed forces, the *Lindh* court stated "[i]t would indeed be absurd for members of a so-called 'regular armed force' to enjoy lawful combatant immunity even though the force had no established command structure and its members wore no recognizable symbol or insignia, concealed their weapons, and did not abide by the customary laws of war. Simply put, the label 'regular armed force' cannot be used to mask unlawful combatant status." *Id.*, at n. 35.

See also Int'l Comm. of the Red Cross, *Commentaries to Article 4(a)(1) Convention (III) relative to the Treatment of Prisoners of War, Geneva, 12 August 1949*, ICRC Database on Int'l Humanitarian Law (*available at* http://www.icrc.org/ihl.nsf/b466ed681ddfcfd241256739003e6368/3ca76fa4dae5b32ec12563ed00425040? Open Document) ("It is the duty of each State to take steps so that members of its armed forces can be immediately recognized as such and to see to it that they are easily distinguishable from members of the enemy armed forces or from civilians."). *See also, generally*, INGRID DETTER, The Law Of War (Cambridge Univ. Press, 2nd ed., 2000), at 136; Christopher Greenwood, *International Law and the War Against Terrorism*, 78 INTERNATIONAL AFFAIRS 301, 316 (2002); Ruth Wedgwood, *Al Qaeda, Terrorism, and Military Commissions*, 96 AM. J. INT'L L. 328, 335 (2002).

Critiques of the United States' Position

International humanitarian and human rights organizations and legal bodies, including the International Committee of the Red Cross ("ICRC"),[101] the Inter-American Court of Human Rights,[102] Amnesty International,[103] the International Commission of Jurists,[104] the Secretary General of the United Nations,[105] the United Nations High Commissioner for Human Rights,[106] as well as certain U.S. and foreign international law scholars[107] have criticized the U.S. position on several grounds.

Article 5 Presumes POW Status Until the Determination of Status by a Competent Tribunal

Critics of the Administration position argue that non-civilian detainees from the War in Afghanistan either clearly qualify as POWs or their POW status is in "doubt." Geneva III mandates that a detainee whose status is in "doubt" must be treated as a POW until his status is decided otherwise by a competent tribunal under Article 5. Indeed, Article 5's presumption that captured combatants are entitled to POW status until their status is determined by a competent tribunal is one that has been

---

[101] ICRC, *Geneva Convention on Prisoners of War* (Feb. 9, 2002) (*available at* http://www.icrc.org/Web/Eng/siteeng().nsf/iwpList454/26D99836025EA80Dc1256B6600610C90) ("International Humanitarian Law foresees that the members of armed forces as well as militias associated to them which are captured by the adversary in an international armed conflict are protected by the Third Geneva Convention. There are divergent views between the United States and the ICRC on the procedures which apply on how to determine that the persons detained are not entitled to prisoner of war status.")

[102] IACHR, DECISION ON REQUEST FOR PRECAUTIONARY MEASURES (DETAINEES AT GUANTANAMO BAY, CUBA), 41 I.L.M. 532, 533 (2002) ("It is . . . well-known that doubt exists as to the legal status of the detainees.")

[103] Amnesty International, *Memorandum to the U.S. Government on the rights of people in U.S. custody in Afghanistan and Guantánamo Bay* (*available at* http://web.amnesty.org/aidoc/aidoc_pdf.nsf/Index/AMR510532002ENGLISH/$File/AMR51 0532.pdf) (The United States' "selective approach to the Geneva Conventions threatens to undermine the effectiveness of international humanitarian law protections for any U.S. or other combatants captured in the future.")

[104] ICJ, *Rule of Law Must be Respected in Relation to Detainees in Guantánamo Bay* (Jan. 17, 2002) (*available at* http://www.icj.org./ews.php?id_article=2612&lang=eng) ("The United States has refused [POW] status to Taliban fighters even though, as members of the armed forces, they are entitled to it.")

[105] Kofi Annan, Press Encounter outside No. 10 Downing Street, London, (Feb. 25, 2002) (unofficial transcript *available at* http://www.un.org/aps/sg/offthecuff.asp?nid=103) ("The Red Cross has indicated that anyone who was arrested in the battlefield, or picked up in the battlefield, is a prisoner of war and they do not make a difference between the al Qaeda and the Taliban. And under the convention, where there is a disagreement, normally you have an independent tribunal to resolve this.").

[106] Mary Robinson, Statement of the High Commissioner for Human Rights on Detention of Taliban and al Qaeda Prisoners at U.S. Base in Guantanamo Bay, Cuba (Jan. 16, 2002) (*available at* http://www.unhchr.ch/hurricane/hurricane.nsf/0/C537C6D4657C7928C1256B43003E7D0B? opendocument) ("All persons detained in this context are entitled to the protection of international human rights law and humanitarian law, in particular the relevant provisions of the International Covenant on Civil and Political Rights (ICCPR) and the Geneva Conventions of 1949.")

[107] *See, generally*, George H. Aldrich, *The Taliban, al Qaeda, and the Determination of Illegal Combatants*, 96 AM. J. INT'L L. 891 (2002); Harold Hongju Koh, *Agora: Military Commissions – The Case Against Military Commissions*, 96 AM. J. INT'L L. 337 (2002); Neil McDonald & Scott Sullivan, *Rational Interpretation in Irrational Times: The Third Geneva Convention and the War on Terror*, 44 HARV. INT'L L.J. 301 (2003); Manooher Mofidi and Amy E. Eckert, *"Unlawful Combatants" or "Prisoners of War": The Law and Politics of Labels*, 36 CORNELL INT'L L.J. 59 (2003); Michael Ratner, *Moving Away from the Rule of Law: Military Tribunals, Executive Detentions and Torture*, 24 CARDOZO L. REV. 1513 (2003).

consistently honored by the U.S. since World War II.[108] Moreover, like Article 5, customary international law also includes the principle that a competent tribunal must resolve any doubt about the status of a captured combatant.[109] We agree with critics of the Administration position that all combatants whose claim to POW status is "in doubt" must be treated as POWs until such doubt has been resolved by a "competent tribunal." Accordingly, since no tribunals have been convened for detainees from the War in Afghanistan, all such detainees must be considered POWs under Geneva III.

The Taliban Detainees Were "Regular Armed Forces" and, Therefore, Are Encompassed by Article 4(A) of Geneva III

Critics of the Administration's position that Taliban fighters are not entitled to POW status because they do not satisfy the requirements of Article 4(a)(2) of Geneva III[110] assert that Taliban captured in the War in Afghanistan are entitled to POW status either under: Article 4(a)(1) because they are "[m]embers of the armed forces" of Afghanistan; or Article 4(a)(3) as they are "[m]embers of regular armed forces who profess allegiance to a government of an authority not recognized by the Detaining Power."[111]

Policy Arguments Favoring Broad Grant of POW Status to Non-Civilian Detainees from the War in Afghanistan

Several policy arguments favor granting POW status liberally even assuming that Geneva III does not apply to Taliban or al Qaeda detainees captured in the War in Afghanistan.

First, depriving Taliban and al Qaeda of POW status because they do not obey the laws of war sets a dangerous precedent, inviting other state parties to claim

---

[108] See JENNIFER ELSEA, Treatment of "Battlefield Detainees" in the War on Terrorism, Cong. Research Serv., RL31367, at 30 (2002) (*available at* http://fpc.state.gov/documents/organization/9655.pdf) (stating that the United States "has in the past interpreted [Article 5] as requiring an individualized assessment of status before privileges can be denied"). *See also* The Judge Advocate General's School, Operational Law Handbook 22 (William O'Brien ed., 2003) (instructing judge advocates to "advise commanders that, regardless of the nature of the conflict, all enemy personnel should initially be accorded the protections of [Geneva III], at least until their status may be determined").

[109] Michael J. Matheson, while serving as Deputy Legal Advisor of the U.S. State Department, stated:

> We [the United States] do support the principle that, should any doubt arise as to whether a person is entitled to combatant status, he be so treated until his status has been determined by a competent tribunal, as well as the principle that if a person who has fallen into the power of an adversary is not held as a prisoner of war and is to be tried for an offense arising out of the hostilities, he should have the right to assert his entitlement before a judicial tribunal and to have that question adjudicated.

Matheson, *supra* note 86.

[110] Some have argued that the Taliban did comply with the requirements for Article 4(a)(2). *See, e.g.,* Robert Goldman and Brian Tittemore, Unprivileged Combatants and the Hostilities in Afghanistan: Their Status and Rights under International Humanitarian Rights Law (The Am. Soc. Of Int'l Law Task Force on Terrorism, Task Force Paper) (*available at* http://asil.org/taskforce/goldman.pdf.)

[111] Not only did the Taliban profess such an allegiance, but they were the strongest military partner in the Alliance, effectively controlling Afghanistan. *See* "Taliban Reach Zenith?," 85 National Defense 10 (Oct. 1, 2000).

that another party is not obeying the rules of war and that they are, therefore, free from the obligations of Geneva III. International humanitarian law applies regardless of whether or not the other party to the conflict respects such laws.[112] Reciprocity arrangements are generally rejected in international humanitarian law as they can so easily be abused at the expense of civilians or persons rendered "hors de combat."[113]

Second, it is in the U.S.'s self-interest to ensure that the Geneva Conventions – a regime of vital importance to the safety of our own armed forces – are interpreted as broadly as possible. Otherwise, an opposing state party could use the argument that the U.S. has violated the laws of war to deny captured U.S. soldiers POW status. In fact, North Korea and Vietnam have already used this argument as a basis to deny captured U.S. prisoners POW protections under the Geneva Conventions.[114] Indeed, it was reportedly these very examples that prompted Colin Powell, out of concern for the safety of U.S. forces, to request that President Bush reconsider the Administration's initial position.[115]

We accordingly urge liberal extension of POW treatment where that would encourage reciprocal treatment of U.S. service personnel and advance more generally foreign policy and national security interests. We further believe that, even to the extent that POW status is denied to detainees, such detainees must be accorded the protections of international criminal law, as well as international human rights and humanitarian law.

GENEVA IV

Geneva IV applies in international armed conflicts to the same extent as Geneva III. It covers "protected persons" defined as "those who, at a given moment and in any manner whatsoever, find themselves, in case of a conflict or occupation, in the hands

---

[112] Article 1 of Geneva III states "The High Contracting Parties undertake to respect and to ensure respect for the present Convention in all circumstances." *See also* Military and Paramilitary Activities (*Nicar. v. U.S.*), 1986 I.C.J. REP. 14, 14 (June 27) (holding that Geneva III applies in all circumstances regardless of the actions of the other party to the conflict). *See also, generally*, Theodor Meron, *The Humanization of Humanitarian Law*, 94 AM. J. INT'L L. 239, 248–249 (2000).

[113] As the ICRC Commentaries on Article 1 state: "it is not merely an engagement concluded on a basis of reciprocity, binding each party to the contract only in so far as the other party observes its obligations. It is rather a series of unilateral engagements solemnly contracted before the world as represented by the other Contracting Parties. Each State contracts obligations 'vis-à-vis' itself and at the same time 'vis-à-vis' the others. The motive of the Convention is so essential for the maintenance of civilization that the need is felt for its assertion, as much out of respect for it on the part of the signatory State itself as in the expectation of such respect from all parties." ICRC *Commentaries to Article 1, Convention (III) relative to the Treatment of Prisoners of War, Geneva, 12 August 1949*, ICRC Database on Int'l Humanitarian Law (*available at* http://www.icrc.org./ihl.nsf/b466ed681ddfcfd241256739003e6368/49cfe5505d5912dlc12563ed00424cdd? Open Document). *See also* Geneva III, Article 13.

[114] George H. Aldrich, *The Taliban, al Qaeda, and the Determination of Illegal Combatants*, 96 AM. J. INT'L L. 891, 895–96 (2002) (noting that North Korea and North Vietnam denied POW status to all American prisoners on the basis of the allegation that they were all war criminals).

[115] Colin Powell apparently made remarks to this effect in a memo leaked to the press on January 27, 2002. *See* Editorial, *Bush's Call on Captives*, The Boston Globe, Jan. 29, 2002, at A10.

of a Party to the conflict or Occupying Power of which they are not nationals." *See* Geneva IV, Article 4.[116]

The fact that a person may have unlawfully participated in a conflict is not relevant to Geneva IV protections, apart from a significant national security exemption. The term "protected persons" includes persons detained as spies or saboteurs as well as other persons suspected of engaging in activities hostile to the security of the detaining power. Specifically, Article 5 provides:

> Where in the territory of a Party to the conflict, the *latter* is satisfied that an individual protected person is definitely suspected of or engaged in activities hostile to the security of the State, such individual person shall not be entitled to claim such rights and privileges under the present Convention as would, if exercised in the favour of such individual person, be prejudicial to the security of such State
>
> . . . .
>
> In each case, such persons shall nevertheless be treated with humanity and, in case of trial, shall not be deprived of the rights of fair and regular trial prescribed by the present Convention. They shall also be granted the full rights and privileges of a protected person under the present Convention at the earliest date consistent with the security of the State or Occupying Power, as the case may be.

As drafted, (*i.e.*, the use of the words "the latter"), it would appear that the national security derogation is available only to the State on whose territory the conflict is occurring (*i.e.*, in the War in Afghanistan, only to the Northern Alliance), and there is no authority whether or not an allied State, such as the United States, can benefit from such exemption.

In an exception of great importance in Afghanistan, given the number of third country participants in the conflict, "protected persons" does not include "[n]ationals of a State which is not bound by the Convention," "[n]ationals of a neutral State who find themselves in the territory of a belligerent State" and "nationals of a co-belligerent State . . . while the State of which they are nationals has normal diplomatic representation in the State in whose hands they are." *See* Geneva IV, Article 4. For example, a Pakistani picked up on the battlefield in Afghanistan would fall within the exceptions to "protected person" status under Geneva IV.

However, in no event would such provision permit the State to commit "grave breaches" as defined in Article 147, which includes torture or inhuman treatment and willfully causing great suffering or serious injury to body or health, upon a "protected person". *See* Geneva IV, Art. 146. Furthermore, to the extent that any physical or moral

---

[116] Legal commentators have argued that persons who have directly participated in the War in Afghanistan and who do not qualify as POWs under Geneva III (*i.e.*, detainees considered to be "unlawful combatants" by the U.S.) should automatically be considered "protected persons" under Geneva IV, unless other exceptions apply. *See, e.g.*, Michael Ratner, *Moving Away from the Rule of Law: Military Tribunals, Executive Detentions and Torture*, 24 CARDOZO L. REV. 1513, 1518–19 (2003) ("There is no gap between the two conventions"). Recent decisions of the International Criminal Tribunal for the Former Yugoslavia (ICTFY) have held that, "if an individual is not entitled to the protections of the Third Convention as a prisoner of war (or of the First or Second Conventions) he or she necessarily falls within the ambit of [Geneva IV]." *See The Prosecutor v. Delalic*, IT-96-21-T, at para. 271 (1998); *see also Prosecutor v. Tadic*, IT-94-I-A, 38 I.L.M. 158 (1999).

coercion (otherwise prohibited by Article 31 of Geneva IV) might fall below the level of "grave breach" and thus be derogable, the ICRC commentary to the national security derogations contained in Article 5 of Geneva IV, involving persons engaged in activities hostile to the security of the state notes that:

> widespread application of the Article may eventually lead to the existence of a category of civilian internees who do not receive the normal treatment laid down by the Convention but are detained under conditions which are almost impossible to check. It must be emphasized most strongly, therefore, that Article 5 can only be applied in individual cases of an exceptional nature, when the existence of specific charges makes it almost certain that penal proceedings will follow. This article should never be applied as a result of mere suspicion.

Like POWs under Geneva III, "protected persons" under Geneva IV cannot be subjected to coercive interrogation tactics. Specifically, Article 31 of Geneva IV provides that "[n]o physical or moral coercion shall be exercised against protected persons, in particular to obtain information from them or from third parties." Article 32 further provides that "any measure of such a character as to the cause the physical suffering or extermination of protected persons" is prohibited and that "[t]his prohibition applies not only to murder, torture, corporal punishments, mutilation and medical or scientific experiments not necessitated by the medical treatment of a protected person, but also to any other measures of brutality, whether applied by civilian or military agents."

By its terms, Geneva IV ceases to apply "on the general close of military operations" in the case of an international conflict. *See* Geneva IV, Art. 6. Whether military operations have reached a "general close" after the establishment of the Karzai government in June 2002 and whether the change in character of the conflict from an international one to a multi national conflict within a single State against non-State opponents terminated application of Geneva IV are issues open to controversy.[117] Thus, the ability of some civilians captured in Afghanistan to claim "protected person" status under Geneva IV today is subject to additional debate. However, regardless of the characterization of the current conflict, torture and inhumane treatment of civilian detainees from the War in Afghanistan or the ongoing conflict in Afghanistan, whether or not they qualify as "protected persons" under Geneva IV, is not permitted. All such persons are still entitled to the protections of international human rights law and to humane treatment under Common Article 3 and Article 75 of Additional Protocol I.

SUMMARY

None of the detainees from the War in Afghanistan or the ongoing conflict in Afghanistan fall outside of international humanitarian law. An individual detained during the armed conflict in Afghanistan – whether considered an international or internal armed conflict – is either protected by Geneva III as a POW, by Geneva IV as a civilian "protected person," or, at the very minimum, by Common Article 3 and Article 75 of Additional Protocol I. Of course, all detainees – regardless of where or when they

---

[117] Such determination does not negate application of Common Article 3 to an "armed conflict not of an international character" or certain other provisions of international humanitarian law and the law of armed conflict.

were captured – are entitled to the protection of human rights law (including CAT and the ICCPR) and customary international law.

Detainees protected as POWs or civilians under Geneva III or Geneva IV cannot be subjected to coercion of any kind. In addition, those detainees whose POW status is in doubt are entitled to interim POW status until a competent tribunal determines otherwise. At least some Afghan detainees are entitled to such tribunals, and the U.S. is long overdue in providing any process whatsoever to detainees, many of whom may simply be innocent non-combatants, wrongfully detained. We, therefore, urge the U.S. to establish proper screening procedures for all detainees.

OTHER INTERNATIONAL LEGAL STANDARDS

The legal standards set forth in the International Covenant on Civil and Political Rights, the American Declaration of the Rights and Duties of Man, and customary international law also apply to the treatment of detainees held by the United States.

THE INTERNATIONAL COVENANT ON CIVIL AND POLITICAL RIGHTS[118]

Relevant Legal Standards

Like CAT, the ICCPR expressly prohibits both torture and CID. Specifically, Article 7 of the ICCPR provides: "No one shall be subjected to torture or to cruel, inhuman or degrading treatment or punishment."[119] However, the ICCPR goes further than CAT in its non-derogability provision, expressly stating that neither torture *nor* CID treatment can be justified by exceptional circumstances such as war, internal political stability or other public emergencies. (*See* ICCPR, Art. 4). Article 10 also provides that: "All persons deprived of their liberty shall be treated with humanity and with respect for the inherent dignity of the human person."

The Human Rights Committee, established under Article 28, adjudicates complaints filed by individuals or states parties alleging violations of the ICCPR. The Committee has found the following conduct to violate Article 7's prohibition against cruel, inhuman or degrading treatment or punishment: threatening a victim with torture, prolonged solitary confinement and incommunicado detention, and repeated beatings.[120] Moreover, the Human Rights Committee has specifically criticized

---

[118] The ICCPR, G.A. Res. 2200A (XXI), U.N. GAOR, 21st Sess., Supp. No. 16, at 52, U.N. Doc. A/6316, 999 U.N.T.S. 171 was adopted in 1966 and came into force in 1976. It was ratified by the United States in 1992, subject to a number of reservations, understandings and declarations. *See* 138 CONG. REC. S4781-01 (1992).

[119] Congressional ratification of the ICCPR with respect to the prohibition against cruel, inhuman or degrading treatment is subject to a reservation mirroring that taken by the U.S. under CAT: "The United States considers itself bound by Article 7 to the extent that 'cruel, inhuman, or degrading treatment or punishment' means the cruel and unusual treatment or punishment prohibited by the Fifth, Eighth and/or Fourteenth Amendments....."*Id.*

[120] *See Floyd Howell v. Jamaica*, Communication No. 798/1998 (20 January 1998), CCPR/C/79/D/798/ 1998; *Victor Alfredo Polay Campos*, Communication No. 577/1994 (6 November 1997), CCPR/C/61/D/ 577/1994; *Dave Marais, Jr. v. Madagascar*, Communication No. 49/1979 (19 April 1979), U.N. Doc. Supp. No. 40 (A/38/40) at 141 (1983); *Raul Sendic Antonaccio v. Uruguay*, Communication No. R.14/63 (28 November 1979), U.N. Doc. Supp. No. 40 (A/37/40) at 114 (1982).

interrogation procedures such as handcuffing, hooding, shaking and sleep deprivation as violations of Article 7 in any circumstances.[121]

Although the ICCPR does not expressly prohibit states parties from "rendering" individuals to countries where they are likely to be mistreated, the Human Rights Committee has explained that, under Article 7, states parties "must not expose individuals to the danger of torture or cruel, inhuman or degrading treatment or punishment upon return to another country by way of their extradition, expulsion or refoulement."[122] Accordingly, the Human Rights Committee has stated that "[i]f a State party extradites a person within its jurisdiction in circumstances such that as a result there is a real risk that his or her rights under the Covenant will be violated in another jurisdiction, the State party itself may be in violation of the Covenant."[123]

Enforcement

U.S. Courts

In ratifying the ICCPR, the U.S. Senate declared that Articles 1 through 27 are not self-executing. Thus, while the Supreme Court has not squarely decided the issue, the majority of federal appeals courts have held that the ICCPR provides no privately enforceable rights and is not binding on federal courts.[124] The Second and Ninth circuit courts, however, have cited the ICCPR as evidence that customary international law prohibits arbitrary arrest, prolonged detention and torture.[125]

The Human Rights Committee

The Human Rights Committee is empowered to: (i) receive state party reports and comment on those reports (*see* ICCPR, Art. 40(4)); (ii) rule on complaints filed by a state party that another state party is not fulfilling its obligations under the ICCPR

---

[121] *See* Concluding Observations of the Human Rights Committee (Israel), CCPR/C/79/Add.93 (1998).
[122] *See* General Comment 20, U.N. GAOR Hum. Rts. Comm., 47th Sess., Supp. No. 40, para. 9, U.N. Doc. A/47/40 (1992).
[123] *Kindler v. Canada*, Communication No. 470/1991, Human Rights Committee, U.N. Doc. CCPR/C/48/D/470/1990 (1993).
[124] *See, e.g., Poindexter v. Nash*, 333 F.3d 372, 379 (2d Cir. 2003); *Bannerman v. Snyder*, 325 F.3d 722, 724 (6th Cir. 2003); *Wesson v. U.S. Penitentiary Beaumont, TX*, 305 F.3d 343, 348 (5th Cir. 2002); *United States v. Duarte-Acero*, 296 F.3d 1277, 1283 (11th Cir. 2002); *Hain v. Gibson*, 287 F.3d 1224, 1243 (10th Cir. 2002); *United States v. Warden, FMC Rochester*, 286 F.3d 1059, 1063 (8th Cir. 2002); *Dutton v. Warden, FCI Estill*, 2002 WL 255520, at *1 (4th Cir. 2002); *Lal v. Roe*, 2002 WL 31356505, at *1 (9th Cir. 2002); *Beazley v. Johnson*, 242 F.3d 248, 267 (5th Cir. 2001); *Kenan v. U.S.P. Lompac*, 2001 WL 1003213, at *1 n.1 (9th Cir. 2001); *Igartua De La Rosa v. United States*, 32 F.3d 8, 10 n.1 (1st Cir. 1994); *see also Beshli v. Dept. of Homeland Security*, 2003 WL 21693668, at *10 (E.D. Pa. July 22, 2003); *Macharia v. United States*, 238 F. Supp. 2d 13, 29–30 (D.D.C. July 30, 2002); *Reaves v. Warden, U.S.P.*, 2002 WL 535398, at *9 (M.D. Pa. Mar. 22, 2002); *Jama v. United States Immigration and Naturalization Service*, 22 F. Supp. 2d 353, 364–65 (D.N.J. 1998).
[125] *See Kim Ho Ma v. Ashcroft*, 257 F.3d 1095, 1114 (9th Cir. 2001) (recognizing that an international prohibition exists against "prolonged and arbitrary detention" and citing, among other sources to ICCPR, Art. 9); *Martinez v. City of Los Angeles*, 141 F.3d 1373, 1383–84 (9th Cir. 1998) (same); *United States v. Romano*, 706 F.2d 370, 375 n.1 (2d Cir. 1983) (citing to ICCPR for articulation of rights of a person charged with a criminal offense); *Filartiga v. Peña-Irala*, 630 F.2d 876, 883–84 (2d Cir. 1980) (citing ICCPR as one example that international law universally rejects torture).

(*see* ICCPR, Art. 41);[126] and (iii) rule on complaints filed by individuals "who claim that any of their rights enumerated in the Covenant have been violated and who have exhausted all available domestic remedies."[127]

ORGANIZATION OF AMERICAN STATES' INSTRUMENTS

Relevant Legal Standards

The U.S. is a member of the Organization of American States (the "OAS"). Article XXV of The American Declaration of the Rights and Duties of Man (the "American Declaration"), which was adopted by the Ninth International Conference of the OAS in 1948, provides:

> Every individual who has been deprived of his liberty has the right to have the legality of his detention ascertained without delay by a court, and the right to be tried without undue delay or, otherwise, to be released. He also has the right to humane treatment during the time he is in custody.

On June 1, 1997, the U.S. signed, but has not yet ratified, the American Convention On Human Rights (1969) (the "American Convention").[128] Article 5 of the American Convention, which sets forth Rights to Humane Treatment, provides:

> 1. Every person has the right to have his physical, mental, and moral integrity respected.

> 2. No one shall be subjected to torture or to cruel, inhuman or degrading punishment or treatment. All persons deprived of their liberty shall be treated with respect for the inherent dignity of the human person.

Moreover, pursuant to Article 27(2) of the American Convention, the Rights to Humane Treatment may not be suspended "[i]n time of war, public danger, or other emergency that threatens the independence or security of a State Party."

With respect to the treatment of detainees, the Inter-American Commission on Human Rights (the "Inter-American Commission") – which represents all member countries of the OAS and was established under Chapter VII of the American Convention – has determined that, "when the State holds a person in detention and under its exclusive control, it becomes the guarantor of that person's safety and rights."[129] In this regard, the Commission has found the following practices to be violations of Article 5 of the American Convention: threats to summon family members and pressure them to "talk"; threats to kill detainees; blindfolding detainees and forcing them to run around; "prolonged isolation and deprivation of communication"; solitary

---

[126] In ratifying the ICCPR, the U.S. Senate declared that "The United States . . . accepts the competence of the Human Rights Committee to receive and consider communications under Article 41 in which a State Party claims that another State Party is not fulfilling its obligations under the Covenant." *See supra* note 118.

[127] *See* Optional Protocol to the International Covenant on Civil and Political Rights, 21 U.N. GAOR Supp. (No. 16) at 59, U.N. Doc. A/6316 (1966), 999 U.N.T.S. 302.

[128] 1144 U.N.T.S. 123, *reprinted in* 9 I.L.M. 101 (1969).

[129] *See Manrique v. Peru*, Report No. 56/98, Inter-Am. C.H.R., OEA/Ser.L/V/II.95 Doc. 7 rev. at 983 (1998).

confinement; confining detainees in small cells with other prisoners; keeping detainees in cells that are damp and/or without adequate ventilation; keeping detainees in cells without beds; forcing detainees to sleep on the floor or on newspaper; depriving detainees of necessary hygiene facilities; beatings with rifles; and kicks in various parts of the body, especially in the stomach.[130]

The Inter-American Court of Human Rights (the "Inter-American Court") – established pursuant to Chapter VIII of the American Convention – has held that, "in order to establish if torture has been inflicted and its scope, all the circumstances of the case should be taken into consideration, such as the nature and context of the respective aggressions, how they were inflicted, during what period of time, the physical and mental effects and, in some case, the sex, age and state of health of the victims."[131] "The violation of the right to physical and psychological integrity of persons is a category of violation that has several gradations and embraces treatment ranging from torture to other types of humiliation or cruel, inhuman or degrading treatment with varying degrees of physical and psychological effects caused by endogenous and exogenous factors which must be proven in each specific situation."[132]

The Inter-American Court has found the following practices to violate Article 5 of the American Convention and/or Article 2 of the Inter-American Convention To Prevent and Punish Torture:[133] forcing detainees to stand blindfolded with their hands cuffed behind their backs; forcing detainees to listen to the cries of others being beaten; threatening detainees with physical torture; restriction of visiting rights; incommunicado detention; incarceration in solitary confinement and/or in a small cell with no ventilation or natural light; prohibiting detainees from engaging in physical exercise or intellectual efforts; deprivation of necessary hygiene facilities; deficient medical treatment; and throwing detainees to the ground.[134] "[A]ccording to international standards for protection, torture can be inflicted not only via physical violence, but also through acts that produce severe physical, psychological or moral suffering in

---

[130] *See, e.g., Request for Advisory Opinion OC-16, by the State of Mexico, of December 10, 1997*, OEA/Ser.L/V/III.39, Doc. 5, at para. 23(d) (1998); *Manrique v. Peru*, Report No. 56/98, Inter-Am. C.H.R., OEA/Ser.L/V/II.95 Doc. 7 rev. at 983, at paras. 87–88 (1998); *Congo v. Ecuador*, Report No. 63/99, Inter-Am. C.H.R., OEQ/Ser.L/V/II.95 Doc. 7 rev. at 475, at paras. 55–59 (1998); *Lucio Parada Cea, et al. v. El Salvador*, Report No. 1/99, Inter-Am. C.H.R., OEA/Ser.L/V/II.95 Doc. 7 rev. at 531, at para. 70 (1998).

[131] *Villagran Morales et al. Case (the "Street Children" Case), Judgment of November 19, 1999*, Inter-Am. Ct. H.R. (Ser. C) No. 63, at para. 74 (1999).

[132] *Loayza-Tamayo Case, Judgment of September 17, 1997*, Inter-Am. Ct. H.R. (Ser. C) No. 33, at para. 57 (1997).

[133] The U.S. is not a signatory to the Inter-American Convention To Prevent and Punish Torture, O.A.S. Treaty Series No. 67. Article 2 of this Convention defines torture as "any act intentionally performed whereby physical or mental pain or suffering is inflicted on a person for purposes of criminal investigation, as a means of intimidation, as personal punishment, as a preventive measure, as a penalty, or for any other purpose. Torture shall also be understood to be the use of methods upon a person intended to obliterate the personality of the victim or to diminish his physical or mental capacities, even if they do not cause physical pain or mental anguish."

[134] *See, e.g., Cantoral Benavides Case, Judgment of August 18, 2000*, Inter-Am. Ct. H.R. (Ser. C) No. 69, at paras. 43(a), 63(e) – (k), 104, 106 (2000); *Loayza-Tamayo Case, Judgment of September 17, 1997*, Inter-Am. Ct. H.R. (Ser. C) No. 33, at para. 58 (1997); *Castillo-Paez Case, Judgment of November 3, 1997*, Inter-Am. Ct. H.R. (Ser. C) No. 34, at para. 66 (1997); *Suarez-Rosero Case, Judgment of November 12, 1997*, Inter-Am. Ct. H.R. (Ser. C) No. 35, at para. 91 (1997).

the victim."[135] The Inter-American Court also has held that: "Prolonged isolation and being held incommunicado constitute, in themselves, forms of cruel and inhuman treatment, harmful to the mental and moral integrity of the person and to the right of all detainees of respect for the inherent dignity of the human being."[136]

Moreover, the Inter-American Court has warned that the fact that a State is confronted with terrorism does not, in itself, warrant the use of force:

> Any use of force that is not strictly necessary, given the behavior of the person detained, constitutes an affront to human dignity... in violation of Article 5 of the American Convention. The need to conduct investigations and the undeniable difficulties inherent to combating terrorism are not grounds for placing restrictions on the protection of the physical integrity of the person.[137]

In a case brought before the Inter-American Commission by detainees alleging violations of the United States' obligations under the American Declaration by U.S. armed forces in Grenada in 1983, *Coard, et al. v. United States*, the Inter-American Commission expressly extended the protections of human rights and humanitarian norms to extraterritorial conduct by U.S. military forces and criticized the U.S. for delay in providing procedure to detainees.[138] Acknowledging the need to balance between public security and individual rights, the Inter-American Commission in *Coard* held that: "What is required when an armed force detains civilians is the establishment of a procedure to ensure that the legality of the detention can be reviewed without delay and is subject to supervisory control.... Control over a detention [cannot] rest exclusively with the agents charged with carrying it out." *Coard*, at paras. 58–59.

Enforcement

The Inter-American Commission has competence with respect to matters relating to the fulfillment of the commitments made by the States Parties to the American

---

[135] *Cantoral Benavides Case, Judgment of August 18, 2000*, Inter-Am. Ct. H.R. (Ser. C) No. 69, at para. 100.

[136] *See Fairen-Garbi and Solis Corrales Case, Judgment of March 15, 1989*, Inter-Am. Ct. H.R. (Ser. C) No. 6, at para 149 (1989); *Godinez-Cruz Case, Judgment of January 20, 1989*, Inter-Am. Ct. H.R. (Ser. C) No. 5, at para. 164 (1989); *Velazquez-Rodriguez Case, Judgment of July 29, 1988*, Inter-Am. Ct. H.R. (Ser. C) No. 4, at para. 156 (1988). In the *Suarez-Rosero* case, the Inter-American Court explained that incommunicado detention is "an exceptional measure" which can cause the detainee to suffer extreme psychological and moral injury. "[I]solation from the outside world produces moral and psychological suffering in any person, places him in a particularly vulnerable position, and increases the risk of aggression and arbitrary acts in prisons." *Suarez-Rosero Case, Judgment of November 12, 1997*, Inter-Am. Ct. H.R. (Ser. C) No. 35, at para. 90 (1997).

[137] *See Castillo-Petruzzi Case, Judgment of May 30, 1999*, Inter-Am. Ct. H.R. (Ser. C) No. 52, at para. 197 (1999).

[138] *Coard, et al. v. United States*, Inter-Am. C.H.R. Report No. 109/99 (Sept. 29, 1999) ("*Coard*"). The *Coard* petitioners alleged that U.S. forces arrested them during the period in which it consolidated control over Grenada; that they were held incommunicado for many days; and that months passed before they were taken to a magistrate, or allowed to consult with counsel. "During this period petitioners were threatened, interrogated, beaten, deprived of sleep and food and constantly harassed." *Coard*, at para. 17. The petitioners alleged that their whereabouts were kept secret, and that requests by lawyers and others to meet with them were rejected. They also alleged that U.S. forces subjected them to threats and physical abuse – including threatening to hand the detainees over to Caribbean authorities and allowing Caribbean authorities to "soften" the detainees. *Coard*, at paras. 18–19.

Convention.[139] "The main function of the Commission" is "to promote respect for and defense of human rights."[140] Any person may lodge a petition with the Commission complaining of violation of the American Convention by a State Party, so long as effective domestic remedies available to the petitioner have been exhausted.[141]

On March 12, 2002, in response to a petition challenging detentions at Guantanamo Bay coordinated by the Center for Constitutional Rights,[142] the Inter-American Commission adopted precautionary measures addressed to the United States concerning the Guantanamo detainees.[143] Specifically, the Commission asked the U.S. "to take the urgent measures necessary to have the legal status of the detainees at Guantanamo Bay determined by a competent tribunal."[144] In so doing, the Inter-American Commission explained:

> Where persons find themselves within the authority and control of a state and where a circumstance of armed conflict may be involved, their fundamental rights may be determined in part by reference to international humanitarian law as well as international human rights law. Where it may be considered that the protections of international humanitarian law do not apply, however, such persons remain the beneficiaries at least of the non-derogable protections under international human rights law. In short, no person under the authority and control of a state, regardless of his or her circumstances, is devoid of legal protection for his or her fundamental and non-derogable human rights.[145]

With regard to the Guantanamo Bay detainees in particular, the Inter-American Commission observed that: "[T]he information available suggests that the detainees remain entirely at the unfettered discretion of the United States government. Absent clarification of the legal status of the detainees, the Commission considers that the rights and protections to which they may be entitled under international or domestic law cannot be said to be the subject of effective legal protection by

---

[139] *See supra* note 128, Art. 33.

[140] *Id.*, Art. 41. The Commission has also been willing to apply other relevant legal standards, including the Geneva Conventions.

[141] *Id.*, Arts. 44 and 46. The Inter-American Court also has competence with respect to matters relating to the fulfillment of the commitments made by the States Parties to the American Convention. *Id.*, Article 33. Only States Parties and the Commission have the right to submit a case to the Inter-American Court, however, and only after the case has been considered by the Inter-American Commission. *Id.*, Art. 61.

[142] A federal habeas corpus petition on behalf of named detainees at Guantanamo which was filed in parallel was dismissed for lack of jurisdiction because "the military base at Guantanamo Bay, Cuba is outside the sovereign territory of the United States." *Rasul v. Bush*, 215 F. Supp. 2d 55, 72 (D.D.C. 2002), *cert. granted*, 2003 WL 22070599 (U.S. Nov. 10, 2003).

[143] *See* Rules of Procedure of the Inter-American Commission on Human Rights, Art. 25(1): "In serious and urgent cases, and whenever necessary according to the information available, the Commission may, on its own initiative or at the request of a party, request that the State concerned adopt precautionary measures to prevent irreparable harm to persons.").

[144] *Ref. Detainees in Guantánamo Bay, Cuba Request for Precautionary Measures*, Inter-Am. C.H.R., Mar. 13, 2002, *reprinted in* 41 I.L.M. 532, 532. The Commission has ruled that OAS member states are subject to an international legal obligation to comply with a request for precautionary measures. *See Fifth Report on the Situation of Human Rights in Guatemala*, Inter-Am. C.H.R. OEA/Ser.L/V/II.111, Doc. 21 rev. (2001), at paras. 71–72 (2001); *Case 12.243*, Inter-Am. C.H.R. OEA/Ser.L/V/II.111, Doc. 21 rev. 1255 (2000), at para. 117.

[145] 41 I.L.M. at 533.

the State."[146] The Inter-American Commission further noted that, regardless of the legal status of the Guantanamo Bay detainees, their legal protections "may in no case fall below the minimal standards of non-derogable rights."[147] Thereafter, the Commission issued a renewed request to the U.S. government for precautionary measures, stating that new factual allegations regarding torture or other ill-treatment of detainees "raise questions concerning the extent to which the United States' policies and practices in detaining and interrogating persons in connection with its anti-terrorist initiatives clearly and absolutely prohibit treatment that may amount to torture or may otherwise be cruel, inhuman or degrading as defined under international norms."[148]

CUSTOMARY INTERNATIONAL LAW AND *JUS COGENS*

Relevant Legal Standards

Customary international law has long prohibited the state practice of torture, without reservation, in peace or in wartime.[149] On December 9, 1975, the United Nations General Assembly adopted by consensus the Declaration on the Protection of All Persons from Being Subjected to Torture and Other Cruel, Inhuman or Degrading

---

[146] *Id.*

[147] *Id.*, at 534. The Inter-American Commission invited the U.S. to provide information concerning compliance with these precautionary measures. In response, the United States argued that: (i) the Commission did not have jurisdiction to apply international humanitarian law, particularly the Geneva Conventions, as well as customary international humanitarian law; (ii) the Commission lacks authority to request precautionary measures with respect to States which are not party to the American Convention; and (iii) in any event, precautionary measures are neither necessary nor appropriate because the detainees are not entitled to prisoner of war status, do not meet Geneva Convention criteria for lawful combatants and are, instead, enemy combatants. *See Response of the United States To Request For Precautionary Measures – Detainees in Guantanamo Bay, Cuba, reprinted in* 41 I.L.M. 1015, 1028–1030 (2002). The U.S. stated, however, that it "is providing the detainees with protections consistent with international humanitarian law." *Id.* at 1031. The U.S. also asserted that it had no obligation to convene a tribunal to determine the detainees' status, and that the detainees had no right to counsel or to have access to courts. *Id.* at 1034. The U.S. Response did not address interrogation techniques. However, on December 2, 2003, the Pentagon announced that U.S. citizen and Taliban soldier Yaser Esam Hamdi would be given access to a lawyer, "as a matter of discretion and military policy," but that the decision "should not be treated as a precedent" and was "subject to appropriate security restrictions." *See* Associated Press Newswires, *Pentagon OKs Lawyer For Terror Suspect*, Dec. 3, 2003; Jerry Markon and Dan Eggen, *U.S. Allows Lawyer For Citizen Held as "Enemy Combatant"*, WASH. POST, Dec. 3, 2003, at A01.

[148] *Ref. Detainees in Guantanamo Bay, Cuba Request for Precautionary Measures*, Inter-Am C.H.R., July 23, 2003, at 5.

[149] In order for a state's practice to be recognized as customary international law, it must fulfill two conditions:

> Not only must the acts concerned amount to a settled practice, but they must also be such, or be carried out in such a way, as to be evidence of a belief that this practice is rendered obligatory by the existence of a rule of law requiring it. The need for such a belief, i.e., the existence of a subjective element, is implicit in the very notion of the *opinion juris sive necessitas*. The States concerned must therefore feel that they are conforming to what amounts to a legal obligation.

North Sea Continental Shelf (*F.R.G. v. Den.*), 1969 I.C.J. 3, 44. *See also* Military and Paramilitary Activities (*Nicar v. U.S.*), 1986 I.C.J. 14, 14; R. JENNINGS & A. WATTS, Oppenheim's International Law, (9th ed. 1996); *The Paquete Habana*, 175 U.S. 677, 700 (1900) (cited with approval in *First Nat'l City Bank v. Banco Para El Comercio Exterior de Cuba*, 462 U.S. 611, 623 (1983)); *U.S. v. Yousef*, 327 F.3d 56, 92 (2d Cir. 2002).

Punishment.[150] The Torture Resolution together with CAT and the ICCPR – ratified by 133 and 151 States, respectively – embody the customary international law obligation to refrain from behavior which constitutes torture.[151] In addition, in 1985 the United Nations Special Rapporteur on Torture, Pieter Koojimans, noted the widespread existing domestic legislation in many countries, including the United States, expressly or by implication prohibiting torture as well as cruel, inhuman and degrading punishment.[152]

The prohibition of torture is, moreover, one of the few norms which has attained peremptory norm or *jus cogens* status, and is recognized as such by United States courts.[153] *Jus cogens* is defined as a peremptory norm "accepted and recognized by the international community of states as a whole as a norm from which no derogation is permitted and which can be modified only by a subsequent norm of general international law having the same character."[154] While many international agreements expressly prohibit both torture and cruel, inhuman and degrading treatment,[155] it remains an open question as to whether *jus cogens* status extends to the prohibition against cruel, inhuman or degrading treatment. What is clear, however, is that cruel, inhuman and degrading treatment or punishment is prohibited by customary international law.

---

[150] GA Res. 3452 (XXX), U.N. GAOR, Supp. No. 34 at 91 (hereinafter the "Torture Resolution").

[151] *See Report by the Special Rapporteur*, U.N. Economic and Social Council, E/CN.4/1986/15, at para. 3. The report details state practice and *opinio juris* with respect to national legislation prohibiting torture. *See also* Herman J. Burgers & Hans Sanelius, The United Nations Convention Against Torture and Other Cruel, Inhuman or Degrading Treatment or Punishment (Martinus Nijhoff Publishers/Kluwer Academic Publishers 1988), at 1–12. The widespread ratification of regional human rights instruments such as the European Convention for the Protection of Human Rights and Fundamental Freedoms, the American Convention on Human Rights and the African Charter on Human and Peoples' Rights further reinforce the argument that torture is prohibited by customary international law.

[152] *Report by the Special Rapporteur, id.*, at paras. 72, 82.

[153] *See* Restatement (Third) of Foreign Relations Law § 702 (1986). *See also Abebe-Jira v. Negewo*, 72 F.3d 844, 847 (11th Cir. 1996); *In re Estate of Ferdinand Marcos, Human Rights Litigation*, 25 F.3d 1467, 1475 (9th Cir. 1994); *Siderman de Blake v. Republic of Argentina*, 965 F.2d 699, 716 (9th Cir. 1992); *Cornejo-Barreto v. Seifert*, 218 F.3d 1004, 1006 (9th Cir. 2000); *Presbyterian Church of Sudan v. Talisman Energy, Inc.*, 244 F. Supp. 2d 289 (S.D.N.Y. 2003); *Mehinovic v. Vuckovic*, 198 Supp. 2d 1322 (N.D. Ga. 2002); *Doe v. Islamic Salvation Front*, 993 F. Supp. 3, 7 (D.D.C. 1998); *Doe v. Unocal*, 963 F. Supp. 880, 890 (C.D. Cal. 1997).

[154] Vienna Convention on the Law of Treaties, 1969, Art. 53, 1155 U.N.T.S. 331.

[155] *See, e.g.*, Universal Declaration of Human Rights, G.A. Res. 217, U.N. GAOR, 3d Sess., Art. 5, U.N. Doc. A/810 (1948) ("no one shall be subjected to torture or to cruel, inhuman or degrading treatment or punishment"); Declaration on the Protection of All Persons from Being Subjected to Torture and Other Cruel, Inhuman or Degrading Treatment or Punishment, G.A. Res. 3452, 30 U.N. GAOR, Supp. No. 34, U.N. Doc. A/10034 (1976), at Article 3 ("Exceptional circumstances such as a state of war or a threat of war, internal political stability or any other public emergency may not be invoked as a justification of torture or other cruel, inhuman or degrading treatment or punishment."); ICCPR, *supra* note 118, at Art. 7 ("no one shall be subjected to torture or to cruel, inhuman or degrading treatment or punishment"); Additional Protocol I, *supra* note 20, at Article 75; Protocol Additional to the Geneva Conventions of 12 August 1949, and Relating to the Protection of Victims of Non-International Armed Conflicts ("Additional Protocol II"), *reprinted in* 16 I.L.M. 1442 (1977), at Article 4; European Convention for the Protection of Human Rights and Fundamental Freedoms, 213 U.N.T.S. 221 (1950), at Art. 3 (declaring that torture and inhuman or degrading treatment or punishment is prohibited); American Convention, *supra* note 128, at Art. 5 (providing that every person retain the right to be free from torture and ill-treatment); African Charter on Human and Peoples' Rights, *reprinted in* 21 I.L.M. 58 (1981), at Article 5 (prohibiting torture and ill-treatment).

U.S. ratification of the ICCPR and CAT are clear pronouncements that we condemn the practice of torture and CID treatment and that we consider ourselves legally bound to prohibit such conduct. Indeed, in 1999, the United States issued a report to the U.N. Committee Against Torture categorically affirming that:

> Every act constituting torture under the Convention constitutes a criminal offense under the law of the United States. No official of the Government, federal, state or local, civilian or military, is authorized to commit or to instruct anyone else to commit torture. Nor may any official condone or tolerate torture in any form. No exceptional circumstances may be invoked as justification for torture. United States law contains no provision permitting otherwise prohibited acts of torture or other cruel, inhuman or degrading treatment or punishment to be employed on grounds of exigent circumstance (for example, during a "state of public emergency") or on orders from a superior officer or public authority, and the protective mechanisms of an independent judiciary are not subject to suspension.[156]

Furthermore, the United States has enacted the Torture Victim Protection Act,[157] has imposed civil liability for acts of torture regardless of where such acts take place,[158] and has enacted the Torture Victims Relief Act, providing for monetary assistance for torture victims.[159] As previously discussed, not only does the U.S. Constitution prohibit cruel and unusual punishment or treatment by state officials (including under the military justice system), but almost all of the U.S. State constitutions have similar prohibitions.[160] Finally, a number of federal judicial proceedings have recognized that the right to be free from torture as well as cruel, inhuman or degrading treatment or punishment is a norm of customary international law.[161]

In the State Department Country Reports On Human Rights Practices, for example, the United States has expressly characterized the following types of conduct – some of which are allegedly occurring at U.S. detention centers – as "torture" or "other abuse": tying detainees in painful positions; forcing detainees to stand for long periods of time; incommunicado detention; depriving detainees of sleep; dousing naked detainees with cold water; denial of access to medical attention; interrogation techniques designed to intimidate or disorient; subjecting a detainee to loud music; forcing a detainee to squat or to assume "stressful, uncomfortable or painful" positions for "prolonged periods of time"; long periods of imprisonment in darkened rooms; verbal threats; and instilling detainees with the false belief that they are to be killed.[162] The following types of conduct have been defined as cruel, inhuman or degrading treatment: stripping;

---

[156] Committee Against Torture, *Consideration of Reports Submitted by States Parties Under Article 19 of the Convention*, United States of America, U.N. Doc. CAT/C/28/Add.5 (2000) ("U.S. Report Under CAT"), at para. 6.

[157] 28 U.S.C. § 1350.

[158] *Id.*

[159] 22 U.S.C. § 2152.

[160] *See* Part I of this Report; U.S. Report Under CAT, at paras. 50, 301–348.

[161] *See Abebe-Jira v. Negero*, 72 F.3d 844 (11th Cir. 1996), *cert. denied*, 519 U.S. 830 (1996); *Najarro de Sanchez v. Banco Central de Nicaragua*, 770 F.2d 1385 (5th Cir. 1985); *Xuncax v. Gramajo*, 886 F. Supp. 162 (D. Mass. 1995); *Paul v. Avril*, 901 F. Supp. 330 (S.D. Fla 1994).

[162] *See* U.S. Dept. of State, Bureau of Democracy, Human Rights and Labor, *Country Reports on Human Rights Practices – 2002* (for Brazil, Burma, China, Egypt, Israel and the occupied territories, Jordan, Kenya, Democratic People's Republic of Korea, Laos, Pakistan, Saudi Arabia, Togo, Turkey and Zimbabwe) (Mar. 31, 2003).

confinement in severely overcrowded cells; beating; imprisonment in small containers; and threats against family members of detainees.[163]

Enforcement

As the Second Circuit stated in *Filartiga v. Peña-Irala*, 630 F.2d 876 (1980), the United States is bound by customary international law. Thus, in cases where jurisdictional hurdles have been met, the bans on torture, arbitrary detention, and at least some aspects of cruel, inhuman and degrading treatment have been enforced by U.S. courts as violations of customary international law.[164]

SHOULD EXCEPTIONS BE MADE FOR THE "WAR ON TERROR"?: THE EXPERIENCE OF OTHER JURISDICTIONS

Notwithstanding the clear legal prohibitions against the use of torture and cruel, inhuman or degrading treatment in U.S. and international law, we considered whether, in a post-September 11 world, the threat posed by terrorists to the United States could ever justify the use of prohibited interrogation practices. We sought to answer the question of whether there are any circumstances in which torture and CID treatment in the interrogation of detainees should be permitted.

For additional guidance in answering these questions, we looked to the experiences of Northern Ireland and Israel, other places where the struggle between fighting terrorism and upholding the rule of law has been waged. Both the European Court of Human Rights and the Israeli Supreme Court have confronted the contradictory demands of national security and human rights against the backdrop of terrorism. The legal debate that infuses these courts' seminal decisions on the use of torture and CID treatment in the interrogation of terrorist suspects offers guidance to the United States in interpreting CAT. These courts have ruled that there are no exceptions to the prohibition against torture and CID treatment. Their rulings express the conviction that the torture and CID treatment of detainees – even when those detainees are suspected terrorists – cannot be justified.

LEGAL CHALLENGES TO INTERROGATION PRACTICES IN NORTHERN IRELAND AND ISRAEL

The Republic of Ireland v. The United Kingdom
The European Convention for the Protection of Human Rights and Fundamental Freedoms (the "European Convention") came into force in 1953.[165] Article 3 of the European Convention provides: "No one shall be subject to torture or to inhuman

---

[163] *Id.* (for Cameroon, Mongolia, Nigeria and Rwanda).
[164] *See, e.g., Filartiga v. Peña-Irala*, 639 F.2d 876 (2d Cir. 1980) (allowing a torture claim to be prosecuted under the Alien Tort Claims Act, 28 U.S.C. § 1350); *see also Forti v. Suarez-Mason*, 672 F. Supp. 1531, 1541–43 (N.D. Cal. 1987) (recognizing torture and arbitrary detention as violations of customary international law, but finding that universal consensus regarding right to be free from cruel, inhuman and degrading treatment had not yet been established).
[165] 213 U.N.T.S. 221.

or degrading treatment or punishment." The judicial body primarily charged with interpreting and enforcing the European Convention is the European Court of Human Rights (the "ECHR"). The ECHR has, in several decisions, applied the European Convention's prohibition against torture and inhuman or degrading treatment to cases involving interrogation of suspected terrorists who pose a threat to national security.

The most important of these decisions is *The Republic of Ireland.*[166] *The Republic of Ireland* case was decided in a legal and political environment conditioned by several years of terrorism in Northern Ireland perpetrated by members of the Irish Republican Army (IRA) and Loyalist groups. By March 1975, over 1,100 people had been killed, over 11,500 injured and £140 million worth of property destroyed.[167] To combat a campaign of violence being carried out by the IRA, in 1971, the Northern Ireland Government introduced regulations providing authorities with extrajudicial powers, including arrest for interrogation purposes and internment.[168]

The Republic of Ireland Decision is a landmark legal discussion of whether specific interrogation practices committed by British security forces against IRA detainees constituted torture or inhuman or degrading treatment. The impetus for the ECHR's decision was the Republic of Ireland's application before the European Commission of Human Rights alleging, among other things, that various interrogation practices – including specific practices referred to as the "five techniques" – amounted to torture and inhuman or degrading treatment, in contravention of Article 3 of the European Convention.[169] The "five techniques" – described by the ECHR as methods of "disorientation" or "sensory deprivation" – include a number of practices allegedly being used today by U.S. interrogators:

- Wall-standing: Forcing a detainee to remain spreadeagled against a wall with his fingers placed high above his head against the wall, his legs spread apart and his feet positioned such that he must stand on his toes with the weight of his body resting on his fingers;
- Hooding: Keeping a dark bag over a detainee's head at all times, except during interrogation;
- Subjection to noise: Holding a detainee in a room where there is a continuous loud and hissing noise;
- Deprivation of sleep; and
- Deprivation of food and drink.[170]

The European Commission of Human Rights unanimously found that the "five techniques" constituted torture, and that other challenged interrogation practices amounted to inhuman and degrading treatment.[171] Although the British Government subsequently discontinued the "five techniques" and did not contest the underlying

---

[166] *The Republic of Ireland v. The United Kingdom*, (1979–80) 2 E.H.R.R. 25.
[167] *Id.*, at 30–31.
[168] *Id.*, at 36.
[169] *Id.*, at 25.
[170] *Id.*, at 59.
[171] *Id.*, at 25.

allegations of the case or the Commission's findings in connection therewith, the Republic of Ireland nevertheless referred the case to the ECHR.[172] The ECHR took the opportunity to rule upon the legality of the "five techniques," citing to the European Court's responsibility "to elucidate, safeguard and develop the rules instituted by the Convention."[173]

In *The Republic of Ireland* decision, the ECHR explained that ill-treatment "had to attain a minimum level of severity to fall within Article 3, the assessment of which was necessarily relative, depending on all the circumstances, including the duration of the treatment, its physical or mental effects and, sometimes, the sex, age or state of health of the victim."[174] The ECHR pointed out that, while the term "torture" attached "a special stigma to deliberate inhuman treatment causing very serious and cruel suffering," the distinction between torture and inhuman or degrading treatment "derived principally from a difference in the intensity of the suffering inflicted."[175] The ECHR held that since the "five techniques were applied in combination, with premeditation and for hours at a time, causing at least intense physical and mental suffering and acute psychiatric disturbances, they amount to inhuman treatment."[176] The ECHR further held that since the "five techniques" aroused "in the victims feelings of fear, anguish and inferiority capable of humiliating and debasing them and possibly breaking their physical or moral resistance, they were also degrading."[177] The ECHR concluded that the "five techniques" violated Article 3's prohibition against inhuman or degrading treatment, but that they did not amount to torture.[178]

---

[172] *Id.*, at 25.

[173] *Id.*, at 75–76.

[174] *Id.*, at 26.

[175] *Id.*, at 26.

[176] *Id.*, at 26.

[177] *Id.*

[178] *Id.*, at 79–80. In separate annexed opinions, Judges Zekia, O'Donoghue and Evrigenis disagreed with the majority's ruling that the five practices did not amount to torture.

In the years since the *Republic of Ireland* decision, neither time nor the ever-expanding threat of terrorism has diminished the ECHR's commitment to maintaining an absolute prohibition against torture and inhuman or degrading treatment. In *Chahal v. United Kingdom*, Case No. 70/1995/576/662 (Nov. 15, 1996), for example, the ECHR rejected Great Britain's argument that national security considerations justified the deportation of an Indian citizen to India on grounds that he was active in extremist Sikh organizations in England and was suspected of planning terrorist and other violent acts in the country. Chahal argued that, if deported, he would be tortured in India. In ruling that Chahal's deportation by the United Kingdom would constitute a violation of Article 3 of the Convention, the ECHR stated:

> Article 3 enshrines one of the most fundamental values of democratic society.... The Court is well aware of the immense difficulties faced by States in modern times in protecting their communities from terrorist violence. However, even in these circumstances, the Convention prohibits in absolute terms torture or inhuman or degrading treatment or punishment, irrespective of the victim's conduct. Unlike most of the substantive clauses of the Convention and of Protocols Nos. 1 and 4, Article 3 makes no provision for exceptions and no derogation from it is permissible under Article 15 even in the event of a public emergency threatening the life of the nation.

Id., at 79. *See also Aksoy v. Turkey*, Case No. 100/1995/606/694 (Dec. 15, 1996), para. 62 (ruling that Turkish security forces' treatment of a detainee suspected of membership and activity on behalf of the PKK, a Kurdish militant organization operating against the Turkish government, constituted torture).

Israeli Supreme Court *Judgment Concerning The Legality Of The General Security Service's Interrogation Methods*

As the Israeli Supreme Court notes at the outset of its *Judgment Concerning The Legality Of The General Security Service's Interrogation Methods*,[179] the State of Israel "has been engaged in an unceasing struggle for both its very existence and security from the day of its founding":

> Terrorist organizations have established as their goal Israel's annihilation. Terrorist acts and the general disruption of order are their means of choice. In employing such methods, these groups do not distinguish between civilian and military targets. They carry out terrorist attacks in which scores are murdered in public areas, public transportation, city squares and centers, theaters and coffee shops. They do not distinguish between men, women and children. They act of cruelty and without mercy.[180]

In 1987, the Landau Commission of Inquiry into the Methods of Investigation of the GSS Regarding Hostile Terrorist Acts (the "Landau Commission") was established to investigate the interrogation practices of the main body responsible for fighting terrorism in Israel, the General Security Service (the "GSS"), and to reach legal conclusions concerning them. The resulting Landau Report[181] concluded: "The effective interrogation of terrorist suspects is impossible without the use of means of pressure, in order to overcome an obdurate will not to disclose information and to overcome the fear of the person under interrogation that harm will befall him from his own organization, if he does not reveal information."[182] The Landau Report explained that: "The means of pressure should principally take the form of non-violent psychological pressure through a vigorous and extensive interrogation, with the use of strategems, including acts of deception. However, when these do not attain their purpose, the exertion of a moderate measure of physical pressure cannot be avoided."[183] The Landau Commission recommended, however, that GSS interrogators should be guided by clear rules "to prevent the use of inordinate physical pressure arbitrarily administered," and formulated a code of guidelines (set forth in a secret part of the Landau Report) which defined, "on the basis of past experience, and with as much precision as possible, the boundaries of what is permitted to the interrogator and mainly what is prohibited to him."[184] The Landau Commission asserted that the latitude it afforded GSS interrogators to use "a moderate measure of physical pressure" did not conflict with the standards set forth in international human rights conventions – such as the UDHR, the ICCPR and the European Convention – which prohibited torture and cruel, inhuman or degrading treatment or punishment.[185]

In 1999, in the *GSS Interrogation Methods Decision*, the Israeli Supreme Court took up the legality of certain interrogation practices employed by the GSS. The

---

[179] *Judgment Concerning The Legality Of The General Security Service's Interrogation Methods*, 38 I.L.M. 1471 (Sept. 9, 1999) (the "GSS Interrogation Methods Decision").
[180] *Id.*, at 1472.
[181] Excerpts printed in 23 Isr. L. Rev. 146 (1989).
[182] *Id.*, at 184.
[183] *Id.*
[184] *Id.*, at 185.
[185] *Id.*, at 186.

Israeli Supreme Court acknowledged that the Landau Commission had approved the use of "a moderate degree of physical pressure," and that the Landau Commission's recommendations had been accepted by the Israeli Government.[186] The interrogation methods considered by the Israeli Supreme Court in the *GSS Interrogation Methods Decision* were:

- Shaking: Forcefully shaking a detainee's upper torso back and forth, repeatedly, and in a manner which causes the neck and head to dangle and vacillate rapidly.
- The "shabach" position: Forcing a detainee who has his hands tied behind his back to sit on a small and low chair whose seat is tilted forward and toward the ground, where one hand is placed inside the gap between the chair's seat and back support, the detainee's head is covered by an opaque sack falling down to his shoulders, and powerfully loud music is played in the room.
- The "frog crouch": Forcing a detainee to crouch on the tips of his/her toes for five minute intervals.
- Excessive tightening of handcuffs: Using particularly small cuffs, ill-fitted in relation to the suspect's arm or leg size.
- Sleep deprivation: A detainee is deprived of sleep as a result of being tied in the "shabach" position, being subjected to powerfully loud music or intense non-stop interrogations.[187]

In examining the legality of these GSS interrogation methods, the Israeli Supreme Court acknowledged that, taken individually, some of the components of the "shabach" position have "legitimate" goals: for example, hooding prevents communication between suspects, the playing of powerfully loud music prevents the passing of information between suspects, the tying of the suspect's hands to a chair protects investigators, and the deprivation of sleep can be necessitated by an interrogation.[188] According to the Israeli Supreme Court, however, there is a necessary balancing process between a government's duty to ensure that human rights are protected and its duty to fight terrorism. The results of that balance, the Israeli Supreme Court stated, are the rules for a "reasonable interrogation" – defined as an interrogation which is: (1) "necessarily one free of torture, free of cruel, inhuman treatment of the subject and free of any degrading handling whatsoever"; and (2) "likely to cause discomfort."[189] "In the end result," the Court noted, "the legality of an investigation is deduced from the propriety of its purpose and from its methods."[190]

---

[186] *GSS Interrogation Methods Decision*, 38 I.L.M. at 1477.
[187] *Id.*, at 1474–76. The Israeli Government argued that such interrogation methods did not need to be outlawed because, before resorting to physical pressure against detainees, GSS interrogators are instructed to "probe the severity of the danger that the interrogation is intending to prevent; consider the urgency of uncovering the information presumably possessed by the suspect in question; and seek an alternative means of preventing the danger." *Id.*, at 1475. The Israeli Government also argued that directives respecting interrogation provide that in cases where shaking – considered the harshest interrogation method of those examined in the *GSS Interrogation Methods Decision* – is to be used, "the investigator must first provide an evaluation of the suspect's health and ensure that no harm comes to him." *Id.*, at 1475.
[188] *Id.*, at 1480–81.
[189] *Id.*, at 1482.
[190] *Id.*

Turning to the specific interrogation methods before it, the Court concluded that shaking, the "frog crouch," the "shabach" position, cuffing causing pain, hooding, the consecutive playing of powerfully loud music and the intentional deprivation of sleep for a prolonged period of time are all prohibited interrogation methods.[191] "All these methods do not fall within the sphere of a 'fair' interrogation. They are not reasonable. They impinge upon the suspect's dignity, his bodily integrity and his basic rights in an excessive manner (or beyond what is necessary). They are not to be deemed as included within the general power to conduct interrogations."[192] The Israeli Supreme Court explained that restrictions applicable to police investigations are equally applicable to GSS investigations, and that there are no grounds to permit GSS interrogators to engage in conduct which would be prohibited in a regular police interrogation.[193]

In so ruling, the Israeli Supreme Court considered the "ticking time bomb" scenario often confronted by GSS interrogators:

> A given suspect is arrested by the GSS. He holds information respecting the location of a bomb that was set and will imminently explode. There is no way to defuse the bomb without this information. If the information is obtained, however, the bomb may be defused. If the bomb is not defused, scores will be killed and maimed. Is a GSS investigator authorized to employ physical means in order to elicit information regarding the location of the bomb in such instances?[194]

The Israeli Supreme Court stated that it was prepared to presume that if a GSS investigator – who applied physical interrogation methods for the purpose of saving human life – is criminally indicted, the "necessity" defense recognized under Israeli Penal Law would be open to him in the appropriate circumstances.[195] The Israeli Supreme Court also acknowledged that the legislature could enact laws permitting the interrogation methods that its decision struck down.[196] However, the Israeli Supreme Court refused to imply from the existence of the "necessity" defense, as the State argued for it to do, "an advance legal authorization endowing the investigator with the capacity to use physical interrogation methods."[197]

THE LEGAL AND MORAL IMPLICATIONS OF THE "TICKING BOMB" SCENARIO

As the *Republic of Ireland and GSS Interrogation Methods Decision* demonstrate, in the face of a terrorist threat there is an inherent tension between obtaining potentially life-saving intelligence information through abusive interrogation of detainees and upholding human rights:

> In crystallizing the interrogation rules, two values or interests clash. On the one hand, lies the desire to uncover the truth, thereby fulfilling the public interest in

---

[191] *Id.*, at 1482–84.
[192] *Id.*, at 1483.
[193] *Id.*, at 1485.
[194] *Id.*
[195] *Id.*, at 1486.
[196] *Id.*, at 1487.
[197] *Id.*, at 1486.

exposing crime and preventing it. On the other hand, is the wish to protect the dignity and liberty of the individual being interrogated.[198]

International and human rights law is clear: torture and cruel, inhuman or degrading treatment of detainees is prohibited. Those who would, nevertheless, support the use of moderate physical force, sensory deprivation or disorientation techniques in the interrogation of terrorist suspects argue that resort to such methods is, at times, the only way to prevent the death of innocent persons and is, therefore, justified in such cases as the "lesser of two evils." Proponents of this view would argue that the legitimacy of an act can be measured by whether its utility exceeds its harm. On this point, the Landau Commission took the following position:

> To put it bluntly, the alternative is: are we to accept the offense of assault entailed in slapping a suspect's face, or threatening him, in order to induce him to talk and reveal a cache of explosive materials meant for use in carrying out an act of mass terror against a civilian population, and thereby prevent the greater evil which is about to occur? The answer is self-evident.

> Everything depends on weighing the two evils against each other.[199]

In the case of detainees being held by the U.S. in connection with the "War on Terror," however, the "ticking bomb" scenario is further complicated. Any utilitarian justification for subjecting these detainees to interrogation practices prohibited by CAT must necessarily be premised on the certainty (or, at least, the substantiated suspicion) that these individuals do, in fact, possess vital intelligence information. But, here, there is no such certainty. Instead, hundreds of detainees at Guantanamo Bay, Bagram Air Force Base and other U.S. detention facilities have been detained for months without any type of hearing or legal challenge permitted to their detention.

Our answer to the question of whether torture of detainees should ever be permitted in a post-September 11 world is that there are no such circumstances. We condemn the use of torture in interrogation of detainees, without exception. By its terms, CAT permits no derogation of the prohibition against torture – stating that "[n]o exceptional circumstances whatsoever, whether a state of war or a threat of war, internal political stability or any other public emergency, may be invoked as a justification of torture."[200] As the Israeli Supreme Court has explained, "A democratic, freedom-loving society does not accept that investigators use any means for the purpose of uncovering the truth. 'The interrogations practices of the police in a given regime are indicative of a regime's very character.'"[201]

We recognize that some legal scholars and ethicists may well argue that circumstances exist (as in the "ticking bomb" scenario) in which torture and CID treatment in the interrogation of detainees should be permitted. However, we stress that torture

---

[198] *Id.*, at 1481.
[199] *See* 23 Isr. L. Rev., at 174.
[200] CAT, Art. 2.
[201] *GSS Interrogation Methods Decision*, 38 I.L.M. at 1481 (internal citations omitted).

of detainees – which is prohibited under international and U.S. law – is never permissible, and should be fully investigated and prosecuted in all cases.

* * *

In summary, the Association makes the following recommendations:

First, we urge the United States to amend 18 U.S.C. § 2340 to encompass the actions of military and intelligence personnel at U.S. facilities overseas, to fully utilize the UCMJ to protect all detainees from abuse and to independently investigate human rights compliance in countries to which we are "rendering" detainees.

Second, U.S. military and intelligence personnel involved in interrogation of terrorist suspects should be educated regarding the prohibition against torture and CID, and should receive training to comply with those rules.

Third, the U.S. should adhere to its commitments under the Geneva Conventions, extend POW treatment to regular force combatants as a matter of policy, and promptly establish proper screening procedures and hearings for all detainees.

Finally, the Association notes that particularly in these times of terrorism and violence, it is important to protect the rule of law and the standards of decency to which our nation and the community of nations are committed. As the Israeli Supreme Court has stated:

> This is the destiny of democracy, as not all means are acceptable to it, and not all practices employed by its enemies are open before it. Although a democracy must often fight with one hand tied behind its back, it nonetheless has the upper hand.[202]

* * *

TABLE OF CONTENTS

---

[202] *Id.*, at 1488.

IV. Should Exceptions be Made for the "War on Terror"?: The Experience
   of Other Jurisdicitons

A. Legal Challenges to Interrogation Practices in Northern Ireland and Israel
   1. *The Republic of Ireland v. The United Kingdom*
   2. Israeli Supreme Court *Judgment Concerning The Legality Of The General
      Security Service's Interrogation Methods*

B. The Legal and Moral Implications of the "Ticking Bomb" Scenario

THE COMMITTEE ON INTERNATIONAL HUMAN RIGHTS

Martin S. Flaherty, Chair*
Scott Horton (Immediate Past Chair)*
Jeanmarie Fenrich, Secretary

Charles Adler
Patricia C. Armstrong
Hon. Deborah A. Batts
Nicole Barrett
Aarthi Belani (student member)*
Seymour H. Chalif
Amy Christina Cococcia
Catherine Daly
Eric O. Darko
Jane M. Desnoyers
Mark K. Dietrich
Fiona M. Doherty
Barbara Fortson (former member)*
Aya Fujimura-Fanselow (student member)
Douglas C. Gray
William M. Heinzen
Alice H. Henkin
Sharon K. Hom
Miranda Johnson (student member)
Anil Kalhan
Mamta Kaushal
Christopher Kean
Elise B. Keppler
Katharine Lauer*
Sara Lesch
Yvonne C. Lodico
Marko C. Maglich
Elisabeth Adams Mason
Nina Massen
Sam Scott Miller

Elena Dana Neacsu
Dyanna C. Pepitone
Marny Requa (student member)
Sidney S. Rosdeitcher**
Margaret L. Satterthwaite*
Joseph H. Saunders
Christopher A. Smith (student member)
Katherine B. Wilmore

THE COMMITTEE ON MILITARY AFFAIRS AND JUSTICE

Miles P. Fischer, Chair*
Michael Mernin, Secretary

Donna Ahlstrand (former member)*
Steven Barrett
Myles Bartley
Philip Blum
Kenneth Carroll
Brian Cogan
Joshua Eisenberg
Matthew Hawkins
Peter Jaensch
Peter Kornman
Peter Langrind
Gerald Lee
Patricia Murphy
Rose Murphy
Harold Nathan
Timothy Pastore
Stanley Paylago*
Visuvanathan Rudrakumaran
Lawrence Sloan

* Members of the Subcommittee who prepared the report.
** Chair of the Subcommittee responsible for preparing the report.

The views expressed herein are solely those of the Association and the participating Committees.

The Committee on International Human Rights and Military Affairs and Justice would like to thank the following persons for their assistance in the preparation of the report: John Cerone (Executive Director, War Crimes Research Office, Washington College of Law, American University); Ken Hurwitz (Human Rights First); Professor Marco Sassòli (University of Geneva, professor of international law); Brigitte Oederlin and Gabor Rona (International Committee of the Red Cross); Paul, Weiss, Rifkind,

Wharton & Garrison LLP ("Paul Weiss") associates Katarina Lawergren and Marc Miller and former Paul Weiss associate Matias Milet; and New York University School of Law students Ari Bassin, Amber A. Baylor, Angelina Fisher, Tzung-lin Fu, David R. Hoffman, Jane Stratton and Stephanie S. Welch; and New York Law School student Holly Higgins. This report could not have been completed without the indefatigable efforts of Paul Weiss associate Liza Velazquez in helping edit the many drafts of the Report and consolidating the many views and comments of the Committees and Subcommittee into a coherent whole.

Appendix A

December 26, 2002

President George W. Bush
The White House
1600 Pennsylvania Avenue, NW
Washington, DC 20500

Dear President Bush:

Human Rights Watch is deeply concerned by allegations of torture and other mistreatment of suspected al Qaeda detainees described in *The Washington Post* ("U.S. Decries Abuse but Defends Interrogations") on December 26. The allegations, if true, would place the United States in violation of some of the most fundamental prohibitions of international human rights law. Any U.S. government official who is directly involved or complicit in the torture or mistreatment of detainees, including any official who knowingly acquiesces in the commission of such acts, would be subject to prosecution worldwide.

Human Rights Watch urges you to take immediate steps to clarify that the use of torture is not U.S policy, investigate *The Washington Post's* allegations, adopt all necessary measures to end any ongoing violations of international law, stop the rendition of detainees to countries where they are likely to be tortured, and prosecute those implicated in such abuse.

I. Prohibitions Against Torture

The Washington Post reports that persons held in the CIA interrogation centers at Bagram air base in Afghanistan are subject to "stress and duress" techniques, including "standing or kneeling for hours" and being "held in awkward, painful positions." *The Post* notes that the detention facilities at Bagram and elsewhere, such as at Diego Garcia, are not monitored by the International Committee of the Red Cross, which has monitored the U.S. treatment of detainees at Guantanamo Bay. Cuba.

The absolute prohibition against torture is a fundamental and well-established precept of customary and conventional international law. Torture is never permissible against anyone, whether in times of peace or of war.

The prohibition against torture is firmly established under international human rights law. It is prohibited by various treaties to which the United States is a party, including the International Covenant on Civil and Political Rights (ICCPR), which the United States ratified in 1992, and the Convention against Torture and Other Cruel, Inhuman or Degrading Treatment or Punishment, which the United States ratified in 1994. Article 7 of the ICCPR states that "No one shall be subjected to torture or to cruel, inhuman or degrading treatment or punishment." The right to be protected from torture is non-derogable, meaning that it applies at all times, including during public emergencies or wartime.

International humanitarian law (the laws of war), which applies during armed conflict, prohibits the torture or other mistreatment of captured combatants and others in captivity, regardless of their legal status. Regarding prisoners-of-war, Article 17 of the Third Geneva Convention of 1949 states: "No physical or mental torture, nor any other form of coercion, may be inflicted on prisoners of war to secure from them information of any kind whatever. Prisoners of war who refuse to answer may not be threatened, insulted, or exposed to any unpleasant or disadvantageous treatment of any kind." Detained civilians are similarly protected by Article 32 of the Fourth Geneva Convention. The United States has been a party to the 1949 Geneva Conventions since 1955.

The United States does not recognize captured al Qaeda members as being protected by the 1949 Geneva Conventions, although Bush administration officials have insisted that detainees will be treated humanely and in a manner consistent with Geneva principles. However, at minimum, all detainees in wartime, regardless of their legal status, are protected by customary international humanitarian law. Article 75 ("Fundamental Guarantees") of the First Additional Protocol to the Geneva Conventions, which is recognized as restating customary International law, provides that "torture of all kinds, whether physical or mental" against "persons who are in the power of a party to the conflict and who do not benefit from more favorable treatment under the [Geneva] Conventions." shall "remain prohibited at any time and in any place whatsoever, whether committed by civilian or military agents." "[C]ruel treatment and torture" of detainees is also prohibited under common Article 3 to the 1949 Geneva Conventions, which is considered indicative of customary international law.

II. Possible U.S. Complicity in Torture

It is a violation of international law not only to use torture directly, but also to be complicit in torture committed by other governments. *The Post* reports being told by U.S. officials that "[t]housands have been arrested and held with U.S. assistance in countries known for brutal treatment of prisoners." The Convention against Torture provides in Article 4 that all acts of torture, including "an act by any person which constitutes complicity or participation in torture," is an offense "punishable by appropriate penalties which take into account their grave nature."

The Post article describes the rendition of captured al Qaeda suspects from U.S. custody to other countries where they are tortured or otherwise mistreated. This might also be a violation of the Convention against Torture, which in Article 3 states: "No State Party shall expel, return ('refouler') or extradite a person to another State where there are substantial grounds for believing that he would be in danger of being subjected to torture.... For the purpose of determining whether there are such grounds, the competent authorities shall take into account all relevant considerations including, where applicable, the existence in the State concerned of a consistent pattern of gross, flagrant or mass violations of human rights."

The U.S. Department of State annual report on human rights practices has frequently criticized torture in countries where detainees may have been sent. These include Uzbekistan, Pakistan, Egypt, Jordan and Morocco. The United States thus could not plausibly claim that it was unaware of the problem of torture in these countries.

III. International Prosecutions for Torture and Command Responsibility

Direct involvement or complicity in torture, as well as the failure to prevent torture, may subject U.S. officials to prosecution under international law.

The wilful torture or inhuman treatment of prisoners-of-war or other detainees, including "wilfully causing great suffering or serious injury to body or health," are "grave breaches" of the 1949 Geneva Conventions, commonly known as war crimes. Grave breaches are subject to universal jurisdiction, meaning that they can be prosecuted in any national criminal court and as well as any international tribunal with appropriate jurisdiction.

The Convention against Torture obligates States Parties to prosecute persons within their jurisdiction who are implicated or complicit in acts of torture. This obligation includes the prosecution of persons within their territory who committed acts of torture elsewhere and have not be extradited under procedures provided in the convention.

Should senior U.S. officials become aware of acts of torture by their subordinates and fail to take immediate and effective steps to end such practices, they too could be found criminally liable under international law. The responsibility of superior officers for atrocities by their subordinates is commonly known as command responsibility. Although the concept originated in military law, it now is increasingly accepted to include the responsibility of civil authorities for abuses committed by persons under their direct authority. The doctrine of command responsibility has been upheld in recent decisions by the international criminal tribunals for the former Yugoslavia and for Rwanda.

There are two forms of command responsibility: direct responsibility for orders that are unlawful and imputed responsibility, when a superior knows or should have known of crimes committed by a subordinate acting on his own initiative and fails to prevent or punish them. All states are obliged to bring such people to justice.

* * *

The allegations made by *The Washington Post* are extraordinarily serious. They have put the United States on notice that acts of torture may be taking place with U.S. participation or complicity. That creates a heightened duty to respond preventively. As an immediate step, we urge that you issue a presidential statement clarifying that it is contrary to U.S. policy to use or facilitate torture. *The Post's* allegations should be investigated and the findings made public. Should there be evidence of U.S. civilian or military officials being directly involved or complicit in torture, or in the rendition of persons to places where they are likely to be tortured, you should take immediate steps to prevent the commission of such acts and to prosecute the individuals who have ordered, organized, condoned, or carried them out. The United States also has a duty to refrain from sending persons to other countries with a history of torture without explicit and verifiable guarantees that no torture or mistreatment will occur.

Thank you for your attention to these concerns.

Sincerely,

Kenneth Roth
Executive Director

Cc: Colin Powell, Secretary of State
Donald Rumsfeld, Secretary of Defense
Condoleezza Rice, National Security Advisor

January 31, 2003

The Honorable George W. Bush
The White House
Washington, DC 20301-1010

Dear President Bush:

We are writing to you on a matter of great concern. As you are no doubt aware, on December 26th *The Washington Post* reported that your Administration has used, tacitly condoned or facilitated torture by third countries in the interrogation of prisoners. These reports are so flagrantly at odds with your many statements about the importance of human rights that we trust that you are equally disturbed by it.

You have repeatedly declared that the United States "will always stand firm for the non-negotiable demands of human dignity." Surely there is no more basic and less negotiable requirement of human dignity than the right to be free of torture or cruel, inhuman or degrading treatment. As you know, under the Torture Convention "no exceptional circumstances whatsoever" may be invoked to justify torture and no party may return or extradite a person to another state where there are "substantial grounds for believing that he would be in danger of being subjected to torture." Likewise, under the Covenant on Civil and Political Rights, "no one shall be subjected to torture or to cruel, inhuman or degrading treatment or punishment."

As you declared in your State of the Union address, these solemn commitments of the United States are non-negotiable; in legal terms, there can be no derogation from them. You may also know that it was your father's Administration that sought and received overwhelming Senate support for the United States to ratify these two treaties.

The Administration's response to the outrageous statements made by numerous unnamed officials to *The Post's* reporters concerning United States use or tolerance of torture and cruel, inhuman and degrading treatment has thus far been wholly inadequate. Whatever the truth of *The Post's* allegations, without a more authoritative response to this high-profile story the world will conclude that the United States is not practicing what it preaches. America's authority as a champion of human rights will be seriously damaged.

What is clearly needed in this instance are unequivocal statements by you and your Cabinet officers that torture in any form or manner will not be tolerated by this Administration, that any US official found to have used or condoned torture will be held accountable, and that the United States would neither seek nor rely upon intelligence obtained through torture in a third country. These statements need to be accompanied by clear written guidance applicable to everyone engaged in the interrogation and rendition of prisoners strictly prohibiting the use or tolerance of torture or cruel, inhuman or degrading treatment of prisoners and mandating full compliance with the Geneva conventions requirements for the treatment of prisoners.

We urge you in the strongest terms to take this opportunity to demonstrate that torture and cruel, inhuman and degrading treatment is, in fact as well as word, non-negotiable.

Sincerely,

William Schulz
Amnesty International USA

Kenneth Roth
Human Rights Watch

Gay McDougall
International Human Rights Law Group

Louise Kantrow
International League for Human Rights

Michael Posner
Lawyers Committee for Human Rights

Robin Phillips
Minnesota Advocates for Human Rights

Len Rubenstein
Physicians for Human Rights

Todd Howland
RFK Memorial Center for Human Rights

NATIONAL CONSORTIUM OF
TORTURE TREATMENT PROGRAMS
74-09 37th Ave. Room 412. Jackson Heights. New York, U.S.A.
Tel: 718-899-1233. Ext. 101; Fax: 718-457-6071

February 5, 2003

President George Bush
Fax 202-456-2461

Dear President Bush:

The National Consortium of Torture Treatment Programs consists of 33 programs through-out the United States that provide medical and mental health care, as well as legal and social services, to survivors of politically motivated torture. I am writing on behalf of our membership to request a dialogue with the Administration regarding recent allegations published in the *Washington Post* that certain U.S. practices, including "stress and duress tactics" and "rendering" of detainees to foreign intelligence services, may amount to or result in torture.

Members of the Consortium commend your strong denunciation of torture in Iraq during this week's State of the Union address. As health professionals caring for torture victims, we have witnessed first-hand the devastating impact torture has on the health and well-being of its victims. Every day we see the after-effects of the abuses you described during your address. We see the scars from shackles, the marks from cigarette burns inflicted during interrogation, the wounds and broken bones from severe beatings, and the disfiguration from acid or flames. We listen to stories of shame and humiliation, of haunting nightmares and memories that will not go away, and of lives shattered by extreme cruelty.

The individuals we care for are among the estimated 500,000 torture survivors now living in the United States. Iraq is only one of 100 countries represented in our client populations last year. Sadly, torture is perpetrated or condoned in nations across the world.

The United States has stated its commitment to end torture in our world, and we commend the Department of State for its continuing efforts in this regard. This nation has also demonstrated its commitment to healing torture survivors who live in this country and abroad through passage of the Torture Victims Relief Act in 1998 and subsequent appropriations to the U.S. Office of Refugee Resettlement, the U.S. Agency for International Development, and the United Nations Voluntary Fund for Victims of Torture.

In order to maintain our country's commitment to end torture and support healing, we are deeply concerned by the allegations published in the *Washington Post*. The National Consortium of Torture Treatment Programs takes no position on the credibility of these allegations. We urge the United States government to fully investigate the allegations of torture of detainees, and to place on the public record our nation's policies and practices with respect to torture.

We request a meeting to discuss a response to the *Washington Post* allegations. We suggest that participants might include Anthony Banbury, William Haynes, William Taft, IV, and

Lorne Craner. I hope a member of your staff will contact my office to schedule such a meeting.

Mr. President, torture undermines the fabric of society through fear and terror. As the U.S. Congress articulated in its resolution of June 20, 2001, "When one individual is tortured, the scars inflicted by such horrific treatment are not only found in the victim but in the global system, as the use of torture undermines, debilitates, and erodes the very essence of that system." We urge you to authorize an investigation of the allegations published in the *Washington Post*, to communicate the results of that investigation to the American people, and to ensure that the United States does not and will not participate in torture.

Respectfully,

Ernest Duff
President
National Consortium of Torture Treatment Programs

cc: Anthony Banbury, Acting Senior Director for Democracy, Human Rights and International Operations, National Security Council, Fax (202) 456-9140
The Honorable Lorne Craner, Assistant Secretary of State for Democracy, Human Rights and Labor, Fax (202) 647-5283
William Haynes, General Counsel, Department of Defense, Fax (703) 693-7278
William Taft, IV, Legal Advisor, Department of State, Fax (202)647-1037

PATRICK LEAHY
VIRMONT

COMMITTEES
AGRICULTURE, NUTRITION, AND
FORESTRY
APPROPRIATIONS
JUDICIARY

UNITED STATES SENATE
WASHINGTON, DC 20510-4502

June 2, 2004

The Honorable Condoleezza Rice
National Security Adviser
The White House
Washington, DC 20500

Dear Dr. Rice:

Over the past several months, unnamed Administration officials have suggested in several press accounts that detainees held by the United States in the war on terrorism have been subjected to "stress and duress" interrogation techniques, including beatings, lengthy sleep and food deprivation, and being shackled in painful positions for extended periods of time. Our understanding is that these statements pertain in particular to interrogations conducted by the Central Intelligence Agency in Afghanistan and other locations outside the United States. Officials have also stated that detainees have been transferred for interrogation to governments that routinely torture prisoners.

These assertions have been reported extensively in the international media in ways that could undermine the credibility of American efforts to combat torture and promote the rule of law, particularly in the Islamic world.

I appreciate President Bush's statement, during his recent meeting with U.N. High Commissioner for Human Rights Sergio De Mello, that the United States does not, as a matter of policy, practice torture. I also commend the Administration for its willingness to meet with and respond to the concerns of leading human rights organizations about reports of mistreatment of detainees. At the same time, I believe the Administration's response thus far, including in a recent letter to Human Rights Watch from Department of Defense General Counsel William Haynes, while helpful, leaves important questions unanswered.

The Administration understandably does not wish to catalogue the interrogation techniques used by U.S. personnel in fighting international terrorism. But it should affirm with clarity that America upholds in practice the laws that prohibit the specific forms of mistreatment reported in recent months. The need for a clear and thorough response from the Administration is all the greater because reports of mistreatment initially arose not from outside complaints, but from statements made by administration officials themselves.

With that in mind, I would appreciate your answers to the following questions:

First, Mr. Haynes' letter states that when questioning enemy combatants, U.S. personnel are required to follow "applicable laws prohibiting torture." What are those laws? Given that the United States has ratified the Convention Against Torture and Other Forms of Cruel, Inhuman or Degrading Treatment or Punishment (CAT), is this Convention one of those laws, and does it bind U.S. personnel both inside and outside the United States?

Second, does the Administration accept that the United States has a specific obligation under the CAT not to engage in cruel, inhuman and degrading treatment?

Third, when the United States ratified the CAT, it entered a reservation regarding its prohibition on cruel, inhuman and degrading treatment, stating that it interprets this term to mean "the cruel, unusual and inhumane treatment or punishment prohibited by the Fifth, Eighth and/or Fourteenth amendments to the Constitution." Are all U.S. interrogations of enemy combatants conducted in a manner consistent with this reservation?

Fourth, in its annual Country Reports on Human Rights Practices, the State Department has repeatedly condemned many of the same "stress and duress" interrogation techniques that U.S. personnel are alleged to have used in Afghanistan. Can you confirm that the United States is not employing the specific methods of interrogation that the State Department has condemned in countries such as Egypt, Iran, Eritrea, Libya, Jordan and Burma?

Fifth, the Defense Department acknowledged in March that it was investigating the deaths from blunt force injury of two detainees who were held at Bagram air base in Afghanistan. What is the status of that investigation and when do you expect it to be completed? Has the Defense Department of the CIA investigated any other allegations of torture or mistreatment of detainees, and if so, with what result? What steps would be taken if any U.S. personnel were found to have engaged in unlawful conduct?

Finally, Mr. Haynes' letter offers a welcome clarification that when detainees are transferred to other countries, "U.S. government instructions are to seek and obtain appropriate assurances that such enemy combatants are not tortured." How does the Administration follow up to determine if these pledges of humane treatment are honored in practice, particularly when the governments in question are known to practice torture?

I believe these questions can be answered without revealing sensitive information or in any way undermining the fight against international terrorism. Defeating terrorism is a national security priority, and no one questions the imperative of subjecting captured terrorists to thorough and aggressive interrogations consistent with the law.

The challenge is to carry on this fight while upholding the values and laws that the distinguish us from the enemy we are fighting. As President Bush has said, America is not merely struggling to defeat a terrible evil, but to uphold "the permanent rights and the hopes of mankind." I hope you agree that clarity on this fundamental question of human rights and human dignity is vital to that larger struggle.

Thank you for your assistance.

Sincerely,

PATRICK LEAHY
United States Senator

*[handwritten note: Condi-I want to make
sure we are on the
right moral plain if an
American is being held
abroad.
Pat]*

THE ASSOCIATION OF THE BAR
OF THE CITY OF NEW YORK
42 WEST 44TH STREET
NEW YORK CITY, NEW YORK 10036-6690

————

STANDING COMMITTEE ON MILITARY AFFAIRS AND JUSTICE

COMMITTEE CHAIR   COMMITTEE SECRETARY
Miles P. Fischer, Esq.   Michael Memin, Esq.
440 E. 79th St., Apt. 14D   Budd Lamer Rosenbaum Greenberg & Sade
New York, NY 10021   150 JFK Pkwy
(212) 838-7380 t   Short Hills, NJ 07078
(212) 838-7463 f   (973) 315-4421 t
                                                      (973) 379-7734 f
mpfischer@aol.com   *mmemin@budd-lamer.com*

June 4, 2003

Scott W. Muller
General Counsel
Central Intelligence Agency
1 George Bush Center
Washington, D.C. 20505

Dear Mr. Muller:

We are writing on behalf of the Committees on International Human Rights and Military Affairs & Justice of the Association of the Bar of the City of New York. Founded in 1870, the Association is an independent non-governmental organization with a membership of more than 22,000 lawyers, judges, law professors and government officials, principally from New York City but also from throughout the United States and from 40 other countries. The Committee on International Human Rights investigates and reports on human rights conditions around the world. The Committee on Military Affairs & Justice engages in matters of policy and law relating to the United States Armed Forces. The two committees are investigating reports about the treatment of detainees subject to CIA interrogation at locations outside of the United States, including the centers at Bagram air base in Afghanistan and on the island of Diego Garcia and at Guantanomo.

Over the past six months, several newspapers (*the Washington Post*, *The New York Times* and *the Wall Street Journal*) have reported allegations of abusive treatment by U.S. interrogators of people detained at Bagram. As described in these reports, some of the abusive treatment would qualify under international law as torture or cruel, inhuman and degrading treatment. In addition, the reports state that in some instances, people suspected of having links to terrorism have been apprehended by U.S. officials outside of the United States and rendered to countries where they can be subject to interrogation tactics – including torture – that are illegal in the United States.

Mr. William J. Haynes II, General Counsel of the Defense Department, recently wrote – in response to a letter from the Executive Director of Human Rights Watch to President Bush raising these issues – that "[w]hen questioning enemy combatants, U.S. personnel are required to follow [United States] policy and applicable laws prohibiting torture." In addition, Mr. Haynes confirmed that in the event of a transfer of "detained enemy combatants to other countries for continued detention on [the U.S. Government's] behalf, U.S. Government instructions are to seek and obtain appropriate assurances that such enemy combatants are not tortured."

Our Committees would like an opportunity to review the Directorate of Operations instructions and any other relevant materials giving guidance to interrogators, so that we may assess the clarity and specificity of the instructions given to U.S. interrogators and other U.S. personnel responsible for handling detainees. It is essential that U.S. personnel understand precisely those actions which are permissible and those which are prohibited by law. Our Committees, therefore, would appreciate it if your office could send us copies of the Directorate of Operations instructions and any other relevant material providing guidance to interrogators.

We are requesting only unclassified materials or classified materials redacted to remove classified information. After we have had an opportunity to review the materials, we would like to arrange a meeting with you to discuss these issues further.

We look forward to hearing from you.

Respectfully,

MILES P. FISCHER, CHAIR
COMMITTEE ON MILITARY AFFAIRS & JUSTICE

SCOTT HORTON, CHAIR
COMMITTEE ON INTERNATIONAL HUMAN RIGHTS

PATRICK LEAHY
VIRMONT

COMMITTEES
AGRICULTURE, NUTRITION, AND
FORESTRY
APPROPRIATIONS
JUDICIARY

UNITED STATES SENATE
WASHINGTON, DC 20510-4502

September 9, 2003

Mr. William J. Haynes, II
General Counsel
Department of Defense
1600 Defense Pentagon
Washington, DC 20301-1600

Dear Mr. Haynes:

Thank you for your June 25, 2003, letter concerning U.S. policy with regard to the treatment of detainees held by the United States.

I very much appreciate your clear statement that it is the policy of the United States to comply with all of its legal obligations under the Convention Against Torture and Other Cruel, Inhuman, or Degrading Treatment or Punishment (CAT). I also welcome your statement that it is United States policy to treat all detainees and conduct all interrogations, wherever they may occur, in a manner consistent with our government's obligation, under Article 16 of the CAT, "to prevent other acts of cruel, inhuman, or degrading treatment or punishment" as prohibited under the Fifth, Eighth, and Fourteenth Amendments to the U.S. Constitution.

This statement of policy rules out the use of many of the "stress and duress" interrogation techniques that have been alleged in press reports over the last several months, including beatings, lengthy sleep and food deprivation, and shackling detainees in painful positions for extended periods of time. It should also go a long way towards answering concerns that have been expressed by our friends overseas about the treatment of detainees in U.S. custody. It should strengthen our nation's ability to lead by example in the protection of human rights around the world, and our ability to protect Americans, including our service members, should they be detained abroad.

At the same time, the ultimate credibility of this policy will depend on its implementation by U.S. personnel around the world. In that spirit, I would appreciate it if you could clarify how the administration's policy to comply with the CAT is communicated to those personnel directly involved in detention and interrogation? As you note in your letter, the U.S. obligation under Article 16 of the CAT is to "undertake...to prevent" cruel, inhuman or degrading treatment or punishment. What is the administration doing to prevent violations? Have any recent directives, regulations or general orders been issued to implement the policy your June 25 letter describes? If so, I would appreciate receiving a copy.

I understand that interrogations conducted by the U.S. military are governed at least in part by Field Manual 34-52, which prohibits "the use of force, mental torture, threats, insults, or exposure to unpleasant and inhumane treatment of any kind." This field manual rightly stresses that "the use of force is a poor technique, as it yields unreliable results, may damage subsequent collection efforts, and can induce the source to say whatever he thinks the interrogator wants to hear." Are there further guidelines that in any way add to, define, or limit the prohibitions contained in this field manual? What mechanisms exist for ensuring compliance with these guidelines?

Most important, I hope you can assure me that interrogators working for other agencies, including the CIA, operate from the same guidelines as the Department of Defense. If CIA or other interrogation guidelines in use by any person working for or on behalf of the U.S. government differ, could you clarify how, and why?

I am pleased that before handing over detainees for interrogation to third countries, the United States obtains specific assurances that they will not be tortured. I remain concerned, however, that mere assurances from countries that are known to practice torture systematically are not sufficient. While you state that the United States would follow up on any credible information that such detainees have been mistreated, how would such information emerge if no outsiders have access to these detainees? Has the administration considered seeking assurances that an organization such as the International Committee for the Red Cross have access to detainees after they have been turned over? If not, I urge you to do so.

Finally, has the administration followed up on specific allegations reported in the press that such detainees may have been tortured, including claims regarding a German citizen sent to Syria in 2001, and statements by former CIA official Vincent Cannistrano concerning an al Qaeda detainee sent from Guantanamo to Egypt (see enclosed articles)?

Thank you again for your response to my last letter.

With best regards,

PATRICK LEAHY
United States Senator

handwritten note: I appreciate your concern.

GENERAL COUNSEL OF THE DEPARTMENT OF DEFENSE
1000 DEFENSE PENTAGON
WASHINGTON, D.C. 30301-1600

April 2, 2003

Mr. Kenneth Roth
Executive Director
Human Rights Watch
350 Fifth Avenue, 34th Floor
New York, NY 10118

Dear Mr. Roth:

This is in response to your December 26, 2002, letter to the President and other letters to senior administration officials regarding detention and questioning of enemy combatants captured in the war against terrorists of global reach after the terrorist attacks on the United States on September 11, 2001.

The United States questions enemy combatants to elicit information they may possess that could help the coalition win the war and forestall further terrorist attacks upon the citizens of the United States and other countries. As the President reaffirmed recently to the United Nations High Commissioner for Human Rights, United States policy condemns and prohibits torture. When questioning enemy combatants, U.S. personnel are required to follow this policy and applicable laws prohibiting torture.

If the war on terrorists of global reach requires transfer of detained enemy combatants to other countries for continued detention on our behalf, U.S. Government instructions are to seek and obtain appropriate assurances that such enemy combatants are not tortured.

U.S. Government personnel are instructed to report allegations of mistreatment of or injuries to detained enemy combatants, and to investigate any such reports. Consistent with these instructions, U.S. Government officials investigate any known reports of mistreatment or injuries to detainees.

The United States does not condone torture. We are committed to protecting human rights as well as protecting the people of the United States and other countries against terrorists of global reach.

Sincerely,

William J. Haynes II

CENTRAL INTELLIGENCE AGENCY
Washington, D.C. 20505

General Counsel   23 June 2003

Miles P. Fischer, Esquire
Scott Horton, Esquire
Association of the Bar
of the City of New York
42 West 44th Street
New York, New York 10036-6690

Dear Messrs, Fischer and Horton:

Thank you for your letter of 4 June regarding the treatment of enemy combatants detained in the wake of the terrorist attacks on the United States of 11 September 2001.

As you know, the Director of Central Intelligence is required by law to protect intelligence sources and methods, 50 U.S.C. 5403-3 (c) (6), and the Central Intelligence Agency (CIA) does not comment on operational activities or practices. I can assure you, however, that in its various activities around the world the CIA remains subject to the requirements of US law. Pursuant to Executive Order 12333, any allegations of unlawful behavior are reported by the CIA to the Department of Justice, and may be investigated both by that Department and by the Agency's own Presidentially appointed, Senate confirmed Inspector General. The Agency also provides the Congressional intelligence oversight committees with briefings and materials about its various activities, as provided by 50 U.S.C. §§ 413a, 413b(b).

I appreciate the concerns raised in your letter as well as the thoughtfulness of your questions. While I acknowledge that this response does not provide you with all the information you have requested, I want you to know that I share your committees' interest in ensuring that US personnel understand their obligations under US law and comply with them.

Sincerely,

Scott W. Muller

GENERAL COUNSEL OF THE DEPARTMENT OF DEFENSE
1600 DEFENSE PENTAGON
WASHINGTON, D.C. 20301-1600

June 25, 2003

The Honorable Patrick J. Leahy
United States Senate
Washington, D.C. 20510

Dear Senator Leahy:

I am writing in response to your June 2, 2003, letter to Dr. Rice raising a number of legal questions regarding the treatment of detainees held by the United States in the wake of the September 11, 2001, attacks on the United States and in this Nation's war on terrorists of global reach. We appreciate and fully share your concern for ensuring that in the conduct of this war against a ruthless and unprincipled foe, the United States does not compromise its commitment to human rights in accordance with the law.

In response to your specific inquiries, we can assure you that it is the policy of the United States to comply with all of its legal obligations in its treatment of detainees, and in particular with legal obligations prohibiting torture. Its obligations include conducting interrogations in a manner that is consistent with the Convention Against Torture and Other Cruel, Inhuman, or Degrading Treatment or Punishment ("CAT") as ratified by the United States in 1994. And it includes compliance with the Federal anti-torture statute, 18 U.S.C. §§ 2340–2340A, which Congress enacted to fulfill U.S. obligations under the CAT. The United States does not permit, tolerate or condone any such torture by its employees under any circumstances.

Under Article 16 of the CAT, the United States also has an obligation to "undertake . . . to prevent other acts of cruel, inhuman, or degrading treatment or punishment which do not amount to torture." As you noted, because the terms in Article 16 are not defined, the United States ratified the CAT with a reservation to this provision. This reservation supplies an important definition for the term "cruel, inhuman, or degrading treatment or punishment." Specifically, this reservation provides that "the United States considers itself bound by the obligation under Article 16 to prevent 'cruel, inhuman or degrading treatment or punishment', only in so far as the term 'cruel inhuman or degrading treatment or punishment' means the cruel, unusual and inhumane treatment or punishment prohibited by the Fifth, Eighth, and/or Fourteenth Amendments to the Constitution of the United States." United States policy is to treat all detainees and conduct all interrogations, wherever they may occur, in a manner consistent with this commitment.

As your letter stated, it would not be appropriate to catalogue the interrogation techniques used by U.S. personnel in fighting international terrorism, and thus we cannot comment on specific cases or practices. We can assure you, however, that credible allegations of illegal conduct by U.S. personnel will be investigated and, as appropriate, reported to proper authorities. In this connection, the Department of Defense investigation into the deaths at Bagram, Afghanistan, is still in progress. Should any investigation indicate that illegal conduct has occurred, the appropriate authorites would have a duty to take action to ensure that any individuals responsible are held accountable in accordance with the law.

With respect to Article 3 of the CAT, the United States does not "expel, return ('refouler') or extradite" individuals to other countries where the U.S. believes it is "more likely than not" that they will be tortured, Should an individual be transferred to another country to be held on behalf of the United States, or should we otherwise deem it appropriate, United States policy is to obtain specific assurances from the receiving country that it will not torture the individual being transferred to that country. We can assure you that the United States would take steps to investigate credible allegations of torture and take appropriate action if there were reason to believe that those assurances were not being honored.

In closing, I want to express my appreciation for your thoughtful questions. We are committed to protecting the people of this Nation as well as to upholding its fundamental values under the law.

Sincerely,

William J. Haynes II

The Mikolashek Report

Department of the Army
The Inspector General
Detainee Operations Inspection

July 21, 2004

Department of the Army
Washington DC 20310

Jul 21 2004

MEMORANDUM FOR CHIEF OF STAFF, ARMY

SUBJECT: Department of the Army Inspector General Inspection Report on Detainee Operations

I approve the Department of the Army Inspector General Inspection Report on Detainee Operations dated 21 July 2004.

I direct :

a. As an exception to policy, the unclassified portion of this report be released, without redactions, through posting on the Army website.

b. Findings and recommendations concerning Central Command be forwarded through the Joint Staff to Central Command for consideration.

c. The Director of the Army Staff task the appropriate Army Staff and major Army commands with implementing the recommendations specified in the inspection report and then track their compliance.

d. The Department of the Army Inspector General disseminate the inspection report to the Army leadership.

R. L. Brownlee
Acting Secretary of the Army

FOREWORD

This inspection report responds to the Acting Secretary of the Army's 10 February 2004 directive to conduct a functional analysis of the Army's conduct of detainee and interrogation operations to identify any capability shortfalls with respect to internment, enemy prisoner of war, detention operations, and interrogation precedures and recommend appropriate resolutions or changes if required.

Based on this inspection:

- the overwhelming majority of our leaders and soldiers understand the requirement to treat detainees humanely and are doing so.
- we were unable to identify system failures that resulted in incidents of abuse. These incidents of abuse resulted from the failure of individuals to follow known standards of discipline and Army Values and, in some cases, the failure of a few leaders to enforce those standards of discipline.
- the current operational enviroment demands that we adapt' our soldiers are adapting, so we must also adapt our doctrine, organization, and training.

We examined the two key components of detainee operations: the capture, security and humane treatment of the detainees; and the conduct of interrogation operations in order to gain useful intelligence. While we did not find any systemic failures that directly led to the abusive situations we reviewed, we have made recommendations to improve the effectiveness of detainee operations.

We found that soldiers are conducting operations under demanding, stressful, and dangerous conditions against an enemy who does not follow the Geneva Conventions. They are in an environment that puts a tremendous demand on human intelligence, particularly, at the tactical level where contact with the enemy and the people are most intense. They do understand their duty to treat detainees humanely and in accordance with laws of land warfare. These soldiers understand their obligation to report incidents of abuse when they do occur, and they do so. Our leaders have been developed, trained and educated to adapt to the enviroment in which they find themselves. They understand their tasks, conditions and standards. The conditions of the current operations have caused them to adapt their tactics, techniques and procedures within their capabilities to accommodate this operational enviroment.

Expanding our doctrine to provide commanders flexibility and adaptability within well-defined principles will better enable them to conduct these operations. Our training and education systems at the individual, unit, and institutional levels must continue to be thorough and realistically simulate the intensity of the environment in which we now operate.

While the primary purpose of this inspection was not to examine specific incidents of abuse, we did analyze reported incidents to determine their root or fundamental causes. To provide a context for the incidents, we noted that an estimated 50,000 individuals were detained for at least some period of time by U.S. Forces during the conduct of **OPERATION ENDURING FREEDOM** and **OPERATION IRAQI FREEDOM**. U.S. Forces' contact with the local populace at checkpoints, on patrols, and in other situations increases the number of contacts well in excess of this 50,000 estimate. As of 9 June 2004, there were 94 cases of confirmed or possible abuse of any type, which include, theft, physical assault, sexual assault, and death.

The abuses that have occurred are not representative of policy, doctrine, or Soldier training. These abuses should be viewed as what they are – unauthorized actions taken by a few individuals, and in some cases, coupled with the failure of a few leaders to provide adequate supervision and leadership. These actions, while regrettable, are aberrations when compared to the actions of fellow soldiers who are serving with distinction.

TABLE OF CONTENTS

Executive Summary   Detainee Operations

1. **Background:** On 10 February 2004, the Acting Secretary of the Army directed the Department of the Army Inspector General (DAIG) to conduct an assessment of detainee operations in Afghanistan and Iraq. In order to satisfy this directive, the DAIG inspected internment, enemy prisoner of war, detention operations, and interrogation procedures in Afghanistan and Iraq. The inspection focused on the adequacy of Doctrine, Organization, Training, Materiel, Leadership, Personnel, and Facilities (DOTMLPF), standards, force structure, and policy in support of these types of operations.

This inspection was not an investigation of any specific incidents or units but rather a comprehensive review of how the Army conducts detainee operations in Afghanistan and Iraq.

The DAIG did not inspect the U.S. military corrections system or operations at the Guantanamo Bay Naval Base during this inspection. Central Intelligence Agency (CIA) and Defense HUMINT Services (DHS) operations were not inspected.

2. **Purpose:** Conduct a functional analysis of the Army's internment, enemy prisoner of war, detention operations, and interrogation procedures, policies, and practices based on current Department of Defense and Army policies and doctrine. The inspection is to identify any capability and systemic shortfalls with respect to internment, enemy prisoner of war, detention operations, and interrogation procedures and recommend appropriate resolutions or changes if required.

3. **Concept:** Two teams conducted inspections of 26 locations in Iraq, Afghanistan, and the Continental United States (CONUS). The CONUS team consisted of seven personnel, including augmentees, and visited 10 locations while the OCONUS team consisted of nine personnel, including augmentees, and inspected 16 locations. We interviewed and surveyed over 650 leaders and soldiers spanning the ranks from Private to Major General. We also reviewed 103 reports of allegations of abuse from Criminal Investigation Division (CID) and 22 unit investigations that covered the period from September 2002 to June 2004.

4. **Objectives:** The DAIG Team had four objectives for the inspection:

a. Assess the adequacy of DOTMLPF of Army Forces for internment, enemy prisoner of war, detention operations, and interrogation procedures.
b. Determine the standards for Army Forces charged with internment, enemy prisoner of war, detention operations and interrogation procedures (e.g., size, equipment, standardization, and training).
c. Assess current and future organizations and structures for Army Forces responsible for internment, enemy prisoner of war, detention operations and interrogation procedures.
d. Identify and recommend any changes in policy related to internment, enemy prisoner of war, detention operations and interrogation procedures.

5. **Synopsis:** In the areas that we inspected, we found that the Army is accomplishing its mission both in the capture, care, and custody of detainees and in its interrogation operations. The overwhelming majority of our leaders and soldiers understand and adhere to the requirement to treat detainees humanely and consistent with the laws of land warfare. Time and again these soldiers, while under the stress of combat operations and prolonged insurgency operations, conduct themselves in a professional and exemplary manner.

The abuses that have occurred in both Afghanistan and Iraq are not representative of policy, doctrine, or soldier training. These abuses were unauthorized actions taken by a few individuals, coupled with the failure of a few leaders to provide adequate monitoring, supervision, and leadership over those soldiers. These abuses, while regrettable, are aberrations when compared to their comrades in arms who are serving with distinction.

The functional analysis of the Army's internment, enemy prisoner of war, detention operations, and interrogation procedures, policies, and practices can be broken down into two main functions: (1) capture, care, and control of detainees, and (2) interrogation operations.

We determined that despite the demands of the current operating environment against an enemy who does not abide by the Geneva Conventions, our commanders have adjusted to the reality of the battlefield and, are effectively conducting detainee operations while ensuring the humane treatment of detainees. The significant findings regarding the capture, care, and control of detainees are:

- All interviewed and observed commanders, leaders, and soldiers treated detainees humanely and emphasized the importance of the humane treatment of detainees.
- In the cases the DAIG reviewed, all detainee abuse occurred when one or more individuals failed to adhere to basic standards of discipline, training, or Army Values; in some cases abuse was accompanied by leadership failure at the tactical level.
- Of all facilities inspected, only Abu Ghraib was determined to be undesirable for housing detainees because it is located near an urban population and is under frequent hostile fire, placing soldiers and detainees at risk.

We determined that the nature of the environment caused a demand for tactical human intelligence. The demands resulted in a need for more interrogators at the tactical level and better training for Military Intelligence officers. The significant findings regarding interrogation are:

- Tactical commanders and leaders adapted their tactics, techniques, and procedures, and held detainees longer than doctrinally recommended due to the demand for timely, tactical intelligence.
- Doctrine does not clearly specify the interdependent, and yet independent, roles, missions, and responsibilities of Military Police and Military Intelligence units in the establishment and operation of interrogation facilities.
- Military Intelligence units are not resourced with sufficient interrogators and interpreters, to conduct timely detainee screenings and interrogations in the current operating environment, resulting in a backlog of interrogations and the potential loss of intelligence.
- Tactical Military Intelligence Officers are not adequately trained to manage the full spectrum of the collection and analysis of human intelligence.
- Officially approved CJTF-7 and CJTF-180 policies and the early CJTF-180 practices generally met legal obligations under U.S. law, treaty obligations and policy, if executed carefully, by trained soldiers, under the full range of safeguards. The DAIG Team found that policies were not clear and contained ambiguities. The DAIG Team found implementation, training, and oversight of these policies was inconsistent; the Team concluded, however, based on a review of cases through 9 June 2004 that no confirmed instance of detainee abuse was caused by the approved policies.

636 The Torture Papers: The Road to Abu Ghraib

We reviewed detainee operations through systems (Policy and Doctrine, Organizational Structures, Training and Education, and Leadership and Discipline) that influence how those operations are conducted, and have identified findings and recommendations in each. While these findings are not critical, the implementation of the corresponding recommendations will better enable our commanders to conduct detainee operations now and into the foreseeable future, decrease the possibility of abuse, and ensure we continue to treat detainees humanely.

The findings and observations from this inspection are separated into the following three chapters: Chapter 3 – Capture, Care, and Control of Detainees, Chapter 4 – Interrogation Operations, and Chapter 5 – Other Observations. A summary of the Capture, Care, and Control of Detainees and the Interrogation Operation findings is provided below.

Capture, Care, and Control of Detainees

Army forces are successfully conducting detainee operations to include the capture, care, and control of detainees. Commanders and leaders emphasized the importance of humane treatment of detainees. We observed that leaders and soldiers treat detainees humanely and understand their obligation to report abuse. In those instances where detainee abuse occurred, individuals failed to adhere to basic standards of discipline, training, or Army Values; in some cases individual misconduct was accompanied by leadership failure to maintain fundamental unit discipline, failure to provide proper leader supervision of and guidance to their soldiers, or failure to institute proper control processes.

We found through our interviews and observations conducted between 7 March 2004 and 5 April 2004 that leaders and soldiers in Afghanistan and Iraq were determined to do what was legally and morally right for their fellow soldiers and the detainees under their care. We found numerous examples of military professionalism, ingrained Army Values, and moral courage in both leaders and soldiers. These leaders and soldiers were self-disciplined and demonstrated an ability to maintain composure during times of great stress and danger. With the nature of the threat in both Afghanistan and Iraq, soldiers are placed in extremely dangerous positions on a daily basis. They face the daily risks of being attacked by detainees, contracting communicable diseases from sick detainees, being taunted or spat upon, having urine or feces thrown upon them, and having to treat a detainee humanely who just attacked their unit or killed a fellow soldier. Despite these challenges, the vast majority of soldiers and other U.S. Military personnel continued to do their duty to care for detainees in a fair and humane manner.

Our review of the detainee abuse allegations attempted to identify underlying causes and contributing factors that resulted in abusive situations. We examined these from the perspective of the Policy and Doctrine, Organizational Structures, Training and Education, and Leadership and Discipline systems. We also examined them in terms of location on the battlefield and sought to determine if there was a horizontal, cross-cutting system failure that resulted in a single case of abuse or was common to all of them. Based on this inspection, we were unable to identify system failures that resulted in incidents of abuse. These incidents of abuse resulted from the failure of individuals to follow known standards of discipline and Army Values and, in some cases, the failure of a few leaders to enforce those standards of discipline. We also found that our policies, doctrine, and training are being continually adapted to address the existing operational environment regarding detainee operations. Commanders adjusted existing doctrinal procedures to accommodate the realities of the battlefield. We expect our leaders to do this and they did. The Army must continue to educate for uncertain environments and develop our leaders to adapt quickly to conditions they confront on the battlefield.

Using a data cut-off of 9 June 2004 we reviewed 103 summaries of Army CID reports of investigation and 22 unit investigation summaries conducted by the chain of command involving detainee death or allegations of abuse. These 125 reports are in various stages of completion. 31 cases have been determined that no abuse occurred; 71 cases are closed; and 54 cases are open or undetermined. Of note, the CID investigates every occurrence of a detainee death regardless of circumstances.

Recognizing that the facts and circumstances as currently known in ongoing cases may not be all-inclusive, and that additional facts and circumstances could change the categorization of a case, the team placed each report in a category for the purposes of this inspection to understand the overall numbers and the facts currently known, and to examine for trends or systemic issues. This evaluation of allegations of abuse reports is not intended to influence commanders in the independent exercise of their responsibilities under the Uniform Code of Military Justice (UCMJ) or other administrative disciplinary actions. As an Inspector General inspection, this report does not focus on individual conduct, but on systems and policies.

This review indicates that as of 9 June 2004, 48% (45 of 94) of the alleged incidents of abuse occurred at the point of capture, where soldiers have the least amount of control of the environment. For this inspection, the DAIG Team interpreted point of capture events as detainee operations occurring at battalion level and below, before detainees are evacuated to doctrinal division forward or central collecting points (CPs). This allowed the DAIG Team to analyze and make a determination to where and what level of possible abuse occurred. The point of capture is the location where most contact with detainees occurs under the most uncertain, dangerous, and frequently violent circumstances.

This review further indicates that as of 9 June 2004, 22% (21 of 94) of the alleged incidents of abuse occurred at Internment/Resettlement (I/R) facilities. This includes the highly publicized incident at Abu Ghraib. Those alleged abuse situations at I/R facilities are attributed to individual failure to abide by known standards and/or individual failure compounded by a leadership failure to enforce known standards, provide proper supervision, and stop potentially abusive situations from occurring. As of 9 June 2004, 20%, (19 of 94) of the alleged incidents of abuse occurred at CPs. For the remaining 10% (9 of 94) of the alleged incidents of abuse, a location could not be determined based on the CID case summaries.

The Army estimates that over 50,000 detainees have been captured or processed. While even one case of abuse is unacceptable, we conclude that given the volume of detainees and the potential for abuse in these demanding circumstances, the

* Note For the purpose of this Inspection, we defined abuse as wrongful death, assault, sexual assaul, and theft.

overwhelming majority of our soldiers and leaders are conducting these operations with due regard for the detainees right to be treated humanely and properly.

Detainee abuse does not occur when individual soldiers remain disciplined, follow known procedures, and understand their duty obligation to report abusive behavior. Detainee abuse does not occur when leaders of those soldiers who deal with detainees enforce basic standards of humane treatment, provide oversight and supervision of detainee operations, and take corrective action when they see potentially abusive situations developing. Our site visits, interviews, sensing sessions, and observations indicate that the vast majority of soldiers and leaders, particularly at the tactical level, understand their responsibility to treat detainees humanely and their duty obligation to report infractions.

We inspected I/R facilities at Bagram, Baghdad, and Camp Bucca and found only Abu Ghraib overcrowded, located near a densely populated urban area, on a dangerous main supply route, and subject to frequent hostile enemy fire from enemy mortars or rockets. The physical design of the camps within the prison was not optimal for the mission: towers were not properly placed to support overlapping fields of fire and cover blind spots; entrance/egress routes were hampered by make-shift gates; and sally ports were not used correctly. The supply of fresh water was difficult to maintain and the food quality was sub-standard. Detainees did not have access to bunkers or shelters with overhead cover to protect them from hostile enemy mortar or rocket fire from outside the walls of Abu Ghraib.

Interrogation Operations

The need for timely, tactical human intelligence is critical for successful military operations particularly in the current environment. Commanders recognized this and adapted by holding detainees longer at the point of capture and collecting points to gain and exploit intelligence. Commanders and interrogators also conducted tactical questioning to gain immediate battlefield intelligence. Commanders and leaders must set the conditions for success, and commanders, leaders, and soldiers must adapt to the ever changing environment in order to be successful.

Of the interviewed point of capture battalion and company leaders, 61% (25 of 41) stated their units established CPs and held detainees at their locations from 12 hours up to 30 days. The primary reason units held detainees at these locations was to conduct screenings and interrogations closer to the point of capture. The result of holding detainees for longer timeframes at all locations was increased requirements in facility infrastructure, medical care, preventive medicine, trained personnel, logistics, and security. Organic unit personnel at these locations did not have the required institutional training and were therefore unaware of or unable to comply fully with Army policies in areas such as detainee processing, confinement operations, security, preventive medicine, and interrogation.

Doctrine does not clearly and distinctly address the relationship between the MP operating I/R facilities and the Military Intelligence (MI) personnel conducting intelligence exploitation at those facilities. Neither MP nor MI doctrine specifically defines the interdependent, yet independent, roles, missions, and responsibilities of the two in detainee operations. MP doctrine states MI may colocate with MP at detention sites to conduct interrogations, and coordination should be made to establish operating procedures. MP doctrine does not, however, address approved and prohibited MI procedures in an MP-operated facility. It also does not clearly establish the role of MPs in the interrogation process. Conversely, MI doctrine does not clearly explain MP internment procedures or the role of MI personnel within an internment setting. Contrary to MP doctrine, FM 34-52, *Intelligence Interrogation*, 28 September 1992, implies an active role for MPs in the interrogation process: "Screeners coordinate with MP holding area guards on their role in the screening process. The guards are told where the screening will take place, how EPWs and detainees are to be brought there from the holding area, and what types of behavior on their part will facilitate the screenings." Subordination of the MP custody and control mission to the MI need for intelligence can create settings in which unsanctioned behavior, including detainee abuse, could occur. Failure of MP and MI personnel to understand each other's specific missions and duties could undermine the effectiveness of safeguards associated with interrogation techniques and procedures.

Doctrine that addresses the establishment and operation of interrogations contains inconsistent guidance on terminology, structure, and function of these facilities. At the time of the inspection there were facilities in **OPERATION ENDURING FREEDOM** and **OPERATION IRAQI FREEDOM** that conducted intelligence exploitation as Joint Interrogation Facilities and as a Joint Interrogation and Debriefing Center. The intelligence sections of each were uniquely structured to meet mission requirements.

Shortfalls in numbers of interrogators and interpreters, and the distribution of these assets within the battlespace, hampered human intelligence (HUMINT) collection efforts. Valuable intelligence – timely, complete, clear, and accurate – may have been lost as a result. Interrogators were not available in sufficient numbers to efficiently conduct screening and interrogations of the large numbers of detainees at collecting points (CPs) and internment/resettlement (I/R) facilities, nor were there enough to man sufficient numbers of Tactical Human Intelligence Teams (THTs) for intelligence exploitation at points of capture. Interpreters, especially those Category II personnel authorized to participate in interrogations, were also in short supply. Units offset the shortage of interrogators with contract interrogators. While these contract interrogators provide a valuable service, we must ensure they are trained in military interrogation techniques and policy.

Due to the demand for immediate tactical intelligence, tactical intelligence officers were conducting interrogations of detainees without thorough training on the management of HUMINT analysis and collection techniques. They were not adequately trained to manage the full spectrum of HUMINT assets being used in the current operating environment. The need for these officers to understand the management of the full spectrum of HUMINT operations is a key for successful HUMINT exploitation in the current operating environment.

Current interrogation doctrine includes 17 interrogation approach techniques. Doctrine recognizes additional techniques may be applied. Doctrine emphasizes that every technique must be humane and be consistent with legal obligations. Commanders in both OEF and OIF adopted additional interrogation approach technique policies. Officially approved CJTF-180 and CJTF -7 generally met legal obligations under U.S. law, treaties and policy, if executed carefully, by trained soldiers, under the full range of safeguards. The DAIG Team found that some interrogators were not trained on the additional techniques in either formal school or unit training programs. Some inspected units did not have the correct command policy in effect at the time of inspection. Based on a review of CID case summaries as of 9 June 2004, the team was unable to establish any direct link between the proper use of an approved approach technique or techniques and a confirmed case of detainee abuse.

6. **Conclusion:** The Army's leaders and soldiers are effectively conducting detainee operations and providing for the care and security of detainees in an intense operational environment. Based on this inspection, we were unable to identify system failures that resulted in incidents of abuse. This report offers 52 recommendations that are designed to improve the ability of the Army to accomplish the key tasks of detainee operations: keep the enemy off the battlefield in a secure and humane manner, and gain intelligence in accordance with Army standards.

Chapter 1 Background and Inspection Concept

1. **Background:** On 10 February 2004, the Acting Secretary of the Army directed the Department of the Army Inspector General (DAIG) to conduct an assessment of detainee operations in Afghanistan and Iraq. In order to satisfy the Acting Secretary of the Army's directive, the DAIG inspected internment, enemy prisoner of war, detention operations, and interrogation procedures in Iraq and Afghanistan. The inspection focused on the adequacy of Doctrine, Organization, Training, Materiel, Leadership, Personnel, and Facilities (DOTMLPF), standards, force structure, and policy.

2. **Inspection Concept:** The detailed concept for this inspection is as follows:

a. **Purpose:** The purpose of this inspection was to conduct a functional analysis of detainee operations based on current Department of Defense (DoD) and Army policy and doctrine.

b. **Objectives:**
   (1) Assess the adequacy of DOTMLPF of Army Forces for internment, enemy prisoner of war, detention operations, and interrogation procedures.
   (2) Determine the standards for Army Forces charged with internment, enemy prisoner of war, detention operations and interrogation procedures (e.g., size, equipment, standardization, and training).
   (3) Assess current and future organizations and structures for Army Forces responsible for internment, enemy prisoner of war, detention operations and interrogation procedures.
   (4) Identify and recommend any changes in policy related to internment, enemy prisoner of war, detention operations and interrogation procedures.

c. **Scope:** Two teams conducted inspections of 25 locations in Iraq, Afghanistan, and the Continental United States (CONUS). The CONUS team consisted of seven personnel, including augmentees, and visited seven locations while the OCONUS team consisted of nine personnel, including augmentees, and inspected 16 locations. We interviewed and surveyed over 650 leaders and soldiers spanning the ranks from Private to Major General. We also reviewed 103 reports of allegations of abuse from Criminal Investigation Division (CID) and 22 unit investigations that cover the period of September 2002 to June 2004.

d. **Focus:** The inspection focused on the functional analysis of the Army's internment, enemy prisoner of war, and detention policies, practices, and procedures as the Army executes its role as the DoD Executive Agent for Enemy Prisoners of War and Detention Program. Numerous DoD Policies, Army Regulations, and Army Field Manuals provided the guiding tenets for this inspection.

e. **Task Organization:** Two teams from the DAIG Inspections Division, with augmentation from the Office of the Provost Marshal General (OPMG), Office of the Judge Advocate General (OTJAG), Office of the Surgeon General (OTSG), U.S. Army Maneuver Support Center (USAMANSCEN), U.S. Army Criminal Investigation Command (USACIC), U.S. Army Special Operations Command (USASOC), and the U.S. Army Intelligence Center (USAIC) conducted the inspection by traveling to 25 locations in CONUS and OCONUS. The composition of these teams was as follows:

Inspector General

CONUS	OCONUS
Team Chief IG	Team Chief IG
Detailed IG	Operation Officer IG
Detailed IG	Detailed IG
Assistant IG	Detailed IG
Expert from OTSG	Expert from USASOC
Expert from OPMG	Expert from OTJAG
Exprt from USACIC (Assistant IG)	Expert from USAIC
	Expert from USAMANSCEN (Assistant IG)
	Expert from OPMG

f. **Inspection Process:**
   (1) Preparation Phase: Research and Training (February–March 2004)
   (2) Execution Phase: On-Site Inspections (March–April 2004)
   (3) Completion Phase: Final Report Preparation (April–June 2004)

g. **Inspection Locations and Schedule:** See Appendix C.

h. **Inspection Approach:** The Inspectors General (IG) for Combined Forces Land Component Command (CFLCC), Combined Joint Task Force-7 (CJTF-7), Combined Joint Task Force-180 (CJTF-180), and local IGs served as coordinating agents for all DAIG inspection activities at those locations. These IGs were telephonically and electronically notified by DAIG with the Notification Memorandum and Detailed Inspection Plan that was sent to all affected Commanders/IGs on 20 February 2004.

i. **Other Reports:** This report mentions the Ryder Report, Miller Report, and Taguba Investigation throughout its inspection results. These two reports and investigation deal with the following: the Ryder Report is an assessment of detention and corrections operations in Iraq; the Miller Report is a classified assessment of the Department of Defense's counter-terrorism interrogation and detention operations in Iraq; and the Taguba Investigation is a classified investigation under Army Regulation 15-6 into the 800th Military Police (MP) Brigade's detention and internment operations.

j. **Definitions:** The DAIG used the following definitions throughout the report.

(1) The DAIG defined the term "detainee operations" as the range of actions taken by soldiers beginning at the point of capture, the movement of detainees through division forward and central collecting points (CPs), to internment at internment/resettlement (I/R) facilities, and release. This includes the administrative and medical processing of detainees, medical treatment of detainees, sanitary conditions at I/R facilities and CPs, and interrogation procedures. The term "detainee operations" does not apply to confined U.S. Military personnel.

(2) Army Regulation (AR) 190-8, *Enemy Prisoners of War, Retained Personnel, Civilian Internees and Other Detainees*, 1 October 1997, defines the term detainee as "any person captured or otherwise detained by an armed force." The DAIG uses the term as defined by AR 190-8 in this report. The term "detainee" includes enemy prisoners of war (EPWs), retained persons (RP), civilian internees (CIs), and other detainees (ODs). When making a differentiation between the different classifications of detainees, the report will specifically mention EPWs, RPs, CIs, or ODs. The report will also point out the use of non-doctrinal terms sometimes used as detainee classifications.

(3) The battlespace of **OPERATION ENDURING FREEDOM** (OEF) and **OPERATION IRAQI FREEDOM** (OIF) included an enemy that deployed asymmetrically with adaptive tactics; a battlespace in which there was not always a clear forward line of troops, massing of forces, or an identifiable rear area to which detainees could be rapidly evacuated. The battlespace of OEF and OIF was non-linear with combat and stability operations taking place simultaneously throughout the areas of operation. Combatants included both uniformed and non-uniformed state and non-state sponsored forces who fought using conventional and non-conventional methods to include terrorist actions against both military and civilian targets. Detainees were, and continue to be, more than compliant civilian internees and enemy prisoners of war. They are primarily a non-compliant hostile population that requires more intensive screening, interrogation and segregation. The Army is in a new and unique operational environment stemming from the need for immediate tactical level intelligence coupled with the significant numbers of non-traditional combatants/detainees encountered.

(4) We define a problem as systemic if it is widespread and presents a pattern. We attempted through observations, sensing sessions, interviews, site visits, surveys, and reviews of documents, other reports, and investigations to identify failures in the systems that comprise detainee operations.

Chapter 2   Inspection Methodology

The Department of the Army Inspector General (DAIG) Team developed a baseline approach to the inspection that focused on gathering information and data from five primary domains: interviews, sensing sessions, document reviews, surveys of commanders, leaders, and soldiers, and site visits. This approach allowed the team to glean perceptions and attitudes about detainee operations from selected individuals and populations; to assess detainee operations in doctrinal manuals, unit policies, unit Standing Operating Procedures (SOPs); and to determine compliance with Department of Defense (DoD) and Army policies. The team visited U.S. Armed Forces-controlled internment/resettlement (I/R) facilities and division central and forward collecting points (CPs), as well as units conducting patrol missions, to gather overall trends and observations on detainee operations from point of capture to the processing conducted at U.S. Armed Forces-controlled I/R facilities.

This baseline methodology afforded the team a standard, systematic approach to conducting an inspection at each location, which proved essential since the DAIG team conducted split operations with two teams that traveled separately to continental United States (CONUS) and outside the continental United States (OCONUS) locations. The team had to tailor their trips to look at units that had already returned from **OPERATION ENDURING FREEDOM** (OEF) and **OPERATION IRAQI FREEDOM** (OIF) as well as those units currently deployed.

The methodology established a three-phase plan for executing the inspection.

a. **Phase 1: Preparation.** This phase included travel planning, pre-deployment training, administrative requirements, a review of documents the team requested in advance from the unit IGs, pre-inspection visits to the National Training Center (NTC) at Fort Irwin and the Joint Readiness Training Center (JRTC) at Fort Polk, and development of a detailed inspection plan.

b. **Phase 2: Execution.** This phase outlined the physical execution of the itinerary developed by the local IG in accordance with the Detailed Inspection Plan. Each visit began with an inbrief to the unit's senior leadership and ended with an outbrief. The DAIG Team conducted interviews, sensing sessions, and a survey of Commanders, leaders and soldiers currently in the area of responsibility (AOR) and those who recently returned from OEF and OIF to determine detainee operations tactics, techniques, and procedures from point of capture to arrival at the CPs; inspected CPs from receipt of detainees to the transfer of detainees to U.S. Armed Forces-controlled I/R facilities; inspected U.S. Armed Forces-controlled I/R facilities and operations; and reviewed policies, plans, records, programs, Standard Operating Procedures (SOPs), and other related documents.

c. **Phase 3: Completion.** The DAIG team returned to home station and conducted post-trip data analyses of the information gathered. The team then crafted detailed trip reports of the visit that captured the critical information gleaned from the trips. These trip reports formed the basis from which the team developed the findings outlined in the report. Additionally, team members cross-walked information and traveled to the MI and MP schools for coordination and confirmation of information used in the findings.

The following section outlines the baseline methodology in detail to include the specific requirements for interviews and sensing sessions based upon the type of unit visited.

a. **Inspection Methodology.** The local IG served as the coordinating agent for all DAIG inspection activities. The coordinating agent worked with his or her respective

DAIG team point of contact (POC) to develop an itinerary for a four-day inspection for CONUS units and a 30-day period for OCONUS. The coordinating agent and DAIG Team POC fine-tuned the itinerary to maximize the team's ability to meet the inspection's baseline requirements.

b. **Personnel Interviewed:**

    (1) OCONUS

        (a) The team conducted interviews at CFLCC, CJTF-7, CJTF-180, U.S. Armed Forces-controlled I/R facilities, and division CPs. The team interviewed selected leaders from CFLCC/CJTF/division/brigade/battalion staffs and company level personnel. Individual interviews occurred in the interviewee's office or in a similar location free from interruptions and telephone calls. The coordinating agent scheduled these interviews to last no more than 1.5 hours. The coordinating agent also considered geographical dispersion and travel times between events. The interviews were conducted by one or two DAIG team members with the unit interviewee.

        (b) The DAIG team conducted sensing sessions at each U.S. Armed Forces-controlled I/R facility, division CPs, and at the company level, one for junior enlisted (Private through Specialist, but not including Corporals) and one for junior non-commissioned officers (Sergeant and Staff Sergeant). Units provided eight to twelve soldiers per session. Each sensing session required a classroom or similar facility that was removed from the unit's normal work location. The area was relatively quiet and free from interruptions and telephone calls. In addition, the room needed no less than 14 chairs or desks formed in a circle or square. The coordinating agent scheduled 1.5-hour time blocks for each sensing session. The sensing sessions were conducted by two DAIG team members with the unit soldiers.

        (c) The coordinating agent adjusted the interview schedule, in coordination with the team, based upon the availability of personnel. The team recognized that only full-time manning personnel might be available in Reserve Component units.

        (d) The matrix below was a strawman that was finalized by the DAIG team POC and the local IG for the OCONUS inspection.

Interviewee/ Sensing Session Requirements	CFLCC	CJTF	DIV COLL Point	BDE COLL Point	Co	MP BDE /BN	US Military Controlled/ Oversight Det Fac
SJA			1			1	1
G2/S2 (for HUMINT purposes)	1	1	1	1		1	1
S1 (if involved with detainee processing)						1	1
SURGEON/MED OFF	1	1	1	1		1	1
PMO	1	1	1				
CHAPLAIN			1	1		1	1
ENGINEER/S4		1	1	1		1	1
CDR/OIC			1	1	1	1	1
1 SG/NCOIC			1	1	1	1	1
S3						1	

INTERROGAT OR (depending where they are located)		3	3		3
GUARD (E1–4) SENSING SESSION		1EA (8–12 SOLDIERS)	1 EA (8–12 SOLDIERS)		1 EA (8–12 SOLDIERS)
GUARD (E5–6) SENSING SESSION		1 EA (8–12 SOLDIERS)	1 EA (8–12 SOLDIERS)		1 EA (8–12 SOLDIERS)
GUARD (NCOIC)		1	1		1
SECURITY FORCE (E1–4) SENSING SESSION					1 EA (8–12 SOLDIERS)
SECURITY FORCE (E5–6) SENSING SESSION					1 EA (8–12 SOLDIERS)
SECURITY FORCE NCOIC					1
INFANTRY BDE XO			1		
INFANTRY BN XO			1		
INFANTRY Co CDR/1SG			1		
PREVENTIVE MED INSP		1	1		1
COLL PT MP PLT LDR		1	1		
COLL PT MP PLT SGT		1	1		
UNIT PLT LDR INVOLVED WITH CAPTURE OF PERSONNEL				2	
UNI PLT SGT INVOLVED WITH CAPTURE OF PERSONNEL				2	
UNIT SOLDIERS INVOLVED WITH CAPTURE OF PERSONNEL (E1–4) SENSING SESSION				2 EA (8–12 SOLDIERS) PER COLLECTING POINT	
UNIT SOLDIERS INVOLVED WITH CAPTURE OF PERSONNEL (E5–6) SENSING SESSION				2 EA (8–12 SOLDIERS) PER COLLECTING POINT	

(2) CONUS

    (a) The team conducted interviews of division, brigade, battalion, and company level personnel. The team interviewed selected leaders from each of these type units. Individual interviews occurred in the interviewee's office or in a similar location that was free from interruptions and telephone calls. The coordinating agent scheduled these interviews to last no more than 1.5 hours. The coordinating agent considered geographical dispersion and travel times between events. The interviews were conducted by one or two team members with the unit interviewee.

    (b) The DAIG team conducted sensing sessions with collecting point and I/R facility guards and with soldiers who captured personnel during OEF and OIF. Sensing sessions included one for junior enlisted (Private through Specialist, but not including Corporals) and one for junior non-commissioned officers (Sergeant and Staff Sergeant). Units provided eight to twelve soldiers per session. Each sensing session required a classroom or similar facility that was removed from the unit's normal work location. The area was relatively quiet and free from interruptions and telephone calls. In addition, the room needed no less than 14 chairs or desks formed in a circle or square. The coordinating agent scheduled 1.5-hour time blocks for each sensing session. The sensing sessions were conducted by two team members with the unit soldiers.

(c) The coordinating agent adjusted the interview schedule, in coordination with the team, based upon the availability of personnel. The team recognized that only full-time manning personnel might be available in Reserve Component units.

(d) The matrix below was a strawman that was finalized by the DAIG team POC and the local IG for the CONUS inspection.

Interviewee/Sensing Session Requirements	DIV/SEP BDE	BDE	BN	Co
INFANTRY CDR			1	1
INFANTRY CSM/1SG			1	1
INFANTRY XO		1		
MP CDR/XO	1		1	
MP S4	1		1	
PMO	1			
COLL PT GUARDS (E1–4) SENSING SESSION				1 EA (8–12 SOLDIERS)
COLL PT GUARDS (E5–6) SENSING SESSION				1 EA (8–12 SOLDIERS)
GUARD (NCOIC)				1
DSA/BSA CDR (if coll pt was is in DSA/BSA)			2	
COLL PT MP PLT LDR				1
COLL PT MP PLT SGT				1
Interviewee/Sensing Session Requirements	DIV/SEP BDE	BDE	BN	Co
UNIT PLT LDR INVOLVED WITH CAPTURE OF PERSONNEL			2	
UNIT PLT SGT INVOLVED WITH CAPTURE OF PERSONNEL			2	
UNIT SOLDIERS INVOLVED WITH CAPTURE OF PERSONNEL (E1–4) SENSING SESSION				2 EA (8–12 SOLDIERS)
UNIT SOLDIERS INVOLVED WITH CAPTURE OF PERSONNEL (E5–6) SENSING SESSION				2 EA (8–12 SOLDIERS)
CHAPLAIN	1	1	1	

d. **Administrative Support Requirements.** The DAIG team conducted this inspection with minimal disruption to ongoing unit missions. The team required special arrangements from the field Inspectors General (IGs), including assistance with country clearances, travel in the AOR, in-country travel, sleeping arrangements, convoy security arrangements, body armor, weapons and ammunition, communications, scheduling of inbriefs and outbriefs, interviews and sensing sessions, and an appropriate work space for up to nine personnel conducting DAIG business.

e. **Documents Reviewed In Advance (OCONUS Only):**
   (1) All inspections related to detainee operations, including command products, Inspector General products, Criminal Investigative Division(CID), legal, etc.
   (2) All case histories of punishment (judicial and non-judicial) relating to detainee abuse.
   (3) Past and current Rules of Engagement (ROE).
f. **Documents Reviewed on Site (OCONUS Only):**
   (1) Unit TACSOPs relating to detainee operations (e.g., 5Ss and T, collecting point procedures, and inventorying EPW belongings).
   (2) U.S. Armed Forces-controlled I/R facility SOPs.
   (3) I/R BDE/BN/CO unit manning documentation.
   (4) DD Form 2745 (EPW Capture Tag) log.
   (5) DD Form 629 (Receipt for Prisoner or Detained Person) log.
   (6) DA Form 4137 (Receipt for Evidence/Property Custody Document) log.
   (7) DD Form 2708 (Receipt of Inmate/Detained Person) log.
   (8) DD Form 1594 (Duty Logs).
   (9) U.S. Armed Forces-controlled I/R facilities reporting system database.
   (10) Facility maintenance and repair documentation.
   (11) Facility security SOP.
   (12) Detainee in/out-processing documentation.
g. **Documents Reviewed During Inspections (CONUS Only):**
   (1) Unit Tactical Standing Operating Procedures (TACSOP) relating to detainee operations (e.g., 5Ss and T, collecting point procedures, and inventorying EPW belongings).
   (2) U.S. Armed Forces-controlled I/R facility SOPs.
   (3) I/R Brigade (BDE)/Battalion (BN)/Company (Co) unit manning documentation.
h. **Inspection Itineraries.** DAIG requested each coordinating agent develop a draft itinerary that met the requirements listed in paragraph b. DAIG requested the coordinating agent include the necessary travel time between scheduled locations. The DAIG team POC and the coordinating agent developed an itinerary that allows the DAIG team to meet the objectives listed in Chapter 1 paragraph 2b. The DAIG team conducted an inbrief with the senior commander/representative at each location.

Chapter 3   Capture, Care, and Control of Detainees

1. **Summary of Findings:** Army forces are successfully conducting detainee operations to include the capture, care, and control of detainees. Commanders and leaders emphasized the importance of humane treatment of detainees and, currently, leaders and soldiers treat detainees humanely and understand their obligation to report abuse. In those instances where detainee abuse occurred, individuals failed to adhere to basic standards of discipline, training, or Army Values; in some cases individual misconduct was accompanied by leadership failure to maintain fundamental unit discipline, failure to provide proper leader supervision of and guidance to their soldiers, or failure to institute proper control processes.

For the purpose of this inspection, we defined abuse as wrongful death, assault, battery, sexual assault, sexual battery, or theft. As of 9 June 2004 we had reviewed 103 summaries of Criminal Investigative Division (CID) reports of investigation and 22 unit investigation summaries conducted by the chain of command involving detainee death or alleged abuse. These 125 reports are in various stages of completion. No abuse was determined to have occurred in 31 cases; 71 cases are closed; and 54 cases are open or undetermined. Of note, the CID investigates every occurrence of a detainee death regardless of circumstances. While recognizing that any abuse incident is one too many, we conducted a review and categorization of the summary reports of the 125 investigations. Based on our review and analysis of reports and case summaries of investigations and our observations and interviews conducted throughout this inspection, we could not identify a systemic cause for the abuse incidents. The DAIG uses the term "systemic" specifically to describe a problem if it is widespread and presents a pattern. As defined by the DAIG in this report, a systemic issue may be found either horizontally across many various types of units, or vertically through many command levels or within systems. The DAIG determined that incidents where detainees were allegedly mistreated occurred as isolated events. In a few incidents, higher ranking individuals up to Lieutenant Colonel were involved; however, the chain of command took action when an allegation of detainee abuse was reported.

Abu Ghraib had problems with deteriorating infrastructure that impacted the clean, safe, and secure working environment for soldiers and living conditions for detainees. Poor food quality and food distribution, lack of laundry capability, and inadequate personal hygiene facilities affected the detainees' living conditions. Overcrowding, frequent enemy hostile fire, and lack of in-depth force protection measures also put soldiers and detainees at risk.

2. **Findings:**

a. **Finding 1:**
   (1) *Finding*: All interviewed and observed commanders, leaders, and soldiers treated detainees humanely and emphasized the importance of the humane treatment of detainees.
   (2) *Standard*: See Appendix E.
   (3) *Inspection Results*: The DAIG team conducted numerous interviews and sensing sessions with leaders and soldiers that revealed most leaders and soldiers have treated detainees humanely and would report detainee abuse if they became aware of it.

For **OPERATION ENDURING FREEDOM** (OEF), Chairman Joint Chiefs of Staff (CJCS) Message dated 211933Z JAN 02, stated that al Qaeda and Taliban would be treated humanely and, to the extent appropriate and consistent with military necessity, in a manner consistent with the principles of the Geneva Conventions. Therefore, most detainees were classified as civilian internees (CIs) (sub-classified for OEF by the following non-doctrinal terms: Persons Under U.S. Control (PUC), Enemy Combatant (EC), and Low-level Enemy Combatant (LLEC)). Interviews, sensing sessions, and document reviews revealed that most soldiers were aware of their requirement to treat detainees humanely. In most cases, the present level of treatment exceeded the

Common Article 3 standard of treatment. Notwithstanding, while detainee abuse had occurred in OEF in the past, the DAIG team observed that units currently conducting detainee operations missions treated detainees humanely.

Many non-commissioned officers (NCOs) stated very clearly that the humane treatment of detainees was paramount to the success of the mission. Another group of junior enlisted soldiers stated that they received substantial training on detainee treatment. They went on to specifically mention that they were taught to treat detainees with dignity and respect. In another sensing session, the NCOs stated that the minimum standard for treating detainees is protection, respect, and humane treatment. Some went on to say that violations are not tolerated by the command or fellow soldiers.

Consistent with these statements, the DAIG team that visited Iraq and Afghanistan discovered no incidents of abuse that had not been reported through command channels; all incidents were already under investigation. The DAIG team that visited units recently returning from Iraq did receive a total of five new allegations of potential abuse that occurred prior to January 2004. The DAIG team immediately turned these over to the chain of command and Army Criminal Investigation Division (CID). There is no evidence of the cover-up of current detainee abuse by U.S. Soldiers. This is consistent with the results of the teams' sensing sessions; all currently deployed soldiers were aware of their responsibility to report abuse and appeared to be willing and able to report any potential abuse.

In OIF, U.S. Forces detained the full spectrum of classes of detainees, but most were classified as EPWs or CIs. Presently, CIs make up the vast majority of the U.S.-controlled detainee population. EPWs are entitled to all the protections in the Geneva Convention Relative to the Treatment of Prisoners of War (GPW), and CIs are entitled to relevant protections in the Geneva Convention Relative to the Protection of Civilian Persons in Time of War (GC). The GPW and GC provide detailed levels and standards of treatment for EPWs and CIs that include treatment during armed conflict and occupation. Most leaders and Soldiers treated EPWs and CIs humanely and consistent with the Geneva Conventions (GPW and GC).

The Army estimates that over 50,000 detainees have been captured or processed. While even one case of abuse is unacceptable, we conclude that given the volume of detainees and the potential for abuse in these demanding circumstances, the overwhelming majority of our soldiers and leaders are conducting these operations with due regard for the detainees right to be treated humanely and properly.

Detainee abuse does not occur when individual soldiers remain disciplined, follow known procedures and understand their duty obligation to report abusive behavior. Detainee abuse does not occur when leaders of those soldiers who deal with detainees enforce basic standards of humane treatment, provide oversight and supervision of detainee operations and take corrective action when they see potentially abusive situations developing. Our site visits, interviews, sensing sessions and observations indicate that the vast majority of soldiers and leaders, particularly at the tactical level, understand their responsibility to treat detainees humanely and their duty obligation to report infractions.

The GC and GPW require that copies of the GC be posted in the detainees' language in facilities that contain EPWs and/or CIs. Only 25% (4 of 16) facilities inspected maintained copies of the Geneva Conventions in the detainees' language. No facilities in Afghanistan complied with this Geneva requirement, while only four facilities in Iraq were compliant. Other specific details of treatment outlined in the GPW and GC are covered elsewhere in this report.

The DAIG Team observed that units made efforts to comply with the DoD requirement to treat the detainees consistent with the Geneva Conventions. Some of the improvements being made by units and resourceful individuals include: increased training for key non-commissioned officers (NCOs) and small unit leaders; developing standing operating procedures (SOPs); and requesting copies of the Geneva Conventions in the detainees' language for posting.

In general, the Miller Report recognized that detainees should be secured in a humane environment and that greater involvement by judge advocates was required. The DAIG team did not observe a dedicated judge advocate for interrogation operations, but did note that the MI brigades, assigned to duty at Abu Ghraib, were each assigned at least one brigade judge advocate. The Ryder Report stated EPWs and CIs should receive the full protections of the Geneva Conventions unless the denial of these protections was due to specifically articulated military necessity.

The Taguba Investigation observed that many soldiers and units upheld the Army Values. The Taguba Investigation also detailed numerous incidents where U.S. soldiers abused detainees, which the investigation characterized as "systemic." As used in the Taguba Investigation, the term "systemic" deals with a subset of the security and interrogation operations at only one interment /resettlement facility and is not theater-wide. However, MG Taguba testified before the Senate Armed Services Committee on 11 May 04, narrowing the extent of the term "systemic" by stating that these particular abuses were individual actions not committed at the direction of the chain of command and that the resulting photos were taken with personal cameras. Additionally, the Taguba Investigation recommended detention facilities make several changes that would help ensure compliance with the Geneva Conventions As stated above, the DAIG uses the term "systemic" specifically to describe a problem if it is widespread and presents a pattern. As defined by the DAIG in this report, a systemic issue may be found either horizontally across many various types of units, or vertically through many command levels from squad through division or higher level. Based on our review and analysis of reports and case summaries of investigations and our observations and interviews conducted throughout this inspection, we could not identify a systemic cause for the abuse incidents.

(4) *Recommendation*: CJTF-7 and CJTF-180 continue to emphasize compliance with the requirements regarding the humane treatment of detainees.

Recommendation: Commanders continue to stress the importance of humane treatment of detainees and continue to supervise and train soldiers on their responsibility to treat detainees humanely and their responsibility to report abuse.

b. **Finding 2:**
   (1) *Finding*: In the cases the DAIG reviewed, all detainee abuse occurred when one or more individuals failed to adhere to basic standards of discipline, training,

> or Army Values; in some cases abuse was accompanied by leadership failure at the tactical level.
> (2) *Standard*: See Appendix E.
> (3) *Inspection Results*: As of 9 June 2004, there were 125 reported cases of detainee abuse (to include death, assault, or indecent assault) that either had been, or were, under investigation.

For the purpose of this inspection, we defined abuse as wrongful death, assault, sexual assault, or theft. As of 9 June 2004 we had reviewed 103 summaries of Criminal Investigation Division (CID) reports of investigation and 22 unit investigation summaries conducted by the chain of command involving detainee death or alleged abuse. These 125 reports are in various stages of completion. No abuse was determined to have occurred in 31 cases; 71 cases are closed; and 54 cases are open or undetermined. Of note, the CID investigates every occurrence of a detainee death regardless of circumstances.

Recognizing that the facts and circumstances as currently known in ongoing cases may not be all inclusive, and that additional facts and circumstances could change the categorization of a case, the team placed each report in a category for the purposes of this inspection to understand the overall numbers and the facts currently known, and to examine for a trend or systemic issue. This evaluation of alleged abuse reports is not intended to, nor should it, influence commanders in the independent exercise of their responsibilities under the Uniform Code of Military Justice (UCMJ) or other administrative disciplinary actions. As an Inspector General inspection, this report does not focus on individual conduct, but on systems and policies.

We separated these 125 cases into two categories:

(1) no abuse occurred
(2) confirmed or possible abuse

In the first category of no abuse occurring, we further separate the reports into deaths (to include death from natural causes and justified homicide as determined by courts martial) and other instances (to include cases where there was insufficient evidence to determine whether abuse occurred or where the leadership determined, through courts martial or investigation, that no abuse occurred). There were a total of 19 natural deaths and justified homicides, and 12 instances of insufficient evidence or determined that no abuse occurred. Deaths occurred at the following locations: 15 at I/R facilities; one at Central Collecting Points (CPs); one at Forward CPs; and two at the point of capture (POC) for a total of 19. Other instances where it was determined that no abuse occurred were at the following locations: two at I/R facilities; one at Central CPs; two at Forward CPs; five at the POC; and two at locations which could not be determined or did not fall into doctrinal categories, for a total of 12.

In the second category of confirmed or possible abuse, we further separated the reports into wrongful deaths, deaths with undetermined causes, and other alleged abuse (e.g., assault, sexual assault, or theft). There were a total of 20 deaths and 74 incidents of other alleged abuse. Deaths occurred at the following locations: 10 at I/R facilities; 0 at Central CPs; five at Forward CPs; and five at the POC, for a total of 20. Other instances of alleged abuse occurred at the following locations: 11 at I/R facilities; three at

Central CPs; 11 at Forward CPs; 40 at the POC; and nine at locations which could not be determined or did not fall into doctrinal categories, for a total of 74.

This review indicates that as of 9 June 2004, 48% (45 of 94) of the alleged incidents of abuse occurred at the point of capture. For this inspection, the DAIG team interpreted point of capture events as detainee operations occurring at battalion level and below, before detainees are evacuated to doctrinal division forward or central collecting points (CPs). This allowed the DAIG team to analyze and make a determination to where and what level of possible abuse occurred. The point of capture is the location where most contact with detainees occurs under the most uncertain, dangerous and frequently violent circumstances. During the period of April–August 2003 when units were most heavily engaged in combat operations, 56% (29 of 52) of point of capture incidents were reported. Even during this period of high intensity combat operations, soldiers and leaders identified incidents that they believe to be abuse and the command took action when reported. Most of the allegations of abuse that occurred at the point of capture were the result of actions by a soldier or soldiers who failed to maintain their self discipline, integrity, and military bearing, when dealing with the recently captured detainees. There are a few incidents that clearly show criminal activity by an individual or individuals with disregard of their responsibility as a soldier.

This review further indicates that as of 9 June 2004, 22% (21 of 94) of the alleged incidents of abuse occurred at I/R facilities. This includes the highly publicized incident at Abu Ghraib. Those alleged abuse situations at the I/R facilities are attributed to: individual failure to abide by known standards and/or individual failure compounded by a leadership failure to enforce known standards, provide proper supervision and stop potentially abusive situations from occurring.

While recognizing that any abuse incident is one too many, through a review of the summary reports of the 125 investigations and categorizing them, the DAIG did not identify a systemic cause for the abuse incidents. The DAIG uses the term "systemic" specifically to describe a problem if it is widespread and presents a pattern. As defined by the DAIG in this report, a systemic issue may be found either horizontally across many various types of units, or vertically through many command levels from squad through division or higher level. The DAIG determined that incidents where detainees were allegedly mistreated occurred as isolated events. In a few incidents, higher ranking individuals up to Lieutenant Colonel were involved; however, the chain of command took action when an allegation of detainee abuse was reported.

Recognizing that the facts and circumstances as currently known in ongoing cases may not be all inclusive, and that additional facts and circumstances could change the categorization of a case, the team placed each report in a category for the purposes of this inspection to understand the overall numbers and the facts currently known, and to examine for a trend or systemic issue. This evaluation of alleged abuse reports is not intended to influence commanders in the independent exercise of their responsibilities under the Uniform Code of Military Justice (UCMJ) or other administrative disciplinary actions.

The DAIG team that visited Iraq and Afghanistan found no incidents of abuse that had not already been reported through command channels; all incidents were already under investigation. The DAIG team that visited units recently returning from Iraq did receive a total of five new allegations of potential abuse that occurred prior to January 2004. In each of these cases, CID and the chain of command were notified of the allegations. There is no evidence of any cover-up of current detainee abuse by U.S. soldiers. This is consistent with the results of the teams' sensing sessions that all currently deployed soldiers were aware of their responsibility to report abuse and appeared to be willing and able to report it.

In studying the actual abuse investigations, the incidents may be broken down into two broad categories. The first category will be referred to as isolated abuse, and the second as progressive abuse. The first are those incidents that appear to be a one-time occurrence. In other words, these are incidents where individual soldiers took inappropriate actions upon the capture of detainees or while holding or interrogating them. The second category of detainee abuse, referred to as progressive abuse because these usually develop from an isolated incident into a more progressive abuse.

There is substantial research on the behavior of guards in prisons and Enemy Prisoner of War (EPW)/Prisoner of War (POW) camps, in addition to the Department of Defense (DoD) experience of running simulated prisoner of war resistance training. Research indicates that regardless of how good the training and oversight, some inappropriate behavior will occur. (For example, one of the seminal studies of prisoner/guard behavior is Haney, C., Banks, C., & Zimbardo, P., *A Study of Prisoners and Guards in a Simulated Prison*, the Office of Naval Research, 1973. For a more recent review, along with significant commentary, see Philip Zimbardo, A Situationalist Perspective on the Psychology of Evil: Understand How Good People are Transformed into Perpetrators, a chapter in Arthur Miller (Ed.) *The social psychology of good and evil: Understanding our capacity for kindness and cruelty*. New York: Guilford, 2004. Also worth reviewing are Stanley Milgram's studies, starting with Obedience to authority, New York: Harper & Row, 1974.) Because of this, the DoD simulated prisoner of war resistance training that prepares service members to resist exploitation, requires intensive oversight to prevent the abuse of soldiers by other soldiers.

Contributing factors to the first category of abuse include poor training (common in the cases the DAIG team reviewed), poor individual discipline, novel situations (to include the stressors involved in combat operations), and a lack of control processes (specific oversight mechanisms). Commander's addressed the first category of abuse through counseling, administrative action, and UCMJ (up to and including courts-martial).

Below are four examples of this first category of detainee abuse from the 125 reported allegations referenced in the first paragraph of the inspection results above.

– One incident occurred at an internment/resettlement (I/R) facility where a Master Sergeant and her three subordinates attempted to beat several detainees as they arrived at the camp. Other soldiers, not in her chain of command, prevented much of the potential abuse and then reported the Master Sergeant to the chain of command who took corrective action. All four soldiers were administratively separated from the Army; three of these soldiers also received non-judicial punishment.

- In another incident a Specialist was threatening detainees by stating he would shoot them. A guard observed him making these threats and immediately turned the Specialist in to his chain of command. The commander took quick action, administering an Article 15, to prevent a recurrence.
- Another example occurred in an internment facility where a Specialist and a Staff Sergeant began to punish a detainee by using excessive force. Another soldier from a different company joined them. The Platoon Sergeant discovered the incident and immediately relieved both of the soldiers in his platoon and pressed charges against all three. All three received field-grade Article 15 punishments.
- Another illustrative incident occurred when an interrogator struck a detainee on the head during questioning. The International Committee of the Red Cross, via the mayor of the detainee's compound, discovered this after the fact. Once he was made aware of the incident, the soldier's commander investigated and ultimately issued a field-grade Article 15. The commander then required two soldiers to be present during every interrogation.

In these examples, abuse was discovered immediately by the command, and corrective actions were taken to prevent a recurrence. One comment made by a non-commissioned officer (NCO) from a unit that did not have any abuse cases was that multiple levels of NCO oversight ensured compliance with the Rules of Engagement (ROE), and the team leaders and Platoon Sergeant maintained strict standards for all Military Police (MP). One interrogator NCO stated that in his unit there would be a number of people in the room during interrogations to ensure that soldiers did not violate the Interrogation ROE.

The psychological research on abuse (see above) suggests that in similar situations, such as prisons, when some relatively minor abusive behavior occurs and corrective action is not taken, there is an escalation of violence. If there is uncorrected abuse and more people become involved, there is a diffusion of responsibility making it easier for individuals to commit abuse. The research further suggests that a moral disengagement occurs which allows individuals to rationalize and justify their behavior. (See Bandura, A., *Moral Disengagement in the Perpetration of Inhumanities*, Personality and Social Psychology Review, 1999.)

In at least 11 of the 125 incidents reviewed by the DAIG team, immediate corrective action was not taken by the chain of command. The reasons for this leadership failure included either a lack of fundamental unit discipline, ambiguous command and control over the facility or individuals involved, ambiguous guidance from command on the treatment of detainees, no control processes in place to provide oversight and notify the command of the incident, or, in very few cases, leader complicity at the Lieutenant Colonel level and below in the actions. This led to the second category of detainee abuse, referred to as progressive abuse because these usually develop from an isolated incident into a more progressive abuse.

Here are five examples of this second category from the 125 reported allegations referenced in the first paragraph of the inspection results above, where actions were not taken until more generalized abuse had occurred.

- The incidents involving Tier 1A at Abu Ghraib began no later than October and continued until December 2003. The degradation of the detainees by the guard force appears to have started out with smaller, less-intensive types of abuse and humiliation, and increased to physical assault and injury. There were no formal control processes, such as a routine inspection of Tier 1A during the night hours or electronic monitoring, in place to easily identify abuse and bring it to the attention of the command. Eventually, a soldier who knew it was wrong was made aware of the abuse and reported it to CID. Charges were preferred on 20 March 2004 against six reserve MP Soldiers for detainee abuse, and further investigation continues.

– In a different incident that resulted in a death, two Warrant Officers appeared to exhibit a pattern of abusive interrogations. A detainee, who was overweight and in poor physical health, died during an interrogation. The CID investigation contained sworn statements indicating that physical beatings at this site were common during this time and alleged that the two Warrant Officers routinely slapped and beat the detainees they were questioning. There were no control processes in place to review the interrogation techniques used in this facility. There was apparently no oversight on the behavior of the interrogators, and, although many of the guard personnel were aware of the techniques being used, the abusive behavior was not reported. There was a perception among the guard personnel that this type of behavior by the interrogators was condoned by their chain of command. Both Warrant Officers received a General Officer Memorandum of Reprimand and further disposition of the case is under review.

– In another incident a platoon detained two individuals, later released them on a bridge, and made them jump into a river below. One of the detainees drowned. Sworn statements indicated the platoon "as a whole" had previously discussed having detainees jump off the bridge, and the planned action apparently had the support of the Platoon Sergeant. There is no evidence to support any previous incidents by this platoon, but these discussions are indicators that junior leader deficiencies at the platoon level contributed to the death of a detainee. CID continues to investigate this incident.

– There was an incident involving a Sergeant First Class (SFC) telling his subordinates to, "rough them up," referring to two detainees in custody. This occurred in the middle of the night without any oversight and at a division collecting point operated by an infantry unit. There are indications that this SFC had given similar guidance earlier. Several of the SFC's subordinates actually performed most of the subsequent beating. There is no evidence that the SFC had abused detainees previously. This incident was adjudicated by both Special and Summary Courts-Martial, with the SFC receiving a reduction to Staff Sergeant (SSG) and a punitive censure. One SSG was reduced to a Specialist and received 30 days confinement; another SSG pled guilty to one specification of violation of a lawful general order and was reduced to the grade of Sergeant. Finally, a Specialist was found guilty at a summary court-martial and his punishment included forfeiture of $1092 and hard labor without confinement for 45 days.

– One final example is an incident where a soldier had been talking extensively with others in his unit about wanting to kill an Iraqi. This soldier later shot and killed an Iraqi detainee who was flexi-cuffed and may have tripped while walking away from the soldier. This incident is currently under investigation.

Although elimination of all abuse is the goal of the DoD Law of War Training several factors prevent the complete elimination of detainee abuse. These include:

a. The psychological process that increases the likelihood of abusive behavior when one person has complete control over another is a major factor. This is the same process that occurs in prisons, in EPW/POW camps, and in DoD resistance training. Even in well-trained and screened populations, it is a constant threat. This threat can be minimized through individual and unit training on proper procedures and standards of behavior and by leader supervision of actual operations.

b. Poor training in the handling of detainees increases the risk of abuse. Although most personnel interviewed had some training in the Law of Land Warfare, many did not have training specific to detainee handling. It was often the case that individuals conducting interrogations were not school-trained as interrogators.

c. Ambiguous instructions concerning the handling of detainees also greatly increase the risk of abuse. Some soldiers believed their command encouraged behavior at the harsher end of the acceptable range of behavior in the treatment of detainees. This can very quickly lead to abusive behavior, even if it is not the intent of the command. The Taguba Investigation makes clear that the 800th MP (I/R) Brigade leadership did not properly communicate to its soldiers the requirements for the treatment of detainees. In order to mitigate the risk of abuse, commanders must give clear, unambiguous guidance, make sure that Soldiers understand the guidance, supervise Soldiers' operations, and then hold their Soldier's accountable for meeting standards.

d. Criminal behavior among a small percentage of soldiers.

e. Combat operations, as a new experience for many soldiers, combined with the above, may lead to soldiers justifying abusive behavior as a result of their exposure to danger. This leads to a moral disengagement where soldiers do not take responsibility for their actions.

f. Poor unit discipline, which is a function of poor leader supervision, allows abusive behavior an opportunity to occur. Again, the Taguba Investigation identified a serious lack of discipline among the units involved in detainee abuse.

The last three of these factors can be best prevented by making sure soldiers understand the standards of behavior expected of them, and by leaders who maintain unit and individual discipline and exercise appropriate supervision of soldiers.

Almost all of the abuse cases studied by the DAIG team were isolated events. The soldiers' chain of command, when notified of the allegation of abuse, took appropriate action and prevented further abusive behavior. The DAIG team found that most abuse incidents were isolated events that, when discovered, were immediately corrected by commanders at battalion level and lower.

Those cases where corrective action did not occur, usually because the chain of command was not aware of the abuse, resulted in a continuation of abuse or a progression from talking about abuse to actually committing abuse. Factors that influenced this progression of abuse and responsive actions taken by units to mitigate these factors were:

a. Poor oversight and poor control mechanisms to inspect and check on soldiers' behavior decreased the likelihood that abuse would be discovered by command.

This led to a breakdown in the command and control of soldiers interacting with detainees. One NCOIC stated that the chain of command did not visit his location very often, and that when they began to receive enemy fire, he did not see the Commander or Command Sergeant Major (CSM). In response, over time, several units developed standing operating procedures that incorporated specific control mechanisms, such as requiring a certain number of personnel to be present during interrogations, having all soldiers sign a document outlining acceptable behavior, and tasking independent officers to monitor all detainee operations, with the ability to observe anything, anytime, within their facility.

b. A command climate that encourages behavior at the harsher end of the acceptable range of behavior towards detainees may unintentionally, increase the likelihood of abuse. One officer interviewed stated that there is often a "do what it takes" mindset. This appeared to be more prevalent in the early days of the war in Iraq. Among other responses, the CJTF-7 Rules for Detainee Operations, published 30 November 2003, states, "Treat all persons with dignity and respect." In addition, on 12 October 2003, CJTF-7 published a memorandum stating all interrogations would be, "applied in a humane and lawful manner with sufficient oversight by trained investigators or interrogators. Interrogators and supervisory personnel will ensure uniform, careful, and safe conduct of interrogations."

c. In the few cases involving the progression to more serious abuse by soldiers, tolerance of inappropriate behavior by any level of the chain of command, even if minor, led to an increase in the frequency and intensity of abuse. In a few cases, the perception, accurate or not, that Other Governmental Agencies(OGA) conducted interrogations using harsher methods than allowed by Army Regulation, led to a belief that higher levels of command condoned such methods. As noted in paragraph b above, CJTF-7 began to publish specific guidance that emphasized the humane treatment of detainees. At the time of the DAIG Team's visit to the theater, leaders and Soldiers uniformly understood the need to treat detainees humanely.

It is evident there were soldiers who knew the right thing to do and reported abuse when they discovered it. soldiers who believed that abusive behavior was not acceptable reported almost all of the abuse incidents. Some of these soldiers stopped other soldiers from hurting detainees, demonstrating moral courage in the face of peer pressure. Others reported serious abuse when it involved their comrades and leaders. This finding on abuse focused on a very small percentage of soldiers who may have committed abusive behavior, and not on the vast majority that, even under the stress of combat and poor living conditions, and presented with sometimes resistant and hostile detainees, have treated all within their care humanely.

(4) *Root Cause*: Detainee abuse was an individual failure to uphold Army Values and in some cases involved a breakdown in the leadership supervision of soldiers' behavior.

(5) *Recommendation*: Commanders enforce the basic fundamental discipline standards of soldiers, provide training, and immediately correct inappropriate behavior of soldiers towards detainees to ensure the proper treatment of detainees.

Recommendation: Commanders assess the quality of leadership in units and replace those leaders who do not enforce discipline and hold soldiers accountable.

Recommendation: TRADOC develop and implement a train-the-trainer package that strongly emphasizes leaders' responsibilities to have adequate supervision and control processes in place to ensure the proper treatment of detainees.

Recommendation: TRADOC integrate training into all Professional Military Education that strongly emphasizes leaders' responsibilities to have adequate supervision and control processes in place to ensure the proper treatment of detainees.

Recommendation: The G3 require pre-deployment training include a strong emphasis on leaders' responsibilities to have adequate supervision and control processes in place to ensure proper treatment of, and prevent abuse of, detainees.

c. **Finding 3:**
    (1) *Finding*: Of all facilities inspected, only Abu Ghraib was determined to be undesirable for housing detainees because it is located near an urban population and is under frequent hostile fire, placing soldiers and detainees at risk.
    (2) *Standard*: See Appendix E.
    (3) *Inspection Results*: Abu Ghraib was overcrowded, located near a densely populated urban area and on a dangerous main supply route, and subject to frequent hostile enemy fire from enemy mortars or rockets. The facility was located approximately 20 miles west of Baghdad. The entire encampment of Abu Ghraib was quite large, covering 280 acres. This facility has had up to 10,000 persons interned there and was considered the most notorious landmark in all of Iraq, made so by the previous regime under Saddam Hussein.

Abu Ghraib consisted of three distinct separate facilities: the hard site prison complex, Camp Vigilant, and Camp Ganci. Except for Tier 1, the rest of the hard site prison complex (Tiers 2 through 7) was under complete control of Iraqi prison guards under supervision of the Coalition Provisional Authority. Criminals were housed there who had committed crimes against other Iraqis. Camp Vigilant was under complete U.S. Armed Forces control. It was the least populated facility of the three at Abu Ghraib, housing several hundred detainees.

The facility employs over 1,500 soldiers and civilians and there is no Post Exchange (PX) within the walls of Abu Ghraib. This was one of the major complaints from soldiers. Routine trips for PX runs did not occur because of the danger in traveling to Camp Victory on the main supply route. Soldiers complained that they could not get necessary clothing and uniform items when needed.

On 19 March 2004, the official detainee headcount in Camps Ganci and Vigilant was 5,967 detainees under U.S. control. This number frequently fluctuated because of releases, transfers, or additional captures of detainees. Including the hard site, there were 7,490 detainees on this date. Only one internment/resettlement (I/R) Military Police battalion was charged with managing, operating, and maintaining security of Camps Ganci and Vigilant. By doctrine an I/R battalion should support the following ratios: up to 4,000 EPWs/CIs; 8,000 dislocated civilians; or 1,500 U.S. Armed Forces prisoners. The Taguba Investigation also addressed the problems of undermanning at Abu Ghraib.

Abu Ghraib also did not have sufficient protection measures in place to protect the detainees from hostile fire. Abu Ghraib was frequently under mortar and small arms fire. Detainees suffered casualties in the past due to enemy hostile fire. Detainees at Camps Vigilant and Ganci did not have access to protective bunkers or shelters, placing them at great risk.

Camp Ganci was overcrowded with a population of over 5,000 detainees at the time of the DAIG inspection. Camp Ganci was designed and built as an Enemy Prisoner of War (EPW) camp, and the camp living environment was not conducive to a criminal or high security population. The population of the camp alone made security and control inherently difficult and dangerous. There were eight compounds in Camp Ganci, and the capacity for each compound was 500. During the inspection, the average population was from 600 to 700 detainees per compound.

Camp Ganci's eight compounds inside of Abu Ghraib had similar problems with the guard towers and perimeter triple-standard concertina wire that the old compounds at Camp Bucca suffered. The overcrowding and cramped conditions at Camp Ganci, and the fact that the distance between each compound was only 30 to 40 feet, compounded the safety and security concerns for soldiers. Detainee rioting had occurred in the past. Lighting at Camp Ganci was poor, especially at compound 6, according to interviewed Soldiers. The physical design of the camps within the facility was not optimal for the mission. The towers, for example, provided limited visibility due to numerous blind spots. Towers supporting Camp Ganci were not placed reasonably well, as they should have been, with good fields of fire. Some towers faced each other, and there were some identified blind spots throughout the compounds according to interviewed Soldiers. Entrance and egress to the compounds were hampered by cumbersome, makeshift gates made of concertina wire and wood that dragged across the ground. This made rapid access very difficult. Sally ports were used primarily as gates or "slow down" barriers.

The Single Channel Ground/Air Radio System (SINCGARS) system used at Abu Ghraib, when operable, was maintained inside the compound for communication with units outside the compound and the roving patrols. Because many units were using the same frequency, crossed radio traffic was common between roving patrols, other outside units, and the Tactical Operations Center (TOC) inside the compound. The facility NCOIC at Abu Ghraib stated there was also a shortfall in radios, which hampered communications and security within the compound. In some instances, the guards in the towers had communication with the TOC, but not with the roving guards on the ground. So, in order to communicate with a tower, the roving guards would have to yell up to them. The guards would also have to yell up to the towers when they wanted to pass information to the TOC. Due to the ineffective communication systems at Abu Ghraib and Camp Bucca, soldiers took it upon themselves to purchase handheld commercial radios to communicate within the camps. Because these radios are unsecured, they pose a communications security (COMSEC) problem; frequencies can be easily monitored by outside forces using the same commercially available radios. The commercial radios were also unable to communicate with the military issue radios.

During sensing sessions, NCOs at Abu Ghraib stated there were no standardized procedures for searching Iraqis entering the compound. The DAIG team's findings are consistent with the Ryder Report that stated, "The lack of policy and standard operating procedures results in inconsistent application of basic security protocols. Visitation is a serious opportunity to introduce security and safety hazards."

Refuse and litter were seen within one of the Ganci compounds. It could not be determined if the trash was actually refuse that had migrated to the surface from an old landfill site on which Camp Ganci was built. There was approximately one portable latrine per 25 detainees, and there was a contract in place to clean the latrines. There was, however, a bad smell throughout the area from sewage because disinfectant chemicals were not replaced in the latrines. According to sensing sessions, there were only 12 showerheads in each Ganci compound for 600 to 700 detainees. The detainees showered every other day, but the guards ran all 600 to 700 detainees through the process in two hours. The lack of laundry capabilities or services for the detainees was similar to the situation at Camp Bucca. Detainees had tubs and soap, but there was no accountability on where the tubs were and how many there were. The unit submitted a contract request to start a laundry service for detainees.

The supply of fresh water was difficult to maintain at the required levels for drinking and personal hygiene for both soldiers and detainees. According to interviews, Abu Ghraib received fresh water from a Baghdad city water main that frequently broke down. A three-day supply (200K gallons) was required to be on-hand. The day before the DAIG team arrived, the reserve water supply was down to 50K gallons. Rationing of fresh water was not uncommon for soldiers and detainees according to leaders and soldiers from interviews and sensing sessions.

Food quality for detainees was a serious issue at Abu Ghraib. Spoiled and contaminated food (rodent droppings and dirt) had been delivered by the contractor for the detainees in the past. Units at Abu Ghraib had to use unit stocks of Meals, Ready to Eat (MREs) to distribute to detainees instead. The unit was working with the contracting officer to remedy the substandard work of the contractor.

Other problems observed included problems with the existing power generators and lack of ventilation for the detainees.

There were planned and ongoing projects at Abu Ghraib. The new Entry Control Point (ECP) was recently completed. This will allow 200 visitations of detainee family members a day and will provide a stand-off of 100 meters for force protection. The project included a new parking lot. Another ongoing project was the new reception center. Besides the ECP and reception center, other projects planned include: perimeter fencing around Abu Ghraib; completion of Camp Avalanche (recently renamed Camp Redemption), a new facility with a capacity of 3,000 detainees; and future plans to upgrade Camps Ganci and Vigilant. Both the Taguba Investigation and Ryder Report mentioned the need for structural improvements and renovations at various facilities. The Taguba Investigation stated the need for structural improvements, including enhancements of perimeter lighting, additional chain link fencing, staking down of all concertina wire, hard site development, and expansion of Abu Ghraib. One recommendation of the Ryder Report included renovation of all available cells at Abu Ghraib to facilitate consolidation and separation of the different categories of detainees. The Ryder Report also recommended modification of the Abu Ghraib master plan that allowed expansion and increased detainee capacity

by means of renovation. All of the improvements mentioned in the Taguba Investigation and Ryder Report are needed at Abu Ghraib if U.S. Forces continue to use
it as an I/R facility. However, because of its location in a densely populated urban
area and the frequent hostile fire, the DAIG team found that the facility should be
phased out as an I/R facility, with Camp Bucca becoming the primary I/R facility in
Iraq.

Abu Ghraib will be the central facility for the Iraqi Prison System after transition
to the interim government. However, Abu Ghraib's location near an urban and hostile
environment goes against doctrine for setting up I/R facilities. The area lends itself
to poor and dangerous living and working conditions. In contrast, Camp Bucca in
southern Iraq is isolated from local Iraqi populations, not frequently attacked, and is
close to vital supply lines and logistical support (Navistar in Kuwait). Camp Bucca
has room to expand if necessary and is already used as an overflow facility for Abu
Ghraib. At the time of the DAIG visit, the detainee population of Camp Bucca was
just over 1,700. The new compounds at Camp Bucca (1 through 6) have a capacity
for 4,500 detainees. If the old compounds (7 through 11) are renovated in the same
manner as the new compounds, Camp Bucca could reasonably expand the population
capacity by several thousand if needed. Once the Camp Bucca expansion is completed
and the "Iraqi on Iraqi "criminal population at Camp Ganci are segregated from other
detainees, a phase out of Abu Ghraib as an I/R facility and complete turnover to the
interim Iraqi government can take place.

    (4) *Root Cause*: Units operating the Abu Ghraib facility were overwhelmed by the
       frequent hostile fire, the overcrowded conditions, and the deteriorating infras-
       tructure.
    (5) *Recommendation*: CJTF-7 expand Camp Bucca as an internment/resettlement
       facility in order to transfer detainees from Camps Ganci and Vigilant, and phase
       out U.S. Armed Forces detainee operations at Abu Ghraib completely.

Chapter 4   Interrogation Operations

1. **Summary of Findings:** Commanders recognized the need for timely, tactical human intelligence and adapted to the environment by keeping detainees longer at the
point of capture and collecting points to gain and exploit intelligence. Commanders
and interrogators conducted tactical questioning to gain immediate battlefield intelligence. Holding detainees longer than 72 hours increased requirements for facility
infrastructure, medical care, preventive medicine, trained personnel, logistics, and
security.

Doctrine does not clearly and distinctly address the relationship between the Military Police (MP) operating I/R facilities and the Military Intelligence (MI) personnel
conducting intelligence exploitation at those facilities. Neither MP nor MI doctrine
specifically defines the distinct but interdependent roles and responsibilities of the
two in detainee operations. MP doctrine states MI may colocate with MP at detention sites to conduct interrogations, and coordination should be made to establish
operating procedures. MP doctrine does not, however, address approved and prohibited MI procedures in an MP-operated facility. It also does not clearly establish the

role of MPs in the interrogation process. Conversely, MI doctrine does not clearly explain MP internment procedures or the role of MI personnel within an internment setting.

There is no DoD or Army policy that addresses the establishment and operation of interrogation facilities, including Joint Interrogation Facilities (JIFs) and Joint Interrogation and Debriefing Centers (JIDCs). Doctrine provided in two field manuals (FMs) dealing with military intelligence, FM 34-52 and FM 3-31, *Joint Force Land Component Commander Handbook* (JFLCC), 13 December 2001, contains inconsistent guidance on terminology, structure, and function of these facilities.

Shortfalls in numbers of interrogators and interpreters, and the distribution of these assets within the battlespace, hampered human intelligence (HUMINT) collection efforts. Valuable intelligence – timely, complete, clear, and accurate – may have been lost as a result. Interrogators were not available in sufficient numbers to efficiently conduct screening and interrogations of the large numbers of detainees at collecting points (CPs) and internment/resettlement (I/R) facilities, nor were there enough to man sufficient numbers of Tactical Human Intelligence Teams (THTs) for intelligence exploitation at points of capture. Interpreters, especially those Category II personnel authorized to participate in interrogations, were also in short supply.

Interviewed MI leaders and soldiers indicated that G2s and S2s were conducting interrogations of detainees without the proper training on the management of HUMINT analysis and collection techniques. They were not adequately trained to manage the full spectrum of HUMINT assets being used in the current operating environment. The need for these officers to understand the management of HUMINT operations is critical to successful HUMINT exploitation in the current operating environment.

Army doctrine found in Field Manual (FM) 34-52, *Intelligence Interrogation*, 28 September 1992, lists 17 accepted interrogations approach techniques. It states that those approach techniques are not inclusive of all possible or accepted techniques. The DAIG team reviewed interrogation approach techniques policy for both OEF and OIF and determined that CJTF-180 and CJTF-7 included additional interrogation approach techniques not found FM 34-52. The DAIG team found that officially approved CJTF-7 and CJTF-180 policies and the early CJTF-180 practices generally met legal obligations under Geneva Convention Relevant to Prisoners of War (GPW), the Geneva Convention Relative to the Protection of Civilian Persons in Time of War (GC), the UN Convention Against Torture and Other Cruel, Inhuman or Degrading Treatment or Punishment (CAT), the U.S. Torture statute, 18 USC §§2034, 2034A, if executed carefully, by trained soldiers, under the full range of safeguards. The DAIG team found that some interrogators may not have received formal instruction from the U.S. Army Military Intelligence Center on interrogation approach techniques not contained in FM 34-52. Additionally, the DAIG team found that while commands published interrogation approach policy, some subordinate units were unaware of the current version of those policies. Content of unit interrogator training programs varied among units in both OEF and OIF. However, no confirmed instance involving the application of approved approach techniques resulted in an instance of detainee abuse.

2. Findings:

a. Finding 4:

 (1) *Finding*: Tactical commanders and leaders adapted to the environment and held detainees longer than doctrinally recommended due to the demand for timely, tactical intelligence.

 (2) *Standard*: See Appendix E.

 (3) *Inspection Results*: In **OPERATION ENDURING FREEDOM** (OEF) and **OPERATION IRAQI FREEDOM** (OIF), company through division units held detainees longer than the doctrinal timeframes. By doctrine, companies and battalions are to evacuate detainees as quickly as possible to a division forward collecting point (CP). Interviewed point of capture battalion and company leaders stated 61% (25 of 41) of their units established CPs and held detainees at their locations from 12 hours up to 30 days. Of the geographically remote inspected companies and battalions, 3 of 3, established CPs at their locations. By doctrine, division forward CPs are located at maneuver brigades and can hold detainees for up to 12 hours before evacuating to division central CPs.

All interviewed leaders from 11 division forward CPs stated their facilities held detainees from 24 hours up to 54 days. By doctrine, division central CPs are located near the division support area (DSA) and can hold detainees for up to 24 hours before evacuating to the corps holding area (CHA) or internment/resettlement (I/R) facility. All interviewed leaders from four central CPs stated their facilities held detainees from 72 hours up to 45 days.

The primary reason units held detainees at these locations was to conduct screenings and interrogations closer to the point of capture. The result of holding detainees for longer timeframes at all locations was increased requirements in facility infrastructure, medical care, preventive medicine, trained personnel, logistics, and security. Organic unit personnel at these locations did not have the required institutional training and were therefore unaware of, or unable, to comply with Army policies in areas such as detainee processing, confinement operations, security, preventive medicine, and interrogation.

Current detainee doctrine is written to apply to a linear battlefield with an identifiable combat zone and rear area, and with the presumption that detainees at the point of capture will normally be enemy prisoners of war (EPWs). EPWs are to be humanely evacuated from the combat zone to internment facilities (normally located in the corps communication zone (COMMZ)). Evacuation is accomplished as quickly as possible for the safety of the EPWs and to ensure operations of the maneuver unit are not hampered. Doctrine assumes EPWs are normally captured forward in the combat zone by company and battalion-sized units. While doctrine does provide for interrogations to be conducted at forward locations, it limits the time detainees should be held at these sites.

By doctrine, EPWs are evacuated from companies and battalions to a division forward CP located in the brigade area of operations. A forward CP is normally a guarded, roped-off area (concertina or razor tape) or a secure fixed facility, with potable water, a latrine, and a trench or cover for protection from indirect fire. A division MP company commander plans for a platoon to operate the forward CP and process EPWs using the STRESS method (search, tag, report, evacuate, segregate, and safeguard). The MP company medical section provides medical support. Additional medical support can be requested by the brigade medical officer from the forward support battalion (FSB). EPWs doctrinally do not remain at a forward CP for more than 12 hours before being escorted to the division central CP.

By doctrine, the division central CP is established near the division support area (DSA). The central CP is larger than the forward CP, contains some type of tentage or uses an existing shelter/structure to protect detainees from the elements. The central CP may have multiple water and latrine sites. A division MP company operates the CP and continues to process EPWs using the STRESS method. The MP company medical section provides medical support. Units within the DSA provide support as stated in the division operations order. EPWs do not remain at a central CP for more than 24 hours before being escorted to the CHA.

By doctrine, a CHA is usually located near a base or base cluster in the corps rear area with one CHA to support each division conducting operations. Normal hold time at the CHA is 72 hours, but the CHA must be prepared to hold EPWs for extended periods until they are evacuated to an internment facility or until hostilities end. A CHA is a semi-permanent facility. The capture rate and captive categories determine the size of the CHA, and it should be divided into two or more compounds for segregation, security, and ease of control. The CHA has areas designated for EPW reception, processing, storage and accountability of detainee property, interrogation, medical facilities, showers, and protection from direct and indirect fire. A corps MP platoon or corps MP company operates a CHA and may be augmented with additional MPs. Support agreements can be arranged between MP headquarters and a base or base cluster where the CHA is located. Class I through Class IX supplies are requested through logistics channels and Class VIII through medical channels.

Doctrine does not address the unique characteristics of OIF and OEF, specifically operations in non-linear battlespaces and large numbers of detainees whose status is not readily identifiable as combatants, criminals, or innocents. In OIF and OEF, units held detainees at division CPs longer than doctrinal timeframes and established CPs at companies and battalions. Commanders held detainees at forward locations to facilitate more effective initial screenings (to determine detainees' status and disposition) and to obtain more timely intelligence than would be obtained from interrogations at I/R facilities. Interviews and sensing sessions with leaders and soldiers indicated a common perception at the unit level that once a detainee was evacuated, interrogations conducted at higher echelon facilities did not return tactical intelligence to the capturing unit. Furthermore, commanders and MI personnel perceived additional value in holding detainees at CPs where they can be segregated and intelligence is less likely to be compromised. Detainees held at CPs were also available for follow-up interrogations and clarifications of details based on the tactical exploitation of intelligence previously provided. Finally, interrogators at CPs are familiar with the unique local characteristics that enable more effective intelligence exploitation, i.e., religious affiliation, tribal affiliation, and regional politics.

Doctrine does not address how to effectively screen and interrogate large numbers of captured persons of undetermined status. Unlike EPWs, detained persons in OIF and OEF did not have a clear status upon capture. Capturing units were attempting to screen persons close to the point of capture to confer status in a timely manner. By doing so, they could quickly release innocent persons with no intelligence value who would otherwise burden the detention system, or detain combatants or persons of potential intelligence value for continued exploitation. In situations where effective screening couldn't be accomplished at the point of capture, companies and battalions established collecting points and held detainees instead of evacuating them to higher echelons. The time detainees were held at company and battalion locations varied from 12 hours up to 30 days based on the number of detainees and the availability of interrogators.

A result of holding detainees at CPs was company, battalion, brigade and divisional units were being required to meet the standards of CHAs without the organic resources (trained personnel, materials, equipment, and facilities) to do so. The DAIG team found most personnel, especially at battalion and brigade CPs, did not have the training to perform the humanitarian, security, and administrative requirements for extended holding times. Because most personnel were not trained in detention operations they were unaware of Army doctrinal requirements, policies, and procedures that address the specific responsibilities for confinement, security, preventive medicine, and interrogation. The DAIG team found most CP operations were conducted using standing operating procedures (SOPs) developed by previous units; internal tactics, techniques, and procedures; common sense; and basic soldier skills and knowledge.

Holding detainees for longer periods of time at CPs increases the infrastructure requirements from those needed for mobile, temporary holding areas to the more substantial demands of semi-permanent facilities. CPs have to provide increased internal and external security to physically contain the detainees. Considerations have to be made for areas designated for detainee reception, processing, storage and accountability of detainee property, interrogation, medical care, latrines, and protection from direct and indirect fire. The medical requirements for the care of detainees increase (e.g., trained personnel, supplies, and equipment), as do the requirements for preventive medicine (e.g., showers, sundry packs, pest control, and facility inspections). Units have increased requirements for logistics (e.g., Class I, Class II (shotguns, restraints, communications, and uniforms), Class III, Class V (non-lethal ammunition), and security (e.g., permanent external guard force and quick reaction force).

Detainee doctrine does not address operations in a non-linear battlespace. Doctrine was written for operations on a linear battlefield on which EPWs were to be quickly evacuated to corps holding areas or I/R facilities. Commanders in OIF and OEF were holding detainees closer to the point of capture to expedite intelligence exploitation. The result of holding detainees forward of I/R facilities was that companies, battalions, brigades and divisions were being required to meet higher standards of detainee humanitarian care when these units are not organically resourced with the trained personnel, materials or equipment to operate semi-permanent facilities. The DAIG team found that battalions, brigades or divisions operating CPs are not trained or resourced to run semi-permanent collection/holding facilities, and no units are fully compliant with Army policy. The DAIG team also found that the inspected units were treating detainees humanely and in accordance with the provisions of the Geneva Conventions. Units continue to physically improve the facilities of the CPs and obtain external support for personnel and resources.

Although the Ryder Report cited changes are required in doctrine and organizational structure related to detention and correction operations, it did not go into specific details. The report did note the wide variance of standards and approaches at collecting points and recommended assessing the tactical feasibility of decreasing the number of collection points.

> (4) *Root Cause*: Units did not comply with doctrine that requires the quick evacuation of detainees to internment facilities. Units held detainees at CPs closer to the point of capture for longer periods of time to conduct more effective interrogation and intelligence exploitation.
>
> (5) *Recommendation*: TRADOC revise doctrine to address the criteria for establishing and operating collecting points to enable commanders to more effectively conduct intelligence exploitation in a non-linear battlespace.

b. **Finding 5:**

> (1) *Finding*: Doctrine does not clearly specify the interdependent, and yet independent, roles, missions, and responsibilities of Military Police and Military Intelligence units in the establishment and operation of interrogation facilities.
>
> (2) *Standard*: See Appendix E.
>
> (3) *Inspection Results*: Doctrine does not provide clear guidance on the relationship between Military Police (MP), responsible for the safekeeping of detainees, and Military Intelligence (MI), responsible for intelligence collection. Neither MP nor MI doctrine clearly defines the distinct but interdependent roles, missions, and responsibilities of the two in detainee operations. MP doctrine states MI may collocate with MP at detention sites to conduct interrogations, and coordination should be made to establish operating procedures. MP doctrine does not, however, address approved and prohibited MI procedures in an MP-operated facility. It also does not clearly establish the role of MPs in the interrogation process. Conversely, MI doctrine does not clearly explain MP internment procedures or the role of MI personnel in an internment setting. Subordination of the MP custody and control mission to the MI need for intelligence can create settings in which unsanctioned behavior, including detainee abuse, could occur. Failure of MP and MI personnel to understand each other's specific missions and duties could undermine the effectiveness of safeguards associated with interrogation techniques and procedures. Failure of MP and MI personnel to understand each other's specific missions and duties could undermine the effectiveness of safeguards associated with interrogation techniques and procedures.

MP doctrine explicitly outlines MP roles and responsibilities in operating collecting points (CPs), corps holding areas (CHAs) and internment/resettlement (I/R) facilities. MP doctrine identifies the priorities of detainee operations as the custody and control of detainees and the security of the facility. MP doctrine states detainees may be interrogated at CPs, CHAs and I/R facilities operated by MPs to facilitate the collection of intelligence information. It highlights the need for coordination between MP and MI to establish operating procedures. MPs are responsible for passively detecting and reporting significant information. MPs can assist MI screeners by identifying captives who may have information that supports Priority Intelligence Requirements (PIRs). MPs can acquire important information through observation and insight even though they are not trained intelligence specialists. MP interaction with detainees is limited, however, to contact necessary for the management of a safe and secure living environment and for security escort functions during detainee movement. Thus, active participation by MPs in the intelligence exploitation process is not within the doctrinal scope of the MP mission.

MI doctrine clearly states MPs command and operate CPs and CHAs, but it does not address operational authority for I/R facilities. MI doctrine specifies MPs conduct detainee receipt, escort, transport, and administrative processing functions, including document handling and property disposition. MI doctrine in FM 34-52, contrary to MP doctrine in FM 3-19.1, contains a passage that implies an active role for MPs in the screening/interrogation process: "Screeners coordinate with MP holding area guards on their role in the screening process. The guards are told where the screening will take place, how EPWs and detainees are to be brought there from the holding area, and what types of behavior on their part will facilitate the screenings." The implication in FM 34-52 that MPs would have an active role in the screening process is in conflict with MP doctrine that states MPs maintain a passive role in both the screening and interrogation processes. This passage could cause confusion with MI personnel as to the role of MPs in screenings and interrogations. The Ryder Report addressed the issue of MPs maintaining a passive role in interrogations, stating that, "Military police, though adept at passive collection of intelligence within a facility, do not participate in Military Intelligence supervised interrogation sessions." The report further states that the active participation of MPs in interrogations could be a source of potential problems: "Such actions generally run counter to the smooth operation of a detention facility, attempting to maintain its population in a compliant and docile state." The Ryder Report recommends establishing "procedures that define the role of military police soldiers securing the compound, clearly separating the actions of the guards from those of the military intelligence personnel."

Additionally, two intelligence oriented field manuals, FM 34-52, *Intelligence Interrogation* (discussed above), and FM 3-31, *Joint Force Land Component Commander Handbook (JFLCC)*, contain inconsistent guidance on terminology, structure, and function of interrogation facilities. Neither field manual address the relationship of MI and MP personnel within those facilities. FM 34-52 describes a Theater Interrogation Facility (TIF). FM 3-31 describes a Joint Interrogation Facility (JIF) and Joint Interrogation and Debriefing Center (JIDC). Interrogation facilities in OEF and OIF identified themselves as JIFs and JIDCs. Commanders and leaders structured the organization and command relationships within these JIFs and JIDCs to meet the unique requirements of their operating environments.

The DAIG team determined MP and MI doctrine did not sufficiently address the interdependent roles of MP and MI personnel in detainee operations in OEF and OIF. Doctrine needs to be updated to clearly specify the roles and responsibilities of MPs in the intelligence exploitation of detainees. It should also clearly specify the roles and responsibilities of MI personnel within MP-operated internment facilities. For example, MP and MI doctrine should address and clarify: (1) command and control relationship of MP and MI personnel within internment facilities; (2) MPs' passive or active role in the collection of intelligence; (3) interrogation techniques and the maintenance of good order within the detention facility; (4) detainee transfer procedures between MP and MI to conduct interrogations, including specific information related to the safety and well-being of the detainee; and (5) locations for conducting interrogations within I/R or other facilities.

> (4) *Root Cause*: Current doctrine does not adequately address or prepare MP or MI units for collaboratively conducting detainee operations and provides inconsistent guidance on terminology, structure, and function of interrogation facilities.
> (5) *Recommendation*: TRADOC develop a single document for detainee operations that identifies the interdependent and independent roles of the Military Police custody mission and the Military Intelligence interrogation mission.

Recommendation: TRADOC establish doctrine to clearly define the organizational structures, command relationships, and roles and responsibilities of personnel operating interrogation facilities.

Recommendation: The Provost Marshal General revise, and the G2 establish, policy to clearly define the organizational structures, command relationships, and roles and responsibilities of personnel operating interrogation facilities.

Recommendation: The G3 direct the incorporation of integrated Military Police and Military intelligence detainee operations into field training exercises, home station and mobilization site training, and combat training center rotations.

c. **Finding 6:**
> (1) *Finding*: Military Intelligence units are not resourced with sufficient interrogators and interpreters, to conduct timely detainee screenings and interrogations in the current operating environment, resulting in a backlog of interrogations and the potential loss of intelligence.
> (2) *Standard*: See Appendix E.
> (3) *Inspection Results*: Shortfalls in numbers of interrogators (Military Occupational Specialty (MOS) 97E and 351E)) and interpreters, and the distribution of these assets within the battlespace, hampered human intelligence (HUMINT) collection efforts. Valuable intelligence – timely, complete, clear, and accurate – may have been lost as a result. Interrogators were not available in sufficient numbers to efficiently conduct screening and interrogations of the large numbers of detainees at collecting points (CPs) and internment/resettlement (I/R) facilities, nor were there enough to man adequate numbers of Tactical Human Intelligence (HUMINT) Teams (THTs) for intelligence exploitation at points of capture. Interpreters, especially those Category II personnel authorized to participate in interrogations, were also in short supply. Interrogations were conducted at locations throughout the battlespace by trained military interrogators, contract interrogators, and, in some forward locations, by leaders and soldiers with no training in military interrogation tactics, techniques, and procedures. Interrogations observed by DAIG team members were conducted in accordance with Army policy and doctrine. Policy and doctrine clearly

reinforce and fully comply with the provisions of the laws of land warfare, and all Army interrogators are trained extensively on approved and prohibited interrogation techniques.

The quantity and distribution of military interrogators were insufficient to conduct timely intelligence exploitation of non-compliant detainees in the current operational environment. 78% (18 of 23) of interviewed S2s and G2s stated the shortage of interrogators at points of capture and company and battalion CPs resulted in untrained combat leaders and soldiers conducting screenings and field interrogations. 89% (17 of 19) of interviewed military interrogators cited a shortage of interrogators, resulting in backlogs of interrogations at I/R facilities. Military interrogators at Abu Ghraib stated there were detainees that had been in custody for as long as 90 days before being interrogated for the first time.

In OEF and OIF, the total number of interrogators varied by unit and location. Each division (1ID, 1AD, 4ID, 1st CAV, 82nd ABN, and 101st ABN) deployed with an MI battalion that was resourced with interrogators. The 519th MI BN of the XVIII ABN Corps, and the 202nd MI BN, echelons above corps, deployed with interrogators. The 30th and 39th Army National Guard (ARNG) Separate Brigades were resourced with interrogators. All of the above units supplemented interrogators with counterintelligence soldiers (MOS 97B and 351B) to increase interrogation capabilities. The 205th MI Brigade, V Corps; 504th MI Brigade, III Corps; and the 902nd MI Group had no interrogators and therefore conducted all interrogations using counterintelligence soldiers. The number of interrogators in the above units varied from four in the ARNG Separate Brigades to 16 in some divisions, to approximately 60 in the 519th MI BN. Military interrogators in OIF were supplemented by 31 contract interrogators. (12 contract interrogators have redeployed for personal reasons since the blanket purchase agreement (contract) was issued 14 August 2003). CJTF-180 was preparing to hire contract interrogators for OEF at the time of the inspection.

Because detainees have varying degrees of intelligence value, there is no doctrinal formula to determine the recommended ratio of interrogators and interpreters to detainees. All detainees require initial screening after capture to determine their status and potential intelligence value. The requirement for interrogation of each detainee is unique and based on potential intelligence yield, the characteristics of the detainee, and the information requirements of the unit. Some detainees may only require a single screening to determine their status and be released, while others will be screened, determined to be of intelligence value, and subsequently interrogated a few times, several times over many weeks, or numerous times over many months. The ratio of interrogators to detainees varied at each facility. At Abu Ghraib there were 120 interrogators for 1,500 detainees determined to be of intelligence value; at Brassfield-Mora there were two interrogators for 50 such detainees; and at Bagram there were 12 interrogators for 192 detainees of intelligence value.

Category II Arabic, Pashtu, and Dari interpreters – interpreters with U.S. citizenship, but no security clearances – were also identified as shortages throughout OEF and OIF. As crucial players in every aspect of operations, skilled interpreters were in high demand. The quality of intelligence derived from an interrogation can depend greatly on the ability of the interpreter to work effectively with the interrogator. An effective interpreter must not only convey the accurate meaning of language, he/she must be able to express the implied message in the demeanor of the interrogator. To function together as a successful team requires specific, individualized training prior to employment in the field, as well as time working to together to maximize their effectiveness. Category II interpreters should be deployed in sufficient numbers to support the commander's intelligence gathering requirements.

Detainee operations in a non-linear battlespace presented a unique challenge, requiring screening operations to be placed closer to points of capture. Using properly trained HUMINT soldiers to screen detainees in the immediate vicinity of the point of capture reduces the number of innocents detained, produces more timely intelligence, and increases the quality of evidence collection and documentation for use in future judicial proceedings. One senior MI officer indicated that his division only had the manpower to utilize THTs at points of capture approximately 10% of the time. Failure to position trained HUMINT soldiers close to points of capture puts a burden on units farther up the chain of custody and delayed the collection of timely intelligence. The backlog of unscreened detainees quickly overwhelmed the internment system in OIF, where I/R facilities were unprepared to deal with such large numbers of detainees. This slowed the process of intelligence exploitation and prevented the timely release of detainees who were apprehended and later found to have no intelligence value and to be of no threat to the Coalition Forces.

If performed by trained interrogators, front-line interrogations offer other advantages. Recently captured persons are less likely to resist the interrogator. They also have not yet entered the general detainee population where they can conspire with others to resist interrogation techniques. In untrained hands, however, these advantages can be lost. To satisfy the need to acquire intelligence as soon as possible following capture, some officers and non-commissioned officers (NCOs) with no training in interrogation techniques began conducting their own interrogation sessions. Inexperienced and untrained persons using unproven interrogation techniques often yield poor intelligence and can harden detainees against future questioning by trained interrogators. The potential for abuse increases when interrogations are conducted in an emotionally-charged environment by untrained personnel who are unfamiliar with the approved interrogation approach techniques. The quality of these interrogations was further eroded by the absence of Category II interpreters. Category I interpreters – local nationals without security clearances – were the only interpreters available in forward locations, and there was no way to guarantee the accuracy or trustworthiness of their work.

The Military Intelligence (MI) School has internally resourced a mobile training team (MTT) to offset the shortage of interrogators in the field. The MTT trains non-MI personnel in the skills and knowledge required to perform basic questioning techniques and operations in order to enhance ongoing HUMINT collection missions at the tactical level. Tactical questioning (TQ) is a critical element of small unit operations. Tactical Questioning (TQ) is defined as the questioning of the local population (non-combatants and enemy prisoners of war (EPWs)/detainees) for information of immediate tactical value. Through TQ, the handling of detainees, and the handling of captured documents, Soldiers serve as the commander's eyes and ears. The information that the Soldiers report as a result of TQ is passed up the chain of command and forms a vital part of planning and operations. The TQ MTT has trained approximately 4,000 soldiers as of March 2004.

Current military interrogation procedures as published in FM 34-52, *Intelligence Interrogations*, 28 September 1992, and taught at the U.S. Army Intelligence Center, Fort Huachuca, remain valid. Interrogation approach techniques, themselves, are addressed in Finding 9. Military interrogators receive 16.5 weeks of intensive training on interrogation procedures and techniques at the Army's Human Intelligence Collector Course. This training includes collection priority, screening, planning and preparation, approaches, questioning, and termination of interrogations. A total of 192 hours of direct and indirect training on the laws of land warfare emphasizes compliance of all military interrogation techniques with the Geneva Conventions and Army policy. Prohibited activities are covered in detail and reinforced in interrogation operation exercises.

Interrogation approach techniques policies were issued for OEF and OIF. The CJTF-7 Commander issued initial interrogation approach techniques policy on 14 September 2003, and amended the interrogation approach techniques policy on 12 October 2003 and 13 May 2004. The CJTF-180 Commander issued approved interrogation approach techniques policy on 16 March 2004.

The DAIG team observed two detainee facilities using digital video recording devices, one in Afghanistan and one in Iraq. Because interrogations are confrontational, a monitored video recording of the process can be an effective check against breaches of the laws of land warfare and Army policy. It further protects the interrogator against allegations of mistreatment by detainees and provides a permanent record of the encounter that can be reviewed to improve the accuracy of intelligence collection. All facilities conducting interrogations would benefit from routine use of video recording equipment.

In summary, the DAIG team found the quantity and distribution of military interrogators were insufficient to conduct timely intelligence exploitation of non-compliant detainees in OEF and OIF. Military interrogators observed in OEF and OIF were performing interrogations of detainees in accordance with doctrine.

(4) *Root Cause*: The shortages of interrogators and interpreters at all echelons caused commanders and other leaders to use untrained personnel to conduct interrogations of detainees. Insufficient numbers of Category II interpreters, especially those with experience working with interrogators, further hampered interrogation operations.

(5) *Recommendation*: TRADOC and G2 ensure documentation of unit organizations meet interrogator personnel manning requirements, authorizations, and capabilities in order to provide commanders with timely intelligence.

Recommendation: The CFLCC contracting officer representative ensure enough Category II interpreters are hired to support timely intelligence exploitation of detainees.

d. **Finding 7:**

(1) *Finding*: Tactical Military Intelligence officers are not adequately trained on how to manage the full spectrum of the collection and analysis of human intelligence.

(2) *Standard*: See Appendix E.

(3) *Inspection Results*: Interviewed Military Intelligence (MI) leaders and soldiers indicated that G2s and S2s were conducting interrogations of detainees without the proper training on the management of Human Intelligence (HUMINT) analysis and collection techniques. They were not adequately trained to manage the full spectrum of HUMINT assets being used in the current operating environment. The counter-intelligence team leaders (TL) interviewed expressed a wish that all G2s and S2s were trained on how to manage the collection and analysis of HUMINT. The need for these officers to understand the management of HUMINT operations is the key for successful HUMINT exploitation in the current operating environment. Battalion commanders, company commanders, and platoon leaders were interrogating detainees at the point of capture according to counter-intelligence TLs interviewed. They complained about this practice because these leaders were not properly trained in interrogation techniques and quite possibly jeopardized the intelligence gathering process to acquire timely intelligence from detainees. Counter-intelligence TLs were told on several occasions by these leaders that they had the interrogations under control and did not require their Military Intelligence (MI) assistance.

Currently, MI officers only receive a general overview of HUMINT during their Professional Military Education (PME) courses. During the Military Intelligence Officer Basic Course (MIOBC), MI officers receive a nine day Intelligence Battlefield Operating System (IBOS) block of instruction which includes a six-hour block on: review/reinforcement of counterintelligence/human intelligence principles; counter-intelligence organizations; Subversion & Espionage Directed Against U.S. Army & Deliberate Security Violations (SAEDA); and the role of the tactical human intelligence teams (THTs). Furthermore, the MIOBC students receive approximately an hour block of instruction from their Stability and Support Operations (SASO) instructor on displaced civilians/refugees on the battlefield.

MI Captain Career Course (MICCC) officers receive a one-hour block of instruction in their intelligence support to brigade operations (ISBO) on imagery intelligence (IMINT), counterintelligence/human intelligence, and signals intelligence (SIGINT). Additionally, during practical exercises the students receive 40 hours of Stability and Support Operations (SASO) training, 32 hours of threat training, and two hours of crime link training from their instructor. Also, during intelligence, surveillance, and reconnaissance planning the basic principles of counter-intelligence/HUMINT are reinforced during practical exercises (30 minutes in length) that addresses IMINT, counter-intelligence/HUMINT, and SIGINT being used on the battlefield to collect intelligence information. During the Intelligence Support Course to division, corps, and joint officers, there is one day of counter-intelligence/HUMINT training. This training includes an overview, specific training, and a practical exercise for counter-intelligence/HUMINT. Additionally, the 35E series (counter-intelligence Officer) course conducts counter-intelligence/HUMINT training for 8 hours, and the Strategic Intelligence Officer Course conducts counter-intelligence /HUMINT training for 5 hours.

Interviewed career course captains with experience in **OPERATION ENDURING FREEDOM** (OEF) and **OPERATION IRAQI FREEDOM** (OIF) from the Military

Intelligence school stated their home station training on detainee operations was limited and concentrated on EPWs or compliant detainee populations. These officers stated the training they received at the MI Basic Course did not provide them with enough training to prepare them to conduct detainee or human intelligence gathering operations.

The G2, in coordination with TRADOC, has created a G2X/S2X Battle Staff Course to begin in July 2004 for MI officers. The G2X/S2X Battle Staff Course will prepare a G2X/S2X staff of a deploying Army division with the capability to synchronize, coordinate, manage and de-conflict counter-intelligence and HUMINT sources within the division's area of responsibility (AOR). The G2X/S2X program of instruction (POI) will be tailored for a staff operating within a Joint or multi national (Coalition) environment which will focus on real world missions, Army-centric, and counter-intelligence/HUMINT tool-specific training. The G2X/S2X curriculum is based upon the counter-intelligence/HUMINT critical tasks and incorporates J2X/G2X/S2X emerging doctrine/methodology and lessons learned. This course will be hands-on and application based. The G2X/S2X Battle Staff Course provides the critical knowledge and skills required to enable the G2X staff to successfully synchronize and monitor asset management to place sources against the combatant commander's target in support of the mission.

The G2, in coordination with the MI School, is currently revising Field Manual (FM) 34-52, *Intelligence Interrogation*, 28 September 1992. Additionally, the G2 is spearheading a coordinated effort with TRADOC and the U.S. Army Military Police School to synchronize between the three disciplines of intelligence, surveillance, and reconnaissance, particularly in the area of detainee handling and internment/resettlement facility management.

Interviewed and sensed leaders and soldiers stated that the Law or War training they received prior to deployment did not differentiate between the different classifications of detainees causing confusion concerning the levels of treatment. Even though this confusion existed, the vast majority of leaders and soldiers treated detainees humanely.

TRADOC, in coordination with the Office of the Judge Advocate General, is currently determining the feasibility of increasing or adjusting Law of War training in the proponent schools to include procedures for handling civilian internees and other non-uniformed personnel on the battlefield.

(4) *Root Cause*: The MI School is not adequately training the management of HUMINT to tactical MI officers. The MI School has no functional training course available to teach the management of HUMINT.

(5) *Recommendation*: TRADOC continue the integration of the G2X/S2X Battle Staff Course for all Military Intelligence officers assigned to G2X/S2X positions.

Recommendation: TRADOC integrate additional training on the collection and analysis of HUMINT into the Military Intelligence Officer Basic Course program of instruction.

e. **Finding 8:**

(1) Finding: The DAIG team found that officially approved CJTF-7 and CJTF-180 policies and the early CJTF-180 practices generally met legal obligations under

U.S. law, treaty obligations and policy, if executed carefully, by trained soldiers, under the full range of safeguards. The DAIG team found that policies were not clear and contained ambiguities. The DAIG team found implementation, training, and oversight of these policies was inconsistent; the Team concluded, however, based on a review of cases through 9 June 2004 that no confirmed instance of detainee abuse resulted from the approved policies.

(2) Standard: See Appendix E.

(3) Inspection Results: Interrogation approach techniques policy is identified by several different titles by the different commands of OEF and OIF. For the purpose of standardization of this report those titles will be referred to collectively as interrogation approach techniques policy.

Army doctrine found in Field Manual (FM) 34-52, *Intelligence Interrogation*, 28 September 1992, lists 17 accepted interrogations approach techniques. It states that those approach techniques are not inclusive of all possible or accepted techniques. The DAIG team reviewed interrogation approach techniques policy for both OEF and OIF and determined that CJTF-180 and CJTF-7 included additional interrogation approach techniques not found FM 34-52. The DAIG team found that officially approved CJTF-7 and CJTF-180 policies and the early CJTF-180 practices generally met legal obligations under Geneva Convention Relevant to Prisoners of War (GPW), the Geneva Convention Relative to the Protection of Civilian Persons in Time of War (GC), the UN Convention Against Torture and Other Cruel, Inhuman or Degrading Treatment or Punishment (CAT), the U.S. Torture statute, 18 USC §§2034, 2034A, if executed carefully, by trained soldiers, under the full range of safeguards. The DAIG team found that some interrogators may not have received formal instruction from the U.S. Army Military Intelligence Center on interrogation approach techniques not contained in FM 34-52. Additionally, the DAIG team found that while commands published interrogation approach policy, some subordinate units were unaware of the current version of those policies. Content of unit interrogator training programs varied among units in both OEF and OIF. However, no confirmed instance involving the application of approved approach techniques resulted in an instance of detainee abuse.

The 17 approved interrogation approach techniques listed in FM 34-52 are direct, incentive, emotional love, emotional hate, fear-up (harsh), fear-up (mild), fear-down, pride and ego-up, pride and ego-down, futility, we know all, file and dossier, establish your identity, repetition, rapid fire, silent, and change of scene. Approach techniques can be used individually or in combination as part of a cohesive, logical interrogation plan. These approach techniques are found in the current training curriculum at the Military Intelligence School. The FM states these approach techniques are "not new nor are all the possible or acceptable techniques discussed. Everything the interrogator says and does must be in concert with the GWS [Geneva Convention For the Amelioration of the Wounded and Sick in Armed Forces in the Field], GPW, GC and UCMJ [Uniform Code of Military Justice]." The FM further states, "Almost any ruse or deception is usable as long as the provisions of the GPW are not violated." Techniques considered to be physical or mental torture and coercion are expressly prohibited, including electric shock, any form of beating, mock execution, and abnormal sleep deprivation.

The FM gives commanders additional guidance in analyzing additional techniques. On page 1-9 it states: "When using interrogation techniques, certain applications of approaches and techniques may approach the line between lawful actions and unlawful actions. It may often be difficult to determine where lawful actions end and unlawful actions begin. In attempting to determine if a contemplated approach or technique would be considered unlawful, consider these two tests: Given all the surrounding facts and circumstances, would a reasonable person in the place of the person being interrogated believe that his rights, as guaranteed under both international and U.S. law, are being violated or withheld if he fails to cooperate. If your contemplated actions were perpetrated by an enemy against U.S. POWs [Prisoners of War], you would believe such actions violate international or U.S. law. If you answer yes to either of these tests, do not engage in the contemplated action. If a doubt still remains as to the legality of the proposed action, seek a legal opinion from your servicing judge advocate."

The FM lists four primary factors that must be considered when selecting interrogation approach techniques:

(1) The person under interrogation's mental or physical state,
(2) The person under interrogation's background and experience,
(3) The objective of the interrogation, and
(4) The interrogator's background and abilities.

The DAIG team found some interrogation approach techniques approved for use at Guantanamo Bay were used in development of policies in OEF and OIF. As interrogation policy was developed for Joint Task Force (JTF) Guantanamo, the Commander, U.S. Southern Command requested additional approach techniques to be approved. A Working Group on Detainee Interrogations in the Global War on Terrorism was convened. This group was required to recommend legal and effective interrogation approach techniques for collection of strategic intelligence from detainees interned at Guantanamo Bay. The working group collected information on 39 existing or proposed interrogation tactics, techniques and procedures from the U.S. Central Command (CENTCOM) and U.S. Southern Command in a 6 March 2003 report. It recommended approval of 26 interrogation approaches.

A memorandum on 16 April 2003, entitled "Counter-Resistance Techniques" approved 26 specific techniques for use only by JTF Guantanamo. It required the use of seven enumerated safeguards in all interrogations. The memorandum stated that the use of any additional interrogation techniques required additional approval. The instructions noted that the intent in all interrogations was to use "the least intrusive method, always applied in a humane and lawful manner with sufficient oversight by trained investigators or interrogators."

Both CJTF-180 and CJTF-7 developed interrogation policies for intelligence exploitation operations in OEF and OIF. All policies contained additional interrogation approach techniques other than those identified in FM 34-52. The DAIG team identified this occurred for three reasons: (1) Drafters referenced the JTF Guantanamo policy memorandum as a basis for development for their policy; (2) In two instances, published policy made reference to the 8 May 1987 version of FM 34-52 which listed a technique that was later removed from the 28 September 1992 revision; and (3) Some intelligence personnel believed that additional interrogation techniques would assist in more effective intelligence exploitation of a non-compliant or hardened detainee population. Both OEF and OIF included safeguards in their policy, although they differed from each other and from the 16 April 2003 memorandum applicable to JTF Guantanamo. Reliance on the Guantanamo policy appears to contradict the terms of the memorandum itself which explicitly states it was applicable to interrogations of unlawful combatants at JTF Guantanamo and failed to take into account that different standards applied to JTF Guantanamo, CJTF-180 and CJTF-7.

The DAIG team found that CJTF-7 issued a series of evolving policy statements, while CJTF-180 only issued one policy. The DAIG team, however, found evidence of practices that had been in effect in Afghanistan since at least early 2003. The DAIG team reviewed the officially approved interrogation approach technique policies for both CJTF-7 and CJTF-180, and the record of practices in use in CJTF-180 prior to adoption of a formal policy. The changes in policies and practices, over time, reflect the struggle that commanders faced in developing approach techniques policies that were both effective and complied generally with legal obligations applicable to the theater. In Iraq, in particular, the commander was faced with a group of detainees that ranged from Enemy Prisoners of War (EPW's). to security internees (SI's) to unlawful combatants. In both theaters, commanders were operating under combat conditions, facing the death and wounding of scores of U.S. soldiers, civilians and other non-combatants on a daily basis. Their decisions and decision-making process must be viewed against this backdrop.

The DAIG team found that officially approved CJTF-7 and CJTF-180 policies and the early CJTF-180 practices generally met legal obligations under U.S. law, treaty obligations and policy, if executed carefully, by trained soldiers, under the full range of safeguards. The approved policies, however, presented significant risk if not executed in strictest compliance with their own safeguards. In this light, the caution noted in FM 34-52 (above) appears applicable, "It may often be difficult to determine where lawful actions end and unlawful actions begin." In a high-stress, high pressure combat environment, soldiers and subordinate leaders require clear, unambiguous guidance well within established parameters that they did not have in the policies we reviewed.

The DAIG team found that the established policies were not clear and contained ambiguity. The absence of clarity could have been mitigated by additional training, detailed planning and brief-backs, detailed case-by-case legal analysis and other command and staff execution safeguards. In the absence of the safeguards, however, the commands could have embarked on high risk interrogation operations without adequate preparation or safeguards. Contributing to the ambiguity were command policies that included both approved techniques and security and safety provisions. While some security provisions provide a secondary benefit to an interrogation, it is not proper to use the security provision solely for the purpose of causing this secondary benefit in the interrogation. Both the CJTF-180 and CJTF-7 policies and the known CJTF-180 practices prior to their first published policy, imprudently mixed discussion of security provisions into interrogation techniques. This added to the possible confusion regarding whether a particular action was truly a security provision or an interrogation technique. While the language of the approved policies could be viewed as a careful attempt to draw the line between lawful and unlawful conduct, the published instructions left considerable room for misapplication, particularly under high-stress combat conditions.

Application of the additional techniques involving higher risk of violations required additional training for interrogators. Formal school training at the U.S. Army Intelligence Center and School (USAICS) for both MOS 97E, Enlisted Human Intelligence Collector, and 351E, Warrant Officer Human Intelligence Collection Technician, provides instruction on the interrogation approach techniques identified in FM 34-52, The DA1G team identified that interrogators only received training on doctrinal approach techniques listed in FM 34-52 from the USAICS, however, some interrogators may have received training on the additional approach techniques at the unit level. Interviewed intelligence personnel stated they were also trained on the additional approaches through mobile training teams. In some organizations, the team found a comprehensive unit training program; in others, the team found no formal or standardized interrogator training program. Inadequately trained interrogators present an increased risk that the approach technique will be improperly applied. The team found no indication that a lack of training resulted in an improper application of any particular technique or techniques; however, it remains critical that units applying any of the additional interrogation approach techniques have a comprehensive training program as a risk mitigation measure for those higher risk techniques.

The DAIG team observed that although both CJTF-180 and CJTF-7 published interrogation approach technique policies, some inspected units were unaware of the correct command policy in effect at the time of inspection. The differences noted were omission of approved approach techniques and failure to note that a particular approach technique required higher command approval. The team was unable to determine if inspected units with incorrect versions of higher headquarters policy had requested authorization to use, or had used, any of the additional techniques. The unit policies did include safeguards consistent with the higher headquarters policy. As with other sensitive changes in unit mission orders, commanders should ensure that they have an effective feedback mechanism to ensure subordinate units receive, acknowledge and comply with changes in approved approach techniques.

Interviews and sworn statements from personnel in both CJTF-180 and CJTF-7 indicated that some of the approach techniques included in their policies, but not listed in FM 34-52, were used by some interrogators. The DAIG team found no indication of the frequency or consistency with which these additional approach techniques were employed. The DAIG team conducted a review of 125 case summaries from the. Criminal Investigation Division (CID) and unit investigations available as of 9 June 2004. Based on a review of case summaries, and despite the significant shortcomings noted in the command policies and practices, the team was unable to establish any direct link between the use of an approved approach technique or techniques and a confirmed case of detainee abuse.

(4) Root Cause: Commanders perceived interrogation approach techniques found in FM 34-52 were insufficient for effective intelligence exploitation of non-compliant detainees in OEF and OIF and published high risk policies that

presented a significant risk of misapplication if not trained and executed carefully. Not all interrogators were trained on all approved approach techniques.

(5) Recommendation: TRADOC, in coordination with G2 and TJAG, revise doctrine to identify interrogation approach techniques that are acceptable, effective and legal for non-compliant detainees.

Recommendation: CJTF-7 and CJTF-180 ensure that standardized policy on interrogation approach techniques are received, understood, trained and enforced by all units.

Chapter 5   Other Observations

1. **Summary of Findings:** We examined seven key systems (Leadership and Discipline, Policy and Doctrine, Military Intelligence/Military Police Relationship, Organizational Structures, Facilities, Resources, and Training and Education) that influence how detainees are handled throughout the detention process, including interrogations. In the course of that examination we identified a number of observations that while not critical, require attention and resolution. None of the findings contributed directly to any specific case of abuse. The recommendations accompanying the 15 following findings are designed to improve our ability to properly conduct detainee operations.

2. **Findings:**

a. **Finding 9:**
   (1) *Finding*: Interviewed leaders and soldiers stated the unit's morale (71%) and command climate (68%) had steadily improved due to competent leadership, caring for soldiers by leaders, and better working and living conditions as the theater matured.
   (2) *Standard*: See Appendix E.
   (3) *Inspection Results*: We attempted to determine the effect of stress and morale on detainee operations and conducted a Combat/Operational Stress Survey. We interviewed or sensed more than 650 leaders and soldiers and received 603 of the surveys back. The DAIG team found that 71 % (428 of 603) of leaders and soldiers surveyed stated the unit's morale, (71 %, 428 of 603) and command climate (68%, 410 of 603) had steadily improved in **OPERATION ENDURING FREEDOM** (OEF) and **OPERATION IRAQI FREEDOM** (OIF). The survey results found that leaders and soldiers perceived that morale and the command climate was good. The results of the survey, interviews, and sensing sessions showed that the morale and command climate improved due to competent leadership, caring for soldiers by leaders, and better working and living conditions as the theater matured. The DAIG team also found that most perceptions of morale and command climate varied widely between senior leaders, junior leaders, and soldiers. The morale and command climate perception was higher for those interviewed and surveyed leaders and soldiers who deployed prior to November 2003 and had redeployed from OEF/OIF than those that were still in country or arrived after the first of the year when living conditions started to improve.

The morale and command climate perceptions varied depending upon the difficulty of the unit's mission and its location. Soldiers conducting detainee operations in remote and dangerous locations complained of very poor to poor morale and command climate due to the lack of higher command involvement and the perception that their leaders did not care. These soldiers stated that the leadership from higher commands hardly ever visited their locations, they were living in much worse conditions than other soldiers, they suffered increased dangers, they were untrained to perform their mission, and the work schedule/lack of personnel depth caused them to "burn out."

Of the soldiers who arrived in theater since November/December 2003 (61%, 194 of 318), expressed morale as good to excellent, while 51% (145 of 285) of soldiers who deployed during the initial stages of OEF/OIF complained of poor morale, but also expressed that it seemed to get better with time.

Most soldiers talked of how morale improved as living and working conditions improved. A majority of soldiers mentioned the arrival of air conditioning, installation of Internet cafes, rest and recuperation (R&R) trips to Qatar, and environmental leave as some of the things that improved morale. Many engaged in Morale, Welfare, and Recreation (MWR) activities, such as weight lifting, basketball, softball, billiards, and ping-pong. Many enjoyed TV, hot meals, satellite phones, volleyball, and MWR bands in some locations. Soldiers were very pleased with how the leaders helped and listened to them more than they had before. The majority of soldiers got more downtime or time off when possible. Most leaders expressed a need to continue to obtain more comfort items sooner to speed up improvements in living conditions as a measure to boost the morale.

The survey was given to every leader and soldier that was interviewed and in sensing sessions both in theater and CONUS. The survey revealed that the majority of leaders and soldiers agreed that unit members can depend, cooperate, and stand up for each other, which are factors of having good unit morale. In addition, leaders and soldiers were told when they were doing a good job, were not embarrassed in front of peers, and were not assigned extra missions by leadership to look good for the chain of command, which are some indicators that there is a perception of a good command climate. Although the morale and command climate was poor under certain conditions, it steadily improved as living conditions in the theater improved over time.

> (4) *Recommendation*: CFLCC, CJTF-7, and CJTF-180 continue to stress the importance of positive unit morale and command climate.

b. **Finding 10:**
   (1) *Finding*: Detainee administration, internment, and intelligence exploitation policy and doctrine does not address detainee operations conducted in the current operating environment, which has a higher demand for human intelligence exploitation at the tactical level and the need for additional classifications of detainees.
   (2) *Standard*: See Appendix E.
   (3) *Inspection Results*:

POLICY

Although classified detainee operations policy has been issued to address individual situations at specific geographic locations, current published detainee operations policy in AR 190-8, *Enemy Prisoners of War, Retained Personnel, Civilian Internees and Other Detainees*, 1 October 1997, does not address additional definitions of detainee designations and related treatment requirements. In addition to enemy prisoners of war (EPWs) in **OPERATION IRAQI FREEDOM** (OIF) and compliant, non-hostile civilian internees (CIs) in **OPERATION ENDURING FREEDOM** (OEF) and OIF, units were faced with capturing, transporting, segregating and controlling other categories of detainees, such as non-state combatants and non-compliant CIs. AR 190-8 also does not address the relationship between mission requirements for reestablishing a civilian prison system and detainee operations. Policy must address requirements for expanded employment of confinement expertise for managing detainee security, custody, and control challenges for a wider array of detainee designations. Policy must also address the confinement expert's role in standing up indigenous prison systems, enabling rapid segregation and transfer of criminal detainee populations from U.S. Forces to indigenous control.

The DAIG team found the addition of new detainee administrative policy classifications of detainees resulted in inconsistent administrative procedures. Current doctrine, regulations, and policy are based on a linear battlefield and a largely compliant population, with the primary goal of removing individuals from the battlefield. In addition to EPWs and compliant, non-hostile CIs, units in OEF and OIF were confronted with capturing, transporting, processing, and confining other classifications of detainees, such as non-state combatants and non-compliant CIs. The nature of the environment in which we now conduct detainee operations requires a more specific classification of the detainees interned, Instead of compliant, non-hostile detainees, units are capturing and transporting non-State combatants, insurgents, criminals, and detainees who are either known or perceived security threats. Policy needs to be updated to address the management of detainees captured and detained primarily for intelligence exploitation, the potential security threat they may pose, or the pending reestablishment of indigenous prison systems.

Army Regulation (AR) 190-8, *Enemy Prisoners of War, Retained Personnel, Civilian Internees and Other Detainees*, 1 October 1997, accords appropriate legal status using four detainee classifications: EPW, Retained Personnel (RP), CI, and Other Detainees (OD). In OEF and OIF, various fragmentary orders, policy memorandums, and unit standing operating procedures utilized several variations on these classifications, including Enemy Combatants, Under-privileged Enemy Combatant, Security Internee, Criminal Detainee, Person Under U.S. Forces Control (PUC), and Low Level Enemy Combatant (LLEC). In accordance with AR 190-8, administrative and treatment requirements are based on the classification assigned to a particular detainee. For example, detainees are to be segregated in facilities according to their status. The development of classifications not correlated to one of the four terms defined in AR 190-8 resulted in confusing and ambiguous requirements for those charged with managing detainees and created the potential for inconsistent treatment. From points of capture to internment/resettlement (I/R) facilities, there are varying degrees of understanding as to which standards apply to the various classifications of detainees in

OEF and OIF. Policy does not specifically address administrative responsibilities related to the timely release of detainees captured and detained primarily for intelligence exploitation and/or the potential security threat they may pose. Administrative processing of detainees by units in OEF and OIF was not standardized or fully compliant with policy and doctrine.

The time between capture and receipt of an Internment Serial Number (ISN) at an I/R facility far exceeded the time specified in policy and doctrine. Once the detainee reached an I/R facility, the required documentation received from collecting points (CPs) was often incomplete. The National Detainee Reporting Center (NDRC) did not receive all mandatory data elements, or in a timely manner, as detainee designation was often not determined until long after capture. From points of capture to corps holding areas, detainees are to be moved "as soon as practical" depending on the condition of the detainee, the threat faced in moving them, and military necessity. The non-linear nature of the battlespace and missions dependent on human intelligence made administrative processing a secondary priority to intelligence exploitation of detainees. This had additional second- and third-order effects on accountability, security, and reporting requirements for detainees. Detaining individuals primarily for intelligence collection or because of their potential security threat, though necessary, presented units with situations not addressed by current policy and doctrine.

Administrative processing is further hampered by the absence of the Branch Prisoner of War Information Center (now called the Theater Detainee Reporting Center (TDRC)), the central agency in theater required by policy to manage information on all EPW, CI and RP and their personal property. This resulted in missing data on individual detainees, poor detainee and property accountability, and the inability of the NDRC to completely and accurately report all required data elements to the DoD, the Army, and other appropriate agencies. Inadequate property accountability could also result in claims against the U.S. government for losses incurred by detainees while in U.S. custody.

According to Department of Defense Directive (DoDD) 2310.1, *DoD Program for Enemy Prisoners of War (EPOW) and Other Detainees*, 18 August 1994, the transfer of detainees to or from the custody and control of U.S. Forces requires the approval of the Assistant Secretary of Defense for International Security Affairs (ASD(ISA)). In OEF, oversight of detainee operations policy was transferred from ASD(ISA) to the Assistant Secretary of Defense for Special Operations and Low Intensity Conflict (ASD(SO/LIC)) in a memorandum dated 17 January 2002, SUBJECT: Responsibility for Detainees in Association with the Global War on Terrorism. In OIF, ASD(ISA) maintained transfer authority under DoDD 2310.1 for most detainees, but ASD(SO/LIC) had authority under the 17 January 2002 memorandum for specific classifications of detainees. Release decisions were made by commanders or review boards at multiple echelons of detention in OIF, from points of capture to the Detainee Release Board (DRB) developed by CJTF-7. The DAIG team did not find evidence of ASD(ISA) oversight of release decisions in OIF.

Complex detainee release mechanisms contributed to overcrowding of I/R facilities. Multiple reviews were required to make release recommendations prior to approval by the release authority. Non-concurrence by area commanders, intelligence organizations or law enforcement agencies resulted in retention of larger numbers of detainees. Interviews with the CJTF-7 Chief Magistrate. Appeal & Review Board members, and Release Review Board members indicated they believed up to 80% of detainees being held for security and intelligence purposes might be eligible for release upon review of their cases with the other 20% either requiring continued detention due to security reasons or continued intelligence requirements. Interviews also indicated area commanders were reluctant to concur with some release decisions out of concern that potential combatants may be reintroduced into their areas of operation. The Ryder Report referenced the overcrowded conditions and recommended holding Iraqi magistrate proceedings at individual facilities, reducing the requirement to manage many detainees centrally. Release of those individuals locally would substantially reduce the detainee population and the related resources and manpower, and would improve the capability to manage the remaining population. The remaining detainee population would be made up of only those criminals awaiting the restoration of the Iraqi prison system, those who are under active or pending interrogation, or those being held for specific security reasons.

During interviews and sensing sessions, the DAIG team noted all Active Component and Reserve Component leaders indicated that current detainee operations policy was not consistent with the requirements of ongoing operations in OEF and OIF. Detainees operations policy must reflect requirements of the Future Force for strategic and operational versatility – conducting combat and stability operations simultaneously – while operating in a joint environment. As Army Transformations continues, detainee operations policy should be appropriate for and responsive to the requirements of non-linear battlespaces. Policy should provide specific guidance for a wider array of detainees who have significantly varying security requirements. This will reduce confusion in relation to the applicability of these requirements to various categories of detainees.

The Ryder Report points to several areas where current policy is not significant for detainee operations. It stated that, "... more detailed instruction in areas such as discipline, instrument of restraint, and treatment of prisoners awaiting trial..." are needed. The report suggested that the 800th MP Brigade's challenges in adapting its organizational structure, training, and equipment resources to expand from a purely EPW operation to also managing Iraqi and third country national detainee populations can be attributed to a lack of policy guidance. The Taguba Investigation also points to a lack of sufficient policy and training on existing policy.

The DAIG team concluded DoD-developed classifications of detainees were different from those found in AR 190-08 and led to inconsistent segregation of these groups as directed by policy. The lack of adequacy system-wide capacity for handling detainees, the lack of specific policy on adequacy of information/evidence collection, and the lack of an operating detainee release process at all echelons, along with the perceived need to conduct interrogations closer to the point of capture, caused units to retain detainees beyond doctrinal time periods and without properly segregation the various classifications of detainees. The decision of capturing of units to hold and interrogate detainees also interfered with the policy requirements for accountability of detainees and their property within the system, leading to the substantial delays in determining an individaul's status and his/her subsequent disposition. Policy must address the appropriate, safe, secure, and humane custody of detainees, the specialized confinement skills required in a high-risk detainee I/R setting, and the need for timely intelligence exploitation of detainees in a non-linear battlespace. Lack of a TDRC contributed to units' failure to administratively process detainees in accordance with all regulations and policy, and the loss theater-wide detainee and property accountability. Incomplete documentation and a cumbersome review process caused detainees to be held for extended periods of time and contributed to the overcrowding of I/R facilities.

DOCTRINE

Current doctrine was designed to quickly evacuate complaint, non-hostile enemy prisoners of war (EPWs) and CIs from point of capture to I/R facilities. It does not envision the demands of gaining immediate, tactical human intelligence, hence the requirements to detain and interrogate at lower levels. The nature of OEF and OIF battlespaces, coupled with the urgent need for human intelligence (HUMINT), compelled many units to adapt their tactics, techniques, and procedures (TTPs) for conducting detainee operations. While the necessary basic skill sets and organizational responsibilities contained in current detainee operations doctrine remain applicable, the procedural timelines for detainee operations processing and movement from the point of capture to the I/R facilities do not consider current operational needs. Also the unit task organizations for detainee processing and movement are not properly resourced to meet many of the challenges faced in OEF and OIF.

During interviews and sensing sessions, the DAIG team noted leaders and soldiers indicated current detainee operations doctrine was not consistent with the requirements of ongoing operations. According to current doctrine, the swift flow of detainees to the rear is critical in getting them to trained interrogators for intelligence exploitation, and to secure them in I/R facilities designed and operated for long-term internment. Under present doctrine, combat units must rely on support elements from other units to perform many mission-related tasks (e.g., MPs to provide escort and guard functions, and Tactical Human Intelligence (HUMINT) Teams (THTs) to screen detainees at points of capture and forward collecting points (CPs)). While current doctrine is meant to relieve combat formations of the significant manpower and logistical requirements for managing detainees before they have a negative impact on combat effectiveness, it has failed to do so in OEF and OIF. Current doctrine does not address a non-linear battlespace where units at division level and below hold detainees for extended periods of time to provide commanders with intelligence for the conduct of effective tactical operations. Traditional task organizations are not properly resourced to meet the needs of this new operating paradigm.

Standing operating procedures (SOPs) for CPs and I/R facilities that were drafted by units prior to deployment (and in accordance with current doctrine) were found early on to be outdated based on the current operating environment for OEF and OIF. Soldiers were required to perform effectively in a variety of missions across a spectrum of operations. Units quickly found themselves taking on roles in detainee operations which were unanticipated. For example, the need for timely intelligence compelled officers and Non-commissioned officers (NCOs) in combat units to conduct tactical questioning even though none had been trained in proper interrogation TTPs.

Manpower shortages at CPs and I/R facilities were satisfied by using in lieu of (ILO) units; most received little or no training in detainee operations.

The limitations of current doctrine meant that mission, enemy, terrain and weather, time, troops available, and civilian (METT-TC) considerations often drove the design and operations of division CPs and battalion and company CPs. This had negative second- and third-order effects on the accountability, intelligence exploitation, security, and safeguarding of detainees. Instead of capturing and rapidly transporting detainees to doctrinal CPs, battalions and companies were holding detainees for up to 30 days without the training, material, or infrastructure for doing so. The desire for timely intelligence, transportation and security concerns, and delays in administrative processing caused units at all echelons to retain detainees for periods of time that exceeded those recommended by doctrine. While adapting and operating outside of established doctrine is necessary and desirable, especially when current doctrine fails to meet the needs of ongoing operations, doing so carries with it a requirement to ensure that mission effectiveness is not hampered while ensuring safeguards are in place to prevent unsanctioned activities and meet other established requirements.

The DAIG team observed and determined through interviews and sensing sessions that capture information was often incomplete when detainees were processed at detention locations. Capturing units lacked knowledge of procedures for information and evidence collection, critical for the accurate disposition of detainees. This was particularly apparent as OIF 2 units began deploying into theater and new commanders were faced with making release decisions based on insufficient information and documentation. The lack of required information and specificity resulted in an administrative processing backlog at all echelons of internment. CPs and I/R facilities now require capturing units to have complete documentation prior to the transfer of a detainee into their custody.

Current interrogation doctrine for intelligence preparation of the battlefield and the composition and structure of interrogation assets does not adequately cover the current operational environment. Field Manual (FM) 34-52, *Intelligence Interrogation*, 28 September 1992, describes military interrogation approaches that remain valid, but the FM may not include all acceptable and effective techniques. Army interrogators receive 16.5 weeks of intensive training on interrogation procedures and techniques at the Human Intelligence Collection Course. This training includes collection priority, screening, planning and preparation, approaches, questioning, and termination of the interrogation. Specific instruction on the laws of land warfare emphasizes compliance of all Army interrogation TTPs with the Geneva Conventions and Army policy. All Army interrogators interviewed in OEF and OIF stated they were performing interrogations of detainees in accordance with policy and doctrine.

The Ryder Report and Taguba Investigation indicated deficiencies in detainee operations doctrine. The Ryder Report noted significant variances from doctrine and highlighted the need for changes in current doctrine to address the "significant paradigm shift" in detainee operations. The report, however, does not provide information on specific instances where doctrine needs to be revised. (The report did state, "the team will forward suggested doctrinal and organizational changes to the appropriate proponent schools for review and action.") The Taguba Investigation of the 800th MP Brigade found, "basic Army doctrine was not widely referenced or utilized to develop the accountability practices throughout the 800th MP Brigade's subordinate units." Procedures were "made up," with "reliance on, and guidance from, junior members of the unit who had civilian corrections experience." The relevance of current doctrine to present and future operations was beyond the scope of the Taguba Investigation. The DAIG team found the statements made in these earlier reports to be consistent with the results of this inspection.

Findings from interviews, sensing sessions, and direct observations of AC and RC units consistently indicated that current doctrine fell short in preparing soldiers to conduct detainee operations in the fluid and dynamic environment of OEF and OIF. Detainee operations doctrine needs to fulfill the requirement of the Future Force for strategic versatility – conducting combat and stability operations simultaneously – while operating in a joint environment with relative independence and at a high operational tempo. As Army Transformation continues, detainee operations doctrine needs to be appropriate for, and responsive to, the requirements of asymmetric battlespaces, the role of non-State belligerents, and modular force structures.

> (4) *Root Cause*: Current doctrine and policy does not provide adequate guidance for detainee operations in OEF and OIF.
> (5) *Recommendation*: TRADOC revise doctrine for the administrative processing of detainees to improve accountability, movement, and disposition in a non-linear battlespace. And further examine processes for capturing and validating lessons learned in order to rapidly modify doctrine and incorporate into training application for soldiers and units.

Recommendation: The Provost Marshal General revise policy for the administrative processing of detainees to improve accountability, movement, and disposition in a non-linear battlespace

Recommendation: The Provost Marshal General, in coordination with the G2, update detainee policy to specifically address the administration, internment/ resettlement, and intelligence exploitation in a non-linear battlespace, enabling commanders to better manage resources, ensure safe and secure custodial environments, and improve intelligence gathering.

c. **Finding 11:**
> (1) *Finding*: Shortfalls in both the Military Police and Military Intelligence organizational structures resulted in the tactical unit commanders adjusting their tactics, techniques, and procedures to conduct detainee operations.
> (2) *Standard*: See Appendix E.
> (3) Inspection Results:

DOCTRINE

Doctrine indicates that Military Police (MP) units accept detainees from capturing units as far forward and as rapidly as possible. MPs operate divisional forward collecting points (CPs), divisional central CPs, and corps holding areas (CHA). MP units operating CPs and CHAs have the responsibilities to sustain, safeguard and ensure sick and wounded detainees receive medical treatment.

A platoon from the division MP company operates the forward CPs and should hold detainees for no more than 12 hours before transporting detainees to the central CP.

The central CP should not hold detainees for more than 24 hours before transporting detainees to the CHA. Units will protect the detainees from enemy attacks and provide medical support, food, potable water, latrine facilities, and shelter. Detainee property is tagged with part C of Department of Defense (DD) Form 2745, Enemy Prisoner of War Capture Tag, and given to the escort guards. The MP leader will request transportation through logistic channels to transfer detainees from the forward CP to the central CP with the same procedures to transport the detainees to the CHA.

The CHA is operated by a platoon or company from a corps MP battalion and should not keep detainees for more than 72 hours. The decision to hold detainees longer is based on mission, enemy, terrain, time, troops available and civilian (METT-TC) considerations and the availability of forces. An MP platoon can guard 500 detainees, while an MP company can guard 2,000 detainees. As the population of the CHA increases, detainee evacuations to the internment/resettlement (I/R) facility also increase. Logistical requirements for food, water, medical care and sanitation must be considered. Locations for use by Military Intelligence (MI) interrogators need to be identified. The MP leader will request transportation through logistic channels to transport detainees from the CHA to the I/R facility.

The I/R facilities provide appropriate segregation, accountability, security, and support of detainees. An I/R facility is semi-permanent and normally consists of one to eight compounds, with each compound capable of interning 500 detainees. The facility is operated by the HHC, MP battalion (I/R) (EPW/CI/DC) which provides command and control, administrative, and logistics functions to operate the facility. The battalion is capable of interning and supporting 4,000 enemy prisoner of war (EPWs) and civilian internees (CIs) or 8,000 dislocated civilians (DCs). An MP company (Guard) is assigned to provide guards for EPWs, CIs, and DCs, at the I/R facility. The company is capable of securing 2,000 EPWs, 2,000 CIs, or 4,000 DCs. The MP company (Escort Guard) provides supervision and security for evacuating and moving EPWs, CIs, DCs and other detained persons via vehicles, trains, aircraft, and road marches. The minimal security requirements for the facility include clear zones, guard towers, lights, sally ports, communications, and patrol roads. The MP and support personnel accepting detainees into the facility will search the detainee, conduct medical screening, perform administrative accountability, photograph and fingerprint as needed, account for personal property, and review records.

Doctrinally the first location an interrogation could take place is at the brigade. The interrogation teams are temporarily attached to the brigade from the division MI battalion interrogation section. The teams at the brigade level are strictly tactical and deal with information of immediate value. Interrogators are not usually assigned below the brigade level unless the combat situation requires limited tactical interrogation at battalion or company. Interrogations below brigade level are brief and concerned with information bearing directly on the combat mission of the capturing unit. This information is immediate tactical intelligence that is necessary for mission accomplishment and permits rapid reaction based on the information obtained.

In addition, MP personnel and MI interrogator teams at CPs and CHAs need to work closely together to determine which detainees, their personal belongings, and completed paperwork will offer intelligence information that would be useful to the command. The MI interrogators must support operations from brigade to theater level. Interrogators have to be highly mobile, and have communication equipment to report timely intelligence information to the supported commander.

Units conducting detainee operations in **OPERATION ENDURING FREEDOM** (OEF) and **OPERATION IRAQI FREEDOM** (OIF) adapted tactics, techniques, and procedures to make up for organizational shortfalls and to fill the void in doctrine resulting from the current operational environment.

OPERATION ENDURING FREEDOM

In OEF, units at point of capture processed their detainees at a non-doctrinal company CPs that held the detainees for up to 72 hours before releasing them or transporting them to higher headquarters. Detainees were held longer than 72 hours if required for intelligence purposes. Battalion Tactical Human Intelligence (HUMINT) Teams (THTs) sent to the company were extremely successful in gathering intelligence information from the detainees. If the THT was not available, the commander determined whether to detain or release a detainee after screening. MP personnel were not assigned to these company CPs, so the forward units had to provide their own guard force for the detainees. This additional duty took soldiers away from performing their combat mission, which decreased the combat effectiveness of the unit. To process a detainee into the CP, the unit had to complete all required paperwork. The unit inventoried and tagged detainee personal property which would accompany the detainee when he was repatriated or transferred to another location. The unit also tracked detainees with a Department of the Army (DA) Form 2708, Receipt of Inmate or Detained Person, when they were transferred to another location. The company CP provided detainees with food, water, shelter, and limited medical treatment.

The battalion CP held anywhere from 11 to 24 detainees for a period of 2 to 30 days. The battalions operating the CPs received sufficient information from the point of capture units to aid in their processing of the detainees. The interrogators examined all evidence before they began interrogating a detainee. When there was no THT present, commanders screened detainees for their intelligence value to determine if they should be released or transferred to the I/R facility. The determination to retain or release detainees at lower levels helped to ease the backlog of detainees requiring screening and questioning at higher locations. There were no MP personnel assigned to the battalions to support the battalion CPs. The battalions drew guards from their subordinate companies to act as a guard force for the detainees. This requirement to guard detainees diverted soldiers from performing their combat mission and decreased the combat effectiveness of the unit. The unit leadership supervised its soldiers to ensure detainees were protected, accounted for, and safeguarded. The unit provided detainees with; food, bottled water, shelter, and limited medical treatment. The unit evacuated detainees by air or tactical vehicles to higher level facilities.

The division central CP at Kandahar was operated by platoons from an MP Company. The MP personnel in-processed the detainees, inventoried their personal property on a DA Form 4137, Evidence/Property Custody Document, placed their items in bags (if they would fit) or large suitcases and other items. A copy of the inventory sheet was placed inside with the property (with the detainee internally generated identification number) and stored the property in a secure area. The detainees were physically searched, checked for injuries, digitally photographed, and if sick or wounded, evacuated to a medical treatment facility (MTF) for treatment. The central CP held anywhere from 23 to 40 detainees. Most detainees were repatriated or transferred within 72 hours of arrival at this location, however detainees could be held longer for intelligence exploitation. MP guards escorted detainees to the interrogators and remained in close proximity during the interrogation. Since the detainees did not leave the facility, there was no custodial transfer of detainees to interrogators. When an interrogator requested to screen detainee personal effects prior to the interrogation, the MP guard would have the interrogator sign for the items prior to releasing them. The unit provided detainees with food, bottled water, shelter, blanket, Our-an, medical treatment and showers for personal hygiene. CP personnel transported detainees by air to the I/R facility.

Detainees were held at the Bagram I/R facility for an unspecified length of time. The facility could house up to 275 detainees and, at the time of the inspection, housed 175. The I/R facility was operated by an MP battalion. The MP battalion did not deploy with two of its organic MP companies, but was augmented with two Reserve Component (RC) MP companies, one company was an MP company (combat support) and the other was an MP company (guard), to aid them with the internment duties. Upon a detainee's arrival, the MPs in-processed the detainee's personal effects and accounted for the items on a DA Form 4137. The evidence custodian signed for the property and stored it in a secure area. The detainee was photographed, received a medical screening including height and weight, was issued a jumpsuit, showered and shaved, and then was photographed again. The MP guards escorted the detainee to the interrogators and remained in close proximity to the interrogation. Since the detainee did not leave the facility there was no custodial transfer of the detainee to the interrogator. If the detainee was transferred outside the facility, a DD Form 2708, Receipt of Inmate or Detained Person, was completed and signed to maintain accountability. Upon return the detainee received a complete medical exam to check for injuries. When an interrogator requested to screen detainee's personal effects prior to the interrogation, the MP guard would have the interrogator sign for the items. The interrogators used the same screening sites they use for interrogations to review personal effects. One MI Officer felt there was a doctrinal shortcoming pertaining to interrogation operations. He felt there should be a standing operating procedure (SOP) for the operations of a joint interrogation facility (JIF) that is standard Army wide. MP personnel provided the detainees with food, bottled water and access to medical treatment. The detainees slept in cells, received blankets and had access to latrines and showers.

OPERATION IRAQI FREEDOM

Based on interviews and sensing sessions with leaders and soldiers in Continental United States (CONUS)/Outside CONUS (OCONUS) the DAIG team found 50% (13 of 26) of interviewed point of capture company leaders stated that their companies had established and operated non-doctrinal company CPs in OIF. These companies detained individuals during their cordon and search operations and raids. The remaining 50% of interviewed point of capture company leaders transported their detainees to the next higher collecting point. The companies held anywhere from 3 to

15 detainees for a period of 12 hours up to 3 days. This was longer than the recommended doctrinal standard of 12 hours. Doctrine also has the MP operating CPs to temporarily secure EPWs/CIs until they can be evacuated to the next higher echelon's holding area. MP personnel are not doctrinally assigned at the company level to collect or guard detainees. The capturing unit had the responsibility to guard their detainees for extended periods of time, which took the soldiers away from performing their combat mission and adversely impacted the combat effectiveness of the unit. The company CPs were established to interrogate detainees closer to the point of capture prior to evacuating the detainee to the next higher level CP. The unit completed the required detainee paperwork at this location. The required paperwork included two sworn statements, the Coalition Provisional Authority Forces Apprehension Form, and DD Form 2745, Enemy Prisoner of War Capture Tag. The unit had to complete this process in order to evacuate the detainees to the next higher location. Units inventoried and bagged the detainees' personal property as part of the paperwork process. Of the interviewed company leaders that had established the company CPs, 62% (16 of 26) said they would interrogate the detainee to gather information while holding them at the company CP. This tactical questioning (TQ) was more than just asking the detainee basic questions (name, age, place of residence, etc); it was an attempt to gather intelligence that might aid the unit in locating other potential targets. In a few cases, when available, units had THTs to conduct initial intelligence screening of detainees. Another 15% (4 of 26) of interviewed company leaders that had established the company CPs, asked detainees basic questions to complete the paperwork. The remaining 23% (6 of 26) of interviewed company leaders that had established the company CPs said they did not conduct interrogations or question detainees at all. The unit leadership did not have the proper training in interrogation procedures and techniques to conduct effective interrogations. Without training, individual conducting interrogation could possibly jeopardize vital intelligence information instead of quickly processing and transporting detainees to an area with trained interrogators. The company CP provided detainees with food bottled water, limited shelter and limited medical treatment. The unit transported detainees to the battalion CP during resupply assets operations for unit security.

Of the interviewed combat arms brigade/battalion leaders who performed cordon and search missions and raids 77% (10 of 13), operated their own non-doctrinal battalion CPs. The remaining three interviewed battalion/brigade leaders said they did not operate CPs but would transport the detainee to the division forward CP. Battalions held 12 to 20 detainees at their CPs for 12 hours up to 14 days, relying on their subordinate units to guard the detainees for extended periods of time. This guard requirement took soldiers away from performing their combat mission and adversely impacted the combat effectiveness of their units. MP personnel are not doctrinally assigned at the company level to collect or guard detainees. The battalions required capturing units to complete all mandatory paperwork (sworn statements, Coalition Provisional Authority Forces Apprehension Form, and DD Form 2745) before accepting the detainees into their battalion CP. The interviewed combat arms brigade/battalion leaders (77%, 10 of 13) said TQ or interrogations of detainees were performed to gather tactical information if there were no trained interrogators at their location. Battalion commanders and S2s did their own interrogations of detainees to ease the backlog of detainees at CPs. Of these battalion commanders 18% (1 of 13) said they had a THT team at their location to conduct interrogation of detainees and 15% (2 of 13) said they did not question detainees. There were not enough interrogators to be pushed down to battalion level to conduct interrogations of detainees. Without trained interrogators at the battalion level and below, the units risked missing intelligence information by holding detainees, instead of quickly processing and transporting them to an area with trained interrogators. The battalion CPs provided detainees with food, water, shelter, blankets, latrines, and limited medical treatment. Battalions transported the detainees to the division forward CP during resupply operations.

Based on interviews with leaders in OCONUS/CONUS who said they operated division forward CPs located in a brigade area, the DAIG team found 45% (5 of 11) were operated by non-MP units during the period of May 03 to April 04. Another 27% (3 of 11) of division MP platoons operating CPs required augmentation from 4 to 14 soldiers from Infantry units to help them with this mission. The remaining 27% (3 of 11) of CPs were operated by MP platoons. The forward CPs held between 4 to 150 (150 detainees in one incident) detainees from 24 hours up to 54 days. The MP platoon provided trained MP personnel to handle, safeguard, and account for detainees. This included reviewing the point of capture unit's paperwork for each detainee, assigning detainees an internally generated detainee number, and a complete inventory of each detainee's personal belongings on a DA Form 4137. The personal belongings were bagged with the DA Form 4137 to include a matched internally generated detainee number and secured in an evidence room, separate cell, small footlocker, container, or tent. If the unit delivering detainees to the forward CP did not have the required paperwork (sworn statements, Coalition Provisional Authority Forces Apprehension Form, and DD Form 2745), the in-processing personnel would not accept the detainee into the CP until the unit completed the paperwork. The paperwork, to include evidence the unit brought in with the detainee, was a critical source of useful information the interrogator could use during their interrogations. The brigades were using their MI interrogators and contracted interpreters to interrogate detainees and gather tactical intelligence information for their units. Personnel operating CPs had different procedures in place for transferring a detainee to an interrogator. If the detainee was not leaving the CP then the guard did not have the interrogator sign for the detainee. When the interrogator was finished with the detainee he would return the detainee to the guard who would then return the detainee to the cell. However, if a detainee was taken outside the CP then the interrogator would sign for the detainee on a DD Form 2708 or DD Form 629, Receipt for Prisoner or Detained Person. Upon the detainee's return, the guards would sign for the detainee and the medic or guard would check the detainee for marks or bruises and then annotate the marks or bruises if any, on an SF 600, Medical Record – Chronological Record of Medical Care. The DAIG team did a sampling of detainee records to include the SF 600 and the team found no annotations of marks or bruises. The detainees were provided; food, bottled water, shelter, blankets, latrines, and medical treatment. The unit transported detainees to the division central CPs by either ground (wheeled convoy) or air (CH-47 helicopter).

Two of the four division central CPs were operated by a platoon from the division MP company, which required augmentation of 7 to 15 soldiers from Infantry or

Engineer units to help them with this mission. The remaining two division central CPs were operated by platoons from a different division or from a company from the MP battalion (Corps). MP platoons provided trained personnel to handle, safeguard, account for, and input information into the Detainee Reporting System (DRS) and or Biometric Automated Tool Set (BATS) system. This included a review of point of capture paperwork for each detainee and an inventory of their personal belongings on DA Form 4137. Once the inventory was complete the evidence custodian locked the detainee's personal property in a separate room. The central CPs used both MI interrogators and contract interrogators and interpreters to interrogate detainees. The MP guards did not have the interrogator sign for the detainee if the interrogator was not departing the CP. Division central CP SOP required the guards to have the interrogators sign a DD Form 629 or DD Form 2708, and enter the information on their DA Form 1594, Daily Staff Journal or Duty Officer's Log, if the detainee departed the CP. Three Provost Marshals said Other Government Agencies (OGAs) did interrogate detainees, however, this required their approval, and the OGAs had to sign for the detainee. Upon their return they were examined and resigned for to regain custody of the detainee. The division central CP held anywhere between 70 to 200 detainees from 72 hours up to 45 days. The division central CP provided the detainees with food, bottled water, shelter, blankets, latrines, and medical treatment. The division central CP transported detainees by ground convoys or helicopter to I/R facilities.

I/R facilities were operated and controlled by MP battalions, MP companies, and in lieu of units (non-MP units). MP personnel processed the detainees into their facilities, which included checking the detainees against the roster for arrival, obtaining weight and height, issuing an Internment Serial Number (ISN), medical screening, inventorying, and tagging property, and review of paperwork (sworn statement, Coalition Provisional Authority Forces Apprehension Form, completed DD Form 2745 verifying that detainee data was entered into the DRS system, and amending and updating the database information as required. The detainee's personal property was annotated on DA Form 4137 and placed in a bag or a box with the detainee's ISN number. The property was then placed in a controlled access evidence room. Each detainee was issued a blanket, jumpsuit, shoes, and a Quran as part of their in-processing.

There was no specific length of time I/R facilities held detainees. The I/R facilities held anywhere from 1,700 detainees up to a maximum of 7,000 detainees depending on the facility. Inside each I/R facility were a series of compounds housing from 450 to 700 detainees each. The operations of I/R facilities and compounds were the responsibility of the MP (Combat Support) battalions who were sometimes not properly equipped with specific items necessary for detainee operations and were not trained specifically on detainee tasks in order to perform this mission. Additionally, in lieu of (ILO) units assigned the guard force (tower) and escort mission for I/R facilities received limited MP training at their Mobilization Site.

Interrogators used the screening procedure to identify a detainee who may have intelligence information. The interrogators screened both the detainee paperwork along with his/her personal effects to determine which individual possessed intelligence information. When an interrogator requested to screen a detainee's personal effects prior to the interrogation, the MP guard would have him sign for the items using DA Form 4137. The MP guard escorted the detainee to the interrogators, and since the detainee was not leaving the facility the interrogator was not required to sign for the detainees. If the detainee was leaving the facility a written authorization was required, and the guard had the individual sign for the detainee on a DD Form 2708 or DD Form 629. The MI units used military and contract interrogators and interpreters to interrogate the detainees. MP personnel provided the detainees with food, water (bottled water or five gallon cans), and access to medical treatment. Each compound had shelter, mats or cots to sleep on, latrines, and showers.

> (4) *Root Cause*: Division level units are not resourced with sufficient numbers of Military Police personnel and Military Intelligence personnel (interrogators) to conduct detainee operations in a non-linear battlespace. Point of capture units did not comply with doctrine that requires the quick evacuation of detainees to internment facilities. Units held detainees at CPs closer to the point of capture for longer periods of time to conduct more effective interrogation and intelligence exploitation so they could obtain time-sensitive tactical intelligence.
>
> (5) *Recommendation*: TRADOC and G3 update the Military Police force structure at the division level and below to support the simultaneous execution of detainee operations and other battlefield missions.

Recommendation: TRADOC and G3 update the Military Intelligence force structure at the division level and below to integrate the requirement for detainee operations that allows for timely intelligence exploitation.

Recommendation: TRADOC update doctrine to integrate tactical interrogation at battalion and company level to assist in the intelligence exploitation of detainees immediately upon capture.

d. **Finding 12:**
> (1) *Finding*: There was no Theater Detainee Reporting Center (TDRC) acting as the central, theater-level agency responsible for detainee accountability, resulting in a lack of detainee personnel and data management.
>
> (2) *Standard*: See Appendix E.
>
> (3) *Inspection Results*: The Office of the Provost Marshal General (OPMG) has redesignated the doctrinal term Prisoner of War Information Center (PWIC) used in the above standards as the TDRC, and the doctrinal term National Prisoner of War Information Center (NPWIC) as the National Detainee Reporting Center (NDRC). The following inspection results will refer to these organizations by their redesignated titles.

The DAIG team found there was no central agency in theater to collect and manage detainee information for **OPERATION ENDURING FREEDOM** (OEF) or **OPERATION IRAQI FREEDOM** (OIF), and no consolidated, comprehensive, and accurate database for detainee accountability. The TDRC that had the doctrinal mission to maintain detainee accountability was not deployed to OIF or OEF during the timeframe of the inspection. In OIF, the TDRC mission of detainee data collection was consolidated at one location in Iraq and was executed as an additional duty by a battalion S1 section. None of the major functions of the TDRC were performed in accordance with policy. Internment facilities were not fully accounting for detainees or property, and they were not meeting policy requirements. There were no procedures to ensure records on detainee disposition, health status, and personal/evidentiary property were adequately accounted for during movement of detainees between collecting points and internment facilities. Capturing units did not have standardized procedures for recording detainee personal and property information or for maintaining accountability. Doctrine and policy for detainee data collection need to be revised to address technological requirements for personnel accountability systems (biometrics) and the processing of non-compliant detainees in the current operating environment.

The TDRC is the specialized unit whose mission is to be the central agency in theater for total detainee and property accountability, from which consolidated detainee data is forwarded to the NDRC. There are two Reserve Component TDRCs, and no Active Component TDRCs, in the Army. TDRCs are structured as 59-Soldier units consisting of a headquarters detachment, operations, record keeping, property accountability, postal operations, public relations, information management, and other staff sections. TDRCs were not used in OIF or OEF. A TDRC was activated and deployed to Kuwait during the mobilization for OIF, but it did not move forward into Iraq in support of detainee operations and was redeployed to Continental United States (CONUS). However, the large numbers of captured detainees, holding detainees longer for intelligence exploitation, and a slow release process resulted in a significantly higher detainee population and a demonstrated need for the TDRC.

In OIF, the TDRC mission of detainee data collection for Iraq was assigned to the MP battalion at Camp Bucca and overseen by the S1 as an additional duty. Detainee data was consolidated as it was received from locations throughout the country and forwarded to the NDRC. Forwarded data was often incomplete, and the S1 lacked the resources to track down missing data from reporting internment facilities. The TDRC responsibilities for detainee property accountability, tracking, records management, and postal operations were not met. The S1 performed as well as could be expected with limited organic assets, but it was impossible to execute the many mission requirements that would normally be executed by a 59-Soldier TDRC. A TDRC was not deployed in OEF. The internment facility at Bagram performed the mission of detainee data collection, consolidation, and reporting. Although information management and property accountability were more consistent in Afghanistan than in Iraq, most TDRC responsibilities were not being performed.

In the absence of a TDRC there were inefficiencies in accounting, reporting and tracking of detainee information from internment/resettlement facilities to the NDRC. The NDRC developed the automated Detainee Reporting System (DRS) as a standardized, automated data system that the TDRC uses to consolidate data from the internment facilities and forward to the NDRC. With no TDRC to provide oversight, OIF and OEF detainee processing centers often used simple spreadsheets or alternate automated data systems (Joint Automated Booking System (JABS) and Biometric Assessment Tool Set (BATS)) with the ability to capture biometric data (e.g., fingerprints), but these applications did not capture other data required by Army policy. Moreover, the alternate data systems were not compatible with DRS and could not transfer information to the NDRC. At the direction of the NDRC, the DRS became the primary automated database that internment facilities were required to use. Concurrently, internment facilities continued to enter data in JABS and BATS due to the inability of DRS to record biometric data. (Note: The DRS is projected to have the capability to collect and store fingerprints by July 2004.) There is a fourth detainee reporting system in place to collect the same data in Arabic for use by the Coalition Provisional Authority (CPA). Because of the use of multiple data systems, incomplete data entry, and the inconsistent implementation of the DRS there are approximately 50,000 missing data points in the NDRC database.

Capturing units did not have standardized procedures for recording detainee personal and property information or for maintaining accountability. In OEF and OIF, units at points of capture and collecting points were not uniformly using DD Form 2745, Enemy Prisoner of War (EPW) Capture Tag. Of the assessed units in Iraq (19%) were using DD Form 2745, compared to 55% in Afghanistan and 30% of units redeploying from both theaters. In Iraq, the Coalition Provisional Authority Forces Apprehension Form was used, a form that is more comprehensive than the EPW Capture Tag. Although the CPA form appears better than DD Form 2745 for the purpose of intelligence exploitation and continued custody determinations, there was no TDRC in theater to manage the use of the form or capture information from the form for forwarding to the NDRC. Units did not uniformly forward documentation (medical, evidence/property, capture, and intelligence documents) when detainees were transferred to other echelons of detention. Furthermore, there was no mechanism during the transfer process to maintain accountability for records that accompanied a particular detainee.

The DAIG concluded the reason for the lack of accountability, standardization and reliability of detainee data is directly related to the absence of the TDRC. The sole purpose of the TDRC, as the field operating agency for the NDRC, is to ensure the accountability of detainees and their property by standardizing practices throughout the theater and implementing DoD and Army policy. An eight-person Camp Liaison Detachment (CLD) was deployed as part of OIF 2 to perform the functions of the TDRC, in addition to numerous other responsibilities. They have received initial training on the DRS, but as a CLD they are not trained on the procedures for executing the other specific TDRC tasks. The CLD may be able to accomplish the TRDC mission if appropriately trained and relieved of additional, unrelated duties, but they lack sufficient manpower to address the backlog of unaccounted-for detainees and property.

(4) *Root Cause*: The TDRC was not deployed for OEF. In OIF, it was initially deployed and subsequently redeployed without moving forward in the theater.
(5) *Recommendation*: CFLCC submit a Request For Forces for the Theater Detainee Reporting Center (TDRC) to meet the requirements for reporting and accountability of detainees and their property.

Recommendation: The Provost Marshal General review the TRDC process, structure, and employment methods for maintaining information on detainees, their property, and other related requirements within an assigned theater of operations and consider the development of an information technology solution.

e. **Finding 13:**
(1) *Finding*: The ongoing Military Intelligence Force Design Update is better suited to conduct simultaneous and sustained human intelligence missions in the current and future operating environment.

(2) *Standard*: See Appendix E.

(3) *Inspection Results*: The DAIG team found the ongoing Military Intelligence – Counter-intelligence/Human Intelligence Force Design Update is better suited than the current Military Intelligence force structure to conduct simultaneous and sustained human intelligence collection and counter-intelligence/force protection missions in the current and future operating environments.

The current Military Intelligence (MI) force structure lacks the necessary 97E – Human Intelligence (HUMINT) Collectors (formerly called interrogators) and 97B – Counter-intelligence personnel to conduct simultaneous and sustained HUMINT collection and counter-intelligence/force protection missions. The current force structure does not allow the commander to employ the doctrinal concept of conducting both HUMINT and counter-intelligence missions simultaneously. Currently the commander must choose which mission is the priority. These items are covered in the Current Military Intelligence Force Structure Section below.

The ongoing Military Intelligence – Counter-intelligence/Human Intelligence (HUMINT) Force Design Update (FDU), provides the necessary 97E and 97B personnel to conduct simultaneous and sustained HUMINT collection and counter-intelligence/force protection missions. Multiple MI initiatives and programs, specifically the Counter-intelligence/HUMINT FDU, are reshaping the MI force structure in a multi-tiered approach, to include: increasing the 97E authorizations, converting 97Bs to 97Es, converting 97L (Translator/Interpreter) to 97E and 97B, rebalancing the Active Component (AC) to Reserve Component (RC) mix to move more personnel to the AC, increasing the number of MI units and the dispersion of Tactical Human Intelligence (HUMINT) Teams (THTs) in the division and Stryker Brigade force structures, and designing Human Intelligence (HUMINT) Collection Teams (HCTs) throughout the Unit of Action (UA), Unit of Employment x (UEx), and Unit of Employment y (UEy) level. These items are addressed in the Military Intelligence – Counter-intelligence/Human Intelligence Force Design Update Section below.

CURRENT MI FORCE STRUCTURE

The MI mission to gain HUMINT information during detainee operations is performed by the 97E. In contrast, the 97B counters the intelligence gathering of foreign intelligence and security services (FIS). Gathering information from detainees focuses the 97Es on their specialty: gathering and developing intelligence from the local environment. The 97E10 is a highly trained soldier who has gone through 82 weeks of training. This soldier has completed language training from the Defense Language Institute, in addition to the required Military Occupational Specialty (MOS) training. Developing this asset is a costly and time-consuming process.

The current force structure does not give the commander on the ground the amount of 97E and 97B expertise required. A divisional MI battalion has all of the 97Es in the division (depending on the type of division, approximately 16 are authorized). The DAIG team visited one division that had six 97Es. In the current operating environment people are the key terrain, but the force structure lacks 97Es and 97Bs at the brigade level.

The average maneuver brigade has an intelligence team consisting of four 97B – Counter-intelligence personnel and three 97E – HUMINT personnel (approximately two Tactical HUMINT Teams (THTs)). These 97Es come from the division MI battalion. The commander must set the intelligence priorities at either HUMINT (gathering intelligence from the local environment and information exploitation from detainees) or at counter-intelligence (denying FIS intelligence on U.S. Forces).

G3 Force Developers stated current rotations in **OPERATION ENDURING FREEDOM** (OEF) and **OPERATION IRAQI FREEDOM** (OIF) require approximately 130 THTs per deployment. There are approximately four personnel per team. The ongoing Counter-intelligence/HUMINT Force Design Update has greatly contributed to meeting the current operational needs. Since 2001, the number of THTs has grown from 300 teams to 450 teams. Even with these changes, the current force structure lacks the depth to meet this doctrinal requirement for a sustained period.

There are usually three 97E HUMINT specialists in the current brigade force structure; they come from the division MI battalion. They gather intelligence on threat forces and capabilities. The 97Es, as part of THTs, accompany patrols, visit communities, talk to local leaders, to gather information on how U.S. Forces are being targeted. The 97Es evaluate the internment/resettlement (I/R) population to identify potential intelligence sources. They conduct interviews and interrogations across the range of detainees, gathering information from civilian internees, enemy prisoners of war (EPWs), and high-risk detainees (HRDs).

Information gathered from detainees is critical to meeting the doctrinal mission of the 97E "to conduct focused collection, analysis, and production on the adversary's composition, strength, dispositions, tactics, equipment, personnel, personalities, capabilities, and intentions". Exploitation of intelligence gathered from EPWs and HRDs is one of the reasons detainees are kept beyond the doctrinal time standard at the point of capture and brigade level. The current force structure of three 97Es in the brigade (division MI battalion assets) provides limited resources to evaluate, gather, and analyze information from detainees.

The 97B counter-intelligence mission requires the intelligence assets of the brigade to cover a large section of the local population. The brigade has a total of four counter-intelligence specialists who gather information on threat forces and foreign intelligence services and their activities and then develop force protection and information denial measures. The 97B focus on denying intelligence to the enemy is based on their ability to stop the following FIS operations: counter-HUMINT, counter-signals intelligence (C-SIGINT), and counter-imagery intelligence (C-IMINT). The 97Bs are not accomplishing their counter-intelligence and force protection missions if they are supporting the HUMINT mission of gathering information from detainees.

The current force structure of the MI is a result of the 1997 Quadrennial Defense Review (QDR) process. The QDR reshaped tactical MI units, relying heavily on the Reserve Component (RC) to carry a large portion of MI personnel. Additionally, in 1994 and 1995, the Army restructured personnel authorizations and sent 97E personnel to the Defense Intelligence Agency.

A substantial number of active component 97Es and 97Bs are in U.S. Army Intelligence and Security Command (INSCOM) Theater Intelligence Brigades (BDEs)/Groups (GPs). Until recently, those personnel were not available to support rotational sourcing.

Some commands were using 97Bs to fill 97E requirements to meet the shortage of personnel who can conduct interrogations of detainees. Commanders who chose the collection and exploitation of information as the priority mission gave up the 97Bs from performing their counter-intelligence/force protection mission. However, force protection is still a critical issue due to the non-linear battlefield. Based on the current force structure, the Army has the ability to support either force protection or HUMINT.

Currently, 60% of the 97E and 97B force structure is in the Reserve Component (RC). Deployment of some units as battalions vs. teams in early rotations to OEF followed by OIF artificially reduced the available population to support subsequent rotations. The buildup of RC THTs prior to OIF met the immediate requirement for tactical intelligence but denied a sustained capability. Additionally, the MOS qualification rate in the RC is at 50%. So even if all RC authorized positions were filled, only one-half of the personnel would be deployable.

The TRADOC proponent (U.S. Army Intelligence Center and Fort Huachuca) developed the Military Intelligence – Counter-intelligence/HUMINT Force Design Update and other initiatives to meet the requirements of the current and future operating environments. G3 Force Management is restructuring the force through redesign of current Modified Tables of Organization and Equipment (MTOEs) of MI units and creation of new MTOEs. The new force structure increases the authorizations for and distribution of 97E and 97B.

MI – COUNTER-INTELLIGENCE/HUMAN INTELLIGENCE FORCE DESIGN UPDATE

The Army recognizes the current force structure does not allow the commander to conduct the doctrinal missions of HUMINT and counter-intelligence simultaneously. Currently, the commander must choose which mission is the priority. The Counter-intelligence/HUMINT FDU was approved on 2 August 2001. Some aspects of the Counter-intelligence/HUMINT FDU and other MI initiatives and programs have assisted the force in current operations, while the majority is still ongoing (as of 21 May 2004). The number of THTs in the Army has increased by 50% since 2001 (300 THTs to 450 THTs).

The main portions of the Counter-intelligence/HUMINT FDU will occur from 2005 to 2009 Total Army Analysis 09 (TAA 09); additional changes will continue in 2007 through 2011 (TAA 11). The changes to the force structure are being documented in the UA, UEx, UEy, templates and in the Stryker Brigades' Modified Tables of Organization and Equipment.

The near-term changes include adding one counter-intelligence company per Theater at Echelon Above Corps Theater Intelligence Groups/Brigades in Fiscal Year (FY) 05–07. The FDU and other initiatives add a variety of active component Counter-intelligence/HUMINT Teams to Theater Intelligence Groups/Brigades for an increase of 400 counterintelligence/HUMINT spaces in FY06. Other changes include revising the MI Corps Support BN (MI-CSB) and changing the MI-CSB allocation from one MI-CSB per Theater to one MI-CSB per Corps. Another Corps-level change is the creation of a "Corps G2X Cell" in the G2 section of the HHC with HUMINT authorizations.

Four counter-intelligence and two HUMINT companies (U.S. Army Reserve) will activate in FY05-07. Finally, the AC/RC mix will rebalance, resulting in activation of two HUMINT companies and one counter-intelligence company (active component) and deactivation of two U.S. Army Reserve counter-intelligence companies.

The design of the HUMINT team will change. Previously, Warrant Officers led HUMINT teams; in the future a Sergeant First Class will lead some HUMINT teams. The current force structure can convert to an enlisted-led team by using currently available NCOs.

The Counter-intelligence/HUMINT FDU is programmed to increase the number of 97E and 97B Soldiers; 97E will increase by 50%. An increase of "in excess of" 1,400 97E and 97B personnel is programmed from FY05-07, including an increase in authorizations for 97E and 97B in the AC. Some of these changes will be the result of rebalancing the AC/RC mix of 97E. The 97E personnel increases have been implemented early and continue to occur. Other changes include the conversion of 460 Compo 2 MOS 97L (Translator/Interpreter) to 97E and 97B authorizations in FY05.

MI Branch will restructure the 97E MOS. 97E10 soldiers will no longer have a language requirement following initial entry training (IET). By removing the language requirement at Skill Level 1 for 97E MOS the MI branch can send 97E10 soldiers directly to units to gain experience. The language requirement will shift to a 97E20 requirement. Currently the 97E10 soldier spends up to 82 weeks post-IET meeting the language requirement.

The Counter-intelligence/HUMINT FDU and other initiatives will support the design of elements within the UEy, UEx, and UA. (The current design of the UEy, UEx, and UA are the base for this section of the report). This increase of counter-intelligence/HUMINT units at each level is significant and is designed to add an intelligence gathering and processing capability at the UA level, as well as at higher levels. The Army's ability to add counter-intelligence/HUMINT resources as it transforms into the Modular Design is based on an increase in the number of 97Es authorizations, which go from the FY04 level of 861 authorizations to the FY 11 projection of 3312 authorizations.

The UEy's Theater Intelligence Brigade will add an Exploitation Battalion and a RC Battalion that are in-Theater assets. The Exploitation Battalion and the RC Battalion will each add a counterintelligence company and a HUMINT company to the Theater, providing an additional two counter-intelligence companies and two HUMINT companies to the commander.

The UEx has a G2X cell designed into its Main HQ staff. The G2X is a new organization not in the current division template. The G2X acts as the single point for all counter-intelligence/HUMINT data. The G2X is a six-person team led by an officer (MAJ/CPT) and contains a CW3 HUMINT Technician, one 97B, and three 97Es. Supplying information to the G2X are the Counterintelligence Control Authority (CICA) and the HUMINT Operations Cell (HOC). The CICA provides the counter-intelligence function with 97Bs while the HOC adds four more 97Es for the HUMINT function. The G2X also contains a Language Coordination Section which sets up contracts for interpreters. The main HUMINT and counter-intelligence gathering capability will exist in the UAs.

There are HUMINT and counter-intelligence gathering capability in both Maneuver UAs (MUA) and Reconnaissance, Surveillance, and Target Acquisition UAs (RSTA UA). In the MUA and the RSTA UA the main HUMINT collection will be conducted by the HUMINT Collection Teams (HCTs) which have taken the place of the Tactical HUMINT Teams (THTs). The HCT is made up of four 97E whose mission is to gather HUMINT. This will eliminate the THTs' requirement of dividing the time among the mission of the 97B and the 97E that made up the THT. The THT currently exists in the division force structure and the Stryker Brigade force structure; THTs are not in the UA or UE force structures.

Each MUA has an S2X in the headquarters, serving the same function as the G2X does at the UEx. The MUA also has an MI company with a robust intelligence gathering capability. The HUMINT platoon contains 26 soldiers focused on gathering HUMINT. The HUMINT platoon has two Operations Management Teams (OMTs) that each manages two HCT. Each OMT also has the ability to serve as a HCT. At the minimum, each MUA has an organic capability to field four HCTs and, if needed, generate two more from the OMTs. This gives the UA commander the ability to put HCTs at the point of capture or where detainees are first encountered.

The RSTA UA has a greater HUMINT capability. The MI battalion in the RTSA UA has a Collection and Exploitation (C&E) company and a counterintelligence/HUMINT company. The C&E Company has 3 HCT platoons (28 Soldiers per platoon) with one OMT and five HCTs per platoon. The C&E Company has a total of 15 HCTs. The counterintelligence/HUMINT company has nine OMTs and 27 HCTs. At the minimum, each RSTA UA will have 42 HCTs on the ground.

The significant difference from the current division force structure is that the average division has all 16 Soldiers with MOS 97E in the division MI battalion. The UEx will deploy into theater with a modular capability that is based on the mission requirements. If the UEx deploys with four MUAs and a RSTA UA, it will have a total of 20 OMTs and 58 HCTs and a robust HUMINT planning, coordination, and analysis capability.

> (4) *Recommendation*: TRADOC and G3 continue to refine and implement the force structure changes in the Military Intelligence – Counter-intelligence/Human Intelligence Force Design Update.

Recommendation: TRADOC integrate the Military Intelligence – Counter-intelligence/Human Intelligence Force Design Updates into the development of Units of Action and Units of Employment.

f. **Finding 14:**
>   (1) *Finding*: The ongoing Military Police Force Design Update provides a force structure for internment/resettlement operations that has the flexibility and is better suited to conduct sustained detainee operations in the current and future operating environment.
>   (2) *Standard*: See Appendix E.
>   (3) *Inspection Results*: The DAIG team found the ongoing Military Police – Internment/Resettlement Battalion Force Design Update provides a force structure for Military Police internment/resettlement operations that has the flexibility and is better suited than the current Military Police force structure to conduct sustained detainee operations in the current and future operating environments, to include control and internment of high-risk detainees.

The current Military Police force structure lacks the 31E (Internment/Resettlement Specialist) personnel to meet the requirements of manning the current detention facilities and conducting sustained detainee operations in the current and future operating environments, to include control and confinement of high-risk detainees. The 31E is the only soldier trained to run a detention facility and specifically deals with controlling and confining high value detainees. The Active Component (AC) 31Es are in the Table of Distribution and Allowance (TDA) that runs the U.S. Military Disciplinary Barracks (USDB), staffs Guantanamo Bay Naval Station (GTMO) and other outside the continental United States (OCONUS)-based confinement facilities, and staff continental United States (CONUS)-based confinement facilities. The Reserve Component (RC) does not have the 31E personnel to provide units to run sustained detainee operations. These items are covered in the Current Military Police Force Structure Section below:

The ongoing Military Police Internment/Resettlement (I/R) Battalion Force Design Update (FDU) standardizes the force structure of Active Component (AC) and Reserve Component (RC) I/R units, converts AC Tables of Distribution and Allowance (TDAs) to I/R Modified Tables of Organization and Equipment (MTOEs), and increases personnel and units throughout the AC and RC force structure. The FDU was approved September 2003, this analysis is based on that data and is current as of 21 May 2004. The increase of deployable 31Es will give Combatant Commanders the flexibility to conduct sustained detainee operations in a non-linear battlefield and the ability to control and confine high-risk detainees (HRDs). The I/R FDU provides the RC force structure necessary to carry out its sustainability mission. Employment of the I/R FDU has been incorporated into the Unit of Employment (UE) design at Unit of Employment y (UEy) level with staff support at Unit of Employment x (UEx) level. These items are covered in the Military Police Internment/Resettlement (I/R) Battalion Force Design Update Section below:

CURRENT MP FORCE STRUCTURE

The current AC TDA organizations, such as the U.S. Army Disciplinary Barracks (USDB) and Regional Correctional Facilities (RCFs) are not deployable, and each has a different force structure. Each facility will convert to at least one I/R company.

The AC 31E population is based out of four installations within CONUS TDA units and two Modified Table of Organization and Equipment (MTOE) MP battalions that are OCONUS. In CONUS, the largest population of 31Es is at the USDB at Fort Leavenworth. Large numbers of 31Es are also assigned to the three Regional Correctional Facilities (RCFs) at Fort Lewis, Fort Sill, and Fort Knox. These are TDA organizations and not designed to deploy, lacking a rotational base to support the TDA corrections mission and other missions such as GTMO. There are 824 AC MOS 31E authorizations in the Army; of these, 770 are directly related to running the current detention facilities. There are 371 31E authorizations at the USDB. The other 31E authorizations are at Fort Lewis (112), Fort Sill (81), Fort Knox (80), and 24 at Navy/Marine facilities (CONUS and OCONUS). The two OCONUS MP battalions contain 31Es in their MTOE, but lack the depth to support rotations; USAREUR has

76 authorizations and USFK has 26 authorizations. The remaining 54 are not directly working with U.S. prisoners or detainees. These soldiers are at the U.S. Army Military Police School (24), recruiting (12), AC/RC support (6), and 12 others throughout the AC force.

The deployable 31Es are in the RC. The RC has 119 31E authorizations, 90 of which were filled as of 22 April 2004. The RC internment/resettlement (I/R) units' missions are to deploy or provide backfill for the AC's 31Es that deploy. However, the RC I/R units lack the qualified personnel to sustain the mission. Additionally, the RC has the only I/R command and control elements, two I/R brigades.

This force structure does not support the policy or doctrine requirement for a deployable, sustainable, and standardized, modular MP I/R battalion force design package that can meet the I/R operations objective of processing, handling, caring for, accounting for, and securing EPWs, CIs, RPs, ODs, DCs, and U.S. Armed Forces prisoners, as well as supporting the global war on terrorism (GWOT) and controlling and confining high-risk detainees. The I/R doctrine is a revision of the old Enemy Prisoner of War concept, reminiscent of Cold War doctrine applicable to a unit that is modular, capabilities-based, and deployable.

The new I/R doctrine adapts well to the Units of Action concept, however, the 31E force structure does not support I/R doctrine. FM 3-19.40, *Military Police Internment/ Resettlement Operations*, 1 August 2001, covers most detainee operations, but at the time the doctrine was written, the MP Corps had not yet developed or defined the term high-risk detainee.

FM 3-19.1 *Military Police Operations*, Change-1, 31 January 2002, and FM 3-19.40, refer to the MPs as having the responsibility for coordinating sustainment for EPW/CI and that I/R battalions are equipped and trained to handle the EPW/CI mission for the long term. This is not true under the current force structure. By doctrine, an I/R battalion should support up to 4,000 EPWs/CIs, 8,000 dislocated civilians, or 1,500 U.S. Armed Forces prisoners. This formula does not address confinement of high-risk detainees. The current MP doctrine only focuses on long-term confinement of U.S. Armed Forces personnel.

The 31E soldier receives his/her MOS training as part of Military Police Advanced Individual Training (AIT). All MP AIT is based on 31B (Military Police) training. There is a split in the MP AIT where 31Es and 31Bs go to different tracks. MOS 31E Soldiers take a four-week Corrections track while the 31B receive four weeks of Law and Order training. The 31B (Military Police) do not receive corrections training. 31Bs receive one day of I/R training in MP AIT. The 31E10 gains MOS experience at a correctional facility or the USDB.

The current Military Police force structure is not designed to support Units of Action. The TDA-based AC units are not flexible, adaptable, or deployable.

The U.S. Army Training and Doctrine Command (TRADOC) proponent (U.S. Army Military Police School) developed an I/R Battalion Force Design Update and which was approved September 2003. G3 Force Management is restructuring the force through redesign of current MTOEs of AC and RC MP units and creation of new MTOEs. The new force structure increases the number of I/R units and 31E authorizations and is covered in the next section of this finding.

MP I/R BATTALION FORCE DESIGN UPDATE SECTION

The ongoing Military Police Internment/Resettlement (I/R) Battalion Force Design Update addresses the flexibility and sustainability of the current MP force structure. The current AC TDA organizations, such as the U.S. Army Disciplinary Barracks (USDB) and Regional Correctional Facilities (RCFs) are not deployable, and each has a different force structure. Each facility will convert to at least one I/R company.

The Director of Force Management approved the I/R Tables of Organization and Equipment (TOEs) on 17 May 2004. The I/R FDU will occur from Fiscal Year (FY04) through FY11. The FDU will standardize the I/R force structures in the AC and RC. The distribution of personnel and units will rebalance between the AC and RC, giving the AC the ability to immediately deploy I/R companies. The RC will have the force structure to accomplish the mission of backfilling Army confinement facilities as well as providing a sustained rotation of deployable units.

The I/R FDU will standardize the force structure and increase the MOS 31E expertise within the units conducting the I/R mission. The I/R battalion will be modular in nature, providing a command and control capability that is flexible and tailorable, that by design supports the Units of Action concept. The MP I/R battalion will be a flexible base that can be tailored to the Theater of Operations and the operating environment.

The I/R battalion Headquarters and Headquarters Detachment (HHD) is a 74-person unit that provides the command and control function and supports a mix of I/R companies, guard companies, and I/R detachments as required. A standard I/R battalion template for deployment could include the battalion HHD, one guard company, one I/R company, and three I/R detachments.

The I/R company is tailored around accomplishing the 31E mission and is the base of the new force structure. It can operate independently or as part of an I/R battalion. The I/R company will have 124 personnel, with 100 31Es. It has the built-in administrative support to conduct detainee operations as well as two internment platoons and a Maximum Security Section. The internment platoons each contain 42 personnel while the Maximum Security Section has 12 personnel. The Maximum Security Section is different from an I/R detachment. The I/R company should have the ability in the short term to control and intern HRDs, a capability that is essential in the current operating environment.

The I/R company can either operate as a standalone organization or operate as part of an I/R battalion. In either mission it provides command and control, staff planning, administration and logistical services (for both assigned personnel and the prisoner population). If the I/R company operates as a standalone unit, it is limited in the detainee operations functions it can perform. The standalone I/R company can operate either a U.S. Armed Forces prisoner confinement facility or a high-risk detainee internment facility.

If the I/R company operates as part of an I/R battalion, it can conduct a wider range of detainee operations due to the support of the I/R battalion's guard company and I/R detachments. When the I/R company operates as part of I/R battalion, it can operate the following types of facilities: high-risk detainee internment facilities; Enemy Prisoner of War/Civilian Internee (EPW/CI) internment facilities; or displaced civilian (DC) resettlement facilities.

The I/R company and I/R battalion force structures are focused on the I/R mission. Any I/R unit will require support from the Command it falls under. I/R units will require engineer support to build facilities, medical support for soldiers and detainees, maintenance support, water purification, and other support as required.

The I/R company's main focus is supporting its two internment platoons and one Maximum Security Section. The I/R company has different capabilities based on whether it is conducting standalone operations or operating as part of an I/R battalion. If operating in the standalone function the I/R company has the capability to confine up to 300 U.S. prisoners or detain up to 100 high-risk detainees. If the I/R company is operating as part of an I/R battalion, the I/R company has the capability to detain up to 300 high-risk detainees when supported by one MP guard company. The I/R company also has the capability to conduct detainee operations for enemy prisoners of war/civilian internees or resettlement operations for dislocated civilians. In these detainee operations, the I/R company will also require support from one MP guard company.

The Maximum Security Section in the I/R company is responsible for detainees/prisoners who require special supervision, control, and discipline. These detainees/prisoners require close and intense management, special precautions, and more stringent confinement, search, and handling measures. The Maximum Security Section is merged with the internment platoons when conducting high-risk detainee operations.

The MP guard company has personnel and equipment resources to provide a perimeter security function as well as a transportation function. Each guard company has three platoons of 31Bs. Each platoon has four 11-man squads. The MP guard company has three light medium tactical vehicle (LMTV) trucks and 16 high mobility multipurpose wheeled vehicle (HMMWV) trucks authorized. This robust guard force and transportation assets will give the I/R battalion the capability to control and transport detainees using internal resources.

The I/R detachment is a 24-person unit that exists only in the RC. The I/R detachment augments an AC or RC I/R battalion HHD. There are no 31Es in an I/R detachment; the detachments support the detainee operations mission by providing 31Bs to act as outside-the-wire security and additional support personnel. The I/R detachment is not designed to detain HRD or U.S. prisoners. The 60 I/R detachments allow a high degree of flexibility in modularizing any organization for a mission. These units are designed to be mobilized and attached to other units as needed.

To meet the requirement for the I/R FDU, G3 plans to increase 31E authorizations through conversion of some 31Bs (Military Police) to 31Es (Internment/Resettlement Specialist), increased recruiting for 31E positions, and a redesignation of RC units to the 31E mission.

The conversion of Active Component MP TDA organizations to an I/R company MTOE has begun. The first AC I/R company will activate in FY04 at Guantanamo Bay (GTMO). A total of 10 AC I/R companies will activate by FY11.

The RC will contain the bulk of the 31E units and personnel. The RC currently contains 119 authorizations. When the I/R battalion FDU is completed in FY11, the RC will contain approximately 1720 31E authorizations, a 14-fold increase in personnel.

The U.S. Army Reserve (USAR) will contain most of the I/R battalions, while the Army National Guard (ARNG) will contain most of the I/R companies. By FY11, the RC will be organized with 20 I/R battalions (17 USAR, 3 ARNG) compared to the AC's one I/R battalion. The RC will have 17 I/R companies (7 USAR, 10 ARNG) compared to the AC's 10 I/R companies. The RC will contain all 60 I/R detachments (51 USAR, 9 ARNG). The I/R sustainment mission will be supplemented by this RC build-up of 17 I/R companies and 60 I/R detachments.

Based on the currently proposed MTOE, the standard I/R battalion will deploy with a battalion HHD, one guard company, one I/R company, and three I/R detachments. The template for a deployed I/R battalion will contain 427 personnel; 101 of them will be 31Es. The I/R company contains the 31E personnel in the two I/R platoons and the Maximum Security Section. The I/R FDU units contain the following personnel:

- I/R battalion HHDs: 74 total personnel (one 31E)
- I/R companies: 124 total personnel (100 31Es)
- I/R platoons: 42 total personnel (41 31Es)
- Maximum Security Sections: 12 total personnel (12 31Es)
- MP guard companies: 157 total personnel (no 31Es)
- I/R detachments (RC only): 24 total personnel (no 31Es)

The I/R FDU is designed to provide I/R units to the UEy that meet the specific requirements of the commander. The primary employment of 31Es will be at the UEy level. They will deploy in the I/R configuration best suited to the mission, whether it be as I/R brigades or I/R battalions. Current planning calls for two 31E NCOs (E-7s) working on the UEx staff, one in the UEx Main and one in the UEx TAC. Both will act as liaisons to the UEy I/R units and as advisors on I/R capabilities at the UEx level. There are no current plans to place 31Es in the Unit of Action (UA) or Stryker Brigades.

A UA will contain a 41-person MP platoon (31Bs). There will be no 31Bs in the Stryker Brigades. In the UEx and UEy, the 31Bs outside of the I/R units will not be primarily tasked with I/R operations.

(4) *Recommendation*: TRADOC and G3 continue to refine and implement the force structure changes in the Military Police – Internment/Resettlement Battalion Force Design Update.

Recommendation: TRADOC integrate the Military Police – Internment/ Resettlement Battalion Force Design Update into the development of Units of Action and Units of Employment.

g. **Finding 15:**
(1) *Finding*: Three of the four inspected internment/resettlement facilities and many of the collecting points, had inadequate force protection measures, Soldier working conditions, detainee living conditions, and did not meet the minimum preventive medicine and medical treatment requirements.
(2) *Standard*: See Appendix E.

(3) *Inspection Results*: The DAIG team inspected four internment/resettlement
(I/R) facilities and 12 forward and central collecting points (CPs). Three of
the four inspected internment/resettlement (I/R) facilities, and three of the 12
(25%) inspected collecting points (CPs), had problems and shortcomings with
deteriorating infrastructure that impacted on having a clean, safe, and secure
working environment for soldiers and living conditions for detainees. Poor food
quality and food distribution, lack of laundry capability, and lack of personal
hygiene facilities at some of these facilities affected the detainees' living conditions. Overcrowding, safety hazards, frequent enemy hostile fire, and lack of
in depth force protection measures also put both soldier and detainee at risk.

Four of 16 (25%) inspected facilities (Camp Bucca, Bagram, Abu Ghraib, and
Brassfield-Mora) were found to have safety hazards that posed risks to soldiers
and detainees. In addition, there was little evidence that units operating facilities
had safety inspection programs in place. Safety programs in just a few facilities
amounted to nothing more than detainee fire evacuation plans, weapons clearing
procedures, and military working dog safety considerations. At the time of the inspection, Camp Cropper, Camp Bucca, and Abu Ghraib did not have finalized and
approved Standing Operating Procedures (SOPs) for their facilities. At the time, units
were busy revising and tailoring their SOPs for the mission. However, during SOP reviews conducted by the DAIG team, there was no evidence that the risk management
process was being incorporated into the working draft SOPs as required. Reviews of
finalized SOPs at other facilities yielded the same results as the working drafts – no
risk management was incorporated into SOPs.

No units fully complied with the medical treatment of detainees or with the sanitary conditions of the detainee facilities. Not all medical personnel supporting division CPs and I/R facilities were aware of detainee medical treatment requirements
or had the proper equipment to treat a detainee population. The medical personnel
interviewed stated that they did not receive any specific training in detainee operations and were not aware of Army Regulation (AR) 190-8, *Enemy Prisoners of War,
Retained Personnel, Civilian Internees and Other Detainees*, 1 October 1997, although
most believed they were required to treat detainees to the same standard of care as
the Coalition Forces. There was a widespread lack of preventive medicine staffing,
supplies, and equipment to meet the needs of CPs and I/R facilities. This shortfall
was compounded by the failure of units to deploy appropriately trained and supplied
field sanitation teams. Medical leaders responsible for direct oversight of preventive
medicine personnel lacked specific training in detainee operations and field sanitation.
I/R facility site selection, design and construction decisions did not incorporate preventive medicine considerations. There was significant variance in the hygiene and
sanitation conditions at CPs and in I/R facilities throughout Afghanistan and Iraq.
While major improvements continue to upgrade conditions at most sites, the process has been hampered by shortages of preventive medicine personnel and materiel,
problems with site selection and design, and detainee populations that exceed the
current system capacity. Lack of trained preventive medicine personnel and required
field sanitation supplies has contributed significantly to deficiencies in hygiene and
sanitation at CPs and I/R facilities.

CAMP BUCCA

Soon after the ground conflict began in Iraq, the Camp Bucca I/R facility was designed and established as an internment facility for Enemy Prisoners of War (EPWs). At the time of the DAIG inspection, Camp Bucca was considered an overflow I/R facility for Abu Ghraib, and all detainees were kept in the old facility, which contained six compounds. The new facility, containing six additional compounds, was in the final stages of completion. The old facility housed a non-compliant Civilian Internee (CI) population, third-country nationals, and a very small number of EPWs. Detainees were not segregated according to category (i.e., EPWs and CIs (to include Security Internees) were housed together in compounds 7 through 11). Compound 12 housed the third-country nationals.

The DAIG team found inadequate security measures at the Camp Bucca. Camp Bucca had two controlled entry points leading into the compound, but blind spots along the perimeter made access possible at other points. The facility had a sally port gate, but it was used as a serpentine instead of a true double-gate security mechanism to control the entrance and exit of personnel and vehicles. The perimeter security consisted of roving guards, a gate guard, and a guard in each of the towers. There were two vehicular security patrols, but they would consistently take the same route, making them vulnerable to enemy attacks and Improvised Explosive Devices (IEDs) placed on the patrol route. The visitation process at Camp Bucca presented security concerns. During visitation hours Iraqi family members were searched at the exterior entry point, but thereafter they were allowed to mingle around guards who were carrying weapons until they were taken inside the compound to visit detained relatives. This posed a major security concern should one or more of the visitors overtake a guard and seize his weapon.

In numerous places at the old facility, the triple-standard concertina wire was over-stretched and not tied down properly, and the short and long U-shaped pickets were not spaced properly. This, and the fact that the detainees vastly outnumbered the guard force, posed a security concern and potentially put soldiers at risk if detainees rushed the wire. There were eight perimeter towers that were not mutually support-ing, creating dead space and blind spots throughout the old compounds. The towers also did not have effective communications with the roving guards. The facility had good lighting according to leaders and soldiers due to recently receiving 32 trailer-mounted portable light stands that can be moved around the facility as needed. The acquired light stands significantly improved the lighting around the compounds. At the time of the Taguba Investigation, the perimeter lighting around Camp Bucca was inadequate and needed to be improved to illuminate dark areas that routinely became avenues of escape. Many of the security concerns due to the wire fences were cor-rected when the detainees were transferred to the six new compounds that have been constructed. The chain link fence at the new compounds was not staked to the ground between fence posts to prevent detainees from slipping through the bottom. However, to overcome this shortcoming, the battalion was placing concertina wire around the inside perimeter of the chain-link fence. This is a significant improvement in security over the old compounds. Detainees were transferred to the new compounds after the DAIG visit. These safety and security concerns were resolved once the detainees were transferred and the old compounds phased out.

According to interviews and sensing sessions at Camp Bucca, soldiers said food is distributed and served in 30 gallon plastic containers, sometimes long after it is prepared. Detainees served themselves by dipping whatever containers they possessed into the food. No utensils were provided, and no portion control measures were in place to ensure that each detainee got the proper amount of food. One leader interviewed stated that serving ladles were on order, but none were on-hand. Food frequently ran out before all detainees had an opportunity to eat. Soldiers stated in sensing sessions that Meals, Ready to Eat (MREs) had to be used to ensure all detainees were fed. The detainees got their drinking water from water spigots at Camp Bucca. It was noted during the walk-through that at least one water source at one of the compounds was located several feet from the human waste dump (septic tank). This problem was eliminated once the detainees were transferred.

There was no laundry service at Camp Bucca to support the detainees so they did their own laundry with the small tubs and soap given them. However, leaders and soldiers said during interviews that they did not know if there were enough washtubs supplied to the detainees. They were not sure how many detainees actually possessed tubs and soap, and where the tubs were located within the six compounds.

Camp Bucca did not routinely receive hostile fire, if at all. However, the compounds did not have adequate force protection measures in place to ensure the safety and protection of detainees and soldiers from potential hostile indirect and small arms fire. There were no bunkers or shelters constructed with overhead cover for detainees to enter if the compounds came under attack. There were also no such bunkers or shelters constructed in the new compounds where the detainees are scheduled to be transferred.

The Taguba Investigation mentioned Camp Bucca as significantly over its intended maximum capacity, with a guard force that is undermanned and underresourced. The DAIG team found that Camp Bucca was not overcrowded nor undermanned because the facility had been scheduled to be discontinued as an I/R facility, and a drawdown in the detainee population had occurred after the investigation was conducted. A decision to use it as an overflow facility for Abu Ghraib kept it operational. The detainee population during the DAIG inspection was 1,769. Capacity for the newly constructed facility is 4,500 according to the command briefing given to the DAIG team.

BAGRAM I/R FACILITY

The Bagram I/R facility was designed and used as a Soviet aircraft maintenance facility that was built in the early 1960s. The DAIG team found several safety hazards at the facility that posed risks to both the soldiers and detainees. Based on the document review and a thorough walk-through of the Bagram I/R facility, there was little evidence of a unit safety program. However, extensive engineering and environmental surveys of the facility, to include contaminated rooms and roof failures, had been recently conducted. At the time of the DAIG inspection, the infrastructure to support the facility was inadequate. Examples included inadequate ventilation/climate control and lighting on the main floor, the electrical distribution system throughout the facility, and non-existent sanitary facilities at the main floor.

In the Bagram I/R facility, there were no handrails and banisters on many of the steep stairwells and landings. The DAIG team determined this was particularly dangerous while soldiers escorted blindfolded detainees up and down the stairs. Team members actually witnessed soldiers escorting blindfolded detainees on these stairs. Some drop-offs from the second floor landings were 5 to 7 feet.

Potential shock hazards existed at the Bagram I/R facility. There were numerous examples of open and exposed electrical wiring around the facility, to include a major electrical panel located in the vicinity of a known roof leak. Throughout the office areas, uncovered receptacles and light switches were found.

Contaminated soil (evidence of heavy metals) was found in the former metal plating rooms. The rooms were previously used as a metal plating facility as part of the Soviet aircraft maintenance facility. The unit requested and received an environmental survey of the rooms, and the conclusion was that the sampled materials represented a health risk. A rough cost estimate ($3-6 million) to remediate the contaminated rooms was cost-prohibitive, and the decision was made to seal the rooms to protect soldiers and detainees from exposure.

According to an interview, lead-based paint was procured from the local economy to paint the interior in various locations in the facility. Lead-based paint had been used in the past and was still being used in the Bagram I/R facility, creating a potential risk to soldiers and detainees.

Concerning the non-existing sanitary system, soldiers were required to remove modified portable latrines from each detainee group cell by hand. These latrines were dragged to a designated location outside the facility where contractors would empty and clean them. After cleaning the latrines, soldiers dragged the latrines back into place in each detainee cell. During interviews and sensing sessions, soldiers stated that human waste spills were frequent on the main floor. There was a project ongoing that will remedy this problem. The project included an installed indoor septic system that consisted of a 4-inch main line running underneath the newly poured concrete pads and along the length of the group cells. Toilets were being installed inside of each cell, and the effluent will flow via gravity to an exterior waste system. The estimated completion date was April or May 2004.

The facility had multiple roof leaks, to include an area that was repaired after damage from aerial bombing. In December 2003, the engineer group conducted a roof inspection and found possible obstructed roof drains and deterioration of parapet walls and flashing. The estimated cost to repair the roof is $350K. This project was not funded at the time of the inspection.

At the time of this inspection, the facility had inadequate personal hygiene facilities for the number of detainees. An ongoing indoor plumbing system project to fix the problem will consist of a newly built shower room with full shower capabilities (10 shower heads) as well as a white water supply system. The fresh water supply will be housed inside of an exterior water system building that must also be designed and built.

The electrical distribution system in place was inadequate, especially to support planned upgrades for the facility that include lighting for new cells and towers and power for the Morale, Welfare, and Recreation room for the soldiers. Current electrical amperage draw is 1279.7 amps. Amperage draw, once the upgrades are complete, will increase by another 340 amps, beyond the current transformer's capability of 1441 amps. The facility engineer was assessing the electrical load and prioritizing electrical distribution throughout the facility, with office air conditioning units and hot water heaters being shut down first during overloads to the system. There was concern that serious overloads to the system will occur this summer. There is a project planned to replace the transformer and renovate the electrical distribution system for the facility, but at the time of the inspection the project had not been funded.

ABU GHRAIB

Abu Ghraib had problems with deteriorating infrastructure that impacted the clean, safe, and secure working environment for soldiers and living conditions for detainees. Poor food quality and food distribution, lack of laundry capability, and inadequate personal hygiene facilities affected the detainees' living conditions. Overcrowding, frequent enemy hostile fire, and lack of in-depth force protection measures also put soldiers and detainees at risk. There is a separate finding concerning Abu Ghraib. See Finding 3 in Chapter 3.

COLLECTING POINTS

Detainees were being held at division forward and central CPs from 1 to 54 days for intelligence exploitation before release or transfer based on interviews and sensing sessions of leaders and soldiers. If detainees are kept longer than doctrinally recommended, then the infrastructure standards for the facilities should be similar to I/R facilities for the security, safety, and wellbeing of the detainee. Three of the 12 (25%) forward and central CPs inspected (Green Zone in Baghdad, Brassfield-Mora in Samarra, and Khost, Afghanistan) were determined to be inadequate to keep detainees for longer than doctrinally recommended due to not having the needed laundry services, personal hygiene facilities, medical care, and adequate shelter from adverse weather conditions and the elements. The division forward collecting point (CP) at Brassfield-Mora was also located within 100 feet of an ammunition holding area and fuel point. Enemy hostile fire targeting these areas could result in detainee casualties due to the close proximity of these sites to the collecting point. There were plans to fix a majority of these shortcomings at these three facilities.

Many forward and central facilities visited had recent improvements and upgrades made to them because of the inadequate facilities and harsh conditions. These improvements included upgrades to supporting infrastructure and expansions to facilities to relieve overcrowding, enhance security, and to provide for better sanitation conditions. Improvements and upgrades at collecting points included (but are not limited to) a completely new facility (construction ongoing) at the Kandahar division central CP; new roof, new interrogation room, new electrical system, installed personal hygiene facility, and additional security lighting at the division forward CP in the Green Zone; security upgrades at the division forward CP at Ar Ramadi; addition of gravel around latrines at the Brassfield-Mora division forward CP to improve drainage; and a repaired guard tower at the division central CP at the Baghdad International Airport.

Planned upgrades and improvements included (but are not limited to) installation of two 500 gallon water tanks, laundry washers, and shower facility at Ar Ramadi; new cells in a hardened facility that will protect detainees from the elements in Khost; and planned security upgrades and construction of new shower facilities for the CP at Brassfield-Mora. All units inspected were placing a great deal of effort on making improvements and upgrades to existing collecting points for the health and welfare of detainees.

PREVENTIVE MEDICINE

Six of the eight inspected units operated CPs and I/R facilities that did not comply with minimum preventive medicine standards established in policy and doctrine. Two of the eight units met or exceeded minimum preventive medicine standards. The DAIG team conducted comprehensive preventive medicine inspections at 8 of the 16 (50%) internment/resettlement (I/R) facilities and collecting points (CPs) visited that were interning detainees.

Leaders and Soldiers from 36 units, both continental U.S. (CONUS) and outside CONUS (OCONUS), were interviewed concerning preventive medicine practices and procedures in detainee operations. There was a widespread lack of preventive medicine staffing, supplies, and equipment to meet the needs of CPs and I/R facilities. This shortfall was compounded by the failure of units to deploy appropriately trained and supplied field sanitation teams. Medical leaders responsible for direct oversight of preventive medicine personnel lacked specific training in detainee operations and field sanitation. I/R facility site selection, design and construction decisions did not incorporate preventive medicine considerations. The capacity of the detainee system was exceeded early in the operations, leading to prolonged holding times at CPs and other areas not prepared for long-term housing of detainees.

There was significant variance in the hygiene and sanitation conditions at CPs and in I/R facilities throughout Afghanistan and Iraq. While major improvements continue to upgrade conditions at most sites, the process has been hampered by shortages of preventive medicine personnel and material, problems with site selection and design, and detainee populations that exceed the current system capacity. As of March 2004, Camp Bucca still had potable water sources within a few feet of exposed fecal material; Abu Ghraib continued to struggle with garbage and rodents in living areas; and Kandahar's food service sanitation was extremely poor. Hand washing stations were still absent from three of the eight (38%) locations inspected, and sanitary orders had not been published and posted at any detainee facilities in accordance with Army Regulation (AR) 190-8, *Enemy Prisoners of War, Retained Personnel, Civilian Internees and Other Detainees*, 1 October 1997.

Lack of trained preventive medicine personnel and required field sanitation supplies contributed significantly to deficiencies in hygiene and sanitation at CPs and I/R facilities. Units (97%, 35 of 36) did not deploy with properly trained and equipped field sanitation teams in accordance with AR 40-5, *Preventive Medicine*, 15 October 1990. Preventive medicine technicians (Military Occupational Specialty 91S) were not deployed in sufficient numbers to support detainee operations, with only one assigned to each Military Police (MP) I/R battalion and none available to support units operating CPs. Preventive medicine detachments at the division level provided support to I/R facilities and CPs when distance and security permitted, but the non-linear battlespace precluded support to the majority of CPs forward of brigade. Shortages of supplies and equipment prohibited preventive medicine personnel from providing complete field sanitation services. Holding times at CPs (up to 54 days; doctrinal maximum is

24 hours) required a more robust infrastructure than units were prepared or resourced to provide.

During interviews and sensing sessions, the DAIG team noted that (86%, 31–36) leaders and soldiers were unaware of the specific hygiene and sanitation requirements for CPs and I/R facilities. They relied on "common sense" and contractors to establish local, often unwritten, standards. All (16 of 16) of the interviewed battalion, brigade, and division surgeons said they were not trained in detainee operations and/or preventive medicine and therefore lacked the knowledge to provide adequate oversight for hygiene and sanitation of CPs and I/R facilities. There were no theater- or unit-level policies that addressed preventive medicine requirements for detainee operations. Additionally, there was no evidence of specific medical planning for field sanitation/preventive medicine support to detainee operations.

Despite the many obstacles, recent (March 2004 timeframe) International Committee of the Red Cross (ICRC) inspections of the U.S.-operated I/R facilities in OIF have indicated general satisfaction with the efforts underway to address persistent problems in hygiene and sanitation (although the slow pace of improvements was criticized). As of March 2004, contractors have assumed responsibility for many sanitation functions, including food and water supplies, latrines, laundry, and waste disposal. The most significant problems that persist include overcrowding and insect/rodent control.

The Ryder Report and the Taguba Investigation indicated deficiencies in preventive medicine aspects of detainee operations. The Ryder Report stated that "significant variance in the health, hygiene and sanitation conditions were observed in the detention facilities throughout Iraq." The report referred to ICRC reports that indicated "major progress" in all areas, and further stated that "most facilities have adequate water supplies, sewage management and appropriate food services to comply with the United Nations guidelines." The deficiencies observed were attributed in this report to "inadequate logistical support for facility operations." The Ryder Report pointed out major sanitation problems at Camps Ganci and Vigilant (compounds at Abu Ghraib). Camp Ganci was littered with trash, had large amounts of standing water around latrines, lacked laundry facilities, had insufficient cleaning supplies, and housed detainees in tents that did not provide adequate protection from severe weather or hostile fire. Camp Vigilant had problems with water supply and latrines. The Taguba Investigation did not look at hygiene and sanitation, but it noted that Abu Ghraib and Camp Bucca were "significantly over their intended maximum capacity", with the overcrowding contributing to "poor living conditions." The DAIG team's findings are consistent with those of the Ryder Report and the Taguba Investigation, but they were not chartered to perform specific evaluations of preventive medicine conditions at U.S.-operated CPs and I/R facilities. While the Ryder Report found most facilities to be in compliance with United Nations guidelines, the DAIG team inspected I/R facilities and CPs against Army standards (AR 190-8, AR 40-5, and FM 21-10).

MEDICAL TREATMENT

No inspected units supporting detainee operations complied with all medical treatment requirements for enemy prisoners of war and civilian internees, such as monthly height/weight screenings, chest X-rays, and tuberculin skin tests. The DAIG team found none of the inspected units were following all the medical requirements in accordance with AR 190-8. However, at the time of the inspection all units were attempting to provide detainees with the same quality of medical treatment as that provided to the Coalition Forces.

AR 190-8 requires an initial medical screening at I/R facilities for both enemy prisoners of war (EPWs) and civilian internees (CIs). At the time of the inspection, all I/R facilities and collecting points (CPs) were performing a medical screening upon initial in processing, but not to standards. At least one I/R facility (Camp Bucca) had previously provided no medical screening, relying on sick call to discover detainees who required medical treatment. The regulation also requires a continuing monthly medical screening, to include weight measurements that ensure detainees are properly nourished. Two of the four I/R facilities (Camp Bucca and the Bagram Internment Facility) were aware of this requirement, and both stated they had started performing these screenings in December 2003. Only two of the four I/R facilities (Camp Cropper and Bagram Internment Facility) conducted a routine, follow-up monthly examination for detainees held over one month as required by regulation.

AR 190-8 also requires CIs be administered a "radioscopic chest examination." None of the facilities had performed this examination. At least one facility (Camp Bucca) had no means of diagnosis for tuberculosis until December 2003. At the time of the inspection, all I/R facilities isolated potentially contagious detainees and provided some preventive measures for soldiers treating these detainees. All I/R facilities and 7 of the 12 (58%) inspected collecting points, established medical records for personnel who required medical treatment. At least three facilities transferred these records with the detainee when they were medically evacuated. Medical personnel at only one facility stated they would provide detainees with their medical records upon release.

Medical personnel at all facilities stated they provided medical care comparable to that afforded to the Coalition Soldiers. The DAIG team found this to be accurate in most cases, with some diagnosis-specific exceptions. The exceptions occurred when treatment required transportation out of the host nation, the patient required significant psychiatric care, or treatment was of an elective nature. Previously, one unit reported there had been some conflict between AR 190-8 and Coalition Provisional Authority treatment policy, which reportedly dictated that U.S. medical care was only available to detainees to prevent loss of life, limb, or eyesight. In these cases Army medical personnel attempted to maintain the higher standard by providing detainees with all necessary care. All interviewed medical providers stated they did not have the proper equipment for treating a detainee population that included older, chronically ill patients. In one I/R facility a senior medical Non-commissioned officer (NCO) stated that over 50% of his population had diabetes, and he had neither glucometers nor insulin. At another location a medical NCO stated that approximately 75% of his detainees had hypertension, and one-third were diabetics. At least four medical personnel and I/R facility commanders described shortfalls in resources to provide adequate psychiatric treatment. At least two I/R facilities had severely ill psychiatric patients (detainees who, in the estimation of the facility's medical personnel, required inpatient treatment) who were being treated pharmacologically by non-psychiatrist physicians.

The medical personnel interviewed stated that they did not receive any specific training in detainee operations or were aware of AR 190-8, although most believed they were required to treat detainees to the same standard of care as the Coalition Forces. All requested additional training. At least one provider requested Mobile Training Teams to provide in-theater training.

The Ryder Report also noted medical personnel lacked adequate training and guidance on the treatment of detainees. Specifically, this report recommended that CJTF-7, "Publish and distribute all new Policies and SOPs to all affected parties and reevaluate the application and adherence to medical practices." It went on to recommend that CJTF-7, "Provide continued in-service training to all newly assigned and/or rotating medical personnel on the provisions, rules and responsibilities stated."

(4) *Root Cause*: Some units did not have thorough plans to upgrade their facilities and in some cases, were not funded for upgrades. Field sanitation teams were not deployed in compliance with AR 40-5 and did not have adequate supplies to provide the services required. None of the units inspected were fully aware of, or trained on the specific medical requirements for detainees in accordance with AR 190-8. Medical leaders were not adequately trained for detainee operations and were unprepared to provide oversight for preventive medicine functions at collecting points and I/R facilities. Preventive medicine aspects of detainee operations were not appropriately incorporated into medical planning processes. Preventive medicine detachments lacked sufficient personnel on their Modified Tables of Organization and Equipment (MTOEs) to adequately inspect all division collecting points and I/R facilities. Units did not have all the necessary medical equipment or supplies to meet the specific requirements contained in AR 190-8.

(5) *Recommendation*: CJTF-7 and CJTF-180 ensure all units meet the guidelines for minimum infrastructure standards supporting detainee operations to allow for adequate facilities to house detainees.

Recommendation: CJTF-7 and CJTF-180 implement a safety inspection program for all facilities that support detainee operations to identify and eliminate hazards to soldiers and detainees.

Recommendation: CJTF-7 and CJTF-180 evaluate current living and working conditions at all facilities housing detainees and take corrective actions to improve the current living and working environment.

Recommendation: CJTF-7 review the physical and operations security requirements and policy/doctrinal procedures to ensure units operating internment/resettlement facilities comply with all requirements.

Recommendation: Force Providers require commanders to have trained and equipped field sanitation teams prior to deployment, and deployed commanders ensure field sanitation teams comply with the Army policy.

Recommendation: TRADOC review the preventive medicine detachment force structure to ensure support to all collecting points and internment/resettlement facilities in a non-linear battlespace.

Recommendation: MEDCOM train all medical personnel in the preventive medicine aspects of detainee operations to ensure compliance with policy and the laws of land warfare.

Recommendation: MEDCOM ensure all health care personnel are trained on the medical treatment requirements for detainees in accordance with Army Regulations and ensure that units have the required medical equipment and supplies for treating detainees.

Recommendation: CJTF-7 and CJTF-180 evaluate current detainee medical capabilities and requirements and take corrective action to ensure detainees receive the required medical screening and care.

h. **Finding 16:**

(1) *Finding*: Two of the four internment/resettlement facilities did not segregate enemy prisoners of war from civilian internees in accordance with legal requirements.

(2) *Standard*: See Appendix E.

(3) *Inspection Results*: The DAIG team observed that two of the four inspected internment/resettlement (I/R) facilities did not segregate enemy prisoners of war (EPWs) from civilian internees (CIs). Inspections of I/R facilities, leader interviews, soldier sensing sessions, and document reviews showed that there were 46 documented EPWs in Iraq, few of which were segregated from the CI population. Units did not segregate EPWs for two reasons: (1) it was too difficult a task because some of the compounds within the internment facility would only have a few EPWs in them, thus wasting space that could be used to house CIs; and (2) they were comingled to support interrogation requirements. Continued failure to segregate EPWs from CIs in Iraq is in contradiction to the legal requirements of GC, Article 84.

The Ryder Report mentioned, "Currently, due to the lack of Iraqi prison facilities and the ongoing consolidation efforts at the Abu Ghraib complex, Iraqi criminals are detained with security internees (generally Iraqi-on-Coalition offenses) and EPWs; though segregated in different cells/compounds. These categories of offenders need to be separated as soon as facility construction and renovation projects permit, especially separating those facilities run by U.S. personnel (for Iraqi criminals). The management of multiple disparate groups of detained persons in a single location by members of the same unit invites confusion about handling, processing, and treatment, and typically facilitates the transfer of information between different categories of detainees. Absent specific mission constraints, intermingling these categories of detainees should be avoided." Abu Ghraib abided by the Ryder Report recommendation regarding segregation of detainees by either releasing EPWs or moving them to other facilities, as the DAIG team observed no EPWs at Abu Ghraib. In addition, the Ryder Report mentions segregation, but not specifically in the context of EPWs and CIs: "Initiate procedures for segregating detainees into separate buildings if and where available, based on category of detainee, sex, untried, or sentenced, and severity of offense."

(4) *Root Cause*: Leaders at all levels were aware of the legal and regulatory requirement to segregate EPWs from CIs. Units did not comply with the segregation standard because they felt it was too difficult a task or they acted to support intelligence requirements.

(5) *Recommendation*: CJTF-7 segregate enemy prisoners of war and civilian internees to ensure compliance with the Geneva Conventions and Army Regulations.

i. **Finding 17:**

(1) *Finding*: Units operating collecting points (42%, 5 of 12), and units operating internment/resettlement facilities (two of the four), were not adequately resourced with communications equipment, shotguns, and non-lethal ammunition.

(2) *Standard*: See Appendix E.

(3) *Inspection Results*: The DAIG team inspected 12 collecting points and four internment/resettlement (I/R) facilities. Five out of 12 (42%) units operating collecting points (CPs), and two of the four (Camp Bucca and Abu Ghraib) units operating I/R facilities experienced equipment shortfalls, including handheld radios for communications between guards, escorts, and towers; weapon systems with non-lethal ammunition; hand and leg restraint devices; and rubber gloves to safely handle detainees.

The Military Police (MP) I/R battalion at Abu Ghraib experienced equipment shortfalls of weapons, radios, and non-lethal ammunition. This problem was compounded because the MP battalion was augmented with in lieu of (ILO) units (a Marine Infantry company and a Field Artillery battery) to perform MP missions. The MP battalion was short radios, so soldiers at Abu Ghraib purchased their own commercial hand-held radios to overcome their shortages. These radios were used primarily for communication between tower guards, roving guards, and for detainee escort missions. Lack of batteries and working radios in the units compounded the problem. Leaders and soldiers stated during interviews and sensing sessions that detainee operations placed additional communication burdens on the units. These commercial handheld radios lacked the range and the communications security (COMSEC) capabilities required to maintain secure communications. According to interviews and sensing sessions, the ILO MP units did not deploy with the authorized number of shotguns, non-lethal ammunition, and radios for guard companies and escort guard companies under the Modified Table of Organization and Equipment (MTO&E) of an I/R battalion.

The situation at Camp Bucca was slightly different. The I/R battalion was augmented by two Field Artillery batteries that were ILO MP units. According to interviewed and sensed leaders and soldiers, the MP battalion, to include the ILO units at Camp Bucca, was short authorized hand and leg restraint devices, radios, shotguns, and non-lethal ammunition. Soldiers at Camp Bucca also purchased commercial handheld radios to overcome unit communication shortages. Like the ILO MP units at Abu Ghraib, the Field Artillery batteries experienced shortages before and after deployment due to MTO&E differences with I/R MP Guard and Guard Escort companies and experienced many of same impacts that the units at Abu Ghraib faced.

Based on interviews and sensing sessions, the collecting points at Baghdad (Green Zone), Tikrit, Baghdad International Airport (BIAP), Brassfield-Mora, and Ar Ramadi all had equipment shortages. Soldiers at the division forward collecting points at Brassfield-Mora and Ar Ramadi said that they did not have enough radios for detainee operations. The forward and central collecting points at the Green Zone, Tikrit, Ar Ramadi, and BIAP experienced shortages in hand and leg restraint devices. Collecting points at the Green Zone and Brassfield-Mora had difficulties in acquiring identification bracelets. All five of the collecting points mentioned above suffered shortages in rubber gloves for the handling of detainees.

  (4) *Root Cause*: Combat support MPs and in lieu of MP units are not adequately equipped to perform detainee operations.
  (5) *Recommendation*: TRADOC identify minimum equipment requirements for detainee operations to ensure successful unit mission accomplishment.

j. **Finding 18:**
  (1) *Finding*: All inspected point of capture units established ad hoc kits containing necessary items and supplies for detainee field processing, but the items they contained and their quantities varied from unit to unit.
  (2) *Standard*: See Appendix E.
  (3) *Inspection Results*: Current operations involving the securing and field processing of detainees require specific equipment and paperwork. A "Detainee Field Processing Kit" would assist all units in processing detainees. Based on leader and soldier interviews, the DAIG team found that capturing units had established some type of ad hoc kit, which included a variety of items required for securing and field processing a detainee, however, the contents and quantities varied from unit to unit. Some units had more complete kits than others.

These kits were put together at unit level with no guidance from higher and no standardization except generally for the type of forms required for field processing. Capturing units developed the kits by trial and error over a period of time to streamline the processing of detainees to the forward collecting points. In some units, leaders and soldiers were not aware of all the processing requirements for detainees for evacuation or transfer to forward collecting points. They expressed concern over not knowing these requirements and felt that if the kit had been established through doctrine, it would have expedited and standardized the field processing of detainees.

Some of the more complete kits contained copies of the required forms from AR 190-8, *Enemy Prisoners of War, Retained Personnel, Civilian Internees and Other Detainees*, 1 October 1997, such as DA Form 4137, Receipt for Evidence/Property Custody Document; DD Form 2745, Enemy Prisoner of War (EPW) Capture Tag; DA Form 2823, Sworn Statement; and the Coalition Provisional Authority (CPA) Forces Apprehension Form (**OPERATION IRAQI FREEDOM** only). Other items generally found in the more complete kits were flexi-cuffs, string or wire (to attach the Capture Tag or CPA Form to the detainee), large plastic bags (to hold evidence, personal effects and other large confiscated items), small zip-lock plastic bags (to hold currency or small valuable items), an instant or digital camera, hearing protection, sandbags, bandages, or blacked-out goggles (to cover eyes), and in times of cold weather, blankets for the detainees.

  (4) *Root Cause*: Capturing units did not have doctrinal guidance to follow in preparing or funding detainee kits that enabled units to safely and efficiently field process detainees.
  (5) *Recommendation*: TRADOC establish and identify resource requirements for a standardized "Detainee Field Processing Kit" that will enable capturing units to properly secure and process detainees quickly, efficiently, and safely.

k. **Finding 19:**

   (1) *Finding*: All inspected units had adequate transportation assets to evacuate and/or transfer detainees from points of capture to collecting points, and eventually to internment/resettlement facilities.

   (2) *Standard*: See Appendix E.

   (3) *Inspection Results*: The DAIG team determined that inspected units had adequate transportation assets to evacuate, transfer, or repatriate detainees. Only a few units experienced minor difficulties arranging transportation, usually during surge periods. These transportation shortages were usually temporary problems that were resolved through coordination with supporting units.

Leaders and soldiers stated that supporting units, such as forward support and main support battalions, were able to assist in providing transportation assets if capturing units were hampered due to other ongoing missions when required.

Capturing units typically transported detainees to the battalion or division forward collecting points in the back of High Mobility MultiWheeled Vehicles or Bradley Fighting Vehicles. Guard ratios and the numbers of accompanying security vehicles were generally well planned out. Most units took advantage of resupply assets to move detainees across the battlefield.

   (4) *Root Cause*: Units were planning for and using transportation assets efficiently to move detainees across the battlefield and through the system.

   (5) *Recommendation*: Commanders continue to stress the importance of planning and providing for adequate transportation assets to support continuing detainee operations.

l. **Finding 20:**

   (1) *Finding*: Common leader training in professional military schools contains only one detainee operations task.

   (2) *Standard*: See Appendix E.

   (3) *Inspection Results*: The DAIG team found that leaders and soldiers from 87% (53 of 61) of the units that commented on Professional Military Education (PME) indicated that their PME common core does not train them to conduct detainee operations. The only PME courses that cover detainee operations training in their common core are during pre-commissioning, Warrant Officer Candidate School and the Primary Leadership Development Course. The Non-commissioned officers (NCOs) interviewed and sensed said they received little detainee operations training in their PME courses. These same NCOs talked more specifically about the Situational Training Exercises (STX) that are conducted at the end of each level of NCOES through the Advanced Non-commissioned Officer Course (ANCOC). Their STX training was force-on-force play using MultiIntegrated Laser Engagement System (MILES), and detainee operations training ceased after the point of capture.

The NCOs experienced difficulty in filling out and completing the required detainee apprehension forms correctly, which included witness statements. They also experienced difficulty in creating a detailed list and accounting for captured detainee property and evidence. The NCOs agreed that there is a training shortfall dealing with detainee classification, and status and treatment afforded to each classification under the provisions of the Geneva Convention. STXs did not cover the classifying of detainees or the paperwork involved in field processing detainees. Their PME training for detainee operations only covered the processing of enemy prisoners of war (EPW). Leaders and soldiers interviewed and sensed indicated a need to incorporate detainee operations tasks into their PME common core programs of instruction (POI). The current operating environment has evolved and soldiers at all levels must have a clear understanding of and how to execute detainee operations in a non-linear battlespace. The PME must apply lessons learned quickly to adjust their training to what is occurring in the current operating environment. Interviewed leaders and soldiers all said that PME is a very important training base, but that it must keep up with current operational lessons-learned and evolving tactics, techniques and procedures.

Interviewed and sensed leaders and soldiers stated that the Law or War training they received prior to deployment did not differentiate between the different classifications of detainees causing confusion concerning the levels of treatment. Even though this confusion existed, most leaders and soldiers treated detainees humanely.

Currently, TRADOC has integrated one detainee operations task into the PME common core: Process Captives, (191-000-0001). The pre-commissioning course, Warrant Officers Candidate School and NCOs at the Primary Leadership Development Course are only courses receiving training on this task.

The U.S. Army Military Police School (USAMPS) has several ongoing initiatives that began in December 2003. USAMPS is currently in the process of creating and revising their detainee operations programs of instruction and training support packages using lessons learned from **OPERATION ENDURING FREEDOM** (OEF) and **OPERATION IRAQI FREEDOM** (OIF). Military Police (MP) NCOs attending the MP NCO Academy receive training on the following new and revised detainee operations tasks:

- Introduction to Detainee operations
- Communication with detainees
- Use of Force and Detainees
- Detainee Frisk, Undress, Cell and area search operations
- Restraint procedures and Detainees
- The Geneva Conventions and detainee operations

USAMPS has currently revised the tasks to provide updated programs of instruction and training support packages to support detainee operations training at all PME schools and colleges.

(4) *Root Cause*: There are currently not enough programs of instruction and training support packages available to the Professional Military Education schools and colleges that support detainee operations training.

(5) *Recommendation*: TRADOC integrate standardized detainee operations training into all Army proponent school common core programs of instruction and training support packages.

m. **Finding 21:**

    (1) *Finding*: Leaders and soldiers assigned to 69% (46 of 67) of inspected units stated they desired additional home station training; and pre- and post mobilization training to assist them in performing detainee operations.

    (2) *Standard*: See Appendix E.

    (3) *Inspection Results*: The DAIG team found that leaders and soldiers assigned to 27 of 39 (69%) of inspected Active Component (AC) units indicated their home station training did not prepare their units to perform detainee operations. Individual and collective training at home station was concentrated on fighting an enemy on a linear battlefield, according to interviewed and sensed leaders and soldiers. Their units did little in the way of training on detainee operations. All inspected units did execute the Common Military Training (CMT) as outlined in Army Regulation 350-1, *Army Training and Education*, 9 April 2003. However, the CMT classes on the Law of War, the Geneva Conventions, and Code of Conduct were generic and did not address the specific application of detainee operations in the current operating environment. These same leaders and soldiers said their detainee operations training only covered field processing of enemy prisoners of war (EPWs) and not other classifications of detainees. The training these units received on field processing of detainees was comprehensive when dealing with EPWs only.

Once deployed in support of **OPERATION ENDURING FREEDOM** (OEF) and **OPERATION IRAQI FREEDOM** (OIF), leaders and soldiers identified a training shortfall dealing with the handling of the different classifications of detainees and their special handling procedures. Units did not have established tactics, techniques, and procedures (TTPs) or standing operating procedures (SOPs) to cover the handling and processing of different classifications of detainees. This lack of training by point of capture units placed a burden on their resources (manpower, logistics and medical). To compound the problem, a number of leaders and soldiers were unaware of the specific Army regulation or field manuals that govern detainee operations.

Soldiers assigned to division MP units told the DAIG team that they did not train at home station on the five MP functional areas that were assigned to the units in theater. One example concerned a division MP platoon conducting maneuver and mobility support training at home station and then being assigned the internment/resettlement (I/R) function after deployment. These soldiers said that their training at home station should include all five of the MP battlefield functions. This agrees with the Taguba Investigation finding that states, "Those military units conducting I/R operations must know of, train on, and constantly reference the applicable Army Doctrine and CJTF command policies."

Reserve Component (RC) leaders and soldiers assigned to 64% (14 of 22) of inspected RC units stated the training they received at their mobilization sites did not prepare them to conduct detainee operations. OEF and OIF experienced RC career course captains, interviewed at the U.S. Army Military Police School (USAMPS), also said their units did not receive adequate training at their mobilization sites to prepare them to conduct detainee operations. Training at some mobilization sites concentrated on improving combat soldiering skills and to pass the Common Task Test (CTT).

Leaders and soldiers were not required to attend deployment briefings at these mobilization sites, also these units maintained no tracking systems to ensure that every
soldier received mandatory training.

Interviewed and sensed leaders and soldiers said they were not given enough time
at the mobilization sites to conduct collective unit level training. Some units had just
enough time to complete their central issue facility (CIF) draw, and complete the soldier readiness checks (SRC) before deploying overseas. Training was considered and
treated like a "revolving door" at some mobilization sites. Interviewed leaders and
soldiers assigned to 64% (14 of 22) of inspected RC stated they were not given a clear
mission statement prior to mobilization and were not notified of their MP mission until after deploying. The units received their MP mission upon their arrival in theater.
Interviewed soldiers gave examples of being placed in stressful situations in intern-
ment/resettlement (I/R) facility with thousands of non-compliant detainees and not
being trained to handle them. The lack of a mission statement limited units in support
of OEF 4 and OIF 1 from training on mission essential tasks at their mobilization site.
This is also supported by the findings in the Taguba Investigation.

Once deployed, these MP units had no means to gain access to the necessary tactics,
techniques, and procedures (TTPs) to train their soldiers on the MP essential tasks
based on their new missions. Regulations and field manuals were digitized, but unit
leaders and soldiers had no access to computers or the Internet. It was very difficult
to train soldiers on MP missions early in their deployment. Interviewed leaders and
soldiers assigned to 64% (14 of 22) of inspected RC units stated they were assigned
battlefield missions that they had never received training on at their home station
or at their mobilization site. Soldiers provided examples of unit training primarily
as an escort or guard MP company, but once deployed the unit was assigned I/R or
law and order missions. A consensus among leaders and soldiers was that their units
should have concentrated their training on all five of the MP functional areas. They
also agreed that all MP units should be resourced to conduct all five MP functional
areas.

Interviewed leaders and soldiers assigned to five of the six inspected in lieu of
(ILO) Military Police (MP) units did not receive detainee operations training at their
mobilization site. These ILO units deployed into theater with little post-mobilization
training on detainee operations and were assigned the ILO MP Security missions. Soldiers assigned to these units had little knowledge on what to do, but just trusted in their
leaders to provide them good guidance. The ILO MP units inspected that deployed in
support of OIF 1 were not given a clear mission statement prior to mobilization and
were not notified of their ILO MP mission until after deploying. The units received
their ILO MP mission upon their arrival in theater and were given just a few days to
conduct a battle-handover with the outgoing units.

Once deployed, the ILO MP units had difficulty in gaining access to the necessary tactics, techniques, and procedures (TTPs) to train their soldiers on the MP
essential tasks based on their new missions. Army regulations and field manuals
were digitized and unit leaders and soldiers had no access to computers or the internet. It was very difficult to train soldiers on MP missions early in their deployment.
During OIF 1 there were no training programs in theater to train units designated
ILO MP before they assumed their ILO MP Security missions. Leaders and soldiers

interviewed and assigned to these ILO MP units were assigned battlefield missions that they had never received training on at their home station or at their mobilization site.

Interviewed and sensed leaders and soldiers stated that the Law or War training they received prior to deployment did not differentiate between the different classifications of detainees, causing confusion concerning the levels of treatment. Even though this confusion existed, most leaders and soldiers treated detainees humanely. Interviewed and sensed leaders and soldiers said the Army has the necessary training tools in place, but doctrine and/or policy needs to address and apply lessons learned more quickly to incorporate changes coming from OEF and OIF. The Common Task Test (CTT) was identified by these leaders and soldiers as an excellent training tool, but the tasks require updating to comply with changes evolving from the current operating environments in OEF and OIF. CTT would be an excellent tool to integrate detainee operations into the force by using a multiechelon training approach. The CMT tasks outlined in AR 350-1 should be updated to address the different classifications of detainees and how to apply the Geneva Conventions and the Law of War to each type of detainee. Interviewed soldiers complained about the lack of detainee operations training their units received during their respective rotations at the National Training Center (NTC) or the Joint Readiness Training Center (JRTC). Soldiers said detainee operations during their rotation at NTC or JRTC was not evaluated beyond the point of capture and lacked realism.

Post-mobilization training for units that deployed in support of OEF 5 and OIF 2 consisted of a comprehensive training program ending in a Mission Rehearsal Exercise (MRX) to assess units' ability to execute wartime missions. Leaders and soldiers interviewed said that all soldiers were required to sign-in for all mandatory training received at the mobilization site. Soldiers deploying in support of OEF 5 and OIF 2 were required to sign a statement acknowledging the training they received at their mobilization site. These soldiers were being tracked by name and by unit. This process ensured that all mobilized leaders and soldiers were accounted for and trained. Mobilization site training was broken down into seven Modules culminating in a Simulation Exercise (SIMEX):

Module 1: Soldier Readiness Packet, Central Issue Facility, Theater Specific Individual Readiness Training briefings

Module 2: NBC survival tasks, Land Navigation, Communications

Module 3: Crew and Individual Basic and Advanced Weapons Qualification Skills, Leader Training & New Equipment Training

Module 4: Specialty Training

Module 5: Squad and Platoon Training

Module 6: Platoon Training

Module 6.1: Combat Support/Combat Service Support training

Module 7: MultiEchelon Training / Support and Stability Operations Training (CAPSTONE)

Brigade SIMEX that covers Battalion and Brigade level collective tasks.

Modules 1 and 2 are augmented with a series of leader and soldier concurrent training on Common Task Test supporting tasks. Leaders and soldiers, deployed in support of OIF 2 and OEF 5, were very complimentary of the training they received at their respective mobilization sites. These training modules provided unit commanders the ability to execute detainee operations training during Modules 4, 5, 6, and 7. Interviewed leaders and soldiers that deployed in support of OIF 2 said that post-mobilization training helped them once they deployed into theater. Forces Command (FORSCOM) issued specific guidance on the collective and individual tasks units must train on prior to deploying in support of OEF and OIF. These tasks did not prepare units to conduct detainee operation in the current operating environment.

The Combat Training Centers (CTC) are using an internal After Action Review (AAR) process in order to continue making improvements to their detainee operations scenario and to include the synchronization and integration of detainee operations into every unit's rotation. NTC's current focus is on conducting detainee operations to the doctrinal standard and by incorporating approved procedures used in OIF. Both JRTC and NTC have incorporated detainee operations into their Mission Rehearsal Exercises (MRXs) and Contemporary Operational Environment High Intensity (COE HI) rotations.

In the future, the Combat Training Centers' (CTCs) detainee operations training during MRX scenarios will be based upon reports and lessons learned from OIF and/or OEF, to include 1st Armored Division SOPs/TTPs, and doctrinal guidelines. All rotating units will be required to establish and operate a collecting point of some kind as part of their rotations. The CTCs are striving to replicate the best scenarios for the current operating environment. The G3, in coordination with TRADOC, the Office of the Provost Marshal General, and the Office of The Judge Advocate General (OTJAG) has initiated a training integration assessment for improving detainee handling from point of capture to repatriation, to include a review of CTT and specialized MP training across the Army during Combat Training Center (CTCs) rotations, MRXs and TRADOC institutional training. This assessment began in December 2003 and is currently ongoing with no projected completion date.

The G3, in coordination with the U.S. Army Training and Doctrine Command (TRADOC), the Office of the Provost Marshal General, and the Office of The Judge Advocate General (OTJAG), has initiated a training integration assessment for improving detainee handling from point of capture to repatriation, to include a review of CTT and specialized MP training across the Army during CTCs rotations, MRXs and TRADOC institutional training. This assessment began in December 2003 and is currently ongoing with no projected completion date.

TRADOC's institutional training assessment is focusing on the Law of War and the 5Ss and T (Search, Silence, Segregate, Safeguard, Speed, and Tag) regarding EPWs throughout the proponent schools. USAMPS has formed an MP subject matter expert team to develop a process to analyze, identify, evaluate, and integrate lessons learned from all CONUS/OCONUS MP operations. TRADOC, in coordination with OTJAG, is currently determining the feasibility of expanding or adjusting Law of War training in the proponent schools to include procedures for handling of detainees.

In January 2004, the U.S. Army Military Police School (USAMPS) sent a Mobile Training Team (MTT) to JRTC to conduct "train-the-trainer" education for their observer controllers (O/Cs) on detainee operations. The MTT training covered detainee operations, personal safety, forced cell movements, restraint procedures, communication with detainees, and case studies. USAMPS is also coordinating with the NTC for a MTT to conduct the same training.

Currently, the USAMPS MTT mission is to train identified CONUS/OCONUS units performing detainee operations or I/R missions in support of OIF 2 on select and approved tasks to enhance their capabilities of mission accomplishment. The 31E detainee operations support and MTT comprises a total of 29 (31E) soldiers. The MTT has trained leaders and soldiers from the following units: 160th MP Battalion (BN), 107th FA Battery, 172nd FA Battery, 391st MP BN, 152nd FA Battery, K 3/24 INF-USMC, 439th CLD, MEK: 336th MP BN, 579th FA Battery, and the 1/124th AR SQ. A total of 565 leaders and Soldiers have been trained as of 7 May 2004. The following units are scheduled: 1st INF DIV (9 May–11 June), 1st CAV DIV (24 May–12 June), 1st MEF (6–30 June), and MNB-N (TF-Olympia) (14–30 June).

(4) *Root Cause*: There is no prescribed detainee operations training program for units to train at home station. A majority of Reserve Component MP Units who deployed in support of OIF 1 were not told of their missions until they arrived into theater and their area of responsibility.

(5) *Recommendation*: The G3 integrate a prescribed detainee operations training program into unit training.

Recommendation: CFLCC and Force Providers coordinate to ensure, where possible, units are aware of their assigned mission upon mobilization so they can train for their specific mission.

Recommendation: FORSCOM integrate a standardized detainee operations training package as part of pre- and post-mobilization training.

Recommendation: CFLCC ensure that ILO MP units are trained before they assume their ILO MP missions.

n. **Finding 22:**
(1) *Finding*: To offset the shortage of interrogators, contractors were employed, however, 35% (11 of 31) of contract interrogators lacked formal training in military interrogation policies and techniques.

(2) *Standard*: See Appendix E.

(3) *Inspection Results*: 35% (11 of 31) Of the contract interrogators in **OPERATION IRAQI FREEDOM** (OIF), 35% (11 of 31) had not received formal training in military interrogation techniques, policy, and doctrine. These personnel conducted interrogations using skill sets obtained in previous occupational specialties such as civilian police interrogator or Military Intelligence (MI) officer. The lack of specific training in military policies and techniques has the potential of placing these interrogators at a higher risk of violating Army policies and doctrine, and decreasing intelligence yield. 65% (20 of 31) of contract interrogators in OIF had previous experience as Army or Marine interrogators (Army 97E military occupational specialty or Marine Corps 0211) where they received formal school training in military interrogation techniques and procedures. These individuals had received formal military interrogation training

an average of 9.5 years prior to employment as interrogators in OIF. The range of time from having completed basic military interrogation training was one to 25 years. Field Manual (FM) 34–52, *Intelligence Interrogation*, 28 September 1992, is the base document for Army interrogation doctrine. Persons trained in interrogation techniques prior to publication of the current version of the FM would have been trained on some doctrinal techniques that are no longer valid.

Contract interrogators were a force multiplier in OIF, supplementing a shortage of military interrogators. Contract interrogators were used to perform screenings and interrogations at collecting points (CPs) and in internment/resettlement (I/R) facilities to free military interrogators and counter intelligence agents to perform tactical missions at points of capture and CPs.

CACI International, Inc. is the civilian company contracted through the Department of the Interior to provide civilian interrogators for OIF. CACI has provided a total of 31 contract interrogators since the blanket purchase agreement (contract) was issued on 14 August 2003. As of 17 May 2004, 19 contract interrogators were deployed in support of OIF, and 12 contract interrogators have returned to the United States citing personal or family reasons.

The CJTF-7 Statement of Work (SOW) required contract interrogators to be the civilian equivalent of military occupational specialty 97E (Human Intelligence Collector) or 351E (Human Intelligence Collection Technician), strategic debriefer (completed the DoD Strategic Debriefing Course), or an individual with a similar skill set. Contract interrogators that only meet the requirements of "strategic debriefer" or "similar skill sets" may not have training in military-specific interrogation techniques and procedures as taught in the 97E and 351E qualification courses. This training is specific to human intelligence exploitation and includes collection priority, battlefield screening, planning and preparation, authorized approaches, methods of questioning, and termination of interrogations. It also includes 192 hours of direct and indirect training on the laws of land warfare, emphasizing compliance of all military interrogation techniques with the Geneva Conventions and Army policy.

The DAIG team inspected the resumes of all 31 individuals hired as contract interrogators by CACI. 65% (20 of 31) were prior service military interrogators who had been awarded the Army 97E MOS or Marine Corps 0211 MOS. These individuals had received formal military interrogation training an average of 9.5 years prior to employment by CACI (range: 1–25 years). Of the contractors without prior military service, 35% (11 of 31) had "similar skill sets" acquired in related military or civilian experience (e.g., military intelligence/counterintelligence agent, police interrogator, intelligence analyst, and police officer).

Prior to May 2004, there was no CACI or CJTF-7 requirement for all contract interrogators to receive formal, comprehensive, military-specific interrogator training prior to performing interrogations in OIF. While in Iraq the DAIG team did not find evidence of a formal training program for contract interrogators. The DAIG team requested from the J2, CJTF-7, both in Iraq and upon return to the United States, a training plan or program of instruction (POI) outlining a formal training program.

On 19 May 2004, the Chief, CJ2X, CJTF-7 provided an email message to the DAIG team stating that prior to February 2004, new contract interrogators working at the Joint Interrogation and Debriefing Center (JIDC) received familiarization training, consisting of briefings on the approved interrogation approach techniques and the Geneva Conventions, "left seat-right seat ride" training, and evaluation by experienced interrogators prior to conducting interrogations. On 21 May 2004, the Chief, CJ2X, CJTF-7 provided an email message stating that in February 2004, the JIDC began a two-part newcomer's training/orientation for all contract interrogators deployed to OIF. This training consisted of an organizational overview, interrogation policy briefing, tour of the facilities, and "left seat-right seat ride" training on interrogation duties and responsibilities. The message stated that documentation of this training began in May 2004.

In interviews conducted during the inspection, when four contract interrogators were asked about in-theater training, there were three different responses. One stated he received no in-theater training of any kind. Two stated training was provided on the Geneva Conventions and the interrogation approach techniques, with some additional time spent observing experienced interrogators. One stated he received two weeks of "right seat" training at Abu Ghraib, followed by one week performing supervised interrogations. Two military interrogators interviewed stated, "While some contract interrogators were fine, some lacked understanding of proper interrogation policies and procedures." In contrast, the DAIG team interviewed five leaders and soldiers who found contract interrogators to be adequate to very good.

Two specific incidents were described to the DAIG team where Army personnel stated they saw contract interrogators using techniques and procedures inconsistent with Army policy and doctrine (e.g., pouring water over detainees' heads while in stress positions); the chain of command was already aware of this incident. In one of these incidents military interrogators at that location were reportedly using the same techniques. The DAIG team did not observe any improper interrogation techniques during the inspection. A DAIG team member observed two contract interrogators performing interrogations; both interrogations were conducted using tactics, techniques, and procedures in accordance with Army policy and doctrine.

The Taguba Investigation cited a contract interrogator who gave an MP non-doctrinal guidance that violated Army policy in order to facilitate conditions for interrogation. The contract interrogator has since requested to return to the United States. A lawyer representing CACI International stated that the Army has not requested, and no contract interrogators in OIF have received, administrative or disciplinary action as a result of improper performance of duties.

At the time of the inspection there were no contract interrogators employed in **OPERATION ENDURING FREEDOM (OEF)**. In March 2004, CJTF-180 contracted with SYTEX, Inc. for four contract interrogators, all of which were assigned to the I/R facility at Bagram, Afghanistan. Two of the four contract interrogators have military interrogation training, and the other two are former police officers. The senior Army interrogator assigned to CJTF-180 stated that upon arrival at Bagram the contract interrogators were provided training on interrogation planning and preparation, interrogation approaches, Geneva Conventions, questioning methods, report writing, and the CJTF-180 interrogation approach techniques. They also underwent left/right seat interrogation training. CJTF-180 provided the DAIG team with a training plan that outlines the above.

In summary, contract interrogators in OIF met the requirements of the CJTF-7 C2 Interrogation Cell SOW. The SOW did not mandate military interrogation training as a prerequisite for employment. While some training may have occurred at Abu Ghraib, there is no evidence of a formalized POI for contract interrogators. All contract interrogators should receive training on specific theater and Army techniques, policies, and doctrine for conducting military interrogations. This requirement should be reflected in the CJTF-7 C2 Interrogation Cell SOW.

>   (4) *Root Cause*: The CJTF-7 C2 Interrogation Cell SOW did not require contract
>   interrogators to be trained in military interrogation procedures, policy, and
>   doctrine. Predeployment and in-theater training for contract interrogators on
>   military interrogation techniques, policy, and doctrine did not occur or was
>   inconsistent.
>   (5) *Recommendation*: The CFLCC contracting officer representative modify the
>   CJTF-7 C2 Interrogation Cell Statement of Work to require civilian interroga-
>   tors to be former military interrogators trained in current interrogation policy
>   and doctrine or receive formal training in current military interrogation policy
>   and doctrine.

o. **Finding 23:**
>   (1) *Finding*: Interviewed leaders and soldiers indicated their Law of War refresher
>   training was not detailed enough to sustain their knowledge obtained during
>   initial and advanced training.
>   (2) *Standard*: See Appendix E.
>   (3) *Inspection Results*: Leaders and soldiers from inspected units who commented
>   on Law of War training stated they did receive some Law of War training prior
>   to deploying, but 57% (272 of 474) of leaders and soldiers indicated that the
>   training was generic and did not prepare them for the current operating envi-
>   ronment. The Level B Law of War training was normally given by the brigade
>   legal advisor. Law of War training is required for leaders and soldiers through-
>   out their military careers commensurate with their duties and responsibilities.
>   There are currently three levels of training for the Law of War. Level A training
>   is conducted during Initial entry training (IET) for all enlisted personnel and
>   during basic courses of instruction for all warrant officers and officers. Level B
>   training is conducted in units for officers, warrant officers noncommissioned
>   officers (NCOs) and enlisted personnel and incorporates the missions of the
>   unit. Level C training is conducted in Professional Military Education (PME).

Currently in IET, Level A Law of Land warfare training is designed to advise the soldier on his rights, duties, and obligations under the Hague Convention of 1907, the Geneva Conventions of 1949, and the customary Law of War. The program of instruction used for this training is dated 1 October 1998, and is scheduled for one hour, which includes 36 minutes of classroom instruction on the principles, spirit, and intent of the Hague and Geneva Conventions; the laws of war prohibiting unnec-essary destruction; and the laws of war requiring humane treatment of prisoners of war (PWs), other captured and detained persons, and civilians. In this portion of the training, soldiers become familiar with their obligations not to commit war crimes and to report all violations of the laws of war, and the significant provisions of the Geneva Convention relative to the treatment of prisoners of war (EPWs). The other 24 minutes consists of a television tape covering the Law of Land Warfare, and emphasizes "honor" and the Army's Values. The tape stresses that each soldier has a personal stake in knowing about these conventions and in understanding how they work. Soldiers are taught to comply with these provisions and that failure may subject them to provisions under the Uniform Code of Military Justice (UCMJ). This program of instruction is given to all IET soldiers who enter the Army.

Level B Law of War training is designed to sustain the training received in IET and PME. Unit commanders are responsible for planning and executing Level B Law of War training. Level B training should reinforce the basic principles set forth in "The Soldiers' Rules." Level B training should be designed around current missions and contingency plans, including anticipated geographical areas of deployment or rules of engagement. Commanders ensure that Law of War training is integrated into unit training activities, field training exercises, and unit external evaluations. There are no Office of The Judge Advocate General (OTJAG) programs of instructions for Level B training. Level B training is designed to be refresher training, used to reinforce previous training and/or to sustain/regain previously acquired skills, knowledge, and experiences. Commanders determine the need for refresher training based on assessment of individual and unit proficiency. Leaders and soldiers complained about the content and quality of their unit level B Law of War training during interviews and sensing sessions. All agreed that their Level B Law of War training needed more structure as part of Common Military Training (CMT) to help them to better function in the current operating environment.

Level C Law of War training is conducted in The Army School System (TASS); TASS is a composite school system consisting of Army National Guard (ARNG), U.S. Army Reserve (USAR), and Active Army institutional training systems. TASS conducts IET; functional training (Military Occupational Specialty (MOS), Area of Concentration (AOC), Additional Skill Identifier (ASI), and Language Identification Code (LIC)); reclassification; and officer, warrant officer, NCO, and DA civilian professional development training and education through both standard resident and distance learning courses. Level C Law of War training emphasizes officer, warrant officer, and NCO responsibilities for their performance of duties in accordance with the Law of War obligations of the United States; Law of War issues in command planning and execution of combat operations; and measures for the reporting of suspected or alleged war crimes committed by or against U.S. or allied personnel. There are currently two PME common core Law of War tasks:

1. Conduct small unit combat operations according to the law of war (Task #181-431-1001) – taught at the Pre-commissioning Course (PRE), the Officer Basic Course (OBC), the Warrant Officer Candidate School (WOCS), the Basic Non-commissioned Officer Course (BNCOC), and the Primary Leadership Development Course (PLDC). This task helps leaders identify key provisions of the Hague and Geneva Conventions and those acts that constitute violations and war crimes against non-combatants,

property, POWs, and medical transports/facilities, and prevent the engagement of unlawful targets and the excessive use of force. This task is designed to be programmed training, with specific learning objectives and an evaluation for proficiency. The task is trained by an instructor/trainer in a structured manner and serves as the foundation for other training. Normally the task is a qualification requirement and is presented and evaluated using the prescribed training conditions and performance standards. This task takes 100 minutes to train.

2. Conduct company level combat operations consistent with the laws of war and laws affecting peacekeeping and peacekeeping operations, rules of engagement, and other legal constraints (Task # 181-433-1001) – taught at the Captain's Career Course (CCC) and the Warrant Officer Advanced Course (WOAC). This task helps leaders prevent law of war violations and war crimes against protected noncombatants, property, POWs, and medical transports/facilities, and prevent engagement of unlawful targets and excessive use of force. This task is designed to be programmed training. This task has specific learning objectives and an evaluation for proficiency; is conducted by an instructor trainer in a structured manner; serves as the foundation for other training; normally is a qualification requirement; and is presented and evaluated using the prescribed training conditions and performance standards. This task also takes 100 minutes to train.

Interviewed and sensed leaders and soldiers stated that the Law or War training they received prior to deployment did not differentiate between the different classifications of detainees, causing confusion concerning the levels of treatment. Even though this confusion existed, most leaders and soldiers treated detainees humanely.

TRADOC, in coordination with the Office of The Judge Advocate General, is currently determining the feasibility of increasing or adjusting Law of War training in the proponent schools to include procedures for handling civilian internees and other non-uniformed personnel on the battlefield.

(4) *Root Cause*: Level B Law of War training is a CMT task, coded "R" (Refresher), that does not require the training to have specific learning objectives and taught by an instructor/trainer in a structured manner.

(5) *Recommendation*: The G3, in coordination with the Office of The Judge Advocate General, mandate that Level B Law of War training have specific learning objectives, be conducted by an instructor/evaluator in a structured manner, and be presented and evaluated annually using the established training conditions and performance standards.

Chapter 6 Summary of Recommendations

1. **Purpose:** The purpose of this chapter is to list all of the recommendations proffered in the report. Some recommendations may be similar to others; however, *all* recommendations are included here.

2. **Recommendation for Implementation:** Director, Army Staff task out appropriate recommendations and track compliance to Department of the Army Staff and

Major Commands. The Acting Secretary of the Army submit appropriate recommendations to the Joint Staff for consideration and implementation as appropriate by units deployed in OPERATION ENDURING FREEDOM and OPERATION IRAQI FREEDOM.

3. **Chapter 3, Capture, Care, and Control of Detainees:**

a. *Recommendation*: CJTF-7 and CJTF-180 continue to emphasize compliance with the requirements regarding the humane treatment of detainees.

b. *Recommendation*: Commanders continue to stress the importance of humane treatment of detainees and continue to supervise and train soldiers on their responsibility to treat detainees humanely and their responsibility to report abuse.

c. *Recommendation*: Commanders enforce the basic fundamental discipline standards of soldiers, provide training, and immediately correct inappropriate behavior of soldiers towards detainees to ensure the proper treatment of detainees.

d. *Recommendation*: Commanders assess the quality of leadership in units and replace those leaders who do not enforce discipline and hold soldiers accountable.

e. *Recommendation*: TRADOC develop and implement a train-the-trainer package that strongly emphasizes leaders' responsibilities to have adequate supervision and control processes in place to ensure the proper treatment of detainees.

f. *Recommendation*: TRADOC integrate training into all Professional Military Education that strongly emphasizes leaders' responsibilities to have adequate supervision and control processes in place to ensure the proper treatment of detainees.

g. *Recommendation*: The G3 require pre-deployment training include a strong emphasis on leaders' responsibilities to have adequate supervision and control processes in place to ensure proper treatment of, and prevent abuse of, detainees.

h. *Recommendation*: CJTF-7 expand Camp Bucca as an internment/resettlement facility in order to transfer detainees from Camps Ganci and Vigilant, and phase out U.S. Armed Forces detainee operations at Abu Ghraib completely.

4. **Chapter 4, Interrogation Operations:**

a. *Recommendation*: TRADOC revise doctrine to address the criteria for establishing and operating collecting points to enable commanders to more effectively conduct intelligence exploitation in a non-linear battlespace.

b. *Recommendation*: TRADOC develop a single document for detainee operations that identifies the interdependent and independent roles of the Military Police custody mission and the Military Intelligence interrogation mission.

c. *Recommendation*: TRADOC establish doctrine to clearly define the organizational structures, command relationships, and roles and responsibilities of personnel operating interrogation facilities.

d. *Recommendation*: The Provost Marshal General revise, and the G2 establish, policy to clearly define the organizational structures, command relationships, and roles and responsibilities of personnel operating interrogation facilities.

e. *Recommendation*: The G3 direct the incorporation of integrated Military Police and Military Intelligence detainee operations into field training exercises, home station and mobilization site training, and combat training center rotations.

f. *Recommendation*: TRADOC and G2 ensure documentation of unit organizations meet interrogator personnel manning requirements, authorizations, and capabilities in order to provide commanders with timely intelligence.

g. *Recommendation*: The CFLCC contracting officer representative ensure enough Category II interpreters are hired to support timely intelligence exploitation of detainees.

h. *Recommendation*: TRADOC continue the integration of the G2X/S2X Battle Staff Course for all Military Intelligence officers assigned to G2X/S2X positions.

i. *Recommendation*: TRADOC integrate additional training on the collection and analysis of HUMINT into the Military Intelligence Officer Basic Course program of instruction.

j. *Recommendation*: TRADOC, in coordination with G2 and TJAG, revise doctrine to identify interrogation approach techniques that are acceptable, effective and legal for non-compliant detainees.

k. *Recommendation*: CJTF-7 and CJTF-180 ensure that standardized policy on interrogation approach techniques are received, understood, trained and enforced by all units.

5. **Chapter 5, Other Observations:**

a. *Recommendation*: CFLCC, CJTF-7, and CJTF-180 continue to stress the importance of positive unit morale and command climate.

b. *Recommendation*: TRADOC revise doctrine for the administrative processing of detainees to improve accountability, movement, and disposition in a non-linear battlespace. And further examine processes for capturing and validating lessons learned in order to rapidly modify doctrine and incorporate into training application for soldiers and units.

c. *Recommendation*: The Provost Marshal General revise policy for the administrative processing of detainees to improve accountability, movement, and disposition in a non-linear battlespace.

d. *Recommendation*: The Provost Marshal General, in coordination with the G2, update detainee policy to specifically address the administration, internment/resettlement, and intelligence exploitation in a non-linear battlespace, enabling commanders to better manage resources, ensure safe and secure custodial environments, and improve intelligence gathering.

e. *Recommendation*: TRADOC and G3 update the Military Police force structure at the division level and below to support the simultaneous execution of detainee operations and other battlefield missions.

f. *Recommendation*: TRADOC and G3 update the Military Intelligence force structure at the division level and below to integrate the requirement for detainee operations that allows for timely intelligence exploitation.

g. *Recommendation*: TRADOC update doctrine to integrate tactical interrogation at battalion and company level to assist in the intelligence exploitation of detainees immediately upon capture.

h. *Recommendation*: CFLCC submit a Request for Forces for the Theater Detainee Reporting Branch Center (TDRC) to meet the requirements for reporting and accountability of detainees and their property.

i. *Recommendation*: The Provost Marshal General review the TDRC process, structure, and employment methods for maintaining information on detainees, their property, and other related requirements within an assigned theater of operations and consider the development of an information technology solution.

j. *Recommendation*: TRADOC and G3 continue to refine and implement the force structure changes in the Military Intelligence – Counterintelligence/Human Intelligence Force Design Update.

k. *Recommendation*: TRADOC integrate the Military Intelligence-Counter Intelligence/ Human Intelligence Force Design Updates into the development of Units of Action and Units of Employment.

l. *Recommendation*: TRADOC and G3 continue to refine and implement the force structure changes in the Military Police – Internment/Resettlement Battalion Force Design Update.

m. *Recommendation*: TRADOC integrate this Force Design Update into the development of Units of Action and Units of Employment.

n. *Recommendation*: CJTF-7 and CJTF-180 ensure all units meet the guidelines for minimum infrastructure standards supporting detainee operations to allow for adequate facilities to house detainees.

o. *Recommendation*: CJTF-7 and CJTF-180 implement a safety inspection program for all facilities that support detainee operations to identify and eliminate hazards to soldiers and detainees.

p. *Recommendation*: CJTF-7 and CJTF-180 evaluate current living and working conditions at all facilities housing detainees and take corrective actions to improve the current living and working environment.

q. *Recommendation*: CJTF-7 review the physical and operations security requirements and policy/doctrinal procedures to ensure units operating internment/resettlement facilities comply with all requirements.

r. *Recommendation*: Force Providers require commanders to have trained and equipped field sanitation teams prior to deployment, and deployed commanders ensure field sanitation teams comply with Army policy.

s. *Recommendation*: TRADOC review the preventive medicine detachment force structure to ensure support to all collecting points and internment/resettlement facilities in a non-linear battlespace.

t. *Recommendation*: MEDCOM train all medical personnel in the preventive medicine aspects of detainee operations to ensure compliance with policy and the laws of land warfare.

u. *Recommendation*: MEDCOM ensure all health care personnel are trained on the medical treatment requirements for detainees in accordance with Army Regulations and ensure that units have the required medical equipment and supplies for treating detainees.

v. *Recommendation*: CJTF-7 and CJTF-180 evaluate current detainee medical capabilities and requirements and take corrective action to ensure detainees receive the required medical screening and care.

w. *Recommendation*: CJTF-7 segregate enemy prisoners of war and civilian internees to ensure compliance with the Geneva Conventions and Army Regulations.

x. *Recommendation*: TRADOC identify minimum equipment requirements for detainee operations to ensure successful unit mission accomplishment.

y. *Recommendation*: TRADOC establish and identify resource requirements for a standardized "Detainee Field Processing Kit" that will enable capturing units to properly secure and process detainees quickly, efficiently, and safely.

z. *Recommendation*: Commanders continue to stress the importance of planning and providing for adequate transportation assets to support continuing detainee operations.

aa. *Recommendation*: TRADOC integrate standardized detainee operations training into all Army proponent school common core programs of instruction and training support packages.

bb. *Recommendation*: The G3 integrate a prescribed detainee operations training program into unit training.

cc. *Recommendation*: CFLCC and Force Providers coordinate to ensure, where possible, units are aware of their assigned mission upon mobilization so they can train for their specific mission.

dd. *Recommendation*: FORSCOM integrate a standardized detainee operations training package as part of pre- and post-mobilization training.

ee. *Recommendation*: CFLCC ensure that ILO MP units are trained before they assume their ILO MP missions.

ff. *Recommendation*: The CFLCC contracting officer representative modify the CJTF-7 C2 Interrogation Cell Statement of Work to require civilian interrogators to be former military interrogators trained in current interrogation policy and doctrine or receive formal training in current military interrogation policy and doctrine.

gg. *Recommendation*: The G3, in coordination with the Office of the Judge Advocate General, mandate that Level B Law of War training have specific learning objectives, be conducted by an instructor/evaluator in a structured manner, and be presented and evaluated annually using the established training conditions and performance standards.

Appendix A References

Reference	Date	Title
AR 1-201	12 January 2004	Army Inspection Policy
AR 25-30	16 March 2004	The Army Publishing Program
AR 27-10	6 September 2002	Military Justice
AR 40-5	15 October 1990	Preventive Medicine
AR 71-32	3 March 1997	Force Development and Documentation-Consolidated Policies
AR 190-5	28 August 1992	Evidence Procedures
AR 190-8	1 October 1997	Enemy Prisoners of War, Retained Personnel, Civilian Internees and Other Detainees
AR 190-11	12 February 1998	Physical Security of Arms, Ammunition and Explosives
AR 190-13	30 September 1993	The Army Physical Security Program
AR 190-14	12 March 1993	Carrying of Firearms and Use of Force for Law Enforcement and Security Duties
AR 190-22	1 February 1983	Searches, Seizures, and Disposition of Property
AR 190-40	30 November 1993	Serious Incident Report
AR 190-47	15 August 1996	The Army Corrections System
AR 350-1	9 April 2003	Army Training and Education
AR 381-20	15 November 1993	The Army Counterintelligence Program
AR 385-10	29 February 2000	The Army Safety Program
AR 420-70	10 October 1997	Buildings and Structures
AR 600-20	13 May 2002	Army Command Policy
AR 735-5	10 June 2002	Policies and Procedures for Property Accountability
ARTEP 19-472-MTP	2 March 2001	Mission Training Plan For The Military Police Combat Support And Internment And Resettlement Brigades And Criminal Investigation Division Groups
ARTEP 19-546-30 MTP	10 April 1999	MTP for HHC MP BN (IR)
ARTEP 19-647-30 MTP	10 April 1999	MTP for MP CO (Escort Guard)
ARTEP 19-667-30 MTP	10 April 1999	MTP for MP CO (Guard)

Reference	Date	Title
CENTCOM REG 27-13	7 February 1995	Captured Persons Determination of Eligibility For Enemy Prisoner of War Status
CFLCC	18 December 2001	OEF Detainee Handling Guidance
CFLCC FRAGO 254 to OPORD 03-032	111800Z April 2003	Subject is Classified Secret
CFLCC FRAGO 501 to OPORD 03-032	241500Z April 2003	Guidance for the Release and Repatriation of EPW.
CJCSI 3290.01A	15 October 2000	Program For Enemy Prisoners Of War, Retained Personnel, Civilian Internees, And Other Detained Personnel (EPW/Detainee Policy)
CJCSI 5810.01B	25 March 2002	Implementation Of The DoD Law Of War Program
CJCS Message	211933ZJan02	Subject is Classified Secret
CJTF-7 CG Memo	14 September 2003	Subject is Classified Secret
CJTF-7 CG Memo	12 October 2003	Subject is Classified Secret
CJTF-7 CG Memo	13 May 2004	Subject is Classified Secret
CJTF-7 FRAGO 209 to CJTF-7 OPORD 03-036	282021D June 2003	Subject is Classified Secret
CJTF-7 FRAGO 368to CJTF-7 OPORD 03-036	141028Z June 2003	Guidance for the Detention, Handling and Release of Individuals Who are Potentially Subject to Prosecution for War Crimes
CJTF-7 FRAGO 415 to CJTF-7 OPORD 03-036	151950D July 2003	Subject is Classified Secret
CJTF-7 FRAGO 455 to CJTF-7 OPORD 03-036	200415D July 2003	Classifying and Processing Enemy Prisoners of War/Detained Persons/Civilian Internees
CJTF-7 FRAGO 749 to CJTF-7 OPORD 03-036	242320D August 2003	Subject is Classified Secret
CJTF-180 SJA Memo	24 January 2004	CJTF180 Interrogation Techniques
CJTF-180 DCG Memo	16 March 2004	Subject is Classified Secret
CJTF-180 DCG Memo	28 March 2004	Consolidated Detainee Operations Standard Operating Procedures

Reference	Date	Title
DA Form 3881	November 1989	Rights Warning Procedure/Waiver Certificate
DA Form 4237-R	August 1985	Detainee Personnel Record
DoD Directive 1325.4	1 December 2003	Confinement of Military Prisoners and Administration of Military Correctional Programs and Facilities
DoD Directive 2310.1	18 August 1994	DoD Program for Enemy Prisoners of War (EPOW) and Other Detainees (Short Title: DoD Enemy POW Detainee Program)
DoD Directive 5100.69	27 December 1972	DoD Program for Prisoners of War and Other Detainees
DoD Directive 5100.77	9 December 1998	DoD Law of War Program
DoD Directive 5210.56	24 January 2002	Use of Deadly Force and the Carrying of Firearms by DoD Personnel Engaged in Law Enforcement and Security Duties
FM 3-0	14 June 2001	Operations
FM 3-31	13 December 2001	Joint Force Land Component Commander Handbook (JFLCC)
FM 3-19.1	31 January 2002	Operations
FM 3-19.4	4 March 2002	Leaders' Handbook
FM 3-19.30	8 January 2001	Physical Security
FM 3-19.40	1 August 2001	Internment/Resettlement Operations
FM 5-34, w/ C3	10 April 2003	Engineer Field Data
FM 6-0	11 August 2003	Mission Command: Command and Control of Army Forces
FM 6-22.5	23 JUNE 2000	Combat Stress
FM 7-0	22 October 2002	Training the Force
FM 22-51	29 September 1994	Leaders' Manual For Combat Stress Control
FM 27-10, w/ C1	15 July 1976	The Law of Land Warfare
FM 27-100	1 March 2000	Legal Support to Operations
FM 34-60	3 October 1995	Counterintelligence
FM 34-52	28 September 1992	Intelligence
FORSCOM Message	162313Z January 2003	Subject is Classified Secret
FORSCOM/ARNG/ USAR Reg 350-2	27 October 1999	Reserve Component Training

Reference	Date	Title
FORSCOM Reg 500-3-1	15 April 1998	FORMDEPS, Volume I, FORSCOM Mobilization Plan (FMP)
FORSCOM Reg 500-3-3	15 July 1999	FORMDEPS Volume III, Reserve Component Unit Commander's Handbook (RCUCH)
Geneva Convention	12 August 1949	Relative to the Treatment of POWs
Geneva Convention	12 August 1949	Amelioration of the Condition of the Wounded, Sick and Shipwrecked Members of Armed Forces at Sea
Geneva Convention	12 August 1949	Amelioration of the Condition of the Wounded and Sick in the Armed Forces in the Field
Geneva Convention	12 August 1949	Protection of War Victims
Geneva Convention	12 August 1949	Relative to the Protections of Civilian Persons in Time of War
Geneva Convention	1967	Relative to the Status of Refugees
Geneva Convention	1951	Relative to the Status of Refugees
Convention Against Torture	1984	Convention Against Torture and Other Cruel, Inhuman or Degrading Treatment or Punishment
Hague Convention No. IV	18 October 1907	Respecting the Laws and Customs of War on Land
JP 1-0	19 November 1998	Doctrine for Personnel Support to Joint Operations
JP 1-02	12 April 2001 (amended through 23 March 04)	Department of Defense Dictionary of Military and Associated Terms
JP 2-01	20 November 1996	Joint Intelligence Support to Military Operations
THIS LINE	INTENTIONALLY	LEFT BLANK
Joint Operations Concepts	November 2003	Joint Operations Concepts
MG Antonio Taguba, AR 15-6 Investigation	14 March 2004	AR 15-6, Investigation of the 800th MP BDE
MG Donald J. Ryder, Provost Marshal Report	6 November 2003	Assessment of Detention and Corrections Operations in Iraq
MG Geoffrey D. Miller, CDR JTF-GTMO, Guantanamo Bay, Cuba Report	9 September 2003	Assessment of DoD Counter Terrorism Interrogation and Detention Operations in Iraq

Reference	Date	Title
ST 2-22.7	11 April 2002	Tactical Human Intelligence and Counter-intelligence Operations
STP 19-95B1-SM	6 August 2002	MOS 95B, Skill Level 1
STP 19-95C14-SM-TG	26 March 1999	MOS 95C, Skill Levels 1/2/3/4
STP 19-95C1-SM	30 September 2003	MOS 95C, Skill Level 1
STP 19-95C24-SM-TG	30 September 2003	MOS 95C, Skill Level 2/3/4
V CORPS FRAGO 006M to V CORPS OPORD 0303-343	190200Z March 2003	Procedures for Handling the Detention of Iraqis in Internment Facilities and Detention Centers
V CORPS FRAGO 312M to V CORPS OPORD FINAL VICTORY	252146D May 2003	Guidance on Tactics, Techniques, and Procedures Designed to Improve the Preservation of Evidence of Crimes Committed by Civilians Detained and Transported to Detention Facilities

Appendix B Acting Secretary of the Army

DIRECTIVE FOR ASSESSMENT OF DETAINEE OPERATIONS

10 February 2004

DEPARTMENT OF THE ARMY

WASHINGTON DC 20310-0200

February 10, 2004

MEMORANDUM FOR THE INSPECTOR GENERAL

SUBJECT: Directive for Assessment of Detainee Operations

You are hereby directed to establish an Assessment Team to complete a Functional Analysis of the Department's internment, enemy prisoner of war, and detention policies, practices, and procedures as the Army executes its role as DOD Executive Agent for Enemy Prisoners of War and Detention Program.

When conducting this assessment, the following terms of reference apply. Use all potential Doctrine, Operations, Training, Materiel, Leadership, Personnel, and Facilities (DOTMLPF) approaches to identify any capability shortfalls with respect to internment, enemy prisoner of war, detention operations, and interrogation procedures and recommend appropriate resolutions or changes if required.

The assessment will focus on the following objectives:

a. Assess the adequacy of DOTMLPF of Army Forces for internment, enemy prisoner of war, detention operations, and interrogation procedures.

b. Determine the standards for Army Forces charged with internment, enemy prisoner of war, detention operations and interrogation procedures (e.g., size, equipment, standardization, and training).

c. Assess current and future organizations and structures for Army Forces responsible for internment, enemy prisoner of war, detention operations and interrogation procedures.

d. Identify and recommend any changes in policy related to internment, enemy prisoner of war, detention operations and interrogation procedures.

You are authorized to task the Army Staff and subordinate headquarters for those resources needed to ensure accomplishment of the detainee operations assessment. You are further authorized access to locations, documents, and personnel across the Army in order to complete your assessment. Coordinate with other Services for assistance, documentation, and information that may assist in completing this assessment.

You will provide me with a report at the conclusion of the assessment.

This assessment is exempt from the HQDA Short Notice Tasking Policy Message, dated 031353Z Jan 01, requiring units to be notified 180 days from execution of tasking and the HQDA memorandum dated January 27, 2004, subject: Travel [Restriction] to Iraq, Afghanistan, Kuwait and Qatar which requires my approval to travel to these countries.

R. L. Brownlee
Acting Secretary of the Army

Appendix C   Locations Visited

February 2004 (CONUS)

JRTC MRX (39th Separate Brigade) (Pre-Inspection)
NTC MRX (81st Separate Brigade) (Pre-Inspection)

March 2004 (Afghanistan)

Bagram (CJTF 180 and 237th MP BN)
Khandahar (274th MP CO, 805th MP CO, and 1/10th MTN DIV)
Gheresk (ODA 312)
Khost (1/501st Parachute Infantry Regiment)

March–April 2004 (Iraq)

Baghdad (CJTF 7, Camp Cropper, Camp Slayer, 1st AD Division Collecting Point, 2/1st AD Brigade Collecting Point)
Camp Bucca (160th MP BN)
Abu Ghraib (504th MI BDE)
Ar Ramadi (1/1st ID Brigade Collecting Point)
Brassfield-Mora (2/1st ID Brigade Collecting Point)
Tikrit (1st ID Division Collecting Point)
Mosul (MND-N Collecting Point and 3/2nd ID Brigade Collecting Point, Battalion Collecting Point)

March–April 2004 (Kuwait)

Camp Doha (CFLCC)
Arifjan (2/4th ID)

March–April 2004 (CONUS)

Fort Dix (310th MP BN and 320th MP BN; at two different times)
Fort Hood (4th ID and 720th MP BN)
Fort Bragg (2/82nd ABN DIV and USASOC SERE Course)
Fort Campbell (3/101st ABN DIV)
Fort Meade (HHC 400th MP BDE)
Owings Mill, MD (433rd MP CO)

June 2004 (CONUS)

Fort Leonard Wood (MP School)
Fort Huachuca (MI School)

Appendix D   Inspection Tools

1. INTERVIEW QUESTIONS:

a. C-4/J-4/G-4

1). Concerning logistical operations, what is your role in the support of (Theater/Division) Detainee Operations?

2). Describe priority of support for Detainee Operations. How does this compete with your other mission requirements? Is the Priority of Support in SOPs, OPORDs/FRAGOs?

3). Describe how subordinate units plan and procure logistical support for Detainee Operations. (Include: transportation, sundry items, subsistence, organizational, and NBC clothing and equipment items, mail collection and distribution, laundry, and bath equipment) Have you ever coordinated for transportation to evacuate Detainees out of the AOR? Who approved the transfer?

4). What are some of the services being contracted out/outsourced to support Detainee Operations in Theater? Are there any issues concerning contracting or budget that you are aware of that impact Detainee Operations? If so, what are they? Who oversees the contracts that support Detainee Operations and where can we find out who the Army Representatives are (CORs)?

5). Are you aware of any Home Station Training that subordinate Combat Service Support units conducted prior to deployment to help them prepare for Detainee Operations? (To include collection point activities, etc) Can you describe it?

6). Have you had the opportunity to personally visit each of the Internment Facilities to determine if units have the necessary support and supplies to run their facilities? If so, what did you find? How about division and brigade Collection Points?

7). What are your challenges/issues in providing daily food rations in sufficient quantity, quality and variety to keep Detainees in good health and IAW with their cultural requirements? What is the schedule for feeding and what are they being fed? Please elaborate

8). How do Detainees receive fresh potable water in your area of responsibility? (Bottled water, Lister bags, running water – if so, is it potable?)

9). What procedures are in place to account for and dispose of captured enemy supplies and equipment?

10). What are your biggest issues concerning adequate facilities for Detainees (tents, cots, etc)?

11). What are your biggest issues concerning logistical support for Detainee Operations?

12). What do you perceive to be doctrinal logistic shortcomings pertaining to Detainee Operations and how would you fix/incorporate into updated doctrine/accomplish differently? How about Force Structure of logistical units that ensures Detainee Operations can be successfully accomplished? What are the shortcomings and how do we fix at the Army-level?

13). Are you aware of your requirement to report abuse or suspected abuse of detainees?

14). What do you perceive as the mission of your unit? Describe the importance of your role in that mission.

15). Describe your working environment and living conditions since being in Theater.

16). Describe the unit command climate and soldier morale. Has it changed or evolved since you have been in Theater?

17). Are you aware of any incidences of detainee or other abuse in your unit?

18). ADVISEMENT OF RIGHTS (For military personnel)
The text of Article 31 provides as follows a. No person subject to this chapter may compel any person to incriminate himself or to answer any questions the answer to which may tend to incriminate him. b. No person subject to this chapter may interrogate or request any statement from an accused or a person suspected of an offense without first informing him of the nature of the accusation and advising him that he does not have to make any statement regarding the offense of which he is accused or suspected, and that any statement made by him may be used as evidence against him in a trial by court-martial. c. No person subject to this chapter may compel any person to make a statement or produce evidence before any military tribunal if the statement or evidence is not material to the issue and may tend to degrade him. d. No statement obtained from any person in violation of this article, or through the use of coercion, unlawful influence, or unlawful inducement, may be received in evidence against him in a trial by court-martial.

19). I am _____ (grade, if any, and name), a member of the (DAIG). I am part of a team inspecting detainee operations, this is not a criminal investigation. I am reading you your rights because of a statement you made causes me to suspect that you may have committed _____. (specify offense, i.e., aggravated assault, assault, murder). Under Article 31, you have the right to remain silent, that is, say nothing at all. Any statement you make, oral or written, may be used as evidence against you in a trial by courts-martial or in other judicial or administrative proceedings. You have the right to consult a lawyer and to have a lawyer present during this interview. You have the right to military legal counsel free of charge. In addition to military counsel, you are entitled to civilian counsel of your own choosing, at your own expense. You may request a lawyer at any time during this interview. If you decide to answer questions, you may stop the questioning at any time. Do you understand your rights? Do you want a lawyer? (If the answer is yes, cease all questions at this point). Are you willing to answer questions?

20). Describe what you understand happened leading up to and during the incident(s) of abuse.

21). Describe soldier morale, feelings and emotional state prior to and after these incidents?

22). Was this incident reported to the chain of command? How, when & what was done? What would you have done?

23). How could the incident have been prevented?

24). Describe any unit training or other programs that you are aware of that teach leaders and soldiers how to recognize and resolve combat stress.

25). What measures are in place to boost morale or to relieve stress?

26). What measures could the command enact to improve the morale and command climate of your unit?

b. PROVOST MARSHAL

1). What references/standards/publications/SOPs do you use to conduct Detainee Operations?

2). What is the C2 structure/organization of internment facilities across Theater? How many internment facilities under U.S. Military Control, do you oversee? How many divisional Central Collection Points? How about Brigade Forward Collection Points? What MP units in Theater operate internment facilities and where are they positioned? (Battalion and Above) Describe the essential organizational requirements to run an internment facility. (Organizational Elements, Manning, Facilities, Equipment). Do you have what you need to accomplish the mission? If not, explain?

3). How do you ensure the units operating these locations/facilities are complying with the provisions of the Geneva Convention and AR 190-8?

4). Are detainees being employed to work? What are the General policy and procedures for the Employment and Compensation of Detainees?

5). Is there a policy on the ratio of guards to Detainees in Theater? If so, what is it? Is this standard being met? If not, what is the shortfall and how are units meeting the challenge to overcome the shortfall?

6). What is your detainee segregation policy? ((EPWs, Females, Juveniles, Civilian Internees (to include those that are security threats, those that are hostile to coalition forces, and possible HTD/HVD, and Retained Persons, Criminals, etc.)) What can you tell me about the categories of Detainees that you are holding? What are they and what are the definitions of the different categories that your organizations detain? How are you organized to handle the different categories of Detainees (EPW, CI, HVD, OD, and refugees?)

7). What is the minimum living space standard for each Detainee? How is it determined and who set the provisions of minimum living space for internment facilities? (when possible, consult the preventative medicine authority in theater for provisions of minimum living space and sanitary facilities). Has a preventative medicine expert given advice on this?

8). Do you use Military Working Dogs (MWD) within internment facilities?

9). How does the command ensure that Detainee Operations is conducted in compliance with the international Law of war? (OPORD/FRAGO, ROE, Interrogation Techniques, general orders, humane treatment, etc)

10). What is the current policy to grant conditional access to the International Red Cross/Crescent to Detainees? Has this always been the policy? Are they the only NGOs that have conditional access? If not, who are the other organizations?

11). What is your responsibility to the National Detainee Reporting Center (NDRC)? What is your relationship with the Theater Detainee Reporting Center (TDRC)? To the best of your knowledge, when were these centers stood up? Describe the Detainee Reporting System? (Software used, DataBase Management, Data Validation, Contingencies, Security and Privacy, etc.) Who has access?

12). What are the policies and procedures for US Forces transferring detainees to other Coalition Forces/Host Nation Forces? Has this been done?

13). What are the procedures that allow other United States Government Agencies (OGA) access and control to Detainees for the purpose of interrogations? What is the process for transfer and accountability of the Detainee? Does the commander of each internment facility have approval authority to transfer to OGAs? How much notice do they have to provide the chain of command for access or request for transfer? Do the same procedures apply when Military Intelligence personnel request access and control?

14). Describe the screening /background checks required prior to hiring interpreters. Are they trusted by U.S. Soldiers?

15). What are your biggest issues concerning adequate facilities for Detainees?

16). Since you have been in your position, what Detention facilities/locations have you visited and inspected for compliance with law, policy, and regulations? What were the results and findings? Can we get copies of your results?

17). What procedures are in place when a detainee in US custody dies?

18). What do you perceive to be doctrinal Military Police shortcomings pertaining to Detainee Operations and how would you fix/incorporate into updated doctrine/accomplish differently? How does your doctrinal law enforcement mission suffer? How about Force Structure of Military Police units that ensures Detainee Operations can be successfully accomplished? What are the shortcomings and how do we fix at the Army-level?

19). Are you aware of your requirement to report abuse or suspected abuse of detainees?

20). What do you perceive as the mission of your unit? Describe the importance of your role in that mission.

21). Describe your working environment and living conditions since being in Theater.

22). Describe the unit command climate and soldier morale. Has it changed or evolved since you have been in Theater?

23). Are you aware of any incidences of detainee or other abuse in your unit?

24). ADVISEMENT OF RIGHTS (For military personnel)

The text of Article 31 provides as follows a. No person subject to this chapter may compel any person to incriminate himself or to answer any questions the answer to which may tend to incriminate him. b. No person subject to this chapter may interrogate or request any statement from an accused or a person suspected of an offense without first informing him of the nature of the accusation and advising him that he does not have to make any statement regarding the offense of which he is accused or suspected, and that any statement made by him may be used as evidence against him in a trial by court-martial. c. No person subject to this chapter may compel any person to make a statement or produce evidence before any military tribunal if the statement or evidence is not material to the issue and may tend to degrade him. d. No statement obtained from any person in violation of this article, or through the use of coercion, unlawful influence, or unlawful inducement, may be received in evidence against him in a trial by court-martial

25). I am _____ (grade, if any, and name), a member of the (DAIG). I am part of a team inspecting detainee operations, this is not a criminal investigation. I am reading you your rights because of a statement you made causes me to suspect that you may have committed _____. (specify offense, i.e. aggravated assault, assault, murder). Under Article 31, you have the right to remain silent, that is, say nothing at all. Any statement you make, oral or written, may be used as evidence against you in a trial by courts-martial or in other judicial or administrative proceedings. You have the right to consult a lawyer and to have a lawyer present during this interview. You have the right to military legal counsel free of charge. In addition to military counsel, you are entitled to civilian counsel of your own choosing, at your own expense. You may request a lawyer at any time during this interview. If you decide to answer questions, you may stop the questioning at any time. Do you understand your rights? Do you want a lawyer? (If the answer is yes, cease all questions at this point). Are you willing to answer questions?

26). Describe what you understand happened leading up to and during the incident(s) of abuse.

27). Describe soldier morale, feelings and emotional state prior to and after these incidents?

28). Was this incident reported to the chain of command? How, when & what was done? What would you have done?

29). How could the incident have been prevented?

30). Describe any unit training or other programs that you are aware of that teach leaders and soldiers how to recognize and resolve combat stress.

31). What measures are in place to boost morale or to relieve stress?

32). What measures could the command enact to improve the morale and command climate of your unit?

c. RED CROSS

1). Which US Military Controlled Internment Facilities have you visited? What did you find?

2). Have you visited any Collection Points in US Army areas? Which ones and what did you find?

3). How often are the US Army collection points/internment facilities inspected? What is the make-up of the team? (Prev Med, Doctors, Psychiatrists/Psychologists, etc) What, specifically do you inspect? What do you do with the results of the inspections? Are the appropriate commanders taking the necessary actions to correct the shortcomings noted during your monthly medical inspections? Have you observed any recurring deficiencies during your inspections? Have you noted improvements and if so, what are the improvements? In what areas can we make improvements and what are those?

4). How often do you or your staff conduct routine medical inspections (examinations) of detainees under US Military control? What does the medical evaluation consist of? What is the purpose of the medical examination? How are the results recorded/reported?

5). Does every US Military Controlled Internment Facility have an infirmary? How adequate is the medical care to the detainees? (Are Retained Persons used?) Do you know of any detainees being denied medical treatment or delayed medical attention? If so, why?

6). Do detainees at US Military Controlled Internment Facilities have access to personal hygiene products?

7). Have you noticed any markings and/or injuries on a detainee at a US Military Controlled Internment Facility that might lead you to believe the detainee was being abused? Did you bring this to the attention of the Facility Commander? Do you know what he did with the information?

8). Are detainees in US Military Controlled Internment Facilities segregated by nationality, language, rank, and sex? Do detainees have the ability to practice their religion? Are detainees able to send and receive mail?

9). Can you describe the living conditions at US Military Controlled Internment Facilities? (Sanitary conditions, heat during the winter, shelter for rain, fire prevention measures, latrines, sleep areas, etc)

10). How do the detainees get fresh water? What kind of meals are they being fed? Do they get enough food?

11). Overall, how do you feel detainees are being treated at US Military Controlled Internment Facilities? What systemic weaknesses have you identified?

d. SJA

1). What specific measures has the commander/unit taken to ensure compliance with the Law of War regarding detainee operations? Individual training events? When? Collective/unit training events? When?

2). What is the minimum standard of treatment that the US must provide any detainee? What policies/procedures do units have in place to support the U.S. General Protection policy relative to the treatment of Detainees in the custody of the US forces?

3). What specific measures did the unit take prior to arrival in the AOR to ensure that subordinate leaders and soldiers know and understand how to treat, handle, and process detainees properly? Do leaders and soldiers know and understand how to apply Detainee Operations doctrine and standards when they arrive in the AOR? Can you provide some examples.

4). How is the issue of classification of detainees being handled? Are any Article 5 tribunals being held or is there a presumption that the insurgents clearly do not meet the Article 4 GC III EPW criteria (commanded by a person responsible for his subordinates, wearing fixed distinctive sign, carrying arms openly, conducting operations in accordance with the laws of war)?

5). Did units receive training on the reporting of Detainee abuse? When did this training occur last and how often is it conducted by the units? Are units reporting Detainee abuse? What is happening to individuals who abuse Detainees? How many cases of detainee abuse have you heard of and or processed since you have been in country? At what point in the detention process are most of the abuses occurring? (point of capture, initial collection point, by guards at internment facility, by interrogators)

6). What control measures are units using to maintain detainee discipline and security in each internment facility/collection point?

7). What are the procedures you follow if you personally notice or if it is reported to you that a detainee is injured and you suspect the detainee has been abused? What training has the unit received regarding reporting procedures for detainee abuse?

8). What are the procedures if a detainee in U.S. custody dies?

9). What are the Theater guidelines for any EPW, CI, and RP claims against the U.S. Government?

10). (Internment facility Judge Advocate only) What is the procedure if an EPW or detainee wants to make a complaint or requests to the camp commander regarding conditions of their internment? How are Detainees complaints and requests to the camp commander processed?

11). Have any detainees refused repatriation? If so, what happened to them?

12). What happens when a detainee is suspected of, or is known to have committed a serious offense while they are being interned at either the collection point or detention facility? Describe the due process available to detainees and rights of the detainee suspected of committing a serious offense. Have you or any Staff Judge Advocate provided legal advice to a detainee who might have committed an offense?

13). What is your feeling on how Detainees are being treated? What do you feel is the primary focus/purpose of detainee operations. (force protection, punishment, rehabilitation, protection, merely a regulatory/legal requirement) No standard. Personnel observations and feelings.

14). What AARs or lessons learned have you written or received regarding detainee operations? Can I get a copy?

15). What do you perceive to be doctrinal legal shortcomings pertaining to Detainee Operations and how would you fix/incorporate into updated doctrine/accomplish differently? How about Force Structure of Staff Judge Advocate to ensure Detainee Operations can be successfully accomplished? What are the shortcomings and how do we fix the problem at the Army-level?

16). What do you perceive as the mission of your unit? Describe the importance of your role in that mission.

17). Describe your working environment and living conditions since being in Theater.

18). Describe the unit command climate and soldier morale. Has it changed or evolved since you have been in Theater?

19). Are you aware of any incidences of detainee or other abuse in your unit?

20). ADVISEMENT OF RIGHTS (For military personnel)
The text of Article 31 provides as follows a. No person subject to this chapter may compel any person to incriminate himself or to answer any questions the answer to which may tend to incriminate him. b. No person subject to this chapter may interrogate or request any statement from an accused or a person suspected of an offense without first informing him of the nature of the accusation and advising him that he does not have to make any statement regarding the offense of which he is accused or suspected, and that any statement made by him may be used as evidence against him in a trial by court-martial. c. No person subject to this chapter may compel any person to make a statement or produce evidence before any military tribunal if the statement or evidence is not material to the issue and may tend to degrade him. d. No statement obtained from any person in violation of this article, or through the use of coercion, unlawful influence, or unlawful inducement, may be received in evidence against him in a trial by court-martial.

21). I am _____ (grade, if any, and name), a member of the (DAIG). I am part of a team inspecting detainee operations, this is not a criminal investigation. I am reading you your rights because of a statement you made causes me to suspect that you may have committed _____. (specify offense, i.e., aggravated assault, assault, murder). Under Article 31, you have the right to remain silent, that is, say nothing at all. Any statement you make, oral or written, may be used as evidence against you in a trial by courts-martial or in other judicial or administrative proceedings. You have the right to consult a lawyer and to have a lawyer present during this interview. You have the right to military legal counsel free of charge. In addition to military counsel, you are entitled to civilian counsel of your own choosing, at your own expense. You may request a lawyer at any time during this interview. If you decide to answer questions, you may stop the questioning at any time. Do you understand your rights? Do you want a lawyer? (If the answer is yes, cease all questions at this point). Are you willing to answer questions?

22). Describe what you understand happened leading up to and during the incident(s) of abuse.

23). Describe soldier morale, feelings and emotional state prior to and after these incidents?

24). Was this incident reported to the chain of command? How, when & what was done? What would you have done?

25). How could the incident have been prevented?

26). Describe any unit training or other programs that you are aware of that teach leaders and soldiers how to recognize and resolve combat stress.

27). What measures are in place to boost morale or to relieve stress?

28). What measures could the command enact to improve the morale and command climate of your unit?

e. STAFF ENGINEER (DIVISION & ABOVE)

1). Describe facilities' overall that infrastructure support Detainee Operations. (Sewer, water distribution, storm drainage, electrical distribution, HVAC systems, and lighting, etc.) What are the problems concerning existing facilities and what is being done to fix?

2). What program is in place in Theater that allows for the maintenance and repair of facilities that house Detainees and their supporting facilities?

3). Are the Corps of Engineers involved in any facility upgrades/improvements in Theater for Detainees? If so, what are some ongoing projects? Can I get a list by Project Number? Who is your POC in USACE? What do you know of the Engineer Corps' Theater Construction Management System (TCSM). Were you aware that they have plans, specifications, and material requirements for Internment Facilities based on Detainee population?

4). Do you have any knowledge as to why U.S. Forces chose existing facilities rather than to use the Theater Construction Management System (TCSM) and build facilities elsewhere? (How and why were facilities picked as Long Term Detention Facilities?)

5). What is your role in determining provisions of minimum living space for Detention Facilities across the AOR? (when possible, consult the preventative medicine authority in theater for provisions of minimum living space and sanitary facilities). What is the minimum living space standard for each Detainee? Has a preventative medicine expert given advice on this?

6). Do engineer officers train and supervise internal and external labor for Detention Facilities? (construction and repair of detention facilities)? If so, describe the work ((construction, maintenance, repair, and operation of utilities (water, electricity, heat, and sanitation.))

7). Are you aware of your requirement to report abuse or suspected abuse of detainees?

8). What do you perceive as the mission of your unit? Describe the importance of your role in that mission.

9). Describe your working environment and living conditions since being in Theater.

10). Describe the unit command climate and Soldier morale. Has it changed or evolved since you have been in Theater?

11). Are you aware of any incidences of detainee or other abuse in your unit?

12). ADVISEMENT OF RIGHTS (For military personnel)
The text of Article 31 provides as follows a. No person subject to this chapter may compel any person to incriminate himself or to answer any questions the answer to which may tend to incriminate him. b. No person subject to this chapter may interrogate or request any statement from an accused or a person suspected of an offense without first informing him of the nature of the accusation and advising him that he does not have to make any statement regarding the offense of which he is accused or suspected, and that any statement made by him may be used as evidence against him in a trial by court-martial. c. No person subject to this chapter may compel any person to make a statement or produce evidence before any military tribunal if the statement or evidence is not material to the issue and may tend to degrade him. d. No statement obtained from any person in violation of this article, or through the use of coercion, unlawful influence, or unlawful inducement, may be received in evidence against him in a trial by court-martial.

13). I am _____ (grade, if any, and name), a member of the (DAIG). I am part of a team inspecting detainee operations, this is not a criminal investigation. I am reading you your rights because of a statement you made causes me to suspect that you may have committed _____. (specify offense, i.e., aggravated assault, assault, murder). Under Article 31, you have the right to remain silent, that is, say nothing at all. Any statement you make, oral or written, may be used as evidence against you in a trial by courts-martial or in other judicial or administrative proceedings. You have the right to consult a lawyer and to have a lawyer present during this interview. You have the right to military legal counsel free of charge. In addition to military counsel, you are entitled to civilian counsel of your own choosing, at your own expense. You may request a lawyer at any time during this interview. If you decide to answer questions, you may stop the questioning at any time. Do you understand your rights? Do you want a lawyer? (If the answer is yes, cease all questions at this point). Are you willing to answer questions?

14). Describe what you understand happened leading up to and during the incident(s) of abuse.

15). Describe soldier morale, feelings and emotional state prior to and after these incidents

16). Was this incident reported to the chain of command? How, when & what was done? What would you have done?

17). How could the incident have been prevented?

18). Describe any unit training or other programs that you are aware of that teach leaders and soldiers how to recognize and resolve combat stress.

19). What measures are in place to boost morale or to relieve stress?

20). What measures could the command enact to improve the morale and command climate of your unit?

f. MI BDE/BN CDR/S-3/CO CDR/1SG

1). (All) What is your overall role in detainee operation process? What involvement do you have in the interrogation process of detainee operations? Do you provide a means to validate detainee's information? Do you provide input as to the disposition of the detainee?

2). (All) What references/standards/publications/SOPs do you use to conduct interrogation Operations?

3). (All) Did your soldiers undergo Level B Law of War training prior to deployment? Explain what training occurred. Is there a plan to train new soldiers (replacements) to the unit? Did this training include the treatment of Detainees? Explain.

4). (All) What training have you received to ensure your knowledge of DO is IAW the provisions under the Geneva Convention?

5). (All) What Home Station/Mob Site Training did your unit conduct prior to deployment to help your unit prepare for Detainee/interrogation Operations? Describe it. How did the training prepare you to conduct Detainee/interrogation Operations for this deployment? How did this training distinguish between the different categories of Detainees (EPWs, RPs, CIs, etc.)?

6). (All) What training did your unit receive on the established Rules of Engagement (ROE)? How often does this occur? Does this training include Rules of Interaction (ROI)?

7). (All) What procedures are in place to ensure your soldiers do not violate the rules of engagement for the interment facility/collection point?

8). (All) What guidance or policies are there to ensure fraternization is not taking place between U.S. military personnel and the detainees?

9). (All) How does the command ensure that interrogation Operations is conducted in compliance with the international Law of war? (OPORD/FRAGO, ROE, Interrogation Techniques, general orders, humane treatment, etc)

10). (All) Have you personally visited each of the interrogation facilities to determine if your unit has the necessary support and supplies to run their facilities? If so, what did you find?

11). (All) What control measures are you using to maintain discipline and security within the interrogation facility?

12). (BN/CO Cdr) Are you receiving sufficient information from the capture paperwork to properly conduct screenings and interrogations? Are the current requirements for documentation of a captured person sufficient or excessive? Did the changes in procedures as far as documenting captured person improve your ability to gather intelligence?

13). (BN/CO Cdr) What are the procedures for the transfer of custody of Detainees from the MP/Guard personnel to Military Intelligence personnel? When the detainee is returned to the guard force, what procedures occur?

14). (CO Cdr/BN S3) Describe the screening /background checks required prior to hiring interpreters. Are they trusted by U.S. soldiers?

15). (All) Do counter-intelligence agents conduct interrogations of detainees? What training have they received for conducting interrogations? What is their understanding of the laws of war as it pertains to interrogating detainees?

16). (All) What do you perceive to be doctrinal shortcomings pertaining to Interrogation Operations? How would you fix/incorporate into updated doctrine/accomplish differently? How about Force Structure to ensure Interrogation Operations can be successfully accomplished? What are the shortcomings and how do we fix the problem at the Army-level?

17). (All) What are the procedures if a detainee in U.S. custody dies?

18). (All) Do you know of the procedures to get stress counseling (Psychiatrist, Chaplain, Medical)? Do your soldiers know of the procedures to get counseling (Psychiatrist, Chaplain, Medical)?

19). (All) Are you aware of your requirement to report abuse or suspected abuse of detainees?

20). (All) Do your subordinates know the reporting procedures if they observe or become aware of a Detainee being abused?

21). (All) What steps would you take if a subordinate reported to you an incident of alleged Detainee abuse?

22). (All) Do you feel you can freely report an incident of alleged Detainee abuse outside Command channels (IG, CID)

23). (All) What procedures do you have to report suspected detainee abuse (IG, CID, Next Level Commander)

24). (All) What procedures are in place for Detainees to report alleged abuse?

25). (All) What do you perceive as the mission of your unit? Describe the importance of your role in that mission.

26). (All) Describe your working environment and living conditions since being in Theater.

27). (All) Describe the unit command climate and soldier morale. Has it changed or evolved since you have been in Theater?

28). (All) Are you aware of any incidences of detainee or other abuse in your unit?

29). ADVISEMENT OF RIGHTS (For military personnel)
The text of Article 31 provides as follows a. No person subject to this chapter may compel any person to incriminate himself or to answer any questions the answer to which may tend to incriminate him. b. No person subject to this chapter may interrogate or request any statement from an accused or a person suspected of an offense without first informing him of the nature of the accusation and advising him that he does not have to make any statement regarding the offense of which he is accused or suspected, and that any statement made by him may be used as evidence against him in a trial by court-martial. c. No person subject to this chapter may compel any person to make a statement or produce evidence before any military tribunal if the statement or evidence is not material to the issue and may tend to degrade him. d. No statement obtained from any person in violation of this article, or through the use of coercion, unlawful influence, or unlawful inducement, may be received in evidence against him in a trial by court-martial.

30). I am _____ (grade, if any, and name), a member of the (DAIG). I am part of a team inspecting detainee operations, this is not a criminal investigation. I am reading you your rights because of a statement you made causes me to suspect that you may have committed _____. (specify offense, i.e., aggravated assault, assault, murder). Under Article 31, you have the right to remain silent, that is, say nothing at all. Any statement you make, oral or written, may be used as evidence against you in a trial by courts-martial or in other judicial or administrative proceedings. You have the right to consult a lawyer and to have a lawyer present during this interview. You have the right to military legal counsel free of charge. In addition to military counsel, you are entitled to civilian counsel of your own choosing, at your own expense. You may request a lawyer at any time during this interview. If you decide to answer questions, you may stop the questioning at any time. Do you understand your rights? Do you want a lawyer? (If the answer is yes, cease all questions at this point). Are you willing to answer questions?

31). (All) Describe what you understand happened leading up to and during the incident(s) of abuse.

32). (All) Describe soldier morale, feelings and emotional state prior to and after these incidents?

33). (All) Was this incident reported to the chain of command? How, when & what was done? What would you have done?

34). (All) How could the incident have been prevented?

35). (All) Describe any unit training or other programs that you are aware of that teach leaders and soldiers how to recognize and resolve combat stress.

36). (All) What measures are in place to boost morale or to relieve stress?

37). (All) What measures could the command enact to improve the morale and command climate of your unit?

g. MP BDE COMMANDER INTERVIEW QUESTIONS

1). What references/standards/publications/SOPs do you require your subordinates to use for Detainee Operations?

2). What MP units under your command operate US military controlled Internment Facilities? (Battalion and Company) How many Internment Facilities under U.S. Military Control, do you operate? Where are they positioned across the Theater? Have you visited any of DIV /BDE Collection Points?

3). What are the policies on the establishment of Internment Facilities? How do you ensure the units are operating these locations/facilities under the provisions of the Geneva Convention and AR 190-8(ROE, Interrogation Techniques, general orders, humane treatment, etc)?

4). Are your operations employing detainees for work? If so, what are the General policy and procedures for the Employment and Compensation of Detainees?

5). Is there (or do you have) a policy on the ratio of guards to Detainees? If so, what is it? Is this standard being met? If not, what is the shortfall and how are your units managing the challenge?

6). What is your detainee segregation policy?

7). What is the minimum living space standard for each Detainee? Who set the provisions of minimum living space for Internment Facilities? (when possible, consult the preventative medicine authority in theater for provisions of minimum living space and sanitary facilities). Has a preventative medicine expert given advice on this?

8). Are the Corps of Engineers involved in any facility upgrades/improvements in Theater for Detainees? If so, what are some ongoing projects? What do you know of the Engineer Corps' Theater Construction Management System (TCSM). Were you aware that they have plans, specifications, and materiel requirements for Internment Facilities based on Detainee population?

9). Do you use Military Working Dogs (MWD) within detention facilities?

10). What is the current policy to grant conditional access to the International Red Cross/Crescent to Detainees? Has this always been the policy? Are they the only NGOs that have conditional access? If not, who are the other organizations?

11). Explain how medical information is kept on each individual Detainee?

12). What is your responsibility to the National Detainee Reporting Center (NDRC)? What is your relationship with the Theater Detainee Reporting Center (TDRC)? To the best of your knowledge, when were these centers stood up? Describe the Detainee Reporting System?

(Software used, DataBase Management, Data Validation, Contingencies, Security and Privacy, etc.) Who has access?

13). When are Detainees assigned Internment Serial Numbers (ISNs) (from point of capture to internment? Are there any reasons why Detainees would not be assigned ISNs?

14). What are the policies and procedures for US Forces transferring detainees to other Coalition Forces/Host Nation Forces? Has this been done?

15). What are the procedures that allow other United States Government Agencies (OGA) access to Detainees? Who is the approval authority? How much notice do they have to provide the chain of command? Do Detainees ever leave U.S. Military Control for interrogation? How about U.S. Military Police control to MI control? What is the process for turnover and accountability of the Detainee? What happens if a detainee is returned to U.S. Military Control from an OGA, and it is determined that abuse has occurred?

16). How are interpreters (linguists/translators) integrated within the Detainee Detention system (within each facility)?

17). What are your biggest issues concerning logistical, contractor, and interpreter support for Detainee Operations?

18). What are your biggest issues concerning adequate facilities for Detainees?

19). Can you describe the in-processing actions required for Detainees? What are some of the reasons that Detainees are not accepted to the internment facility? Are capturing units/subordinate units properly processing Detainees? If not, what are they doing wrong? Is it administrative in nature or in the physically handling of Detainees?

20). What is the process to account for and dispose of weapons and contraband confiscated from Detainees? What happens to personal property? (Is it disposed of/tagged along with the Detainee and is it stored properly and accounted for?) Why is the DD Form 2745 (Capture Tag) not being used? What are units using in lieu of (if any)? ((Detainee Capture Card found in draft MTTP, Detainee Ops – this card does not require near as much data as DD 2745 (). The CPA Apprehension Form helps offset the lack of info on the Detainee, however it is usually filled out in a single copy (not the three required))) Who decided on the use of the Coalition Provisional Authority Apprehension Form and why?

21). Does the current force structure meet the requirements to run Internment Facilities? If not why? What recommendations can you can you provide? Do your units have what they need to accomplish the mission (personnel/equipment) without additional support? If not, explain? What do you perceive to be doctrinal shortcomings pertaining to Detainee Operations and how would you fix/incorporate into updated doctrine and accomplish differently?

22). What is the ROE concerning Detainees? How do you ensure that this ROE is being followed and understood by all soldiers in your command that have any contact with Detainees? What is the policy to train on the established Rules of Engagement (ROE)? How often does this occur? Does this training include Rules of Interaction (ROI)?

23). What procedures are in place when a detainee in US custody dies?

24). What are the procedures for repatriation?

25). What religious activities are permitted?

26). Are you aware of your requirement to report abuse or suspected abuse of detainees?

27). Do your subordinates know the reporting procedures if they observe or become aware of a Detainee being abused?

28). What steps would you take if a subordinate reported to you an incident of alleged Detainee abuse?

29). Do you feel you can freely report an incident of alleged Detainee abuse outside Command channels (IG, CID)?

30). What procedures do you have to report suspected detainee abuse (IG, CID, Next Level Commander)?

31). What procedures are in place for Detainees to report alleged abuse?

32). What do you perceive as the mission of your unit? Describe the importance of your role in that mission.

33). Describe your working environment and living conditions since being in Theater.

34). Describe the unit command climate and soldier morale. Has it changed or evolved since you have been in Theater?

35). Are you aware of any incidences of detainee or other abuse in your unit?

36). ADVISEMENT OF RIGHTS (For military personnel)
The text of Article 31 provides as follows a. No person subject to this chapter may compel any person to incriminate himself or to answer any questions the answer to which may tend to incriminate him. b. No person subject to this chapter may interrogate or request any statement from an accused or a person suspected of an offense without first informing him of the nature of the accusation and advising him that he does not have to make any statement regarding the offense of which he is accused or suspected, and that any statement made by him may be used as evidence against him in a trial by court-martial. c. No person subject to this chapter may compel any person to make a statement or produce evidence before any military tribunal if the statement or evidence is not material to the issue and may tend to degrade him. d. No statement obtained from any person in violation of this article, or through the use of coercion, unlawful influence, or unlawful inducement, may be received in evidence against him in a trial by court-martial.

37). I am____(grade, if any, and name), a member of the (DAIG). I am part of a team inspecting detainee operations, this is not a criminal investigation. I am reading you your rights because of a statement you made causes me to suspect that you may have committed_____. (specify offense, i.e., aggravated assault, assault, murder). Under Article 31, you have the right to remain silent, that is, say nothing at all. Any statement you make, oral or written, may be used as evidence against you in a trial by courts-martial or in other judicial or administrative proceedings. You have the right to consult a lawyer and to have a lawyer present during this interview. You have the right to military legal counsel free of charge. In addition to military counsel, you are entitled to civilian counsel of your own choosing, at your own expense. You may request a lawyer at any time during this interview. If you decide to answer questions, you may stop the questioning at any time. Do you understand your rights? Do you want a lawyer? (If the answer is yes, cease all questions at this point). Are you willing to answer questions?

38). Describe what you understand happened leading up to and during the incident(s) of abuse.

39). Describe soldier morale, feelings and emotional state prior to and after these incidents?

40). Was this incident reported to the chain of command? How, when & what was done? What would you have done?

41). How could the incident have been prevented?

42). Describe any unit training or other programs that you are aware of that teach leaders and soldiers how to recognize and resolve combat stress.

43). What measures are in place to boost morale or to relieve stress?

44). What measures could the command enact to improve the morale and command climate of your unit?

h. CDR/OIC & SGM/NCOIC INTERNMENT FACILITY

1). Can you tell me what basic publications you use for Detainee Operations (doctrine and standards)?

2). What standards were used in establishing this facility?

3). What procedures do you have in place to ensure soldiers and leaders understand the use of force and rules of engagement for the interment facility?

4). How did you prepare yourself and your junior leaders to become familiar with and understand the applicable regulations, OPORDS/FRAGOs, directives, international laws and administrative procedures to operate an I/R facility?

5). How did Home Station/Mob Site Training prepare you to conduct Detainee Operations at this facility? What training have you and your soldiers received to ensure your knowledge of DO is IAW the Geneva Convention and DoD/Army policy? (Did this include Law of War and treatment of Detainees training.)?

6). Describe the training the guard force received to prepare them for their duties.

7). How does your unit conduct sustainment training for Detainee Operations or training for newly assigned personnel? When did your unit last conduct this training?

8). Describe some of the basic operations of the camp relating to detainee segregation, captured medical/religious personnel, feeding, sanitation, etc? Where do you maintain copies of the Geneva Convention around the facility? (Is it posted in the detainee's home language within the facilities)? Are camps segregating Detainees by nationality, language, rank, and sex? How are captured Medical personnel and Chaplains being used in the camps? What provisions are in place for the receipt and distribution of Detainee correspondence/mail? Are the daily food rations sufficient in quantity or quality and variety to keep detainees in good health? Are personal hygiene items and needed clothing being supplied to the Detainees? Are the conditions within the camp sanitary enough to ensure a clean and healthy environment free from disease and epidemics? Is there an infirmary located within the camp?

9). How are you organized to handle the different categories of personnel (EPW, CI, OD, females, JVs, and refuges)? How about female Detainees? How and where do you house them? Do you maintain a separate site for sick or wounded Detainees? If so where is it and how does your unit maintain the security and safeguarding of Detainees there?

10). Describe the procedures you use when you inprocess a detainee. (CPA Forces Apprehension Form, two sworn statements, EPW tag, where do you store Detainees' confiscated
personal effects (if any) and how are they accounted for (are they tagged with DD Form
2745)? How is evidence tagged? What procedures are in place to dispose of captured enemy supplies and equipment?) How is the transfer of Detainees handled between different
services and Other Governmental Organizations?

11). Where do you store Detainees' confiscated personal effects (if any) and how are they
accounted for? (Are they tagged with DD Form 2745)?

12). What are the procedures for the interrogation/questioning of Detainees?

13). What are the procedures for the transfer of custody of Detainees from the MP/Guard
personnel to Military Intelligence personnel? When the detainee is returned to the guard
force, what procedures occur? (what info is passed on to the Guard Force (type of
reward?)? . . . Observation report, paper trail audit)

14). What control measures do you use to maintain discipline and security in the facility?

15). What MP units (guards, escort, detachments) do you have at your disposal to operate
and maintain this Internment Facility? Do you have any shortages? How do these shortages
impact your mission? What non-MP units are you using to help operate this facility? Do
you have any shortages? How do these shortages impact your mission?

16). What kind of security lighting do you have that ensures you have a safe and secure
operation at night? How do you provide heat to detainees during the winter? What fire
prevention/safety measures do you have?

17). Are you employing detainees for work? What are the General policy and procedures
for the Employment and Compensation of Detainees?

18). What type of Medical assets are present in support of medical treatment of detainees?

19). What kind of stress counseling do you provide to Soldiers/Guards?

20). Are Detainees allowed to practice their religion? Is there a chaplain available to minister to the detainees? Is the chaplain a Retained Personnel, US Forces, or a civilian?

21). Describe the latrine facilities for Detainees' use (do they have access to it day and night
and does it conform to the rules of hygiene and do females have separate facilities). How
are they cleaned and how often and by whom? Where do they bathe and conduct other
personal hygiene (this will depend how long it takes to evacuate Detainees to U.S. Military
Controlled Detention Facilities – 12 hours is the standard)?

22). Describe how the unit plans and procures logistical support to include: transportation,
subsistence, organizational, and NBC clothing and equipment items, mail collection and
distribution, laundry, and bath equipment ISO DO. What logistical support do you receive
to run this Facility? What types of supplies is greater in-demand for the unit during detainee
operations? What are your shortfalls?

23). How do the Detainees receive fresh water (Bottled water or Lister bag)?

24). What personnel or equipment USR shortages are affecting your ability to perform
detainee operations?

25). What do you perceive to be doctrinal shortcomings pertaining to Detainee Operations
and how would you fix/incorporate into updated doctrine/accomplish differently? How

about Force Structure to ensure Detainee Operations can be successfully accomplished? What are the shortcomings and how do we fix the problem at the Army-level?

26). What are the procedures if an EPW or RP in U.S. custody dies?

27). What AARs or lessons learned have you written or received regarding detainee operations? Can I get a copy?

28). Are you aware of your requirement to report abuse or suspected abuse of detainees?

29). Do your subordinates know the reporting procedures if they observe or become aware of a Detainee being abused?

30). What steps would you take if a subordinate reported to you an incident of alleged Detainee abuse?

31). Do you feel you can freely report an incident of alleged Detainee abuse outside Command channels (IG, CID)?

32). What procedures do you have to report suspected detainee abuse (IG, CID, Next Level Commander)?

33). What procedures are in place for Detainees to report alleged abuse?

34). What do you perceive as the mission of your unit? Describe the importance of your role in that mission.

35). Describe your working environment and living conditions since being in Theater.

36). Describe the unit command climate and Soldier morale. Has it changed or evolved since you have been in Theater?

37). Are you aware of any incidences of detainee or other abuse in your unit?

38). ADVISEMENT OF RIGHTS (For military personnel)
    The text of Article 31 provides as follows a. No person subject to this chapter may compel any person to incriminate himself or to answer any questions the answer to which may tend to incriminate him. b. No person subject to this chapter may interrogate or request any statement from an accused or a person suspected of an offense without first informing him of the nature of the accusation and advising him that he does not have to make any statement regarding the offense of which he is accused or suspected, and that any statement made by him may be used as evidence against him in a trial by court-martial. c. No person subject to this chapter may compel any person to make a statement or produce evidence before any military tribunal if the statement or evidence is not material to the issue and may tend to degrade him. d. No statement obtained from any person in violation of this article, or through the use of coercion, unlawful influence, or unlawful inducement, may be received in evidence against him in a trial by court-martial.

39). I am_____(grade, if any, and name), a member of the (DAIG). I am part of a team inspecting detainee operations, this is not a criminal investigation. I am reading you your rights because of a statement you made causes me to suspect that you may have committed _____.(specify offense, i.e., aggravated assault, assault, murder). Under Article 31, you have the right to remain silent, that is, say nothing at all. Any statement you make, oral or written, may be used as evidence against you in a trial by courts-martial or in other judicial or administrative proceedings. You have the right to consult a lawyer and to have a lawyer present during this interview. You have the right to military legal counsel free of charge. In addition to military counsel, you are entitled to civilian counsel of your own choosing, at your own expense. You may request a lawyer at any time during this interview. If you decide to answer questions. you may stop the questioning at any time. Do you understand your rights? Do you want a lawyer? (If the answer is yes, cease all questions at this point). Are you willing to answer questions?

40). Describe what you understand happened leading up to and during the incident(s) of abuse.

41). Describe soldier morale, feelings and emotional state prior to and after these incidents?

42). Was this incident reported to the chain of command? How, when & what was done? What would you have done?

43). How could the incident have been prevented?

44). Describe any unit training or other programs that you are aware of that teach leaders and soldiers how to recognize and resolve combat stress.

45). What measures are in place to boost morale or to relieve stress?

46). What measures could the command enact to improve the morale and command climate of your unit?

i. MANEUVER BDE/BN XO

1). What are your responsibilities concerning detainee operations?

2). (BDE XO) What are your responsibilities concerning the Forward Collection Point in the BSA? What is your relationship with the Forward Collection Point OIC?

3). Can you tell me what basic publications you use for Detainee Operations?

4). How did you prepare yourself and your junior leaders to become familiar with and understand the applicable regulations, OPORDS/FRAGOs directives, international laws and administrative procedures to support Detainee Operations?

5). How did Home Station/Mob Site Training prepare you to conduct Detainee Operations?

6). Can you describe the process of getting a Detainee to the Forward Collection Point in the BSA beginning with the point of Capture? How long do detainees stay in the company holding area before being transported to the BDE Forward Collection Point?

7). (BN XO) How do your companies integrate the security and defense of the company holding areas into their perimeter defense? What is your normal ratio of guards to detainees in the holding area? Is this ratio the proper mix for you to perform your mission? If not, what are the shortfalls? How do these shortfalls impact your mission

8). Are you experiencing any transportation problems to move detainees, and if so what? What is the number of personnel needed to move prisoners internally or externally (i.e., from the BN holding areas to the Forward Collection Point, for medical evacuation, etc?

9). What personnel or equipment USR shortages are affecting your ability to support detainee operations? What are your resource shortfalls to support this operation? What types of supplies is greater in-demand for the unit during detainee operations?

10). What do you perceive to be doctrinal shortcomings pertaining to Detainee Operations and how would you fix/incorporate into updated doctrine/accomplish differently? How about Force Structure to ensure Detainee Operations can be successfully accomplished? What are the shortcomings and how do we fix the problem at the Army-level?

11). What procedures are in place to ensure soldiers and leaders understand the use of force and rules of engagement?

12). What kind of stress counseling are Soldiers/Guards provided?

13). What are the procedures for evacuating a sick or wounded Detainee? How does your unit maintain the security and safeguarding of sick or wounded Detainees while in transport?

14). Describe how the unit plans and procures logistical support to include: subsistence, organizational, and NBC clothing and equipment items, mail collection and distribution, laundry, and bath equipment ISO DO.

15). (BN XO) How do you provide your unit holding area with water? (Bottled water or bulk water)?

16). What are the procedures if a detainee in U.S. custody dies?

17). What AARs or lessons learned have you written or received regarding detainee operations? Can I get a copy?

18). Are you aware of your requirement to report abuse or suspected abuse of detainees?

19). What procedures do you have to report suspected detainee abuse? Who can you report abuse/suspected abuse to?

20). Do your subordinates know the reporting procedures if they observe or become aware of a Detainee being abused?

21). What steps would you take if a subordinate reported to you an incident of alleged Detainee abuse?

22). What do you perceive as the mission of your unit? Describe the importance of your role in that mission.

23). Describe your working environment and living conditions since being in Theater.

24). Describe the unit command climate and Soldier morale. Has it changed or evolved since you have been in Theater?

25). Are you aware of any incidences of detainee or other abuse in your unit?

26). ADVISEMENT OF RIGHTS (For military personnel)
The text of Article 31 provides as follows a. No person subject to this chapter may compel any person to incriminate himself or to answer any questions the answer to which may tend to incriminate him. b. No person subject to this chapter may interrogate or request any statement from an accused or a person suspected of an offense without first informing him of the nature of the accusation and advising him that he does not have to make any statement regarding the offense of which he is accused or suspected, and that any statement made by him may be used as evidence against him in a trial by court-martial. c. No person subject to this chapter may compel any person to make a statement or produce evidence before any military tribunal if the statement or evidence is not material to the issue and

may tend to degrade him. d. No statement obtained from any person in violation of this article, or through the use of coercion, unlawful influence, or unlawful inducement, may be received in evidence against him in a trial by court-martial.

27). I am_____(grade, if any, and name), a member of the (DAIG). I am part of a team inspecting detainee operations, this is not a criminal investigation. I am reading you your rights because of a statement you made causes me to suspect that you may have committed _____. (specify offense, i.e., aggravated assault, assault, murder). Under Article 31, you have the right to remain silent, that is, say nothing at all. Any statement you make, oral or written, may be used as evidence against you in a trial by courts-martial or in other judicial or administrative proceedings. You have the right to consult a lawyer and to have a lawyer present during this interview. You have the right to military legal counsel free of charge. In addition to military counsel, you are entitled to civilian counsel of your own choosing, at your own expense. You may request a lawyer at any time during this interview. If you decide to answer questions, you may stop the questioning at any time. Do you understand your rights? Do you want a lawyer? (If the answer is yes, cease all questions at this point). Are you willing to answer questions?

28). Describe what you understand happened leading up to and during the incident(s) of abuse.

29). Describe soldier morale, feelings and emotional state prior to and after these incidents?

30). Was this incident reported to the chain of command? How, when & what was done? What would you have done?

31). How could the incident have been prevented?

32). Describe any unit training or other programs that you are aware of that teach leaders and soldiers how to recognize and resolve combat stress.

33). What measures are in place to boost morale or to relieve stress?

34). What measures could the command enact to improve the morale and command climate of your unit?

j. OIC & NCOIC COLLECTION POINT

1). Can you tell me what sources that you use to get policy, doctrine and standards for Detainee Operations? (What doctrine was used in setting up the collection point?) Describe the basic principles of detainee operations and how you are applying them.

2). How did you prepare yourself and your junior leaders/soldiers to understand applicable regulations, OPORD/FRAGO, directives, international laws and administrative procedures to operate a Collection Point?

3). How did Home Station/Mob Site Training prepare you to conduct Detainee Operations? (Did this include Law of War and treatment of Detainees training.)?

4). Describe the training the guard force received to prepare them for their duties.

5). How does your unit conduct sustainment training for Detainee Operations or training for newly assigned personnel? (How often does this occur and please describe it?) When did your unit last conduct this training?

6). What kind of security lighting do you have that ensures you have a safe and secure operation at night? How do you provide heat to detainees during the winter? What fire prevention/safety measures do you have?

7). In relation to where the detainees are housed, how far away are your ammunition and fuel storage sites? Where is your screening site where MI Soldiers interrogate Detainees?

8). Describe some of the basic operations of the collection point relating to detainee segregation, captured medical/religious personnel, feeding, sanitation, etc? (Do you segregate Detainees by nationality, language, religion, rank, and sex? How are captured Medical personnel and Chaplains being used? Are the daily food rations sufficient in quantity or quality and variety to keep detainees in good health? Are personal hygiene items and needed clothing being supplied to the Detainees? Are the conditions within the collection point sanitary enough to ensure a clean and healthy environment free from disease and epidemics)?

9). What control measures do you use to maintain detainee discipline and security in the collection point?

10). What are the procedures for the transfer of Detainees from the collection points to US Military controlled detention facilities? How is the transfer of Detainees handled between coalition forces/host nation?

11). What transportation problems do you experience moving detainees during the operation?

12). Describe the procedures you use when you inprocess a detainee. (CPA Forces Apprehension Form, two sworn statements, EPW tag, where do you store Detainees' confiscated personal effects (if any) and how are they accounted for (are they tagged with DD Form 2745)? How is evidence tagged? What procedures are in place to dispose of captured enemy supplies and equipment? Do you medically screen detainees?)

13). What MP units (platoon, guards, escort, detachments) do you have at your disposal to operate and maintain the collection point? Do you have any shortages? How do these shortages impact your mission? What non-MP units are you using to help operate the collection point? Do you have any shortages? How do these shortages impact your mission?

14). What is your normal ratio of guards to detainees in the collection point? Is this ratio the proper mix for you to perform your mission? If not, what are the shortfalls? Why are their shortfalls? How do these shortfalls impact your mission?

15). What is the number of personnel that is needed to move prisoners internally and externally (i.e., to the internment facility, from the BN Collection Points, for medical, evacuation, etc.

16). What personnel shortages do you have? What issues, if any, do you feel your unit has regarding manning or personnel resourcing in conducting Detention Operations?

17). What equipment shortages (USR) are affecting your ability to perform detainee operations? What other equipment is the unit experiencing as a shortfall concerning detainee operations, (i.e., restraints, uniforms, CIF items, weapons, etc.)? What major shortfalls has the unit encountered in regards to material and supply distribution?

18). Describe how the unit plans and procures logistical support to include: transportation, subsistence, organizational, and NBC clothing and equipment items, mail collection and distribution, laundry, and bath equipment ISO DO.

19). What logistical support do you receive to run this Facility? What types of supplies is greater in-demand for the unit during detainee operations? And are these items regularly filled?

20). What procedures do you have in place to ensure soldiers and leaders understand the use of force and rules of engagement for the collection point?

21). What are the unit's procedures for the interrogation/questioning of Detainees?

22). What kind of stress counseling are Soldiers/Guards provided?

23). Do you maintain a separate site for sick or wounded Detainees? If so where is it and how does your unit maintain the security and safeguarding of Detainees there? How about female Detainees? How and where do you house them?

24). What type of Medical personnel/units are available in support of medical treatment of detainees?

25). Are Detainees given the latitude to practice their religion? Is there a chaplain available to minister to the detainees? Is the chaplain a Retained Personnel, US Forces, or a civilian?

26). Describe the latrine facilities for Detainees' use (do they have access to it day and night and does it conform to the rules of hygiene and do females have separate facilities). How are they cleaned and how often and by whom? Where do they bathe and conduct other personal hygiene (this will depend how long it takes to evacuate Detainees to U.S. Military Controlled Detention Facilities – 12 hours is the standard)?

27). How do the Detainees receive fresh water (Bottled water or Lister bag)?

28). What are the procedures if a detainee in U.S. custody dies?

29). What AARs or lessons learned have you written or received regarding detainee operations? Can I get a copy?

30). Are you aware of your requirement to report abuse or suspected abuse of detainees?

31). Do your subordinates know the reporting procedures if they observe or become aware of a Detainee being abused?

32). What steps would you take if a subordinate reported to you an incident of alleged Detainee abuse?

33). Do you feel you can freely report an incident of alleged Detainee abuse outside Command channels (IG, CID)?

34). What procedures do you have to report suspected detainee abuse (IG, CID, Next Level Commander)?

35). What systems are in place for detainees to report alleged abuse?

36). What do you perceive as the mission of your unit? Describe the importance of your role in that mission.

37). Describe your working environment and living conditions since being in Theater.

38). Describe the unit command climate and Soldier morale. Has it changed or evolved since you have been in Theater?

39). Are you aware of any incidences of detainee or other abuse in your unit?

40). ADVISEMENT OF RIGHTS (For military personnel)
The text of Article 31 provides as follows a. No person subject to this chapter may compel any person to incriminate himself or to answer any questions the answer to which may tend to incriminate him. b. No person subject to this chapter may interrogate or request any statement from an accused or a person suspected of an offense without first informing him of the nature of the accusation and advising him that he does not have to make any statement regarding the offense of which he is accused or suspected, and that any statement made by him may be used as evidence against him in a trial by court-martial. c. No person subject to this chapter may compel any person to make a statement or produce evidence before any military tribunal if the statement or evidence is not material to the issue and may tend to degrade him. d. No statement obtained from any person in violation of this article, or through the use of coercion, unlawful influence, or unlawful inducement, may be received in evidence against him in a trial by court-martial.

41). I am____(grade, if any, and name), a member of the (DAIG). I am part of a team inspecting detainee operations, this is not a criminal investigation. I am reading you your rights because of a statement you, made causes me to suspect that you may have committed _____. (specify offense, i.e., aggravated assault, assault, murder). Under Article 31, you have the right to remain silent, that is, say nothing at all. Any statement you make, oral or written, may be used as evidence against you in a trial by courts-martial or in other judicial or administrative proceedings. You have the right to consult a lawyer and to have a lawyer present during this interview. You have the right to military legal counsel free of charge. In addition to military counsel, you are entitled to civilian counsel of your own choosing, at your own expense. You may request a lawyer at any time during this interview. If you decide to answer questions, you may stop the questioning at any time. Do you understand your rights? Do you want a lawyer? (If the answer is yes, cease all questions at this point). Are you willing to answer questions?

42). Describe what you understand happened leading up to and during the incident(s) of abuse.

43). Describe soldier morale, feelings and emotional state prior to and after these incidents?

44). Was this incident reported to the chain of command? How, when & what was done? What would you have done?

45). How could the incident have been prevented?

46). Describe any unit training or other programs that you are aware of that teach leaders and soldiers how to recognize and resolve combat stress.

47). What measures are in place to boost morale or to relieve stress?

48). What measures could the command enact to improve the morale and command climate of your unit?

k. INTERROGATOR OIC/NCOIC

1). What references/standards/publications/SOPs do you use to conduct interrogation Operations?

2). How does the command ensure that interrogation Operations is conducted in compliance with the international Law of war? (OPORD/FRAGO, ROE, Interrogation Techniques, general orders, humane treatment, etc).

3). Did you and your soldiers undergo Level B Law of War training prior to deployment? Explain what training occurred. Is there a plan to train new Soldiers (replacements) to the unit? Did this training include the treatment of Detainees? Explain.

4). What Home Station/Mob Site Training did you and your soldiers receive prior to deployment to help your unit prepare for Detainee/interrogation Operations? Describe it. How did the training prepare you to conduct Detainee/interrogation Operations for this deployment? How did this training distinguish between the different categories of Detainees (EPWs. RPs, CIs, etc.)?

5). What training did you receive on the established Rules of Engagement (ROE)? How often does this occur? Does this training include Rules of Interaction (ROI)?

6). What procedures are in place to ensure your soldiers do not violate the rules of engagement for the interment facility/collection point?

7). What guidance or policies are there to ensure fraternization is not taking place between U.S. military personnel and the detainees?

8). What training have you and your subordinates received to ensure your knowledge of DO is IAW the provisions under the Geneva Convention?

9). What is the OIC/NCOICs overall role in detainee operation process? What involvement do the OIC/NCOICs have in the interrogation process of detainee operations? Do the OIC/NCOICs provide a means to validate detainee's information? Do the OIC/NCOICs provide input as to the disposition of the detainee?

10). Where are your screening sites located (where detainees are interrogated and screened)? Are these facilities adequate for your needs? Do you have enough interrogators for your operation needs? What are your personnel shortfalls?

11). What is the procedure on how to identify a detainee who may have intelligence information? Who performs this procedure? Are MPs involved in the decision-making? Are PIRs used as a basis for the identification of detainees of interest, personality lists used, etc?

12). Have you personally observed the interrogation operations at this Facility to determine if your unit has the necessary support and supplies to run the facilities? If so, what did you find?

13). What control measures are you using to maintain discipline and security within the interrogation facility?

14). How many people are authorized to be present in the room when interrogating/screening a detainee? Under what circumstances are you required and authorized to have more people?

15). Are the personal effects of a detainee released to the interrogator or is the interrogator allowed to examine the items?

16). Are you receiving sufficient information from the capture paperwork to properly conduct screenings and interrogations? Are the current requirements for documentation of a captured person sufficient or excessive? Did the changes in procedures as far as documenting captured person improve your ability to gather intelligence?

17). What are the procedures for the transfer of custody of Detainees from the MP/Guard personnel to Military Intelligence personnel? When the detainee is returned to the guard force, what procedures occur?

18). Describe the screening /background checks required prior to hiring interpreters. Are they trusted by U.S. Soldiers?

19). What is your perception of the contract interrogators training and capabilities to conduct proper interrogations of detainees?

20). How are translators/linguists used during the screening/interrogation process? Do you trust the interpreter? How are MPs/Guards used during this process?

21). Do counterintelligence agents conduct interrogations of detainees? What training have they received for conducting interrogations? What is their understanding of the laws of war as it pertains to interrogating detainees?

22). What do you perceive to be doctrinal shortcomings pertaining to Interrogation Operations? How would you fix/incorporate into updated doctrine/accomplish differently? How about Force Structure to ensure Interrogation Operations can be successfully accomplished? What are the shortcomings and how do we fix the problem at the Army-level?

23). What are the procedures if a detainee in U.S. custody dies?

24). Do you know of the procedures to get stress counseling (Psychiatrist, Chaplain, Medical)? Do your Soldiers know of the procedures to get counseling (Psychiatrist, Chaplain, Medical)?

25). Are you aware of your requirement to report abuse or suspected abuse of detainees?

26). Do your subordinates know the reporting procedures if they observe or become aware of a Detainee being abused?

27). What steps would you take if a subordinate reported to you an incident of alleged Detainee abuse?

28). Do you feel you can freely report an incident of alleged Detainee abuse outside Command channels (IG, CID)?

29). What procedures do you have to report suspected detainee abuse (IG, CID, Next Level Commander)?

30). What procedures are in place for Detainees to report alleged abuse?

31). What do you perceive as the mission of your unit? Describe the importance of your role in that mission.

32). Describe your working environment and living conditions since being in Theater.

33). Describe the unit command climate and soldier morale. Has it changed or evolved since you have been in Theater?

34). Are you aware of any incidences of detainee or other abuse in your unit?

35). ADVISEMENT OF RIGHTS (For military personnel)
    The text of Article 31 provides as follows a. No person subject to this chapter may compel any person to incriminate himself or to answer any questions the answer to which may tend to incriminate him. b. No person subject to this chapter may interrogate or

request any statement from an accused or a person suspected of an offense without first informing him of the nature of the accusation and advising him that he does not have to make any statement regarding the offense of which he is accused or suspected, and that any statement made by him may be used as evidence against him in a trial by court-martial. c. No person subject to this chapter may compel any person to make a statement or produce evidence before any military tribunal if the statement or evidence is not material to the issue and may tend to degrade him. d. No statement obtained from any person in violation of this article, or through the use of coercion, unlawful influence, or unlawful inducement, may be received in evidence against him in a trial by court-martial.

36). I am_____(grade, if any, and name), a member of the (DAIG). I am part of a team inspecting detainee operations, this is not a criminal investigation. I am reading you your rights because of a statement you made causes me to suspect that you may have committed _____.(specify offense, i.e., aggravated assault, assault, murder). Under Article 31, you have the right to remain silent, that is, say nothing at all. Any statement you make, oral or written, may be used as evidence against you in a trial by courts-martial or in other judicial or administrative proceedings. You have the right to consult a lawyer and to have a lawyer present during this interview. You have the right to military legal counsel free of charge. In addition to military counsel, you are entitled to civilian counsel of your own choosing, at your own expense. You may request a lawyer at any time during this interview. If you decide to answer questions, you may stop the questioning at any time. Do you understand your rights? Do you want a lawyer? (If the answer is yes, cease all questions at this point). Are you willing to answer questions?

37). Describe what you understand happened leading up to and during the incident(s) of abuse.

38). Describe soldier morale, feelings and emotional state prior to and after these incidents?

39). Was this incident reported to the chain of command? How, when & what was done? What would you have done?

40). How could the incident have been prevented?

41). Describe any unit training or other programs that you are aware of that teach leaders and soldiers how to recognize and resolve combat stress.

42). What measures are in place to boost morale or to relieve stress

43). What measures could the command enact to improve the morale and command climate of your unit?

l. INTERROGATOR QUESTIONS

1). What references/standards/publications/SOPs do you use to conduct interrogation Operations?

2). What training have you received to ensure your knowledge of DO is IAW the provisions under the Geneva Convention?

3). Did your unit undergo Level B Law of War training prior to deployment? Explain what training occurred. Is there a plan to train new soldiers (replacements) to the unit? Did this training include the treatment of Detainees? Explain.

4). What training did your unit receive on the established Rules of Engagement (ROE)? How often does this occur? Does this training include Rules of Interaction (ROI)?

5). What is the procedure on how to identify a detainee who may have intelligence information? Who performs this procedure? Are MPs involved in the decision-making? Are PIRs used as a basis for the identification of detainees of interest, personality lists used, etc?

6). What is the Rules of Engagement (ROE)/Rules of Interaction (ROI) when interrogating a detainee?

7). What is the maximum amount of time allowed a detainee could be interrogated during one session? Where is this standard located?

8). What is the procedure in determining how long to hold a detainee at this level for interrogation once he refuses to cooperate?

9). How many people are authorized to be present in the room when interrogating/ screening a detainee? Under what circumstances are you required and authorized to have more people?

10). Who may allow an interrogator to question a detainee if he is wounded or sick? (Medical personnel)

11). What types of restraining devices are authorized on the detainee during the interrogation? What type and/or amount of physical constraints are interrogators authorized to place on an unruly detainee during interrogation?

12). Where are your screening sites located (where detainees are interrogated and screened)? Are these facilities adequate for your needs? Do you have enough interrogators for your operation needs? What are your personnel shortfalls?

13). Are you receiving sufficient information from the capture paperwork to properly conduct screenings and interrogations? Are the current requirements for documentation of a captured person sufficient or excessive? Did the changes in procedures as far as documenting captured person improve your ability to gather intelligence?

14). What are the procedures for the transfer of custody of Detainees from the MP/Guard personnel to Military Intelligence personnel? When the detainee is returned to the guard force, what procedures occur? (what info is passed on to the Guard Force (type of reward?)... observation report, paper trail audit)

15). Are the personal effects of a detainee released to the interrogator or is the interrogator allowed to examine the items?

16). How are translators/linguists used during the screening/interrogation process? Do you trust the interpreter? How are MPs/Guards used during this process?

17). What is your perception of the contract interrogators training and capabilities to conduct proper interrogations of detainees?

18). What do you perceive to be doctrinal shortcomings pertaining to Interrogation Operations? How would you fix/incorporate into updated doctrine/accomplish differently? How about Force Structure to ensure Interrogation Operations can be successfully accomplished? What are the shortcomings and how do we fix the problem at the Army-level?

19). Do you know of the procedures to get stress counseling (Psychiatrist, Chaplain, Medical)? Do your soldiers know of the procedures to get counseling (Psychiatrist, Chaplain, Medical)?

20). What is considered abuse to a detainee during interrogation?

21). Are you aware of your requirement to report abuse or suspected abuse of detainees?

22). Do your subordinates know the reporting procedures if they observe or become aware of a Detainee being abused?

23). What steps would you take if a subordinate reported to you an incident of alleged Detainee abuse?

24). Do you feel you can freely report an incident of alleged Detainee abuse outside Command channels (IG, CID)?

25). What procedures do you have to report suspected detainee abuse (IG, CID, Next Level Commander)?

26). What procedures are in place for Detainees to report alleged abuse?

27). What do you perceive as the mission of your unit? Describe the importance of your role in that mission.

28). Describe your working environment and living conditions since being in Theater.

29). Describe the unit command climate and Soldier morale. Has it changed or evolved since you have been in Theater?

30). Are you aware of any incidences of detainee or other abuse in your unit?

31). ADVISEMENT OF RIGHTS (For military personnel)
The text of Article 31 provides as follows a. No person subject to this chapter may compel any person to incriminate himself or to answer any questions the answer to which may tend to incriminate him. b. No person subject to this chapter may interrogate or request any statement from an accused or a person suspected of an offense without first informing him of the nature of the accusation and advising him that he does not have to make any statement regarding the offense of which he is accused or suspected, and that any statement made by him may be used as evidence against him in a trial by court-martial. c. No person subject to this chapter may compel any person to make a statement or produce evidence before any military tribunal if the statement or evidence is not material to the issue and may tend to degrade him. d. No statement obtained from any person in violation of this article, or through the use of coercion, unlawful influence, or unlawful inducement, may be received in evidence against him in a trial by court-martial.

32). I am_____(grade, if any, and name), a member of the (DAIG). I am part of a team inspecting detainee operations, this is not a criminal investigation. I am reading you your rights because of a statement you made causes me to suspect that you may have committed _____.(specify offense, i.e., aggravated assault, assault, murder). Under Article 31, you have the right to remain silent, that is, say nothing at all. Any statement you make, oral or written, may be used as evidence against you in a trial by courts-martial or in other judicial or administrative proceedings. You have the right to consult a lawyer and to have a lawyer present during this interview. You have the right to military legal counsel free of charge. In addition to military counsel, you are entitled to civilian counsel of your own choosing, at your own expense. You may request a lawyer at any time during this interview. If you decide to answer questions, you may stop the questioning at any time. Do you understand your rights? Do you want a lawyer? (If the answer is yes, cease all questions at this point). Are you willing to answer questions?

33). Describe what you understand happened leading up to and during the incident(s) of abuse.

34). Describe soldier morale, feelings and emotional state prior to and after these incidents?

35). Was this incident reported to the chain of command? How, when & what was done? What would you have done?

36). How could the incident have been prevented?

37). Describe any unit training or other programs that you are aware of that teach leaders and soldiers how to recognize and resolve combat stress.

38). What measures are in place to boost morale or to relieve stress?

39). What measures could the command enact to improve the morale and command climate of your unit?

m. Chaplain

1). Are Detainees allowed to practice their religion? Is there a chaplain available to minister to the detainees? Is the chaplain a Retained Personnel, US Forces chaplain, or a civilian?

2). What are your unit ministry team's responsibilities as part of the cadre for the detainees at this collection point / internment facility? (Looking for contraband the detainee might have hidden in their Koran?)

3). What are the procedures to bring local religious clergy members into the collection point or facility to help ministry to detainees?

4). Are you aware of your requirement to report abuse or suspected abuse of detainees?

5). Has any service member spoken with you about abusing detainees or seeing detainees being abused? If yes, can you provide details without violating your privilege information/ confidentially status between you and the service member? (We do not want names).

6). How many times have you heard about detainees being abused or mistreated? What did you hear?

7). Have you made the Chain of Command aware of these allegations of abuse and have you seen the Chain of Command do anything about correcting detainee abuse?

8). What is your feeling on how Detainees are being treated? No standard. Personnel observations and feelings.

9). What do you perceive as the mission of your unit? Describe the importance of your role in that mission.

10). Describe your working environment and living conditions since being in Theater.

11). Describe the unit command climate and soldier morale. Has it changed or evolved since you have been in Theater?

12). Are you aware of any incidences of detainee or other abuse in your unit?

13). ADVISEMENT OF RIGHTS (For military personnel)
The text of Article 31 provides as follows a. No person subject to this chapter may compel any person to incriminate himself or to answer any questions the answer to which may tend to incriminate him. b. No person subject to this chapter may interrogate or request any statement from an accused or a person suspected of an offense without first informing him of the nature of the accusation and advising him that he does not have to make any statement regarding the offense of which he is accused or suspected, and that any statement made by him may be used as evidence against him in a trial by court-martial. c. No person subject to this chapter may compel any person to make a statement or produce evidence before any military tribunal if the statement or evidence is not material to the issue and may tend to degrade him. d. No statement obtained from any person in violation of this article, or through the use of coercion, unlawful influence, or unlawful inducement, may be received in evidence against him in a trial by court-martial.

14). I am_____(grade, if any, and name), a member of the (DAIG). I am part of a team inspecting detainee operations, this is not a criminal investigation. I am reading you your rights because of a statement you made causes me to suspect that you may have committed _____. (specify offense, i.e., aggravated assault, assault, murder). Under Article 31, you have the right to remain silent, that is, say nothing at all. Any statement you make, oral or written, may be used as evidence against you in a trial by courts-martial or in other judicial or administrative proceedings. You have the right to consult a lawyer and to have a lawyer present during this interview. You have the right to military legal counsel free of charge. In addition to military counsel, you are entitled to civilian counsel of your own choosing, at your own expense. You may request a lawyer at any time during this interview. If you decide to answer questions, you may stop the questioning at any time. Do you understand your rights? Do you want a lawyer? (If the answer is yes, cease all questions at this point). Are you willing to answer questions?

15). Describe what you understand happened leading up to and during the incident(s) of abuse.

16). Describe soldier morale, feelings and emotional state prior to and after these incidents?

17). Was this incident reported to the chain of command? How, when & what was done? What would you have done?

18). How could the incident have been prevented?

19). Describe any unit training or other programs that you are aware of that teach leaders and soldiers how to recognize and resolve combat stress.

20). What measures are in place to boost morale or to relieve stress?

21). What measures could the command enact to improve the morale and command climate of your unit

m. S-4 (INTERNMENT FACILITY)

1). Concerning logistical operations, what is your role in the support of (Theater/Division) Detainee Operations?

2). What references/standards/publications do you use to conduct Detainee Operations or does your operation depend solely on existing SOPs, OPORDs, FRAGOs, supply/logistic requests?

3). What Home Station Training did your unit conduct prior to deployment to help the unit (and you) prepare for this mission? Describe it.

4). Describe how your unit plans and procures logistical support for Detainee Operations. (include: transportation, subsistence, organizational, and NBC clothing and equipment items, distribution, laundry, and bath equipment) What are the procedures for transporting and evacuating Detainees? Have you ever coordinated for transportation to evacuate Detainees out of the AOR? Who approved the transfer?

5). Do you have any responsibilities for feeding the detainees? If so, are the daily food rations sufficient in quantity and quality and variety to keep Detainees in good health and LAW with their cultural requirements? How and what are they being fed? Please elaborate.

6). Do detainees have adequate furnishings for sleeping and eating (does it include bedding/blankets)? Is the supply system in place allowing you to replace or procure necessary furnishings? Is there a means to launder clothing items for the Detainees here at this facility

7). How do Detainees receive fresh potable water in your area of responsibility? (Bottled water, Lister bags, running water – if so, is it potable)?

8). What procedures are in place to account for and dispose of captured enemy supplies and equipment?

9). How are personal hygiene items and needed clothing being supplied to the Detainees? What precisely are provided to them? Do detainees have access to sundry items?

10). What do you perceive to be doctrinal logistic shortcomings pertaining to Detainee Operations and how would you fix/incorporate into updated doctrine/accomplish differently?

11). What are your biggest issues concerning logistical support for Detainee Operations?

12). What are your biggest issues concerning adequate facilities for Detainees? Who provides engineer support to this facility? What is your relationship with the engineer? (If the S-4 provides engineer support, then ask the Engineer Support to Internment Facility Questions.)

13). Are you aware of your requirement to report abuse or suspected abuse of detainees?

14). Do your subordinates know the reporting procedures if they observe or become aware of a Detainee being abused?

15). What steps would you take if a subordinate reported to you an incident of alleged Detainee abuse?

16). Do you feel you can freely report an incident of alleged Detainee abuse outside Command channels (IG, CID)?

17). What procedures do you have to report suspected detainee abuse (IG, CID, Next Level Commander)?

18). What procedures are in place for Detainees to report alleged abuse?

19). What do you perceive as the mission of your unit? Describe the importance of your role in that mission.

20). Describe your working environment and living conditions since being in Theater.

21). Describe the unit command climate and Soldier morale. Has it changed or evolved since you have been in Theater?

22). Are you aware of any incidences of detainee or other abuse in your unit?

23). ADVISEMENT OF RIGHTS (For military personnel)
The text of Article 31 provides as follows a. No person subject to this chapter may compel any person to incriminate himself or to answer any questions the answer to which may tend to incriminate him. b. No person subject to this chapter may interrogate or request any statement from an accused or a person suspected of an offense without first informing him of the nature of the accusation and advising him that he does not have to make any statement regarding the offense of which he is accused or suspected, and that any statement made by him may be used as evidence against him in a trial by court-martial. c. No person subject to this chapter may compel any person to make a statement or produce evidence before any military tribunal if the statement or evidence is not material to the issue and may tend to degrade him. d. No statement obtained from any person in violation of this article, or through the use of coercion, unlawful influence, or unlawful inducement, may be received in evidence against him in a trial by court-martial.

24). I am_____(grade, if any, and name), a member of the (DAIG). I am part of a team inspecting detainee operations, this is not a criminal investigation. I am reading you your rights because of a statement you made causes me to suspect that you may have committed_____.(specify offense, i.e., aggravated assault, assault, murder). Under Article 31, you have the right to remain silent, that is, say nothing at all. Any statement you make, oral or written, may be used as evidence against you in a trial by courts-martial or in other judicial or administrative proceedings. You have the right to consult a lawyer and to have a lawyer present during this interview. You have the right to military legal counsel free of charge. In addition to military counsel, you are entitled to civilian counsel of your own choosing, at your own expense. You may request a lawyer at any time during this interview. If you decide to answer questions, you may stop the questioning at any time. Do you understand your rights? Do you want a lawyer? (If the answer is yes, cease all questions at this point). Are you willing to answer questions?

25). Describe what you understand happened leading up to and during the incident(s) of abuse.

26). Describe soldier morale, feelings and emotional state prior to and after these incidents?

27). Was this incident reported to the chain of command? How, when & what was done? What would you have done?

28). How could the incident have been prevented?

29). Describe any unit training or other programs that you are aware of that teach leaders and soldiers how to recognize and resolve combat stress.

30). What measures are in place to boost morale or to relieve stress?

31). What measures could the command enact to improve the morale and command climate of your unit?

n. CID Special Agent

1). What is your involvement with detainee abuse investigations? Please provide a general description of the quantity and type of investigations that you were involved in?

2). Can you list the detainee facilities that these incidents occurred?

3). During those investigations did you establish the motives for soldiers that abused detainees? If so, please list the motives you uncovered and explain each individually in as much detail as possible.

4). During those investigations, did you establish any deficiencies regarding training of those persons who committed abuse? If so, please explain?

5). During those investigations, did you establish any deficiencies in regards to the leadership of those who committed abuse? If so, please explain?

6). During those investigations, did you establish if the environmental factors (length of work day, shift schedule, living conditions, weather, food, etc . . .) might have been the cause of abuse? If so, explain?

7). During those investigations, did you determine if combat stress was a cause of the abuse? If so, please explain.

8). During those investigations did you establish if the assignment of MOS' that do not normally deal with detainee operations had an impact on those soldiers abusing detainees. If so, please explain.

9). During these investigations did you establish any patterns as far as one unit having more soldiers who abused detainees, or a specific MOS that had more soldiers who abused detainees. Did you see any specific patterns?

10). Is there anything else that you may have observed that you felt was the cause of those soldiers abusing detainees?

11). What do you perceive as the mission of your unit? Describe the importance of your role in that mission.

12). Describe your working environment and living conditions since being in Theater.

13). Describe the unit command climate and Soldier morale. Has it changed or evolved since you have been in Theater?

14). Are you aware of any incidences of detainee or other abuse in your unit?

15). ADVISEMENT OF RIGHTS (For military personnel)
The text of Article 31 provides as follows a. No person subject to this chapter may compel any person to incriminate himself or to answer any questions the answer to which may tend to incriminate him. b. No person subject to this chapter may interrogate or request any statement from an accused or a person suspected of an offense without first informing him of the nature of the accusation and advising him that he does not have to make any statement regarding the offense of which he is accused or suspected, and that any statement made by him may be used as evidence against him in a trial by court-martial. c. No person subject to this chapter may compel any person to make a statement or produce evidence before any military tribunal if the statement or evidence is not material to the issue and may tend to degrade him. d. No statement obtained from any person in violation

of this article, or through the use of coercion, unlawful influence, or unlawful inducement, may be received in evidence against him in a trial by court-martial.

16). I am_____(grade, if any, and name), a member of the (DAIG). I am part of a team inspecting detainee operations, this is not a criminal investigation. I am reading you your rights because of a statement you made causes me to suspect that you may have committed_____. (specify offense, i.e., aggravated assault, assault, murder). Under Article 31, you have the right to remain silent, that is, say nothing at all. Any statement you make, oral or written, may be used as evidence against you in a trial by courts-martial or in other judicial or administrative proceedings. You have the right to consult a lawyer and to have a lawyer present during this interview. You have the right to military legal counsel free of charge. In addition to military counsel, you are entitled to civilian counsel of your own choosing, at your own expense. You may request a lawyer at any time during this interview. If you decide to answer questions, you may stop the questioning at any time. Do you understand your rights? Do you want a lawyer? (If the answer is yes, cease all questions at this point). Are you willing to answer questions?

17). Describe what you understand happened leading up to and during the incident(s) of abuse.

18). Describe soldier morale, feelings and emotional state prior to and after these incidents?

19). Was this incident reported to the chain of command? How, when & what was done? What would you have done?

20). How could the incident have been prevented?

21). Describe any unit training or other programs that you are aware of that teach leaders and soldiers how to recognize and resolve combat stress.

22). What measures are in place to boost morale or to relieve stress

23). What measures could the command enact to improve the morale and command climate of your unit?

n. ENGINEER SUPPORT TO INTERNMENT FACILITIES (MP BDE/BN)

1). What is your role in assisting this unit to maintain the security and safeguarding of Detainees at this interment facility?

2). What is the maximum capacity for this particular facility? What is the current Detainee population? What is your plan for surge? (tentage, latrines, etc)

3). What standards were used in establishing this internment facility? What standards do you use in providing engineer support for this facility? Have any facility standards been waived, and if so, by whom, and why?

4). Why was this facility picked as an internment facility (permanent)? What makes this the place of choice? Who decided the location of this facility?

5). What are some of the services being contracted out/outsourced to support Detainee Operations in Theater? (Custodial, Garbage, etc.) What are issues concerning contracting or budget that you are aware of that impact Detainee Operations? If so, what are they? Who oversees these contracts that support Detainee Operations (CORs)?

6). What do you know about the Engineer Corps' Theater Construction Management System (TCSM). Were you aware that they have plans, specifications, and materiel requirements for Internment Facilities based on Detainee population?

7). What is the minimum living space standard for each Detainee? Who set the provisions of minimum living space for this facility (Engineers are managers of real property) (when possible, consult the preventative medicine authority in theater for provisions of minimum living space and sanitary facilities). What is your relationship with the preventive medicine expert? Has a preventative medicine expert given advice on this?

8). Describe the latrine facilities for Detainees' use (do they have access to it day and night and does it conform to the rules of hygiene and do females have separate facilities. Are they serviced with running water)? How are they cleaned and how often, and by whom (Contracted?)? Where do they bathe and conduct other personal hygiene? How recently has a preventative medicine expert inspected the latrine and personal hygiene facilities?

9). Is the sewage system intact? If not, what are the problems and what is being done to fix. What is used in lieu of?

10). Describe your lighting system for the internment facility. How does it enhance the security of the facility? Does the facility have emergency lighting/power capability? Describe the system. How about the electrical distribution system? What are your problems with the system?

11). How do the Detainees receive fresh potable water (Bottled water, Lister bags, running water – if so, is it potable)? How reliable is the (running) water distribution system (any breakdowns and if so, how often)?

12). How about heating during the winter? What fire prevention/safety measures are in place? Describe major problems in these areas.

13). Describe the facilities where the Detainees eat? (Is there a kitchen facility), what equipment do you have in place?

14). Do you train and supervise internal and external labor (CIs) (construction and repair of facilities)? If so, describe the work ((construction, maintenance, repair, and operation of utilities (water, electricity, heat, and sanitation.)

15). How do you prioritize your maintenance and repair? What is your backlog on work orders? Are there any future plans for this facility in terms of renovation or expansion? Please describe (how will they use swing space).

16). Are you aware of your requirement to report abuse or suspected abuse of detainees?

17). Do your subordinates know the reporting procedures if they observe or become aware of a Detainee being abused?

18). What steps would you take if a subordinate reported to you an incident of alleged Detainee abuse?

19). Do you feel you can freely report an incident of alleged Detainee abuse outside Command channels (IG, CID)

20). What procedures do you have to report suspected detainee abuse (IG, CID, Next Level Commander)

21). What procedures are in place for Detainees to report alleged abuse?

22). What do you perceive as the mission of your unit? Describe the importance of your role in that mission

23). Describe your working environment and living conditions since being in Theater.

24). Describe the unit command climate and Soldier morale. Has it changed or evolved since you have been in Theater?

25). Are you aware of any incidences of detainee or other abuse in your unit?

26). ADVISEMENT OF RIGHTS (For military personnel)
The text of Article 31 provides as follows a. No person subject to this chapter may compel any person to incriminate himself or to answer any questions the answer to which may tend to incriminate him. b. No person subject to this chapter may interrogate or request any statement from an accused or a person suspected of an offense without first informing him of the nature of the accusation and advising him that he does not have to make any statement regarding the offense of which he is accused or suspected, and that any statement made by him may be used as evidence against him in a trial by court-martial. c. No person subject to this chapter may compel any person to make a statement or produce evidence before any military tribunal if the statement or evidence is not material to the issue and may tend to degrade him. d. No statement obtained from any person in violation of this article, or through the use of coercion, unlawful influence, or unlawful inducement, may be received in evidence against him in a trial by court-martial.

27). I am_____(grade, if any, and name), a member of the (DAIG). I am part of
    a team inspecting detainee operations, this is not a criminal investigation. I am reading you your rights because of a statement you made causes me to suspect that you may have committed_____. (specify offense, i.e., aggravated assault, assault, murder). Under Article 31, you have the right to remain silent, that is, say nothing at all. Any statement you make, oral or written, may be used as evidence against you in a trial by courts-martial or in other judicial or administrative proceedings. You have the right to consult a lawyer and to have a lawyer present during this interview. You have the right to military legal counsel free of charge. In addition to military counsel, you are entitled to civilian counsel of your own choosing, at your own expense. You may request a lawyer at any time during this interview. If you decide to answer questions, you may stop the questioning at any time. Do you understand your rights? Do you want a lawyer? (If the answer is yes, cease all questions at this point). Are you willing to answer questions?

28). Describe what you understand happened leading up to and during the incident(s) of abuse.

29). Describe soldier morale, feelings and emotional state prior to and after these incidents?

30). Was this incident reported to the chain of command? How, when & what was done? What would you have done?

31). How could the incident have been prevented?

32). Describe any unit training or other programs that you are aware of that teach leaders and soldiers how to recognize and resolve combat stress.

33). What measures are in place to boost morale or to relieve stress?

34). What measures could the command enact to improve the morale and command climate of your unit?

o. MEDICAL OFFICER / PREVENTIVE MEDICAL OFFICER

1). What medical requirements in support of the detainee program were identified in the medical annexes of relevant OPLANs, OPORDs, and other contingency planning documents? What identified requirements were actually allocated? What procedures were specified in these documents

2). What training, specific to detainee medical operations, did you receive prior to this deployment? What training have you received during this deployment?

3). What are the minimum medical care and field sanitation standards for collection points/internment facilities? What have you observed when detainees are received at collection points/internment facilities? (Describe the process)

4). How often are the collection points/internment facilities inspected (PVNTMED inspections)? Who performs the inspections (field sanitation team, PVNTMED detachment)? What do the inspections consist of? What do you do with the results of the inspections? Are the appropriate commanders taking the necessary actions to correct the shortcomings noted during your monthly medical inspections? Have you observed any recurring deficiencies during your inspections?

5). How do you ensure that each unit has a field sanitation team and all necessary field sanitation supplies? What PVNTMED personnel are assigned to MP units responsible for detention operations?

6). How are detainees initially evaluated (screened) and treated for medical conditions (same as US)? Who performs the screening? What do you do if a detainee is suspected of having a communicable disease (isolated)?

7). How often do you or your staff conduct routine medical inspections (examinations) of detainees? What does the medical evaluation consist of? What is the purpose of the medical examination? How are the results recorded/reported?

8). Does every internment facility have an infirmary? If not, why not? How do (detainees request medical care? What are the major reasons detainees require medical care? Have any detainees been denied medical treatment or has medical attention been delayed? If so, why?

9). How do detainees obtain personal hygiene products?

10). What are the procedures for the transfer of custody of detainees to/from the infirmary for medical treatment? How is security maintained when a detainee is transferred to a medical facility? (Database, form, etc)

11). What are the procedures for repatriation of sick and wounded detainees? Who is eligible for repatriation based on a medical condition? How do you interact with the Mixed Medical Commission (EPW/RP only)?

12). Who maintains medical records of detainees? How are these maintained and accessed? What is kept in the medical record? Who collects, analyzes, reports, and responds to detainee DNBI data?

13). What are the standards for detainee working conditions? Who monitors and enforces them? Who administers the safety program? What is included in the safety program? How does a detainee apply for work-related disability compensation?

14). How are retained medical personnel identified? What special conditions apply to them? How are they employed in the care of detainees? How are they certified as proficient? Who supervises them?

15). What measures are taken to protect US personnel from contracting diseases carried by detainees? Who monitors/enforces these procedures?

16). What kind of stress counseling do you provide to Soldiers/Guards of detainees?

17). What are the procedures if a detainee in U.S. custody dies?

18). What do you perceive to be doctrinal medical shortcomings pertaining to detainee operations? How would you fix/incorporate into updated doctrine/accomplish differently? Does the current force structure of the Medical/MS/SP Corps support the successful accomplishment of detainee operations? What are the shortcomings, and how do we fix the problem at the Army level?

19). If you noticed any markings and/or injuries on a detainee that might lead you to believe the detainee was being abused, what would you do with the information? Do your subordinates know the reporting procedures if they observe or become aware of a detainee being abused?

20). Overall, how do you feel detainees are being treated at the infirmary, collection points and/or detention facilities? What systemic weaknesses have you identified?

21). What AARs or lessons learned have you written or received regarding detainee operations? Can I get a copy?

22). What do you perceive as the mission of your unit? Describe the importance of your role in that mission.

23). Describe your working environment and living conditions since being in Theater.

24). Describe the unit command climate and Soldier morale. Has it changed or evolved since you have been in Theater?

25). Are you aware of any incidences of detainee or other abuse in your unit?

26). ADVISEMENT OF RIGHTS (For military personnel)
The text of Article 31 provides as follows a. No person subject to this chapter may compel any person to incriminate himself or to answer any questions the answer to which may tend to incriminate him. b. No person subject to this chapter may interrogate or request any statement from an accused or a person suspected of an offense without first informing him of the nature of the accusation and advising him that he does not have to make any statement regarding the offense of which he is accused or suspected, and that any statement made by him may be used as evidence against him in a trial by court-martial. c. No person subject to this chapter may compel any person to make a statement or produce evidence before any military tribunal if the statement or evidence is not material to the issue and may tend to degrade him. d. No statement obtained from any person in violation of this article, or through the use of coercion, unlawful influence, or unlawful inducement, may be received in evidence against him in a trial by court-martial.

27). I am_____(grade, if any, and name), a member of the (DAIG). I am part of a team inspecting detainee operations, this is not a criminal investigation. I am reading you your rights because of a statement you made causes me to suspect that you may have committed_____. (specify offense, i.e., aggravated assault, assault, murder). Under Article 31, you have the right to remain silent, that is, say nothing at all. Any statement you make, oral or written, may be used as evidence against you in a trial by courts-martial or in other judicial or administrative proceedings. You have the right to consult a lawyer and to have a lawyer present during this interview. You have the right to military legal counsel free of charge. In addition to military counsel, you are entitled to civilian counsel of your own choosing, at your own expense. You may request a lawyer at any time during this interview. If you decide to answer questions, you may stop the questioning at any time. Do you understand your rights? Do you want a lawyer? (If the answer is yes, cease all questions at this point). Are you willing to answer questions?

28). Describe what you understand happened leading up to and during the incident(s) of abuse.

29). Describe soldier morale, feelings and emotional state prior to and after these incidents?

30). Was this incident reported to the chain of command? How, when & what was done? What would you have done?

31). How could the incident have been prevented?

32). Describe any unit training or other programs that you are aware of that teach leaders and soldiers how to recognize and resolve combat stress.

33). What measures are in place to boost morale or to relieve stress?

34). What measures could the command enact to improve the morale and command climate of your unit?

p. NCOIC GUARD FORCE COLLECTION POINT & INTERNMENT FACILITY

1). How did you prepare yourself and your soldiers to become familiar with and understand the applicable regulations, OPORDS/FRAGOs directives, international laws and administrative procedures to operate an I/R facility or Collection Point?

2). Did you and all of your soldiers undergo Law of War training prior to deployment? Explain what training occurred. What is your plan to train new soldiers (replacements) to the unit? Did this training include the treatment of Detainees? Explain.

3). What policies/procedures does your unit have in place to support the U.S. policy relative to the humane treatment of Detainees?

4). Does your unit have a formal training program for the care and control of Detainees? Describe what it includes. (For Permanent Internment Facilities only)

5). What training did your unit receive on the established Rules of Engagement (ROE)? How often does this occur? Does this training include Rules of Interaction (ROI)?

6). What procedures do you have in place to ensure soldiers understand the use of force and rules of engagement for the interment facility/collection point?

7). What guidance or policies do you have to ensure fraternization is not taking place between U.S. military personnel and the detainees?

8). Describe the training the guard force received to prepare them for their duties (5Ss & T)) How does your unit conduct sustainment training for Detainee Operations in Theater? How often does this occur and please describe it? When did your unit last conduct this training?

9). What Home Station/Mob Site Training did your unit conduct prior to deployment to help your unit prepare for Detainee Operations? Describe it. How did the training prepare you to conduct Detainee Operations for this deployment? What are your unit's strengths and weaknesses? How did this training distinguish between the different categories of Detainees (EPWs, RPs, CIs, etc.)?

10). Describe the training you received during your last Military Institutional School (BNCOC/ANCOC) in handling/processing Detainees. How was it helpful in preparing you for Detainee Operations? How would you improve the training at the schoolhouse?

11). What are some of the basic operations of the collection point/internment facility? Is there a copy of the Geneva Convention posted in the detainee's home language within these camps? Are camps segregating Detainees by nationality, language, rank, and sex? How are captured Medical personnel and Chaplains being used in the camps? What provisions are in place for the receipt and distribution of Detainee correspondence/mail? Are the daily food rations sufficient in quantity or quality and variety to keep detainees in good health? Are personal hygiene items and needed clothing being supplied to the Detainees? Are the conditions within the camp sanitary enough to ensure a clean and healthy environment free from disease and epidemics? Is there an infirmary located within the camp?

12). What control measures are your unit using to maintain discipline and security in the collection point/internment facility?

13). What procedures are in place to account for and dispose of captured enemy supplies and equipment? What procedures are in place to process personnel, equipment, and evidence?

14). What is your ratio of guards to detainees in your collection point/internment facility? Is this ratio the proper mix for you to perform your mission? If not, what are the shortfalls? Why are their shortfalls? How do these shortfalls impact your mission?

15). How are you organized to handle the different categories of personnel (EPW, CI, OD, females, juveniles and refugees)? Do you maintain a separate site for sick or wounded Detainees? If so where is it and how does your unit maintain the security and safeguarding of Detainees there?

16). What is the number of personnel needed to escort prisoners internally and externally? (i.e. for medical, evacuation, etc.)?

17). What are the procedures for transporting and evacuating detainees? What are the procedures for transferring Detainees from the collection points to US Military controlled detention facilities? How is the transfer of Detainees handled between different services?

18). What are the procedures for the transfer of custody of Detainees from the collection points/internment facility to Military Intelligence/OGA personnel? When the detainee is returned to the guard force, what procedures occur with the detainee? (in processing, medical screening, suicide watch, observation report DD Form 2713?, etc)

19). What MP units (guards, escort, detachments) do you have at your disposal to operate and maintain this collection point/internment facility? What non-MP units are you using to help operate this collection point/internment facility? If you do not use MP teams, what forces are required to operate the Collection Point (guard, security etc)? Do you have any shortfalls in performing the Collection Point mission? How does this affect your doctrinal mission? How long are you holding Detainees at the collection point? Is holding the detainees longer than the 12/24 hours impacting on your units' ability to perform its mission? Why?

20). Describe how this unit is able to maintain the security and safeguarding of Detainees at this interment facility/collection point. Describe your security requirements. (What are your clear zones? How do your Guard Towers permit an unobstructed view of the clear zone and how do they allow for overlapping fields of fire? Describe your perimeter security.

21). How do you maintain a high state of discipline with your soldiers to enhance the internal and external security of the internment facility/Collection Point?

22). Does this facility include Sally Ports? Describe the system in place.

23). What do you have in place for communications (between guards/towers and the TOC/C^2)? What problems do you have? How do you overcome them?

24). Describe the latrine facilities for Detainees' use (do they have access to it day and night and does it conform to the rules of hygiene and do females have separate facilities). How are they cleaned and how often and by whom? Where do they bathe and conduct other personal hygiene (this will depend how long it takes to evacuate Detainees to U.S. Military Controlled Detention Facilities – 12/24 hours is the standard)?

25). How do the Detainees receive fresh water (Bottled water or Lister bag)?

26). Can you give some examples of contraband? What are the procedures when you find contraband?? (i.e., knives, narcotics, weapons, currency)

27). Describe your lighting systems at the Facility/Collection Point (how does it affect security?). How about heating during the winter? What fire prevention/safety measures are in place?

28). How are Detainee complaints and requests to the camp commander processed?

29). What are your shortcomings/problems in feeding the population? What is the menu of the population?

30). What problems, if any, do you feel the unit has regarding manning or personnel resourcing in conducting Detention Operations? What about the number of personnel to control the detention operation in regards to riot control?

31). What personal equipment is the unit experiencing as a shortfall concerning detainee operations, (i.e., restraints, uniforms, CIF items, weapons, etc?

32). What types of supplies is greater in-demand for the unit during detainee operations? And are these items regularly filled? What major shortfalls has the unit encountered in regard to material and supply distribution?

33). What transportation problems is the unit experiencing to move detainees during the operation?

34). What safety programs/policies are currently being used in the Detainee camps?

35). Do you know of the procedures to get stress counseling (Psychiatrist, Chaplain, Medical)? Do your soldiers know of the procedures to get counseling (Psychiatrist, Chaplain, Medical)?

36). Are you aware of your requirement to report abuse or suspected abuse of detainees?

37). Do your subordinates know the reporting procedures if they observe or become aware of a Detainee being abused?

38). What steps would you take if a subordinate reported to you an incident of alleged Detainee abuse?

39). Do you feel you can freely report an incident of alleged Detainee abuse outside Command channels (IG, CID)?

40). What procedures do you have to report suspected detainee abuse (IG, CID, Next Level Commander)?

41). What systems are in place for detainees to report alleged abuse?

42). What do you perceive as the mission of your unit? Describe the importance of your role in that mission.

43). Describe your working environment and living conditions since being in Theater.

44). Describe the unit command climate and soldier morale. Has it changed or evolved since you have been in Theater?

45). Are you aware of any incidences of detainee or other abuse in your unit?

46). ADVISEMENT OF RIGHTS (For military personnel)
The text of Article 31 provides as follows a. No person subject to this chapter may compel any person to incriminate himself or to answer any questions the answer to which may tend to incriminate him. b. No person subject to this chapter may interrogate or request any statement from an accused or a person suspected of an offense without first informing him of the nature of the accusation and advising him that he does not have to make any statement regarding the offense of which he is accused or suspected, and that any statement made by him may be used as evidence against him in a trial by court-martial. c. No person subject to this chapter may compel any person to make a statement or produce evidence before any military tribunal if the statement or evidence is not material to the issue and may tend to degrade him. d. No statement obtained from any person in violation of this article, or through the use of coercion, unlawful influence, or unlawful inducement, may be received in evidence against him in a trial by court-martial.

47). I am_____(grade, if any, and name), a member of the (DAIG). I am part of a team inspecting detainee operations, this is not a criminal investigation. I am reading you your rights because of a statement you made causes me to suspect that you may have committed_____. (specify offense, i.e., aggravated assault, assault, murder). Under Article 31, you have the right to remain silent, that is, say nothing at all. Any statement you make, oral or written, may be used as evidence against you in a trial by courts-martial or in other judicial or administrative proceedings. You have the right to consult a lawyer and to have a lawyer present during this interview. You have the right to military legal counsel free of charge. In addition to military counsel, you are entitled to civilian counsel of your own choosing, at your own expense. You may request a lawyer at any time during this interview. If you decide to answer questions, you may stop the questioning at any time. Do you understand your rights? Do you want a lawyer? (If the answer is yes, cease all questions at this point). Are you willing to answer questions?

48). Describe what you understand happened leading up to and during the incident(s) of abuse.

49). Describe soldier morale, feelings and emotional state prior to and after these incidents?

50). Was this incident reported to the chain of command? How, when & what was done? What would you have done?

51). How could the incident have been prevented?

52). Describe any unit training or other programs that you are aware of that teach leaders and soldiers how to recognize and resolve combat stress.

53). What measures are in place to boost morale or to relieve stress

54). What measures could the command enact to improve the morale and command climate of your unit?

q. POINT OF CAPTURE–CDR/1SG/PL/PS

1). How did you prepare yourself and your junior leaders to become familiar with and understand the applicable regulations, OPORDS/FRAGOs directives, international laws and administrative procedures to operate a unit Collection Point?

2). Did you and all of your soldiers undergo Law of War training prior to deployment? Explain what training occurred. Did this training include the treatment of Detainees? Is there a plan to train new Soldiers (replacements) to the unit? Explain.

3). What Home Station/Mob Site Training did your unit conduct prior to deployment to help your unit prepare for Detainee Operations? Describe it. How did the training prepare you to conduct Detainee Operations for this deployment? How did this training distinguish between the different categories of Detainees (EPWs, RPs, CIs, etc.)?

4). What training did you receive on the established Rules of Engagement (ROE)? How often does this occur? Does this training include Rules of Interaction (ROI)?

5). Describe the training you received at the last Professional Military Education on handling/processing Detainees. How was it helpful in preparing you for Detainee Operations? How would you improve the training at the schoolhouse?

6). Describe the training the guard force received to prepare them for their duties. How do you ensure your guards understand their orders?

7). How does your unit conduct sustainment training for Detainee Operations? How often does this occur and please describe it? When did your unit last conduct this training?

8). (CDR/1SG) What are your policies on the establishment of a unit holding area? How do you ensure that these areas operate IAW Law of War?

9). (PL/PS) What is the units' policy on the establishment of a unit holding area? How do you know that you are operating the holding areas IAW Law of War? ?

10). How do you administratively process each detainee, (i.e., tagging pax and equipment, evidence, witness statements, etc.)?

11). How do you maintain good morale and discipline with soldiers and leaders to enhance the security of the unit collection point?

12). What procedures do you have in place to ensure soldiers and leaders understand the use of force and rules of engagement for the unit collection point? (ROE Card, sustainment tng, etc)

13). What procedures are in place to dispose of captured contraband (enemy supplies and equipment)?

14). (CDR/1SG) What policies/procedures do you have in place to ensure that all Detainees are protected, safeguarded, and accounted for (5Ss & T)? What policies/procedures does your unit have to ensure the humane treatment of Detainees?

15). What are your procedures for questioning Detainees? (Is interrogation taking place?) Who is interrogating the detainees?

16). What are your procedures to evacuate a detainee from the point of capture to the Battalion/Brigade collection point? What transportation problems is the unit experiencing either to move troops or detainees during the operation? How do you process detainees too sick or wounded to be evacuated?

17). What is the number of personnel that is needed to move prisoners within the holding area and then to higher? (i.e., for medical sick call, evacuation, etc.)?

18). What medical personnel are available to support DO?

19). What procedures are in place when a detainee in US custody dies?

20). What equipment is the unit experiencing as a shortfall concerning detainee operations, (i.e., restraints, uniforms, CIF items, radios, weapons, etc.)?

21). (CDR) Are any of these USR shortages and if so are you reporting them on your USR?

22). What types of supplies is greater in-demand for the unit during detainee operations? What about health and comfort items? And are these items regularly filled?

23). What duties put the most stress on soldiers in terms of personnel resources?

24). What is the most important factor that you would address in terms of personnel resources in regard to a successful detainee operation?

25). What AARs or lessons learned have you written or received regarding detainee operations? Can I get a copy?

26). Do you know of the procedures to get stress counseling (Psychiatrist, Chaplain, Medical)? Do your soldiers know of the procedures to get counseling (Psychiatrist, Chaplain, Medical)?

27). Are you aware of your requirement to report abuse or suspected abuse of detainees?

28). Do your subordinates know the reporting procedures if they observe or become aware of a Detainee being abused?

29). What steps would you take if a subordinate reported to you an incident of alleged Detainee abuse?

30). Do you feel you can freely report an incident of alleged Detainee abuse outside Command channels (IG, CID)?

31). What procedures do you have to report suspected detainee abuse (IG, CID, Next Level Commander)?

32). What systems are in place for detainees to report alleged abuse?

33). What do you perceive as the mission of your unit? Describe the importance of your role in that mission.

34). Describe your working environment and living conditions since being in Theater.

35). Describe the unit command climate and soldier morale. Has it changed or evolved since you have been in Theater?

36). Are you aware of any incidences of detainee or other abuse in your unit?

37). ADVISEMENT OF RIGHTS (For military personnel)
The text of Article 31 provides as follows a. No person subject to this chapter may compel any person to incriminate himself or to answer any questions the answer to which may tend to incriminate him. b. No person subject to this chapter may interrogate or request any statement from an accused or a person suspected of an offense without first informing him of the nature of the accusation and advising him that he does not have to make any statement regarding the offense of which he is accused or suspected, and that any statement made by him may be used as evidence against him in a trial by court-martial. c. No person subject to this chapter may compel any person to make a statement or produce evidence before any military tribunal if the statement or evidence is not material to the issue and may tend to degrade him. d. No statement obtained from any person in violation of this article, or through the use of coercion, unlawful influence, or unlawful inducement, may be received in evidence against him in a trial by court-martial.

38). I am_____(grade, if any, and name), a member of the (DAIG). I am part of a team inspecting detainee operations, this is not a criminal investigation. I am reading you your rights because of a statement you made causes me to suspect that you may have committed_____. (specify offense, i.e., aggravated assault, assault, murder). Under Article 31, you have the right to remain silent, that is, say nothing at all. Any statement you make, oral or written, may be used as evidence against you in a trial by courts-martial or in other judicial or administrative proceedings. You have the right to consult a lawyer and to have a lawyer present during this interview. You have the right to military legal counsel free of charge. In addition to military counsel, you are entitled to civilian counsel of your own choosing, at your own expense. You may request a lawyer at any time during this interview. If you decide to answer questions, you may stop the questioning at any time. Do you understand your rights? Do you want a lawyer? (If the answer is yes, cease all questions at this point). Are you willing to answer questions?

39). Describe what you understand happened leading up to and during the incident(s) of abuse.

40). Describe soldier morale, feelings and emotional state prior to and after these incidents?

41). Was this incident reported to the chain of command? How, when & what was done? What would you have done?

42). How could the incident have been prevented?

43). Describe any unit training or other programs that you are aware of that teach leaders and soldiers how to recognize and resolve combat stress.

44). What measures are in place to boost morale or to relieve stress?

45). What measures could the command enact to improve the morale and command climate of your unit?

r. DETAINEE ADMINISTRATION COLLECTION POINT/INTERNMENT FACILITY

1). Can you tell me what basic publications that you use to get doctrine and standards for Detainee Operations? How are you applying standards/doctrine to your processing of Detainees?

2). How often does your immediate supervisor/commander come here to ensure that Detainee Operations is conducted in compliance with the international Law of war? How about other commanders in your chain of command?

3). Describe the in processing for Detainees at this Collection Point/Internment Facility. (tagging, equipment, evidence, sworn statements, etc)? By what means are they transported here? ? How long do Detainees typically stay here (12/24 hours is the standard for each location of captivity until they get to the Long Term Detention Facility)? How long does it typically take Detainees to get here after capture? How are they out-processed and where do they go? How are they transported to the next higher level facility/Collection Point? (What is the documentation required for the transfer of prisoners/Civilian Internees? (What is the documentation required for the transfer of Detainees to other locations or to either MI Soldiers or other U.S. Government Agencies?)

4). What are the procedures for the transfer of custody of Detainees from the MP/Guard personnel to Military Intelligence personnel? When the detainee is returned to the guard force, what procedures occur? (what info is passed on to the Guard Force (type of reward?) . . . observation report, paper trail audit?)

5). What is your Detainee segregation policy? (EPWs, Females, Juveniles, Civilian Internees (to include those that are security threats, those that are hostile to coalition forces, and possible HTD/HVD), and Retained Persons, Criminals, etc.)) What can you tell me about the categories of Detainees that you are holding? What are they and what are the definitions of the different categories that you detain? How are you organized to handle the different categories of Detainees (EPW, CI, HVD, OD, and refugees?)

6). What happens to weapons/contraband confiscated from Detainees? What happens to personal property? (Is it disposed of/tagged along with the Detainee and is it stored properly and accounted for?) Why is the DD Form 2745 (Capture Tag) not being used in country? Who gave the authority not to use this form? What are units using in lieu of (if any)? ((Detainee Capture Card found in draft MTTP, Detainee Ops – this card does not require near as much data as DD 2745. The CPA Apprehension Form helps offset the lack of info on the Detainee, however it is in single copy (not the three required))) Who decided on the use of the Coalition Provisional Authority Apprehension Form? Why and under whose authority?

7). How are interpreters (linguists/translators) used in this Collection Point/Internment Facility? How many do you have at your disposal? How do you obtain them? Do you and your soldiers trust them?

8). (Collecting Point Only) Are the daily food rations sufficient in quantity or quality and variety to keep detainees in good health (How Much Food Do They Get)? Are personal hygiene items and needed clothing being supplied to the Detainees if they are kept longer than 12/24 hours here? Explain?

9). Are you aware of your requirement to report abuse or suspected abuse of detainees?

10). Do your subordinates know the reporting procedures if they observe or become aware of a Detainee being abused?

11). What steps would you take if a subordinate reported to you an incident of alleged Detainee abuse? Do you feel you can freely report an incident of alleged Detainee abuse outside Command channels (IG, CID)

12). What procedures do you have to report suspected detainee abuse (IG, CID, Next Level Commander)

13). What procedures are in place for Detainees to report alleged abuse?

14). What do you perceive as the mission of your unit? Describe the importance of your role in that mission.

15). Describe your working environment and living conditions since being in Theater.

16). Describe the unit command climate and soldier morale. Has it changed or evolved since you have been in Theater?

17). Are you aware of any incidences of detainee or other abuse in your unit?

18). ADVISEMENT OF RIGHTS (For military personnel) The text of Article 31 provides as follows a. No person subject to this chapter may compel any person to incriminate himself or to answer any questions the answer to which may tend to incriminate him. b. No person subject to this chapter may interrogate or request any statement from an accused or a person suspected of an offense without first informing him of the nature of the accusation and advising him that he does not have to make any statement regarding the offense of which he is accused or suspected, and that any statement made by him may be used as evidence against him in a trial by court-martial. c. No person subject to this chapter may compel any person to make a statement or produce evidence before any military tribunal if the statement or evidence is not material to the issue and may tend to degrade him. d. No statement obtained from any person in violation of this article, or through the use of coercion, unlawful influence, or unlawful inducement, may be received in evidence against him in a trial by court-martial.

19). I am _____ (grade, if any, and name), a member of the (DAIG). I am part of a team inspecting detainee operations, this is not a criminal investigation. I am reading you your rights because of a statement you made causes me to suspect that you may have committed _____. (specify offense, i.e., aggravated assault, assault, murder). Under Article 31, you have the right to remain silent, that is, say nothing at all. Any statement you make, oral or written, may be used as evidence against you in a trial by courts-martial or in other judicial or administrative proceedings. You have the right to consult a lawyer and to have a lawyer present during this interview. You have the right to military legal counsel free of charge. In addition to military counsel, you are entitled to civilian counsel of your own choosing, at your own expense. You may request a lawyer at any time during this interview. If you decide to answer questions, you may stop the questioning at any time. Do you understand your rights? Do you want a lawyer? (If the answer is yes, cease all questions at this point). Are you willing to answer questions?

20). Describe what you understand happened leading up to and during the incident(s) of abuse.

21). Describe soldier morale, feelings and emotional state prior to and after these incidents?

22). Was this incident reported to the chain of command? How, when & what was done? What would you have done?

23). How could the incident have been prevented?

24). Describe any unit training or other programs that you are aware of that teach leaders and soldiers how to recognize and resolve combat stress.

25). What measures are in place to boost morale or to relieve stress?

26). What measures could the command enact to improve the morale and command climate of your unit?

2. SENSING SESSION QUESTIONS

a. NCO (Point of Capture)

1). What regulations, directives, policies, are you aware of that deal with detainee operations?

2). Did you and all of your soldiers undergo Law of War/Geneva Convention training prior to deployment? Explain what training occurred. Did this training include the treatment of Detainees? What is your plan to train new soldiers (replacements) to the unit? Explain.

3). What training did your unit receive on the established Rules of Engagement (ROE)? How often does this occur? Does this training include Rules of Interaction (ROI) (How can you interact with the detainees)?

4). Does your unit conduct sustainment training for Detainee Operations? How often does this occur and please describe it? When did your unit last conduct this training?

5). What Home Station/Mob Site Training did your unit conduct prior to deployment to help your unit prepare for Detainee Operations? Describe it. How did the training prepare you to conduct Detainee Operations for this deployment? What are your unit's strengths and weaknesses? How did this training distinguish between the different categories of Detainees (EPWs, RPs, CIs, etc.)?

6). Describe the training you received During PLDC/BNCOC/ANCOC in handling/processing Detainees. How was it helpful in preparing you for Detainee Operations? How would you improve the training at the schoolhouse?

7). What procedures are in place to ensure soldiers understand the use of force and rules of engagement? (ROE Card? Etc)

8). How do you maintain discipline and security until the detainees are handed off to higher? Describe the training/GUIDANCE the guard force received to prepare them for their duties?

9). What is the minimum standard of treatment US soldiers must provide detainees? What policies/procedures does your unit have to ensure the humane treatment of Detainees? What procedures does your unit have in place to ensure that Detainees are protected, safeguarded, and accounted for?

10). How do you tag detainees for processing? (CPA Forces Apprehension Form, two sworn statements, EPW tag) What procedures do you go through? How do you tag equipment? (are they tagged with DD Form 2745)? What about evidence? What procedures do you use to process equipment/evidence? What about confiscated personal effects? Where do you store Detainees' confiscated personal effects (if any)?

11). What is your ratio of guards to detainees? Is this ratio the proper mix for you to perform your mission? If not, what are the shortfalls? Why are their shortfalls? How do these shortfalls impact your mission?

12). What is the number of personnel needed to maintain security for the detainees until they are processed to a higher collection point?

13). What is the number of personnel needed to move prisoners within the holding area (i.e., from one point to another, for medical, evacuation, etc.)?

14). How long do you keep detainees at the unit collection point? In relation to the Collection Point, how far away are your ammunition and fuel storage sites? Where is your Tactical Operation Center (TOC)? Where is your screening site where MI Soldiers interrogate Detainees?

15). Do you maintain a separate site for sick or wounded Detainees? If so, where is it and how does your unit maintain the security and safeguarding of Detainees there? How about female Detainees? How and where do you house them?

16). What are the procedures for transporting and evacuating detainees? What procedures are in place to account for or dispose of captured enemy supplies and equipment?

17). What transportation problems is the unit experiencing either to move troops or detainees during the operation?

18). What is the most important factor that you would address in terms of personnel resources in regards to a successful detainee operation?

19). What equipment is the unit experiencing as a shortfall concerning detainee operations, (i.e., restraints, uniforms, CIF items, weapons, etc)?

20). How do the Detainees receive fresh water (Bottled water or Lister bag)?

21). What types of supplies is greater in-demand for the unit during detainee operations? And are these items regularly filled?

22). What procedures are in place when a detainee in U S custody dies?

23). Do you know of the procedures to get stress counseling (Psychiatrist, Chaplain, Medical)? Do your soldiers know of the procedures to get counseling (Psychiatrist, Chaplain, Medical)?

24). Are you aware of your requirement to report abuse or suspected abuse of detainees?

25). Do your subordinates know the reporting procedures if they observe or become aware of a Detainee being abused?

26). What steps would you take if a subordinate reported to you an incident of alleged Detainee abuse?

27). Do you feel you can freely report an incident of alleged Detainee abuse outside Command channels (IG, CID)?

28). What procedures do you have to report suspected detainee abuse (IG, CID, Next Level Commander)?

29). What procedures are in place for detainees to report alleged abuse?

30). What do you perceive as the mission of your unit? Describe the importance of your role in that mission.

31). Describe your working environment and living conditions since being in Theater.

32). Describe the unit command climate and soldier morale. Has it changed or evolved since you have been in Theater?

33). Please provide by show of hands if you aware of any incidences of detainee or other abuse in your unit? (Those that raise their hands, need to be noted and interviewed individually afterward using the abuse questionnaire)

b. SOLDIER (Point of Capture)

1). Did you undergo Law of War training prior to deployment? Explain what training occurred. Did this training include the treatment of Detainees? Explain.

2). Describe the training/guidance you received to prepare you for handling/guarding the detainees. Does your unit conduct sustainment training for Detainee Operations in Theater? How often does this occur and please describe it? When did your unit last conduct this training?

3). What Home Station/Mob Site Training did your unit conduct prior to deployment to help your unit prepare for Detainee Operations? Describe it (5Ss & T). How did the training prepare you to conduct Detainee Operations for this deployment? What are your unit's strengths and weaknesses? How did this training distinguish between the different categories of Detainees (EPWs, RPs, CIs, etc.)? What training have you received to ensure your knowledge of DO is IAW the provisions under the Geneva Convention?

4). Describe the training you received during Basic Training in handling/processing Detainees. How was it helpful in preparing you for Detainee Operations? How would you improve the training at the schoolhouse?

5). How does your unit train on the established Rules of Engagement (ROE)? How often does this occur? Does this training include Rules of Interaction (ROI)? What about

Standards of Conduct? (How can you interact with the detainees)? What guidance or policies have you been trained/briefed on to ensure you understand interaction/ fraternization and that it is not taking place between U.S. military personnel and the detainees?

6). What procedures has your leadership developed to ensure you understand the use of force and the rules of engagement?

7). How is your unit ensuring that all Detainees are protected, safeguarded, and accounted for IAW the 5Ss & T?

8). How do you tag detainees for processing (CPA Form, DD Form 2745)? What procedures do you go through? How do you tag equipment (DD Form 2745, DA Form 4137)? What about evidence(DD Form 2745, DA Form 4137)? What procedures do you use to process equipment/evidence? What about confiscated personal effects? Where do you store Detainees' confiscated personal effects (if any)?

9). What are the procedures for transporting and evacuating detainees?

10). What transportation problems is the unit experiencing either to move troops or detainees during the operation?

11). What is the ratio of guards to detainees? Is this ratio the proper mix for you to perform your mission? If not, what are the shortfalls? Why are their shortfalls? How do these shortfalls impact your mission?

12). What equipment is the unit experiencing as a shortfall concerning detainee operations, (i.e., restraints, uniforms, CIF items, weapons, etc.)?

13). Describe the latrine facilities for Detainees' use (do they have access to it day and night and does it conform to the rules of hygiene and do females have separate facilities). How are they cleaned and how often and by whom? Where do they bathe and conduct other personal hygiene (this will depend how long it takes to evacuate Detainees to CO/BN?

14). How do the Detainees receive fresh water (Bottled water or Lister bag)?

15). Do you know of the procedures to get stress counseling (Psychiatrist, Chaplain, Medical)?

16). Are you aware of your requirement to report abuse or suspected abuse of detainees?

17). Do you feel you can freely report an incident of alleged Detainee abuse outside Command channels (IG, CID)?

18). What procedures do you have to report suspected detainee abuse (IG, CID, Next Level Commander)?

19). What procedures are in place for detainees to report alleged abuse?

20). What do you perceive as the mission of your unit? Describe the importance of your role in that mission.

21). Describe your working environment and living conditions since being in Theater. (Identify physical and psychological impact on soldier's attitude).

22). Describe the unit command climate and soldier morale. Has it changed or evolved since you have been in Theater?

23). Please provide by show of hands if you aware of any incidences of detainee or other abuse in your unit. (Those that raise their hands, need to be noted and interviewed individually afterwards using the abuse questionnaire)

c. GUARD FORCE (NCO) COLLECTION POINT & INTERNMENT FACILITY

1). How did you prepare yourself and your soldiers to become familiar with and understand the applicable regulations, OPORDS/FRAGOs directives, international laws and administrative procedures to operate an I/R facility or Collection Point?

2). Did you and all of your soldiers undergo Law of War training prior to deployment? Explain what training occurred. What is your plan to train new soldiers (replacements) to the unit? Did this training include the treatment of Detainees? Explain.

3). What policies/procedures does your unit have in place to support the U.S. policy relative to the humane treatment of Detainees?

4). Does your unit have a formal training program for the care and control of Detainees? Describe what it includes. (For Permanent Internment Facilities only)

5). What training did your unit receive on the established Rules of Engagement (ROE)? How often does this occur? Does this training include Rules of Interaction (ROI)?

6). What procedures do you have in place to ensure soldiers understand the use of force and rules of engagement for the interment facility/collection point? What guidance or policies do you have to ensure fraternization is not taking place between U.S. military personnel and the detainees?

7). Describe the training the guard force received to prepare them for their duties (5Ss & T)) How does your unit conduct sustainment training for Detainee Operations in Theater? How often does this occur and please describe it? When did your unit last conduct this training?

8). What Home Station/Mob Site Training did your unit conduct prior to deployment to help your unit prepare for Detainee Operations? Describe it. How did the training prepare you to conduct Detainee Operations for this deployment? What are your unit's strengths and weaknesses? How did this training distinguish between the different categories of Detainees (EPWs, RPs, CIs, etc.)?

9). Describe the training you received during your last Military Institutional School (BNCOC/ANCOC) in handling/processing Detainees. How was it helpful in preparing you for Detainee Operations? How would you improve the training at the schoolhouse?

10). What are some of the basic operations of the collection point/internment facility? Is there a copy of the Geneva Convention posted in the detainee's home language within these camps? Are camps segregating Detainees by nationality, language, rank, and sex? How are captured Medical personnel and Chaplains being used in the camps? What provisions are in place for the receipt and distribution of Detainee correspondence/mail? Are the daily food rations sufficient in quantity or quality and variety to keep detainees in good health? Are personal hygiene items and needed clothing being supplied to the Detainees? Are the conditions within the camp sanitary enough to ensure a clean and healthy environment free from disease and epidemics? Is there an infirmary located within the camp?

11). What control measures are your unit using to maintain discipline and security in the collection point/internment facility?

12). What procedures are in place to account for and dispose of captured enemy supplies and equipment? What procedures are in place to process personnel, equipment, and evidence?

13). What is your ratio of guards to detainees in your collection point/internment facility? Is this ratio the proper mix for you to perform your mission? If not, what are the shortfalls? Why are their shortfalls? How do these shortfalls impact your mission?

14). How are you organized to handle the different categories of personnel (EPW, CI, OD, females, juveniles and refugees)? Do you maintain a separate site for sick or wounded Detainees? If so where is it and how does your unit maintain the security and safeguarding of Detainees there?

15). What is the number of personnel needed to escort prisoners internally and externally? (i.e., for medical, evacuation, etc.)?

16). What are the procedures for transporting and evacuating detainees? What are the procedures for transferring Detainees from the collection points to US Military controlled detention facilities? How is the transfer of Detainees handled between different services?

17). What are the procedures for the transfer of custody of Detainees from the collection points/internment facility to Military Intelligence/OGA personnel? When the detainee is returned to the guard force, what procedures occur with the detainee? (in processing, medical screening, suicide watch, observation report DD Form 2713?, etc)

18). What MP units (guards, escort, detachments) do you have at your disposal to operate and maintain this collection point/internment facility? What non-MP units are you using to help operate this collection point/internment facility? If you do not use MP teams, what forces are required to operate the Collection Point (guard, security etc)? Do you have any shortfalls in performing the Collection Point mission? How does this affect your doctrinal mission? How long are you holding Detainees at the collection point? Is holding the detainees longer than the 12/24 hours impacting on your units' ability to perform its mission? Why

19). Describe how this unit is able to maintain the security and safeguarding of Detainees at this interment facility/collection point. Describe your security requirements. (What are your clear zones?) How do your Guard Towers permit an unobstructed view of the clear zone and how do they allow for overlapping fields of fire? Describe your perimeter security.

20). How do you maintain a high state of discipline with your soldiers to enhance the internal and external security of the internment facility/Collection Point?

21). Does this facility include Sally Ports? Describe the system in place.

22). What do you have in place for communications (between guards/towers and the TOC/C^2)? What problems do you have? How do you overcome them?

23). Describe the latrine facilities for Detainees' use (do they have access to it day and night and does it conform to the rules of hygiene and do females have separate facilities). How are they cleaned and how often and by whom? Where do they bathe and conduct other personal hygiene (this will depend how long it takes to evacuate Detainees to U.S. Military Controlled Detention Facilities – 12/24 hours is the standard)?

24). How do the Detainees receive fresh water (Bottled water or Lister bag)?

25). Can you give some examples of contraband? What are the procedures when you find contraband?? (i.e., knives, narcotics, weapons, currency)

26). Describe your lighting systems at the Facility/Collection Point (how does it affect security?). How about heating during the winter? What fire prevention/safety measures are in place?

27). How are Detainee complaints and requests to the camp commander processed?

28). What are your shortcomings/problems in feeding the population? What is the menu of the population?

29). What problems, if any, do you feel the unit has regarding manning or personnel resourcing in conducting Detention Operations? What about the number of personnel to control the detention operation in regards to riot control?

30). What personal equipment is the unit experiencing as a shortfall concerning detainee operations, (i.e., restraints, uniforms, CIF items, weapons, etc.)?

31). What types of supplies is greater in-demand for the unit during detainee operations? And are these items regularly filled? What major shortfalls has the unit encountered in regard to material and supply distribution?

32). What transportation problems is the unit experiencing to move detainees during the operation?

33). What safety programs/policies are currently being used in the Detainee camps?

34). Do you know of the procedures to get stress counseling (Psychiatrist, Chaplain, Medical)? Do your soldiers know of the procedures to get counseling (Psychiatrist, Chaplain, Medical)?

35). Are you aware of your requirement to report abuse or suspected abuse of detainees?

36). Do your subordinates know the reporting procedures if they observe or become aware of a Detainee being abused?

37). What steps would you take if a subordinate reported to you an incident of alleged Detainee abuse?

38). Do you feel you can freely report an incident of alleged Detainee abuse outside Command channels (IG, CID)?

39). What procedures do you have to report suspected detainee abuse (IG, CID, Next Level Commander)?

40). What systems are in place for detainees to report alleged abuse?

41). What do you perceive as the mission of your unit? Describe the importance of your role in that mission.

42). Describe your working environment and living conditions since being in Theater.

43). Describe the unit command climate and soldier morale. Has it changed or evolved since you have been in Theater?

44). Please provide by show of hands if you aware of any incidences of detainee or other abuse in your unit? (Those that raise their hands, need to be noted and interviewed individually afterwards using the abuse questionnaire).

d. GUARD FORCE (ENLISTED) COLLECTION POINT & INTERNMENT FACILITY

1). Did all of you undergo Law of War training prior to deployment? Explain what training occurred. Is there a plan to train new soldiers (replacements) to the unit? Did this training include the treatment of Detainees? Explain.

2). What training have you received to ensure your knowledge of DO is IAW the provisions under the Geneva Convention? (5Ss & T)

3). What training did your unit receive on the established Rules of Engagement (ROE)? How often does this occur? Does this training include Rules of Interaction (ROI)?

4). Describe the training the guard force received to prepare them for their duties.

5). How does your unit conduct sustainment training for Detainee Operations here in Theater? How often does this occur and please describe it? When did your unit last conduct this training?

6). (For Permanent Internment Facilities only) Does your unit have a formal training program for the care and control of Detainees? Describe what it includes.

7). What Home Station/Mob Site Training did your unit conduct prior to deployment to help your unit prepare for Detainee Operations? Describe it. How did the training prepare you to conduct Detainee Operations for this deployment? How did this training distinguish between the different categories of Detainees (EPWs, RPs, CIs, etc).

8). What are some of the basic operations of the collection point/facility? Is there a copy of the Geneva Convention posted in the detainee's home language within these camps? Are camps segregating Detainees by nationality, language, rank, and sex? What provisions are in place for the receipt and distribution of Detainee correspondence/mail? Are personal hygiene items and needed clothing being supplied to the Detainees? Are the conditions within the camp sanitary enough to ensure a clean and healthy environment free from disease and epidemics? Is there an infirmary located within the camp?

9). What is the maximum capacity for this particular collection point/facility? What is the current Detainee population? What is your ratio of guards to detainees in the collection point/facility? Is this ratio the proper mix for you to perform your mission? If not, what are the shortfalls? Why are their shortfalls? How do these shortfalls impact your mission?

10). What control measures are units using to maintain discipline and security in each collection point/facility?

11). Describe how this unit is able to maintain the security and safeguarding of Detainees at this collection point/interment facility. Describe your security requirements. (What are your clear zones)? How do your Guard Towers permit an unobstructed view of the clear zone and how do they allow for overlapping fields of fire? Describe your perimeter security.

12). What MP units (guards, escort, detachments) do you have at your disposal to operate and maintain this collection point/facility? What non-MP units are you using to help operate this collection point/facility?

13). What is the number of personnel that is needed to move prisoners internally and externally, (i.e., for medical, evacuation, etc.)?

14). How are you organized to handle the different categories of personnel (EPW, CI, OD, and refuges)? How many female Detainees are housed here? How and where do you house them? How do you maintain separation from the male population (during the day or during recreational activities)? What about other categories (juveniles, CI, RP, etc)? What about other categories (juveniles, CI, RP, etc)? Do you maintain a separate site for sick or wounded Detainees? If so where is it and how does your unit maintain the security and safeguarding of Detainees there?

15). (Collection Point only) How long are you holding Detainees at the collection point? Is holding the detainees longer than the 12 hours (FWD CP) or 24 hours (Central CP) impacting on your units' ability to perform its mission? Why?

16). What procedures are in place to account for and dispose of captured enemy supplies and equipment?

17). Can you give some examples of contraband? What are the procedures when you find contraband?? (i.e., knives, narcotics, weapons, currency)

18). (Collection Point only) What are the procedures for transporting and evacuating detainees?

19). What are the procedures for the transfer of Detainees from the collection points to US Military controlled detention facilities? How is the transfer of Detainees handled between different services?

20). What are the procedures for the transfer of custody of Detainees from the collection points/internment facility to Military Intelligence/OGA personnel? When the detainee is returned to the guard force, what procedures occur with the detainee? (inprocessing, medical screening, suicide watch, observation report DD Form 2713?, etc.)

21). Does this facility include Sally Ports? Describe the system in place.

22). What do you have in place for communications (between guards/towers and the TOC/C^2)? What problems do you have?

23). How do the Detainees receive fresh water (Bottled water or Lister bag)?

24). How are Detainee complaints and requests to the internment facility commander processed?

25). What safety programs/policies are currently being used in the internment facilities?

26). What personal equipment is the unit experiencing as a shortfall concerning detainee operations, (i.e., restraints, uniforms, CIF items, weapons, etc.)?

27). What transportation problems is the unit experiencing either to move troops or detainees during the operation?

28). What problems, if any, do you feel the unit has regarding manning or personnel resourcing in conducting Detention Operations?

29). Do you know of the procedures to get stress counseling (Psychiatrist, Chaplain, Medical)?

30). Are you aware of your requirement to report abuse or suspected abuse of detainees?

31). Do you feel you can freely report an incident of alleged Detainee abuse outside Command channels (IG, CID)?

32). What procedures do you have to report suspected detainee abuse (IG, CID, Next Level Commander)

33). What procedures are in place for detainees to report alleged abuse?

34). What do you perceive as the mission of your unit? Describe the importance of your role in that mission.

35). Describe your working environment and living conditions since being in Theater.

36). Describe the unit command climate and soldier morale. Has it changed or evolved since you have been in Theater?

37). Please provide by show of hands if you aware of any incidences of detainee or other abuse in your unit? (Those that raise their hands, need to be noted and interviewed individually afterwards using the abuse questionnaire).

e. ABUSE QUESTIONNAIRE.

1). What do you perceive as the mission of your unit? Describe the importance of your role in that mission.

2). Describe your working environment and living conditions since being in Theater.

3). Describe the unit command climate and soldier morale. Has it changed or evolved since you have been in Theater

4). Are you aware of any incidences of detainee or other abuse in your unit?

5). ADVISEMENT OF RIGHTS (For military personnel)
    The text of Article 31 provides as follows a. No person subject to this chapter may compel any person to incriminate himself or to answer any questions the answer to which may tend to incriminate him. b. No person subject to this chapter may interrogate or request any statement from an accused or a person suspected of an offense without first informing him of the nature of the accusation and advising him that he does not have to make any statement regarding the offense of which he is accused or suspected, and that any statement made by him may be used as evidence against him in a trial by court-martial. c. No person subject to this chapter may compel any person to make a statement or produce evidence before any military tribunal if the statement or evidence is not material to the issue and may tend to degrade him. d. No statement obtained from any person in violation of this article, or through the use of coercion, unlawful influence, or unlawful inducement, may be received in evidence against him in a trial by court-martial. (1.2, 1.6)

6). I am _____ (grade, if any, and name), a member of the (DAIG). I am part of a team inspecting detainee operations, this is not a criminal investigation. I am reading you your rights because of a statement you made causes me to suspect that you may have committed _____. (specify offense, i.e., aggravated assault, assault, murder). Under Article 31, you have the right to remain silent, that is, say nothing at all. Any statement you make, oral or written, may be used as evidence against you in a trial by courts-martial or in other judicial or administrative proceedings. You have the right to consult a lawyer and to have a lawyer present during this interview. You have the right to military legal counsel free of charge. In addition to military counsel, you are entitled to civilian counsel of your own choosing, at your own expense. You may request a lawyer at any time during this interview. If you decide to answer questions, you may stop the questioning at any time. Do you understand your rights? Do you want a lawyer? (If the answer is yes, cease all questions at this point). Are you willing to answer questions?

7). Describe what you understand happened leading up to and during the incident(s) of abuse.

8). Describe soldier morale, feelings and emotional state prior to and after these incidents?

9). Was this incident reported to the chain of command? How, when & what was done? What would you have done?

10). How could the incident have been prevented?

11). Describe any unit training or other programs that you are aware of that teach leaders and soldiers how to recognize and resolve combat stress.

12). What measures are in place to boost morale or to relieve stress?

13). What measures could the command enact to improve the morale and command climate of your unit?

3. INSPECTION TOOLS.

a. Receipt at the US Military Controlled Detention Facilities Worksheet

UNIT: _____ DATE: _____ NAME: _____

Receipt at the US Military Controlled Detention Facilities:
1. What means of transportation are Detainees delivered to the Detention Facility? How are they subdued? Are detainees receiving humane treatment? Are they immediately screened and searched upon arrival? Who is in Charge? (What Unit?)
Remarks:
2. Describe in Detail what the In-Processing Procedures are.
Remarks:
3. Describe in Detail what the Out-Processing Procedures are.
Remarks:
4. Describe security at the Interment Facility. What is the Guard to Detainee Ratio? Describe the Facility in Detail?
Remarks:

5. Is the Facility using DA Form 2674-R (Strength Report) to maintain accountability of detainees	Yes	No	Are the detainees' names listed on this form?	Yes	No
Remarks:					
6. Is the DA 4237-R used for Protected Persons?	Yes	No	Are there children annotated on the form?	Yes	No
Remarks: ((Ask if there compassionate Detainees? (children?))					

7. What paperwork follows the Detainee?: Is it completed to standard?: If not, why? If not to standard, what happens?
Remarks:

8. Did you witness anyone taking photos or films of detainees outside the parameters of internment facilities administration or for intelligence/ counterintelligence purposes?	Yes	No
Remarks:		
9. Are sick or wounded detainees kept separately and in the same manner as US Forces? Does the Facility have an Infirmary? Describe in detail.	Yes	No
Remarks:		
10. Do detainees enjoy the latitude in the exercise of their religious practices?	Yes	No
Remarks:		
11. Are there interpreters at the Internment Facility? How many? What background checks are conducted?	Yes	No
Remarks:		
12. Are the following forms/requirements being used properly for Civilian Detainees?	Yes	No
a. DA Form 1132 (Prisoners Personal Property)	Yes	No
b. DA Form 2677-R (Civilian Internee Identification Card)	Yes	No
c. Are Internment Serial Numbers assigned to each Civilian Internee?	Yes	No
d. DA Form 2678-R (Civilian Internee Notification of Address)	Yes	No
e. DA Form 2663-R (Fingerprint Card) or (BAT Process)	Yes	No
f. or any other forms used (possibly in lieu of) IAW local SOPs or Policy (CPA Apprehension Form?)	Yes	No
Remarks:		
13. What type of unit is in charge of operating the Internment Facility? Is there an adequate number of personnel running the Facility?	Yes	No
Remarks:		
14. Describe physical security at and around the Facility? Describe lighting systems. How about Sally Ports?		
Remarks:		

15. Describe the latrine facilities for Detainees' use. (Do they have access to it day and night and does it conform to the rules of hygiene and do females have separate facilities?). How are they cleaned and how often and by whom?
Remarks:
16. Describe the furnishings for sleeping and eating (does it include bedding/blankets)? Is there a means to launder clothing items for the Detainees at the Facility
Remarks:
17. Describe the Facility's Infrastructure.
a. Electrical Distribution and Lighting.
Remarks:
b. Sewer or Sanitation System (Waste Water, if any).
Remarks:
c. Potable Water Supply (drinking).
Remarks:
d. Water for bathing and laundry.
Remarks:
e. Heating and Ventilation.
Remarks:
f Fire Prevention Measures.
Remarks:
g. Segregation based on Detainee Classification.
Remarks:
h. Vector/Animal/Pest Control.
Remarks:
18. Preventative Medicine Remarks.
Remarks:

	Yes	No
19. Are Medical Records Maintained for each Detainee? Where are they kept?		
Remarks:		

20. Where is the screening site? Where are detainees interrogated? Who interrogates/questions the detainees?
Remarks:
19. General Observations: (Include sketch of location/facility area).
SAFETY PROGRAM
SCREENING/INTERROGATION SITE
ADD RECEIVING/INPROCESSING STATION
ADD INTERROGATION LOCATION, IF APPLICABLE

b. Receipt at the (BDE/DIV) Collection Point to Evacuation to US Military Controlled Detention Facilities Worksheet.

UNIT: _____ DATE: _____ NAME: _____

Receipt at the (BDE/DIV) Collection Point to Evacuation to US Military Controlled Detention Facilities					
1. Describe security at the Collection Point. What is the Guard to Detainee Ratio?				Ratio:	
Remarks:					
2. Is the Collection point using DD Form 629 to maintain accountability of detainees?	Yes	No	Are the detainees' names listed on this list?	Yes	No
Remarks:					
3. Did you witness anyone taking photos or films of detainees outside the parameters of internment facilities administration or for intelligence/ counterintelligence purposes?				Yes	No
Remarks:					
4. Describe the Collection Point? Is it located near ammunition sites, fuel facilities, communications equipment, or other potential targets?				Yes	No
5. Are sick or wounded detainees evacuated separately and in the same manner as US Forces? Are they classified by qualified medical personnel (walking wounded, litter, non-walking wounded)?				Yes	No
Remarks:					
6. Do detainees enjoy the latitude in the exercise of their religious practices?				Yes	No
Remarks:					
7. How long are detainees kept in the Collection point?					
Remarks:					
8. Are escorts provided a DD Form 629 with all the escorted detainees' names listed while evacuating them to US Military Controlled Detention facilities?					
Remarks:					
9. Are there interpreters at the Collection Point?				Yes	No
Remarks:					
10. Are detainees being evacuated to US Military Controlled Detention facilities? How soon after arrival at the CP? Can you describe the process of evacuation?				Yes	No
Remarks:					

11. Is DA Form 4137 being used to account for the detainee's personal property?	Yes	No
Remarks:		

12. What type of unit is in charge of operating the Collection Point (MPs or other)? What type of unit does the guard force consist of (MPs or others)? Is there an adequate number of personnel running the Collection Point?	Yes	No
Remarks:		

13. Describe your lighting systems at the Collection Point. How about heating during the winter? What fire prevention/safety measures are in place?
Remarks:

14. Describe the latrine facilities for Detainees' use. (Do they have access to it day and night and does it conform to the rules of hygiene and do females have separate facilities). How are they cleaned and how often and by whom? Where do they bathe and conduct other personal hygiene (this will depend how long it takes to evacuate Detainees to U.S. Military Controlled Detention Facilities – 12 hours is the standard)?
Remarks:

15. Describe the furnishings for sleeping and eating (does it include bedding/blankets)? Is there a means to launder clothing items for the Detainees at this Collection Point (this will depend how long it takes to evacuate Detainees to U.S. Military Controlled Detention Facilities – 12 Hours is the standard).
Remarks:

16. How do the Detainees receive fresh water (Bottled water or Lister bag)? How are they fed (how often and what)?
Remarks:

17. What is the overall Description of the Collection Point? (Hardened Facility, tents, etc)
Remarks:

18. Where is the screening site? Where are detainees interrogated? Who interrogates/questions the detainees?
Remarks:

19. Describe Receiving/In-processing Station.
Remarks:

20. General Observations: (Include sketch of location/facility area).

c. From Capture to the Collection Point Worksheet

UNIT: _____ **DATE**: _____ **NAME**: _____

From Capture to the Collection Point						
1. Are detainees receiving humane treatment?					Yes	No
Remarks:						
2. Were detainees searched immediately upon capture?					Yes	No
Remarks:						
3. Was currency confiscated?	Yes	No	Did a commissioned officer approve the confiscation?		Yes	No
Remarks:						
4. Were detainees able to keep some personal effects, such as jewelry, protective mask and garments, helmets, clothing, ID Cards, badges of rank/nationality, etc?					Yes	No
Remarks:						
5. Were the detainees tagged using DD Form 2745? Was the required information entered onto the form (date of capture, grid coordinates of capture, capturing unit, and how the detainee was captured)?					Yes	No
Remarks:						
6. Is the DD Form 2745 properly divided into Parts A (attached to the detainee), B (retained by the capturing unit), and C (attached to the property of the detainee)?					Yes	No
Remarks:						
7. What other Forms and in-processing techniques are used and for what (CPA Apprehension Form)?						
Remarks:						
8. Are the detainees being interrogated/questioned soon after being captured? By Whom?					Yes	No
Remarks:						
9. Are wounded detainees receiving medical treatment?					Yes	No
Remarks:						
10. How are detainees evacuated to the Collection Points and how soon after capture?						
Remarks:						
11. General Observations:						

d. PREVENTIVE MEDICINE SITE ASSESSMENT TOOL (FOR COLLECTION POINTS / INTERNMENT FACILITIES)

NAME OF CP / FACILITY: _____ TYPE OF CP / FACILITY: _____

LOCATION (TOWN/CITY, COUNTRY): _____

DETAINEE POPULATION: MEN _____   WOMEN _____

PERSONAL HYGIENE SHOWERS
  NUMBER OF SHOWERS: _____
  SOAKAGE PITS / GOOD DRAINAGE / NO STANDING WATER: Y   N
  NON-POTABLE WATER SIGNS POSTED IN LOCAL LANGUAGE: Y   N
  SOAP / SHAMPOO & TOWELS PRESENT: Y   N
  CLEANLINESS: POOR   FAIR   GOOD   EXCELLENT
  FREQUENCY OF INSPECTION: DAILY   WEEKLY   MONTHLY
  COMMENTS: _____

HAND WASHING STATIONS
  OUTSIDE ALL LATRINES   Y   N
  IN FOOD SERVICE AREA: Y   N
  SOAKAGE PITS / GOOD DRAINAGE / NO STANDING WATER: Y   N
  SOAP & TOWELS PRESENT: Y   N
  NON-POTABLE WATER SIGNS POSTED IN LOCAL LANGUAGE: Y   N
  CLEANLINESS: POOR   FAIR   GOOD   EXCELLENT
  FREQUENCY OF INSPECTION: DAILY   WEEKLY   MONTHLY
  COMMENTS: _____

LAUNDRY FACILITIES   PRESENT   ABSENT
  SOAKAGE PITS / GOOD DRAINAGE / NO STANDING WATER: Y   N
  NON-POTABLE WATER SIGNS POSTED IN LOCAL LANGUAGE: Y   N
  CLEANLINESS: POOR   FAIR   GOOD   EXCELLENT
  FREQUENCY OF INSPECTION: DAILY   WEEKLY   MONTHLY
  COMMENTS: _____

POTABLE WATER SUPPLY
  QUANTITY AVAILABLE PER PERSON PER DAY (GALLONS): POTABLE _____
    3–4 gal/person/day potable; 3–15 gal/person/day non-potable   NON-POTABLE ?
  WATER SOURCE(S):   SURFACE   GROUND   RAIN   ROWPU
  WATER CONTAINERS: 5-GAL CANS   FABRIC DRUM   TRAILER
  SOAKAGE PITS / GOOD DRAINAGE / NO STANDING WATER: Y   N
  ALL SPIGOTS FUNCTIONAL: Y   N
  POTABLE WATER SIGNS POSTED IN LOCAL LANGUAGE: Y   N
  CONTAINER CLEANLINESS: POOR   FAIR   GOOD   EXCELLENT
  FREQUENCY OF INSPECTION: DAILY   WEEKLY   MONTHLY
  COMMENTS: _____

FOOD SERVICE SANITATION

    TYPE OF MEALS PROVIDED: MREs   A/B/T RATIONS   PREPARED

    NUMBER OF MEALS SERVED PER DAY: _____

    TRANSPORT VEHICLE CLEAN & COMPLETELY COVERED: Y   N

    FACILITY CLEANLINESS: POOR   FAIR   GOOD   EXCELLENT

    FREQUENCY OF INSPECTION: DAILY   WEEKLY   MONTHLY

    COMMENTS: _____

    _____

IF HOT MEALS PREPARED:

REFRIG AT 45°F OR BELOW:	Y	N
ICE: APPROVED SOURCE / IN APPROPRIATE CONTAINER:	Y	N
FOOD CONTAINERS CLEAN & INSULATED:	Y	N
PALLETS FOR DRY STORAGE:	Y	N
FOOD NOT CONTAMINATED DURING PREP & SERVING:	Y	N
FOOD MAINTAINED AT CORRECT TEMP:	Y	N
(COLD < 45°F, HOT > 140°F)		
LEFTOVERS PROPERLY DISPOSED:	Y	N
NO EVIDENCE OF SPOILAGE:	Y	N
FOOD THERMOMETERS USED:	Y	N
DISHWASHING THOROUGH & AT RIGHT TEMPS:	Y	N

    WASTE CONTAINERS: COVERED / CLEAN / VERMIN-PROOF /
                                    EMPTIED OFTEN

    FOOD SERVERS

PROPERLY TRAINED & DOCUMENTED:	Y	N
EVIDENCE OF COMMUNICABLE DISEASE:	Y	N
(SKIN INFECTION, RASH, CUT, BURN, RESP SYMPTOMS)		
HANDS WASHED & GLOVED:	Y	N
HAIR RESTRAINTS (HATS / NETS):	Y	N

    COMMENTS: _____

    _____

WASTE

    NUMBER OF LATRINES: MALE _____

    (FM 4-25.12: 1 per 25 males, 1 per 17 females)   FEMALE _____

                                              NOT SEPARATED _____

    TYPE(S) OF LATRINES: CHEMICAL   TRENCH/PIT   BURN-OUT

    OTHER

    LATRINES LOCATED 100 YDS DOWNWIND OF FOOD SERVICE: Y   N

    LATRINES LOCATED 100 FT FROM GROUND WATER SOURCE(S):   Y   N

    CLEANLINESS: POOR   FAIR   GOOD   EXCELLENT

    FREQUENCY OF INSPECTION: DAILY   WEEKLY   MONTHLY

    COMMENTS: _____

    _____

    GARBAGE STORED 100 FT FROM ANY WATER SOURCE: Y   N

    GARBAGE IS: BURIED   INCINERATED   HAULED AWAY

    CLEANLINESS: POOR   FAIR   GOOD   EXCELLENT

FREQUENCY OF INSPECTION: DAILY   WEEKLY   MONTHLY
COMMENTS: _____

PEST CONTROL

SITE ON HIGH, WELL-DRAINED GROUND:	Y	N
SITE AT LEAST 1 MILE FROM STANDING WATER:	Y	N
BILLETS SCREENED:	Y	N
PESTICIDES AVAILABLE: Y N USED:	Y	N
INSECT REPELLENT AVAILABLE:	Y	N
SIGHTINGS OF LIVE OR DEAD RODENTS:	Y	N
DROPPINGS, GNAWINGS, BURROWS/HOLES, ODORS:	Y	N
EVIDENCE OF TRAPS, BAITS, OTHER CONTROLS:	Y	N

PRESENCE OF INSECTS: NONE   FEW   MANY
TYPE(S) OF INSECTS PRESENT: FLIES   MOSQUITOES   SAND FLIES
FREQUENCY OF INSPECTION: DAILY   WEEKLY   MONTHLY
COMMENTS: _____

WORK CONDITIONS

DETAINEES OBSERVED WORKING:	Y	N
IF YES: CLOTHING/PROTECTIVE EQUIPMENT APPROPRIATE:	Y	N

WET BULB MONITORED BY: UNIT   PVNTMED
METEOROLOGICAL SERVICE

WORK/REST CYCLES FOLLOWED:	Y	N

COMMENTS: _____

QUARTERS (INTERIOR & EXTERIOR)

ADEQUATE SPACE, LIGHTING, CLIMATE CONTROL:	Y	N
ADEQUATE LIGHTING:	Y	N
ADEQUATE CLIMATE CONTROL:	Y	N
EVIDENCE OF RODENTS:	Y	N
FOOD DEBRIS/TRASH PRESENT:	Y	N
STANDING WATER PRESENT:	Y	N
VEGETATION WITHIN XX FT OF QUARTERS:	Y	N

CLEANLINESS: POOR   FAIR   GOOD   EXCELLENT
FREQUENCY OF INSPECTION: DAILY   WEEKLY   MONTHLY
COMMENTS: _____

FIELD SANITATION TEAM

APPOINTED: Y   N   TRAINED: Y   N
SUPPLIES: Y   N   PERFORMING DUTIES: Y   N
COLLECT COPIES OF (MOST RECENT? LAST 3?) PVNTMED INSPEC-
TION REPORTS, INCLUDING SITE SURVEYS, FOOD SERVICE SANITATION
INSPECTIONS, WATER ANALYSIS, PEST SURVEYS

e. COMBAT / OPERATIONAL STRESS QUESTIONNAIRE

Please answer all questions completely and honestly. Your responses will remain anonymous.

1. Rank   E1–4   E5–6   E7–9   O1–3   O4–6
2. Type of UnitPLT   CO   BN   BDE   Other

Rate the following statements regarding morale and unit cohesion (1 = strongly disagree, 5 = strongly agree):

3. The members of my unit know that they can depend on each other   1 2 3 4 5
4. The members of my unit are cooperative with each other   1 2 3 4 5.
5. The members of my unit stand up for each other   1 2 3 4 5.
6. The members of my unit were adequately trained for this mission   1 2 3 4 5

Rate the following statements regarding your unit's leadership (1 = never, 5 = always):
7. In your unit, how often do NCOs/officers tell soldiers when they have done a good job?   1 2 3 4 5
8. In your unit, how often do NCOs/officers embarrass soldiers in front of other soldiers?   1 2 3 4 5
9. In your unit, how often do NCOs/officers try to look good to higher-ups by assigning extra missions or details to soldiers?   1 2 3 4 5
10. In your unit, how often do NCOs/officers exhibit clear thinking and reasonable action under stress?   1 2 3 4 5

Rate the following statements regarding access to mental health care (1 = strongly disagree, 5 = strongly agree):

11. I don't know where to get help   1 2 3 4 5
12. It is difficult to get an appointment   1 2 3 4 5
13. It's too difficult to get to the location where the mental health specialist is 1 2 3 4 5
14. I don't trust mental health professionals   1 2 3 4 5
15. My leadership would treat me differently   1 2 3 4 5
16. My leaders would blame me for the problem   1 2 3 4 5
17. I would be seen as weak   1 2 3 4 5

Rate the following statements regarding personal issues at home (1 = strongly disagree, 5 = strongly agree):

18. My relationship with my spouse is very stable   1 2 3 4 5
19. My relationship with my spouse makes me happy   1 2 3 4 5
20. Do you and/or your spouse have any plans to separate or divorce?   Y   N
21. My unit's rear detachment supports my family   1 2 3 4 5
22. My unit's family readiness group supports my family   1 2 3 4 5

Combat exposure:

23. How many times have you been attacked or ambushed? Never 1–5 times 6–10 times >10 times
24. How many times have you received small arms fire? Never 1–5 times 6–10 times >10 times
25. How many times have you seen dead bodies or human remains? Never 1–5 times 6–10 times >10 times

26. How many times have you cleared/searched buildings or homes? Never 1–5 times 6–10 times >10 times
27. How many times have you been responsible for the death of an enemy combatant? Never 1–5 times 6–10 times >10 times

Rate the level of concern you have regarding the following (1 = not concerned at all, 5 = very concerned):

28. Being separated from family   1 2 3 4 5
29. Uncertain redeployment date   1 2 3 4 5
30. Duration of deployment   1 2 3 4 5
31. Lack of privacy   1 2 3 4 5
32. Boring and repetitive work   1 2 3 4 5
33. Living conditions   1 2 3 4 5

Rate the following statements regarding stress management training (1 = strongly disagree, 5 = strongly agree):
34. My training in handling the stresses of deployment was adequate   1 2 3 4 5
35. My training in recognizing stress in other soldiers was adequate   1 2 3 4 5

Thank you for your honest responses.

Appendix E   Standards

a. **Finding 1:**
   (1) *Finding*: All interviewed and observed commanders, leaders, and soldiers treated detainees humanely and emphasized the importance of the humane treatment of detainees.
   (2) *Standard*: Standard of treatment for detainees in OPERATION ENDURING FREE-DOM (OEF): Chairman, Joint Chiefs of Staff (CJCS) message dated 211933Z JAN 02 states that members of the Taliban militia and members of al Qaeda under the control of US Forces would be treated humanely and, to the extent appropriate and consistent with military necessity, in a manner consistent with the principles of the Geneva Conventions of 1949. The DAIG has therefore used the provisions of the Geneva Conventions as a benchmark against which to measure the treatment pro-vided to detainees by U.S. Forces to determine if detainees were treated humanely. The use of these standards as benchmarks does not state or imply a position for the United States or U.S. Army on the legal status of its operations in OEF.

The DAIG refers to three key documents in this report. CJCS Message dated 211933Z JAN 02, provides the determination regarding the humane treatment of al Qaeda and Taliban detainees. *Convention Relative to the Treatment of Prisoners of War of August 12, 1949* (GPW) is the international treaty that governs the treatment of prisoners of war, and *Geneva Convention Relative to the Protection of Civilian Persons in Time of War (GC)*, 12 August 1949, is the international treaty that governs the treatment of civilian persons in time of war.

As the guidance did not define "humane treatment" but did state that the US would treat members of the Taliban militia and al Qaeda in a manner consistent with the Geneva Conventions, the DAIG determined that it would use Common Article 3 of the GCs as its floor measure of humane treatment, but would also include provisions of the Geneva

Convention on the Treatment of Prisoners of War (GPW) and Geneva Convention Relative to the Protection of Civilian Persons in Time of War (GC) as other relevant indicia of "humane treatment." The use of this standard does not state or imply a position for the United States or U.S. Army on the legal status of its operations in OEF.

Standard of treatment for detainees in OPERATION IRAQI FREEDOM (OIF): OIF was an international armed conflict and therefore the provisions of the Geneva Conventions applied. Additionally, the United States was an occupying power and has acted in accordance with the obligations of an occupying power described in the *Hague Convention No. IV Respecting the Laws and Customs of War on Land (H.IV)*, 18 October 1907, including, but not limited to, Articles 43–46 and 50; *Geneva Convention Relative to the Treatment of Prisoners of War of August 12, 1949 (GPW)*, *Geneva Convention Relative to the Protection of Civilian Persons in Time of War (GC)*, 12 August 1949. The GC supplements H.IV, providing the general standard of treatment at Article 27 and specific standards in subsequent Articles.

The minimum treatment provided by Common Article 3 of the Geneva Conventions is: 1) No adverse distinction based upon race, religion, sex, etc.; 2) No violence to life or person; 3) No taking hostages; 4) No degrading treatment; 5) No passing of sentences in absence of fair trial, and; 6) The wounded and sick must be cared for.

The specific language in the CJCS Message for OEF and the GPW/GC and H.IV follows: CJCS Message dated 211933Z JAN 02, "Paragraph 3. The combatant commanders shall, in detaining al Qaeda and Taliban individuals under the control of the Department of Defense, treat them humanely and, to the extent appropriate and consistent with military necessity, in a manner consistent with the principles of the Geneva Conventions of 1949."

GPW/GC, Article 3 (Common Article 3) – "In the case of armed conflict not of an international character occurring in the territory of one of the High Contracting Parties, each party to the conflict shall be bound to apply, as a minimum, the following provisions:

1. Persons taking no active part in the hostilities, including members of armed forces who have laid down their arms and those placed hors de combat by sickness, wounds, detention, or any other cause, shall in all circumstances be treated humanely, without any adverse distinction founded on race, color, religion or faith, sex, birth or wealth, or any other similar criteria.

To this end the following acts are and shall remain prohibited at any time and in any place whatsoever with respect to the above-mentioned persons:

(a) Violence to life and person, in particular, murder of all kinds, mutilation, cruel treatment and torture;
(b) Taking of hostages;
(c) Outrages upon personal dignity, in particular, humiliating and degrading treatment;
(d) The passing of sentences and the carrying out of executions without previous judgment pronounced by a regularly constituted court affording all the judicial guarantees which are recognized as indispensable by civilized peoples.

2. The wounded and sick shall be collected and cared for. An impartial humanitarian body, such as the International Committee of the Red Cross, may offer its services to the Parties to the conflict. The Parties to the conflict should further endeavour to bring into force, by means of special agreements, all or part of the other provisions of the present Convention. The application of the preceding provisions shall not affect the legal status of the Parties to the conflict."

H.IV, Article 43 – "The authority of the legitimate power having in fact passed into the hands of the occupant, the latter shall take all the measures in his power to restore, and ensure, as far as possible, public order and safety, while respecting, unless absolutely prevented, the laws in force in the country.

H.IV, Article 44 – A belligerent is forbidden to force the inhabitants of territory occupied by it to furnish information about the army of the other belligerent, or about its means of defense.

H.IV, Article 45 – It is forbidden to compel the inhabitants of occupied territory to swear allegiance to the hostile Power.

H.IV, Article 46 – Family honour and rights, the lives of persons, and private property, as well as religious convictions and practice, must be respected. Private property cannot be confiscated.

H.IV, Article 47 – Pilage is formally forbidden.

H.IV, Article 50 – No general penalty, pecuniary or otherwise, shall be inflicted upon the population on account of the acts of individuals for which they cannot be regarded as jointly and severally responsible.

GPW, Article 13 – Prisoners of war must at all times be humanely treated. Any unlawful act or omission by the Detaining Power causing death or seriously endangering the health of a prisoner of war in its custody is prohibited, and will be regarded as a serious breach of the present Convention. In particular, no prisoner of war may be subjected to physical mutilation or to medical or scientific experiments of any kind which are not justified by the medical, dental or hospital treatment of the prisoner concerned and carried out in his interest. Likewise, prisoners of war must at all times be protected, particularly against acts of violence or intimidation and against insults and public curiosity.

GPW, Article 14 – Prisoners of war are entitled in all circumstances to respect for their persons and their honour. Women shall be treated with all the regard due to their sex and shall in all cases benefit by treatment as favourable as that granted to men. Prisoners of war shall retain the full civil capacity which they enjoyed at the time of their capture. The Detaining Power may not restrict the exercise, either within or without its own territory, of the rights such capacity confers except in so far as the captivity requires.

GPW, Article 15 – The Power detaining prisoners of war shall be bound to provide free of charge for their maintenance and for the medical attention required by their state of health.

GPW, Article 16 – Taking into consideration the provisions of the present Convention relating to rank and sex, and subject to any privileged treatment which may be accorded to them by reason of their state of health, age or professional qualifications, all prisoners of war shall be treated alike by the Detaining Power, without any adverse distinction based on race, nationality, religious belief or political opinions, or any other distinction founded on similar criteria.

GPW, Article 39 – Every prisoner of war camp shall be put under the immediate authority of a responsible commissioned officer belonging to the regular armed forces of the Detaining Power. Such officer shall have in his possession a copy of the present Convention; he shall ensure that its provisions are known to the camp staff and the guard and shall be responsible, under the direction of his government, for its application. Prisoners of war, with the exception of officers, must salute and show to all officers of the Detaining Power the external marks of respect provided for by the regulations applying in their own forces. Officer prisoners of war are bound to salute only officers of a higher rank of the Detaining Power; they must, however, salute the camp commander regardless of his rank.

GPW, Article 41 – In every camp the text of the present Convention and its Annexes and the contents of any special agreement provided for in Article 6, shall be posted, in the prisoners' own language, at places where all may read them. Copies shall be supplied, on request, to the prisoners who cannot have access to the copy which has been posted. Regulations, orders, notices and publications of every kind relating to the conduct of prisoners of war shall be issued to them in a language which they understand. Such regulations, orders and publications shall be posted in the manner described above and copies shall be handed to the prisoners' representative. Every order and command addressed to prisoners of war individually must likewise be given in a language which they understand.

GC, Article 27 – Protected persons are entitled, in all circumstances, to respect for their persons, their honour, their family rights, their religious convictions and practices, and their manners and customs. They shall at all times be humanely treated, and shall be protected especially against all acts of violence or threats thereof and against insults and public curiosity. Women shall be especially protected against any attack on their honour, in particular, against rape, enforced prostitution, or any form of indecent assault. Without prejudice to the provisions relating to their state of health, age and sex, all protected persons shall be treated with the same consideration by the Party to the conflict in whose power they are, without any adverse distinction based, in particular, on race, religion or political opinion. However, the Parties to the conflict may take such measures of control and security in regard to protected persons as may be necessary as a result of the war.

GC, Article 31 – No physical or moral coercion shall be exercised against protected persons, in particular to obtain information from them or from third parties.

GC, Article 32 – The High Contracting Parties specifically agree that each of them is prohibited from taking any measure of such a character as to cause the physical suffering or extermination of protected persons in their hands. This prohibition applies not only to murder, torture, corporal punishments, mutilation and medical or scientific experiments not necessitated by the medical treatment of a protected person, but also to any other measures of brutality whether applied by civilian or military agents.

GC, Article 37 – Protected persons who are confined pending proceedings or subject to a sentence involving loss of liberty, shall during their confinement be humanely treated."

GC, Article 41 – Should the Power, in whose hands protected persons may be, consider the measures of control mentioned in the present Convention to be inadequate, it may not have recourse to any other measure of control more severe than that of assigned residence or internment, in accordance with the provisions of Articles 42 and 43. In applying the provisions of Article 39, second paragraph, to the cases of persons required to leave their usual places of residence by virtue of a decision placing them in assigned residence, by virtue of a decision placing them in assigned residence, elsewhere, the Detaining Power shall be guided as closely as possible by the standards of welfare set forth in Part III, Section IV of this Convention.

GC, Article 42 – The internment or placing in assigned residence of protected persons may be ordered only if the security of the Detaining Power makes it absolutely necessary. If any person, acting through the representatives of the Protecting Power, voluntarily demands internment, and if his situation renders this step necessary, he shall be interned by the Power in whose hands he may be.

GC, Article 43 – Any protected person who has been interned or placed in assigned residence shall be entitled to have such action reconsidered as soon as possible by an appropriate court or administrative board designated by the Detaining Power for that purpose. If the internment or placing in assigned residence is maintained, the court or administrative board shall periodically, and at least twice yearly, give consideration to his or her case, with a view to the favorable amendment of the initial decision, if circumstances permit. Unless the protected persons concerned object, the Detaining Power shall, as rapidly as possible, give the Protecting Power the names of any protected persons who have been interned or subjected to assigned residence, or who have been released from internment or assigned residence. The decisions of the courts or boards mentioned in the first paragraph of the present Article shall also, subject to the same conditions, be notified as rapidly as possible to the Protecting Power."

GC, Article 68 – Protected persons who commit an offence which is solely intended to harm the Occupying Power, but which does not constitute an attempt on the life or limb of members of the occupying forces or administration, nor a grave collective danger, nor seriously damage the property of the occupying forces or administration or the installations used by them, shall be liable to internment or simple imprisonment, provided the duration of such internment or imprisonment is proportionate to the offence committed. Furthermore, internment or imprisonment shall, for such offences, be the only measure adopted for depriving protected persons of liberty. The courts provided for under Article 66 of the present Convention may at their discretion convert a sentence of imprisonment to one of internment for the same period.

The penal provisions promulgated by the Occupying Power in accordance with Articles 64 and 65 may impose the death penalty on a protected person only in cases where the person is guilty of espionage, of serious acts of sabotage against the military installations of the Occupying Power or of intentional offences which have caused the death of one or more persons, provided that such offences were punishable by death under the law of the occupied territory in force before the occupation began.

The death penalty may not be pronounced on a protected person unless the attention of the court has been particularly called to the fact that since the accused is not a national of the Occupying Power, he is not bound to it by any duty of allegiance.

In any case, the death penalty may not be pronounced on a protected person who was under eighteen years of age at the time of the offence.

GC, Article 78 – If the Occupying Power considers it necessary, for imperative reasons of security, to take safety measures concerning protected persons, it may, at the most, subject them to assigned residence or to internment. Decisions regarding such assigned residence or internment shall be made according to a regular procedure to be prescribed by the Occupying Power in accordance with the provisions of the present Convention. This procedure shall include the right of appeal for the parties concerned. Appeals shall be decided with the least possible delay. In the event of the decision being upheld, it shall be subject to periodical review, if possible every six months, by a competent body set up by the said Power. Protected persons made subject to assigned residence and thus required to leave their homes shall enjoy the full benefit of Article 39 of the present Convention.

GC, Article 79 – The Parties to the conflict shall not intern protected persons, except in accordance with the provisions of Articles 41, 42, 43, 68 and 78.

GC, Article 80 – Internees shall retain their full civil capacity and shall exercise such attendant rights as may be compatible with their status.

GC, Article 82 – The Detaining Power shall, as far as possible, accommodate the internees according to their nationality, language and customs. Internees who are nationals of the same country shall not be separated merely because they have different languages. Throughout the duration of their internment, members of the same family, and in particular, parents and children, shall be lodged together in the same place of internment, except when separation of a temporary nature is necessitated for reasons of employment or health or for the purposes of enforcement of the provisions of Chapter IX of the present Section. Internees may request that their children who are left at liberty without parental care shall be interned with them. Wherever possible, interned members of the same family shall be housed in the same premises and given separate accommodation from other internees, together with facilities for leading a proper family life.

GC, Article 83 – The Detaining Power shall not set up places of internment in areas particularly exposed to the dangers of war. The Detaining Power shall give the enemy Powers, through the intermediary of the Protecting Powers, all useful information regarding the geographical location of places of internment. Whenever military considerations permit, internment camps shall be indicated by the letters IC, placed so as to be clearly visible in the daytime from the air. The Powers concerned may, however, agree upon any other system of marking. No place other than an internment camp shall be marked as such.

GC, Article 84 – Internees shall be accommodated and administered separately from prisoners of war and from persons deprived of liberty for any other reason.

GC, Article 85 – The Detaining Power is bound to take all necessary and possible measures to ensure that protected persons shall, from the outset of their internment, be accommodated in buildings or quarters which afford every possible safeguard as regards hygiene and health, and provide efficient protection against the rigours of the climate and the effects of the war. In no case shall permanent places of internment be situated in unhealthy areas or in districts, the climate of which is injurious to the internees. In all cases where the district, in which a protected person is temporarily interned, is an unhealthy area or has a climate which is harmful to his health, he shall be removed to a more suitable place of internment as rapidly as circumstances permit. The premises shall be fully protected from dampness, adequately heated and lighted, in particular, between dusk and lights out. The sleeping quarters shall be sufficiently spacious and well ventilated, and the internees shall have suitable bedding and sufficient blankets, account being taken of the climate, and the age, sex, and state of health of the internees. Internees shall have for their use, day and night, sanitary conveniences which conform to the rules of hygiene, and are constantly maintained in a state of cleanliness. They shall be provided with sufficient water and soap for their daily personal toilet and for washing their personal laundry; installations and facilities necessary for this purpose shall be granted to them. Showers or baths shall also be available. The necessary time shall be set aside for washing and for cleaning. Whenever it is necessary, as an exceptional and temporary measure, to accommodate women internees who are not members of a family unit in the same place of internment as men, the provision of separate sleeping quarters and sanitary conveniences for the use of such women internees shall be obligatory.

GC, Article 86 – The Detaining Power shall place at the disposal of interned persons, of whatever denomination, premises suitable for the holding of their religious services.

GC, Article 88 – In all places of internment exposed to air raids and other hazards of war, shelters adequate in number and structure to ensure the necessary protection shall be installed. In case of alarms, the internees shall be free to enter such shelters as quickly as possible, excepting those who remain for the protection of their quarters against the aforesaid hazards. Any protective measures taken in favour of the population shall also apply to them. All due precautions must be taken in places of internment against the danger of fire.

GC, Article 89 – Daily food rations for internees shall be sufficient in quantity, quality and variety to keep internees in a good state of health and prevent the development of nutritional deficiencies. Account shall also be taken of the customary diet of the internees. Internees shall also be given the means by which they can prepare for themselves any additional food in their possession. Sufficient drinking water shall be supplied to internees. The use of tobacco shall be permitted. Internees who work shall receive additional rations in proportion to the kind of labour which they perform. Expectant and nursing mothers and children under fifteen years of age, shall be given additional food, in proportion to their physiological needs.

GC, Article 90 – When taken into custody, internees shall be given all facilities to provide themselves with the necessary clothing, footwear and change of underwear, and later on, to procure further supplies, if required. Should any internees not have sufficient clothing, account being taken of the climate, and be unable to procure any, it shall be provided free of charge to them by the Detaining Power. The clothing supplied by the Detaining

Power to internees and the outward markings placed on their own clothes shall not be ignominious nor expose them to ridicule. Workers shall receive suitable working outfits, including protective clothing, whenever the nature of their work so requires.

GC, Article 93 – Internees shall enjoy complete latitude in the exercise of their religious duties, including attendance at the services of their faith, on condition that they comply with the disciplinary routine prescribed by the detaining authorities.

GC, Article 97 – Internees shall be permitted to retain articles of personal use. Monies, cheques, bonds, etc., and valuables in their possession may not be taken from them except in accordance with the established procedure. Detailed receipts shall be given thereof. The amounts shall be paid into the account of every internee as provided for in Article 98. Such amounts may not be converted into any other currency unless legislation in force in the territory in which the owner is interned so requires or the internee gives his consent. Articles which have above all a personal or sentimental value may not be taken away. A woman internee shall not be searched except by a woman. On release or repatriation, internees shall be given all articles, monies or other valuables taken from them during internment and shall receive in currency the balance of any credit to their accounts kept in accordance with Article 98, with the exception of any articles or amounts withheld by the Detaining Power by virtue of its legislation in force. If the property of an internee is so withheld, the owner shall receive a detailed receipt. Family or identity documents in the possession of internees may not be taken away without a receipt being given. At no time shall internees be left without identity documents. If they have none, they shall be issued with special documents drawn up by the detaining authorities, which will serve as their identity papers until the end of their internment. Internees may keep on their persons a certain amount of money, in cash or in the shape of purchase coupons, to enable them to make purchases.

GC, Article 99 – Every place of internment shall be put under the authority of a responsible officer, chosen from the regular military forces or the regular civil administration of the Detaining Power. The officer in charge of the place of internment must have in his possession a copy of the present Convention in the official language, or one of the official languages, of his country and shall be responsible for its application. The staff in control of internees shall be instructed in the provisions of the present Convention and of the administrative measures adopted to ensure its application. The text of the present Convention and the texts of special agreements concluded under the said Convention shall be posted inside the place of internment, in a language which the internees understand, or shall be in the possession of the Internee Committee. Regulations, orders, notices and publications of every kind shall be communicated to the internees and posted inside the places of internment in a language which they understand. Every order and command addressed to internees individually must, likewise, be given in a language which they understand.

GC, Article 100 – The disciplinary regime in places of internment shall be consistent with humanitarian principles, and shall in no circumstances include regulations imposing on internees any physical exertion dangerous to their health or involving physical or moral victimization. Identification by tattooing or imprinting signs or markings on the body, is prohibited. In particular, prolonged standing and roll-calls, punishment drill, military drill and manoeuvres, or the reduction of food rations, are prohibited.

Army Regulation 190–8, *Enemy Prisoners of War, Retained Personnel, Civilian Internees and Other Detainees*, 1 October 1997, Chapter 1, paragraph 1-1, subparagraphs a and b. This regulation is a multiservice regulation implementing DOD Directive 2310.1 and incorporates Army Regulation 190-8 and 190-57 and SECNAV Instruction 3461.3, and Air Force Joint Instruction 31-304 and outlines policies, procedures, and responsibilities for treatment of enemy prisoners of war (EPW), retained personnel (RP), civilian internees (CI), and other detainees (OD) and implements international law for all military operations. The specific language in the regulation follows:

"1–1. Purpose

a. This regulation provides policy, procedures, and responsibilities for the administration, treatment, employment, and compensation of enemy prisoners of war (EPW), retained personnel (RP), civilian internees (CI) and other detainees (OD) in the custody of U.S. Armed Forces. This regulation also establishes procedures for transfer of custody from the United States to another detaining power.

b. This regulation implements international law, both customary and codified, relating to EPW, RP, CI, and ODs which includes those persons held during military operations other than war."

b. **Finding 2:**

(1) *Finding*: In the cases the DAIG reviewed, all detainee abuse occurred when one or more individuals failed to adhere to basic standards of discipline, training, or Army Values; in some cases abuse was accompanied by leadership failure at the tactical level.

(2) *Standard*: Standard of treatment for detainees in OPERATION ENDURING FREEDOM (OEF): Guidance was provided stating that members of the Taliban militia and members of al Qaeda under the control of U.S. Forces would be treated humanely and, to the extent appropriate and consistent with military necessity, in a manner consistent with the principles of the Geneva Conventions of 1949. The DAIG has therefore used the provisions of the Geneva Conventions as a benchmark against which to measure the treatment provided to detainees by U.S. Forces to determine if detainees were treated humanely. The use of these standards as benchmarks does not state or imply a position for the United States or U.S. Army on the legal status of its operations in OEF.

Chairman, Joint Chiefs of Staff (CJCS) Message dated 211933Z JAN 02, provides the determination regarding the humane treatment of al Qaeda and Taliban detainees. *Convention Relative to the Treatment of Prisoners of War of August 12, 1949* (GPW) is the international treaty that governs the treatment of prisoners of war, and *Geneva Convention Relative to the Protection of Civilian Persons in Time of War (GC)*, August 12, 1949 is the international treaty that governs the treatment of civilian persons in time of war.

As the guidance did not define "humane treatment" but did state that the U.S. would treat members of the Taliban militia and al Qaeda in a manner consistent with the Geneva Conventions, the DAIG determined that it would use Common Article 3 of the GCs as its floor measure of humane treatment, but would also include provisions of the Geneva Convention on the Treatment of Prisoners of War (GPW) and Geneva Convention Relative to the Protection of Civilian Persons in Time of War (GC) as other relevant indicia of "humane treatment" The use of this standard does not state or imply a position for the United States or U.S. Army on the legal status of its operations in OEF.

Standard of treatment for detainees in OPERATION IRAQI FREEDOM (OIF): OIF was an international armed conflict and therefore the provisions of the Geneva Conventions applied. Additionally, the United States was an occupying power and has acted in accordance with the obligations of an occupying power described in the *Hague Convention No. IV Respecting the Laws and Customs of War on Land (H.IV)*, Oct. 18, 1907, including, but not limited to, Articles 43–46 and 50; *Geneva Convention Relative to the Treatment of Prisoners of War of August 12, 1949* (GPW); and *Geneva Convention Relative to the Protection of Civilian Persons in Time of War (GC)*, August 12, 1949. The GC supplements H.IV, providing the general standard of treatment at Article 27 and specific standards in subsequent Articles.

The minimum treatment provided by Common Article 3 of the Geneva Conventions is: (1) No adverse distinction based upon race, religion, sex, etc.; (2) No violence to life or person; (3) No taking hostages; (4) No degrading treatment; (5) No passing of sentences in absence of fair trial, and; (6) The wounded and sick must be cared for.

The specific language in the CJCS Message for OEF and the GPW/GC and H.IV follows:

CJCS Message dated 211933Z JAN 02, "Paragraph 3. The combatant commanders shall, in detaining al Qaeda and Taliban individuals under the control of the Department of Defense, treat them humanely and, to the extent appropriate and consistent with military necessity, in a manner consistent with the principles of the Geneva Conventions of 1949."

GPW/GC, Article 3 (Common Article 3) – "In the case of armed conflict not of an international character occurring in the territory of one of the High Contracting Parties, each party to the conflict shall be bound to apply, as a minimum, the following provisions:

1. Persons taking no active part in the hostilities, including members of armed forces who have laid down their arms and those placed hors de combat by sickness, wounds, detention, or any other cause, shall in all circumstances be treated humanely, without any adverse distinction founded on race, color, religion or faith, sex, birth or wealth, or any other similar criteria.

To this end the following acts are and shall remain prohibited at any time and in any place whatsoever with respect to the above-mentioned persons:

(a) Violence to life and person, in particular, murder of all kinds, mutilation, cruel treatment and torture;
(b) Taking of hostages;
(c) Outrages upon personal dignity, in particular, humiliating and degrading treatment;
(d) The passing of sentences and the carrying out of executions without previous judgment pronounced by a regularly constituted court affording all the judicial guarantees which are recognized as indispensable by civilized peoples.

2. The wounded and sick shall be collected and cared for. An impartial humanitarian body, such as the International Committee of the Red Cross, may offer its services to the Parties to the conflict. The Parties to the conflict should further endeavour to bring into force, by means of special agreements, all or part of the other provisions of the present Convention. The application of the preceding provisions shall not affect the legal status of the Parties to the conflict."

GPW, Article 13 – "Prisoners of war must at all times be humanely treated. Any unlawful act or omission by the Detaining Power causing death or seriously endangering the health of a prisoner of war in its custody is prohibited, and will be regarded as a serious breach of the present Convention. In particular, no prisoner of war may be subjected to physical mutilation or to medical or scientific experiments of any kind which are not justified by the medical, dental or hospital treatment of the prisoner concerned and carried out in his interest. Likewise, prisoners of war must at all times be protected, particularly against acts of violence or intimidation and against insults and public curiosity."

GPW, Article 14 – Prisoners of war are entitled in all circumstances to respect for their person and their honour. Women shall be treated with all the regard due to their sex and shall in all cases benefit by treatment as favourable as that granted to men. Prisoners of war shall retain the full civil capacity which they enjoyed at the time of their capture. The Detaining Power may not restrict the exercise, either within or without its own territory, of the rights such capacity confers except in so far as the captivity requires.

GPW, Article 15 – The Power detaining prisoners of war shall be bound to provide free of charge for their maintenance and for the medical attention required by their state of health.

GPW, Article 16 – Taking into consideration the provisions of the present Convention relating to rank and sex, and subject to any privileged treatment which may be accorded to them by reason of their state of health, age or professional qualifications, all prisoners of war shall be treated alike by the Detaining Power, without any adverse distinction based on race, nationality, religious belief or political opinions, or any other distinction founded on similar criteria.

GPW, Article 39 – "Every prisoner of war camp shall be put under the immediate authority of a responsible commissioned officer belonging to the regular armed forces of the Detaining Power. Such officer shall have in his possession a copy of the present Convention; he shall ensure that its provisions are known to the camp staff and the guard and shall be responsible, under the direction of his government, for its application. Prisoners of war, with the exception of officers, must salute and show to all officers of the Detaining Power the external marks of respect provided for by the regulations applying in their own forces. Officer prisoners of war are bound to salute only officers of a higher rank of the Detaining Power; they must, however, salute the camp commander regardless of his rank."

GPW, Article 41 – "In every camp the text of the present Convention and its Annexes and the contents of any special agreement provided for in Article 6, shall be posted, in the prisoners' own language, at places where all may read them. Copies shall be supplied, on request, to the prisoners who cannot have access to the copy which has been posted. Regulations, orders, notices and publications of every kind relating to the conduct of prisoners of war shall be issued to them in a language which they understand. Such regulations, orders and publications shall be posted in the manner described above and copies shall be handed to the prisoners' representative. Every order and command addressed to prisoners of war individually must likewise be given in a language which they understand."

GC, Article 27 – "Protected persons are entitled, in all circumstances, to respect for their persons, their honour, their family rights, their religious convictions and practices, and their manners and customs. They shall at all times be humanely treated, and shall be protected especially against all acts of violence or threats thereof and against insults and public curiosity. Women shall be especially protected against any attack on their honour, in particular, against rape, enforced prostitution, or any form of indecent assault. Without prejudice to the provisions relating to their state of health, age and sex, all protected persons shall be treated with the same consideration by the Party to the conflict in whose power they are, without any adverse distinction based, in particular, on race, religion or political opinion. However, the Parties to the conflict may take such measures of control and security in regard to protected persons as may be necessary as a result of the war."

GC, Article 31 – No physical or moral coercion shall be exercised against protected persons, in particular to obtain information from them or from third parties.

GC, Article 32 – The High Contracting Parties specifically agree that each of them is prohibited from taking any measure of such a character as to cause the physical suffering or extermination of protected persons in their hands. This prohibition applies not only to murder, torture, corporal punishments, mutilation and medical or scientific experiments not necessitated by the medical treatment of a protected person, but also to any other measures of brutality whether applied by civilian or military agents.

GC, Article 37 – "Protected persons who are confined pending proceedings or subject to a sentence involving loss of liberty, shall during their confinement be humanely treated."

GC, Article 41 – Should the Power, in whose hands protected persons may be, consider the measures of control mentioned in the present Convention to be inadequate, it may not have recourse to any other measure of control more severe than that of assigned residence or internment, in accordance with the provisions of Articles 42 and 43. In applying the provisions of Article 39, second paragraph, to the cases of persons required to leave their usual places of residence by virtue of a decision placing them in assigned residence, by virtue of a decision placing them in assigned residence, elsewhere, the Detaining Power shall be guided as closely as possible by the standards of welfare set forth in Part III, Section IV of this Convention.

GC, Article 42 – The internment or placing in assigned residence of protected persons may be ordered only if the security of the Detaining Power makes it absolutely necessary. If any person, acting through the representatives of the Protecting Power, voluntarily demands internment, and if his situation renders this step necessary, he shall be interned by the Power in whose hands he may be.

GC, Article 43 – Any protected person who has been interned or placed in assigned residence shall be entitled to have such action reconsidered as soon as possible by an appropriate court or administrative board designated by the Detaining Power for that purpose. If the internment or placing in assigned residence is maintained, the court or administrative board shall periodically, and at least twice yearly, give consideration to his or her case, with a view to the favorable amendment of the initial decision, if circumstances permit. Unless the protected persons concerned object, the Detaining Power shall, as rapidly as possible, give the Protecting Power the names of any protected persons who have been interned or subjected to assigned residence, or who have been released from internment or assigned residence. The decisions of the courts or boards mentioned in the first paragraph of the present Article shall also, subject to the same conditions, be notified as rapidly as possible to the Protecting Power.

GC, Article 68 – "Protected persons who commit an offence which is solely intended to harm the Occupying Power, but which does not constitute an attempt on the life or limb of members of the occupying forces or administration, nor a grave collective danger, nor seriously damage the property of the occupying forces or administration or the installations used by them, shall be liable to internment or simple imprisonment, provided the duration of such internment or imprisonment is proportionate to the offence committed. Furthermore, internment or imprisonment shall, for such offences, be the only measure adopted for depriving protected persons of liberty. The courts provided for under Article 66 of the present Convention may at their discretion convert a sentence of imprisonment to one of internment for the same period.

The penal provisions promulgated by the Occupying Power in accordance with Articles 64 and 65 may impose the death penalty on a protected person only in cases where the person is guilty of espionage, of serious acts of sabotage against the military installations of the Occupying Power or of intentional offences which have caused the death of one or more persons, provided that such offences were punishable by death under the law of the occupied territory in force before the occupation began.

The death penalty may not be pronounced on a protected person unless the attention of the court has been particularly called to the fact that since the accused is not a national of the Occupying Power, he is not bound to it by any duty of allegiance.

In any case, the death penalty may not be pronounced on a protected person who was under eighteen years of age at the time of the offence."

GC, Article 78 – If the Occupying Power considers it necessary, for imperative reasons of security, to take safety measures concerning protected persons, it may, at the most, subject them to assigned residence or to internment. Decisions regarding such assigned residence or internment shall be made according to a regular procedure to be prescribed by the Occupying Power in accordance with the provisions of the present Convention. This procedure shall include the right of appeal for the parties concerned. Appeals shall be decided with the least possible delay. In the event of the decision being upheld, it shall be subject to periodical review, if possible every six months, by a competent body set up by the said Power. Protected persons made subject to assigned residence and thus required to leave their homes shall enjoy the full benefit of Article 39 of the present Convention.

GC, Article 79 – The Parties to the conflict shall not intern protected persons, except in accordance with the provisions of Articles 41, 42, 43, 68 and 78.

GC, Article 80 – Internees shall retain their full civil capacity and shall exercise such attendant rights as may be compatible with their status.

GC, Article 82 – "The Detaining Power shall, as far as possible, accommodate the internees according to their nationality, language and customs. Internees who are nationals of the same country shall not be separated merely because they have different languages. Throughout the duration of their internment, members of the same family, and in particular, parents and children, shall be lodged together in the same place of internment, except when separation of a temporary nature is necessitated for reasons of employment or health or for the purposes of enforcement of the provisions of Chapter IX of the present Section. Internees may request that their children who are left at liberty without parental care shall be interned with them. Wherever possible, interned members of the same family shall be housed in the same premises and given separate accommodation from other internees, together with facilities for leading a proper family life.

GC, Article 83 – The Detaining Power shall not set up places of internment in areas particularly exposed to the dangers of war. The Detaining Power shall give the enemy Powers, through the intermediary of the Protecting Powers, all useful information regarding the geographical location of places of internment. Whenever military considerations permit, internment camps shall be indicated by the letters IC, placed so as to be clearly visible in the daytime from the air. The Powers concerned may, however, agree upon any other system of marking. No place other than an internment camp shall be marked as such.

GC, Article 84 – Internees shall be accommodated and administered separately from prisoners of war and from persons deprived of liberty for any other reason.

GC, Article 85 – The Detaining Power is bound to take all necessary and possible measures to ensure that protected persons shall, from the outset of their internment, be accommodated in buildings or quarters which afford every possible safeguard as regards hygiene and health, and provide efficient protection against the rigours of the climate and the effects of the war. In no case shall permanent places of internment be situated in unhealthy areas or in districts, the climate of which is injurious to the internees. In all cases where the district, in which a protected person is temporarily interned, is an unhealthy area or has a climate which is harmful to his health, he shall be removed to a more suitable place of internment as rapidly as circumstances permit. The premises shall be fully protected from dampness, adequately heated and lighted, in particular, between dusk and lights out. The sleeping quarters shall be sufficiently spacious and well ventilated, and the internees shall have suitable bedding and sufficient blankets, account being taken of the climate, and the age, sex, and state of health of the internees. Internees shall have for their use, day and night, sanitary conveniences which conform to the rules of hygiene, and are constantly maintained in a state of cleanliness. They shall be provided with sufficient water and soap for their daily personal toilet and for washing their personal laundry; installations and facilities necessary for this purpose shall be granted to them. Showers or baths shall also be available. The necessary time shall be set aside for washing and for cleaning. Whenever it is necessary, as an exceptional and temporary measure, to accommodate women internees who are not members of a family unit in the same place of internment as men, the pro-vision of separate sleeping quarters and sanitary conveniences for the use of such women internees shall be obligatory.

GC, Article 86 – The Detaining Power shall place at the disposal of interned per-sons, of whatever denomination, premises suitable for the holding of their religious services."

GC, Article 88 – "In all places of internment exposed to air raids and other hazards of war, shelters adequate in number and structure to ensure the necessary protection shall be installed. In case of alarms, the internees shall be free to enter such shelters as quickly as possible, excepting those who remain for the protection of their quarters against the aforesaid hazards. Any protective measures taken in favour of the population shall also apply to them. All due precautions must be taken in places of internment against the danger of fire.

GC, Article 89 – Daily food rations for internees shall be sufficient in quantity, quality and variety to keep internees in a good state of health and prevent the development of nutritional deficiencies. Account shall also be taken of the customary diet of the internees. Internees shall also be given the means by which they can prepare for themselves any additional food in their possession. Sufficient drinking water shall be supplied to internees. The use of tobacco shall be permitted. Internees who work shall receive additional rations in proportion to the kind of labour which they perform. Expectant and nursing mothers and children under fifteen years of age, shall be given additional food, in proportion to their physiological needs.

GC, Article 90 – When taken into custody, internees shall be given all facilities to provide themselves with the necessary clothing, footwear and change of underwear, and later on, to procure further supplies, if required. Should any internee not have sufficient clothing, account being taken of the climate, and be unable to procure any, it shall be provided free of charge to them by the Detaining Power. The clothing supplied by the Detaining Power to internees and the outward markings placed on their own clothes shall not be ignominious nor expose them to ridicule. Workers shall receive suitable working outfits, including protective clothing, whenever the nature of their work so requires."

GC, Article 93 – "Internees shall enjoy complete latitude in the exercise of their religious duties, including attendance at the services of their faith, on condition that they comply with the disciplinary routine prescribed by the detaining authorities."

GC, Article 97 – "Internees shall be permitted to retain articles of personal use. Monies, cheques, bonds, etc., and valuables in their possession may not be taken from them except in accordance with established procedure. Detailed receipts shall be given thereof. The amounts shall be paid into the account of every internee as provided for in Article 98. Such amounts may not be converted into any other currency unless legislation in force in the territory in which the owner is interned so requires or the internee gives his consent. Articles which have above all a personal or sentimental value may not be taken away. A woman internee shall not be searched except by a woman. On release or repatriation, internees shall be given all articles, monies or other valuables taken from them during internment and shall receive in currency the balance of any credit to their accounts kept in accordance with Article 98, with the exception of any articles or amounts withheld by the Detaining Power by virtue of its legislation in force. If the property of an internee is so withheld, the owner shall receive a detailed receipt. Family or identity documents in the possession of internees may not be taken away without a receipt being given. At no time shall internees be left without identity documents. If they have none, they shall be issued with special documents drawn up by the detaining authorities, which will serve as their identity papers until the end of their internment. Internees may keep on their persons a certain amount of money, in cash or in the shape of purchase coupons, to enable them to make purchases."

GC, Article 99 – "Every place of internment shall be put under the authority of a responsible officer, chosen from the regular military forces or the regular civil administration of the Detaining Power. The officer in charge of the place of internment must have in his possession a copy of the present Convention in the official language, or one of the official languages, of his country and shall be responsible for its application. The staff in control of internees shall be instructed in the provisions of the present Convention and of the administrative measures adopted to ensure its application. The text of the present Convention and the texts of special agreements concluded under the said Convention shall be posted inside the place of internment, in a language which the internees understand, or shall be in the possession of the internee Committee. Regulations, orders, notices and publications of every kind shall be communicated to the internees and posted inside the places of internment in a language which they understand. Every order and command addressed to internees individually must, likewise, be given in a language which they understand."

GC, Article 100 – "The disciplinary regime in places of internment shall be consistent with humanitarian principles, and shall in no circumstances include regulations imposing on internees any physical exertion dangerous to their health or involving physical or moral victimization. Identification by tattooing or imprinting signs or markings on the body, is prohibited. In particular, prolonged standing and roll-calls, punishment drill, military drill and manoeuvres, or the reduction of food rations, are prohibited."

H.IV, Article 43 – "The authority of the legitimate power having in fact passed into the hands of the occupant, the latter shall take all the measures in his power to restore, and ensure, as far as possible, public order and safety, while respecting, unless absolutely prevented, the laws in force in the country.

H.IV, Article 44 – A belligerent is forbidden to force the inhabitants of territory occupied by it to furnish information about the army of the other belligerent, or about its means of defense.

H.IV, Article 45 – It is forbidden to compel the inhabitants of occupied territory to swear allegiance to the hostile Power.

H.IV, Article 46 – Family honour and rights, the lives of persons, and private property, as well as religious convictions and practice, must be respected. Private property cannot be confiscated.

H.IV, Article 47 – Pillage is formally forbidden."

H.IV, Article 50 – "No general penalty, pecuniary or otherwise, shall be inflicted upon the population on account of the acts of individuals for which they cannot be regarded as jointly and severally responsible."

Army Regulation (AR) 190–8, *Enemy Prisoners of War, Retained Personnel, Civilian Internees and Other Detainees*, 1 October 1997, Chapter 1, paragraphs 1–5, subparagraphs *a*, *b*, and *c*; paragraph 2–1, subparagraph a (1)(*d*); and paragraph 5–1, subparagraph (6), provides instruction on the overall treatment of detainees. This regulation is a multiservice regulation implementing DOD Directive 2310.1 and incorporates Army Regulation 190–8 and 190–57 and SECNAV Instruction 3461.3, and Air Force Joint Instruction 31–304 and outlines policies, procedures, and responsibilities for treatment of enemy prisoners of war (EPW), retained personnel (RP), civilian internees (CI), and other detainees (OD) and implements international law for all military operations. The specific language in the regulation follows:

"1–5. General protection policy

a. U.S. policy, relative to the treatment of EPW, CI and RP in the custody of the U.S. Armed Forces, is as follows:

(1) All persons captured, detained, interned, or otherwise held in U.S. Armed Forces custody during the course of conflict will be given humanitarian care and treatment from the moment they fall into the hands of U.S. forces until final release or repatriation."

"(4) The inhumane treatment of EPW, CI, RP is prohibited and is not justified by the stress of combat or with deep provocation. Inhumane treatment is a serious and punishable violation under international law and the Uniform Code of Military Justice (UCMJ)."

"*b.* All prisoners will receive humane treatment without regard to race, nationality, religion, political opinion, sex, or other criteria. The following acts are prohibited: murder, torture, corporal punishment, mutilation, the taking of hostages, sensory deprivation, collective punishments, execution without trial by proper authority, and all cruel and degrading treatment.

c. All persons will be respected as human beings. They will be protected against all acts of violence to include rape, forced prostitution, assault and theft, insults, public curiosity, bodily injury, and reprisals of any kind. They will not be subjected to medical or scientific experiments. This list is not exclusive. EPW/RP is to be protected from all threats or acts of violence."

"2–1. a. (1)(*d*) Prisoners may be interrogated in the combat zone. The use of physical or mental torture or any coercion to compel prisoners to provide information is prohibited. . . . Prisoners may not be threatened, insulted, or exposed to unpleasant or disparate treatment of any kind because of their refusal to answer questions."

"5–1 (6) The following acts are specifically prohibited:

(a) Any measures of such character as to cause the physical suffering or extermination of the CI. This prohibition applies not only to murder, torture, corporal punishment, mutilation, and medical or scientific experiments, but also to any other measure of brutality.
(b) Punishment of the CI for an offense they did not personally commit.
(c) Collective penalties and all measures of intimidation and terrorism against the CI.
(d) Reprisals against the CI and their property.
(e) The taking and holding of the CI as hostages."

AR 600–20, *Army Command Policy*, Chapter 1, paragraph 1–5, subparagraph c (1), and (4), prescribes the policies and responsibilities of command. The specific language in the regulation follows:

"c. Characteristics of command leadership.

The commander is responsible for establishing leadership climate of the unit and developing disciplined and cohesive units. This sets the parameters within which command will be exercised and, therefore, sets the tone for social and duty relationships within the command. Commanders are also responsible for the professional development of their soldiers. To this end, they encourage self-study, professional development, and continued growth of their subordinates' military careers.

(1) Commanders and other leaders committed to the professional Army ethic promote a positive environment. If leaders show loyalty to their soldiers, the Army, and the Nation, they earn the loyalty of their soldiers. If leaders consider their soldiers' needs and care for their well-being, and if they demonstrate genuine concern, these leaders build a positive command climate."

"(4) Professionally competent leaders will develop respect for their authority by-

(*a*) Striving to develop, maintain, and use the full range of human potential in their organization. This potential is a critical factor in ensuring that the organization is capable of accomplishing its mission.

(b) Giving troops constructive information on the need for and purpose of military discipline. Articles in the UCMJ which require explanation will be presented in such a way to ensure that soldiers are fully aware of the controls and obligations imposed on them by virtue of their military service. (See Art 137, UCMJ.)

(c) Properly training their soldiers and ensuring that both soldiers and equipment are in the proper state of readiness at all times. Commanders should assess the command climate periodically to analyze the human dimension of combat readiness. Soldiers must be committed to accomplishing the mission through the unit cohesion developed as a result of a healthy leadership climate established by the command. Leaders at all levels promote the individual readiness of their soldiers by developing competence and confidence in their subordinates. In addition to being mentally, physically, tactically, and technically competent, soldiers must have confidence in themselves, their equipment, their peers, and their leaders. A leadership climate in which all soldiers are treated with fairness, justice, and equity will be crucial to development of this confidence within soldiers. Commanders are responsible for developing disciplined and cohesive units sustained at the highest readiness level possible."

c. **Finding 3:**
   (1) *Finding*: Of all facilities inspected, only Abu Ghraib was determined to be undesirable for housing detainees because it is located near an urban population and is under frequent hostile fire, placing soldiers and detainees at risk.
   (2) *Standard*: *Hague Convention No. IV Respecting the Laws and Customs of War on Land (H.IV)*, Oct. 18, 1907, Articles 43–46 and 50; and *Geneva Convention Relative to the Protection of Civilian Persons in Time of War (GC)*, Aug 12, 1949, Articles 81, 83, 85, 88, 89, and 91 discuss the requirement to accommodate detainees in buildings or quarters which afford every possible safeguard regarding health and hygiene and the effects of war. The specific language in the GC follows:

GC Article 81 – "Parties to the conflict who intern protected persons shall be bound to provide free of charge for their maintenance, and to grant them also the medical attention required by their state of health. No deduction from the allowances, salaries or credits due to the internees shall be made for the repayment of these costs.

GC, Article 83 – "The Detaining Power shall not set up places of internment in areas particularly exposed to the dangers of war. . . .

GC, Article 84 – Internees shall be accommodated and administered separately from prisoners of war and from persons deprived of liberty for any other reason.

GC, Article 85 – The Detaining Power is bound to take all necessary and possible measures to ensure that protected persons shall, from the outset of their internment, be accommodated in buildings or quarters which afford every possible safeguard as regards hygiene and health, and provide efficient protection against the rigors of the climate and the effects of the war. In no case shall permanent places of internment be situated in unhealthy areas or in districts, the climate of which is injurious to the internees. In all cases where the district, in which a protected person is temporarily interned, is an unhealthy area or has a climate which is harmful to his health, he shall be removed to a more suitable place of internment as rapidly as circumstances permit. The premises shall be fully protected from dampness, adequately heated and lighted, in particular, between dusk and lights out. The sleeping quarters shall be sufficiently spacious and well ventilated, and the internees shall have suitable bedding and sufficient blankets, account being taken of the climate, and the age, sex, and state of health of the internees. Internees shall have for their use, day and night, sanitary conveniences which conform to the rules of hygiene, and are constantly maintained in a state of cleanliness. They shall be provided with sufficient water and soap for their daily personal toilet and for washing their personal laundry; installations and facilities necessary for this purpose shall be granted to them. Showers or baths shall also be available. The necessary time shall be set aside for washing and for cleaning. Whenever it is necessary, as an exceptional and temporary measure, to accommodate women internees who are not members of a family unit in the same place of internment as men, the provision of separate sleeping quarters and sanitary conveniences for the use of such women internees shall be obligatory."

GC, Article 88 – "In all places of internment exposed to air raids and other hazards of war, shelters adequate in number and structure to ensure the necessary protection shall be installed.

GC, Article 89 – Daily food rations for internees shall be sufficient in quantity, quality and variety to keep internees in a good state of health and prevent the development of nutritional deficiencies. Account shall also be taken of the customary diet of the internees. Internees shall also be given the means by which they can prepare for themselves any additional food in their possession. Sufficient drinking water shall be supplied to internees. . . ."

GC Article 91 – "Every place of internment shall have an adequate infirmary, under the direction of a qualified doctor, where internees may have the attention they require, as well as appropriate diet. Isolation wards shall be set aside for cases of contagious or mental diseases. Maternity cases and internees suffering from serious diseases, or whose condition requires special treatment, a surgical operation or hospital care, must be admitted to any institution where adequate treatment can be given and shall receive care not inferior to that provided for the general population. Internees shall, for preference, have the attention of medical personnel of their own nationality. Internees may not be prevented from presenting themselves to the medical authorities for examination. The medical authorities of the Detaining Power shall, upon request, issue to every internee who has undergone treatment an official certificate showing the nature of his illness or injury, and the duration and nature of the treatment given. A duplicate of this certificate shall be forwarded to the Central Agency provided for in Article 140 Treatment, including the provision of any apparatus necessary for the maintenance of internees in good health, particularly dentures and other artificial appliances and spectacles, shall be given free of charge to the internee."

Army Regulation 190–8, *Enemy Prisoners of War, Retained Personnel, Civilian Internees and Other Detainees*, 1 October 1997, Chapter 5, paragraph 5–2, subparagraph a, states that a safety program for civilian internees (CIs) will be established. Chapter 6, paragraph 6–1, subparagraphs a & b, (1) through (4), states commanders' responsibilities regarding housing, caring for, and safeguarding CIs in facilities. This regulation is a multiservice regulation implementing DOD Directive 2310.1 and incorporates Army Regulation 190–8 and 190–57 and SECNAV Instruction 3461.3, and Air Force Joint Instruction 31–304 and outlines policies, procedures, and responsibilities for treatment of enemy prisoners of war (EPW), retained personnel (RP), civilian internees (CI), and other detainees (OD) and implements international law for all military operations. The specific language in the regulation follows: "a. Establishment. A safety program for the CI will be established and administered in accordance with the policies prescribed in AR 385–10 and other pertinent safety directives.

"6–1. Internment Facility

a. Location. The theater commander will be responsible for the location of the CI internment facilities within his or her command. The CI retained temporarily in an unhealthy area or where the climate is harmful to their health will be removed to a more suitable place of internment as soon as possible.

b. Quarters. Adequate shelters to ensure protection against air bombardments and other hazards of war will be provided and precautions against fire will be taken at each CI camp and branch camp.

(1) All necessary and possible measures will be taken to ensure that CI shall, from the outset of their internment, be accommodated in buildings or quarters which afford every possible safeguard as regards hygiene and health, and provide efficient protection against the rigors of the climate and the effects of war. In no case shall permanent places of internment be placed in unhealthy areas, or in districts the climate of which is injurious to CI.

(2) The premises shall be fully protected from dampness, adequately heated and lighted, in particular, between dusk and lights out. The sleeping quarters shall be sufficiently spacious and well ventilated, and the internees shall have suitable bedding and sufficient blankets, account being taken of the climate, and the age, sex and state of health of the internees.

(3) Internees shall have for their use, day and night, sanitary conveniences which conform to the rules of hygiene and are constantly maintained in a state of cleanliness. They shall be provided with sufficient water and soap for their daily personal hygiene and for washing their personal laundry; installations and facilities necessary for this purpose shall be provided. Showers or baths shall also be available. The necessary time shall be set aside for washing and for cleaning.

(4) CI shall be administered and housed separately from EPW/RP. Except in the case of families, female CI shall be housed in separate quarters and shall be under the direct supervision of women."

Field Manual (FM) 3-19.1, *Military Police Operations*, 31 January 2002, Chapter 4, paragraph 4-44, describes the capability of a modular internment/resettlement (I/R) Military Police (MP) battalion that is trained and equipped for an I/R mission. The specific language in the field manual follows:

"4-44. Although the CS MP unit initially handles EPWs/CIs, modular MP (I/R) battalions with assigned MP guard companies and supporting MWD teams are equipped and trained to handle this mission for the long term. A properly configured modular MP (I/R) battalion can support, safeguard, account for, guard, and provide humane treatment for up to 4,000 EPWs/CIs; 8,000 dislocated civilians; or 1,500 US military prisoners."

FM 3-19.40, *Military Police Internment/Resettlement Operations*, 1 August 2001, Chapter 6, paragraphs 6-2 and 6–3, discuss the considerations of choosing sites for I/R facilities. The specific language in the field manual follows:

"6-2. The MP coordinate the location with engineers, logistical units, higher headquarters, and the HN. The failure to properly consider and correctly evaluate all factors may increase the logistical and personnel efforts required to support operations. If an I/R facility is improperly located, the entire internee population may require movement when resources are scarce. When selecting a site for a facility, consider the following:

- Will the interned population pose a serious threat to logistical operations if the tactical situation becomes critical?
- Is there a threat of guerrilla activity in the area?
- What is the attitude of the local population?
- What classification of internees will be housed at the site?
- What type of terrain surrounds the site, and will it help or hinder escapes?
- What is the distance from the MSR to the source of logistical support?
- What transportation methods are required and available to move internees, supplies, and equipment?

6–3. In addition, consider the –

- METT-TC.
- Proximity to probable target areas.
- Availability of suitable existing facilities (avoids unnecessary construction).
- Presence of swamps, mosquitoes, and other factors (including water drainage) that affect human health.
- Existence of an adequate, satisfactory source of potable water. The supply should meet the demands for consumption, food sanitation, personal hygiene, and sewage disposal.
- Availability of electricity. Portable generators can be used as standby and emergency sources of electricity.
- Distance to work if internees are employed outside the facility.
- Availability of construction material.
- Soil drainage."

d. **Finding 4:**

(1) *Finding*: Tactical commanders and leaders adapted to the environment and held detainees longer than doctrinally recommended due to the demand for timely, tactical intelligence.

(2) *Standard*: Army Regulation (AR) 190–8, *Enemy Prisoners of War, Retained Personnel, Civilian Internees and Other Detainees*, 1 October 1997, Chapter 2, paragraph 2–1, subparagraph a (d), states that prisoners may be interrogated in the combat zone; subparagraph a (e) states that prisoners will be evacuated as quickly as possible from the collecting points (CPs) to the Corps Holding Area (CHA). If evacuation is delayed the detaining force will increase the level of humanitarian care provided at the CP. Chapter 3, paragraph 3–2, subparagraph b, states that CPs will operate under conditions similar to those prescribed for internment camps; paragraph 3–4, subparagraph e, requires enemy prisoners of war (EPWs) and retained persons (RP) to be housed under the same conditions as U.S. Forces residing in the same area; subparagraph i requires EPW/RP facilities to ensure a clean and healthy environment for detainees. Chapter 6, paragraph 6–1, subparagraph b, requires that internment facilities for CIs provide a safe and sanitary environment; paragraph 6–6, subparagraph g, requires facilities housing Civilian Internees (CI) to provide hygiene and sanitation measures in accordance with AR 40–5, *Preventive Medicine*. This regulation is a multiservice regulation implementing DOD Directive 2310.1 and incorporates Army Regulation 190–8 and 190–57 and SECNAV Instruction 3461.3, and Air Force Joint Instruction 31–304 and outlines policies, procedures, and responsibilities for treatment of EPW, RP, CI, and other detainees (OD) and implements international law for all military operations. The specific language in the regulation follows:

2–1. a. (d) – "Prisoners may be interrogated in the combat zone.

2–1. a. (e) – "Prisoners will be humanely evacuated from the combat zone and into appropriate channels as quickly as possible. . . . When military necessity requires delay in evacuation beyond a reasonable period of time, health and comfort items will be issued, such as food, potable water, appropriate clothing, shelter, and medical attention.

3–2. b. – ". . . Transit camps or collecting points will operate under conditions similar to those prescribed for permanent prisoner of war camps, and the prisoners will receive the same treatment as in permanent EPW camps.

3–4. e. – "EPW/RP will be quartered under conditions as favorable as those for the force of the detaining power billeted in the same area. The conditions shall make allowance for the habits and customs of the prisoners and shall in no case be prejudicial to their health. The forgoing shall apply in particular to the dormitories of EPW/RP as it regards both total surface and minimum cubic space and the general installation of bedding and blankets. Quarters furnished to EPW/RP must be protected from dampness, must be adequately lit and heated. (particularly between dusk and lights-out), and must have adequate precautions taken against the dangers of fire. In camps accommodating both sexes, EPW/RP will be provided with separate facilities for women.

Field Manual (FM) 3-19.40, *Military Police Internment/Resettlement Operations*, 1 August 2001, Introduction, explains the role of MPs in establishing CPs. Chapter 3, paragraph 3-1, further explains the MP role in establishing CPs and CHAs; paragraph 3–3, states that MPs and MI interrogation teams should work closely at CPs and CHAs to make a determination of the potential intelligence value of detainees; paragraphs 3-37, 3-45 and 3-54, state that divisions will operate forward and central CPs as temporary holding areas until detainees are removed from the battlefield and transferred to the CHA. Doctrine states that detainees should remain at a forward CP no longer than 12 hours, and a central CP no longer than 24 hours. Paragraphs 3-41 to 3-43 identify planning considerations for division forward and central CPs. Doctrine identifies divisions providing minimum medical, preventive medical, logistics, personnel and infrastructure support to hold detainees for 12 hours at forward CPs and for 24 hours at central CPs. Paragraph 3-49 describes the Preventive Medicine (PVNTMED) support to a central CP. Paragraph 3-55 states that CHAs are more permanent than CPs and must be prepared to hold detainees for 72 hours. External support is required if CHAs are required to hold detainees for more than 72 hours. Chapter 5, paragraph 5-52, describes the sanitation requirements for Civilian Internee (CI) populations. The specific language in the field manual follows:

Introduction – "A large number of captives on the battlefield hampers maneuver units as they move to engage and destroy an enemy. To assist maneuver units in performing their mission —

- Division MP units operate CPs in the division AO.
- Corps MP units operate holding areas in the corps AO."

"3.1. The MP units accept captives from capturing units as far forward as possible, and captives are held in CPs and CHAs until they are removed from the battlefield. Normally, CPs are operated in the division AO and CHAs are operated in the corps AO; but they can be operated anywhere they are needed. The CPs and CHAs sustain and safeguard captives and ensure a minimum level of field processing and accountability. Wounded and sick captives receive medical treatment, and captives who require lifesaving medical attention are evacuated to the nearest medical facility.

3.3. The MP work closely with military intelligence (MI) interrogation teams at CPs and CHAs to determine if captives, their equipment, and their weapons have intelligence value. This process is accelerated when MI interrogation teams can observe captives during arrival and processing, and interrogators can also be used as interpreters during this phase. Before a captive is interviewed by MI personnel, he must have a Department of Defense (DD) Form 2745 (Figure 3-1) attached to him and be accounted for on DD Form 2708.

3-37. A division operates two types of CPs-forward and central. A division MP company operates forward CPs in each maneuver brigade AO and a central CP in the division rear area. Both CPs are temporary areas designed to hold captives until they are removed from the battlefield. Forward CPs are positioned as far forward as possible to accept captives from maneuver elements. Central CPs accept captives from forward CPs and local units.

3-41. Medical support is provided by the MP company medical section. Additional medical support can be requested through the forward support battalion (FSB) to the brigade medical officer. The brigade OPORD includes specific actions and support (operational requirements) needed from non-MP units.

3-42. When a division MP company commander is tasked with planning and operating a forward CP, he-

- Coordinates with the unit responsible for the area.
- Conducts a recon of the area before selecting a location.
- Locates it far enough from the fighting to avoid minor shifts in the main battle area (MBA) (normally 5 to 10 kilometers).
- Notifies the BSA tactical operations center (TOC) and the PM operations section of the selected location (grid coordinates). The BSA TOC reports the location to the brigade TOC, and the brigade TOC notifies subordinate units.
- Coordinates with MI on co-locating an MI interrogation team at the CP.
- Provides potable water and, if required, food for captives.

3-43. A forward CP is seldom located near the indigenous population to prevent problems caused by the presence of captives in the area. A forward CP is usually a guarded, roped-off area (concertina or razor tape) or a secure, fixed facility. The capture rate and the captive categories determine the size of forward CP.

3-45. Captives should not remain at a forward CP more than 12 hours before being escorted to the central CP.

3-49. The division PVNTMED section supports the central CP by –

- Monitoring drinking water and advising on disinfection procedures.
- Controlling animals and insects that carry disease.
- Ensuring that captives help prevent illness by –
- Drinking enough water.
  - Wearing clothing that is suited for the weather and the situation.
  - Handling heating fuels carefully.
  - Avoiding contact of exposed skin to cold metal.
  - Using insect repellent, netting, and insecticides.
  - Taking approved preventive medication.
  - Using purification tablets when water quality is uncertain.
  - Disposing of bodily wastes properly.
  - Practicing personal hygiene.

3-54. Captives should not remain at the central CP more than 24 hours before being evacuated to the CHA.

3-55. A CHA (Figure 3-4) can hold more captives for longer periods of times than a central CP. Depending on the availability of MP units to establish I/R facilities, corps MP units must be prepared to hold captives at the CHA more than 72 hours. If the CHA keeps captives more than 72 hours, MP must plan and coordinate for the increased logistics and personnel required to operate a long-term facility. The decision to hold captives longer is based on METT-TC and the availability of forces. Captives remain in the CHA until they are evacuated to an I/R facility or until hostilities end."

e. **Finding 5:**
   (1) *Finding*: Doctrine does not clearly specify the interdependent, and yet independent, roles, missions, and responsibilities of Military Police and Military Intelligence units in the establishment and operation of interrogation facilities.

(2) *Standard*: Department of Defense Directive (DoDD) 2310. 1, *DoD Program for Enemy Prisoners of War (EPOW) and Other Detainees*, 18 August 1994, Paragraph 3.4, outlines the disposition of persons captured or detained and indicates who should operate collecting points, other holding facilities and installations. The specific language in the directive follows:

"Persons captured or detained by the U.S. Military Services shall normally be handed over for safeguarding to U.S. Army Military Police, or to detainee collecting points or other holding facilities and installations operated by U.S. Army Military Police as soon as practical. Detainees may be interviewed for intelligence collection purposes at facilities and installations operated by U.S. Army Military Police."

Joint Publication (JP) 1-02, *Department of Defense Dictionary of Military and Associated Terms*, 12 April 2001 (as amended through 23 March 2004), defines "tactical control", often abbreviated by the acronym "TACON". The specific language in the joint publication follows:

"Tactical control – Command authority over assigned or attached forces or commands, or military capability or forces made available for tasking, that is limited to the detailed direction and control of movements or maneuvers within the operational area necessary to accomplish missions or tasks assigned. Tactical control is inherent in operational control. Tactical control may be delegated to, and exercised at any level at or below the level of combatant command. When forces are transferred between combatant commands, the command relationship the gaining commander will exercise (and the losing commander will relinquish) over these forces must be specified by the Secretary of Defense. Tactical control provides sufficient authority for controlling and directing the application of force or tactical use of combat support assets within the assigned mission or task. Also called TACON."

JP 2-01, *Joint Intelligence Support to Military Operations*, 20 November 1996, Appendix G, paragraph 1, subparagraph d, describes the organization and function of the Joint Interrogation and Debriefing Center (JIDC). The specific language in the joint publication follows:

"Joint Interrogation and Debriefing Center. The JFC normally tasks the Army component commander to establish, secure, and maintain an EPW camp system. Under some circumstances, particularly during MOOTW, the JFC may designate another component commander to be responsible for the EPW camp system. The subordinate joint force J-2 establishes a JIDC for follow-on exploitation. The establishment (when, where, and how) of the JIDC is highly situation dependent, with the main factors being the geographic nature of the JOA, the type and pace of military operations, the camp structure, and the number and type of the sources. The JIDC may be a central site where appropriate EPW are segregated for interrogation, or it may be more of a clearinghouse operation for dispatch of interrogators or debriefers to other locations.

- Organization. The JIDC interrogation and debriefing activities are managed by the subordinate joint force HUMINT staff section or HOC. The HOC will coordinate with the TFCICA within the J-2X for CI [counter-intelligence] augmentation for exploitation of those personnel of CI [counter-intelligence] interest, such as civil and/or military leadership, intelligence or political officers and terrorists. The staff is augmented by deployed DHS personnel, linguists and, as required, component personnel. The HUMINT appendix of Annex B (Intelligence) to the OPLAN or CONPLAN contains JIDC planning considerations.
- Responsibilities. Service component interrogators collect tactical intelligence from EPWs based on joint force J-2 criteria. EPWs (i.e., senior level EPWs) are screened by

the components and those of further intelligence potential are identified and processed for follow-on interrogation and debriefing by the JIDC to satisfy theater strategic and operational requirements. In addition to EPW, the JIDC may also interrogate civilian detainees, and debrief refugees as well as other non-prisoner sources for operational and strategic information."

FM 3-31, *Joint Force Land Component Commander Handbook (JFLCC)*, 13 December 2001, Appendix A, paragraph A-11, describes the roles of the Joint Interrogation Facility (JIF) and the Joint Interrogation and Debriefing Center (JIDC). The specific language in the field manual follows:

"The following may be established or requested by the JFLCC in addition to the J-2X [J-2 CI [counter-intelligence] and HUMINT Support Element] and JACE [Joint Analysis and Control Element]:

Joint Interrogation Facility (JIF). JIF conducts initial screening and interrogation of EPWs, translation and exploitation of captured adversary documents, and debriefing of captured or detained US personnel released or escaped from adversary control. It coordinates exploitation of captured equipment with the JCMEC [Joint Captured Material Exploitation Center], documents with the JDEC [Joint Document Exploitation Center], and human sources with the JIDC [Joint Interrogation and Debriefing Center]. More than one JIF may be established in the JOA depending upon the anticipated number of EPWs.

JIDC. JIDC conducts follow-on exploitation of EPWs. EPWs are screened by the JIFs, and those of further intelligence potential are identified and forwarded to the JIDC for follow-on interrogation and debriefing in support of JTF and higher requirements. Besides EPWs, the JIDC may also interrogate civilian detainees, refugees, and other non-prisoner sources. JIDC activities are managed by the J-2X HOC [HUMINT Operations Cell]."

FM 34-52, *Intelligence Interrogation*, 28 September 1992, Preface, establishes this FM as the doctrinal foundation for interrogations of detainees. Chapter 1 defines and explains the purpose of interrogation. Chapter 2 describes the organization and operation of the Theater Interrogation Facility (TIF). The specific language in the field manual follows:

Preface – "This manual provides doctrinal guidance, techniques, and procedures governing employment of interrogators as human intelligence (HUMINT) collection assets in support of the commander's intelligence needs. It outlines the interrogator's role within the intelligence collection effort and the supported unit's day-to-day operations.

This manual is intended for use by interrogators as well as commanders, staff officers, and military intelligence (MI) personnel charged with the responsibility of the interrogation collection effort."

Chapter 1 – "Interrogation is the process of questioning a source to obtain the maximum amount of usable information. The goal of any interrogation is to obtain reliable information in a lawful manner, in a minimum amount of time, and to satisfy intelligence requirements of any echelon of command.

A good interrogation produces needed information, which is timely, complete, clear, and accurate."

Chapter 2 – "At echelons above corps (EAC), the MI company (I&E), MI battalion (C&E) or (I&E), MI brigade (EAC), will form the Theater Interrogation Facility (TIF). The TIF, which is commanded by an MI captain, provides interrogation support to the theater or joint command and to national level intelligence agencies. The TIF will –

- Be located within the main theater EPW internment facility.
- Be tailored organizationally to meet requirements of the theater and situation.

- Include interrogators, CI [counter-intelligence] personnel, and intelligence analysts from the Army, Air Force, Marine Corps, and, in some cases, the Navy.
- Be organized similarly to the CIF; that is, by function.
- Have intelligence analysts to handle requirements and keep interrogators informed of changes in the operational or strategic situation.
- Maintain the capability to deploy "GO" teams to multiple theater EPW camps, as well as to forward deploy them to corps and ECB as needed.
- Provide experienced senior interrogation warrant officers and NCOs who are graduates of the Department of Defense (DOD) Strategic Debriefer Course (additional skill identifier 9N or N7) and physical plant for the Joint Debriefing Center (JDC), where exploitation of high-level (Category A) sources takes place on operational and strategic topics."

"THEATER INTERROGATION FACILITY

The EAC interrogation facility will normally be designated as the TIF. A TIF is staffed by US Army interrogators and analysts, with support from Air Force, Navy, Marine Corps, and other US national agencies as required. In a multinational operation, a combined interrogation facility may be established with allied interrogator augmentation. In addition to conventional theater Army operations, a TIF may be established to support a joint or unified command to meet theater requirements during crisis or contingency deployments. MI battalion companies, MI brigade (EAC) provide US Army interrogation support to the EAC TIF. The mission of the TIF is to –

- Establish liaison with host nation (HN) commanders to achieve critical intelligence information in response to theater and national level intelligence collection requirements.
- Ensure communication between HN and US military TF commanders, and establish rapport with HN interrogation activities.
- Coordinate for national level collection requirements.
- Interrogate PWs, high-level political and military personnel, civilian internees, defectors, refugees, and displaced persons.
- Participate in debriefings of US and allied personnel who have escaped after being captured, or who have evaded capture.
- Translate and exploit selected CEDs.
- Assist in technical support activity (TSA) operations (see FM 34-5(S)).

The MI battalion (I&E) has an HHC for C³, and three interrogation companies, of which one is Active Component (AC) and the other two are RC. The companies consist of two MI companies, I&E (EPW support) and one MI company, I&E (GS-EAC).

The two MI companies support EPW compound operations. Their elements are primarily for GS at EAC, but may be deployed for DS at corps and division. The MI company (I&E) (GS-EAC) provides priority interrogation and DOCEX support to corps and divisions, to the TIF, and to temporary EPW compounds as required.

A TIF is organized into a headquarters section, operations section, and two interrogation and DOCEX sections. It will normally have an attached TSA section from Operations Group, and a liaison team from the Joint Captured Materiel Exploitation Center (JCMEC). The JCMEC liaison team assists in exploiting sources who have knowledge of captured enemy weapons and equipment.

The headquarters section provides all command, administrative, logistical, and maintenance support to the TIF. It coordinates with –

- Commander, MI Battalion (I&E) for personnel status, administrative support, and logistical support prior to deployment.
- Battalion S3 for deployment of interrogation assets.
- Theater J2 for reporting procedures, operational situation update, and theater and national level intelligence requirements.
- Provost marshal for location of theater EPW camps, and for procedures to be followed by interrogators and MP for processing, interrogating, and internment.
- Commanders of theater medical support units and internment facility for procedures to treat, and clear for questioning, wounded EPWs.
- Commander, CI [counter-intelligence] company, for CI [counter-intelligence] requirements and joint interrogation and CI [counter-intelligence] procedures.

OPERATIONS SECTION

This section (where ideally the officer in charge [OIC] has the 3Q additional skill identifier) is organized into the operations, OB, and communications elements. The operations section –

- Designates work areas for all TIF elements.
- Establishes and maintains TIF functional files.
- Establishes interrogation priorities.
- Maintains a daily log and journal.
- Disseminates incoming and outgoing distribution.
- Conducts liaison with local officials, adjacent and subordinate intelligence activities, CI [counter-intelligence], MP, PSYOP, the JCMEC, Plans and Policy Directorate (J5), and provost marshal.
- Conducts coordination with holding area OIC or enclosure commander for screening site, medical support, access, movement, and evacuation procedures for EPWs.
- Conducts operations briefings when required.
- Manages screening operations.
- Manages EPW access for intelligence collection.
- Assigns control numbers (see DIAM 58–13).
- Supervises all intelligence collection activities within the TIF."

Army Regulation (AR) 190-8, *Enemy Prisoners of War, Retained Personnel, Civilian Internees and Other Detainees*, 1 October 1997, Chapter 2, paragraph 2-1, provides the regulatory guidance for interrogation of detainees in a combat zone. This regulation is a multiservice regulation implementing DOD Directive 2310.1 and incorporates Army Regulation 190-8 and 190-57 and SECNAV Instruction 3461.3, and Air Force Joint Instruction 31-304 and outlines policies, procedures, and responsibilities for treatment of enemy prisoners of war (EPW), retained personnel (RP), civilian internees (CI), and other detainees (OD) and implements international law for all military operations. The specific language in the regulation follows:

"(d) Prisoners may be interrogated in the combat zone. The use of physical or mental torture or any coercion to compel prisoners to provide information is prohibited. Prisoners may voluntarily cooperate with PSYOP personnel in the development, evaluation, or dissemination of PSYOP messages or products. Prisoners may not be threatened, insulted, or exposed to unpleasant or disparate treatment of any kind because of their refusal to answer questions. Interrogations will normally be performed by intelligence or counter-intelligence personnel."

Field Manual (FM) 3–19.1, *Military Police Operations*, 31 January 2002, Chapter 4, paragraphs 4-42 and 4-43, describe the role of MP units in detainee operations and references MI. The specific language in the field manual follows:

"4-42. The Army is the Department of Defense's (DoD's) executive agent for all EPW/CI operations. Additionally, the Army is DoD's executive agent for long-term confinement of US military prisoners. Within the Army and through the combatant commander, the MP is tasked with coordinating shelter, protection, accountability, and sustainment for EPWs/CIs. The I/R function addresses MP roles when dealing with EPWs/CIs, dislocated civilians, and US military prisoners.

4-43. The I/R function is of humane as well as tactical importance. In any conflict involving US forces, safe and humane treatment of EPWs/CIs is required by international law. Military actions on the modern battlefield will result in many EPWs/CIs. Entire units of enemy forces, separated and disorganized by the shock of intensive combat, may be captured. This can place a tremendous challenge on tactical forces and can significantly reduce the capturing unit's combat effectiveness. The MP supports the battlefield commander by relieving him of the problem of handling EPWs/CIs with combat forces. The MP performs their I/R function of collecting, evacuating, and securing EPWs throughout the AO. In this process, the MP coordinates with MI to collect information that may be used in current or future operations."

FM 3-19.40, *Military Police Internment/Resettlement Operations*, 1 August 2001, Preface, establishes this FM as the doctrinal foundation for detainee operations. Chapter 2, paragraph 2-1, describes the role of the MP Battalion Commander. Chapter 3, paragraph 3-3, states the need for MP and MI to work closely, and paragraphs 3-64 to 3-66 describe the MP-MI interaction at collecting points (CPs) and corps holding areas (CHAs). The specific language in the field manual follows:

"Field Manual (FM) 3-19.40 depicts the doctrinal foundation, principles, and processes that MP will employ when dealing with enemy prisoners of war (EPWs), civilian internees (CIs), US military prisoner operations, and MP support to civil-military operations (populace and resource control [PRC], humanitarian assistance [HA], and emergency services [ES]).

2-1. An MP battalion commander tasked with operating an I/R facility is also the facility commander. As such, he is responsible for the safety and well-being of all personnel housed within the facility. Since an MP unit may be tasked to handle different categories of personnel (EPW, CI, OD, refugee, and US military prisoner), the commander, the cadre, and support personnel must be aware of the requirements for each category.

3-3. The MP work closely with military intelligence (MI) interrogation teams at CPs and CHAs to determine if captives, their equipment, and their weapons have intelligence value.

3-64. To facilitate collecting enemy tactical information, MI may collocate interrogation teams at CPs and CHAs. This provides MI with direct access to captives and their equipment and documents. Coordination is made between MP and MI to establish operating procedures that include accountability. An interrogation area is established away from the receiving/processing line so that MI personnel can interrogate captives and examine their equipment and documents. If a captive or his equipment or documents are removed from the receiving/processing line, account for them on DD Form 2708 and DA Form 4137.

3-65. The MI interrogation teams screen captives at CPs and CHAs, looking for anyone who is a potential source of information. Screeners observe captives from an area close to the dismount point or processing area. As each captive passes, MI personnel examine the capture tag and look for branch insignias that indicate a captive with information to support command priority intelligence requirements (PIR) and information requirements (IR). They also look for captives who are willing or attempting to talk to guards; joining the wrong group intentionally; or displaying signs of nervousness, anxiety, or fear.

3-66. The MP assist MI screeners by identifying captives who may have answers that support PIR and IR. Because MP are in constant contact with captives, they see how certain captives respond to orders and see the type of requests they make. The MP ensure that searches requested by MI are conducted out of sight of other captives and that guards conduct same-gender searches."

FM 6-0, *Mission Command: Command and Control of Army Forces*, 11 August 2003, Appendix D, paragraph D-114, describes the responsibilities of the Provost Marshal (PM). The specific language in the field manual follows: "PM responsibilities include –

- Internment and resettlement of EPWs and civilian internees, dislocated civilians, and US military prisoners, including their –
  - Collection
  - Detention and internment
  - Protection
  - Sustainment
  - Evacuation
- Coordinating for all logistic requirements relative to EPW and civilian internees, US military prisoners, and dislocated civilians (with the G-4).
- Coordinating on EPW and civilian internee pay support, and financial aspects of weapons bounty programs (with the finance officer and RM)."

FM 34-52, *Intelligence Interrogation*, 28 September 1992, Preface, establishes this FM as the doctrinal foundation for interrogations of detainees. Chapter 1 defines and explains the purpose of interrogation. Chapter 2 describes the role of MPs in the operation of CPs and CHAs. Chapter 3 describes the role of MPs in the MI screening process. Chapter 4 allows MI to assume control of detainees from MP for interrogation. The specific language in the field manual follows:

Preface – "This manual provides doctrinal guidance, techniques, and procedures governing employment of interrogators as human intelligence (HUMINT) collection assets in support of the commander's intelligence needs. It outlines the interrogator's role within the intelligence collection effort and the supported unit's day-to-day operations.

This manual is intended for use by interrogators as well as commanders, staff officers, and military intelligence (MI) personnel charged with the responsibility of the interrogation collection effort."

"Chapter 1 – Interrogation is the process of questioning a source to obtain the maximum amount of usable information. The goal of any interrogation is to obtain reliable information in a lawful manner, in a minimum amount of time, and to satisfy intelligence requirements of any echelon of command.

A good interrogationindexInterrogation produces needed information, which is timely, complete, clear, and accurate."

"Chapter 2 – The division's central EPW collecting point is operated by division MP under the supervision of the division provost marshal.

The capturing unit escorts or transports EPWs or detainees to the nearest collecting point, and turns them over to the MP. Interrogators in DS of the brigade will screen and categorize all EPWs or detainees, question them, and report information obtained in response to brigade PIR, IR, and SIR.

The corps MP commander operates the corps EPW holding area and provides escort guard support to divisions for EPW evacuation in routine or medical channels.

"Chapter 3 – Screeners coordinate with MP holding area guards on their role in the screening process. The guards are told where the screening will take place, how EPWs and detainees are to be brought there from the holding area, and what types of behavior on their part will facilitate the screenings."

"Chapter 4 – MI assumes control from the MP when interrogators determine a captured item or EPW is of intelligence value."

f. **Finding 6:**
  (1) *Finding*: Military Intelligence units are not resourced with sufficient interrogators and interpreters, to conduct timely detainee screenings and interrogations in the current operating environment, resulting in a backlog of interrogations and the potential loss of intelligence.
  (2) *Standard*: Army Regulation (AR) 190-8, *Enemy Prisoners of War, Retained Personnel, Civilian Internees and Other Detainees*, 1 October 1997, Chapter 2, paragraph 2-1, provides the regulatory guidance for interrogation of detainees in a combat zone. This regulation is a multiservice regulation implementing DOD Directive 2310.1 and incorporates Army Regulation 190-8 and 190-57 and SECNAV Instruction 3461.3, and Air Force Joint Instruction 31-304 and outlines policies, procedures, and responsibilities for treatment of enemy prisoners of war (EPW), retained personnel (RP), civilian internees (CI), and other detainees (OD) and implements international law for all military operations. The specific language in the regulation follows:

"(d) Prisoners may be interrogated in the combat zone. The use of physical or mental torture or any coercion to compel prisoners to provide information is prohibited. Prisoners may voluntarily cooperate with PSYOP personnel in the development, evaluation, or dissemination of PSYOP messages or products. Prisoners may not be threatened, insulted, or exposed to unpleasant or disparate treatment of any kind because of their refusal to answer questions. Interrogations will normally be performed by intelligence or counterintelligence personnel."

Field Manual (FM) 3-19.40, *Military Police Internment/Resettlement Operations*, 1 August 2001, Chapters 2 and 3, paragraphs 2-48, 3-3, 3-13, 3-65 to 3-68, describe doctrine for Military Intelligence (MI) operations in internment/resettlement (I/R) facilities. The specific language in the field manual follows:

"2-48. Personnel assigned or attached to I/R facilities are trained on the care and control of housed personnel. They are fully cognizant of the provisions of the Geneva and UN Conventions and applicable regulations as they apply to the treatment of housed personnel. A formal training program should include –

- Principles and laws of land warfare, specifically provisions of Geneva and UN Conventions and HN laws and customs.
- Supervisory and human relations techniques.
- Methods of self-defense.
- The use of force, the ROE, and the ROI.
- Firearms qualification and familiarization.
- Public relations, particularly CONUS operations.
- First aid.
- Stress management techniques.
- Facility regulations and SOPs.

- Intelligence and counter-intelligence techniques.
- Cultural customs and habits of internees."

"3-3. The MP work closely with military intelligence (MI) interrogation teams at CPs and CHAs to determine if captives, their equipment, and their weapons have intelligence value. This process is accelerated when MI interrogation teams can observe captives during arrival and processing, and interrogators can also be used as interpreters during this phase. Before a captive is interviewed by MI personnel, he must have a Department of Defense (DD) Form 2745 (Figure 3-1) attached to him and be accounted for on DD Form 2708.

3-13. The MP coordinate with MI interrogation teams to determine which confiscated items have intelligence value. Personal items (diaries, letters from home, and family pictures) can be taken by MI teams for review and then returned to the proper owner via MP."

"INTERROGATION TEAMS

"3-65. The MI interrogation teams screen captives at CPs and CHAs, looking for anyone who is a potential source of information. Screeners observe captives from an area close to the dismount point or processing area. As each captive passes, MI personnel examine the capture tag and look for branch insignias that indicate a captive with information to support command priority intelligence requirements (PIR) and information requirements (IR). They also look for captives who are willing or attempting to talk to guards; joining the wrong group intentionally; or displaying signs of nervousness, anxiety, or fear.

3-66. The MP assist MI screeners by identifying captives who may have answers that support PIR and IR. Because MP are in constant contact with captives, they see how certain captives respond to orders and see the type of requests they make. The MP ensure that searches requested by MI are conducted out of sight of other captives and that guards conduct same-gender searches.

3-67. The MI screeners examine captured documents, equipment and, in some cases, personal papers (journals, diaries, and letters from home). They are looking for information that identifies a captive and his organization, mission, and personal background (family, knowledge, and experience). Knowledge of a captive's physical and emotional status or other information helps screeners determine his willingness to cooperate.

LOCATION

3-68. Consider the following when planning an MI screening site:

- The site is located where screeners can observe captives as they are segregated and processed. It is shielded from the direct view of captives and is far enough away that captives cannot overhear screeners' conversations.
- The site has an operation, administrative, and interrogation area. The interrogation area accommodates an interrogator, a captive, a guard, and an interpreter as well as furniture. Lights are available for night operations.
- Procedures are implemented to verify that sick and wounded captives have been treated and released by authorized medical personnel.
- Guards are available and procedures are implemented for escorting captives to the interrogation site.
- Procedures are published to inform screeners who will be moved and when they will be moved.
- Accountability procedures are implemented and required forms are available."

FM 3-31, *Joint Force Land Component Commander Handbook (JFLCC)*, 13 December 2001, Appendix A, paragraph A-11, describes the role of the Joint Interrogation and Debriefing Center (JIDC). The specific language in the field manual follows:

"JIDC conducts follow-on exploitation of EPWs. EPWs are screened by the JIFs, and those of further intelligence potential are identified and forwarded to the JIDC for follow-on interrogation and debriefing in support of JTF and higher requirements. Besides EPWs, the JIDC may also interrogate civilian detainees, refugees, and other nonprisoner sources. JIDC activities are managed by the J-2X HOC."

FM 27-10, *The Law of Land Warfare*, 18 July 1956 (change 1, 15 July 1976), Paragraph 93, describes guidelines for the questioning of enemy prisoners of war (EPWs). The specific language in the field manual follows:

"Every prisoner of war, when questioned on the subject, is bound to give only his surname, first names and rank, date of birth, and army, regimental, personal or serial number, or failing this equivalent information. If he wilfully infringes this rule, he may render himself liable to a restriction of the privileges accorded to his rank or status. Each Party to a conflict is required to furnish the persons under its jurisdiction who are liable to become prisoners of war, with an identity card showing the owner's surname, first names, rank, army, regimental, personal or serial number or equivalent information, and date of birth. The identity card may, furthermore, bear the signature or the fingerprints, or both, of the owner, and may bear, as well, any other information the Party to the conflict may wish to add concerning persons belonging to its armed forces. As far as possible the card shall measure 6.5 × 10 cm. and shall be issued in duplicate. The identity card shall be shown by the prisoner of war upon demand, but may in no case be taken away from him. No physical or mental torture, nor any other form of coercion, may be inflicted on prisoners of war to secure from them information of any kind whatever. Prisoners of war who refuse to answer may not be threatened, insulted, or exposed to unpleasant or disadvantageous treatment of any kind."

FM 34–52, *Intelligence Interrogation*, 28 September 1992, Chapter 1, defines and explains the purpose of interrogation. The specific language in the field manual follows: "Interrogation is the process of questioning a source to obtain the maximum amount of usable information. The goal of any interrogation is to obtain reliable information in a lawful manner, in a minimum amount of time, and to satisfy intelligence requirements of any echelon of command.

A good interrogation produces needed information, which is timely, complete, clear, and accurate."

Special Text (ST) 2-22.7 (FM 34-7-1), *Tactical Human Intelligence and Counterintelligence Operations*, 11 April 2002, Chapter 1, paragraphs 1-19, 1-21 to 1-25, provides the doctrinal basis for the structure and utilization of tactical human intelligence assets. The specific language in the special text follows:

"1-19. The requirement for collectors is based on the density of the potential source pool. The basic methodology of collection does not change in the urban environment; however, the density of the population results in a proportional increase in the number of collectors required. This need for additional assets has been illustrated by recent operations in Somalia, Haiti, Bosnia, and Kosovo."

"ARMY CORPS AND BELOW

1-21. Army HUMINT and CI assets organic at corps and below are uniquely qualified to be the primary collection asset in many of our future conflicts. They are organic to –

• Tactical exploitation battalions (TEBs) and the corps support battalions (CSBs) at the Corps MI brigade.

- MI battalions at division.
- MI companies at armored cavalry regiments (ACRs) and separate brigades (SEP BDEs).
- MI elements at Special Forces Groups (SFGs).

1-22. Army HUMINT and CI assets provide technologically enhanced exploitation of human sources and media. This exploitation provides valuable intelligence to meet the critical requirements affecting the MDMP. The simultaneous digital interaction between operational HUMINT and CI teams and analytical elements provides the deployed commander with near-instantaneous information. This rapid transmission of critical intelligence to the user gives the supported command an information edge and a more complete vision of the battlespace.

INTERIM BRIGADE COMBAT TEAM

1-23. The brigade's intelligence system is a flexible force of Intelligence, Surveillance, and Reconnaissance (ISR) personnel, organizations, and equipment. Individually and collectively, these assets provide commanders throughout the brigade with the capability to plan and direct ISR operations, collect and process information, produce relevant intelligence, and disseminate combat information and intelligence to those who need it, when they need it. The brigade and its subordinate units possess organic ISR assets that enable the above actions. Based on METT-TC considerations the brigade task organizes its organic ISR assets for the operation and, in addition, may receive additional ISR assets from corps, joint, and national organizations.

1-24. The brigade's tactical HUMINT assets include an S2X team, a tactical HUMINT platoon with two operational management teams (OMTs) and tactical HUMINT teams, and troop HUMINT collectors in the reconnaissance, surveillance, and target acquisition (RSTA) squadron. The functions and responsibilities of these assets are the same as at higher echelons. The mission of the Troop HUMINT collector is limited to providing tactical questioning and DOCEX in support of the squadron's multidimensional reconnaissance and surveillance (R&S) mission and identifying possible sources of interest for the tactical HUMINT platoon. The functions of the different teams and offices in tactical HUMINT are similar through the echelons where tactical HUMINT is conducted.

RESERVE COMPONENT INTEGRATION

1-25. Given the Army's current operational tempo and force structure, the integration of RC forces into the AC is a near certainty for future operational deployments. Commanders must identify their requirements early and establish proactive coordination (both in garrison and while deployed) with their RC counterparts to fully integrate them during all phases of training and operations."

ST 2–91.6 *Small Unit Support to Intelligence*, March 2004, Chapter 2, paragraphs 2-13 to 2-17, explains the use of interpreters in tactical interrogations. The specific language in the special text follows:

"2-13. The use of interpreters is an integral part of the information collection effort. Use of an interpreter is time consuming and potentially confusing. Proper use and control of an interpreter is a skill that must be learned and practiced to maximize the potential of collection.

2-14. Perhaps the most important guideline to remember is that an interpreter is essentially your mouthpiece; he says what you say, but in a different language. This sounds simple, but for those who have never worked with interpreters, problems can quickly develop.

2-15. Upon meeting your interpreter, it is important that you assess his proficiency in English. You need an interpreter with a firm grasp of English and the terminology you may encounter.

2-16. Interpreters are categorized as to capability and clearance they have been granted. The categories below are more fully detailed in Interpreter Ops, Multiservice Reference Manual for Interpreter Operations, February 2004. This manual can be obtained from the Air Land Sea Application (ALSA) Center.

CATEGORIES OF INTERPRETERS

- CAT I Linguists – Locally hired personnel with an understanding of the English language. These personnel are screened and hired in-theater and do not possess a security clearance. During most operations, CAT I linguists are required to be re screened by CI personnel on a scheduled basis. CAT I linguists should not be used for HUMINT collection operations.
- CAT II Linguists – CAT II linguists are United States citizens who have native command of the target language and near-native command of the English language. These personnel undergo a screening process, which includes a background check. Upon favorable findings, these personnel are granted an equivalent of a Secret Collateral clearance.
- CAT III Linguists – CAT III linguists are United States citizens who have native command of the target language and native command of the English language. These personnel undergo a screening process, which includes a special background check. Upon favorable findings, these personnel are granted an equivalent of a Top Secret (TS) clearance. CAT III linguists are used mostly for high-ranking official meetings and by strategic collectors.

2–17. The following are several tips that should prove useful when working with an interpreter. Placement

- When standing, the interpreter should stand just behind you and to the side.
- When sitting, the interpreter should sit right beside you but not between you and the individual.

Body Language and Tone

- Have the interpreter translate your message in the tone you are speaking.
- Ensure the interpreter avoids making gestures.

Delivery

- Talk directly to the person with whom you are speaking, not the interpreter.
- Speak as you would in a normal conversation, not in the third person. For example, do not say, "Tell him that...." Rather say, "I understand that you..." and instruct the interpreter to translate as such.
- Speak clearly, avoid acronyms or slang, and break sentences uniformly to facilitate translation.

- Some interpreters will begin to translate while you are still speaking. This is frustrating for some people. If so, discuss the preference of translation with the interpreter.
- The most important principle to obey while using an interpreter is to remember that you control the conversation, not the interpreter.

Security

- Work on the premise that the interpreter is being debriefed by a threat intelligence service.
- Always assume the worst.
- Avoid careless talk.
- Avoid giving away personal details.
- Do not become emotionally involved!

Interpreter Checklist for Patrolling

- Tell the interpreter what you expect of him, and how you want him to do it.
- Tell the interpreter exactly what you want translated. The interpreter should translate all conversation between you and the individual without adding anything on his own.
- Just as questioning should be conducted in such a way as to disguise the true intent of the questioning from the source, you should not reveal intelligence requirements (FFIR, IR, or essential elements of friendly information [EEFI]) to the interpreter. Brief the interpreter on actions to take at the halt or in the event of enemy contact."

g. **Finding 7:**
   (1) *Finding*: Tactical Military Intelligence officers are not adequately trained on how to manage the full spectrum of the collection and analysis of human intelligence.
   (2) *Standard*: Army Regulation 350–1, *Army Training and Education*, 9 April 2003, Chapter 3, paragraph 3–2, requires that TRADOC establish training and education goals and objectives for all Army personnel. The specific language in the regulation follows:

"Training proponents. These would include TRADOC schools and colleges, USAJFKSWC&S and AMEDDC&S and would perform the following.

a. Develop courses based on established training and education goals and objectives as well as the duties, responsibilities, and missions their graduates will be assigned.
b. Develop, evaluate, and train leader, technical, and tactical tasks that focus on missions for the size or type units to which graduates will be assigned.
c. Provide progressive and sequential training.
d. Provide personnel serving at the same organizational level with training consisting of the same tasks, conditions, and standards.
e. Provide leader, technical, and tactical training that affords soldiers and DA civilians an opportunity to acquire the skills and knowledge needed to perform more complex duties and missions of greater responsibility."

Field Manual (FM) 7–0, *Training the Force*, 22 October 2002, Chapter 1, paragraph 1–29, gives overall guidance for the implementation of Professional Military Education (PME). The specific language in the field manual follows:

"Professional Military Education – PME develops Army leaders. Officer, warrant officer, and NCO training and education is a continuous, career-long, learning process that integrates structured programs of instruction – resident at the institution and non-resident via distributed learning at home station. PME is progressive and sequential, provides a doctrinal foundation, and builds on previous training, education and operational experiences.

PME provides hands-on technical, tactical, and leader training focused to ensure leaders are prepared for success in their next assignment and higher-level responsibility.

- Officer Education System (OES). Army officers must lead and fight; be tactically and technically competent; possess leader skills; understand how the Army operates as a service, as well as a component of a joint, multinational, or interagency organization; demonstrate confidence, integrity, critical judgment, and responsibility; operate in a complex, uncertain, and rapidly changing environment; build effective teams amid continuous organizational and technological change; and solve problems creatively. OES develops officers who are self-aware and adaptive to lead Army units to mission success.
- Warrant Officer Education System (WOES). Warrant officers are the Army's technical experts. WOES develops a corps of highly specialized experts and trainers who are fully competent and proficient operators, maintainers, administrators, and managers of the Army's equipment, support activities, and technical systems.
- NCO Education System (NCOES). NCOES trains NCOs to lead and train soldiers, crews, and subordinate leaders who work and fight under their leadership. NCOES provides hands-on technical, tactical, and leader training focused to ensure that NCOs are prepared for success in their next assignment and higher-level responsibility.
- Functional Training. In addition to the preceding PME courses, there are functional courses available in both resident and non-resident distributed learning modes that enhance functional skills for specific duty positions. Examples are Battalion S2, Battalion Motor Officer, First Sergeant, Battle Staff NCO, and Airborne courses."

FM 34-52, *Intelligence Interrogation*, 28 September 1992, Chapter 1, Intelligence Disciplines, states that the Intelligence Electronic Warfare (IEW) system includes three MI disciplines. The specific language in the field manual follows:
"HUMINT –
HUMINT is obtained from information collected from human sources and consists of the following intelligence collection operations. Interrogation of EPWs, civilian detainees, insurgents, defectors, refugees, displaced persons and agents and suspected agents.

- Long-range surveillance patrols.
- Strategic debriefing
- Controlled collection operations
- Open-source exploitation, to include publications and broadcasts.
- Reports of contact from forward units.
- Observation and listening posts
- Low-level source operations (LLSO)
- HUMINT liaison contacts

HUMINT is vital in all combat operations, regardless of echelon or intensity of conflict. By nature, HUMINT lends itself to the collection of information about the enemy's thought processes and intentions. HUMINT can provide information on almost any topic of intelligence interest, including order of battle (OB) factors, as well as scientific and technical (S&T) intelligence subjects. During Operation Desert Storm, interrogators collected information which helped to –

- Develop a plan to breach Iraqi defensive belts.
- Confirm Iraqi supply line interdiction by coalition air strikes.
- Identify diminishing Iraqi troop morale.
- Identify a US Prisoner of war captured during the battle of Kanji."

h. **Finding 8:**

(1) *Finding*: The DAIG team found that officially approved CJTF-7 and CJTF-180 policies and the early CJTF-180 practices generally met legal obligations under US law,
treaty obligations and policy, if executed carefully, by trained soldiers, under the full
range of safeguards. The DAIG team found that policy was not clear and contained
ambiguity. The DAIG team found implementation, training, and oversight of these
policies was inconsistent; the team concluded, however, based on a review of cases
through 9 June 2004 that no confirmed instance of detainee abuse resulted from
the approved policies.

(2) *Standard*: Standard of treatment for detainees in OPERATION ENDURING FREE-
DOM (OEF): The Secretary of Defense determined that members of the Taliban
militia and members of al Qaeda under the control of US Forces would be treated
humanely and, to the extent appropriate and consistent with military necessity, in
a manner consistent with the principles of the Geneva Conventions of 1949. The
DAIG has therefore used the provisions of the Geneva Conventions as a benchmark
against which to measure the treatment provided to detainees by U.S. Forces to
determine if detainees were treated humanely. The use of these standards as benchmarks does not state or imply a position for the United States or U.S. Army on the
legal status of its operations in OEF.

Chairman, Joint Chiefs of Staff *(CJCS) Message dated 211933Z JAN 02*, provides the
determination regarding the humane treatment of al Qaeda and Taliban detainees. *Convention Relative to the Treatment of Prisoners of War of August 12, 1949* (GPW) is the international treaty that governs the treatment of prisoners of war, and *Geneva Convention
Relative to the Protection of Civilian Persons in Time of War (GC)*, August 12, 1949, is the
international treaty that governs the treatment of civilian persons in time of war.

As the guidance did not define "human treatment" but did state that the US would
treat members of the Taliban militia and al Qaeda in a manner consistent with the Geneva
Conventions, the DAIG determined that it would use Common Article 3 of the GCs as
its floor measure of humane treatment, but would also include provisions of the Geneva
Convention on the Treatment of Prisoners of War (GPW) and Geneva Convention Relative
to the Protection of Civilian Persons in Time of War (GC) as other relevant indicia of
"humane treatment." The use of this standard does not state or imply a position for the
United States or U.S. Army on the legal status of its operations in OEF.

Standard of treatment for detainees in OPERATION IRAQI FREEDOM (OIF): OIF was
an international armed conflict and therefore the provisions of the Geneva Conventions applied. Additionally, the United States was an occupying power and has acted in accordance
with the obligations of an occupying power described in the *Hague Convention No. IV Respecting the Laws and Customs of War on Land (H.IV)*, 18 October 1907, including, but not
limited to, Articles 43–46 and 50; *Geneva Convention Relative to the Treatment of Prisoners
of War of August 12, 1949* (GPW), *Geneva Convention Relative to the Protection of Civilian
Persons in Time of War (GC)*, 12 August 1949. The GC supplements H.IV, providing the
general standard of treatment at Article 27 and specific standards in subsequent Articles.

The minimum treatment provided by Common Article 3 of the Geneva Conventions
is: 1) No adverse distinction based upon race, religion, sex, etc.; 2) No violence to life or
person; 3) No taking hostages; 4) No degrading treatment; 5) No passing of sentences in
absence of fair trial, and; 6) The wounded and sick must be cared for.

The specific language in the CJCS Message for OEF and the GPW/GC and H.IV follows:
CJCS Message dated 211933Z JAN 02, "Paragraph 3. The combatant commanders shall, in
detaining al Qaeda and Taliban individuals under control of the Department of Defense,

treat them humanely and, to the extent appropriate and consistent with military necessity, in a manner consistent with the principles of the Geneva Conventions of 1949."

GPW/GC, Article 3 (Common Article 3) – "In the case of armed conflict not of an international character occurring in the territory of one of the High Contracting Parties, each party to the conflict shall be bound to apply, as a minimum, the following provisions:

1. Persons taking no active part in the hostilities, including members of armed forces who have laid down their arms and those placed hors de combat by sickness, wounds, detention, or any other cause, shall in all circumstances be treated humanely, without any adverse distinction founded on race, color, religion or faith, sex, birth or wealth, or any other similar criteria.

To this end the following acts are and shall remain prohibited at any time and in any place whatsoever with respect to the above-mentioned persons:

(a) Violence to life and person, in particular murder of all kinds, mutilation, cruel treatment and torture;
(b) Taking of hostages;
(c) Outrages upon personal dignity, in particular, humiliating and degrading treatment;
(d) The passing of sentences and the carrying out of executions without previous judgment pronounced by a regularly constituted court affording all the judicial guarantees which are recognized as indispensable by civilized peoples.

2. The wounded and sick shall be collected and cared for. An impartial humanitarian body, such as the International Committee of the Red Cross, may offer its services to the Parties to the conflict. The Parties to the conflict should further endeavour to bring into force, by means of special agreements, all or part of the other provisions of the present Convention. The application of the preceding provisions shall not affect the legal status of the Parties to the conflict."

Geneva Convention Relative to the Treatment of Prisoners of War, 12 August 1949, Part II, Article 13, requires that enemy prisoners of war (EPWs) be treated humanely at all times; Part III, Section I, Articles 13, 14, and 17, explain the protections afforded EPWs. The specific language in the convention follows:

"Article 13
Prisoners of war must at all times be humanely treated. Any unlawful act or omission by the Detaining Power causing death or seriously endangering the health of a prisoner of war in its custody is prohibited, and will be regarded as a serious breach of the present Convention. In particular, no prisoner of war may be subjected to physical mutilation or to medical or scientific experiments of any kind which are not justified by the medical, dental or hospital treatment of the prisoner concerned and carried out in his interest.

Likewise, prisoners of war must at all times be protected, particularly against acts of violence or intimidation and against insults and public curiosity. Measures of reprisal against prisoners of war are prohibited.

Article 14
Prisoners of war are entitled in all circumstances to respect for their persons and their honour. Women shall be treated with all the regard due to their sex and shall in all cases benefit by treatment as favourable as that granted to men. Prisoners of war shall retain the full civil capacity which they enjoyed at the time of their capture. The Detaining Power may not restrict the exercise, either within or without its own territory, of the rights such capacity confers except in so far as the captivity requires."

Article 17

Every prisoner of war, when questioned on the subject, is bound to give only his sur-name, first names and rank, date of birth, and army, regimental, personal or serial number, or failing this, equivalent information. If he wilfully infringes this rule, he may render him-self liable to a restriction of the privileges accorded to his rank or status.

Each Party to a conflict is required to furnish the persons under its jurisdiction who are liable to become prisoners of war, with an identity card showing the owner's surname, first names, rank, army, regimental, personal or serial number or equivalent information, and date of birth. The identity card may, furthermore, bear the signature or the fingerprints, or both, of the owner, and may bear, as well, any other information the Party to the conflict may wish to add concerning persons belonging to its armed forces. As far as possible the card shall measure 6.5 × 10 cm. and shall be issued in duplicate. The identity card shall be shown by the prisoner of war upon demand, but may in no case be taken away from him.

No physical or mental torture, nor any other form of coercion, may be inflicted on prisoners of war to secure from them information of any kind whatever. Prisoners of war who refuse to answer may not be threatened, insulted, or exposed to any unpleasant or disadvantageous treatment of any kind.

Prisoners of war who, owing to their physical or mental condition, are unable to state their identity, shall be handed over to the medical service. The identity of such prison-ers shall be established by all possible means, subject to the provisions of the preceding paragraph.

The questioning of prisoners of war shall be carried out in a language which they understand."

Geneva Convention Relative to the Protection of Civilian Persons in Time of War, 12 August 1949, Part

III, Section I, Articles 31 32, and 100, prohibit coercion and abuse of civilian internees. The specific language in the convention follows:

"Article 31

No physical or moral coercion shall be exercised against protected persons, in particular to obtain information from them or from third parties.

Article 32

The High Contracting Parties specifically agree that each of them is prohibited from taking any measure of such a character as to cause the physical suffering or extermination of protected persons in their hands. This prohibition applies not only to murder, torture, corporal punishment, mutilation and medical or scientific experiments not necessitated by the medical treatment of a protected person but also to any other measures of brutality whether applied by civilian or military agents."

"Article 100

The disciplinary regime in places of internment shall be consistent with humanitarian principles, and shall internees any physical exertion dangerous to their health or involving physical or moral victimization. Identification by tattooing or imprinting signs or markings on the body, is prohibited. In particular, prolonged standing and roll-calls, punishment drill, military drill and manoeuvres, or the reduction of food rations, are prohibited."

Convention Against Torture and Other Cruel, Inhuman or Degrading Treatment or Pun-ishment, 10 December 1984, Part I, Articles 1,2, 10, 11 and 16(1) define torture (1), the basic responsibilities of states under the convention (2), the requirement for training personnel on this convention (10), the need to conduct systematic reviews of interrogations rules, in-structions, methods and practices (11), and the requirement to prevent acts not amounting to "torture" committed with consent or acquiescence of a public official or other person in an official capacity (16). The specific language in the convention follows:

"Article 1

1. For the purposes of this Convention, the term "torture" means any act by which severe pain or suffering, whether physical or mental, is intentionally inflicted on a person for such purposes as obtaining from him or a third person information or a confession, punishing him for an act he or a third person has committed or is suspected of having committed, or intimidating or coercing him or a third person, or for any reason based on discrimination of any kind, when such pain or suffering is inflicted by or at the instigation of or with the consent or acquiescence of a public official or other person acting in an official capacity. It does not include pain or suffering arising only from, inherent in or incidental to lawful sanctions.

2. This article is without prejudice to any international instrument or national legislation which does or may contain provisions of wider application.

Article 2

1. Each State Party shall take effective legislative, administrative, judicial or other measures to prevent acts of torture in any territory under its jurisdiction.

2. No exceptional circumstances whatsoever, whether a state of war or a threat of war, internal political in stability or any other public emergency, may be invoked as a justification of torture.

3. An order from a superior officer or a public authority may not be invoked as a justification of torture.

Article 10

1. Each State Party shall ensure that education and information regarding the prohibition against torture are fully included in the training of law enforcement personnel, civil or military, medical personnel, public officials and other persons who may be involved in the custody, interrogation or treatment of any individual subjected to any form of arrest, detention or imprisonment.

2. Each State Party shall include this prohibition in the rules or instructions issued in regard to the duties and functions of any such person.

Article 11

Each State Party shall keep under systematic review interrogation rules, instructions, methods and practices as well as arrangements for the custody and treatment of persons subjected to any form of arrest, detention or imprisonment in any territory under its jurisdiction, with a view to preventing any cases of torture.

Article 16 (1)

Each State Party shall undertake to prevent in any territory under its jurisdiction other acts of cruel, inhuman or degrading treatment or punishment which do not amount to torture as defined in Article I, when such acts are committed by or at the instigation of or with the consent or acquiescence of a public official or other person acting in an official capacity. In particular, the obligations contained in Articles 10, 11, 12 and 13 shall apply with the substitution for references to torture of references to other forms of cruel, inhuman or degrading treatment or punishment.

US Reservations, Declarations and Understandings the Convention Against Torture. The United States Senate ratified the Convention Against Torture subject to certain reservations, declarations and understandings. Pertinent reservations and understandings are as follow:

Senate Reservations: (136 Cong Rec S 17486):

The Senate's advice and consent is subject to the following reservations:

(1) That the United States considers itself bound by the obligation under Article 16 to prevent 'cruel, inhuman or degrading treatment or punishment', only insofar as the term 'cruel, inhuman or degrading treatment or punishment' means the cruel, unusual and inhumane treatment or punishment prohibited by the Fifth, Eighth, and/or Fourteenth Amendments to the Constitution of the United States. Senate Understandings (136 Cong Rec S 17486):

The Senate's advice and consent is subject to the following understandings, which shall apply to the obligations of the United States under this Convention:

(1) (a) That with reference to Article 1, the United States understands that, in order to constitute torture, an act must be specifically intended to inflict severe physical or mental pain or suffering and that mental pain or suffering refers to prolonged mental harm caused by or resulting from (1) the intentional infliction or threatened, infliction of severe physical pain or suffering; (2) the administration or application, or threatened administration or application, of mind-altering substances or other procedures calculated to disrupt profoundly the senses or the personality; (3) the threat of imminent death; or (4) the threat that another person will imminently be subjected to death, severe physical pain or suffering, or the administration or application of mind-altering substances or other procedures calculated to disrupt profoundly the senses or personality.
(b) That the United States understands that the definition of torture in Article 1 is intended to apply only to acts directed against persons in the offender's custody or physical control.
(c) That with reference to Article 1 of the Convention, the United States understands that 'sanctions' includes judicially-imposed sanctions and other enforcement actions authorized by United States law or by judicial interpretation of such law provided that such sanctions or actions are not clearly prohibited under international law.
(d) That with reference to Article 1 of the Convention, the United States understands that the term 'acquiescence' requires that the public official, prior to the activity constituting torture, have awareness of such activity and thereafter breach his legal responsibility to intervene to prevent such activity.
(e) That with reference to Article 1 of the Convention, the Unites States understands that non-compliance with applicable legal procedural standards does not per se constitute torture.

Domestic Criminal Law: US Domestic Criminal law reflects treaty obligations and ratification reservations and understandings regarding torture in the adoption of 18 USCS §§ 2340, 2340A, which state:

18 USC§ 2340 Definitions

As used in this chapter [18 USCS §§2340 et seq.]

(1) "torture" means an act committed by a person acting under the color of law specifically intended to inflict severe physical or mental pain or suffering (other than pain or suffering incidental to lawful sanctions) upon another person within his custody or physical control;

(2) "severe mental pain or suffering" means the prolonged mental harm caused by or resulting from-

(A) the intentional infliction or threatened infliction of severe physical pain or suffering;

(B) the administration or application, or threatened administration or application, of mind-altering substances or other procedures calculated to disrupt profoundly the senses or the personality;

(C) the threat of imminent death;

(D) the threat that another person will imminently be subjected to death, severe physical pain or suffering, or the administration or application of mind-altering substances or other procedures calculated to disrupt profoundly the senses or personality; and

(3) "United States" includes all areas under the jurisdiction of the United States including any of the places described in sections 5 and 7 of this title and section 46501(2) of title 49.

§ 2340A. Torture

(a) Offense. Whoever outside the United States commits or attempts to commit torture shall be fined under this title or imprisoned not more than 20 years, or both, and if death results to any person from conduct prohibited by this subsection, shall be punished by death or imprisoned for any term of years or for life.

(b) Jurisdiction. There is jurisdiction over the activity prohibited in subsection (a) if –

(1) the alleged offender is a national of the United States; or

(2) the alleged offender is present in the United States, irrespective of the nationality of the victim or alleged offender.

(c) Conspiracy. A person who conspires to commit an offense under this section shall be subject to the same penalties (other than the penalty of death) as the penalties prescribed for the offense, the commission of which was the object of the conspiracy.

Field Manual (FM) 34-52, *Intelligence Interrogation*, 28 September 1992, Chapter 1, explains the prohibitions against use of torture or coercion. Chapter 3 describes the interrogation approaches and techniques used by trained Army interrogators. The specific language in the field manual follows:

Chapter 1 – "One of the significant means used by the intelligence staff is the interrogation of the following:

- EPWs
- Captured insurgents
- Civilian internees
- Other captured, detained, or retained persons
- Foreign deserters or other persons of intelligence interest

These persons are protected by the Geneva Conventions for the Protection of War Victims of August 12, 1949, as they relate to captured wounded and sick enemy personnel (GWS), retained enemy medical personnel and chaplains (GWS), enemy prisoners of war (EPW), and civilian internees (CI). Captured insurgents and other detained personnel whose status is not clear, such as suspected terrorists, are entitled to PW protection until their precise status has been determined by competent authority.

In conducting intelligence interrogations, the J2, G2, or S2 has primary staff responsibility to ensure these activities are performed in accordance with the GWS, GPW, and GC, as well as US policies, regarding the treatment and handling of the above-mentioned persons.

The GWS, GPW, GC, and US policy expressly prohibit acts of violence or intimidation, including physical or mental torture, threats, insults, or exposure to inhumane treatment as a means of or aid to interrogation.

Such illegal acts are not authorized and will not be condoned by the US Army. Acts in violation of these prohibitions are criminal acts punishable under the UCMJ. If there is doubt as to the legality of a proposed form of interrogation not specifically authorized in this manual, the advice of the command judge advocate should be sought before using the method in question. Experience indicates that the use of prohibited techniques is not necessary to gain the cooperation of interrogation sources. Use of torture and other illegal methods is a poor technique that yields unreliable results, may damage subsequent collection efforts, and can induce the source to say what he thinks the interrogator wants to hear.

Revelation of use of torture by US personnel will bring discredit upon the US and its armed forces while undermining domestic and international support for the war effort. It also may place US and allied personnel in enemy hands at a greater risk of abuse by their captors. Conversely, knowing the enemy has abused US and allied PWs does not justify using methods of interrogation specifically prohibited by the GWS, GPW, or GC, and US policy.

Limitations on the use of methods identified herein as expressly prohibited should not be confused with psychological ploys, verbal trickery, or other non-violent or non-coercive ruses used by the interrogator in the successful interrogation of hesitant or uncooperative sources.

The psychological techniques and principles in this manual should neither be confused with, nor construed to be synonymous with, unauthorized techniques such as brainwashing, physical or mental torture, or any other form of mental coercion to include drugs that may induce lasting and permanent mental alteration and damage.

Physical or mental torture and coercion revolve around eliminating the source's free will, and are expressly prohibited by GWS, Article 13; GPW, Articles 13 and 17; and GC, Articles 31 and 32. Torture is defined as the infliction of intense pain to body or mind to extract a confession or information, or for sadistic pleasure.

Examples of physical torture include –

- Electric shock
- Infliction of pain through chemicals or bondage (other than legitimate use of restraints to prevent escape)
- Forcing an individual to stand, sit, or kneel in abnormal positions for prolonged periods of time
- Food deprivation
- Any form of beating Examples of mental torture include
- Mock executions
- Abnormal sleep deprivation
- Chemically induced psychosis

Coercion is defined as actions designed to unlawfully induce another to compel an act against one's will. Examples of coercion include –

- Threatening or implying physical or mental torture to the subject, his family, or others to whom he owes loyalty.

- Intentionally denying medical assistance or care in exchange for the information sought or other cooperation.
- Threatening or implying that other rights guaranteed by the GWS, GPW, or GC will not be provided unless cooperation is forthcoming.

Chapter 3 – "The number of approaches used is limited only by the interrogator's skill. Almost any ruse or deception is usable as long as the provisions of the GPW, as outlined in Figure 1-4, are not violated.

An interrogator must not pass himself off as a medic, chaplain, or as a member of the Red Cross (Red Crescent or Red Lion). To every approach technique, there are literally hundreds of possible variations, each of which can be developed for a specific situation or source. The variations are limited only by the interrogator's personality, experience, ingenuity, and imagination.

3-7 There are four primary factors that must be considered when selecting tentative approaches:

- The source's mental and physical state. Is the source injured, angry, crying, arrogant, cocky, or frightened? If so, how can this state be best exploited during interrogation.
- The source's background. What is the source's age and level of military or civilian experience.
- The objective of the interrogation. How much time is available for the interrogation? Is the commander interested only in specific areas (PIR, IR, SIR)? Is this source knowledgeable enough to require a full OB interrogation?
- The interrogator himself. What abilities does he have that can be brought into play? What weaknesses does he have that may interfere with the interrogation? Can his personality adapt to the personality of the source?

APPROACH COMBINATIONS

With the exception of the direct approach, no other approach is effective by itself. Interrogators use different approach techniques or combine them into a cohesive, logical technique. Smooth transitions, sincerity, logic, and conviction almost always make a strategy work. The lack of will undoubtedly dooms it to failure. Some examples of combinations are –

Direct—futility—incentive
Direct—futility—love of comrades
Direct—fear-up (mild)—incentive

The number of combinations are unlimited. Interrogators must carefully choose the approach strategy in the planning and preparation phase and listen carefully to what the source is saying (verbally or non-verbally) for leads the strategy chosen will not work. When this occurs, the interrogator must adapt to approaches he believes will work in gaining the source's cooperation.

The approach techniques are not new nor are all the possible or acceptable techniques discussed below. Everything the interrogator says and does must be in concert with the GWS, GPW, GC, and UCMJ. The approaches which have proven effective are –

- Direct
- Incentive
- Emotional
- Increased fear-up
- Pride and ego

Direct Approach

The interrogator asks questions directly related to information sought, making no effort to conceal the interrogation's purpose. The direct approach, always the first to be attempted, is used on EPWs or detainees who the interrogator believes will cooperate.

This may occur when interrogating an EPW or detainee who has proven cooperative during initial screening or first interrogation. It may also be used on those with little or no security training. The direct approach works best on lower enlisted personnel, as they have little or no resistance training and have had minimal security training.

The direct approach is simple to use, and it is possible to obtain the maximum amount of information in the minimum amount of time. It is frequently employed at lower echelons when the tactical situation precludes selecting other techniques, and where the EPW's or detainee's mental state is one of confusion or extreme shock. Figure C-3 contains sample questions used in direct questioning.

The direct approach is the most effective. Statistics show in World War II, it was 90 percent effective. In Vietnam and OPERATIONS URGENT FURY, JUST CAUSE, and DESERT STORM, it was 95 percent effective.

Incentive Approach

The incentive approach is based on the application of inferred discomfort upon an EPW or detainee who lacks willpower. The EPW or detainee may display fondness for certain luxury items such as candy, fruit, or cigarettes. This fondness provides the interrogator with a positive means of rewarding the EPW or detainee for cooperation and truthfulness, as he may give or withhold such comfort items at his discretion. Caution must be used when employing this technique because –

- Any pressure applied in this manner must not amount to a denial of basic human needs under any circumstances. [NOTE: Interrogators may not withhold a source's rights under the GPW, but they can withhold a source's privileges.] Granting incentives must not infringe on these rights, but they can be things to which the source is already entitled. This can be effective only if the source is unaware of his rights or privileges.
- The EPW or detainee might be tempted to provide false or inaccurate information to gain the desired luxury item or to stop the interrogation.

The GPW, Article 41, requires the posting of the convention contents in the EPW's' own language. This is an MP responsibility.

Incentives must seem to be logical and possible. An interrogator must not promise anything that cannot be delivered. Interrogators do not make promises, but usually infer them while sidestepping guarantees.

For example, if an interrogator made a promise he could not keep and he or another interrogator had to talk with the source again, the source would not have any trust and would probably not cooperate. Instead of clearly promising a certain thing, such as political asylum, an interrogator will offer to do what he can to help achieve the source's desired goal, as long as the source cooperates.

As with developing rapport, the incentive approach can be broken down into two incentives. The determination rests on when the source expects to receive the incentive offered.

- Short term – received immediately; for example, letter home, seeing wounded buddies.
- Long term – received within a period of time; for example, political asylum.

Emotional Approach

Through EPW or detainee observation, the interrogator can often identify dominant emotions which motivate. The motivating emotion may be greed, love, hate, revenge, or others.

The interrogator employs verbal and emotional ruses in applying pressure to the EPW's or detainee's dominant emotions.

One major advantage of this technique is it is versatile and allows the interrogator to use the same basic situation positively and negatively.

For example, this technique can be used on the EPW who has a great love for his unit and fellow soldiers. The interrogator may take advantage of this by telling the EPW that by providing pertinent information, he may shorten the war or battle in progress and save many of his comrades' lives, but his refusal to talk may cause their deaths. This places the burden on the EPW or detainee and may motivate him to seek relief through cooperation.

Conversely, this technique can also be used on the EPW or detainee who hates his unit because it withdrew and left him to be captured, or who feels he was unfairly treated in his unit. In such cases, the interrogator can point out that if the EPW cooperate and specifies the unit's location, the unit can be destroyed, thus giving the EPW an opportunity for revenge. The interrogator proceeds with this method in a very formal manner.

This approach is likely to be effective with the immature and timid EPW.

Emotional Love Approach. For the emotional love approach to be successful, the interrogator must focus on the anxiety felt by the source about the circumstances in which he finds himself. The interrogator must direct the love the source feels toward the appropriate object: family, homeland, or comrades. If the interrogator can show the source what the source himself can do to alter or improve his situation, the approach has a chance of success.

This approach usually involves some incentive such as communication with the source's family or a quicker end to the war to save his comrades' lives. A good interrogator will usually orchestrate some futility with an emotional love approach to hasten the source's reaching the breaking point.

Sincerity and conviction are critical in a successful attempt at an emotional love approach as the interrogator must show genuine concern for the source, and for the object at which the interrogator is directing the source's emotion.

If the interrogator ascertains the source has great love for his unit and fellow soldiers, the interrogator can effectively exploit the situation. This places a burden on the source and may motivate him to seek relief through cooperation with the interrogator.

Emotional Hate Approach. The emotional hate approach focuses on any genuine hate, or possibly a desire for revenge, the source may feel. The interrogator must ascertain exactly what it is the source may hate so the emotion can be exploited to override the source's rational side. The source may have negative feelings about his country's regime, immediate superiors, officers in general, or fellow soldiers.

This approach is usually most effective on members of racial or religious minorities who have suffered discrimination in military and civilian life. If a source feels he has been treated unfairly in his unit, the interrogator can point out that, if the source cooperates and divulges the location of that unit, the unit can be destroyed, thus affording the source revenge.

By using a conspiratorial tone of voice, the interrogator can enhance the value of this technique. Phrases, such as "You owe them no loyalty for the way they treated you," when used appropriately, can expedite the success of this technique.

Do not immediately begin to berate a certain facet of the source's background or life until your assessment indicates the source feels a negative emotion toward it.

The emotional hate approach can be used more effectively by drawing out the source's negative emotions with questions that elicit a thought-provoking response. For example, "Why do you think they allowed you to be captured?" or "Why do you think they left you to die?" Do not berate the source's forces or homeland unless certain negative emotions surface.

Many sources may have great love for their country, but may hate the regime in control. The emotional hate approach is most effective with the immature or timid source who may have no opportunity up to this point for revenge, or never had the courage to voice his feelings.

Fear-Up Approach

The fear-up approach is the exploitation of a source's preexisting fear during the period of capture and interrogation. The approach works best with young, inexperienced sources, or sources who exhibit a greater than normal amount of fear or nervousness. A source's fear may be justified or unjustified. For example, a source who has committed a war crime may justifiably fear prosecution and punishment. By contrast, a source who has been indoctrinated by enemy propaganda may unjustifiably fear that he will suffer torture or death in or hand if captured.

This approach has the greatest potential to violate the law of war. Great care must be taken to avoid threatening or coercing a source which is in violation of the GPW, Article 17. It is critical the interrogator distinguish what the source fears in order to exploit that fear. The way in which the interrogator exploits the source's fear depends on whether the source's fear is justified or unjustified.

Fear-Up (Harsh). In this approach, the interrogator behaves in an overpowering manner with a loud and threatening voice. The interrogator may even feel the need to throw objects across the room to heighten the source's implanted feelings of fear. Great care must be taken when doing this so any actions would not violate the prohibition on coercion and threats contained in the GPW, Article 17.

This technique is to convince the source he does indeed have something to fear; that he has no option but to cooperate. A good interrogator will implant in the source's mind that the interrogator himself is not the object to be feared, but is a possible way out of the trap.

Use the confirmation of fear only on sources whose fear is justified. During this approach, confirm to the source that he does indeed have a legitimate fear. Then convince the source that you are the source's best or only hope in avoiding or mitigating the object of his fear, such as punishment for his crimes.

You must take great care to avoid promising actions that are not in your power to grant. For example, if the source has committed a war crime, inform the source that the crime has been reported to the appropriate authorities and that action is pending. Next, inform the source that, if he cooperates and tells the truth, you will report that he cooperated and told the truth to the appropriate authorities. You may add that you will also report his lack of cooperation. You may not promise that the charges against him will be dismissed because you have no authority to dismiss the charges.

Fear-Up (Mild). This approach is better suited to the strong, confident type of interrogator; there is generally no need to raise the voice or resort to heavy-handed, table-banging.

For example, capture may be a result of coincidence – the soldier was caught on the wrong side of the border before hostilities actually commenced (he was armed, he could be a terrorist) — or as a result of his actions (he surrendered contrary to his military oath and now a traitor to his country, and his forces will take care of the disciplinary action).

The fear-up (mild) approach must be credible. It usually involves some logical incentive. In most cases, a loud voice is not necessary. The actual fear is increased by helping the source realize the unpleasant consequences the facts may cause and by presenting an alternative, which, of course, can be brought about by answering some simple questions.

The fear-up (harsh) approach is usually a dead-end, and a wise interrogator may want to keep it in reserve as a trump card. After working to increase the source's fear, it would be difficult to convince him everything will be all right if the approach is not successful.

Fear-Down Approach

This technique is nothing more than calming the source and convincing him he will be properly and humanely treated, or telling him the war for him is mercifully over and he need not go into combat again. When used with a soothing, calm tone of voice, this often creates rapport and usually nothing else is needed to get the source to cooperate.

While calming the source, it is a good idea to stay initially with nonpertinent conversation and to avoid the subject which has caused the source's fear. This works quickly in developing rapport and communication, as the source will readily respond to kindness.

When using this approach, it is important the interrogator relate to the source at his perspective level and not expect the source to come up to the interrogator's level.

If the EPW or detainee is so frightened he has withdrawn into a shell or regressed to a less threatening state of mind, the interrogator must break through to him. The interrogator can do this by putting himself on the same physical level as the source; this may require some physical contact. As the source relaxes and begins to respond to kindness, the interrogator can begin asking pertinent questions.

This approach technique may backfire if allowed to go too far. After convincing the source he has nothing to fear, he may cease to be afraid and may feel secure enough to resist the interrogator's pertinent question. If this occurs, reverting to a harsher approach technique usually will bring the desired result quickly.

The fear-down approach works best if the source's fear is unjustified. During this approach, take specific actions to reduce the source's unjustified fear. For example, if the source believes that he will be abused while in your custody, make extra efforts to ensure that the source is well cared for, fed, and appropriately treated.

Once the source is convinced that he has no legitimate reason to fear you, he will be more inclined to cooperate. The interrogator is under no duty to reduce a source's unjustified fear. The only prohibition is that the interrogator may not say or do anything that directly or indirectly communicates to the source that he will be harmed unless he provides the requested information.

These applications of the fear approach may be combined to achieve the desire effect. For example, if a source has justified and unjustified fears, you may initially reduce the source's unfounded fears, and then confirm his legitimate fears. Again, the source should be convinced the interrogator is his best or only hope in avoiding or mitigating the object of his fear.

Pride and Ego Approach

The strategy of this approach is to trick the source into revealing desired information by goading or flattering him. It is effective with sources who have displayed weakness or feelings of inferiority. A real or imaginary deficiency voiced about the source, loyalty to his organization, or any other feature can provide a basis for this technique.

The interrogator accuses the source of weakness or implies he is unable to do a certain thing. This type of source is also prone to excuses and reasons why he did or did not do a certain thing, often shifting the blame to others. An example is opening the interrogation with the question, "Why did you surrender so easily when you could have escaped by crossing the nearby ford in the river?"

The source is likely to provide a basis for further questions or to reveal significant intelligence information if he attempts to explain his surrender in order to vindicate himself. He may give an answer such as, "No one could cross the ford because it is mined."

This technique can also be employed in another manner – by flattering the source into admitting certain information in order to gain credit. For example, while interrogating a suspected saboteur, the interrogator states: "This was a smooth operation. I have seen many previous attempts fail. I bet you planned this. Who else but a clever person like you would have planned it? When did you first decide to do the job?"

This technique is especially effective with the source who has been looked down upon by his superiors. The source has the opportunity to show someone he is intelligent.

A problem with the pride and ego approach is it relies on trickery. The source will eventually realize he has been tricked and may refuse to cooperate further. If this occurs, the interrogator can easily move into a fear-up approach and convince the source the questions he has already answered have committed him, and it would be useless to resist further.

The interrogator can mention it will be reported to the source's forces that he has cooperated fully with the enemy, will be considered a traitor, and has much to fear if he is returned to his forces.

This may even offer the interrogator the option to go into a love-of-family approach where the source must protect his family by preventing his forces from learning of his duplicity or collaboration. Telling the source you will not report that he talked or that he was a severe discipline problem is an incentive that may enhance the effectiveness of the approach.

Pride and Ego-Up Approach. This approach is most effective on sources with little or no intelligence, or on those who have been looked down upon for a long time. It is very effective on low-ranking enlisted personnel and junior grade officers, as it allows the source to finally show someone he does indeed have some "brains."

The source is constantly flattered into providing certain information in order to gain credit. The interrogator must take care to use a flattering somewhat-in-awe tone of voice, and speak highly of the source throughout this approach. This quickly produces positive feelings on the source's part, as he has probably been looking for this type of recognition all of his life.

The interrogator may blow things out of proportion using items from the source's background and making them seem noteworthy or important. As everyone is eager to hear praise, the source will eventually reveal pertinent information to solicit more laudatory comments from the interrogator.

Effective targets for a successful pride and ego-up approach are usually the socially accepted reasons for flattery, such as appearance and good military bearing. The interrogator should closely watch the source's demeanor for indications the approach is working. Some indications to look for are –

- Raising of the head
- A look of pride in the eyes
- Swelling of the chest
- Stiffening of the back

Pride and Ego-Down Approach. This approach is based on attacking the source's sense of personal worth. Any source who shows any real or imagined inferiority or weakness about himself, loyalty to his organization, or captured under embarrassing circumstances, can be easily broken with this approach technique.

The objective is for the interrogator to pounce on the source's sense of pride by attacking his loyalty, intelligence, abilities, leadership qualities, slovenly appearance, or any other perceived weakness. This will usually goad the source into becoming defensive, and he will try to convince the interrogator he is wrong. In his attempt to redeem his pride, the source will usually involuntarily provide pertinent information in attempting to vindicate himself.

A source susceptibie to this approach is also prone to make excuses and give reasons why he did or did not do a certain thing, often shifting the blame to others. If the interrogator uses a sarcastic, caustic tone of voice with appropriate expressions of distaste or disgust, the source will readily believe him. Possible targets for the pride and ego-down approach are the source's –

- Loyalty
- Technical competence
- Leadership abilities
- Soldierly qualities
- Appearance

The pride and ego-down approach is also a dead-end in that, if unsuccessful, it is difficult for the interrogator to recover and move to another approach and reestablish a different type of rapport without losing all credibility.

Futility

In this approach, the interrogator convinces the source that resistance to questioning is futile. When employing this technique, the interrogator must have factual information. These facts are presented by the interrogator in a persuasive, logical manner. He should be aware of and able to exploit the source's psychological and moral weaknesses, as well as weaknesses inherent in his society.

The futility approach is effective when the interrogator can play on doubts that already exist in the source's mind. There are different variations of the futility approach. For example:

- Futility of the personal situation – "You are not finished here until you answer the question."
- Futility in that "everyone talks sooner or later."
- Futility of the battlefield situation.
- Futility in the sense if the source does not mind talking about history, why should he mind talking about his missions, they are also history.

If the source's unit had run out of supplies (ammunition, food, or fuel), it would be somewhat easy to convince him all of his forces are having the same logistical problems. A soldier who has been ambushed may have doubts as to how he was attacked so suddenly. The interrogator should be able to talk him into believing that the interrogator's forces knew of the EPW's unit location, as well as many more units.

The interrogator might describe the source's frightening recollections of seeing death on the battlefield as an everyday occurrence for his forces. Factual or seemingly factual information must be presented in a persuasive, logical manner, and in a matter-of-fact tone of voice.

Making the situation appear hopeless allows the source to rationalize his actions, especially if that action is cooperating with the interrogator. When employing this technique, the interrogator must not only have factual information but also be aware of and exploit the source's psychological, moral, and sociological weaknesses.

Another way of using the futility approach is to blow things out of proportion. If the source's unit was low on, or had exhausted, all food supplies, he can be easily led to believe all of his forces had run out of food. If the source is hinging on cooperating, it may aid the interrogation effort if he is told all the other source's have cooperated.

The futility approach must be orchestrated with other approach techniques (for example, love of comrades). A source who may want to help save his comrades' lives may be convinced the battlefield situation is hopeless and they will die without his assistance. The futility approach is used to paint a bleak picture for the prisoner, but it is not effective in and of itself in gaining the source's cooperation.

We Know All

This approach may be employed in conjunction with the "file and dossier" technique (discussed below) or by itself. If used alone, the interrogator must first become thoroughly familiar with available data concerning the source. To begin the interrogation, the interrogator asks questions based on this known data. When the source hesitates, refuses to answer, or provides an incorrect or incomplete reply, the interrogator provides the detailed answer.

When the source begins to give accurate and complete information, the interrogator interjects questions designed to gain the needed information. Questions to which answers are already known are also asked to test the source's truthfulness and to maintain the deception that the information is already known. By repeating this procedure, the interrogator convinces the source that resistance is useless as everything is already known.

After gaining the source's cooperation, the interrogator still tests the extent of cooperation by periodically using questions to which he has the answers; this is very necessary. If the interrogator does not challenge the source when he is lying, the source will know everything is not known, and he has been tricked. He may then provide incorrect answers to the interrogator's questions.

There are some inherent problems with the use of the "we know all" approach. The interrogator is required to prepare everything in detail, which is time consuming. He must commit much of the information to memory, as working from notes may show the limits of the information actually known.

File and Dossier

The file and dossier approach is used when the interrogator prepares a dossier containing all available information obtained from documents concerning the source or his organization. Careful arrangement of the material within the file may give the illusion it contains more data than actually there. The file may be padded with extra paper, if necessary. Index tabs with titles such as education, employment, criminal record, military service, and others are particularly effective.

The interrogator confronts the source with the dossiers at the beginning of the interrogation and explains intelligence has provided a complete record of every significant happening in the source's life; therefore, it would be useless to resist. The interrogator may read a few selected bits of known data to further impress the source.

If the technique is successful, the source will be intimidated by the size of the file, conclude everything is known, and resign himself to complete cooperation. The success of this technique is largely dependent on the naiveté of the source, volume of data on the subject, and skill of the interrogator in convincing the source.

Establish Your Identity

This approach is especially adaptable to interrogation. The interrogator insists the source has been correctly identified as an infamous individual wanted by higher authorities on serious charges, and he is not the person he purports to be. In an effort to clear himself of this allegation, the source makes a genuine and detailed effort to establish or substantiate his true identity. In so doing, he may provide the interrogator with information and leads for further development.

The "establish your identity" approach was effective in VietNam with the Viet Cong and in OPERATIONS JUST CAUSE and DESERT STORM.

This approach can be used at tactical echelons. The interrogator must be aware if it is used in conjunction with the file and dossier approach, as it may exceed the tactical interrogator's preparation resources.

The interrogator should initially refuse to believe the source and insist he is the criminal wanted by the ambiguous higher authorities. This will force the source to give even more detailed information about his unit in order to convince the interrogator he is who he says he is. This approach works well when combined with the "futility" or "we know all" approach.

Repetition

This approach is used to induce cooperation from a hostile source. In one variation of this approach, the interrogator listens carefully to a source's answer to a question, and then repeats the question and answer several times. He does this with each succeeding question until the source become so thoroughly bored with the procedure he answers questions fully and candidly to satisfy the interrogator and gain relief from the monotony of this method.

The repetition technique must be judiciously used, as it will generally be ineffective when employed against introverted sources or those having great self-control. In fact, it may provide an opportunity for a source to regain his composure and delay the interrogation. In this approach, the use of more than one interrogator or a tape recorder has proven effective.

Rapid Fire

This approach involves a psychological ploy based upon the principles that —

- Everyone likes to be heard when he speaks.
- It is confusing to be interrupted in mid-sentence with an unrelated question.

This approach may be used by one or simultaneously by two or more interrogators in questioning the same source. In employing this technique, the interrogator asks a series of questions in such a manner that the source does not have time to answer a question completely before the next one is asked.

This confuses the source and he will tend to contradict himself, as he has little time to formulate his answers. The interrogator then confronts the source with the inconsistencies causing further contradictions.

In many instances, the source will begin to talk freely in an attempt to explain himself and deny the interrogator's claims of inconsistencies. In this attempt, the source is likely to reveal more than he intends, thus creating additional leads for further exploitation. This approach may be orchestrated with the pride and ego-down or fear-up approaches.

Besides extensive preparation, this approach requires an experienced and competent interrogator, with comprehensive case knowledge and fluency in the source's language.

Silent

This approach may be successful when used against the nervous or confident source. When employing this technique, the interrogator says nothing to the source, but looks him squarely in the eye, preferably with a slight smile on his face. It is important not to look away from the source but force him to break eye contact first.

The source may become nervous, begin to shift in his chair, cross and recross his legs, and look away. He may ask questions, but the interrogator should not answer until he is ready to break the silence. The source may blurt out questions such as, "Come on now, what do you want with me?"

When the interrogator is ready to break silence, he may do so with some nonchalant questions such as, "You planned this operation for a long time, didn't you? Was it your idea?" The interrogator must be patient when using this technique. It may appear the technique is not succeeding, but usually will when given a reasonable chance.

Change of Scene

The idea in using this approach is to get the source away from the atmosphere of an interrogation room or setting. If the interrogator confronts a source who is apprehensive or frightened because of the interrogation environment, this technique may prove effective.

In some circumstances, the interrogator may be able to invite the source to a different setting for coffee and pleasant conversation. During the conversation in this more relaxed environment, the interrogator steers the conversation to the topic of interest. Through this somewhat indirect method, he attempts to elicit the desired information. The source may never realize he is being interrogated.

Another example in this approach is an interrogator poses as a compound guard and engages the source in conversation, thus eliciting the desired information."

i. **Finding 9:**
   (1) *Finding*: Interviewed leaders and soldiers stated the unit's morale (71%) and command climate (68%) had steadily improved due to competent leadership, caring of soldiers by leaders, and better working and living conditions as the theater matured.
   (2) *Standard*: Army Regulation (AR) 600–20, *Army Command Policy*, 13 May 2002, Chapter 1, paragraph 1-5, subparagraph c (1) and (4)(c), prescribes the policies and responsibilities of command. The specific language in the regulation follows:

"c. Characteristics of command leadership.

(1) Commanders and other leaders committed to the professional Army ethic promote a positive environment. If leaders show loyalty to their soldiers, the Army, and the Nation, they earn the loyalty of their soldiers. If leaders consider their soldiers' needs and care for their well-being, and if they demonstrate genuine concern, these leaders build a positive command climate.

"(4) Professionally competent leaders will develop respect for their authority by –

"(c) Properly training their soldiers and ensuring that both soldiers and equipment are in the proper state of readiness at all times. Commanders should assess the command climate periodically to analyze the human dimension of combat readiness. Soldiers must be committed to accomplishing the mission through the unit cohesion developed as a result of a healthy leadership climate established by the command. Leaders at all levels promote the individual readiness of their soldiers by developing competence and confidence in their subordinates. In addition to being mentally, physically, tactically, and technically competent, soldiers must have confidence in themselves, their equipment, their peers, and their leaders. A leadership climate in which all soldiers are treated with fairness, justice, and equity will be crucial to development of this confidence within soldiers. Commanders are responsible for developing disciplined and cohesive units sustained at the highest readiness level possible."

j.　**Finding 10:**

(1) *Finding*: Detainee administration, internment, and intelligence exploitation policy and doctrine does not address detainee operations conducted in the current operating environment, which has a higher demand for human intelligence exploitation at the tactical level and the need for additional classifications of detainees.

(2) *Standard*: Standard of treatment for detainees in OPERATION ENDURING FREEDOM (OEF): Chairman, Joint Chiefs of Staff (CJCS) message dated 211933Z JAN 02 states that members of the Taliban militia and members of al Qaeda under the control of US Forces would be treated humanely and, to the extent appropriate and consistent with military necessity, in a manner consistent with the principles of the Geneva Conventions of 1949. The DAIG has therefore used the provisions of the Geneva Conventions as a benchmark against which to measure the treatment provided to detainees by U.S. Forces to determine if detainees were treated humanely. The use of these standards as benchmarks does not state or imply a position for the United States or U.S. Army on the legal status of its operations in OEF.

CJCS Message dated 211933Z JAN 02, provides the determination regarding the humane treatment of al Qaeda and Taliban detainees. *Convention Relative to the Treatment of Prisoners of War of August 12, 1949* (GPW) is the international treaty that governs the treatment of prisoners of war; and *Geneva Convention Relative to the Protection of Civilian Persons in Time of War (GC), August 12, 1949* is the international treaty that governs the treatment of civilian persons in time of war.

As the guidance did not define "humane treatment" but did state that the US would treat members of the Taliban militia and al Qaeda in a manner consistent with the Geneva Conventions, the DAIG determined that it would use Common Article 3 of the GCs as its floor measure of humane treatment, but would also include provisions of the Geneva Convention on the Treatment of Prisoners of War (GPW) and Geneva Convention Relative to the Protection of Civilian Persons in Time of War (GC) as other relevant indicia of "humane treatment." The use of this standard does not state or imply a position for the United States or U.S. Army on the legal status of its operations in OEF.

Standard of treatment for detainees in OPERATION IRAQI FREEDOM (OIF): OIF was an international armed conflict and therefore the provisions of the Geneva Conventions applied. Additionally, the United States was an occupying power and has acted in accordance with the obligations of an occupying power described in the *Hague Convention No. IV Respecting the Laws and Customs of War on Land (H.IV), Oct. 18, 1907*, including, but not limited to Articles 43-46 and 50; *Geneva Convention Relative to the Treatment of Prisoners of War of August 12, 1949* (GPW), *Geneva Convention Relative to the Protection of Civilian Persons in Time of War (GC), August 12, 1949*. The GC supplements H.IV, providing the general standard of treatment at Article 27 and specific standards in subsequent Articles.

The minimum treatment provided by Common Article 3 of the Geneva Conventions is: (1) No adverse distinction based upon race, religion, sex, etc.; (2) No violence to life or person; (3) No taking hostages; (4) No degrading treatment; (5) No passing of sentences in absence of fair trial, and; (6) The wounded and sick must be cared for.

The specific language in the CJCS Message for OEF and the GPW/GC and H.IV follows:

CJCS Message dated 211933Z JAN 02, "Paragraph 3. The combatant commanders shall, in detaining al Qaeda and Taliban individuals under the control of the Department of Defense, treat them humanely and, to the extent appropriate and consistent with military necessity, in a manner consistent with the principles of the Geneva Conventions of 1949."

GPW/GC, Article 3 (Common Article 3) – "In the case of armed conflict not of an international character occurring in the territory of one of the High Contracting Parties, each party to the conflict shall be bound to apply, as a minimum, the following provisions:

1. Persons taking no active part in the hostilities, including members of armed forces who have laid down their arms and those placed hors de combat by sickness, wounds, detention, or any other cause, shall in all circumstances be treated humanely, without any adverse distinction founded on race, color, religion or faith, sex, birth or wealth, or any other similar criteria.

To this end the following acts are and shall remain prohibited at any time and in any place whatsoever with respect to the above-mentioned persons:

(a) Violence to life and person, in particular, murder of all kinds, mutilation, cruel treatment and torture;
(b) Taking of hostages;
(c) Outrages upon personal dignity, in particular, humiliating and degrading treatment;
(d) The passing of sentences and the carrying out of executions without previous judgment pronounced by a regularly constituted court affording all the judicial guarantees which are recognized as indispensable by civilized peoples.

2. The wounded and sick shall be collected and cared for. An impartial humanitarian body, such as the International Committee of the Red Cross, may offer its services to the Parties to the conflict. The Parties to the conflict should further endeavour to bring into force, by means of special agreements, all or part of the other provisions of the present Convention. The application of the preceding provisions shall not affect the legal status of the Parties to the conflict."

The following specific provisions of GPW and GC apply:

"Article 18 – All effects and articles of personal use, except arms, horses, military equipment and military documents, shall remain in the possession of prisoners of war, likewise their metal helmets and gas masks and like articles issued for personal protection. Effects and articles used for their clothing or feeding shall likewise remain in their possession, even if such effects and articles belong to their regulation military equipment. At no time should prisoners of war be without identity documents. The Detaining Power shall supply such documents to prisoners of war who possess none. Badges of rank and nationality, decorations and articles having above all a personal or sentimental value may not be taken from prisoners of war. Sums of money carried by prisoners of war may not be taken away from them except by order of an officer, and after the amount and particulars of the owner have been recorded in a special register and an itemized receipt has been given, legibly inscribed with the name, rank and unit of the person issuing the said receipt. Sums in the currency of the Detaining Power, or which are changed into such currency at the prisoner's request, shall be placed to the credit of the prisoner's account as provided in Article 64. The Detaining Power may withdraw articles of value from prisoners of war only for reasons of security; when such articles are withdrawn, the procedure laid down for sums of money impounded shall apply. Such objects, likewise sums taken away in any currency other than that of the Detaining Power and the conversion of which has not been asked for by the owners, shall be kept in the custody of the Detaining Power and shall be returned in their initial shape to prisoners of war at the end of their captivity.

Article 19 – Prisoners of war shall be evacuated, as soon as possible after their capture, to camps situated in an area far enough from the combat zone for them to be out of danger. Only those prisoners of war who, owing to wounds or sickness, would run greater risks by being evacuated than by remaining where they are, may be temporarily kept back in a danger zone. Prisoners of war shall not be unnecessarily exposed to danger while awaiting evacuation from a fighting zone."

Department of Defense Directive (DoDD) 2310.1, *DoD Program for Enemy Prisoners of War (EPOW) and Other Detainees*, 18 August 1994, Paragraph 3.3, requires the application of appropriate legal status, transfer and release authority and authorization. Paragraph 3.4 directs the handing over of detainees to Military Police and provides for intelligence collection. Paragraph 4.4 assigns responsibility for treatment, classification, administrative processing, and custody for detainees. The specific language in the directive follows:

"3.3 Captured or detained personnel shall be accorded an appropriate legal status under international law. Persons captured or detained may be transferred to or from the care, custody, and control of the U.S. Military Services only on approval of the Assistant Secretary of Defense for International Security Affairs (ASD(ISA)) and as authorized by the Geneva Conventions Relative to the Treatment of Prisoners of War and for the Protection of Civilian Persons in Time of War (references (d) and (e)).

3.4 Persons captured or detained by the U.S. Military Services shall normally be handed over for safeguarding to U.S. Army Military Police, or to detainee collecting points or other holding facilities and installations operated by U.S. Army Military Police as soon as practical. Detainees may be interviewed for intelligence collection purposes at facilities and installations operated by U.S. Army Military Police."

"4.4. The Commanders of the Unified Combatant Commands shall:

4.4.2. Provide for the proper treatment, classification, administrative processing and custody of those persons captured or detained by the Military Services under their command and control. "Department of Defense Directive (DoDD) 2310.1, *DoD Program for Enemy Prisoners of War (EPOW) and Other Detainees*, 18 August 1994, Paragraph 1.1, reissues responsibility, specifically assigning the Army as Executive Agent for the DoD Program for Enemy Prisoners of War (EPOW) and Other Detainees. The specific language in the directive follows:

"1.1. Reissues reference (a) to update policy and responsibilities within the Department of Defense for a program to ensure implementation of the international law of war, both customary and codified, about EPOW, to include the enemy sick or wounded, retained personnel, civilian internees (Cls), and other detained personnel (detainees). Detainees include, but are not limited to, those persons held during operations other than war."

Under Secretary of Defense Memorandum, *SUBJECT: Responsibility for Detainees in Association with the Global War on Terrorism*, 17 January 2002, assigns the Assistant Secretary of Defense for Special Operations and Low Intensity Conflict (ASD(SO/LIC)) responsibility for DoD policies and plans related to persons detained in the Global War on Terrorism. The specific language in the memorandum follows:

"Effective immediately, ASD(SO/LIC) assumes responsibility for overall development, coordination, approval and promulgation of major DoD policies and plans related to persons detained in association with the Global War on Terrorism. This includes development, coordination, approval, and promulgation of major DoD policies, and new courses of action with DoD Components and other Federal Agencies as necessary.

DoD Directive 2310.1 will be adjusted to reflect this decision."

Army Regulation (AR) 25-30, *The Army Publishing Program*, 16 March 2004, Glossary, defines the term Army regulation and field manual The specific language in the regulation follows:

"Army regulation

A directive that sets forth missions, responsibilities, and policies, delegates authority, sets objectives, and prescribes mandated procedures to ensure uniform compliance with those policies. Mandated procedures in Army regulations are required and authoritative instructions that contain the detail needed to make sure basic policies are carried out uniformly throughout the Army. These mandated procedures also ensure uniform implementation of public law, policy guidance, and instructions from higher headquarters or other Government agencies such as the JCP, OMB, or Department of Defense."

"Field manual

A DA publication that contains doctrine and training principles with supporting tactics, techniques, and/or procedures and describes how the Army and its organizations function in terms of missions, organizations, personnel, and equipment. FMs implement ratified international standardization agreements. FMs may also contain informational or reference material relative to military operations and training and may be used to publish selected alliance doctrinal publications that are not readily integrated into other doctrinal literature."

AR 190-8, *Enemy Prisoners of War, Retained Personnel, Civilian Internees and Other Detainees*, 1 October 1997, Chapter 1, paragraph 1-1, subparagraphs a and b, implement DoDD 2310.1 and incorporates Army Regulation 190-8 and 190-57 and SECNAV Instruction 3461.3, and Air Force Joint Instruction 31-304. It establishes policies and planning guidance for the treatment, care, accountability, legal status, and administrative procedures for Enemy Prisoners of War, Civilian Internees, Retained Persons, and Other Detainees and implements international law for all military operations. The specific language in the regulation follows:

"Summary. This regulation implements Department Of Defense Directive 2310.1 and establishes policies and planning guidance for the treatment, care, accountability, legal status, and administrative procedures for Enemy Prisoners of War, Civilian Internees, Retained Persons, and Other Detainees. This regulation is a consolidation of Army Regulation 190-8 and Army Regulation 190-57 and incorporates SECNAV Instruction 3461.3 and Air Force Joint Instruction 31-304. Policy and procedures established herein apply to the services and their capabilities to the extent that they are resourced and organized for enemy prisoner of war operations.

Applicability. This is a multiservice regulation. It applies to the Army, Navy, Air Force and Marine Corps and to their Reserve components when lawfully ordered to active duty under the provisions of Title 10 United States Code.

"a. This regulation provides policy, procedures, and responsibilities for the administration, treatment, employment, and compensation of enemy prisoners of war (EPW), retained personnel (RP), civilian internees (CI) and other detainees (OD) in the custody of U.S. Armed Forces. This regulation also establishes procedures for transfer of custody from the United States to another detaining power.

b. This regulation implements international law, both customary and codified, relating to EPW, RP, CI, and ODs, which includes those persons, held during military operations other than war. The principal treaties relevant to this regulation are:

(1) The 1949 Geneva Convention Relative to the Amelioration of the Condition of the Wounded and Sick in Armed Forces in the Field (GWS).

(2) The 1949 Geneva Convention for the Amelioration of the Condition of Wounded, Sick and Shipwrecked Members of Armed Forces at Sea (GWS SEA).

(3) The 1949 Geneva Convention Relative to the Treatment of Prisoners of War (GPW).

(4) The 1949 Geneva Convention Relative to the Protection of Civilian Persons in Time of War (GC), and in the event of conflicts or discrepancies between this regulation and the Geneva Conventions, the provisions of the Geneva Conventions take precedence."
  Field Manual (FM) 3-19.1, *Military Police Operations*, 31 January 2002, Chapter 4, paragraphs 4-42 to 4-45, describe the role of MP units in detainee operations. The specific language in the field manual follows:
  "4-42. The Army is the Department of Defense's (DOD's) executive agent for all EPW/CI operations. Additionally, the Army is DOD's executive agent for long-term confinement of US military prisoners. Within the Army and through the combatant commander, the MP are tasked with coordinating shelter, protection, accountability, and sustainment for EFWs/CIs. The I/R function addresses MP roles when dealing with EPWs/CIs, dislocated civilians, and US military prisoners.
  4-43. The I/R function is of humane as well as tactical importance. In any conflict involving US forces, safe and humane treatment of EPWs/CIs is required by international law. Military actions on the modern battlefield will result in many EPWs/CIs. Entire units of enemy forces, separated and disorganized by the shock of intensive combat, may be captured. This can place a tremendous challenge on tactical forces and can significantly reduce the capturing unit's combat effectiveness. The MP support the battlefield commander by relieving him of the problem of handling EPWs/CIs with combat forces. The MP perform their I/R function of collecting, evacuating, and securing EPWs throughout the AO. In this process, the MP coordinate with MI to collect information that may be used in current or future operations.
  4-44. Although the CS MP unit initially handles EPWs/CIs, modular MP (I/R) battalions with assigned MP guard companies and supporting MWD teams are equipped and trained to handle this mission for the long term. A properly configured modular MP (I/R) battalion can support, safeguard, account for, guard, and provide humane treatment for up to 4,000 EPWs/CIs; 8,000 dislocated civilians; or 1,500 US military prisoners.

EPW/CI HANDLING

4-45. The MP are tasked with collecting EPWs/CIs from combat units as far forward as possible. The MP operate collection points and holding areas to temporarily secure EPWs/CIs until they can be evacuated to the next higher echelon's holding area. The MP escort-guard company assigned to the MP brigade (I/R) evacuate the EPWs/CIs from the corps's holding area to the COMMZ's internment facilities. The MP safeguard and maintain accountability, protect, and provide humane treatment for all personnel under their care."
  FM 3-19.4, *Military Police Leaders' Handbook*, 2 August 2002, Preface, addresses detainee operations doctrine at the platoon level. The specific language in the field manual follows:
  "This field manual (FM) addresses military police (MP) maneuver and mobility support (MMS), area security.(AS), internment and resettlement (I/R), law and order (L&O), and

police intelligence operations (PIO) across the full spectrum of Army operations. Although this manual includes a discussion of corps and division MP elements, it primarily focuses on the principles of platoon operations and the tactics, techniques, and procedures (TTP) the platoon uses to accomplish its mission."

FM 3-19.40, *Military Police Internment/Resettlement Operations*, 1 August 2001, Preface, establishes this FM as the doctrinal foundation for detainee operations. Chapter 2, paragraph 2-1, explains the role of the MP battalion commander. Chapter 3, paragraphs 3-1 to 3-3, 3-5, and 3-6, describe the basic requirements for the handling, securing, and accounting for EPWs and CIs; paragraphs 3-14 to 3-17 describe the procedures for handling property and tagging EPWs and CIs. Chapter 4 describes detailed administrative procedures for enemy prisoners of war (EPWs), including evacuation, receiving, processing, personnel files, internment serial number (ISN) issuance, information flow, facility assignment, classification, control and discipline, transfer between facilities, host nation or allied forces, and repatriation; the introduction outlines this content. Chapter 5 describes procedures for civilian internees (CIs), including specifying who is a CI, general protection requirements, authorization to intern, administrative responsibilities, receiving, processing, flow of information, security, control and discipline; the introduction explains the difference between CIs and EPWs. The specific language in the field manual follows:

"Field Manual (FM) 3-19.40 depicts the doctrinal foundation, principles, and processes that MP will employ when dealing with enemy prisoners of war (EPWs), civilian internees (CIs), US military prisoner operations, and MP support to civil-military operations (populace and resource control [PRC], humanitarian assistance [HA], and emergency services [ES])."

"2-1. An MP battalion commander tasked with operating an I/R facility is also the facility commander. As such, he is responsible for the safety and well-being of all personnel housed within the facility. Since an MP unit may be tasked to handle different categories of personnel (EPW, CI, OD, refugee, and US military prisoner), the commander, the cadre, and support personnel must be aware of the requirements for each category.

3-1. The MP units accept captives from capturing units as far forward as possible, and captives are held in CPs and CHAs until they are removed from the battlefield. Normally, CPs are operated in the division AO and CHAs are operated in the corps AO; but they can be operated anywhere they are needed. The CPs and CHAs sustain and safeguard captives and ensure a minimum level of field processing and accountability. Wounded and sick captives receive medical treatment, and captives who require lifesaving medical attention are evacuated to the nearest medical facility.

3-2. The MP establishes listening posts (LPs), observation posts (OPs), guard posts, and fighting positions to protect captives and prevent their escape. Captured soldiers are trained to believe that escape from captivity is their duty; therefore, they must be closely guarded. Consider the morale and physical condition of captives when determining the number of guards needed. Guards must be prepared to use and maintain firm control and security.

3-3. The MP work closely with military intelligence (MI) interrogation teams at CPs and CHAs to determine if captives, their equipment, and their weapons have intelligence value. This process is accelerated when MI interrogation teams can observe captives during arrival and processing, and interrogators can also be used as interpreters during this phase. Before a captive is interviewed by MI personnel, he must have a Department of Defense (DD) Form 2745 (Figure 3-1) attached to him and be accounted for on DO Form 2708.

3-5. Processing begins when US forces capture or detain an individual. The processing is accomplished in the CZ for security, control, intelligence, and the welfare of captives in evacuation channels. This is referred to *as field processing*. The capturing unit begins field processing by using the Five Ss and T procedure (search, segregate, silence, speed, safeguard, and tag). At the CP or the CHA, MP continue processing with the principles of STRESS (search, tag, report, evacuate, segregate, and safeguard).

3-6. After receiving a captive from a capturing unit, MP are responsible for safeguarding and accounting for the captive at each stage of his removal from the battlefield. The processing procedure begins upon capture and continues until the captive reaches the I/R facility and is released. The process of identifying and tagging a captive helps US forces control and account for him as they move rearward from the battlefild. Before a captive is interned, repatriated, or released, MP at the I/R facility must provide full-scale processing.

3-14: Property Accountability. When seizing property from a captive –

- Bundle it or place it in a bag to keep it intact and separate from other captives' possessions.
- Prepare DA Form 4137 for confiscated and impounded property.
- Prepare a receipt for currency and negotiable instruments to be signed by the captive and the receiver. Use cash collection vouchers so that the value can be credited to each captive's account. List currency and negotiable instruments on the captive's personal-property list, but treat them as impounded property.
- Keep the original receipt with the property during evacuation. Give the captive a copy of the receipt, and tell him to keep it to expedite the return of his property.
- Have MI sign for property on DA Form 4137 and for captives on DD Form 2708.
- Return confiscated property to supply after it is cleared by MI teams. Items kept by MI because of intelligence value are forwarded through MI channels.
- Evacuate retained items with the captive when he moves to the next level of internment.
- Maintain controlled access to confiscated and impounded property.
- 3-15. Tag each captive with a DD Form 2745. The MP at CPs and CHAs check each tag for the –
- Date and time of capture.
- Capturing unit.
- Place of capture.
- Circumstances of the capture.

The remaining information on the tag is included as it becomes available.

3-16. A DD Form 2745 is a perforated, three-part form that is individually serial-numbered. It is constructed of durable, waterproof, tear-resistant material with reinforced eyeholes on Parts A and C. Part A is attached to the captive with wire or string, Part B is maintained by the capturing unit for their records, and Part C is attached to confiscated property so that the owner can be identified later.

3-17. The MP at division CPs ensure that a DD Form 2745 is placed on each captive who arrives at the CP without one. They may direct the capturing unit to complete a capture tag before accepting the prisoner into the CP. The MP –

- Make a statement on the tag if the captive arrived without it.
- Instruct the captive not to remove or alter the tag.
- Annotate the tag's serial number and the captive's name on a locally developed manifest."

Chapter 4, Introduction – "The MP are responsible for evacuating EPWs from division CPs to HAs and then to internment facilities (normally located in the COMMZ). This chapter addresses procedures for properly handling, processing, and safeguarding EPWs. The procedures outlined in this chapter are also applicable to RPs.

Chapter 5, Introduction – "A CI internment facility runs parallel to an EPW internment facility, with some differences.

A CI –

- Is protected under the provisions of the GC.
- Does not meet the criteria for classification as an EPW or an RP.
- Is considered a security risk.
- Needs protection because he committed an offense against the detaining power (insurgents, criminals, or other persons)."

FM 34-52, *Intelligence Interrogation*, 28 September 1992, Preface, establishes this FM as the doctrinal foundation for interrogations of detainees. The specific language in the field manual follows:

"This manual provides doctrinal guidance, techniques, and procedures governing employment of interrogators as human intelligence (HUMINT) collection assets in support of the commander's intelligence needs. It outlines the interrogator's role within the intelligence collection effort and the supported unit's day-to-day operations.

This manual is intended for use by interrogators as well as commanders, staff officers, and military intelligence (MI) personnel charged with the responsibility of the interrogation collection effort."

ARTEP 19-546-MTP, *Mission Training Plan for the Headquarters and Headquarters Company Military Police Battalion Internment/Resettlement)*, 10 April 1999, Chapter 1, paragraph 1-4, subparagraph a, outlines training doctrine for I/R battalions. The specific language in the ARTEP follows:

"1-4. *Mission and Tasks.*
a. The battalion's critical mission is to provide command, staff planning, administration, and logistical support for the operation of an Internment/Resettlement facility for either Enemy Prisoner of War/Civilian Internees (EPW/CI), or US Military Prisoners. It also provides direct supervision of battalion functions: Personnel, Medical, Supply, and Food Services. This MTP is composed of major activities that the unit must execute to accomplish the mission."

k. **Finding 11:**
  (1) *Finding*: Shortfalls in both the Military Police and Military Intelligence organizational structures resulted in the tactical unit commanders adjusting their tactics, techniques, and procedures to conduct detainee operations.
  (2) *Standard*: Field Manual (FM) 3-19.1, *Military Police Operations*, 31 January 2002, Chapter 7, paragraph 7-9, requires corps augmentation for sustained operations and for special operations such as dealing with dislocated civilians, and refugee internment or resettlement. Paragraphs 7-13, 7-14, 7-17, 7-21, and paragraph 7-26 discusses the employment of the different division Military Police companies, by the type of division to which they are assigned. The specific language in the field manual follows:

"7-9. In the division (where flexible support of an austere force is crucial), the division PM must have a clear understanding of situational awareness. To obtain current information for projecting MP needs in the division area, he must be mobile and be able to conduct split-cell operations. The assets available to the PM include the division MP company and at least one corps MP company. Corps augmentation is required for sustained operations and for special operations such as river crossings, dealing with dislocated civilians, and refugee internment or resettlement. The division PM coordinates with the corps PM and the MP brigade or CID commanders for—● Evacuating and guarding EPWs/CIs from division to corps."

"7-13. The Army of Excellence (AOE) heavy division MP company has six platoons. Three platoons provide support to each maneuver brigade and are designated as DS. The other three platoons are designated as GS platoons. One MP platoon provides security for the division main CP; one provides security for the division's EPW central collection point; and one performs other MP operations within the division rear.

7-14. The GS MP platoons' AOs are configured based on METT-TC and the availability of MP augmentation from the corps. The DS MP platoons' AOs coincide with the supported maneuver brigade's boundary. Each platoon headquarters locates within its brigade's support area or any other area where it can best provide and receive support. To accomplish its mission, each DS platoon requires a minimum of two squads, each with three teams. One squad operates the EPW/CI collection point. The other squads perform MMS and AS operations. All MP platoons are capable of performing all five MP functions. However, performance of these functions is prioritized based on METT-TC and the division commander's concept of operations. The division PM, the company commander, and METT-TC dictate how these platoons should be tasked-organized to accomplish the mission."

"7-17. The company has three GS platoons to support the division. No platoons are provided to the maneuver brigade. One platoon is normally located in the vicinity of the division main CP so that its resources can help support CP security. Another platoon locates in the DSA and operates the division EPW/ CI collection point. The last platoon has an AO configured according to METT-TC and the commander's priority of MP missions. Each GS MP platoon has a headquarters and three squads, each with two teams. The PM section is located in the vicinity of the division main CP. The exact location is based on the current operational status and on METT- TC.

"7-21. The nature of airborne operations makes the capture of EPWs likely. Therefore, during the first stage of the assault phase, the priority of MP support is given to EPW operations. After assembling the DZ or LZ, the MP collect EPWs captured during the assault. Combat elements are relieved of EPWs as far forward as possible. In airborne operations, EPWs are held for later movement to a central collection point. During the first stage of the assault, the MP perform limited straggler and refugee control and undertake AS operations, when possible.

"7-26. When possible, habitually aligned platoons remain with their brigades, and corps assets perform GS missions. However, when no corps assets are available and two division platoons are employed as stated above, the two remaining platoons conduct division EPW collection-point operations and other MP functions based on METT-TC. Normally, the EPW platoon and the MP company headquarters colocate in the DSA. As required (and based on METT-TC), airflow planning includes EPW/CI evacuation from the AATF/FOB collection point back to the DSA. The PM section operates from the division rear CP to facilitate I/R operations and to coordinate MMS and AS with key logistical staff. Due to potentially extreme distances on the air assault battlefield, the DPM normally locates with the division main CP to serve as a key G3 battle-staff member and to coordinate PIO with the G2."

FM, 3-19.40, *Military Police Internment/Resettlement Operations*, 1 August 2001, Chapter 3, addresses the responsibility of division Military Police (MP) units to operate collecting points and to assist maneuver units as they move through the battlefield and perform their mission. Paragraph 3-1 assigns MP units the responsibility to accept captives from capturing units as far forward as possible, but allowing them to operate anywhere they are needed. Paragraph 3-3 describes how MP personnel work closely with the Military Intelligence (MI) interrogators to determine if detainees and their possessions have any intelligence value. Paragraph 3-5 outlines the beginning of detainee processing when U.S. Armed Forces detain an individual in the combat zone. Paragraph 3-64 provides information to facilitate collecting enemy tactical information and how MI may collocate interrogation teams at collecting points and Corps Holding Area to collect intelligence information. The specific language in the field manual follows:

"A large number of captives on the battlefield hampers maneuver units as they move to engage and destroy an enemy. To assist maneuver units in performing their mission–
• Division MP units operate CPs in the division AO.• Corps MP units operate holding areas in the corps AO."

"3-1. The MP units accept captives from capturing units as far forward as possible, and captives are held in CPs and CHAs until they are removed from the battlefield. Normally, CPs are operated in the division AO and CHAs are operated in the corps AO; but they can be operated anywhere they are needed. The CPs and CHAs sustain and safeguard captives and ensure a minimum level of field processing and accountability. Wounded and sick captives receive medical treatment, and captives who require lifesaving medical attention are evacuated to the nearest medical facility."

"3-3. The MP work closely with military intelligence (MI) interrogation teams at CPs and CHAs to determine if captives, their equipment, and their weapons have intelligence value. This process is accelerated when MI interrogation teams can observe captives during arrival and processing, and interrogators can also be used as interpreters during this phase. Before a captive is interviewed by MI personnel, he must have a Department of Defense (DD) Form 2745 (Figure 3-1) attached to him and be accounted for on DD Form 2708."

"3-5. Processing begins when US forces capture or detain an individual. The processing is accomplished in the CZ for security, control, intelligence, and the welfare of captives in evacuation channels. This is referred to as field processing. The capturing unit begins field processing by using the Five Ss and T procedure (search, segregate, silence, speed, safeguard, and tag). At the CP or the CHA, MP continue processing with the principles of STRESS (search, tag, report, evacuate, segregate, and safeguard)."

"3-64. To facilitate collecting enemy tactical information, MI may colocate interrogation teams at CPs and CHAs. This provides MI with direct access to captives and their equipment and documents. Coordination is made between MP and MI to establish operating procedures that include accountability. An interrogation area is established away from the receiving/processing line so that MI personnel can interrogate captives and examine their equipment and documents. If a captive or his equipment or documents are removed from the receiving/processing line, account for them on DD Form 2708 and DA Form 4137."

FM, 34-52, *Intelligence Interrogation*, 28 September 1992, Chapter 1, definition of Interrogation, pages 1–6 and 1–7, Objective, pages 1–7, discuss the interrogator should not concentrate on the objective to the extent he overlooks or fails to recognize and exploit other valuable information extracted from the source. Chapter 2, page 2–1, Composition and Structure, discusses that the interrogation architecture is a seamless system that supports operations from brigade to theater level. Page 2–2, Interrogation below division, addresses the first interrogation could take place at brigade level to receive tactical information that will provide immediate value to the unit on the ground. Page 2–3, Division interrogation assets, provides an overview of the capabilities a division Military Intelligence battalion provides to a division. Page 2–4, Interrogation Teams, provides the composition of an interrogation team and is normally employed as part of the MI company teams. Page 2–12, Interrogation at Brigade and Below, describes that an MI battalion interrogator can be attached temporarily to the committed battalion to assist in exploiting information immediately from the enemy prisoner of war (EPW). Page 2–22, Theater Interrogation Facility, describe the purpose of the Theater Interrogation Facility and that it is staffed by U.S. Army interrogators, with support from Air Force, Navy, Marine Corps, and other U.S. national agencies as required. Page 3–1, provides the criteria for selecting personnel to be interrogated. Page 3–2, Screening, explains the screening to select a source to interrogate. Page 3-2, Prepare to conduct screenings, describe the coordination and roles between the screeners and MP holding area guards. Page 3–2, Document Screening, outlines when examining documents, the screener should identify topics on which EPWs and detainees have pertinent information that may contain indications of pertinent knowledge and potential cooperation. Page 3-2, Personnel Screening, recommends if time permits, that screeners should question holding area personnel about the EPWs and detainees who might identify sources or answer the supported commander's priority intelligence requirements (PIR) and intelligence requirements (IR). Page 3-29, Interrogation with an Interpreter, provides what needs to take place before, during, and after an interrogation. Page 3-30, Conduct the Interrogation, outlines the steps the interrogators need to take when an interpreter does not follow the guidance of the interrogator during an interrogation. The specific language in the field manual follows:

Page 1-6. "Definition of Interrogation. Interrogation is the process of questioning a source to obtain the maximum amount of usable information. The goal of any interrogation is to obtain reliable information in a lawful manner, in a minimum amount of time, and satisfy intelligence requirements of any echelon of command. Sources may be – civilian internees, insurgents, EPWs, defectors, refugees, displaced persons, agents or suspected agents, other non-US personnel. A good interrogation produces needed information which is timely, complete, clear, and accurate. An interrogation involved the interaction of two personalities-the source and the interrogator."

Page 1-7. "Objective. Each interrogation must be conducted for a definite purpose. The interrogator must keep this purpose firmly in mind as he proceeds to obtain usable information to satisfy the assigned requirement, and thus contribute to the success of the unit's mission.... In either case, the interrogator must use the objective as a basis for planning and conducting the interrogation. He should attempt to prevent the source from becoming aware of the true objective of the interrogation. The interrogator should not concentrate on the objective to the extent he overlooks or fails to recognize and exploit other valuable information extracted from the source."

Page 2-1. "Composition and Structure. The interrogation architecture (interrogators and interrogation units) is a seamless system that supports operations from brigade to theater level. The dynamic warfighting doctrine requires interrogation units be highly mobile and have automation and communication equipment to report information to the supported commander. The MI commander must ensure interrogators have the necessary equipment to accomplish their wartime mission. The MI commander retains overall responsibility for interrogators assigned to his unit. The manner in which these interrogators are controlled depends on how the MI unit is task organized for combat."

Page 2-2, "Interrogation Below Division. The first interrogation could take place at brigade. Interrogation teams are attached temporarily to brigades in enemy contact when determined appropriate by the Division G2. These teams come from the interrogation section of the parent division. Interrogation personnel are organic to separate brigades and armored cavalry regiments (ACRs). Interrogation at brigade level is strictly tactical and deals with information of immediate value.

Interrogation personnel in DS to brigade will be colocated or immediately adjacent to the division forward EPW collecting point in the brigade support area (BSA). For MI units to receive S2 support, the collecting point and interrogation site will be colocated and accessible to the command post (CP)."

Page 2-3, "Division Interrogation Assets. An MI battalion is organic to each division. It provides combat intelligence, EW, and OPSEC support to light or heavy infantry and airborne or air assault division. The MI battalion provides special support the G2 needs to produce combat intelligence. Interrogation personnel organic to the MI battalions compose the interrogation support element."

Page 2-4, "Interrogation Teams. Each interrogation team consists of a team leader (warrant officer), NCO assistant team leader, and three team members. Teams are normally employed as part of the MI company teams which provide IEW support to the brigades."

Page 2-12. "Interrogation at Brigade and Below. Interrogators are not usually attached below brigade level unless the combat situation requires limited tactical interrogation at battalion or lower. In this event, skilled interrogators from the MI battalion will be attached temporarily to committed battalions. They will assist in exploiting EPW immediately upon capture to extract information needed in support of the capturing unit.

Interrogations at battalion or lower are brief and concerned only with information bearing directly on the combat mission of the capturing unit. The following are examples of circumstance warranting an interrogation:

- A unit or landing force assigned an independent mission in which the S2 is primarily responsible for collecting information necessary to fulfill the unit's mission. Immediate tactical intelligence is necessary for mission accomplishment.
- There is a definite need for interrogation at the lower level to permit rapid reaction based on information obtained.
- It is advantageous to have an EPW point out enemy defense and installation from observation points in forward areas."

Page 2-22. "Theater Interrogation Facility. The EAC interrogation facility will normally be designated as the TIF. A TIF is staffed by US Army interrogators and analysts, with support from Air Force, Navy, Marine Corps, and other US national agencies as required. In a multinational operation, a combined interrogation facility may be established with allied interrogators augmentation. In addition to conventional theater Army operations, a TIF may be established to support a joint or unified command to meet theater requirements during crisis or contingency deployments.

MI battalion companies, MI brigade (EAC) provide us Army interrogation support to the EAC TIF. The mission of the TIF is to –

- Interrogate PWs, high-level political and military personnel, civilian internees, defectors, refugees, and displace persons."

"A TIF is organized into a headquarters section, operations section, and two interrogation and DOCEX sections. It will normally have an attached TSA section from Operations Group, and a liaison team from the Joint Captured Materiel Exploitation Center (JCMEC). The JCMEC liaison team assists in exploiting sources who have knowledge of captured enemy weapons and equipment.

- Provost marshal for location of theater EPW camps, and for procedures to be followed by interrogators and MP for processing, interrogating, and internment."

Page 3-1. "Interrogation Process. Criteria for selecting personnel to be interrogated vary with the – commander's collection requirements. Time limitations. Number and types of potential sources available. Exact circumstance surrounding the employment of US Forces. In this regard, source selection is important in conducting interrogation at tactical echelons of command because of the proximity to enemy elements, number and conditions of detainees, and time restrictions."

Page 3-2. "Screening. Screening is the selection of sources for interrogation. It must be conducted at every echelon to – Determine source cooperativeness and knowledgeability. Determine which sources can best satisfy the commander's PIR and IR in a timely manner."

Page 3-2. "Prepare to Conduct Screenings. Screeners coordinate MP holding area guards on their role in the screening process. The guards are told where the screening will take place, how EPWs, and detainees are to be brought there from the holding area, and what types of behavior on their part will facilitate the screening."

Page 3-2. "Document Screening. If time permits, screeners should go to the holding area and examine all available documents pertaining to the EPWs and detainees. They should look for signs that certain EPWs and detainees are willing, or can be induced, to cooperate with the interrogators. Previous screening and interrogation reports and EPW personnel records are important."

Page 3-2. "Personnel Screening. If time permits, screeners should question holding area personnel about the EPWs and detainees. Since these personnel are in almost constant contact with the EPWs and detainees, their descriptions of specific ones can help identify sources who might answer the supported commander's PIR and IR. Screeners should identify and note those EPWs and detainees whose appearance and behavior indicate they are willing to cooperate immediately or are unlikely to cooperate ever."

Page 3-29. "Interrogation With an Interpreter. Interrogation through an interpreter is time consuming because the interpreter must repeat everything said by the interrogator and source.

The interrogator must brief the interpreter before the interrogation can begin. An interrogation with an interpreter will go through all five phases of the interrogation process. After the interrogation is over, the interrogator will evaluate the interpreter."

Page 3-30. "Conduct the Interrogation. During the interrogation, the interrogator corrects the interpreter if he violates any standards on which he was briefed. For example, if the interpreter injects his own ideas into the interrogation he must be corrected.

"Corrections should be made in a low-key manner. At no time should the interrogator rebuke his interpreter sternly or loudly while they are with the source. The interrogator should never argue with the interpreter in the presence of the source. If a major correction must be made, the interrogator and the interpreter should leave the interrogation site temporarily, and only when necessary."

l.   **Finding 12:**
    (1) *Finding*: There was no Theater Detainee Reporting Center (TDRC) acting as the central, theater-level agency responsible for detainee accountability, resulting in a lack of detainee personnel and data management.
    (2) *Standard*: Standard of treatment for detainees in OPERATION ENDURING FREE-DOM (OEF): Chairman, Joint Chiefs of Staff (CJCS) message dated 211933Z JAN 02 states that members of the Taliban militia and members of al Qaeda under the control of US Forces would be treated humanely and, to the extent appropriate and consistent with military necessity, in a manner consistent with the principles of the Geneva Conventions of 1949. The DAIG has therefore used the provisions of the Geneva Conventions as a benchmark against which to measure the treatment provided to detainees by U.S. Forces to determine if detainees were treated humanely. The use of these standards as benchmarks does not state or imply a position for the United States or U.S. Army on the legal status of its operations in OEF.

CJCS Message dated 211933Z JAN 02, provides the determination regarding the humane treatment of al Qaeda and Taliban detainees. *Convention Relative to the Treatment of Prisoners of War of August 12, 1949* (GPW) is the international treaty that governs the treatment of prisoners of war; and *Geneva Convention Relative to the Protection of Civilian Persons in Time of War (GC), August 12,1949* is the international treaty that governs the treatment of civilian persons in time of war.

As the guidance did not define "humane treatment" but did state that the US would treat members of the Taliban militia and al Qaeda in a manner consistent with the Geneva Conventions, the DAIG determined that it would use Common Article 3 of the GCs as its floor measure of humane treatment, but would also include provisions of the Geneva Convention on the Treatment of Prisoners of War (GPW) and Geneva Convention Relative to the Protection of Civilian Persons in Time of War (GC) as other relevant indicia of "humane treatment." The use of this standard does not state or imply a position for the United States or U.S. Army on the legal status of its operations in OEF.

Standard of treatment for detainees in **OPERATION IRAQI FREEDOM (OIF):** OIF was an international armed conflict and therefore the provisions of the Geneva Conventions applied. Additionally, the United States was an occupying power and has acted in accordance with the obligations of an occupying power described in the *Hague Convention No. IV Respecting the Laws and Customs of War on Land (H.IV), Oct. 18. 1907.* including, but not limited to Articles 43-46 and 50; *Geneva Convention Relative to the Treatment of Prisoners of War of August 12, 1949* (GPW), *Geneva Convention Relative to the Protection of Civilian Persons in Time of War (GC), August 12, 1949.* The GC supplements H.lV, providing the general standard of treatment at Article 27 and specific standards in subsequent Articles.

The minimum treatment provided by Common Article 3 of the Geneva Conventions is: (1) No adverse distinction based upon race, religion, sex, etc.; (2) No violence to life or person; (3) No taking hostages; (4) No degrading treatment; (5) No passing of sentences in absence of fair trial, and; (6) The wounded and sick must be cared for.

The specific language in the CJCS Message for OEF and the GPW/GC and H.lV follows: CJCS Message dated 211933Z JAN 02, "Paragraph 3. The combatant commanders shall, in detaining al Qaeda and Taliban individuals under the control of the Department of Defense, treat them humanely and, to the extent appropriate and consistent with military necessity, in a manner consistent with the principles of the Geneva Conventions of 1949."

GPW/GC, Article 3 (Common Article 3) – "In the case of armed conflict not of an international character occurring in the territory of one of the High Contracting Parties, each party to the conflict shall be bound to apply, as a minimum, the following provisions:

1. Persons taking no active part in the hostilities, including members of armed forces who have laid down their arms and those placed hors de combat by sickness, wounds, detention, or any other cause, shall in all circumstances be treated humanely, without any adverse distinction founded on race, color, religion or faith, sex, birth or wealth, or any other similar criteria.

To this end the following acts are and shall remain prohibited at any time and in any place whatsoever with respect to the above-mentioned persons:

(a) Violence to life and person, in particular, murder of all kinds, mutilation, cruel treatment and torture;
(b) Taking of hostages;
(c) Outrages upon personal dignity, in particular, humiliating and degrading treatment;
(d) The passing of sentences and the carrying out of executions without previous judgment pronounced by a regularly constituted court affording all the judicial guarantees which are recognized as indispensable by civilized peoples.

2. The wounded and sick shall be collected and cared for. An impartial humanitarian body, such as the International Committee of the Red Cross, may offer its services to the Parties to the conflict. The Parties to the conflict should further endeavour to bring into force, by means of special agreements, all or part of the other provisions of the present Convention. The application of the preceding provisions shall not affect the legal status of the Parties to the conflict."

The following specific provisions of GPW and GC apply:

"Article 18 – All effects and articles of personal use, except arms, horses, military equipment and military documents, shall remain in the possession of prisoners of war, likewise their metal helmets and gas masks and like articles issued for personal protection. Effects and articles used for their clothing or feeding shall likewise remain in their possession, even if such effects and articles belong to their regulation military equipment. At no time should prisoners of war be without identity documents. The Detaining Power shall supply such documents to prisoners of war who possess none. Badges of rank and nationality, decorations and articles having above all a personal or sentimental value may not be taken from prisoners of war. Sums of money carried by prisoners of war may not be taken away from them except by order of an officer, and after the amount and particulars of the owner have been recorded in a special register and an itemized receipt has been given, legibly inscribed with the name, rank and unit of the person issuing the said receipt. Sums in the currency of the Detaining Power, or which are changed into such currency at the prisoner's request, shall be placed to the credit of the prisoner's account as provided in Article 64. The Detaining Power may withdraw articles of value from prisoners of war only for reasons of security; when such articles are withdrawn, the procedure laid down for sums of money impounded shall apply. Such objects, likewise sums taken away in any currency other than that of the Detaining Power and the conversion of which has not been asked for by the owners, shall be kept in the custody of the Detaining Power and shall be returned in their initial shape to prisoners of war at the end of their captivity.

Article 19 – Prisoners of war shall be evacuated, as soon as possible after their capture, to camps situated in an area far enough from the combat zone for them to be out of danger. Only those prisoners of war who, owing to wounds or sickness, would run greater risks by being evacuated than by remaining where they are, may be temporarily kept back in a danger zone. Prisoners of war shall not be unnecessarily exposed to danger while awaiting evacuation from a fighting zone."

Department of Defense Directive (DoDD), 2310.1, *DoD Program for Enemy Prisoners of War (EPOW) and Other Detainees*, 18 August 1994, Paragraph 1.2, designates the Secretary of the Army as Executive Agent for detainee operations; paragraph 4.2.5 establishes information coordination requirements for the Executive Agent for detainee operations. The specific language in the directive follows:

"1.2. Designates the Secretary of the Army as the Executive Agent for the Department of Defense for the administration of the DoD EPOW Detainee Program.

"4.2.5. Provide, in coordination with the ASD(ISA), appropriate reports to the OSD, the Chairman of the Joint Chiefs of Staff, and information or reports to other U.S. Government Agencies or Components, to include the Congress of the United States, or to the International Committee of the Red Cross."

Army Regulation (AR) 190-8, *Enemy Prisoners of War. Retained Personnel. Civilian internees and Other Detainees*, 1 October 1997, Chapter 1, paragraph 1-7, subparagraph b, requires specific data elements to be collected and stored by the National Prisoner of War Information Center (NPWIC, now called the National Detainee Recording Center (NDRC)). Paragraph 1-8, subparagraphs a and b, assigns the Branch Prisoner of War Information Center (Branch PWIC, now called the Theater Detainee Reporting Center (TDRC)) as the field agency for maintaining information on persons and property within an assigned theater of operations or in Continental United States (CONUS) and outlines the Branch PWIC's primary responsibilities. Chapter 2, paragraph 2-1, subparagraph a (1) (b), explains how prisoners are to be tagged. Paragraph 2-2, subparagraph b (1), requires the use of DA Form 4137 for accounting for large sums of money and property taken from captured persons. This regulation is a multi-service regulation implementing DOD Directive 2310.1 and incorporates Army Regulation 190-8 and 190-57 and SECNAV Instruction 3461.3, and Air Force Joint Instruction 31-304 and outlines policies, procedures, and responsibilities for treatment of enemy prisoners of war (EPW), retained personnel (RP), civilian internees (CI), and other detainees (OD) and implements international law for all military operations. The specific language in the regulation follows:

1-7. b. – "Obtain and store information concerning EPW, CI and RP, and their confiscated personal property. Information will be collected and stored on each EPW, CI, and RP captured and detained by U.S. Armed Forces. This includes those EPW, RP, who were captured by the United States but are in custody of other powers and those who have been released or repatriated. EPW, CI and RP cannot be forced to reveal any information however they are required to provide their name, rank, serial number and date of birth. The Geneva Convention requires the NPWIC to collect and store the following information for EPW, RP:

(1) Complete name.
(2) ISN.
(3) Rank.
(4) Serial number.
(5) Date of birth.
(6) City of birth.
(7) Country of birth.
(8) Name and address of next of kin.
(9) Date of capture.
(10) Place of capture.
(11) Capturing unit.
(12) Circumstances of capture.
(13) Location of confiscated personal property.
(14) Nationality.
(15) General statement of health.
(16) Nation in whose armed services the individual is serving.
(17) Name and address of a person to be notified of the individual's capture.
(18) Address to which correspondence may be sent.
(19) Certificates of death or duly authenticated lists of the dead.
(20) Information showing the exact location of war graves together with particulars of the dead.
(21) Notification of capture.
(22) List of personal articles of value not restored upon repatriation."

1-8. a. – "The Branch PWIC functions as the field operations agency for the NPWIC. It is the central agency responsible to maintain information on all EPW, CI and RP and their personal property within an assigned theater of operations or in CONUS.

1-8. b. – The Branch PWIC serves as the theater repository for information pertaining to:

(1) Accountability of EPW, CI, and RP and implementation of DOD policy.

(2) Providing initial and replacement block ISN assignments to theater EPW, CI and RP processing organizations, and requests replacement ISN's from the NPWIC.

(3) Obtaining and storing information concerning all EPW, CI and RP, in the custody of U.S. Armed Forces, those captured by U.S. Armed Forces and transferred to other powers for internment (either temporarily or permanently), those EPW and RP transferred to CONUS for internment, and EPW, CI and RP released or repatriated. Obtaining and storing information about CI kept in the custody of U.S. Armed Forces within its assigned theater of operations who are subjected to assigned residence, interned, or released."

2-1. a. (1) (b) – "All prisoners of war and retained persons will, at the time of capture, be tagged using DD Form 2745.

2-2. b. (1) – Appropriate intelligence sources will be notified when EPW and RP are found in possession of large sums of U.S. or foreign currency. A receipt DA Form 4137 will be prepared to account for all property that is taken from the EPW. Copies of DD Form 629 (Receipt for Prisoner or Detained Person) and DA Form 4137 will be maintained to establish positive accountability of the EPW and their property and can be used to substantiate proper care and treatment at a later time. DA Form 4137 will be used to account for property released before final disposition is ordered. Records of disposition of property will be evacuated with prisoners for inclusion in their personnel records."

Field Manual (FM) 3-19.40, *Military Police Internment/Resettlement Operations*, 1 August 2001, Chapter 3, paragraphs 3-45 and 3-54, establish the 12-hour forward collecting point and 24-hour central collecting point doctrine. The specific language in the field manual follows:

"3-45. Captives should not remain at a forward CP more than 12 hours before being escorted to the central CP.

3-54. Captives should not remain at the central CP more than 24 hours before being evacuated to the CHA."

m. **Finding 13:**

  (1) *Finding*: The ongoing Military Intelligence Force Design Update is better suited to conduct simultaneous and sustained human intelligence missions in the current and future operating environment.

  (2) *Standard*: Army Regulation (AR) 71-32, *Force Development and Documentation – Consolidated Policies*, 3 March 1997, Paragraph 2-1, subparagraph f, establishes the Deputy Chief of Staff for Operations and Plans (DCSOPS) responsibility for The Army Authorization Documents System-Redesign (TAADS-R) systems, which provides Army Modified Table of Organization and Equipment (MTOE) and Table of Distribution and Allowance (TDA) units with authorization documents containing the HQDA-approved organizational structure, personnel and equipment requirements and authorizations. Paragraph 2-2, subparagraph x, directs the Commander of U.S. Army Force Management Support Agency (USAFMSA) to act as executive agent for TAADS-R and review, develop, and publish MTOEs and TDAso Paragraph 2-26, subparagraphs a-c, requires the Commander of U.S. Army Training and Doctrine Command (TRADOC) to develop and validate battlefield requirements and use the force design update process to document needed changes. TRADOC develops organizational concepts and designs. TRADOC provides USAFMSA the approved organization designs for the development of a Table of Organization and Equipment (TOE). Paragraph 4-1, subparagraphs b, c. and e, describe the TOE as the result of the combat development process and documents wartime capabilities, organizational structure, personnel and equipment. Paragraph 4-4 describes the

concept for TOE review and revision. In this case the TOE revision documents a more effective organizational design. The specific language in the regulation follows:

"2-1. Deputy Chief of Staff for Operations and Plans (DCSOPS) The DCSOPS will –

"*f*. Have HQDA responsibility for TAADS-R and, after appropriate HQDA coordination, will –

"(2) Develop and manage the Army force structure.

"(4) In coordination with the DCSPER and the DCSLOG publish and enforce policy and procedures to document requirements for and authorization of, organizations. personnel, and equipment.

"(6) Serve as the final HQDA approval authority for authorization documents.

"2-2. CDR, U.S. Army Force Management Support Agency (USAFMSA) CDR, US-AFMSA will —

"*x*. Act as executive agent for the operation of the TAADS-R and perform the following:

"(9) Perform technical review of Active Army and Reserve Component (RC) MTOE and TDA.

(10) Develop MTOEs for all Active Army and RC MTOE organizations under the CEN-DOC concept.

(11) Provide a foundation for manning the force, quantitatively and qualitatively, principally through detailed manpower requirements determination programs such as MARC, manpower staffing guides, organizational and manpower studies, and the MS3.

"(17) Maintain and distribute current files of all authorization documents (MTOEs and TOEs). Furnish authorization documentation data to HQDA and agencies/activities using TAADS.

"2-26. CG, U.S. Army Training and Doctrine Command (TRADOC)

In addition to the responsibilities in paragraph 2-19, the CG, TRADOC will –

a. Lead the Army in developing and validating battlefield requirements and use the force design update (FDU) process as the semiannual Army process to update organizational concepts and designs.

b. Develop organizational concepts and designs.

c. Provide USAFMSA completed unit reference sheets for FDU approved organization designs as the basis for TOE development.

"4-1. Concepts

"*b.* The TOE is the end-product document of the Army's combat development process. It merges, in one document, the results of the requirements determination process . . .

"*c.* TOEs are the primary basis for stating Army requirements. This document heavily impacts the budget, the training base, efficiency, operational readiness, and overall management of Army resources.

"*e.* The TOE system is characterized by incremental TOEs that prescribe the wartime mission, capabilities, organizational structure, and minimum mission essential personnel and equipment requirements for military units. They portray the doctrinal modernization path (MODPATH) of a unit over time from the least modernized configuration to the most modernized.

"4-4. TOE review and revision

TOEs are normally revised as required to accommodate changes to doctrine, introduction of new equipment, or to incorporate more effective designs. Some TOEs are replaced by new organizations. Those TOEs that do not fall into the above categories will be reviewed not less than every three years from the date of approval."

AR 381-20, *The Army Counterintelligence Program*, 15 November 1993, Glossary, defines the terms counterintelligence, counterintelligence operations, and counterintelligence special agent. The term Military Occupational Specialty (MOS) refers to the type of training and skills of a soldier in a specific specialty. In this report the DAIG Team uses the abbreviation CI to refer to Civilian Internees; the Military Intelligence mission of counterintelligence will not be abbreviated as CI except when quoted directly from Military Intelligence policy/doctrine paragraph(s) referring to counterintelligence, as in the following. The specific language in the regulation follows:

"counterintelligence

1. Information gathered and activities conducted to protect against espionage, other intelligence activities, sabotage or assassinations conducted for or on behalf of foreign powers, organizations, or persons, or international terrorist activities, but not including personnel, physical, document or communications security programs. Synonymous with foreign counterintelligence. (ICS Glossary)

2. Those activities which are concerned with identifying and counteracting the threat to security posed by foreign intelligence services or organizations, or by individuals engaged in espionage, sabotage, sedition, subversion or terrorism.

"counterintelligence operations

Activities taken to hinder the multidisciplinary activities of foreign intelligence and security services, and to cause FIS to doubt the validity of its own analysis.

"counterintelligence special agent

Soldiers holding the SSI 35E, MOS 351B or 97B, and civilian employees in the GS-0132 career field, who have successfully completed a CI [counterintelligence] officer/agent course, who are authorized USAI badges and credentials, and who are assigned to conduct CI [counterintelligence] investigations and operations. Also known as CI [counterintelligence] agent or MI agent."

Field Manual (FM) 34-60, *Counterintelligence*, 3 October 1995, Chapter 1, describes the Army counterintelligence mission as preventing other organizations and agencies from gathering information on Army organizations and agencies. Counterintelligence operations is a force protection factor and includes counter-human intelligence (C-HUMINT), counter-signals intelligence (C-SIGINT), and counter-imagery intelligence (C-IMINT) functions. In this report the DAIG team uses the abbreviation CI to refer to Civilian Internees; the Military Intelligence mission of counterintelligence will not be abbreviated as CI except when quoted directly from Military Intelligence policy/doctrine paragraph(s) referring to counterintelligence, as in the following. The specific language in the field manual follows:

"MISSION

The CI [counterintelligence] mission is authorized by Executive Order (EO) 12333, implemented by AR 381-20. The Army conducts aggressive, comprehensive, and coordinated CI (counterintelligence) activities worldwide. The purpose is to detect, identify, assess, counter, neutralize, or exploit threat intelligence collection efforts. This mission is accomplished during peacetime and all levels of conflict. Many CI [counterintelligence] functions, shown in Figure 1-1, are conducted by echelons above corps (EAC); some by echelons corps and below (ECB); and some are conducted by both. Those CI [counterintelligence] assets found at ECB respond to tactical commanders. EAC assets respond primarily to commanders of intelligence units while supporting all commanders within their theater or area of operations (AO).

"The essence of the Army's CI [counterintelligence] mission is to support force protection. By its nature, CI [counterintelligence] is a multidiscipline (C-HUMINT, C-SIGINT, and C-IMINT) function designed to degrade threat intelligence and targeting capabilities. Multidiscipline counterintelligence (MDCI) is an integral and equal part of intelligence and electronic warfare (IEW). MDCI operations support force protection through OPSEC, deception, and rear area operations across the range of military operations. For more information on IEW operations, see FM 34-1."

ST 2-22.7, *Tactical Human Intelligence and Counterintelligence Operations*, 11 April 2002, Paragraphs 1-1 and 1-7, describe the relationship between human intelligence (HUMINT) and counterintelligence and the function of Tactical HUMINT. Paragraph 1-10 defines the term HUMINT Collector. Additionally, the unit's counterintelligence mission is a force protection factor. In this report the DAIG team uses the abbreviation CI to refer to Civilian Internees; Military Intelligence mission of counterintelligence will not be abbreviated as CI except when quoted directly from Military Intelligence policy/doctrine paragraph(s) referring to counterintelligence, as in the following. The specific language in the manual follows:

"1-1. HUMINT and CI [counterintelligence] have distinctly different missions. HUMINT collectors gather information to answer intelligence and information requirements while CI [counterintelligence] personnel help protect the force from an adversary's intelligence collection efforts. HUMINT collectors and CI [counterintelligence] personnel bring unique sets of skills to any mission. At times each discipline may uncover information relating to the other's primary mission. Although HUMINT collectors and CI [counterintelligence] personnel appear to have similar functions, because the common denominator is human interaction, each discipline has its own area of expertise.

"1-7. Tactical HUMINT is the task organization of HUMINT collection assets and CI [counterintelligence] assets into combined teams to accomplish the mission of both disciplines at the tactical level (echelon corps and below). This task organization supports the force protection plan and answers the commander's intelligence requirements by employing –

- "CI [counterintelligence] agents to conduct focused identification, collection, analysis, recommendation of countermeasures, and production against FISS technical means and other adversary intelligence collection threats.
- "HUMINT collectors to conduct focused collection, analysis, and production on the adversary's composition, strength, dispositions, tactics, equipment, personnel, personalities, capabilities, and intentions.

"1-10. HUMINT collectors are personnel who, by training or in certain specific positions, are tasked with collecting information for intelligence use from people or related documents. A HUMINT source is any person who can provide information to answer collection requirements. [Unless otherwise noted in this manual, the term "HUMINT collector" refers to personnel in MOSs 351 E and 97E. The term "CI [counterintelligence] collector" or "CI [counterintelligence] agent" refers to 35E, 351B, and 97B personnel] The HUMINT and CI [counterintelligence] force is organized, trained, and equipped to provide timely and relevant answers to information requirements at each echelon. While HUMINT and CI [counterintelligence] have a different focus, in most deployment scenarios they work best in a collaborative effort."

n. **Finding 14:**

   (1) *Finding*: The ongoing Military Police Force Design Update provides a force structure for internment/resettlement operations that has the flexibility and is better suited

to conduct sustained detainee operations in the current and future operating environments.

(2) *Standard*: Army Regulation (AR) 71-32, *Force Development and Documentation – Consolidated Policies*, 3 March 1997, Paragraph 2-1, subparagraph f, establishes the Deputy Chief of Staff for Operations and Plans (DCSOPS) responsibility for The Army Authorization Documents System-Redesign (TAADS-R) systems, which provides Army Modified Table of Organization and Equipment (MTOE) and Table of Distribution and Allowance (TDA) units with authorization documents containing the HQDA-approved organizational structure, personnel and equipment requirements and authorizations. Paragraph 2-2, subparagraph f, requires Commander of U.S. Army Force Management Support Agency (USAFMSA) to review, evaluate, and coordinate all changes to force structure documents with affected Major Commands (MACOMs) and the U.S. Army Training and Doctrine Command (TRADOC) proponent. Paragraph 2-26, subparagraphs a-c, requires the Commander of U.S. Army Training and I Doctrine Command (TRADOC) to develop and validate battlefield requirements and use the force design update process to document needed changes. TRADOC develops organizational concepts and designs. TRADOC provides USAFMSA the approved organization designs for the development of a Table of Organization and Equipment (TOE). Paragraph 4-1, subparagraphs b, c, and e, describe the TOE as the result of the combat development process and documents wartime capabilities, organizational structure, personnel and equipment. Paragraph 4-4 describes the concept for TOE review and revision. In this case the TOE revision documents a more effective organizational design. Paragraph 8-4, Table 8-1, gives the characteristics of an MTOE: a unit or organization with the ability to perform sustained Combat, Combat Support (CS), or Combat Service Support (CSS) missions; and the characteristics of a TDA: a unit or organization performing a mission at a fixed location. The Active Component (AC) units qualified to conduct internment/resettlement (I/R) operations are organized in TDAs and are not designed for deployment. Reserve Component (RC) units conducting I/R operations are organized in MTOEs for deployment. The specific language in the regulation follows:

"2-1. Deputy Chief of Staff for Operations and Plans (DCSOPS) The DCSOPS will –

"*f*. Have HQDA responsibility for TAADS-R and, after appropriate HQDA coordination, will —

"(2) Develop and manage the Army force structure.

"(4) In coordination with the DCSPER and the DCSLOG publish and enforce policy and procedures to document requirements for and authorization of, organizations, personnel, and equipment.

"(6) Serve as the final HQDA approval authority for authorization documents.

"2-2. CDR, U.S. Army Force Management Support Agency (USAFMSA) CDR, USAFMSA will –

"*f*. Review and evaluate ali proposed TOE changes. Coordinate requests for TOE changes with the affected MACOM and proponent schools. Recommend approval to HQDA if appropriate.

"2-26. CG, U.S. Army Training and Doctrine Command (TRADOC) In addition to the responsibilities in paragraph 2-19, the CG, TRADOC will –

"*a*. Lead the Army in developing and validating battlefield requirements and use the force design update (FDU) process as the semi-annual Army process to update organizational concepts and designs.

b. Develop organizational concepts and designs.

c. Provide USAFMSA completed unit reference sheets for FDU approved organization designs as the basis for TOE development.

"4-1. Concepts

"*b*. The TOE is the end-product document of the Army's combat development process. It merges, in one document, the results of the requirements determination process…

"*c*. TOEs are the primary basis for stating Army requirements. This document heavily impacts the budget, the training base, efficiency, operational readiness, and overall management of Army resources.

"*e*. The TOE system is characterized by incremental TOEs that prescribe the wartime mission, capabilities, organizational structure, and minimum mission essential personnel and equipment requirements for military units. They portray the doctrinal modernization path (MODPATH) of a unit over time from the least modernized configuration to the most modernized.

"4-4. TOE review and revision

TOEs are normally revised as required to accommodate changes to doctrine, introduction of new equipment, or to incorporate more effective designs. Some TOEs are replaced by new organizations. Those TOEs that do not fall into the above categories will be reviewed not less than every three years from the date of approval.

"8-4. Type of organization

Criteria in Table 8-1 will be used to determine whether an organization should be documented as a MTOE, TDA, or AUGTDA.

"MTOE – The unit or organization is required to perform combat, CS, or CSS missions on a continuing basis.

"TDA – The unit or organization is part of a fixed support establishment, for example, installation, garrison."

AR 190-8, *Enemy Prisoners of War, Retained Personnel, Civilian Internees and Other Detainees*, 1 October 1997, Paragraph 1-1, subparagraph a, establishes the regulation as the source for policy for enemy prisoners of war (EPW), retained personnel (RP), civilian internees (CI) and other detainees (OD). The policy (written in 1997) is based on the Cold War model of an organized EPW population that is cooperative. The policy does not address the confinement of high-risk detainees. Paragraph 1-4, subparagraph g, establishes that EPW, RP, CI, and OD will be handed over to the Military Police (MP) or facilities run by the MPs. The regulation states that MPs have units specifically organized to perform the long-term functions associated with EPW/CI internment. The force structure of MP units does not support this requirement. The Glossary, Section II, defines the following terms: EPW, RP, CI, OD, and Detainee. The MP Corps has not yet developed or defined the term High Risk Detainee. This regulation is a multiservice regulation implementing DOD Directive 2310.1 and incorporates Army Regulation 190-8 and 190-57 and SECNAV Instruction 3461.3, and Air Force Joint Instruction 31-304 and outlines policies, procedures, and responsibilities for treatment of EPWs, RPs, CIs, and ODs and implements international law for all military operations. The specific language in the regulation follows:

"1-1. Purpose

a. This regulation provides policy, procedures, and responsibilities for the administration, treatment, employment, and compensation of enemy prisoners of war (EPW), retained personnel (RP), civilian internees (CI) and other detainees (OD) in the custody of U.S. Armed Forces. This regulation also establishes procedures for transfer of custody from the United States to another detaining power.

"1-4. Responsibilities

"g. Combatant Commanders, Task Force Commanders and Joint Task Force Commanders.
Combatant Commanders, Task Force Commanders and Joint Task Force Commanders
have the overall responsibility for the EPW, CI and RP program, operations, and contingency plans in the theater of operation involved to ensure compliance with international
law of war. DOD Directive 2310.1 provides that persons captured or detained by the U.S.
Military Services shall normally be handed over for safeguarding to U.S. Army Military
Police, or to detainee collecting points or other holding facilities and installations operated by U.S. Army Military Police as soon as practical. U.S. Army Military Police have
units specifically organized to perform the long-term functions associated with EPW/CI
internment.

"GLOSSARY

"Section II Terms

"Civilian Internee(s). A civilian who is interned during armed conflict or occupation for
security reasons or for protection or because he has committed an offense against the
detaining power.
     "Detainee. A term used to refer to any person captured or otherwise detained by an
armed force.
     "Enemy Prisoner of War. A detained person as defined in Articles 4 and 5 of the Geneva
Convention Relative to the Treatment of Prisoners of War of August 12, 1949. In particular,
one who, while engaged in combat under orders of his or her government, is captured by
the armed forces of the enemy. As such, he or she is entitled to the combatant's privilege
of immunity from the municipal law of the capturing state for warlike acts which do not
amount to breaches of the law of armed conflict. For example, a prisoner of war may be, but
is not limited to, any person belonging to one of the following categories who has fallen into
the power of the enemy: a member of the armed forces, organized militia or volunteer corps;
a person who accompanies the armed forces without actually being a member thereof; a
member of a merchant marine or civilian aircraft crew not qualifying for more favorable
treatment; or individuals who, on the approach of the enemy, spontaneously take up arms
to resist invading forces.
     "Other Detainee (OD). Persons in the custody of the U.S. Armed Forces who have not
been classified as an EPW (Article 4, GPW), RP (Article 33, GPW), or CI (Article 78, GC),
shall be treated as EPWs until a legal status is ascertained by competent authority."
     Field Manual (FM) 3-19.1, *Military Police Operations*, 31 January 2002, Paragraph 1-3,
describes the doctrine review process the MP Corps underwent in 1996 and establishes
and separates the internment and resettlement (I/R) function from the EPW mission.
Paragraph 4-42 requires the Army to act as the Department of Defense's (DoD) Executive Agent for long-term confinement of U.S. Armed Forces prisoners. The paragraph
goes on to address the MPs role in I/R functions, but does not address long-term confinement as an I/R function. The MP Corps does not address the doctrinal requirement for
long-term I/R confinement or confinement of high-risk detainees. Paragraph 4-44 states
the ratios by type of detainee that an MP (I/R) Battalion can support. This formula does
not address confinement of high-risk detainees. The specific language in the field manual
follows:
     "1-3. In 1996, the MP Corps went through a doctrinal review process to determine if it
was properly articulating its multiple performance capabilities in support of US forces deployed worldwide (see Appendix B). The review process identified the need to restructure

and expand the EPW mission to include handling US military prisoners and all dislocated civilians. This new emphasis transformed the EPW mission into the internment and resettlement (I/R) function. The review process also identified the need to shift from missions to functions. In the past, the four battlefield missions adequately described MP capabilities in a mature theater against a predictable, echeloned threat. However, that landscape is no longer valid. Accordingly, the four MP battlefield missions have become the following five MP functions:

- Maneuver and mobility support (MMS).
- AS.
- L&O.
- I/R.
- Police intelligence operations (PIO).

"4-42. The Army is the Department of Defense's (DOD's) executive agent for all EPW/CI operations. Additionally, the Army is DOD's executive agent for long-term confinement of US military prisoners. Within the Army and through the combatant commander, the MP are tasked with coordinating shelter, protection, accountability, and sustainment for EPWs/CIs. The I/R function addresses MP roles when dealing with EPWs/CIs, dislocated civilians, and US military prisoners.

"4-44. Although the CS MP unit initially handles EPWs/CIs, modular MP (I/R) battalions with assigned MP guard companies and supporting MWD teams are equipped and trained to handle this mission for the long term. A properly configured modular MP (I/R) battalion can support, safeguard, account for, guard, and provide humane treatment for up to 4,000 EPWs/CIs; 8,000 dislocated civilians; or 1,500 US military prisoners."

FM 3-19.40, *Military Police Internment/Resettlement Operations*, 1 August 2001, Paragraph 1-13, states the objectives of I/R operations and the types of detainees expected. The terms refer to EPW, CI, RP, OD, dislocated civilian (DC), and U.S. Armed Forces prisoners. At the time this doctrine was written (August 2001) the MP Corps had not yet developed or defined the term high-risk detainee. The specific language in the field manual follows:

"1-13. The objectives of I/R operations are to process, handle, care for, account for, and secure –

- EPWs.
- CIs.
- RPs.
- ODs.
- DCs.
- US military prisoners."

o. **Finding 15:**

   (1) *Finding*: Three of the four inspected internment/resettlement facilities, and many of the collecting points, had inadequate force protection measures, Soldier working conditions, detainees living conditions, and did not meet the minimum preventive medical treatment requirements.

   (2) *Standard*: Standard of treatment for detainees in OPERATION ENDURING FREEDOM (OEF): CJCS message dated 211933Z JAN 02 states that members of the Taliban militia and members of al Qaeda under the control of U.S. Forces would be treated humanely and, to the extent appropriate and consistent with military necessity, in a manner consistent with the principles of the Geneva Conventions of 1949. The DAIG has therefore used the provisions of the Geneva Conventions as a benchmark against which to measure the treatment provided to detainees by U.S.

Forces to determine if detainees were treated humanely. The use of these standards as benchmarks does not state or imply a position for the United States or U.S. Army on the legal status of its operations in OEF.

CJCS Message dated 211933Z JAN 02, provides the determination regarding the humane treatment of al Qaeda and Taliban detainees. *Convention Relative to the Treatment of Prisoners of War of August 12, 1949* (GPW) is the international treaty that governs the treatment of prisoners of war, and *Geneva Convention Relative to the Protection of Civilian Persons in Time of War (GC)*, August 12, 1949, is the international treaty that governs the treatment of civilian persons in time of war.

As the guidance did not define "humane, treatment" but did state that the U.S. would treat members of the Taliban militia and al Qaeda in a manner consistent with the Geneva Conventions, the DAIG determined that it would use Common Article 3 of the GCs as its floor measure of humane treatment, but would also include provisions of the Geneva Convention on the Treatment of Prisoners of War (GPW) and Geneva Convention Relative to the Protection of Civilian Persons in Time of War (GC) as other relevant indicia of "humane treatment." The use of this standard does not state or imply a position for the United States or U.S. Army on the legal status of its operations in OEF.

Standard of treatment for detainees in **OPERATION IRAQI FREEDOM (OIF)**: OIF was an international armed conflict and therefore the provisions of the Geneva Conventions applied. Additionally, the United States was an occupying power and has acted in accordance with the obligations of an occupying power described in the *Hague Convention No. IV Respecting the Laws and Customs of War on Land (H.IV), Oct. 18, 1907*, including, but not limited to, Articles 43-46 and 50; *Geneva Convention Relative to the Treatment of Prisoners of War of August 12, 1949* (GPW); and *Geneva Convention Relative to the Protection of Civilian Persons in Time of War (GC)*, August 12, 1949. The GC supplements H.IV, providing the general standard of treatment at Article 27 and specific standards in subsequent Articles.

The minimum treatment provided by Common Article 3 of the Geneva Conventions is: (1) No adverse distinction based upon race, religion, sex, etc.; (2) No violence to life or person; (3) No taking hostages; (4) No degrading treatment; (5) No passing of sentences in absence of fair trial, and; (6) The wounded and sick must be cared for.

The specific language in the CJCS, Message for OEF and the GPW/GC and H.IV follows: CJCS Message dated 211933Z JAN 02, "Paragraph 3. The combatant commanders shall, in detaining al Qaeda and Taliban individuals under the control of the Department of Defense, treat them humanely and, to the extent appropriate and consistent with military necessity, in a manner consistent with the principles of the Geneva Conventions of 1949."

GPW/GC, Article 3 (Common Article 3) – "In the case of armed conflict not of an international character occurring in the territory of one of the High Contracting Parties, each party to the conflict shall be bound to apply, as a minimum, the following provisions:

1. Persons taking no active part in the hostilities, including members of armed forces who have laid down their arms and those placed hors de combat by sickness, wounds, detention, or any other cause, shall in all circumstances be treated humanely, without any adverse distinction founded on race, color, religion or faith, sex, birth or wealth, or any other similar criteria.

To this end the following acts are and shall remain prohibited at any time and in any place whatsoever with respect to the above-mentioned persons:

(a) Violence to life and person, in particular, murder of all kinds, mutilation, cruel treatment and torture;

(b) Taking of hostages;

(c) Outrages upon personal dignity, in particular, humiliating and degrading treatment;

(d) The passing of sentences and the carrying out of executions without previous judgment pronounced by a regularly constituted court affording all the judicial guarantees which are recognized as indispensable by civilized people."

2. The wounded and sick shall be collected and cared for. An impartial humanitarian body, such as the International Committee of the Red Cross, may offer its services to the Parties to the conflict. The Parties to the conflict should further endeavour to bring into force, by means of special agreements, all or part of the other provisions of the present Convention. The application of the preceding provisions shall not affect the legal status of the Parties to the conflict."

Hague Convention No. IV Respecting the Laws and Customs of War on Land (H.IV.), Oct. 18, 1907, Articles 43-46 and 50; and *Geneva Convention Relative to the Protection of Civilian Persons in Time of War (GC)*, Aug 12, 1949, Articles 81, 83, 85, 88, 89, and 91 discuss the requirement to accommodate detainees in buildings or quarters which afford every possible safeguard regarding health and hygiene and the effects of war. The specific language in the GC follows:

GC Article 81 – "Parties to the conflict who intern protected persons shall be bound to provide free of charge for their maintenance, and to grant them also the medical attention required by their state of health. No deduction from the allowances, salaries or credits due to the internees shall be made for the repayment of these costs."

GC, Article 83 – "The Detaining Power shall not set up places of internment in areas particularly exposed to the dangers of war. . . . "

GC, Article 85 – "The Detaining Power is bound to take all necessary and possible measures to ensure that protected persons shall, from the outset of their internment, be accommodated in buildings or quarters which afford every possible safeguard as regards hygiene and health, and provide efficient protection against the rigors of the climate and the effects of the war. In no case shall permanent places of internment be situated in unhealthy areas or in districts, the climate of which is injurious to the internees. In all cases where the district, in which a protected person is temporarily interned, is an unhealthy area or has a climate which is harmful to his health, he shall be removed to a more suitable place of internment as rapidly as circumstances permit. The premises shall be fully protected from dampness, adequately heated and lighted, in particular, between dusk and lights out. The sleeping quarters shall be sufficiently spacious and well ventilated, and the internees shall have suitable bedding and sufficient blankets, account being taken of the climate, and the age, sex, and state of health of the internees. Internees shall have for their use, day and night, sanitary conveniences which conform to the rules of hygiene, and are constantly maintained in a state of cleanliness. They shall be provided with sufficient water and soap for their daily personal toilet and for washing their personal laundry; installations and facilities necessary for this purpose shall be granted to them. Showers or baths shall also be available. The necessary time shall be set aside for washing and for cleaning. Whenever it is necessary, as an exceptional and temporary measure, to accommodate women internees who are not members of a family unit in the same place of internment as men, the provision of separate sleeping quarters and sanitary conveniences for the use of such women internees shall be obligatory."

GC, Article 88 – "In all places of internment exposed to air raids and other hazards of war, shelters adequate in number and structure to ensure the necessary protection shall be installed. . . . "

GC, Article 89 – "Daily food rations for internees shall be sufficient in quantity, quality and variety to keep internees in a good state of health and prevent the development of nutritional deficiencies. Account shall also be taken of the customary diet of the internees. Internees shall also be given the means by which they can prepare for themselves any additional food in their possession. Sufficient drinking water shall be supplied to internees...."

GC Article 91 – "Every place of internment shall have an adequate infirmary, under the direction of a qualified doctor, where internees may have the attention they require, as well as appropriate diet. Isolation wards shall be set aside for cases of contagious or mental diseases. Maternity cases and internees suffering from serious diseases, or whose condition requires special treatment, a surgical operation or hospital care, must be admitted to any institution where adequate treatment can be given and shall receive care not inferior to that provided for the general population. Internees shall, for preference, have the attention of medical personnel of their own nationality. Internees may not be prevented from presenting themselves to the medical authorities for examination. The medical authorities of the Detaining Power shall, upon request, issue to every internee who has undergone treatment an official certificate showing the nature of his illness or injury, and the duration and nature of the treatment given. A duplicate of this certificate shall be forwarded to the Central Agency provided for in Article 140 Treatment, including the provision of any apparatus necessary for the maintenance of internees in good health, particularly dentures and other artificial appliances and spectacles, shall be free of charge to the internee."

GPW, Article 29 – "The Detaining Power shall be bound to take all sanitary measures necessary to ensure the cleanliness and healthfulness of the camps and to prevent epidemics.

Prisoners of war shall have for their use, day and night, conveniences which conform to the rules of hygiene and are maintained in a constant state of cleanliness. In any camps in which women prisoners of war are accommodated, separate conveniences shall be provided for them.

Also, apart from the baths and showers with which the camps shall be furnished, prisoners of war shall be provided with sufficient water and soap for their personal toilet and for washing their personal laundry; the necessary installations, facilities and time shall be granted them for that purpose."

Army Regulation (AR) 40-5, *Preventive Medicine*, 15 October 1990, Chapter 14, paragraph 14-3, subparagraph a, requires field sanitation teams at all company-level units. The specific language in the regulation follows:

"a. Functions. As a minimum, units deploying to the field will –

(1) Before deployment, appoint a field sanitation team with responsibilities defined in b below.
(2) Before deployment, incorporate PMM into SOPs.
(3) Have the capability to use pesticides and vegetation controls.
(4) Bury and/or burn wastes to prevent the breeding of insects and rodents. Consult the environmental coordinator or PVNTMED personnel to ensure compliance with local environmental regulations and laws during field exercises.
(5) Protect food during storage and preparation to prevent contamination (TB MED 530).
(6) Monitor unit water sources to assure adequate supplies and disinfection.
(7) Arrange for maintenance of immunizations and prophylaxis.
(8) Use other appropriate measures under FM 21-10/ AFM 161-10.
(9) Assure command supervision of individual PMM.
(10) Request assistance for problems exceeding unit capabilities.
(11) Deploy to the field with field sanitation equipment listed in table 14-1."

Army Regulation (AR) 190-8, *Enemy Prisoners of War Retained Personnel, Civilian Internees and Other Detainees*, 1 October 1997, Chapter 1, paragraph 1-4, subparagraph g (6) (a), discusses sanitary aspects of food service and the need to provide potable water and vector control. Chapter 3, paragraph 3-2, subparagraph b, requires internment/resettlement (I/R) facilities and collecting points (CPs) to operate under the same standards of hygiene and sanitation. Paragraph 3-4, subparagraph e, requires enemy prisoners of war/retained personnel (EPW/RP) to be housed under the same conditions as US forces residing in the same area; subparagraph i requires EPW/RP facilities to ensure a clean and healthy environment for detainees. Chapter 5, paragraph 5-2, subparagraph a, states that a safety program for civilian internees (CIs) will be established. Chapter 6, paragraph 6-1, subparagraph b, discusses minimum standards to house (CIs). Paragraph 6-5 discusses subsistence requirement for CIs, and paragraph 6-6 covers medical care and sanitation. This regulation is a multiservice regulation implementing DoD Directive 2310.1 and incorporates Army Regulation 190-8 and 190-57 and SECNAV Instruction 3461.3, and Air Force Joint Instruction 31-304 and outlines policies, procedures, and responsibilities for treatment of enemy prisoners of war (EPW), retained personnel (RP), civilian internees (CI), and other detainees (OD) and implements international law for all military operations. The specific language in the regulation follows:

3-2. b. – "Prisoners will not normally be interned in unhealthy areas, or where the climate proves to be injurious to them, and will be removed as soon as possible to a more favorable climate. Transit camps or collecting points will operate under conditions similar to those prescribed for permanent prisoner of war camps, and the prisoners will receive the same treatment as in permanent EPW camps.

3-4. e. – "EPW/RP will be quartered under conditions as favorable as those for the force of the detaining power billeted in the same area. The conditions shall make allowance for the habits and customs of the prisoners and shall in no case be prejudicial to their health. The foregoing shall apply in particular to the dormitories of EPW/RP as it regards both total surface and minimum cubic space and the general installation of bedding and blankets. Quarters furnished to EPW/RP must be protected from dampness, must be adequately lit and heated (particularly, between dusk and lights-out), and must have adequate precautions taken against the dangers of fire. In camps accommodating both sexes, EPW/RP will be provided with separate facilities for women.

3-4.i. – "Hygiene and medical care:

(1) The United States is bound to take all sanitary measures necessary to ensure clean and healthy camps to prevent epidemics. EPW/RP will have access, day and night, to latrines that conform to the rules of hygiene and are maintained in a constant state of cleanliness. In any camps in which women EPW/RP are accommodated, separate latrines will be provided for them. EPW/RP will have sufficient water and soap for their personal needs and laundry. "(6) Identify requirements and allocations for Army Medical units in support of the EPW, CI and RP Program, and ensure that the medical annex of OPLANs, OPORDs and contingency plans includes procedures for treatment of EPW, CI, RP, and ODs. Medical support will specifically include:

(a) First aid and all sanitary aspects of food service including provisions for potable water, pest management, and entomological support.

"5-2. Civilian Internee Safety Program

a. Establishment. A safety program for the CI will be established and administered in accordance with the policies prescribed in AR 385-10 and other pertinent safety directives.

"6-1. Internment Facility

a. Location. The theater commander will be responsible for the location of the CI internment facilities within his or her command. The CI retained temporarily in an unhealthy area or where the climate is harmful to their health will be removed to a more suitable place of internment as soon as possible.

b. Quarters. Adequate shelters to ensure protection against air bombardments and other hazards of war will be provided and precautions against fire will be taken at each CI camp and branch camp.

(1) All necessary and possible measures will be taken to ensure that CI shall, from the outset of their internment, be accommodated in buildings or quarters which afford every possible safeguard as regards hygiene and health, and provide efficient protection against the rigors of the climate and the effects of war. In no case shall permanent places of internment be placed in unhealthy areas, or in districts the climate of which is injurious to CI.

(2) The premises shall be fully protected from dampness, adequately heated and lighted, in particular, between dusk and lights out. The sleeping quarters shall be sufficiently spacious and well ventilated, and the internees shall have suitable bedding and sufficient blankets, account being taken of the climate, and the age, sex and state of health of the internees.

(3) Internees shall have for their use, day and night, sanitary conveniences which conform to the rules of hygiene and are constantly maintained in a state of cleanliness. They shall be provided with sufficient water and soap for their daily personal hygiene and for washing their personal laundry; installations and facilities necessary for this purpose shall be provided. Showers or baths shall also be available. The necessary time shall be set aside for washing and for cleaning.

(4) CI shall be administered and housed separately from EPW/RP. Except in the case of families, female CI shall be housed in separate quarters and shall be under the direct supervision of women.
"6-5. Supplies.
"b. Food.
(1) Subsistence for the CI will be issued on the basis of a master CI menu prepared by the theater commander. Preparation of the menu will include the following:
(a) The daily individual food ration will be sufficient in quantity, quality, and variety to maintain the CI in good health and to prevent nutritional deficiencies.
"6-6. Medical Care and Sanitation.
a. General
"(2) A medical officer will examine each CI upon arrival at a camp and monthly thereafter. The CI will not be admitted into the general population until medical fitness is determined. These examinations will detect vermin infestation and communicable diseases especially tuberculosis, malaria, and venereal disease. They will also determine the state of health, nutrition, and cleanliness of each CI. During these examinations, each CI will be weighed, and the weight will be recorded on DA Form 2664-R."
AR 385-10, *The Army Safety Program*, 29 February 2000, Chapter 1, paragraph 1-4, paragraph n, subparagraph (1) (a), discusses commanders' responsibilities in implementing the Army Safety Program. Paragraph 1-5, subparagraph b, states that all decision makers will employ the risk management process. Chapter 2, paragraph 2-2, subparagraph b, states that the risk management process will be incorporated into SOPs. Paragraph 2-3, subparagraph d, discusses that, as a minimum requirement, annual inspections or surveys will

be conducted on facilities – more inspections may be required based on risk. The specific language in the regulation follows:

"n. MACOM commanders will – (1) Ensure the full and effective implementation of the Army safety and OH program throughout their MACOM. This includes – (a) Providing a safe and healthful workplace and environment.

"b. Decision makers at every level will employ the risk management process, as specified in paragraph 2-3d of this regulation, to avoid unnecessary residual risk to missions, personnel, equipment, and the environment.

"2-2. Operational procedures. Leaders and managers are responsible for integrating risk management into all Army processes and operations. Safety and occupational health staffs will provide risk management training, tools and other related assistance. Leaders and managers will –

"b. Ensure that the risk management process is incorporated in regulations, directives, SOPs, special orders, training plans, and operational plans to minimize accident risk and that SOPs are developed for all operations entailing risk of death, serious injury, occupational illness or property loss.

"2-3. Prevention program procedures. a. Inspections and surveys. Inspections and surveys of operations and facilities will be conducted annually or more often (chap 4).

"d. Risk management. Risk Management is the Army's principal risk reduction process to assist leaders in identifying and controlling hazards and making informed decisions. (1) Every commander, leader and manager is responsible for protecting the force and persons affected by Army operations. The five-step process is the commander's principal risk reduction process to identify and control hazards and make informed decisions. (a) Identify hazards. (b) Assess hazards. (c) Develop controls and make risk decisions. (d) Implement controls. (e) Supervise and evaluate."

AR 420-70, *Buildings and Structures*, 10 October 1997, Chapter 2, paragraph 2-10, subparagraph a, states that lead-based paint will not be used in Army facilities. The specific language in the regulation follows:

"a. Lead-based paint (LBP). LBP will not be applied to any Army facility."

Field Manual (FM) 3-19.4, *Military Police Leaders' Handbook*, 4 March 2002, Chapter 7, paragraph 7-8, states that detainees do not remain at forward collecting points more than 12 hours before moving to the central collecting point. Paragraph 7-9 states that existing structures should be used when possible. Paragraph 7-29 discusses safeguarding and protecting detainees from attack. Paragraph 7-30 discusses GS MPs and their role in establishing division central collecting points. Paragraph 7-33 discusses MP roles in escorting detainees from forward collecting points to division central collecting points within 12 hours. Paragraph 7-58, discusses the physical criteria for collecting points. The specific language in the field manual follows:

"7-8. . . . Units needed to support the division forward collecting point should be specifically tasked in the brigade OPORD. MP leaders operating the division forward collecting point will –

- Ensure that captives do not remain at the division forward collecting point more than 12 hours before being escorted to the division central collecting point.

7-9. A forward collecting point (Figure 7-1, page 7-6) should not be set up near local inhabitants. Existing structures like vacant schools, apartments, or warehouses should be used when possible. This reduces construction requirements and minimizes logistical requirements. If existing structures are not used, detainees, except officers, can be tasked to help construct the collecting point. Prisoners may dig or build cover to protect themselves from artillery, mortar, or air attack. There is no set design for a forward collecting point. It can be anything from a guarded, roped-off area to a secured, existing structure. The collecting point is built to suit the climate, the weather, and the situation. When selecting a collecting point, consider the following:

- The security of the detainees. The perimeters of the enclosure must be clearly defined and understood by the detainees.
- First aid. Injured or ill detainees require the same treatment that would be given to US casualties.
- Food and water. Detainees may have been without food or water for a long time before capture.
- Latrine facilities.
- Field sanitation. If possible, have detainees wash with soap and water to reduce the likelihood of disease.
- Shelter and cover.
- Language barriers. Provide interpreters and/or instructional graphic training aids (GTAs) in the EPW native language to compensate for the language differences.

"7-29. Protecting detainees from attack, preventing their escape, and quickly removing them from the battle area further safeguards them. Detainees should not remain at the division forward collecting point more than 12 hours, if possible. MP from the division central collecting point move forward to escort detainees back to the central collecting points.

7-30. MP in GS are responsible for establishing and maintaining the division central collecting point. They collect detainees from the forward collecting points, then process and secure them until corps MP come forward to evacuate them to the rear. Detainees should be transferred to the corps holding area or directly to an internment facility within 24 hours, if possible. One or more GS MP platoons operate the division central collecting point. The MP platoons are augmented by the division band and/or by the corps MP. Augmentation is based on the number and rate of captives expected.

"7-33. The MP platoon charged with operating the division central collecting point sends MP forward to the division forward collecting point to escort detainees back to the central collecting point. EPWs or CIs must be evacuated from the division forward collecting point as soon as possible, preferably within 12 hours. Before evacuating the detainees, MP checks with MI interrogation teams for any property to be returned to, or evacuated with, the detainees before they are moved.

"7-58. The size of the facility is based on the number of prisoners being detained. It may be a room or a tent, as long as it provides shelter equal to that offered to other soldiers in the combat zone. The physical criteria for permanent and temporary structures are the same. MP use existing structures if you can. Otherwise, they use tents. . . .

FM 3-19.40, *Military Police Internment/Resettlement Operations*, 1 August 2001, Chapter 2, paragraph 2-1, discusses the Military Police Battalion Commander's responsibilities. Paragraph 2-1 states the role of the MP battalion commander, paragraph 2-17 discusses the requirement for a safety program for I/R facilities, and paragraph states the engineer officer's responsibilities. Paragraph 2-37 states the responsibility of the engineer officer. Chapter 6, paragraphs 6-2 and 6-3 discuss the considerations of choosing sites for Internment/Resettlement (I/R) facilities. The specific language in the field manual follows:

"2-1. An MP battalion commander tasked with operating an I/R facility is also the facility commander. As such, he is responsible for the safety and well-being of all personnel housed within the facility. Since an MP unit may be tasked to handle different categories of personnel (EPW, CI, OD, refugee, and US military prisoner), the commander, the cadre, and support personnel must be aware of the requirements for each category.

"2-17. Set up and administer a safety program for housed personnel in each I/R facility. Follow the procedures outlined in AR 385-10 and associated circulars and pamphlets to establish the safety program. Maintain records and reports for the internee safety program separate from those for the Army safety program.

"2-37. The engineer officer is a captain in a brigade and a lieutenant in a battalion. He trains and supervises internees who perform internal and external labor (construction and repair of facilities). The engineer officer is responsible for –

- Construction, maintenance, repair, and operation of utilities (water, electricity, heat, and sanitation).
- Construction support.
- Fire protection.
- Insect and rodent control and fumigation.

"6-2. The MP coordinate the location with engineers, logistical units, higher headquarters, and the HN. The failure to properly consider and correctly evaluate all factors may increase the logistical and personnel efforts required to support operations. If an I/R facility is improperly located, the entire internee population may require movement when resources are scarce. When selecting a site for a facility, consider the following:

- Will the interned population pose a serious threat to logistical operations if the tactical situation becomes critical?
- Is there a threat of guerrilla activity in the area?
- What is the attitude of the local population?
- What classification of internees will be housed at the site?
- What type of terrain surrounds the site, and will it help or hinder escapes?
- What is the distance from the MSR to the source of logistical support?
- What transportation methods are required and available to move internees, supplies, and equipment?

6-3. In addition, consider the –

- METT-TC.
- Proximity to probable target areas.
- Availability of suitable existing facilities (avoids unnecessary construction).
- Presence of swamps, mosquitoes, and other factors (including water drainage) that affect human health.
- Existence of an adequate, satisfactory source of potable water. The supply should meet the demands for consumption, food sanitation, personal hygiene, and sewage disposal.
- Availability of electricity. Portable generators can be used as standby and emergency sources of electricity.
- Distance to work if internees are employed outside the facility.
- Availability of construction material.
- Soil drainage."

p. **Finding 16:**

   (1) *Finding*: Two of the four internment/resettlement facilities did not segregate enemy prisoners of war from civilian internees in accordance with legal requirements.

(2) *Standard*: Standard of treatment for detainees in OPERATION ENDURING FREE-
DOM (OEF): CJCS message dated 211933Z JAN 02 states that members of the
Taliban militia and members of al Qaeda under the control of U.S. Forces would
be treated humanely and, to the extent appropriate and consistent with military
necessity, in a manner consistent with the principles of the Geneva Conventions of
1949. The DAIG has therefore used the provisions of the Geneva Conventions as a
benchmark against which to measure the treatment provided to detainees by U.S.
Forces to determine if detainees were treated humanely. The use of these standards
as benchmarks does not state or imply a position for the United States or U.S. Army
on the legal status of its operations in OEF.

CJCS Message dated 211933Z JAN 02, provides the determination regarding the humane treatment of al Qaeda and Taliban detainees. *Convention Relative to the Treatment
of Prisoners of War of August 12, 1949* (GPW) is the international treaty that governs the
treatment of prisoners of war), and *Geneva Convention Relative to the Protection of Civilian
Persons in Time of War (GC)*, August 12, 1949, is the international treaty that governs the
treatment of civilian persons in time of war.

As the guidance did not define "humane treatment" but did state that the U.S. would
treat members of the Taliban militia and al Qaeda in a manner consistent with the
Geneva Conventions, the DAIG determined that it would use Common Article 3 of the
GCs as its floor measure of humane treatment, but would also include provisions of the
Geneva Convention on the Treatment of Prisoners of War (GPW) and Geneva Convention Relative to the Protection of Civilian Persons in Time of War (GC) as other relevant indicia of "humane treatment." The use of this standard does not state or imply a position for the United States or U.S. Army on the legal status of its operations
in OEF.

Standard of treatment for detainees in OPERATION IRAQI FREEDOM (OIF): OIF was
an international armed conflict and therefore the provisions of the Geneva Conventions
applied. Additionally, the United States was an occupying power and has acted in accordance with the obligations of an occupying power described in the *Hague Convention No.
IV Respecting the Laws and Customs of War on Land (H.IV)*, Oct. 18, 1907, including, but
not limited to, Articles 43-46 and 50; *Geneva Convention Relative to the Treatment of Prisoners of War of August 12, 1949*(GPW); and *Geneva Convention Relative to the Protection of
Civilian Persons in Time of War (GC)*, August 12, 1949. The GC supplements H.IV, providing the general standard of treatment at Article 27 and specific standards in subsequent
Articles.

The minimum treatment provided by Common Article 3 of the Geneva Conventions
is: (1) No adverse distinction based upon race, religion, sex, etc.; (2) No violence to life or
person; (3) No taking hostages; (4) No degrading treatment; (5) No passing of sentences in
absence of fair trial, and; (6) The wounded and sick must be cared for.

The specific language in the CJCS Message for OEF and the GPW/GC and H.IV follows:

CJCS Message dated 211933Z JAN 02, "Paragraph 3. The combatant commanders shall,
in detaining al Qaeda and Taliban individuals under the control of the Department of
Defense, treat them humanely and, to the extent appropriate and consistent with military necessity, in a manner consistent with the principles of the Geneva Conventions
of 1949."

GPW/GC, Article 3 (Common Article 3) – "In the case of armed conflict not of
an international character occurring in the territory of one of the High Contracting
Parties, each party to the conflict shall be bound to apply, as a minimum, the following
provisions:

1. Persons taking no active part in the hostilities, including members of armed forces who have laid down their arms and those placed hors de combat by sickness, wounds, detention, or any other cause, shall in all circumstances be treated humanely, without any adverse distinction founded on race, color, religion or faith, sex, birth or wealth, or any other similar criteria.

To this end the following acts are and shall remain prohibited at any time and in any place whatsoever with respect to the above-mentioned persons:

(a) Violence to life and person, in particular, murder of all kinds, mutilation, cruel treatment and torture;
(b) Taking of hostages;
(c) Outrages upon personal dignity, in particular, humiliating and degrading treatment;
(d) The passing of sentences and the carrying out of executions without previous judgment pronounced by a regularly constituted court affording all the judicial guarantees which are recognized as indispensable by civilized peoples.

2. The wounded and sick shall be collected and cared for. An impartial humanitarian body, such as the International Committee of the Red Cross, may offer its services to the Parties to the conflict. The Parties to the conflict should further endeavour to bring into force, by means of special agreements, all or part of the other provisions of the present Convention. The application of the preceding provisions shall not affect the legal status of the Parties to the conflict."

Geneva Convention Relative to the Protection of Civilian Persons in Time of War (GC), Article 84; and *Geneva Convention Relative to the Treatment of Prisoners of War (GPW)*, Article 17. The specific language in the Geneva Conventions follows:

GC, Article 84 – "Internees shall be accommodated and administered separately from prisoners of war and from persons deprived of liberty for any other reason."

GPW, Article 17 – "Every prisoner of war, when questioned on the subject, is bound to give only his surname, first names and rank, date of birth, and army, regimental, personal or serial number, or failing this, equivalent information. If he wilfully infringes this rule, he may render himself liable to a restriction of the privileges accorded to his rank or status. Each Party to a conflict is required to furnish the persons under its jurisdiction who are liable to become prisoners of war, with an identity card showing the owner's surname, first names, rank, army, regimental, personal or serial number or equivalent information, and date of birth. The identity card may, furthermore, bear the signature or the fingerprints, or both, of the owner, and may bear, as well, any other information the Party to the conflict may wish to add concerning persons belonging to its armed forces. As far as possible the card shall measure 6.5 × 10 cm. and shall be issued in duplicate. The identity card shall be shown by the prisoner of war upon demand, but may in no case be taken away from him. No physical or mental torture, nor any other form of coercion, may be inflicted on prisoners of war to secure from them information of any kind whatever. Prisoners of war who refuse to answer may not be threatened, insulted, or exposed to any unpleasant or disadvantageous treatment of any kind. Prisoners of war who, owing to their physical or mental condition, are unable to state their identity, shall be handed over to the medical service. The identity of such prisoners shall be established by all possible means, subject to the provisions of the preceding paragraph. The questioning of prisoners of war shall be carried out in a language which they understand."

q. **Finding 17:**
   (1) *Finding*: Units operating collecting points (42%, 5 of 12), and two of the four units operating internment/resettlement facilities, were not adequately resourced with communications equipment, shotguns, and non-lethal ammunition.

(2) *Standard*: Army Regulation (AR) 190-8, *Enemy Prisoners of War, Retained Personnel, Civilian Internees and Other Detainees*, 1 October 1997, Chapter 1, paragraph 1-4, subparagraph e, states that the G4 is responsible for logistics. Paragraph 1-4, sub-paragraph g (2), states that Combatant Commanders, Task Force Commanders, and Joint Task Force Commanders have overall responsibility for civilian internee (CI) programs and in the planning and procuring for logistical support. This regulation is a multiservice regulation implementing DOD Directive 2310.1 and incorporates Army Regulation 190-8 and 190-57 and SECNAV Instruction 3461.3, and Air Force Joint Instruction 31-304 and outlines policies, procedures, and responsibilities for treatment of enemy prisoners of war (EPW), retained personnel (RP), civilian internees (CI), and other detainees (OD) and implements international law for all military operations. The specific language in the regulation follows:

"e. Deputy Chief of Staff for Logistics (DCSLOG). The DCSLOG will ensure logistical resources are available to support EPW operations."

"g. Combatant Commanders, Task Force Commanders and Joint Task Force Commanders. Combatant Commanders, Task Force Commanders and Joint Task Force Commanders have the overall responsibility for the EPW, CI and RP program, operations, and contingency plans in the theater of operation involved to ensure compliance with international law of war."

"(2) Plan and procure logistical support to include: transportation, subsistence, personal, organizational and Nuclear, Biological & Chemical (NBC) clothing and equipment items, mail collection and distribution, laundry, and bath for EPW, CI and RP." Field Manual (FM) 3-19.40, *Military Police Internment/Resettlement Operations*, 1 August 2001, Chapter 6, paragraph 6-7, discusses the importance of good communication within a facility. The specific language in the field manual follows:

"6-7.

- Communications. Ensure that communication between towers and operation head-quarters is reliable. Telephones are the preferred method; however, ensure that alternate forms of communication (radio and visual or sound signals) are available in case telephones are inoperable."

r. **Finding 18:**
  (1) *Finding*: All inspected point of capture units established ad hoc kits containing necessary items and supplies for detainee field processing, but the items they contained and their quantities varied from unit to unit.
  (2) (2) *Standard*: There is no regulatory standard for a detainee field processing kit for capturing units. Army Regulation (AR) 190-8, *Enemy Prisoners of War, Retained Personnel, Civilian Internees and Other Detainees*, 1 October 1997, Chapter 1, paragraph 1-4, subparagraph g (2), states that Combatant Commanders, Task Force Commanders, and Joint Task Force Commanders have overall responsibility for civilian internee (CI) programs and in the planning and procuring for logistical support. Chapter 2, paragraph 2-1, subparagraph a (1) (a) & (b), requires a capturing unit to document confiscated currency and to tag all captured prisoners. This regulation is a multiservice regulation implementing DOD Directive 2310.1 and incorporates Army Regulation 190-8 and 190-57 and SECNAV Instruction 3461.3, and Air Force Joint Instruction 31-304 and outlines policies, procedures, and responsibilities for treatment of enemy prisoners of war (EPW), retained personnel (RP), civilian internees (CI), and other detainees (OD) and implements international law for all military operations. The specific language in the regulation follows:

"g. Combatant Commanders, Task Force Commanders and Joint Task Force Commanders. Combatant Commanders, Task Force Commanders and Joint Task Force Commanders have the overall responsibility for the EPW, CI and RP program, operations, and contingency plans in the theater of operation involved to ensure compliance with international law of war."

"(2) Plan and procure logistical support to include: transportation, subsistence, personal, organizational and Nuclear, Biological & Chemical (NBC) clothing and equipment items, mail collection and distribution, laundry, and bath for EPW, CI and RP."

"a. Each EPW/RP will be searched immediately after capture. . . . Currency will only be confiscated on the order of a commissioned officer and will be receipted for using a DA Form 4137 (Evidence/Property Custody Document).

b. All prisoners of war and retained persons will, at the time of capture, be tagged using DD Form 2745. They will be searched for concealed weapons and items of intelligence. All equipment, documents, and personal property confiscated during the search must be tagged and administratively accounted for by the capturing unit. Capturing units must provide the: date of capture, location of capture (how the EPW was captured). The remaining information will be included on the tag as it becomes available."

s. **Finding 19:**

  (1) *Finding*: All inspected units had adequate transportation assets to evacuate and/or transfer detainees from points of capture to collecting points, and eventually to internment/resettlement facilities.

  (2) *Standard*: Army Regulation 190-8, *Enemy Prisoners of War, Retained Personnel, Civilian Internees and Other Detainees*, 1 October 1997, Chapter 1, paragraph 1-4, subparagraph g (2) and (5), states that Combatant Commanders, Task Force Commanders, and Joint Task Force Commanders have overall responsibility for civilian internee (CI) programs and in the planning and procuring for logistical support, to include transportation. This regulation is a multiservice regulation implementing DOD Directive 2310.1 and incorporates Army Regulation 190-8 and 190-57 and SECNAV Instruction 3461.3, and Air Force Joint Instruction 31-304 and outlines policies, procedures, and responsibilities for treatment of enemy prisoners of war (EPW), retained personnel (RP), civilian internees (CI), and other detainees (OD) and implements international law for all military operations. The specific language in the regulation follows:

"(2) Plan and procure logistical support to include: transportation, subsistence, personal, organizational and Nuclear, Biological & Chemical (NBC) clothing and equipment items, mail collection and distribution, laundry, and bath for EPW, CI and RP."

"(5) Establish guidance for the use, transport, and evacuation of EPW, CI, RP, and ODs in logistical support operations."

Field Manual 3-19.40, *Military Police Internment/Resettlement Operations*, 1 August 2001, Chapter 3, paragraph 3-7, states that the basic principle of speed is the responsibility of the capturing unit, who moves the detainee to the collecting point (CP). Paragraph 3-18 states that the number of detainees at the CP must be reported through MP channels to assist in the transportation planning. Paragraph 3-26 states who is responsible for moving detainees from CPs to the internment/resettlement facility. Paragraph 3-33 states the ratio of MP guards to detainees for movement. Paragraph 3-34 states that detainees cannot be moved with MP organic assets. Paragraph 3-35 states that the preferred method of detainee movement is by using the backhaul system. The specific language in the field manual follows:

"3-7. The Five Ss and T procedure is performed by the capturing unit. The basic principles are search, segregate, silence, speed, safeguard, and tag."

"3-18. Report the number of captives at each CP through MP channels. This aids in the transportation and security planning processes."

"3-26. Remove captives from the CZ as quickly as possible. The intent is to move them from division CPs to an I/R facility. The goal is for higher-level echelons to go forward to lower echelons and evacuate captives to the rear as follows:

- Division MP move forward to the forward CP to escort captives to the central CP.
- Corps MP move forward to the central CP to escort captives to the CHA.
- Echelons above corps (EAC) MP move forward to the CHA to escort captives to the I/R facility."

"3-33. The MP guard able-bodied captives during movement to prevent escape, liberation, or injury. A general planning consideration when determining the number of MP necessary is one for every five to ten captives.

3-34. When moving forward to escort captives to the rear area, MP responsibilities begin at the CP or the CHA where custody is accepted. Verify the method of moving captives, the location and time of pick-up, and the number of captives contained in orders from higher headquarters. The MP units cannot transport captives with organic assets.

3-35. The preferred method for moving captives through a battlefield is the backhaul system. This transportation system relies on assets that have delivered their primary cargo and are available to move personnel and materials to another location. The availability of vehicles will vary, depending on the cargo delivered to the area. The command and control (C2) element of MP unit tasked with evacuation arranges transportation through the local MCO."

t. **Finding 20:**
    (1) *Finding*: Common leader training in professional military school contains only one detainee operations task.
    (2) *Standard*: Army Regulation 350-1, *Army Training and Education*, 9 April 2003, Chapter 3, paragraph 3–2, requires that TRADOC establish training and education goals and objectives for all Army personnel. The specific language in the regulation follows:

"Training proponents. These would include TRADOC schools and colleges, USAJFK-SWC&S and AMEDDC&S and would perform the following:

(a) Develop courses based on established training and education goals and objectives as well as the duties, responsibilities, and missions their graduates will be assigned.
(b) Develop, evaluate, and train leader, technical, and tactical tasks that focus on missions for the size or type units to which graduates will be assigned.
(c) Provide progressive and sequential training.
(d) Provide personnel serving at the same organizational level with training consisting of the same tasks, conditions, and standards.
(e) Provide leader, technical, and tactical training that affords soldiers and DA civilians an opportunity to acquire the skills and knowledge needed to perform more complex duties and missions of greater responsibility."

Field Manual (FM) 7-0, *Training the Force*, 22 October 2002, Chapter 1, paragraph 1-29, provides overall guidance for the implementation of Professional Military Education (PME). The specific language in the field manual follows:

"Professional Military Education – PME develops Army leaders. Officer, warrant officer, and NCO training and education is a continuous, career-long, learning process that integrates structured programs of instruction – resident at the institution and non-resident via distributed learning at home station. PME is progressive and sequential, provides a doctrinal foundation, and builds on previous training, education and operational experiences. PME provides hands-on technical, tactical, and leader training focused to ensure leaders are prepared for success in their next assignment and higher-level responsibility.

- Officer Education System (OES). Army officers must lead and fight; be tactically and technically competent; possess leader skills; understand how the Army operates as a service, as well as a component of a joint, multinational, or interagency organization; demonstrate confidence, integrity, critical judgment, and responsibility; operate in a complex, uncertain, and rapidly changing environment; build effective teams amid continuous organizational and technological change; and solve problems creatively. OES develops officers who are self-aware and adaptive to lead Army units to mission success.
- Warrant Officer Education System (WOES). Warrant officers are the Army's technical experts. WOES develops a corps of highly specialized experts and trainers who are fully competent and proficient operators, maintainers, administrators, and managers of the Army's equipment, support activities, and technical systems.
- NCO Education System (NCOES). NCOES trains NCOs to lead and train soldiers, crews, and subordinate leaders who work and fight under their leadership. NCOES provides hands-on technical, tactical, and leader training focused to ensure that NCOs are prepared for success in their next assignment and higher-level responsibility.
- Functional Training. In addition to the preceding PME courses, there are functional courses available in both resident and non-resident distributed learning modes that enhance functional skills for specific duty positions. Examples are Battalion S2, Battalion Motor Officer, First Sergeant, Battle Staff NCO, and Airborne courses."

u. **Finding 21:**
    (1) *Finding*: Leaders and soldiers assigned to 69% (46 of 67) of inspected units stated they desired additional home station training; and pre- and post mobilization training to assist them in performing detainee operations.
    (2) *Standard*: Training on standard of treatment for detainees in OPERATION ENDURING FREEDOM (OEF): Guidance was provided stating that members of the Taliban militia and members of al Qaeda under the control of U.S. Forces would be treated humanely and, to the extent appropriate and consistent with military necessity, in a manner consistent with the principles of the Geneva Conventions of 1949. The DAIG has therefore used the provisions of the Geneva Conventions as a benchmark against which to measure the treatment provided to detainees by U.S. Forces to determine if detainees were treated humanely and if the corresponding training was consistent with this obligation. The use of these standards as benchmarks does not state or imply a position for the United States or U.S. Army on the legal status of its operations in OEF.

Chairman, Joint Chiefs of Staff (CJCS) Message dated 211933Z JAN 02, provides the determination regarding the humane treatment of al Qaeda and Taliban detainees. *Convention Relative to the Treatment of Prisoners of War of August 12, 1949* (GPW) is the international treaty that governs the treatment of prisoners of war), and *Geneva Convention Relative to the Protection of Civilian Persons in Time of War (GC)*, August 12, 1949, is the international treaty that governs the treatment of civilian persons in time of war.

As the guidance did not define "humane treatment" but did state that the U.S. would treat members of the Taliban militia and al Qaeda in a manner consistent with the Geneva

Conventions, the DAIG determined that it would use Common Article 3 of the GCs as its floor measure of humane treatment and corresponding training, but would also include provisions of the Geneva Convention on the Treatment of Prisoners of War (GPW) and Geneva Convention Relative to the Protection of Civilian Persons in Time of War (GC) as other relevant indicia of "humane treatment." The use of this standard does not state or imply a position for the United States or U.S. Army on the legal status of its operations in OEF.

Standard of treatment for detainees in OPERATION IRAQI FREEDOM (OIF): OIF was an international armed conflict and therefore the provisions of the Geneva Conventions applied.

The minimum treatment provided by Common Article 3 of the Geneva Conventions is: (1) No adverse distinction based upon race, religion, sex, etc.; (2) No violence to life or person; (3) No taking hostages; (4) No degrading treatment; (5) No passing of sentences in absence of fair trial, and; (6) The wounded and sick must be cared for.

The specific language in the CJCS Message for OEF and the GPW/GC and H.IV follows:

CJCS Message dated 211933Z JAN 02, "Paragraph 3. The combatant commanders shall, in detaining al Qaeda and Taliban individuals under the control of the Department of Defense, treat them humanely and, to the extent appropriate and consistent with military necessity, in a manner consistent with the principles of the Geneva Conventions of 1949."

GPW/GC, Article 3 (Common Article 3) – "In the case of armed conflict not of an international character occurring in the territory of one of the High Contracting Parties, each party to the conflict shall be bound to apply, as a minimum, the following provisions:

1. Persons taking no active part in the hostilities, including members of armed forces who have laid down their arms and those placed hors de combat by sickness, wounds, detention, or any other cause, shall in all circumstances be treated humanely, without any adverse distinction founded on race, color, religion or faith, sex, birth or wealth, or any other similar criteria.

To this end the following acts are and shall remain prohibited at any time and in any place whatsoever with respect to the above-mentioned persons:

(a) Violence to life and person, in particular, murder of all kinds, mutilation, cruel treatment and torture;
(b) Taking of hostages;
(c) Outrages upon personal dignity, in particular, humiliating and degrading treatment;
(d) The passing of sentences and the carrying out of executions without previous judgment pronounced by a regularly constituted court affording all the judicial guarantees which are recognized as indispensable by civilized peoples.

2. The wounded and sick shall be collected and cared for. An impartial humanitarian body, such as the International Committee of the Red Cross, may offer its services to the Parties to the conflict. The Parties to the conflict should further endeavour to bring into force, by means of special agreements, all or part of the other provisions of the present Convention. The application of the preceding provisions shall not affect the legal status of the Parties to the conflict."

GPW Article 127 and GC Article 144 establish a requirement for signatories to the treaties to train their military on the obligations under the conventions. The specific standards follow:

"GC Article 127 – The High Contracting Parties undertake, in time of peace as in time of war, to disseminate the text of the present Convention as widely as possible in their respective countries, and, in particular, to include the study thereof in their programmes of military and, if possible, civil instruction, so that the principles thereof may become known to all their armed forces and to the entire population. Any military or other authorities, who in time of war assume responsibilities in respect of prisoners of war, must possess the text of the Convention and be specially instructed as to its provisions.

GC Article 144 – The High Contracting Parties undertake, in time of peace as in time of war, to disseminate the text of the present Convention as widely as possible in their respective countries, and, in particular, to include the study thereof in their programmes of military and, if possible, civil instruction, so that the principles thereof may become known to the entire population. Any civilian, military, police or other authorities, who in time of war assume responsibilities in respect of protected persons, must possess the text of the Convention and be specially instructed as to its provisions."

Army Regulation 350-1, *Army Training and Education*, 9 April 2003, Chapter 1, paragraph 1-8, subparagraph 2d, establishes Home Station Training priorities for all Army personnel. Chapter 4, paragraph 4-5, outlines training requirements for Common Military Training for all Army personnel. Appendix G, paragraph G-1, subparagraph(s) b-c, outlines an overview of the Common Military Training program. Table G-1, provides examples of military training requirements in units. The specific language in the regulation follows:

"2d. Training will be the top priority for all commanders – To prepare individuals and units for immediate deployment and organizations for employment in support of operational missions, Army individual, collective, and modernization training provides for –

(1) Unit training that develops the critical components of combat readiness. These include development of –

(a) Soldiers, leaders, and units capable of deploying, executing assigned missions, and redeploying.
(b) Effective combined arms teams consisting of integrated combat, combat support (CS), combat service support, and close air support.

(2) An individual training system that –

(a) Produces initial entry soldiers who are highly motivated, disciplined, physically fit, and skilled in common soldier and basic branch tasks.
(b) Provides a training base of Army schools that prepares soldiers and DA civilian employees for more complex duties and progressively higher positions of responsibility.
(c) Produces soldiers capable of performing military occupational specialty (MOS), Area of Concentration (AOC), additional skill identifier (ASI), skill identifier (SI), special qualification identifier (SQI), and language identification code (LIC) tasks. Prior service Reserve Component (RC) and Active Army personnel receive required training through The Army Training System courses (TATS-C) or proponent-approved formal on-the-job training (OJT). TATS courses are designed to train the same MOS, AOC, skill level, SQI, ASI, LIC, and SI within the Army. TATS also includes MOS qualification (reclassification), Army leadership, and professional development courses.
(d) Provides reclassification training for changing an enlisted or warrant officer MOS, or to qualify an officer in a new branch. Reclassification training will be accomplished in accordance with Army Regulation (AR) 140-1, AR 614-200, and AR 611-1.

(3) Active Army, Department of the Army civilians, and RC forces able to mobilize rapidly, deploy, and perform their operational missions.

(4) Standardization of tasks and performance standards across the Army. Units and soldiers performing the same tasks will be trained to the same standard.

(5) Efficient and effective internal and external evaluation procedures that improve training, sustain required readiness levels, and control or reduce costs.

(6) A training system that supports peacetime requirements and transitions smoothly at mobilization."

"4-5. Common military training and common task training –

(a) CMT program identifies common military training requirements for unit commanders' planning and training programs because of their importance to individual soldier and unit readiness. Common military training is required for all leaders and soldiers at specific organizational levels, and proficiency in those subject areas is necessary, regardless of branch or career field or rank or grade. Common military training requirements are limited to those subject areas directed by law and HQDA. The HQDA, DCS, G-3, maintains centralized control over CMT directed training requirements and validates these requirements biennially."

"G-1. Overview –

(b) MACOM commanders have a degree of latitude in adding to or emphasizing certain training requirements; however, care should be taken not to degrade battle-focused training.

(c) Successful CMT programs are measured by performance to standard and not adherence to rosters or hours scheduled."

"Table G-1, Common military training requirements in units – Weapons Qualification, Civil disturbance, Anti-terrorism and Force Protection, Code of Conduct/ SERE, Law of War..."

Field Manual (FM) 3-19.4, *Military Police Leaders' Handbook*, 4 March 2002, Chapter 1, paragraph 1-4, outlines the 5 Military Police Functional Areas. The specific language in the field manual follows:

"b. Military Police Functional Areas –

(1-4) with the old battlefield missions, the term "operations" was used extensively and carried too broad of a meaning. To clarify the specific tasks of the MP, the battlefield missions have been redefined into the following five functional areas:

- MMS (Maneuver and Mobility Support)
- AS (Area Security)
- I/R (Internment and Resettlement)
- L&O (Law and Order)
- PIO (Police Intelligence Operations)"

FORSCOM Regulation 500-3-1, *FORSCOM MOBILIZATION and DEPLOYMENT PLANNING SYSTEM (FORMDEPS), Volume 1, FORSCOM MOBILIZATION PLAN (FMP)*, 15 April 1998, Annex O, paragraph 2.4.4, defines additional training requirements at mobilization sites. The specific language in the regulation follows: "Mobilized Unit Commanders –

(2) Commanders will additionally concentrate on training on soldier/leader skills. This training will be designed to make best use of time available after unit equipment is shipped and will include the following as a minimum:

(a) Physical fitness. Its importance cannot be overstated. Training should be conducted in accordance with AR 350-15 and FM 21-20.

(b) Common Task Test. Testing is most often practiced in a sterile, "round robin" setting using the tasks, conditions and standards provided in the STP 21-series Soldier's Manual of Common Tasks Testing should include an element of tactical realism to cause soldiers, as members of teams, crews, sections, and squads to think and react instinctively.

(c) The NBC Training. The following tasks are of paramount importance:
1. Recognize/react to chemical/ biological hazards.
2. Don Mission-Oriented Protection Posture (MOPP) gear.
3. Detect and identify chemical agents using M8/M9 paper.
4. Administer nerve agent antidote to self (self-aid) and to a nerve agent casualty (buddy-aid).
5. Decon skin and personal equipment using the M258A 1 decon kit, the M291 skin decon kit, and the M295 equipment decon kit.
6. Drink from a canteen while wearing a protective mask.
7. Maintain and use the M40 series protective mask with hood.

(d) Care and maintenance of CTA 50–900 series and MTO&E equipment.
(e) Force protection to include terrorist threat. (See Appendix 1)
(f) Hazards and survival.
(g) Individual and crew served weapons proficiency.
(h) First Aid – Combat Lifesavers.
(i) Rules of Engagement.
(j) Personal hygiene.
(k) Threat and allied equipment recognition
(l) An orientation on the area of probable operations to include language, customs, courtesies, etc."

v. **Finding 22:**
(1) *Finding*: To offset the shortage of interrogators, contractors were employed, however, 35% (11 of 31) of contract interrogators lacked formal training in military interrogation policies and techniques.
(2) *Standard*: Army Regulation (AR) 190-8, *Enemy Prisoners of War, Retained Personnel, Civilian Internees and Other Detainees*, 1 October 1997, Chapter 2, paragraph 2-1, provides the regulatory guidance for interrogation of detainees in a combat zone. This regulation is a multiservice regulation implementing DOD Directive 2310.1 and incorporates Army Regulation 190-8 and 190-57 and SECNAV Instruction 3461.3, and Air Force Joint Instruction 31–304 and outlines policies, procedures, and responsibilities for treatment of enemy prisoners of war (EPW), retained personnel (RP), civilian internees (CI), and other detainees (OD) and implements international law for all military operations. The specific language in the regulation follows:

"(d) Prisoners may be interrogated in the combat zone. The use of physical or mental torture or any coercion to compel prisoners to provide information is prohibited. Prisoners may voluntarily cooperate with PSYOP personnel in the development, evaluation, or dissemination of PSYOP messages or products. Prisoners may not be threatened, insulted, or exposed to unpleasant or disparate treatment of any kind because of their refusal to answer questions. Interrogations will normally be performed by intelligence or counterintelligence personnel."

Field Manual (FM) 27-10, *The Law of Land Warfare*, 18 July 1956 (change 1, 15 July 1976), Chapter 3, section IV, paragraph 93, describes guidelines for the questioning of

EPWs. The specific language in the field manual follows:

"No physical or mental torture, nor any other form of coercion, may be inflicted on prisoners of war to secure from them information of any kind whatever. Prisoners of war who refuse to answer may not be threatened, insulted, or exposed to unpleasant or disadvantageous treatment of any kind."

FM 34-52, *Intelligence Interrogation*, 28 September 1992, Chapter 1, defines and explains the purpose of interrogation. The specific language in the field manual follows:

"Interrogation is the process of questioning a source to obtain the maximum amount of usable information. The goal of any interrogation is to obtain reliable information in a lawful manner, in a minimum amount of time, and to satisfy intelligence requirements of any echelon of command.

A good interrogation produces needed information, which is timely, complete, clear, and accurate." *CJTF-7 C2 Interrogation Cell Statement of Work*, CACI International, Inc., 14 August 2003, Paragraphs 7 (c) and 9 (c) describe the requirements for contract interrogators hired to man the theater and division interrogations support cells in OIF. The specific language in the statement of work follows:

"Identified interrogators should be the civilian equivalent to one of the following: 97E, 351E, Strategic Debriefer or an individual with a similar skill set, and US Citizens with a Secret clearance."

w. **Finding 23:**

   (1) *Finding*: Interviewed leaders and soldiers indicated their Law of War refresher training was not detailed enough to sustain their knowledge obtained during initial and advanced training.

   (2) *Standard*: Training on standard of treatment for detainees in OPERATION ENDURING FREEDOM (OEF):

   Guidance was provided stating that members of the Taliban militia and members of al Qaeda under the control of U.S. Forces would be treated humanely and, to the extent appropriate and consistent with military necessity, in a manner consistent with the principles of the Geneva Conventions of 1949. The DAIG has therefore used the provisions of the Geneva Conventions as a benchmark against which to measure the treatment provided to detainees by U.S. Forces to determine if detainees were treated humanely and if the corresponding training was consistent with this obligation. The use of these standards as benchmarks does not state or imply a position for the United States or U.S. Army on the legal status of its operations in OEF.

Chairman, Joint Chiefs of Staff (CJCS) Message dated 211933Z JAN 02, provides the determination regarding the humane treatment of al Qaeda and Taliban detainees. *Convention Relative to the Treatment of Prisoners of War of August 12, 1949* (GPW) is the international treaty that governs the treatment of prisoners of war), and *Geneva Convention Relative to the Protection of Civilian Persons in Time of War (GC)*, August 12, 1949, is the international treaty that governs the treatment of civilian persons in time of war.

As the guidance did not define "humane treatment" but did state that the U.S. would treat members of the Taliban militia and al Qaeda in a manner consistent with the Geneva Conventions, the DAIG determined that it would use Common Article 3 of the GCs as its floor measure of humane treatment and corresponding training, but would also include provisions of the Geneva Convention on the Treatment of Prisoners of War (GPW) and Geneva Convention Relative to the Protection of Civilian Persons in Time of War (GC) as other relevant indicia of "humane treatment." The use of this standard does not state or imply a position for the United States or U.S. Army on the legal status of its operations in OEF.

Standard of treatment for detainees in OPERATION IRAQI FREEDOM (OIF): OIF was an international armed conflict and therefore the provisions of the Geneva Conventions applied.

The minimum treatment provided by Common Article 3 of the Geneva Conventions is: (1) No adverse distinction based upon race, religion, sex, etc.; (2) No violence to life or person; (3) No taking hostages; (4) No degrading treatment; (5) No passing of sentences in absence of fair trial, and; (6) The wounded and sick must be cared for.

The specific language in the CJCS Message for OEF and the GPW/GC and H.IV follows:

CJCS Message dated 211933Z JAN 02, "Paragraph 3. The combatant commanders shall, in detaining al Qaeda and Taliban individuals under the control of the Department of Defense, treat them humanely and, to the extent appropriate and consistent with military necessity, in a manner consistent with the principles of the Geneva Conventions of 1949."

GPW/GC, Article 3 (Common Article 3) – "In the case of armed conflict not of an international character occurring in the territory of one of the High Contracting Parties, each party to the conflict shall be bound to apply, as a minimum, the following provisions:

1. Persons taking no active part in the hostilities, including members of armed forces who have laid down their arms and those placed hors de combat by sickness, wounds, detention, or any other cause, shall in all circumstances be treated humanely, without any adverse distinction founded on race, color, religion or faith, sex, birth or wealth, or any other similar criteria.

To this end the following acts are and shall remain prohibited at any time and in any place whatsoever with respect to the above-mentioned persons:

(a) Violence to life and person, in particular, murder of all kinds, mutilation, cruel treatment and torture;
(b) Taking of hostages;
(c) Outrages upon personal dignity, in particular, humiliating and degrading treatment;
(d) The passing of sentences and the carrying out of executions without previous judgment pronounced by a regularly constituted court affording all the judicial guarantees which are recognized as indispensable by civilized peoples.

2. The wounded and sick shall be collected and cared for. An impartial humanitarian body, such as the International Committee of the Red Cross, may offer its services to the Parties to the conflict. The Parties to the conflict should further endeavour to bring into force, by means of special agreements, all or part of the other provisions of the present Convention. The application of the preceding provisions shall not affect the legal status of the Parties to the conflict."

GPW Article 127 and GC Article 144 establish a requirement for signatories to the treaties to train their military on the obligations under the conventions. The specific standards follow:

"GC Article 127 – The High Contracting Parties undertake, in time of peace as in time of war, to disseminate the text of the present Convention as widely as possible in their respective countries, and, in particular, to include the study thereof in their programmes of military and, if possible, civil instruction, so that the principles thereof may become known to all their armed forces and to the entire population. Any military or other authorities, who in time of war assume responsibilities in respect of prisoners of war, must possess the text of the Convention and be specially instructed as to its provisions.

GC Article 144 – The High Contracting Parties undertake, in time of peace as in time of war, to disseminate the text of the present Convention as widely as possible in their respective countries, and, in particular, to include the study thereof in their programmes of military and, if possible, civil instruction, so that the principles thereof may become known to the entire population. Any civilian, military, police or other authorities, who in time of war assume responsibilities in respect of protected persons, must possess the text of the Convention and be specially instructed as to its provisions."

Department of Defense Directive (DoDD) 2310.1, *DoD Program for Enemy Prisoners of War (EPOW) and Other Detainees*, 18 August 1994, Section 3. provides DoD policy for training on the Geneva Conventions. The specific language in the directive follows:

"3. Policy, It is DoD policy that:

3.1. The U.S. Military Services shall comply with the principles, spirit, and intent of the international law of war, both customary and codified, to include the Geneva Conventions (references (b) through (e)).

3.2. The U.S. Military Services shall be given the necessary training to ensure they have knowledge of their obligations under the Geneva Conventions (references (b) through (e)) and as required by DoD Directive 5100.77 (reference (f)) before an assignment to a foreign area where capture or detention of enemy personnel is possible.

3.3. Captured or detained personnel shall be accorded an appropriate legal status under international law. Persons captured or detained may be transferred to or from the care, custody, and control of the U.S. Military Services only on approval of the Assistant Secretary of Defense for International Security Affairs (ASD(ISA)) and as authorized by the Geneva Conventions Relative to the Treatment of Prisoners of War and for the Protection of Civilian Persons in Time of War (references (d) and (e)).

3.4. Persons captured or detained by the U.S. Military Services shall normally be handed over for safeguarding to U.S. Army Military Police, or to detainee collecting points or other holding facilities and installations operated by U.S. Army Military Police as soon as practical. Detainees may be interviewed for intelligence collection purposes at facilities and installations operated by U.S. Army Military Police."

Department of Defense Directive (DoDD) 5100.77, *DoD Law of War Program*, 9 December 1998, Section 5.5, provides DoD policy for Law of War policy and training. The specific language in the directive follows:

"5.5. The Secretaries of the Military Departments shall develop internal policies and procedures consistent with this Directive in support of the DoD Law of War Program to:

5.5.1. Provide directives, publications, instructions, and training so that the principles and rules of the law of war will be known to members of their respective Departments, the extent of such knowledge to be commensurate with each individual's duties and responsibilities.

5.5.2. Ensure that programs are implemented in their respective Military Departments to prevent violations of the law of war, emphasizing any types of violations that have been reported under this Directive.

5.5.3. Provide for the prompt reporting and investigation of reportable incidents committed by or against members of their respective Military Departments, or persons accompanying them, in accordance with directives issued under paragraph 5.8.4., below.

5.5.4. Where appropriate, provide for disposition, under the Uniform Code of Military Justice (reference (i)), of cases involving alleged violations of the law of war DODD 5100.77, December 9, 1998 4 by members of their respective Military Departments who are subject to court-martial jurisdiction.

5.5.5. Provide for the central collection of reports and investigations of reportable incidents alleged to have been committed by or against members of their respective Military Departments, or persons accompanying them.

5.5.6. Ensure that all reports of reportable incidents are forwarded to the Secretary of the Army in his or her capacity as the DoD Executive Agent under subsection 5.6., below."

Army Regulation (AR) 350-1, *Army Training and Education*, 9 April 2003, Section 4-14, sets the guidelines for Law of War training. The specific language in the regulation follows: "4–14. Law of war training

a. Soldiers and leaders require law of war training throughout their military careers commensurate with their duties and responsibilities. Prescribed subject matter for training at the following levels is specified in paras 4-14b-d of this regulation.
   (1) Level A training is conducted during IET for all enlisted personnel and during basic courses of instruction for all warrant officers and officers.
   (2) Level B training is conducted in units for officers, warrant officers, NCOs and enlisted personnel commensurate with the missions of the unit.
   (3) Level C training is conducted in The Army School System (TASS).

b. Level A training provides the minimum knowledge required for all members of the Army. The following basic law of war rules (referred to as "The Soldier's Rules," which stresses the importance of compliance with the law of war) will be taught during level A training:
   (1) Soldiers fight only enemy combatants.
   (2) Soldiers do not harm enemies who surrender. They disarm them and turn them over to their superior.
   (3) Soldiers do not kill or torture enemy prisoners of war.
   (4) Soldiers collect and care for the wounded, whether friend or foe.
   (5) Soldiers do not attack medical personnel, facilities, or equipment.
   (6) Soldiers destroy no more than the mission requires.
   (7) Soldiers treat civilians humanely.
   (8) Soldiers do not steal. Soldiers respect private property and possessions.
   (9) Soldiers should do their best to prevent violations of the law of war.
   (10) Soldiers report all violations of the law of war to their superior.

c. Unit commanders will plan and execute level B law-of-war training based on the following:
   (1) Training should reinforce the principles set forth in The Soldier's Rules.
   (2) Training will be designed around current missions and contingency plans (including anticipated geographical areas of deployment or rules of engagement).
   (3) Training will be integrated into unit training activities, field training exercises and unit external evaluations (EXEVAL). Maximum combat realism will be applied to tactical exercises consistent with good safety practices.

d. Army schools will tailor law of war training to the tasks taught in those schools. Level C training will emphasize officer, warrant officer, and NCO responsibilities for:
   (1) Their performance of duties in accordance with the law of war obligations of the United States.
   (2) Law of war issues in command planning and execution of combat operations.
   (3) Measures for the reporting of suspected or alleged war crimes committed by or against U.S. or allied personnel."

Appendix F Abbreviations and Acronyms

AAR	After Action Review
ABN	Airborne
AC	Active Component
AD	Armored Division
ANCOC	Advanced Noncommissioned Officer Course
AOC	Area of Concentration
AOR	Area of Responsibility
AR	Army Regulation
ARNG	Army National Guard
ASD(ISA)	Assistant Secretary of Defense for International Security Affairs
ASD(SO/LIC)	Assistant Secretary of Defense for Special Operations and Low Intensity Conflict
ASI	Additional Skill Identifier
BATS	Biometric Assessment Tool Set
BIAP	Baghdad International Airport
BDE	Brigade
BN	Battalion
CAT	and Other Cruel, Inhuman or Degrading Treatment or Punishment
CAV	Cavalry
CCC	Captain's Career Course
C&E	Collection and Exploitation
CENTCOM	U.S. Central Command
CFLCC	Combined Forces Land Component Command
CHA	Corps Holding Area
CI	Civilian Detainee
CID	Criminal Investigation Division
CIF	Central Issue Facility
C-IMINT	Counter-Imagery Intelligence
CJCS	Chairman of the Joint Chiefs of Staff
CJTF-7	Combined Joint Task Force-7
CJTF-180	Combined Joint Task Force-180
CMT	Common Military Training
CO	Company
COE HI	Contemporary Operational Environment High Intensity
COMMZ	Communication Zone
COMSEC	Communications Security
CONUS	Continental United States
CP	Collecting Points
CPA	Coalition Provisional Authority
C-SIGINT	Counter-Signals Intelligence
CSM	Command Sergeant Major
CTC	Combat Training Center
CTT	Common Task Training
DAIG	Department of the Army Inspectors General
DD FORM	Department of Defense Form
DOD	Department of Defense

DOTMLPF	Doctrine, Organization, Training, Materiel, Leadership, Personnel, and Facilities
DRB	Detainee Release Board
DSA	Division Support Area
EC	Enemy Combatant
EPW	Enemy Prisoners of War
FDU	Force Design Update
FM	Field Manual
FORSCOM	Forces Command
FSB	Forward Support Battalion
FY	Fiscal Year
GC	Geneva Convention Relative to the Protection of Civilian Persons in Time of War
GPW	Geneva Convention Relative to the Treatment of Prisoners of War
HHD	Headquarters and Headquarters Detachment
HMMWV	High Mobility Multipurpose Wheeled Vehicle
HRD	High Risk Detainee
HUMINT	Human Intelligence
IBOS	Intelligence Battlefield Operating System
ICRC	International Committee of the Red Cross
ID	Infantry Division
IED	Improvised Explosive Device
IET	Initial Entry Training
IG	Inspectors General
ILO	In Lieu Of
IMINT	Imagery Intelligence
IN	Infantry
I/R	Internment/Resettlement
JABS	Joint Automated Booking System
JFLCC	Joint Force Land Component Commander
JIDC	Joint Interrogation and Debriefing Center
JIF	Joint Interrogation Facility
JRTC	Joint Readiness Training Center
JTF	Joint Task Force
LLEC	Low Level Enemy Combatant
LMTV	Light Medium Tactical Vehicle
METT-TC	Mission, Enemy, Terrain and Weather, Time, Troops Available, and Civilian
MG	Major General
MI	Military Intelligence
MICCC	Military Intelligence Captain Career Course
MI-CSB	Military Intelligence Corps Support Battalion
MILES	Multi-Integrated Laser Engagement System
MIOBC	Military Intelligence Officer Basic Course
MOS	Military Occupational Specialty
MP	Military Police
MRE	Meal Ready to Eat
MRX	Mission Rehearsal Exercise
MTOE	Modified Tables of Organization and Equipment

MTT	Mobile Training Team
MUA	Maneuver Unit of Action
MWR	Morale, Welfare, and Recreation
NCO	Noncommissioned Officer
NCOIC	Noncommissioned Officer in Charge
NDRC	National Detainee Reporting Center
NPWIC	National Prisoner of War Information Center
NTC	National Training Center
OCONUS	Outside the Continental United States
OD	Other Detainee
OEF	OPERATION ENDURING FREEDOM
OGA	Other Government Organization
OIF	OPERATION IRAQI FREEDOM
OMT	Operations Management Team
OPMG	Office of the Provost Marshal General
OTJAG	Office of The Judge Advocate General
OTSG	Office of the Surgeon General
PLDC	Primary Leadership Development Course
PME	Professional Military Education
POC	Point of Contact
POI	Program of Instruction
PUC	Person Under U.S. Control
PWIC	Prisoner of War Information Center
PX	Post Exchange
QDF	Quadrennial Defense Review
RC	Reserve Component
RCF	Regional Correctional Facility
ROE	Rules of Engagement
RP	Retained Person
R&R	Rest and Recuperation
RSTA UA	Reconnaissance, Surveillance, and Target Acquisition Unit of Action
SAEDA	Subversion & Espionage Directed Against U.S. Army & Deliberate Security Violation
SASO	Stability and Support Operation
SF	Standard Form
SFC	Sergeant First Class
SIMEX	Simulation Exercise (SIMEX)
SINCGARS	Single Channel Ground/Air Radio System
SOP	Standing Operating Procedure
SOW	Statement of Work
SRC	Soldier Readiness Checks
SSG	Staff Sergeant
STX	Situational Training Exercises
TAA	Total Army Analysis
TACSOP	Tactical Standing Operating Procedure
TDA	Table of Distribution and Allowance
TDRC	Theater Detainee Reporting Center
THT	Tactical Human Intelligence Team
TIF	Theater Interrogation Center

TOC	Tactical Operations Center
TOE	Table of Organization and Equipment
TRADOC	Training and Doctrine Command
TTP	Tactics, Techniques, and Procedures
UA	Unit of Action
UCMJ	Uniform Code of Military Justice
UEX	Unit of Employment x
UEY	Unit of Employment y
USACIC	U.S. Army Criminal Investigation Command
USAIC	U.S. Army Intelligence Center
USAICS	U.S. Army Intelligence Center and School
USAMANSCEN	U.S. Army Maneuver Support Center
USAMPS	U.S. Army Military Police School
USAR	U.S. Army Reserve
USASOC	U.S. Army Special Operations Command
USDB	U.S. Military Disciplinary Barracks
WOAC	Warrant Officer Advanced Course
WOCS	Warrant Officer Candidate School
2X	Human Intelligence / Counterintelligence Personnel
31B	Enlisted Military Occupational Specialty – Military Police
31E	Enlisted Military Occupational Specialty – Internment/ Resettlement
97B	Enlisted Military Occupational Specialty – Counterintelligence Personnel
97E	Enlisted Military Occupational Specialty – Human Intelligence (HUMINT) Collector
351E	Warrant Officer Human Intelligence Collection Technician

The Schlesinger Report

Final Report of the Independent Panel to Review
DoD Detention Operations

The Independent Panel to Review Department of Defense
Detention Operations

August 2004

TABLE OF CONTENTS

TABLE OF APPENDICES

President of the United States Memorandum, February 7, 2002 – Appendix C

Interrogation Policies – Appendix D

Evolution of Interrogation Techniques – Appendix E

Timeline, Major Detention Events – Appendix F

Psychological Stresses – Appendix G

Ethical Issues – Appendix H

EXECUTIVE SUMMARY

OVERVIEW

The events of October through December 2003 on the night shift of Tier 1 at Abu Ghraib prison were acts of brutality and purposeless sadism. We now know these abuses occurred at the hands of both military police and military intelligence person- nel. The pictured abuses, unacceptable even in wartime, were not part of authorized interrogations nor were they even directed at intelligence targets. They represent de- viant behavior and a failure of military leadership and discipline. However, we do know that some of the egregious abuses at Abu Ghraib which were not photographed did occur during interrogation sessions and that abuses during interrogation sessions occurred elsewhere.

In light of what happened at Abu Ghraib, a series of comprehensive investigations has been conducted by various components of the Department of Defense. Since the beginning of hostilities in Afghanistan and Iraq, U.S. military and security operations have apprehended about 50,000 individuals. From this number, about 300 allega- tions of abuse in Afghanistan, Iraq or Guantanamo have arisen. As of mid-August 2004, 155 investigations into the allegations have been completed, resulting in 66 substantiated cases. Approximately one-third of these cases occurred at the point of capture or tactical collection point, frequently under uncertain, dangerous and violent circumstances.

Abuses of varying severity occurred at differing locations under differing circum- stances and context. They were widespread and, though inflicted on only a small per- centage of those detained, they were serious both in number and in effect. No approved procedures called for or allowed the kinds of abuse that in fact occurred. There is no evidence of a policy of abuse promulgated by senior officials or military authorities. Still, the abuses were not just the failure of some individuals to follow known stan- dards, and they are more than the failure of a few leaders to enforce proper discipline. There is both institutional and personal responsibility at higher levels.

Secretary of Defense Donald Rumsfeld appointed the members of the Independent Panel to provide independent professional advice on detainee abuses, what caused them and what actions should be taken to preclude their repetition. The Panel re- viewed various criminal investigations and a number of command and other major investigations. The Panel also conducted interviews of relevant persons, including the Secretary and Deputy Secretary of Defense, other senior Department of Defense officials, the military chain-of-command and their staffs and other officials directly and indirectly involved with Abu Ghraib and other detention operations. However, the Panel did not have full access to information involving the role of the Central Intelligence Agency in detention operations; this is an area the Panel believes needs further investigation and review. It should be noted that information provided to the Panel was that available as of mid-August 2004. If additional information becomes available, the Panel's judgments might be revised.

POLICY

With the events of September 11, 2001, the President, the Congress and the American people recognized we were at war with a different kind of enemy. The terrorists who flew airliners into the World Trade Center and the Pentagon were unlike enemy combatants the U.S. has fought in previous conflicts. Their objectives, in fact, are to kill large numbers of civilians and to strike at the heart of America's political cohesion and its economic and military might. In the days and weeks after the attack, the President and his closest advisers developed policies and strategies in response. On September 18, 2001, by a virtually unanimous vote, Congress passed an Authorization for Use of Military Force. Shortly thereafter, the U.S. initiated hostilities in Afghanistan and the first detainees were held at Mazar-e-Sharrif in November 2001.

On February 7, 2002, the President issued a memorandum stating that he determined the Geneva Conventions did not apply to the conflict with al Qaeda, and although they did apply in the conflict with Afghanistan, the Taliban were unlawful combatants and therefore did not qualify for prisoner of war status (see Appendix C). Nonetheless, the Secretary of State, Secretary of Defense, and the Chairman of the Joint Chiefs of Staff were all in agreement that treatment of detainees should be consistent with the Geneva Conventions. The President ordered accordingly that detainees were to be treated "...humanely and, to the extent appropriate and consistent with military necessity, in a manner consistent with the principles of Geneva." Earlier, the Department of State had argued the Geneva Conventions in their traditional application provided a sufficiently robust legal construct under which the Global War on Terror could effectively be waged. The Legal Advisor to the Chairman, Joint Chiefs of Staff, and many of the military service attorneys agreed with this position.

In the summer of 2002, the Counsel to the President queried the Department of Justice Office of Legal Counsel (OLC) for an opinion on the standards of conduct for interrogation operations conducted by U.S. personnel outside of the U.S. and the applicability of the Convention Against Torture. The OLC responded in an August 1, 2002 opinion in which it held that in order to constitute torture, an act must be specifically intended to inflict severe physical or mental pain and suffering that is difficult to endure.

Army Field Manual 34-52 (FM 34-52), with its list of 17 authorized interrogation methods, has long been the standard source for interrogation doctrine within the Department of Defense (see Appendix D). In October 2002, authorities at Guantanamo requested approval of stronger interrogation techniques to counter tenacious resistance by some detainees. The Secretary of Defense responded with a December 2, 2002 decision authorizing the use of 16 additional techniques at Guantanamo (see Appendix E). As a result of concerns raised by the Navy General Counsel on January 15, 2003, Secretary Rumsfeld rescinded the majority of the approved measures in the December 2, 2002, authorization. Moreover, he directed the remaining more aggressive techniques could be used only with his approval (see Appendix D).

At the same time, he directed the Department of Defense (DoD) General Counsel to establish a working group to study interrogation techniques. The Working Group was headed by Air Force General Counsel Mary Walker and included wide membership from across the military legal and intelligence communities. The Working Group also relied heavily on the OLC. The Working Group reviewed 35 techniques and after a very extensive debate ultimately recommended 24 to the Secretary of Defense. The study led to the Secretary of Defense's promulgation on April 16, 2003, of a list of approved techniques strictly limited for use at Guantanamo. This policy remains in force at Guantanamo (see Appendix E).

In the initial development of these Secretary of Defense policies, the legal resources of the Services' Judge Advocates General and General Counsels were not utilized to their full potential. Had the Secretary of Defense had a wider range of legal opinions and a more robust debate regarding detainee policies and operations, his policy of April 16, 2003 might well have been developed and issued in early December 2002. This would have avoided the policy changes which characterized the December 2, 2002, to April 16, 2003 period.

It is clear that pressures for additional intelligence and the more aggressive methods sanctioned by the Secretary of Defense memorandum, resulted in stronger interrogation techniques that were believed to be needed and appropriate in the treatment of detainees defined as "unlawful combatants." At Guantanamo, the interrogators used those additional techniques with only two detainees, gaining important and time-urgent information in the process.

In Afghanistan, from the war's inception through the end of 2002, all forces used FM 34-52 as a baseline for interrogation techniques. Nonetheless, more aggressive interrogation of detainees appears to have been on-going. On January 24, 2003, in response to a data call from the Joint Staff to facilitate the Working Group efforts, the Commander Joint Task Force-180 forwarded a list of techniques being used in Afghanistan, including some not explicitly set out in FM 34-52. These techniques were included in a Special Operation Forces (SOF) Standard Operating Procedures document published in February 2003. The 519th Military Intelligence Battalion, a company of which was later sent to Iraq, assisted in interrogations in support of SOF and was fully aware of their interrogation techniques.

Interrogators and lists of techniques circulated from Guantanamo and Afghanistan to Iraq. During July and August 2003, the 519th Military Intelligence Company was sent to the Abu Ghraib detention facility to conduct interrogation operations. Absent any explicit policy or guidance, other than FM 34-52, the officer in charge prepared draft interrogation guidelines that were a near copy of the Standard Operating Procedure created by SOF. It is important to note that techniques effective under carefully controlled conditions at Guantanamo became far more problematic when they migrated and were not adequately safeguarded.

Following a CJTF-7 request, Joint Staff tasked SOUTHCOM to send an assistance team to provide advice on facilities and operations, specifically related to screening, interrogations, HUMINT collection, and inter-agency integration in the short and long term. In August 2003, MG Geoffrey Miller arrived to conduct an assessment of DoD counter-terrorism interrogation and detention operations in Iraq. He was to discuss current theater ability to exploit internees rapidly for actionable intelligence. He brought the Secretary of Defense's April 16, 2003, policy guidelines for Guantanamo with him and gave this policy to CJTF-7 as a possible model for the command-wide policy that he recommended be established. MG Miller noted that it applied to unlawful combatants at Guantanamo and was not directly applicable to Iraq where the Geneva Conventions applied. In part as a result of MG Miller's call for strong, command-wide interrogation policies and in part as a result of a request for guidance coming up from the 519th at Abu Ghraib, on September 14, 2003, LTG Sanchez signed a memorandum authorizing a dozen interrogation techniques beyond Field Manual 34-52 – five beyond those approved for Guantanamo (see Appendix D).

MG Miller had indicated his model was approved only for Guantanamo. However, CJTF-7, using reasoning from the President's Memorandum of February 7, 2002, which addressed "unlawful combatants," believed additional, tougher measures were warranted because there were "unlawful combatants" mixed in with Enemy Prisoners of War and civilian and criminal detainees. The CJTF-7 Commander, on the advice of his Staff Judge Advocate, believed he had the inherent authority of the Commander in a Theater of War to promulgate such a policy and make determinations as to the categorization of detainees under the Geneva Conventions. CENTCOM viewed the CJTF-7 policy as unacceptably aggressive and on October 12, 2003 Commander CJTF-7 rescinded his September directive and disseminated methods only slightly stronger than those in Field Manual 34-52 (see Appendix D). The policy memos promulgated at the CJTF-7 level allowed for interpretation in several areas and did not adequately set forth the limits of interrogation techniques. The existence of confusing and inconsistent interrogation technique policies contributed to the belief that additional interrogation techniques were condoned.

DETENTION AND INTERROGATION OPERATIONS

From his experience in Guantanamo, MG Miller called for the military police and military intelligence soldiers to work cooperatively, with the military police "setting the conditions" for interrogations. This MP role included passive collection on detainees as well as supporting incentives recommended by the military interrogators. These collaborative procedures worked effectively in Guantanamo, particularly in light of the high ratio of approximately 1 to 1 of military police to mostly compliant detainees. However, in Iraq and particularly in Abu Ghraib the ratio of military police to repeatedly unruly detainees was significantly smaller, at one point 1 to about 75 at Abu Ghraib, making it difficult even to keep track of prisoners. Moreover, because Abu Ghraib was located in a combat zone, the military police were engaged in force protection of the complex as well as escorting convoys of supplies to and from the prison. Compounding these problems was the inadequacy of leadership, oversight and support needed in the face of such difficulties.

At various times, the U.S. conducted detention operations at approximately 17 sites in Iraq and 25 sites in Afghanistan, in addition to the strategic operation at Guantanamo. A cumulative total of 50,000 detainees have been in the custody of U.S. forces since November 2001, with a peak population of 11,000 in the month of March 2004.

In Iraq, there was not only a failure to plan for a major insurgency, but also to quickly and adequately adapt to the insurgency that followed after major combat operations. The October 2002 CENTCOM War Plan presupposed that relatively benign stability and security operations would precede a handover to Iraq's authorities. The contingencies contemplated in that plan included sabotage of oil production facilities and large numbers of refugees generated by communal strife.

Major combat operations were accomplished more swiftly than anticipated. Then began a period of occupation and an active and growing insurgency. Although the removal of Saddam Hussein was initially welcomed by the bulk of the population, the occupation became increasingly resented. Detention facilities soon held Iraqi and foreign terrorists as well as a mix of Enemy Prisoners of War, other security detainees, criminals and undoubtedly some accused as a result of factional rivalries. Of the 17 detention facilities in Iraq, the largest, Abu Ghraib, housed up to 7,000 detainees in October 2003, with a guard force of only about 90 personnel from the 800th Military Police Brigade. Abu Ghraib was seriously overcrowded, under-resourced, and under continual attack. Five U.S. soldiers died as a result of mortar attacks on Abu Ghraib. In July 2003, Abu Ghraib was mortared 25 times; on August 16, 2003, five detainees were killed and 67 wounded in a mortar attack. A mortar attack on April 20, 2004, killed 22 detainees.

Problems at Abu Ghraib are traceable in part to the nature and recent history of the military police and military intelligence units at Abu Ghraib. The 800th Military Police Brigade had one year of notice to plan for detention operations in Iraq. Original projections called for approximately 12 detention facilities in non-hostile, rear areas with a projection of 30,000 to 100,000 Enemy Prisoners of War. Though the 800th had planned a detention operations exercise for the summer of 2002, it was cancelled because of the disruption in soldier and unit availability resulting from the mobilization of Military Police Reserves following 9/11. Although its readiness was certified by U.S. Army Forces Command, actual deployment of the 800th Brigade to Iraq was chaotic. The "Time Phased Force Deployment List," which was the planned flow of forces to the theater of operations, was scrapped in favor of piecemeal unit deployment orders based on actual unit readiness and personnel strength. Equipment and troops regularly arrived out of planned sequence and rarely together. Improvisation was the order of the day. While some units overcame these difficulties, the 800th was among the lowest in priority and did not have the capability to overcome the shortfalls it confronted.

The 205th MI Brigade, deployed to support Combined Joint Task Force-7 (CJTF-7), normally provides the intelligence capability for a Corps Headquarters. However, it was insufficient to provide the kind of support needed by CJTF-7, especially with regard to interrogators and interpreters. Some additional units were mobilized to fill in the gaps, but while these MI units were more prepared than their military police counterparts, there were insufficient numbers of units available. Moreover, unit cohesion was lacking because elements of as many as six different units were assigned to the interrogation mission at Abu Ghraib. These problems were heightened by friction between military intelligence and military police personnel, including the brigade commanders themselves.

ABUSES

As of the date of this report, there were about 300 incidents of alleged detainee abuse across the Joint Operations Areas. Of the 155 completed investigations, 66 have resulted in a determination that detainees under the control of U.S. forces were abused. Dozens of non-judicial punishments have already been awarded. Others are in various stages of the military justice process.

Of the 66 already substantiated cases of abuse, eight occurred at Guantanamo, three in Afghanistan and 55 in Iraq. Only about one-third were related to interrogation, and two-thirds to other causes. There were five cases of detainee deaths as a result of abuse by U.S. personnel during interrogations. Many more died from natural causes and enemy mortar attacks. There are 23 cases of detainee deaths still under investigation; three in Afghanistan and 20 in Iraq. Twenty-eight of the abuse cases are alleged to include Special Operations Forces (SOF) and, of the 15 SOF cases that have been closed, 10 were determined to be unsubstantiated and five resulted in disciplinary action. The Jacoby review of SOF detention operations found a range of abuses and causes similar in scope and magnitude to those found among conventional forces.

The aberrant behavior on the night shift in Cell Block 1 at Abu Ghraib would have been avoided with proper training, leadership and oversight. Though acts of abuse occurred at a number of locations, those in Cell Block 1 have a unique nature fostered by the predilections of the non-commissioned officers in charge. Had these non-commissioned officers behaved more like those on the day shift, these acts, which one participant described as "just for the fun of it," would not have taken place.

Concerning the abuses at Abu Ghraib, the impact was magnified by the fact the shocking photographs were aired throughout the world in April 2004. Although CENT-COM had publicly addressed the abuses in a press release in January 2004, the photographs remained within the official criminal investigative process. Consequently, the highest levels of command and leadership in the Department of Defense were not adequately informed nor prepared to respond to the Congress and the American public when copies were released by the press.

POLICY AND COMMAND RESPONSIBILITIES

Interrogation policies with respect to Iraq, where the majority of the abuses occurred, were inadequate or deficient in some respects at three levels: Department of Defense, CENTCOM/CJTF-7, and Abu Ghraib Prison. Policies to guide the demands for actionable intelligence lagged behind battlefield needs. As already noted, the changes in DoD interrogation policies between December 2, 2002, and April 16, 2003, were an element contributing to uncertainties in the field as to which techniques were authorized.

Although specifically limited by the Secretary of Defense to Guantanamo, and requiring his personal approval (given in only two cases), the augmented techniques for Guantanamo migrated to Afghanistan and Iraq where they were neither limited nor safeguarded.

At the operational level, in the absence of specific guidance from CENTCOM, interrogators in Iraq relied on Field Manual 34-52 and on unauthorized techniques that had migrated from Afghanistan. On September 14, 2003, CJTF-7 signed the theater's first policy on interrogation, which contained elements of the approved Guantanamo policy and elements of the SOF policy (see Appendix D). Policies approved for use on al Qaeda and Taliban detainees, who were not afforded the protection of the Geneva Conventions, now applied to detainees who did fall under the Geneva Convention protections.

CENTCOM disapproved the September 14, 2003 policy, resulting in another policy signed on October 12, 2003, which essentially mirrored the outdated 1987 version of the FM 34-52 (see Appendix D). The 1987 version, however, authorized interrogators to control all aspects of the interrogation, "to include lighting and heating, as well as food, clothing, and shelter given to detainees." This was specifically left out of the current 1992 version. This clearly led to confusion on what practices were acceptable. We cannot be sure how much the number and severity of abuses would have been curtailed had there been early and consistent guidance from higher levels. Nonetheless, such guidance was needed and likely would have had a limiting effect.

At the tactical level we concur with the Jones/Fay investigation's conclusion that military intelligence personnel share responsibility for the abuses at Abu Ghraib with the military police soldiers cited in the Taguba investigation. The Jones/Fay Investigation found 44 alleged instances of abuse, some which were also considered by the Taguba report. A number of these cases involved MI personnel directing the actions of MP personnel. Yet it should be noted that of the 66 closed cases of detainee abuse in Guantanamo, Afghanistan and Iraq cited by the Naval Inspector General, only one-third were interrogation related.

The Panel concurs with the findings of the Taguba and Jones investigations that serious leadership problems in the 800th MP Brigade and 205th MI Brigade, to include the 320th MP Battalion Commander and the Director of the Joint Debriefing and Interrogation Center (JDIC), allowed the abuses at Abu Ghraib. The Panel endorses the disciplinary actions taken as a result of the Taguba Investigation. The Panel anticipates that the Chain of Command will take additional disciplinary action as a result of the referrals of the Jones/Fay investigation.

We believe LTG Sanchez should have taken stronger action in November when he realized the extent of the leadership problems at Abu Ghraib. His attempt to mentor BG Karpinski, though well-intended, was insufficient in a combat zone in the midst of a serious and growing insurgency. Although LTG Sanchez had more urgent tasks than dealing personally with command and resource deficiencies at Abu Ghraib, MG Wojdakowski and the staff should have seen that urgent demands were placed to higher headquarters for additional assets. We concur with the Jones findings that LTG Sanchez and MG Wojdakowski failed to ensure proper staff oversight of detention and interrogation operations.

We note, however, in terms of its responsibilities, CJTF-7 was never fully resourced to meet the size and complexity of its mission. The Joint Staff, CJTF-7 and CENTCOM took too long to finalize the Joint Manning Document (JMD). It was not finally approved until December 2003, six months into the insurgency. At one point, CJTF-7 had only 495 of the 1,400 personnel authorized. The command was burdened with additional complexities associated with its mission to support the Coalition Provisional Authority.

Once it became clear in the summer of 2003 that there was a major insurgency growing in Iraq, with the potential for capturing a large number of enemy combatants, senior leaders should have moved to meet the need for additional military police forces. Certainly by October and November when the fighting reached a new peak, commanders and staff from CJTF-7 all the way to CENTCOM to the Joint Chiefs of Staff should have known about and reacted to the serious limitations of the battalion of the 800th Military Police Brigade at Abu Ghraib. CENTCOM and the JCS should have at least considered adding forces to the detention/interrogation operation mission. It is the judgment of this panel that in the future, considering the sensitivity of this kind of mission, the OSD should assure itself that serious limitations in detention/interrogation missions do not occur.

Several options were available to Commander CENTCOM and above, including reallocation of U.S. Army assets already in the theater, Operational Control (OPCON) of other Service Military Police units in theater, and mobilization and deployment of additional forces from the continental United States. There is no evidence that any of the responsible senior officers considered any of these options. What could and should have been done more promptly is evidenced by the fact that the detention/interrogation operation in Iraq is now directed by a Major General reporting directly to the Commander, Multi-National Forces Iraq (MNFI). Increased units of Military Police, fully manned and more appropriately equipped, are performing the mission once assigned to a single under-strength, poorly trained, inadequately equipped and weakly-led brigade. In addition to the already cited leadership problems in the 800th MP Brigade, there were a series of tangled command relationships. These ranged from an unclear military intelligence chain of command, to the Tactical Control (TACON) relationship of the 800th with CJTF-7 which the Brigade Commander apparently did not adequately understand, and the confusing and unusual assignment of MI and MP responsibilities at Abu Ghraib. The failure to react appropriately to the October 2003 ICRC report, following its two visits to Abu Ghraib, is indicative of the weakness of the leadership at Abu Ghraib. These unsatisfactory relationships were present neither at Guantanamo nor in Afghanistan.

RECOMMENDATIONS

Department of Defense reform efforts are underway and the Panel commends these efforts. They are discussed in more detail in the body of this report. The Office of the Secretary of Defense, the Joint Chiefs of Staff and the Military Services are conducting comprehensive reviews on how military operations have changed since the end of the Cold War. The Military Services now recognize the problems and are studying force compositions, training, doctrine, responsibilities and active duty/reserve and guard/contractor mixes which must be adjusted to ensure we are better prepared to succeed in the war on terrorism. As an example, the Army is currently planning and developing 27 additional MP companies.

The specific recommendations of the Independent Panel are contained in the Recommendations section, beginning on page 87.

CONCLUSION

The vast majority of detainees in Guantanamo, Afghanistan and Iraq were treated appropriately, and the great bulk of detention operations were conducted in compliance with U.S. policy and directives. They yielded significant amounts of actionable intelligence for dealing with the insurgency in Iraq and strategic intelligence of value in the Global War on Terror. For example, much of the information in the recently released 9/11 Commission's report, on the planning and execution of the attacks on the World Trade Center and Pentagon, came from interrogation of detainees at Guantanamo and elsewhere.

Justice Sandra Day O'Connor, writing for the majority of the Supreme Court of the United States in *Hamdi v. Rumsfeld* on June 28, 2004, pointed out that "The purpose of detention is to prevent captured individuals from returning to the field of battle and taking up arms once again." But detention operations also serve the key purpose of intelligence gathering. These are not competing interests but appropriate objectives which the United States may lawfully pursue.

We should emphasize that tens of thousands of men and women in uniform strive every day under austere and dangerous conditions to secure our freedom and the freedom of others. By historical standards, they rate as some of the best trained, disciplined and professional service men and women in our nation's history.

While any abuse is too much, we see signs that the Department of Defense is now on the path to dealing with the personal and professional failures and remedying the underlying causes of these abuses. We expect any potential future incidents of abuse will similarly be discovered and reported out of the same sense of personal honor and duty that characterized many of those who went out of their way to do so in most of these cases. The damage these incidents have done to U.S. policy, to the image of the U.S. among populations whose support we need in the Global War on Terror and to the morale of our armed forces, must not be repeated.

INTRODUCTION – CHARTER AND METHODOLOGY

The Secretary of Defense chartered the Independent Panel on May 12, 2004, to review Department of Defense (DoD) Detention Operations (see Appendix A). In his memorandum, the Secretary tasked the Independent Panel to review Department of Defense investigations on detention operations whether completed or ongoing, as well as other materials and information the Panel deemed relevant to its review. The Secretary asked for the Panel's independent advice in highlighting the issues considered most important for his attention. He asked for the Panel's views on the causes and contributing factors to problems in detainee operations and what corrective measures would be required.

Completed investigations reviewed by the Panel include the following:

- Joint Staff External Review of Intelligence Operations at Guantanamo Bay, Cuba, September 28, 2002 (Custer Report)
- Joint Task Force Guantanamo assistance visit to Iraq to assess intelligence operations, September 5, 2003 (Miller Report)
- Army Provost Marshal General assessment of detention and corrections operations in Iraq, November 6, 2003 (Ryder Report)
- Administrative investigation under Army Regulation 15-6 (AR 15-6) regarding Abu Ghraib, June 8, 2004 (Taguba Report)
- Army Inspector General assessment of doctrine and training for detention operations, July 23, 2004 (Mikolashek Report)
- The Fay investigation of activities of military personnel at Abu Ghraib and related LTG Jones investigation under the direction of GEN Kern, August 16, 2004
- Naval Inspector General's review of detention procedures at Guantanamo Bay, Cuba and the Naval Consolidated Brig, Charleston, South Carolina (A briefing was presented to the Secretary of Defense on May 8, 2004.)
- Naval Inspector General's review of DoD worldwide interrogation operations, due for release on September 9, 2004
- Special Inspection of Detainee Operations and Facilities in the Combined Forces Command-Afghanistan AOR (CFC-A), June 26, 2004 (Jacoby Report).
- Administrative Investigation of Alleged Detainee Abuse by the Combined Joint Special Operations Task Force – Arabian Peninsula (Formica Report) Due for release in August, 2004. Assessment not yet completed and not reviewed by the Independent Panel
- Army Reserve Command Inspector General Assessment of Military Intelligence and Military Police Training (due for release in December 2004)

Panel interviews of selected individuals either in person or via video-teleconference:

June 14, 2004:

- MG Keith Dayton, Director, Iraq Survey Group (ISG), Baghdad, Iraq
- MG Geoffrey Miller, Director, Detainee Operations, CJTF-7, Baghdad, Iraq
- Hon Donald Rumsfeld, Secretary of Defense
- Hon Steve Cambone, Under Secretary of Defense for Intelligence
- MG Walter Wojdakowski, Deputy Commanding General, V Corps, USAREUR and 7th Army
- MG Donald Ryder, Provost Marshal, U.S. Army/Commanding General, U.S. Army Criminal Investigation Command, Washington, D.C.
- COL Thomas Pappas, Commander, 205th Military Intelligence Brigade, V Corps, USAREUR and 7th Army

June 24, 2004:

- LTG David McKiernan, Commanding General, Third U.S. Army, U.S. Army Forces Central Command, Coalition Forces Land Component Command
- MG Barbara Fast, CJTF-7 C-2, Director for Intelligence, Baghdad, Iraq

- MG Geoffrey Miller, Director, Detainee Operations, CJTF-7, Baghdad, Iraq
- LTG Ricardo Sanchez, Commanding General, CJTF-7, Commanding General, V Corps, USAREUR and 7th Army in Iraq
- Mr. Daniel Dell'Orto, Principal Deputy General Counsel, DoD
- LTG Keith Alexander, G-2, U.S. Army, Washington, D.C.
- LTG William Boykin, Deputy Undersecretary of Defense for Intelligence, Intelligence and Warfighting Support, Office of the Under Secretary of Defense for Intelligence
- Hon Douglas Feith, Under Secretary of Defense for Policy

July 8, 2004:

- COL Marc Warren, Senior Legal Advisor to LTG Sanchez, Iraq
- BG Janis Karpinski, Commander (TPU), 800th Military Police Brigade, Uniondale, NY
- Hon Paul Wolfowitz, Deputy Secretary of Defense
- Hon William Haynes, General Counsel DoD
- Mr. John Rizzo, CIA Senior Deputy General Counsel
- GEN John Abizaid, Commander, U.S. Central Command
- MG George Fay, Deputy to the Army G2, Washington, D.C.
- VADM Albert Church III, Naval Inspector General

July 22, 2004:

- Hon Donald Rumsfeld, Secretary of Defense

The Panel did not conduct a case-by-case review of individual abuse cases. This task has been accomplished by those professionals conducting criminal and commander-directed investigations. Many of these investigations are still on-going. The Panel did review the various completed and on-going reports covering the causes for the abuse. Each of these inquiries or inspections defined abuse, categorized the abuses, and analyzed the abuses in conformity with the appointing authorities' guidance, but the methodologies do not parallel each other in all respects. The Panel concludes, based on our review of other reports to date and our own efforts that causes for abuse have been adequately examined.

The Panel met on July 22 and again on August 16 to discuss progress of the report. Panel members also reviewed sections and versions of the report through July and mid-August.

An effective, timely response to our requests for other documents and support was invariably forthcoming, due largely to the efforts of the DoD Detainee Task Force. We conducted reviews of multiple classified and unclassified documents generated by DoD and other sources.

Our staff has met and communicated with representatives of the International Committee of the Red Cross and with the Human Rights Executive Directors' Coordinating Group.

It should be noted that information provided to the Panel was that available as of mid-August 2004. If additional information becomes available, the Panel's judgments might be revised.

THE CHANGING THREAT

The date September 11, 2001, marked an historic juncture in America's collective sense of security. On that day our presumption of invulnerability was irretrievably shattered. Over the last decade, the military has been called upon to establish and maintain the peace in Bosnia and Kosovo, eject the Taliban from Afghanistan, defeat the Iraqi Army, and fight ongoing insurgencies in Iraq and Afghanistan. Elsewhere it has been called upon to confront geographically dispersed terrorists who would threaten America's right to political sovereignty and our right to live free of fear.

In waging the Global War on Terror, the military confronts a far wider range of threats. In Iraq and Afghanistan, U.S. forces are fighting diverse enemies with varying ideologies, goals and capabilities. American soldiers and their coalition partners have defeated the armored divisions of the Republican Guard, but are still under attack by forces using automatic rifles, rocket-propelled grenades, roadside bombs and surface-to-air missiles. We are not simply fighting the remnants of dying regimes or opponents of the local governments and coalition forces assisting those governments, but multiple enemies including indigenous and international terrorists. This complex operational environment requires soldiers capable of conducting traditional stability operations associated with peacekeeping tasks one moment and fighting force-on-force engagements normally associated with war-fighting the next moment.

Warfare under the conditions described inevitably generates detainees – enemy combatants, opportunists, trouble-makers, saboteurs, common criminals, former regime officials and some innocents as well. These people must be carefully but humanely processed to sort out those who remain dangerous or possess militarily-valuable intelligence. Such processing presents extraordinarily formidable logistical, administrative, security and legal problems completely apart from the technical obstacles posed by communicating with prisoners in another language and extracting actionable intelligence from them in timely fashion. These activities, called detention operations, are a vital part of an expeditionary army's responsibility, but they depend upon training, skills, and attributes not normally associated with soldiers in combat units.

Military interrogators and military police, assisted by front line tactical units, found themselves engaged in detention operations with detention procedures still steeped in the methods of World War II and the Cold War, when those we expected to capture on the battlefield were generally a homogenous group of enemy soldiers. Yet this is a new form of war, not at all like Desert Storm nor even analogous to Vietnam or Korea.

General Abizaid himself best articulated the current nature of combat in testimony before the U.S. Senate Armed Services Committee on May 19, 2004:

> Our enemies are in a unique position, and they are a unique brand of ideological extremists whose vision of the world is best summed up by how the Taliban ran Afghanistan. If they can outlast us in Afghanistan and undermine the legitimate government there, they'll once again fill up the seats at the soccer stadium and force people to watch executions. If, in Iraq, the culture of intimidation practiced by our enemies is allowed to win, the mass graves will fill again. Our enemies kill without remorse, they challenge our will through the careful manipulation of

propaganda and information, they seek safe havens in order to develop weapons of mass destruction that they will use against us when they are ready. Their targets are not Kabul and Baghdad, but places like Madrid and London and New York. While we can't be defeated militarily, we're not going to win this thing militarily alone. . . . As we fight this most unconventional war of this new century, we must be patient and courageous.

In Iraq the U.S. commanders were slow to recognize and adapt to the insurgency that erupted in the summer and fall of 2003. Military police and interrogators who had previous experience in the Balkans, Guantanamo and Afghanistan found themselves, along with increasing numbers of less-experienced troops, in the midst of detention operations in Iraq the likes of which the Department of Defense had not foreseen. As Combined Joint Task Force-7 (CJTF-7) began detaining thousands of Iraqis suspected of involvement in or having knowledge of the insurgency, the problem quickly surpassed the capacity of the staff to deal with and the wherewithal to contain it.

Line units conducting raids found themselves seizing specifically targeted persons, so designated by military intelligence; but, lacking interrogators and interpreters to make precise distinctions in an alien culture and hostile neighborhoods, they reverted to rounding up any and all suspicious-looking persons – all too often including women and children. The flood of incoming detainees contrasted sharply with the trickle of released individuals. Processing was overwhelmed. Some detainees at Abu Ghraib had been held 90 days before being interrogated for the first time.

Many interrogators, already in short supply from major reductions during the post-Cold War drawdown, by this time, were on their second or third combat tour. Unit cohesion and morale were largely absent as under-strength companies and battalions from across the United States and Germany were deployed piecemeal and stitched together in a losing race to keep up with the rapid influx of vast numbers of detainees.

As the insurgency reached an initial peak in the fall of 2003, many military policemen from the Reserves who had been activated shortly after September 11, 2001, had reached the mandatory two-year limit on their mobilization time. Consequently, the ranks of soldiers having custody of detainees in Iraq fell to about half strength as MPs were ordered home by higher headquarters.

Some individuals seized the opportunity provided by this environment to give vent to latent sadistic urges. Moreover, many well-intentioned professionals, attempting to resolve the inherent moral conflict between using harsh techniques to gain information to save lives and treating detainees humanely, found themselves in uncharted ethical ground, with frequently changing guidance from above. Some stepped over the line of humane treatment accidentally; some did so knowingly. Some of the abusers believed other governmental agencies were conducting interrogations using harsher techniques than allowed by the Army Field Manual 34–52, a perception leading to the belief that such methods were condoned. In nearly 10 percent of the cases of alleged abuse, the chain of command ignored reports of those allegations. More than once a commander was complicit.

The requirements for successful detainee operations following major combat operations were known by U.S. forces in Iraq. After Operations Enduring Freedom and earlier phases of Iraqi Freedom, several lessons learned were captured in official reviews and were available on line to any authorized military user. These lessons included the need for doctrine tailored to enable police and interrogators to work together effectively; the need for keeping MP and MI units manned at levels sufficient to the task; and the need for MP and MI units to belong to the same tactical command. However, there is no evidence that those responsible for planning and executing detainee operations, in the phase of the Iraq campaign following the major combat operations, availed themselves of these "lessons learned" in a timely fashion.

Judged in a broader context, U.S. detention operations were both traditional and new. They were traditional in that detainee operations were a part of all past conflicts. They were new in that the Global War on Terror and the insurgency we are facing in Iraq present a much more complicated detainee population.

Many of America's enemies, including those in Iraq and Afghanistan, have the ability to conduct this new kind of warfare, often referred to as "asymmetric" warfare. Asymmetric warfare can be viewed as attempts to circumvent or undermine a superior, conventional strength, while exploiting its weaknesses using methods the superior force neither can defeat nor resort to itself. Small unconventional forces can violate a state's security without any state support or affiliation whatsoever. For this reason, many terms in the orthodox lexicon of war – e.g., state sovereignty, national borders, uniformed combatants, declarations of war, and even war itself, are not terms terrorists acknowledge.

Today, the power to wage war can rest in the hands of a few dozen highly motivated people with cell phones and access to the Internet. Going beyond simply terrorizing individual civilians, certain insurgent and terrorist organizations represent a higher level of threat, characterized by an ability and willingness to violate the political sovereignty and territorial integrity of sovereign nations.

Essential to defeating terrorist and insurgent threats is the ability to locate cells, kill or detain key leaders, and interdict operational and financial networks. However, the smallness and wide dispersal of these enemy assets make it problematic to focus on signal and imagery intelligence as we did in the Cold War, Desert Storm, and the first phase of Operation Iraqi Freedom. The ability of terrorists and insurgents to blend into the civilian population further decreases their vulnerability to signal and imagery intelligence. Thus, information gained from human sources, whether by spying or interrogation, is essential in narrowing the field upon which other intelligence gathering resources may be applied. In sum, human intelligence is absolutely necessary, not just to fill these gaps in information derived from other sources, but also to provide clues and leads for the other sources to exploit.

Military police functions must also adapt to this new kind of warfare. In addition to organizing more units capable of handling theater-level detention operations, we must also organize those units, so they are able to deal with the heightened threat environment. In this new form of warfare, the distinction between front and rear becomes more fluid. All forces must continuously prepare for combat operations.

THE POLICY PROMULGATION PROCESS

Although there were a number of contributing causes for detainee abuses, policy processes were inadequate or deficient in certain respects at various levels: Department of Defense (DoD), CENTCOM, Coalition Forces Land Component Command (CFLCC),

CJTF-7, and the individual holding facility or prison. In pursuing the question of the extent to which policy processes at the DoD or national level contributed to abuses, it is important to begin with policy development as individuals in Afghanistan were first being detained in November 2001. The first detainees arrived at Guantanamo in January 2002.

In early 2002, a debate was ongoing in Washington on the application of treaties and laws to al Qaeda and Taliban. The Department of Justice, Office of Legal Counsel (OLC) advised DoD General Counsel and the Counsel to the President that, among other things:

- Neither the Federal War Crimes Act nor the Geneva Conventions would apply to the detention conditions of al Qaeda prisoners,
- The President had the authority to suspend the United States treaty obligations applying to Afghanistan for the duration of the conflict should he determine Afghanistan to be a failed state,
- The President could find that the Taliban did not qualify for Enemy Prisoner of War (EPW) status under Geneva Convention III.

The Attorney General and the Counsel to the President, in part relying on the opinions of OLC, advised the President to determine the Geneva Conventions did not apply to the conflict with al Qaeda and the Taliban. The Panel understands DoD General Counsel's position was consistent with the Attorney General's and the Counsel to the President's position. Earlier, the Department of State had argued that the Geneva Conventions in their traditional application provided a sufficiently robust legal construct under which the Global War on Terror could effectively be waged.

The Legal Advisor to the Chairman, Joint Chiefs of Staff and many service lawyers agreed with the State Department's initial position. They were concerned that to conclude otherwise would be inconsistent with past practice and policy, jeopardize the United States armed forces personnel, and undermine the United States military culture which is based on a strict adherence to the law of war. At the February 4, 2002, National Security Council meeting to decide this issue, the Department of State, the Department of Defense, and the Chairman of the Joint Chiefs of Staff were in agreement that all detainees would get the treatment they are (or would be) entitled to under the Geneva Conventions.

On February 7, 2002, the President issued his decision memorandum (see Appendix B). The memorandum stated the Geneva Conventions did not apply to al Qaeda and therefore they were not entitled to prisoner of war status. It also stated the Geneva Conventions did apply to the Taliban but the Taliban combatants were not entitled to prisoner of war status as a result of their failure to conduct themselves in accordance with the provisions of the Geneva Conventions. The President's memorandum also stated: "As a matter of policy, United States Armed Forces shall continue to treat detainees humanely and, to the extent appropriate and consistent with military necessity, in a manner consistent with the principles of Geneva."

Regarding the applicability of the Convention Against Torture and Other Cruel Inhumane or Degrading Treatment, the OLC opined on August 1, 2002, that interrogation methods that comply with the relevant domestic law do not violate the Convention. It held that only the most extreme acts, that were specifically intended to inflict severe pain and torture, would be in violation; lesser acts might be "cruel, inhumane, or degrading" but would not violate the Convention Against Torture or domestic statutes. The OLC memorandum went on to say, as Commander in Chief exercising his wartime powers, the President could even authorize torture, if he so decided.

Reacting to tenacious resistance by some detainees to existing interrogation methods, which were essentially limited to those in Army Field Manual 34-52 (see Appendix E), Guantanamo authorities in October 2002 requested approval of strengthened counter-interrogation techniques to increase the intelligence yield from interrogations. This request was accompanied by a recommended tiered list of techniques, with the proviso that the harsher Category III methods (see Appendix E) could be used only on "exceptionally resistant detainees" and with approval by higher headquarters.

This Guantanamo initiative resulted in a December 2, 2002, decision by the Secretary of Defense authorizing, "as a matter of policy," the use of Categories I and II and only one technique in Category III: mild, non-injurious physical contact (see Appendix E). As a result of concern by the Navy General Counsel, the Secretary of Defense rescinded his December approval of all Category II techniques plus the one from Category III on January 15, 2003. This essentially returned interrogation techniques to FM 34-52 guidance. He also stated if any of the methods from Categories II and III were deemed warranted, permission for their use should be requested from him (see Appendix E).

The Secretary of Defense directed the DoD General Counsel to establish a working group to study interrogation techniques. The working group was headed by Air Force General Counsel Mary Walker and included wide membership from across the military, legal and intelligence communities. The working group also relied heavily on the OLC. The working group reviewed 35 techniques, and after a very expansive debate, ultimately recommended 24 to the Secretary of Defense. The study led to the Secretary's promulgation on April 16, 2003, of the list of approved techniques. His memorandum emphasized appropriate safeguards should be in place and, further, *"Use of these techniques is limited to interrogations of unlawful combatants held at Guantanamo Bay, Cuba."* He also stipulated that four of the techniques should be used only in case of military necessity and that he should be so notified in advance. If additional techniques were deemed essential, they should be requested in writing, with "recommended safeguards and rationale for applying with an identified detainee."

In the initial development of these Secretary of Defense policies, the legal resources of the Services' Judge Advocates and General Counsels were not utilized to their fullest potential. Had the Secretary of Defense had the benefit of a wider range of legal opinions and a more robust debate regarding detainee policies and operations, his policy of April 16, 2003, might well have been developed and issued in early December 2002. This could have avoided the policy changes which characterized the December 2, 2002, to April 16, 2003, period.

It is clear that pressure for additional intelligence and the more aggressive methods sanctioned by the Secretary of Defense memorandum resulted in stronger interrogation techniques. They did contribute to a belief that stronger interrogation methods were needed and appropriate in their treatment of detainees. At Guantanamo, the interrogators used those additional techniques with only two detainees, gaining important and time-urgent information in the process.

In Afghanistan, from the war's inception through the end of 2002, all forces used FM 34-52 as a baseline for interrogation techniques. Nonetheless, more aggressive interrogation of detainees appears to have been ongoing. On January 24, 2003, in response to a data call from the Joint Staff to facilitate the Secretary of Defense-directed Working Group efforts, the Commander Joint Task Force-180 forwarded a list of techniques being used in Afghanistan, including some not explicitly set out in FM 34-52. These techniques were included in a Special Operations Forces (SOF) Standard Operating Procedures document published in February 2003. The 519th Military Intelligence Battalion, a Company of which was later sent to Iraq, assisted in interrogations in support of SOF and was fully aware of their interrogation techniques.

In Iraq, the operational order from CENTCOM provided the standard FM 34-52 interrogation procedures would be used. Given the greatly different situations in Afghanistan and Iraq, it is not surprising there were differing CENTCOM policies for the two countries. In light of ongoing hostilities that monopolized commanders' attention in Iraq, it is also not unexpected that the detainee issues were not given a higher priority.

Interrogators and lists of techniques circulated from Guantanamo and Afghanistan to Iraq. During July and August 2003, a Company of the 519th MI Battalion was sent to the Abu Ghraib detention facility to conduct interrogation operations. Absent guidance other than FM 34-52, the officer in charge prepared draft interrogation guidelines that were a near copy of the Standard Operating Procedure created by SOF. It is important to note that techniques effective under carefully controlled conditions at Guantanamo became far more problematic when they migrated and were not adequately safeguarded.

In August 2003, MG Geoffrey Miller arrived to conduct an assessment of DoD counterterrorism interrogation and detention operations in Iraq. He was to discuss current theater ability to exploit internees rapidly for actionable intelligence. He brought to Iraq the Secretary of Defense's April 16, 2003, policy guidelines for Guantanamo – which he reportedly gave to CJTF-7 as a potential model – recommending a commandwide policy be established. He noted, however, the Geneva Conventions did apply to Iraq. In addition to these various printed sources, there was also a store of common lore and practice within the interrogator community circulating through Guantanamo, Afghanistan and elsewhere.

At the operational level, in the absence of more specific guidance from CENTCOM, interrogators in Iraq relied on FM 34-52 and on unauthorized techniques that had migrated from Afghanistan. On September 14, 2003, Commander CJTF-7 signed the theater's first policy on interrogation which contained elements of the approved Guantanamo policy and elements of the SOF policy. Policies approved for use on al Qaeda and Taliban detainees who were not afforded the protection of EPW status under the Geneva Conventions now applied to detainees who did fall under the Geneva Convention protections. CENTCOM disapproved the September 14, 2003, policy resulting in another policy signed on October 12, 2003, which essentially mirrored the outdated 1987 version of the FM 34-52. The 1987 version, however, authorized interrogators to control all aspects of the interrogation, "to include lighting and heating, as well as food, clothing, and shelter given to detainees." This was specifically left out of the 1992 version, which is currently in use. This clearly led to confusion on what practices were acceptable. We cannot be sure how much the number and severity of abuses would have been curtailed had there been early and consistent guidance from higher levels. Nonetheless, such guidance was needed and likely would have had a limiting effect.

At Abu Ghraib, the Jones/Fay investigation concluded that MI professionals at the prison level shared a "major part of the culpability" for the abuses. Some of the abuses occurred during interrogation. As these interrogation techniques exceeded parameters of FM 34-52, no training had been developed. Absent training, the interrogators used their own initiative to implement the new techniques. To what extent the same situation existed at other prisons is unclear, but the widespread nature of abuses warrants an assumption that at least the understanding of interrogations policies was inadequate. A host of other possible contributing factors, such as training, leadership, and the generally chaotic situation in the prisons, are addressed elsewhere in this report.

PUBLIC RELEASE OF ABUSE PHOTOS

In any large bureaucracy, good news travels up the chain of command quickly; bad news generally does not. In the case of the abuse photos from Abu Ghraib, concerns about command influence on an ongoing investigation may have impeded notification to senior officials.

Chronology of Events

On January 13, 2004, SPC Darby gave Army criminal investigators a copy of a CD containing abuse photos he had taken from SPC Graner's computer. CJTF-7, CENT-COM, the Chairman of the Joint Chiefs of Staff and the Secretary of Defense were all informed of the issue. LTG Sanchez promptly asked for an outside investigation, and MG Taguba was appointed as the investigating officer. The officials who saw the photos on January 14, 2004, not realizing their likely significance, did not recommend the photos be shown to more senior officials. A CENTCOM press release in Baghdad on January 16, 2004, announced there was an ongoing investigation into reported incidents of detainee abuse at a Coalition Forces detention facility.

An interim report of the investigation was provided to CJTF-7 and CENTCOM commanders in mid-March 2004. It is unclear whether they saw the Abu Ghraib photos, but their impact was not appreciated by either of these officers or their staff officers who may have seen the photographs, as indicated by the failure to transmit them in a timely fashion to more senior officials. When LTG Sanchez received the Taguba report, he immediately requested an investigation into the possible involvement of military intelligence personnel. He told the panel that he did not request the photos be disseminated beyond the criminal investigative process because commanders are prohibited from interfering with, or influencing, active investigations. In mid-April, LTG McKiernan, the appointing official, reported the investigative results through his chain of command to the Department of the Army, the Army Judge Advocate General, and the U.S. Army Reserve Command. LTG McKiernan advised the panel that he did not send a copy of the report to the Secretary of Defense, but forwarded it through his chain of command. Again the reluctance to move bad news farther up the chain of command probably was a factor impeding notification of the Secretary of Defense.

Given this situation, GEN Richard Myers, the Chairman of the Joint Chiefs of Staff, was unprepared in April 2004 when he learned the photos of detainee abuse were to be aired in a CBS broadcast. The planned release coincided with particularly intense fighting by Coalition forces in Fallujah and Najaf. After a discussion with GEN Abizaid, GEN Myers asked CBS to delay the broadcast out of concern that the lives of the Coalition soldiers and the hostages in Iraq would be further endangered. The story of the abuse itself was already public. Nonetheless, both GEN Abizaid and GEN Myers understood the pictures would have an especially explosive impact around the world.

Informing Senior Officials

Given the magnitude of this problem, the Secretary of Defense and other senior DoD officials need a more effective information pipeline to inform them of high-profile incidents which may have a significant adverse impact on DoD operations. Had such a pipeline existed, it could have provided an accessible and efficient tool for field commanders to apprise higher headquarters, the Joint Chiefs of Staff, and the Office of the Secretary of Defense, of actual or developing situations which might hinder, impede, or undermine U.S. operations and initiatives. Such a system could have equipped senior spokesmen with the known facts of the situation from all DoD elements involved. Finally, it would have allowed for senior official preparation and Congressional notification.

Such a procedure would make it possible for a field-level command or staff agency to alert others of the situation and forward the information to senior officials. This would not have been an unprecedented occurrence. For example, in December 2002, concerned Naval Criminal Investigative Service agents drew attention to the potential for abuse at Guantanamo. Those individuals had direct access to the highest levels of leadership and were able to get that information to senior levels without encumbrance. While a corresponding flow of information might not have prevented the abuses from occurring, the Office of the Secretary of Defense would have been alerted to a festering issue, allowing for an early and appropriate response.

Another example is the Air Force Executive Issues Team. This office has fulfilled the special information pipeline function for the Air Force since February 1998. The team chief and team members are highly trained and experienced field grade officers drawn from a variety of duty assignments. The team members have access to information flow across all levels of command and staff and are continually engaging and building contacts to facilitate the information flow. The information flow to the team runs parallel and complementary to standard reporting channels in order to avoid bypassing the chain of command yet ensures a rapid and direct flow of relevant information to Air Force Headquarters.

A proper, transparent posture in getting the facts and fixing the problem would have better enabled the DoD to deal with the damage to the mission of the U.S. in the region and to the reputation of the U.S. military.

COMMAND RESPONSIBILITIES

Although the most egregious instances of detainee abuse were caused by the aberrant behavior of a limited number of soldiers and the predilections of the non-commissioned officers on the night shift of Tier 1 at Abu Ghraib, the Independent Panel finds that commanding officers and their staffs at various levels failed in their duties and that such failures contributed directly or indirectly to detainee abuse. Commanders are responsible for all their units do or fail to do, and should be held accountable for their action or inaction. Command failures were compounded by poor advice provided by staff officers with responsibility for overseeing battlefield functions related to detention and interrogation operations. Military and civilian leaders at the Department of Defense share this burden of responsibility.

Commanders

The Panel finds that the weak and ineffectual leadership of the Commanding General of the 800th MP Brigade and the Commanding Officer of the 205th MI Brigade allowed the abuses at Abu Ghraib. There were serious lapses of leadership in both units from junior non-commissioned officers to battalion and brigade levels. The commanders of both brigades either knew, or should have known, abuses were taking place and taken measures to prevent them. The Panel finds no evidence that organizations above the 800th MP Brigade-or the 205th MI Brigade-level were directly involved in the incidents at Abu Ghraib. Accordingly, the Panel concurs in the judgment and recommendations of MG Taguba, MG Fay, LTG Jones, LTG Sanchez, LTG McKiernan, General Abizaid and General Kern regarding the commanders of these two units. The Panel expects disciplinary action may be forthcoming.

The Independent Panel concurs with the findings of MG Taguba regarding the Director of the Joint Interrogation and Debriefing Center (JIDC) at Abu Ghraib. Specifically, the Panel notes that MG Taguba concluded that the Director, JIDC made material misrepresentations to MG Taguba's investigating team. The panel finds that he failed to properly train and control his soldiers and failed to ensure prisoners were afforded the protections under the relevant Geneva Conventions. The Panel concurs with MG Taguba's recommendation that he be relieved for cause and given a letter of reprimand and notes that disciplinary action may be pending against this officer.

The Independent Panel concurs with the findings of MG Taguba regarding the Commander of the 320th MP Battalion at Abu Ghraib. Specifically, the Panel finds that he failed to ensure that his subordinates were properly trained and supervised and that he failed to establish and enforce basic soldier standards, proficiency and accountability. He was not able to organize tasks to accomplish his mission in an appropriate manner. By not communicating standards, policies and plans to soldiers, he conveyed a sense of tacit approval of abusive behavior towards prisoners and a lax and dysfunctional command climate took hold. The Panel concurs with MG Taguba's recommendation that he be relieved from command, be given a General Officer Memorandum of reprimand, and be removed from the Colonel/O-6 promotion list.

The Independent Panel finds that BG Karpinski's leadership failures helped set the conditions at the prison which led to the abuses, including her failure to establish appropriate standard operating procedures (SOPs) and to ensure the relevant Geneva Conventions protections were afforded to prisoners, as well as her failure to take appropriate actions regarding ineffective commanders and staff officers. The Panel notes the conclusion of MG Taguba that she made material misrepresentations to his investigating team regarding the frequency of her visits to Abu Ghraib. The Panel concurs with MG Taguba's recommendation that BG Karpinski be relieved of command and given a General Officer Letter of Reprimand.

Although LTG Sanchez had tasks more urgent than dealing personally with command and resource deficiencies and allegations of abuse at Abu Ghraib, he should have ensured his staff dealt with the command and resource problems. He should have assured that urgent demands were placed for appropriate support and resources through Coalition Forces Land Component Command (CFLCC) and CENTCOM to the Joint Chiefs of Staff. He was responsible for establishing the confused command relationship at the Abu Ghraib prison. There was no clear delineation of command responsibilities between the 320th MP Battalion and the 205th MI Brigade. The situation was exacerbated by CJTF-7 (Fragmentary Order (FRAGO) 1108 issued on November 19, 2003, that appointed the commander of the 205th MI Brigade as the base commander for Abu Ghraib, including responsibility for the support of all MPs assigned to the prison. In addition to being contrary to existing doctrine, there is no evidence the details of this command relationship were effectively coordinated or implemented by the leaders at Abu Ghraib. The unclear chain of command established by CJTF-7, combined with the poor leadership and lack of supervision, contributed to the atmosphere at Abu Ghraib that allowed the abuses to take place.

The unclear command structure at Abu Ghraib was further exacerbated by the confused command relationship up the chain. The 800th MP Brigade was initially assigned to the Central Command's Combined Forces Land Component Commander (CFLCC) during the major combat phase of Operation Iraqi Freedom. When CFLCC left the theater and returned to Fort McPherson Georgia, CENTCOM established Combined Joint Task Force-Seven (CJTF-7). While the 800th MP Brigade remained assigned to CFLCC, it essentially worked for CJTF-7. LTG Sanchez delegated responsibility for detention operations to his Deputy, MG Wojdakowski. At the same time, intelligence personnel at Abu Ghraib reported through the CJTF-7 C-2, Director for Intelligence. These arrangements had the damaging result that no single individual was responsible for overseeing operations at the prison.

The Panel endorses the disciplinary actions already taken, although we believe LTG Sanchez should have taken more forceful action in November when he fully comprehended the depth of the leadership problems at Abu Ghraib. His apparent attempt to mentor BG Karpinski, though well-intended, was insufficient in a combat zone in the midst of a serious and growing insurgency.

The creation of the Joint Interrogation and Debriefing Center (JIDC) at Abu Ghraib was not an unusual organizational approach. The problem is, as the Army Inspector General assessment revealed, joint doctrine for the conduct of interrogation operations contains inconsistent guidance, particularly with regard to addressing the issue of the appropriate command relationships governing the operation of such organizations as a JIDC. Based on the findings of the Fay, Jones and Church investigations, SOUTHCOM and CENTCOM were able to develop effective command relationships for such centers at Guantanamo and in Afghanistan, but CENTCOM and CJTF-7 failed to do so for the JIDC at Abu Ghraib.

Staff Officers

While staff officers have no command responsibilities, they are responsible for providing oversight, advice and counsel to their commanders. Staff oversight of detention and interrogation operations for CJTF-7 was dispersed among the principal and special staff. The lack of one person on the staff to oversee detention operations and facilities complicated effective and efficient coordination among the staff.

The Panel finds the following:

- The CJTF-7 Deputy Commander failed to initiate action to request additional military police for detention operations after it became clear that there were insufficient assets in Iraq.
- The CJTF-7 C-2, Director for Intelligence failed to advise the commander properly on directives and policies needed for the operation of the JIDC, for interrogation techniques and for appropriately monitoring the activities of Other Government Agencies (OGAs) within the Joint Area of Operations.
- The CJTF-7 Staff Judge Advocate failed to initiate an appropriate response to the November 2003 ICRC report on the conditions at Abu Ghraib.

Failure of the Combatant Command to Adjust the Plan

Once it became clear in July 2003 there was a major insurgency growing in Iraq and the relatively benign environment projected for Iraq was not materializing, senior leaders should have adjusted the plan from what had been assumed to be a stability operation and a benign handoff of detention operations to the Iraqis. If commanders and staffs at the operational level had been more adaptive in the face of changing conditions, a different approach to detention operations could have been developed by October 2003, as difficulties with the basic plan were readily apparent by that time. Responsible leaders who could have set in motion the development of a more effective alternative course of action extend up the command chain (and staff), to include the Director for Operations, Combined Joint Task Force 7 (CJTF-7); Deputy Commanding General, CJTF-7; Commander CJTF-7; Deputy Commander for Support, CFLCC; Commander, CFLCC; Director for Operations, Central Command (CENTCOM); Commander, CENTCOM; Director for Operations, Joint Staff; the Chairman of the Joint Chiefs of Staff; and the Office of the Secretary of Defense. In most cases these were errors of omission, but they were errors that should not go unnoted.

There was ample evidence in both Joint and Army lessons learned that planning for detention operations for Iraq required alternatives to standard doctrinal approaches. Reports from experiences in Operation Enduring Freedom and at Guantanamo had already recognized the inadequacy of current doctrine for the detention mission and the need for augmentation of both MP and MI units with experienced confinement officers and interrogators. Previous experience also supported the likelihood that detainee population numbers would grow beyond planning estimates. The relationship between MP and MI personnel in the conduct of interrogations also demanded close, continuous coordination rather than remaining compartmentalized. "Lessons learned" also reported the value of establishing a clear chain of command subordinating MP and MI to a Joint Task Force or Brigade Commander. This commander would be in charge of all aspects of both detention and interrogations just as tactical combat forces are subordinated to a single commander. The planners had only to search the lessons learned databases (available on line in military networks) to find these planning insights. Nevertheless, CENTCOM's October 2002 planning annex for detention operations reflected a traditional doctrinal methodology.

The change in the character of the struggle signaled by the sudden spike in U.S. casualties in June, July and August 2003 should have prompted consideration of the need for additional MP assets. GEN Abizaid himself signaled a change in operations when he publicly declared in July that CENTCOM was now dealing with a growing "insurgency," a term government officials had previously avoided in characterizing the war. Certainly by October and November when the fighting reached a new peak, commanders and staffs from CJTF-7 all the way to CENTCOM and the Joint Chiefs of Staff knew by then the serious deficiencies of the 800th MP Brigade and should have at least considered reinforcing the troops for detention operations. Reservists, some of whom had been first mobilized shortly after September 11, 2001, began reaching a two-year mobilization commitment, which, by law, mandated their redeployment and deactivation.

There was not much the 800th MP Brigade (an Army Reserve unit), could do to delay the loss of those soldiers, and there was no individual replacement system or a unit replacement plan. The MP Brigade was totally dependent on higher headquarters to initiate action to alleviate the personnel crisis. The brigade was duly reporting readiness shortfalls through appropriate channels. However, its commanding general was emphasizing these shortfalls in personal communications with CJTF-7 commanders and staff as opposed to CFLCC. Since the brigade was assigned to CFLCC, but under the Tactical Control (TACON) of CJTF-7, her communications should been with CFLCC. The response from CJTF-7's Commander and Deputy Commander was that the 800th MP Brigade had sufficient personnel to accomplish its mission and that it needed to reallocate its available soldiers among the dozen or more detention facilities it was operating in Iraq. However, the Panel found the further deterioration in the readiness condition of the brigade should have been recognized by CFLCC and CENTCOM by late summer 2003. This led the Panel to conclude that CJTF-7, CFLCC and CENTCOM failure to request additional forces was an avoidable error.

The Joint Staff recognized intelligence collection from detainees in Iraq needed improvement. This was their rationale for sending MG Miller from Guantanamo to assist CJTF-7 with interrogation operations. However, the Joint Staff was not paying sufficient attention to evidence of broader readiness issues associated with both MP and MI resources.

We note that CJTF-7 Headquarters was never fully resourced to meet the size and complexity of its mission. The Joint Staff, CJTF-7 and CENTCOM took too long to finalize the Joint Manning Document (JMD) which was not finally approved until December 2003 – six months into the insurgency. At one point, CJTF-7 Headquarters had only 495 of the 1,400 personnel authorized. The command was burdened with additional complexities associated with its mission to support the Coalition Provisional Authority.

Finally, the Joint Staff failed to recognize the implications of the deteriorating manning levels in the 800th MP Brigade; the absence of combat equipment among detention elements of MP units operating in a combat zone; and the indications of deteriorating mission performance among military intelligence interrogators owing to the stress of repeated combat deployments.

When CJTF-7 did realize the magnitude of the detention problem, it requested an assistance visit by the Provost Marshal General of the Army, MG Ryder. There seemed to be some misunderstanding of the CJTF-7 intent, however, since MG Ryder viewed his visit primarily as an assessment of how to transfer the detention program to the Iraqi prison system.

In retrospect, several options for addressing the detention operations challenge were available. CJTF-7 could have requested a change in command relationships to place the 800th MP Brigade under Operational Control of CJTF-7 rather than Tactical Control. This would have permitted the Commander of CJTF-7 to reallocate tactical assets under his control to the detention mission. While other Military Police units in Iraq were already fully committed to higher-priority combat and combat support missions, such as convoy escort, there were non-MP units that could have been reassigned to help in the conduct of detention operations. For example, an artillery brigade was tasked to operate the CJTF-7 Joint Visitors Center in Baghdad. A similar tasking could have provided additional troop strength to assist the 800th MP Brigade at Abu Ghraib. Such a shift would have supplied valuable experienced sergeants, captains and lieutenant colonels sorely lacking in both the MI and MP units at Abu Ghraib. A similar effect could have been achieved by CENTCOM assigning USMC, Navy and Air Force MP and security units to operational control of CJTF-7 for the detention operations mission.

Mobilization and deployment of additional forces from CONUS was also a feasible option. A system is in place for commands such as CJTF-7, CFLCC, and CENTCOM to submit a formal Request for Forces (RFF). Earlier, CJTF-7 had submitted a RFF for an additional Judge Advocate organization, but CENTCOM would not forward it to the Joint Chiefs of Staff. Perhaps this experience made CJTF-7 reluctant to submit a RFF for MP units, but there is no evidence that any of the responsible officers considered any option other than the response given to BG Karpinski to "wear her stars" and reallocate personnel among her already over-stretched units.

While it is the responsibility of the JCS and services to provide adequate numbers of appropriately trained personnel for missions such as the detention operations in Iraq, it is the responsibility of the combatant commander to organize those forces in a manner to achieve mission success. The U.S. experience in the conduct of post-conflict stability operations has been limited, but the impact of our failure to conduct proper detainee operations in this case has been significant. Combatant commanders and their subordinates must organize in a manner that affords unity of command, ensuring commanders work for commanders and not staff.

The fact that the detention operation mission for all of Iraq is now commanded by a two-star general who reports directly to the operational commander, and that 1,900 MPs, more appropriately equipped for combat, now perform the mission once assigned to a single under-strength, poorly trained, inadequately equipped, and weakly-led brigade, indicate more robust options should have been considered sooner.

Finally, the panel notes the failure to report the abuses up the chain of command in a timely manner with adequate urgency. The abuses at Abu Ghraib were known and under investigation as early as January 2004. However, the gravity of the abuses was not conveyed up the chain of command to the Secretary of Defense. The Taguba report, including the photographs, was completed in March 2004. This report was transmitted to LTG Sanchez and GEN Abizaid; however, it is nuclear whether they ever saw the Abu Ghraib photos. GEN Myers has stated he knew of the existence of the photos as early as January 2004. Although the knowledge of the investigation into Abu Ghraib was widely known, as we noted in the previous section, the impact of the photos was not appreciated by any of these officers as indicated by the failure to transmit them in a timely fashion to officials at the Department of Defense. (See Appendix A for the names of persons associated with the positions cited in this section.)

MILITARY POLICE AND DETENTION OPERATIONS

In Operation Enduring Freedom in Afghanistan and Operation Iraqi Freedom, commanders should have paid greater attention to the relationship between detainees and military operations. The current doctrine and procedures for detaining personnel are inadequate to meet the requirements of these conflicts. Due to the vastly different circumstances in these conflicts, it should not be surprising there were deficiencies in the projected needs for military police forces. All the investigations the Panel reviewed highlight the urgency to augment the prior way of conducting detention operations. In particular, the military police were not trained, organized, or equipped to meet the new challenges.

The Army IG found that the morale was high and command climate was good throughout forces deployed in Iraq and Afghanistan with one noticeable exception. Soldiers conducting detainee operations in remote or dangerous locations complained of very poor morale and command climate due to the lack of higher command involvement and support and the perception that their leaders did not care. At Abu Ghraib, in particular, there were many serious problems, which could have been avoided, if proper guidance, oversight and leadership had been provided.

Mobilization and Training

Mobilization and training inadequacies for the MP units occurred during the various phases of employment, beginning with peacetime training, activation, arrival at the mobilization site, deployment, arrival in theater and follow-on operations.

Mobilization and Deployment

Problems generally began for the MP units upon arrival at the mobilization sites. As one commander stated, "Anything that could go wrong went wrong." Preparation was not consistently applied to all deploying units, wasting time and duplicating efforts already accomplished. Troops were separated from their equipment for excessive periods of time. The flow of equipment and personnel was not coordinated. The

Commanding General of the 800th MP Brigade indicated the biggest problem was getting MPs and their equipment deployed together. The unit could neither train at its stateside mobilization site without its equipment nor upon arrival overseas, as two or three weeks could go by before joining with its equipment. This resulted in assigning equipment and troops in an *ad hoc* manner with no regard to original unit. It also resulted in assigning certain companies that had not trained together in peacetime to battalion headquarters. The flow of forces into theater was originally planned and assigned on the basis of the Time Phased Force Deployment List (TPFDL). The TPFDL was soon scrapped, however, in favor of individual unit deployment orders assigned by U.S. Army Forces Command based on unit readiness and personnel strength. MP Brigade commanders did not know who would be deployed next. This method resulted in a condition wherein a recently arrived battalion headquarters would be assigned the next arriving MP companies, regardless of their capabilities or any other prior command and training relationships.

Original projections called for approximately 12 detention facilities with a projection of 30,000 to 100,000 enemy prisoners of war. These large projections did not materialize. In fact, the initial commanding general of the 800th MP brigade, BG Hill, stated he had more than enough MPs designated for the Internment/Resettlement (I/R – hereafter called detention) mission at the end of the combat phase in Iraq. This assessment radically changed following the major combat phase, when the 800th moved to Baghdad beginning in the summer of 2003 to assume the detention mission. The brigade was given additional tasks assisting the Coalition Provisional Authority (CPA) in reconstructing the Iraqi corrections system, a mission they had neither planned for nor anticipated.

Inadequate Training for the Military Police Mission

Though some elements performed better than others, generally training was inadequate. The MP detention units did not receive detention-specific training during their mobilization period, which was a critical deficiency. Detention training was conducted for only two MP detention battalions, one in Afghanistan and elements of the other at Camp Arifjan, Kuwait. The 800th MP Brigade, prior to deployment, had planned for a major detention exercise during the summer of 2002; however, this was cancelled due to the activation of many individuals and units for Operation Noble Eagle following the September 11, 2001 attack. The Deputy Commander of one MP brigade stated "training at the mobilization site was wholly inadequate." In addition, there was no theater-specific training.

The Army Inspector General's investigators also found that training at the mobilization sites failed to prepare units for conducting detention operations. Leaders of inspected reserve units stated in interviews that they did not receive a clear mission statement prior to mobilization and were not notified of their mission until after deploying. Personnel interviewed described being placed immediately in stressful situations in a detention facility with thousands of non-compliant detainees and not being trained to handle them. Units arriving in theater were given just a few days to conduct a handover from the outgoing units. Once deployed, these newly arrived units had difficulty gaining access to the necessary documentation on tactics, techniques, and procedures to train their personnel on the MP essential tasks of their new mission.

A prime example is that relevant Army manuals and publications were available only on line, but personnel did not have access to computers or the Internet.

Force Structure Organization

The current military police organizational structure does not address the detention mission on the nonlinear battlefield characteristic of the Global War on Terror.

Current Military Police Structure

The present U.S. Army Reserve and Army National Guard system worked well for the 1991 Gulf War for which large numbers of reserve forces were mobilized, were deployed, fought, and were quickly returned to the United States. These forces, however, were not designed to maintain large numbers of troops at a high operational tempo for a long period of deployment as has been the case in Afghanistan and Iraq.

Comments from commanders and the various inspection reports indicated the current force structure for the MPs is neither flexible enough to support the developing mission, nor can it provide for the sustained detainee operations envisioned for the future. The primary reason is that the present structure lacks sufficient numbers of detention specialists. Currently, the Army active component detention specialists are assigned in support of the Disciplinary Barracks and Regional Correctional Facilities in the United States, all of which are non-deployable.

New Force Structure Initiatives

Significant efforts are currently being made to shift more of the MP detention requirements into the active force structure. The Army's force design for the future will standardize detention forces between active and reserve components and provide the capability for the active component to immediately deploy detention companies.

The Panel notes that the Mikolashek inspection found significant shortfalls in training and force structure for field sanitation, preventive medicine and medical treatment requirements for detainees.

Doctrine and Planning

Initial planning envisaged a conflict mirroring operation Desert Storm; approximately 100,000 enemy prisoners of war were forecast for the first five days of the conflict. This expectation did not materialize in the first phase of Operation Iraqi Freedom. As a result, there were too many MP detention companies. The reverse occurred in the second phase of Iraqi Freedom, where the plan envisaged a reduced number of detention MPs on the assumption the initial large numbers of enemy prisoners of war would already have been processed out of the detention facilities. The result was that combat MPs were ultimately reassigned to an unplanned detention mission.

The doctrine of yesterday's battlefield does not satisfy the requirements of today's conflicts. Current doctrine assumes a linear battlefield and is very clear for the handling of detainees from the point of capture to the holding areas and eventually to the detention facilities in the rear. However, Operations Enduring Freedom and Iraqi Freedom, both occurring where there is no distinction between front and rear areas, forced organizations to adapt tactics and procedures to address the resulting voids. Organizations initially used standard operating procedures for collection points and detention facilities. These procedures do not fit the new environment, generally because there are no safe areas behind "friendly lines" – there *are* no friendly lines. The inapplicability of current doctrine had a negative effect on accountability, security, safeguarding of detainees, and intelligence exploitation. Instead of capturing and rapidly moving detainees to secure collection points as prescribed by doctrine, units tended to retain the detainees and attempted to exploit their tactical intelligence value without the required training or infrastructure.

Current doctrine specifies that line combat units hold detainees no longer than 12–24 hours to extract immediately useful intelligence. Nonetheless, the Army IG inspection found detainees were routinely held up to 72 hours. For corps collection points, doctrine specifies detainees be held no longer than three days; the Army IG found detainees were held from 30 to 45 days.

Equipment Shortfalls

The current force structure for MP detention organizations does not provide sufficient assets to meet the inherent force protection requirement on battlefields likely to be characteristic of the future. Detention facilities in the theater may have to be located in a hostile combat zone, instead of the benign secure environment current doctrine presumes.

MP detention units will need to be equipped for combat. Lack of crew-served weapons, e.g., machine guns and mortars, to counter external attacks resulted in casualties to the detainee population as well as to the friendly forces. Moreover, Army-issued radios were frequently inoperable and too few in number. In frustration, individual soldiers purchased commercial radios from civilian sources. This improvisation created an unsecured communications environment that could be monitored by any hostile force outside the detention facility.

Detention Operations and Accountability

Traditionally, military police support the Joint Task Force (JTF) by undertaking administrative processing of detention operations, thereby relieving the war-fighters of concern over prisoners and civilian detainees. The handling of detainees is a tactical and operational consideration the JTF addresses during planning to prevent combat forces from being diverted to handle large numbers of detainees. Military police are structured, therefore, to facilitate the tempo of combat operations by providing for the quick movement of prisoners from the battle area to temporary holding areas and thence to detention facilities.

However, the lack of relevant doctrine meant the design and operation of division, battalion, and company collection points were improvised on an *ad hoc* basis, depending on such immediate local factors as mission, troops available, weather, time, etc. At these collection points, the SOPs the units had prior to deployment were outdated or ill-suited for the operating environment of Afghanistan and Iraq. Tactical units found themselves taking on roles in detainee operations never anticipated in their prior training. Such lack of proper skills had a negative effect on the intelligence exploitation, security, and safeguarding of detainees.

The initial point of capture may be at any time or place in a military operation. This is the place where soldiers have the least control of the environment and where most contact with the detainees occurs. It is also the place where, in or immediately after battle, abuse may be most likely. And it is the place where the detainee, shocked by capture, may be most likely to give information. As noted earlier, instead of capturing and rapidly transporting detainees to collection points, battalions and companies were holding detainees for excessive periods, even though they lacked the training, materiel, or infrastructure for productive interrogation. The Naval IG found that approximately one-third of the alleged incidents of abuse occurred at the point of capture.

Detention

The decision to use Abu Ghraib as the primary operational level detention facility happened by default. Abu Ghraib was selected by Ambassador Bremer who envisioned it as a temporary facility to be used for criminal detainees until the new Iraqi government could be established and an Iraqi prison established at another site. However, CJTF-7 saw an opportunity to use it as an interim site for the detainees it expected to round up as part of Operation Victory Bounty in July 2003. CJTF-7 had considered Camp Bucca but rejected it, as it was 150 miles away from Baghdad where the operation was to take place.

Abu Ghraib was also a questionable facility from a standpoint of conducting interrogations. Its location, next to an urban area, and its large size in relation to the small MP unit tasked to provide a law enforcement presence, made it impossible to achieve the necessary degree of security. The detainee population of approximately 7,000 outmanned the 92 MPs by approximately a 75:1 ratio. The choice of Abu Ghraib as the facility for detention operations placed a strictly detention mission-driven unit – one designed to operate in a rear area – smack in the middle of a combat environment.

Detainee Accountability and Classification

Adequate procedures for accountability were lacking during the movement of detainees from the collection points to the detainee facilities. During the movement, it was not unusual for detainees to exchange their identification tags with those of other detainees. The diversity of the detainee population also made identification and classification difficult. Classification determined the detainee assignment to particular cells/blocks, but individuals brought to the facility were often a mix of criminals and security detainees. The security detainees were either held for their intelligence value or presented a continuing threat to Coalition Forces. Some innocents were also included in the detainee population. The issue of unregistered or "ghost" detainees presented a limited, though significant, problem of accountability at Abu Ghraib.

Detainee Reporting

Detainee reporting lacked accountability, reliability and standardization. There was no central agency to collect and manage detainee information. The combatant commanders and the JTF commanders have overall responsibility for the detainee programs to ensure compliance with the international law of armed conflict, domestic law and applicable national policy and directives. The reporting system is supposed to process all inquiries concerning detainees and provide accountability information to the International Committee of the Red Cross. The poor reporting system did not meet this obligation.

Release Procedures

Multiple reviews were required to make release recommendations prior to approval by the release authority. Non-concurrence by area commanders, intelligence organizations, or law enforcement agencies resulted in retention of ever larger numbers of detainees. The Army Inspector General estimated that up to 80 percent of detainees being held for security and intelligence reasons might be eligible for release upon proper review of their cases with the other 20 percent either requiring continued detention on security grounds or uncompleted intelligence requirements. Interviews indicated area commanders were reluctant to concur with release decisions out of concern that potential combatants would be reintroduced into their areas of operation or that the detainees had continuing intelligence value.

INTERROGATION OPERATIONS

Any discussion of interrogation techniques must begin with the simple reality that their purpose is to gain intelligence that will help protect the United States, its forces and interests abroad. The severity of the post-September 11, 2001, terrorist threat and the escalating insurgency in Iraq make information gleaned from interrogations especially important. When lives are at stake, all legal and moral means of eliciting information must be considered. Nonetheless, interrogations are inherently unpleasant, and many people find them objectionable by their very nature.

The relationship between interrogators and detainees is frequently adversarial. The interrogator's goal of extracting useful information likely is in direct opposition to the detainee's goal of resisting or dissembling. Although interrogators are trained to stay within the bounds of acceptable conduct, the imperative of eliciting timely and useful information can sometimes conflict with proscriptions against inhumane or degrading treatment. For interrogators in Iraq and Afghanistan, this tension is magnified by the highly stressful combat environment. The conditions of war and the dynamics of detainee operations carry inherent risks for human mistreatment and must be approached with caution and careful planning and training.

A number of interrelated factors both limited the intelligence derived from interrogations and contributed to detainee abuse in Operations Enduring Freedom and Iraqi Freedom. A shortfall of properly trained human intelligence personnel to do tactical interrogation of detainees existed at all levels. At the larger detention centers, qualified and experienced interrogators and interpreters were in short supply. No doctrine existed to cover segregation of detainees whose status differed or was unclear, nor was there guidance on timely release of detainees no longer deemed of intelligence interest. The failure to adapt rapidly to the new intelligence requirements of the Global War on

Terror resulted in inadequate resourcing, inexperienced and untrained personnel, and a backlog of detainees destined for interrogation. These conditions created a climate not conducive to sound intelligence-gathering efforts.

The Threat Environment

The Global War on Terror requires a fundamental reexamination of how we approach collecting intelligence. Terrorists present new challenges because of the way they organize, communicate, and operate. Many of the terrorists and insurgents are geographically dispersed non-state actors who move across national boundaries and operate in small cells that are difficult to surveil and penetrate.

Human Intelligence from Interrogations

The need for human intelligence has dramatically increased in the new threat environment of asymmetric warfare. Massed forces and equipment characteristic of the Cold War era, Desert Storm and even Phase I of Operation Iraqi Freedom relied largely on signals and imagery intelligence. The intelligence problem then was primarily one of monitoring known military sites, troop locations and equipment concentrations. The problem today, however, is discovering new information on widely dispersed terrorist and insurgent networks. Human intelligence often provides the clues to understand these networks, enabling the collection of intelligence from other sources. Information derived from interrogations is an important component of this human intelligence, especially in the Global War on Terror.

The interrogation of al Qaeda members held at Guantanamo has yielded valuable information used to disrupt and preempt terrorist planning and activities. Much of the 9/11 Commission's report on the planning and execution of the attacks on the World Trade Center and Pentagon came from interrogation of detainees. In the case of al Qaeda, interrogations provided insights on organization, key personnel, target selection, planning cycles, cooperation among various groups, and logistical support. This information expanded our knowledge of the selection, motivation, and training of these groups. According to Congressional testimony by the Under Secretary of Defense for Intelligence, we have gleaned information on a wide range of al Qaeda activities, including efforts to obtain weapons of mass destruction, sources of finance, training in use of explosives and suicide bombings, and potential travel routes to the United States.

Interrogations provide commanders with information about enemy networks, leadership, and tactics. Such information is critical in planning operations. Tactically, detainee interrogation is a fundamental tool for gaining insight into enemy positions, strength, weapons, and intentions. Thus, it is fundamental to the protection of our forces in combat. Notably, Saddam Hussein's capture was facilitated by interrogation-derived information. Interrogations often provide fragmentary pieces of the broader intelligence picture. These pieces become useful when combined with other human intelligence or intelligence from other sources.

Pressure on Interrogators to Produce Actionable Intelligence

With the active insurgency in Iraq, pressure was placed on the interrogators to produce "actionable" intelligence. In the months before Saddam Hussein's capture, inability to determine his whereabouts created widespread frustration within the intelligence community. With lives at stake, senior leaders expressed, forcibly at times, their needs for better intelligence. A number of visits by high-level officials to Abu Ghraib undoubtedly contributed to this perceived pressure. Both the CJTF-7 commander and his intelligence officer, CJTF-7 C2, visited the prison on several occasions. MG Miller's visit in August/September, 2003 stressed the need to move from simply collecting tactical information to collecting information of operational and strategic value. In November 2003, a senior member of the National Security Council Staff visited Abu Ghraib, leading some personnel at the facility to conclude, perhaps incorrectly, that even the White House was interested in the intelligence gleaned from their interrogation reports. Despite the number of visits and the intensity of interest in actionable intelligence, however, the Panel found no undue pressure exerted by senior officials. Nevertheless, their eagerness for intelligence may have been perceived by interrogators as pressure.

Interrogation Operations Issues

A number of factors contributed to the problems experienced in interrogation operations. They ranged from resource and leadership shortfalls to doctrinal deficiencies and poor training.

Inadequate Resources

As part of the peace dividend following the Cold War much of the human intelligence capability, particularly in the Army, was reduced. As hostilities began in Afghanistan and Iraq, Army human intelligence personnel, particularly interrogators and interpreters, were ill-equipped to deal with requirements at both the tactical level and at the larger detention centers. At the tactical level, questioning of detainees has been used in all major conflicts. Knowledge of the enemy's positions, strength, equipment and tactics is critical in order to achieve operational success while minimizing casualties. Such tactical questioning to gain immediate battlefield intelligence is generally done at or near the point of capture. In Iraq, although their numbers were insufficient, some of the more seasoned MIs from the MI units supporting Abu Ghraib were assigned to support the Army Tactical HUMINT teams in the field.

In both Afghanistan and Iraq, tactical commanders kept detainees longer than specified by doctrine in order to exploit their unique local knowledge such as religious and tribal affiliation and regional politics. Remaining with the tactical units, the detainees could be available for follow-up questioning and clarification of details. The field commanders were concerned that information from interrogations, obtained in the more permanent facilities, would not be returned to the capturing unit. Tactical units, however, were not properly resourced to implement this altered operating arrangement. The potential for abuse also increases when interrogations are conducted in an emotionally charged field environment by personnel unfamiliar with approved techniques.

At the fixed detention centers such as Abu Ghraib, lack of resources and shortage of more experienced senior interrogators impeded the production of actionable intelligence. Inexperienced and untrained personnel often yielded poor intelligence. Interpreters, particularly, were in short supply, contributing to the backlog of detainees to be interrogated. As noted previously, at Abu Ghraib for instance, there were detainees who had been in custody for as long as 90 days before being interrogated for the first time.

Leadership and Organization Shortfalls at Abu Ghraib

Neither the leadership nor the organization of Military Intelligence at Abu Ghraib was up to the mission. The 205th MI Brigade had no organic interrogation elements; they had been eliminated by the downsizing in the 1990s. Soldiers from Army Reserve units filled the ranks, with the consequence that the Brigade Commander had to rely on disparate elements of units and individuals, including civilians, which had never trained together. The creation of the Joint Interrogation and Debriefing Center (JIDC) introduced another layer of complexity into an already stressed interrogations environment. The JIDC was an ad hoc organization made up of six different units lacking the normal command and control structure, particularly at the senior non-commissioned officer level. Leadership was also lacking, from the Commander of the 800th MP Brigade in charge of Abu Ghraib, who failed to ensure that soldiers had appropriate SOPs for dealing with detainees, to the Commander of the 205th MI Brigade, who failed to ensure that soldiers under his command were properly trained and followed the interrogation rules of engagement. Moreover, the Director of the JIDC was a weak leader who did not have experience in interrogation operations and who ceded the core of his responsibilities to subordinates. He failed to provide appropriate training and supervision of personnel assigned to the Center. None of these leaders established the basic standards and accountability that might have served to prevent the abusive behaviors that occurred.

Interrogation Techniques

Interrogation techniques intended only for Guantanamo came to be used in Afghanistan and Iraq. Techniques employed at Guantanamo included the use of stress positions, isolation for up to 30 days and removal of clothing. In Afghanistan techniques included removal of clothing, isolating people for long periods of time, use of stress positions, exploiting fear of dogs, and sleep and light deprivation. Interrogators in Iraq, already familiar with some of these ideas, implemented them even prior to any policy guidance from CJTF-7. Moreover, interrogators at Abu Ghraib were relying on a 1987 version of FM 34-52, which authorized interrogators to control all aspects of the interrogation to include light, heating, food, clothing and shelter given to detainees.

A range of opinion among interrogators, staff judge advocates and commanders existed regarding what techniques were permissible. Some incidents of abuse were clearly cases of individual criminal misconduct. Other incidents resulted from misinterpretations of law or policy or confusion about what interrogation techniques were permitted by law or local SOPs. The incidents stemming from misinterpretation or confusion occurred for several reasons: the proliferation of guidance and information from other theaters of operation; the interrogators' experiences in other theaters; and the failure to distinguish between permitted interrogation techniques in other theater environments and Iraq. Some soldiers or contractors who committed abuse may honestly have believed the techniques were condoned.

Use of Contractors as Interrogators

As a consequence of the shortage of interrogators and interpreters, contractors were used to augment the workforce. Contractors were a particular problem at Abu Ghraib. The Army Inspector General found that 35 percent of the contractors employed did not receive formal training in military interrogation techniques, policy, or doctrine. The Naval Inspector General, however, found some of the older contractors had backgrounds as former military interrogators and were generally considered more effective than some of the junior enlisted military personnel. Oversight of contractor personnel and activities was not sufficient to ensure intelligence operations fell within the law and the authorized chain of command. Continued use of contractors will be required, but contracts must clearly specify the technical requirements and personnel qualifications, experience, and training needed. They should also be developed and administered in such as way as to provide the necessary oversight and management.

Doctrinal Deficiencies

At the tactical level, detaining individuals primarily for intelligence collection or because they constitute a potential security threat, though necessary, presents units with situations not addressed by current doctrine. Many units adapted their operating procedures for conducting detainee operations to fit an environment not contemplated in the existing doctrinal manuals. The capturing units had no relevant procedures for information and evidence collection, which were critical for the proper disposition of detainees.

Additionally, there is inconsistent doctrine on interrogation facility operations for the fixed detention locations. Commanders had to improvise the organization and command relationships within these elements to meet the particular requirements of their operating environments in Afghanistan and Iraq. Doctrine is lacking to address the screening and interrogation of large numbers of detainees whose status (combatants, criminals, or innocents) is not easily ascertainable. Nor does policy specifically address administrative responsibilities related to the timely release of detainees captured and detained primarily for intelligence exploitation or for the security threat they may pose.

Role of CIA

CIA personnel conducted interrogations in DoD detention facilities. In some facilities these interrogations were conducted in conjunction with military personnel, but at Abu Ghraib the CIA was allowed to conduct its interrogations separately. No memorandum of understanding existed on interrogations operations between the CIA and CJTF-7, and the CIA was allowed to operate under different rules. According to the Fay investigation, the CIA's detention and interrogation practices contributed to a loss of accountability at Abu Ghraib. We are aware of the issue of unregistered detainees, but the Panel did not have sufficient access to CIA information to make any determinations in this regard.

THE ROLE OF MILITARY POLICE AND MILITARY INTELLIGENCE IN DETENTION OPERATIONS

Existing doctrine does not clearly address the relationship between the Military Police (MP) operating detention facilities and Military Intelligence (MI) personnel conducting intelligence exploitation at those facilities. The Army Inspector General report states neither MP nor MI doctrine specifically defines the distinct, but interdependent, roles and responsibilities of the two elements in detainee operations.

In the Global War on Terror, we are dealing with new conditions and new threats. Doctrine must be adjusted accordingly. MP doctrine currently states intelligence personnel may collaborate with MPs at detention sites to conduct interrogations, with coordination between the two groups to establish operating procedures. MP doctrine does not, however, address the subject of approved and prohibited MI procedures in an MP-operated facility. Conversely, MI doctrine does not clearly explain MP detention procedures or the role of MI personnel within a detention setting.

GUANTANAMO

The first detainees arrived at Guantanamo in January 2002. The SOUTHCOM Commander established two joint task forces at Guantanamo to execute the detention operations (JTF-160) and the interrogation operations (JTF-170). In August of that year, based on difficulties with the command relationships, the two JTFs were organized into a single command designated as Joint Task Force Guantanamo. This reorganization was conceived to enhance unity of command and direct all activities in support of interrogation and detention operations.

On November 4, 2002, MG Miller was appointed Commander of Joint Task Force Guantanamo. As the joint commander, he called upon the MP and MI soldiers to work together cooperatively. Military police were to collect passive intelligence on detainees. They became key players, serving as the eyes and ears of the cellblocks for military intelligence personnel. This collaboration helped set conditions for successful interrogation by providing the interrogator more information about the detainee – his mood, his communications with other detainees, his receptivity to particular incentives, etc. Under the single command, the relationship between MPs and MIs became an effective operating model.

AFGHANISTAN

The MP and MI commands at the Bagram Detention Facility maintained separate chains of command and remained focused on their independent missions. The Combined Joint Task Force-76 Provost Marshal was responsible for detainee operations. He designated a principal assistant to run the Bagram facility. In parallel fashion, the CJTF-76 Intelligence Officer was responsible for MI operations in the facility, working through an Officer-in-Charge to oversee interrogation operations. The two deputies worked together to coordinate execution of their respective missions. A dedicated judge advocate was assigned full time to the facility, while the CJTF-76 Inspector General provided independent oversight. Based on information from the Naval Inspector General investigation, this arrangement in Afghanistan worked reasonably well.

ABU GHRAIB, IRAQ

The Central Confinement Facility is located near the population center of Baghdad. Abu Ghraib was selected by Ambassador Bremer who envisioned it as a temporary facility to be used for criminal detainees until the new Iraqi government could be established and an Iraqi prison established at another site. Following operations during the summer of 2003, Abu Ghraib also was designated by CJTF-7 as the detention center for security detainees. It was selected because it was difficult to transport prisoners, due to improvised explosives devices (IEDs) and other insurgent tactics, to the more remote and secure Camp Bucca, some 150 miles away.

Request for Assistance

Commander CJTF-7 recognized serious deficiencies at the prison and requested assistance. In response to this request, MG Miller and a team from Guantanamo were sent to Iraq to provide advice on facilities and operations specific to screening, interrogations, HUMINT collection and interagency integration in the short- and long-term. The team arrived in Baghdad on August 31, 2003. MG Miller brought a number of recommendations derived from his experience at Guantanamo to include his model for MP and MI personnel to work together. These collaborative procedures had worked well at Guantanamo, in part because of the high ratio of approximately one-to-one of military police to mostly compliant detainees. However, the guard-to-detainee ratio at Abu Ghraib was approximately 1 to 75, and the Military Intelligence and the Military Police had separate chains of command.

MG Ryder, the Army Provost Marshal, also made an assistance visit in mid-October 2003. He conducted a review of detainee operations in Iraq. He found flawed operating procedures, a lack of training, an inadequate prisoner classification system, understrength units and a ratio of guard to prisoners designed for "compliant" prisoners of war and not for criminals or high-risk security detainees. However, he failed to detect the warning signs of potential and actual abuse that was ongoing during his visit. The assessment team members did not identify any MP units purposely applying inappropriate confinement practices. The Ryder report continues that "Military Police, though adept at passive collection of intelligence within a facility, do not participate in Military Intelligence-supervised interrogation sessions. The 800th MP Brigade has not been asked to change its facility procedures to set the conditions for MI interviews, nor participate in those interviews."

Prevailing Conditions

Conditions at Abu Ghraib reflected an exception to those prevailing at other theater detainee facilities. U.S. forces were operating Tiers 1A and 1B, while Tiers 2 through 7 were under the complete control of Iraqi prison guards. Iraqis who had committed crimes against other Iraqis were intended to be housed in the tiers under Iraqi control. The facility was under frequent hostile fire from mortars and rocket-propelled grenades. Detainee escape attempts were numerous and there were several riots. Both MI and MP units were seriously under-resourced and lacked unit cohesion and mid-level leadership. The reserve MP units had lost senior non-commissioned officers and other personnel through rotations back to the U.S. as well as reassignments to other missions in the theater.

When Abu Ghraib opened, the first MP unit was the 72nd MP Company, based in Henderson, Nevada. Known as "the Nevada Company," it has been described by many involved in investigations concerning Abu Ghraib as a very strong unit that kept tight rein on operational procedures at the facility. This company called into question the interrogation practices of the MI brigade regarding nakedness of detainees. The 72nd MP Company voiced and then filed written objections to these practices.

The problems at Abu Ghraib intensified after October 15, 2003, when the 372nd Military Police Company took over the facility. The 372nd MP Company had been given the most sensitive mission: control of Tier 1A and Tier 1B, where civilian and military intelligence specialists held detainees identified for interrogations as well as "high-risk" detainees. An "MI hold" was anyone of intelligence interest and included foreign and Iraqi terrorists, as well as individuals possessing information regarding foreign fighters, infiltration methods, or pending attacks on Coalition forces. The "high-risk" troublemakers were held in Tier 1B. The prison cells of Tiers 1A and 1B were collectively known as "the hard site." The 372nd soldiers were not trained for prison guard duty and were thinly stretched in dealing with the large number of detainees. With little experience to fall back on, the company commander deferred to non-commissioned officers who had civilian correctional backgrounds to work the night shift. This deference was a significant error in judgment.

Leadership Shortfalls

At the leadership level, there was friction and a lack of communication between the 800th MP Brigade and the 205th MI Brigade through the summer and fall of 2003. There was no clear delineation of responsibility between commands and little coordination at the command level. Both the Director of the Joint Interrogation and Debriefing Center (JIDC) and the Commander of the 320th MP Battalion were weak and ineffective leaders. Both failed to ensure their subordinates were properly trained and supervised. They failed to establish and enforce basic soldier standards, proficiency, and accountability. Neither was able to organize tasks to accomplish their missions in an appropriate manner. By not communicating standards, policies, and plans to soldiers, these leaders conveyed a sense of tacit approval of abusive behaviors toward prisoners. This was particularly evident with respect to prisoner-handling procedures and techniques, including unfamiliarity with the Geneva Conventions. There was a lack of discipline and standards of behavior were not established nor enforced. A lax and dysfunctional command climate took hold.

In November 2003, the 205th MI Brigade Commander was assigned as the Forward Operation Base Commander, thus receiving responsibility for Abu Ghraib. This assignment was made as a result of CJTF-7 Commander's concern over force protection at the prison. The Fay investigation found this did not change the relationship of MP and MI units in day-to-day operations at the facility, although the Commander of the 800th MP Brigade says she was denied access to areas of Abu Ghraib for which she was doctrinally responsible. Key leaders did not seem to recognize or appreciate psychological stressors associated with the detention mission. MG Taguba concluded these factors included "differences in culture, soldiers' quality of life, and the real presence of mortal danger over an extended time period. The failure of commanders to recognize these pressures contributed to the pervasive atmosphere existing at Abu Ghraib Detention Facility."

Military Working Dogs at Abu Ghraib

The Military Police directives give guidance for the use of military working dogs. They are used to provide an effective psychological and physical deterrent in the detention facility, offering an alternative to using firearms. Dogs are also used for perimeter security, inspections and patrols. MG Miller had recommended dogs as beneficial for detainee custody and control during his visit in August/September 2003. However, he never recommended, nor were dogs used for interrogations at Guantanamo. The working dog teams were requested by the Commander 205th MI Brigade who never understood the intent as described by MG Miller. It is likely the confusion about using dogs partially stems from the initial request for dog teams by military intelligence and not military police.

The working dogs arrived at Abu Ghraib in mid-November 2003. The two Army teams were assigned primarily to security of the compound while the three Navy teams worked inside at the entry control point. The senior Army and Navy dog handlers indicated they had not previously worked in a prison environment and received only a one-day training session on scout and search for escaped Enemy Prisoners of War. The Navy handler stated that upon arrival at Abu Ghraib he had not received an orientation on what was expected from his canine unit nor what was authorized or not authorized. He further stated he had never received instruction on the use of force in the compound, but he acknowledged he knew a dog could not be used on a detainee if the detainee posed no threat.

Guidance provided by the CJTF-7 directive of September 14, 2003, allowed working dogs to be used as an interrogation technique with the CJTF-7 Commander's approval. This authorization was updated by the October 12, 2003, memorandum, which allowed the presence of dogs during interrogation as long as they were muzzled and under control of the handler at all times but still required approval. The Taguba and Jones/Fay investigations identified a number of abuses related to using muzzled and unmuzzled dogs during interrogations. They also identified some abuses involving dog-use unrelated to interrogations, apparently for the sadistic pleasure of the MPs involved in these incidents.

MP/MI Relationship

It is clear, with these serious shortfalls and lack of supervision, the model MG Miller presented for the effective working relationship between MI and MP was neither understood nor could it have been successfully implemented. Based on the Taguba and Jones/Fay investigations, "setting favorable conditions" had some basis in fact at Abu Ghraib, but it was also used as an excuse for abusive behavior toward detainees.

The events that took place at Abu Ghraib are an aberration when compared to the situations at other detention operations. Poor leadership and a lack of oversight set the stage for abuses to occur.

LAWS OF WAR/GENEVA CONVENTIONS

American military culture, training, and operations are steeped in a long-held commitment to the tenets of military and international law as traditionally codified by the world community. Department of Defense Directive 5100.77, DoD Law of War Program, describes the law of war as:

> That part of international law that regulates the conduct of armed hostilities. It is often called the law of armed conflict. The law of war encompasses all international law for the conduct of hostilities binding on the United States or its individual citizens, including treaties and international agreements to which the United States is a party, and applicable customary international law.

The law of war includes, among other agreements, the Geneva Conventions of 1949. The Geneva Conventions set forth the rights and obligations which govern the treatment of civilians and combatants during periods of armed conflict. Specifically, Geneva Convention III addresses the treatment of prisoners of war; and Geneva Convention IV addresses the treatment of civilians.

Chairman of the Joint Chiefs of Staff Instruction 5810.01B, Implementation of the DoD Law of War Program, reiterates U.S. policy concerning the law of war: "The Armed Forces of the United States will comply with the law of war during all armed conflicts, however such conflicts are characterized. . . ."

The United States became engaged in two distinct conflicts, Operation Enduring Freedom (OEF) in Afghanistan and Operation Iraqi Freedom (OIF) in Iraq. As a result of a Presidential determination, the Geneva Conventions did not apply to al Qaeda and Taliban combatants. Nevertheless, these traditional standards were put into effect for OIF and remain in effect at this writing. Some would argue this is a departure from the traditional view of the law of war as espoused by the ICRC and others in the international community.

Operation Enduring Freedom

On October 17, 2001, pursuant to the commencement of combat operations in OEF, the Commander, CENTCOM, issued an order instructing the Geneva Conventions were to be applied to all captured individuals in accordance with their traditional interpretation. Belligerents would be screened to determine whether or not they were entitled to prisoner of war status. If an individual was entitled to prisoner of war status, the protections of Geneva Convention III would apply. If armed forces personnel were in doubt as to a detained individual's status, Geneva Convention III rights would be accorded to the detainee until a Geneva Convention III Article 5 tribunal made a definitive status determination. If the individual was found not to be entitled to Geneva Convention III protections, he or she might be detained and processed under U.S. criminal code, a procedure consistent with Geneva Convention IV.

A policy debate concerning the application of treaties and laws to al Qaeda and Taliban detainees then began taking shape. The Department of Justice Office of Legal Counsel (OLC) provided opinions to Counsel to the President and Department of Defense General Counsel concluding the Geneva Conventions did not protect members of the al Qaeda organization, and the President could decide that Geneva Conventions did not protect Taliban militia. Counsel to the President and the Attorney General so advised the President.

On February 7, 2002 the President issued a memorandum stating, in part,

> ...the war against terrorism ushers in a new paradigm.... Our nation recognizes that this new paradigm – ushered in not by us, but by terrorists – requires new thinking in the law of war, but thinking that should nevertheless be consistent with the principles of Geneva.

Upon this premise, the President determined the Geneva Conventions did not apply to the U.S. conflict with al Qaeda, and that Taliban detainees did not qualify for prisoner of war status. Removed from the protections of the Geneva Conventions, al Qaeda and Taliban detainees have been classified variously as "unlawful combatants," "enemy combatants," and "unprivileged belligerents."

The enemy in the Global War on Terror is one neither the United States nor the community of nations has ever before engaged on such an extensive scale. These far-reaching, well-resourced, organized, and trained terrorists are attempting to achieve their own ends. Such terrorists are not of a nation state such as those who are party to the agreements which comprise the law of war. Neither do they conform their actions to the letter or spirit of the law of war.

The Panel accepts the proposition that these terrorists are not combatants entitled to the protections of Geneva Convention III. Furthermore, the Panel accepts the conclusion the Geneva Convention IV and the provisions of domestic criminal law are not sufficiently robust and adequate to provide for the appropriate detention of captured terrorists.

The Panel notes the President qualified his determination, directing that United States policy would be "consistent with the principles of Geneva." Among other things, the Geneva Conventions adhere to a standard calling for a delineation of rights for all persons, and humane treatment for all persons. They suggest that no person is "outlaw," that is, outside the laws of some legal entity.

The Panel finds the details of the current policy vague and lacking. Justice Sandra Day O'Connor, writing for the majority in *Hamdi v Rumsfeld*, June 28, 2004 points out "the Government has never provided any court with the full criteria that it uses in classifying individuals as [enemy combatants]." Justice O'Connor cites several authorities to support the proposition that detention "is a clearly established principle of the law of war," but also states there is no precept of law, domestic or international, which would permit the indefinite detention of any combatant.

As a matter of logic, there should be a category of persons who do not comply with the specified conditions and thus fall outside the category of persons entitled to EPW status. Although there is not a particular label for this category in law of war conventions, the concept of "unlawful combatant" or "unprivileged belligerent" is a part of the law of war.

Operation Iraqi Freedom

Operation Iraqi Freedom is wholly different from Operation Enduring Freedom. It is an operation that clearly falls within the boundaries of the Geneva Conventions and the traditional law of war. From the very beginning of the campaign, none of the senior leadership or command considered any possibility other than that the Geneva Conventions applied.

The message in the field, or the assumptions made in the field, at times lost sight of this underpinning. Personnel familiar with the law of war determinations for OEF in Afghanistan tended to factor those determinations into their decision-making for military actions in Iraq. Law of war policy and decisions germane to OEF migrated, often quite innocently, into decision matrices for OIF. We noted earlier the migration of interrogation techniques from Afghanistan to Iraq. Those interrogation techniques were authorized only for OEF. More important, their authorization in Afghanistan and Guantanamo was possible only because the President had determined that individuals subjected to these interrogation techniques fell outside the strict protections of the Geneva Conventions.

One of the more telling examples of this migration centers around CJTF-7's determination that some of the detainees held in Iraq were to be categorized as unlawful combatants. "Unlawful combatants" was a category set out in the President's February 7, 2002 memorandum. Despite lacking specific authorization to operate beyond the confines of the Geneva Conventions, CJTF-7 nonetheless determined it was within their command discretion to classify, as unlawful combatants, individuals captured during OIF. CJTF-7 concluded it had individuals in custody who met the criteria for unlawful combatants set out by the President and extended it in Iraq to those who were not protected as combatants under the Geneva Conventions, based on the OLC opinions. While CJTF-7's reasoning is understandable in respect to unlawful combatants, nonetheless, they understood there was no authorization to suspend application of the Geneva Conventions, in letter and spirit, to all military actions of Operation Iraqi Freedom. In addition, CJTF-7 had no means of discriminating detainees among the various categories of those protected under the Geneva Conventions and those unlawful combatants who were not.

THE ROLE OF THE INTERNATIONAL COMMITTEE OF THE RED CROSS

Since December 2001, the International Committee of the Red Cross (ICRC) has visited U.S. detention operations in Guantanamo, Iraq, and Afghanistan numerous times. Various ICRC inspection teams have delivered working papers and reports of findings to U.S. military leaders at different levels. While the ICRC has acknowledged U.S. attempts to improve the conditions of detainees, major differences over detainee status as well as application of specific provisions of Geneva Conventions III and IV remain. If we were to follow the ICRC's interpretations, interrogation operations would not be allowed. This would deprive the U.S. of an indispensable source of intelligence in the war on terrorism.

The ICRC is an independent agency whose activities include observing and reporting on conditions in wartime detention camps and facilities. During visits, it attempts to register all prisoners, inspect facilities, and conduct private interviews with detainees to discuss any problems concerning detainee treatment or conditions; it also provides a means for detainees to contact their families. While the ICRC has no enforcing authority and its reports are supposedly confidential, any public revelation regarding standards of detainee treatment can have a substantial effect on international opinion.

The ICRC seeks to handle problems at the lowest level possible. When a team conducts an inspection, it provides a briefing, and sometimes a report, to the local commander. Discrepancies and issues are presented to the detaining authorities, and follow-up visits are made to monitor compliance with recommendations. The commander may or may not implement the recommendations based on either resource constraint or his interpretation of applicable law. These constraints can make complete implementation of ICRC recommendations either difficult or inappropriate. If recommendations are not implemented, the ICRC may address the issue with higher authorities. The ICRC does not expect to receive, nor does the DoD have a policy of providing, a written response to ICRC reports. However, DoD elements do attempt to implement as many of the recommendations as practicable, given security and resource constraints.

One important difference in approach between the U.S. and the ICRC is the interpretation of the legal status of terrorists. According to a Panel interview with CJTF-7 legal counsel, the ICRC sent a report to the State Department and the Coalition Provisional Authority in February 2003 citing lack of compliance with Protocol 1. But the U.S. has specifically rejected Protocol 1 stating that certain elements in the protocol, that provide legal protection for terrorists, make it plainly unacceptable. Still the U.S. has worked to preserve the positive elements of Protocol 1. In 1985, the Secretary of Defense noted that "certain provisions of Protocol 1 reflect customary international law, and others appear to be positive new developments. We therefore intend to work with our allies and others to develop a common understanding or declaration of principles incorporating these positive aspects, with the intention they shall, in time, win recognition as customary international law." In 1986 the ICRC acknowledged that it and the U.S. government had "agreed to disagree" on the applicability of Protocol 1. Nevertheless, the ICRC continues to presume the United States should adhere to this standard under the guise of customary international law.

This would grant legal protections to terrorists equivalent to the protections accorded to prisoners of war as required by the Geneva Conventions of 1949 despite the fact terrorists do not wear uniforms and are otherwise indistinguishable from non-combatants. To do so would undermine the prohibition on terrorists blending in with the civilian population, a situation which makes it impossible to attack terrorists without placing non-combatants at risk. For this and other reasons, the U.S. has specifically rejected this additional protocol.

The ICRC also considers the U.S. policy of categorizing some detainees as "unlawful combatants" to be a violation of their interpretation of international humanitarian law. It contends that Geneva Conventions III and IV, which the U.S. has ratified, allow for only two categories of detainees: (1) civilian detainees who must be charged with a crime and tried and (2) enemy combatants who must be released at the cessation of hostilities. In the ICRC's view, the category of "unlawful combatant" deprives the detainees of certain human rights. It argues that lack of information regarding the reasons for detention and the conditions for release are major sources of stress for detainees.

However, the 1949 Geneva Conventions specify conditions to qualify for protected status. By logic, then, if detainees do not meet the specific requirements of privileged status, there clearly must be a category for those lacking in such privileges. The ICRC does not acknowledge such a category of "unprivileged belligerents," and argues that it is not consistent with its interpretation of the Geneva Conventions.

Regarding the application of current international humanitarian law, including Geneva Conventions III and IV, the ICRC has three concerns: (1) gaining access to and ascertaining the status of all detainees in U.S. custody; (2) its belief that linking detention with interrogations should not be allowed which follows from its refusal to recognize the category of unprivileged combatants and (3) they also worry about losing their effectiveness.

Although the ICRC found U.S. forces generally cooperative, it has cited occasions when the forces did not grant adequate access to detainees, both in Iraq and Afghanistan. Of particular concern to the ICRC, however, has been the existence of "ghost detainees," detainees who were kept from ICRC inspectors. While the Panel has not been able to ascertain the number of ghost detainees in the overall detainee population, several investigations cite their existence. Both the Taguba and Jones/Fay reports cite instances of ghost detainees at Abu Ghraib. Secretary Rumsfeld publicly declared he directed one detainee be held secretly at the request of the Director of Central Intelligence.

On balance, the Panel concludes there is value in the relationship the Department of Defense historically has had with the ICRC. The ICRC should serve as an early warning indicator of possible abuse. Commanders should be alert to ICRC observations in their reports and take corrective actions as appropriate. The Panel also believes the ICRC, no less than the Defense Department, needs to adapt itself to the new realities of conflict, which are far different from the Western European environment from which the ICRC's interpretation of Geneva Conventions was drawn. The Department of Defense has established an office of detainee affairs and should continue to reshape its operational relationship with the ICRC.

RECOMMENDATIONS

Department of Defense reform efforts are underway and the Panel commends these efforts. The Office of the Secretary of Defense, the Joint Chiefs of Staff and the Military Services are conducting comprehensive reviews on how military operations have changed since the end of the Cold War. The military services now recognize the problems and are studying how to adjust force compositions, training, doctrine and responsibilities for active/reserve/guard and contractor mixes to ensure we are better prepared to succeed in the war on terrorism.

The Panel reviewed various inspections, investigations and assessments that produced over 300 recommendations for corrective actions to address the problems identified with DoD detention operations. For the most part the Panel endorses their recommendations. In some areas the recommendations do not go far enough and we augment them. We provide additional recommendations to address relevant areas not covered by previous analysis.

The Independent Panel provides the following additional recommendations:

1. The United States should further define its policy, applicable to both the Department of Defense and other government agencies, on the categorization and status of all detainees as it applies to various operations and theaters. It should define their status and treatment in a way consistent with U.S. jurisprudence and military doctrine and with U.S. interpretation of the Geneva Conventions. We recommend that additional operational, support and staff judge advocate personnel be assigned to appropriate commands for the purpose of expediting the detainee release review process.

2. The Department of Defense needs to address and develop joint doctrine to define the appropriate collaboration between military intelligence and military police in a detention facility. The meaning of guidance, such as MPs "setting the conditions" for interrogation, needs to be defined with precision. MG Taguba argued that all detainee operations be consolidated under the responsibility of a single commander reporting directly to Commander CJTF-7. This change has now been accomplished and seems to be working effectively. Other than lack of leadership, training deficiencies in both MP and MI units have been cited most often as the needed measures to prevent detainee abuse. We support the recommendations on training articulated by the reports published by the various other reviews.

3. The nation needs more specialists for detention/interrogation operations, including linguists, interrogators, human intelligence, counter-intelligence, corrections police and behavioral scientists. Accompanying professional development and career field management systems must be put in place concurrently. The Panel agrees that some use of contractors in detention operations must continue into the foreseeable future. This is especially the case with the need for qualified interpreters and interrogators and will require rigorous oversight.

4. Joint Forces Command should chair a Joint Service Integrated Process Team to develop a new Operational Concept for Detention Operations in the new era of warfare, covering the Global War on Terror. The team should place special and early emphasis on detention operations during Counter-Insurgency campaigns and Stability Operations in which familiar concepts of front and rear areas may not apply. Attention should also be given to preparing for conditions in which normal law enforcement has broken down in an occupied or failed state. The Panel recommends that the idea of a deployable detention facility should be studied and implemented as appropriate.

5. Clearly, force structure in both MP and MI is inadequate to support the armed forces in this new form of warfare. Every investigation we reviewed refers to force structure deficiencies in some measure. There should be an active and reserve component mix of units for both military intelligence and military police. Other forces besides the Army are also in need of force structure improvements. Those forces have not been addressed adequately in the reports reviewed by the Panel, and we recommend that the Secretaries of the Navy and Air Force undertake force structure reviews of their own to improve the performance of their Services in detention operations.

6. Well-documented policy and procedures on approved interrogation techniques are imperative to counteract the current chilling effect the reaction to the abuses have had on the collection of valuable intelligence through interrogations. Given the critical role of intelligence in the Global War on Terror, the aggressiveness of interrogation techniques employed must be measured against the value of intelligence sought, to include its importance, urgency and relevance. A policy for interrogation operations should be promulgated early on and acceptable interrogation techniques for each operation must be clearly understood by all interrogation personnel.

7. All personnel who may be engaged in detention operations, from point of capture to final disposition, should participate in a professional ethics program that would equip them with a sharp moral compass for guidance in situations often riven with conflicting moral obligations. The development of such a values-oriented ethics program should be the responsibility of the individual services with assistance provided by the Joint Chiefs of Staff.

8. Clearer guidelines for the interaction of CIA with the Department of Defense in detention and interrogation operations must be defined.

9. The United States needs to redefine its approach to customary and treaty international humanitarian law, which must be adapted to the realities of the nature of conflict in the 21st century. In doing so, the United States should emphasize the standard of reciprocity, in spite of the low probability that such will be extended to United States Forces by some adversaries, and the preservation of United States societal values and international image that flows from an adherence to recognized humanitarian standards.

10. The Department of Defense should continue to foster its operational relationship with the International Committee of the Red Cross. The Panel believes the International Committee of the Red Cross, no less than the Defense Department, needs to adapt itself to the new realities of conflict which are far different from the Western European environment from which the ICRC's interpretation of Geneva Conventions was drawn.

11. The assignment of a focal point within the office of the Under Secretary for Policy would be a useful organizational step. The new focal point for Detainee Affairs should be charged with all aspects of detention policy and also be responsible for oversight of DoD relations with the International Committee of the Red Cross.

12. The Secretary of Defense should ensure the effective functioning of rapid reporting channels for communicating bad news to senior Department of Defense leadership without prejudice to any criminal or disciplinary actions already underway. The Panel recommends consideration of a joint adaptation of procedures such as the Air Force special notification process.

13. The Panel notes that the Fay investigation cited some medical personnel for failure to report detainee abuse. As noted in that investigation, training should include the obligation to report any detainee abuse. The Panel also notes that the Army IG found significant shortfalls in training and force structure for field sanitation, preventive

medicine and medical treatment requirements for detainees. As the DoD improves detention operations force structure and training, it should pay attention to the need for medical personnel to screen and monitor the health of detention personnel and detainees.

14. The integration of the recommendations in this report and all the other efforts underway on detention operations will require further study. Analysis of the dynamics of program and resource implications, with a view to assessing the trade-offs and opportunity costs involved, must be addressed.

Appendices
Glossary

Army Regulation 15-6	AR 15-6	Army regulation which specifies procedures for command investigations. The common name for both formal and informal command investigations.
Active Component	AC	Active military component of the Army, Navy, Air Force or Marines.
Abuse Cases		An incident or allegation of abuse, including, but not limited to death, assault, sexual assault, and theft, that triggers a CID investigation, which may involve multiple individuals.
Behavioral Science Coordination Team	BSCT	Team comprising medical and other specialized personnel that provides support to special operations forces.
Civilian Internees	CI	Designation of civilians encountered and detained in the theater of war.
Criminal Investigation Command	CID	Investigative agency of the U. S. Army responsible for conducting criminal investigations to which the Army is or may be a party.
Collection Points	CP	Forward locations where prisoners are collected, processed and prepared for movement to the detention center.
Coalition Provisional Authority	CPA	Interim government of Iraq, in place from May 2003 through June 2004.
Convention Against Torture and Other Cruel Inhumane or Degrading Treatment		An international treaty brought into force in 1987 which seeks to define torture and other cruel, inhuman or degrading treatment or punishment and provides a mechanism for punishing those who would inflict such treatment on others.
Enemy Prisoner of War	EPW	International Committee of the Red Cross term for prisoners of war; this status bestows certain rights to the individual in the Geneva Conventions.

Force Design Update	FDU	The Army process to review and restructure forces.
Fragmentary Order	FRAGO	An abbreviated form of an operation order (verbal, written or digital) usually issued on a day-to-day basis that eliminates the need for restarting information contained in a basic operation order.
Army Field Manual 34–52 "Intelligence Interrogation"	FM 34–52	Current manual for operations and training in interrogation techniques. The edition dated 1987 was updated in 1992.
Geneva Conventions	GC	The international treaties brought into force in August 1949. These conventions extend protections to, among others, prisoners of war and civilians in time of war.
Global War on Terror	GWOT	Worldwide operation to eradicate individuals and groups that participate in and sponsor terrorism.
Internment/Resettlement	I/R	Internment/resettlement mission assigned to specific US Army Military Police units who are responsible for the detention of Enemy Prisoners of War during armed conflict.
International Committee of the Red Cross	ICRC	Non-governmental organization that seeks to help victims of war and internal violence.
In Lieu Of	ILO	When used in reference to manning, indicates that forces were used in a manner other than originally specified.
Initial Point of Capture	IPOC	Location where an enemy prisoner or internee is captured.
Iraq Survey Group	ISG	Organization located in Iraq with the mission to find weapons of mass destruction.
Joint Manning Document	JMD	Master document covering personnel requirements for the joint theater.
Navy Criminal Investigative Service	NCIS	Investigative service for the US Navy and Marine Corps
National Detainee Reporting Center	NDRC	Agency charged with accounting for and reporting all EPW, retained personnel, civilian internees and other detainees during armed conflict.
Operation Enduring Freedom	OEF	Military operation in Afghanistan
Other Government Agencies	OGA	Refers to non-Department of Defense agencies operating in theaters of war.
Operation Iraqi Freedom	OIF	Military operation in Iraq.
Office of Legal Counsel	OLC	Refers to the Department of Justice Office of Legal Counsel.

Operation Noble Eagle	ONE	Operation to activate and deploy forces for homeland defense and civil support in response to the attacks of September 11, 2001.
Operation Victory Bounty	OVB	CJTF-7 operation to sweep Baghdad area for remaining elements of the Saddam Fedayeen in 2003.
Operational Control	OPCON	Command authority over all aspects of military operations.
Republican Guard	RG	Elite Iraqi military forces under the regime of Saddam Hussein.
Reserve Component	RC	Army, Navy, Air Force and Marine Reserves and Army and Air National Guard
Request for Forces	RFF	Commanders request for additional forces to support the mission.
Standing Operating Procedure	SOP	A set of instructions covering those features of operations which lend themselves to a definite or standardized procedures without loss of effectiveness. The procedure is applicable unless ordered otherwise.
Tactical Control	TACON	Command authority to control and task forces for maneuvers within an area of operations.
Tactical Human Intelligence Team	THT	Forward deployed intelligence element providing human intelligence support to maneuver units.
Time Phased Force Deployment List	TPFDL	Identifies the units needed to support an operational plan and specifies their order and method of deployment.
Army Regulation 15-6	AR 15-6	Army regulation which specifies procedures for command investigations. The common name for both formal and informal command investigations.
Active Component	AC	Active military component of the Army, Navy, Air Force or Marines.
Abuse Cases		An incident or allegation of abuse, including, but not limited to death, assault, sexual assault, and theft, that triggers a CID investigation, which may involve multiple individuals.
Behavioral Science Coordination Team	BSCT	Team comprising medical and other specialized personnel that provides support to special operations forces.
Civilian Internees	CI	Designation of civilians encountered and detained in the theater of war.
Criminal Investigation Command	CID	Investigative agency of the U. S. Army responsible for conducting criminal investigations to which the Army is or may be a party.

Collection Points	CP	Forward locations where prisoners are collected, processed and prepared for movement to the detention center.
Coalition Provisional Authority	CPA	Interim government of Iraq, in place from May 2003 through June 2004.
Convention Against Torture and Other Cruel Inhumane or Degrading Treatment		An international treaty brought into force in 1987 which seeks to define torture and other cruel, inhuman or degrading treatment or punishment and provides a mechanism for punishing those who would inflict such treatment on others.
Enemy Prisoner of War	EPW	International Committee of the Red Cross term for prisoners of war; this status bestows certain rights to the individual in the Geneva Conventions.
Force Design Update	FDU	The Army process to review and restructure forces.
Fragmentary Order	FRAGO	An abbreviated form of an operation order (verbal, written or digital) usually issued on a day-to-day basis that eliminates the need for restarting information contained in a basic operation order.
Army Field Manual 34-52 "Intelligence Interrogation"	FM 34-52	Current manual for operations and training in interrogation techniques. The edition dated 1987 was updated in 1992.
Geneva Conventions	GC	The international treaties brought into force in August 1949. These conventions extend protections to, among others, prisoners of war and civilians in time of war.
Global War on Terror	GWOT	Worldwide operation to eradicate individuals and groups that participate in and sponsor terrorism.
Internment/Resettlement	I/R	Internment/resettlement mission assigned to specific US Army Military Police units who are responsible for the detention of Enemy Prisoners of War during armed conflict.
International Committee of the Red Cross	ICRC	Non-governmental organization that seeks to help victims of war and internal violence.
In Lieu Of	ILO	When used in reference to manning, indicates that forces were used in a manner other than originally specified.
Initial Point of Capture	IPOC	Location where an enemy prisoner or internee is captured.
Iraq Survey Group	ISG	Organization located in Iraq with the mission to find weapons of mass destruction.
Joint Manning Document	JMD	Master document covering personnel requirements for the joint theater.

Navy Criminal Investigative Service	NCIS	Investigative service for the US Navy and Marine Corps
National Detainee Reporting Center	NDRC	Agency charged with accounting for and reporting all EPW, retained personnel, civilian internees and other detainees during armed conflict.
Operation Enduring Freedom	OEF	Military operation in Afghanistan
Other Government Agencies	OGA	Refers to non-Department of Defense agencies operating in theaters of war.
Operation Iraqi Freedom	OIF	Military operation in Iraq.
Office of Legal Counsel	OLC	Refers to the Department of Justice Office of Legal Counsel.
Operation Noble Eagle	ONE	Operation to activate and deploy forces for homeland defense and civil support in response to the attacks of September 11, 2001.
Operation Victory Bounty	OVB	CJTF-7 operation to sweep Baghdad area for remaining elements of the Saddam Fedayeen in 2003.
Operational Control	OPCON	Command authority over all aspects of military operations.
Republican Guard	RG	Elite Iraqi military forces under the regime of Saddam Hussein.
Reserve Component	RC	Army, Navy, Air Force and Marine Reserves and Army and Air National Guard
Request for Forces	RFF	Commanders request for additional forces to support the mission.
Standing Operating Procedure	SOP	A set of instructions covering those features of operations which lend themselves to a definite or standardized procedures without loss of effectiveness. The procedure is applicable unless ordered otherwise.
Tactical Control	TACON	Command authority to control and task forces for maneuvers within an area of operations.
Tactical Human Intelligence Team	THT	Forward deployed intelligence element providing human intelligence support to maneuver units.
Time Phased Force Deployment List	TPFDL	Identifies the units needed to support an operational plan and specifies their order and method of deployment.

Guantanamo

			Commander
United States Southern Command	USSOUTHCOM	One of nine Unified Combatant Commands with operational control of U.S. military forces. Area of responsibility includes Guantanamo Bay, Cuba.	GEN James Hill
Joint Task Force 160	JTF-160	Initially responsible for detention operations at Guantanamo, merged in JTF-G 11/4/02.	
Joint Task Force 170	JTF-170	Initially responsible for interrogation operations at Guantanamo, merged in JTF-G 11/4/02.	
Joint Task Force Guantanamo	JTF-G	Joint task force for all operations at Guantanamo, formed 11/4/02.	

Afghanistan

United States Central Command	USCENTCOM	One of nine Unified Commands with operational control of U.S. military forces. Area of responsibility includes Afghanistan and Iraq.	GEN John Abizaid
Coalition Forces Land Component Command	CFLCC	Senior headquarters element for multinational land forces in both Iraq and Afghanistan.	LTG David McKiernan
Combined Joint Task Force 180	CJTF-180	Forward deployed headquarters for Afghanistan.	

Iraq

United States Central Command	USCENTCOM	One of nine Unified Commands with operational control of U.S. military forces. Area of responsibility includes Afghanistan and Iraq.	GEN John Abizaid
Coalition Forces Land Component Command	CFLCC	Senior headquarters element for multinational land forces in both Iraq and Afghanistan.	LTG David McKiernan
Combined Joint Task Force 7	CJTF-7	Forward deployed headquarters for Operation Iraqi Freedom. Replaced in May 04 by Multi-National Force – Iraq and Multi-National Corps – Iraq	LTG Ricardo Sanchez
Combined Joint Task Force 7 Intelligence Staff	CJTF-7 C2	Intelligence staff support to CJTF-7	MG Barbara Fast

800th Military Police Brigade	800th MP BDE	U.S. Army Reserve Military Police Brigade, responsible for all internment facilities in Iraq, and assistance to CPA Minister of Justice.	BG Janis Karpinski
Joint Interrogation and Detention Center	JDIC	Element of CJTF-7 for interrogation mission at Abu Ghraib.	LTC Steven Jordan
320th Military Police Battalion	320th MP BN	Element of 800th Bde; assigned to Abu Ghraib.	LTC Jerry Phillabaum
372nd Military Police Company	372nd MP CO	Element of 320th Bn; assigned to Abu Ghraib in October 2003.	CPT Donald Reese
72nd Military Police Company	72nd MP CO	Nevada National Guard MP Company, assigned to Abu Ghraib prior to 372nd MP Co.	
205th Military Intelligence Brigade	205th MI BDE	Military Intelligence Brigade responsible for multiple Army intelligence missions throughout Iraq.	COL Thomas Pappas
519th Military Intelligence Battalion	519th MI BN	Tactical exploitation element of 525 MI Bde; Company A was located at Abu Ghraib.	MAJ Michnewicz

Other

| United States Army Forces Command | FORSCOM | U.S. Army major command responsible for training, readiness and deployment. | |

SECRETARY OF DEFENSE
1000 DEFENSE PENTAGON
WASHINGTON, DC 20301-1000

MAY 12 2004

MEMORANDUM FOR THE HONORABLE JAMES R. SCHLESINGER,
CHAIRMAN
THE HONORABLE HAROLD BROWN
THE HONORABLE TILLIE K. FOWLER
GENERAL CHARLES A. HORNER, USAF (RET.)

SUBJECT: Independent Panel to Review DoD Detention Operations

Various organizations of the Department of Defense have investigated, or will investigate, various aspects of allegations of abuse at DoD Detention Facilities and other matters related to detention operations. Thus far these inquiries include the following:

– Criminal investigations into individual allegations
– Army Provost Marshal General assessment of detention and corrections operations in Iraq
– Joint Task Force Guantanamo assistance visit to Iraq to assess intelligence operations
– Administrative Investigation under AR 15-6 regarding Abu Ghraib operations
– Army Inspector General assessment of doctrine and training for detention operations
– Commander, Joint Task Force-7 review of activities of military intelligence personnel at Abu Ghraib
– Army Reserve Command Inspector General assessment of training of Reserve units regarding military intelligence and military police
– Naval Inspector General review of detention procedures at Guantanamo Bay, Cuba, and the Naval Consolidated Brig, Charleston, South Carolina

I have been or will be briefed on the results of these inquiries and the corrective actions taken by responsible officials within the Department.

It would be helpful to me to have your independent, professional advice on the issues that you consider most pertinent related to the various allegations, based on your review of completed and pending investigative reports and other materials and information. I am especially interested in your views on the cause of the problems and what should be done to fix them. Issues such as force structure, training of regular and reserve personnel, use of contractors, organization, detention policy and procedures, interrogation policy and procedures, the relationship between detention and interrogation, compliance with the Geneva Conventions, relationship with the International Committee of the Red Cross, command relationships, and operational practices may be contributing factors you might wish to review. Issues of personal accountability will be resolved through established military justice and administrative procedures, although any information you may develop will be welcome.

I would like your independent advice orally and in writing, preferably within 45 days after you begin your review. DoD personnel will collect information for your review and assist you as you deem appropriate. You are to have access to all relevant DoD investigations and other DoD information unless prohibited by law. Reviewing all written materials relevant to these issues may be sufficient to allow you to provide your advice. Should you believe it necessary to travel or conduct interviews, the Director of Administration and Management will make appropriate arrangements.

I intend to provide your report to the Committees on Armed Services, the Secretaries of the Military Departments, the Chairman of the Joint Chiefs of Staff, the Commanders of the Combatant Commands, the Directors of the Defense Agencies, and others as appropriate. If your report contains classified information, please also provide an unclassified version suitable for public release.

By copy of this memorandum, I request the Director of Administration and Management to secure the necessary technical, administrative and legal support for your review from the Department of Defense Components. I appoint you as full-time employees of this Department without pay under 10 U.S.C. §1583. I request all Department of Defense personnel to cooperate fully with your review and to make available all relevant documents and information at your request.

cc: SECRETARIES OF THE MILITARY DEPARTMENTS
  CHAIRMAN OF THE JOINT CHIEFS OF STAFF
  UNDER SECRETARIES OF DEFENSE
  DIRECTOR, DEFENSE RESEARCH AND ENGINEERING
  ASSISTANT SECRETARIES OF DEFENSE
  GENERAL COUNSEL OF THE DEPARTMENT OF DEFENSE
  INSPECTOR GENERAL OF THE DEPARTMENT OF DEFENSE
  DIRECTOR, OPERATIONAL TEST AND EVALUATION
  ASSISTANTS TO THE SECRETARY OF DEFENSE
  DIRECTOR, ADMINISTRATION AND MANAGEMENT
  DIRECTOR, FORCE TRANSFORMATION
  DIRECTOR, NET ASSESSMENT
  DIRECTOR, PROGRAM ANALYSIS AND EVALUATION
  DIRECTORS OF THE DEFENSE AGENCIES
  DIRECTORS OF THE DOD FIELD ACTIVITIES

THE WHITE HOUSE
WASHINGTON

February 7, 2002

MEMORANDUM FOR THE VICE PRESIDENT
               THE SECRETARY OF STATE
               THE SECRETARY OF DEFENSE
               THE ATTORNEY GENERAL
               CHIEF OF STAFF TO THE PRESIDENT
               DIRECTOR OF CENTRAL INTELLIGENCE
               ASSISTANT TO THE PRESIDENT FOR NATIONAL
                   SECURITY AFFAIRS
               CHAIRMAN OF THE JOINT CHIEFS OF STAFF

SUBJECT: Humane Treatment of al Qaeda and Taliban Detainees

1. Our recent extensive discussions regarding the status of al Qaeda and Taliban detainees confirm that the application of the Geneva Convention Relative to the Treatment of Prisoners of War of August 12, 1949 (Geneva) to the conflict with al Qaeda and the Taliban involves complex legal questions. By its terms, Geneva applies to conflicts involving "High Contracting Parties," which can only be states. Moreover, it assumes the existence of "regular" armed forces fighting on behalf of states. However, the war against terrorism ushers in a new paradigm, one in which groups with broad, international reach commit horrific acts against innocent civilians, sometimes with the direct support of states. Our Nation recognizes that this new paradigm – ushered in not by us, but by terrorists – requires new thinking in the law of war, but thinking that should nevertheless be consistent with the principles of Geneva.

2. Pursuant to my authority as Commander in Chief and Chief Executive of the United States, and relying on the opinion of the Department of Justice dated January 22, 2002, and on the legal opinion rendered by the Attorney General in his letter of February 1, 2002, I hereby determine as follows:

    a. I accept the legal conclusion of the Department of Justice and determine that none of the provisions of Geneva apply to our conflict with al Qaeda in Afghanistan or elsewhere throughout the world because, among other reasons, al Qaeda is not a High Contracting Party to Geneva.

    b. I accept the legal conclusion of the Attorney General and the Department of Justice that I have the authority under the Constitution to suspend Geneva as between the United States and Afghanistan, but I decline to exercise that authority at this time. Accordingly, I determine that the provisions of Geneva will apply to our present conflict with the Taliban. I reserve the right to exercise this authority in this or future conflicts.

    c. I also accept the legal conclusion of the Department of Justice and determine that common Article 3 of Geneva does not apply to either al Qaeda or Taliban detainees, because, among other reasons, the relevant conflicts are international in scope and common Article 3 applies only to "armed conflict not of an international character."

    d. Based on the facts supplied by the Department of Defense and the recommendation of the Department of Justice, I determine that the Taliban detainees are unlawful combatants and, therefore, do not qualify as prisoners of war under Article 4 of

Geneva. I note that, because Geneva does not apply to our conflict with al Qaeda, al Qaeda detainees also do not qualify as prisoners of war.

3. Of course, our values as a Nation, values that we share with many nations in the world, call for us to treat detainees humanely, including those who are not legally entitled to such treatment. Our Nation has been and will continue to be a strong supporter of Geneva and its principles. As a matter of policy, the United States Armed Forces shall continue to treat detainees humanely and, to the extent appropriate and consistent with military necessity, in a manner consistent with the principles of Geneva.

4. The United States will hold states, organizations, and individuals who gain control of United States personnel responsible for treating such personnel humanely and consistent with applicable law.

5. I hereby reaffirm the order previously issued by the Secretary of Defense to the United States Armed Forces requiring that the detainees be treated humanely and, to the extent appropriate and consistent with military necessity, in a manner consistent with the principles of Geneva.

6. I hereby direct the Secretary of State to communicate my determinations in an appropriate manner to our allies, and other countries and international organizations cooperating in the war against terrorism of global reach.

Interrogation Policies in Guantanamo, Afghanistan and Iraq

Number of Authorized Techniques	Notes	Policy	Date	Number of Authorized Techniques	Notes	Policy	Date	Number of Authorized Techniques	Policy	Date	Notes
17		FM 34-52 (1992)	Jan 02-01 Dec 02	17		FM 34-52 (1992)	27 Oct 01-24 Jan 03	17	FM 34-52 (1992)		
33	1	Secretary of Defense Approved Tiered System	02 Dec 02-15 Jan 03	33	1, 3, 6	CJTF 180 Response to Director, Joint Staff	24-Jan-03	29	CJTF-7 Signed Policy	14-Sep-03	1
20		FM 34-52 (1992) with 3 Cat I Techniques	16 Jan 03-15 Apr 03	32	1	CJTF 180 Detainee SOP	27-Mar-04	19	CJTF-7 Signed Policy	12-Oct-03	4
24	1,2	Secretary of Defense Memo	16 Apr 03-Present	19	4	CJTF-A Rev 2 Guidance	Jun-04	19	CJTF-7 Signed Policy	13-May-04	4

1 Some techniques specifically delineated in this memo are inherent to techniques contained in FM 34-52, e.g., Yelling as a component of Fear Up

2 Five Approved Techniques require SOUTHCOM approval and SECDEF notification.

3 Figure includes techniques that were not in current use but requested for future use.

4 Figure includes one technique which requires CG approval.

5 Memorandum cited for Afghanistan and Iraq are classified.

6 Figure includes the 17 techniques of FM-34-52, although they are not specified in the Memo.

Appendix D
Source: Naval IG Investigation

Evolution of Interrogation Techniques – GTMO

Interrogation Techniques	FM 34-52 (1992) Jan 02-01 Dec 02	Secretary of Defense Approved Tiered System 02 Dec 02-15 Jan 03	FM 34-52 (1992) with some Cat I 16 Jan 03-15 Apr 03	Secretary of Defense Memo 16 Apr 03-Present
Direct questioning	x	x	x	x
Incentive/removal of incentive	x	x	x	x
Emotional love	x	x	x	x
Emotional hate	x	x	x	x
Fear up harsh	x	x	x	x
Fear up mild	x	x	x	x
Reduced fear	x	x	x	x
Pride and ego up	x	x	x	x
Pride and ego down	x	x	x	x
Futility	x	x	x	x
We know all	x	x	x	x
Establish your identity	x	x	x	x
Repetition approach	x	x	x	x
File and dossier	x	x	x	x
Mutt and Jeff				x*
Rapid Fire	x	x	x	x
Silence	x	x	x	x
Change of Scene	x	x	x	x
Yelling		x (Cat I)	x	

Evolution of Interrogation Techniques – GTMO

Interrogation Techniques	FM 34-52 (1992) Jan 02-01 Dec 02	Secretary of Defense Approved Tiered System 02 Dec 02-15 Jan 03	FM 34-52 (1992) with some Cat I 16 Jan 03-15 Apr 03	Secretary of Defense Memo 16 Apr 03-Present
Deception		x (Cat I)		
Multiple interrogators		x (Cat I)	x	
Interrogator identity		x (Cat I)	x	
Stress positions, like standing		x (Cat II)		
False documents/reports		x (Cat II)		
Isolation for up to 30 days		x (Cat II)		x*
Deprivation of light/auditory stimuli		x (Cat II)		
Hooding (transportation & questioning)		x (Cat II)		
20-interrogations		x (Cat II)		
Removal of ALL comfort items, including religious items		x (Cat II)		
MRE-only diet		x (Cat II)		x*
Removal of clothing		x (Cat II)		
Forced grooming		x (Cat II)		
Exploiting individual phobias, e.g., dogs		x (Cat II)		
Mild, non-injurious physical contact, e.g., grabbing, poking or light pushing		x (Cat III)		
Environmental manipulation				x
Sleep adjustment				x
False flag				x

* Techniques require SOUTHCOM approval and SECDEF notification.

Source: Naval IG Investigation
Appendix E

Major Deten

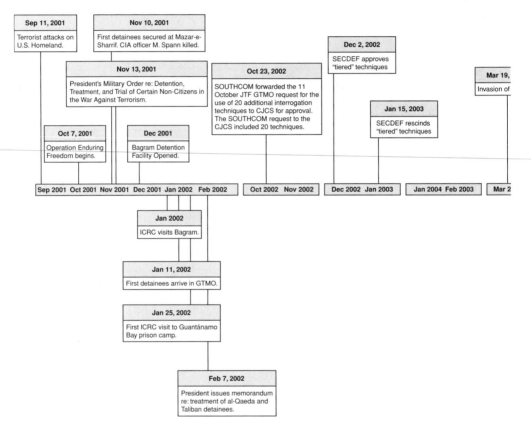

tion Events

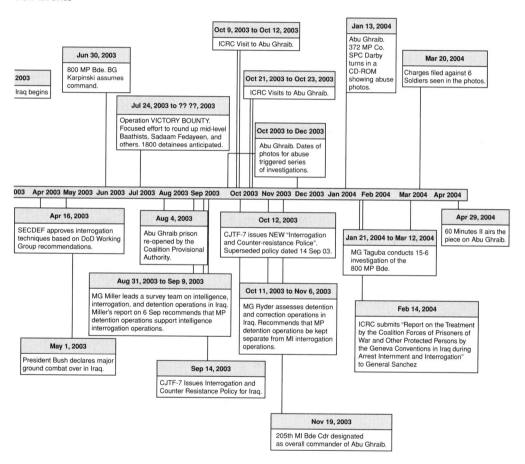

PSYCHOLOGICAL STRESSES

The potential for abusive treatment of detainees during the Global War on Terrorism was entirely predictable based on a fundamental understanding of the principle of social psychology principles coupled with an awareness of numerous known environmental risk factors. Most leaders were unacquainted with these known risk factors, and therefore failed to take steps to mitigate the likelihood that abuses of some type would occur during detainee operations. While certain conditions heightened the possibility of abusive treatment, such conditions neither excuse nor absolve the individuals who engaged in deliberate immoral or illegal behaviors.

The abuse the detainees endured at various places and times raises a number of questions about the likely psychological aspects of inflicting such abuses. Findings from the field of social psychology suggest that the conditions of war and the dynamics of detainee operations carry inherent risks for human mistreatment, and therefore must be approached with great caution and careful planning and training.

The Stanford Prison Experiment

In 1973, Haney, Banks and Zimbardo (1) published their landmark Stanford study, "Interpersonal Dynamics in a Simulated Prison." Their study provides a cautionary tale for all military detention operations. The Stanford Experiment used a set of tested, psychologically sound college students in a benign environment. In contrast, in military detention operations, soldiers work under stressful combat conditions that are far from benign.

The Stanford Prison Experiment (SPE) attempted to "create a prison-like situation" and then observe the behavior of those involved. The researchers randomly assigned 24 young men to either the "prisoner" or "guard" group. Psychological testing was used to eliminate participants with overt psychopathology, and extensive efforts were made to simulate actual prison conditions. The experiment, scheduled to last two weeks, was cancelled after only six days due to the ethical concerns raised by the behaviors of the participants. The study notes that while guards and prisoners were free to engage in any form of interpersonal interactions, the "characteristic nature of their encounters tended to be negative, hostile, affrontive and dehumanizing."

The researchers found that both prisoners and guards exhibited "pathological reactions" during the course of the experiment. Guards fell into three categories: (1) those who were "tough but fair," (2) those who were passive and reluctant to use coercive control and, of special interests, (3) those who "went far beyond their roles to engage in creative cruelty and harassment." With each passing day, guards "were observed to generally escalate their harassment of the prisoners." The researchers reported: "We witnessed a sample of normal, healthy American college students fractionate into a group of prison guards who seemed to derive pleasure from insulting, threatening, humiliating, and dehumanizing their peers."

Because of the random assignment of subjects, the study concluded the observed behaviors were the result of situational rather than personality factors:

> The negative, anti-social reactions observed were not the product of an environment created by combining a collection of deviant personalities, but rather, the result of an intrinsically pathological situation which could distort and rechannel the behaviour of essentially normal individuals. The abnormality here resided in the psychological nature of the situation and not in those who passed through it.

The authors discussed how prisoner-guard interactions shaped the evolution of power use by the guards:

> The use of power was self-aggrandizing and self-perpetuating. The guard power, derived initially from an arbitrary label, was intensified whenever there was any perceived threat by the prisoners and this new level subsequently became the baseline from which further hostility and harassment would begin. The most hostile guards on each shift moved spontaneously into the leadership roles of giving orders and deciding on punishments. They became role models whose behaviour was emulated by other members of the shift. Despite minimal contact between the three separate guard shifts and nearly 16 hours a day spent away from the prison, the absolute level of aggression as well as the more subtle and "creative" forms of aggression manifested, increased in a spiraling function. Not to be tough and arrogant was to be seen as a sign of weakness by the guards and even those "good" guards who did not get as drawn into the power syndrome as the others respected the implicit norm of never contradicting or even interfering with an action of a more hostile guard on their shift.

In an article published 25 years after the Stanford Prison Experiment, Haney and Zimbardo noted initial study "underscored the degree to which institutional settings can develop a life of their own, independent of the wishes, intentions, and purposes of those who run them." They highlighted the need for those outside the culture to offer external perspectives on process and procedures. (2)

Social Psychology: Causes of Aggression and Inhumane Treatment

The field of social psychology examines the nature of human interactions. Researchers in the field have long been searching to understand why humans sometimes mistreat fellow humans. The discussions below examine the factors behind human aggression and inhumane treatment, striving to impart a better understanding of why detainee abuses occur.

Human Aggression
Research has identified a number of factors that can assist in predicting human aggression. These factors include:

- **Personality traits.** Certain traits among the totality of an individual's behavioral and emotional make-up predispose to be more aggressive than other individuals.

- **Beliefs.** Research reveals those who believe they can carry out aggressive acts, and that such acts will result in a desired outcome, are more likely to be aggressive than those who do not hold these beliefs.

- **Attitudes.** Those who hold more positive attitudes towards violence are more likely to commit violent acts.

- **Values.** The values individuals hold vary regarding the appropriateness of using violence to resolve interpersonal conduct.

- **Situational Factors.** Aggressive cues (the presence of weapons), provocation (threats, insults, aggressive behaviors), frustration, pain and discomfort (hot temperatures, loud noises, unpleasant odors), and incentives can all call forth aggressive behaviors.

- **Emotional factors.** Anger, fear, and emotional arousal can heighten the tendency to act out aggressively.

The personality traits, belief systems, attitudes, and values of those who perpetrated detainee abuses can only be speculated upon. However, it is reasonable to assume, in any given population, these characteristics will be distributed along a bell curve, which will predispose some more than others within a group to manifest aggressive behaviors. These existing traits can be affected by environmental conditions, which are discussed later.

Abusive Treatment

Psychologists have attempted to understand how and why individuals and groups who usually act humanely can sometimes act otherwise in certain circumstances. A number of psychological concepts explain why abusive behavior occurs. These concepts include:

Deindividuation. Deindividuation is a process whereby the anonymity, suggestibility, and contagion provided in a crowd allows individuals to participate in behavior marked by the temporary suspension of customary rules and inhibitions. Individuals within a group may experience reduced self-awareness which can also result in disinhibited behavior.

Groupthink. Individuals often make very uncharacteristics decisions when part of a group. Symptoms of groupthink include: (1) Illusion of invulnerability – group members believe the group is special and morally superior; therefore its decisions are sound; (2) Illusion of unanimity in which members assume all are in concurrence, and (3) Pressure is brought to bear on those who might dissent.

Dehumanization. Dehumanization is the process whereby individuals or groups are viewed as somehow less than fully human. Existing cultural and moral standards are often not applied to those who have been dehumanized.

Enemy Image. Enemy image describes the phenomenon wherein both sides participating in a conflict tend to view themselves as good and peace-loving people, while the enemy is seen as evil and aggressive.

Moral Exclusion. Moral exclusion is a process whereby one group views another as fundamentally different, and therefore prevailing moral rules and practices apply to one group but not the other.

Abuse and Inhumane Treatment in War

Socialization to Evil and Doubling. Dr. Robert Jay Lifton has extensively examined the nature of inhumane treatment during war. Dr. Lifton suggested that ordinary people can experience "socialization to evil," especially in a war environment. Such people often experience a "doubling." They are socialized to evil in one environment and act accordingly within that environment, but they think and behave otherwise when removed from that environment. For example, doctors committed unspeakable acts while working in Auschwitz, but would go home on weekends and behave as "normal" husbands and fathers.

Moral Disengagement. Moral disengagement occurs when normal self-regulatory mechanisms are altered in a way that allows for abusive treatment and similar immoral behaviors. Certain conditions, identified by Bandura and his colleagues (3), can lead to moral disengagement, such as:

- **Moral Justification.** Misconduct can be justified if it is believed to serve a social good.

- **Euphemistic Language.** Language affects attitudes and beliefs, and the use of euphemistic language such as "softening up" (and even "humane treatment") can lead to moral disengagement.

- **Advantageous Comparison.** "Injurious conduct can be rendered benign" when compared to more violent behaviors. This factor is likely to occur during war. Essentially, abusive behaviors may appear less significant and somehow justifiable when compared to death and destruction.

- **Displacement of Responsibility.** "People view their actions as springing from the social pressures or dictates of others rather than as something for which they are socially responsible." This is consistent with statements from those under investigation for abuses.

- **Diffusion of Responsibility.** Group decisions and behaviors can obscure responsibility: "When everyone is responsible, no one really feels responsible."

- **Disregarding or Distorting the Consequences of Actions.** Harmful acts can be minimized or ignored when the harm is inflicted for personal gain or because of social inducements.

- **Attribution of Blame.** "Victims get blamed for bringing suffering on themselves."

Detainee and interrogation operations consist of a special subset of human interactions, characterized by one group which has significant power and control over another group which must be managed, often against the will of its members. Without proper oversight and monitoring, such interactions carry a higher risk of moral disengagement on the part of those in power and, in turn, are likely to lead to abusive behaviors.

Environmental Factors

The risk of abusive behaviors is best understood by examining both psychological and environmental risk factors. A cursory examination of situational variables present at Abu Ghraib indicates the risk for abusive treatment was considerable. Many of the problematic conditions at Abu Ghraib are discussed elsewhere in this report, to include such factors as poor training, under nearly daily attack, insufficient staffing, inadequate oversight, confused lines of authority, evolving and nuclear policy, and a generally poor quality of life. The stresses of these conditions were certainly exacerbated by delayed troop rotations and by basic issues of safety and security. Personnel needed to contend with both internal threats from volatile and potentially dangerous prisoners and external threats from frequent mortar fire and attacks on the prison facilities.

The widespread practice of stripping detainees, another environmental factor, deserves special mention. The removal of clothing interrogation technique evolved into something much broader, resulting in the practice of groups of detainees being kept naked for extended periods at Abu Ghraib. Interviews with personnel at Abu Ghraib indicated that naked detainees were a common sight within the prison, and this was understood to be a general part of interrogation operations.

While the removal of clothing may have been intended to make detainees feel more vulnerable and therefore more compliant with interrogations, this practice is likely to have had a psychological impact on guards and interrogators as well. The wearing of clothes is an inherently social practice, and therefore the stripping away of clothing may have had the unintended consequence of dehumanizing detainees in the eyes of those who interacted with them. As discussed earlier, the process of dehumanization lowers the moral and cultural barriers that usually preclude the abusive treatment of others.

(1) Haney, C., Banks, C., and Zimbardo, P., Interpersonal Dynamics in a Simulated Prison, *International Journal of Criminology and Penology*, 1973, 1, 69–97.
(2) Haney, C. and Zimbardo, P., The Past and Future of U.S. Prison Policy, Twenty-Five Years after the Stanford Prison Experiment, *American Psychologist*, July 1998, 709–27.

Appendix G

(3) Bandura, A., Barbaranelli, C., Caprara, G., and Pastorelli, C., Mechanisms of Moral Disengagement in the Exercise of Moral Agency, *Journal of Personality and Social Psychology*, Vol. 71(2), August 1996, 364–74.

ETHICAL ISSUES

Introduction

For the United States and other nations with similar value systems, detention and interrogation are themselves ethically challenging activities. Effective interrogators must deceive, seduce, incite, and coerce in ways not normally acceptable for members of the general public. As a result, the U. S. places restrictions on who may be detained and the methods interrogators may employ. Exigencies in the Global War on Terror have stressed the normal American boundaries associated with detention and interrogation. In the ensuing moral uncertainty, arguments of military necessity make the ethical foundation of our soldiers especially important.

Ethical Foundations of Detention and Interrogation

Within our values system, consent is a central moral criterion on evaluating our behavior toward others. Consent is the manifestation of the freedom and dignity of the person and, as such, plays a critical role in moral reasoning. Consent *restrains*, as well as *enables*, humans in their treatment of others. Criminals, by not respecting the rights of others, may be said to have consented – in principle – to arrest and possible imprisonment. In this construct – and due to the threat they represent – insurgents and terrorists "consent" to the possibility of being captured, detained, interrogated, or possibly killed.

Permissions and Limits on Detentions

This guideline of implied consent for the U.S. first limits who may be detained. Individuals suspected of insurgent or terrorist activity may be detained to prevent them from conducting further attacks and to gather intelligence to prevent other insurgents and terrorists from conducting attacks. This suggests two categories of persons who may be detained and interrogated: (1) persons who have engaged in or assisted those who engage in terrorist or insurgent activities; and (2) persons who have come by information regarding insurgent and terrorist activity.

By engaging in such activities, persons in the first category may be detained as criminals or enemy combatants, depending on the context. Persons in the second category may be detained and questioned for specific information, but if they do not represent a continuing threat, they may be detained only long enough to obtain the information.

Permissions and Limits on Interrogation Techniques

For the U.S., most cases for permitting harsh treatment of detainees on moral grounds begin with variants of the "ticking time bomb" scenario. The ingredients of such scenarios usually include an impending loss of life, a suspect who knows how to prevent it – and in most versions is responsible for it – and a third party who has no humane alternative to obtain the information in order to save lives. Such cases raise a perplexing moral problem: Is it permissible to employ inhumane treatment when it is believed to be the only way to prevent loss of lives? In periods of emergency, and especially in combat, there will always be a temptation to override legal and moral norms for morally good ends. Many in Operations Enduring Freedom and Iraqi Freedom were not well prepared by their experience, education, and training to resolve such ethical problems.

A morally consistent approach to the problem would be to recognize there are occasions when violating norms in understandable but not necessarily correct – that is, we can recognize that a good person might, in good faith, violate standards. In principle, someone who, facing such a dilemma, committed abuse should be required to offer his actions up for review and judgment by a competent authority. An excellent example is the case of a 4th Infantry Division battalion commander who permitted his men to beat a detainee whom he had good reason to believe had information about future attacks against his unit. When the beating failed to produce the desired results, the commander fired his weapon near the detainee's head. The technique was successful and the lives of U.S. servicemen were likely saved. However, his actions clearly violated the Geneva Conventions and he reported his actions knowing he would be prosecuted by the Army. He was punished in moderation and allowed to retire.

In such circumstances interrogators must apply a "minimum harm" rule by not inflicting more pressure than is necessary to get the desired information. Further, any treatment that causes permanent harm would not be permitted, as this surely consititutes torture. Moreover, any pain inflicted to teach a lesson or after the interrogator has determined he cannot extract information is morally wrong.

National security is an obligation of the state, and therefore the work of interrogators carries a moral justification. But the methods employed should reflect this nation's commitment to our own values. Of course the tension between military necessity and our values will remain. Because of this, military professionals must accept the reality that during crises they may find themselves in circumstances where lives will be at stake and the morally appropriate methods to preserve those lives may not be obvious. This should not preclude action, but these professionals must be prepared to accept the consequences.

Ethics Education

The instances of detainee abuse in Iraq and Afghanistan do indicate a review of military ethics education programs is needed. This is not to suggest that more adequate ethics education will necessarily prevent abuses. Major service programs such as the Army's "core values," however, fail to adequately prepare soldiers working in detention operations.

While there are numerous ethics education programs throughout the services, almost all refer to certain "core values" as their foundation. Core-values programs are grounded in organizational efficacy rather than the moral good. They do not address humane treatment of the enemy and non-combatants, leaving military leaders and educators an incomplete tool box with which to deal with "real-world" ethical problems. A professional ethics program addressing these situations would help equip them with a sharper moral compass for guidance in situations often riven with conflicting moral obligations.

Appendix H

Presenter: Vice Admiral Albert T. Church, III, Naval Inspector General   Wednesday, May 12, 2004

Media Availability with Vice Admiral Church

ADMIRAL CHURCH: I'm Vice Admiral Albert T. I usually go by Tom Church, I'm the Naval Inspector General. Okay, let's start. I was directed by the Secretary of Defense last week to go down to Guantanamo Bay, and my specific direction task was to ensure that his orders, DoD orders with respect to detainees at GTMO and Charleston were being carried out. Let me emphasize a couple things as I start out here. As I told the secretary, this was a review. We were on the ground for about two days. So this was not an inspection, either by length of time or by scope. Neither was it an investigation because we had no allegation for investigating any incident or any person. On second thing was this—this was a snapshot of current existing conditions. There was insufficient time to do what I'll call reach-back, which is to look at all the things that might or might not have happened since 9-11. And I'll talk to you about most of the large for example, we've been here nine or 10 months. So, this is just a snapshot. I think I did enough to give him a high degree of confidence of what I found.

What I also told him is you can't be 100% confident of what your findings are when you have that little time to do the job. Finally, this is a compliance look I did not, it was not my charter to look at Geneva as it applies to GTMO and try to determine how that applies. It was not my idea to review all the interrogation phone calls and see if those were wrecked [phonetic]. My job was to see if the orders specific, specifically directed to JTF Commander in GTMO and to Charleston were being carried out. So, having listened to the previous conversation, I think it's important you understand that what this is and what it was not.

Okay, the [inaudible] line was received by direction the night of 3 May. I assembled a team of about 15 on Tuesday, the 4th of May. We traveled onto Wednesday the 5th. Got a command brief. I was on station Thursday/Friday 6 to 7. My military assistant Brigadier General Dwayne Deeson [phonetic] drove up on Thursday, went into Charleston to take a look at the brig there. We got back on Saturday and started analyzing the results of our visit.

MALE VOICE: You didn't go to prison [inaudible].

ADMIRAL CHURCH: I did not have, we just didn't have the time to [inaudible]. I did talk about the team compositions. Had a number of lawyers, I had a doctor, I had some folks to take foreign testimony. I had some folks who served there before from the previous X.O., a member of Naval Criminal Investigative Service. I had a former interrogator. So I had a as good a cross-section of folks I could get to [inaudible]. Here's what we did our two days. We observed interrogations, we watched the detainee movements, we observed the M.P. force and their procedures. We reviewed as much documentation as we could absorb, including the standard operating procedures. All incident reports, all unit punishment logs. We got a hold of some ICRC reports and records of meetings with General Miller, during the outbriefs. We looked very closely at all detainee medical records—excuse me—100 detainee medical records to see if that would shed any light on any potential abuse. We did over 100 interviews, and we did 43 selected at random testimonies under oath. Forty-three under oath testimonies, including interrogators, guards, military civilians, contractor, and we asked them a pretty full range of questions. Have you seen any abuse, have you heard of any abuse, do you know anybody who has seen abuse, would you report abuse if you saw it, would you feel free to come forward if you see anything that doesn't look right. So that's the nature of the questions that we asked those 43 people.

MALE VOICE: [Inaudible] military civilians.

ADMIRAL CHURCH: We did a range of some military civilians, contractors, some analysts, I think there were nine interrogators and nine military police if I remember. I'm not sure of those numbers exact but they're approximate. This is a summation of what I told the Secretary I found. There is a very, we have a very professional organization in place. With very detailed and understood roles and responsibilities. Strong leadership, strong chain of command, and a very positive command climate. The directions to the Secretary of Defense with respect to humane treatment of detainees and the interrogation techniques were being carried out as best we could determine. We found minor infractions involving contact with detainees, and we documented eight of those.

MALE VOICE: Physical contact?

ADMIRAL CHURCH: Some with physical contact. Let me come back to that in the Q & A. Cover that and make sure I get that correct. And we found some of minor items that require some follow-on resolution, and I think it's supposedly a matter of interpretation primarily. We looked at the training records in depth. And I said we looked at standard operating procedures. And I found those to be in my view, very effective. I covered the eight minor infractions, as I like to call them. I also asked the JTF GTMO commander to tell me what the amount of abuse that the guards were taking, and he told me there were about an average of 14 a week. Abuse against the guards, incidents against a guard, verbal harassment, throwing of excrement, that type of thing. We noted that there are a number of outstanding ICRC issues. I also noticed General Miller seemed to take those seriously and appeared to be working on those.

MALE VOICE: General Miller?

ADMIRAL CHURCH: Previously General Miller, General Hood currently.

MALE VOICE: Who is General Hood?

ADMIRAL CHURCH: General Hood, Jeff Hood is—I'm sorry, Jay Hood, is currently the JTF GTMO commander. That's a good question. He was wearing one star. He may be a selectee, I don't know. We found no evidence of current abuse in our underlying currents because the people we talked to had been there nine, 10 months. They're ending their rotations. Specifically we recommend areas of follow-up based on the fact that we really didn't have a great deal of time on station. The first of those would be the reach-back, if you want better assurance that there were no incidents early on, you need to probably go back in and look at the, talk to people who have since rotated out. But based on what I saw, the people who were currently there, I wasn't able to [inaudible].

MALE VOICE: [inaudible] abuse [inaudible] administrative punishment there have been two, there were two prison guards [inaudible].

ADMIRAL CHURCH: [inaudible] the eight. There's actually more than two.

MALE VOICE: Who actually were punished and reduced in rank and what-not.

ADMIRAL CHURCH: There's more than eight. There's more than two.

MALE VOICE: How many?

ADMIRAL CHURCH: Well, let's do that now. There was documented eight, eight minor infractions going back as far as we can get the records, I think to 2002. The, as I remember, four were, involved guards, three involved interrogators, and one involved a barber. Those numbers are from my memory. They're roughly correct.

MALE VOICE: [inaudible]?

ADMIRAL CHURCH: A barber. And, the specific incident was an unauthorized haircut. To a detainee.

MALE VOICE: [inaudible]. A haircut?

ADMIRAL CHURCH: It was, it was a haircut. Now. What I know Secretary's...

MALE VOICE: [interposing] [inaudible].

ADMIRAL CHURCH: I think it was a Mohawk. I guess I'm on the record, so I don't have that in front of me.

FEMALE VOICE: Unauthorized haircut?

ADMIRAL CHURCH: I would phrase it as an unauthorized haircut. Now I characterized this to the Secretary as generally good news, because it was clear to me that the incidents are being reported, number one. Number two, the chain of command was taking swift and effective action. And in every case, the punishments ranged from admonishment to reduction in rate, and some cases maybe more. In fact, one individual went to Court-Martial.

MALE VOICE: So all eight have been acted on already?

ADMIRAL CHURCH: All eight were acted on very swiftly.

MALE VOICE: Inaudible.

ADMIRAL CHURCH: I'm not sure. But all of these were reported through the chain of command.

MALE VOICE: [inaudible]

ADMIRAL CHURCH: Oh yeah, I'd say, you know, roughly two years. A year and a half to two years.

MALE VOICE: [inaudible]

ADMIRAL CHURCH: No, and in fact, that's what gives me a great deal of confidence in my findings, is the 43 people taken under oath and specifically asked the kinds of questions we asked them, given that combined with the reports, the incidents we've seen reported and acted on, I'm pretty confident that there's no abuse currently going on, or that there's been any in recent past that has gone unreported.

MALE VOICE: [inaudible] allegations [inaudible].

ADMIRAL CHURCH: With a high level of confidence, but I'll take you back to my initial statement. When you interview 43, there's still a low probability that something's slipped through the cracks.

MALE VOICE: Clearly, you didn't interview 100 detainees, you looked at their medical records.

ADMIRAL CHURCH: We looked at over just over 100 medical records.

MALE VOICE: [inaudible]?

ADMIRAL CHURCH: We did not interview detainees, no. No.

MALE VOICE: Did you say that you recommended it to the Secretary that a more in depth look be looked, be taken as to what happened [inaudible].

ADMIRAL CHURCH: I made, I said he should consider several things for follow-up. Should he decide to do that, one would be to look a little bit more at the ICRC reports. Apparently there's a new one forthcoming we tried to get. We were not able to get that. And the resolution process for that, that they might go back and take some more sworn testimony, in case there were some gaps. Although we feel pretty confident that with 43, we hit a pretty wide range of personnel. And the third thing that he might want to reach back and talk to people who were there at the earlier stages of Task Force 160 and 170, before they combined them into JTF GTMO, see if there may have been prior incidents that either did or did not go reported. We just didn't have the capabilities to talk to them, to re-track that far.

MALE VOICE: [inaudible] characterize in some way.

ADMIRAL CHURCH: I'll give you one. I think this was in the press. We had a guard, they had to do what they call an IRF, Immediate Response Force for a disturbance in a cell, one of the guards was bitten. In order to free himself, he hit the detainee with his walkie-talkie. They were able to free him. Subsequent to that, the detainee was cuffed. After he was cuffed, the detainee—I'm sorry, the military police punched the detainee. He was taken to Article 15. Not the first incident, which was determined to be self-defense, but the follow-on incident, which was a violation of standard operating procedures, and a standard operating procedures are unambiguous and adhered to. And he was reduced in rate.

MALE VOICE: Rate? Or rank?

ADMIRAL CHURCH: Rank.

MALE VOICE: Rank.

ADMIRAL CHURCH: Rating, or rank.

MALE VOICE: Oh, I see, sorry. [inaudible].

ADMIRAL CHURCH: There was, I don't know if I'd characterize it as more serious. That was probably about as serious I could think.

MALE VOICE: Is there a way to characterize the pending issues with the first ICRC report? What are the things that need to be solved from the first one?

ADMIRAL CHURCH: The reason I said that they need to do little more in depth look at the ICRC, we didn't have the time. Really to get that involved in it, or to, I mean I read, I read the transcripts of the minutes that General Miller had the last two visits. It was clear to me that they're working on the issues. But there's a wide range of issues dealing with, you know, the relatively, let's say lesser important from the speed of which mail was processed, up to the more lasting issues, which are things like the whole legal framework, the long-term and uncertain duration of the [inaudible], some of which we talked about earlier today, and some of which, obviously I wasn't involved. I think the, I think the Secretary may already be looking at a process.

FEMALE VOICE: [inaudible] parameters on these eight incidences. I mean, is that haircut, is that a violation because the detainee was humiliated, or does this run from humiliation to minor physical abuse but that didn't result in severe injuries?

ADMIRAL CHURCH: [interposing] That's a good characterization. Humiliation to mild physical contact. There is one issue...

MALE VOICE: [inaudible] humiliation described by [inaudible]?

FEMALE VOICE: That is a clear violation of [inaudible].

STAFF MALE VOICE: I know, but in the current context, humiliation has a new standard, and it's important to see description that Admiral will provide and the context was understood at the time.

MALE VOICE: [inaudible]?

ADMIRAL CHURCH: Not in the last 35 years.

MALE VOICE: What about another incident where a guard had sprayed a detainee with a water hose?

ADMIRAL CHURCH: Well, [inaudible] coming back to me, that was, as I, I won't recall the details exactly, but as I remember, the guard was passing through, and I'm not certain what was thrown on him, whether it was toilet water or excretement (phonetic), and he did a shot of pepper spray, which was determined to be premature and in violation to standard operating procedures, and military justice was swift.

MALE VOICE: [inaudible] military police and military intelligence, and what is the [inaudible]?

ADMIRAL CHURCH: What I saw was...

MALE VOICE: Did you investigate this incident or element?

ADMIRAL CHURCH: I looked at the organization. It's very clear to me that CJTF GTMO, who is General Hood, previously General Miller, as a very tight organization where everybody reports to and through him. So military police, it's called JDOG, Detention Operations Group, and the Joint Intelligence Group must report directly to him, for all matters relating to what goes on in the camp.

MALE VOICE: Sorry, I wanted to get his name for, and his name and rank?

ADMIRAL CHURCH: Brigadier General Jay Hood. He was [inaudible].

MALE VOICE: J-A-Y?

ADMIRAL CHURCH: J-A-Y? Like [inaudible]. He was our—I'm sorry. There may have been a second part to the question.

MALE VOICE: As far as the organization [inaudible] at the top, but if there's any interaction, what's the organizational interaction between the MPs and [inaudible]?

ADMIRAL CHURCH: They, they do what I would call a coordinating role. Military police, it's very clearly laid out in standard operating procedures. It's all passive. They monitor the detainees, they monitor their behavior, they monitor who the leaders are, who the followers are, they monitor what is said and they ask for an interpreter it there's a lot of conversation going on. They'll know eating habits, and they'll record this in a management information system, which could be useful to the intelligence group, during the interrogations. The only physical thing they do is they escort the detainees to the interrogation. They escort them back, and they monitor the interrogations in a side room. So you have interrogators, the analysts, linguists, the guards are monitoring outside the room what's going on, in case they need to get in there.

MALE VOICE: All [inaudible] interrogation [inaudible] present, sir?

ADMIRAL CHURCH: I was inside the room. I watched [inaudible].

FEMALE VOICE: [interposing] [inaudible] one-way glass?

ADMIRAL CHURCH: Yes, there's a, on the one-way glass.

MALE VOICE: [inaudible]

ADMIRAL CHURCH: That wasn't my charter.

MALE VOICE: [inaudible]

ADMIRAL CHURCH: [inaudible] the Secretary of Defense go down to see if my orders are being carried out. I don't need to interview detainees to do that in my view.

MALE VOICE: What's the approximate number of hours in a week that a detainee might get interrogated?

ADMIRAL CHURCH: I don't know that. It varies. I know the interrogation protocol varies based on what their intelligence value is. It's all laid out in a plan. Here's a good point of clarification. I didn't look at the plan. It wasn't my job to see whether I agree or disagree with the plan. I wanted to make sure the plans were done, they were approved by proper authority procedures involved.

MALE VOICE: [inaudible] taped incidents?

MALE VOICE: Most are hall guards, not interrogators.

ADMIRAL CHURCH: No. As I remember, there were four guards, three interrogators, and a barber.

MALE VOICE: Oh, I'm sorry. You went through that.

ADMIRAL CHURCH: Yeah, it may be three or four the other way, but it's split about even.

MALE VOICE: What does it say about this critical Red Cross report that the Secretary referred to?

ADMIRAL CHURCH: Not much because first of all, it's classified as far as I know. Secondly, I haven't seen it. We tried to get it when we were down there, and we couldn't get it.

MALE VOICE: What do you mean you couldn't get it?

ADMIRAL CHURCH: Well, it hadn't, it hadn't been made available to us.

STAFF MALE VOICE: [interposing] [inaudible] recently, it was our understanding that they've been provided to some officials of the State Department. State Department officials shared it just last night, yesterday, and there's been no opportunity to get it this way.

FEMALE VOICE: Total number of guards on the staff, total? Do you have a ballpark [inaudible]?

ADMIRAL CHURCH: Well, there's, depends on how you define staff.

FEMALE VOICE: Well, I was told that you interviewed 43 out of how large a sample?

ADMIRAL CHURCH: Oh, actually, that's a very small sample. There are six MP companies there are probably close to 600 guards. There is a batallion guarding the exterior perimeter, but they're not involved in the process. The number of interrogators I have to get back to.

MALE VOICE: A hundred?

ADMIRAL CHURCH: I have to get back you. I don't think it's quite that high.

FEMALE VOICE: [inaudible]?

ADMIRAL CHURCH: I learned it on Monday night. I think he learned of it, about the same time I did. [inaudible] we arranged travel [inaudible].

MALE VOICE: Eight guards have received reductions in rank? There were two guards that...

ADMIRAL CHURCH: [interposing] No, no, no, no.

MALE VOICE: How many guards received...

ADMIRAL CHURCH: I documented eight minor infractions during my visit, all of which have been reported to higher authority.

MALE VOICE: Over a period of time.

ADMIRAL CHURCH: Over a period of between 18 months and two years. As I remember there were four guards, three interrogators, and a barber. All were investigated. Disciplinary action was taken quickly. All were reported through the chain of command. And in my view, that was good news because obviously people felt free to report, which is what I was looking for. And there was swift disciplinary action taken by a strong chain of command, which is another thing I was looking for.

MALE VOICE: It ranged from reprimands [inaudible].

ADMIRAL CHURCH: [inaudible].

MALE VOICE: Yeah. Reprimands to reductions in rank. [inaudible]

ADMIRAL CHURCH: [interposing] Yeah, there were reductions in rank to admonitions. Let's say that.

MALE VOICE: [inaudible] Court-Martials [inaudible] Court-Martial result?

ADMIRAL CHURCH: He was acquitted.

MALE VOICE: [inaudible] punish [inaudible].

ADMIRAL CHURCH: [inaudible] yeah, but you see the, you see the stress regards work under and the discipline and the whole procedures down there, I think I was very impressed, particularly when you look at the other side, the 14 incidents against the guards weekly.

MALE VOICE: [inaudible] recommend any substance [inaudible] Secretary in treatment or procedure?

ADMIRAL CHURCH: No. It wasn't my job to do that. I did recommend some follow-up areas where he might consider looking into. My job was to see that his orders were being carried out. I did that to the best of my ability.

FEMALE VOICE: You feel that they are?

ADMIRAL CHURCH: Yes. With a high level of confidence, based on what I was able to do in 48 hours.

MALE VOICE: [inaudible] with respect to...

ADMIRAL CHURCH: With respect to specific areas of interrogation, orders on humane treatment that were passed down, as you mentioned, reviewed by the lawyers and passed down to the commander on the scene.

MALE VOICE: Thanks a lot [inaudible].

MALE VOICE: Thank you.

[Editor's note: The Associated Press asked the Department of Defense for its response to the allegations of abuse of prisoners at Guantanamo Bay and Abu Ghraib which were noted both in the Schlesinger report and in Vice Admiral Church's press briefing. Their response is below.]

Following is our response to the Schlesinger report GTMO allegations of abuse incidents (finally).

Earlier this year, both the Schlesinger Report and the press briefing provided by Vice Admiral A.T. Church III, cited eight "substantiated cases" regarding appropriate treatment of detainees at Guantanamo.

The Department takes all allegations of abuse seriously. Credible allegations of abuse made by detainees or reported by JTF GTMO officials are investigated. Those who are found to have committed unlawful acts are immediately removed from further contact with detainees and are disciplined as the circumstances warrant.

The following are the details of those infractions and how they were resolved.

1) A guard was charged with assault against a detainee for actions during an incident in September 2002. During that incident, detainees in a detention block were protesting and one detainee threw food out of his cell window (the portal in the door through which food and books are passed). The window was closed by a guard, and during a later check on the detainee, the detainee threw what was believed to be water from the toilet on the guard. The guard then attempted to spray the detainee with a hose. The guard received non-judicial punishment pursuant to an Article 15, Uniform Code of Military Justice (UCMJ). He was reduced in rank to E-3 (suspended) and given 7 days restriction. He was reassigned to other duties at Guantanamo.

2) A guard was charged with dereliction of duty and assault on a detainee following an incident in April of 2003 that involved a disturbance in one of the detention blocks. One detainee who was already out of his cell assaulted another guard, and while the detainee was being subdued, the detainee bit the guard. After the detainee was subdued, the guard struck the detainee with his fist in which he held a handheld radio. He received non-judicial punishment pursuant to an Article 15 in May 2003. The guard was reduced in rank to E-3, given 45 days of extra duty and was reassigned.

3) In April 2003, during the approach phase of an interrogation, a female interrogator took off her uniform top (her brown T-shirt was still worn), ran her fingers through the detainee's hair and sat on his lap. A supervisor monitoring the interrogation immediately terminated the session. The interrogator was given a written reprimand for her conduct and received additional training before being allowed to continue duties as an interrogator.

4) In early 2003 a female interrogator (different interrogator than incident 3) wiped dye from red magic marker on detainees' shirt after detainee spit on her. She told the detainee the stain was blood. The interrogator received a verbal reprimand for inappropriate contact/interrogation technique.

5) An interrogator in April 2003 used a "fear-up/harsh" technique by directing MPs to repeatedly bring the detainee from a standing to prone position and back. A review of medical records indicated superficial bruising to the detainee's knees. The interrogator was issued a written reprimand. Maj. Gen. Miller, JTF Commander at the time of this incident, prohibited further use of the "fear-up/harsh" technique and specifically prohibited MPs from involvement during interrogation.

6) In February 2004, an MP was joking with a detainee and dared the detainee to throw water on him. The detainee did so and the MP squirted the detainee with water from a water bottle. The MP also engaged in inappropriate casual conversation with detainee. The MP's behavior described above was in violation of JTF Guantanamo Standard Operating Procedures (SOP). The MP was reassigned to other duties at Guantanamo.

7) In March 2003, an MP sprayed pepper spray on a detainee who was preparing to throw unidentified liquid on another MP during an Initial Response Force response. The MP was alleged to have used the spray in violation of the JTF Guantanamo SOP. The MP turned down an Article 15 (non-judicial punishment) and instead requested a court-martial proceeding. He was acquitted by members at a Special Court Martial in June 2003.

8) In February 2004, a Camp barber intentionally gave two unusual haircuts, in an effort to frustrate detainee requests for similar haircuts, as a sign of detainee unity. The barber and his company commander were counseled by their battalion commander, and the barber was required to re-cut the detainees' hair appropriately.

The Fay-Jones Report

Investigation of Intelligence Activities at Abu Ghraib

Investigation of the Abu Ghraib Prison and 205th Military Intelligence Brigade, LTG Anthony R. Jones

Investigation of the Abu Ghraib Detention Facility and 205th Military Intelligence Brigade, MG George R. Fay

August 2004

Executive Summary

Investigation of Intelligence Activities At Abu Ghraib

AR 15-6 Investigation of the Abu Ghraib Prison and 205th Military
  Intelligence Brigade
LTG Anthony R. Jones

AR 15-6 Investigation of the Abu Ghraib Detention Facility and 205th
  Military Intelligence Brigade
MG George R. Fay

EXECUTIVE SUMMARY

Investigation of Intelligence Activities At Abu Ghraib

Background

This investigation was ordered initially by LTG Ricardo S. Sanchez, Commander, Combined Joint Task Force Seven (CJTF-7). LTG Sanchez appointed MG George R. Fay as investigating officer under the provisions of Army Regulation 381-10, Procedure 15. MG Fay was appointed to investigate allegations that members of the 205th Military Intelligence Brigade (205 MI BDE) were involved in detainee abuse at the Abu Ghraib Detention Facility. Specifically, MG Fay was to determine whether 205 MI BDE personnel requested, encouraged, condoned, or solicited Military Police (MP) personnel to abuse detainees and whether MI personnel comported with established interrogation procedures and applicable laws and regulations.

On 16 June 2004, Acting Secretary of the Army R. L. Brownlee appointed General Paul J. Kern, Commander, US Army Material Command (AMC), as the new Procedure 15 appointing authority. On 25 June 2004, GEN Kern appointed LTG Anthony R. Jones, Deputy Commanding General, US Army Training and Doctrine Command, as an additional Procedure 15 investigating officer. MG Fay was retained as an investigating officer.

Without reinvestigating areas reviewed by MG Fay, LTG Jones was specifically directed to focus on whether organizations or personnel higher than the 205th MI BDE chain of command, or events and circumstances outside of the 205th MI Brigade, were involved, directly or indirectly, in the questionable activities regarding alleged detainee abuse at Abu Ghraib prison.

The investigative teams conducted a comprehensive review of all available background documents and statements pertaining to Abu Ghraib from a wide variety of sources. These sources included the reports written by MG Geoffrey Miller, MG Donald Ryder, MG Antonio Taguba and the Department of Army Inspector General. LTG Jones interviewed LTG Sanchez and MG Barbara Fast, the CJTF-7 Senior Intelligence Staff Officer. MG Fay's team conducted over 170 interviews concerning the interviewees' knowledge of interrogation and detention operations at Abu Ghraib and/or their knowledge of and involvement in detainee abuse. MG Fay's interviews included interviews with MG Fast, MG Walter Wojdakowski, MG Geoffrey Miller, MG Thomas Miller, and BG Janis Karpinski.

Operational Environment

The events at Abu Ghraib cannot be understood in a vacuum. Three interrelated aspects of the operational environment played important roles in the abuses that occurred at Abu Ghraib. First, from the time V Corps transitioned to become CJTF-7, and throughout the period under investigation, it was not resourced adequately to accomplish the missions of the CJTF: stability and support operations (SASO) and support to the Coalition Provisional Authority (CPA). The CJTF-7 headquarters lacked adequate personnel and equipment. In addition, the military police and military intelligence units at Abu Ghraib were severely under-resourced. Second, providing support to the Coalition Provisional Authority (CPA) required greater resources than envisioned in operational plans. Third, operational plans envisioned that CJTF-7 would execute SASO and provide support to the CPA in a relatively non-hostile environment. In fact, opposition was robust and hostilities continued throughout the period under investigation. Therefore, CJTF-7 had to conduct tactical counter-insurgency operations, while also executing its planned missions.

These three circumstances delayed establishment of an intelligence architecture and degraded the ability of the CJTF-7 staff to execute its assigned tasks, including oversight of interrogation and detention operations at Abu Ghraib.

When hostilities were declared over, US forces had control of only 600 Enemy Prisoners of War (EPW) and Iraqi criminals. In the fall of 2003, the number of detainees rose exponentially due to tactical operations to capture counter-insurgents dangerous to U.S. forces and Iraqi civilians. At that time, the CJTF-7 commander believed he had no choice but to use Abu Ghraib as the central detention facility.

Command and staff actions and inaction must be understood in the context of the operational environment discussed above. In light of the operational environment, and CJTF-7 staff and subordinate unit's under-resourcing and increased missions, the CJTF-7 Commander had to prioritize efforts. CJTF-7 devoted its resources to fighting the counter-insurgency and supporting the CPA, thereby saving Coalition and civilian

Iraqi lives and assisting in the transition to Iraqi self-rule. In the overall scheme of OIF, the CJTF-7 Commander and staff performed above expectations.

Abuse

Clearly abuses occurred at the prison at Abu Ghraib. There is no single, simple explanation for why this abuse at Abu Ghraib happened. The primary causes are misconduct (ranging from inhumane to sadistic) by a small group of morally corrupt soldiers and civilians, a lack of discipline on the part of the leaders and Soldiers of the 205th MI BDE and a failure or lack of leadership by multiple echelons within CJTF-7. Contributing factors can be traced to issues affecting Command and Control, Doctrine, Training, and the experience of the Soldiers we asked to perform this vital mission.

For purposes of this report, abuse is defined as treatment of detainees that violated U.S. criminal law or international law or treatment that was inhumane or coercive without lawful justification. Whether the Soldier or contractor knew, at the time of the acts, that the conduct violated any law or standard, is not an element of the definition.

The abuses at Abu Ghraib primarily fall into two categories: a) intentional violent or sexual abuse and, b) abusive actions taken based on misinterpretations or confusion regarding law or policy.

LTG Jones found that while senior level officers did not commit the abuse at Abu Ghraib they did bear responsibility for lack of oversight of the facility, failing to respond in a timely manner to the reports from the International Committee of the Red Cross and for issuing policy memos that failed to provide clear, consistent guidance for execution at the tactical level.

MG Fay has found that from 25 July 2003 to 6 February 2004, 27 205 MI BDE Personnel allegedly requested, encouraged, condoned or solicited Military Police (MP) personnel to abuse detainees and/or participated in detainee abuse and/or violated established interrogation procedures and applicable laws and regulations during interrogation operations at Abu Ghraib.

Most, though not all, of the violent or sexual abuses occurred separately from scheduled interrogations and did not focus on persons held for intelligence purposes. No policy, directive or doctrine directly or indirectly caused violent or sexual abuse. In these cases, Soldiers knew they were violating the approved techniques and procedures.

Confusion about what interrogation techniques were authorized resulted from the proliferation of guidance and information from other theaters of operation; individual interrogator experiences in other theaters; and, the failure to distinguish between interrogation operations in other theaters and Iraq. This confusion contributed to the occurrence of some of the non-violent and non-sexual abuses.

MG Taguba and MG Fay reviewed the same photographs as supplied by the US Army Criminal Investigation Command (CID). MG Fay identified one additional photograph depicting abuse by MI personnel that had not been previously identified by MG Taguba. MG Fay also identified other abuse that had not been photographed.

Alleged incidents of abuse by military personnel have been referred to the CID for criminal investigation and the chain of command for disciplinary action. Alleged incidents of abuse by civilian contractors have been referred through the Department of Defense to the Department of Justice.

Discipline and Leadership

Military Intelligence and Military Police units had missions throughout the Iraqi Theater of Operations (ITO), however, 205th MI Brigade and 800th Military Police Brigade leaders at Abu Ghraib failed to execute their assigned responsibilities. The leaders from units located at Abu Ghraib or with supervision over Soldiers and units at Abu Ghraib, failed to supervise subordinates or provide direct oversight of this important mission. These leaders failed to properly discipline their Soldiers. These leaders failed to learn from prior mistakes and failed to provide continued mission-specific training. The 205th MI Brigade Commander did not assign a specific subordinate unit to be responsible for interrogations at Abu Ghraib and did not ensure that a Military Intelligence chain of command at Abu Ghraib was established. The absence of effective leadership was a factor in not sooner discovering and taking actions to prevent both the violent/sexual abuse incidents and the misinterpretation/confusion incidents.

Neither Department of Defense nor Army doctrine caused any abuses. Abuses would not have occurred had doctrine been followed and mission training conducted. Nonetheless, certain facets of interrogation and detention operations doctrine need to be updated, refined or expanded, including, the concept, organization, and operations of a Joint Interrogation and Debriefing Center (JIDC); guidance for interrogation techniques at both tactical and strategic levels; the roles, responsibilities and relationships between Military Police and Military Intelligence personnel at detention facilities; and, the establishment and organization of a Joint Task Force structure and, in particular, its intelligence architecture.

Other Contributing Factors

Demands on the Human Intelligence (HUMINT) capabilities in a counter-insurgency and in the future joint operational environment will continue to tax tactical and strategic assets. The Army needs trained and experienced tactical HUMINT personnel.

Working alongside non-DOD organizations/agencies in detention facilities proved complex and demanding. The perception that non-DOD agencies had different rules regarding interrogation and detention operations was evident. Interrogation and detention policies and limits of authority should apply equally to all agencies in the Iraqi Theater of Operations.

"Ghost Detainees"

The appointing authority and investigating officers made a specific finding regarding the issue of "ghost detainees" within Abu Ghraib. It is clear that the interrogation practices of other government agencies led to a loss of accountability at Abu Ghraib. DoD must document and enforce adherence by other government agencies with established DoD practices and procedures while conducting detainee interrogation operations at DoD facilities. This matter requires further investigation and, in accordance with the provisions of AR 381-10, Part 15, is being referred to the DoD Inspector General, as the DoD liaison with other government agencies for appropriate investigation and evaluation. Soldiers/Sailors/Airmen/Marines should never be put in a position that potentially puts them at risk for non-compliance with the Geneva Convention or Laws of Land Warfare.

Conclusion

Leaders and Soldiers throughout Operation Iraqi Freedom were confronted with a complex and dangerous operations environment. Although a clear breakdown in dicipline and leadership, the events at Abu Ghraib should not blind us from the noble conduct of the vast majority of our Soldiers. We are a values based profession in which the clear majority of our Soldiers and leaders take great pride.

A clear vote of confidence should be extended by the senior leadership to the leaders and Soldiers who continue to perform extraordinarily in supporting our Nation's wartime mission. Many of our Soldiers have paid the ultimate sacrifice to preserve the freedoms and liberties that America and our Army represent throughout the world.

23 August 2004

AR 15-6 Investigation
of the Abu Ghraib Prison
and 205th Military Intelligence Brigade

LTG Anthony R. Jones

(U) TABLE OF CONTENTS

(U) AR 15–6 Investigation of the
Abu Ghraib Detention Facility
and 205th MI Brigade

1. (U) EXECUTIVE SUMMARY

a. (U) Appointment, Charter and Investigative Activity

(1) (U) On 24 June 2004, Acting Secretary of the Army R. L. Brownlee notified me that I was selected to serve as the Senior Investigating Officer in the investigation of the 205th Military Intelligence Brigade. GEN Paul Kern was the appoining authority and in a memorandum, dated 25 June 2004, formally designated me Senior Investigating Officer. MG George Fay, who had been investigating the 205th MI BDE since his appointment by LTG Ricardo Sanchez on 31 March 2004, would continue as an investigating officer. Without reinvestigating areas reviewed by MG Fay, I was specifically directed to focus on whether organizations or personnel higher than the 205th Military Intelligence (MI) Brigade chain of command, or events and circumstances outside of the 205th MI Brigade, were involved, directly or indirectly, in the questionable activities regarding alleged detainee abuse at Abu Ghraib prison.

(2) (U) During the course of my investigation, I interviewed LTG Ricardo Sanchez, the Commander of Combined Joint Task Force-7 (CJTF-7)[1] during the period under investigation, and the senior intelligence officer on his staff, MG Barbara Fast (the "C2"). In addition, I reviewed witness statements that MG Fay's investigation team had collected; assessment and investigation reports written by MG Geoffrey Miller, MG Donald Ryder, MG Antonio Taguba and the Department of the Army Inspector General (DAIG); and other written materials including relevant law, doctrine, organizational documents, policy, directives, and U.S. Central Command (CENTCOM) and CJTF-7 operational orders (OPORDS) and fragmentary orders (FRAGOs).

b. (U) Background and Operational Environment

(1) (U) The events at Abu Ghraib cannot be understood in a vacuum. Three interrelated aspects of the operational environment played important roles in the abuses that occurred at Abu Ghraib. First, from the time V Corps transitioned to become CJTF-7, and throughout the period under investigation, it was not resourced adequately to accomplish the missions of the CJTF: stability and support operations (SASO) and support to the Coalition Provisional Authority (CPA). The CJTF-7 headquarters lacked adequate personnel and equipment. In addition, the military police and military intelligence units at Abu Ghraib were severely under-resourced. Second, providing support to the Coalition Provisional Authority (CPA) required greater resources than envisioned in operational plans. Third, operational plans envisioned that CJTF-7 would execute SASO and provide support to the CPA in a relatively non-hostile environment. In fact, opposition was robust and hostilities continued throughout the period under investigation. Therefore, CJTF-7 had to conduct tactical counter-insurgency operations, while also executing its planned missions.

(2) (U) These three circumstances delayed establishment of an intelligence architecture and degraded the ability of the CJTF-7 staff to execute its assigned tasks, including oversight of interrogation and detention operations at Abu Ghraib.

---

[1] CJTF-7 was the higher headquarters to which the 205th MI Brigade reported.

(3) (U) When hostilities were declared over, U.S. forces had control of only 600 Enemy Prisoners of War (EPWs) and Iraqi criminals. In the fall of 2003, the number of detainees rose exponentially due to tactical operations to capture counter-insurgents dangerous to U.S. forces and Iraqi civilians. At this time, the CJTF-7 commander believed he had no choice but to use Abu Ghraib as the central detention facility.

c. (U) Abuse at Abu Ghraib

(1) (U) Clearly abuses occurred at the prison at Abu Ghraib. For purposes of this report, I defined abuse as treatment of detainees that violated U.S. criminal law or international law or treatment that was inhumane or coercive without lawful justification. Whether the Soldier or contractor knew, at the time of the acts, that the conduct violated any law or standard, is not an element of the definition. MG Fay's portion of this report describes the particular abuses in detail.

(2) (U) I found that no single, or simple, explanation exists for why some of the Abu Ghraib abuses occurred. For clarity of analysis, my assessment divides abuses at Abu Ghraib into two different types of improper conduct: First, intentional violent or sexual abuses and, second, actions taken based on misinterpretations of or confusion about law or policy.

(3) (U) Intentional violent or sexual abuses include acts causing bodily harm using unlawful force as well as sexual offenses including, but not limited to rape, sodomy and indecent assault. No Soldier or contractor believed that these abuses were permitted by any policy or guidance. If proven, these actions would be criminal acts. The primary causes of the violent and sexual abuses were relatively straight-forward-individual criminal misconduct, clearly in violation of law, policy, and doctrine and contrary to Army values.

(4) (U) Incidents in the second category resulted from misinterpretations of law or policy or resulted from confusion about what interrogation techniques were permitted. These latter abuses include some cases of clothing removal (without any touching) and some uses of dogs in interrogations (uses without physical contact or extreme fear). Some of these incidents may have violated international law. At the time the Soldiers or contractors committed the acts, however, some of them may have honestly believed the techniques were condoned.

d. (U) Major Findings

(1) (U) The chain of command directly above the 205th MI Brigade was not directly involved in the abuses at Abu Ghraib. However, policy memoranda promulgated by the CJTF-7 Commander led indirectly to some of the non-violent and non-sexual abuses. In addition, the CJTF-7 Commander and Deputy Commander failed to ensure proper staff oversight of detention and interrogation operations. Finally, CJTF-7 staff elements reacted inadequately to earlier indications and warnings that problems existed at Abu Ghraib.

Command and staff actions and inaction must be understood in the context of the operational environment discussed above. In light of the operational environment, and CJTF-7 staff and subordinate unit's under-resourcing and increased missions, the CJTF-7 Commander had to prioritize efforts. CJTF-7 devoted its resources to fighting the counter-insurgency and supporting the CPA, thereby saving Coalition and civilian Iraqi lives and assisting in the transition to Iraqi self-rule. I find that the CJTF-7 Commander and staff performed above expectations, in the overall scheme of OIF.

(2) (U) Most, though not all, of the violent or sexual abuses occurred separately from scheduled interrogations and did not focus on persons held for intelligence purposes. No policy, directive or doctrine directly or indirectly caused violent or sexual abuse. Soldiers knew they were violating the approved techniques and procedures.

(3) (U) Confusion about what interrogation techniques were authorized resulted from the proliferation of guidance and information from other theaters of operation; individual interrogator experiences in other theaters; and, the failure to distinguish between interrogation operations in other theaters and Iraq. This confusion contributed to the occurrence of some of the non-violent and non-sexual abuses.

(4) (U) Military Intelligence and Military Police units also had missions throughout the Iraqi Theater of Operations (ITO), however, 205th MI Brigade and 800th Military Police Brigade leaders at Abu Ghraib failed to execute their assigned responsibilities. The leaders from these units located at Abu Ghraib or with supervision over Soldiers and units at Abu Ghraib, failed to supervise subordinates or provide direct oversight of this important mission. These leaders failed to properly discipline their Soldiers. These leaders failed to learn from prior mistakes and failed to provide continued mission-specific traning. The 205th MI Brigade Commander did not assign a specific subordinate unit to be responsible for interrogations at Abu Ghraib and did not ensure that a Military Intelligence chain of command at Abu Ghraib was established. The absence of effective leadership was a factor in not sooner discovering and taking actions to prevent both the violent/sexual abuse incidents and the misinterpretation/confusion incidents.

(5) (U) Neither Defense nor Army doctrine caused any abuses. Abuses would not have occurred had doctrine been followed and mission training conducted. Nonetheless, certain facets of interrogation and detention operations doctrine need to be updated, refined or expanded, including, the concept, organization, and operations of a Joint Interrogation and Debriefing Center (J1DC); guidance for interrogation techniques at both tactical and strategic levels; the roles, responsibilities and relationships between Military Police and Military Intelligence personnel at detention facilities; and, the establishment and organization of a Joint Task Force structure and in particular, its intelligence architecture.

(6) (U) No single or simple theory can explain why some of the abuses at Abu Ghraib occurred. In addition to individual criminal propensities, leadership failures and,

multiple policies, many other factors contributed to the abuses occurring at Abu Ghraib, including:

- Safety and security conditions at Abu Ghraib;
- Multiple agencies/organizations involvement in interrogation operations at Abu Ghraib;
- Failure to effectively screen, certify, and then integrate contractor interrogators/analysts/linguists;
- Lack of a clear understanding of MP and MI roles and responsibilities in interrogation operations.
- Dysfunctional command relationships at brigade and higher echelons, including the tactical control (TACON) relationship between the 800th MP Brigade and CJTF-7.

(7) (U) Demands on the Human Intelligence (HUMINT) capabilities in a counter-insurgency and in the future joint operational environment will continue to tax tactical and strategic assets. The Army needs trained and experienced tactical HUMINT personnel.

(8) (U) Working alongside non-DOD organizations/agencies in detention facilities proved complex and demanding. The perception that non-DOD agencies had different rules regarding interrogation and detention operations was evident, Interrogation and detention policies and limits of authority should apply equally to all agencies in the Iraqi Theater of Operations.

(9) (U) Leaders and Soldiers throughout Operation Iraqi Freedom were confronted with a complex and dangerous operational environment. Although a clear breakdown in discipline and leadership, the events at Abu Ghraib should not blind us from the noble conduct of the vast majority of our Soldiers. We are a values based profession in which the clear majority of our Soldiers and leaders take great pride.

(10) (U) A clear vote of confidence should be extended by the senior leadership to the leaders and Soldiers who continue to perform extraordinarily in supporting our Nation's wartime mission. Many of our Soldiers have paid the ultimate sacrifice to preserve the freedoms and liberties that America and our Army represent throughout the world.

2. (U) CHARTER AND INVESTIGATIVE ACTIVITY

a. (U) On 24 June 2004, Acting Secretary of the Army, R. L. Brownlee, notified me that I was selected to serve as the Senior Investigating Officer in the investigation of the 205th Military Intelligence Brigade. GEN Paul Kern was the appointing authority and in a memorandum dated 25 June 2004, formally designated me Senior Investigating Officer. MG George Fay, who had been investigating the 205th MI BDE since his appointment by LTG Ricardo Sanchez on 31 March 2004, would continue as an investigating officer.

b. (U) My specific duties were to focus on whether organizations or personnel higher than the 205th Military Intelligence (MI) Brigade chain of command, or events

and circumstances outside of the 205th MI Brigade, were involved, directly or indirectly, in the questionable activities regarding alleged detainee abuse at Abu Ghraib
prison.

c. (U) In accordance with guidance from the Appointing Authority, I would interview
LTG Ricardo Sanchez and other Combined Joint Task Force-7 (CJTF-7) staff, as required, to obtain information to make findings and recommendations to GEN Kern on
the culpability of senior leaders who had responsibility for interrogation and detainee
operations in Iraq. My directions were to not reinvestigate the areas that MG Fay had
already reviewed. Rather, I was to look at operational and strategic level events that
occurred prior to and during the period under investigation and determine their relationship, if any, to the abuses that occurred while the 205th MI Brigade was involved
in interrogations and intelligence analysis at Abu Ghraib.

d. (U) During the course of my investigation, I interviewed LTG Ricardo Sanchez,
the Commander of Combined Joint Task Force-7 (CJTF-7) during the period under investigation, and the senior intelligence officer on his staff, MG Barbara Fast
(the "C2"). In addition, I reviewed witness statements that MG Fay's investigation
team had collected; reviewed the assessment and investigation reports written by MG
Geoffrey Miller, MG Donald Ryder, MG Antonio Taguba, and the Department of the
Army Inspector General; and reviewed other written materials including relevant law,
doctrine, organizational documents, policy, directives, and U.S. Central Command
(CENTCOM) and CJTF-7 Operational Orders (OPORDS) and Fragmentary Orders
(FRAGOs).

3. (U) BACKGROUND: OPERATION IRAQI FREEDOM DURING THIS PERIOD

4. (U) OPERATIONAL ENVIRONMENT

a. (U) Before deciding to centralize detainees at Abu Ghraib, major organizational
changes were ongoing in the structure of U.S. Forces fighting the Iraqi campaign.
Following major ground operations and declaration of the end of hostilities, the U.S.
Army V Corps transitioned to become the CJTF-7. Also during this period, then-MG
Sanchez was promoted to Lieutenant General and assumed command of V Corps,
replacing LTG Wallace who led Phase III, Decisive Operations, in Iraq. LTG Sanchez
transitioned from commanding a division, consisting of approximately 15,000 Soldiers, to commanding V Corps. The U.S. Third Army, or ARCENT, was designated
the Combined Forces Land Component Command under the U.S. Central Command
during the initial phases of OW. When V Corps transitioned to the CJTF-7, the new
command assumed responsibility for the Combined Forces Land Component Command (CFLCC) missions and operations in the Iraqi Theater of Operations (IT 0). The
Forces under the command of LTG Sanchez grew to approximately 180,000 U.S. and
Coalition forces. In addition, the new CJTF-7 was directed to transition to Phase IV
of the Iraqi campaign. Phase IV operations were envisioned as stability and support
operations (SASO) and direct support to the CPA. CJTF-7 assistance to the CPA was
essential to help the CPA succeed in recreating essential government departments under the control of Iraqi leaders. CJTF-7 would also help the CPA transition control

of critical government organizations, strategic communications, reconstruction contracts, and lines of operation necessary to enable Iraqi self-rule.

b. (U) In actuality, LTG Sanchez and his V Corps staff rapidly realized that the war
had not ended. They were in a counter-insurgency operation with a complex, adaptive
enemy that opposed the rule of law and ignored the Geneva Conventions. This enemy
opposed the transition of the new Iraqi governing councils that would enable self-rule,
and opposed any occupation by U.S. or coalition forces. The hostilities continued.
Operations were planned and executed to counter the insurgency.

c. (U) In June 2003, when the CJTF-7 organization was established, a vast increase in
responsibilities began. A Joint Manning Document (JMD) was developed to delineate
the specific skill sets of personnel needed to perform the increased roles and functions
of this new headquarters. After multiple reviews, the JMD for the CJTF-7 HQ5 was
formally approved for 1,400 personnel in December 2003. That JMD included personnel needed to support the Coalition Provisional Authority (CPA), staff the functional
elements needed to focus at joint operational and strategic levels, and specifically augment areas such as intelligence, operations, and logistics. Building a coherent, focused
team was essential to the success of Phase IV operations.

d. (U) CJTF-7 remained in the direct chain of command of the U.S. Central Command,
but was also charged with a direct support role to the CPA. Command relationships
of subordinate tactical commands previously under V Corps remained as previously
outlined in Operational Orders. Therefore, the divisions' and Corps' separate brigades,
which included the 205th MI Brigade, remained under the CJTF-7. The level of authority and responsibilities of a command of this magnitude is normally vested in
a four-star level Army Service Component Command under a Regional Combatant
Commander, Of the 1,400 personnel required on the JMD, the V Corps staff transitioned to only 495, or roughly a third, of the manning requirements. The new JMD also
required that key staff positions be manned by general officers rather than the normal
colonel level positions on a Corps staff. Although the JMD was properly staffed and
approved, personnel and equipment shortages impacted on CJTF-7's ability to execute
the mission and remained a critical issue throughout the period in question. The JMD
had 169 positions earmarked for support of operations at Abu Ghraib.

(1) (S/NF)

(2) (U) The 800th MP Brigade remained TACON to the CJTF-7 throughout this period.
With the essential task and responsibility for all EPW and confinement operations
transferring from CFLCC to CJTF-7, this unit would have been more appropriately
designated as OPCON instead of TACON to the CJTF. Tactical Control (TACON) allows
commanders the detailed and usually local direction and control of movements and
maneuver necessary to accomplish missions and tasks. Whereas, Operational Control
(OPCON) provides full authority to organize commands and forces and employ them
as the commander considers necessary to accomplish assigned missions. The 800th
MP Brigade's parent unit in the area of operations remained the 377th Theater Support
Command, located in Kuwait. In accordance with the CENTCOM OPLAN, CFLCC
(ARCENT) had to provide operational logistic support to Army Forces employed from

Kuwait. The TACON relationship of the 800th MP Brigade with CJTF-7 resulted in disparate support from the CJTF-7 staff, lower priority in meeting resource needs for detention facilities, and the lack of intrusive, aggressive oversight of the unit by CJTF-7 leadership. No attempt was made by the CJTF-7 or ARCENT Staff to coordinate a change in this command relationship.

e. (U) Following the period of major ground hostilities in Phase III operations, the infrastructure of the country remained in desperate need of reconstruction. In addition to battle damage, looting, pillaging, and criminal actions had decimated the government buildings and infrastructure necessary to detain enemy prisoners of war or criminals.

f. (U) The logistics system, including local contracted support, to support units in Iraq was slowly catching up to the priority requirements that needed to be executed. Improving living conditions and basic support for Soldiers, as well as ensuring the safety and security of all forces, remained priorities, especially with the advent of the counter-insurgency. Quality of life for Soldiers did not improve in many locations until December of 2003.

g. (U) Prior to the beginning of hostilities, planners estimated 30-100 thousand enemy prisoners of war would need to be secured, segregated, detained, and interrogated. The 800th MP Brigade was given the mission to establish as many as 12 detention centers, to be run by subordinate battalion units. As of May 2003, BG Hill reported that only an estimated 600 detainees were being held in a combination of enemy prisoners and criminals. As a result, additional military police units previously identified for deployment were demobilized in CONUS. The original plan also envisioned that only the prisoners remaining from the initial major combat operations would require detention facilities, and they would eventually be released or turned over to the Iraqi authorities once justice departments and criminal detention facilities were re-established,

h. (U) As major counter-insurgency operations began in the July 2003 timeframe, the demands on the CJTF-7 commander and staff, the CPA, the subordinate units, the Iraqi interim government, and Soldiers at all levels increased dramatically. Decisions were made to keep some units in-country to fight the insurgency. Pressure increased to obtain operational intelligence on the enemy's identity, support systems, locations, leadership, intelligence sources, weapons and ammunition caches, and centers of gravity. In addition, the location of Saddam Hussein and information of WMD remained intelligence priorities. The complexity of missions being conducted by CJTF-7 and subordinate units increased and placed a high demand on leadership at all levels. Leaders had to adapt to the new environment and prosecute hostilities, while at the same time exercising appropriate compassion for non-combatants and protecting the people who were trying to do what was right for their country. Operations were planned to pursue the various factions of the counter-insurgency based on intelligence developed with the Iraqi people and Coalition Forces. A rapid increase in the number of detainees (due to the apprehension of counter-insurgents who posed a security risk to our Soldiers and to the Iraqi people, members of criminal factions, and personnel of intelligence value) demanded a decision on a detention facility and a need to rapidly expand interrogation operations.

i. (U) Throughout the Iraqi Theater of Operations (ITO), synchronization of force protection and security operations between operational forces and forward operating bases, such as Abu Ghraib, demanded more focus by brigade-level leadership. Supported-to-supporting relationships were blurred due to the large geographical areas given to tactical units. At Abu Ghraib, outside-the-wire responsibilities during the period in question were the responsibility of the 3d Armored Cavalry Regiment and then the 82d Airborne Division. Force Protection and security for the Abu Ghraib forward operating base was an implied task for the 320th MP Battalion initially, and then, after the 19 November FRAGO, a specified task for the 205th MI Brigade Commander. The defense and security of the Abu Ghraib forward operating base, to include engaging the communities outside of the base for information, was a key concern of LTG Sanchez during his visits and led to the decision to place the 205th MI Brigade commander in charge of forces at Abu Ghraib for force protection and defense of the base in November 2003.

j. (U) Interrogating detainees was a massive undertaking. In accordance with the doctrine, unit level personnel would gather initial battlefield intelligence at the point of apprehension. Tactical interrogations would continue at designated collection points (CP) at Brigade and Division levels. Then a more detailed interrogation to get operational and strategic intelligence was to be conducted at a designated central detention facility. The location and facility for this detention and interrogation was Abu Ghraib. Abu Ghraib was selected by Ambassador Bremer after consultation with his staff and LTG Sanchez. Abu Ghraib was envisioned as a temporary facility to be used for criminal detainees until the new Iraqi government could be established and an Iraqi prison established at another site. Following operations during the summer of 2003, Abu Ghraib also was designated by CJTF-7 as the detention center for security detainees. The population of criminals, security detainees, and detainees with potential intelligence value grew to an estimated 4,000-5,000 personnel in the fall of 2003.

k. (U) The 800th MP Brigade was designated the responsible unit for the Abu Ghraib detention facility and for securing and safeguarding the detainees. The 205th MI Brigade was given responsibility for screening and interrogating detainees at Abu Ghraib. The 320th MP battalion was the unit specifically charged with operating the Abu Ghraib detainee facility by the 800th MP Brigade. Initially, the 205th MI Brigade commander did not specify an MI unit or organization for interrogation operations at Abu Ghraib. Interrogators, analysts, and linguists arrived at Abu Ghraib from multiple units and locations within the 205th MI Brigade.

Contractor personnel were also later used to augment interrogation, analyst, and linguist personnel at Abu Ghraib.

5. (U) ASSESSMENTS AND VISITS TO IMPROVE INTELLIGENCE, DETENTION AND INTERROGATION OPERATIONS

a. (U) As commanders at all levels sought operational intelligence, it became apparent that the intelligence structure was undermanned, underequipped, and inappropriately organized for counter-insurgency operations. Upon arrival in July 2003, MG Barbara Fast was tasked to do an initial assessment of the intelligence architecture needed to execute the CJTF-7 mission in Iraq. Technical intelligence collection means alone were insufficient in providing the requisite information on an enemy that had adapted to the environment and to a hightech opponent. Only through an aggressive structure of human intelligence (HUMINT) collection and analysis could the requisite information be obtained. Communications equipment, computers, and access to sufficient bandwidth to allow reachback capabilities to national databases were needed to assist in the fusion and collaboration of tactical through strategic intelligence data. Disparate cells of different agencies had to be co-located to allow access to respective databases to assist in the fusion and collaboration effort. Interrogation reports had to be standardized and rapidly reviewed to allow dissemination to subordinate tactical units, coalition allies, Iraqis, and other personnel at the unclassified level.

b. (U) Following MG Fast's initial assessment and report to CENTCOM headquarters, changes began to take place to put the right architecture in place. An Intelligence Fusion Cell was established, as were a Joint Inter-Agency Task Force and expanded JC2X HUMINT Management Cell, at CJTF-7 headquarters. The CPA staff was augmented with military personnel from the CJTF-7 intelligence staff. With the assistance of the Department of the Army Staff, CJTF-7 obtained needed communications equipment, computers, and reachback access to the Information Dominance Center (IDC) to collaborate intelligence information. The focus of the previous V Corps staff, which formed the nucleus of the initial CJTF-7 staff, rapidly changed from a tactical focus to a joint operational and strategic level focus. The subsequent successes of this new intelligence architecture created by MG Fast and her team exponentially improved the intelligence process and saved the lives of Coalition Forces and Iraqi civilians. HUMINT operations and the fusion of intelligence led to the capture of key members of the former regime, and ultimately, to the capture of Saddam Hussein himself. During the time period of the Abu Ghraib abuses, the intelligence focus was on Saddam Hussein's capture and exploitation of documents related to Saddam Hussein, preparation for Ramadan, and large scale enemy activity at Fallujah and Najaf. The effort to expand the intelligence organization, obtain operational intelligence about the counter-insurgency, and support the CPa consumed the efforts of the CJTF-7 staff. Responsibilities for oversight of tactical interrogation procedures, Intel analysis, and reporting at Abu Ghraib as throughout the ITO, were entrusted to the commanders in the field.

c. (U) Due to the expanded scope of the mission for this new organization, the need to gain operational intelligence about the counter-insurgency, and the rapid and unexpected number of detainees, assistance was requested to help inform the leadership on proper procedures, techniques, and changes needed for success. The assessment visit by MG Ryder greatly assisted the review and improvement of detention operations. Ryder's recommendations to automate the in-processing and accountability of detainees using the Biometrics Automated Tool Set (BATS), to discipline the audit trail of detainees from the point of capture to the central detention facility, and to properly segregate different groups, were implemented.

d. (S/NF)

e. (U) MG Fast's initial assessment and report on the intelligence organization and the needed systems architecture to support the mission was invaluable to establishing a roadmap for needed intelligence resources. LTG Alexander, the DA G2, was instrumental in providing needed equipment and guidance to improve the intelligence collection and fusion capabilities in Iraq. LTG Alexander was specifically helpful in getting the equipment necessary to support the intelligence architecture from the tactical to the strategic fusion levels.

6. (U) INDICATIONS AND WARNINGS

a. (U) In retrospect, indications and warnings had surfaced at the CJTF-7 level that additional oversight and corrective actions were needed in the handling of detainees from the point of capture through the central collection facilities, to include Abu Ghraib. Examples of these indications and warnings include: the investigation of an incident at Camp Cropper, the International Committee of the Red Cross (ICRC) reports on handling of detainees in subordinate units, ICRC reports on Abu Ghraib detainee conditions and treatment, CID investigations and disciplinary actions being taken by commanders, the death of an OGA detainee at Abu Ghraib, the lack of an adequate system for identification and accountability of detainees, and division commanders' continual concerns that intelligence information was not returning to the tactical level once detainees were evacuated to the central holding facility. The Commander, CJTF-7, recognized the need to place emphasis on proper handling of detainees and proper treatment of the Iraqi people in close proximity to operations. In October and December 2003, CDR, CJTF-7 published two policy memos entitled "Proper treatment of the Iraqi people during combat operations" and "Dignity and respect while conducting operations." Reports from the assessments of MG Miller and MG Ryder clearly confirmed the CJTF-7 Commander's instincts that action was needed to improve procedures and set the conditions for success in intelligence and detention operations. The report from the CID in January 2004 and subsequent investigation by MG Taguba confirmed that abuses occurred at Abu Ghraib during the period under investigation.

b. (U) I would be remiss if I did not reemphasize that the 180,000 U.S. and coalition forces, under all echelons of command within the CJTF-7, were prosecuting this complex counter-insurgency operation in a tremendously horrid environment, and were performing above all expectations. Leaders and Soldiers confronted a faceless enemy whose hatred of the United States knew no limits. The actions of a few undisciplined Soldiers at Abu Ghraib have overshadowed the selfless service demonstrated every day, 24 hours a day, by the vast majority of our Soldiers and civilians on the battlefield. We, as a Nation, owe a debt of gratitude to our service members who have answered our Nation's call and are in harm's way, every day. This fact became perfectly clear to me as I conducted my investigation.

7. (U) DOCTRINE, ORGANIZATIONAL STRUCTURE AND POLICY CHALLENGES IN THE IRAQI THEATER OF OPERATIONS

a. (U) Doctrine and Organizational Structures

(1) (U) Doctrine could not provide quick solutions for all the situations that confronted CJTF-7. In many cases, the situation, mission, and environment dictated the decisions and the actions taken by the CJTF leadership. This situation is not uncommon. Rarely

does war follow the pre-planned strategy. As the V Corps staff morphed to form the nucleus of the CJTF-7 staff, doctrine was not available to prescribe a detailed sequence to efficiently and effectively execute the transition. The new JMD focused on supplementing the V Corps headquarters structure to perform the expected mission in the Iraqi environment stability and support operations and support of the CPA.

(2) (U) *Joint Interrogation and Debriefing Center*. In accordance with JP 2.01, the use of a JIDC by a JTF is situation-dependent. No defined organization exists for implementing the JIDC concept. At Abu Ghraib, a JIDC was established based on the recommendation of MG Miller during his assessment. At the time, Abu Ghraib had only a few hundred detainees. LTC Jordan was sent to Abu Ghraib to oversee the establishment of the JIDC. On 19 November 2003, when COL Thomas Pappas assumed the role of commander of the forward operating base, he directed activities of the JIDC and LTC Jordan became the deputy director of the JIDC. There are conflicting statements regarding who had the responsibilities to implement and oversee the JIDC at Abu Ghraib. In accordance with doctrine, the CJTF-7 C2, MG Fast, through her JC2-X staff, provided priority intelligence requirements for the interrogators and analysts in the J1IDC. A portion of the approved CJTF-7 JMD earmarked 169 personnel for the interrogation operations and analysis cells in the JIDC. Many of these positions were later filled with contractor personnel. Although a senior officer was directed to be the Chief, JIDC, the establishment and efficient operation of the JIDC was further complicated by the lack of an organizational MI unit and chain of command at Abu Ghraib solely responsible for MI personnel and intelligence operations.

(3) (U) *MI & MP Responsibilities at Abu Ghraib*. The delineation of responsibilities for interrogations between the military intelligence and military police may not have been understood by some Soldiers and some leaders. The doctrinal implications of this issue are discussed later in this report. At Abu Ghraib, the lack of an MI commander and chain of command precluded the coordination needed for effective operations. At the same time, LTC Jordan failed to execute his responsibilities as Chief, JIDC. Tactical doctrine states that interrogators should specify to the guards what types of behavior on their part will facilitate screening of detainees. Normally, interrogation facilities are colocated with detention facilities, requiring close coordination between the MPs who are responsible for detention operations, and the MI personnel who are responsible for screening and interrogations. Both doctrinal manuals, for military police and military intelligence operations, clearly provide that Soldiers and units must obey rules of land warfare and, specifically, the Geneva Conventions when handling detainees. At Abu Ghraib, the delineation of responsibilities seems to have been blurred when military police Soldiers, untrained in interrogation operations, were used to enable interrogations. Problems arose in the following areas: use of dogs in interrogations, sleep deprivation as an interrogation technique and use of isolation as an interrogation technique.

(4) (U) *CJTF-7 Staff Responsibility*. CJTF-7 responsibility for staff oversight of detention operations, facilities, intelligence analysis and fusion, and limits of authority of interrogation techniques was dispersed among the principal and special staff. Overall responsibility for detention operations was vested in the C3, MG Tom Miller, with

further delegation to the Provost Marshal. Support of facilities was a C4 responsibility, with priorities of work established by the DCG, MG Walter Wojdakowski. MG Wojdakowski also had direct responsibility and oversight of the separate brigades assigned or TACON to CJTF-7. Priorities for intelligence collection, analysis and fusion were the responsibility of the C2, MG Fast. Lastly, LTG Sanchez used his Staff Judge Advocate, Colonel Marc Warren, to advise him on the limits of authority for interrogation and compliance with the Geneva Conventions for the memos published. The lack of one person on the staff to oversee detention operations and facilities, and the responsibilities of all units at a detention facility complicated effective and efficient coordination among the staff. Subordinate brigade commanders and their staffs also had to coordinate different actions for support with the various staff sections responsible for the support requested.

b. (U) Policy

(1) (U) *Policy Guidance.* DOD-wide, formal written policies for interrogation techniques have been prescribed by various levels of command and authority. In most cases, the doctrinal reference is FM 34-52, Intelligence Interrogation, dated September 1992. As stated, this manual is currently under revision by the proponent. During the period under investigation, there was confusing and sometimes conflicting guidance resulting from the number of policy memos and the specific areas of operation the various policies were intended to cover. Each theater's techniques for interrogation and counter-resistance were reviewed by appropriate legal authorities and subjected to external assessments before commanders were advised of their acceptability. In the wartime settings of each theater, commanders were satisfied that appropriate oversight had been conducted for procedures being used for interrogations. However, when reviewing the various reports on the number of abuses in the ITO, it became clear there is no agreed upon definition of abuse among all legal, investigating and oversight agencies.

(2) (U) Interrogation techniques, including Counter-Resistance Techniques, were developed and approved for the detainees in Guantanamo and Afghanistan who were determined not to be EPWs or protected persons under the Geneva Conventions of 1949. The OSD memo promulgated in December 2002, approving techniques and safeguards for interrogation of unlawful combatants in GTMO, included the use of dogs to induce stress and the removal of clothing as Counter-Resistance Techniques. This memo was rescinded in January 2003. A General Counsel Interrogation Working Group was subsequently formed and published a revised memo in April 2003 under the signature of the SECDEF on Counter-Resistance Techniques. This memo produced by the Working Group and the techniques outlined in FM 34-52 were referenced by Colonel Warren and his staff to develop the limits of authority memo for LTG Sanchez. The provisions of Geneva Convention IV, Relative to Protection of Civilian Persons in Time of War, did apply to detainees in Iraq.

(3) (U) Initially, no theater-specific guidance on approved interrogation techniques was published by CJTF-7 for the ITO. Thus, LTG Sanchez reemphasized the limits of authority for interrogations in his memos dated 14 September 2003 and 12 October 2003.

The first was rescinded, and the second addressed only security detainees and, inadvertently, left certain issues for interpretation: namely, the responsibility for clothing the detainees, the use of dogs in interrogation, and applicability of techniques to detainees who were not categorized as "security detainees." Furthermore, some military intelligence personnel executing their interrogation duties at Abu Ghraib had previously served as interrogators in other theaters of operation, primarily Afghanistan and GTMO. These prior interrogation experiences complicated understanding at the interrogator level. The extent of "word of mouth" techniques that were passed to the interrogators in Abu Ghraib by assistance teams from Guantanamo, Fort Huachuca, or amongst themselves due to prior assignments is unclear and likely impossible to definitively determine. The clear thread in the CJTF-7 policy memos and published doctrine is the humane treatment of detainees and the applicability of the Geneva Conventions. Experienced interrogators will confirm that interrogation is an art, not a science, and knowing the limits of authority is crucial. Therefore, the existence of confusing and inconsistent interrogation technique policies contributed to the belief that additional interrogation techniques were condoned in order to gain intelligence.

8. (U) SPECIFIC COMMENTS ON ABUSE AT ABU GHRAIB

a. (U) This report, so far, has discussed the OPLAN background, operational environment, and policy, doctrine and structural decisions that created conditions which allowed the abuses at Abu Ghraib to occur. The earlier investigations aptly described what happened at Abu Ghraib. MG Taguba found that "numerous incidents of sadistic, blatant, and wanton criminal abuses were inflicted on detainees." MG Fay identified 44 incidents of detainee abuse and his report describes the particular abuses in detail. In this section, I rely on the statements and other investigative activity from MG Fay. The conclusions, however, are my own. Clearly, shameful events occurred at the detention facility of Abu Ghraib and the culpable MI and MP Soldiers and leaders should be held responsible. In this section, I set forth an analytical framework for categorizing the abuses, propose causes for the incidents of abuse, and also discuss the culpability of organizations and personnel higher than the 205th MI Brigade Commander.

b. (U) For purposes of this report, I defined abuse as treatment of detainees that violated U.S. criminal law (including the Uniform Code of Military Justice (UCMJ)) or international law, or treatment that was inhumane or coercive without lawful justification. Whether the Soldier or contractor knew, at the time of the acts, that the conduct violated any law or standard, is not an element of the definition. In other words, conduct that met the definition would be "abuse" independent of the actor's knowledge that the conduct violated any law or standard.

c. (U) For clarity of analysis, my assessment divides abuses at Abu Ghraib into two different types of improper conduct: first, intentional violent or sexual abuses and, second, actions taken based on misinterpretation of or confusion about law or policy.

(1) (U) *Intentional violent or sexual abuses*, for purposes of this report, include acts causing bodily harm using unlawful force as well as sexual offenses including, but

not limited to rape, sodomy and indecent assault.[2] These incidents of physical or sexual abuse are serious enough that no Soldier or contractor believed the conduct was based on official policy or guidance. If proven, these actions would be criminal acts. I found that no policy, directive, or doctrine caused the violent or sexual abuse incidents. Soldiers knew they were violating the approved techniques and procedures. The primary causes of these actions were relatively straight-forward individual criminal misconduct, clearly in violation of law, policy, and doctrine and contrary to Army values.

(2) (U) The second category of abuse consists of *incidents that resulted from misinterpretations of law or policy* or resulted from confusion about what interrogation techniques were permitted by law or local SOPs. I found that misinterpretation as to accepted practices or confusion occurred due to the proliferation of guidance and information from other theaters of operation; individual interrogator experiences in other theaters; and, the failure to distinguish between permitted interrogation techniques in other theater environments and Iraq. These abuses include some cases of clothing removal (without any touching), some use of dogs in interrogations (uses without physical contact or extreme fear) and some instances of improper imposition of isolation. Some of these incidents involve conduct which, in retrospect, violated international law. However, at the time some of the Soldiers or contractors committed the acts, they may have honestly believed the techniques were condoned. Some of these incidents either took place during interrogations or were related to interrogation. Often, these incidents consisted of MP Soldiers, rather than MI personnel, implementing interrogation techniques.

d. (U) Some abuses may in fact fall in between these two categories or have elements of both. For instance, some Soldiers under the guise of confusion or misinterpretation may actually have intentionally violated approved interrogation techniques. For example, a Soldier may know that clothing removal is prohibited, but still removed some of a detainee's clothing to try to enhance interrogation techniques. This Soldier can later claim to have believed the actions were condoned. Soldier culpability in this area is best left to individual criminal or command investigations. While no analytical scheme can aptly categorize all misconduct, I think using the two categories set forth above helps explain *why* the entire range of abuses occurred.

e. (U) The appointment memo directed me to determine whether organizations or personnel higher than the 205th MI Brigade chain of command were involved directly or indirectly, in the questionable activities regarding alleged detainee abuse at Abu Ghraib prison.

(1) (U) I find no organization or individual higher in the chain of command of the 205th MI Brigade were directly involved in the questionable activities regarding alleged detainee abuse at Abu Ghraib prison.

(2) (U) CJTF-7 leaders and staff actions, however, contributed indirectly to the questionable activities regarding alleged detainee abuse at Abu Ghraib.

---

[2] As those offenses are defined in the Uniform Code of Military Justice.

(a) (U) Policy memoranda promulgated by the CJTF-7 Commander led indirectly to some of the non-violent and non-sexual abuses. The policy memos promulgated at the CJTF-7 level allowed for interpretation in several areas, including use of dogs and removal of clothing. Particularly, in light of the wide spectrum of interrogator qualifications, maturity, and experiences (i.e., in GTMO and Afghanistan), the memos did not adequately set forth the limits on interrogation techniques. Misinterpretations of CJTF policy memos led to some of the abuses at Abu Ghraib, but did not contribute to the violent or sexual abuses.

(b) (U) Inaction at the CJTF-7 staff level may have also contributed to the failure to discover and prevent abuses before January 2004. As discussed above, staff responsibility for detention and interrogation operations was dispersed among the Deputy Commanding General, C2, C3, C4 and SJA. The lack of a single CJTF-7 staff proponent for detention and interrogation operations resulted in no individual staff member focusing on these operations. As discussed in Section V, certain warning signs existed. In addition, there is sufficient evidence to reasonably believe that personnel in the CJTF-7 staff, principally in the OSJA and JC2X had knowledge of potential abuses and misconduct in violation of the Geneva Conventions at Abu Ghraib. This knowledge was not presented to the CJTF-7 leadership. Had the pace of combat operations and support to the CPA not been so overwhelming, the CJTF-7 staff may have provided additional oversight to interrogation operations at Abu Ghraib. The Commander, CJTF-7 had to prioritize efforts and CJTF-7, by necessity, devoted its resources to fighting the counter-insurgency and supporting the CPA, thereby saving U.S. and civilian Iraqi lives and assisting in the transition to Iraqi self-rule. Further, LTG Sanchez and MG Wojdakowski relied upon two senior officer Brigade Commanders (BG Janice Karpinski and COL Pappas) to run detention and interrogation operations at Abu Ghraib. In my professional opinion, in light of all the circumstances, the CJTF-7 staff did everything they could have reasonably been expected to do to successfully complete all their assigned missions.

f. (U) Assessing the materials from MG Fay and from MG Taguba, I agree that leadership failure, at the brigade level and below, clearly was a factor in not sooner discovering and taking actions to prevent both the violent/sexual abuse incidents and the misinterpretation/confusion incidents. At Abu Ghraib, interrogation operations were also plagued by a lack of an organizational chain of command presence and by a lack of proper actions to establish standards and training by the senior leaders present.

(1) (U) The leaders from 205th MI and 800th MP Brigades located at Abu Ghraib or with supervision over Abu Ghraib, failed to supervise subordinates or provide direct oversight of this important mission. The lack of command presence, particularly at night, was clear.

(2) (U) The 205th Brigade Commander did not specifically assign responsibility for interrogation operations to a specific subordinate MI unit at Abu Ghraib and did not ensure that a chain of command for the interrogation operations mission was established at Abu Ghraib. The presence of a clear chain of Military Intelligence command and associated responsibilities would have enhanced effective operations.

(3) (U) The leaders from 205th MI and 800th MP Brigades located at Abu Ghraib or with supervision over Soldiers and units at Abu Ghraib, failed to properly discipline their Soldiers and failed to develop and learn from AARs and lessons learned.

(4) (U) These leaders failed to provide adequate mission-specific training to execute a mission of this magnitude and complexity.

(5) (U) A dysfunctional command relationship existed between the MI Brigade and the MP Brigade, including:

(a) Failure to coordinate and document specific roles and responsibilities;

(b) Confusion at the Soldier level concerning the clarity of the MP role in interrogations.

(6) (U) Despite these leadership deficiencies, the primary cause of the most egregious violent and sexual abuses was the individual criminal propensities of the particular perpetrators. These individuals should not avoid personal responsibility, despite the failings of the chain of command.

g. (U) Other Contributing Factors. No single, or simple, cause explains why some of the Abu Ghraib abuses happened. In addition to the leadership failings discussed above, other contributing factors include:

(1) (U) Safety and security conditions at Abu Ghraib. Resources that might otherwise have been put toward detention operations instead had to be dedicated to force protection. In addition, the difficult circumstances for Soldiers, including a poor quality of life and the constant threat of death or serious injury, contributed to Soldiers' frustrations and increased their levels of stress. Facilities at Abu Ghraib were poor. Working and living conditions created a poor climate to conduct interrogation and detention operations to standard.

(2) (U) The lack of clear and consistent guidance, promulgated at the CJTF level on interrogation procedures coupled with the availability of information on Counter-Resistance Techniques used in other theaters.

(3) (U) Soldier knowledge of interrogation techniques permitted in GTMO and Afghanistan and failure to distinguish between those environments and Iraq.

(4) (U) Interaction with OGA and other agency interrogators who did not follow the same rules as U.S. Forces. There was at least the perception, and perhaps the reality, that non-DOD agencies had different rules regarding interrogation and detention operations. Such a perception encouraged Soldiers to deviate from prescribed techniques.

(5) (U) Integration of some contractors without training, qualifications, and certification created ineffective interrogation teams and the potential for non-compliance with doctrine and applicable laws.

(6) (U) Under-resourcing of personnel in both the 800th MP BDE (including the inability to replace personnel leaving theater) and in the 205th MI Brigade, specifically

in the interrogator, analyst, and linguist fields. (Under-resourcing at the CJTF-7 level also contributed and was previously discussed.)

(7) (U) Lack of a clear understanding of MP and MI roles and responsibilities by some Soldiers and leaders.

(8) (U) Lack of clear roles and responsibilities for tactical, as opposed to, strategic interrogation.

9. (U) ASSESSMENTS AS THE SENIOR INVESTIGATING OFFICER

a. (U) Introduction. Due to the previous assessments and investigations conducted on Abu Ghraib, I was able to develop my own assessments based on interviews I conducted, the findings and conclusions in the earlier reports, as well as the materials in MG Fay's report. The following assessments provide insight on the challenges that CJTF-7 faced, as well as areas that need to be addressed by our military in the near future. The specific investigations and assessments were provided by the reports of MG Miller, MG Ryder, MG Taguba, the DAIG, and MG Fay.

b. (U) Charters. MG Miller's and MG Ryder's assessments were conducted on interrogation and detention operations as a result of the request and/or discussions by the CJTF Commander and the Commander, CENTCOM. MG Taguba and MG Fay were directed to investigate personnel in the MP Brigade and the MI Brigade after the discovery of abuses at Abu Ghraib. The DAIG was specifically tasked to conduct an assessment of Detainee Operations as the Army executes its role as DOD Executive Agent for Enemy Prisoners of War and Detention Program.

c. (U) Summaries of assessment visits. The assistance visits by MG Miller and MG Ryder, discussed briefly above, confirmed the instincts of the Commander, CJTF-7, and provided solid recommendations for improving procedures. MG Miller's assessment set forth what had to be done to synchronize intelligence efforts, and provided different techniques in interrogation and analysis. MG Ryder provided processes for more efficient and effective chain of custody of, and accountability for, detainees. MG Taguba's and MG Fay's investigative reports confirmed that abuses occurred and assigned specific responsibility for the actions. The DAIG report provided insights across doctrine, organizations, training, material, leadership, personnel and facilities (DOTMLPF) and on capability and standards shortfalls. I found that the assistance visits by senior leaders with experience in detention and interrogation operations, subject matter experts, and mobile training teams were extremely helpful in validating needed procedures and increasing the effectiveness of interrogation and detention operations. The investigative reports and DAIG findings will be used to fix deficiencies that have been found in current operations.

d. (U) Doctrine.

(1) (U) Doctrine is meant to be a guideline to focus efforts in a specific area. Doctrine is the culmination of years of experience, doctrine allows leaders at all levels to adapt to the different environments and situations that their units may encounter.

When prosecuting hostilities, doctrine does not replace the inherent responsibilities of commanders to execute their missions, care for the safety and security of their Soldiers, train their Soldiers and their organizations to be competent and confident in their assigned duties and responsibilities, or uphold the rule of law and legal authority such as the Geneva Convention. An overarching doctrine allows commanders the latitude to develop tactics, techniques, and procedures, as well as unit standard operating procedures, to focus Soldier and unit operations. Commander policies and directives often supplement or emphasize specific items that the commander wants to ensure are clearly understood within their command.

(2) (U) Basic Army and Joint doctrine for detention and interrogation operations served as a guideline for operations in OIF. Doctrine did not cause the abuses at Abu Ghraib. Had Army doctrine and training been followed, the abuses at Abu Ghraib would not have occurred. Several areas, however, need to be updated, refined or expanded: roles, responsibilities and relationships between MP and MI personnel; the concept, structure, and organization of a JIDC; the transition to and organization of a JTF structure and in particular, the intelligence organization within the JTF headquarters.

(a)(U) *Roles, responsibilities and relationships between MP and MI personnel.* The various investigations indicate that the delineation of responsibilities for interrogations between the military intelligence and military police may not have been understood by some Soldiers and some leaders. At Abu Ghraib, non-violent and non-sexual abuses may have occurred as a result of confusion in three areas of apparent MI/MP overlap: use of dogs during interrogations, nudity, and implementation of sleep deprivation. Doctrinal manuals prescribe responsibilities for military intelligence and military police personnel at detention facilities. These manuals do not address command or support relationships. Subordinate units of the military intelligence brigade of a Corps are normally tasked with running the Corps Interrogation Facility (CIF). Centralized EPW collection and holding areas, as well as detention centers, are the responsibility of the Military Police with staff oversight by the Provost Marshal. FM 34-52, Intelligence Interrogation, does state that in the screening process of EPWs, MPs and MI Soldiers should coordinate roles.

(b)(U) Relationships between MP and MI personnel and leadership responsibilities at a detention facility of this magnitude need to be more prescriptive. Doctrine establishes the need for coordination and designates detention operations as a military police responsibility. Responsibility for interrogation of detainees remains with the military intelligence community. Doctrine for Interrogation operations states that MPs can enable, in coordination with MI personnel, a more successful interrogation. Exact procedures for how MP Soldiers assist with informing interrogators about detainees or assist with enabling interrogations can be left to interpretation. Our doctrinal manuals are clear on humane treatment of detainees and compliance with the Geneva Conventions by MI, MP and all U.S. Forces. The current version of FM 34-52, Intelligence Interrogation, is under revision to incorporate lessons learned in ongoing theaters of operations. Lessons learned have also resulted in changes to programs of instruction by military police and military intelligence proponents.

My assessment is that the ongoing revision of Intelligence Interrogation manuals will assist in clarification of roles and responsibilities. At Abu Ghraib, doctrinal issues did not preclude onsite leaders from taking appropriate action to execute their missions.

(c)(U) *The Joint Interrogation and Debriefing Center.* The JIDC was formed at Abu Ghraib by personnel from a number of organizations, creating an ad hoc relationship. Further, the establishment of the JIDC at Abu Ghraib, coupled with implementing the new Tiger Team approach to interrogations (where an interrogator, analyst, and linguist operate as a team) were new to Abu Ghraib personnel and demanded creation of a detailed standard operating procedure (SOP). A SOP was initially developed and published in October 2003 by MI personnel at the facility. Joint doctrine needs to expand on the operation and organization for a JIDC at centralized detention facilities. A template for a JIDC needs to be developed, to include identifying Joint and other agency resources with strategic interrogation expertise, to provide insight for combatant commanders in specific areas of operation.

(d)(U) Joint doctrine and policy should also address the roles of military personnel and other agencies in colocated detention and interrogation facilities. All detainees must be in-processed, medically screened, accounted for, and properly documented when interned in a military facility. This did not happen at Abu Ghraib.

(3) (U) *Transition to and Organization of JTF Structure and its Intelligence Architecture.* The intelligence architecture for the missions tasked to the CJTF-7 was inadequate due to the expanded mission and continuation of hostilities in theater. Several reports stated that lack of manning provided significant challenges due to the increased mission work load and the environment. Certainly, the V Corps Headquarters was not trained, manned or equipped to assume the role of a CJTF. Although the mission was initially considered to be SASO, in fact hostilities continued. CI/HUMINT capabilities in current force structure, among all services, needs a holistic review. The Army has significantly reduced tactical interrogators since Desert Shield/Desert Storm. Creation of the Defense HUMINT Service and worldwide demands for these skills has depleted the number of experienced interrogators that may be needed in the future joint operational environment. The HUMINT management organization within the Intelligence Staff of a JTF needs to be institutionalized and resourced. Specifically, work needs to be done to institutionalize the personnel and equipment needs for future command and control headquarters to include the JIATF and C2X cells within a JTF intelligence staff.

(4) (U) In addition, the ongoing review by the Army and Joint Forces Command to create JTF capable headquarters and Standing Joint Task Force Headquarters organic to combatant commands should be expedited and resourced. Such efforts may have helped transition V Corps to the CJTF-7 staff more rapidly by assigning a Standing Joint Task Force to the CJTF-7. Similarly, the Army's initiative to develop standalone command and control headquarters, currently known as Units of Employment, that are JTF-capable would have greatly facilitated the transition of the V Corps staff to the new organization.

e. (U) Policy and Procedures

(1) (U) *Detention Operations*. At first, at Abu Ghraib and elsewhere in Iraq, the handling of detainees, appropriately documenting their capture, and identifying and accounting for them, were all dysfunctional processes, using little or no automation tools. The assistance visits by MG Miller and MG Ryder revealed the need to adhere to established policies and guidance, discipline the process, properly segregate detainees, and use better automation techniques to account for detainees and to provide timely information.

(2) (U) *Interrogation Techniques Policy*. A review of different theaters' interrogation technique policies reveals the need for clear guidance for interrogation techniques at both the tactical and strategic levels, especially where multiple agencies are involved in interrogation operations. The basic Field Manuals provide guidance for Soldiers conducting interrogations at the tactical level. Different techniques and different authorities currently exist for other agencies. When Army Soldiers and other agency personnel operate in the same areas, guidelines become blurred. The future joint operational environment presents a potential for a mix of lawful and unlawful combatants and a variety of different categories of detainees. Techniques used during initial battlefield interrogations as opposed to at a central detention facility differ in terms of tactical versus more strategic level information collection. The experience, maturity, and source of interrogators at each of these locations may also dictate a change in techniques. In each theater, commanders were seeking guidance and information on the applicability of the articles of the Geneva Conventions to specific population sets and on what techniques could be used to improve intelligence production and remain within the limits of lawful authorities.

(a)(U) At Abu Ghraib, the lack of consistent policy and command oversight regarding interrogation techniques, coupled with changing policies, contributed to the confusion concerning which techniques could be used, which required higher level approval, and what limits applied to permitted techniques. Initially, CJTF-7 had no theater-specific guidance other than the basic Field Manuals which govern Intelligence Interrogations and Internment and Resettlement operations. Policies for interrogation techniques including policies for Counter-Resistance Techniques, were provided for different theaters of operation – namely Guantanamo, Afghanistan, and Iraq. Some interrogators conducting operations at Abu Ghraib had experience in different theaters and used their experiences to develop procedures at Abu Ghraib. An example of this is the SOP for the JIDC created by personnel of the 519th MI Battalion.

(b)(U) When policies, SOPs, or doctrine were available, Soldiers were inconsistently following them. In addition, in some units, training on standard procedures or mission tasks was inadequate. In my assessment, I do not believe that multiple policies resulted in the violent or sexual abuses discovered at Abu Ghraib. However, confusion over policies contributed to some of the non-violent and non-sexual abuses. There is a need, therefore, to further refine interrogation techniques and limits of authority at the tactical versus the strategic level, and between Soldiers and other agency personnel.

(3) (U) *Use of Military Detention Centers by Other Agencies*. In joint military detention centers, service members should never be put in a position that potentially puts them at risk for non-compliance with the Geneva Conventions or Laws of Land Warfare. At Abu Ghraib, detainees were accepted from other agencies and services without proper in-processing, accountability, and documentation. These detainees were referred to as "ghost detainees." Proper procedures must be followed, including, segregating detainees of military intelligence value and properly accounting and caring for detainees incarcerated at military detention centers. The number of ghost detainees temporarily held at Abu Ghraib, and the audit trail of personnel responsible for capturing, medically screening, safeguarding and properly interrogating the "ghost detainees," cannot be determined.

f. (U) *Training*. The need for additional training during the mobilization phase or in-country on unit and specific individual tasks was clearly an issue in the reports and assessments. Some military police units found themselves conducting detention operations which was not a normal unit mission essential task, and those units needed additional training to properly accomplish the missions they were given. The collocation and mixture of other agency and civilian personnel conducting detention and interrogation operations became confusing for junior leaders and Soldiers not normally accustomed to working with other organizations. Collective training to standard by MP and MI units in combined scenarios as rigorous as the situations faced in OIF is needed to prepare for the future.

In addition, V Corps personnel, to include commanders and staff, were not trained to execute a JTF mission. The transition from major combat operations to a headquarters focused on SASO and support to the Coalition Provisional Authority was a major transition which the unit did not have time to train or prepare. Most importantly, we must continue to place rigor and values in our training regimen. Our values are non-negotiable for members of our profession. They are what a professional military force represents to the world. As addressed before, leaders need rigorous training to be able to adapt to this level of complexity.

g. (U) *Material*. Priorities for logistical support remained with the operational units who were conducting combat operations and providing force protection and security of U.S. and coalition forces. Creating an intelligence organization to provide tactical through strategic intelligence in a seamless manner and the dramatic increase in detention operations demanded communications, computers, and a network to support operations. The concept of a Joint Logistics Command should be further examined using lessons learned from OIF/OEF. Automation equipment needed to provide seamless connectivity of intelligence information from tactical through strategic levels, and enable an Intelligence Fusion Center in a JTF should be documented and embedded in JTF capable headquarters. Equipment currently undergoing research and development and commercial off–the-shelf solutions which enable CI/HUMINT operations and enable Soldiers to serve as sensors and collectors should be rapidly pursued. The process of accounting for detainees, their equipment, and their personal property, and documenting their intelligence value, should be automated from the tactical level to the centralized detention facilities.

h. (U) *Leader Development*. The OIF environment demanded adaptive, confident, and competent leadership at all echelons. Leaders must set the example and be at the critical centers of gravity for their respective operations. Leaders set the example in a values-based profession. The risk to Soldiers and the security of all personnel demanded continued leader involvement in operations, planning, after-action reviews, and clear dissemination of lessons learned, to adapt to the dynamics of the counter-insurgency. Successful leaders were involved in their operations and were at the tip of the spear during critical periods. Leadership failure was seen when leaders did not take charge, failed to provide appropriate guidance, and did not conduct continual training. In some cases, leaders failed to accept responsibility or apply good judgment in executing assigned responsibilities. This latter fact is evident in the lack of a coordinated defense at Abu Ghraib, inconsistent training and standards, and lack of discipline by Soldiers. Commanders and leaders at all levels remain responsible for execution of their mission and the welfare of their Soldiers, In Iraq, leaders had to adapt to a new complex operational environment. Some of our leaders adapted faster than others. We must continue to put rigor in our leader and unit training. Leaders must be trained for certainty and educated for uncertainty. The ability to know how to think rather than what to think is critical in the future Joint Operational Environment. Specific leader and Soldier failures in the 800th MP Brigade and the 205th MI Brigade are identified in the investigative reports by MG Taguba and MG Fay. As discussed above, my review of echelons above brigade revealed that CJTF-7 leaders were not directly involved in the abuses at Abu Ghraib. Their actions and inaction did indirectly contribute to the non-sexual and non-violent abuses.

i. (U) *Facilities*. Facilities and quality of life for Soldiers and detainees were representative of the conditions throughout the AOR initially. Only when the logistics system became responsive to the needs of units and Soldiers, contracting mechanisms were put in place to support operations, and the transportation system matured to move supplies, were improvements seen in facilities and quality of life. The conditions at Abu Ghraib were representative of the conditions found throughout the country during post Phase III, Decisive Operations. The slow process of developing the logistics system and providing secure lines of communication directly impeded Soldier security and quality of life.

10. (U) CONCLUDING FINDINGS AND RECOMMENDATIONS

a. (U) **SUMMARY AS SENIOR INVESTIGATING OFFICER.** I derived these findings and recommendations from the observations and assessments discussed in Sections 2-9, from the interviews I conducted, and from the documents I have reviewed. Furthermore, I support the recommendations of the Fay and Taguba Reports concerning individual culpability for actions that violated U.S. criminal law (including the Uniform Code of Military Justice (UCMJ)) or international law, or that was inhumane or coercive without lawful justification. The personnel who committed these acts did not act in accordance with the discipline and values that the U.S. Army represents. Leaders who had direct responsibilities for the actions of these individuals failed to adequately exercise their responsibilities in the execution of this mission.

b. (U) **RESPONSIBILITY ABOVE 205TH MI BRIGADE**

(1) (U)Findings:

(a) (U) I find that the chain of command above the 205th MI Brigade was not directly involved in any of the abuses that occurred at Abu Ghraib.

(b) (U) I find that the chain of command above the ₂0Sth MI Brigade promulgated policy memoranda that, inadvertently, left room for interpretation and may have indirectly led to some of the non-violent and non-sexual abuse incidents.

(c) (U) I find that LTG Sanchez, and his DCG, MG Wojdakowski, failed to ensure proper staff oversight of detention and interrogation operations. As previously stated, MG Wojdakowski had direct oversight of two new Brigade Commanders. Further, staff elements of the CJTF-7 reacted inadequately to some of the Indications and Warnings discussed above. However, in light of the operational environment, and CJTF-7's under-resourcing and unplanned missions, and the Commander's consistent need to prioritize efforts, I find that the CJTF-7 Commander and staff performed above expectations, in the overall scheme of OIF.

(d) (U) I find that the TACON relationship of the 800th MP Brigade to the CJTF-7 created a dysfunctional relationship for proper oversight and effective detention operations in the Iraqi Theater of Operations (ITO). In addition, the relationship between leaders and staff of the 205th MI Brigade and 800th MP Brigade was ineffective as they failed to effect proper coordination of roles and responsibilities for detention and interrogation operations.

(e) (U) I find that a number of causes outside of the control of CJTF-7 also contributed to the abuses at Abu Ghraib. These are discussed in Section 8 and include, individuals' criminal propensity; Soldier knowledge of interrogation techniques permitted in GTMO and Afghanistan and failure to distinguish between those environments and Iraq; interaction with OGA and other agency interrogators who did not follow the same rules as U.S. Forces; integration of some contractors without training, qualifications, and certification; under-resourcing of personnel in both the 800th MP BDE (including the inability to replace personnel leaving theater) and in the 205th MI Brigade, specifically in the interrogator, analyst, and linguist fields.

(2) (U) Recommendations:

(a) (U) That CJTF-7 designate a single staff proponent for Detention and Interrogation Operations. The grade of this officer should be commensurate with the level of responsibilities of the particular operation. Further, that the Army in concert with JFCOM should review the concept and clarify responsibilities for a single staff position for Detention and Interrogation operations as part of a JTF capable organization.

(b) (U) That CJTF-7 in concert with CENTCOM publish clear guidance that applies to all units and agencies on roles and responsibilities for Detention and Interrogation Operations, and publish clear guidance on the limits of interrogation authority for interrogation techniques as pertains to the detainee population in the ITO.

(c) (U) That CENTCOM review command relationship and responsibilities for the 800th MP Brigade with CJTF-7 in the conduct of detention operations in the ITO.

(d) (U) That the CJTF-7 Inspector General be designated the staff proponent to rapidly investigate ICRC allegations. That the CJTF-7 Inspector General periodically conduct unscheduled inspections of detention and interrogation operations providing direct feedback to the commander.

c. (U) DOCTRINE

(1) (U) Finding: Army and Joint doctrine did not directly contribute to the abuses found at Abu Ghraib. Abuses would not have occurred had doctrine been followed. Nonetheless, certain areas need to updated, expanded or refined.

(2) (U) Recommendations:

(a) (U) That JFCOM in concert with the Army update Joint and Army publications to clearly address the concept, organization and operations of a Joint Interrogation and Debriefing Center in a future joint operational environment.

(b) (U) That the Army update interrogation operations doctrine to clarify responsibilities for interrogation techniques at both tactical and strategic levels. The ongoing revision and update of FM 34-52, Intelligence Interrogations, should clarify the roles and responsibilities of MP and MI units at centralized detention facilities.

(c)(U) That DOD assess the impact of current policies on Detention and Interrogation Operations. That DOD review the limits of authority for interrogation techniques and publish guidance that applies to all services and agencies.

d. (U) V CORPS TRANSITION TO CJTF

(1) (U)Findings:

(a)(U) V Corps was never adequately resourced as a CJTF. The challenge of transitioning from V Corps HQ5 to CJTF-7 without adequate personnel, equipment, and intelligence architecture, severely degraded the commander and staff during transition. Personnel shortages documented in the JMD continued to preclude operational capabilities.

(b)(U) Command and control headquarters that can perform as a Joint Task Force in a joint operational environment will be the norm for the future. This fact warrants action by supporting commands and services to resource and train JTF capable headquarters for success.

(2) (U) Recommendations:

(a)(U) That the Army expedite the development and transition of Corps-level command and control headquarters into JTF-capable organizations.

(b)(U) That the Army in concert with JFCOM institutionalize and resource the personnel and equipment needs of future JTF-capable headquarters, including the intelligence architecture of such headquarters.

e. (U) **INTELLIGENCE ARCHITECTURE** and **INTELLIGENCE PERSONNEL RESOURCES**

(I) (U)Findings:

(a)(U) Demands on the HUMINT capabilities in a counter-insurgency and in the future joint operational environment will continue to tax tactical and strategic assets. An Intelligence Fusion Center, a Joint Inter-agency Task Force and a JC2X are essential to provide seamless tactical through strategic level intelligence in a JTF headquarters.

(b)(U) Future land forces, especially the Army, need trained and experienced tactical HUMINT personnel to operate in the future Joint Operational Environment,

(2) (U) Recommendations:

(a) (U) That the Army conduct a holistic review of the CIIHUMINT intelligence force structure and prioritize needs for the future joint operational environment. The review should consider the personnel, equipment and resources needed to provide a seamless intelligence capability from the tactical to the strategic level to support the combatant commander.

(b) (U) That the Army align and train HUMINT assets geographically to leverage language skills and knowledge of culture.

(c) (U) That land forces, particularly MI and MP personnel, conduct rigorous collective training to replicate the complex environment experienced in OIF and in likely future areas of conflict.

f. (U) **FACILITIES**

(1) (U) Finding: Abu Ghraib detention facility was inadequate for safe and secure detention and interrogation operations. CJTF-7 lacked viable alternatives due to the depleted infrastructure in Iraq.

(2) (U) Recommendation: That the Army review the concept of detainee contingency facilities that can be rapidly deployed and established to safeguard and secure detainees, while providing necessary facilities to conduct screening and interrogations (similar to the concept of the Force Provider or Red Horse contingency facilities, where pre-fabricated buildings can be set up quickly). Adopting this recommendation would provide commanders an option for rapidly deploying and establishing detention facilities.

g. (U) **OTHER GOVERNMENT AGENCIES**

(1) (U) Findings:

(a) (U) Working alongside non-military organizations/agencies to jointly execute missions for our Nation, proved to be complex and demanding on military units at the tactical level. There was at least the perception that non-DOD agencies had different rules regarding interrogation and detention operations. Policies and specific limits of authority need review to ensure applicability to all organizations operating in the designated theater of operations.

(b) (U) Seamless sharing of operational intelligence was hindered by lack of a fusion center that received, analyzed, and disseminated all intelligence collected by CJTF-7 units and other agencies/units outside of the CJTF-7 chain of command.

(c) (U) Proliferation of Interrogation and Counter-Resistance Technique memorandums, with specific categorization of unlawful combatants in various theaters of operations, and the intermingling of tactical, strategic, and other agency interrogators at the central detention facility of Abu Ghraib, provided a permissive and compromising climate for Soldiers.

(d) (U) Soldiers/Sailors/Airmen/Marines should never be put in a position that potentially puts them at risk for non-compliance with the Geneva Conventions or Laws of Land Warfare

(2) (U) Recommendations:

(a)(U) That DOD review inter-agency policies to ensure that all parties in a specific theater of operations are required to adhere to the same guidance and rules in the use of military Interrogation and Detention Facilities, including limits of authority for interrogation techniques.

(b)(U) That CENTCOM publish guidance for compliance by all agencies/organizations utilizing military detention facilities in the Iraqi theater of operation.

(c)(U) That DOD review the responsibilities for interrogations by other agencies and other agencies responsibilities to the combatant commander to provide intelligence information and support.

(d)(U) That DOD assess the impact of current policies and guidance on unlawful combatants in the conduct of Detention and Interrogation Operations. And, that DOD review the limits of authority for use of interrogation techniques and publish guidance that is applicable to all parties using military facilities.

h. (U) LEADERSHIP and SUCCESSES

(1) (U) Findings:

(a) (U) Leaders throughout Operation Iraqi Freedom were confronted with a complex operational environment. The speed at which leaders at all echelons adapted to this environment varied based on level of training, maturity in command, and ability to see the battlefield. The adaptability of leaders in future operational environments will be critical.

(b) (U) In Operation Iraqi Freedom, as the Intelligence architecture matured and became properly equipped and organized, and close working relationships with all intelligence agencies and other OIF forces developed, there were clear successes in obtaining intelligence.

(c) (U) HUMINT management and Intelligence Fusion were essential to enable success in this complex operational environment.

(2) (U) Recommendations.

(a) (U) That rigorous leader training in our institutions, at home stations, and at the Army's Training Centers (Joint Readiness Training Center, National Training Center, Combat Maneuver Training Center, and Battle Command Training Program) continue.

(b) (U) That DOD/CENTCOM and the senior leaders of all services recognize and provide a vote of confidence to our military's leaders and Soldiers executing the OIF mission and supporting the Iraqi people.

AR 15-6 INVESTIGATION OF THE
ABU GHRAIB DETENTION FACILITY AND
205th MILITARY INTELLIGENCE BRIGADE (U)

MG GEORGE R. FAY
INVESTIGATINIG OFFICER

SUBJECT: (U) AR 15-6 Investigation of the Abu Ghraib Detention Facility and
            205th MI Brigade

TABLE OF CONTENTS

1. (U) APPOINTING OFFICIALS' INSTRUCTIONS AND INVESTIGATIVE METHODOLOGY

a. (U) Appointing Officials' Instruction.

(1) (U) On 31 March 2004, LTG Ricardo S. Sanchez, Commander, Combined Joint Task Force 7 (CJTF-7), appointed MG George R. Fay as an Army Regulation (AR) 381-10 Procedure 15 Investigating Officer. LTG Sanchez determined, based upon MG Antonio Taguba's out brief of the results of an Article 15-6 investigation of the Abu Ghraib Detention Facility in Iraq, that another investigation was warranted. MG Fay was to investigate allegations that members of the 205th Military Intelligence Brigade were involved in detainee abuse at the Abu Ghraib Detention Facility.

(a) (U) MG Fay was instructed as follows: Pursuant to AR 381-10, Procedure 15, you are hereby appointed as an investigating officer to conduct an investigation in accordance with (IAW) Army Regulation (AR) 15-6 into all the relevant facts and circumstances surrounding the alleged misconduct on the part of personnel assigned and/or attached to the 205th Military Intelligence (MI) Brigade, to include civilian interrogators and/or interpreters, from 15 August 2003, to 1 February 2004, at the Abu Ghraib (AG) Detention Facility.

(b) (U) Specifically, you will investigate the following areas:

[1] (U) Whether 205th MI Brigade personnel requested, encouraged, condoned, or solicited Military Police (MP) personnel to abuse detainees at AG as preparation for interrogation operations.

[2] (U) Whether 205th MI Brigade personnel comported with established interrogation procedures and applicable laws and regulations when questioning Iraqi security internees at the Joint Interrogation and Debriefing Center.

(2) (U) The Commander, United States Central Command (CENTCOM) requested a new appointing authority and investigating officer be assigned to the investigation. On 14 June 2004, Secretary of Defense (SECDEF) Donald Rumsfeld requested the Acting Secretary of the Army (SECARMY) R.L.Brownlee assign an "officer senior to LTG Sanchez" to assume his duties as appointing authority, and a new or additional investigating officer should one be required. SECDEF provided the following additional guidance to the Acting SECARMY:

(U) The new appointing authority shall refer recommendations concerning issues at the Department of the Army level to the Department of the Army and recommendations concerning issues at the Department of Defense (DoD) level to the Department of Defense for appropriate action. The appointing authority shall refer the completed report to the Commander, United States Central Command for further action as appropriate, including forwarding to the ATSD(IO) [Assistant to the Secretary of Defense for Intelligence Oversight] in accordance with DoD Directive 5240.1-R and CJCS-I 5901.01. Matters concerning accountability, if any, should be referred by the appointing authority, without recommendation, to the appropriate level of the chain of command for disposition.

(3) (U) On 16 June 2004, Acting SECARMY Brownlee designated GEN Paul J. Kern, Commander of the US Army Material Command, as the new Procedure 15 appointing authority. Acting SECARMY Brownlee's instructions included the following:

(a) (U) I am designating you as the appointing authority. Major General Fay remains available to perform duties as the investigating officer. If you determine, however, after reviewing the status of the investigation, that a new additional investigating officer is necessary, please present that request to me.

(b) (U) Upon receipt of the investigation, you will refer all recommendations concerning issues at the Department of the Army level to me and all recommendations concerning issues at the Department of Defense level to the Secretary of Defense for appropriate action. You will refer the completed report to the Commander, United States Central Command, for further action as appropriate, including forwarding to ATSD(IO) IAW DoD Directive 5240.1-R and CJCS-I 5901.01. Finally, you should refer matters concerning accountability, if any, without recommendation, to the appropriate level of the chain of command for disposition. If you determine that you need further legal resources to accomplish this mission, you should contact the Judge Advocate General.

(4) (U) On 25 June 2004, GEN Kern appointed LTG Anthony R. Jones, Deputy Commanding General, US Army Training and Doctrine Command (TRADOC), as an additional Procedure 15 investigating officer. GEN Kern's instructions to LTG Jones included the following:

(a) (U) Pursuant to AR 381-10, Procedure 15, and AR 15-6, you are hereby appointed as an investigating officer to conduct an investigation of alleged misconduct involving personnel assigned or attached to the 205th Military Intelligence Brigade at the Abu Ghraib Detention Facility. Your appointment is as an additional investigating officer. MG Fay and his investigative team are available to assist you.

(b) (U) Specifically, the purpose of the investigation is to determine the facts and to determine whether the questionable activity at Abu Ghraib is legal and is consistent with applicable policy. In LTG Sanchez's 31 March 2004, appointment letter to MG Fay, which I have adopted, he specified three areas into which the investigation was to look: whether the 205th Military Intelligence Brigade had been involved in Military Police detainee abuse at Abu Ghraib; whether 205th Military Intelligence Brigade personnel complied with established procedures, regulations, and laws when questioning internees at the Joint Interrogation and Debriefing Center; and the facts behind several identified sworn statements. In addition, your investigation should determine whether organizations or personnel higher in the chain of command of the 205th Military Intelligence Brigade were involved directly or indirectly in any questionable activities regarding alleged detainee abuse at Abu Ghraib.

b. (U) Investigative Methodology.

(1) (U) The investigative team conducted a comprehensive and exhaustive review of available background documents and statements pertaining to the operations of the 205th Military Intelligence (MI) Brigade (205 MI BDE) at Abu Ghraib from a wide variety of sources, to include all previous investigations. Where possible, coordination was established with other ongoing investigations of the same nature.

(2) (U) Over 170 personnel were interviewed (some multiple times) during the course of the investigation (Reference Annex B, Appendix 1). These interviews included personnel assigned or attached to the 205 MI BDE, the 800th Military Police (MP) Brigade (800 MP BDE), CJTF-7, Joint Task Force Guantanamo (JTF-GTMO), 28th Combat Support Hospital (CSH), the United States Army Intelligence Center (USAIC), the United States Navy, Titan Corporation, CACI International, Inc., and three detainees at Abu Ghraib. Written sworn statements were prepared as a result of these interviews. Several personnel invoked their rights under Article 31, Uniform Code of Military Justice (UCMJ) and the Fifth Amendment of the US Constitution. In these cases and in cases where no sworn statements were collected, Memoranda for Record (MFR) were prepared to describe the nature of and information addressed in the interview.

(3) (U) Over 9,000 documents were collected, catalogued and archived into a database. Advanced analytic tools were used to organize, collate, and analyze this data as well as all collected interview data. Other analytical tools were used to prepare graphic representations of the data.

(4) (U) The investigative team consisted of 26 personnel to include investigators, analysts, subject matter experts and legal advisors.

2. (U) EXECUTIVE SUMMARY

a. (U) Background.

(1) (U) This investigation was ordered initially by LTG Ricardo S. Sanchez, Commander, CJTF-7. LTG Sanchez appointed MG George R. Fay as investigating officer under the provisions of AR 381-10. MG Fay was appointed to investigate allegations that members of the 205 MI BDE were involved in detainee abuse at the Abu Ghraib Detention Facility. Specifically, he was to determine whether 205 MI BDE personnel requested, encouraged, condoned, or solicited MP personnel to abuse detainees and whether MI personnel comported with established interrogation procedures and applicable laws and regulations. The investigative team conducted a comprehensive review of all available background documents and statements pertaining to Abu Ghraib from a wide variety of sources. Over 170 persons were interviewed concerning their knowledge of interrogation and detention operations at Abu Ghraib and/or their knowledge of and involvement in detainee abuse. On 16 June 2004, GEN Paul J. Kern, Commander, US Army Material Command (AMC), was appointed as the new Procedure 15 appointing authority. On 25 June 2004, GEN Kern appointed LTG Jones, Deputy Commanding General, TRADOC, as an additional Procedure 15 investigating officer. MG Fay was retained as an investigating officer.

(2) (U) This investigation identified forty-four (44) alleged instances or events of detainee abuse committed by MP and MI Soldiers, as well as civilian contractors. On sixteen (16) of these occasions, abuse by the MP Soldiers was, or was alleged to have been, requested, encouraged, condoned, or solicited by MI personnel. The abuse, however, was directed on an individual basis and never officially sanctioned or approved. MI solicitation of MP abuse included the use of isolation with sensory deprivation, removal of clothing and humiliation, the use of dogs as an interrogation tool to induce fear, and physical abuse. In eleven (11) instances, MI personnel were found to be directly involved in the abuse. MI personnel were also found not to have fully comported with established interrogation procedures and applicable laws and regulations. Theater Interrogation and Counter-Resistance Policies (ICRP) were found to be poorly defined, and changed several times. As a result, interrogation activities sometimes crossed into abusive activity.

(3) (U) This investigation found that certain individuals committed offenses in violation of international and US law to include the Geneva Conventions and the UCMJ and violated Army Values. Leaders in key positions failed properly to supervise the interrogation operations at Abu Ghraib and failed to understand the dynamics created at Abu Ghraib. Leaders also failed to react appropriately to those instances where detainee abuse was reported, either by other service members, contractors, or by the International Committee of the Red Cross (ICRC). Fifty-four (54) MI, MP, and Medical Soldiers, and civilian contractors were found to have some degree of responsibility or complicity in the abuses that occurred at Abu Ghraib. Twenty-seven (27) were cited

in this report for some degree of culpability and seventeen (17) were cited for misunderstanding of policy, regulation or law. Three (3) MI Soldiers, who had previously
received punishment under UCMJ, were recommended for additional investigation.
Seven (7) MP Soldier identified in the MG Taguba Report and currently under criminal investigation and/or charges are also central figures in this investigation and are
included in the above numbers. One (1) person cited in the MG Taguba Report was
exonerated.

(4) (U) Looking beyond personal responsibility, leader responsibility and command
responsibility, systemic problems and issues also contributed to the volatile environment in which the abuse occurred. These systemic problems included: inadequate
interrogation doctrine and training, an acute shortage of MP and MI Soldiers, the
lack of clear lines of responsibility between the MP and MI chains of command, the
lack of a clear interrogation policy for the Iraq Campaign, and intense pressure felt
by the personnel on the ground to produce actionable intelligence from detainees.
Twenty-four (24) additional findings and two (2) observations regarding systemic failures are included in the final investigative report. These findings ranged from doctrine
and policy concerns, to leadership and command and control issues, to resource and
training issues.

b. (U) Problems: Doctrine, Policy, Training, Organization, and Other Government
Agencies.

(1) (U) Inadequacy of doctrine for detention operations and interrogation operations
was a contributing factor to the situations that occurred at Abu Ghraib. The Army's
capstone doctrine for the conduct of interrogation operations is Field Manual (FM)
34-52, Intelligence Interrogation, dated September 1992. Non-doctrinal approaches,
techniques, and practices were developed and approved for use in Afghanistan and
GTMO as part of the Global War on Terrorism (GWOT). These techniques, approaches,
and practices became confused at Abu Ghraib and were implemented without proper
authorities or safeguards. Soldiers were not trained on non-doctrinal interrogation
techniques such as sleep adjustment, isolation, and the use of dogs. Many interrogators and personnel overseeing interrogation operations at Abu Ghraib had prior exposure to or experience in GTMO or Afghanistan. Concepts for the non-doctrinal,
non field-manual approaches and practices came from documents and personnel in
GTMO and Afghanistan. By October 2003, interrogation policy in Iraq had changed
three times in less than 30 days and it became very confusing as to what techniques could be employed and at what level non-doctrinal approaches had to be
approved.

(2) (U) MP personnel and MI personnel operated under different and often incompatible rules for treatment of detainees. The military police referenced DoD-wide
regulatory and procedural guidance that clashed with the theater interrogation and
counter-resistance policies that the military intelligence interrogators followed. Further, it appeared that neither group knew or understood the limits imposed by the
other's regulatory or procedural guidance concerning the treatment of detainees, resulting in predictable tension and confusion. This confusion contributed to abusive
interrogation practices at Abu Ghraib. Safeguards to ensure compliance and to protect

against abuse also failed due to confusion about the policies and the leadership's failure to monitor operations adequately.

(3) (U) By December 2003, the JIDC at Abu Ghraib had a total of approximately 160 personnel with 45 interrogators and 18 linguists/translators assigned to conduct interrogation operations. These personnel were from six different MI battalions and groups – the 519 MI BN, 323 MI BN, 325 MI BN, 470 MI GP, the 66th MI GP, the 500 MI GP. To complicate matters, interrogators from a US Army Intelligence Center and School, Mobile Training Team (MTT) consisting of analysts and interrogators, and three interrogation teams consisting of six personnel from GTMO, came to Abu Ghraib to assist in improving interrogation operations. Additionally, contract interrogators from CACI and contract linguists from Titan were hired in an attempt to address shortfalls. The JIDC was created in a very short time period with parts and pieces of various units. It lacked unit integrity, and this lack was a fatal flaw.

(4) (U) The term Other Government Agencies (OGA) most commonly referred to the Central Intelligence Agency (CIA). The CIA conducted unilateral and joint interrogation operations at Abu Ghraib. The CIA's detention and interrogation practices contributed to a loss of accountability and abuse at Abu Ghraib. No memorandum of understanding existed on the subject of interrogation operations between the CIA and CJTF-7, and local CIA officers convinced military leaders that they should be allowed to operate outside the established local rules and procedures. CIA detainees in Abu Ghraib, known locally as "Ghost Detainees," were not accounted for in the detention system. With these detainees unidentified or unaccounted for, detention operations at large were impacted because personnel at the operations level were uncertain how to report or classify detainees.

c. (U) Detainee Abuse at Abu Ghraib.

(1) (U) Physical and sexual abuses of detainees at Abu Ghraib were by far the most serious. The abuses spanned from direct physical assault, such as delivering head blows rendering detainees unconscious, to sexual posing and forced participation in group masturbation. At the extremes were the death of a detainee in OGA custody, an alleged rape committed by a US translator and observed by a female Soldier, and the alleged sexual assault of a female detainee. These abuses are, without question, criminal. They were perpetrated or witnessed by individuals or small groups. Such abuse can not be directly tied to a systemic US approach to torture or approved treatment of detainees. The MPs being prosecuted claim their actions came at the direction of MI. Although self-serving, these claims do have some basis in fact. The environment created at Abu Ghraib contributed to the occurrence of such abuse and the fact that it remained undiscovered by higher authority for a long period of time. What started as nakedness and humiliation, stress and physical training (exercise), carried over into sexual and physical assaults by a small group of morally corrupt and unsupervised Soldiers and civilians.

(2) (U) Abusing detainees with dogs started almost immediately after the dogs arrived at Abu Ghraib on 20 November 2003. By that date, abuses of detainees was already occurring and the addition of dogs was just one more device. Dog Teams were brought

to Abu Ghraib as a result of recommendations from MG G. Miller's assessment team from GTMO. MG G. Miller recommended dogs as beneficial for detainee custody and control issues. Interrogations at Abu Ghraib, however, were influenced by several documents that spoke of exploiting the Arab fear of dogs. The use of dogs in interrogations to "fear up" detainees was utilized without proper authorization.

(3) (U) The use of nudity as an interrogation technique or incentive to maintain the cooperation of detainees was not a technique developed at Abu Ghraib, but rather a technique which was imported and can be traced through Afghanistan and GTMO. As interrogation operations in Iraq began to take form, it was often the same personnel who had operated and deployed in other theaters and in support of GWOT, who were called upon to establish and conduct interrogation operations in Abu Ghraib. The lines of authority and the prior legal opinions blurred. They simply carried forward the use of nudity into the Iraqi theater of operations. The use of clothing as an incentive (nudity) is significant in that it likely contributed to an escalating "de-humanization" of the detainees and set the stage for additional and more severe abuses to occur.

(4) (U) There was significant confusion by both MI and MPs between the definitions of "isolation" and "segregation." LTG Sanchez approved the extended use of isolation on several occasions, intending for the detainee to be kept apart, without communication with their fellow detainees. His intent appeared to be the segregation of specific detainees. The technique employed in several instances was not, however, segregation but rather isolation – the complete removal from outside contact other than required care and feeding by MP guards and interrogation by MI. Use of isolation rooms in the Abu Ghraib Hard Site was not closely controlled or monitored. Lacking proper training, clear guidance, or experience in this technique, both MP and MI stretched the bounds into further abuse; sensory deprivation and unsafe or unhealthy living conditions. Detainees were sometimes placed in excessively cold or hot cells with limited or poor ventilation and no light.

3. (U) BACKGROUND AND ENVIRONMENT

a. (U) Operational Environment

(1) (U) The Global War on Terrorism began in earnest on 11 September 2001 (9/11). Soon after 9/11 attacks, American forces entered Afghanistan to destroy the primary operating and training base of al Qaeda. Prisoners collected in these and other global counter-terrorist operations were transferred to Guantanamo Naval Base, Cuba. Two Task Forces were formed at JTF-GTMO to manage intelligence collection operations with the newly captured prisoners. Military and civilian interrogators, counterintelligence agents, analysts, and other intelligence personnel from a variety of services and agencies manned the task forces and exploited the captured personnel for information.

(2) (U) US and coalition partners attacked Iraq on 20 March 2003, and soon after toppled Saddam Hussein's regime. The Iraq conflict transitioned quickly and unexpectedly to an insurgency environment. Coalition forces began capturing and interrogating alleged insurgents. Abu Ghraib prison, opened after the fall of Saddam to house criminals, was soon used for collecting and interrogating insurgents and other persons

of intelligence interest. The unit responsible for managing Abu Ghraib interrogations was the 205 MI BDE.

b. (U) Law, Policy, Doctrine and Training

(1) (U) Applicable Law

(a) (U) Military Order of November 13 2001 – Detention, Treatment and Trial of Certain Non-Citizens in the War Against Terrorism (Reference Annex J, Appendix 1).

(b) (U) Geneva Convention (IV) Relative to the Protection of Civilian Persons in Time of War, 12 August 1949 (Reference Annex J, Appendix 5).

(c) (U) AR 190-8 / OPNAVINST 3461.6 / AFJI 31-302/MCO 3461.1, Enemy Prisoners of War, Retained Personnel, Civilian Internees and other Detainees, 1 October 1997 (Reference Annex M, Appendix 2).

(d) (U) FM 34-52, Intelligence Interrogation, 28 September 1992 (Reference Annex M, Appendix 3).

(e) (U) Classification of Detainees. The overwhelming evidence in this investigation shows that most "detainees" at Abu Ghraib were "civilian internees." Therefore, this discussion will focus on "civilian internees."

[1] (U) Detainee. AR 190-8 defines a detainee as any person captured or otherwise detained by an armed force. By this definition, a detainee could be an Enemy Prisoner of War (EPW), a Retained Person, such as a doctor or chaplain, or a Civilian Internee. The term "detainee" is a generic one with no specific implied rights or protections being afforded to the individual; however, it is almost exclusively used by the Soldiers and other individuals interviewed in this investigation to refer to the individuals interned at Abu Ghraib. In order to understand the rights and protections that need to be provided to a "detainee," further classification is necessary.

[2] (U) Civilian Internee. Using Geneva Convention IV (GC IV), Article 78, as further defined by AR 190-8, a "Civilian Internee" is someone who is interned during armed conflict or occupation for security reasons or for protection or because he has committed an offense against the detaining power. (Reference Annex H, Appendix 1, FRAGO 749 to CJTF-7 OPORD 03-036). The overwhelming evidence in this investigation shows that all "detainees" at Abu Ghraib were civilian internees. Within the confinement facility, however, there were further sub-classifications that were used, to include criminal detainee, security internee, and MI Hold.

[a] (U) Criminal Detainee. A person detained because he/she is reasonably suspected of having committed a crime against Iraqi Nationals or Iraqi property or a crime not related to the coalition force mission (Reference Annex H, Appendix 1, FRAGO 749 to CJTF-7 OPORD 03-036).

[b] (U) Security Internee. Civilians interned during conflict or occupation for their own protection or because they pose a threat to the security of coalition forces, or its mission, or are of intelligence value. This includes persons detained for committing

offenses (including attempts) against coalition forces (or previous coalition forces), members of the Provisional Government, Non-Government Organizations, state infrastructure, or any person accused of committing war crimes or crimes against humanity. Security internees are a subset of civilian internees (Reference Annex H, Appendix 1, FRAGO 749 to CJTF-7 OPORD 03-036).

[c] (U) MI Hold. A directive to hold and not release a detainee/internee in the custody of the Coalition Forces, issued by a member or agent of a US Military Intelligence Organization (Reference Annex H, Appendix 1, FRAGO 749 to CJTF-7 OPORD 03-036).

[d] (U) Most detainees located within Abu Ghraib, to include those in Tier 1A and 1B (Reference Annex F, Appendix 1, Abu Ghraib Overhead with Organizational Layout), were Civilian Internees and therefore, entitled to protections under GC IV. In addition to applicable international laws, ARs, and the FMs on Intelligence Interrogations further clarify US Policy regarding the protections afforded to Civilian Internees.

(f) (U) Geneva Convention Relative to the Protection of Civilians in Time of War. GC IV provides protections for civilians in time of war. The US is bound by the Geneva Conventions; therefore, any individual acting on behalf of the US during an armed conflict is also bound by Geneva Conventions. This includes not only members of the armed forces, but also civilians who accompany or work with the US Armed Forces. The following are some relevant articles to the discussion on detainee abuse:

[1] (U) Article 5. Where in the territory of a Party to the conflict, the latter is satisfied that an individual protected person is definitely suspected of or engaged in activities hostile to the security of the State, such individual person shall not be entitled to claim such rights and privileges under the present Conventions as would, if exercised in the favor of such individual person, be prejudicial to the security of such State. Where in occupied territory an individual protected person is detained as a spy or saboteur, or as a person under definite suspicion of activity hostile to the security of the Occupying Power, such person shall, in those cases where absolute military security so requires, be regarded as having forfeited rights of communication under the present Conventions. In each case, such persons shall nevertheless be treated with humanity and, in case of trial, shall not be deprived of the rights of fair and regular trial prescribed by the present [convention].

[2] (U) Article 27. Protected persons are entitled, in all circumstances, to respect for their persons, their honor, their family rights, their religious convictions and practices, and their manner and customs. They shall at all times be humanely treated, and shall be protected against all acts of violence or threats thereof and against insults and public curiosity.

[3] (U) Article 31. No physical or moral coercion shall be exercised against protected persons, in particular to obtain information from them or from third parties.

[4] (U) Article 32. The [Parties to the Convention] agree that each of them is prohibited from taking any measure of such a character as to cause the physical suffering or extermination of protected persons in their hands. This prohibition applies not

only to murder, torture, corporal punishments, mutilation and medical and scientific experiments not necessitated by the medical treatment of a protected person, but also to any other measures of brutality whether applied by civilian or military agents.

[5] (U) Article 37. Protected persons who are confined pending proceedings or serving a sentence involving loss of liberty, shall during their confinement be humanely treated.

[6] (U) Article 100. The disciplinary regime in places of internment shall be consistent with humanitarian principles, and shall in no circumstances include regulation imposing on internees any physical exertion dangerous to their health or involving physical or moral victimization. Identification by tattooing or imprinting signs on the body is prohibited. In particular, prolonged standing and roll-calls, punishment drills, military drill and maneuver, or the reduction of food rations, are prohibited.

[7] (U) Article 143. Representatives or delegates of the Protecting Powers shall have permission to go to all places where protected persons are, particularly to places of internment, detention and work. They shall have access to all premises occupied by protected persons and shall be able to interview the latter without witnesses, personally or through an interpreter. Such visits may not be prohibited except for reasons of military imperative, and then only as an exceptional and temporary measure. Their duration and frequency shall not be restricted. Such representatives and delegates shall have full liberty to select the places they wish to visit. The Detaining or Occupying Power, the Protecting Power, and when occasion arises the Power of origin of the persons to be visited, may agree that compatriots of the internees shall be permitted to participate in the visits. The delegates of the International Committee of the Red Cross shall also enjoy the above prerogatives. The appointment of such delegates shall be submitted for the approval of the Power governing the territories where they will carry out their duties.

(2) (U) AR 190-8, Enemy Prisoners of War, Retained Personnel, Civilian Internees and other Detainees is a joint publication between all services of the Armed Forces (Reference Annex M, Appendix 2).

(a) (U) US Policy Overview. The regulation (Reference Annex M, Appendix 2, AR 190-8, Paragraph 1-5) sets out US Policy stating that "US policy, relative to the treatment of EPW, Civilian Internees and RP in the custody of the US Armed Forces, is as follows: All persons captured, detained, interned, or otherwise held in US Armed Forces custody during the course of conflict will be given humanitarian care and treatment from the moment they fall into the hands of the US forces until final release and repatriation." The regulation further defines this policy.

(b) (U) Inhumane Treatment. Specifically, inhumane treatment of detainees is prohibited and is considered a serious and punishable offense under international law and the UCMJ. The following acts are prohibited: murder, torture, corporal punishment, mutilation, the taking of hostages, sensory deprivation, collective punishment, execution without trial, and all cruel and degrading treatment. (Reference Annex M, Appendix 2, AR 190-8, Paragraph 1-5(b)).

(c) (U) Protection from Certain Acts. All detainees will be protected against all acts of violence to include rape, forced prostitution, assault and theft, insults, public curiosity, bodily injury, and reprisals of any kind. (Reference Annex M, Appendix 2, AR 190-8, Paragraph 1-5(c)). This is further reinforced in FM 34-52 (Reference Annex M, Appendix 3), which states that the Geneva Conventions and US policy expressly prohibit acts of violence or intimidation, including physical or mental torture, threats, insults, or exposure to inhumane treatment as a means of or aid to interrogation.

(d) (U) Photographs. Photographs of detainees are strictly prohibited except for internal administrative purposes of the confinement facility. (Reference Annex M, Appendix 2, AR 190-8, Paragraph 1-5(d)).

(e) (U) Physical torture or moral coercion. No form of physical or moral coercion will be exercised against the Civilian Internee. (Reference Annex M, Appendix 2, AR 190-8, Paragraph 1-5(a)(1)).

(f) (U) At all times, the Civilian Internee will be humanely treated and protected against all acts of violence or threats and insults and public curiosity. The Civilian Internee will be especially protected against all acts of violence, insults, public curiosity, bodily injury, reprisals of any kind, sexual attacks such as rape, forced prostitution, or any form of indecent assault. (Reference Annex M, Appendix 2, AR 190-8, Paragraph 1-5(a)(2) & (3)).

(3) (U) Military Intelligence Doctrine and Training

(a) (U) Doctrine.

[1] (U) The Army's capstone doctrine for the conduct of interrogation operations is FM 34-52, Intelligence Interrogation, dated September, 1992. This doctrine provides an adequate basis for the training of interrogators at the Soldier level (e.g., in the art of tactical interrogation and the Geneva Conventions); however, it is out of date with respect to the management and conduct of detainee operations. Joint Doctrine on the conduct of detainee operations is sparse even though the Army has operated JIDCs since 1989 in Operation Just Cause, and because the Army is normally tasked by the Joint Force Commander to establish and manage EPW/Detainee operations for the deployed force (Reference Annex M, Appendix 1, APPENDIX G-3, Joint Publication 2-01, Joint Intelligence Support to Military Operations). National level doctrine, in the form of a Defense Intelligence Agency Manual (DIAM), also contains very little doctrinal basis for the conduct and management of joint interrogation operations. A critical doctrinal gap at the joint and service level is the role of national level agencies (e.g., other governmental agencies [OGA]) in detainee operations to include appropriate protocols for sharing valuable intelligence assets. The Center for Army Lessons Learned (CALL) reported the following in a recent assessment of Operation Iraqi Freedom detainee and interrogation operations (Reference Annex C, Appendix 5):

> MP and MI doctrine at division and below must be modified for stability operations and support operations to reflect the need for long-term detention facilities and interrogation of captives at the tactical level.

[2] (U) It is possible that some of the unauthorized interrogation techniques employed in Iraq may have been introduced through the use of an outdated training manual (FM 34-52 dated 1987 vice FM 34-52 dated 1992). The superseded version (FM 34-52, dated 1987) has been used at various locations in OIF. In a prior AR 15-6 investigation of Camp Cropper (Reference Annex C, Appendix 2), the 1987 version was again used as the reference (Reference Annex M, Appendix 3). On 9 June 2004, CJTF-7 published an email (Reference Annex L, Appendix 4, email) that indicated the May 1987 version was used as CJTF-7's primary reference. The section encapsulated below from the 1987 version has been removed from the 1992 version of FM 34-52. To the untrained, the reference in the outdated version could appear as a license for the interrogator to go beyond the current doctrine as established in the current FM 34-52. The 1987 version suggests the interrogator controls lighting, heating, and configuration of the interrogation room, as well as the food, shelter, and clothing given to the source. The section from the 1987 version that could be misunderstood is from Chapter 3 and reads as follows:

> FM 34-52 (1987) Chapter 3, Establish and Maintain Control. The interrogator should appear to be the one who controls all aspects of the interrogation to include the lighting, heating, and configuration of the interrogation room, as well as the food, shelter, and clothing given to the source. The interrogator must always be in control, he must act quickly and firmly. However, everything that he says and does must be within the limits of the Geneva and Hague Conventions, as well as the standards of conduct outlined in the UCMJ.

[3] (U) Doctrine provides the foundation for Army operations. A lack of doctrine in the conduct of non-conventional interrogation and detainee operations was a contributing factor to the abuses at Abu Ghraib.

(b) (U) Training

[1] (U) Formal US Army interrogation training is conducted at the Soldier level, primarily as part of a Soldier's Initial Entry Training (IET). There is no formal advanced interrogation training in the US Army. Little, if any, formal training is provided to MI leaders and supervisors (Commissioned Officers, Warrant Officers, and Non-Commissioned Officers) in the management through assignments to an interrogation unit, involvement in interrogation training exercises, or on deployments. Unfortunately, unit training and exercises have become increasingly difficult to conduct due to the high pace of deployments of interrogation personnel and units. With very few exceptions, combined MI and MP training on the conduct of detainee operations is non-existent.

[2] (U) The IET course at the USAIC, Fort Huachuca, AZ, provides a 16.5 week course of instruction. The course consists of 758.2 hours of academic training time that includes collection prioritization, screening, planning and preparation, approaches, questioning, termination of interrogations, and report writing in the classroom and practical exercise environments. The course focuses on the conduct of tactical interrogations in conventional war. Each student receives eight hours of classroom training on AR 381-10, Army Intelligence Activities (Reference Annex M, Appendix 2) and FM 27-10, Law of Land Warfare (Reference Annex M, Appendix 3) and 184 hours of practical

exercise. The student's understanding of the Geneva Conventions and Law of Land Warfare is continually evaluated as a critical component. If at any time during an exercise, the student violates the Geneva Conventions, they will fail the exercise. A failure does not eliminate the student from the course. Students are generally given the chance to recycle to the next class; however, egregious violations could result in dismissal from the course.

[3] (U) The reserve components use the same interrogator program of instruction as does the active component. They are exposed to the same classes and levels of instruction. Like the active component, the reserve components' training opportunities prior to deployment in recent years have been minimal, if any. Those slated for deployment to the JTF-GTMO attend the Intelligence Support to Counter Terrorism (ISCT) Course.

[4] (U) Army Regulations require interrogators to undergo refresher training on the Geneva Conventions annually. Units are also expected to conduct follow-up training for Soldiers to maintain and improve their interogation skills. This becomes difficult given that Soldiers fresh from the basic interrogation course are deployed almost as soon as they arrive to their unit of assignment. This leaves little, if any, time to conduct that follow-on training with their unit to hone the skills they have learned in school. In addition to the unit deployments, the individual interrogators find themselves deployed to a wide variety of global engagements in a temporary duty status – not with their units of assignments. It is not uncommon for an individual to be deployed two or three times in the course of a year (e.g., the Balkans, Cuba [JTF-GTMO], Afghanistan, Iraq, or in support of Special Operations Forces [SOF]).

[5] (U) There is no formal advanced interrogation training in the US Army. The DoD manages a Strategic Debriefing Course for all services. While some of the skills are similar, the Strategic Debriefing Course is not an advanced interrogation course. Further, only interrogators being assigned to strategic debriefing assignments are authorized to attend this course. This prevents the tactical interrogator, the operator at Abu Ghraib, from further developing skills. Junior NCOs receive only limited interrogation-related training during his or her advanced NCO courses – the Basic Non-Commissioned Officers Course (BNCOC) and the Advanced Non-Commissioned Officer's Course (ANCOC). This limited training is restricted to the management of interrogation operations. The amount of time spent on the Geneva Conventions training during either of these courses is minimal. Officers receive limited training in interrogation or interrogation management in their entry level and advanced level courses. Like BNCOC and ANCOC, this training is focused on management and not the intricacies of interrogation operations or the legal restrictions applicable to interrogation operations.

[6] (U) Very little training is available or conducted to train command and staff elements on the conduct, direction, and oversight of interrogation operations. To address a portion of this shortfall, USAIC is standing up a course to teach the management of Human Intelligence to MI officers. A pilot course is scheduled and is designed to prepare the intelligence staffs (G2, S2) of a deploying Army Division with the capability to synchronize, coordinate, manage and de-conflict Counterintelligence and Human Intelligence (HUMINT) operations within the division's area of responsibility.

[7] (U) Most interrogator training that occurred at Abu Ghraib was on-the-job-training. The JIDC at Abu Ghraib conducted Interrogation Rules of Engagement (IROE) and interrogation operations training. The fast paced and austere environment limited the effectiveness of any training. After mid-September 2003, all Soldiers assigned to Abu Ghraib had to read a memorandum titled IROE, acknowledging they understood the ICRP, and sign a confirmation sheet indicating they had read and understood the ICRP. Most Soldiers have confirmed they received training on the IROE. See attached CJTF-7 IROE standard signature sheet (Reference Annex J, Appendix 4) to view an example.

[8] (U) MG G. Miller led an assessment team to Abu Ghraib in early September 2003. This was followed by a training team from 2 October – 2 December 2003. There is no indication that the training provided by the JTF-GTMO Team led to any new violations of the Geneva Conventions and the law of land warfare. Training focused on screening, the use of pocket litter during interrogations, prioritization of detainees, planning and preparation, approaches, questioning, interpreter control, deception detection, reporting, automation, and interrogation booths. The training provided at Abu Ghraib did not identify the abuses that were ongoing as violations of regulations or law, nor did it clarify issues involving detainee abuse reporting.

[9] (U) Interrogators learn as part of their training that the MPs provide the security for and run detention operations at the Collection Points (CPs), Corps Holding Areas (CHAs), and Internment/Resettlement (IR) facilities. The interrogator's mission is only to collect intelligence from prisoners or detainees. Interaction with the MPs is encouraged to take advantage of any observations the MPs/guards might have concerning a particular prisoner or detainee. While the USAIC includes this in the interrogator's training, very little time is spent training MI/MP detention operations. In the past, the Army conducted large EPW/Detainee exercises (the Gold Sword and Silver Sword series) that provided much of the training critical to MPs' and Interrogators' understanding of their respective roles and responsibilities. These exercises were discontinued in the mid-1990s due to frequent deployments and force structure reductions, eliminating an excellent source of interoperability training. The increase in op-tempo since 9/11 has further exacerbated the unit training and exercise problem.

[10] (U) Contract Training.

[a] (U) The US Army employs contract linguists/translators and contract interrogators in military operations. Some IET is provided to familiarize military interrogators in the conduct of interrogations using translators. No training is conducted at any level (enlisted, NCO, Warrant Officer, or Officer) on the employment of contract interrogators in military operations. The use of contract interrogators and linguists at Abu Ghraib was problematic (See paragraph 4.g.) from a variety of perspectives. JIDC interrogators, analysts, and leaders were unprepared for the arrival of contract interrogators and had no training to fall back on in the management, control, and discipline of these personnel.

[b] (U) No doctrine exists to guide interrogators and their intelligence leaders (NCO, Warrant Officer, and Officer) in the contract management or command

and control of contractors in a wartime environment. These interrogators and leaders faced numerous issues involving contract management: roles and responsibilities of JIDC personnel with respect to contractors; roles, relationships, and responsibilities of contract linguists and contract interrogators with military personnel; and the methods of disciplining contractor personnel. All of these need to be addressed in future interrogation and interrogation management training.

[11] (U) Soldier interrogator training is adequate with respect to interrogation techniques and procedures for conventional warfare. It is far less suited to the realities of the GWOT and Stability and Support Operations (SASO) and contract management. Despite the emphasis on the Geneva Conventions, it is clear from the results at Abu Ghraib (and elsewhere in operations in support of the GWOT) that Soldiers on the ground are confused about how they apply the Geneva Conventions and whether they have a duty to report violations of the conventions. Most Abu Ghraib interrogators performed their duties in a satisfactory manner without incident or violation of training standards. Some interrogators (See paragraph 5.e.-5.h., below), however, violated training standards in the performance of selected interrogations. Army training at USAIC never included training on interrogation techniques using sleep adjustment, isolation, segregation, environmental adjustment, dietary manipulation, the use of military working dogs, or the removal of clothing. These techniques were introduced to selected interrogators who worked at Abu Ghraib from sources other than official Army training.

(4) (U) Military Police Doctrine and Training

(a) (U) DoD Directives 2310.1, DoD Program for Enemy Prisoners of War and Other Detainees, and 5100.77, DoD Law of War Program, require that the US military services comply with the principles, spirit, and intent of international laws of war, that the DoD observes and enforces the US obligations under the laws of war, that personnel know the laws of war obligations, and that personnel promptly report incidents violating the laws of war and that the incidents be throughly investigated.

(b) (U) AR 190-8, "Enemy Prisoner of War, Retained Personnel Civilian Internees and other Detainees," is a multi-service policy that incorporates the directives from the DoD publications above. The regulation addresses the military police treatment of civilian internees, and directs that:

- No physical or moral coercion be used
- Internees be treated with respect for their person, honor, manner, and customs
- Internees be protected against violence, insults, public curiosity, bodily injury, or any form of indecent assault

It specifically prohibits:

- Measures causing physical suffering, to include corporal punishment, and other measures of brutality

It specifies that disciplinary measures NOT:

- Be inhumane, brutal, or dangerous to health
- Include imprisonment in a place without daylight

The authorized disciplinary punishments include:

- Discontinuance of privileges granted over and above the treatment provided for by regulation
- Confinement, not to exceed 30 consecutive days

(Reference Annex M, Appendix 2, AR 190-8)

(c) (U) AR 190-12, Military Working Dog Program, notes that military police may potentially use dogs for EPW control, but limits their use against people to instances when the responsible commander determines it absolutely necessary that there have been reasonable efforts to use all lesser means of force. (Reference Annex M, Appendix 2, AR 190-12)

(d) (U) Procedural guidance, found in FM 3-19.40 and the MP Standard Operating Procedure (SOP) for Abu Ghraib (400th MP BN SOP for Camp Vigilant Detention Center), consistently follow directly from the DoD directives and applicable ARs. The procedural guidance provides military police clear-cut guidance for permissible and impermissible practices during Internment Operations. (Reference Annex M, Appendix 3, FM 3-19.40; Annex J, Appendix 4, 400 MP BN SOP Camp Vigilant Detention Center)

(5) (U) Intelligence and Interrogation Policy Development.

(a) (U) National Policy.

(1) (U) US forces and intelligence officials deployed to Afghanistan and elsewhere to conduct military operations pursuant to GWOT. Specific regulatory or procedural guidance concerning either "humane" treatment or "abuse" was not available in the context of GWOT and the recently promulgated national policies. Military and civilian intelligence agencies, to include the 519th MI Battalion (519 MI BN) in late 2002, conducted interrogations in Afghanistan in support of GWOT. As a result, deployed military interrogation units and intelligence agencies in Afghanistan developed certain practices. Later, some of these same techniques surfaced as interrogation techniques in Iraq. Prior to these deployments, US Army interrogators used the doctrine found in FM 34-52. The 1992 FM was what military interrogators at Abu Ghraib were trained on, and it contained the techniques and the restrictions they had been taught. (Reference Annex M, Appendix 3; FM 34-52, Interrogation Operations, [1987 and 1992 versions])

(2) (S//NF)

(3) (S//NF)

(4) (S//NF)

(5) (U) On 16 April 2003, SECDEF approved approaches for use on the Guantanamo "unlawful" combatants, as defined by the President's Military Order of 13 November 2001, and reiterated in the 7 February 2002, memorandum to DoD. Once this document was signed, it became policy at JTF-GTMO, and later became the bedrock on which the CJTF-7 policies were based. The first 18 approaches listed in the 16 April 2003, memo from the SECDEF all appear in the current, 1992, FM 34-52, except the Mutt-and-Jeff approach, which was derived from the superseded 1987 FM 34-52. The remaining approaches, similar to the ones identified in the OGC working group's memorandum derived from the CJTF-180 memorandum and the JTF-GTMO request, included:

Change of Scenery Down
Dietary Manipulation
Environmental Manipulation
Sleep Adjustment
False Flag
Isolation

Although approving all approaches for use, the SECDEF required that he be notified prior to implementing the following approaches:

Incentive/Removal of Incentive	Mutt and Jeff
Pride and Ego Down	Isolation

(Reference Annex J, Appendix 2, Counter-Resistance Techniques)

(6) (U) No regulatory guidance exists for interrogators aside from DoD Directives 2310.1, DoD Program for Enemy Prisoners of War and Other Detainees and 5100.77, DoD Law of War Program. The most current interrogation procedural guidance is in the 1992 FM 34-52. (Reference Annex M, Appendix 1, DoD Directive 2310.1; Annex M, Appendix 1, DoD Directive 5100.77).

(b) (U) Development of Intelligence and Interrogation Policy in Iraq and Abu Ghraib.

(1) (U) In July 2003, the 519 MI BN, veterans of Afghanistan already at the BIAP facility, simultaneously conducted interrogations of the detainees with possible information of intelligence value and began to develop IROE for interrogators to meet the newly-focused mission. No known documentation exists concerning specific approaches and techniques used before September 2003.

(2) (S//NF)

(3) (U) Meanwhile, at Headquarters, CJTF-7, as the need for actionable intelligence rose, the realization dawned that pre-war planning had not included planning for detainee operations. Believing that FM 34-52 was not sufficiently or doctrinally clear for the situation in Iraq, CJTF-7 staff sought to synchronize detainee operations, which ultimately resulted in a methodology and structure derived from the JTF-GTMO system as presented by MG G. Miller. At the same time, LTG Sanchez directed that an interrogation policy be established that would address "permissible techniques and safeguards for interrogators" for use in Iraq. The CJTF-7 staff relied heavily on the series of SOPs which MG G. Miller provided to develop not only the structure, but also

the interrogation policies for detainee operations (Reference Annex B, Appendix 1, SANCHEZ).

(4) (U) On 10 September 2003, CPT Fitch, assigned to the 205 MI BDE as the Command Judge Advocate, was tasked by COL Marc Warren, the Staff Judge Advocate (SJA) for CJTF-7, to work with MAJ Daniel Kazmier and MAJ Franklin D. Raab from the CJTF-7 Office of the Staff Judge Advocate (OSJA) to produce a set of interrogation rules. The OSJA identified interrogation policies from the SECDEF 16 April 2003, memo for JTF-GTMO operations. OSJA provided CPT Fitch the 16 April 2003, SECDEF memorandum, which he copied almost verbatim onto a document entitled CJTF-7 Interrogation and Counter-Resistance Policy (ICRP). This document was developed without reference to the 519 MI BN's July 2003 and August 2003 memos. CPT Fitch sent the policy memo to the 519 MI BN for coordination, and the 519 MI BN added the use of dogs, stress positions, sleep management, sensory deprivation, and yelling, loud music and light control from its 27 August 2003, memo. The use of all the techniques was to apply to interrogations of detainees, security internees, and EPWs. CPT Fitch finalized the combined memo and sent it back to the CJTF-7 SJA. It also went to the CJ-2, CJ-3, and the Commander, 205 MI BDE, who until that point had apparently not been involved in drafting or approving the policy. (Reference Annex B, Appendix 1, FITCH, KAZMIER; Annex J, Appendix 3, CJTF-7 Interrogation and Counter-Resistance Policy, [1st Draft], Annex J, Appendix 3, CJTF-7 Interrogation and Counter-Resistance Policy, [2nd Draft])

(5) (U) Between 10 and 14 September 2003, the OSJA at CJTF-7 changed the 10 September 2003, memo to reflect the addition of the techniques that were not included in the JTF-GTMO policy; i.e., the use of dogs, stress positions, and yelling, loud music, and light control. Upon the guidance and recommendation of the SJA staff, it was decided that LTG Sanchez would approve the use of those additional methods on a case-by-case basis.

(6) (S//NF)

(7) (S//NF)

(8) (S//NF)

(9) (S//NF)

(10) (U) The 12 October 2003, policy significantly changed the tone and substance of the previous policy. It removed any approach not listed in the 1987 FM 34-52. While acknowledging the applicability of the Geneva Conventions and the duty to treat all detainees humanely, it also cited Articles 5 and 78 noting specifically that those "detainees engaged in activities hostile to security of coalition forces had forfeited their Geneva Convention rights of communication." It also included provisions found in the superseded 1987 FM 34-52 that authorized interrogators to control all aspects of the interrogation, "to include lighting, and heating, as well as food, clothing and shelter given to detainees." This phrase was specifically left out of the 1992 version (See section 3a(2), above). The 12 October 2003, policy also deleted references to EPWs and specified the policy was for use on civilian security internees.

(11) (S//NF)

(12) (S//NF)

(13) (S//NF)

(14) (S//NF)

(15) (U) On 16 October 2003, the JIDC Interrogation Operations Officer, CPT Carolyn A. Wood, produced an "Interrogation Rules of Engagement" chart as an aid for interrogators, graphically portraying the 12 October 2003 policy. It listed the approved approaches, and identified the approaches which had been removed as authorized interrogation approaches, which nonetheless could be used with LTG Sanchez's approval. The chart was confusing, however. It was not completely accurate and could be subject to various interpretations. For example, the approved approaches list left off two techniques which previously had been included in the list (the Pride and Ego Down approach and the Mutt and Jeff approach). The right side of the chart listed approaches that required LTG Sanchez's prior approval. What was particularly confusing was that nowhere on the chart did it mention a number of techniques that were in use at the time: removal of clothing, forced grooming, hooding, and yelling, loud music and light control. Given the detail otherwise noted on the aid, the failure to list some techniques left a question of whether they were authorized for use without approval. (Reference Annex J, Appendix 4, CJTF-7 IROE training card)

(16) (U) By mid-October, interrogation policy in Iraq had changed three times in less than 30 days. Various versions of each draft and policy were circulated among Abu Ghraib, 205 MI BDE, CJTF-7 C2, and CJTF-7 SJA. Anecdotal evidence suggests that personnel were confused about the approved policy from as early as 14 September 2003. The SJA believed that the 14 September 2003 policy was not to be implemented until CENTCOM approved it. Meanwhile, interrogators in Abu Ghraib began operating under it immediately. It was not always clear to JIDC officers what approaches required LTG Sanchez's approval, nor was the level of approval consistent with requirements in other commands. The JIDC October 2003 SOP, likewise created by CPT Wood, was remarkably similar to the Bagram (Afghanistan) Collection Point SOP. Prior to deployment to Iraq, CPT Wood's unit (A/519 MI BN) allegedly conducted the abusive interrogation practices in Bagram resulting in a Criminal Investigation Command (CID) homicide investigation. The October 2003 JIDC SOP addressed requirements for monitoring interrogations, developing detailed interrogation plans, delegating interrogation plan approval authority to the Interrogation Officer in Charge (OIC), and report writing. It failed to mention details concerning ICRP, approval requirements or procedures. Interrogators, with their section leaders' knowledge, routinely utilized approaches/techniques without obtaining the required authority, indicating confusion at a minimum of two levels of supervision. (Reference Annex J, Appendix 4, JIDC Interrogation SOP; Annex J, Appendix 4, CJTF-180 Bagram Collection Point SOP)

(17) (U) Concepts for the non-doctrinal, non-field manual approaches and practices clearly came from documents and personnel in Afghanistan and Guantanamo. The techniques employed in JTF-GTMO included the use of stress positions, isolation for up to 30 days, removal of clothing, and the use of detainees' phobias (such as the

use of dogs) as the 2 December 2002 Counter-Resistance memo, and subsequent statements demonstrate. As the CID investigation mentioned above shows, from December 2002, interrogators in Afghanistan were removing clothing, isolating people for long periods of time, using stress positions, exploiting fear of dogs and implementing sleep and light deprivation. Interrogators in Iraq, already familiar with the practice of some of these new ideas, implemented them even prior to any policy guidance from CJTF-7. These practices were accepted as SOP by newly-arrived interrogators. Some of the CJTF-7 ICRPs neither effectively addressed these practices, nor curtailed their use. (Annex J, Appendix 2, Tab A, Counter-Resistance Techniques; Annex J, Appendix 2, Interrogation Techniques; Annex E, Appendix 4, CID Report)

(18) ~~(S//REL TO USA and MCFI)~~

(6) (U) Other Regulatory Procedural Guidance

(a) (U) On 13 November 2001, the President issued a military order entitled the Detention, Treatment and Trial of Certain Non-Citizens in the War Agains Terrorism. The order authorized US military forces to detain non-US citizens suspected of terrorism, and try them for violations of the law of war and other applicable laws. The order also authorized the SECDEF to detain individuals under such conditions he may prescribe and to issue related orders and regulations as necessary. (Reference Annex J, Appendix 1, Presidential Military Order)

(b) ~~(S//NF)~~

(c) (U) The MP personnel and the MI personnel operated under different and often incompatible rules for treatment of detainees. The MPs referenced DoD-wide regulatory and procedural guidance that clashed with the theater interrogation and counter-resistance policies that the MI interrogators followed. Further, it appears that neither group knew or understood the limits imposed by the other's regulatory or procedural guidance concerning the treatment of detainees, resulting in predictable tension and confusion.

(d) (U) For instance, a MI order to strip a detainee as an interrogation process conflicted with the AR 190-8 directive to treat detainees with respect for their person and honor (Reference Annex M, Appendix 2, AR 190-8, paragraph 5-1a(2)); or to protect detainees against violence, insults, public curiosity, or any form of indecent assault (Reference Annex M, Appendix 2, AR 190-8, paragraph 5-1a(3)); and FM 3-19.40 (Reference Annex M, Appendix 3) (which specifically directs that internees will retain their clothing). A MI order to place a detainee in isolation violated the AR 190-8 directive to not imprison a detainee in a place without daylight (Reference Annex M, Appendix 2, AR 190-8, paragraph 6-11a(5)); to not confine for more than 30 consecutive days, (Reference Annex M, Appendix 2, AR 190-8, paragraph 6-12d(1)); and FM 3-19.40 which specifically directs that the facility commander must authorize any form of punishment. Finally, when interrogators ordered the use of dogs as an interrogation technique, the order violated the policy and intent of AR 190-12. (Reference Annex M, Appendix 2)

4. (U) SUMMARY OF EVENTS AT ABU GHRAIB

a. (U) Military Intelligence Organization and Resources

(1) (U) Task Organization

(a) (U) The 205 MI BDE was organizationally, and geographically, the size of two MI Brigades. It was composed of four Active and three Reserve Battalions. The 205 MI BDE possessed no organic interrogation elements or personnel. All HUMINT assets (units and personnel) assigned to the 205 MI BDE were from other organizations. Major subordinate elements of the 205 MI BDE included three Tactical Exploitation Battalions (HUMINT and Counterintelligence), one Aerial Exploitation Battalion (Signal Intelligence [SIGINT]) and Imagery Intelligence (IMINT), an Operations Battalion (ANALYSIS), a Linguist Battalion (HUMINT Support) and a Corps Support Battalion (HUMINT). Elements of the Brigade were located throughout Iraq supporting a wide variety of combat operations. (Reference Annex H, Appendix 6, Tab C, 205 MI BDE Command Brief).

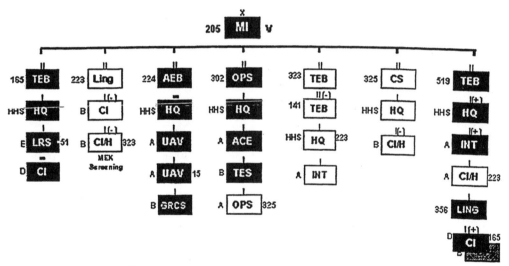

205th MI Brigade Task Organization (August 2003)

(b) (U) The 205 MI BDE Commander, COL Thomas Pappas, had a reputation for being an excellent MI officer with a great background and experience before being selected for command. He took command of the 205 MI BDE on 1 July 2003, while the unit was already deployed in Iraq. His performance as Brigade Commander prior to the Abu Ghraib incidents was "outstanding" according to his rater, MG Wojdakowski, DCG, V Corps/CJTF-7 (Reference Annex B, Appendix 1, WOJDAKOWSKI). LTG Sanchez also believed COL Pappas was an excellent and dedicated officer (Reference Annex B, Appendix 1, SANCHEZ). Other key members of COL Pappas' staff included MAJ Potter, Deputy Commander; MAJ M. Williams, Brigade Operations Officer (S-3); and CPT Fitch, Command Judge Advocate.

(2) (U) Resources

(a) (U) As hostilities began to shift from a tactical fight to an insurgency, so did intelligence priorities. Iraq quickly became a HUMINT-focused environment in support of SASO with interrogation operations representing the intelligence 'Center of Gravity' (Reference Annex B, Appendix 1, SANCHEZ). Beginning in July 2003, demands placed upon interrogation operations were growing rapidly from both the tactical commanders as well as from the CJTF-7. The 205 MI BDE had the missions of providing Tactical HUMINT Teams (THT – small elements consisting of an interrogator, a linguist, and several combat arms Soldiers attached to maneuver elements to conduct tactical interrogations at "the point of the spear") to forward-deployed combat forces as well as operating a Joint Interrogation and Debriefing Center (JIDC).

(b) (U) As previously mentioned, the 205 MI BDE had no organic interrogation capability. Those assets were eliminated from the active force structure during the downsizing of the Army in the 1990s. The interrogation assets available to COL Pappas when he first took Command were A/519 MI BN and interrogation sections from the 325th MI Battalion (325 MI BN), US Army Reserve (USAR), and 323rd MI Battalion (323 MI BN), USAR. Because both of the USAR units were significantly under strength before being deployed to Iraq, they received many Soldiers from other USAR units countrywide to fill up their ranks. This process is known as "cross-leveling." Although it has the benefit of filling the ranks, it has the disadvantage of inserting Soldiers into units shortly before deployment who had never trained with those units. The Soldiers did not know the unit. The unit and the unit leadership did not know the Soldiers. The Army has always stressed "you train as you fight." As COL Pappas began to focus his efforts on interrogation operations, all he had were disparate elements of units and individuals, including civilians, that had never trained together, but now were going to have to fight together.

(c) (U) Interestingly, and as a matter of comparison, Iraqi Survey Group (ISG) interrogation operations of high-level detainees at BIAP suffered no such shortages of interrogators. Roughly the same level of personnel supported the ISG interrogation operations at BIAP, even though the ISG facility had an order of magnitude less of detainees of intelligence interest to exploit than did the 205 MI BDE (100 at BIAP vs. over a 1,000 at Abu Ghraib). Unfortunately, these much needed resources were unavailable for support to critical CJTF-7 mission needs (Reference Annex B, Appendix 1, SANCHEZ).

(d) (U) The number of interrogators initially assigned to the 205 MI BDE was sufficient for a small detainee population of only several hundred. In late July 2003, only 14 interrogation personnel were present in the 205 MI BDE to support interrogation operations at Abu Ghraib. All of these personnel were from one unit – A/519 MI BN. By December 2003, Abu Ghraib (the JIDC) had approximately 160 205 MI BDE personnel with 45 interrogators and 18 linguists/translators assigned to conduct interrogation operations. These personnel were from six different MI battalions and groups – the 519 MI BN, the 323 MI BN (USAR), the 325 MI BN (USAR), the 470th MI Group (470 MI GP), the 66th MI Group (66 MI GP), the 500th MI Group (500 MI GP).

Additional resources in the form of interrogators from one MTT consisting of analysts and interrogators, and at just about the same time, three "Tiger Teams" consisting of six personnel from JTF-GTMO, came to Abu Ghraib to assist in improving interrogation operations (See paragraph 4.j.(2)). Still short of resources, the Army hired contract interrogators from CACI International, and contract linguists from Titan Corporation in an attempt to address shortfalls (See paragraph 4.g.). Some units, such as the A/519 MI BN, had personnel who had been deployed to combat operations in theater in excess of 400 days so they also faced a rotation of selected personnel home with the resulting personnel turmoil.

b. (U) Establishment of the Prison at Abu Ghraib

(1) (U) The Coalition Provisional Authority (CPA) made the initial decision to use Abu Ghraib Prison as a criminal detention facility in May 2003 (Reference Annex B, Appendix 1, SANCHEZ). Abu Ghraib began receiving criminal prisoners in June 2003. There were no MI Holds or security detainees in the beginning. All such categories of detainees were sent to Camp Cropper (located at BIAP) or to the other existing facilities throughout the country such as Camp Bucca (Reference Annex F, Appendix 1, AG Overhead Photo).

(2) (S//NF)

(3) (U) The Hard Site permanent building facilities at Abu Ghraib were not open for occupancy until 25 August 2003. The opening of the Hard Site was important because it marked the beginning of the serious abuses that occurred. CPT Wood, A/519 MI BN, believed that, based on her experience, the availability of an isolation area to house detainees determined to be of MI value would enhance results. She initiated the request through the 205 MI BDE to CPA for use of part of the Hard Site building for that purpose. Her request received strong support from the 205 MI BDE, specifically from its Operations Officer, MAJ Williams. The 519 MI BN was then granted use of Tier 1A (Reference Annex F, Appendix 1, AG Overview Briefing for diagram) to house detainees.

c. (U) Detention Operations and Release Procedures

(1) (S//NF)

(2) (S//NF)

(3) (S//NF)

(4) (S//NF)

(5) (S//NF)

(6) (U) The problems cited above contributed significantly to the overcrowding at Abu Ghraib. Overcrowding was even further exacerbated with the transfer of detainees from Camp Bucca to Abu Ghraib. The physical plant was totally inadequate in size and the construction and renovations that were underway were incomplete. Scarcity

of resources – both personnel and equipment – to conduct effective confinement or interrogation operations made the situation worse.

(7) (U) There was general consensus (Reference Annex B, Appendix 1, FAST, CIVILIAN-12, LYONS, WOOD, SOLDIER 14, SANCHEZ) that as the pace of operations picked up in late November – early December 2003, it became a common practice for maneuver elements to round up large quantities of Iraqi personnel in the general vicinity of a specified target as a cordon and capture technique. Some operations were conducted at night resulting in some detainees being delivered to collection points only wearing night clothes or under clothes. SGT Jose Garcia, assigned to the Abu Ghraib Detainee Assessment Board, estimated that 85%–90% of the detainees were of no intelligence value based upon board interviews and debriefings of detainees. The Deputy C2X, CJTF-7, CIVILIAN-12, confirmed these numbers. (Reference Annex B, Appendix 1, GARCIA, CIVILIAN-12). Large quantities of detainees with little or no intelligence value swelled Abu Ghraib's population and led to a variety of overcrowding difficulties. Already scarce interrogator and analyst resources were pulled from interrogation operations to identify and screen increasing numbers of personnel whose capture documentation was incomplete or missing. Complicated and unresponsive release procedures ensured that these detainees stayed at Abu Ghraib – even though most had no value.

(8) (U) To make matters worse, Abu Ghraib increasingly became the target of mortar attacks (Reference Annex F, Appendix 3 shows an image of mortar round strikes at Abu Ghraib prior to February 2004 and the times of mortar strikes from January-April 2004) which placed detainees – innocent and guilty alike – in harms way. Force protection was a major issue at Abu Ghraib. The prison is located in a hostile portion of Iraq, adjacent to several roads and highways, and near population centers. BG Karpinski recognized Abu Ghraib's vulnerabilities and raised these concerns frequently to both MG Wojdakowski and LTG Sanchez (Reference Annex B, Appendix 1, KARPINSKI). LTG Sanchez was equally concerned with both the inherent vulnerability of Abu Ghraib and frustrated with the lack of progress in establishing even rudimentary force protection measures and plans (Reference Annex B, Appendix 1, SANCHEZ). LTG Sanchez directed that measures be taken to improve the force protection situation even to the point of having the 82nd Airborne Division Commander meet with Abu Ghraib officers concerning the issue. But, little progress was made and the mortar attacks continued. In an effort to improve force protection at Abu Ghraib, LTG Sanchez directed COL Pappas assume Tactical Control (TACON) of the Abu Ghraib Forward Operating Base (FOB) (Reference Annex H, Appendix 1, FRAGO 1108) on 19 November 2003. COL Pappas devoted considerable energy to improving security, even to the point of bringing a subordinate battalion commander to Abu Ghraib to coordinate force protection plans and operations. In spite of these efforts, the mortar attacks continued and culminated in an attack in April 2004 killing 22 detainees and wounding approximately 80 others, some seriously. This highlights the critical need for adequate force protection for a detainee center.

(9) (U) The Security Internee Review and Appeal Board was established on 15 August 2003. It served as the release authority for security internees and/or those on MI Hold

who were deemed to be of no security threat or (further) intelligence value. It consisted of three voting members – the C2, CJTF-7 (MG Fast), the Commander 800 MP BDE (BG Karpinski), and the CJTF-7 SJA (COL Warren), and two non-voting members (a SJA recorder and a MI assistant recorder). When first instituted, it was to meet on an "as required" basis; however, it appeared to be difficult to balance the schedules of three senior officers and the necessary support staff on a recurring, regular basis. Due to poor record keeping, accurate detainee release statistics are not available. We do know that by 2 October 2003, only 220 files had been reviewed by the board (Reference Annex H, Appendix 9, 031002 Oct CJTF7 JA Memo for CG). A preliminary screening board (Appellate Review Panel) at a level of authority below the General Officers on the Security Internee Review and Appeal Board was established to speed up the review of files by the General Officers. In the October – November 2003 timeframe, only approximately 100 detainee files a week were considered for release (Reference Annex B, Appendix 1, SUMMERS). As the detainee population increased, it became necessary to have the meetings on a much more frequent basis – initially twice a week. In the January 2004 timeframe, the board was meeting six times a week (Reference Annex B, Appendix 1, FAST). By February 2004, a standing board was established to deal with the ever increasing backlog. Even with more frequent meetings, the release of detainees from Abu Ghraib did not keep pace with the inflow. BG Karpinski believed that MG Fast was unreasonably denying detainees' release. By 11 January 2004, 57 review boards had been held and 1,152 detained personnel had been released out of a total of 2,113 considered. From February 2004 on, the release flow increased. (Reference Annex C, Appendix 1, Tab B, Annex 104)

(10) (U) As of late May 2004, over 8,500 detainees had been reviewed for release, with 5300 plus being released and 3,200 plus being recommended for continued internment. (Reference Annex H, Appendix 9, CJTF-7 C2X email). Even those that were initially deemed of no intelligence value and those that had been drained of intelligence information were not released on a timely basis – not as the result of any specific policy, but simply because the system that supported the release board (screening, interviews, availability of accurate records, and coordination) and the release board itself could not keep up with the flow of detainees into Abu Ghraib. Even with these long release delays (often six months and longer), there were concerns between the intelligence and tactical sides of the house. Combat Commanders desired that no security detainee be released for fear that any and all detainees could be threats to coalition forces. On occasion, Division Commanders overturned the recommendations of Division Staffs to release some detainees at the point of capture (Reference Annex B, Appendix 1, PHILLABAUM). The G2, 4 ID informed MG Fast that the Division Commander did not concur with the release of any detainees for fear that a bad one may be released along with the good ones. MG Fast described the 4ID's response to efforts to coordinate the release of selected detainees, "…we wouldn't have detained them if we wanted them released." (Reference Annex B, Appendix 1, FAST, CIVILIAN-12). MG Fast responded that the board would ultimately release detainees if there was no evidence provided by capturing units to justify keeping them in custody.

(11) (U) The chart below depicts the rise in detainee 'MI Hold' population (those identified by the "system" to be deemed of intelligence interest) (Reference Annex H,

Appendix 5). SOLDIER-14, the officer at Abu Ghraib primarily responsible for managing collection requirements and intelligence reporting, estimated that only 10-15% of the detainees on MI Hold were of actual intelligence interest. (Reference Annex B, Appendix 1, SOLDIER-14)

AG MI Hold Population

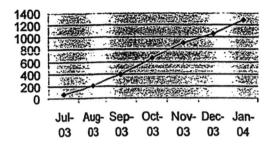

(12) (U) Interrogation operations in Abu Ghraib suffered from the effects of a broken detention operations system. In spite of clear guidance and directives, capturing units failed to perform the proper procedures at the point-of-capture and beyond with respect to handling captured enemy prisoners of war and detainees (screening, tactical interrogation, capture cards, sworn statements, transportation, etc.). Failure of capturing units to follow these procedures contributed to facility overcrowding, an increased drain on scarce interrogator and linguist resources to sort out the valuable detainees from innocents who should have been released soon after capture, and ultimately, to less actionable intelligence.

d. (U) Establishment of MP Presence at Abu Ghraib. The first Army unit to arrive was the 72nd MP Company (72 MP CO), Nevada Army National Guard. When first assigned to Abu Ghraib, the 72 MP CO was a subordinate unit of the 400th MP Battalion (400 MP BN) headquartered at BIAP. The 320th MP Battalion (320 MP BN) advance party was the next to arrive at Abu Ghraib on 24 July 2003. The rest of the 320 MP BN Headquarters, commanded by LTC Phillabaum arrived on 28 July 2003. With the 320 MP BN came one of its subordinate units, the 447th MP Company (447 MP CO). The 72 MP CO was then reassigned from the 400 MP BN to the 320 MP BN. The next unit to arrive was the 229th MP Company (229 MP CO) on or about 3 August 2003. On 1 October 2003, SSG Frederick, CPL Graner and other MPs who have allegedly abused detainees, arrived as part of the 372 MP CO. The rest of the 320 MP CO arrived in late October 2003, followed by the 870th MP Company (870 MP CO) and 670 MP Company (670 MP CO) on approximately 14 November 2003.

e. (U) Establishment of MI Presence at Abu Ghraib

(1) (U) The first MI unit to arrive at Abu Ghraib was a detachment from A/519 MI BN on 25 July 2003. The person in charge of that contingent was 1SGT McBride. Soldiers from the 519 MI BN had been sent there to prepare for OVB. CPT Wood arrived at Abu Ghraib on 4 August 2003, to assume the duties of Interrogation Operations OIC. MAJ

Thompson arrived on or about 10 September 2003, along with elements of the 325 MI BN. MAJ Thompson was sent by COL Pappas to set up the JIDC at Abu Ghraib. LTC Jordan arrived at Abu Ghraib on 17 September 2003, to become the Director of the JIDC. MAJ Price and elements of the 323 MI BN arrived at the end of September 2003. MAJ Price had been the OIC of the interrogation operation at Camp Bucca. He became the Operations Officer of the JIDC, working closely with MAJ Thompson and CPT Wood. Most of the personnel from the 323 MI BN element that arrived with MAJ Price were used as the Headquarters element and did not directly participate in interrogations.

(2) (U) Civilian CACI contract interrogators began to arrive in late September 2003. There are a number of shortfalls connected to this issue (See paragraph 4.g., below). It was another complicating factor with respect to command and control. CPT Wood relied on the CACI site manager, CIVILIAN-18, to interview contractors as they arrived and to assign them based on his interviews. She knew little of their individual backgrounds or experience and relied on "higher headquarters" to screen them before arrival. Such screening was not occurring.

(3) (U) During October 2003, in addition to the elements of the already mentioned MI units and the Titan and CACI civilians, elements of the 470 MI GP, 500 MI GP, and 66 MI GP appeared. These units were from Texas, Japan, and Germany, and were part of the US Army Intelligence and Security Command (INSCOM), which tasked those subordinate units to send whatever interrogator and analyst support they had available. MAJ Thompson rotated back to the US on 15 November 2003. CPT Wood left on emergency leave on 4 December 2003, and never returned. MAJ Price, then, was the only commissioned officer remaining in the Operations Section.

(4) (U) It is important to understand that the MI units at Abu Ghraib were far from complete units. They were small elements from those units. Most of the elements that came to Abu Ghraib came without their normal command structure. The unit Commanders and Senior NCOs did not go to Abu Ghraib but stayed with the bulk of their respective units. The bringing together of so many parts of so many units, as well as civilians with very wide backgrounds and experience levels in a two-month time period, was a huge challenge from a command and control perspective.

f. (U) Establishment, Organization, and Operation of the Joint Interrogation Debriefing Center (JIDC)

(1) (U) The idea for the creation of the JIDC came about after a number of briefings and meetings were held among LTG Sanchez, MG Fast, COL Pappas, and COL Steven Boltz, Assistant C2, CJTF-7. These meetings and briefings occurred about mid-August 2003 through early September 2003. They partially coincided with MG G. Miller's arrival from GTMO. He and his team provided an assessment of detainee operations in Iraq from 31 August to 9 September 2003 (See Paragraph 4.j.(1)). MG G. Miller's discussions with the CJTF personnel and the 205 MI BDE personnel influenced the decision to create a JIDC and how it would be organized, but those discussions were already underway before his arrival. The objective for the establishment of the JIDC

was to enhance the interrogation process with a view toward producing better, timelier, actionable intelligence (actionable intelligence provides commanders and Soldiers a high level of situational understanding, delivered with speed, accuracy, and timeliness, in order to conduct successful operations).

(2) (U) On 6 September 2003, COL Pappas briefed LTG Sanchez on a plan to improve interrogation operations resulting from a 31 August 2003 meeting (Reference Annex H, Appendix 10). LTG Sanchez approved the concept and directed COL Pappas to accelerate all aspects of the plan. This decision established the JIDC and modified previous interrogation operations at Abu Ghraib. COL Pappas decided when standing up the JIDC not to make it a battalion operation (Reference Annex B, Appendix 1, WILLIAMS), therefore deciding not to place one of his battalion commanders in charge of the JIDC but instead rely upon staff personnel to manage the entire operation. The current operation would be transitioned to a JIDC by personnel already assigned at Abu Ghraib with additional manning provided by the consolidation of security detainee interrogation operations from other locations (e.g., Camp Cropper). LTC Jordan would become the Director of the JIDC on 17 September 2003. Other key JIDC personnel included CPT Wood (OIC ICE), MAJ Thompson (JIDC Operations Officer), MAJ Price (JIDC Operations Officer), SOLDIER-14 and SOLDIER-23 (Interrogation Technicians). CJTF-7 decided to use the JTF-GTMO Tiger Team concept which uses an interrogator, an intelligence analyst, and an interpreter on each team. A re-organization of the JIDC took place in the late September to October 2003 timeframe which divided Tiger Teams into functional categories.

(3) (U) The reorganization introduced another layer of complexity into an already stressed Abu Ghraib interrogation operations environment. The Tiger Team worked well at GTMO. JTF-GTMO's target population and mission, however, were different from what was faced in Iraq. The Tiger Team method was designed to develop strategic level information from the GTMO detainees who were primarily captured in Afghanistan. By the time they reached GTMO any tactical value they may have had was gone. The same is true for Abu Ghraib relative to Iraq. The best place to collect tactical intelligence from interrogations is at the tactical level. Tactical intelligence is the most perishable, and the faster you harvest it the more useful it will be to help that tactical unit. JIDC personnel at Abu Ghraib believed the thirst for intelligence reporting to feed the national level systems was driving the train. There was then a focus to fill that perceived void and feed that system. LTG Sanchez did not believe significant pressure was coming from outside of CJTF-7, but does confirm that there was great pressure placed upon the intelligence system to produce actionable intelligence (Reference Annex B, Appendix 1, SANCHEZ). The Tiger Team concept should have only been used at Abu Ghraib for any high value targets identified. Those targets should receive careful planning and preparation, and be interrogated by the most experienced interrogators, analysts, and interpreters. Using a Tiger Team at Corps (the JIDC) for developing tactical intelligence did not work.

(4) (U) The JIDC is a non-doctrinal organization. Initially, there was no joint manning document for the JIDC (though one was developed by the 205 MI BDE over time and was submitted to CJTF-7). There was no approved structure for the JIDC. The

manning document was being created as the JIDC was already operating (Reference Annex B, Appendix 1, WILLIAMS, Maurice). Because there is no JIDC doctrine (or training), procedures were ad hoc in nature – adapted from FM 34-52 where possible, though most processes and procedures were developed on the fly based upon the needs of the situation. The organization of the JIDC changed often (Reference Annex H, Appendix 6, Tab B) and contributed to the general state of turmoil at Abu Ghraib. Interrogators were not familiar with the new working arrangements (e.g., working with analysts) and were only slightly trained on the conduct of interrogations using translators. Note that most interrogators are only trained in conducting tactical interrogations in a conventional war environment (See paragraph 3.b.(3)). In spite of this turmoil, lack of training and doctrine, and shortages, the JIDC did mature over time and improved intelligence production derived from interrogations at Abu Ghraib.

(5) (U) Early in the formation of the JIDC, COL Pappas requested COL Boltz provide him with a Lieutenant Colonel to run the new organization because the responsibilities would require someone of that rank and commensurate experience. LTC Jordan had just arrived in Iraq four days earlier. He was originally sent to be COL Boltz's Deputy C2 but then a decision was made to upgrade the C2 position from a COL to a MG. MG Fast was sent to CJTF-7 to be the C2, COL Boltz became the Deputy C2 and LTC Jordan became excess. Since LTC Jordan was available, COL Boltz assigned him to Abu Ghraib to run the JIDC. COL Boltz expected LTC Jordan to report to COL Pappas because COL Pappas had command responsibility for the JIDC. LTC Jordan was assigned to the JIDC verbally. He states that he never received orders (Reference Annex B, Appendix 1, JORDAN, BOLTZ).

(6) (U) There is a significant difference between what LTC Jordan claims he was told when he was sent to Abu Ghraib and what COL Pappas and COL Boltz say he was told. LTC Jordan says he was sent to be a "liaison" officer between CJTJ-7 and the JIDC. COL Pappas and COL Boltz say he was sent there to be in charge of it. Reference to titles is useless as a way to sort through this because there was no actual manning document for reference; people made up their own titles as things went along. Some people thought COL Pappas was the Director; some thought LTC Jordan was the Director. A major shortcoming on the part of COL Pappas and LTC Jordan was the failure to do a formal Officer Evaluation Report (OER) support form, Department of Army (DA) Form 67-8-1, to clearly delineate LTC Jordan's roles and responsibilities. It is clear that both had their own ideas as to roles and responsibilities, and an initial goal-setting session formalized via the support form would have forced both parties to deal in specifics. Such sessions are frequently done after the fact; especially in stress-filled combat situations. The less organized the situation, however, the more such a process is needed in order to sort out the boundaries and lanes in the road. Abu Ghraib was certainly a place and a situation that required both clear boundaries and clear lanes in the road. LTC Jordan did provide a support form that he said he did some weeks after his assignment to Abu Ghraib and which he sent to COL Boltz. COL Boltz claims he never received it. LTC Jordan never received a signed copy back from COL Boltz and never followed up to get one. Even if LTC Jordan had sent the support form a few weeks later as he states, it was by then too late. The confusion/damage had been done.

The early stages of the Abu Ghraib operation were the most critical to the disastrous end results (Reference Annex B, Appendix 1 BOLTZ, PAPPAS, JORDAN).

(7) (U) The preponderance of evidence supports the COLs Pappas/Boltz position that LTC Jordan was sent to run the JIDC. (Reference Annex B, Appendix 1, PAPPAS and BOLTZ). MAJ M. Williams, Operations Officer of the 205 MI BDE, and MAJ L. Potter, Deputy Commander of the 205 MI BDE, were adamant that LTC Jordan was sent for that reason. LTC Phillabaum believed LTC Jordan was in charge once he arrived at Abu Ghraib and started dealing directly with him. In all but one important aspect, interrogation operations, LTC Jordan began to act as if he were in charge.

(8) (U) As is now evident, LTC Jordan was a poor choice to run the JIDC. He was a Civil Affairs officer. He was an MI officer early in his career, but transferred to Civil Affairs in 1993. The MI experience he did have had not been in interrogation operations. LTC Jordan left the actual management, organization, and leadership of the core of his responsibilities to MAJ Thompson and CPT Wood. The reality of the situation was that MAJ Thompson and CPT Wood were overwhelmed by the huge demands of trying to organize, staff, equip, and train the JIDC while at the same time answering incessant requests for information from both the 205 MI BDE as well as from CJTF-7. What the JIDC needed in the beginning, more than ever, was a trained, experienced MI LTC. COL Pappas was correct in his assessment of what was required. In the critical early stages of the JIDC, as it was being formed, Abu Ghraib needed a LTC to take total control. The need was for a leader to get the JIDC organized, to set standards, enforce discipline, create checks and balances, establish quality controls, communicate a zero tolerance for abuse of detainees, and enforce that policy by quickly and efficiently punishing offenders so that the rest of the organization clearly understood the message. Well-disciplined units that have active, involved leaders both at the NCO and Officer level are less likely to commit abuses or other such infractions. If such instances do occur, they are seldom repeated because those leaders act aggressively to deal with the violators and reemphasize the standards (Reference Annex B, Appendix 1, BOLTZ, PAPPAS, JORDAN).

(9) (U) LTC Jordan gravitated to what he knew, and what he was comfortable with, rather than filling the void noted above. He was actually a very hard working officer who dedicated himself to improving life for all of the Soldiers at Abu Ghraib. He is physically brave, volunteered for Iraq, and was wounded in action at Abu Ghraib during the mortar attack on 20 September 2003. He addressed shortcomings in the mess situation, lack of exercise equipment, protective gear, living conditions, and communications. He also enforced stricter adherence to the uniform policies and the wearing of protective gear by Soldiers and contractors. Many of the Soldiers that we spoke to, both MPs and MI, considered LTC Jordan the "go to guy" to get the types of things just enumerated done. BG Karpinski even remarked once to LTC Jordan during one of her visits "Do you ever sleep?" (Reference Annex B, Appendix 2, KARPINSKI). Unfortunately, all of the issues he was addressing should have been left to the staffs of the 205 MI BDE and the 320 MP BN. He was not the FOB Commander. LTC Phillabaum was the FOB Commander until the 19 November 2003, FRAGO. (Annex B, Appendix 1, JORDAN).

(10) (U) LTC Jordan became fascinated with the "Other Government Agencies," a term used mostly to mean Central Intelligence Agency (CIA), who were operating at Abu Ghraib. The OGA "Ghost Detainee" issue (housing of detainees not formally accounted for) was well known within both the MI and MP communities and created a mystique about what "they" were doing (See paragraph 4.h.). LTC Jordan allowed OGA to do interrogations without the presence of Army personnel (Reference Annex B, Appendix 1, WOOD, THOMPSON, and PRICE). Prior to that time, JIDC policy was that an Army interrogator had to accompany OGA if they were interrogating one of the detainees MI was also interrogating. As noted above, LTC Jordan was little involved in the interrogation operations, but in this aspect he did become involved and it did not help the situation. The lack of OGA adherence to the practices and procedures established for accounting for detainees eroded the necessity in the minds of Soldiers and civilians for them to follow Army rules.

(11) (U) LTC Jordan and 10 other Soldiers were wounded in the mortar attack that occurred on 20 September 2003. Two Soldiers died in that attack. LTC Jordan was extremely traumatized by that attack, especially by the two deaths and the agony suffered by one of those Soldiers before his death. He was still very emotional about that attack when interviewed for this investigation on 27 May 2004. He said he thinks about the attack and the deaths daily. That attack also had an impact on a number of other Soldiers at Abu Ghraib as did the very frequent mortar attacks that occurred at Abu Ghraib during this entire period. The Soldiers' and civilians' morale at Abu Ghraib suffered as the attacks continued. Additionally, there was a general feeling by both MI and MP personnel that Abu Ghraib was the forgotten outpost receiving little support from the Army. (Reference Annex F, Appendix 3, Mortar Attacks). The frequency of these attacks and the perceived lack of aggressive action to prevent them were contributing factors to the overall poor morale that existed at Abu Ghraib.

(12) (U) COL Pappas perceived intense pressure for intelligence from interrogations. This began soon after he took Command in July 2003. In fact, as the time progressed from July 2003 through January 2004, interrogation operations at Abu Ghraib became the central focus of his efforts despite the fact that he was in command of the entire MI Brigade. That pressure for better results was passed from COL Pappas to the rest of the JIDC leadership (including MAJ Thompson, MAJ Price, CPT Wood, SOLDIER-23, and SOLDIER-14) and from them to the interrogators and analysts operating at Abu Ghraib. Pressure consisted in deviation from doctrinal reporting standards (pressure to report rapidly any and all ifnormation in non-standard formats such as Interrogator Notes in lieu of standard intelligence reports), directed guidance and prioritization from "higher," outside of doctrinal or standard operating procedures, to pursue specific lines of questioning with specific detainees, and high priority 'VFR Direct' taskings to the lowest levels in the JIDC. This pressure should have been expected in such a critical situation, but was not managed by the leadership and was a contributing factor to the environment that resulted in abuses. (Reference Annex B, Appendix 1, PAPPAS, BOLTZ, LYONS, WOOD, JORDAN, WILLIAMS, Maurice, POTTER, THOMAS, PRICE; and Annex B, Appendix 2, FAST, GEOFFREY MILLER, THOMAS MILLER).

(13) (U) The most critical period of time for Abu Ghraib was when COL Pappas committed a critical error in judgment by failing to remove LTC Jordan as soon as his shortcomings were noted, on approximately 10 October 2003. Very shortly after LTC Jordan's arrival at Abu Ghraib, on or about 17 September 2003, the 205 MI BDE Staff began to note LTC Jordan's involvement in staff issues and his lack of involvement in interrogation operations. The situation as described above would have been a daunting challenge for the most experienced, well trained, MI Officer. COL Pappas knew LTC Jordan was not who was needed to fulfill the JIDC functions early on, but nevertheless chose to see if LTC Jordan could work out over time. COL Pappas made more frequent visits during this time period both because he was receiving increasing pressure for results but also because he could rely on LTC Jordan to run the entire operation.

(14) (U) As pointed out clearly in the MG Taguba report, MP units and individuals at Abu Ghraib lacked sufficient training on operating a detainment/interrogation facility. MI units and individuals also lacked sufficient, appropriate, training to cope with the situation encountered at Abu Ghraib (See Paragraph 3.b.(4)). An insurgency is HUMINT intensive. The majority of that HUMINT comes from interrogations and debriefings. Yet at the JIDC, which was set up to be the focal point for interrogation operations, there was only one officer, CPT Wood, with significant interrogation operations experience. There were four MI Warrant Officers but all were used for staff functions rather than directly supervising and observing interrogations. There was a shortage of trained NCOs at the E-7/E-6 level. Each Section Leader had four or five Tiger Teams, too many to closely observe, critique, counsel, consult, and supervise. One Section Leader was an E-5. Several of the interrogators were civilians and about half of those civilians lacked sufficient background and training. Those civilians were allowed to interrogate because there were no more military assets to fill the slots. (Reference Annex B, Appendix 1, PAPPAS). Such a mixture together with constant demands for reports and documentation overwhelmed the Section Leaders. The analysts assigned to Tiger Teams were not all trained 96Bs, but were a mixture of all available intelligence Military Occupational Specialities (MOS). Many of those assigned as analysts had never been trained nor had they ever served as analysts.

(15) (U) Guard and interrogation personnel at Abu Ghraib were not adequately trained or experienced and were certainly not well versed in the cultural understanding of the detainees. MI personnel were totally ignorant of MP lanes in the road or rules of engagement. A common observation was that MI knew what MI could do and what MI couldn't do; but MI did not know what the MPs could or could not do in their activities. The same was true of MP ignorance of MI operational procedures. Having two distinct command channels (MI and MP – see Command and Control) in the same facility with little understanding of each other's doctrinal and regulatory responsibilities caused uncertainty and confusion. There was a perception among both MI and MP personnel that the other group was not doing its fair share in mutually supportive tasks of running the physical plant. CIVILIAN-12 (Assistant CJTF-7 C2X) observed that confusion seemed to be the order of the day at Abu Ghraib. There was hostility between MI and MP personnel over roles and responsibilities (Reference Annex B,

Appendix 1, CIVILIAN-12). There was a distinct lack of experience in both camps. Except for some of the Reserve Component MPs who had civilian law enforcement experience, most of the MPs were never trained in prison operations. Because of the shortage of MPs, some MI personnel had to assume detainee escort duties, for which they received only the most rudimentary training.

(16) (U) Abu Ghraib rapidly evolved from a tactical interrogation operation in July 2003 to a JIDC beginning in September 2003. Doctrine, SOPs, and other tactics, techniques and procedures (TTP) for a JIDC were initially non-existent. The personnel manning the JIDC came from numerous units, backgrounds, and experiences. Equipment such as computer, software, IT infrastructure (networks, data storage), and connectivity to relevant intelligence databases was very limited. Even file cabinets were in short supply which resulted in lost documents. One JIDC Soldier stated, "I can believe them (files for requests for exceptions to policy) getting lost because we often lost complete files. Our filing system was not the best. We did not have serviceable file cabinets and teams were given approval to place files in cardboard boxes." (Reference Annex B, Appendix 1, ADAMS) Initially there was only one computer available for every four interrogators. Ad hoc databases were built, employed, and modified as requirements dictated. Data connectivity between interrogators and analysts was established using "thumb drives." Forms, intelligence products, and database formats came and went based upon their immediate utility – many times dictated by the changing structure of the JIDC itself as directed by leadership. Critical records regarding each detainee were located in several electronic and hardcopy locations – the operations officers maintained some files, others were maintained by section leaders, others by collection management personnel, and others by Detainee Release Board (DRB) personnel. Some interrogation related information was recorded on a whiteboard which was periodically erased. No centralized management system existed to manage interrogation operations. One result was that detainee records critical to the evaluation of prisoners for a variety of reasons (for intelligence value assessment, release, medical evaulation, etc.) were difficult to find or construct. MP records at Abu Ghraib were equally primitive. These documentation shortfalls not only hindered effective interrogation operations and information sharing, but also hindered the ability of the Security Internee Review and Appeal Board (which relied upon records reviews to make decisions to release or retain detainees). As addressed earlier, many detainees arrived at Abu Ghraib with little or no documentation from capturing units. Follow-on records maintained by the MP and MI personnel at Abu Ghraib would be sparse if the detainee had not been thoroughly interrogated. DRBs were reluctant to release a detainee if they knew little about him. MG Fast noted that one detainee file that was reviewed by the release board was completely empty. Even detainee medical records that should have been created and stored (Reference Annex H, Appendix 8) were not maintained appropriately. Medical doctors on site at Abu Ghraib claim that excellent medical records were maintained on detainees (Reference Annex B, Appendix 1, ACKERSON). Only a few detainee medical records could be found, indicating that they are not being maintained IAW AR 40-66 (Medical Records Administration and Healthcare Documentation).

g. (U) Contract Interrogators and Linguists

(1) (U) Contracting-related issues contributed to the problems at Abu Ghraib prison. Several of the alleged perpetrators of the abuse of detainees were employees of government contractors. Two contractual arrangements were involved: one with CACI, for interrogators and several other intelligence-related occupational categories; and one with BTG, for linguists. Since 28 November 2001, BTG has been part of Titan Corporation. The contract is still in the name of BTG. Most people have referred to it as the Titan Contract. A brief description of these two contractual arrangements follows:

(a) (U) Linguist contract- Titan, Inc. - Contract DASC01-99-D-0001.
[1] (U) The need to supplement the Army's capacity for linguists was first raised to the Vice Chief of Staff of the Army in a 1997 "Foreign Language Lay down." It was proposed to establish a contract with the private sector to provide linguists, as needed, for contingencies and current intelligence operations.

[2] (U) As a result of this perceived need, INSCOM awarded Contract DASC01-99-D-0001 to Titan, in March 1999. The contract called for Titan initially to develop a plan to provide and manage linguists throughout the world, and later, implement the plan as required. The contract called for three levels of linguists - some were required to obtain security clearances and some were not. The linguist candidates were subject to some level of background investigations, based on individual requirements for security clearances. Since the award of the contract, hundreds of linguists have been provided, with generally positive results. It is noted that the contract calls for translation services only, and makes no mention of contractor employees actually conducting interrogations. Since the statement of work is limited to translation services, the linguists apparently were not required to review and sign the IROE at Abu Ghraib. A recent review of the contract indicated that the current contract ceiling is approximately $650 million. Other agencies can order linguist services under this contract. For the most part, the ordering activity also provides the funds for these delivery orders. The contract contains a clause that allows the Contracting Officer to direct the contractor to remove linguists from the theater in which they are performing. This clause has been invoked on occasion for misconduct.

(b) Interrogator contract-CACI, Inc.
[1] (U) The second contractual arrangement is a series of Delivery Orders awarded to CACI, in August 2003, which call for the provision of numerous intelligence-related services such as "Interrogator Support," "Screening Cell Support," "Open Source Intelligence," "Special Security Office," "HUMINT Augmentee Contractors" (which includes "Interrogation Support," "Junior Interrogators," "Senior and Junior Counter-Intelligence Agents," and "Tactical/Strategic Interrogators").

[2] (U) These Delivery Orders were awarded under a Blanket Purchase Agreement (BPA) (NBCHA01-0005) with the National Business Center (NBC), a fee for service activity of the Interior Department. The BPA between CACI and NBC set out the ground rules for ordering from the General Services Administration (GSA) pursuant to

GSA Schedule Contract GS-35F-5872H, which is for various Information Technology (IT) Professional Services. Approximately 11 Delivery Orders were related to services in Iraq. While CJTF-7 is the requiring and funding activity for the Delivery Orders in question, it is not clear who, if anyone, in Army contracting or legal channels approved the use of the BPA, or why it was used.

[3] (U) There is another problem with the CACI contract. A CACI employee, Thomas Howard, participated with the COR, LTC Brady, in writing the Statement of Work (SOW) prior to the award of the contract (Reference Annex B, Appendix 1, BOLTZ). This situation may violate the provisions of Federal Acquisition Regulation (FAR) 9.505-2 (b) (1).

[4] (U) On 13 May 2004, the Deputy General Counsel (Acquisition) of the Army issued an opinion that all Delivery Orders for Interrogator Services should be cancelled immediately as they were beyond the scope of the GSA Schedule contract.

(2) (U) Although intelligence activities and related services, which encompass interrogation services, should be performed by military or government civilian personnel wherever feasible, it is recognized that contracts for such services may be required in urgent or emergency situations. The general policy of not contracting for intelligence functions and services was designed in part to avoid many of the problems that eventually developed at Abu Ghraib, i.e., lack of oversight to insure that intelligence operations continued to fall within the law and the authorized chain of command, as well as the government's ability to oversee contract operations.

(3) (U) Performing the interrogation function in-house with government employees has several tangible benefits for the Army. It enables the Army more readily to manage the function if all personnel are directly and clearly subject to the chain of command, and other administrative and/or criminal sanctions, and it allows the function to be directly accessible by the commander/supervisor without going through a Contracting Officer Representative (COR). In addition, performing the function in-house enables Army Commanders to maintain a consistent approach to training (See Paragraph 3.b.(3)) and a reliable measure of the qualifications of the people performing the function.

(4) (U) If it is necessary to contract for interrogator services, Army requiring activities must carefully develop the applicable SOW to include the technical requirements and requisite personnel qualifications, experience, and training. Any such contracts should, to the greatest extent possible, be awarded and administered by an Army contracting activity in order to provide for the necessary oversight, management, and chain of command. Use of contracting vehicles such as GSA Federal Supply Schedule (FSS) contracts should be carefully scrutinized given the complexity and sensitivities connected to interrogation operations.

(5) (U) Some of the employees at Abu Ghraib were not DoD contractor employees. Contractor employees under non-DoD contracts *may* not be subject to the Military Extraterritorial Jurisdiction Act (18 US Code 3261 - 3267). The Act allows DoD contractor employees who are "accompanying the Armed Forces outside the United States" to be subject to criminal prosecution if they engage in conduct that would constitute

an offense punishable by imprisonment for more than one year if the conduct had occurred within the jurisdiction of the United States.

(6) (U) In the performance of such sensitive functions as interrogation, the Army needs to maintain close control over the entire operation. If a decision is made to contract for these services, the most effective way to do that and maintain a direct chain of command is to award, administer, and manage the contract with Army personnel. As learned in the current situation, it is very difficult, if not impossible, to effectively administer a contract when the COR is not on site.

(7) (U) The Army needs to improve onsite contract monitoring by government employees (using CORs) to insure that the Army's basic interests are protected. The inadequacy of the onsite contract management at Abu Ghraib is best understood by reviewing the statement of CPT Wood (Reference Annex B, Appendix 1, WOOD), the Interrogation OIC, who indicated she never received any parameters or guidance as to how the CACI personnel were to be utilized. She also indicates that her primary point of contact (POC) on matters involving the CACI Delivery Orders was the CACI onsite manager. There is no mention of a COR. Another indication of the inadequacy of the contract management is reflected in the statement of SOLDIER14 (Reference Annex B, Appendix 1, SOLDIER-14), who indicated he was never informed that the Government could reject unsatisfactory CACI employees. It would appear that no effort to familiarize the ultimate user of the contracted services of the contract's terms and procedures was ever made. In order to improve this situation, training is required to ensure that the COR is thoroughly familiar with the contract and gains some level of familiarity with the Geneva Conventions standards. It needs to be made clear that contractor employees are bound by the requirements of the Geneva Conventions.

(8) (U) If it is necessary to contract for interrogator services, more specific training requirements and personnel standards must be incorporated into the solicitation/ contract to insure that the contractor hires properly trained and qualified personnel.

(9) (U) Emerging results from a DA Inspector General (DAIG) Investigation indicate that approximately 35% of the contract interrogators lacked formal military training as interrogators. While there are specific technical requirements in the linguist contract, the technical requirements for the interrogator contract were not adequate. It appears that the only mention of qualifications in the contract stated merely that the contractor employee needs to have met the requirements of one of two MOS, 97E or 351E, or "equivalent". Any solicitation/contract for these services needs to list specific training, if possible, not just point to an MOS. If the training from the MOS is what is required, those requirements should be listed in the solicitation/contract in full, not just referenced. Perhaps the best way of insuring that contractor interrogators receive adequate training would be to utilize existing government training. For example, prospective contractor employees could be sent, at contractor expense, to the Tactical Human Intelligence Course for the 97E MOS, "Human Intelligence Collector." Such a step would likely require some adjustments to the current program of instruction. Prospective contract interrogators could be given the course tests on Interrogation and the Geneva Conventions. If they can pass the examinations, no further training would be required. After a reasonable training period, prospective

contractor interrogators who are unable to pass the exam would be rejected. There are, of course other training possibilities. The key point would be agreement on some standardization of the training of contractor interrogators. The necessity for some sort of standard training and/or experience is made evident by the statements of both contractor employees and military personnel. CIVILIAN-21 (CACI) seemingly had little or no interrogator experience prior to coming to Abu Ghraib (Reference Annex B, Appendix 1, CIVILIAN-21, ADAMS), even though he was a Navy Reserve Intelligence Specialist. Likewise, numerous statements indicated that little, if any, training on Geneva Conventions was presented to contractor employees (Reference Annex B, Appendix 1, SOLDIER-25, CIVILIAN-10, CIVILIAN-21 and CIVILIAN-11). Prior to deployment, all contractor linguists or interrogators should receive training in the Geneva Conventions standards for the treatment of detainees/prisoners. This training should include a discussion of the chain of command and the establishment of some sort of "hotline" where suspected abuses can be reported in addition to reporting through the chain of command. If the solicitation/contract allows "equivalent" training and experience, the Contracting Officer, with the assistance of technical personnel, must evaluate and assess the offerors'/contractor's proposal/written rationale as to why it believes that the employee has "equivalent" training. It appears that under the CACI contract, no one was monitoring the contractor's decisions as to what was considered "equivalent."

(10) (U) In addition, if functions such as these are being contracted, MI personnel need to have at least a basic level of contract training so they can protect the Army's interests. Another indication of the apparent inadequacy of onsite contract management and lack of contract training is the apparent lack of understanding of the appropriate relationship between contractor personnel, government civilian employees, and military personnel. Several people indicated in their statements that contractor personnel were "supervising" government personnel or *vice versa*. SGT Adams indicated that CACI employees were in positions of authority, and appeared to be supervising government personnel. She indicated a CACI employee named "First Name" was listed as being in charge of screening. CIVILIAN-08 (CACI) was in charge of "B Section" with military personnel listed as subordinates on the organization chart. SOLDIER-14 also indicated that CIVILIAN-08 was a supervisor for a time. CPT Wood stated that CACI "supervised" military personnel in her statement, but offered no specifics. Finally, a government organization chart (Reference Annex H, Appendix 6, Tab B) showed a CIVILIAN-02 (CACI) as the Head of the DAB. CIVILIAN-02 is a CACI employee. On the other side of the coin, CIVILIAN-21 indicated in his statement that the Non-Commissioned Officer in Charge (NCOIC) was his supervisor. (Reference Annex B, Appendix 1, SOLDIER-14, CIVILIAN-21, ADAMS, WOOD)

(11) (U) Given the sensitive nature of these sorts of functions, it should be required that the contractor perform some sort of background investigation on the prospective employees. A clause that would allow the government to direct the contractor to remove employees from the theater for misconduct would seem advisable. The need for a more extensive pre-performance background investigation is borne out by the allegations of abuse by contractor personnel.

(12) (U) An important step in precluding the recurrence of situations where contractor personnel may engage in abuse of prisoners is to insure that a properly trained COR is onsite. Meaningful contract administration and monitoring will not be possible if a small number of CORs are asked to monitor the performance of one or more contractors who may have 100 or more employees in the theater, and in some cases, perhaps in several locations (which seems to have been the situation at Abu Ghraib). In these cases, the CORs do well to keep up with the paper work, and simply have no time to actively monitor contractor performance. It is apparent that there was no credible exercise of appropriate oversight of contract performance at Abu Ghraib.

(13) (U) Proper oversight did not occur at Abu Ghraib due to a lack of training and inadequate contract management and monitoring. Failure to assign and adequate number of CORs to the area of contract performance puts the Army at risk of being unable to control poor performance or become aware of possible misconduct by contractor personnel. This lack of monitoring was a contributing factor to the problems that were experienced with the performance of the contractors at Abu Ghraib. The Army needs to take a much more aggressive approach to contract administration and management if interrogator services are to be contracted. Some amount of advance planning should be utilized to learn from the mistakes made at Abu Ghraib.

h. (U) Other Government Agencies and Abu Ghraib

(1) (U) Although the FBI, JTF-121, Criminal Investigative Task Force, ISG and the Central Intelligence Agency (CIA) were all present at Abu Ghraib, the acronym "Other Government Agency" (OGA) referred almost exclusively to the CIA. CIA detention and interrogation practices led to a loss of accountability, abuse, reduced interagency cooperation, and an unhealthy mystique that further poisoned the atmosphere at Abu Ghraib.

(2) (U) CIA detainees in Abu Ghraib, known locally as "Ghost Detainees," were not accounted for in the detention system. When the detainees were unidentified or un-accounted for, detention operations at large were impacted because personnel at the operations level were uncertain how to report them or how to classify them, or how to database them, if at all. Therefore, Abu Ghraib personnel were unable to respond to requests for information about CIA detainees from higher headquarters. This confusion arose because the CIA did not follow the established procedures for detainee in-processing, such as fully identifying detainees by name, biometric data, and Internee Serial Number (ISN) number.

(3) (U) DETAINEE-28, suspected of having been involved in an attack against the ICRC, was captured by Navy SEAL Team 7 during a joint TF-121/CIA mission. He reportedly resisted arrest, so a SEAL Team member butt-stroked DETAINEE-28 on the side of the head to subdue him. CIA representatives brought DETAINEE-28 into Abu Ghraib early in the morning of 4 November 2003, sometime around 0430 to 0530 hours. Under a supposed verbal agreement between the JIDC and the CIA, the CIA did not announce its arrival to JIDC Operations. SPC Stevanus, the MP on duty at the Hard Site at the time, observed the two CIA representatives come in with DETAINEE-28

and place him in a shower room in Tier 1B. About 30 to 45 minutes later, SPC Stevanus was summoned to the shower stall and when he arrived, DETAINEE-28 appeared to be dead. Removing the sandbag covering DETAINEE-28's head, SPC Stevanus checked DETAINEE-28's pulse. Finding none, he called for medical assistance, and notified his chain of command. LTC Jordan arrived on site at approximately 0715 hours, and found several MPs and US medical staff with DETAINEE-28 in the Tier 1B shower stall, face down, handcuffed with his hands behind his back. CIVILIAN-03, an Iraqi prison medical doctor, informed him DETAINEE-28 was dead. "OTHER AGENCY EMPLOYEE01," a CIA representative, uncuffed DETAINEE-28 and turned his body over. Where DETAINEE-28's head had lain against the floor, LTC Jordan noted a small spot of blood. LTC Jordan notified COL Pappas (205 MI BDE Commander), and "OTHER AGENCY EMPLOYEE01" said he would notify "OTHER AGENCY EMPLOYEE02," his CIA supervisor. Once "OTHER AGENCY EMPLOYEE02" arrived, he requested that the Hard Site hold DETAINEE28's body until the following day. DETAINEE-28's body was placed in a body bag, packed in ice, and stored in the shower area. CID was notified. The next day, DETAINEE-28's body was removed from Abu Ghraib on a litter, to make it appear as if he were only ill, so as not to draw the attention of the Iraqi guards and detainees. The body was transported to the morgue at BIAP for an autopsy, which concluded that DETAINEE-28 died of a blood clot in the head, likely a result of injuries he sustained during apprehension. (Reference Annex B, Appendix 1, JORDAN, PAPPAS, PHILLABAUM, SNIDER, STEVANUS, THOMPSON; Annex I, Appendix 1, photographs C5-21, D5-11, M65-69)

(4) (U) The systemic lack of accountability for interrogator actions and detainees plagued detainee operations in Abu Ghraib. It is unclear how and under what authority the CIA could place prisoners like DETAINEE-28 in Abu Ghraib because no memorandums of understanding existed on the subject between the CIA and CJTF-7. Local CIA officers convinced COL Pappas and LTC Jordan that they should be allowed to operate outside the established local rules and procedures. When COL Pappas raised the issue of CIA use of Abu Ghraib with COL Boltz, COL Boltz encouraged COL Pappas to cooperate with the CIA because everyone was all one team. COL Boltz directed LTC Jordan to cooperate. (Reference Annex B, Appendix 1, PAPPAS, BOLTZ)

(5) (U) In many instances, failure to adhere to in-processing procedures caused confusion and acrimony between the Army and OGA, and in at least one instance, acrimony between the US and Saudi Arabian entities. (Reference Annex K, Appendix 3, emails) For example, the CIA interned three Saudi national medical personnel working for the coalition in Iraq. CIA officers placed them in Abu Ghraib under false names. The Saudi General in charge of the men asked US authorities to check the records for them. A search of all databases using their true names came back negative. Ambassador Bremer then requested a search, which produced the same results. The US Embassy in Riyadh also requested a search, which likewise produced no information. Ultimately, the Secretary of State, Colin Powell, requested a search, and as with the other requestors, had to be told that the three men were not known to be in US custody. Shortly after the search for the Secretary of State, a JIDC official recalled that CIA officers once brought three men together into the facility. A quick discussion with the detainees disclosed their true names, which matched the name search

requests, and the men were eventually released. (Reference Annex B, Appendix 1, CIVILIAN-12)

(6) (U) Another instance showing lack of accountability to the procedures or rules involved a CIA officer who entered the interrogation room after a break in the interrogation, drew his weapon, chambered a round, and placed the weapon in his holster. This action violated the rule that no weapons be brought into an interrogation room, especially weapons with live rounds. Detainees who have been interrogated by CIA officers have alleged abuse. (Reference Annex B, Appendix 1, CIVILIAN-12)

(7) (U) The death of DETAINEE-28 and incidents such as the loaded weapon in the interrogation room, were widely known within the US community (MI and MP alike) at Abu Ghraib. Speculation and resentment grew over the lack of personal responsibility, of some people being above the laws and regulations. The resentment contributed to the unhealthy environment that existed at Abu Ghraib. The DETAINEE-28 death remains unresolved. CIA officers operating at Abu Ghraib used alias' and never revealed their true names. "OTHER AGENCY EMPLOYEE01" (alias) was the CIA officer with DETAINEE-28 on the morning of his death. "OTHER AGENCY EMPLOYEE02" (alias) was not directly involved in DETAINEE-28's death, but participated in the discussions after his death. Had the CIA followed established Army procedures and in-processed DETAINEE-28 in accordance with those procedures, DETAINEE-28 would have been medically screened.

(8) (U) OGA never provided results of their abuse investigations to Commander, CJTF-7. This resulted in a total lack of visibility over OGA interaction with detainees held in CJTF-7 spaces. Additionally, the CJTF-7 charter provided no oversight or control over the ISG. LTG Sanchez could neither leverage ISG interrogation assets to assist the detainee operations in Abu Ghraib, nor could he compel ISG to share substantive intelligence reports with CJTF-7. (Reference Annex B, Appendix 1, SANCHEZ)

i. (U) The Move of the 205 MI BDE Commander to Abu Ghraib.

(1) (U) In September 2003, COL Pappas began visiting Abu Ghraib two or three times per week as opposed to once every week or two, his previous routine. He was also beginning to stay overnight occasionally. His visit schedule coincided with the increased emphasis being placed on interrogation operations and the newly formed JIDC. (Reference Annex B, Appendix 1, PAPPAS)

(2) (U) On 16 November 2003, COL Pappas took up full-time residence at Abu Ghraib after once again speaking with LTG Sanchez and MG Fast and deciding that he needed to be there. He was appointed FOB Commander on 19 November 2003, in FRAGO 1108. The issuance of FRAGO 1108 has been pointed to and looked upon by many as being a significant change and one that was a major factor in allowing the abuses to occur. It was not. The abuses and the environment for them began long before FRAGO 1108 was ever issued. That FRAGO appointed the Commander, 205 MI BDE, the Commander FOB Abu Ghraib for Force Protection and Security of Detainees. COL Pappas then had TACON of the 320 MP BN. TACON has been misinterpreted by some to mean that COL Pappas then took over the running of the prison, or what has been referred

to as Warden functions. COL Pappas never took over those functions, and LTC Phill-abaum agrees that the running of the prison was always his responsibility. LTG San-chez has stated that he never intended to do anything except improve the Force Pro-tection posture of the FOB. That improved force protection posture would have thus improved the security of detainees as well. COL Pappas' rater, MG Wojdakowski, also stated that COL Pappas was never given responsibility for running the prison, but that the MPs retained that responsibility. It would appear from MG Taguba's investigation and the interview for this investigation that BG Karpinski was the only person among the Army leadership involved at the time who interpreted that FRAGO differently. (Re-ference Annex B, Appendix 1, KARPINSKI and Annex B, Appendix 2, KARPINSKI)

(3) (U) Upon being appointed FOB Commander, COL Pappas brought in one of his subordinate units, the 165th MI Battalion (165 MI BN) to enhance base security and to augment forces providing perimeter security as well as to conduct reconnaissance and surveillance outside the perimeter. That unit had reconnaissance and surveillance elements similar to line combat units that the MP Battalions did not possess. COL Pap-pas, on 8 December 2003, requested additional forces to support his force protection mission (Reference Annex H, Appendix 6, TAB – Request for Forces (RFF)). Requested forces included personnel for additional guards and a rapid reaction force.

(4) (U) The fact that COL Pappas did not have control of the MP force after the 19 November 2003 FRAGO regarding prison operations is further supported by the fact that at some point near the end of November 2003, the MPs stopped escorting detainees from the camps to the interrogation sites due to personnel shortages. This required MI to take over this function despite their protests that they were neither trained nor manned to do it. COL Pappas would have ordered the MPs to continue the escorts if he had had such authority (See paragraph 4.c.)

(5) (U) A milestone event at Abu Ghraib was the shooting incident that occurred in Tier 1A on 24 November 2003 (See paragraph 5.e.). COL Pappas was by then in residence at Abu Ghraib. LTC Jordan displayed personal bravery by his direct involvement in the shoot-out, but also extremely poor judgment. Instead of ordering the MPs present to halt their actions and isolate the tier until the 320 MP BN Commander and COL Pappas could be notified, he became directly involved. As the senior officer present, LTC Jordan became responsible for what happened. Eventually, COL Pappas was notified, and he did visit the scene. By then the shooting was over, and the MPs were searching the cells. COL Pappas did not remain long but admits to being told by SOLDIER-23 that the Iraqi Police were being interrogated by MI personnel. COL Pappas left LTC Jordan in charge of the situation after the shooting which came to be known as the IP Roundup. The IP Roundup was, by all accounts chaotic. The Iraqi Police, hence the name "IP," became detainees and were subjected to strip searching by the MPs in the hallway, with female Soldiers and at least one female interpreter present. The IP were kept in various stages of dress, including nakedness, for prolonged periods as they were interrogated. This constitutes humiliation, which is detainee abuse. Military working dogs were being used not only to search the cells, but also to intimidate the IPs during interrogation without authorization. There was a general understanding among the MI personnel present that LTG Sanchez had authorized

suspending existing ICRP (known by the Abu Ghraib personnel locally as the IROE) because of the shooting (Reference Annex C, Appendix 1, Tab B, Annex 8, AR 15-6 Investigation, 24 November 2003). Nobody is sure where that information came from, but LTG Sanchez never gave such authorization (Reference Annex B, Appendix 1, SANCHEZ). LTC Jordan and the Soldiers should have known the Interrogation Rules would not and could not have been suspended. LTC Jordan should have controlled the situation and should have taken steps to reinforce proper standards at a time when emotions were likely high given the circumstances. LTC Jordan is responsible for allowing the chaotic situation, the unauthorized nakedness and resultant humiliation, and the military working dog abuses that occurred that night. LTC Jordan should have obtained any authorizations to suspend ICRP in writing, via email, if by no other means. The tone and the environment that occurred that night, with the tacit approval of LTC Jordan, can be pointed to as the causative factor that set the stage for the abuses that followed for days afterward related to the shooting and the IP Roundup. COL Pappas is also responsible and showed poor judgment by leaving the scene before normalcy returned, as well as for leaving LTC Jordan in charge.

(6) (U) The small quantity of MI personnel had a difficult time managing the large number of MI holds which moved from the hundreds to over a thousand by December 2003 (See paragraph 4.c.(12)). In December 2003, COL Pappas, in his role as FOB Commander, requested additional forces be allocated to support the difficult and growing force protection mission. Prior to his designation as FOB Commander, COL Pappas had requested additional forces to support the JIDC mission. One of the reasons he cited in the December request was that the mixing of MI and MP functions was worsening the already difficult personnel resource situation.

j. (U) Advisory and Training Team Deployments

(1) (U) MG Geoffrey Miller Visit

(a) (U) MG G. Miller's visit was in response to a J3, JCS, request to SOUTHCOM for a team to assist CENTCOM and ISG in theater (Reference Annex L, Appendix 1, Electrical Message, DTG: 181854Z Aug 03, FM JOINT STAFF WASHINGTON DC // J3). The team was directed to assist with advice on facilities and operations specific to screening, interrogations, HUMINT collection, and interagency integration in the short and long term. MG G. Miller was tasked as the result of a May 2003 meeting he had with MG Ronald Burgess, J2, JCS. MG Burgess indicated there were some challenges in CJTF-7 with the transition from major combat operations to SASO in the areas of intelligence, interrogation, and detention (Reference Annex B, Appendix 1, MILLER). COL Boltz believed LTG Sanchez had requested the support (Reference Annex B, Appendix 1, BOLTZ).

(b) (U) From 31 August to 9 September 2003, MG G. Miller led a team to Iraq to conduct an "Assessment of DoD Counterterrorism Interrogation and Detention Operations in Iraq." Specifically, MG G. Miller's team was to conduct assistance visits to CJTF-7, TF-20, and the ISG to discuss current theater ability to exploit internees rapidly for actionable intelligence. MG G. Miller and his team of 17 experts assessed three major areas of concern: intelligence integration, synchronization, and fusion; interrogation operations; and detention operations. The team's assessment (Reference Annex L, Appendix 1, MG Miller's Report, Assessment of DoD Counterterrorism Interrogation and Detention Operations in Iraq, undated, and MG Miller's Briefing of his findings, dated 6 September 2003) identified several areas in need of attention: the interrogators didn't have the authorities and procedures in place to effect a unified strategy to detain, interrogate, and report information from detainees in Iraq; the information needs required an in-theater analysis capability integrated in the interrogation operations to allow for access/leverage of the worldwide intelligence databases; and the detention operations function must support the interrogation process.

(c) (U) MG G. Miller's visit also introduced written GTMO documentation into the CJTF-7 environment. LTG Sanchez recalled MG G. Miller left behind a whole series of SOPs that could be used as a start point for CJTF-7 interrogation operations. It was clear that these SOPs had to be adapted to the conditions in Iraq and that they could not be implemented blindly. LTG Sanchez was confident the entire CJTF-7 staff understood that the conditions in GTMO were different than in Iraq, because the Geneva Conventions applied in the Iraqi theater.

(d) (U) The assessment team essentially conducted a systems analysis of the intelligence mission in Iraq and did not concentrate on specific interrogation techniques. While no "harsh techniques" were briefed, COL Pappas recalled a conversation with MG G. Miller regarding the use of military working dogs to support interrogations (See paragraph 5.f.). According to COL Pappas, MG G. Miller said they, GTMO, used military working dogs, and that they were effective in setting the atmosphere for interrogations (Reference Annex B, Appendix 2, PAPPAS). MG G. Miller contradicted COL Pappas in his statement (Reference Annex B, Appendix 1, MILLER), saying he only discussed using military working dogs to help the MPs with detainee custody and control issues. According to MG G. Miller, the dogs help provide a controlled atmosphere (not interrogations as recalled by COL Pappas) that helps reduce risk of detainee demonstrations or acts of violence. According to MG G. Miller, his team recommended a strategy to work the operational schedule of the dog teams so the dogs were present when the detainees were awake, not when they are sleeping.

(e) (U) Several things occurred subsequent to MG G. Miller's visit to Abu Ghraib. The JIDC was established. The use of Tiger Teams was implemented based on the JTF-GTMO model, which teamed an interrogator and an analyst together, giving each team an organic analytical capability. There was also a moderate increase in the number of interrogators reassigned to the Abu Ghraib operation. This increase was probably not connected to MG G. Miller's visit as much as to the arrival of elements of the 325 MI BN which began to arrive 10 September 2003 – the same day MG G. Miller departed Iraq. Prior to their arrival, the interrogation assets consisted of one OIC (captain), one technician (chief warrant officer), 12 HUMINT collectors (MOS 97E/97B), an analyst, and a communications team. While the number of interrogators increased, the JIDC requirements for a staff and leadership also increased. Those positions were filled from within the assigned units. It is indeterminate what impact the MG G. Miller Team's concepts had on operations at Abu Ghraib. There was an increase in intelligence reports after the visit but that appears more likely due to the assignment of trained interrogators and an increased number of MI Hold detainees to interrogate.

(2) JTF-GTMO Training Team.

(a) (U) Subsequent to MG G. Miller's visit, a team of subject matter experts was dispatched from JTF-GTMO to Abu Ghraib (approximately 4 October to 2 December 2003) to assist in the implementation of the recommendations identified by MG G. Miller. The JTF-GTMO Team included three interrogators and three analysts, organized into three teams, with one interrogator and one analyst on each, which is the GTMO "Tiger Team" concept. The JTF GTMO Team included SOLDIER28 (351E Team Chief), SOLDIER27, CIVILIAN-14 (97E), SOLDIER-03 (97E), SSG Miller (96B), and SOLDIER-11 (96B). The Team Chief understood his task was to assist CJTF-7 for a period not to exceed 90 days with the mission of building a robust and effective JIDC, and identifying solutions and providing recommendations for the JIDC (Reference Annex B, Appendix 1, SOLDIER-28). Upon arrival at Abu Ghraib, SOLDIER-28 and SOLDIER-27, both of whom had been on the original MG G. Miller assessment visit, concentrated on establishing the various JIDC elements. Particular emphasis was given to formalizing the JIDC staff and the collection, management and dissemination (CM&D) function at Abu Ghraib, to alleviate many of the information distribution issues surfaced during MG G. Miller's visit. Some interrogation policies were already in place. Consistent with its charter to assist in establishment of a GTMO-like operation, the team provided copies of the current JTF-GTMO policies, SOPs (Reference, Annex L, Appendix 2, SOP for JTF-GTMO, Joint Intelligence Group [JIG], Interrogation Control Element [ICE], Guantanamo Bay, CU, dated 21 January 2003, revised 12 June 2003), and the SECDEF Letter (Reference, Annex J, Appendix 2, MEMORANDUM FOR COMMANDER, US SOUTHERN COMMAND, Subject: Counter-Resistance Techniques in the War on Terrorism (S), dated 16 April 2003) outlining the techniques authorized for use with the GTMO detainees. The four other JTF-GTMO team members were split up and integrated into interrogation operations as members/leaders of the newly formed Tiger Teams under the ICE. SOLDIER-28 and SOLDIER-27 did not directly participate in any interrogation operations and reported that they never observed, or heard about, any detainee abuse or mistreatment. SOLDIER-28's assertion as regards knowledge of abuses is contradicted by one of his Soldiers (Reference Annex B, Appendix 1, SOLDIER-03) (See paragraphs 4.j.(2)(c) and 4.j.(2)(d), below).

(b) (U) While the JTF-GTMO team's mission was to support operations and assist in establishment of the JIDC, there was a great deal of animosity on the part of the Abu Ghraib personnel, especially some A/519 MI BN Personnel. This included an intentional disregard for the concepts and techniques the GTMO Team attempted to instill, as well as contempt for some of the team's work ethic, professional judgment, and ideas. Because of this, the GTMO Team's ability to effect change at Abu Ghraib may have been severely limited. This information was obtained during a review of email exchanged between SOLDIER-14, CW2 Grace, CW3 Sammons, SFC McBride, with info copies to CPT Wood and SOLDIER-23. It should be noted that senior managers at Abu Ghraib thought highly of the JTF-GTMO team and believed they positively impacted the operations.

(c) (U) SOLDIER-11, a JTF-GTMO analyst assigned to the "Former Regime Loyalists" Tiger Team, stated that he witnessed and reported two incidents of abuse (Reference Annex B, Appendix 1, SOLDIER-11). In his first report, SOLDIER-11 reported that he was observing an interrogation being conducted by SOLDIER 19 A/519 MI BN. As SOLDIER-11 observed from behind a glass, SOLDIER-19 directed a detainee to roll his jumpsuit down to his waist and insinuated that the detainee would be stripped further if he did not cooperate. The interrogation ended abruptly when the translator objected to the tactic and refused to continue. SOLDIER-11 reported the incident to both SOLDIER-16, his Tiger Team Leader, and to SOLDIER-28, his JTF GTMO Team Chief. SOLDIER-16 invoked her rights under UCMJ and chose not to make any statement regarding this or any other matters (Reference Annex B, Appendix 1SOL-DIER16). When asked, SOLDIER-28 stated that he could not recall what SOLDIER11 reported to him regarding the rolling down of the detainee's jumpsuit, but does recall a conversation about a translator walking out of an interrogation due to a "cultural difference" (Reference Annex B, Appendix 1, SOLDIER-28). SOLDIER-11 is adamant that he reported the incident in detail (Reference Annex B, Appendix 1, SOLDIER-11) and that he never used the phrase "cultural difference."

(d) (U) In another report to SOLDIER-28, SOLDIER-11 reported a second incident. SOLDIER-11 and SOLDIER-19 were conducting an interrogation around mid-October 2003. The detainee was uncooperative and was not answering questions. SOLDIER19 became frustrated and suggested to SOLDIER11 that the detainee be placed in solitary. SOLDIER-11 did not agree with the recommendation and suggested it would be counterproductive. About 15 minutes later (two hours into the interrogation), SOLDIER-19 exercised his authority as the lead interrogator and had the detainee placed in solitary confinement. About a half an hour later, SOLDIER-11 and SOLDIER-19 went to the Hard Site to see the detainee, and found him lying on the floor, completely naked except for a hood that covered his head from his upper lip, whimpering. SOLDIER-11 and SOLDIER-19 had the MPs redress the detainee before escorting him back to the general population. SOLDIER-11 was disturbed by what he had seen and considered reporting it to several different people. Ultimately, SOLDIER-11 reported this incident to SOLDIER-28 (Reference Annex B, Appendix 1, SOLDIER-11). SOLDIER-11 added that SOLDIER-28 accepted the report and indicated he would surface the issue to COL Pappas (not due to return to Abu Ghraib for 2/3 days). Also according to SOLDIER-11, SOLDIER-28 was very ill and placed on 30 days quarters shortly after SOLDIER-11 made his report. When asked, SOLDIER-28 could not recall such a report being made to him (Reference Annex B, Appendix 1, SOLDIER-28).

(e) (U) SSG Miller does not recall the JTF-GTMO team ever discussing specific interrogation techniques employed, abuse, or unauthorized interrogation methods. He observed only approved interrogation techniques in line with FM 34-52, and never saw any detainee abuse, mistreatment, or nakedness (Reference Annex B, Appendix 1, MILLER).

(f) (U) CIVILIAN-14 never observed any activity or training event that was not in compliance with basic human rights and the Geneva Conventions. CIVILIAN-14 did, however, notice "a lot of detainee nakedness at Abu Ghraib," possibly, he speculated, attributable to the lack of available clothing. There was nothing he observed or heard that he considered detainee abuse. Relating to his JTF-GTMO experience/training, CIVILIAN-14 believed the removal of clothing for interrogation purposes was an option available with the appropriate approvals; however, it was rarely used at JTF-GTMO. This misunderstanding of the rules and regulations was evident in his reaction to the detainee nakedness at Abu Ghraib. Clearly CIVILIAN-14 was not aware of the fact the SECDEF had withdrawn that authority. (Reference Annex B, Appendix 1, CIVILIAN-14)

(g) (U) In reviewing his activities while at Abu Ghraib, SOLDIER-03 recalled his team submitted two requests to use techniques requiring approvals beyond the team level. In cases requiring such approvals, the request went to the Operations Officer (either MAJ Thompson or MAJ Price) (Operations Officer) and they would approve or disapprove the technique. Those requests requiring a CJTF-7 approval level went to CPT Wood who would forward them for approval. SOLDIER-03 recalled submitting the requests several days in advance of the interrogation to ensure it was approved or disapproved before the interrogation began. His first request (detainee sitting against a wall) was initiated by SOLDIER-21 (analyst) and SOLDIER-30 (interrogator). SOLDIER-03 reviewed the request and forwarded it for approval (SOLDIER-03 could not recall to whom he submitted the request or who had approved it). The request was approved and was implemented. After "observing for a couple of minutes," SOLDIER-03 ended the interrogation. In preparation for another interrogation, the same two females (SOLDIER-21 and SOLDIER-30) submitted a request to interrogate a detainee naked. The request was reviewed by SOLDIER-03 and forwarded to MAJ Price. MAJ Price denies ever approving a naked interrogation. SOLDIER-03 recalled that the technique had been approved, but could not recall by whom. As with the above interrogation, SOLDIER-03 observed the interrogation. After about 15 minutes, he determined the nudity was not a productive technique and terminated the session. SOLDIER-03 never discussed this incident with SOLDIER-28. In his opinion, he had obtained the appropriate authorities and approvals for an "acceptable technique." When asked, SOLDIER-03 recalled hearing about nakedness at GTMO, but never employed the technique. (Reference Annex B, Appendix 1, SOLDIER-03, PRICE).

(h) (U) The JTF-GTMO Team viewed itself as having the mission of setting up and organizing an effective and efficient JIDC staff, and assisting in establishing the Tiger Team concept based on the GTMO model and experience. They did not veiw their mission as being for training specific interrogation techniques. This is contrary to MG G. Miller's understanding of the mission. There is no evidence that the JTF-GTMO team intentionally introduced any new/prohibited interrogation techniques. Clearly, however, they were operating without a full understanding of the current JTF-GTMO ICRP.

(i) (U) According to SOLDIER-28, no After Action Report (AAR) was prepared for this mobile training team's effort. He provided a post-mission briefing to MG G. Miller upon his return to GTMO. The team's mission was not clearly defined until they arrived at Abu Ghraib. According to MAJ Price (Reference Annex B, Appendix 1, PRICE), the

JTF-GTMO Team arrived without a defined charter; however, in his opinion, the team's suggestions were very good and exactly what the Abu Ghraib operation needed. MAJ Price felt that the real changes began to show after COL Pappas arrived on or about 16 November 2003.

(3) (U) Fort Huachuca Mobile Training Team

(a) (U) From 7 to 21 October 2003, a five-person ISCT MTT from the USAIC, Fort Huachuca, AZ, was dispatched to conduct an overall assessment of interrogation operations, present training, and provide advice and assistance at the Abu Ghraib JIDC. This course was developed in response to requirements surfaced during interrogation operations at JTF-GTMO, specifically to prepare reserve interrogators and order of battle analysts for deployment to JTF-GTMO. The course consists of a refresher in interrogation procedures and an introduction to strategic debriefing procedures (Reference Annex L, Appendix 4, ISCT POI; ISCT MTT AAR). The MTT consisted of a team chief, CW3 Norris (351B), three 97E interrogators, MSG Filhanessian, SFC Fierro and SFC Walters, and one analyst (96B) SOLDIER-56. The MTT spent the first few days at Abu Ghraib observing ongoing JIDC interrogation operations and establishing a training schedule based on their observations. The training phase lasted approximately five days and focused on interrogation skills and elicitation techniques, cultural awareness, collection management, and use of interpreters. The team discussed the use of Tiger Teams, but did not conduct any training in their use. The Tiger Team concept of teaming an Interrogator and an Analyst together had been previously recommended by the GTMO Assessment Team and was already being employed at Abu Ghraib when the ISCT MTT arrived. Following the training, at least two ISCT MTT Interrogators participated in approximately 19 interrogations and observed several others. The MTT prepared an After Action Report (Reference Annex L, Appendix 4, ISCT MTT AAT, Joint Detainee Interrogation Center, CJTF-7, Abu Ghurayb (sic), Iraq, dated 3 November 2003), which noted 11 issues and provided recommendations for each. The issues mainly concerned screening procedures, interrogation planning and preparation, approaches, questioning, interpreter control, deception detection, and administrative and reporting issues. SFC Filhanessian did recall they had access to the 16 April 2003 SECDEF Memorandum and devoted some time to discussing approach strategies outside the ones mentioned in FM 34-52, Intelligence Interrogations, 28 September 1992, like the issue of military working dogs, sleep deprivation, etc., (Reference Annex B, Appendix 1, FILHANESSIAN). According to SOLDIER-25 (Reference Annex B, Appendix 1, SOLDIER25), "A team from Fort Huachuca . . . gave us three days of classes, including rules of engagement and the use of sleep deprivation and sleep management." The ISCT MTT AAR did not note any incidents of detainee abuse or mistreatment. Three interviewed ISCT MTT members stated that they did not witness, or hear of any incidents of detainee abuse or mistreatment. Neither did they observe or know of any incidents where MI instructed or insinuated that the MP should abuse detainees. Further, MTT members stated that the 519 MI BN interrogators at Abu Ghraib demonstrated experience, "did things by the book," and used techniques that were within the limitations established by FM 34-52 (Interrogation Operations). Some team members, however, expressed some concerns about what appeared to them to be a lack of experience with some of the civilian contracted

CACI Interrogators, and the fact that the MTT did not have the opportunity to train and work with some newly arriving contractors (Reference Annex B, Appendix 1, WALTERS; CIVILIAN-07; and FIERRO).

(b) (U) On 21 June 2004, SFC Walters contacted the investigative team via email and indicated he wanted to make additions to his statement (Reference Annex B, Appendix 1, WALTERS 20040621, email). SFC Walters was concerned that as a member of the ISCT MTT, he may have contributed to the abuse at Abu Ghraib. When questioned by CACI employee CIVILIAN-21 for ideas to use to get these prisoners to talk, SFC Walters related several stories about the use of dogs as an inducement, suggesting he (CIVILIAN-21) talk to the MPs about the possibilities. SFC Walters further explained that detainees are most susceptible during the first few hours after capture. "The prisoners are captured by Soldiers, taken from their familiar surroundings, blindfolded and put into a truck and brought to this place (Abu Ghraib); and then they are pushed down a hall with guards barking orders and thrown into a cell, naked; and that not knowing what was going to happen or what the guards might do caused them extreme fear." SFC Walters also suggested CIVILIAN-21 could take some pictures of what seemed to be guards being rough with prisoners . . . so he could use them to scare the prisoners. Lastly, SFC Walters also shared what he described as a formal, professional prisoner in-processing as he observed it in Bagram (a reference to the detainee operations that had taken place Afghanistan).

(c) (U) On 26 June 2004, during a follow-on interview (Reference Annex B, Appendix 1, WALTERS); SFC Walters confirmed the information he provided in his email. He clarified that his conversation with CIVILIAN-21 occurred before the training was conducted and that he was certain CIVILIAN-21 clearly understood the rules with regard to interrogations. SFC Walters was adamant he had stressed the need to obtain the appropriate authorities before using any of the techniques discussed. SFC Walters knew of no other "off line" conversations between the MTT members and assigned interrogators. SFC Walters said he had related stories he had heard, but did not personally observe. In addressing the ISCT MTT training objectives, SFC Walters noted they (ISCT MTT) did not agree with the JTF-GTMO modus operandi. The (ISCT MTT) felt the use of Tiger Teams wasted limited analytical support. Analysts should support interrogation teams and not be part of the interrogation. This mirrors the opinions of the Abu Ghraib team (Reference Annex B, Appendix 1, WOOD).

(d) (U) Throughout OIF I, USAIC assisted in sending MTTs to all divisional locations within Iraq in order to provide instruction on THT operations, G2X staff functions, and tactical questioning for non-military intelligence Soldiers. Prior to this training, a separate team traveled to Afghanistan and Iraq to provide similar training at Bagram Airfield and Abu Ghraib Detention Facility. This training was the same training provided to OIF units in Iraq that also incorporated lessons learned during that MTT.

k. (U) International Committee of the Red Cross (ICRC)

(1) (U) The ICRC visits to Abu Ghraib have been the source of great concern since the abuses at Abu Ghraib became public knowledge. The ICRC are independent observers

who identified abuses to the leadership of Abu Ghraib as well as to CJTF-7. Their allegations were not believed, nor were they adequately investigated.

(2) (U) During the 9-12 and 21-23 October 2003, visits to Abu Ghraib, the ICRC noted that the ill treatment of detainees during interrogation was not systemic, except with regard to persons arrested in connection with suspected security offenses or deemed to have an "intelligence value." These individuals were probably the MI holds. "In these cases, persons deprived of their liberty [and] under supervision of the Military Intelligence were at high risk of being subjected to a variety of harsh treatments. These ranged from insults, threat and humiliations, to both physical and psychological co-ercion (which in some cases was tantamount to torture) in order to force cooperation with their interrogators (Reference Annex G, Appendix 1, Executive Summary)." The ICRC noted that some detainees in Tier 1A were held naked in their cells, with meals ready to eat (MRE) packing being used to cover their nudity. The ICRC immediately informed the authorities, and the detainees received clothes for the remainder of the ICRC visit. Additionally, the ICRC complained about MI-imposed restrictions on vis-iting certain security detainees in Camp Vigilant and in Tier 1A. Red Cross delegates were informed they could visit those areas the following day and then only on the basis of a list of detainees and tasks agreed on with Abu Ghraib officials. (Reference Annex G, Appendix 1, TAB B)

(3) (U) The ICRC found a high level of depression, feelings of helplessness, stress, and frustration, especially by those detainees in isolation. Detainees made the following allegations during interviews with the ICRC: threats during interrogation; insults and verbal insults during transfer in Tier 1A; sleep deprivation; walking in the corridors handcuffed and naked, except for female underwear over the head; handcuffing either to the upper bed bars or doors of the cell for 3-4 hours. Some detainees presented physical marks and psychological symptoms which were compatible with these alle-gations. Also noted were brutality upon capture, physical or psychological coercion during interrogation, prolonged isolation, and excessive and disproportionate use of force. (Reference Annex G, Appendix 1, TAB B)

(4) (U) The ICRC made a number of recommendations after the October 2003 visits, including: grant ICRC full and unimpeded access to all detainees; improve the security related to the accommodation structure; clarify and improve conditions of detention and treatment; distribute hygiene items, spare clothes, blankets, etc.; inform detainees of the reason for their detention; implement regular family visits for detainees; and increase recreational and educational activities. (Reference Annex G, Appendix 1, Tab B, ICRC Working Paper, dated 6 November 2003).

(5) (U) LTC Phillabaum, regarding the 9–12 October 2003 visit, stated he was told of naked detainees by the ICRC and immediately contacted LTC Jordan. The two went to see the situation first hand. LTC Phillabaum claimed that LTC Jordan acknowledged that it was common practice for some of the detainees to be kept naked in their cells. In November 2003, after having received the written ICRC report, CJTF-7 sent an Australian Judge Advocate officer, MAJ George O'Kane, to Abu Ghraib to meet with LTC Jordan and other officers to craft a response to the ICRC memo. (Reference Annex B, Appendices 1 and 2, PHILLABAUM)

(6) (U) Stemming from those October 2003 visits, the ICRC also made the following request of the Coalition Forces: respect at all times the human dignity, physical integrity, and cultural sensitivity of detainees; set up a system of notification of arrest to the families of detainees; prevent all forms of ill-treatment; respect and protect the dignity of detainees; allow sufficient time for outside activity and exercise; define and apply regulations compatible with international Humanitarian Law; thoroughly investigate violation of international Humanitarian Law; ensure that capturing forces and internment facility personnel are trained to function in a proper manner without resorting to ill-treatment of detainees. (Reference ANNEX G, Appendix 1, Tab A, ICRC Report February 2004)

(7) (U) COL Warren, the CJTF-7 SJA, stated that neither he nor anyone else from CJTF-7 Headquarters was present at Abu Ghraib during the ICRC visit in October 2003. Throughout 2003, all ICRC reports were addressed to the commander or subordinate commanders of the 800 MP BDE. The OSJA received a copy of the reports. Letters on specific topics addressed to LTG Sanchez were given to COL Warren and he would prepare the response for LTG Sanchez. MAJ O'Kane prepared an analysis of the report on 25 November 2003 and the draft was sent to CJTF-7 C2 and the 800 MP BDE for review. On 4 December 2003, a meeting was held at Abu Ghraib, attended by MP, MI, and legal personnel, in order to discuss the report. In mid-December, the draft response was sent by OSJA to the 800 MP BDE for review and coordination. BG Karpinski signed the response, dated 24 December 2003. (Reference Annex G, Appendix 3, KARPINSKI Letter)

(8) (U) During the 4–8 January 2004 visit, the ICRC expressed special concern over being informed by COL Pappas and COL Warren that they were invoking Article 143 of Geneva Convention IV, thereby denying the ICRC access to eight of the detainees in the interrogation section. Of particular interest was the status of detainee DETAINEE-14, a Syrian national and self-proclaimed Jihadist, who was in Iraq to kill coalition troops. DETAINEE-14 was detained in a totally darkened cell measuring about two meters long and less than a meter across, devoid of any window, latrine or water tap, or bedding. On the door the ICRC delegates noticed the inscription "the Gollum," and a picture of the said character from the film trilogy "Lord of the Rings." During the 14–18 March 2004 visit, the ICRC was once again denied access to nine detainees, including DETAINEE-14. They noted that DETAINEE-14 was no longer in the same cell as he was previously, but was still in one of the more "difficult" cells. (Reference Annex G, Appendix 1, ICRC Working Paper, dated 6 November 2003; Appendix 2, ICRC Letter dated February 2004; Appendix 2, Tab B, ICRC Letter dated 25 March 2004)

(9) (U) Article 143, Fourth Geneva Convention, reads in part "Such visits may be prohibited except for reasons of imperative military necessity, and then only for an exceptional and temporary measure." COL Warren and COL Pappas both acknowledge denying access to specified detainees by the ICRC on each of two occasions (in January and March 2004), invoking the above cited provision. The ICRC, in their memorandum of 25 March 2004, acknowledged the right of COL Warren and COL Pappas to invoke the "imperative military necessity clause." It questioned the "exceptional and temporary" nature of the denial of access to DETAINEE-14 on both occasions,

however, given that DETAINEE-14 (by the time of the second visit) had been under interrogation for some four months. This was the same DETAINEE-14 that was
viewed a "special project" and who was abused by the use of dogs. (See paragraph
5.f.) (Reference Annex B, Appendix 1, PAPPAS, WARREN)

(10) (U) COL Pappas acknowledges in his statement that the ICRC visited Abu Ghraib
twice (January and March 2004). He received a copy of the results and noted there
were allegations of maltreatment and detainees wearing women's underwear on their
heads. He did not believe it. He recalled he might have related to the staff that "this
stuff couldn't have been happening." He added that when the ICRC came by the second
time (March 2004), he invoked Article 143, preventing the eight detainees in Tier 1A
from talking to the ICRC while undergoing active interrogation. COL Pappas states:
"COL Warren informed me that I had the authority to do this." (Reference Annex B,
Appendices 1 and 2, PAPPAS)

(11) (U) COL Warren also stated that when he saw the ICRC report on naked detainees
and detainees wearing women's underwear, he couldn't believe it. He saw the report
when he returned to CJTF-7 from leave on 30 November 2003. His office probably
had received the report on 16 November 2003. He regrets not having taken the report
earlier to LTG Sanchez or MG Wojadakowski. While this would not have prevented the
abuse they subsequently discovered (because it had taken place in November 2003),
it may have resulted in CID beginning an investigation a month earlier than they did.
During the ICRC's next visit to Abu Ghraib, during the period 4–8 January 2004, COL
Warren states they invoked Article 143 of the Fourth Geneva Conventions and did not
allow the ICRC to have private interviews with eight detainees who were undergoing
active interrogations. He did allow the ICRC delegate to see the detainees, observe the
conditions of their detention, and obtain their names and Internee Serial Numbers."
(Reference Annex B, Appendix 1, WARREN)

(12) (U) LTC Chew, Commander of the 115th MP Battalion (115 MP BN), has stated
that although he attended the ICRC out-brief, after the 21–23 October 2003 visits, he
never saw or heard of any detainees being stripped or held naked, nor did he ever see
a written report from the ICRC. He stated that a doctor with the ICRC team provided
information concerning a few detainees having psychological problems and stating
that they should be evaluated. ICRC also related charges of handcuffing, nakedness,
wearing of female underwear, and sleep deprivation. The ICRC also complained about
lack of access to certain detainees, and he discussed the matter with LTC Jordan. He
also discussed the allegations made by the ICRC with MAJ Potter, BG Karpinski, and
MAJ Cavallero. BG Karpinski does not recall hearing about the report until early
December 2003 when it was discussed at CJTF-7 Headquarters with COL Warren.
(Reference Annex B, Appendix 1, CHEW, KARPINSKI)

(13) (U) LTC Jordan has stated that after the ICRC visited Abu Ghraib, COL Pappas and
BG Karpinski received the final report, but that he did not see the report. When asked
by COL Pappas if he had ever seen or heard any rumors of abuse, LTC Jordan told COL
Pappas that he (LTC Jordan) had not. He was not aware of COL Pappas ever doing
anything concerning the ICRC allegations (Reference Annex B, Appendix 1, JORDAN
and Annex B, Appendix 2, JORDAN).

(14) (U) The only response to the ICRC was a letter signed by BG Karpinski, dated 24 December 2003. According to LTC Phillabaum and COL Warren (as quoted above) an Australian Judge Advocated officer, MAJ O'Kane, was the principal drafter of the letter. Attempts to interview MAJ O'Kane were unsuccessful. The Australian Government agreed to have MAJ O'Kane respond to written questions, but as of the time of this report, no response has been received. The section of the BG Karpinski letter pertaining to Abu Ghraib primarily addresses the denial of access to certain detainees by the ICRC. It tends to gloss over, close to the point of denying the inhumane treatment, humiliation, and abuse identified by the ICRC. The letter merely says: Improvement can be made for the provision of clothing, water, and personal hygiene items. (Reference Annex G, Appendix 3, KARPINSKI Letter)

5. SUMMARY OF ABUSES AT ABU GHRAIB

a. (U) Several types of detainee abuse were identified in this investigation: physical and sexual abuse; improper use of military working dogs; humiliating and degrading treatments; and improper use of isolation.

(1) (U) Physical Abuse. Several Soldiers reported that they witnessed physical abuse of detainees. Some examples include slapping, kicking, twisting the hands of a detainee who was handcuffed to cause pain, throwing balls at restrained internees, placing gloved hand over the nose and mouth of an internee to restrict breathing, "poking" at an internee's injured leg, and forcing an internee to stand while handcuffed in such a way as to dislocate his shoulder. These actions are clearly in violation of applicable laws and regulations.

(2) (U) Use of Dogs. The use of military working dogs in a confinement facility can be effective and permissible under AR 190-12 as a means of controlling the internee population. When dogs are used to threaten and terrify detainees, there is a clear violation of applicable laws and regulations. One such impermissible practice was an alleged contest between the two Army dog handlers to see who could make the internees urinate or defecate in the presence of the dogs. An incident of clearly abusive use of the dogs occurred when a dog was allowed in the cell of two male juveniles and allowed to go "nuts." Both juveniles were screaming and crying with the youngest and smallest trying to hide behind the other juvenile. (Reference Annex B, Appendix 1, SOLDIER-17)

(3) (U) Humiliating and Degrading Treatments. Actions that are intended to degrade or humiliate a detainee are prohibited by GC IV, Army policy and the UCMJ. The following are examples of such behavior that occurred at Abu Ghraib, which violate applicable laws and regulations.

(4) (U) Nakedness. Numerous statements, as well as the ICRC report, discuss the seemingly common practice of keeping detainees in a state of undress. A number of statements indicate that clothing was taken away as a punishment for either not cooperating with interrogators or with MPs. In addition, male internees were naked in the presence of female Soldiers. Many of the Soldiers who witnessed the nakedness

were told that this was an accepted practice. Under the circumstances, however, the nakedness was clearly degrading and humiliating.

(5) (U) Photographs. A multitude of photographs show detainees in various states of undress, often in degrading positions.

(6) (U) Simulated Sexual Positions. A number of Soldiers describe incidents where detainees were placed in simulated sexual positions with other internees. Many of these incidents were also photographed.

(7) (U) Improper Use of Isolation. There are some legitimate purposes for the segregation (or isolation) of detainees, specifically to prevent them from sharing interrogation tactics with other detainees or other sensitive information. Article 5 of Geneva Convention IV supports this position by stating that certain individuals can lose their rights of communication, but only when absolute military security requires. the use of isolation at Abu Ghraib was often done as punishment, either for a disciplinary infraction or for failure to cooperate with an interrogation. These are improper uses of isolation and depending on the circumstances amounted to violation of applicable laws and regulations. Isolation could properly be a sanction for a disciplinary infraction if applied through the proper process set out in AR 190-8 and the Geneva Conventions.

(8) (U) Failure to Safeguard Detainees. The Geneva Conventions and Army Regulations require that detainees be "protected against all acts of violence and threats thereof and against insults and public curiosity." Geneva Convention IV, Article 27 and AR 190-8, paragraph 5-1(a)(2). The duty to protect imposes an obligation on an individual who witnesses an abusive act to intervene and stop the abuse. Failure to do so may be a violation of applicable laws and regulations.

(9) (U) Failure to Report Detainee Abuse. The duty to report detainee abuse is closely tied to the duty to protect. The failure to report an abusive incident could result in additional abuse. Soldiers who witness these offenses have an obligation to report the violations under the provision of Article 92, UCMJ. Soldiers who are informed of such abuses also have a duty to report violations. Depending on their position and their assigned duties, the failure to report detainee abuse could support a charge of dereliction of duty, a violation of the UCMJ. Civilian contractors employed as interrogators and translators would also have a duty to report such offenses as they are also bound by the Geneva Conventions and are charged with protecting the internees.

(10) (U) Other traditional prison guard issues were far less clear. MPs are responsible for the clothing of detainees; however, MI interrogators started directing nakedness at Abu Ghraib as early as 16 September 2003, to humiliate and break down detainees. MPs would also sometimes discipline detainees by taking away clothing and putting detainees in cells naked. A severe shortage of clothing during the September, October, November 2003, time frame was frequently mentioned as the reason why people were naked. Removal of clothing and nakedness were being used to humiliate detainees at the same time there was a general level of confusion as to what was allowable in terms of MP disciplinary measures and MI interrogation rules, and what clothing was

available. This contributed to an environment that would appear to condone depravity and degradation rather than the humane treatment of detainees.

b. (U) The original intent by MI leadership (205 MI BDE) was for Tier 1A to be reserved for MI Holds only. In fact, CPT Wood states in an email dated 7 September 2003, during a visit from MG Miller and BG Karpinski, that BG Karpinski confirmed "we (MI) have all the iso (Isolation) cells in the wing we have been working. We only had 10 cells to begin with but that has grown to the entire wing." LTC Phillabaum also thought that MI had exclusive authority to house MI holds in Tier 1A. The fact is, however, that a number of those cells were often used by the MPs to house disciplinary problems. That fact is supported by the testimony of a large number of people who were there and further supported by the pictures and the detainee records. In fact, 11 of a total of 25 detainees identified by the CID as victims of abuse were not MI holds and were not being interrogated by MI. The MPs put the problem detainees (detainees who required separation from the general population for disciplinary reasons) in Tier 1A because there was no other place available to isolate them. Neither CPT Wood nor MAJ Williams appreciated the mixing because it did not allow for a pure MI environment, but the issue never made its way up to either LTC Phillabaum or to BG Karpinski.

c. (U) The "sleep adjustment" technique was used by MI as soon as the Tier 1A block opened. This was another source of confusion and misunderstanding between MPs and MI which contributed to an environment that allowed detainee abuse, as well as its perpetuation for as long as it continued. Sleep adjustment was brought with the 519 MI BN from Afghanistan. It is also a method used at GTMO. (See paragraph 3.b.(5)). At Abu Ghraib, however, the MPs were not trained, nor informed as to how they actually should do the sleep adjustment. The MPs were just told to keep a detainee awake for a time specified by the interrogator. The MPs used their own judgment as to how to keep them awake. Those techniques included taking the detainees out of their cells, stripping them and giving them cold showers. CPT Wood stated she did not know this was going on and thought the detainees were being kept awake by the MPs banging on the cell doors, yelling, and playing loud music. When one MI Soldier inquired about water being thrown on a naked detainee he was told that it was an MP discipline technique. Again, who was allowed to do what and how exactly they were to do it was totally unclear. Neither of the communities (MI and MP) knew what the other could and could not do. (Reference Annex B, Appendix 1, WOOD, JOYNER)

d. (U) This investigation found no evidence of confusion regarding actual physical abuse, such as hitting, kicking, slapping, punching, and foot stomping. Everyone we spoke to knew it was prohibited conduct except for one Soldier. (Reference Annex B, Appendix 1, SOLDIER-29). Physical discomfort from exposure to cold and heat or denial of food and water is not as clear-cut and can become physical or moral coercion at the extreme. Such abuse did occur at Abu Ghraib, such as detainees being left naked in their cells during severe cold weather without blankets. In Tier 1A some of the excesses regarding physical discomfort were being done as directed by MI and some were being done by MPs for reasons not related to interrogation. (See paragraph 5.e.-h.).

e. (U) The physical and sexual abuses of detainees at Abu Ghraib are by far the most serious. The abuses spanned from direct physical assault, such as delivering head blows rendering detainees unconscious, to sexual posing and forced participation in group masturbation. At the extremes were the death of a detainee in OGA custody, an alleged rape committed by a US translator and observed by a female Soldier, and the alleged sexual assault of an unknown female. They were perpetrated or witnessed by individuals or small groups. Such abuse can not be directly tied to a systemic US approach to torture or approved treatment of detainees. The MPs being investigated claim their actions came at the direction of MI. Although self-serving, these claims do have some basis in fact. The climate created at Abu Ghraib provided the opportunity for such abuse to occur and to continue undiscovered by higher authority for a long period of time. What started as undressing and humiliation, stress and physical training (PT), carried over into sexual and physical assaults by a small group of morally corrupt and unsupervised Soldiers and civilians. Twenty-four (24) serious incidents of physical and sexual abuse occurred from 20 September through 13 December 2003. The incidents identified in this investigation include some of the same abuses identified in the MG Taguba investigation; however, this investigation adds several previously unreported events. A direct comparison cannot be made of the abuses cited in the MG Taguba report and this one.

(1) (U) **Incident #1**. On 20 September 2003, two MI Soldiers beat and kicked a passive, cuffed detainee, suspected of involvement in the 20 September 2003, mortar attack on Abu Ghraib that killed two Soldiers. Two Iraqis (male and female) were detained and brought to Abu Ghraib immediately following the attack. MI and the MP Internal Reaction Force (IRF) were notified of the apprehension and dispatched teams to the entry control point to receive the detainees. Upon arrival, the IRF observed two MI Soldiers striking and yelling at the male detainee whom the subsequently "threw" into the back of a High-Mobility Multipurpose Wheeled Vehicle (HMMWV). 1LT Sutton, 320th MP BN IRF intervened to stop the abuse and was told by the MI Soldiers "we are the professionals; we know what we are doing." They refused 1LT Sutton's lawful order to identify themselves. 1LT Sutton and his IRF team (SGT Spiker, SFC Plude) immediately reported this incident, providing sworn statements to MAJ Dinenna, 320 MP BN S3 and LTC Phillabaum, 320 MP BN Commander. 1SG McBride, A/205 MI BN interviewed and took statements from SGT Lawson, identified as striking the detainee, and each MI person present: SSG Hannifan, SSG Cole, SGT Claus, SGT Presnell. While the MP statements all describe abuse at the hands of an unidentified MI person (SGT Lawson), the MI statements all deny any abuse occurred. LTC Phillabaum subsequently reported the incident to the CID who determined the allegation lacked sufficient basis for prosecution. The detainee was interrogated and released that day (involvement in the mortar attack was unlikely); therefore, no detainee is available to confirm either the MP or MI recollection of events. This incident was not further pursued based on limited data and the absence of additional investigative leads. (Reference Annex B, Appendix 1, DINENNA, LAWSON, MCBRIDE, PHILLABAUM, PLUDE, SPIKER, SUTTON; Annex B, Appendix 2, DINENNA, PHILLABAUM, PLUDE; Annex B, Appendix 3, PLUDE, SPIKER)

(2) (U) **Incident #2**. On 7 October 2003, three MI personnel allegedly sexually assaulted female DETAINEE-29. CIVILIAN-06 (Titan) was the assigned interpreter, but there is no indication he was present or involved. DETAINEE-29 alleges as follows:

First, the group took her out of her cell and escorted her down the cellblock to an empty cell. One unidentified Soldier stayed outside the cell (SOLDIER33, A/519 MI BN); while another held her hands behind her back, and the other forcibly kissed her (SOLDIER32, A/519 MI BN). She was escorted downstairs to another cell where she was shown a naked male detainee and told the same would happen to her if she did not cooperate. She was then taken back to her cell, forced to kneel and raise her arms while one of the Soldiers (SOLDIER31, A/519 MI BN) removed her shirt. She began to cry, and her shirt was given back as the Soldier cursed at her and said they would be back each night. CID conducted an investigation and SOLDIER33, SOLDIER32, and SOLDIER31 invoked their rights and refused to provide any statements. DETAINEE-29 identified the three Soldiers as SOLDIER33, SOLDIER32, and SOLDIER31 as the Soldiers who kissed her and removed her shirt. Checks with the 519 MI BN confirmed no interrogations were scheduled for that evening. No record exists of MI ever conducting an authorized interrogation of her. The CID investigation was closed. SOLDIER33, SOLDIER32, and SOLDIER31 each received non-judicial punishment, Field Grade Article 15's, from the Commander, 205 MI BDE, for failing to get authorization to interrogate DETAINEE-29. Additionally, COL Pappas removed them from interrogation operations. (Reference Annex B, Appendix 1, PAPPAS; Annex B, Appendix 2, PAPPAS; Annex B, Appendix 3, DETAINEE-29).

(3) **Incident #3**. On 25 October 2003, detainees DETAINEE-31, DETAINEE-30, and DETAINEE-27 were stripped of their clothing, handcuffed together nude, placed on the ground, and forced to lie on each other and simulate sex while photographs were taken. Six photographs depict this abuse. Results of the CID investigation indicate on several occasions over several days, detainees were assaulted, abused and forced to strip off their clothing and perform indecent acts on each other. DETAINEE-27 provided a sworn statement outlining these abuses. Those present and/or participating in the abuse were CPL Graner, 372 MP CO, SSG Frederick, 372 MP CO, SPC England, 372 MP CO, SPC Harman, 372 MP CO, SOLDIER34, 372 MP CO, CIVILIAN-17, Titan Corp., SOLDIER-24, B/325 MI BN, SOLDIER19, 325 MI BN, and SOLDIER10, 325 MI BN. SOLDIER-24 claimed he accompanied SOLDIER10 to the Hard Site the evening of 25 October 2003, to see what was being done to the three detainees suspected of raping a young male detainee. SOLDIER-10 appeared to have foreknowledge of the abuse, possibly from his friendship with SPC Harman, a 372 MP CO MP. SOLDIER-24 did not believe the abuse was directed by MI and these individuals were not interrogation subjects. PFC England, however, claimed "MI Soldiers instructed them (MPs) to rough them up." When SOLDIER-24 arrived the detainees were naked, being yelled at by an MP through a megaphone. The detainees were forced to crawl on their stomachs and were handcuffed together. SOLDIER-24 observed SOLDIER-10 join in the abuse with CPL Graner and SSG Frederick. All three made the detainees act as though they were having sex. He observed SOLDIER-19 dump water on the detainees from a cup and throw a foam football at them. SOLDIER-24 described what he saw to SOLDIER-25, B/321 MI BN, who reported the incident to SGT Joyner, 372 MP CO. SGT Joyner advised SOLDIER-25 he would notify his NCOIC and later told SOLDIER-25 "he had taken care of it." SOLDIER-25 stated that a few days later both she and SOLDIER24 told SOLDIER-22 of the incident. SOLDIER-22 subsequently failed to report what he

was told. SOLDIER-25 did not report the abuse through MI channels because she felt it was an MP matter and would be handled by them.

(U) This is a clear incident of direct MI personnel involvement in detainee abuse; however, it does not appear to be based on MI orders. The three detainees were incarcerated for criminal acts and were not of intelligence interest. This incident was most likely orchestrated by MP personnel (CPL Graner, SSG Frederick, SOLDIER34, SPC Harman, PFC England), with the MI personnel (SOLDIER-19, SOLDIER-10, and SOLDIER-24, CIVILIAN-17, and another unidentified interpreter) joining in and/or observing the abuse. (Reference Annex B, Appendix 1, JOYNER, SOLDIER-19, CIVILIAN-17, SOLDIER-25; Annex B, Appendix 3, SOLDIER34, ENG-LAND, HARMAN, DETAINEE-31, DETAINEE-30, DETAINEE-27; Annex I, Appendix 1, Photographs M36-41).

(4) (U) **Incident #4.** DETAINEE-08, arrived at Abu Ghraib on 27 October 2003, and was subsequently sent to the Hard Site. DETAINEE-08 claims when he was sent to the Hard Site, he was stripped of his clothing for six days. He was then given a blanket and remained with only the blanket for three more days. DETAINEE-08 stated the next evening he was transported by CPL Graner, 372 MP CO MP, to the shower room, which was commonly used for interrogations. When the interrogation ended, his female interrogator left, and DETAINEE-08 claims CPL Graner and another MP, who meets the description of SSG Fredrick, then threw pepper in DETAINEE-08's face and beat him for half an hour. DETAINEE-08 recalled being beaten with a chair until it broke, hit in the chest, kicked, and choked until he lost consciousness. On other occasions DETAINEE-08 recalled that CPL Graner would throw his food into the toilet and say "go take it and eat it." DETAINEE-08's claims of abuse do not involve his interrogator(s) and appear to have been committed by CPL Graner and SSG Frederick, both MPs. Reviewing the interrogation reports; however, suggests a correlation between this abuse and his interrogations. DETAINEE-08's interrogator for his first four interrogations was SOLDIER-29, a female, and almost certainly the interrogator he spoke of. Her analyst was SOLDIER-10. In the first interrogation report they concluded he was lying and recommended a "fear up" approach if he continued to lie. Following his second interrogation it was recommended DETAINEE-08 be moved to isolation (the Hard Site) as he continued "to be untruthful." Ten days later, a period roughly correlating with DETAINEE-08's claim of being without clothes and/or a blanket for nine days before his beating, was interrogated for a third time. The interrogation report references his placement in "the hole," a small lightless isolation closet, and the "Mutt and Jeff" interrogation technique being employed. Both techniques as they were used here were abusive and unauthorized. According to the report, the interrogators "let the MPs yell at him" and upon their return, "used a fear down," but "he was still holding back." The following day he was interrogated again and the report annotates "use a direct approach with a reminder of the unpleasantness that occurred the last time he lied." Comparing the interrogation reports with DETAINEE-08's recollections, it is likely the abuse he describes occurred between his third and forth interrogations and that his interrogators were aware of the abuse, the "unpleasantness." SGT Adams stated that SOLDIER-29 and SSG Frederick had a close personal relationship and it is plausible she had CPL Graner and SSG Frederick "soften up this detainee" as

they have claimed "MI" told them to do on several, unspecified, occasions (Reference Annex B, Appendix 1, ADAMS, SOLDIER-29; Annex B, Appendix 3, DETAINEE-08; Annex I, Appendix 4, DETAINEE-08).

(5) (U) **Incident #5**. In October 2003, DETAINEE-07, reported alleged multiple incidents of physical abuse while in Abu Ghraib. DETAINEE-07 was an MI Hold and considered of potentially high value. He was interrogated on 8, 21, and 29 October; 4 and 23 November and 5 December 2003. DETAINEE-07's claims of physical abuse (hitting) started on his first day of arrival. He was left naked in his cell for extended periods, cuffed in his cell in stressful positions ("High cuffed"), left with a bag over his head for extended periods, and denied bedding or blankets. DETAINEE-07 described being made to "bark like a dog, being forced to crawl on his stomach while MPs spit and urinated on him, and being struck causing unconsciousness." On another occasion DETAINEE-07 was tied to a window in his cell and forced to wear women's underwear on his head. On yet another occasion, DETAINEE-07 was forced to lie down while MPs jumped onto his back and legs. He was beaten with a broom and a chemical light was broken and poured over his body. DETAINEE-04 witnessed the abuse with the chem-light. During this abuse a police stick was used to sodomize DETAINEE-07 and two female MPs were hitting him, throwing a ball at his penis, and taking photographs. This investingation surfaced no photographic evidence of the chemical light abuse or sodomy. DETAINEE-07 also alleged that CIVILIAN-17, MP Interpreter, Titan Corp., hit DETAINEE-07 once, cutting his ear to an extent that required stitches. He told SOLDIER-25, analyst, B/321 MI BN, about this hitting incident during an interrogation. SOLDIER-25 asked the MPs what had happened to the detainee's ear and was told he had fallen in his cell. SOLDIER-25 did not report the detainee's abuse. SOLDIER-25 claimed the detainee's allegation was made in the presence of CIVILIAN-21, Analyst/Interrogator, CACI, which CIVILIAN-21 denied hearing this report. Two photos taken at 2200 hours, 1 November 2003, depict a detainee with stitches in his ear; however, we could not confirm the photo was DETAINEE-07. Based on the details provided by the detainee and the close correlation to other known MP abuses, it is highly probable DETAINEE-07's allegations are true. SOLDIER-25 failed to report the detainee's allegation of abuse. His statements and available photographs do not point to direct MI involvement. However, MI interest in this detainee, his placement in Tier 1A of the Hard Site, and initiation of the abuse once he arrived there, combine to create a circumstantial connection to MI (knowledge of or implicit tasking of the MPs to "set conditions") which are difficult to ignore. MI should have been aware of what was being done to this detainee based on the frequency of interrogations and high interest in his intelligence value. (Reference Annex B, Appendix 1, SOLDIER-25, CIVILIAN-21; Annex B, Appendix 3, DETAINEE-04, DETAINEE-07; Annex I, Appendix 1, Photographs M54-55).

(6) (U) **Incident #6**. DETAINEE-10 and DETAINEE-12 claimed that they and "four Iraqi Generals, were abused upon their arrival at the Hard Site. DETAINEE-10 was documented in MP records as receiving a 1.5 inch laceration on his chin, the result of his resisting an MP transfer. His injuries are likely those captured in several photographs of an unidentified detainee with a lacerated chin and bloody clothing which were taken on 14 November, a date coinciding with his transfer. DETAINEE-12

claimed he was slammed to the ground, punched, and forced to crawl naked to his cell with a sandbag over his head. These two detainees as well as the other four (DETAINEE-20, DETAINEE-19, DETAINEE-22, DETAINEE-21) were all high value Iraqi General Officers or senior members of the Iraqi Intelligence Service. MP logs from the Hard Site indicate they attempted to incite a riot in Camp Vigilant while being transferred to the Hard Site. There is no documentation of what occurred at Camp Vigilant or of detainees receiving injuries. When DETAINEE-10 was in-processed into the Hard Site, he was resisting and was pushed against the wall. At that point the MPs noticed blood coming from under his hood and they discovered the laceration on his chin. A medical corpsman was immediately called to suture the detainee's chin. These events are all documented, indicating the injury occurred before the detainee's arrival at the Hard Site and that he received prompt medical attention. When, where, and by whom this detainee suffered his injuries could not be determined nor could an evaluation be made of whether it constituted "reasonable force" in conjunctions with a riot. Our interest in this incident stems from MP logs concerning DETAINEE-10 indicating MI provided direction about his treatment. CPL Graner wrote an entry indicating he was told by SFC Joyner, who was in turn told by LTC Jordan, to "Strip them out and PT them." Whether "strip out" meant to remove clothing or to isolate we couldn't determine. Whether "PT them" meant physical stress or abuse can't be determined. The vagueness of this order could, however, have led to any subsequent abuse. The alleged abuse, injury, and harsh treatment correlating with the detainees' transfer to MI hold also suggest MI could have provided direction or MP could have been given the perception they should abuse or "soften up detainees," however, there is no clear proof. (Reference Annex B, Appendix 1, JORDAN, JOYNER; Annex C).

(7) (U) **Incident #7**. On 4 November 2003, a CIA detainee, DETAINEE-28 died in custody in Tier 1B. Allegedly, a Navy SEAL Team had captured him during a joint TF-121/CIA mission. DETAINEE-28 was suspected of having been involved in an attack against the ICRC and had numerous weapons with him at the time of his apprehension. He was reportedly resisting arrest, and a SEAL Team member butt-stroked him on the side of the head to suppress the threat he posed. CIA representatives brought DETAINEE-28 into Abu Ghriab sometime around 0430 to 0530 without notifying JIDC Operations, in accordance with a supposed verbal agreement with the CIA. While all the details of DETAINEE-28's death are still not known (CIA, DOJ, and CID have yet to complete and release the results of their investigations), SPC Stevanus, an MP on duty at the Hard Site at the time DETAINEE-28 was brought in, stated that two CIA representatives came in with DETAINEE-28 and he was placed in a shower room (in Tier 1B). About 30 to 45 minutes later, SPC Stevanus was summoned to the shower stall, and when he arrived, DETAINEE-28 appeared to be dead. SPC Stevanus removed the sandbag which was over DETAINEE-28's head and checked for the detainee's pulse. He found none. He uncuffed DETAINEE-28 called for medical assistance, and notified his chain of command. LTC Jordan stated that he was informed of the death shortly thereafter, at approximately 0715 hours. LTC Jordan arrived at the Hard Site and talked to CIVILIAN03, an Iraqi prison medical doctor, who informed him DETAINEE-28 was dead. LTC Jordan stated that DETAINEE-28 was in the Tier 1B shower stall, face down, handcuffed with his hands behind his back. LTC Jordan's version of the

handcuffs conflicts with SPC Stevanus' account that he uncuffed DETAINEE-28. This incident remains under CID and CIA investigation.

(U) A CIA represeentative identified only as "OHTER AGENCY EMPLOYEE-01" was present, along with several MPs and US medical staff. LTC Jordan recalled that it was "OTHER AGENCY EMPLOYEE-01" who uncuffed DETAINEE-28 and the body was turned over. LTC Jordan stated that he did not see any blood anywhere, except for a small spot where DETAINEE-28's head was touching the floor. LTC Jordan notified COL Pappas (205 MI BDE Commander), and "OTHER AGENCY EMPLOYEE-01" said he would notify "OTHER AGENCY EMPLOYEE-02" his CIA supervisor. Once "OTHER AGENCY EMPLOYEE-02" arrived, he stated he would call Washington, and also requested that DETAINEE-28's body be held in the Hard Site until the following day. The body was placed in a body bag, packed in ice, and stored in the shower area. CID was notified and the body was removed from Abu Ghraib the next day on a litter to make it appear as if DETAINEE-28 was only ill, thereby not drawing the attention of the Iraqi guards and detainees. The body was transported to the morgue at BIAP for an autopsy, which concluded that DETAINEE-28 died of a blood clot in the head, a likely result of injuries he sustained while resisting apprehension. There is no indication or accusations that MI personnel were involved in this incident except for the removal of the body. (Reference Annex B, Appendix 1, JORDAN, PAPPAS, PHILL-ABAUM, SNIDER, STEVANUS, THOMPSON; Annex I, Appendix 1, Photographs C5–21, D5–11, M65–69).

(8) (U) **Incident #8**. On 20 October 2003, DETAINEE-03, was allegedly stripped and physically abused for sharpening a toothbrush to make a shank (knife-like weapon). DETAINEE-03 claimed the toothbrush was not his. An MP log book entry by SSG Frederick, 372 MPs, directed DETAINEE-03 to be stripped in his cell for six days. DETAINEE-03 claimed he was told his clothing and mattress would be taken away as punishment. The next day he claims he was cuffed to his cell door for several hours. He claims he was taken to a closed room where he had cold water poured on him and his face was forced into someone's urine. DETAINEE-03 claimed he was then beaten with a broom and spat upon, and a female Soldier stood on his legs and pressed a broom against his anus. He described getting his clothes during the day from SGT Joyner and having them taken away each night by CPL Graner for the next three days. DETAINEE-03 was an MI Hold but was not interrogated between 16 September and 2 November 2003. It is plausible his interrogators would be unaware of the alleged abuse and DETAINEE-03 made no claim he informed them (Reference Annex B, Appednix 3, DETAINEE-03).

(9) (U) **Incident #9**. Three photographs taken on 25 October 2003, depicted PFC England, 372 MP CO, holding a leash which was wrapped around an unidentified detainee's neck. Present in the photograph is SPC Ambuhl who was standing to the side watching. PFC England claimed in her initial statement to CID that CPL Graner had placed the tie-down strap around the detainee's neck and then asked her to pose for the photograph. There is no indication of MI involvement or knowledge of this incident (Reference Annex E, CID Report and Reference Annex I, Appendix 1, Photographs M33-35).

(10) (U) **Incident #10**. Six Photographs of DETAINEE-15, depict him standing on a box with simulated electrical wires attached to his fingers and a hood over his head. These photographs were taken between 2145 and 2315 on 4 November 2003. DETAINEE-15 described a female making him stand on the box, telling him if he fell off he would be electrocuted, and a "tall black man" as putting the wires on his fingers and penis. From the CID investigation into abuse at Abu Ghraib it was determined SGT J. Davis, SPC Harman, CPL Graner, and SSG Frederick, 372 MP CO, were present during this abuse. DETAINEE-15 was not an MI Hold and it is unlikely MI had knowledge of this abuse (Reference Annex B, Appendix 3, DETAINEE-15; Annex I, Appendix 1, Photographs C1–2, D19–21, M64).

(11) (U) **Incident #11**. Twenty-nine photos taken between 2315 and 0024, on 7 and 8 November 2003, depict seven detainees (DETAINEE-17, DETAINEE-16, DETAINEE-24, DETAINEE-23, DETAINEE-26, DETAINEE-1, DETAINEE-18) who were physically abused, placed in a pile and forced to masturbate. Present in some of these photographs are CPL Graner and SPC Harman. The CID investigation into these abuses identified SSG Frederick, CPL Graner, SGT J. Davis, SPC Ambuhl, SPC Harman, SPC Sivits, and PFC England; all MPs, as involved in the abuses which occurred. There is no evidence to support MI personnel involvement in this incident. CID statements from PFC England, SGT J. Davis, SPC Sivits, SPC Wisdom, SPC Harman, DETAINEE-17, DETAINEE-01, and DETAINEE-16 detail that the detainees were stripped, pushed into a pile, and jumped on by SGT J. Davis, CPL Graner, and SSG Frederick. They were photographed at different times by SPC Harman, SPC Sivits, and SSG Frederick. The detainees were subsequently posed sexually, forced to masturbate, and "ridden like animals." CPL Graner knocked at least one detainee unconscious and SSG Frederick punched one so hard in the chest that he couldn't breathe and a medic was summoned. SSG Frederick initiated the masturbation and forced the detainees to hit each other. PFC England stated she observed SSG Frederick strike a detainee in the chest during these abuses. The detainee had difficulty breathing and a medic, SOLDIER-01, was summoned. SOLDIER-01 treated the detainee and while in the Hard Site observed the "human pyramid" of naked detainees with bags over their heads. SOLDIER-01 failed to report this abuse. These detainees were not MI Holds and MI involvement in this abuse has not been alleged nor is it likely. SOLDIER-29 reported seeing a screen saver for a computer in the Hard Site that depicted several naked detainees stacked in a "pyramid." She also once observed, unrelated to this incident, CPL Graner slap a detainee. She stated that she didn't report the picture of naked detainees to MI because she did not see it again and also did not report the slap because she didn't consider it abuse (Reference Annex B, Appendix 1, SOLDIER-29; Annex B, Appendix 3, DETAINEE-01, DETAINEE-17, DETAINEE-16, ENGLAND, DAVIS, HARMAN, SIVITS, WISDOM; Annex B, Appendix 3, TAB A, SOLDIER-01, and Annex I, Appendix 1, Photographs C24-42, D22-25, M73-77, M87).

(12) (U) **Incident #12**. A photograph taken circa 27 December 2003, depicts a naked DETAINEE-14, apparently shot with a shotgun in his buttocks. This photograph could not be tied to a specific incident, detainee, or allegation and MI involvement is indeterminate (Reference Annex I, Appendix 1, Photographs D37-38, H2, M111).

(13) (U) **Incident #13**. Three photographs taken on 29 November 2003, depict an unidentified detainee dressed only in his underwear, standing with each foot on a separate box, and bent over at the waist. This photograph could not be tied to a specific incident, detainee, or allegation and MI involvement is indeterminate. (Reference Annex I, Appendix 1, Photographs D37-38, M111)

(14) (U) **Incident #14**. An 18 November 2003 photograph depicts a detainee dressed in a shirt or blanket lying on the floor with a banana inserted into his anus. This as well as several others show the same detainee covered in feces, with his hands encased in sandbags, or tied in foam and between two stretchers. These are all identified as DETAINEE-25 and were determined by CID investigation to be self-inflicted incidents. Even so, these incidents constitute abuse; a detainee with a known mental condition should not have been provided the banana or photographed. The detainee has a severe mental problem and the restraints depicted in these photographs were allegedly used to prevent the detainee from sodomizing himself and assaulting himself and others with his bodily fluids. He was known for inserting various objects into his rectum and for consuming and throwing his urine and feces. MI had no association with this detainee (Reference Annex C; Annex E; Annex I, Appendix 1, Photographs, C22-23, D28-36, D39, M97-99, M105-110, M131-133).

(15) (U) **Incident #15**. On 26 or 27 November 2003, SOLDIER-15, 66 MI GP, observed CIVILIAN-11, a CACI contractor, interrogating an Iraqi policeman. During the interrogation, SSG Frederick, 372 MP CO, alternated between coming into the cell and standing next to the detainee and standing outside the cell. CIVILIAN-11 would ask the policeman a question stating that if he did not answer, he would bring SSG Frederick back into the cell. At one point, SSG Frederick put his hand over the policeman's nose, not allowing him to breathe for a few seconds. At another point SSG Frederick used a collapsible nightstick to push and possibly twist the policeman's arm, causing pain. When SSG Frederick walked out of the cell, he told SOLDIER-15 he knew ways to do this without leaving marks. SOLDIER-15 did not report the incident. The interpreter utilized for this interrogation was CIVILIAN-16. (Reference Annex B, Appendix 1, SOLDIER-15)

(16) (U) **Incident #16**. On an unknown date, SGT Hernandez, an analyst, observed CIVILIAN-05, a CACI contractor, grab a detainee from the back of a High-Mobility, Multipurpose, Wheeled Vehicle (HMMWV) and drop him on the ground. CIVILIAN-05 then dragged the detainee into an interrogation booth. The detainee was handcuffed the entire time. When the detainee tried to get up to his knees, CIVILIAN-05 would force him to fall. SGT Hernandez reported the incident to CID but did not report it in MI channels. (Reference Annex B, Appendix 1, HERNANDEZ)

(17) (U) **Incident #17**. A 30 November 2003, MP Log entry described an unidentified detainee found in a cell covered in blood. This detainee had assaulted CPL Graner, 372 MP CO, while they moved him to an isolation cell in Tier 1A. CPL Graner and CPL Kamauf, subdued the detainee, placed restraints on him and put him in an isolation cell. At approximately 0320 hours, 30 November 2003, after hearing banging on the isolation cell door, the cell was checked and the detainee was found in the cell standing by the door covered in blood. This detainee was not an MI Hold and there is no record

of MI association with this incident or detainee. (Reference Annex I, Appendix 1, Photographs M115–129, M134).

(18) (U) **Incident #18**. On approximately 12 or 13 December 2003, DETAINEE-06 claimed numerous abuse incidents against US Soldiers. DETAINEE-06 was a Syrian foreign fighter and self-proclaimed Jihadist who came to Iraq to kill Coalition troops. DETAINEE-06 stated the Soldiers supposedly retaliated against him when he returned to the Hard Site after being released from the hospital following a shooting incident in which he attempted to kill US Soldiers. DETAINEE-06 had a pistol smuggled into him by an Iraqi Policeman and used that pistol to try to kill US personnel working in the Hard Site on 24 November 2003. An MP returned fire and wounded DETAINEE-06. Once DETAINEE-06 ran out of ammunition, he surrendered and was transported to the hospital. DETAINEE-06 claimed CIVILIAN-21 visited him in the hospital and threatened him with terrible torture upon his return. DETAINEE-06 claimed that upon his return to the Hard Site, he was subjected to various threats and abuses which included Soldiers threatening to torture and kill him, being forced to eat pork and having liquor put in his mouth, having a "very hot" substance put in his nose and on his forehead, having the guards hit his "broken" leg several times with a solid plastic stick, being forced to "curse" his religion, being urinated on, being hung by handcuffs from the cell door for hours, being "smacked" on the back of the head, and "allowing dogs to try to bite" him. This claim was substantiated by medic, SOLDIER-20, who was called to treat a detainee (DETAINEE-06) who had been complaining of pain. When SOLDIER-20 arrived DETAINEE-06 was cuffed to the upper bunk so that he could not sit down and CPL Graner was poking at his wounded legs with an asp with DETAINEE-06 crying out in pain. SOLDIER-20 provided pain medication and departed. He returned the following day to find DETAINEE-06 again cuffed to the upper bunk and a few days later returned to find him cuffed to the cell door with a dislocated shoulder. SOLDIER-20 failed to either stop or report this abuse. DETAINEE-06 also claimed that prior to the shooting incident, which he described as when "I got shot with several bullets" without mentioning that he ever fired a shot, he was threatened "every one or two hours . . . with torture and punishment", was subjected to sleep deprivation by standing up "for hours and hours", and had a "black man" tell him he would rape DETAINEE-06 on two occasions. Although DETAINEE-06 stated that CPL Graner led "a number of Soldiers" into his cell, he also stated that he had never seen CPL Graner beat a prisoner. These claims are from a detainee who attempted to kill US service members. While it is likely some Soldiers treated DETAINEE-06 harshly upon his return to the Hard Site, DETAINEE-06'S accusations are potentially the exaggerations of a man who hated Americans. (Reference Annex B, Appendix 3, DETAINEE-06, SOLDIER-20).

(19) (U) **Incident #19**. SGT Adams, 470 MI GP, stated that sometime between 4 and 13 December 2003, several weeks after the shooting of "a detainee who had a pistol" (DETAINEE-06), she heard he was back from the hospital, and she went to check on him because he was one of the MI Holds she interrogated. She found DETAINEE-06 without clothes or blanket, his wounds were bleeding and he had a catheter on without a bag. The MPs told her they had no clothes for the detainee. SGT Adams ordered the MPs to get the detainee some clothes and went to the medical site to get the doctor on

duty. The doctor (Colonel) asked what SGT Adams wanted and was asked if he was aware the detainee still had a catheter on. The Colonel said he was, the Combat Army Surgical Hospital (CASH) had made a mistake, and he couldn't remove it because the CASH was responsible for it. SGT Adams told him this was unacceptable, he again refused to remove it and stated the detainee was due to go back to the CASH the following day. SGT Adams asked if he had ever heard of the Geneva Conventions, and the Colonel responded "Fine Sergeant, you do what you have to do, I am going back to bed."

(U) It is apparent from this incident that DETAINEE06 did not receive proper medical treatment, clothing or bedding. The "Colonel" has not been identified in this investigation, but efforts continue. LTC Akerson was chief of the medical team for "security holds" at Abu Ghraib from early October to late December 2003. He treated DETAINEE06 following his shooting and upon his return from the hospital. He did not recall such an incident or DETAINEE06 having a catheter. It is possible SGT Adams was taken to a different doctor that evening. She asked and was told the doctor was a Colonel, not a Lieutenant Colonel and is confident she can identify the Colonel from a photograph. LTC Akerson characterized the medical records as being exceptional at Abu Ghraib, however, the records found by this investigation were poor and in most cases non-existent. (Reference Annex B, Appendix 1, ADAMS, AKERSON; Annex B, Appendix 3, DETAINEE-06).

(20) (U) **Incident #20**. During the fall of 2003, a detainee stated that another detainee, named DETAINEE-09, was stripped, forced to stand on two boxes, had water poured on him and had his genitals hit with a glove. Additionally, the detainee was handcuffed to his cell door for a half day without food or water. The detainee making the statement did not recall the exact date or participants. Later, "Assad" was identified as DETAINEE-09, who stated that on 5 November 2003, he was stripped naked, beaten, and forced to crawl on the floor. He was forced to stand on a box and was hit in his genitals. The participants in this abuse could not be determined. MI involvement is indeterminate. (Reference Annex B, Appendix 3, DETAINEE-09; Annex I, Appendix 1, Photographs D37-38, M111)

(21) (U) **Incident #21**. Circa October 2003, CIVILIAN-17, an interpreter of the Titan Corporation, observed the following incident: CPL Graner, 372 MP CO, pushed a detainee, identified as one of the "three stooges" or "three wise men", into a wall, lacerating the detainee's chin. CIVILIAN-17 specifically stated the detainee was pushed into a wall and "busted his chin." A medic, SGT Wallin, stated he was summoned to stitch the detainee and treated a 2.5 inch laceration on the detainee's chin requiring 13 stitches. SGT Wallin did not know how the detainee was injured. Later that evening, CPL Graner took photos of the detainee. CPL Graner was identified in another incident where he stitched an injured detainee in the presence of medics. There is no indication of MI involvement, knowledge, or direction of this abuse. (Reference Annex B, Appendix 1, CIVILIAN-17; Annex B, Appendix 3, CIVILIAN-17, WALLIN, DETAINEE-02; Annex I, Appendix 1, Photographs M88-96).

(22) (U)**Incident #22**. On an unknown date, an interpreter named "CIVILIAN-01" allegedly raped a 15-18 year old male detainee according to DETAINEE-05.

heard screaming and climbed to the top of his cell door to see over a sheet covering the door of the cell where the abuse was occurring. DETAINEE-05 observed CIVILIAN-01, who was wearing a military uniform, raping the detainee. A female Soldier was taking pictures. DETAINEE-05 described CIVILIAN-01 as possibly Egyptian, "not skinny or short," and effeminate. The date and participants of this alleged rape could not be confirmed. No other reporting supports DETAINEE-05's allegation, nor have photographs of the rape surfaced. A review of all available records could not identify a translator by the name of CIVILIAN-01. DETAINEE-05's description of the interpreter partially matches CIVILIAN-17, Interpreter, Titan Corp. CIVILIAN-17 is a large man, believed by several witnesses to be homosexual, and of Egyptian extraction. CIVILIAN-17 functioned as an interpreter for a Tactical HUMINT Team at Abu Ghraib, but routinely provided translation for both MI and MP. CID has an open investigation into this allegation. (Reference Annex B, Appendix 3, DETAINEE-05)

(23) (U) **Incident #23**. On 24 November 2003, a US Army officer, CPT Brinson, MP, allegedly beat and kicked a detainee. This is one of three identified abuses associated with the 24 November shooting. A detainee obtained a pistol from Iraqi police guards, shot an MP and was subsequently shot and wounded. During a subsequent search of the Hard Site and interrogation of detainees, SGT Spiker, 229 MP CO, a member of the Abu Ghraib Internal Reaction Force (IRF), observed an Army Captain dragging an unidentified detainee in a choke hold, throwing him against a wall, and kicking him in the mid-section. SPC Polak, 229 MP CO, IRF was also present in the Hard Site and observed the same abuse involving two Soldiers and a detainee. The detainee was lying on his stomach with his hands cuffed behind his back and a bag over his head. One Soldier stood next to him with the barrel of a rifle pressed against the detainee's head. The other Soldier was kneeling next to the detainee punching him in the back with a closed fist. The Soldier then stood up and kicked the detainee several times. The Soldier inflicting the beating was described as a white male with close cropped blond hair. SPC Polak saw this Soldier a few days later in full uniform, identifying him as a Captain, but could not see his name. Both SPC Polak and SGT Spiker reported this abuse to their supervisors, SFC Plude and 1LT Sutton, 372 MP CO. Photos of company grade officers at Abu Ghraib during this time were obtained and shown to SPC Polak and SGT Spiker, who positively identified the "Captain" as CPT Brinson. This incident was investigated by CID and the assault was determined to be unfounded; a staged event to protect the fact the detainee was a cooperative MP Source. (Reference Annex B, Appendix 1, PLUDE, POLAK, SPIKER, SUTTON; Annex B, Appendix 3, PLUDE, SUTTON; Annex E, Appendix 5, CID Report of Investigation 0005-04-CID 149-83131)

(24) (U) **Incident #24**. A photograph created circa early December 2003 depicts an unidentified detainee being interrogated by CIVILIAN-11, CACI, Interrogator, and CIVILIAN-16, Titan, linguist. The detainee is squatting on a chair which is an unauthorized stress position. Having the detainee on a chair which is a potentially unsafe situation, and photographing the detainee are violations of the ICRP. (Reference Annex I, Appendix 2, Photograph "Stress Position").

f. (U) Incidents of Detainee Abuse Using Dogs. (U) Abusing detainees with dogs started almost immediately after the dogs arrived at Abu Ghraib on 20 November 2003. By that date, abuses of detainees was already occurring and the addition of dogs was just one more abuse device. Dog Teams were brought to Abu Ghraib as a result of recommendations from MG G. Miller's assessment team from JTF-GTMO. MG G. Miller recommended dogs as beneficial for detainee custody and control issues, especially in instances where there were large numbers of detainees and few guards to help reduce the risk of detainee demonstrations or acts of violence, as at Abu Ghraib. MG G. Miller never recommended, nor were dogs used for interrogations at GTMO. The dog teams were requested by COL Pappas, Commander, 205 MI BDE. COL Pappas never understood the intent as described by MG G. Miller. Interrogations at Abu Ghraib were also influenced by several documents that spoke of exploiting the Arab fear of dogs: a 24 January 2003 "CJTF 180 Interrogation Techniques," an 11 October 2002 JTF 170 "Counter-Resistance Strategies," and a 14 September 2003 CJTF-7 ICRP. Once the dogs arrived, there was controversy over who "owned" the dogs. It was ultimately decided that the dogs would be attached to the Internal Reaction Force (IRF). The use of dogs in interrogations to "fear up" detainees was generally unquestioned and stems in part from the interrogation techniques and counter-resistance policy distributed from CJTF 180, JTF 170 and CJTF-7. It is likely the confusion about using dogs partially stems from the initial request for dog teams by MI, not MPs, and their presence being associated with MG G. Miller's visit. Most military intelligence personnel believed that the use of dogs in interrogations was a "non-standard" technique which required approval, and most also believed that approval rested with COL Pappas. COL Pappas also believed, incorrectly, that he had such authority delegated to him from LTG Sanchez. COL Pappas's belief likely stemmed in part from the changing ICRP. The initial policy was published on 14 September 2003 and allowed the use of dogs subject to approval by LTG Sanchez. On 12 October 2003, these were amended to eliminate several techniques due to CENTCOM objections. After the 12 October 2003 amendment, the ICRP safeguards allowed that dogs present at interrogations were to be muzzled and under the control of a handler. COL Pappas did not recall how he got the authority to employ dogs; just that he had it. (Reference Annex B, Appendix 1, G. MILLER and PAPPAS, and Annex J, Appendix 3)

(U) SFC Plude stated the two Army dog teams never joined the Navy teams as part of the IRF and remained separate and under the direct control of MAJ Dinenna, S3, 320 MP BN. These teams were involved in all documented detainee abuse involving dogs; both MP and MI directed. The Navy dog teams were properly employed because of good training, excellent leadership, personal moral character, and professionalism exhibited by the Navy Dog Handlers, MA1 Kimbro, MA1 Clark, and MA2 Pankratz, and IRF personnel. The Army teams apparently agreed to be used in abusive situations by both MPs and MI in contravention to their doctrine, training, and values. In an atmosphere of permissiveness and absence of oversight or leadership the Army dog teams became involved in several incidents of abuse over the following weeks (Reference Annex B, Appendix 1, KIMBRO, PLUDE; Annex B, Appendix 2, PLUDE; Annex B, Appendix 3, PLUDE).

(1) (U) **Incident #25**. The first documented incident of abuse with dogs occurred on 24 November 2003, just four days after the dogs teams arrived. An Iraqi detainee was smuggled a pistol by an Iraqi Police Guard. While attempting to confiscate the weapon, an MP was shot and the detainee was subsequently shot and wounded. Following the shooting, LTC Jordan ordered several interrogators to the Hard Site to screen 11 Iraqi Police who were detained following the shooting. The situation at the Hard Site was described by many as "chaos," and no one really appeared to be in charge. The perception was that LTG Sanchez had removed all restrictions that night because of the situation; however, that was not true. No one is able to pin down how that perception was created. A Navy Dog Team entered the Hard Site and was instructed to search for additional weapons and explosives. The dogs searched the cells, no explosives were detected and the Navy Dog Team eventually completed their mission and left. Shortly thereafter, MA1 Kimbro, USN, was recalled when someone "needed" a dog. MA1 Kimbro went to the top floor of Tier 1B, rather than the MI Hold area of Tier 1A. As he and his dog approached a cell door, he heard yelling and screaming and his dog became agitated. Inside the cell were CIVILIAN-11 (CACI contract interrogator), a second unidentified male in civilian clothes who appeared to be an interrogator and CIVILIAN16 (female contract interpreter), all of whom were yelling at a detainee squatting in the back right corner. MA1 Kimbro's dog was barking a lot with all the yelling and commotion. The dog lunged and MA1 Kimbro struggled to regain control of it. At that point, one of the men said words to the effect "You see that dog there, if you don't tell me what I want to know, I'm gonna get that dog on you!" The three began to step out of the cell leaving the detainee inside and MA1 Kimbro backed-up to allow them to exit, but there was not much room on the tier. After they exited, the dog lunged and pulled MA1 Kimbro just inside the cell. He quickly regained control of his dog, and exited the cell. As CIVILIAN-11, CIVILIAN-16, and the other interrogator re-entered the cell, MA1 Kimbro's dog grabbed CIVILIAN-16's forearm in its mouth. It apparently did not bite through her clothes or skin and CIVILIAN-16 stated the dog did not bite her. Realizing he had not been called for an explosives search, MA1 Kimbro departed the area with his dog and as he got to the bottom of the tier stairs, he heard someone calling for the dog again, but he did not return. No record of this interrogation exists, as was the case for the interrogations of Iraqi Police in the hours and days following the shooting incident. The use of dogs in the manner directed by CIVILIAN-11 was clearly abusive and unauthorized (Reference Annex B, Appendix 1, SOLDIER-11, KIMBRO, PAPPAS, CIVILIAN-11; Annex B, Appendix 2, PAPPAS).

(U) Even with all the apparent confusion over roles, responsibilities and authorities, there were early indications that MP and MI personnel knew the use of dog teams in interrogations was abusive. Following this 24 November 2003, incident the three Navy dog teams concluded that some interrogators might attempt to misuse Navy Dogs to support their interrogations. For all subsequent requests they inquired what the specific purpose of the dog was and when told "for interrogation" they explained that Navy dogs were not intended for interrogations and the request would not be fulfilled. Over the next few weeks, the Navy dog teams received about eight similar calls, none of which were fulfilled. In the later part of December 2003, COL Pappas summoned MA1 Kimbro and wanted to know what the Navy dogs's capabilities were. MA1 Kimbro explained Navy dog capabilities and provided the Navy Dog Use SOP. COL Pappas never asked if they could be used in interrogations and following that meeting the Navy Dog teams received no additional requests to support interrogations.

(2) (U) **Incident #26**. On or about 8 January 2004, SOLDIER-17 was conducting an interrogation of a Baath Party General Officer in the shower area of Tier 1B of the Hard Site. Tier 1B was the area of the Hard Site dedicated to female and juvenile detainees. Although Tier 1B was not the normal location for interrogations, due to a space shortage in Tier 1A, SOLDIER-17 was using this area. SOLDIER-17 witnessed an MP guard and an MP Dog Handler, whom SOLDIER-17 later identified from photographs as SOLDIER27, enter Tier 1B with SOLDIER-27's black dog. The dog was on a leash, but was not muzzled. The MP guard and MP Dog Handler opened a cell in which two juveniles, one known as "Casper," were housed. SOLDIER-27 allowed the dog to enter the cell and "go nuts on the kids," barking at and scaring them. The juveniles were screaming and the smaller one tried to hide behind "Casper." SOLDIER-27 allowed the dog to get within about one foot of the juveniles. Afterward, SOLDIER-17 overheard SOLDIER-27 say that he had a competition with another handler (likely SOLDIER-08, the only other Army dog handler) to see if they could scare detainees to the point that they would defecate. He mentioned that they had already made some detainees urinate, so they appeared to be raising the competition. This incident has no direct MI involvement; however, SOLDIER-17 failed to properly report what he observed. He stated that he went to bed and forgot the incident until asked about misuse of dogs during this ivestigation (Reference Annex B, Appendix 1, SOLDIER-17).

(3) (U) **Incident #27**. On 12 December 2003, an MI Hold detainee named DETAINEE-11, was recommended by MI (SOLDIER-17) for an extended stay in the Hard Site because he appeared to be mentally unstable. He was bitten by a dog in the Hard Site, but at the time he was not undergoing an interrogation and no MI personnel were present. DETAINEE-11 told SOLDIER-17 that a dog had bitten him and SOLDIER-17 saw dog bite marks on DETAINEE-11's thigh. SOLDIER-08, who was the dog handler of the dog that bit DETAINEE-11, stated that in December 2003 his dog bit a detainee and he believed that MPs were the only personnel around when the incident occurred, but he declined to make further statements regarding this incident to either the MG Taguba inquiry or to this inquiry. SOLDIER-27, another Army dog handler, also stated that SOLDIER-08's dog had bitten someone, but did not provide further information. This incident was captured on digital photograph 0178/CG LAPS and appears to be the result of MP harassment and amusement, no MI involvement is suspected (Reference Annex B, Appendix 1,SOLDIER-17; Annex B, Appendix 2, SOLDIER-08, SMITH; Annex I, Appendix 1, Photographs, D45-54, M146-171).

(4) (U) **Incident #28**. In an apparent MI directed use of dogs in detainee abuse, circa 18 December 2003, a photograph depicts a Syrian detainee (DETAINEE-14) kneeling on the floor with his hands bound behind his back. DETAINEE-14 was a "high value" detainee who had arrived at Abu Ghraib in December 2003, from a Navy ship. DETAINEE-14 was suspected to be involved with al-Qaeda. Military Working Dog

Handler SOLDIER-27 is standing in front of DETAINEE-14 with his black dog a few feet from DETAINEE-14's face. The dog is leashed, but not muzzled. SGT Eckroth was DETAINEE-14's interrogator from 18 to 21 December 2003, and CIVILIAN-21, CACI contract interrogator, assumed the lead after SGT Eckroth departed Abu Ghraib on 22 December 2003. SGT Eckroth identified DETAINEE14 as his detainee when shown a photo of the incident. CIVILIAN-21 claimed to know nothing about this incident; however, in December 2003 he related to SSG Eckroth he was told by MPs that DETAINEE-14's bedding had been ripped apart by dogs. CIVILIAN-21 was characterized by SOLDIER-25 as having a close relationship with the MPs, and she was told by SGT Frederick about dogs being used when CIVILIAN-21 was there. It is highly plausible that CIVILIAN-21 used dogs without authorization and directed the abuse in this incident as well as others related to this detainee (Reference Annex B, Appendix 1, ECKROTH, SOLDIER25, CIVILIAN-21; Annex I, Appendix 1, Photographs Z1-6).

(5) (U) **Incident #29**. On or about 14-15 December 2003, dogs were used in an interrogation. SPC Aston, who was the Section Chief of the Special Projects team, stated that on 14 December, one of his interrogation teams requested the use of dogs for a detainee captured in conjunction with the capture of Saddam Hussein on 13 December 2003. SPC Aston verbally requested the use of dogs from COL Pappas, and COL Pappas stated that he would call higher to request permission. This is contrary to COL Pappas' statement that he was given authority to use dogs as long as they were muzzled. About one hour later, SPC Aston received approval. SPC Aston stated that he was standing to the side of the dog handler the entire time the dog was used in the interrogation. The dog never hurt anyone and was always muzzled, about five feet away from the detainee (Reference Annex B, Appendix 1, ASTON, PAPPAS).

(6) (U) **Incident #30**. On another occasion, SOLDIER-26, an MI Soldier assigned to the S2, 320 MP BN, was present during an interrogation of a detainee and was told the detainee was suspected to have al Qaeda affiliations. Dogs were requested and approved about three days later. SOLDIER-26 didn't know if the dog had to be muzzled or not, likely telling the dog handler to unmuzzle the dog, in contravention to CJTF-7 policy. The interrogators were CIVILIAN-20, CACI, and CIVILIAN-21 (CACI), SOLDIER-14, Operations Officer, ICE stated that CIVILIAN-21, used a dog during one of his interrogations and this is likely that occasion. According to SOLDIER-14, CIVILIAN-21 had the dog handler maintain control of the dog and did not make any threatening reference to the dog, but apparently "felt just the presence of the dog would be unsettling to the detainee." SOLDIER-14 did not know who approved the procedure, but was verbally notified by SOLDIER-23, who supposedly received the approval from COL Pappas. CIVILIAN-21 claimed he once requested to use dogs, but it was never approved. Based on the evidence, CIVILIAN-21 was deceitful in his statement (Reference Annex B, Appendix 1, SOLDIER-14, SOLDIER-26, CIVILIAN-21).

(7) (U) **Incident #31**. In a 14/15 December 2003 interrogation, military working dogs were used but were deemed ineffective because the detainee had little to no response to them. CIVILIAN-11, SOLDIER-05 and SOLDIER-12, all who participated in the interrogation, believed they had authority to use the dogs from COL Pappas or from

LTG Sanchez; however, no documentation was found showing CJTF7 approval to use dogs in interrogations. It is probable that approval was granted by COL Pappas without such authority. LTG Sanchez stated he never approved the use of dogs. (Reference Annex B, Appendix 1, CIVILIAN-11, SOLDIER-12, SOLDIER-14, PAPPAS, SOLDIER-23, CIVILIAN-21, SANCHEZ).

(8) (U) **Incident #32**. In yet another instance, SOLDIER-25, an interrogator, stated that when she and SOLDIER-15 were interrogating a female detainee in the Hard Site, they heard a dog barking. The female detainee was frightened by dogs, and SOLDIER-25 and SOLDIER-15 returned her to her cell. SOLDIER-25 went to see what was happening with the dog barking and saw a detainee in his underwear on a mattress on the floor of Tier 1A with a dog standing over him. CIVILIAN-21 was upstairs giving directions to SSG Fredrick (372 MP Co), telling him to "take him back home." SOLDIER-25 opined it was "common knowledge that CIVILIAN-21 used dogs while he was on special projects, working directly for COL Pappas after the capture of Saddam on 13 December 2003." SOLDIER25 could not identify anyone else specifically who knew of this "common knowledge." It appeared CIVILIAN-21 was encouraging and even directing the MP abuse with dogs; likely a "softening up" technique for future interrogations. The detainee was one of CIVILIAN-21's. SOLDIER-25 did not see an interpreter in the area, so it is unlikely that CIVILIAN-21 was actually doing an interrogation.

(9) (U) SOLDIER-25 stated that SSG Frederick would come into her office every other day or so and tell her about dogs being used while CIVILIAN-21 was present. SSG Fredrick and other MPs used to refer to "doggy dance" sessions. SOLDIER-25 did not specify what "doggy dance" was (Reference Annex B, Appendix 1, SOLDIER-25), but the obvious implication is that it referred to an unauthorized use of dogs to intimidate detainees.

g. (U) Incidents of Detainee Abuse Using Humiliation. Removal of clothing was not a technique developed at Abu Ghraib, but rather a technique which was imported and can be traced through Afghanistan and GTMO. The 1987 version of FM 34-52, Interrogation, talked about "controlling all aspects of the interrogation to include . . . clothing given to the source," while the current 1992 version does not. The 1987 version was, however, cited as the primary reference for CJTF-7 in Iraq, even as late as 9 June 2004. The removal of clothing for both MI and MP objectives was authorized, approved, and employed in Afghanistan and GTMO. At GTMO, the JTF 170 "Counter-Resistance Strategy," documented on 11 October 2002, permitted the removal of clothing, approved by the interrogation officer-in-charge, as an incentive in detention operations and interrogations. The SECDEF granted this authority on 2 December 2002, but it was rescinded six weeks later in January 2003. This technique also surfaced in Afghanistan. The CJTF-180 "Interrogation Techniques," documented on 24 January 2003, highlighted that deprivation of clothing had not historically been included in battlefield interrogations. However, it went on to recommend clothing removal as an effective technique that could potentially raise objections as being degrading or inhumane, but for which no specific written legal prohibition existed. As interrogation operations in Iraq began to take form, it was often the same personnel who had operated and deployed in other theaters and in support of GWOT, who were called upon to establish and conduct interrogation operations in Abu Ghraib. The lines of authority and the prior legal opinions blurred. Soldiers simply carried forward the use of nudity into the Iraqi theater of operations.

(U) Removal of clothing is not a doctrinal or authorized interrogation technique but appears to have been directed and employed at various levels within MI as an "ego down" technique. It was also employed by MPs as a "control" mechanism. Individual observation and/or understanding of the use and approval of clothing removal varied in each interview conducted by this investigation. LTC Jordan was knowledgeable of naked detainees and removal of their clothing. He denied ordering it and blamed it on the MPs. CPT Wood and SOLDIER-14 claimed not to have observed nudity or approved clothing removal. Multiple MPs, interrogators, analysts, and interpreters observed nudity and/or employed clothing removal as an incentive, while an equal number didn't. It is apparent from this investigation that removal of clothing was employed routinely and with the belief it was not abuse. SOLDIER-03, GTMO Tiger Team believed that clothing as an "ego down" technique could be employed. He thought, mistakenly, that GTMO still had that authority. Nudity of detainees throughout the Hard Site was common enough that even during an ICRC visit they noted several detainees without clothing, and CPT Reese, 372 MP CO, stated upon his initial arrival at Abu Ghraib, "There's a lot of nude people here." Some of the nudity was attributed to a lack of clothing and uniforms for the detainees; however, even in these cases we could not determine what happened to the detainee's original clothing. It was routine practice to strip search detainees before their movement to the Hard Site. The use of clothing as an incentive (nudity) is significant in that it likely contributed to an escalating "de-humanization" of the detainees and set the stage for additional and more severe abuses to occur (Reference Annex I, Appendix I, Photographs D42-43, M5-7, M17-18, M21, M137-141).

(1) (U) **Incident #33**. There is also ample evidence of detainees being forced to wear women's underwear, sometimes on their heads. These cases appear to be a form of humiliation, either for MP control or MI "ego down." DETAINEE-07 and DETAINEE-05 both claimed they were stripped of their clothing and forced to wear women's underwear on their heads. CIVILIAN-15 (CACI) and CIVILIAN-19 (CACI), a CJTF-7 analyst, alleged CIVILIAN-21 bragged and laughed about shaving a detainee and forcing him to wear red women's underwear. Several photographs include unidentified detainees with underwear on their heads. Such photos show abuse and constitute sexual humiliation of detainees (Reference Annex B, Appendix 1, SOLDIER-03, SOLDIER-14, JORDAN, REESE, CIVILIAN-21, WOOD; Annex B, Appendix 3, DETAINEE-05,CIVILIAN-15, CIVILIAN-19, DETAINEE-07; Annex C; Annex G; Annex I, Appendix 1, photographs D12, D14, M11-16).

(2) (U) **Incident #34**. On 16 September 2003, MI directed the removal of a detainee's clothing. This is the earliest incident we identified at Abu Ghraib. An MP log indicated a detainee "was stripped down per MI and he is neked (sic) and standing tall in his cell." The following day his interrogators, SPC Webster and SSG Clinscales, arrived at the detainee's cell, and he was unclothed. They were both surprised. An MP asked SSG

Clinscales, a female, to stand to the side while the detainee dressed and the detainee appeared to have his clothing in his cell. SSG Clinscales was told by the MP the detainee had voluntarily removed his clothing as a protest and, in the subsequent interrogation, the detainee did not claim any abuse or the forcible removal of his clothing. It does not appear the detainee was stripped at the interrogator's direction, but someone in MI most likely directed it. SPC Webster and SOLDIER-25 provided statements where they opined SPC Claus, in charge of in-processing MI Holds, may have directed removal of detainee clothing on this and other occasions. SPC Claus denies ever giving such orders (Reference Annex B, Appendix 1, CLAUS, CLINSCALES, SOLDIER-25, WEBSTER).

(3) (U) **Incident #35**. On 19 September 2003, an interrogation "Tiger Team" consisting of SOLDIER-16, SOLDIER-07, and a civilian contract interpreter identified only as "Maher" (female), conducted a late night/early morning interrogation of a 17-year old Syrian foreign fighter. SOLDIER-16 was the lead interrogator. SOLDIER-07 was told by SOLDIER-16 that the detainee they were about to interrogate was naked. SOLDIER-07 was unsure if SOLDIER-16 was simply passing along that fact or had directed the MPs to strip the detainee. The detainee had fashioned an empty "Meals-Ready-to-Eat" (MRE) bag to cover his genital area. SOLDIER-07 couldn't recall who ordered the detainee to raise his hands to his sides, but when he did, the bag fell to the floor exposing him to SOLDIER-07 and the two female interrogation team members. SOLDIER-16 used a direct interrogation approach with the incentive of getting back clothing, and the use of stress positions.

(U) There is no record of an Interrogation Plan or any approval documents which would authorize these techniques. The fact these techniques were documented in the Interrogation Report suggests, however, that the interrogators believed they had the authority to use clothing as an incentive, as well as stress positions, and were not attempting to hide their use. Stress positions were permissible with Commander, CJTF-7 approval at that time. It is probable that use of nudity was sanctioned at some level within the chain-of-command. If not, lack of leadership and oversight permitted the nudity to occur. Having a detainee raise his hands to expose himself in front of two females is humiliation and therefore violates the Geneva Conventions (Reference Annex B, Appendix 1, SOLDIER-07, SOLDIER-14, SOLDIER-16, SOLDIER-24, WOOD).

(4) (U) **Incident #36**. In early October 2003, SOLDIER-19 was conducting an interrogation and ordered a detainee to roll his orange jumpsuit down to his waist, insinuating to the detainee that he would be further stripped if he did not cooperate. SOLDIER-19's interpreter put up his hand, looked away, said that he was not comfortable with the situation, and exited the interrogation booth. SOLDIER-19 was then forced to stop the interrogation due to lack of language support. SOLDIER-11, an analyst from a visiting JTF GTMO Tiger Team, witnessed this incident through the booth's observation window and brought it to the attention of SOLDIER-16, who was SOLDIER-19's Team Chief and first line supervisor. SOLDIER-16 responded that SOLDIER-19 knew what he was doing and did not take any action regarding the matter. SOLDIER-11 reported the same information to SOLDIER-28, his JTF GTMO Tiger Team Chief,

who, according to SOLDIER-11, said he would "take care of it." SOLDIER-28 recalled a conversation with SOLDIER-11 concerning an interpreter walking out of an interrogation due to a "cultural difference," but could not remember the incident. This incident has four abuse components: the actual unauthorized stripping of a detainee by SOLDIER-19, the failure of SOLDIER-10 to report the incident he witnessed, the failure of SOLDIER-16 to take corrective action, reporting the incident up the chain of command, and the failure of SOLDIER-28 to report. (Reference Annex B, Appendix 1, SOLDIER-11, SOLDIER-16, SOLDIER-19, SOLDIER-28)

(5) (U) **Incident #37**. A photograph taken on 17 October 2003, depicts a naked detainee chained to his cell door with a hood on his head. Several other photographs taken on 18 October 2003, depict a hooded detainee cuffed to his cell door. Additional photographs on 19 October 2003, depict a detainee cuffed to his bed with underwear on his head. A review of available documents could not tie these photos to a specific incident, detainee or allegation, but these photos reinforce the reality that humiliation and nudity were being employed routinely enough that photo opportunities occurred on three successive days. MI involvement in these apparent abuses cannot be confirmed. (Reference Annex I, Appendix 1, Photographs D12, D14, D42-44, M5-7, M17-18, M21, M11-16, M137-141)

(6) (U) **Incident #38**. Eleven photographs of two female detainees arrested for suspected prostitution were obtained. Identified in these photographs are SPC Harman and CPL Graner, both MPs. In some of these photos, a criminal detainee housed in the Hard Site was shown lifting her shirt with both her breasts exposed. There is no evidence to confirm if these acts were consensual or coerced; however in either case sexual exploitation of a person in US custody constitutes abuse. There does not appear to be any direct MI involvement in either of the two incidents above. (Reference Annex I, Appendix 1, Photographs M42-52)

(7) (U) **Incident #39**. On 16 November 2003, SOLDIER-29 decided to strip a detainee in response to what she believed was uncooperative and physically recalcitrant behavior. She had submitted an Interrogation Plan in which she planned to use the "Pride and Ego Down," technique but did not specify that she would strip the detainee as part of that approach. SOLDIER-29 felt the detainee was "arrogant," and when she and her analyst, SOLDIER-10, "placed him against the wall" the detainee pushed SOLDIER-10. SOLDIER-29 warned if he touched SOLDIER-10 again, she would have him remove his shoes. A bizarre tit-for-tat scenario then ensued where SOLDIER-29 would warn the detainee about touching SOLDIER-10, the detainee would "touch" SOLDIER-10, and then had his shirt, blanket, and finally his pants removed. At this point, SOLDIER-29 concluded that the detainee was "completely uncooperative" and terminated the interrogation. While nudity seemed to be acceptable, SOLDIER-29 went further than most when she walked the semi-naked detainee across the camp. SGT Adams, SOLDIER-29's supervisor, commented that walking a semi-naked detainee across the camp could have caused a riot. CIVILIAN-21, a CACI contract interrogator, witnessed SOLDIER-29 and SOLDIER-10 escorting the scantily clad detainee from the Hard Site back to Camp Vigilant, wearing only his underwear

and carrying his blanket. CIVILIAN-21 notified SGT Adams, who was SOLDIER-29's section chief, who in turn notified CPT Wood, the ICE OIC. SGT Adams immediately called SOLDIER-29 and SOLDIER-10 into her office, counseled them, and removed them from interrogation duties.

(U) The incident was relatively well known among JIDC personnel and appeared in several statements as second-hand information when interviewees were asked if they knew of detainee abuse. LTC Jordan temporarily removed SOLDIER-29 and SOLDIER-10 from interrogation duties. COL Pappas left the issue for LTC Jordan to handle. COL Pappas should have taken sterner action such as an Article 15, UCMJ. His failure to do so did not send a strong enough message to the rest of the JIDC that abuse would not be tolerated. CPT Wood had recommended to LTC Jordan that SOLDIER-29 receive an Article 15 and SFC Johnson, the interrogation NCOIC, recommended she be turned over to her parent unit for the non-compliance. (Reference Annex B, Appendix 1, ADAMS, CIVILIAN-04, JORDAN, PAPPAS, SOLDIER-29, CIVILIAN-21, WOOD; Annex B, Appendix 2, JORDAN).

(8) (U) **Incident #40**. On 24 November 2003, there was a shooting of a detainee at Abu Ghraib in Tier 1A. DETAINEE-06, had obtained a pistol. While the MPs attempted to confiscate the weapon, an MP and DETAINEE-06 were shot. It was alleged that an Iraqi Police Guard had smuggled the pistol to DETAINEE-06 and in the aftermath of the shooting 43 Iraqi Police were screened and 11 subsequently detained and interrogated. All but three were released following intense questioning. A fourth did not report for work the next day and is still at large. The Iraqi guard detainees admitted smuggling the weapons into the facility hiding them in an inner tube of a tire and several of the Iraqi guards were identified as Fedayeen trainers and members. During the interrogations of the Iraqi Police, harsh and unauthorized techniques were employed to include the use of dogs, discussed earlier in this report, and removal of clothing (See paragraph 5.e(18), above). Once detained, the police were strip-searched, which was a reasonable precaution considering the threat of contraband or weapons. Following such search, however, the police were not returned their clothes before being interrogated. This is an act of humiliation and was unauthorized. It was the general understanding that evening that LTG Sanchez and COL Pappas had authorized all measures to identify those involved, however, that should not have been construed to include abuse. LTC Jordan was the senior officer present at the interrogations and is responsible for the harsh and humiliating treatment of the police (Reference Annex B, Appendix 1, JORDAN, PAPPAS; Annex B, Appendix 2, JORDAN, PAPPAS, Annex B, Appendix 1, DETAINEE-06).

(9) (U) **Incident #41**. On 4 December 2003, documentation in the MP Logs indicated that MI leadership was aware of clothing removal. An entry indicated "Spoke with LTC Jordan (205 MI BDE) about MI holds in Tier 1A/B. He stated he would clear up with MI and let MPs run Tiers 1A/B as far as what inmate gets (clothes)." Additionally, in his statement, LTC Phillabaum claims he asked LTC Jordan what the situation was with naked detainees, and LTC Jordan responded with, "It was an interrogation technique." Whether this supports allegations of MI involvement in the clothing and stripping of detainees is uncertain, but it does show that MI at least knew of the practice and was

willing to defer decisions to the MPs. Such vague guidance, if later combined with an implied tasking from MI, or perceived tasking by MP, potentially contributed to the subsequent abuse (Reference Annex B, Appendix 2, PHILLABAUM).

h. (U) Incidents of Detainee Abuse Using Isolation. Isolation is a valid interrogation technique which required approval by the CJTF-7 Commander. We identified documentation of four instances where isolation was approved by LTG Sanchez. LTG Sanchez stated he had approved 25 instances of isolation. This investigation, however, found numerous incidents of chronic confusion by both MI and MPs at all levels of command, up through CJTF-7, between the definitions of "isolation" and "segregation." Since these terms were commonly interchanged, we conclude Segregation was used far more often than Isolation. Segregation is a valid procedure to limit collaboration between detainees. This is what was employed most often in Tier 1A (putting a detainee in a cell by himself vice in a communal cell as was common outside the Hard Site) and was sometimes incorrectly referred to as "isolation." Tier 1A did have isolation cells with solid doors which could be closed as well as a small room (closet) which was referred to as the isolation "Hole." Use of these rooms should have been closely controlled and monitored by MI and MP leaders. They were not, however, which subjected the detainees to excessive cold in the winter and heat in the summer. There was obviously poor air quality, no monitoring of time limits, no frequent checks on the physical condition of the detainee, and no medical screening, all of which added up to detainee abuse. A review of interrogation reports identified 10 references to "putting people in the Hole," "taking them out of the Hole," or consideration of isolation. These occurred between 15 September 2003 and 3 January 2004. (Reference Annex B, Appendix 1, SANCHEZ)

(1) (U) **Incident #42**. On 15 September 2003, at 2150 hours, unidentified MI personnel, using the initials CKD, directed the use of isolation on a unidentified detainee. The detainee in cell #9 was directed to leave his outer cell door open for ventilation and was directed to be taken off the light schedule. The identification of CKD, the MI personnel, or the detainee could not be determined. This information originated from the prison log entry and confirms the use of isolation and sensory deprivation as interrogation techniques. (Reference MP Hard Site log book entry, 15 September 2003).

(2) (U) **Incident #43**. In early October 2003, SOLDIER-11 was interrogating an unidentified detainee with SOLDIER-19, an interrogator, and an unidentified contract interpreter. About an hour and 45 minutes into the interrogation, SOLDIER-19 turned to SOLDIER-11 and asked if he thought they should place the detainee in solitary confinement for a few hours, apparently because the detainee was not cooperating or answering questions. SOLDIER-11 expressed his misgivings about the tactic, but deferred to SOLDIER-19 as the interrogator. About 15 minutes later, SOLDIER-19 stopped the interrogation, departed the booth, and returned about five minutes later with an MP, SSG Frederick. SSG Frederick jammed a bag over the detainee's head, grabbed the handcuffs restraining him and said something like "come with me piggy", as he led the detainee to solitary confinement in the Hard Site, Tier 1A of Abu Ghraib.

(U) About half an hour later, SOLDIER-19 and SOLDIER-11 went to the Hard Site without their interpreter, although he was available, if needed. When they arrived at the detainee's cell, they found him lying on the floor, completely naked except for a hood that covered his head from his upper lip, whimpering, but there were no bruises or marks on him. SSG Frederick then met SOLDIER-19 and SOLDIER-11 at the cell door. He started yelling at the detainee, "You've been moving little piggy, you know you shouldn't move", or words to that effect, and yanked the hood back down over the detainee's head. SOLDIER-19 and SOLDIER-11 instructed other MPs to clothe the detainee, which they did. SOLDIER-11 then asked SOLDIER-19 if he knew the MPs were going to strip the detainee, and SOLDIER-19 said that he did not. After the detainee was clothed, both SOLDIER-19 and SOLDIER-11 escorted him to the general population and released him without interrogating him again. SSG Frederick made the statement "I want to thank you guys, because up until a week or two ago, I was a good Christian." SOLDIER-11 is uncertain under what context SSG Frederick made this statement. SOLDIER-11 noted that neither the isolation technique, nor the "striping incident" in the cell, was in any "interrogator notes" or "interrogation plan."

(U) More than likely, SOLDIER-19 knew what SSG Frederick was going to do. Given that the order for isolation appeared to be a spontaneous reaction to the detainee's recalcitrance and not part of an orchestrated Interrogation Plan; that the "isolation" lasted only approximately half an hour; that SOLDIER-19 chose to re-contact the detainee without an interpreter present; and that SOLDIER-19 was present with SSG Frederick at another incident of detainee abuse; it is possible that SOLDIER-19 had a prearranged agreement with SSG Frederick to "soften up" uncooperative detainees and directed SSG Frederick to strip the detainee in isolation as punishment for being uncooperative, thus providing the detainee an incentive to cooperate during the next interrogation. We believe at a minimum, SOLDIER-19 knew or at least suspected this type of treatment would take place even without specific instructions (Reference Annex B, Appendix 1,SOLDIER-11, SOLDIER-19, PAPPAS, SOLDIER-28).

(3) (U) **Incident(s) #44**. On 13 November 2003, SOLDIER-29 and SOLDIER-10, MI interrogators, noted that a detainee was unhappy with his stay in isolation and visits to the hole.

(U) On 11, 13, and 14 November 2003, MI interrogators SOLDIER-04, SOLDIER-09, SOLDIER-02, and SOLDIER-23 noted that a detainee was "walked and put in the Hole," "pulled out of extreme segregation," "did not seem to be bothered to return to the Hole," "Kept in the Hole for a long time unless he started to talk," and "was in good spirits even after three days in the Hole." (Reference Annex I, Appendix 3, Photo of "the Hole").

(U) A 5 November 2003 interrogation report indicates in the recommendations/future approaches paragraph: "Detainee has been recommended for the hole in ISO. Detainee should be treated harshly because friendly treatment has not been productive and because COL Pappas wants fast resolution, or he will turn the detainee over to someone other than the 205th [MI]."

(U) On 12 November 2003, MI interrogators SOLDIER-18 and SOLDIER13 noted that a detainee "feared the isolation Hole, and it made him upset, but not enough to break."

(U) On 29 November 2003, MI interrogators SOLDIER-18 and SOLDIER-06 told a detainee that "he would go into the Hole if he didn't start cooperating."

(U) On 8 December 2003, unidentified interrogators told a detainee that he was "recommended for movement to ISO and the Hole - he was told his sun [sunlight] would be taken away, so he better enjoy it now."

(U) These incidents all indicate the routine and repetitive use of total isolation and light deprivation. Documentation of this technique in the interrogation reports implies those employing it thought it was authorized. The manner it was applied is a violation of the Geneva Conventions, CJTF-7 policy, and Army policy (Reference Annex M, Appendix 2, AR 190-8). Isolation was being employed without proper approval and with little oversight, resulting in abuse (Reference Annex I, Appendix 4, DETAINEE-08).

i. (U) Several alleged abuses were investigated and found to be unsubstantiated. Others turned out to be no more than general rumor or fabrication. This investigation established a threshold below which information on alleged or potential abuse was not included in this report. Fragmentary or difficult to understand allegations or information at times defied our ability to investigate further. One such example is contained in a statement from an alleged abuse victim, DETAINEE-13, who claimed he was always treated well at Abu Ghraib but was abused earlier by his captors. He potentially contradicts that claim by stating his head was hit into a wall. The detainee appears confused concerning the times and locations at which he was abused. Several incidents involved numerous victims and/or occurred during a single "event," such as the Iraqi Police Interrogations on 24 November 2003. One example receiving some visibility was a report by SOLDIER-22 who overheard a conversation in the "chow hall" between SPC Mitchell and his unidentified "friends." SPC Mitchell was alleged to have said: "MPs were using detainees as practice dummies. They would hit the detainees as practice shots. They would apply strikes to their necks and knock them out. One detainee was so scared; the MPs held his head and told him everything would be alright, and then they would strike him. The detainees would plead for mercy and the MPs thought it was all funny." SPC Mitchell was interviewed and denied having knowledge of any abuse. He admitted that he and his friends would joke about noises they heard in the Hard Site and say things such as "the MPs are doing their thing." SPC Mitchell never thought anyone would take him seriously. Several associates of SPC Mitchell were interviewed (SPC Griffin, SOLDIER-12, PVT Heidenreich). All claimed their discussions with SPC Mitchell were just rumor, and they didn't think anyone would take him seriously or construe he had personal knowledge of abuse. SPC Mitchell's duties also make it unlikely he would have witnessed any abuse. He arrived at Abu Ghraib as an analyst, working the day shift, in late November 2003. Shortly after his arrival, the 24 November "shooting incident" occurred and the following day, he was moved to Camp Victory for three weeks. Upon his return, he was transferred to guard duty at Camp Wood and Camp Steel and never returned to the Hard Site. This alleged abuse is likely an individual's boastful exaggeration of a rumor which was rampant throughout Abu Ghraib, nothing more (Reference Annex B, Appendix 1, SOLDIER-12, GRIFFIN, HEIDENREICH, MITCHELL, SOLDIER-22).

Allegations of Abuse Incidents, the Nature of Reported Abuse, and Associated Personnel

Note: The chart lists all allegations considered. The specific abuse claimed and entities involved are not confirmed in all cases. The category of abuse are underlined. (See paragraph 5e-h, above)

Date/Time	Incident	Nature of Alleged Abuse						Comments
		Nudity/ Humiliation	Assault	Sexual Assault	Use of Dogs	The "Hole"	Other	
15 SEP 03/2150	Use of Isolation. Incident #42.					MI/MP		MP log entry confirms MI use of isolation and sensory deprivation as an interrogation technique
16 SEP 03/1315–1445	MI Directs Removal of Clothing. Incident #34.	MI/MP						MPs respond to MI tasking. Detainee apparently stripped upon arrival to Hard Site at MI direction.
19–20 SEP 03	Naked Detainee During Interrogation. Incident #35.	MI/MP						
20 SEP 03	Two MI Soldiers Beat and Kicked a Cuffed Detainee. Incident #1.		MI					CID investigated and referred the case back to the command.
7 OCT 03	Unauthorized Interrogation and Alleged Assault of a Female Detainee. Incident #2.	MI		MI				Unauthorized interrogation. MI personnel received Field Grade Article 15s.
Early OCT 03	Interrogator Directs Partial Removal of Clothing/Failure to Report. Incident #36.	MI						

Allegations of Abuse Incidents, the Nature of Reported Abuse, and Associated Personnel

Note: The chart lists all allegations considered. The specific abuse claimed and entities involved are not confirmed in all cases. The category of abuse are underlined. (See paragraph 5e-h, above)

Date/Time	Incident	Nature of Alleged Abuse						Comments
		Nudity/ Humiliation	Assault	Sexual Assault	Use of Dogs	The "Hole"	Other	
Early OCT 03	Interrogator Directs Unauthorized Solitary Confinement/Military Police Stripping of Detainee/Failure to Report. Incident #**43**.	MP	MP			*MI/MP*		MI directed the MP place the detainee in solitary confinement (apparently the "Hole") for a few hours. The MPs carried out the request, stripped and hooded the detainee.
17 OCT 03-19 Oct 03	Photos Depicting a Naked Hooded Detainee Cuffed to His Cell Door. Detainee Cuffed to His Bed with Underwear on his Head. Incident #**37**.	*UNK*						Nudity, hooding, and restraint. No indication of association with MI.
20 OCT 03	Detainee Was Stripped and Abused for Making a Shank from a Toothbrush. Incident #**8**.	MP	*MP*	*MP*				No indication of association with MI.
25 OCT 03/2015 (est)	Photos of a Naked Detainee on a Dog Leash. Incident #**9**.	MP		*MP*				Humiliation and degradation. No indication of association with MI.

1097

Date	Incident	MI/MP	MI/MP	MI/MP		Notes
25 OCT 03/2300–2317 (est)	Three Naked Detainees Handcuffed Together and Forced to Simulate Sex While Photographed and Abused. Incident #**3**.	MI/MP	MI/MP	MI/MP		Incident not associated with interrogation operations. MI personnel observed and participated as individuals.
28 OCT 03	Photographs of Female Detainees. Incident #**38**.	*MP*		MP		MPs took many photos of two female detainees. One detainee photographed exposing her breasts.
OCT 03	Abuse and Sodomy of a Detainee (Chem Light Incident). Incident #**5**.	MP	*MP*	MP		Detainee on MI Hold. No other indication of association with MI.
OCT 03	Detainee's Chin Lacerated. Incident #**21**.		*MP*			No indication of association with MI. Assailant unknown.
4 NOV 03/2140–2315	Detainee Forced to Stand on a Box With Simulated Electrical Wires Attached to his Fingers and Penis. Incident # **10**.	MP	*MP*			No indication of association with MI. Attached wire to penis. Threatened detainee with electrocution
4 NOV 03	CIA Detainee Dies in Custody. Incident #**7**.		*CIA*			SEAL Team involved in apprehending detainee. MPs photographed body. Tampered with evidence

(Cont.)

Allegations of Abuse Incidents, the Nature of Reported Abuse, and Associated Personnel

Note: The chart lists all allegations considered. The specific abuse claimed and entities involved are not confirmed in all cases. The category of abuse are underlined. (See paragraph 5e-h, above)

Date/Time	Incident	Nature of Alleged Abuse						Comments
		Nudity/ Humiliation	Assault	Sexual Assault	Use of Dogs	The "Hole"	Other	
5 NOV 03	Detainee Forced to Stand on Boxes, Water is Poured on Him, His Genitals are Hit. Incident #20.	MP	MP	MP				Detainee on MI Hold. No other indication of association with MI.
7-8 NOV 03/2315-0024 (est)	Naked Dog pile and Forced Masturbation of Detainees Following the 6 NOV 03 Riot at Camp Vigilant. Incident #11.	MP	MP	MP				
13 NOV 03	Detainee Claim of MP Abuse Corresponds with Interrogations. Incident #4.	MP	MP					Interrogation reports suggest MI directed abuse. Withholding of bedding
14 NOV 03	MP Log-Detainees Were Ordered "PT'd" By MI. Incident#6.	MP	MP					MPs performed unauthorized medical procedures – stitching detainee wounds
16 NOV 03	Stripping of Detainee During Interrogation. Incident#39.	MI						MI interrogator counseled and removed as lead interrogator.

Date	Incident			
18 NOV 03	Photo Depicting Detainee on the Floor with a Banana Inserted into his Anus. Incident#**14**.	*MP*		Detainee had an apparent mental disorder. Photos were taken of him on other dates including showing him naked, praying upside down or covered in feces; blood on a door from an apparently self-inflicted wound; and efforts to restrain him. Appropriate psychiatric care and facilities apparently were not available.
24 NOV 03	MP CPT Beat and Kicked a Detainee. Incident#**23**.	*MP*		Subsequent investigation determined to be a staged event and not an abusive incident.
24 NOV 03	Interrogator Threatens Use of Military Working Dog. Incident #**25**.	*MI/MP*	*MP/MI*	
24 NOV 03	The use of dogs and humiliation (clothing removal) was approved by MI. Incident #**40**.	*MI/MP*	*MI/MP*	COL Pappas authorized, and LTC Jordan supervised, the harsh treatment of Iraqi Police during interrogations, to include humiliation (clothing removal) and the use of dogs.

(Cont.)

Allegations of Abuse Incidents, the Nature of Reported Abuse, and Associated Personnel

Note: The chart lists all allegations considered. The specific abuse claimed and entities involved are not confirmed in all cases. The category of abuse are underlined. (See paragraph 5e-h, above)

Date/Time	Incident	Nature of Alleged Abuse						Comments
		Nudity/ Humiliation	Assault	Sexual Assault	Use of Dogs	The "Hole"	Other	
26 or 27 Nov 03	MI/MP Abuse During an Interrogation of Iraqi Policeman. Incident **#15**.		*MI/MP*					MP cut off air supply by covering nose and mouth of detainee and twisted his arm at direction of the contract interrogator during interrogation of Iraqi policeman.
29 NOV 04	Photo Depicting a detainee in his underwear standing on a box. Incident **#13**.	UNK	*UNK*					Photo could not be tied to any specific incident, detainee, or allegation and MI involvement is indeterminate.
30 NOV 03	MP Log Entry-Detainee Was Found in Cell Covered in Blood. Incident #**17**.		*UNK*					Wounds apparently self-inflicted. No indication of association with MI.
Circa Dec 03	Photo Depicting detainee in stress position on chair. Incident #**24.**		*MI*					Photo shows detainee kneeling on a chair with Interrogators watching. No associated interrogation summaries to ID detainee

Date	Incident				Notes
4 DEC 03	MP Log-Determination of Inmate Clothing by MI. Incident #41.	*MI/MP*			Suggests MI direction to remove selected detainee's clothing, with MP collaboration.
12-13 DEC 03 (est)	Detainee Involved in Attempted Murder of MPs Claims Retaliatory Acts Upon Return to the Hard Site. Incident #18.	*MP*		MP	Detainee allegations may have been exaggerated. MP – Forced him to eat pork and forced alcohol in his mouth. MPs may have retaliated in response to the detainee shooting an MP on 24 NOV 03.
4-13 DEC 03 (est)	Withholding of Clothing, Bedding, and Medical Care. Incident #19.	MP	*UNK*		MI Soldier discovered and attempted to rectify the situation. A U/I COL or LTC medical officer refused to remove a catheter when notified by MI.
12 DEC 03	Dog Bites Iranian Detainee. Incident #27.	MP	MP	*MP*	Detainee on MI Hold. No other indication of association with MI.
14/15 DEC 03	MI Uses Dog in Interrogation. Incident #29.			*MI/MP*	Used allegedly in response to COL Pappas's blanket approval for use of harsher techniques against Saddam associates.
14/15 DEC 03	MI Uses Dog in Interrogation. Incident #31.			*MI/MP*	Interrogation report indicates dogs used with little effect during an interrogation.

(Cont.)

Allegations of Abuse Incidents, the Nature of Reported Abuse, and Associated Personnel

Note: The chart lists all allegations considered. The specific abuse claimed and entities involved are not confirmed in all cases. The category of abuse are underlined. (See paragraph 5e-h, above)

Date/Time	Incident	Nature of Alleged Abuse						Comments
		Nudity/ Humiliation	Assault	Sexual Assault	Use of Dogs	The "Hole"	Other	
Late DEC 03	Contract Interrogator Possibly Involved in Dog Use on Detainee. Incident #**32**.				*MI/MP*			
18 DEC 03 or later	Dog Handler Uses Dog on Detainee. Incident #**28**.				*MP*			Photos of incident show only MP personnel; however, it is possible MI directed the dogs to prepare the detainee for interrogation.
27 DEC 03 (est)	Photo Depicting Apparent Shotgun Wounds on Detainee's Buttocks. Incident #**12**.	UNK	*UNK*					Detainee apparently shot by MP personnel with shotgun using less-than-lethal rounds. Nudity may have been required to have medics observe and treat wounds. No indication of association with MI.

Date	Incident	Category	Remarks
8 JAN 04 (Estimated)	Dog Used to Scare Juvenile Inmates. Incident #26.	MP	MI Soldier observed the event while in the area during an interrogation. MP motivation unknown. MI Soldier failed to report it.
Unspecified	Unmuzzled dog used during an interrogation. Incident #30.	MI/MP	MI approved the use of dogs during an interrogation. The dog was unmuzzled without such approval.
Unspecified	Possible Rape of a Detainee by a US Translator. Incident #22.	MI	
Unspecified	Civilian Interrogator Forcibly Pulls Detainee from Truck and Drags Him Across Ground. Incident #16.	MI	The incident was reported by MI, but CID apparently did not pursue the case.
Various Dates	MI Use of Isolation as an Interrogation Technique. Incident #44.	MI/MP	Seven detainees are associated with this line item.
Various Dates	MI Forces Detainee to Wear Women's Underwear on his Head. Incident #33.	MI/MP	MPs may have performed two of the incidents identified in photos, and may have no MI association.

6. (U) FINDINGS AND RECOMMENDATIONS

a. (U) Major Finding: From 25 July 2003 to 6 February 2004, twenty-seven (27) 205 MI BDE personnel alegedly:

– Requested, encouraged, condoned, or solicited MP personnel to abuse detainees or;
– Participated in detainee abuse or;
– Violated established interrogation procedures and applicable laws and regulations as preparation for interrogation operations at Abu Ghraib.

(U) **Explanation**: Some MI personnel encouraged, condoned, participated in, or ignored abuse. In a few instances, MI personnel acted alone in abusing detainees. MI abuse and MI solicitation of MP abuse included the use of isolation with sensory deprivation ("the Hole"), removal of clothing and humiliation, the use of dogs to "fear up" detainees, and on one occasion, the condoned twisting of a detainee's cuffed wrists and the smothering of this detainee with a cupped hand in MI's presence. Some MI personnel violated established interrogation practices, regulations, and conventions which resulted in the abuse of detainees. While Interrogation and Counter-Resistance Policies (ICRP) were poorly defined and changed several times, in most cases of detainee abuse the MI personnel involved knew or should have known what they were doing was outside the bounds of their authority. Ineffective leadership at the JIDC failed to detect violations and discipline those responsible. Likewise, leaders failed to provide adequate training to ensure Soldiers understood the rules and complied.

(U) **Recommendation**: The Army needs to re-emphasize Soldier and leader responsibilities in interrogation and detention operations and retrain them to perform in accordance with law, regulations, and Army values and to live up to the responsibilities of their rank and position. Leaders must also provide adequate training to ensure Soldiers understand their authorities. The Army must ensure that future interrogation policies are simple, direct and include safeguards against abuse. Organizations such as the JIDC must possess a functioning chain of command capable of directing interrogation operations.

b. (U) Other Findings and Recommendations.

(1) (U) **Finding**: There was a lack of clear Command and Control of Detainee Operations at the CJTF-7 level.

(U) **Explanation**: COL Pappas was rated by MG Wojdakowski, DCG, V Corps/CJTF-7. MG Wojdakowski, however, was not directly involved with interrogation operations. Most of COL Pappas' direction was coming from LTG Sanchez directly as well as from MG Fast, the C2. BG Karpinski was rated by BG Diamond, Commander, 377th Theater Support Command (377 TSC). However, she testified that she believed her rater was MG Wojdakowski and in fact it was he she received her direction from the entire time she was in Iraq (Reference Annex B, Appendix 1, KARPINSKI). The 800 MP BDE was TACON to CJTF-7. Overall responsibility for detainee operations never came together under one person short of LTG Sanchez himself until the assignment of MG G. Miller in April 2004.

(U) **Recommendation**: There should be a single authority designated for command and control for detention and interrogation operations. (DoD/DA)

(2) (U) **Finding**: FRAGO 1108 appointing COL Pappas as FOB Commander at Abu Ghraib was unclear. This issue did not impact detainee abuse.

(U) **Explanation**: Although FRAGO 1108 appointing COL Pappas as FOB Commander on 19 November 2003 changed the command relationship, it had no specific effect on detainee abuses at Abu Ghraib. The FRAGO giving him TACON of the 320 MP BN did not contain any specified or implied tasks. The TACON did not include responsibility for conducting prison or "Warden" functions. Those functions remained the responsibility of the 320 MP BN. This FRAGO has been cited as a significant contributing factor that allowed the abuses to happen, but the abuses were already underway for two months before CJTF-7 issued this FRAGO. COL Pappas and the Commander of the 320 MP BN interpreted that FRAGO strictly for COL Pappas to exercise the external Force Protection and Security of Detainees. COL Pappas had a Long Range Reconnaissance Company in the 165 MI BN that would augment the external protection of Abu Ghraib. The internal protection of detainees, however, still remained the responsibility of the 320 MP BN. The confusion and disorganization between MI and MPs already existed by the time CJTF-7 published the FRAGO. Had there been no change of FOB Command, it is likely abuse would have continued anyway.

(U) **Recommendation**: Joint Task Forces such as CJTF-7 should clearly specify relationships in FRAGOs so as to preclude confusion. Terms such as Tactical Control (TACON) should be clearly defined to identify specific command relationships and preclude confusion. (DoD/CJTF-7)

(3) (U) **Finding**: The JIDC was manned with personnel from numerous organizations and consequently lacked unit cohesion. There was an absence of an established, effective MI chain of command at the JIDC.

(U) **Explanation**: A decision was made not to run the JIDC as a unit mission. The JIDC was manned, led and managed by staff officers from multiple organizations as opposed to a unit with its functioning chain of command. Responsibilities for balancing the demands of managing interrogation operations and establishing good order and discipline in this environment were unclear and lead to lapses in accountability.

(U) **Recommendation**: JIDCs need to be structured, manned, trained and equipped as standard military organizations. These organizations should be certified by TRADOC and/or JFCOM. Appropriate Army and Joint doctrine should be developed defining JIDCs' missions and functions as separate commands. (DoD/DA/CJTF-7)

(4) (U) **Finding**: Selecting Abu Ghraib as a detention facility placed soldiers and detainees at an unnecessary force protection risk.

(U) **Explanation**: Failure adequately to protect and house detainees is a violation of the Third and Fourth Geneva Conventions and AR 190-8. Therefore, the selection of Abu

Ghraib as a detention facility was inappropriate because of its inherent indefensibility and poor condition. The selection of Abu Ghraib as a detention center was dictated by the Coalition Provisional Authority officials despite concerns that the Iraqi people would look negatively on Americans interning detainees in a facility associated with torture. Abu Ghraib was in poor physical condition with buildings and sections of the perimeter wall having been destroyed, resulting in completely inadequate living conditions. Force protection must be a major consideration in selecting any facility as a detention facility. Abu Ghraib was located in the middle of the Sunni Triangle, an area known to be very hostile to coalition forces. Further, being surrounded by civilian housing and open fields and encircled by a network of roads and highways, its defense presented formidable force protection challenges. Even though the force protection posture at Abu Ghraib was compromised from the start due to its location and poor condition, coalition personnel still had a duty and responsibility to undertake appropriate defensive measures. However, the poor security posture at Abu Ghraib resulted in the deaths and wounding of both coalition forces and detainees.

(U) Recommendations:

– Detention centers must be established in accordance with AR 190-8 to ensure safety and compliance with the Geneva Conventions. (DoD/DA/CJTF-7).

– As a matter of policy, force protection concerns must be applicable to any detention facility and all detention operations. (DoD/DA/CJTF-7)

– Protect detainees in accordance with Geneva Convention IV by providing adequate force protection. (DoD/DA/CJTF-7)

(5) (U) **Finding**: Leaders failed to take steps to effectively manage pressure placed upon JIDC personnel.

(U) **Explanation**: During our interviews, leaders within the MI community commented upon the intense pressure they felt from higher headquarters, to include CENTCOM, the Pentagon, and DIA for timelier, actionable intelligence (Reference Annex B, Appendix 1, WOOD, PAPPAS, and PRICE). These leaders have stated that this pressure adversely affected their decision making. Requests for information were being sent to Abu Ghraib from a number of headquarters without any prioritization. Based on the statements from the interrogators and analysts, the pressure was allowed to be passed down to the lowest levels.

(U) **Recommendation**: Leaders must balance mission requirements with unit capabilities, soldier morale and effectiveness. Protecting Soldiers from unnecessary pressure to enhance mission effectiveness is a leader's job. Rigorous and challenging training can help prepare units and soldiers for the stress they face in combat. (DoD/DA/CENTCOM/CJTF-7)

(6) (U) **Finding**: Some capturing units failed to follow procedures, training, and directives in the capture, screening, and exploitation of detainees.

(U) **Explanation**: The role of the capturing unit was to conduct preliminary screening of captured detainees to determine if they posed a security risk or possessed information of intelligence value. Detainees who did not pose a security risk and possessed no intelligence value should have been released. Those that posed a security risk and possessed no intelligence value should have been transferred to Abu Ghraib as a security hold. Those that possessed intelligence information should have been interrogated within 72 hours at the tactical level to gather perishable information of value to the capturing unit. After 72 hours, these personnel should have been transferred to Abu Ghraib for further intelligence exploitation as an MI hold. Since most detainees were not properly screened, large numbers of detainees were transferred to Abu Ghraib, who in some cases should not have been sent there at all, and in almost all cases, were not properly identified or documented in accordance with doctrine and directives. This failure led to the arrival of a significant number of detainees at Abu Ghraib. Without proper detainee capture documentation, JIDC interrogators were diverted from interrogation and intelligence production to screening operations in order to assess the value of the incoming detainees (no value, security hold, or MI Hold). The overall result was that less intelligence was produced at the JIDC than could have been if capturing forces had followed proper procedures.

(U) **Recommendation**: Screening, interrogation and release procedures at the tactical level need to be properly executed. Those detainees who pose no threat and are of no intelligence value should be released by capturing units within 72 hours. Those detainees thought to be a threat but of no further intelligence value should be sent to a long term confinement facility. Those detainees thought to possess further intelligence value should be sent to a Corps/Theater Interrogation Center. (DA/CENTCOM/CJTF-7)

(7) (U) **Finding**: DoD's development of multiple policies on interrogation operations for use in different theaters or operations confused Army and civilian Interrogators at Abu Ghraib.

(U) **Explanation**: National policy and DoD directives were not completely consistent with Army doctrine concerning detainee treatment or interrogation tactics, resulting in CJTF-7 interrogation and counter-resistance policies and practices that lacked basis in Army interrogation doctrine. As a result, interrogators at Abu Ghraib employed non-doctrinal approaches that conflicted with other DoD and Army regulatory, doctrinal and procedural guidance.

(U) **Recommendation**: Adopt one DoD policy for interrogation, within the framework of existing doctrine, adhering to the standards found in doctrine, and enforce that standard policy across DoD. Interrogation policy must be simple and direct, with reference to existing doctrine, and possess effective safeguards against abuse. It must be totally understandable by the interrogator using it. (DoD/DA/CJTF-7)

(8) (U) **Finding**: There are an inadequate number of MI units to satisfy current and future HUMINT missions. The Army does not possess enough interrogators and linguists to support interrogation operations.

(U) **Explanation**: The demand for interrogators and linguists to support tactical screening operations at the point-of-capture of detainees, tactical HUMINT teams, and personnel to support interrogation operations at organizations like the JIDC cannot be supported with the current force structure. As a result, each of these operations in Iraq was undermanned and suffered accordingly.

(U) **Recommendation**: The Army must increase the number of HUMINT units to overcome downsizing of HUMINT forces over the last 10 years and to address current and future HUMINT requirements.

(9) (U) **Finding**: The JIDC was not provided with adequate personnel resources to effectively operate as an interrogation center.

(U) **Explanation**: The JIDC was established in an ad hoc manner without proper planning, personnel, and logistical support for the missions it was intended to perform. Interrogation and analyst personnel were quickly kluged together from a half dozen units in an effort to meet personnel requirements. Even at its peak strength, interrogation and analyst manpower at the JIDC was too shorthanded to deal with the large number of detainees at hand. Logistical support was also inadequate.

(U) **Recommendation**: The Army and DoD should plan on operating JIDC organizations in future operational environments, establish appropriate manning and equipment authorizations for the same. (DoD/DA)

(10) (U) **Finding**: There was/is a severe shortage of CAT II and CAT III Arab linguists available in Iraq.

(U) **Explanation**: This shortage negatively affected every level of detainee operations from point-of-capture through detention facility. Tactical units were unable to properly screen detainees at their levels not only because of the lack of interrogators but even more so because of the lack of interpreters. The linguist problem also existed at Abu Ghraib. There were only 20 linguists assigned to Abu Ghraib at the height of operations. Linguists were a critical node and limited the maximum number of interrogations that could be conducted at any time to the number of linguists available.

(U) **Recommendation**: Army and DoD need to address the issue of inadequate linguist resources to conduct detention operations. (DA/DoD)

(11) (U) **Finding**: The cross leveling of a large number of Reserve Component (RC) Soldiers during the Mobilization process contributed to training challenges and lack of unit cohesion of the RC units at Abu Ghraib.

(U) **Recommendation**: If cross leveling of personnel is necessary in order to bring RC units up to required strength levels, then post mobilization training time should be extended. Post mobilization training should include unit level training in addition to Soldier training to ensure cross leveled Soldiers are made part of the team. (DA)

(12) (U) **Finding**: Interrogator training in the Laws of Land Warfare and the Geneva Conventions is ineffective.

(U) **Explanation**: The US Army Intelligence Center and follow-on unit training provided interrogators with what appears to be adequate curriculum, practical exercises and man-hours in Law of Land Warfare and Geneva Conventions training. Soldiers at Abu Ghraib, however, remained uncertain about what interrogation procedures were authorized and what proper reporting procedures were required. This indicates that Initial Entry Training for interrogators was not sufficient or was not reinforced properly by additional unit training or leadership.

(U) **Recommendation**: More training emphasis needs to be placed on Soldier and leader responsibilities concerning the identification and reporting of detainee abuse incidents or concerns up through the chain of command, or to other offices such as CID, IG or SJA. This training should not just address the rules, but address case studies from recent and past detainee and interrogation operations to address likely issues interrogators and their supervisors will encounter. Soldiers and leaders need to be taught to integrate Army values and ethical decision-making to deal with interrogation issues that are not clearly prohibited or allowed. Furthermore, it should be stressed that methods employed by US Army interrogators will represent US values.

(13) (U) **Finding**: MI, MP, and Medical Corps personnel observed and failed to report instances of Abuse at Abu Ghraib. Likewise, several reports indicated that capturing units did not always treat detainees IAW the Geneva Convention.

(U) **Recommendation**: DoD should improve training provided to *all* personnel in Geneva Conventions, detainee operations, and the responsibilities of reporting detainee abuse. (DoD)

(14) (U) **Finding**: Combined MI/MP training in the conduct of detainee/interrogation operations is inadequate.

(U) **Explanation**: MI and MP personnel at Abu Ghraib had little knowledge of each other's missions, roles and responsibilities in the conduct of detainee/interrogation operations. As a result, some "lanes in the road" were worked out "on the fly." Other relationships were never fully defined and contributed to the confused operational environment.

(U) **Recommendation**: TRADOC should initiate an effort to develop a cross branch training program in detainee and interrogation operations training. FORSCOM should reinstitute combined MI/MP unit training such as the Gold Sword/Silver Sword Exercises that were conducted annually. (DA)

(15) (U) **Finding**: MI leaders do not receive adequate training in the conduct and management of interrogation operations.

(U) **Explanation**: MI Leaders at the JIDC were unfamiliar with and untrained in interrogation operations (with the exception of CPT Wood) as well as the mission and purposes of a JIDC. Absent any knowledge from training and experience in interrogation operations, JIDC leaders had to rely upon instinct to operate the JIDC. MTTs and Tiger Teams were deployed to the JIDC as a solution to help train interrogators and leaders in the management of HUMINT and detainee/interrogator operations.

(U) **Recommendation**: MI Officer, NCO and Warrant Officer training needs to include interrogation operations to include management procedures, automation support, collection management and JIDC operations. Officer and senior NCO training should also emphasize the potential for abuse involved in detention and interrogation operations. (DA)

(16) (U) **Finding**: Army doctrine exists for both MI interrogation and MP detainee operations, but it was not comprehensive enough to cover the situation that existed at Abu Ghraib.

(U) **Explanation**: The lines of authority and accountability between MI and MP were unclear and undefined. For example, when MI would order sleep adjustment, MPs would use their judgment on how to apply that technique. The result was MP taking detainees from their cells stripping them and giving them cold showers or throwing cold water on them to keep them awake.

(U) **Recommendation**: DA should conduct a review to determine future Army doctrine for interrogation operations and detention operations. (DA)

(17) (U) **Finding**: Because of a lack of doctrine concerning detainee and interrogation operations, critical records on detainees were not created or maintained properly thereby hampering effective operations.

(U) **Explanation**: This lack of record keeping included the complete life cycle of detainee records to include detainee capture information and documentation, prison records, medical records, interrogation plans and records, and release board records. Lack of record keeping significantly hampered the ability of this investigation to discover critical information concerning detainee abuse.

(U) **Recommendation**: As TRADOC reviews and enhances detainee and interrogation operations doctrine, it should ensure that record keeping and information sharing requirements are addressed. (DA)

(18) (U) **Finding**: Four (4) contract interrogators allegedly abused detainees at Abu Ghraib.

(U) **Explanation**: The contracting system failed to ensure that properly trained and vetted linguist and interrogator personnel were hired to support operations at Abu Ghraib. The system also failed to provide useful contract management functions in support of the facility. Soldiers and leaders at the prison were unprepared for the arrival, employment, and oversight of contract interrogators.

(U) **Recommendations**: The Army should review the use contract interrogators. In the event contract interrogators must be used, the Army must ensure that they are properly qualified from a training and performance perspective, and properly vetted. The Army should establish standards for contract requirements and personnel. Additionally, the Army must provide sufficient contract management resources to monitor contracts and contractor performance at the point of performance.

(19) (U) **Observation**: MG Miller's visit did not introduce "harsh techniques" into the Abu Ghraib interrogation operation.

(U) **Explanation**: While there was an increase in intelligence reports after the visit, it appears more likely it was due to the assignment of trained interrogators and an increased number of MI Hold detainees to interrogate. This increase in production does not equate to an increase in quality of the collected intelligence. MG G.

Miller's visit did not introduce "harsh techniques" into the Abu Ghraib interrogation operation.

(20) (U) **Finding**: The JTF-GTMO training team had positive impact on the operational management of the JIDC; however, the JTF-GTMO training team inadvertently validated restricted interrogation techniques.

(U) **Explanation**: The JTF-GTMO team stressed the conduct of operations with a strategic objective, while the Abu Ghraib team remained focused on tactical operations. Instead of providing guidance and assistance, the team's impact was limited to one-on-one interaction during interrogations. Clearly a significant problem was the JTF-GTMO's lack of understanding of the approved interrogation techniques, either for GTMO or CJTF-7 or Abu Ghraib. When the training team composed of the experts from a national level operation failed to recognize, object to, or report detainee abuse, such as the use of nudity as an interrogation tactic, they failed as a training team and further validated the use of unacceptable interrogation techniques.

(U) **Recommendation**: TRADOC should initiate an Army-wide effort to ensure all personnel involved in detention and interrogation operations are properly trained with respect to approved doctrine. There should be a MTT to assist ongoing detention operations. This MTT must be of the highest quality and understand the mission they have been sent to support. They must have clearly defined and unmistakable objectives. Team members with varied experience must be careful to avoid providing any training or guidance that contradicts local or national policy. (DA/DoD)

(21) (U) **Finding**: The Fort Huachuca MTT failed to adapt the ISCT training (which was focused upon improving the JTF-GTMO operational environment) to the mission needs of CJTF-7 and JIDC; however, actions of one team member resulted in the inadvertent validation of restricted interrogation techniques.

(U) **Explanation**: Although the Fort Huachuca Team (ISCT) team was successful in arranging a few classes and providing some formal training, to include classes on the Geneva Conventions, both the JIDC leadership and the ISCT team failed to include/require the contract personnel to attend the training. Furthermore, the training that was given was ineffective and certainly did nothing to prevent the abuses occurring at Abu Ghraib, e.g., the "Hole," nakedness, withholding of bedding, and the use of dogs to threaten detainees. The ISCT MTT members were assigned to the various Tiger Teams/sections to conduct interrogations. The ISCT team's lack of understanding of approved doctrine was a significant failure. This lack of understanding was evident in SFC Walters' "unofficial" conversation with one of the Abu Ghraib interrogators (CIVILIAN21). SFC Walters related several stories about the use of dogs as an inducement, suggesting the interrogator talk to the MPs about the possibilities. SFC Walters noted that detainees are most susceptible during the first few hours after capture. "The prisoners are captured by Soldiers, taken from their familiar surroundings, blindfolded and put into a truck and brought to this place (Abu Ghraib); and then they are pushed down a hall with guards barking orders and thrown into a cell, naked; and that not knowing what was going to happen or what the guards might do caused them extreme fear." It was also suggested that an interrogator could take some pictures of what seemed to be guards being rough with prisoners so he could use them to scare the prisoners. This conversation certainly contributed to the abusive environment at Abu Ghraib. The team validated the use of unacceptable interrogation techniques. The ISCT team's Geneva Conventions training was not effective in helping to halt abusive techniques, as it failed to train Soldiers on their responsibilities for identifying and reporting those techniques.

(U) **Recommendation**: TRADOC should initiate an Army-wide effort to ensure all personnel involved in detention and interrogation operations are properly trained with respect to approved doctrine. There should be a MTT to assist ongoing detention operations. This MTT must be of the highest quality and understand the mission they have been sent to support. They must have clearly defined and unmistakable objectives. Team members with varied experience must be careful to avoid providing any training or guidance that contradicts local or national policy. (DA/DoD)

(22) (U) **Finding**: Other Government Agency (OGA) interrogation practices led to a loss of accountability at Abu Ghraib.

(U) **Explanation**: While the FBI, JTF-121, Criminal Investigative Task Force, Iraq Survey Group, and the CIA were all present at Abu Ghraib, the acronym "Other Government Agency" referred almost exclusively to the CIA. Lack of military control over OGA interrogator actions or lack of systemic accountability for detainees plagued detainee operations in Abu Ghraib almost from the start. Army allowed CIA to house "Ghost Detainees" who were unidentified and unaccounted for in Abu Ghraib. This procedure created confusion and uncertainty concerning their classification and subsequent DoD reporting requirements under the Geneva Conventions. Additionally, the treatment and interrogation of OGA detainees occurred under different practices and procedures which were absent any DoD visibility, control, or oversight. This separate grouping of OGA detainees added to the confusion over proper treatment of detainees and created a perception that OGA techniques and practices were suitable and authorized for DoD operations. No memorandum of understanding on detainee accountability or interrogation practices between the CIA and CJTF-7 was created.

(U) **Recommendation**: DoD must enforce adherence by OGA with established DoD practices and procedures while conducting detainee interrogation operations at DoD facilities.

(23) (U) **Finding**: There was neither a defined procedure nor specific responsibility within CJTF-7 for dealing with ICRC visits. ICRC recommendations were ignored by MI, MP and CJTF-7 personnel.

(U) **Explanation**: Within this investigation's timeframe, 16 September 2003 through 31 January 2004, the ICRC visited Abu Ghraib three times, notifying CJTF-7 twice of their visit results, describing serious violations of international Humanitarian Law and of the Geneva Conventions. In spite of the ICRC's role as independent observers, there seemed to be a consensus among personnel at Abu Ghraib that the allegations were not true. Neither the leadership, nor CJTF-7 made any attempt to verify the allegations.

(U) **Recommendation**: DoD should review current policy concerning ICRC visits and establish procedures whereby findings and recommendations made by the ICRC are investigated. Investigation should not be done by the units responsible for the facility in question. Specific procedures and responsibilities should be developed for ICRC visits, reports, and responses. There also needs to be specific inquiries made into ICRC allegations of abuse or maltreatment by an independent entity to ensure that an unbiased review has occurred. (DoD/CJTF-7)

(24) (U) **Finding**: Two soldiers that the 519 MI BN had reason to suspect were involved in the questionable death of a detainee in Afghanistan were allowed to deploy and continue conducting interrogations in Iraq. While in Iraq, those same soldiers were alleged to have abused detainees.

(U) **Recommendation**: Once soldiers in a unit have been identified as possible participants in abuse related to the performance of their duties, they should be suspended from such duties or flagged.

(25) (U) **Observation**: While some MI Soldiers acted outside the scope of applicable laws and regulations, most Soldiers performed their duties in accordance with the Geneva Conventions and Army Regulations.

(U) **Explanation**: MI Soldiers operating the JIDC at Abu Ghraib screened thousands of Iraqi detainees, conducted over 2,500 interrogations, and produced several thousand valuable intelligence products supporting the war fighter and the global war on terrorism. This great effort was executed in difficult and dangerous conditions with inadequate physical and personnel resources.

c. (U) Individual Responsibility for Detainee Abuse at Abu Ghraib.

(1)(U) **Finding**: *COL Thomas M. Pappas, Commander, 205 MI BDE.* A preponderance of evidence supports that COL Pappas did, or failed to do, the following:

- Failed to insure that the JIDC performed its mission to its full capabilities, within the applicable rules, regulations and appropriate procedures.
- Failed to properly organize the JIDC.
- Failed to put the necessary checks and balances in place to prevent and detect abuses.
- Failed to ensure that his Soldiers and civilians were properly trained for the mission.
- Showed poor judgment by leaving LTC Jordan in charge of the JIDC during the critical early stages of the JIDC.
- Showed poor judgment by leaving LTC Jordan in charge during the aftermath of a shooting incident known as the Iraqi Police Roundup (IP Roundup).
- Improperly authorized the use of dogs during interrogations. Failed to properly supervise the use of dogs to make sure they were muzzled after he improperly permitted their use.
- Failed to take appropriate action regarding the ICRC reports of abuse.

- Failed to take aggressive action against Soldiers who violated the ICRP, the CJTF-7 interrogation and Counter-Resistance Policy and the Geneva Conventions.
- Failed to properly communicate to Higher Headquarters when his Brigade would be unable to accomplish its mission due to lack of manpower and/or resources. Allowed his Soldiers and civilians at the JIDC to be subjected to inordinate pressure from Higher Headquarters.
- Failed to establish appropriate MI and MP coordination at the brigade level which would have alleviated much of the confusion that contributed to the abusive environment at Abu Ghraib.
- The significant number of systemic failures documented in this report does not relieve COL Pappas of his responsibility as the Commander, 205th MI BDE for the abuses that occurred and went undetected for a considerable length of time.

(U) **Recommendation**: This information should be forwarded to COL Pappas' chain of command for appropriate action.

(2) (U) **Finding**: *LTC Stephen L. Jordan, Director, Joint Interrogation Debriefing Center.* A preponderance of evidence supports that LTC Jordan did, or failed to do, the following:

- Failed to properly train Soldiers and civilians on the ICRP.
- Failed to take full responsibility for his role as the Director, JIDC.
- Failed to establish the necessary checks and balances to prevent and detect abuses.
- Was derelict in his duties by failing to establish order and enforce proper use of ICRP during the night of 24 November 2003 (IP Roundup) which contributed to a chaotic situation in which detainees were abused.
- Failed to prevent the unauthorized use of dogs and the humiliation of detainees who were kept naked for no acceptable purpose while he was the senior officer-in-charge in the Hard Site.
- Failed to accurately and timely relay critical information to COL Pappas, such as:
  - The incident where a detainee had obtained a weapon.
  - ICRC issues.
- Was deceitful during this, as well as the MG Taguba, investigations. His recollection of facts, statements, and incidents were always recounted to avoid blame or responsibility. His version of events frequently diverged from most others.
- Failed to obey a lawful order to refrain from contacting anyone except his attorney regarding this investigation. He conducted an e-mail campaign soliciting support from others involved in the investigation.

(U) **Recommendation**: This information should be forwarded to LTC Jordan's chain of command for appropriate action.

(3) (U) **Finding**: *MAJ David M. Price, Operations Officer, Joint Interrogation and Debriefing Center, 141st MI Battalion.* A preponderance of evidence indicates that MAJ Price did, or failed to do, the following:

- Failed to properly train Soldiers and civilians on the ICRP.

- Failed to understand the breadth of his responsibilities as the JIDC Operations Officer. Failed to effectively assess, plan, and seek command guidance and assistance regarding JIDC operations.
- Failed to intervene when the Interrogation Control Element (ICE) received pressure from Higher Headquarters.
- Failed to plan and implement the necessary checks and balances to prevent and detect abuses.
- Failed to properly review interrogation plans which clearly specified the improper use of nudity and isolation as punishment.

(U) **Recommendation:** This information should be forwarded to MAJ Price's chain of command for appropriate action.

(4) (U) **Finding:** *MAJ Michael D. Thompson, Deputy Operations Officer,* **Joint Interrogation and Debriefing Center, 325 MI BN.** A preponderance of evidence supports that MAJ Thompson failed to do the following:

- Failed to properly train Soldiers and civilians on the ICRP.
- Failed to understand the breadth of his responsibilities as the JIDC Deputy Operations Officer. Failed to effectively assess, plan, and seek command guidance and assistance regarding JIDC operations.
- Failed to intervene when the ICE received pressure from Higher Headquarters.
- Failed to plan and implement the necessary checks and balances to prevent and detect abuses.
- Failed to properly review interrogation plans which clearly specified the improper use of nudity and isolation as punishment.

(U) **Recommendation:** This information should be forwarded to MAJ Thompson's chain of command for appropriate action.

(5) (U) **Finding:** *CPT Carolvn A. Wood. Officer in Charge, Interrogation* *Control Element (ICE), Joint Interrogation and Debriefing Center, 519 MI BDE.* A preponderance of evidence supports that CPT Wood failed to do the following:

- Failed to implement the necessary checks and balances to detect and prevent detainee abuse. Given her knowledge of prior abuse in Afghanistan, as well as the reported sexual assault of a female detainee by three 519 MI BN Soldiers working in the ICE, CPT Wood should have been aware of the potential for detainee abuse at Abu Ghraib. As the Officer-in-Charge (OIC) she was in a position to take steps to prevent further abuse. Her failure to do so allowed the abuse by Soldiers and civilians to go undetected and unchecked.
- Failed to assist in gaining control of a chaotic situation during the IP Roundup, even after SGT Eckroth approached her for help.
- Failed to provide proper supervision. Should have been more alert due to the following incidents:
  - An ongoing investigation on the 519 MI BN in Afghanistan.
  - Prior reports of 519 MI BN interrogators conducting unauthorized interrogations.

- SOLDIER-29's reported use of nudity and humiliation techniques.
- Quick Reaction Force (QRF) allegations of detainee abuse by 519th MI Soldiers.
- Failed to properly review interrogation plans which clearly specified the improper use of nudity and isolation in interrogations and as punishment.
- Failed to ensure that Soldiers were properly trained on interrogation techniques and operations.
- Failed to adequately train Soldiers and civilians on the ICRP.

(U) **Recommendation:** This information should be forwarded to CPT Wood's chain of command for appropriate action.

(6) (U) **Finding:** *SOLDIER-28, Guantanamo Base Team Chief, 260th MI Battalion.* A preponderance of evidence supports that SOLDIER-28 did, or failed to do, the following:

- Failed to report detainee abuse when he was notified by SOLDIER-11 that a detainee was observed in a cell naked, hooded, and whimpering, and when SOLDIER-11 reported an interrogator made a detainee pull his jumpsuit down to his waist.

(U) **Recommendation:** This information should be forwarded to SOLDIER-28's chain of command for appropriate action.

(7) (U) **Finding:** *SOLDIER-23, Operations Section, ICE, JIDC, 325 MI BN.* A preponderance of evidence supports that SOLDIER-23 did, or failed to do, the following:

- Failed to prevent detainee abuse and permitted the unauthorized use of dogs and unauthorized interrogations during the IP Roundup. As the second senior MI officer during the IP Roundup, his lack of leadership contributed to detainee abuse and the chaotic situation during the IP Roundup.
- Failed to properly supervise and ensure Soldiers and civilians followed the ICRP.
- Failed to properly review interrogation plans which clearly specified the improper use of nudity and isolation as interrogation techniques and punishment.

(U) **Recommendation:** This information should be forwarded to SOLDIER-23' chain of command for appropriate action.

(8) (U) **Finding:** *SOLDIER-14, Night Shift OIC, ICE, JIDC, 519 MI BN.* A preponderance of evidence supports that SOLDIER-14 did, or failed to do, the following:

- Failed to properly supervise and ensure Soldiers and civilians followed the ICRP.
- Failed to provide proper supervision. SOLDIER-14 should have been aware of the potential for detainee abuse at Abu Ghraib: The following incidents should have increased his diligence in overseeing operations:
  - An ongoing investigation of the 519 MI BN in Afghanistan.
  - Allegations by a female detainee that 519 MI BN interrogators sexually assaulted her. The Soldiers received non-judicial punishment for conducting unauthorized interrogations.
  - SOLDIER-29's reported use of nudity and humiliation techniques.
  - Quick Reaction Force (QRF) allegations of detainee abuse by 519 MI BN Soldiers.

- Failed to properly review interrogation plans which clearly specified the improper use of nudity and isolation as punishment.

(U) **Recommendation:** This information should be forwarded to SOLDIER-14's chain of command for appropriate action.

(9) (U) **Finding: *SOLDIER-15, Interrogator, 66 MI GP.*** A preponderance of evidence supports that SOLDIER-15 did, or failed to do, the following:

- Failed to report detainee abuse. He witnessed SSG Frederick twisting the handcuffs of a detainee causing pain and covering the detainee's nose and mouth to restrict him from breathing.
  - Witnessed during that same incident, CIVILIAN-11 threaten a detainee by suggesting he would be turned over to SSG Frederick for further abuse if he did not cooperate.

(U) **Recommendation:** This information should be forwarded to SOLDIER-15's chain of command for appropriate action.

(10) (U) **Finding: *SOLDIER-22, 302d MI Battalion.*** A preponderance of evidence supports that SOLDIER-22 did, or failed to do, the following:

- Failed to report detainee abuse.
  - He was made aware by SOLDIER-25 of an incident where three detainees were abused by MPs (Reference Annex I, Appendix l, Photographs M36-37, M39-41).
  - He was made aware by SOLDIER-25 of the use of dogs to scare detainees.
  - He overheard Soldiers stating that MPs were using detainees as "practice dummies;" striking their necks and knocking them unconscious.
  - He was made aware of MPs conducting "PT" (Physical Training) sessions with detainees and MI personnel participating.
- Failed to obey a direct order. He interfered with this investigation by talking about the investigation, giving interviews to the media, and passing the questions being asked by investigators to others via a website.

(U) **Recommendation:** This information should be forwarded to SOLDIER-22's chain of command for appropriate action.

(11) (U) **Finding: *SOLDIER-10, Analyst, 325 MI BN (currently attached to HHC, 504 MI BDE).*** A preponderance of evidence supports that SOLDIER-10 did, or failed to do, the following:

- Actively participated in abuse when he threw water on three detainees who were handcuffed together and made to lie on the floor of the detention facility (Reference Annex I, Appendix 1, Photographs M36-37).
- Failed to stop detainee abuse in the above incident and in the incident when SOLDIER-29 stripped a detainee of his clothes and walked the detainee naked from an interrogation booth to Camp Vigilant during a cold winter day.
- Failed to report detainee abuse.

(U) **Recommendation:** This information should be forwarded to SOLDIER-10's chain of command for appropriate action.

(12) (U) **Finding:** *SOLDIER-17, Interrogator, 2d MI Battalion.* A preponderance of evidence supports that SOLDIER-17 did, or failed to do, the following:

- Failed to report the improper use of dogs. He saw an unmuzzled black dog go into a cell and scare two juvenile detainees. The dog handler allowed the dogs to "go nuts" on the juveniles (Reference Annex I, Appendix 1, Photograph D-48).
- Failed to report inappropriate actions of dog handlers. He overheard Dog Handlers state they had a competition to scare detainees to the point they would defecate. They claimed to have already made several detainees urinate when threatened by their dogs.

(U) **Recommendation:** This information should be forwarded to SOLDIER-17's chain of command for appropriate action.

(13) (U) **Finding:** *SOLDIER-19, Interrogator, 325 MI BN.* A preponderance of evidence supports that SOLDIER-19 did, or failed to do, the following:

- Abused detainees:
  - Actively participated in the abuse of three detainees depicted in photographs (Reference Annex I, Appendix 1, Photographs M36-37, M39-41). He threw a Foam-ball at their genitals and poured water on the detainees while they were bound, nude, and abused by others.
  - Turned over a detainee to the MPs with apparent instructions for his abuse. He returned to find the detainee naked and hooded on the floor whimpering.
  - Used improper interrogation techniques. He made a detainee roll down his jumpsuit and threatened the detainee with complete nudity if he did not cooperate.
- Failed to stop detainee abuse in the above incidents.
- Failed to report detainee abuse for the above incidents.

(U) **Recommendation:** This information should be forwarded to SOLDIER-19's chain of command for appropriate action.

(14) (U) **Findings:** *SOLDIER-24, Analyst, 325 MI BN (currently attached to HHC, 504 MI BDE).* A preponderance of evidence supports that SOLDIER-24 did, or failed to do, the following:

- Failed to report detainee abuse. He was present during the abuse of detainees depicted in photographs (Reference Annex I, Appendix 1, Photographs M36-37, M39, M41).
- Failed to stop detainee abuse.

(U) **Recommendation:** This information should be forwarded to SOLDIER-24's chain of command for appropriate action.

(15) (U) **Findings: *SOLDIER-25, Interrogator, 321st MI BN.*** A preponderance of evidence supports that SOLDIER-25 did, or failed to do, the following:

- Failed to report detainee abuse.
  - She saw Dog Handlers use dogs to scare detainees. She "thought it was funny" as the detainees would run into their cells from the dogs.
  - She was told by SOLDIER-24 that the detainees who allegedly had raped another detainee were handcuffed together, naked, in contorted positions, making it look like they were having sex with each other.
  - She was told that MPs made the detainees wear women's underwear.
- Failed to stop detainee abuse.

(U) **Recommendation:** This information should be forwarded to SOLDIER-25's chain of command for appropriate action.

(16) (U) **Finding: *SOLDIER-29, Interrogator, 66 MI GP.*** A preponderance of evidence supports that SOLDIER-29 did, or failed to do, the following:

- Failed to report detainee abuse.
  - She saw CPL Graner slap a detainee.
  - She saw a computer screen saver depicting naked detainees in a "human pyramid."
  - She was aware MPs were taking photos of detainees.
  - She knew MPs had given a detainee a cold shower, made him roll in the dirt, and stand outside in the cold until he was dry. The detainee was then given another cold shower.
- Detainee abuse (Humiliation). She violated interrogation rules of engagement by stripping a detainee of his clothes and walking him naked from an interrogation booth to Camp Vigilant on a cold winter night.
- Gave MPs instruction to mistreat/abuse detainees.
  - SOLDIER-29's telling MPs (SSG Frederick) when detainees had not cooperated in an interrogation appeared to result in subsequent abuse.
  - One of the detainees she interrogated was placed in isolation for several days and allegedly abused by the MPs. She annotated in an interrogation report (IN-AG00992-DETAINEE-08-04) that a "direct approach" was used with "the reminder of the unpleasantness that occurred the last time he lied to us."

(U) **Recommendation:** This information should be forwarded to SOLDIER-29's chain of command for appropriate action.

(17) (U) **Findings: *SOLDIER-08, Dog Handler, Abu Ghraib, 42 MP Detachment, 16 MP BDE (ABN).*** A preponderance of evidence supports that SOLDIER-08 did, or failed to do, the following:

- Inappropriate use of dogs. Photographs (Reference Annex I, Appendix 1, D46, D52, M149-151) depict SOLDIER-08 inappropriately using his dog to terrorize detainees.

- Abused detainees. SOLDIER-08 had an ongoing contest with SOLDIER-27, another dog handler, to scare detainees with their dogs in order to see who could make the detainees urinate and defecate first.

(U) **Recommendation:** This information should be forwarded to SOLDIER-08's chain of command for appropriate action.

(18) (U) **Findings: *SOLDIER34, 372 MP CO.*** A preponderance of evidence supports that SOLDIER-34 did, or failed to do, the following:

- Failed to report detainee abuse. He was present during the abuse of detainees depicted in photographs (Reference Annex I, Appendix 1, Photographs M36-37, M39-41).
- Failed to stop detainee abuse.

(U) **Recommendation:** This information should be forwarded to SOLDIER-34's chain of command for appropriate action.

(19) (U) **Findings: *SOLDIER-27, 372 MP CO.*** A preponderance of evidence supports that SOLDIER-27 did, or failed to do, the following:

- Actively participated in detainee abuse.
  - During the medical treatment (stitching) of a detainee, he stepped on the chest of the detainee (Reference Annex I, Appendix 1, Photograph M163).
  - He participated in the abuse of naked detainees depicted in photographs (Reference Annex I, Appendix 1, Photographs M36-37, M39-41).
- Failed to stop detainee abuse.

(U) **Recommendation:** This information should be forwarded to SOLDIER-27's chain of command for appropriate action.

(20) (U) **Findings: *SOLDIER-27, Dog Handler, Abu Ghraib, 523 MP Detachment.*** A preponderance of evidence supports that SOLDIER-27 did, or failed to do, the following:

- Inappropriate use of dogs. Photographs (Reference Annex I, Appendix 1, Photographs D46, D48, M148, M150, M151, M153, Z1, Z3-6) depict SOLDIER-27 inappropriately using his dog terrorizing detainees.
- Detainee abuse. SOLDIER-27 had an ongoing contest with SOLDIER-08, another dog handler, to scare detainees with their dogs and cause the detainees to urinate and defecate.
- Led his dog into a cell with two juvenile detainees and let his dog go "nuts." The two juveniles were yelling and screaming with the youngest one hiding behind the oldest.

(U) **Recommendation:** This information should be forwarded to SOLDIER-27's chain of command for appropriate action.

(21) (U) **Finding: *SOLDIER-20, Medic, 372 MP CO.*** A preponderance of evidence supports that SOLDIER-20 did, or failed to do, the following:

- Failed to report detainee abuse.

- When called to assist a detainee who had been shot in the leg, he witnessed CPL Graner hit the detainee in his injured leg with a stick.
- He saw the same detainee handcuffed to a bed over several days, causing great pain to the detainee as he was forced to stand.
- He saw the same detainee handcuffed to a bed which resulted in a dislocated shoulder.
- He saw pictures of detainees being abused (stacked naked in a "human pyramid").

(U) **Recommendation:** This information should be forwarded to SOLDIER-20's chain of command for appropriate action.

(22) (U) **Finding: *SOLDIER-01, Medic, Abu Ghraib.*** A preponderance of evidence supports that SOLDIER-01 did, or failed to do, the following:

- Failed to report detainee abuse. She saw a "human pyramid" of naked Iraqi prisoners, all with sandbags on their heads when called to the Hard Site to provide medical treatment.

(U) **Recommendation:** This information should be forwarded to SOLDIER-01's chain of command for appropriate action.

(23) (U) **Finding: *CIVILIAN-05, CACI employee.*** A preponderance of evidence supports that CIVILIAN-05 did, or failed to do, the following:

- He grabbed a detainee (who was handcuffed) off a vehicle and dropped him to the ground. He then dragged him into an interrogation booth and as the detainee tried to get up, CIVILIAN-05 would yank the detainee very hard and make him fall again.
- Disobeyed General Order Number One; drinking alcohol while at Abu Ghraib.
- Refused to take instructions from a Tiger Team leader and refused to take instructions from military trainers.
  - When confronted by SSG Neal, his Tiger Team leader, about his inadequate interrogation techniques, he replied, "I have been doing this for 20 years and I do not need a 20-year old telling me how to do my job."
  - When placed in a remedial report writing class because of his poor writing, he did not pay attention to the trainer and sat in the back of the room facing away from the trainer.

(U) **Recommendation:** This information should be forwarded to the Army General Counsel for determination of whether CIVILIAN-05 should be referred to the Department of Justice for prosecution. This information should be forwarded to the Contracting Officer (KO) for appropriate contractual action.

(24) (U) **Finding: *CIVILIAN-10, Translator, Titan employee.*** After a thorough investigation, we found no direct involvement in detainee abuse by CIVILIAN-10. Our investigation revealed CIVILIAN-10 had a valid security clearance until it was suspended.

(U) **Recommendation:** This information should be forwarded to Titan via the KO. CIVILIAN-10 is cleared of any wrongdoing and should retain his security clearance.

(25) (U) **Finding: *CIVILIAN-11, Interrogator, CACI employee.*** A preponderance of evidence supports that CIVILIAN-11 did, or failed to do, the following:

- Detainee abuse.
    - He encouraged SSG Frederick to abuse Iraqi Police detained following a shooting incident (IP Roundup). SSG Frederick twisted the handcuffs of a detainee being interrogated; causing pain.
    - He failed to prevent SSG Frederick from covering the detainee's mouth and nose restricting the detainee from breathing:
- Threatened the Iraqi Police "with SSG Frederick." He told the Iraqi Police to answer his questions or he would bring SSG Frederick back into the cell.
- Used dogs during the IP Roundup in an unauthorized manner. He told a detainee, "You see that dog there, if you do not tell me what I want to know, I'm going to get that dog on you."
- Placed a detainee in an unauthorized stress position (Reference Annex I, Appendix 2, Photograph "Stress Positions"). CIVILIAN-11 is photographed facing a detainee who is in a stress position on a chair with his back exposed. The detainee is in a dangerous position where he might fall back and injure himself.
- Failed to prevent a detainee from being photographed.

(U) **Recommendation:** This information should be forwarded to the Army General Counsel for determination of whether CIVILIAN-11 should be referred to the Department of Justice for prosecution. This information should be forwarded to the KO for appropriate contractual action.

(26) (U) **Finding: *CIVILIAN-16, Translator, Titan employee.*** A preponderance of evidence supports that CIVILIAN-16 did, or failed to do, the following:

- Failed to report detainee abuse.
    - She participated in an interrogation during the IP Roundup, where a dog was brought into a cell in violation of approved ICRP.
    - She participated in the interrogation of an Iraqi Policeman who was placed in a stress position; squatting backwards on a plastic lawn chair. Any sudden movement by the IP could have resulted in injury (Reference Annex I, Appendix 2, Photograph "Stress Positions").
    - She was present during an interrogation when SSG Frederick twisted the handcuffs of a detainee, causing the detainee pain.
    - She was present when SSG Frederick covered an IP's mouth and nose, restricting the detainee from breathing.
- Failed to report threats against detainees.
    - She was present when CIVILIAN-11 told a detainee, "You see that dog there, if you do not tell me what I want to know, I'm going to get that dog on you."
    - She was present when CIVILIAN-11 threatened a detainee "with SSG Frederick."

(U) **Recommendation:** This information should be forwarded to the Army General Counsel for determination of whether CIVILIAN-16 should be referred to the Department of Justice for prosecution. This information should be forwarded to the KO for appropriate contractual action.

(27) (U) **Finding: *CIVILIAN-17, Interpreter, Titan employee.*** A preponderance of evidence supports that CIVILIAN-17 did, or failed to do, the following:

- Actively participated in detainee abuse.
  - He was present during the abuse of detainees depicted in photographs (Reference Annex I, Appendix 1, Photographs M36-37, M39, M41).
  - A detainee claimed that CIVILIAN-17 (sic), an interpreter, hit him and cut his ear which required stitches.
  - Another detainee claimed that someone fitting CIVILIAN-17's description raped a young detainee.
- Failure to report detainee abuse.
- Failure to stop detainee abuse.

(U) **Recommendation:** This information should be forwarded to the Army General Counsel for determination of whether CIVILIAN-17 should be referred to the Department of Justice for prosecution. This information should be forwarded to the KO for appropriate contractual action.

(28) (U) ***Finding: CIVILIAN-21, Interrogator, CACI employee.*** A preponderance of evidence supports that CIVILIAN-21 did, or failed to do, the following:

- Inappropriate use of dogs. SOLDIER-26 stated that CIVILIAN-21 used a dog during an interrogation and the dog was unmuzzled. SOLDIER-25 stated she once saw CIVILIAN-21 standing on the second floor of the Hard Site, looking down to where a dog was being used against a detainee, and yelling to the MPs "Take him home." The dog had torn the detainee's mattress. He also used a dog during an interrogation with SSG Aston but stated he never used dogs.
- Detainee abuse. CPT Reese stated he saw "NAME" (his description of "NAME"" matched CIVILIAN-21) push (kick) a detainee into a cell with his foot.
- Making false statements. During questioning about the use of dogs in interrogations, CIVILIAN-21 stated he never used them.
- Failed to report detainee abuse. During an interrogation, a detainee told SOLDIER-25 and CIVILIAN-21 that CIVILIAN-17, an interpreter, hit him and cut his ear which required stitches. SOLDIER-25 stated she told CIVILIAN-21 to annotate this on the interrogation report. He did not report it to appropriate authorities.
- Detainee Humiliation.
  - CIVILIAN-15 stated he heard CIVILIAN-21 tell several people that he had shaved the hair and beard of a detainee and put him in red women's underwear. CIVILIAN-21 was allegedly bragging about it.
  - CIVILIAN-19 stated he heard OTHER AGENCY EMPLOYEE02 laughing about red panties on detainees.

(U) **Recommendation:** This information should be forwarded to the Army General Counsel for determination of whether CIVILIAN-21 should be referred to the

Department of Justice for prosecution. This information should be forwarded to the KO for appropriate contractual action.

(29) (U) **Finding:** There were several personnel who used clothing removal, improper isolation, or dogs as techniques for interrogations in violation of the Geneva Conventions. Several interrogators documented these techniques in their interrogation plans and stated they received approval from the JIDC, Interrogation Control Element. The investigative team found several entries in interrogation reports which clearly specified clothing removal; however, all personnel having the authority to approve interrogation plans claim they never approved or were aware of clothing removal being used in interrogations. Also found were interrogation reports specifying use of isolation, "the Hole." While the Commander, CJTF-7 approved "segregation" on 25 occasions, this use of isolation sometimes trended toward abuse based on sensory deprivation and inhumane conditions. Dogs were never approved, however on several occasions personnel thought they were. Personnel who committed abuse based on confusion regarding approvals or policies are in need of additional training.

(U) **Recommendation:** This information should be forwarded to the Soldiers' chain of command for appropriate action.

> CIVILIAN-14 (formally with 368 Military Intelligence Battalion)
> SOLDIER-04, 500 Military Intelligence Group
> SOLDIER-05, 500 Military Intelligence Group
> SOLDIER-03, GTMO Team, 184 Military Intelligence Company
> SOLDIER-13, 66 Military Intelligence Group
> SOLDIER-18, 66 Military Intelligence Group
> SOLDIER-02, 66 Military Intelligence Group
> SOLDIER-11 6 Battalion 98 Division (IT)
> SOLDIER-16, 325 Military Intelligence Battalion
> SOLDIER-30, 325 Military Intelligence Battalion
> SOLDIER-26, 320 Military Police Battalion
> SOLDIER-06, 302 Military Intelligence Battalion
> SOLDIER-07, 325 Military Intelligence Battalion
> SOLDIER-21, 325 Military Intelligence Battalion
> SOLDIER-09, 302 Military Intelligence Battalion
> SOLDIER-12, 302 Military Intelligence Battalion
> CIVILIAN-20, CACI Employee

(30) (U) **Finding:** In addition to SOLDIER-20 and SOLDIER-01, medical personnel may have been aware of detainee abuse at Abu Ghraib and failed to report it. The scope of this investigation was MI personnel involvement. SOLDIER-20 and SOLDIER-01 were cited because sufficient evidence existed within the scope of this investigation to establish that they were aware of detainee abuse and failed to report it. Medical records were requested, but not obtained, by this investigation. The location of the records at the time this request was made was unknown.

(U) **Recommendation:** An inquiry should be conducted into 1) whether appropriate medical records were maintained, and if so, were they properly stored and collected and 2) whether medical personnel were aware of detainee abuse and failed to properly document and report the abuse.

(31) (U) **Finding:** A preponderance of the evidence supports that SOLDIER-31, SOLDIER-32, and SOLDIER-33 participated in the alleged sexual assault of a female detainee by forcibly kissing her and removing her shirt (Reference CID Case-0216-03-CID259-6121). The individuals received non-judicial punishment for conducting an unauthorized interrogation, but were not punished for the alleged sexual assault.

(U) **Recommendation:** CID should review case # 0216-03-CID259-61211 to determine if further investigation is appropriate. The case should then be forwarded to the Soldiers' chain of command for appropriate action.

(32) (U) **Finding:** An unidentified person, believed to be a contractor interpreter, was depicted in six photographs taken on 25 October 2003, showing the abuse of three detainees. The detainees were nude and handcuffed together on the floor. This investigation could not confirm the identity of this person; however, potential leads have been passed to and are currently being pursued by CID.

(U) **Recommendation:** CID should continue to aggressively pursue all available leads to identify this person and determine the degree of his involvement in detainee abuse.

7. (U) Personnel Listing. Deleted in accordance with the Privacy Act and 10 USC §130b

8. (U) TASK FORCE MEMBERS.

LTG Anthony R. CIVILIAN-08 Command	Investigating Officer	HQs, Training and Doctrine
MG George R. Fay	Investigating Officer	HQs, Dept of the Army, G2
Mr. Thomas A. Gandy	Deputy	HQs, Dept of the Army, G2
LTC Phillip H. Bender	Chief Investigator	HQs, Dept of the Army, G2
LTC Michael Benjamin	Legal Advisor	TJAG
MAJ(P) Maricela Alvarado	Executive Officer	HQs, Dept of the Army, G2
CPT Roseanne M. Bleam	Staff Judge Advocate, CJTF-7	CJTF-7 (MNF-I) SJA
CW5 Donald Marquis	SME – Training & Doctrine	HQs, US Army Intelligence Center
CW3 Brent Pack	CID Liaison	US Army CID Command
CW2 Mark Engan	Investigator – Baghdad Team	HQs, 308th MI Bn, 902nd MI Group

SGT Patrick D. Devine	All Source Analyst	ACIC, 310th MI Bn, 9022nd MI Group
CPL Ryan Hausterman	Investigator – Baghdad Team	HQs, 310th MI Bn, 9022nd MI Group
Mr. Maurice J. Sheley	Investigator	HQs, US Army INSCOM
Mr. Michael P. Scanland	Investigator	HQs, 9022nd MI Group
Mr. Claude B. Benner	Investigative Review	ACIC, 9022nd MI Group
Mr. Michael Wright	Investigator	HQs, 308th MI Bn, 9022nd MI Group
Mr. Scott Robertson	Investigator	HQs, Dept of the Army, G2
Mr. Paul Stark	Chief of Analysis	ACIC, 310th MI Bn, 9022nd MI Group
Mr. Kevin Brucie	Investigator – Baghdad Team	Det 13, FCA, 9022nd MI Group
Ms. Linda Flanigan	Analyst	ACIC, 310th MI Bn, 9022nd MI Group
Mr. Albert Scott	Cyber-Forensic Analyst	HQs, 310th MI Bn, 9022nd MI Group
Ms. Saoirse Spain	Analyst	ACIC, 310th MI Bn, 9022nd MI group
Mr. Albert J. McCarn Jr.	Chief of Logistics	HQs, Dept of the Army, G2
Ms. Cheryl Clowser	Administrator	HQs, Dept of the Army, G2
Mr. Alfred Moreau	SME – Contract Law	HQs, Dept of the Army, OTJAG
Mr. Rudolph Garcia	Senior Editor	HQs, Dept of the Army, G2

Contract Services provided by Object Sciences Corp. and SYTEX

9. (U) Acronyms.

2 MI BN	2d Military Intelligence Battalion
B/321 MI BN	B Company, 321st Military Intelligence Battalion
B/325 MI BN	B Company, 325th Military Intelligence Battalion
A/205 MI BN	A Company, 205th Military Intelligence Battalion
115 MP BN	115th Military Police Battalion
165 MI BN	165th Military Intelligence Battalion
205 MI BDE	205th Military Intelligence Brigade
229 MP CO	229th Military Police Battalion
320 MP BN	320th Military Police Battalion
320 MP CO	320th Military Police Company
323 MI BN	323d Military Intelligence Battalion
325 MI BN	325th Military Intelligence Battalion
372 MP CO	372d Military Police Company
377 TSC	377th Theater Support Command
400 MP BN	400th Military Police Battalion

470 MI GP	470th Military Intelligence Group
447 MP CO	447th Military Police Company
500 MI GP	500th Military Intelligence Group
504 MI BDE	504th Military Intelligence Battalion
519 MI BN	519th Military Intelligence Battalion
66 MI GP	66th Military Intelligence Group
670 MP CO	670th Military Police Company
72 MP CO	72d Military Police Company
800 MP BDE	800th Military Police Brigade
870 MP CO	870th Military Police Company
1SG	First Sergeant
A/519 MI BN	A Company, 519th Military Intelligence Battalion
AAR	After Action Report
AFJI	Air Force Joint Instructor
AG	Abu Ghraib
ANCOC	Advanced Non-Commission Officer's Course
AR	Army Regulation
ATSD (IO)	Assistant to the Secretary of Defense for Intelligence Oversight
BDE	Brigade
BG	Brigadier General
BIAP	Baghdad International Airport
BN	Battalion
BNCOC	Basic Non-Commission Officer's Course
BPA	Blanket Purchase Agreement
C2X	Command and Control Exercise
CALL	Center for Army Lessons Learned
CENTCOM	US Central Command
CG	Commanding General
CHA	Corps Holding Area
CIA	Central Intelligence Agency
CID	Criminal Investigation Command
CJCS-I	Chairman, Joint Chief of Staff Instruction
CJTF-7	Combined Joint Task Force 7
CM&D	Collection Management and Dissemination
COL	Colonel
COR	Contracting Officers Representative
CP	Collection Point
CPA	Coalition Provisional Authority
CPL	Corporal
CPT	Captain
CSH	Combat Support Hospital
DA	Department of the Army
DAIG	Department of the Army Inspector General
DCI	Director of Central Intelligence
DCG	Deputy Commanding General
DIAM	Defense Intelligence Agency Manual
DoD	Department of Defense
1LT	First Lieutenant
CASH	Combat Army Surgical Hospital
DIA	Defense Intelligence Agency

KO	Contracting Officer
DOJ	Department of Justice
DRA	Detention Review Authority
DRB	Detainee Release Branch
EPW	Enemy Prisoner of War
FM	Field Manual
FOB	Forward Operating Base
FRAGO	Fragmentary Order
G-3	Army Training Division
GCIV	Geneva Conventions IV
GP	Group
GSA	General Services Administration
GTMO	Guantanamo Naval Base, Cuba
GWOT	Global War On Terrorism
HQ	Headquarters
HUMINT	Human Intelligence
IAW	In Accordance With
ICE	Interrogation and Control Element
ICRC	International Committee of the Red Cross
ICRP	Interrogation and Counter-Resistance Policies
IET	Initial Entry Training
ID	Infantry Division
IG	Inspector General
IMINT	Imagery Intelligence
INSCOM	Intelligence and Security Command
IP	Iraqi Police
IR	Internment/Resettlement
IROE	Interrogation Rules Of Engagement
ISCT	Interrogation Support to Counterterrorism
ISG	Iraqi Survey Group
JA	Judge Advocate
JCS	Joint Chiefs of Staff
JIDC	Joint Interrogation and Detention Center
JTF-GTMO	Joint Task Force Guantanamo
MAJ	Major
MCO	Marine Corps Order
LTC	Lieutenant Colonel
LTG	Lieutenant General
MFR	Memorandum For Record
MG	Major General
MI	Military Intelligence
MIT	Mobile Interrogation Team
MOS	Military Occupational Specialty
MOU	Memorandum of Understanding
MP	Military Police
MRE	Meals Ready to Eat
MSC	Major Subordinate Command
MSG	Master Sergeant
MTT	Mobile Training Team
NCO	Non-Commissioned Officer

NCOIC	Non-Commissioned Officer In Charge
OER	Officer Evaluation Report
OGA	Other Government Agency
OGC	Office Of General Counsel
OIC	Officer In Charge
OIF	Operation Iraqi Freedom
OPORD	Operations Order
OPNAVINST	Office of the Chief of Naval Operations Instructions
OSJA	Office Of the Staff Judge Advocate
OVB	Operation Victory Bounty
RP	Retained Personnel
SASO	Stability And Support Operations
SECARMY	Secretary of the Army
SECDEF	Secretary of Defense
SFC	Sergeant First Class
SGT	Sergeant
SIGINT	Signals Intelligence
SITREP	Situation Report
HMMWV	High-Mobility, Multipurpose Wheeled Vehicle
PFC	Private First Class
MA1	Master at Arms 1
MA2	Master at Arms 2
PVT	Private
QRF	Quick Reaction Force
SJA	Staff Judge Advocate
SOF	Special Operations Forces
SOP	Standard Operating Procedure
SOUTHCOM	US Southern Command
SOW	Statement of Work
SSG	Staff Sergeant
TACON	Tactical Control
THT	Tactical HUMINT Team
TRADOC	Training and Doctrine Command
TTP	Tactics, Techniques, and Procedures
UCMJ	Uniform Code Of Military Justice
USAIC	US Army Intelligence Center
USAR	US Army Reserve
VFR	Visual Flight Rules
E-6	Enlisted Grade 6 (Staff Sergeant)
E-7	Enlisted Grade 7 (Sergeant First Class)
E-5	Enlisted Grade 5 (Sergeant)
96B	Intelligence Analyst
NBC	National Business Center
FSS	Federal Supply Schedule
POC	Point of Contact
DAIG	Department of the Army Inspector General
97E	Human Intelligence Collector
351E	Interrogation Warrant Officer
FBI	Federal Bureau of Investigation
ISN	Internee Serial Number

JTF-21	Joint Task Force – 21
TF-121	Task Force – 121
SEAL	Sea, Air, Land
SPC	Specialist
RFF	Request for Forces
TF-20	Task Force – 20
97B	Counterintelligence Agent
CM&D	Collection, Management and Dissemination
JIG	Joint Intelligence Group
351B	Counterintelligence Warrant Officer
PT	Physical Training
IRF	Internal Reaction Force

American Bar Association
Report to the House of Delegates

August 2004

REVISED 10-B

Adopted by Voice Vote
August 9, 2004

AMERICAN BAR ASSOCIATION

ASSOCIATION OF THE BAR OF THE CITY OF NEW YORK
TASK FORCE ON TREATMENT OF ENEMY COMBATANTS
CRIMINAL JUSTICE SECTION
SECTION OF INDIVIDUAL RIGHTS AND RESPONSIBILITIES
SECTION OF INTERNATIONAL LAW AND PRACTICE
SECTION OF LITIGATION
CENTER FOR HUMAN RIGHTS
BEVERLY HILLS BAR ASSOCIATION
BAR ASSOCIATION OF SAN FRANCISCO
NATIONAL ASSOCIATION OF CRIMINAL DEFENSE LAWYERS
SECTION OF ADMINISTRATIVE LAW AND REGULATORY PRACTICE
SECTION OF BUSINESS LAW
NEW YORK STATE BAR ASSOCIATION
VIRGIN ISLANDS BAR ASSOCIATION
NEW YORK COUNTY LAWYERS' ASSOCIATION

REPORT TO THE HOUSE OF DELEGATES

RECOMMENDATION

RESOLVED, That the American Bar Association condemns any use of torture or other cruel, inhuman or degrading treatment or punishment upon persons within the custody or under the physical control of the United States government (including its contractors) and any endorsement or authorization of such measures by government lawyers, officials and agents;

FURTHER RESOLVED, That the American Bar Association urges the United States government to comply fully with the Constitution and laws of the United States and treaties to which the United States is a party, including the Geneva Conventions of August 12, 1949, the International Covenant on Civil and Political Rights, the Convention Against Torture and Other Cruel, Inhuman or Degrading Treatment or Punishment, and related customary international law, including Article 75 of the 1977 Protocol I to the Geneva Conventions, to take all measures necessary to ensure that no person within the custody or under the physical control of the United States government is subjected to torture or other cruel, inhuman or degrading treatment or punishment;

FURTHER RESOLVED, That the American Bar Association urges the United States government to: (a) comply fully with the four Geneva Conventions of August 12, 1949, including timely compliance with all provisions that require access to protected persons by the International Committee of the Red Cross; (b) observe the minimum protections of their common Article 3 and related customary international law; and (c) enforce such compliance through all applicable laws, including the War Crimes Act and the Uniform Code of Military Justice;

FURTHER RESOLVED, That the American Bar Association urges the United States government to take all measures necessary to ensure that all foreign persons captured, detained, interned or otherwise held within the custody or under the physical control of the United States are treated in accordance with standards that the United States would consider lawful if employed with respect to an American captured by a foreign power;

FURTHER RESOLVED, That the American Bar Association urges the United States government to take all measures necessary to ensure that no person within the custody or under the physical control of the United States is turned over to another government when the United States has substantial grounds to believe that such person will be in danger of being subjected to torture or other cruel, inhuman or degrading treatment or punishment;

FURTHER RESOLVED, That the American Bar Association urges that 18 U.S.C. §§ 2340(1) and 2340A be amended to encompass torture wherever committed, and regardless of the underlying motive or purpose;

FURTHER RESOLVED, That the American Bar Association urges the United States government to pursue vigorously (1) the investigation of violations of law, including the War Crimes Act and the Uniform Code of Military Justice, with respect to the mistreatment or rendition of persons within the custody or under the physical control of the United States government, and (2) appropriate proceedings against persons who may have committed, assisted, authorized, condoned, had command responsibility for, or otherwise participated in such violations;

FURTHER RESOLVED, That the American Bar Association urges the President and Congress, in addition to pending congressional investigations, to establish an independent, bipartisan commission with subpoena power to prepare a full account of detention and interrogation practices carried out by the United States, to make public findings, and to provide recommendations designed to ensure that such practices adhere faithfully to the Constitution and laws of the United States and treaties to which the United States is a party, including the Geneva Conventions, the International Covenant on Civil and Political Rights, and the Convention against Torture and Other Cruel, Inhuman or Degrading Treatment or Punishment, and related customary international law, including Article 75 of the 1977 Protocol I to the Geneva Conventions;

FURTHER RESOLVED, That the American Bar Association urges the United States government to comply fully and in a timely manner with its reporting obligations as a Sate Party to the Convention Against Torture and Other Cruel, Inhuman or Degrading Treatment or Punishment;

FURTHER RESOLVED, That the American Bar Association urges that, in establishing and executing national policy regarding the treatment of persons within the custody or under the physical control of the United States government, Congress and the Executive Branch should consider how United States practices may affect (a) the treatment of United States persons who may be captured and detained by other nations and (b) the credibility of objections by the United States to the use of torture or other cruel, inhuman or degrading treatment or punishment against United States persons.

REPORT

INTRODUCTION

The use of torture and cruel, inhuman or degrading treatment by United States personnel in the interrogation of prisoners captured in the Afghanistan and Iraq conflicts has brought shame on the nation and undermined our standing in the world. While the U.S. government has acknowledged, and is moving to punish, the acts at Abu Ghraib that have been documented on videotape, this does not address the substantial, fundamental concerns regarding U.S. interrogation policy and the treatment of detainees.

The U.S. government maintains that its policies comport with the requirements of law, and that the violations at Abu Ghraib represent isolated instances of individual misconduct. But there apparently has been a widespread pattern of abusive detention methods. Executive Branch memoranda were developed to justify interrogation procedures that are in conflict with long-held interpretations and understandings of the reach of treaties and laws governing treatment of detainees. Whether and to what extent the memoranda were relied upon by U.S. officials may be open to question, but it is clear that those legal interpretations do not represent sound policy, risk undercutting the government's ability to assert any high moral ground in its "war on terrorism", and put Americans at risk of being tortured or subjected to cruel, inhuman or degrading treatment by governments and others willing to cite U.S. actions as a pretext for their own misconduct.

The American public still has not been adequately informed of the extent to which prisoners have been abused, tortured, or rendered to foreign governments which are known to abuse and torture prisoners. There is public concern that the investigations under way to identify those accountable for prisoner abuse are moving slowly, and are too limited in scope. We do not yet know who is being detained, where they are, what are the conditions of their detention and interrogation, which agencies and personnel are exercising authority over them, who made the decisions regarding

U.S. detention policy, and what, precisely, is the U.S. policy toward treatment of detainees.

It is incumbent upon this organization, which makes the rule of law its touchstone, to urge the U.S. government to stop the torture and abuse of detainees, investigate violations of law and prosecute those who committed, authorized or condoned those violations, and assure that detention and interrogation practices adhere faithfully to the Constitution, laws and treaties of the United States and related customary international law.

BACKGROUND

In conducting military operations in Afghanistan and Iraq, and in undertaking other acts related to the "war on terrorism", the United States has detained large numbers of persons believed to be involved in activities in furtherance of terrorism or in opposition to U.S. military actions. There was great interest in obtaining information from these detainees regarding upcoming actions against U.S. forces and planned terrorist attacks. From the outset, questions were raised regarding the lengths to which United States personnel could go to extract information from detainees[1]. High-level legal memoranda dating from early 2002[2] sketched out the legal positions which could be advanced to defend interrogation techniques which had not previously been considered legal or appropriate for use by U.S. personnel and were beyond standard military doctrine.[3]

Allegations of the use of interrogation techniques long considered to be torture or cruel, inhuman or degrading treatment began to surface in connection with interrogations of persons captured during the conflict in Afghanistan. The first public acknowledgement of these allegations came in December 2002, when the U.S. military announced that it had begun a criminal investigation into the death of a 22-year old Afghan farmer and part-time taxi driver who had died of "blunt force injuries to lower extremities complicating coronary artery disease" while in U.S. custody at Bagram Air Force Base in Afghanistan.[4]

The American public has now learned that in December 2002, Secretary of Defense Rumsfeld approved a series of harsh questioning techniques for use in Guantanamo; novel techniques, including use of dogs to scare prisoners, were authorized in Iraq; and only after the Abu Ghraib scandal brought U.S. interrogation procedures into

---

[1] *See, e.g.,* Dana Priest & Bradley Graham, *U.S. Struggled Over How Far to Push Tactics,* WASH. POST, June 24, 2004, at A01 (hereinafter *"U.S. Struggled"*).

[2] *See* Memorandum from John Yoo, Deputy Assistant Attorney General, to William J. Haynes, General Counsel, DOD (January 9, 2002)

[3] *See* Douglas Jehl, *Detainee Treatment; U.S. Rules on Prisoners Seen as a Back and Forth of Mixed Messages to G.I. 's,* N.Y. TIMES, June 22, 2004 at A1 (hereinafter, *"Detainee Treatment"*); *U.S. Struggled,* supra note 1.

[4] Carlotta Gall, *U S. Military Investigating Death of Afghan In Custody,* N.Y. TIMES, Mar. 4, 2003, at A14. According to the *New York Times,* another Afghan man died of a pulmonary embolism or a blood clot in the lung while in U.S. custody at Bagram on December 3, 2002. Both men died within days of arriving at Bagram. Human Rights Watch criticized the U.S. government for failing, one year after the first two deaths at Bagram – which were classified as homicides, to release the results of its investigation. *See* Press Releases & Documents, Voice of America, Rights Group Criticizes U.S. Military for Treatment of Afghan Detainees (Dec. 1, 2003) (printed at 2003 WL 66801402).

public view was there a substantial scaling back of the authorized techniques in Iraq.[5] In addition, while the Department of Defense ("DOD") exercises control over thousands of detainees, the Central Intelligence Agency ("CIA") is conducting a secret detention operation, including an extensive program in Afghanistan.[6] While the details of this operation are not being disclosed, Secretary of Defense Donald Rumsfeld has admitted to keeping the identity of a suspect secret, and hiding him from the International Committee of the Red Cross ("ICRC"), at the request of the CIA.[7] The ICRC has criticized the U.S. for not providing the ICRC with notification of, or access to, other persons in U.S. custody.[8]

Allegations of abusive techniques reportedly being practiced by DOD and CIA personnel and U.S. government contractors at U.S. detention facilities in Iraq and Afghanistan include: forcing detainees to stand or kneel for hours in black hoods or spray-painted goggles, 24-hour bombardment with lights, "false-flag" operations meant to deceive a captive about his whereabouts, withholding painkillers from wounded detainees, confining detainees in tiny rooms, binding in painful positions, subjecting detainees to loud noises, and sleep deprivation.[9] In addition, the U.S. is reportedly "rendering" suspects to the custody of foreign intelligence services in countries where the practice of torture and cruel, inhuman or degrading treatment during interrogation is well-documented.[10]

The abusive treatment of detainees became consistent front-page news in April 2004, when videotapes circulated showing extensive torture and abusive treatment by United States personnel of detainees in the Abu Ghraib prison in Baghdad. These disclosures were followed by further charges of severe mistreatment by former detainees in Afghanistan, Iraq and the Guantanamo Naval Base. Military sources indicate that over 30 prisoners have died in U.S. custody[11] and military officials have acknowledged two prisoner deaths they consider to be homicides and are investigating another 12 deaths.[12] Prison guards charged that intelligence officers told them to "soften up"

---

[5] *See, e.g., U.S. Struggled*, supra note 1; Editorial, *Torture Policy*, WASH. POST, June 16, 2004, at A26; Julian Coman, *Interrogation abuses were 'approved at highest levels'*, London Daily Telegraph, June 13, 2004 (www.portal.telegraph.co.uk/core/Content/displayPrintable.jhtml?xml=/news/2004/06).

[6] *See* Dana Priest & Joe Stephens, *Secret World of U.S. Interrogation; Long History of Tactics in Overseas Prisons in Coming to Light*, WASH. POST, May 11, 2004, ar A01; Seymour M. Hersh, *Annals of National Security; The Gray Zone*, NEW YORKER, May 24, 2004 (*www.newyorker.com/printable/?fact/040524fa fact*).

[7] *See U.S. Struggled*, supra note 1.

[8] *See U.S. Hiding Terror Suspects? Red Cross Wants Access to Detainees*, ASSOC. PRESS, June 13, 2004.

[9] *See, e.g.,* Dana Priest & Barton Gellman, *U.S. Decries Abuse but Defends Interrogations*; *"Stress and Duress" Tactics used on Terrorism Suspects Held in Secret Overseas Facilities*, WASH. POST, Dec. 26, 2002, at A01 (hereinafter "U.S. Decries Abuse"); Eric Lichtblau & Adam Liptak, *Questioning to Be Legal, Humane and Aggressive, The White House Says Now*, N.Y. TIMES, Mar. 4, 2003, at A13; Jess Bravin & Gary Fields, *How do U.S. Interrogators Make A Captured Terrorist Talk*, WALL ST. J., Mar 4, 2003, at B 1; Tania Branigan, *Ex-Prisoners Allege Rights Abuses By U.S. Military*, WASH. POST, Aug. 19, 2003, at A02.

[10] Captives have reportedly been "rendered" by the U.S. to Jordan, Egypt, Morocco, Saudi Arabia and Syria, in secret and without resort to legal process. *See, e.g.,* Peter Finn, *Al Qaeda Recruiter Reportedly Tortured; Ex-Inmate in Syria Cites Others' Accounts*, WASH. POST, Jan. 31, 2003, at A14; *U.S. Decries* Abuse, supra note 8; Rajiv Chandrasekaran & Peter Finn, *US. Behind Secret Transfer of Terror Suspects*, WASH. POST, Mar. 11, 2002, at A01.

[11] *New Probes Of Prison Deaths*, CBSNEWS.com, June 30, 2004.

[12] *14 prisoner deaths under investigation*, MSNBC (www.msnbc.msn.com/id/4901264), May 5, 2004.

the Iraqi prisoners, with no explanation as to what that meant.[13] Over 100 cases of misconduct in Iraq and Afghanistan have now been reported.[14]

As the Department of Defense and the CIA were preparing and implementing their approach to interrogations, a series of memoranda were being prepared by various high-ranking legal officials in the Executive Branch which appear designed to provide a legal basis for going beyond established policies with regard to treatment of detainees. These memoranda set out a series of arguments for restrictive interpretation of the laws and treaties relevant to the subject, so as to greatly curb their effect. One example, in the August 1, 2002 memorandum from the Department of Justice Office of Legal Counsel to Alberto R. Gonzales, Counsel to the President, (recently rescinded by the Justice Department) concluded that for an act to constitute torture as defined in 18 U.S.C. § 2340, "it must inflict pain that is difficult to endure", "equivalent in intensity to the pain accompanying serious physical injury, such as organ failure, impairment of bodily function, or even death."[15]

Beyond their strained interpretation of the law, the memoranda attempted to craft an overall insulation from liability by arguing that the President has the authority to ignore any law or treaty that he believes interferes with the President's Article II power as Commander-in-Chief. In one such example, government lawyers argued that, for actions taken with respect to "the President's inherent constitutional authority to manage a military campaign, 18 U.S.C. § 2340A (the prohibition against torture) must be construed as inapplicable to interrogations undertaken pursuant to his Commander-in-Chief authority."[16]

These documents,[17] which were released publicly after they were widely leaked, purported to provide authority for an aggressive effort to extract information from detainees using means not previously sanctioned. We do not construe the giving of good faith legal advice to constitute endorsement or authorization of torture. Moreover, it is unclear to what extent these memoranda represented or formed the basis for official policy. However, what does seem clear is that the memoranda and the decisions of high U.S. officials at the very least contributed to a culture in which prisoner abuse became widespread.

The Administration has acknowledged that the conduct that was featured in the Abu Ghraib tapes violated the law, and pledged that those who committed the violations would be brought to justice. In addition, at least six investigations are under way with regard to the abuse of detainees.[18] It is important these investigations be thorough and timely, and that they be conducted by officers and agencies with the scope and authority to reach all those who should be held responsible.

---

[13] *See Detainee Treatment*, supra note 3.

[14] Editorial, *Remedies for Prisoner Abuse*, WASH. POST, June 7, 2004, at A18.

[15] Memorandum, at 1. It should be noted there are JAG officers who have expressed concerns regarding the approach of DOD and that outlined in these internal memoranda with regard to compliance with the Geneva Conventions and the methods used to interrogate detainees. *See, e.g.*, Adam Liptak, *U.S. Barred Legal Review of Detentions, Lawyer Says*, N.Y. TIMES, May 19, 2004, at A14.

[16] *Working Group Report on Detainee Interrogations in the Global War on Terrorism: Assessment of Legal, Historical, Policy, and Operational Considerations, 6 March 2003*, at 21 (hereinafter *Working Group Report*).

[17] *See* A Guide to the Memos on Torture, www.nytimes.com/ref/international/24MEMO-GUIDE.html (posted June 26, 2004).

[18] *See "Detainee Treatment"*, supra note 3.

LEGAL STANDARDS

The Convention Against Torture

The United States' obligation to prohibit and prevent the torture and cruel, inhuman or degrading treatment of detainees in its custody is set forth in the Convention Against Torture And Other Cruel, Inhuman, or Degrading Treatment ("CAT"), to which the U.S. is a party.[19] Under CAT, there are no exceptional circumstances that warrant torture, and extradition or other rendering of a person to a country that would likely subject that person to torture is prohibited. The United Nations Committee Against Torture, created by CAT, monitors implementation of CAT, considers country reports and issues decisions.

When the U.S. ratified CAT in 1994, it did so subject to a reservation providing that the U.S. would prevent "cruel, inhuman or degrading treatment" insofar as such treatment is prohibited under the Fifth, Eighth, and/or Fourteenth Amendments.[20] Thus, the U.S. is obligated to prevent not only torture, but also conduct considered cruel, inhuman or degrading under international law if such conduct is also prohibited by the Fifth, Eighth and Fourteenth Amendments.

In interpreting U.S. obligations, we look to the U.N. Committee Against Torture's interpretations of CAT as well as U.S. case law decided in the immigration and asylum law context, under the Alien Tort Claims and Torture Victim Protection Acts and concerning the treatment of detainees and prisoners under the Fifth, Eighth or Fourteenth Amendments. Under these interpretations, measures such as severe sleep deprivation, the threat of torture, and forcing someone to sleep on the floor of a cell while handcuffed following interrogation constitutes torture[21] The U.N. Committee found that such measures as physical restraints in very painful conditions, being hooded, and using cold air to chill – all measures of which United States interrogators are accused of using – constitute cruel, inhuman or degrading treatment.[22]

The United States' attempt to comply with its obligation under CAT to criminalize torture is codified in 18 U.S.C. § 2340A. Section 2340A criminalizes conduct by a U.S. national or a foreign national present in the U.S. who, acting under color of law, commits or attempts to commit torture outside the United States. The statute is exclusively criminal and may not be construed as creating any right enforceable in a civil proceeding. It is also narrower in scope than CAT. Section 2340A generally applies to acts committed by U.S. nationals overseas (everywhere *except* "all areas under the jurisdiction of the United States, including any of the places described in sections 5 and 7 of this title and § 46501(2) of Title 49.") When the section was enacted the reach of the cross-referenced provisions, notably 18 U.S.C. § 7, was uncertain.[23] However, § 7

---

[19] Convention Against Torture and Other Cruel, Inhuman or Degrading Treatment or Punishment, *opened for signature* Feb. 4, 1985, G.A. Res. 46, U.N. GAOR 39th Sess., Supp. No. 51, at 197, U.N. Doc. A/RES/39/708 (1984), *reprinted in* 23 I.L.M. 1027 (1984) ("CAT").

[20] 136 Cong. Rec. S17486-01, 1990 WL 168442.

[21] Concluding Observations concerning Republic of Korea (1996), U.N. Doc. No. a/52/44, at para. 56; Concluding Observations concerning New Zealand (1993), U.N. Doc. No. A/48/44, at para. 148; *See* Inquirey under Article 20: Committee Against Torture, Findings concerning Peru (2001), U.N. Doc. No. A/56/44, at para. 35.

[22] Concluding Observations concerning Israel (1997), U.N. Doc. No. A/52/44, at para. 257.

[23] *Compare U.S. v. Gatlin*, 216 F.3d 207 (2d Cir 2000) *with U.S. v. Corey*, 232 F.3d 1166 (9th Cir 2000). However, the question was substantially mooted for most purposes by the passage of the Military

was broadened in the USA PATRIOT Act to clarify jurisdiction over crimes committed against U.S. citizens on U.S. property abroad by extending U.S. criminal jurisdiction over certain crimes committed at its foreign diplomatic, military and other facilities (which would encompass extraterritorial detention centers under U.S. jurisdiction) and by cross-reference excluded those places from the reach of § 2340A.

Section 2340A defines torture to be any "act committed by a person acting under color of law specifically intended to inflict severe physical or mental pain..." The Administration has interpreted this "specific intent" language to virtually eliminate its use against torturers: [E]ven if the defendant knows that severe pain will result from his actions, if causing such harm is not his objective, he lacks the requisite specific intent even though the defendant did not act in good faith."[24] So long as the purpose is to get information, this interpretation suggests that any means may be used. This language clearly needs to be restricted to facilitate meaningful enforcement of CAT by the United States. The U.S. did not enact a specific criminal statute outlawing torture within the United States, out of deference to federal-state relations and because it determined that existing federal and state criminal law was sufficient to cover any domestic act that would qualify as torture under CAT.[25]

The Uniform Code of Military Justice may be used to prosecute in courts-martial certain acts of ill-treatment carried out, whether in the United States or overseas, by American military personnel and possibly certain civilians, such as CIA agents, accompanying such personnel. The UCMJ is the most substantively extensive body of federal criminal law relating to interrogation of detainees by U.S. military personnel. The UCMJ prohibits such persons from subjecting detainees to torture and "cruelty and maltreatment" regardless of the applicability of the constitutional rights exception to CAT.[26] There is no civilian parallel to the provisions of the UCMJ. Recent events make a persuasive case that the inapplicability of state law to U.S. facilities abroad and the lack of other federal criminal law comparable to § 2340A leaves a gap in anti-torture law that should be filled.

Unfortunately the U.S. has never enforced 18 U.S.C. § 2340A, and has thereby fallen far short of its obligations under international law and its professed ideals. It has failed to utilize the statute to prosecute either U.S. agents suspected of committing torture outside the jurisdiction of the U.S. or foreign torturers living within the United States.[27] In addition, the United States is out of compliance with the requirement under Article 19 of CAT that it report to the United Nations Committee Against Torture every four years on measures taken to give effect to its undertakings under the

Extraterritorial Jurisdiction Act of 2000, Pub. L. 106-503, 112 Stat. 2488, which subjects persons accompanying the armed forces abroad to U.S. civilian criminal jurisdiction, even if outside the "special maritime and territorial jurisdiction."
[24] *Working Group Report*, supra note 15, at 9.
[25] *See* U.S. Dept. of State, Initial Report of the United States of America to the U.N. Committee against Torture, U.N. Doc. CAT/C/28/Add.5 (1999), at para. 178.
[26] 10 U.S.C.§ 893.
[27] *Amnesty International Report Charges U.S. is "Safe Haven" for Torturers Fleeing Justice; Eight Years On, U.S. Has Failed to Prosecute Single Individual for Torture*, Amnesty International Press Release (2002) (*available at* http://www.amnestyusa.org/news/2002/usa04102002.html). See also William J. Aceves United States of America: A Safe Haven For Torturers (Amnesty International USA Publications 2002), at 50.

Convention. The Second report was due in 1999, and the U.N. Committee has written to the United States asking for submission of the overdue report by October 1, 2004.

The Geneva Conventions

Geneva Convention III Relative to the Treatment of Prisoners of War ("Geneva III") flatly prohibits "any form of coercion" of POWs in interrogation – the most protective standard of treatment found in international law. Geneva Convention IV Relative to the Protection of Civilian Persons in Time of War ("Geneva IV") protects "civilian" detainees who qualify as "protected persons" from "coercion."[28]

The U.S., Iraq and Afghanistan are all parties to the Geneva Conventions. Article 2 common to all four Conventions provides that the Conventions "apply to all cases of declared war or of any other armed conflict" between two or more parties to the Conventions so long as a state of war is recognized by a party to the conflict. The Conventions also apply to all cases of partial or total occupation of the territory of a signatory, even if the occupation meets with no armed resistance. *See* Geneva Conventions, Article 2. Signatories to the Conventions are bound by its terms regardless of whether any other party to the conflict is a signatory. *Id.*

The requirements of humane treatment embodied in Common Article 3 of the Geneva Conventions and Article 75 of Additional Protocol I protect all detainees captured in situations of international or internal armed conflict, regardless of "legal" status.[29] Of course, all detainees – including those captured outside of Afghan territory or in connection with the "War on Terror" – are entitled to the

---

[28] *See* Section II(C) for a discussion of who qualifies as a "protected person" under Geneva IV.

[29] "Common Article 3" provides that detainees "shall in all circumstances be treated humanely" and prohibits the following acts "at any time and in any place whatsoever": "violence to life and person, in particular murder of all kinds, mutilation, cruel treatment and torture;" and "outrages upon personal dignity, in particular humiliating or degrading treatment." Common Article 3 also provides that the "wounded and sick shall be collected and cared for."

Although neither the United States nor Afghanistan is a party to Additional Protocol I, it is generally acknowledged that relevant sections of Protocol I constitute either binding customary international law or good practice, in particular the minimum safeguards guaranteed by Article 75(2). See Michael J. Matheson, *Remarks on the United States Position on the Relation of Customary International Law to the 1977 Protocols Additional to the 1949 Geneva Conventions, reprinted in The Sixth Annual American Red Cross-Washington College of Law Conference on International Humanitarian Law: A Workshop on Customary International Law and the 1977 Protocols Additional to the 1949 Geneva Conventions*, 2 AM. U. J. INT'L L. & POL'Y 415, 425-6 (1987).

Article 75 provides that "persons who are in the power of a Party to the conflict and who do not benefit from more favourable treatment under the Conventions" "shall be treated humanely in all circumstances" and that each state Party "shall respect the person, honour, convictions and religious practices of all such persons." Paragraph 2 of Article 75 prohibits, "at any time and in any place whatsoever, whether committed by civilian or military agents": "violence to the life, health, or physical or mental well-being of persons, in particular... torture of all kinds, whether physical or mental," "corporal punishment," and "mutilation"; "outrages upon personal dignity, in particular humiliating and degrading treatment... and any form of indecent assault"; and "threats to commit any of the foregoing acts."

The U.S. rejection of Additional Protocol I was explained in a presidential note to the Senate in the following terms: "Protocol I... would grant combatant status to irregular forces even if they do not satisfy the traditional requirements to distinguish themselves from the civilian population and otherwise comply with the laws of war. This would endanger civilians among whom terrorists and other irregulars attempt to conceal themselves. These problems are so fundamental in character that they cannot be remedied through reservations...." *See* 1977 U.S.T. LEXIS 465.

protection provided by human rights law, including CAT, the ICCPR and customary international law.

The Administration's official position is that the Geneva Conventions apply to the War in Afghanistan[30] and the occupation of Iraq,[31] but do not apply to al Qaeda detainees, and that neither the Taliban nor al Qaeda detainees are entitled to prisoner of war ("POW") status thereunder. Initially, the Administration's position was that the Geneva Convention did not apply to the Taliban, but it relented, except with regard to withholding POW status.[32] The legal underpinning of this approach is found in the internal government documents dating from early 2002 cited above.[33] The stated purposes of this analysis were to preserve maximum flexibility with the least restraint by international law and to immunize government officials from prosecution under the War Crimes Act, which renders certain violations of the Geneva Conventions violations of U.S. criminal law.

The Administration has stated that it is treating Taliban and al Qaeda detainees "humanely and, to the extent appropriate and consistent with military necessity, in a manner consistent with the principles of the Third Geneva Convention of 1949," and that the detainees "will not be subjected to physical or mental abuse or cruel treatment."[34] However, the Administration has never explained how it determines what interrogation techniques are "appropriate" or "consistent with military necessity," or how it squares that determination with U.S. obligations under human rights and customary international law.

Furthermore, the Administration's approach raises serious issues regarding the application of the Geneva Conventions to the War on Terror, notably the minimal protections of Common Article 3 and the actual standards applied in the field. The internal Administration memoranda argue that Common Article 3 does not apply at all to al Qaeda's activities in the Afghanistan conflict because, inasmuch as al Qaeda operated cross-border and with support from persons in countries outside Afghanistan, that conflict is not an armed conflict of a non-international character within the meaning of Article 3. In fact, the Geneva Conventions are structured in terms of international armed conflicts (between State parties) and non-international (non-inter-State) conflict. There is no indication that there is any category of armed conflict that is not covered by the Geneva Conventions.[35] The Geneva Conventions

---

[30] See, e.g., Sean D. Murphy, Contemporary Practice of the United States Relating to International Law, 96 AM. J. INT'L L. 461, 476-77 (2002).

[31] S.C. Res. 1483, U.N. Doc s/Res/1483 (2003).

[32] See White House Fact Sheet: Status of Detainees at Guantanamo (February 7, 2002) (available at http://www.whitehouse.gov/news/releases/2002/02/print/20020207-13.html).

[33] See, e.g., Michael Isikoff, "Double Standards? A Justice Department memo proposes that the United States hold others accountable for international laws on detainees – but that Washington did not have to follow them itself" Newsweek, May 22, 2004, available at <www.msnbc.msn.com/id/5032094/site/newsweek/>.

[34] See White House Fact Sheet: Status of Detainees at Guantánamo (Feb. 7, 2002) (available at http://www.whitehouse.gov/news/releases/2002/02/print/20020207-13.html).

[35] The authoritative ICRC Commentary refers to the application of the Conventions "to all cases of armed conflict, including internal ones" at 26 (italics in original). Whether a particular event is "armed conflict" is another question. There is no doubt that initial U.S. air and ground operations in Afghanistan and certainly the invasion of Iraq were armed conflict. In circumstances not constituting armed conflict, other legal standards apply, including CAT and the International Covenant on Civil and Political Rights ("ICCPR"), as more fully discussed in the Report.

apply to the totality of a conflict including the regular forces, irregulars (whether or not privileged combatants) and civilians.

With respect to interrogation in armed conflict, Common Article 3 requires humane treatment generally and specifically forbids "cruel treatment and torture" or "outrages upon personal dignity, in particular humiliating and degrading treatment." Such provisions were violated not only by the conduct photographed at Abu Ghraib, but also by practices reported to have been engaged in at other U.S. facilities in Iraq, and, if reports are accurate, also in Afghanistan.

The U.S. has acknowledged that its presence in Iraq is an "occupation" within the meaning of Geneva IV.[36] The U.S., as occupying power, is consequently subject to provisions for the benefit of "protected persons,"[37] including Article 31's prohibition of "physical or moral coercion to obtain information from them or third parties".[38] Should the occupation be considered terminated, in any armed conflict that may continue between remaining U.S. armed forces in Iraq and Iraqi resistance – a non-international (non-state) armed conflict – the minimal protections of Common Article 3 of the Geneva Conventions would apply.

It is clear that not only the abuses in Abu Ghraib but also certain practices contemplated by the "Interrogation Rules of Engagement"[39] – such as extended sleep deprivation and stressful positions – amount to "physical or moral coercion" and are, therefore, violations of Geneva IV.[40]

U.S. military authorities maintain that interrogation of certain detainees possessing "high value intelligence" does not have to comply with certain restrictions of Geneva IV because of an exception provided in Article 5 of Geneva IV with

---

[36] Security Council Resolution 1483, passed on May 22, 2003, constitutes a formal recognition by the UN of the occupation. *See* S.C. Res. 1483, U.N. Doc S/Res/1483 (2003). This resolution also notes the letter from the Permanent Representatives of the U.S. and U.K. to the President of the Security Council, which formally announced to the UN the creation of the Coalition Provisional Authority "to exercise powers of government temporarily." *See Letter from the Permanent Representatives of the UK and the US to the UN addressed to the President of the Security Council*, U.N. Doc. S/2003/538 (May 8, 2003).

[37] On the Geneva Conventions and Geneva IV generally, *see* Part II of our Report.

[38] The ICRC Report also cites Articles 5, 27, 32 and 33 of Geneva IV. *See ICRC Report* at ¶8.

[39] In Senate hearings the Pentagon disclosed "Interrogation Rules of Engagement", which listed certain interrogation practices and specified a second group of practices that required approval of the Commanding General (Lt. Gen. Ricardo Sanchez). This second group included: "Isolation [solitary confinement] for longer than 30 days, Presence of Mil [Military] Working Dogs, Sleep Management (72 hrs max), Sensory Deprivation (72 hours max), Stress Positions (No longer than 45 min)". A week following the disclosure of this document, General Sanchez announced that none of the practices in this second group, except for isolation, would now be permitted.

  Such form of Rules of Engagement is understood to be one of at least four versions adopted at various times in the fall of 2003 for use in one or more Coalition facilities. It is cited here as illustrative of the approach taken to interrogation standards.

[40] A February 2004 report of the International Committee of the Red Cross ("ICRC"), only recently disclosed, describes abuses that are "part of the process" in the case of persons arrested in connection with suspected security offenses or deemed to have "intelligence value." *Report of the International Committee of the Red Cross (ICRC) on the Treatment by the Coalition Forces of Prisoners of War and Other Protected Persons by the Geneva Conventions in Iraq during Arrest, Internment and Interrogation*, February 2004 ("ICRC Report") www.derechos.ore/nizkor/us/doc/icrc-prisoner-report-feb-2004.pdf.

respect to persons who threaten the security of a state so-called "security detainees".[41] This view is based on a misinterpretation of the plain meaning and purpose of Article 5.

Article 5 provides for two categories of temporary exceptions to certain of its standards in the case of detainees who are definitely suspected of being threats to the security of a Party. The first paragraph of Article 5 provides that "where in the territory of a Party to the conflict," that Party determines that an individual protected person is definitely suspected of, or engaged in, activities hostile to the security of the State, the Party can suspend that person's rights and privileges under Geneva IV, where the exercise of such rights are prejudicial to the security of the State.[42] The plain language of this paragraph limits a Party's ability to suspend certain protections of Geneva IV to situations where a party to the conflict determines that a protected person is posing a security risk in that party's territory. Accordingly, this paragraph plainly has no application to protected persons detained by the U.S. in Iraq, because such detainees are not persons posing a security risk in the territory of the United States.[43]

The second exception[44] applicable to occupation permits the Occupying Power, where absolute military necessity so requires, to temporarily deny "rights of communication" – but no other rights – for a person detained as a spy or saboteur or as a threat to the security of the Occupying Power. Therefore, during occupation, even detainees who pose a security risk to the Occupying Power have the same protection against coercion as any other detainee.

---

[41] For example, in a December 24, 2003 Letter from Brigadier General Janis L. Karpinski to the ICRC regarding ICRC's visits to Camp Cropper and Abu Ghraib in October 2003, General Karpinski states: "[W]hile the armed conflict continues, and where 'absolute military security so requires' security internees will not obtain full GC protection as recognized in GCIV/5, although such protection will be afforded as soon as the security situation in Iraq allows it." *See also* Douglas Jehl & Neil A. Lewis, *U.S. Disputed Protected Status of Iraq Inmates*, May 24, 2004.

[42] Specifically, Article 5 provides in part:

> Where *in the territory of a Party to the conflict, the latter* is satisfied that an individual protected person is definitely suspected of or engaged in activities hostile to the security of the State, such individual person shall not be entitled to claim such rights and privileges under the present Convention as would, if exercised in the favour of such individual person, be prejudicial to the security of such State . . .

See Geneva IV, Art. 5 (emphasis added).

[43] Even in a case covered by paragraph I of Article 5, the detainee must be treated "with humanity." *See* the definition of humane treatment in Common Article 3 of the Geneva Conventions quoted and discussed below, which would clearly exclude the abuses found at Abu Ghraib and probably a number of the practices contemplated by the "Interrogation Rules of Engagement." If the first paragraph's broad right of derogation were interpreted to apply to occupied territory, it would make the second paragraph's narrow derogation superfluous, contrary to principles of interpretation that seek to give meaning to all provisions.

[44] The second paragraph of Article 5 provides, in part:

> Where in occupied territory an individual protected person is detained as a spy or saboteur, or as a person under definite suspicion of activity hostile to the security of the Occupying Power, such person shall, in those cases where absolute military security so requires, be regarded as having forfeited rights of communication under the present Convention.

Application of Geneva Conventions and the Anti-Torture Statute to Civilians

The War Crimes Act[45] criminalizes as a "war crime" the commission in the U.S. or abroad of a "grave breach" of the Geneva Conventions, violation of Common Article 3, and certain other international offenses, where the perpetrator or the victim is a member of the Armed Forces or a U.S. national. (With respect to the military, given the other recourse against active service members, the statute applies only to those who may have been discharged before prosecution and therefore were outside the jurisdiction of courts martial or who are being prosecuted jointly with civilians.)

The jurisdictional basis for enforcing the War Crimes Act against civilian contractors or others "accompanying" the Armed Forces outside the U.S. is likely to be the Military Extraterritorial Jurisdiction Act ("MEJA").[46] Indeed, the Department of Justice has recently announced that it is asserting jurisdiction over, and is prosecuting, a civilian contractor in Iraq.[47] A significant issue under MEJA is whether a contractor was "employed" by the Armed Forces (expressly covered by the Act), was employed by a contractor serving the Armed Forces or was employed by the CIA. In the latter cases, the reach of MEJA would depend on whether the defendant was "accompanying" the Armed Forces, a factual matter to be determined on a case-by-case basis.

Other International Legal Standards that Bind the United States

International law offers guidance in interpreting CAT. Some of these international legal standards are, without question, binding on the U.S., such as: the International

---

[45] 18 U.S.C. § 2441 (2004) provides, in relevant part:

> (a) Offense. Whoever, whether inside or outside the United States, commits a war crime, in any of the circumstances described in subsection (b), shall be fined under this title or imprisoned for life or any term of years, or both, and if death results to the victim, shall also be subject to the penalty of death.

> (b) Circumstances. The circumstances referred to in subsection (a) are that the person committing such war crime or the victim of such war crime is a member of the Armed Forces of the United States or a national of the United States . . .

> (c) Definition. As used in this section, the term "war crime" means any conduct -

> (1) defined as a grave breach in any of the international conventions signed at Geneva 12 August 1949, or any protocol to such convention to which the United States is a party . . .

> . . . (3) which constitutes a violation of common Article 3 of the international conventions signed at Geneva, 12 August 1949, or any protocol to such convention to which the United States is a party and which deals with non-international armed conflict . . .

See 18 U.S.C. § 2441. An internal Administration document referenced above argued against application of the Geneva Conventions specifically to develop a defense against application of the War Crimes Act, in case government officials were alleged to have committed grave breaches of the Geneva Conventions and other offenses thereunder.

[46] The Military Extraterritorial Jurisdiction Act provides, in relevant part:

> (a) Whoever engages in conduct outside the United States that would constitute an offense punishable by imprisonment for more than one year if the conduct had been engaged in within the special maritime and territorial jurisdiction of the United States –

> (1) while employed by or accompanying the Armed Forces outside the United States; or

> (2) while a member of the Armed Forces subject to Chapter 47 of title 10 (the Uniform Code of Military Justice), shall be punished as provided for that offense.

See 18 U.S.C. § 3261. Application to members of the Armed Forces is, however, limited to those no longer subject to the UCMJ (usually because of discharge) or accused of committing an offense with civilian defendants.

[47] David Kravets, *Patriot Act used to prosecute U.S. civilian*, CLEVE. PLAIN DEALER, June 19, 2004.

Covenant on Civil and Political Rights (the "ICCPR"),[48] the law of *jus cogens* and customary international law. The Human Rights Committee established under the ICCPR has found prolonged solitary confinement, threatening a victim with torture, and repeated beatings to violate the Covenant's prohibition against cruel, inhuman or degrading treatment or punishment.[49] Other sources, such as the European Convention for the Protection of Human Rights and Fundamental Freedoms,[50] also provide guidance.

Customary international law has long prohibited the state practice of torture, without reservation, in peace or in wartime.[51] In 1975, the United Nations General Assembly adopted by consensus the Declaration on the Protection of All Persons from Being Subjected to Torture and Other Cruel, Inhuman or Degrading Punishment.[52] The Torture Resolution together with CAT and the ICCPR – ratified by 133 and 151 States, respectively – embody the customary international law obligation to refrain from behavior which constitutes torture.[53] The prohibition of torture is, moreover, one of the few norms which has attained peremptory norm or *jus cogens* status, and is recognized as such by United States courts.[54] *Jus cogens* is

---

[48] G.A. Res. 2200A (XXI), U.N. GAOR, 21st Sess., Supp. No. 16, at 52, U.N. Doc. A/6316.

[49] *See Floyd Howell v. Jamaica*, Communication No. 798/1998 (20 January 1998), CCPR/C/79/D/798/ 1998; *Victor Alfredo Polay Campos*, Communication No. 577/1994 (6 November 1997), CCPR/C/61/D/ 577/1994; *Dave Marais, Jr. v. Madagascar*, Communication No. 49/1979 (19 April 1979), U.N. Doc. Supp. No. 40 (A/38/40) at 141 (1983); *Raul Sendic Antonaccio v. Uruguay*, Communication No. R. 14/63 (28 November 1979), U.N. Doc. Supp. No. 40 (A/37/40) at 114 (1982). In ratifying the ICCPR, the U.S. Senate declared that the Articles 1 through 27 (which cover the subject at hand) are not self-executing.

[50] 213 U.N.T.S. 221.

[51] In order for a state's practice to be recognized as customary international law, it must fulfill two conditions:

> Not only must the acts concerned amount to a settled practice, but they must also be such, or be carried out in such a way, as to be evidence of a belief that this practice is rendered obligatory by the existence of a rule of law requiring it. The need for such a belief, *i.e.*, the existence of a subjective element, is implicit in the very notion of the *opinio juris sive necessitas*. The States concerned must therefore feel that they are conforming to what amounts to a legal obligation.

North Sea Continental Shelf (*F.R.G. v. Den.*), 1969 I.C.J. 3, 44. *See also* Military and Paramilitary Activities (*Nicar v. U.S.*), 1986 I.C.J. 14, 14; R. Jennings & A. Watts, Oppenheim's International Law, (9th ed. 1996); *The Paquete Habana*, 175 U.S. 677, 700 (1900) (cited with approval in *First Nat'l City Bank v. Banco Para El Comercio Exterior de Cuba*, 462 U.S. 611, 623 (1983)); *U.S. v. Yousef*, 327 F.3d 56, 92 (2d Cir. 2002).

[52] GA Res. 3452 (XXX), U.N. GAOR, Supp. No. 34 at 91 (hereinafter the "Torture Resolution").

[53] *See Report by the Special Rapporteur*, U.N. Economic and Social Council, E/CN.4/1986/15, at para. 3. The report details state practice and *opinio juris* with respect to national legislation prohibiting torture. *See also* Herman J. Burgers & Hans Sanelius, The United Nations Convention Against Torture and Other Cruel, Inhuman or Degrading Treatment or Punishment (Martinus Nijhoff Publishers/Kluwer Academic Publishers 1988), at 1-12. The widespread ratification of regional human rights instruments such as the European Convention for the Protection of Human Rights and Fundamental Freedoms, the American Convention on Human Rights and the African Charter on Human and Peoples' Rights further reinforce the argument that torture is prohibited by customary international law.

[54] See Restatement (Third) of Foreign Relations Law § 702 (1986). See also Abebe-Jira v. Negewo, 72 F.3d 844, 847 (11th Cir. 1996); In re Estate of Ferdinand Marcos, Human Rights Litigation, 25 F.3d 1467, 1475 (9th Cir. 1994); Siderman de Blake v. Republic of Argentina, 965 F.2d 699, 716 (9th Cir. 1992); Cornejo-Barreto v. Seifert, 218 F.3d 1004, 1006 (9th Cir. 2000); Presbyterian Church of Sudan v. Talisman Energy, Inc., 244 F. Supp. 2d 289 (S.D.N.Y. 2003); Mehinovic v. Vuckovic, 198 Supp. 2d

defined as a peremptory norm "accepted and recognized by the international community of states as a whole as a norm from which no derogation is permitted and which can be modified only by a subsequent norm of general international law having the same character."[55] While many international agreements expressly prohibit *both* torture and cruel, inhuman and degrading treatment,[56] it remains an open question as to whether *jus cogens* status extends to the prohibition against cruel, inhuman or degrading treatment. What is clear, however, is that cruel, inhuman and degrading treatment or punishment is prohibited by customary international law.

RECOMMENDATIONS

The above facts and law support the Recommendations, which address the following issues:

1. The United States must condemn the torture and abusive treatment of detainees within the custody or under the physical control of the U.S. government, including U.S. government contractors. Abuses at Abu Ghraib and elsewhere are strong evidence that in the war on terror this nation's detention policies have lost their moral compass. Rather than seek to excuse or minimize these failings, the U.S. must take responsibility for violations of treaties and international law, condemn those violations, investigate all plausible allegations of violations, and punish all those responsible, no matter how high ranking. It is vital to ensure that this disgraceful behavior does not happen again. Any individual who alleges that he or she has been subjected to torture must be provided with a meaningful opportunity to complain to, and to have his/her case promptly and impartially examined by, competent authorities. Steps must be taken to ensure that the complainant and witnesses are protected against ill-treatment and intimidation.

2. The U.S. government must ensure compliance with the Geneva Conventions, the Convention against Torture and Other Cruel, Inhuman or Degrading Treatment or Punishment, and related customary international law. In doing so, it should

---

1322 (N.D. Ga. 2002); Doe v. Islamic Salvation Front, 993 F. Supp. 3, 7 (D.D.C. 1998); Doe v. Unocal, 963 F. Supp. 880, 890 (C.D. Cal. 1997).

[55] Vienna Convention on the Law of Treaties, 1969, Art. 53, 1155 U.N.T.S. 331.

[56] *See, e.g.*, Universal Declaration of Human Rights, G.A. Res. 217, U.N. GAOR, 3d Sess., Art. 5, U.N. Doc. A/810 (1948) ("no one shall be subjected to torture or to cruel, inhuman or degrading treatment or punishment"); Declaration on the Protection of All Persons from Being Subjected to Torture and Other Cruel, Inhuman or Degrading Treatment or Punishment, G.A. Res. 3452, 30 U.N. GAOR, Supp. No. 34, U.N. Doc. A/10034 (1976), at Article 3 ("Exceptional circumstances such as a state of war or a threat of war, internal political stability or any other public emergency may not be invoked as a justification of torture or other cruel, inhuman or degrading treatment or punishment."); ICCPR, *supra* note 118, at Article 7 ("no one shall be subjected to torture or to cruel, inhuman or degrading treatment or punishment"); Additional Protocol I, *supra* note 20, at Article 75; Protocol Additional to the Geneva Conventions of 12 August 1949, and Relating to the Protection of Victims of Non-International Armed Conflicts ("Additional Protocol II"), *reprinted in* 16 I.L.M. 1442 (1977), at Article 4; European Convention for the Protection of Human Rights and Fundamental Freedoms, 213 U.N.T.S. 221 (1950), at Article 3 (declaring that torture and inhuman or degrading treatment or punishment is prohibited); American Convention, *supra* note 128, at Article 5 (providing that every person retain the right to be free from torture and ill-treatment); African Charter on Human and Peoples' Rights, *reprinted in* 21 I.L.M. 58 (1981), at Article 5 (prohibiting torture and ill-treatment).

accept the time-honored interpretations of these instruments. They were designed to stop torture, not to stimulate an effort to narrow their scope beyond common sense meaning. The U.S. government should fully renounce the misguided interpretations found in its internal memoranda and clearly state a policy for treatment of detainees that would restore this nation's standing among the countries of the world.

3. The U.S. government must honor and implement fully the four Geneva Conventions. It must acknowledge the applicability of Common Article 3 to all armed conflicts. There are no "black holes" in the Conventions' scheme. Similarly, the Administration must acknowledge the very limited reach of the security exception of Article 5, and understand that the protections in the Convention are substantial, such that no POW's may be coerced in any way. The United States should adhere to Geneva III's requirement that any detainee whose POW status is in "doubt" is entitled to POW status – and, therefore, cannot be subjected to coercive treatment – until a competent tribunal, which must be convened promptly, determines otherwise.[57]

4. The U.S. government should recognize its responsibility to treat detainees in accordance with standards it would consider legal if perpetrated against an American prisoner. Before adopting restrictive interpretations of binding prohibitions against torture or other cruel, inhuman or degrading treatment, it should consider how such interpretations would affect captured U.S. service members or others serving abroad were such interpretations to be adopted by our adversaries.

5. The United States must not render detainees to nations that it has reason to believe would subject them to torture or other cruel, inhuman or degrading treatment. Rendition not only violates all basic humanitarian standards, but violates treaty obligations which make clear that a nation cannot avoid its obligations by having other nations conduct unlawful interrogations in its stead.

6. 18 U.S.C. § 2340 should be amended in two significant ways. First, the definition of torture in § 2340(1) should be revised to apply to all acts of torture regardless of the underlying motive or purpose of the perpetrator. This change would prevent this or any future administration from again arguing that the required showing of "specific intent" means that a jailer or interrogator should not be found liable under the statute when his underlying motive or purpose was not to inflict severe physical or mental pain or suffering but only to extract information. That interpretation truly makes a mockery of all the United States purports to stand for regarding human rights. Second, consistent with its obligation under Article 4 of CAT to ensure that all acts of torture are offenses under its criminal law, the U.S. must expand the geographic reach of § 2340 so that the prescriptions of CAT are applicable to torture and cruel, inhuman or degrading treatment wherever committed.

7. The U.S. government must investigate violations of law with regard to mistreatment of persons under its control and bring appropriate proceedings against those responsible.

---

[57] Geneva III, Article 5.
[58] Geneva III, Article 5.
[59] *Id.*, Art. 4.

8. The extent of the prisoner abuse scandal is so great, and its ramifications so broad and lasting, that an independent investigation is necessary to identify how these practices evolved and their extent, and to make recommendations to assure they will not recur. This investigation should not be confined to allegations of criminal behavior. Rather, it should extend to all actions, decisions and policy development regarding the interrogation of detainees in the post-September 11 "war on terrorism" that played even a small part in creating a culture that could allow such extensive abuse to happen.

9. The United States, as a State Party to the Convention Against Torture and Other Cruel, Unusual or Degrading Treatment or Punishment, must fulfill its requirement under Article 19 of the Convention to report to the United Nations Committee Against Torture every four years on measures taken to give effect to its undertakings under the Convention.

10. The actions urged by these recommendations are necessary to protect American troops who may be detained by other nations that would be disinclined to honor their treaty commitments in light of the U.S. government's failure to honor its own. Furthermore, these actions are necessary to re-establish the nation's credibility in asserting the rights of people everywhere. The world's most powerful nation must exercise its power while demonstrating its respect for the rule of law.

CONCLUSION

Al Qaeda and other terrorist organizations pose a real threat to the United States and other nations. That threat creates a tension between the need to obtain potentially life-saving information through interrogation and the legal standards banning torture and other cruel, inhuman or degrading treatment. But as a nation long pledged to the rule of law, we cannot resolve the tension by seeking to overcome that threat by violations of law. Condoning torture under any circumstances erodes one of the most basic principles of international law and human rights, places captured U.S. personnel at inordinate risk, and contradicts the basic values of a democratic state. Moreover, these violations feed terrorism by painting the United States as an arrogant nation above the law. The American Bar Association must go on record as supporting adherence to the rule of law as a fundamental principle, for when the rule of law suffers all who claim its benefits are less secure.

Respectfully submitted,

Bettina B. Plevan, President
Association of the Bar of the City of New York

Neal R. Sonnett, Chair
ABA Task Force on Treatment of Enemy Combatants

August 2004

GENERAL INFORMATION FORM

Submitting Entities : Association of the Bar of the City of New York
                     Bettina B. Plevan, President

                     Task Force on Treatment of Enemy Combatants
                     Neal R. Sonnett, Chair

1. *Summary of Recommendation(s).*

Through these Recommendations, the American Bar Association expresses its condemnation of any use of torture or other cruel, inhuman or degrading treatment or punishment upon persons within the custody or under the physical control of the United States government (including its contractors) and any approval or condoning of such measures by government lawyers, officials and agents.

The Recommendations urge the government to fully comply with the Constitution and laws of the United States and treaties to which the United States is a party, to ensure that no such person is subjected to such treatment or is turned over to another government when the United States has substantial grounds to believe that the person will be in danger of being subjected to such treatment.

The Recommendations also call for the amendment of 18 U.S.C. 2340 to encompass torture wherever committed, and whenever intentionally inflicted, without requiring proof of specific intent to torture, and urges the United States government to pursue vigorously the investigation of violations of law and bring appropriate proceedings against persons who may have committed, assisted, authorized, condoned, had command responsibility for, or otherwise participated in such violations.

The Recommendations call for an independent, bipartisan commission with subpoena power to prepare a full account of detention and interrogation practices carried out by the United States, to make public findings, and to provide recommendations designed to ensure that such practices adhere faithfully to the Constitution and laws of the United States and treaties to which the United States is a party.

Finally, the Recommendations urge that, in establishing and executing national policy regarding the treatment of persons within the custody or under the physical control of the United States government, Congress and the Executive Branch should consider how U.S. practices may affect the treatment of United States persons who may be captured and detained by other nations and the credibility of United States objection to such treatment against United States persons.

2. *Approval by Submitting Entity.*

This Recommendation and Report has been approved by the submitting entities, the Association of the Bar of the City of New York and the ABA Task Force on Treatment of Enemy Combatants. In addition, it has been approved by the governing bodies of the original cosponsors, the Criminal Justice Section, the Section of Individual Rights and Responsibilities, the Section of International Law and Practice, the Section of

Litigation, the Center for Human Rights, the Beverly Hills Bar Association, and the Bar Association of San Francisco.

3. *Has this or a similar recommendation been submitted to the House or Board previously?*

No similar Recommendations are known to have been previously submitted.

4. *What existing Association policies are relevant to this recommendation and how would they be affected by its adoption?*

The ABA has a long history of advocating respect for the rule of law and treaties to which the United States is a party, including the Geneva Conventions of August 12, 1949, the International Covenant on Civil and Political Rights, the Convention Against Torture and Other Cruel, Inhuman or Degrading Treatment or Punishment, and related customary international law, including Article 75 of the 1977 Protocol I to the Geneva Conventions,

This Recommendation would complement and extend those existing policies by urging that persons within the custody or under the physical control of the United States government (including its contractors) are not subjected to torture or other cruel, inhuman or degrading treatment or punishment, that such treatment is not approved or condoned by government lawyers, officials and agents, and that our nation fully respects and complies with its obligations under the Constitution, laws, and treaties of the United States.

5. *What urgency exists which requires action at this meeting of the House?*

Recent reports regarding the use of torture and cruel, inhuman or degrading treatment by United States personnel in the interrogation of prisoners captured in the Afghanistan and Iraq conflicts have brought international condemnation and undermined our standing in the world. United States interrogation policies and treatment of detainees present substantial, fundamental concerns that are currently being addressed by the Congress, and the American Bar Association should be heard on these critical issues.

6. *Status of Legislation.*

On May 6, 2004, House passed H. Res. 627, deploring the abuse of prisoners in the custody of the United States in Iraq and urging the Secretary of the Army to bring to swift justice any member of the Armed forces who has violated the Uniform Code of Military Justice.

On May 10, 2004, the Senate passed S. Res. 356, condemning the abuse of Iraq prisoners at Abu Ghraib prison, urging a full and complete investigation to ensure justice is served, and expressing support for all Americans serving nobly in Iraq.

On June 16, 2004, the United States Senate approved an amendment introduced by Senator Richard Durbin (D-IL) to S. 2400, the Defense Authorization bill for Fiscal

Year 2005, which passed the Senate as amended on June 23, 2004. That amendment reaffirms the American commitment to refrain from engaging in torture or cruel, inhuman, or degrading treatment or punishment. It would require the Defense Secretary to issue guidelines to ensure compliance with this standard, provide these guidelines to Congress, and report to Congress any suspected violations of the prohibition on torture or cruel, inhuman or degrading treatment.

On June 23, 2004, Rep. Edward Markey (D-MA) introduced HR 4674, a bill to prohibit rendition of terrorism suspects to nations known to practice torture, which was referred to the House International Relations Committee.

On June 25, 2004, Rep. John Conyers (D-MI) introduced H. Res. 700, directing the Attorney General to transmit to the House of Representatives documents in his possession relating to the treatment of prisoners and detainees in Iraq, Afghanistan, and Guantanamo Bay. H. Res. 700 was scheduled for markup by the House Judiciary Committee on July 21, 2004.

On July 14, 2004, Rep. Duncan Hunter (D-CA) introduced H. Con. Res. 472, expressing the sense of Congress that the apprehension, detention, and interrogation of terrorists are fundamental elements in the successful prosecution of the Global War on Terrorism and the protection of the lives of United States citizens at home and abroad.

7. *Cost to the Association.*

The adoption of the Recommendation would not result in any direct costs to the Association. The only anticipated costs would be indirect costs that might be attributable to lobbying to have the Recommendations adopted and implemented by Congress and the Executive Branch. Such costs should be negligible since lobbying efforts would be conducted by existing staff members who already are budgeted to lobby on behalf of Association policies.

8. *Disclosure of Interest. (If applicable)*

No known conflict of interest exists.

9. *Referrals.*

Concurrently with submission of this report to the ABA Policy Administration Office, it is being circulated to the following entities in addition to the listed sponsors:

Standing Committees/Task Forces:
    Law and National Security
Sections, Divisions and Forums:
    Administrative Law
    Government and Public Sector Lawyers
    Judicial Division
        National Conference of Federal Trial Judges
    Law Student Division
    Litigation
    Young Lawyers Division

Affiliated Organizations:
    The American Judicature Society
    The Federal Bar Association
    The National Conference of Bar Presidents

Other Entities:
    United States Department of Defense
    United States Department of Justice
    United States Department of State

10. *Contact Persons (Prior to the meeting).*

Alan Rothstein
The Association of the Bar of the City of New York
42 West 44th Street
New York, NY 10036
Phone: 212-382-6623
Fax: 212-398-6634
Email: arothstein@abcny.org

Neal R. Sonnett, Chair
Task Force on Treatment of Enemy Combatants
Two South Biscayne Boulevard, Suite 2600
Miami, FL 33131-1804
Tel: 305-358-2000
Fax: 305-358-1233
Email: nrs@sonnett.com

Mark D. Agrast, Immediate Past Chair
Section of Individual Rights and Responsibilities
805 Fifteenth Street, N.W., Suite 400
Washington, D.C. 20005
Tel: 202-682-1611
Fax: 202-682-1867
Email: magrast@americanprogress.org

Jerome J. Shestack, Chair
Center for Human Rights
Wolf Block Schorr & Solis-Cohen
1650 Arch Street, 22nd Floor
Philadelphia, PA 19103-2097
Tel: 215-977-2290
Fax: 215-977-2787
Email: jshestack@wolfblock.com

Stephen Saltzburg, Delegate
Criminal Justice Section
George Washington University School of Law
2000 H Street, NW - Room 301

Washington, DC 20052
Tel: 202-994-7089
Fax: 202-994-7143
Email: ssaltz@law.gwu.edu

C. Elisia Frazier, Delegate,
Section of Individual Rights and Responsibilities
1310 W. Lexington Avenue
Fort Wayne, IN 46807
Tel: 260-745-3044
Fax: 260-455-5403
Email: cefl938@comcast.com

William M. Hannay III, Delegate
Section of International Law and Practice
Schiff Hardin & Waite
233 S. Wacker Drive
Chicago, IL 60606-6306
Tel: 312-258-5617
Fax: 312-258-5700
Email: whannay@schiffhardin.com

Albert J Krieger, Delegate
National Association of Criminal Defense Lawyers
1899 South Bayshore Drive
Miami, FL 33133-3307
Tel: 305-854-0050
Fax: 305-285-1761
Email: ajkrieger@ajkriegerlaw.com

11. *Contact Persons (Who will present the report to the House)*

Bettina B. Plevan, President
The Association of the Bar of the City of New York
42 West 44th Street
New York, NY 10036
Tel: 212-382-6700 (ABCNY) or 212-969-2900 (Office)
Fax: 212-768-8116
Email: bplevan@proskauer.com

Neal R. Sonnett, Chair
Task Force on Treatment of Enemy Combatants
Two South Biscayne Boulevard, Suite 2600
Miami, FL 33131-1804
Tel: 305-358-2000
Fax: 305-358-1233
Email: nrs@sonnett.com

Mark D. Agrast, Immediate Past Chair
Section of Individual Rights and Responsibilities
805 Fifteenth Street, N.W., Suite 400
Washington, D.C. 20005
Tel: 202-682-1611
Fax: 202-682-1867
Email: magrast@americanprogress.org

Jerome J. Shestack, Chair
Center for Human Rights
Wolf Block Schorr & Solis-Cohen
1650 Arch Street, 22nd Floor
Philadelphia, PA 19103-2097
Tel: 215-977-2290
Fax: 215-977-2787
Email: jshestack@wolfblock.com

Stephen Saltzburg, Delegate
Criminal Justice Section
George Washington University School of Law
2000 H Street, NW - Room 301
Washington, DC 20052
Tel: 202-994-7089
Fax: 202-994-7143
Email: ssaltz@law.gwu.edu

C. Elisia Frazier, Delegate,
Section of Individual Rights and Responsibilities
1310 W. Lexington Avenue
Fort Wayne, IN 46807
Tel: 260-745-3044
Fax: 260-455-5403
Email: cefl 938@comcast.com

William M. Hannay III, Delegate
Section of International Law and Practice
Schiff Hardin & Waite
233 S. Wacker Drive
Chicago, IL 60606-6306
Tel: 312-258-5617
Fax: 312-258-5700
Email: whannay@schiffhardin.com

Albert J Krieger, Delegate
National Association of Criminal Defense Lawyers
1899 South Bayshore Drive

Miami, FL 33133-3307
Tel: 305-854-0050
Fax: 305-285-1761
Email: ajkrieger@ajkriegerlaw.com

Supplement

Human Rights Standards Applicable To The United States' Interrogation of Detainees

Recent Developments

Following the issuance of the Committees' Report in the last week of April, 2004[1], we and all Americans were stunned to learn of the abuses at Abu Ghraib Prison in Iraq. Disclosures since then include allegations of more widespread abuses of detainees in both Iraq and from the conflict in Afghanistan. The scope and causes of these known and alleged abuses and issues of responsibility and accountability are now the subject of investigation by Congress, the Departments of Defense and Justice and the military. At the same time, these recent events and disclosures raise additional legal questions concerning the legal standards applicable to the conflict in Afghanistan and the occupation of Iraq which were not thoroughly addressed in our original Report. It is the purpose of this Supplement to address those questions. We therefore examine the following questions:

(1) What standards are applicable to treatment of detainees during the occupation in Iraq and what standards apply when the occupation ends?

(2) What is the scope of any exceptions to the standards of the Geneva Conventions for interrogation of detainees in Iraq who pose a security threat and/or are suspected of possessing "high value intelligence"?

(3) To what extent do the Geneva Conventions apply to the detainees from the conflict in Afghanistan?

(4) How and to what extent can CIA personnel and civilian contractors be held accountable for any violations of international law resulting from their participation in any abuses in Iraq?

Application of the Geneva Conventions to the Occupation of Iraq

The U.S. acknowledges that its presence in Iraq is an "occupation" within the meaning of Geneva IV.[2] The U.S., as occupying power, is consequently subject to provisions

---

Certain terms are used in this Supplement as defined in our Report.

[1] The Report was submitted to the General Counsels of the Department of Defense and the Central Intelligence Agency, the Legal Adviser to the National Security Counsel, and Counsel to the Joint Chiefs of Staff, and the Chair and Ranking Member of the committees for the Armed Services, Foreign Relations, Intelligence and the Judiciary of the Senate and the House of Representatives. These committees have held and are holding hearings on aspects of the Abu Ghraib abuses within their respective jurisdiction.

[2] Security Council Resolution 1483, passed on May 22, 2003, constitutes a formal recognition by the UN of the occupation. See S.C. Res. 1483, U.N. Doc S/Res/1483 (2003). This resolution also notes the letter from the Permanent Representatives of the U.S. and U.K. to the President of the Security

for the benefit of "protected persons,"[3] including Article 31's prohibition of "physical or moral coercion to obtain information from them or third parties".[4] It is clear that not only the abuses in Abu Ghraib but also certain practices contemplated by the "Interrogation Rules of Engagement"[5] – such as extended sleep deprivation and stressful positions – amount to "physical or moral coercion" and are, therefore, violations of Geneva IV. [6]

Who Are Protected Persons? As noted in the Report at footnote 116, Geneva IV benefits all persons in the hands of an Occupying Power, with exceptions only for nationals of that Power and its allies, nationals of certain neutrals and persons protected by other Geneva Conventions, such as prisoners of war. There is no blanket exception for so-called "unlawful combatants"[7] who fail to qualify as POWs under Geneva III. Once disqualified from POW status, such detainees become protected persons under Geneva IV.

Are There Exceptions To The Geneva Conventions For "Security" Detainees Or Detainees Who Possess "High Value Intelligence"?[8]

U.S. military authorities maintain that interrogation of certain detainees possessing "high value intelligence" does not have to comply with certain restrictions of Geneva IV because of an exception provided in Article 5 of Geneva IV with respect to persons who threaten the security of a state – so-called "security detainees".[9]

Council, which formally announced to the UN the creation of the Coalition Provisional Authority "to exercise powers of government temporarily." *See Letter from the Permanent Representatives of the UK and the US to the UN addressed to the President of the Security Council*, U.N. Doc. S/2003/538 (May 8, 2003).

[3] On the Geneva Conventions and Geneva IV generally, *see* Part II of our Report.

[4] The ICRC Report also cites Articles 5, 27, 32 and 33 of Geneva IV. *See ICRC Report* at ¶8.

[5] In Senate hearings the Pentagon disclosed "Interrogation Rules of Engagement", attached to this Supplement as Appendix A which listed certain interrogation practices and specified a second group of practices that required approval of the Commanding General (Lt. Gen. Ricardo Sanchez). This second group included: "Isolation [solitary confinement] for longer than 30 days, Presence of Mil [Military] Working Dogs, Sleep Management (72 hrs max), Sensory Deprivation (72 hours max), Stress Positions (No longer than 45 min)". A week following the disclosure of this document, General Sanchez announced that all of the practices in this second group, other than isolation, would not be permitted.

Such form of Rules of Engagement is understood to be one of at least four versions adopted at various times in the fall of 2003 for use in one or more Coalition facilities. It is cited here as illustrative of the approach taken to interrogation standards.

[6] A February 2004 report of the International Committee of the Red Cross ("ICRC"), only recently disclosed, describes abuses that are "part of the process" in the case of persons arrested in connection with suspected security offenses or deemed to have "intelligence value." *Report of the International Committee of the Red Cross (ICRC) on the Treatment by the Coalition Forces of Prisoners of War and Other Protected Persons by the Geneva Conventions in Iraq during Arrest, Internment and Interrogation*, February 2004 ("ICRC Report") www.derechos.org/nizkor/us/doc/icrc-prisoner-report-feb-2004.pdf.

[7] *See* Report, fn. 7.

[8] On May 23, 2004, it was disclosed that the Coalition response to the ICRC communication cited above asserted that certain detainees in question were "security detainees" not subject to the full obligations of Geneva IV. *See* Douglas Jehl and Neil A. Lewis, "The Reach of War: The Prisoners," N.Y. TIMES, May 23, 2004, at A12.

[9] For example, in a December 24, 2003 Letter from Brigadier General Janis L. Karpinski to the ICRC regarding ICRC's visits to Camp Cropper and Abu Ghraib in October 2003 , General Karpinski states: "[W]hile the armed conflict continues, and where 'absolute military security so requires' security

This view is based on a misinterpretation of the plain meaning and purpose of Article 5.

Article 5 provides for two categories of temporary exceptions to certain of its standards in the case of detainees who are definitely suspected of being threats to the security of a Party. The first paragraph of Article 5 provides that "where in the territory of a Party to the conflict," that Party determines that an individual protected person is definitely suspected of, or engaged in, activities hostile to the security of the State, the Party can suspend that person's rights and privileges under Geneva IV, where the exercise of such rights are prejudicial to the security of the State.[10] The plain language of this paragraph limits a Party's ability to suspend certain protections of Geneva IV to situations where a party to the conflict determines that a protected person is posing a security risk in that party's territory. Accordingly, this paragraph plainly has no application to protected persons detained by the U.S. in Iraq, because such detainees are not persons posing a security risk in the territory of the United States.[11] Rather, the United States, as an Occupying Power, is subject to the provisions of a separate paragraph of Article 5 applicable to occupation. That separate paragraph[12] applicable to occupation permits the Occupying Power, where absolute military necessity so requires, temporarily to deny "rights of communication" – but no other rights – for a person detained as a spy or saboteur or as a threat to the security of the Occupying Power. Therefore, during occupation, even detainees who pose a security risk to the Occupying Power have the same protection against coercion as any other detainee.

What Standards Apply When The Occupation Ends? The occupation will continue under Article 6 as long as *de facto* the U.S. "exercises the functions of government" in Iraq. This result cannot be varied by agreement with Iraqi "authorities." Article 47 provides that agreements between the authorities of the occupied territories and the Occupying Power are not effective to deprive protected persons of the protections of Geneva IV. The ICRC Commentary confirms that Article 47 applies where the Occupying Power has installed and maintained a government in power. For the occupation

---

internees will not obtain full GC protection as recognized in GCIV/5, although such protection will be afforded as soon as the security situation in Iraq allows it."

[10] Specifically, Article 5 provides in part:

> Where *in the territory of a Party to the conflict, the latter* is satisfied that an individual protected person is definitely suspected of or engaged in activities hostile to the security of the State, such individual person shall not be entitled to claim such rights and privileges under the present Convention as would, if exercised in the favour of such individual person, be prejudicial to the security of such State ...

See Geneva IV, Art. 5 (emphasis added).

[11] Even in a case covered by paragraph 1 of Article 5, the detainee must be treated "with humanity." *See* the definition of humane treatment in Common Article 3 of the Geneva Conventions quoted and discussed below, which would clearly exclude the abuses found at Abu Ghraib and probably a number of the practices contemplated by the "Interrogation Rules of Engagement." If the first paragraph's broad right of derogation were interpreted to apply to occupied territory, it would make the second paragraph's narrow derogation superfluous, contrary to principles of interpretation that seek to give meaning to all provisions.

[12] The second paragraph of Article 5 provides, in part:

> Where in occupied territory an individual protected person is detained as a spy or saboteur, or as a person under definite suspicion of activity hostile to the security of the Occupying Power, such person shall, in those cases where absolute military security so requires, be regarded as having forfeited rights of communication under the present Convention.

to end there must be an independent national government internationally recognized exercising the full functions of government. The establishment of a transitional regime that failed to exercise the full functions of government would not terminate the occupation. When the occupation does end, Article 31 will no longer apply. However, in any armed conflict that may continue between remaining U.S. armed forces in Iraq and Iraqi resistance – a non-international (non-state) armed conflict – the minimal protections of Common Article 3 of the Geneva Conventions would apply.

The Applicability of the Minimal Safeguards of Common Article 3 of the Geneva Conventions

Working documents dating from early 2002 have recently become public exposing internal dialogue within the Administration about the application of the Geneva Conventions to the Afghan conflict.[13] White House counsel, the Office of the Vice President, the Department of Justice and Department of Defense civilian attorneys, over the objections of Secretary of State Powell and the Joint Chiefs of Staff, argued that the Geneva Conventions did not apply to detainees from the Afghan conflict. The purposes of this interpretation were to preserve maximum flexibility with the least restraint by international law and to immunize government officials from prosecution under the War Crimes Act, which renders certain violations of the Geneva Conventions violations of U.S. criminal law.

Ultimately, the President accepted application of the Geneva Conventions in principle to the conflict with the Taliban, while asserting that Taliban personnel did not qualify under Geneva III for status as prisoners of war. However, the Administration denied that the Geneva Conventions applied at all to al Qaeda and to the broader War on Terror, although it announced that it would adhere to comparable humanitarian standards. (*See* Report at text accompanying footnote 95, *et seq.*) Official correspondence from the General Counsel of the Department of Defense dated June 25, 2003, appended to our Report, stated that the U.S. would comply with applicable international law, including the Convention Against Torture And Other Cruel, Inhuman, or Degrading Treatment ("CAT").

Notwithstanding those assurances, the foregoing raises serious issues regarding the application of the Geneva Conventions in the War on Terror, notably the minimal protections of Common Article 3 and the actual standards applied in the field.

Each of the four Geneva Conventions has a "Common Article 3", which provides a safety net in non-international armed conflicts (not between State parties) which are not covered by the full protection of the Conventions.[14] The prime example

---

[13] *See, e.g.*, Michael Isikoff, "Double Standards? A Justice Department memo proposes that the United States hold others accountable for international laws on detainees – but that Washington did not have to follow them itself." *Newsweek*, May 22, 2004, *available at* <www.msnbc.msn.com/id/5032094/site/newsweek/>.

[14] Article 3 provides, in pertinent part:

> In the case of armed conflict not of an international character occurring in the territory of one of the High Contracting Parties, each Party to the conflict shall be bound to apply, as a minimum, the following provisions:
>
> (1) *Persons taking no active part in the hostilities, including members of armed forces who have laid down their arms and those placed hors de combat by* sickness, wounds, *detention*, or any other cause,

is an armed conflict not between nation-state parties to the Conventions, but between one state-party and non-state forces occurring on the territory of a party to the Geneva Conventions, as in the case of the conflict in Afghanistan after the formation of the Karzai government. In such conflicts, Article 3 expressly applies to armed forces who have "laid down their arms" (surrendered) or been detained. Its broad terms cover all detainees including captured unprivileged or "unlawful" combatants.[15]

The internal Administration memoranda mentioned above argue that Common Article 3 does not apply at all to al Qaeda's activities in the Afghanistan conflict because, inasmuch as al Qaeda operated cross-border and with support from persons in countries outside Afghanistan, that conflict is not an armed conflict of a non-international character within the meaning of Article 3. According to a Justice Department memorandum of January 2002 by then Justice Department official and now Professor John Yoo, and his recent op-ed article[16], Article 3 was intended to apply only to large-scale and entirely internal civil wars, for which it cites the example of the Spanish Civil War of the 1930's.[17] In fact, the Geneva Conventions are structured in terms of international armed conflicts (between State parties) and non-international (non-inter-State) conflict. There is no indication that there is any category of armed conflict that is not covered by the Geneva Conventions.[18] Nor should the different status of the Taliban

---

shall in all circumstances be treated humanely, without any adverse distinction founded on race, colour, religion or faith, sex, birth or wealth, or any other similar criteria.

To this end the following acts are and shall remain prohibited at any time and in any place whatsoever with respect to the above-mentioned persons:

(a) violence to life and person, in particular murder of all kinds, mutilation, *cruel treatment and torture;*

...(c) *outrages upon personal dignity, in particular humiliating and degrading treatment;*

See Geneva Conventions, Art. 3 (emphasis added).

[15] In classic inter-state conflicts, combatants might qualify for prisoner of war status under Geneva III or, if disqualified from that status, be subject to the lesser, but significant, protections of Geneva IV. In other armed conflicts, all combatants are covered by Common Article 3.

[16] *See* John Yoo, "Terrorists Have No Geneva Rights," THE WALL STREET JOURNAL, May 26, 2004, at A16.

[17] The Spanish Civil War is an ironic example for the Administration to rely on given the internationalization of that conflict with the indirect involvement of the governments of the Soviet Union on one side and Germany and Italy on the other, and including the commitment of a covert Luftwaffe unit, the Kondor Legion, and the Italian Legione Aviazione but without overt State conflict. It is inconceivable that the drafters of the Geneva Convention would have favored less humanitarian protection for a non-State armed conflict that crossed borders than for either a strictly internal conflict or a classic State conflict; yet that is the position advocated within the Administration.

[18] The authoritative ICRC Commentary refers to the application of the Conventions "to *all* cases of armed conflict, including internal ones" at 26 (italics in original). Whether a particular event is "armed conflict" is another question. There is no doubt that initial U.S. air and ground operations in Afghanistan and certainly the invasion of Iraq were armed conflict. Whether other operations in the "War on Terror" constitute armed conflict is beyond the scope of this Supplement, but to the extent that the Administration characterizes a particular event as armed conflict in order to invoke indefinite detention of combatants or trial by military commission under the law of armed conflict, it cannot disclaim the application of the entire law of armed conflict, including the Geneva Conventions, when compliance becomes inconvenient. *See* President's Military Order of November 23, 2001 (declaring the attacks by al Qaeda to be "on a scale that created a state of armed conflict").

In circumstances not constituting armed conflict, other legal standards apply, including CAT and the International Covenant on Civil and Political Rights ("ICCPR"), as more fully discussed in the Report.

and al Qaeda in the conflict in Afghanistan affect the question of whether the Geneva Conventions apply to that armed conflict, as Professor Yoo argues. Although their different status may affect *how* the Geneva Conventions apply to these different groups, it does not affect the question of *whether* the Geneva Conventions apply. The Geneva Conventions apply to the totality of a conflict including the regular forces, irregulars (whether or not privileged combatants) and civilians.

With respect to interrogation in armed conflict, Common Article 3 requires humane treatment generally and specifically forbids "cruel treatment and torture" or "outrages upon personal dignity, in particular humiliating and degrading treatment." Such provisions were violated not only by the conduct photographed at Abu Ghraib, but also by practices reported to have been engaged in at other U.S. facilities not only in Iraq, but, if reports are accurate, also from the conflict in Afghanistan.

Enforcement of the Geneva Conventions and the Anti-Torture Statute against Civilians

Our Report fully described the provisions of the Uniform Code of Military Justice defining the standard of treatment for military detainees and providing for criminal enforcement through courts martial of the Geneva Conventions, as applied by regulations and orders, and defining other offenses that would be violated by abuse of detainees.

Because the Congressional investigation and news reports have noted the possible involvement of civilian contractors and CIA personnel in the Abu Ghraib abuses and elsewhere, it is appropriate to consider further the enforcement of such standards against civilians, as well as the military. The War Crimes Act[19] criminalizes as a "war crime" the commission in the U.S. or abroad of a "grave breach" of the Geneva Conventions, violation of Common Article 3, and certain other international offenses, where the perpetrator or the victim is a member of the Armed Forces or a U.S. national. (With respect to the military, given the other recourse against active service members, the statute applies only to those who may have been discharged before prosecution and therefore were outside the jurisdiction of courts martial or who are being prosecuted jointly with civilians.)

---

[19] 18 U.S.C. § 2441 (2004) provides, in relevant part:

(a) Offense. Whoever, whether inside or outside the United States, commits a war crime, in any of the circumstances described in subsection (b), shall be fined under this title or imprisoned for life or any term of years, or both, and if death results to the victim, shall also be subject to the penalty of death.

(b) Circumstances. The circumstances referred to in subsection (a) are that the person committing such war crime or the victim of such war crime is a member of the Armed Forces of the United States or a national of the United States . . .

(c) Definition. As used in this section, the term "war crime" means any conduct –

(1) defined as a grave breach in any of the international conventions signed at Geneva 12 August 1949, or any protocol to such convention to which the United States is a party . . .

. . . (3) which constitutes a violation of common Article 3 of the international conventions signed at Geneva, 12 August 1949, or any protocol to such convention to which the United States is a party and which deals with non-international armed conflict . . .

See 18 U.S.C. § 2441. An internal Administration document referenced above argued against application of the Geneva Conventions specifically to develop a defense against application of the War Crimes Act, in case government officials were alleged to have committed grave breaches of the Geneva Conventions and other offenses thereunder.

The jurisdictional basis for enforcing the War Crimes Act against civilian contractors or others "accompanying" the Armed Forces outside the U.S. is likely to be the Military Extraterritorial Jurisdiction Act ("MEJA") cited in our Report at footnotes 66 and 72.[20] Indeed, the Department of Justice has recently announced that it is asserting jurisdiction under this statute to open a criminal investigation regarding a civilian contractor in Iraq. MEJA provides federal court jurisdiction over federal offenses with a penalty of more than one year, thus excluding an offense like simple assault, while including violation of the War Crimes Act or the anti-torture statute implementing CAT, 18 U.S.C. § 2340A[21], both of which provide for life imprisonment or even capital punishment in crimes causing death. A significant issue under MEJA is whether a contractor was "employed" by the Armed Forces (expressly within the Act), was employed by a contractor serving the Armed Forces or was employed by the CIA. In the latter cases, the reach of MEJA would depend on whether the defendant was "accompanying" the Armed Forces, a factual matter in the circumstances.

Conclusion

Disclosures since we issued our Report indicate violations of the Geneva Conventions in Iraq, where the Administration acknowledges they apply, and a mistaken belief that they have no application at all to detainees in the War on Terror, such as suspected al Qaeda detainees from the conflict in Afghanistan. Investigations by Congress, the Justice Department, and the military must be pursued vigorously to uncover any violations of international and U.S. law, to prosecute any violations of the War Crimes Act or the Uniform Code of Military Justice, and to determine accountability not merely of subordinate personnel who engaged in such conduct, but of all those in the civilian and military hierarchy who may have authorized or condoned unlawful conduct.

Misinterpretations of the Geneva Convention and CAT must be corrected. It appears that Article 5 of Geneva IV is being misused to evade the protections against coercive interrogations to obtain information from detainees with "high value intelligence." Furthermore, the protections of Common Article 3 are claimed not to apply to detainees from the armed conflict in Afghanistan at Guantanamo, Bagram and elsewhere, although the Administration claims to have assured comparable humane standards. The photographs from Abu Ghraib show that detainees in Iraq have been

---

[20] The Military Extraterritorial Jurisdiction Act provides, in relevant part:

(a) Whoever engages in conduct outside the United States that would constitute an offense punishable by imprisonment for more than one year if the conduct had been engaged in within the special maritime and territorial jurisdiction of the United States –

(1) while employed by or accompanying the Armed Forces outside the United States; or

(2) while a member of the Armed Forces subject to Chapter 47 of title 10 (the Uniform Code of Military Justice), shall be punished as provided for that offense.

See 18 U.S.C. § 3261. Application to members of the Armed Forces is, however, limited to those no longer subject to the UCMJ (usually because of discharge) or accused of committing an offense with civilian defendants.

[21] As noted in the Report at the text accompanying footnote 66, enforcement of 18 U.S.C. § 2340A was severely limited as to the offenses committed at U.S. military or government facilities by the technical effect of an amendment in the USA Patriot Act. The Report recommends legislation to correct that presumably inadvertent nullification of this important criminal statute.

deprived of CAT's protections against both torture and cruel, inhuman and degrading treatment that also amounts to cruel and inhuman treatment under the U.S. Constitution and of the standard of treatment established for the military under the UCMJ, and allegations have been made of violations of such standards in Afghanistan and elsewhere. We urge the Administration to re-examine its positions and live up to the legal obligations clearly imposed upon it by the Geneva Conventions, CAT and the UCMJ.

We again urge, as we did in our Report, that civilian and military personnel engaged in the detention and interrogation of detainees in Iraq, Guantanamo and elsewhere receive thorough education, training and clear instructions concerning their obligations under international and U.S. law.

We also urge the restoration of the role of Judge Advocate Officers in advising on, and monitoring, interrogations on site.[22]

Finally, we recommend that gaps in U.S. law to punish violations of our international legal obligations under the Geneva Conventions and CAT be remedied by Congress. Our Report discusses the need to cure deficiencies in 18 U.S.C. § 2340A, which criminalizes torture. The Military Extraterritorial Jurisdiction Act should be amended to extend jurisdiction over violations of U.S. law committed by all persons employed by, or serving at the direction of, any U.S. intelligence agency, not merely those that "accompany" the Armed Forces.

Above all, we urge all those who set the tone and climate for our military and civilian government personnel to establish respect for our treaty obligations and the rule of law in the treatment of detainees.

Dated: New York, New York.
June 4, 2004

The Committee on International Human Rights

Martin S. Flaherty, Chair*
Scott Horton (Immediate Past Chair)*
Jeanmarie Fenrich, Secretary

Charles Adler
Patricia C. Armstrong
Hon. Deborah A. Batts
Nicole Barrett
Aarthi Belani (student member)*
Seymour H. Chalif
Amy Christina Cococcia
Catherine Daly
Eric O. Darko
Jane M. Desnoyers
Mark K. Dietrich
Fiona M. Doherty

---

[22] A member of a participating Committee was recently advised by senior JAG officers that the prior practice of having JAG officers monitor interrogations in the field for compliance with law and regulations had been curtailed at the direction of senior officials.

Barbara Fortson (former member)*
Aya Fujimura-Fanselow (student member)
Douglas C. Gray
William M. Heinzen
Alice H. Henkin
Sharon K. Hom
Miranda Johnson (student member)
Anil Kalhan
Mamta Kaushal
Christopher Kean
Elise B. Keppler
Katharine Lauer*
Sara Lesch
Yvonne C. Lodico
Marko C. Maglich
Elisabeth Adams Mason
Nina Massen
Sam Scott Miller
Elena Dana Neacsu
Dyanna C. Pepitone
Elizabeth Quinlan
Marny Requa (student member)
Sidney S. Rosdeitcher**
Margaret L. Satterthwaite*
Joseph H. Saunders
Christopher A. Smith (student member)
Katherine B. Wilmore

The Committee on Military Affairs and Justice

Miles P. Fischer, Chair*
Michael Mernin, Secretary

Steven Barrett
Myles Bartley
Philip Blum
Kenneth Carroll***
Brian Cogan***
Joshua Eisenberg
Matthew Hawkins***
Peter Jaensch
Peter Langrind
Gerald Lee
Patricia Murphy
Rose Murphy
Harold Nathan
Timothy Pastore
Stanley Paylago*
Visuvanathan Rudrakumaran
Lawrence Sloan

   * Members of the Subcommittee who prepared the Supplement
  ** Chair of the Subcommittee responsible for preparing the Supplement
 *** Members dissenting from the Supplement

The Committees wish to thank Liza Velazquez for her invaluable contribution to this Supplement.

SUPPLEMENT APPENDIX A

INTERROGATION RULES OF ENGAGEMENT

Approved approaches for All detainees:	*Require CG's Approval: Requests must be submitted in writing*
Direct	Change of scenery down
Incentive	Dietary Manip (monitored by med)
Incentive Removal	Environmental Manipulation
Emotional Love/Hate	Sleep Adjustment (reverse sched)
Fear Up Harsh	Isolation for longer than 30 days
Fear Up Mild	Presence of Mil Working Dogs
Reduced Fear	Sleep Management (72 hrs max)
Pride & Ego Up	Sensory Deprivation (72 hrs max)
Futllity	Stress Positions (no longer than 45 min)
We Know All	
Establish Your ldentity	*Safeguards:*
Repetition	~Techniques must be annotated in questioning strategy
File & Dossier	~Approaches must always be humane and lawful
Rapid Fire	~Detainees will NEVER be touched in a malicious or
Silence	unwanted manner
	~Wounded or medically burdened detainees must be
	medically cleared prior to interrogation
	~The Geneva Conventions apply within CJTF-7

EVERYONE IS RESPONSIBLE FOR ENSURING COMPLIANCE TO THE IROE. VIOLATIONS MUST BE REPORTED IMMEDIATELY TO THE OIC.

The use of the techniques are subject to the general safeguard as provided as well as specific guidelines implemented by the 205th Ml Cdr. FM 34-52, and the Commanding General, CJTF-7

Afterword

As this volume goes to press, additional materials on Abu Ghraib and new materials on Guantánamo are daily finding their way into the public arena via the media, human rights groups and indefatigable researchers. Included are a select few of those documents, brought to light by the American Civil Liberties Union. They include reports on detainee mistreatment and abuse and discussions among the FBI, the Department of Defense, and the White House.

Following the newly released ACLU documents is a statement from David Hicks, a detainee at Guantánamo. Hicks is an Australian citizen.

INFO MEMO

S-0517/DR   June 25, 2004

FOR: UNDER SECRETARY OF DEFENSE FOR INTELLIGENCE

FROM: L. E. Jacoby, Vice Admiral, USN, Director, Defense Intelligence Agency

Subject: (S//NF) Alleged Detainee Abuse by TF 62-6 Personnel

(S//NF) During the afternoon of 24 June 2004, we were notified that DIA
personnel serving with TF 6-26 in Baghdad had informed their ISG seniors of the
following:

- (S//NF) Two DIA, Directorate for Human Intelligence (DIA/DH)
  interrogators/debriefers assigned to support TF 6-26 (SOF) have observed:

  - Prisoners arriving at the Temporary Detention Facility in Baghdad with
    burn marks on their backs. Some have bruises, and some have complained
    of kidney pain.

  - One of the two DIA/DH interrogators/debriefers witnessed TF 6-26 officers
    punch a prisoner in the face to the point the individual needed medical
    attention. This record of treatment was not recorded by TF 6-26 personnel.
    In this instance, the debriefer was ordered to leave the room.

  - One DIA/DH interrogator/debriefer took pictures of the injuries and
    showed them to his TF 62-6 supervisor, who immediately confiscated them.

- (S//NF) TF 6-26 personnel have taken the following actions with regards to
  DIA/DH interrogators/debriefers:

  - Confiscated vehicle keys

  - Instructed them not to leave the compound without specific permission,
    even to get a haircut at the PX

  - Threatened them

- Informed them that their e-mails were being screened

- Ordered them not to talk to anyone in the US

- (S//NF) The two DH strategic debriefers assigned to TF 62-6 reported the above information to the Operations Officer. He immediately contacted DIA IG Forward and asked that both individuals be interviewed. The IG representative made the recommendation that VADM Church's group be immediately apprised in order to get this into official IG channels as the issue fell directly under its charter. The Church IG Team senior investigating officer is conducting interviews of the interrogators/debriefers today. The DIA IG was informed and concurred with this course of action.

- (S//NF) The ISG Operations Officer contacted and briefed the Director of the ISG, who was in Qatar attending a Commander's Conference. The ISG Director informed the Deputy Commander for Detainee Affairs, MNF-I. He subsequently contacted the Commander of TF 6-26 and directed him to investigate this situation. In turn the TF 6-26 Commander informed his superior, the Commander JSOC. The Commander, CENTCOM has also been informed of this situation.

- (S//NF) The two interrogators/debriefers were directed to return to the ISG compound at Camp Slayer due to these events.

(b)(3)

UNITED STATES GOVERNMENT

memorandum

DATE: 10 June, 2004

REPLY TO ████████████████████████   (b)(3)
ATTN OF: ████████████████ •

SUBJECT: Memorandum for Record - Report of Violations of The Geneva Conventions and the International Laws of Land Warfare (U).

TO: ██████████████████████

1. (S) From ██████████████████████████ I was employed by the Defense Intelligence Agency as an Intelligence Officer assigned and under the operational control to ████████████████████████ I have been in the civilian employment of the   (b)(1) Department of Defense in the capacity of intelligence officer for approximately 14 years. I have received specialized on-the-job-training in HUMINT operations, to include interrogation. I spoke about the incidents reported in the document during a meeting with ████████████████████████ at approximately 12:15 pm. Present at the meeting were ██   (b)(6)

(U) This statement is in support of the following:

   a. (U) Two counts of violations of The Geneva Convention as it pertains to detainee abuse.

   b. (U) One count of violations of The Geneva Convention as it pertains to the illegal detainment of non-combatants.

3. (U) Details:

   a. (S//NF) (1ˢᵗ count, ref para 2.a.) On or about 11 May 2004, in Baghdad, Iraq, I witnessed the mistreatment of a TF 6-26 detainee during the initial interrogation after his capture. During the interrogation, conducted by a US Army interrogator, four or five non-interrogator personnel from the Task Force entered the room and began slapping the detainee while he was attempting to respond to the questioning. After approximately 15 minutes, a senior NCO, going by call sign "XO3" entered the room and asked most of the personnel to leave, to include ALL of the interrogators. I am not aware of what specifically occurred during my absence. ████████████████████ officer assigned   (b)(3) to the Task Force, was present as well and witness the incident. ████████ was observing the interrogation and I was assisting the lead interrogator. A 1ˢᵗ SF Group interrogator also augmenting the unit. I am not aware if this matter has been previously reported.

√ FROM: DH HUMINT SCG, SEP 03
DECL ON: X1

1169

b. (S//NF) 12th count, ref para 2.a.) During another TF 6-26 operation in Baghdad, a ███████████████████ of the Coalition Provisional Authority's Counterintelligence office PA-CI) was arrested during a raid targeting an al-Qaida facilitator. ████████ and two male family members were detained and moved to the TF 6-26 screening facility. ████████ and his family members were released and during the initial debriefing of ████████ he (b)(1) reported to TF 6-26 and CPA-CI handlers that he had been "slapped around" during initial interrogation at the place of his capture. The matter was reported in an internal TF contract report to the B Squadron commander by the DIA handling officer. ████████ ██████████ (b)(1)

c. (S//NF) (Ref para 2.b.) On 9 May 2004, TF 6-26 personnel detained the wife of a suspected Iraqi terrorist, in Tarmiya, Iraq. The 28-year-old woman had three young children at the house, one being as young as six months and still nursing. Her husband was the primary target of the raid, with other suspect personnel subject to detainment as well. The house belonged to the primary target's in-laws, and it was believed his wife and children would be there as well. During the pre-operation brief it was recommended by TF personnel that if the wife were present, she be detained and held in order to leverage the primary target's surrender. I objected to the detainment of the young mother to the raid team leader, "XO3". I believed it was a dead issue, since I would be on-target and responsible for screening the occupants of the house for suspects to detain. During my initial screening of the occupants at the target house, I determined that the wife could provide no actionable intelligence leading to the arrest her husband. Despite my protest, ₃ raid team leader detained her anyway. I concurred with the arrest of one of her ⌐rothers, who had been identified as likely having knowledge of the primary target's location. I reported the incident to the HUMINT support element operations officer, ████ (b)(3) ████████ as I understand it, the matter was in turn reported to the Task Force HQ. Approximately two day later, the wife and her brother were released into the custody of their tribal sheikh.

4. (U) Concluding statement: The tactical interrogation report is a record of the interrogation and is more often then not the only written record forwarded with the detainees as they are moved through the detention system from screening facilities to final detention centers. Since those interrogation reports, as a matter of record, contain the names of the interrogators, any mistreatment of detainees, whether in the presence of the interrogator or not, reflects adversely and directly on the interrogator named in the report. This is a liability to the DHS collector and the DIA. It is my recommendation that any direct interrogation support to a DoD element by DHS be supported with an MOU clearly defining DoD interrogation and detainee treatment policies.

(b)(3)

✓ FROM: DH HUMINT SCG, SEP 03
⌐ECL ON: X1

PTP0943

SECRET   PTP0943 RELEASED IN PART

PAGE 01   ISLAMA 00295 01 OF 02 170633Z   B1, 1.4(D)

@INFO: CIAE(01) D(01)   DODE(01) INR(01)
        NSCE(01) P(01)   S(01)   SA(01)   SPX(01)
        SS(01)   SSO(01) SSOX(01) T(01)   TF1(01)
==================== 170155L JAN 02 DJB (TOTAL COPIES:014)

@COMMENT: TOPAR 147; NSC/DOD FOR ADDRESSEES AS LISTED

@INFO: SWO(00)
==================== 170629Z JAN 02 STePS (TOTAL COPIES:000)

ACTION NODS-00

INFO LOG-00   CCOE-00 SAS-00   /000W
                      ------------------58FB9C 170633Z /38   (PBA)
O 170619Z JAN 02
FM AMEMBASSY ISLAMABAD
TO SECSTATE WASHDC IMMEDIATE 2758
NSC WASHDC IMMEDIATE
SECDEF WASHINGTON DC IMMEDIATE
INFO USCINCCENT MACDILL AFB FL IMMEDIATE

S E C R E T SECTION 01 OF 02 ISLAMABAD 000295

NODIS   DECAPTIONED

FROM USLO KABUL #0050

FROM SPECIAL PRESIDENTIAL ENVOY ZAL KHALILZAD

SECSTATE FOR SECRETARY POWELL AND A/S ROCCA

NSC FOR NSA RICE AND HADLEY

SECDEF FOR RUMSFELD AND WOLFOWITZ

E.O. 12958: DECL:01/16/22
TAGS: PREL, PGOV, PROP, PTER, PINS, AF
SUBJECT: VISIT TO QANDAHAR:FOCUS ON DETAINEES

SECTION 01 OF 02 Islamabad 295

SUBJECT: USLO-KABUL #0050 QANDAHAR DETAINEES

Classified by Special Presidential Envoy Zal Khalilzad.
Reason 1.5 (b) and (d).

SUMMARY
----

1. (S) Accompanied by my delegation members, I called on
[   ]   B1
with a report on detainees as well as an assessment of the
ground situation. As a part of the briefing, I visited the
airport holding facility for the Cuba-bound al Qaida and
Taliban detainees. End Summary.

OBJECTIVES
----

2. (S) [   ]has three principal
objectives - to process and transport the detainees, to
clean up weapons and munitions caches and to support
Special Forces operations - tasks made all the more

difficult because of the estimated 19,000 Taliban and al
Qaida soldiers in the hills surrounding Qandahar as well as
in the city itself. While the Taliban pose a concern to
the base - both because of the possibility of an attack on
the U.S. military camp, either with a terrorist motive or
in an attempt to free the captives - General Mattis told me
that his primary concern relates to landmines and
unexploded ordinance. He explained that the Taliban have
re-mined areas that were marked as mine free. The General
told me that several Marines and a number of local fighters
had been seriously injured in land-mine incidents.

3. (C)   with
regard to access to detainees for interrogation purposes,
cooperation is also excellent between USG and foreign
agencies seeking information.

DETAINEES
----

5. (S) There are currently 380 prisoners from a number of
countries,
                                        Some European detainees have
told their interrogators that they joined the Taliban/al
Qaida for the adventure. Others say hate for the U.S. led
them to the Taliban. Most of the prisoners are between 20-
30 years of age, but several appear to be in their sixties.
The detainees are held in groups of twenty in razor wired
pens. There is no privacy and even calls of nature are
performed in public, a practice aimed at preventing suicide
or escapes during the unsupervised periods. The only
prisoners not held in open pens are those who are located
in a small hangar, either for interrogation or because they
are high-ranking and need to be separated from others for
interrogation purposes.

6. (S) Walking through the detention center, I observed
the detainees, uniformly attired in blue coveralls, seated
in pens and sleeping or reading the Koran, the only book
they are allowed. Several detainees were carrying the
honey buckets for disposal across the compound. Each
prisoner had two blankets (purchased locally to boost the
economy the General said).

7. (S) We also visited the field hospital where detainees

                            SECRET

SECTION 02 OF 02 Islamabad 295

are treated by the same military doctors who treat the
American soldiers. The doctors explained that the
detainees generally arrive with severe gastroenteritis
complicated by malnutrition. A few have serious battle
injuries, including some which require below the knee
amputations. Respecting a policy of informed consent, the
doctors said that no detainee has agreed to an amputation,
preferring to rely on various temporary measures that will
not save the limb but will prolong the situation. The
doctors told me these detainees believe that their limbs
will be repaired once they reach their next destination,
perhaps the U.S. As a part of a delousing program, the

military has had to shave off the beards of some of the
Cuba-bound detainees, a practice the Red Cross has
approved.

8. (S) Detainees eat MREs (Meals Ready to Eat) just like
their captors although all pork products have been removed.
The plastic spoons also are removed from the packets since
the detainees might sharpen them and use the implements as
weapons or a tool for suicide.

9. (S) Detainees are allowed to talk to residents in their
own pen, but large groups are not allowed. They are not
allowed to talk to prisoners in other pens. The General's
assessment of the detainees is based on interaction with
them over an extended period. He considers them hostile
and dangerous. They shout epithets at their captors,
including threats against the female relatives of the
soldiers guarding them, knee Marines in the groin, and say
that they will escape and kill "more Americans and Jews."
The General is all business. There is a risk that the
detainees may try to throw their blankets over the razor
wire and make a run for it.

10. (S) The General does not consider the Taliban and al
Qaida to be particularly devout and cites as an example the
defiled mosque at the airport. Littered with garbage and
piles of human excrement, the General said people who would
desecrate their own religious sites in this way were hardly
religious.

11. (C) Another part of the General's job is to clean up
weapons and ammunition caches. The triage process involves
sorting by category, removing those items which are of
interest to the USG and shipping them back to the U.S., and
destroying the rest. When I asked if we had considered
turning these over to the Interim Authority, the General
said that the items thus far were degraded to a point where
they were no longer useful.

12. (C) Due to scheduling problems, I was unable to meet
local officials but hope to return on January 18.
CHAMBERLIN

SECRET

NODIS

200201625

UNCLASSIFIED

United States Department of State

Washington, D.C. 20520

JAN 24 2002

RELEASED IN PART
B6

INFORMATION MEMORANDUM
S/ES

SECRET/NOFORN
DECL: 1/24/12

TO: The Deputy Secretary

FROM: PM - Gregory M. Suchan, Acting

SUBJECT: Nationalities at Bagram

You asked for information regarding the nationalities of the prisoners held at the Bagram facility. The CWG has collected the following information:

Bagram is a temporary "collection center" where some detainees stop over enroute to their permanent location. The conditions at Bagram are stable. Plans are to construct accommodations for 75 detainees. Currently there are 27 detainees at this location.

Detainees at the Bagram Facility

Country	No. of Detainees
Yemeni	10
Afghani	4
Pakistani	1
Kuwaiti	2
Saudi	5
Tunisian	2
Egyptian	1
Palestinian	1
Morrocan	1

Attachment:
    Tab 1- List of Detainees (in detail)

SECRET
Classified by PM A/S Gregory M. Suchan, Acting
Reasons: E.O. 12958, 1.5 (b) and (d)

UNCLASSIFIED

1174

LE98

NotesTele.TXT

UNCLASSIFIED
TELEGRAM

March 24, 2004

To: SECSTATE WASHDC - PRIORITY

RELEASED IN PART
B6

Action: IO

From: USMISSION GENEVA (GENEVA 824 - PRIORITY)

TAGS: PHUM

Captions: None

Subject: LETTER FROM SPECIAL RAPPORTEUR ON TORTURE TO AMBASSADOR
         BREMMER REGARDING FOUR MEN BEING HELD IN BASRA, IRAQ

Ref: None

---

1. Mission has received a letter dated March 12, 2004 from
Theo van Boven, Special Rapporteur on Torture regarding the
detention of four individuals in Basra, Iraq.

2. Begin text of letter:

Excellency,

I have the honour to address you in my capacity as Special
Rapporteur on torture pursuant to Commission on Human Rights
resolution 2001/62.

In this connection, I would like to draw the attention of
your Excellency's Government to information I have received
regarding

B6

          The four men are reportedly held incommunicado
detention at the "Intelligence Directorate" in Basra; Basra
being currently under control of the United Kingdom military.

Page 1

1175

NotesTele.TXT

The "Intelligence Directorate" was reportedly formed a few months ago by the Badr organization, the alleged armed wing of the political group, the Supreme Council for the Islamic Revolution in Iraq. Several people are said to have been held incommunicado and tortured at the directorate's headquarters in Basra. The methods of torture reportedly include lashing on various parts of the body, specifically on the back with an iron stick inserted inside a plastic pipe.

In view of their alleged incommunicado detention, it is feared that they may be at risk of torture or ill-treatment.

Without in any way implying any determination of the facts of the case, I should like to appeal to your Excellency to seek clarification of the circumstances with a view to ensuring that the right to physical and mental integrity of the above-named persons is protected. Under Articles 3 and 4 of the 1949 Geneva Convention relative to the Protection of Civilian Persons in Time of War, the Coalition Provisional Authority, as the occupying power is obliged to respect the rights of civilians in occupied territories, including the prohibition of cruel treatment, torture, and humiliating and degrading treatment. Moreover, this is set forth, inter alia, in the Universal Declaration of Human Rights, the International Covenant on Civil and Political Rights and the Declaration on the Protection of All Persons from being subjected to Torture and Other Cruel, Inhuman or Degrading Treatment or Punishment. I would also like to draw your Excellency's attention to Commission on Human Rights resolution 2001/62 and 2003/32 which remind all States that "prolonged incommunicado detention may facilitate the perpetration of torture and can in itself constitute a form of cruel, inhuman or degrading treatment, and urges all States to respect the safeguards concerning the liberty, security and dignity of the person." (paras 10 and 14 respectively).

I would greatly appreciate receiving information from your Excellency's Government concerning the steps taken by the competent authorities in compliance with the provisions contained in the international legal instruments referred to above, as they apply to the aforementioned persons.

Accept, Excellency, the assurances of my highest consideration.

Theo van Boven

Page 2

$S25B$

CONFIDENTIAL

~PAGE 01   KABUL   01012   00 OF 02   181302Z

@INFO: G(00)   P(00)   PRS(00) R(00)   SCT(00)
        SP(00)   SRPP(00) SSO(00) SSO(00)
        SS(00)   SWCI(00) USNW(00) USNW(00)
        WO(00)
================== 181319Z APR 03 STePS (TOTAL COPIES:000)

ACTION SWCI-00

INFO LOG-00   AID-00   SRPP-00 EB-00   EUR-00   TEDE-00 INR-00
      IO-00   L-00   NEA-00   NSAE-00 OIC-02   PM-00   PRS-00
      P-00   SCT-00   SP-00   SSO-00   SS-00   STR-00   TRSE-00
      USIE-00 SA-00   PMB-00   PRM-00   DRL-01   G-00   SAS-00
      /003W

------------------57EC4F 181318Z /45
O 180811Z APR 03
FM AMEMBASSY KABUL
TO SECSTATE WASHDC IMMEDIATE 7196
INFO FBI WASHDC PRIORITY
GENEVA USMISSION PRIORITY
AMEMBASSY ASHGABAT
AMEMBASSY DUSHANBE
AMEMBASSY ISLAMABAD
AMEMBASSY TASHKENT
AMCONSUL KARACHI
AMCONSUL PESHAWAR
NSC WASHDC
DIA WASHDC
CIA WASHDC
JOINT STAFF WASHDC//J5/UNMA//
JOINT STAFF WASHINGTON DC//J-3//
CJCS WASHINGTON DC
USMISSION USUN NEW YORK
COMCJTF 180 BAGRAM AFG//CG/C3/C9/POLAD//
SECDEF WASHDC//USDP/J3//
USCINCCENT MACDILL AFB FL//CCJ3/CCJ4/CCJ5/POLAD//
USCINCSOC MACDILL AFB FL

C O N F I D E N T I A L KABUL 001012

NSC FOR ZKHALILZAD, JDWORKEN, HMANN, RHANSON, DSEDNEY
PACOM FOR POLAD
CENTCOM FOR POLAD

E.O. 12958: DECL: 04/17/2013
TAGS: PREL, PHUM, PTER, KAWC, AF, PK

SUBJECT: IMPROVED CONDITIONS AT SHIBERGHAN PRISON

REF: STATE 95030 (NOTAL)

Classified By: AMBASSADOR ROBERT P. FINN FOR REASONS 1.5

(B) AND (D)

1.   (C) Summary. The prison in the provincial (Jowzjan) capital of Shiberghan has the largest population of Taliban prisoners in Afghanistan. Shortly after the fall of the Taliban the prison suffered from over-crowding as well as shortages of food and medicine. A site visit on April 17 revealed a significantly better life for the prisoners with one-third the population of a year ago and sufficient nutrition and medical care. End Summary.

2.   (C) Mazar-e Sharif-based Poloff conducted a site visit accompanied by a military civil affairs team with expertise in preventative medicine and prison assessment. A citizen soldier provided prison assessment expertise from the U.S. Army Civil Affairs Unit. Prior to being called to active duty in Afghanistan,

B6

3.   (C) The delegation interviewed the prison warden, Akhtar Khan and   prior to inspecting the grounds, medical facility, and interviewing 13 prisoners.

B1

4.   (C) The warden reported this is a 43-year-old prison built to support 1000 inmates. In January 2002, the population swelled to 3478 as Taliban forces surrendered or were captured. Local forces were taxed to their capacity to care for the prisoners and requested assistance from the International Committee of the Red Cross (ICRC) for supplemental feeding assistance, prisoner registration, as well as, humanitarian medical and sanitation assistance.

5.   (C) The picture is now better in April 2003 with a prison population of 1088, comprised of 564 Pakistani and 524 Afghan prisoners. Most of the prisoners have been in confinement for one and a half years. there are 75 known Taliban commanders and 35 inmates convicted of civil crimes such as murder, robbery, gambling, and sexual abuse. The population was reduced by over 1000 through a series of amnesty decrees from President Karzai during Eid celebrations; others were released after investigation by the intelligence agencies. A small number of prisoners were transferred to U.S. control for detention elsewhere.

6.   (C) The health of the prisoners has improved dramatically in the past year. There were three patients in the 14-bed sick ward with mild respiratory difficulties compared to an overflowing combat casualty ward in 2002. The humanitarian NGO Emergencies provides all the medicine and a medical staff of three. The physicians interviewed confirmed additional assistance is provided by the Shiberghan city public health hospital primarily to treat the 108 cases of tuberculosis (TB). There are 25 contagious TB patients housed in a stark but uncrowded TB isolation cellblock close to the infirmary and away from the prison population. The

balance of the TB patients have been treated, do not have active TB and have been returned to the prison population. The medical facility is clean and provides a higher standard of care than the Balkh and Mazar regional clinics for Afghan citizens. The warden and medical staff reported one death in 2003 compared to 36 in 2002. There no longer is concern with dysentery or jaundice in the prison population. The ICRC has assisted in upgrading the sanitation system of the prison and the medical staff provides health education. Periodic outbreaks of lice and scabies are treated with appropriate medication and are not prevalent. The prisoner,s clothes

and bodies appeared as clean as the Afghan population we observe daily in Mazar and the Afghan countryside.

7.   (C) The diet of the prisoners has steadily improved as the population decreased to a more manageable level. The ICRC provided a supplemental feeding program during the winter of 2002-2003 to ensure adequate nutrition. This was discontinued as the three meals currently provide sufficient calories. The diet includes bread and sugar for breakfast, rice for lunch and beans for dinner. Drinking water is from a tap in the cellblock.

8.   (C) Poloff did not observe outward signs of physical mistreatment of the prisoners. Except for a walk through of the central courtyard where prisoners could be seen from behind locked gates and 13 randomly selected interviews with inmates, the delegation members did not go into the cellblocks for their own protection. Prison officials wanted to offer access but were correctly concerned about a spontaneous uprising of passionate Taliban and suspected al-Qa'ida prisoners against an American official. The ICRC _____ conduct bi-weekly visits to this prison with unfettered access to all prisoners. All the prisoners interviewed by the delegation said they had spoken with an ICRC representative and some have received and sent letters and had visits from relatives as a result of registration.

9.   (C) The prisoners rotate for exercise by cellblock. The cells are emptied, scrubbed down, and bedding is aired out during their exercise rotation. Prisoners may flow between the interior and exterior courtyards during this time. Non-compliant prisoners are isolated or have their movement restricted. Prisoners may have visitors for five minutes on Mondays and Thursdays and may receive packages from family and friends.

10. (C) Comment: Following a January 2002 visit by Physicians for Human Rights (PHR) to Shiberghan prison, PHR released a report documenting the poor conditions there. Shiberghan became a synonym for misery. Human rights and press reporting since then have continued to feed off the PHR report that is now over a year old and out of date. Lodging and food at Shiberghan are on par with those of most Afghans who are not in prison. The medical facility and treatment is

superior to what is available to citizens in the region. We saw no overt signs of animosity directed by the prison staff toward the prisoners, and the prisoners did not appear to be afraid of the guard staff. While conditions at Shiberghan are not ideal, prison officials working with IOs and NGOs have clearly improved prison standards and reduced the misery that was so evident in January 2002. End comment.
FINN

UNCLASSIFIED

2 00330899

United States Department of State

Ambassador-at-Large for
War Crimes Issues   S34
Washington, D.C. 20520

December 12, 2003

RELEASED IN PART
B6

Yvan Peeters

B6

2003 DEC 22 AM 10:22

Dear Ms. Peeters:

Thank you for your letter of October 12 to Secretary Powell expressing concern related to juveniles detainees held under U.S. control at a U.S. Naval Base located in Guantanamo Bay, Cuba. Secretary Powell has asked me to respond to your letter on his behalf.

The detention of juveniles in accordance with the laws and customs of war is consistent with U.S. obligations under the Convention on the Rights of the Child. As with all detainees, these individuals are being held because they are enemy combatants who pose a threat to United States forces. The United States recognizes the special needs of younger detainees and the difficult circumstances surrounding their situation, and is treating young enemy combatants in a manner appropriate to their status and age.

Sincerely,

Pierre Prosper

UNCLASSIFIED

1181

United States Department of State

Ambassador-at-Large for
War Crimes Issues
Washington, D.C. 20520

February 23, 2004

Tausif Paracha

RELEASED IN PART   B6
B6

Dear Mr. Paracha:

Thank you for your letter to Secretary Powell expressing concern related to a detainee held under U.S. control at an airbase in Afghanistan.

The United States and its Coalition partners are at war with the al Qaida network and remnants of the Taliban who continue to support them. The al Qaida network today is a multinational enterprise with operations in more than 60 countries. Active hostilities are ongoing daily in Afghanistan and around the world. We continue to fight against enemy combatants who are planning and conducting attacks against the international community. In this context, operational and security concerns compel me to refrain from confirming or commenting on the circumstances of capture, transfer or detention of specific individuals believed to be held as enemy combatants in the course of that conflict.

Let me assure you, however, that President Bush has affirmed on any number of occasions that al Qaida and Taliban detainees are treated humanely, and, to the extent consistent with military necessity, in a manner consistent with the principles of the Third Geneva Convention of 1949. As a result, representatives of the International Committee of the Red Cross (ICRC) routinely visit detainees individually and privately. United States Government personnel are not permitted to torture detainees or participate in torture by others. Torture is a violation of the laws of the United States. Allegations of torture will be thoroughly investigated. In cases where the United States Government transfers detainees to other countries for detention or questioning on our behalf, we seek and receive assurances that the detainees will not be tortured and will be treated humanely.

The authority to detain enemy combatants for the duration of hostilities exists in law independent of the civil or criminal justice system. In this war, as in every war, enemy combatants are not provided counsel or access to courts for the purpose of challenging their detention while hostilities are ongoing. While some enemy combatants may face criminal prosecution before the end of hostilities, nations at war traditionally have waited until hostilities cease to bring such charges. If and when an enemy is charged with a crime, he would then be entitled to access to counsel and be afforded other privileges necessary to receive a fair trial.

Sincerely,

Pierre-Richard Prosper

UNCLASSIFIED

S 35A

Tausif Paracha

2004 JAN 9 PM 2 18

RELEASED IN PART
B6

B(

November 3, 2003

RE: Illegal Detainment of Saifullah Paracha

Dear Mr. Powell

I hope you recover well from your surgery and wish you a Merry Christmas. This letter is in regards to my uncle.

Kidnapping, torture, use of chemicals, would you ever think the United States of America would be involved in this. My uncle is living proof of this. The US government on July 5th kidnapped him. My family was literally begging the US government to let us know if he was just alive, and they refused to comment. We found out about two months after he was kidnapped. We received a letter from the International Red Cross that he is in US custody in Afghanistan.

As newspapers and well-known magazines like Time, Guardian, Newsweek state, torture and use of chemicals takes place at the US base on detainees in Afghanistan. How can the US be involved in such atrocious behavior. Nothing justifies kidnapping and torturing people. How can a country such as the US who has always supported Human Rights be involved in such uncivilized actions.

I myself am a 9/11 survivor; I was in front of the WTC on Sept 11th. I am pleading for you to help us in our cause. We just want the US government to act civilized. If the US government has proof of my uncle being involved in something unjust, bring him into the legal process. Bring him to a court and provide him an attorney as amendment VI of the Bill of Rights state.

Everything the government is doing to my uncle is against the US constitution, International law, and Universal Declaration of Human Rights. There is a legal system the US follows; all we want is to have America follow that.

Amendment VI

In all criminal prosecutions, the accused shall enjoy the right to a speedy and public trial, by an impartial jury of the state and district wherein the crime shall have been committed, which district shall have been previously ascertained by law, and to be informed of the nature and cause of the accusation; to be confronted with the witnesses against him; to have compulsory process for obtaining witnesses in his favor, and to have the assistance of counsel for his defense.

Amendment VIII

Excessive bail shall not be required, nor excessive fines imposed, nor cruel and unusual punishments inflicted.

UNIVERSAL DECLARATION OF HUMAN RIGHTS

Article 5.

No one shall be subjected to torture or to cruel, inhuman or degrading treatment or punishment.

Article 6.

Everyone has the right to recognition everywhere as a person before the law.

Article 7.

All are equal before the law and are entitled without any discrimination to equal protection of the law. All are entitled to equal protection against any discrimination in violation of this Declaration and against any incitement to such discrimination.

Article 8.

Everyone has the right to an effective remedy by the competent national tribunals for acts violating the fundamental rights granted him by the constitution or by law.

Article 9.

No one shall be subjected to arbitrary arrest, detention or exile.

Article 10.

Everyone is entitled in full equality to a fair and public hearing by an independent and impartial tribunal, in the determination of his rights and obligations and of any criminal charge against him.

Article 11.

(1) Everyone charged with a penal offence has the right to be presumed innocent until proved guilty according to law in a public trial at which he has had all the guarantees necessary for his defense.

(2) No one shall be held guilty of any penal offence on account of any act or omission which did not constitute a penal offence, under national or international law, at the time when it was committed. Nor shall a heavier penalty be imposed than the one that was applicable at the time the penal offence was committed.

Everyone of these laws are being violated, on a national and international level.

I am a US citizen and have lived in New York my entire life.

I am again pleading for your assistance, if you can help in anyway it will be greatly appreciated.

Respectfully yours,
Tausif Paracha
President
Verticity

UNCLASSIFIED

RELEASED IN FULL   PRM   Y2

United States Department of State

Washington, D.C. 20520

JUN -1 2004

Dear Mr. Skelton:

In your letter to Dr. Rice dated May 20, you asked "when was Secretary Powell or his staff at the State Department given a copy of the ICRC report?" Similar questions were asked about when the President, the Secretary of Defense, and others were given the report. Dr. Rice has replied on behalf of the President. As she noted in her May 20 response to you, the U.S. Mission in Geneva obtained a copy, and transmitted it to the Department on March 5. The NSC was provided a copy of the ICRC report the same day. The Secretary of State received an internal memorandum describing the allegations of the report on March 11.

We hope this information is helpful to you. If we can be of further assistance, please do not hesitate to contact us again.

Sincerely,

Paul V. Kelly
Assistant Secretary
Legislative Affairs

The Honorable
Ike Skelton,
House of Representatives.

UNCLASSIFIED

H2004 0525=009

3386

THE WHITE HOUSE
WASHINGTON
May 20, 2004

MEMORANDUM FOR THE SECRETARY OF STATE
                  THE SECRETARY OF DEFENSE

SUBJECT: Letter from Representative Skelton regarding
                  February 2004 Report of the International
                  Committee of the Red Cross

Representative Skelton wrote the President on May 10, 2004, to
ask, among other things, when the Departments of State and
Defense became aware of the February 2004 Report of the
International Committee of the Red Cross (Tab B). I have
provided a response to Representative Skelton on behalf of the
President (Tab A). I request that each of you provide a response
to Representative Skelton on behalf of your departments.

Condoleezza Rice
Assistant to the President
    for National Security Affairs

Attachments
Tab A   Copy of Rice Letter to Representative Skelton
Tab B   Copy of Incoming Correspondence from
           Representative Skelton

UNCLASSIFIED

RELEASED IN FULL

Y 2E-

THE WHITE HOUSE

WASHINGTON
May 20, 2004

Dear Representative Skelton:

I am responding to your letter to the President dated May 10, 2004.

Before the date of your letter, neither the President nor I were given a copy of the International Committee of the Red Cross (ICRC) February 2004 report on Iraq. The ICRC did not provide a copy of the report to the White House. When ICRC President Kellenberger met with me on January 15, he did not raise the issue of mistreatment of detainees in Iraq nor did he mention that ICRC was preparing a report.

National Security Council staff learned in mid-February that ICRC officials had provided a report about ill-treatment of Iraqi detainees to CPA officials in Baghdad. Our staff inquired with DOD officials in Washington about the ICRC report and were told that DOD officials were generally aware of the allegations, were seeking more information about them, and that military authorities were investigating them. The Secretary of Defense had already informed the President that the Department of Defense was investigating allegations of mistreatment of detainees in Iraq.

National Security Council staff sought and eventually received a copy of the ICRC report from the State Department in early March. Our staff was told that the State Department's Mission in Geneva had obtained a copy of the report from ICRC officials in Geneva. Our staff was also told by State Department officials that the ICRC was reluctant to share the report with Washington because the issues were being handled between local ICRC officials and United States Government authorities in Baghdad with whom the ICRC had a positive working relationship that the ICRC did not wish to jeopardize. Finally, NSC staff were told that the ICRC had told the State Department that ICRC officials in Baghdad were pleased with the initial response by United States Government officials in Baghdad and with steps already taken by United States Government authorities to respond positively to the report. National Security Council staff were

UNITED STATES DEPARTMENT OF STATE
REVIEW AUTHORITY: WILLIAM E LANDFAIR
DATE/CASE ID: 26 OCT 2004　200303827

UNCLASSIFIED

informed that the ICRC had told the State Department that ICRC
planned to conduct another round of inspections soon and
expected to be able to report substantial improvements. Upon
receiving the report, NSC staff asked appropriate DOD officials
to review the issues raised in the report.

You also asked when Secretaries Powell and Rumsfeld or their
staffs were given copies of the ICRC report. In order to
provide a rapid response to your letter, I have provided you
information about when the NSC was informed about the ICRC
report. Secretaries Powell and Rumsfeld have asked their
departments to collect information about the handling of the
ICRC report in their departments, and I have asked them to reply
to you directly as soon as that information is available.

Finally, you have asked why the ICRC report was not shared with
the Congress. ICRC reports are generally provided to the
Departments of State and Defense and are not routinely shared
with the White House. Accordingly, the Departments of State and
Defense are in the best position to provide you information
about their practices for handling ICRC reports. It is my
understanding, however, that ICRC practice is to limit
dissemination of their reports and often to provide copies only
to local military commanders in order to maintain a confidential
working relationship with the military units responsible for
detention of prisoners of war and other detainees.

                              Sincerely,

                              Condoleezza Rice
                              Assistant to the President
                                for National Security Affairs

The Honorable Ike Skelton
House of Representatives
Washington, D.C. 20515-2504

RELEASED IN FULL Y3

TIME OF TRANSMISSION: TIME OF RECEIPT:

2004 MAY 20 AM 10: 0

| WHITE HOUSE |
| SITUATION ROOM |

MAY 20 A 10: 25

PRECEDENCE	CLASSIFICATION:	RELEASER:	(signature)
PRIORITY	**UNCLASSIFIED**	DATE/TIME:	
		MESSAGE #:	1216

| FROM: | NSC | PH: **456-9425** | ROOM: **WWD** |
| SUBJECT: | LETTER FROM REP SKELTON RE FEB 04 REPORT OF THE INTL COMMITTEE OF THE RED CROSS | PAGES: **5** | |

PLEASE DELIVER TO:

LOCATION	DELIVER TO	ROOM	PHONE
STATE	COLIN POWELL SECRETARY OF STATE		
DEFENSE	DONALD RUMSFELD SECRETARY OF DEFENSE		

SPECIAL DELIVERY INSTRUCTIONS/REMARKS:

1190

UNCLASSIFIED

(THU)MAY 20 2004 9:55/ST. 9:55/NO. 6160085854 P

RELEASED IN PART
B5

5-10-04

IKE SKELTON
4TH DISTRICT, MISSOURI

2206 RAYBURN HOUSE OFFICE BUILDING
WASHINGTON, DC 20515-2504
TELEPHONE: (202) 225-2876
website: www.house.gov/skelton

B5

Congress of the United States
House of Representatives
Washington, DC 20515-2504
May 10, 2004

B5

Y2F

The President
The White House
Washington, DC 20500

Dear Mr. President:

I have a copy of the February 2004 Report of the International Committee of the Red Cross (ICRC) on the Treatment By the Coalition Forces of Prisoners of War and Other Protected Persons by the Geneva Conventions in Iraq During Arrest, Internment, and Interrogation.

As this report was dated February 2004 and Members of Congress did not find out about the issue of prisoner mistreatment until early May by way of the media, my question is three-fold:

1) When was the President or his Administration given a copy of the ICRC report?

2) When was Secretary Powell or his staff at the State Department given a copy of the ICRC report?

3) When was Secretary Rumsfeld or his staff at the Department of Defense given a copy of the ICRC report?

According to an article by David S. Cloud in today's Wall Street Journal entitled, "Red Cross Cited Detainee Abuse Over a Year Ago,"

"It could not be learned last night how widely read the ICRC report was among senior Bush administration officials. U.S. officials said yesterday that Secretary of State Colin Powell, for instance, had raised the problems with detention procedures at several high-level administration meetings this year. A State Department official said last night that he couldn't say when Mr. Powell first saw the report. But he noted that the ICRC had been making recommendations and raising concerns for a long time, and that Mr. Powell and other administration officials had been aware of that."

Please explain why this issue was not brought to the attention of Members of Congress whose committee responsibilities include oversight of the U.S. military and U.S. foreign affairs.

Sincerely,

IKE SKELTON
Member of Congress

IS:lb

UNCLASSIFIED

From:
To:
Date: Mon, Dec 16, 2002 3:23 PM   b6 -1
Subject: Fwd: GTMO matters   b7C -1

Looks like we are stuck in the mud with the interview approach of the military vrs. law enforcement. We need to establish a Bureau policy laying out the boundaries for the interview process Apparently, CITF is formulating a policy for their agents.

The attached is a draft that is being worked on down at GTMO   b5 -1
                                                                                                b6 -1
                                                                                                b7C -1

Let me know what you think.

                          b6 -1
                          b7C -1
CC:

DETAINEES-2859

FD-302 (REv. 10-6-95)

FEDERAL BUREAU OF INVESTIGATION

Date of transcription   11/25/2002

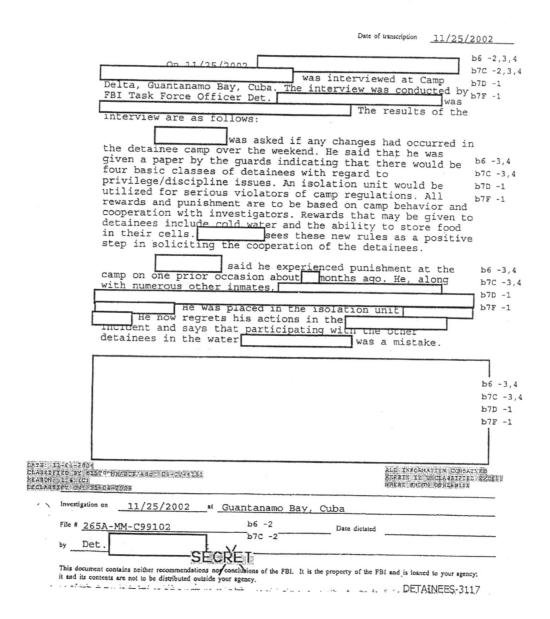

On 11/25/2002 [   ] was interviewed at Camp
Delta, Guantanamo Bay, Cuba. The interview was conducted by
FBI Task Force Officer Det. [   ] was
interview are as follows: The results of the

[   ] was asked if any changes had occurred in
the detainee camp over the weekend. He said that he was
given a paper by the guards indicating that there would be
four basic classes of detainees with regard to
privilege/discipline issues. An isolation unit would be
utilized for serious violators of camp regulations. All
rewards and punishment are to be based on camp behavior and
cooperation with investigators. Rewards that may be given to
detainees include cold water and the ability to store food
in their cells. [   ] sees these new rules as a positive
step in soliciting the cooperation of the detainees.

[   ] said he experienced punishment at the
camp on one prior occasion about [   ] months ago. He, along
with numerous other inmates, [   ]
[   ] He was placed in the isolation unit [   ]
[   ] He now regrets his actions in the
incident and says that participating with the other
detainees in the water [   ] was a mistake.

b6 -2,3,4
b7C -2,3,4
b7D -1
b7F -1

b6 -3,4
b7C -3,4
b7D -1
b7F -1

b6 -3,4
b7C -3,4
b7D -1
b7F -1

b6 -3,4
b7C -3,4
b7D -1
b7F -1

Investigation on   11/25/2002   at Guantanamo Bay, Cuba

File # 265A-MM-C99102   b6 -2   Date dictated
                               b7C -2

by   Det. [   ]

This document contains neither recommendations nor conclusions of the FBI. It is the property of the FBI and is loaned to your agency;
it and its contents are not to be distributed outside your agency.

DETAINEES-3117

1193

FD-302a (Rev. 10-6-95)

265A-MM-C99102

Continuation of FD-302 of _____ , On 11/25/2002 , Page __2__

b6 -3,4
b7C -3,4
b7D -1
b7F -1

b6 -3,4,5
b7C -3,4,5
b7D -1
b7F -1
b1

(S)

      The interviewer probed _____ on his guilt or innocence based on the facts of his detainment. It was mentioned that if _____ was truly innocent, he should have no hesitation answering any questions posed by interviewers. If, on the other hand, _____ was guilty of some crime, _____ should admit his mistake(s) and move ahead with his life in the hopes of one day being released from custody. _____ volunteered that he has not been overly enthusiastic about being interviewed during Ramadan. With 10 days of Ramadan left, _____ _____ promised that he would be willing to answer any questions that this interviewer poses to him, without an "R.T.N." response, after Ramadan ends. _____ was told that no promises could be made to him at this time with regard to when he is called for his next interview.

b6 -3,4
b7C -3,4
b7D -1
b7F -1

b6 -3,4,5
b7C -3,4,5
b7D -1
b7F -1

SECRET

DETAINEES-3118

1194

FD-302a (Rev. 10-6-95)

265A-MM-C99102

b6 -3,4
b7C -3,4
b7D -1
b7F -1

Continuation of FD-302 of _____ , On 11/25/2002 , Page 3

b6 -3,4
b7C -3,4
b7D -1
b7F -1

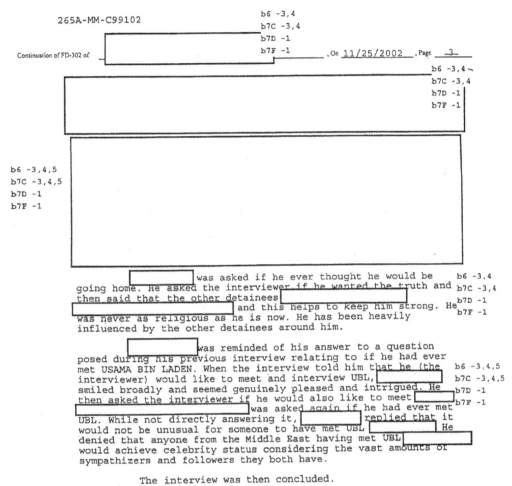

b6 -3,4,5
b7C -3,4,5
b7D -1
b7F -1

_____ was asked if he ever thought he would be   b6 -3,4
going home. He asked the interviewer if he wanted the truth and b7C -3,4
then said that the other detainees _____   b7D -1
_____ and this helps to keep him strong. He b7F -1
was never as religious as he is now. He has been heavily
influenced by the other detainees around him.

_____ was reminded of his answer to a question
posed during his previous interview relating to if he had ever
met USAMA BIN LADEN. When the interview told him that he (the   b6 -3,4,5
interviewer) would like to meet and interview UBL, _____   b7C -3,4,5
smiled broadly and seemed genuinely pleased and intrigued. He   b7D -1
then asked the interviewer if he would also like to meet _____   b7F -1
_____ was asked again if he had ever met
UBL. While not directly answering it, _____ replied that it
would not be unusual for someone to have met UBL _____   He
denied that anyone from the Middle East having met UBL _____
would achieve celebrity status considering the vast amounts of
sympathizers and followers they both have.

        The interview was then concluded.

1195

FEDERAL BUREAU OF INVESTIGATION

Precedence: DEADLINE 10/24/2003   Date: 10/21/2003

To: _ Counterterrorism _____ Attn: A/SC [   ]   b6 -1
                                          ITOS II Rm 4972 JEH   b7C -1
                                          SA [   ]
                                          Conus II Rm 5432 JEH

     Counterintelligence   Attn: SSA [   ]
                                          Eurasian, CD-IC, Rm 4323 JEH

     Baltimore   Attn: SA [   ]
     Buffalo   Attn: SA [   ]
     Cincinatti   Attn: SA [   ]
     New York   Attn: SA [   ] DT-2
     Washington Field   Attn: [   ] CI-19

From: CIRG
       NCAVC/BAU I   b2 -1
       Contact: SSA [   ]   b6 -1
                                                                       b7C -1

Approved By: [   ]
                                      b6 -1
                                      b7C -1
Drafted By: [   ]

Case ID #: 1V-IR-A-6033-NCAVC   (Pending)

Title: INTERVIEW AND INTERROGATION
        OF EXTREMISTS WORKING GROUP
        CRITICAL INCIDENT RESPONSE GROUP (CIRG)
        NATIONAL CENTER FOR THE ANALYSIS OF VIOLENT CRIME (NCAVC)
        BEHAVIORAL ANALYSIS UNIT I (BAU I)
        11/04-07/2003

Synopsis: The purpose of this working group is to bring together
personnel with background in terrorist investigations and incorporate
this information into a practical guide for personnel involved in
conducting interviews both in the field and in controlled
environments such as in Guantanamo Bay.

Details: The Behavioral Analysis Unit I (BAU I) is one of several
National Center for the Analysis of Violent Crime (NCAVC) units
within the Critical Incident Response Group (CIRG) in Quantico,
Virginia, providing support to field offices as well as to state,
local, and foreign police. Although the NCAVC is best known for
providing behavioral analyses on violent crime cases, ie., serial
murder, sexual assault and child abduction, stalking, etc., the NCAVC
has considerable experience in the area of terrorism and threat
assessment. In recognition of the changing nature of FBI priorities,
and in order to be more responsive to requesting offices, the NCAVC

DETAINEES-2743

recently reorganized and established a unit (BAU I) which focuses on matters involving terrorism and threat assessment. Services offered by BAU I will continue to include crime scene analysis, personality assessment, interview strategies, analysis of threatening communications and investigative suggestions

Of particular interest and concern to BAU I, especially amidst our war on terrorism, is how the FBI can best obtain information from those involved in terrorist activities. The FBI has successfully investigated a wide range of domestic and international terrorist groups throughout the years and a host of dangerous domestic terrorist groups The recent attacks against U.S. interests and citizens in New York, Virginia, Lebanon, Saudi Arabia, East Africa, Indonesia, Baghdad, and other places, highlight the need to better understand, not only the mindset of those terrorists, but also the cultural, political, and economic influences which may have contributed to their decision to align themselves with extremist causes. More important, BAU I is interested in learning how we can better elicit information from these individuals either as sources, subjects, suspects, witnesses or victims.

Of the thousands of persons involved in terrorist investigations, the above-listed individuals have come to the attention of BAU I as a sample of those who have been particularly successful in obtaining information from terrorists and their associates or in developing excellent sources. Although, ideally, BAU I would like to include all personnel who have had successes in the terrorist arena, it is believed that the use of a small working group, initially, will be more conducive to capturing the understanding and organizing a voluminous amount of information.

BAU I is inviting these individuals to the CIRG facility in Stafford, Virginia, for a two-day working group on 11/05-06/2003, in order to debrief them in detail about their successes and failures and to better understand the elements of their personality experiences, approaches, and other factors which contributed to their overall success The ultimate objective of BAU I is to organize this information and, hopefully, incorporate it into a practical guide for individuals involved in conducting interviews both in the field and in controlled environments such as in Guantanamo Bay Although a comprehensive guide may not be possible as a result of one seminar, BAU I believes this is a first step in collecting important details from the recent valuable experiences and insights from these individuals to benefit future investigative and operational requirements.

(Rev. 01-31-2003)

FEDERAL BUREAU OF INVESTIGATION

Precedence: ROUTINE   Date: 10/06/2003

To: Counterterrorism   Attn: SC. Frankie Battle
                                     Rm 4712 JEH
                                     UC
                                     Rm 5382 JEH
                                     SA
                                     Rm 1B223 JEH
                                     SA
                                     Rm 4383 JEH
                                     SA
                                     Rm 5999 JEH
                                     SA
                                     Rm 5258 JEH
                                     SA
                                     Rm 8672 JEH
                                     IOS
                                     Rm 8672 JEH

    Security   Attn: SA
                                 Polygraph Unit, GRB 2

    CIRG   Attn: UC   BAU I   b6 -1
                                 UC   BAU II   b7C -1
                                 UC   BAU III
                                 SSA   BAU I
                                 IRS   BAU I
                                 MA   BAU III
                                 MA   BAU I

    Baltimore   Attn: SA
    Chicago   Attn: SA
    Miami   Attn: SA
    Milwaukee   Attn: SA
                                 Madison RA
    New York   Attn: SA
                                 SA
                                 SA
                                 SA
                                 SA
                                 SA
                                 SA
                                 SA
    Philadelphia   Attn: SA
    Pittsburgh   Attn: IOS
    Phoenix   Attn: SA
                                 SA
    San Diego   Attn: SA
    Seattle   Attn: SA

    From: CIRG

DETAINEES-2746

Questions Concerning FBI Personnel Activities at Abu Ghurayb Prison - IRAQ

Time period: October 2003 - December 2003

1   Did you observe any misconduct or mistreatment of prisoners at any time during your presence at Abu Ghurayb prison?   *No*

2   Did you have any reason to believe that any misconduct or mistreatment of detainees at Abu Ghurayb was occurring? These reasons could include casual   *No* observations, prisoner appearance or demeanor, or conversations with prison personnel

3   Did interviews conducted by you and members of your team comport with prescribed Department of Justice and/or FBI protocols?   *Yes*

4   Please identify where the interviews occurred in the prison

5   Were they ever held in Unit 1A or 1B (where the abuses occurred)?

6   Did you have any substantive contact with Military Police personnel in charge of the prison? If so, who?

7   Please explain the roles of members which comprised your interview team?   *N/A*

8   During your interviews did any interviewee bring to your attention any acts of   *No* misconduct or mistreatment by U S personnel?

9   Are you in possession of any pictures, video tapes, or notes of actions depicting misconduct or inappropriate behavior by U S personnel against detainees? Are you aware of anyone else who is in possession of such items?   *No*

10 What, if any, was your understanding of Department of Defense and/or Department of Justice authorization for the permitted use of certain interrogation techniques?

11 If you were aware of any mistreatment or abuse of detainees, did you document or   *would* report it to anyone?   *have reported*

12 Do you have any additional information relating to the abuse/mistreatment of detainees?

DETAINEES-3514

1199

On May 17, 2004, SA [redacted] was contacted
telephonically at the Little Rock Division's EL Dorado RA, by SSA
[redacted] concerning FBI personnel activities at Abu
Ghurayb Prison to which he provided the following information.

     b6 -1
     b7C -1

SA [redacted] advised that during the course of the
interviews he conducted of [redacted] and [redacted]
[redacted] at no time did he observe any misconduct or
mistreatment of prisoners at any time during his presence at ABU
Ghurayb prison

     b6 -1,4
     b7C -1,4
     b7D -1
     b7F -1

SA [redacted] advised that he did not have reason to
believe that any misconduct or mistreatment of detainees at ABU
Ghurayb was occurring nor did anyone ever volunteer any
information to him that any mistreatment of prisoners had
occurred. He further stated that all interviews conducted by him
and/or members of his team comported with FBI protocols

     b6 -1
     b7C -1

SA [redacted] advised the interview conducted by him of
[redacted] took place in an isolated area of the prison
whereas the interview of [redacted] took place in the office of
the Military Intelligence (MI). During the interviews SA [redacted]
was assisted by [redacted] (MI) and SSG [redacted]
U.S. Army and a translator

     b6 -1,2,4
     b7C -1,2,4
     b7D -1
     b7F -1

SA [redacted] advised that he never felt a need to have an
understanding of Department of Defense and/or Department of
Justice authorization for permitted use of certain interrogation
techniques. That was because he was a bomb technician and he was
there for "Intel" and evaluation. He also stated that he does
not have any pictures, video tapes, or notes of actions depicting
misconduct or inappropriate behavior by U.S. personnel against
detainees or was not aware of anyone else who was in possession
of such items.

     b6 -1
     b7C -1

SA [redacted] advised that if he was aware of any
mistreatment or abuse of detainees, he would have reported the
inappropriate actions to the authorities.

     b6 -1
     b7C -1

DETAINEES-3463

297-HQ-A13276697-E
HGB·hq

1

On May 18, 2004, SA [ ] was contacted
telephonically [ ] at the [ ] in DOHA
QATAR by SSA [ ] concerning FBI personnel
activities at Abu Ghurayb Prison to which he provided the
following information:

        SA [ ] advised that during his time at the ABU
Ghurayb Prison his role was to only process and fingerprint
prisoners and at no time did he observe any misconduct or
mistreatment of prisoners at any time during his presence at ABU
Ghurayb prison. SA [ ] processed prisoners at two separate
locations, on two occasions he processed detainees inside the ABU
Ghurayb prison in a side storage room off to the side of the
prison cell block. He didn't recall if that area actually had a
particular name. The second location where he processed the
majority of the detainees was outside in a tent on the ABU
Ghurayb prison grounds SA [ ] stated the processing of the
detainees occurred around October 2003, generally between the
hours of 10am to 5pm, two to three times per week. SA [ ]
further reiterated that he did not interview any of the
detainees.

        SA [ ] advised that he did not have reason to
believe that any misconduct or mistreatment of detainees at ABU
Ghurayb was occurring in Unit 1A or 1B nor did anyone ever
volunteer any information to him that any mistreatment of
prisoners had occurred

        SA [ ] advised that he never felt a need to have an
understanding of Department of Defense and/or Department of
Justice authorization for permitted use of certain interrogation
techniques. That was because he was only at the prison to pro
and fingerprint prisoners. He also stated that he does not have
any pictures, video tapes, or notes of actions depicting
misconduct or inappropriate behavior by U.S. personnel against
detainees or was not aware of anyone else who was in possession
of such items.

        SA [ ] advised that he had no additional
information relating to the abuse of detainees and if he had been
aware of any mistreatment or abuse he would have reported the
inappropriate actions to the authorities.

b2 -1
b6 -1
b7C -1

b6 -1
b7C -1

b6 -1
b7C -1

b6 -1
b7C -1

b6 -1
b7C -1

DETAINEES-3464

ALL INFORMATION CONTAINED
HEREIN IS UNCLASSIFIED
DATE 10-07-2004 BY 61572DNH/3-575/G 04-CV-415

1201

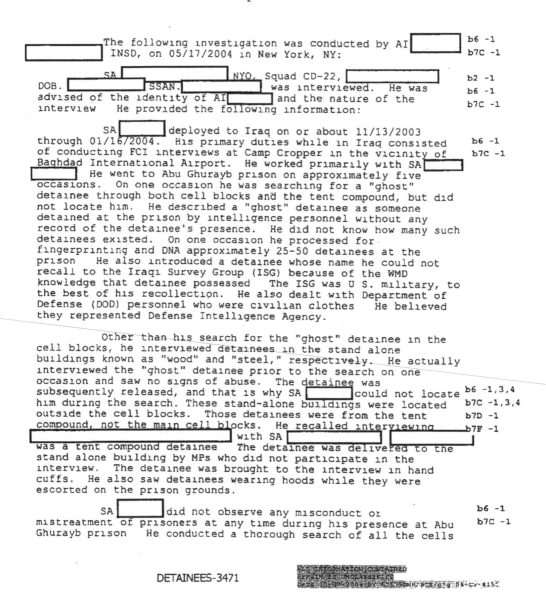

The following investigation was conducted by AI [____]   b6 -1
INSD, on 05/17/2004 in New York, NY: b7C -1

      SA [_____] NYO, Squad CD-22, [_____]   b2 -1
DOB. [_____] SSAN. [_____] was interviewed. He was   b6 -1
advised of the identity of AI [_____] and the nature of the   b7C -1
interview   He provided the following information:

      SA [_____] deployed to Iraq on or about 11/13/2003
through 01/16/2004. His primary duties while in Iraq consisted   b6 -1
of conducting FCI interviews at Camp Cropper in the vicinity of   b7C -1
Baghdad International Airport. He worked primarily with SA [_____]
[_____]   He went to Abu Ghurayb prison on approximately five
occasions. On one occasion he was searching for a "ghost"
detainee through both cell blocks and the tent compound, but did
not locate him. He described a "ghost" detainee as someone
detained at the prison by intelligence personnel without any
record of the detainee's presence. He did not know how many such
detainees existed. On one occasion he processed for
fingerprinting and DNA approximately 25-50 detainees at the
prison   He also introduced a detainee whose name he could not
recall to the Iraqi Survey Group (ISG) because of the WMD
knowledge that detainee possessed   The ISG was U S. military, to
the best of his recollection. He also dealt with Department of
Defense (DOD) personnel who were civilian clothes   He believed
they represented Defense Intelligence Agency.

      Other than his search for the "ghost" detainee in the
cell blocks, he interviewed detainees in the stand alone
buildings known as "wood" and "steel," respectively. He actually
interviewed the "ghost" detainee prior to the search on one
occasion and saw no signs of abuse. The detainee was
subsequently released, and that is why SA [_____] could not locate   b6 -1,3,4
him during the search. These stand-alone buildings were located   b7C -1,3,4
outside the cell blocks. Those detainees were from the tent   b7D -1
compound, not the main cell blocks. He recalled interviewing   b7F -1
[_____] with SA [_____] [_____]
was a tent compound detainee   The detainee was delivered to the
stand alone building by MPs who did not participate in the
interview. The detainee was brought to the interview in hand
cuffs. He also saw detainees wearing hoods while they were
escorted on the prison grounds.

      SA [_____] did not observe any misconduct or   b6 -1
mistreatment of prisoners at any time during his presence at Abu   b7C -1
Ghurayb prison   He conducted a thorough search of all the cells

in the prison for the "ghost" detainee and saw no evidence of any mistreatment or misconduct.

b6 -1

SA ____ had no reason to believe that any misconduct b7C -1
or mistreatment of detainees was occurring at the prison. While processing numerous (25-50) detainees for fingerprints and DNA samples, he noticed no marks or signs of abuse on the prisoners. He did not recall meeting the guards who were depicted in the media allegedly abusing prisoners in the prison.

b6 -1

SA ____ advised his interviews conducted at Camp b7C -1
Cropper and Abu Ghurayb prison were reported via EC He did not advise detainees of their Miranda Warning rights, and could not recall why. His interviews always took place in the stand alone buildings previously described and none of his interviewees were housed in units 1A or 1B. He had no substantive contact with Military Police personnel in charge of the prison. The only b6 -1
other member of his interview team at the prison was SA ____ b7C -1
He did not recall a translator being present because the subject of the interview spoke English.

During his interviews, no interviewee brought to his attention any acts of misconduct or mistreatment by U.S personnel He was in possession of no pictures, video tapes, or notes of actions depicting misconduct or inappropriate behavior by U.S. personnel against detainees. He was not aware of anyone in possession of such items. He had no knowledge of DOD or DOJ authorization for the use of certain interrogation techniques. He and other interviewers, including the MI handlers, would discuss interview strategies as to whether or not the interview would use a positive, rapport building tone, or an accusatorial, negative tone No discussion or thought was given to using physical interrogation techniques during any interview. He had no knowledge of sleep deprivation or isolation used on detainees. He had no additional information relating to the abuse/mistreatment of detainees.

DETAINEES-3472

1

The following investigation was conducted by
Supervisory Special Agent (SSA) [ ] in Portland,
Oregon on May 18, 2004

b6 -1
b7C -1

Special Agent (SA) [ ] assigned to the
Fly Away/Rapid Deployment Team at FBI Headquarters (FBIHQ)
provided the following information:

b6 -1
b7C -1

SA [ ] started work with the FBI on [ ]
His FBIHQ extension is [ ] and cell phone is [ ]
In his capacity as an SA assigned to the Fly Away Team, he
served in Iraq from 11/05/2003 until 01/30/2004. As one of
his duties in Iraq, he interviewed detainees at Abu Ghurayb
Prison. As a result, the following questions were posed to SA
[ ]

b2 -1
b6 -1
b7C -1

1 Did you observe any misconduct or mistreatment
of prisoners at any time during your presence at Abu Ghurayb
prison?

Response: SA [ ] stated he did not observe any
mistreatment of the nature, or extent, as recently reported by
the media. SA [ ] stated he observed three incidents that
caught his attention. On one occasion at Abu Ghurayb Prison,
SA [ ] observed military personnel restraining a detainee.
The detainee was spread eagle on a mattress on the floor and
yelling and flailing The military personnel advised SA [ ]
the detainee was mentally ill. The detainee was covered with
a blanket. SA [ ] also thinks he remembers observing an IV
bag for the detainee. SA [ ] stated his observations were
consistent with military personnel attempting to assist a
mentally ill person. SA [ ] also noted the prison held
numerous mentally ill detainees.

b6 -1
b7C -1

The second incident consisted of a detainee, either
naked or wearing boxer shorts, lying prone on the wet floor
There was one military person in the vicinity, but no one was
interacting with the detainee.

The third incident consisted of a detainee standing
on the second floor of the prison and handcuffed to a waist
high railing. An empty green nylon sand bag was placed over
the detainee's head The prisoner was draped in a shower
curtain. The military personnel advised SA [ ] the detainee
was being subjected to sleep deprivation. SA [ ] observed a
military policeman (MP) lightly slap the detainee on his back.

b6 -1
b7C -1

The slap was not hard, and consistent with someone trying to assure the detainee did not fall asleep.

    2. Did you have any reason to believe that any misconduct or mistreatment of detainees at Abu Ghurayb was occurring? These reasons could include casual observations, prisoner appearance or demeanor, or conversations with prison personnel.

    Response: No, other than the limited observations documented in the response to question number one. SA [   ] noted there was documentation and limited conversation related to "Ego Up and Ego Down," and "Fear Up and Fear Down," referring to the detainees Before SA [   ] was able to conduct interviews in the prison, he was required to sign a Military Intelligence (MI) document delineating the interview techniques allowed, and those requiring specific approval The document appeared to be a standard form, and applicable to agencies wanting to conduct interviews of detainees. SA [   ] thinks the document specifically mentioned "Ego Up and Ego Down," as well as "Fear Up and Fear Down " SA [   ] noted sleep deprivation was not on the list of permissible interview activities, but required a specific request. SA [   ] stated he generally discussed the form, read the form, and signed the form. He did not maintain a copy of the form.

b6 -1
b7C -1

    3. Did interview conducted by you and members of your team comport with prescribed Department of Justice and/or FBI protocols?

    Response: Yes. SA [   ] noted he was not aware of any specific DOJ or FBI protocols established for the detainee interviews. He said he did not give the detainees Miranda rights, but stated he was conducting the interview for intelligence information. SA [   ] added that he, and his associates, treated the interviewees professionally and humanely at all times.

b6 -1
b7C -1

    4 Please identify where the interviews occurred in the prison.

    Response· SA [   ] stated each of his interviews was conducted in an interview facility called the "wood site." It was called the wood site because it was a structure built of wood. It was located approximately 150 yards from the security cell block portion of the main prison. The "wood site" consisted of six interview rooms. Each room held a plastic table and plastic or metal chairs. Each room also had

b6 -1
b7C -1

one door, a one way glass/mirror for persons outside the room
to observe the interview, and an air conditioning/heating
unit

SA [____] stated the interviewees would be removed
from the main prison and escorted to the interview site, the
"wood site." Per prison regulations. the prisoners were
escorted in handcuffs and hoods. For the first interviews
conducted by SA [____] the detainee was escorted by MI or
other military police personnel. Later, SA [____] sometimes
escorted the detainee from the cell area to the interview
site.

b6 -1
b7C -1

5. **Were they ever held in Units 1A or 1B (where the abuses occurred)?**

Response: SA [____] stated he was not aware of the
1A or 1B classification for areas of the prison, nor was he
aware of the specific area in question. He stated he obtained
his detainees from the last wing of the prison. To get to the
wing holding his detainees, he would enter the front of the
prison building and walk down the center corridor. Four or
five wings, on both sides of the central corridor, spoked off
from the main corridor. SA [____] stated he walked to the last
set of wings, and passed all the wings while traveling to his
destination. On one occasion when SA [____] interviewed
detainee [____] unidentified military personnel brought the
detainee to SA [____] SA [____] thought the detainee was in
Camp Vigilant, the open air detention camp next to the Abu
Ghurayb Prison From the wing holding SA [____] interview
subjects, SA [____] escorted them out the back door to the
interview building.

b6 -1,3,4
b7C -1,3,4
b7D -1
b7F -1

6. **Did you have any substantive contact with Military Police personnel in charge of the prison? If so, who?**

Response: SA [____] stated his conversations with
Military Police personnel in charge of the prison were
frequent, but not substantive nor related to interviews other
than in general terms. Relative to Military Intelligence
personnel, SA [____] noted he met Colonel [____] on one
occasion. He did not hold any substantive conversation with
the Colonel

b6 -1,2
b7C -1,2

SA [____] met Lt. Colonel [____] on several
occasions On at least one occasion, they discussed general
security issues because of attempted prison escapes, prisoner

b6 -1,2
b7C -1,2

DETAINEES-3486

uprisings, a shooting incident inside the high security
cellblock, and attacks on the prison from the surrounding
village. They did not discuss interview techniques.

SA⬚ met both Captain⬚ and Major
⬚ SA⬚ thinks Captain⬚ was in charge of the MI
interview teams SA⬚ conversed with both officers on
several occasions, but did not discuss specific interview
techniques. SA⬚ noted he knew how he was going to
proceed on his interviews, and knew his procedures were within
DOJ and FBI parameters. SA⬚ stated he introduced other
interviewers to Major⬚

b6 -1,2
b7C -1,2

SA⬚ said his primary prison contact person was
Chief Warrant Officer⬚ Chief⬚ supervised the
Sgts. and Specialists responsible for scheduling and
monitoring interviews. On several occasions, SA⬚
discussed his proposed interview approaches for specific
detainees, with Chief⬚ SA⬚ indicated his intent,
to Chief⬚ to pursue a lengthy and professional series of
interviews with a detainee. At no time did Chief⬚
suggest a more aggressive approach for the interviews.

b6 -1,2
b7C -1,2

7. Please explain the roles of members which
comprised your interview team.

Response: SA⬚ said he primarily interviewed
detainee⬚ SA⬚ primary
counterpart in the interviews was SA⬚ SA
⬚ served as a translator and co-interviewer After SA
⬚ left the country, ⬚ served as a
translator in the interviews. On one occasion, Intelligence
Analyst⬚ served as an observer and note taker.
On one occasion, ⬚ served as a linguist during an
interview On another occasion, SA⬚ served as a co-
interviewer with SA⬚

b6 -1,3,4
b7C -1,3,4
b7D -1
b7F -1

8. During your interviews, did any interviewee
bring to your attention any acts of misconduct or mistreatment
by U S personnel?

Response· No, During the first interviews with
detainee⬚ complained of commotion
and screaming at night. SA⬚ said he interpreted the
detainee's statements as possible surmise on the detainee's
part that other detainees might be subject to torture. SA
⬚ said the detainee was in a cell with a solid door and
walls, so was unable to report on anything he observed SA

b6 -1,3,4
b7C -1,3,4
b7D -1
b7F -1

_____ also perceived the detainee's complaint of hearing
screams as "posturing" to support his early anti U.S.
position, as well as a complaint regarding lack of sleep. SA
_____ noted the prison was a very noisy environment with
frequent wailing and/or yelling. SA_____ does not recall his
interview subjects complaining of abuse to themselves, or to
anyone else in the prison At one point, detainee_____
complained of not being able to see a doctor. SA_____
arranged for doctor visits to detainee_____

     9 Are you in possession of any pictures, video
tapes, or notes of actions depicting misconduct or
inappropriate behavior by U.S. personnel against detainees?
Are you aware of anyone else who is in possession of such
items?

     Response· No / No

     10. What, if any, was your understanding of
Department of Defense and/or Department of Justice
authorization for the permitted use of certain interrogation
techniques?

     Response· SA_____ stated that other than the
initial DOD form he signed prior to conducting interviews, he
was not aware of DOD authorizations or techniques regarding
interviews. SA_____ said the DOD techniques were irrelevant
to his interviews. SA_____ stated he did not have any
understanding of altered DOJ interview standards, other than
not utilizing Miranda warnings

     11. If you were aware of any mistreatment or abuse
of detainees, did you document or report it to anyone?

     Response: Not Applicable

     12 Do you have any additional information relating
to the abuse/mistreatment of detainees?

     Response· No. SA_____ wanted to note the
difference in his interview techniques between detainee_____
_____ and detainee_____ SA_____ noted detainee_____
was a potential long term interview subject with information
of possible value over a period of time. Conversely, detainee
_____ was thought to hold information of immediate value
only. As a result, the interview technique with detainee
_____ was more aggressive. The techniques included yelling
and hitting the table SA_____ stated they did not, at any

b6 -1,3,4
b7C -1,3,4
b7D -1
b7F -1

b6 -1
b7C -1

b6 -1,3,4
b7C -1,3,4
b7D -1
b7F -1

time, threaten the detainees with abuse or harm, or harm a
detainee

SA [   ] noted he provided amenities to one
detainee/interviewee. SA [   ] brought a light bulb for the
detainee's cell, provided him with polypropolene underwear and
sandals, and provided him a copy of the Koran. SA [   ]   b6 -1
requested the prison guards to treat one detainee, of   b7C -1
interview interest, very professionally · Specifically, SA
[   ] requested the prison personnel to not ridicule or
humiliate the detainee, and to respect his needs for prayer
time.

DETAINEES-3489

The following investigation was conducted by SSA
[redacted] on 05/21/2004. The information was gathered   b6 -1
from a telephonic follow up interview, of SA [redacted]   b7C -1
to a personal interview between SSA [redacted] and SA
[redacted] on 05/18/2004.

SA [redacted] provided information concerning
the reference, from his prior conversation with SSA [redacted] to   b6 -1
his request that prison guards not "ridicule or humiliate" a   b7C -1
specific detainee. SA [redacted] stated he did not observe any
physical harassment of detainees, other than the examples he
previously noted. He observed the prison guards verbally
harassing and ridiculing the detainees. It was never
aggressive, but was degrading

As an example, SA [redacted] observed the guards give the
detainees cleaning supplies and ordered them to scrub the   b6 -1
floors. He observed the orders given in a "theatrical and   b7C -1
humiliating" manner, that is the guards ordered the detainees
to clean "their" (meaning the guard's) floor and repeatedly
yelled orders to the detainees. SA [redacted] described the
treatment as constant verbal haranguing SA [redacted] noted the
treatment was not unlike treatment he had observed in U.S.
prisons/jails.

SA [redacted] stated he requested the guards spare the
specific detainee the "ridicule and humiliation" not because   b6 -1
SA [redacted] was concerned for the safety of the detainee, but   b7C -1
because SA [redacted] wanted the detainee to think SA [redacted] had the
power to change the detainee's environment. SA [redacted]
requested the guards call the specific detainee by his true
name

297-HQ-A1327669-E-3
ELM elm

-1-

On 05/18/2004, Language Specialist (LS) [_____] EOD [_____]   b2 -1
telephone number [_____] assigned to FBI Houston, was contacted by SSA [____]   b6 -1
[_____] at the J Edgar Hoover Building, FBIHQ, Washington, D C , regarding his knowledge   b7C -1
concerning FBI personnel activities at Abu Ghurayb Prison, Baghdad, IRAQ [_____]
provided the following information

[_____] stated that between 09/12/2003 through 11/11/2003, he served as an
interpreter at the Abu Ghurayb prison During that time, he did not observe any misconduct of
mistreatment of prisoners [_____] stated that on one occasion, he witnessed one military   b6 -1
police (MP) officer yelling in the face of a prisoner who did not understand the directions of the   b7C -1
MP This particular incident stood out because several agents, and MPs were around and
witnessed the MP shouting and "talking down" to the prisoner However, no observations of
physical contact or abuse were noted

[_____] advised that he was part of interview teams that consisted of at least
two FBI agents, two HRT members, and him The agents, [_____] (phonetic), from FBI El
Paso, and [____] LNU, from FBI Los Angeles were [_____] primary team members [____]
[_____] stated that all contact with the prisoners was conducted in either an office outside the cell   b6 -1
blocks, an air conditioned tent, or a fixed office building (similar to a trailer) detached from the   b7C -1
cell blocks, but on the Abu Ghurayb Prison compound [_____] stated that all prisoners were
afforded water, restroom breaks, and chairs Detainees were placed in comfortable settings and
agents went out of their way to treat all detainees with dignity and respect On several
occasions, FBI agents delivered messages to family members of detainees All interviews were
conducted in a professional manner and in accordance with Department of Defense and/or
Department of Justice protocols [_____] stated that FBI employees went out of their way to
ensure each detainee was treated with dignity and respect

[_____] stated that during his interviews with detainees, on three occasions,
prisoners brought to his team's attention acts of abuse had taken place prior to arriving at Abu
Ghurayb Prison [_____] stated that his interviews determined those acts of abuse occurred
during arrests by military personnel further described as non-American (presumed to be Iraqi
Military) Examples of the reported acts of abuse included being kicked in the stomach, electric   b6 -1
shock, threats to harm family members, and one burn victim The burn victim, an Iraqi   b7C -1
Intelligence Officer (IO) was the only individual [_____] recalled contacting outside the
prisons compound This individual was a patient in a Baghdad hospital and was contacted there
several times by himself and SA [_____] stated that FBI Agents took pictures of all
injuries, even those which occurred prior to the incarcerations at the AGP These findings were
documented on the FD-302's of interviewing agents

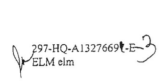

DETAINEES-3493

[_____] advised that he had limited contact with MPs. Aside from FBI personnel, his other contact would have been with individuals [_____] who accompanied him to a few interviews. [_____] stated that only agents had direct contact with MPs. His role as the translator did not lend itself to other outside contacts. [_____] advised that during the time in Abu Ghurayb Prison, he did not record, photograph, or video tape any instances of abuse nor did he have the same in his possession. Other than what was reported above, [_____] was not aware of any improprieties resulting in the abuse of prisoners as described on television today.

b1
b6 -1
b7C -1

(S)

SECRET   DETAINEES-3494

1212

(1)
5/17/x

1. ~~STATE~~ NO MISCONDUCT OR MISTREATMENT.
3-4 TIMES. DETAINEE ORDERED TO STRIP
& PLACED IN ISOLATION CELL W/NO CLOTHES

2. ~~ALL~~ YES. ONE INSTANCE IN WHICH DETAINEE
COMPLAINED ABOUT BEING STRIPPED NAKED,
KEPT NAKED AND SLEEP DEPRIVATION BY GUARDS
& STILL ROUGHED UP. DETAINEE WAS
INTERVIEWED BY ANOTHER PERSON WHO WERE
NOT IN MILITARY UNIFORMS WHO MISTREATED
HIM. DETAINEE WAS INTERVIEWED ABOUT
8 TIMES, DURING, & ALL WAS DOCUMENTED ON ITS

TO [REDACTED] FILE [REDACTED]

ANSSAR AL ISLAM - NO MARKS.

CLASSIFIED TERRORIST GROUP OPERATING
IN IRAQ, ASSOCIATION TIES W/ AL QAEDA.

5A [REDACTED] - FEW TOO - ISIS?

3. ADVISORY:

4. INTERROGATION ROOMS
2 DIFFERENT WOODEN BUILDINGS WITHIN PRISON
COMPOUND, 1 CLOSE TO ISOLATION CELL,
OUTSIDE BY NEW PERMUTATION.
6 ROOMS IN ONE BUILDING
2 ROOMS ON ONE SIDE W/WINDOWS
SEPARATED BY HALLS.

DETAINEES-3502

1213

L.S.

EOD.   7/14/03   7/8/03   Houston, Texas
Houston, SS -

Time in Baghdad

1. Observed yelling in face + prisoner not understanding shouting at prisoners face — no physical contact
   " Talking down — Don't eyeball me — Used loud voices " — One of the military guys.

   (Only eating from 5 whs) — 2 - HRT

   3A

   —E (Prior
   (A) former
   C.S.

   NO — Other than above

   b6 -1
   b7C -1

2. NO — (End of Oct) HRT Transferred prisoners

3. Yes - Very pol. water, chair, comfortable out of their way. — At sea

torture
before
arrival
Najaf P.D.

① One prisoner — _____ Al Najaf Bombing suspect described he was tortured Badaar group (non-Amer). Burned w/ Elec. shocks + talking info how they kept his man
   NO Amer - Individual

   b6 -3,4
   b7C -3,4
   b7D -1
   b7F -1

② _____ UN Bomb suspect - that FBI released
   ✱ said when he was arrested he was kicked in stomach by military Brokejaws house.

   ✱ ③ Hospital Al-Cassi IRAQI I.D. — Burns over body told Come during arrest in Baghdad

DETAINEES-3515

1214

of Hanover — which was hot & could burn near body — Legat took picture

SA [REDACTED] El Paso — Determined Suicidal fires, (Suspect & I.D.)

[REDACTED] dic. & sent 302 re: this matter

X Prof team in dealing w/ prisoners — all props of SA — Very respectful. Accm. needs messages to family

[REDACTED] Always outside prison — Outside of cells

4. In a room located in tent — Bungalo
   Trailer — Perma.
   fixture w/ interviews
   Rooms & air
   Pleasant to them.

5. Don't know — Not sure where there are
   Rooms on TV are similar. But not sure.

6. Very minimal contact. Agents w/ PP.

7. LS, 2-3 agents } Prisoners w/ 2 people
   did 'Al Anai (Hosp) } HRT outside

DETAINEES-3516

1215

8. NO — Other before.

9. NO - 2: NO ⟩ nothing from him or people
                              talking

10. Don't recall anything other than sleep. at
    that time he didn't know. at time
    their interviewers were "Good Guys."

11. Others were there no need to report
    Everything was shared to agents

12. NO — Muslims - taking clothes off
         not sure of truth or not

b6 -1
b7C -1

5/21

True in theory
observed theard

harassing + ridiculing in work

name calling + verbal harassment

not aggressive — but degrading
to inmates

because I wanted detainee to
know I had power to change
his environment

asked they call him by true name
+ allow dignity —
was when I gave light bulbs

not observed physical harassment
of detainee

saw guards frequently request
detainee to clean scrub cells
but in humiliating way —
guards give cleaning supplies +
almost in theatrical manner
yell to ensure my floor
was clean. Inmate appeared
humiliated by constant orders +

b6 -1
b7C -1

| | (INSD) (FBI) |

From	
Sent.	Saturday, May 22, 2004 12 23 PM
To·	Caproni, Valerie E (OGC) (FBI)
Cc·	(INSD) (FBI), (INSD) (FBI)
Subject	RE Post report

b6 -1
b7C -1

UNCLASSIFIED
NON-RECORD

Valerie, We are ready to launch on the other interviews and as you know there is zero indication of this thus far

-----Original Message-----
From: Caproni, Valerie E. (Div09) (FBI)
Sent: Saturday, May 22, 2004 12 17 PM
To: CHANDLER, CASSANDRA M. (Div00) (FBI), KALISCH, ELENI P. (Div00) (FBI), WAINSTEIN, KENNETH L. (Div00) (FBI), MUELLER, ROBERT S. III (Div00) (FBI), MCCRAW, STEVEN C.; GEBHARDT, BRUCE J. (Div00) (FBI)
Cc: BRIESE, M C. (Div13) (FBI); HARRINGTON, T J (Div13) (FBI)
Subject: Post report

UNCLASSIFIED
NON-RECORD

According to the Washington Post, one of the MPs that gave a statement in the Abu Ghraib prison investigation said that FBI was involved in the abuse We are going to try to get a copy of the statement and see if there is anything we can do to follow up As of right now, my information is that because of the danger at the prison, our people never spent the night

UNCLASSIFIED

UNCLASSIFIED

From:
Sent: Thursday, May 13, 2004 3:42 PM   b6 -1
To: (IR) (FBI)   ·b7C -1.
Subject: current events

for a better understanding of the issue we spoke about, one should read not
only the bau ec, but the attachments as well.

____ is here with me and should anyone be interested , he could illuminate   b6 -1
a lot about gen miller's views on interrogation. ___ was the the miami case   b7C -1
agent for 14 months.

from what cnn reports , gen karpinsky at abu gharib said that gen miller
came to the prison several months ago and told her they wanted to "gimotize"
abu gharib. i am not sure what this means. however, if this refers to intell
gathering as i suspect, it suggests he has continued to support interrogation
strategies we not only advised against, but questioned in terms of.
effectiveness.

yesterday, however, we were surprised to read an article in stars and stripes,   b6 -1
in which gen miller is quoted as saying that he believes in the   b7C -1
rapport-building approach. this is not what he was saying at gitmo when i was
there. ___ and i did cart wheels. the battles fought in gitmo while gen
miller he was there are on the record.

check out not onlythe bau ec but one written by miami division. ____   b6 -1,2.
should know about this as should _____ in san francisco. its a must read. b7C -1,2
_____ knows these issue quite well and has also fought
battles. has anyone checked with _____?

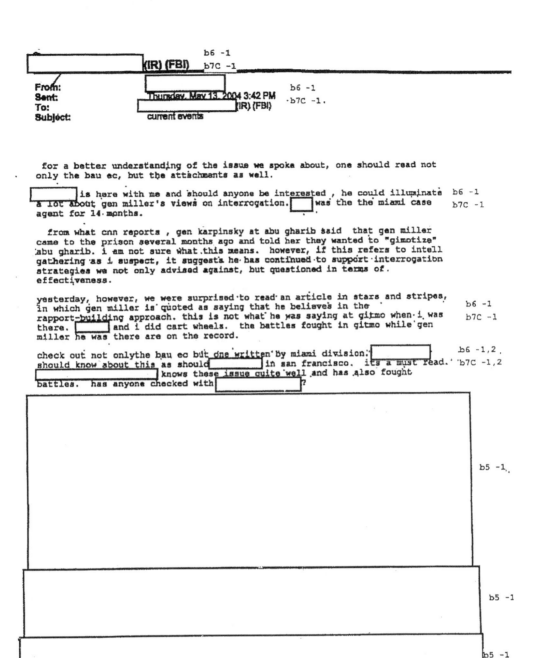

b5 -1.

b5 -1

b5 -1

SECRET

_____(IR) (FBI)   b6 -1
                                       b7C -1

From: _____(Div13) (FBI)
Sent: Monday, May 10, 2004 12:26 PM   b6 -1
To: HARRINGTON, T J. (Div13) (FBI)   b7C -1
Cc: BATTLE, FRANKIE (Div13) (FBI); _____(IR) (FBI);
    _____(Div13) (FBI); _____(Div13) (FBI); _____(Div13) (FBI);
    CUMMINGS, ARTHUR M. (Div13) (FBI)

Subject: Instructions to GTMO interrogators.

SECRET//ORCON,NOFORN
RECORD 315N-MM-C99102

TJ,

I will have to do some digging into old files_____
_____. We did advise each supervisor that went to GTMO to stay in line with Bureau policy and not
deviate from that_____. I went to
GTMO with_____early on and we discussed the effectiveness_____with   b5 -1
the SSA. We (BAU and ITOS1) had also met with General's Dunlevey & Miller explaining our position (Law   b6 -1,2
Enforcement techniques) vs. DoD. Both agreed the Bureau has their way of dong business and DoD has their   b7C -1,2
marching orders from the Sec Def. Although the two techniques differed drastically, both Generals believed they
had a job to accomplish. It was our mission to gather critical intelligence and evidence_____
_____in furtherance of FBI cases. In my weekly meetings with DOJ we often discussed_____
techniques and how they were not effective or producing Intel that was reliable. _____(SES),_____
_____(SES)_____(now SES)_____at the time) and_____(SES Appointee) all from DOJ
Criminal Division attended meetings with FBI. We all agreed_____were going to be an issue in the military
commission cases. I know_____brought this to the attention of_____

                One specific example was_____ Once the Bureau provide DoD with the findings_____
b5 -1   _____they wanted to pursue expeditiously their methods to get "more out of him"._____We
b6 -1,4,5   were given a so called deadline to use our traditional methods. Once our timeline_____was
b7C -1,4,5   up_____took the reigns. We stepped out of the picture and_____ran the operation_____FBI did not
b7D -1   participate at the direction of myself,_____and BAU UC_____ We would receive IIRs on the results
b7F -1   of the process.   (S)

I went to GTMO on one occasion to specifically address the information coming from_____
_____We (DoD 3 Star Geoff Miller, FBI, CITF_____etc) had a VTC with the Pentagon Detainee Policy Committee.
During this VTC I voiced concerns that the intel produced was nothing more than what FBI got using simple
investigative techniques (following the trail of the detainee in and out of the US compared to the trail of_____
_____was
providing)_____portion of the briefing._____was present at the Pentagon side of
the VTC. After allowing_____to produce nothing, I finally voiced my opinion concerning the   b5 -1
information. The conversations were somewhat heated._____agreed with me._____finally admitted the   b6 -1,2,5
information was the same info the Bureau obtained. It still did not prevent them from continuing the_____   b7C -1,2,5
methods". DOJ was with me at GTMO_____during that time.

Bottom line is FBI personnel have not been involved in any methods of interrogation that deviate from our policy.
The specific guidance we have given has always been no Miranda, otherwise, follow FBI/DOJ policy just as you
would in your field office. Use common sense. Utilize our methods that are proven (Reed school, etc).

If you would like to call me to discuss this on the telephone I can be reached at_____   b2 -1

-----Original Message-----

SECRET

9/26/2004

DETAINEES-2709

From: HARRINGTON, T J. (Div13) (FBI)
Sent: Monday, May 10, 2004 9:21 AM
To: [   ] (Div13) (FBI)   b6 -1
Subject: RE: pls confirm   b7C -1

SENSITIVE BUT UNCLASSIFIED
NON-RECORD

                                            Referral/Direct

We have this information, now we are trying to go beyond, did we ever put into writing, in an EC, memo, note or briefing paper to our personnel our position [   ] that we were pursuing our traditional methods of building trust and a relationship with subjects. Tom

-----Original Message-----
From: [   ] (Div13) (FBI)   b6 -1
Sent: Monday, May 10, 2004 10:52 AM   b7C -1
To: HARRINGTON, T J. (Div13) (FBI)
Cc: [   ] (Div13) (FBI); BATTLE, FRANKIE (Div13) (FBI); BOWMAN, MARION E. (Div09) (FBI)
Subject: RE: pls confirm

SENSITIVE BUT UNCLASSIFIED
NON-RECORD

BAU at the request of the then (GTMO Task Force, ITOS1) wrote an EC (quite long) explaining the   b5 -1
Bureau way of interrogation vs. DoDs methodology. Our formal guidance has always been that all   b6 -2
personnel conduct themselves in interviews in the manner that they would in the field. [   ]   b7C -2
[   ] along with FBI advised that the LEA (Law Enforcement Agencies) at
GTMO were not in the practice of the using [   ] and were of the opinion results
obtained from these interrogations were [   ] BAU explained [   ] FBI has been   b5 -1
successful for many years obtaining confessions via non-confrontational interviewing techniques.   b6 -2

We spoke to FBI OGC with our concerns. I also brought these matters to the attention of DOJ   b7C -2
during detainee meetings with [   ] express their concerns to

[   ] has a copy of all the information regarding the BAU LHM. I believe she has provided that to   b6 -1
TJ Harrington.   b7C -1

I may have more specific information in my desk at HQ. I will search what I have when I return (5/17).

-----Original Message-----
From: HARRINGTON, T J. (Div13) (FBI)
Sent: Monday, May 10, 2004 4:33 AM
To: BATTLE, FRANKIE (Div13) (FBI); [   ] (Div13) (FBI) [   ]   b6 -1
[   ] (Div13) (FBI)   b7C -1
Subject: FW: pls confirm

SENSITIVE BUT UNCLASSIFIED
NON-RECORD

Please review our control files, did we produce anything on paper???
-----Original Message-----
From: Caproni, Valerie E. (Div09) (FBI)
Sent: Sunday, May 09, 2004 2:31 PM   b6 -1
To: [   ] (Div09) (FBI); HARRINGTON, T J. (Div13) (FBI) [   ]   b7C -1

SECRET

9/26/2004

Referral/Direct

DETAINEES-2710

1221

b6 -1
(IR) (FBI) b7C -1

From:	(Div13) (FBI)
Sent:	Wednesday, May 05, 2004 8:50 AM
To:	(Div13) (FBI); (Div13) (FBI) b6 -1
	(Div13) (FBI); (Div13) (FBI); (Div13)(FBI); b7C -1
	(Div13) (FBI) (Div13) (FBI)
Cc:	(Div13) (FBI) (Div09) (FBI);
	(IR) (FBI)

Subject: RE: Detainee abuse claims

SENSITIVE BUT UNCLASSIFIED
NON-RECORD

ALCON,
Based on Rumsfeld's public statements, DoD is against hooding prisoners, threats of violence and techniques meant to humiliating detainees (there is a list of these I have seen)
b5 -1
An EC outlining these b6 -1,4
was done by MLDU in November 2003 as to FBI's dissaproval b7C -1,4
regardless of whether they were approved by the Deputy Secretary Defense. DAD Harrington has b7F -1
also been interested in following up on this.

where does that stand?

SSA   b6 -1
CTD/ORS/MLDU   b7C -1
JEH, Room 5382
                                 b2 -1

-----Original Message-----
From: (Div13) (FBI)
Sent: Wednesday, May 05, 2004 8:23 AM
To: (Div13) (FBI) (Div13) (FBI); Div13)
(FBI); (Div13) (FBI) Div13)(FBI); b6 -1
(Div13) (FBI); (Div13) (FBI) b7C -1
Cc: (Div13) (FBI); (Div09) (FBI);
(IR) (FBI)
Subject: RE: Detainee abuse claims
Importance: High

We need to be very careful here. Everyone should pay particular attention to the distinctions between allegations of abuse and the use of techniques which fall outside of FBI/DOJ training and policy. As I stated in my email yesterday, I am not aware of any credible allegations of abuse by anyone in GTMO.

b5 -1
b6 -4
b7C -4
b7F -1

9/26/2004   DETAINEES-2715

Our Behavioral Assessment Unit (BAU) disagreed with the use of specific techniques in the case of ☐ as they opined that the techniques would not be successful and they could produce   b6 -4
unreliable results. BAU did not make any allegations of abuse that I am aware of.   b7C -4
                                                                                              b7F -1

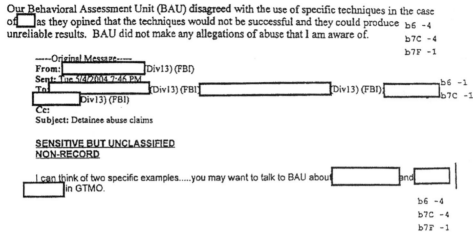

-----Original Message-----
From: ☐ (Div13) (FBI)
Sent: Tue 5/4/2004 7:46 PM
To: ☐ (Div13) (FBI) ☐ (Div13) (FBI) ☐   b6 -1
☐ (Div13) (FBI)   b7C -1
Cc:
Subject: Detainee abuse claims

SENSITIVE BUT UNCLASSIFIED
NON-RECORD

I can think of two specific examples.....you may want to talk to BAU about ☐ and ☐
☐ in GTMO.
                                                                                              b6 -4
                                                                                              b7C -4
                                                                                              b7F -1

SENSITIVE BUT UNCLASSIFIED

SENSITIVE BUT UNCLASSIFIED

To· Counterterrorism From Counterterrorism
Re (U): 315N-HQ-C1409646-E, 02/28/2004

b6 -3,4
b7C -3,4
b7D -1
b7F -1

(U) ---

b6 -3,4
b7C -3,4
b7D -1
b7F -1

(U)   was then asked if he had heard of UBL, KSM,
Al Qaeda,   appeared uncomfortable
with this line of questioning and continued to deny any knowledge
of the above. When reminded that he had been shown a video of
the 09/11/2001 terror attacks that explained the relevance of
UBL, KSM and Al Qaeda,   said he had first heard of these
matters from his interrogators When reminded that writer had
posed this exact question to him just one week prior,
appeared confused and stated he was losing his mind while in
custody   went on to state that all he can think of is his
family and returning home to them   then stated if the
writer went to his village of   the writer would be moved
to tears by the desperate·situation there. When told it was
difficult to believe no one ever discussed UBL whether in his
home village or while in custody at Bagram,   stated no one is
allowed to speak inside the BCP and therefor none of his fellow
PUC's discuss terrorism or terrorist activities

b6 -3,4
b7C -3,4
b7D -1
b7F -1

(U) ---

b6 -3,4
b7C -3,4
b7D -1
b7F -1

2

DETAINEES-1989

1664

1224

Sub - 281

SECRET

SECRET

FEDERAL BUREAU OF INVESTIGATION

(Rev 08-28-2000)

Precedence: ROUTINE   Date: 04/09/2004

To: Counterterrorism   Attn: ITOS1, UC
                                  TRRS, IOS   b6 -1
                                  ITOS2, UC   b7C -1
                                  ITOS2, IOS
                                  ITOS2, UC
                                  ITOS2, Iran Unit

From: Counterterrorism
      ORS/MLDU/Bagram, Afghanistan
      Contact: TDY-SA   b2 -1
                                                               b6 -1
Approved By: b7C -1

Drafted By:

Case ID #: (U) ☒ 315N-HQ-C1409646-E   (Pending)

Title: (U) ☒ GTMO TASK FORCE,
              BAGRAM AFGHANISTAN

Synopsis: (U) ☒ Provide results of interviews conducted   b6 -1,2,3,4
and [   ] with Person Under Control (PUC)   b7C -1,2,3,4
                                                        Writer   b7D -1
conducted the interviews with the assistance of US Army Major   b7F -1
[   ] and [   ] [   ] Linguist [   ]

        ☒ Derived From: G-3 ··· (U)
           Declassify On: X1

Administrative: ☒ As a result of meetings conducted by Bagram
b1   SSA [   ] with representatives of the Department of
b6 -1   Defense [   ] the FBI is now
b7C -1 permitted to release the following information to the USIC   (S)

Details: (U) ☒ [   ]
                                                               b6 -3,4,5
                                                               b7C -3,4,5
                                                               b7D -1
                                                               b7F -1

SECRET

ALL INFORMATION CONTAINED
HEREIN IS UNCLASSIFIED EXCEPT
WHERE SHOWN OTHERWISE

CLASSIFIED BY 6152 DMH/DCB/JSS/27484 04 CV 4151
REASON 1.4 (C)
DECLASSIFY ON: 03-07-2032

SECRET

DETAINEES-1991

1667

b6 -3,4,5
b7C -3,4,5
b7D -1
b7F -1

(U) ☒

When asked what [ ] he himself
understood [ ] stated that even though he can conduct basic
conversations in [ ] he is unable to read it. When asked why
he spends so much time with [ ] Koran in his cell, [ ]
responded that he essentially is just looking at the words but is
unable to comprehend them [ ] said he was not familiar himself
with the content of the Koran other than what he had been told by
others. Additionally, [ ] did not know the Koran has been
published in [ ] English and several other languages. When
asked if he would like to receive a copy of the Koran in [ ]
[ ] became excited at the possibility

b6 -3,4
b7C -3,4
b7D -1
b7F -1

(U) ☒ Note: Writer believes [ ] would be an excellent
candidate for an ideological/theological approach by an Islamic
scholar that speaks [ ] He appears to be a genuinely
religious individual that is easily influenced by persons that
hold positions of authority within Islam.

b6 -3,4
b7C -3,4
b7D -1
b7F -1

(U) ☒ The subject then provided the following information
regarding the day he was captured by coalition forces [ ]

b6 -3,4,5
b7C -3,4,5
b7D -1
b7F -1

(U) ☒

b6 -3,4,5
b7C -3,4,5
b7D -1
b7F -1

1668

To: Counterterrorism From: Counterterrorism.
Re: (U) ☒ 315N-HQ-C1409646-E, 04/09/2004

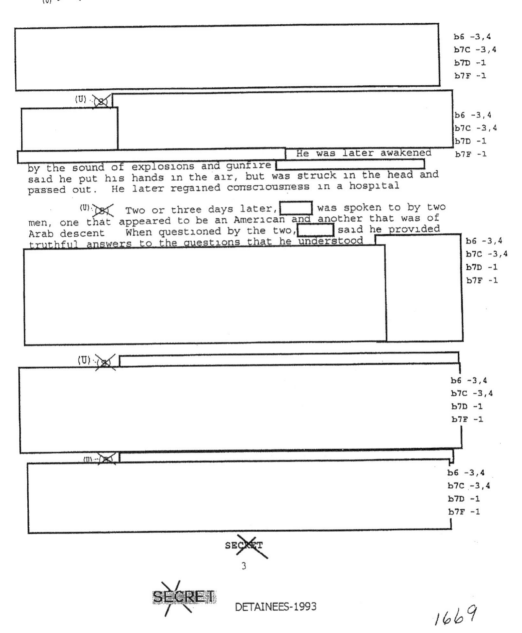

b6 -3,4
b7C -3,4
b7D -1
b7F -1

(U) ☒

b6 -3,4
b7C -3,4
b7D -1
b7F -1

He was later awakened
by the sound of explosions and gunfire said he put his hands in the air, but was struck in the head and passed out. He later regained consciousness in a hospital

(U) ☒ Two or three days later, [ ] was spoken to by two
men, one that appeared to be an American and another that was of
Arab descent   When questioned by the two, [ ] said he provided
truthful answers to the questions that he understood

b6 -3,4
b7C -3,4
b7D -1
b7F -1

(U) ☒

b6 -3,4
b7C -3,4
b7D -1
b7F -1

(U) ☒

b6 -3,4
b7C -3,4
b7D -1
b7F -1

3

DETAINEES-1993

1669

To: Counterterrorism   From   Counterterrorism
Re: ~~(S)~~   315N-HQ-C1409646-E, 04/09/2004
(U)

b6 -3,4
b7C -3,4
b7D -1
b7F -1

(U) ~~(S)~~ When questioned, ☐ said he was familiar with Mir Amal Kansi, a Pakistani that was convicted for murdering two CIA employees outside of CIA headquarters ☐ said he did not know him personally, but was aware of his case because it had garnered so much media attention ☐ said he was not familiar with Ramzi Yousef. ☐

b6 -3,4
b7C -3,4
b7D -1
b7F -1

(U) ~~(S)~~ When asked what he would like more than anything, ☐ said he wanted to know what his punishment was going to be When asked why he picked that over seeing his family or going home, ☐ said he knows he is going to be in American custody for a long time and that he will eventually be turned over to the ☐ authorities when the US is done with him. When asked why the ☐ would want him, ☐ replied that it is because he is a ☐ citizen and has a case pending against him in ☐ went on to explain that he has a ☐ case pending ☐

b6 -3,4
b7C -3,4
b7D -1
b7F -1

(U) ~~(S)~~ ☐

b6 -3,4,5
b7C -3,4,5
b7D -1
b7F -1

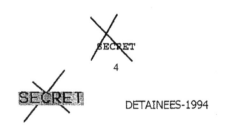

SECRET   DETAINEES-1994

1670

1228

Sub E 315

~~SECRET~~/NOFORN

FEDERAL BUREAU OF INVESTIGATION

Precedence: ROUTINE   Date: 05/02/2004

To: Counterterrorism   Attn: ITOS1, CONUS1, SSA
                                   ITOS1, CONUS1, IOS
                                   TRRS, IOS   b6 -1,5
                                   TRRS, IOS   b7C -1,5
         Islamabad   Legat
         New York   SA
                                   Det

From: Counterterrorism
         ORS/MLDU/TDY Bagram, Afghanistan
         Contact: TDY-SSA   b6 -1
                                                                b7C -1
Approved By:

Drafted By:

Case ID #: (S) 315N-NY-285984
           (U) (S) 315N-HQ-C1406946-E   b6 -3,4
                                         b7C -3,4
Title: (S)   b7D -1
     (U) ✗   IT-OTHER   b7F -1

    (U) ~~(S)~~   GTMO TASK FORCE;
                  FBIHQ-AFGHANISTAN   b6 -3,4
                                                                b7C -3,4
          (U)   b7D -1
Synopsis: ✗ Documentation of   b7F -1
interviews of   at Bagram Air Field (BAF),
Afghanistan.

          (S)   ~~Derived From : G-3~~   (U)
                ~~Declassify On: X1~~

          (U) ✗   b6 -1,2,3,4
Details: (S/NF) On   Supervisory   b7C -1,2,3,4
Special Agent (SSA   and Sgt   b7D -1
USA, Military Intelligence (MI), interviewed   b7F -1
           hereafter referred to as

          (U) (S/NF) On   was asked whether he had   b6 -3,4
thought about Interviewing Agents comments regarding a need to be b7C -3,4
truthful and candid in all aspects of interviews   stated b7D -1
                                                                   b7F -1
                  ~~SECRET~~/NOFORN

DETAINEES-1997

1683

1229

To· Counterterrorism From· Counterterrorism
Re (U) 315N-NY-285984, 05/02/2004

that he had been completely candid and that he could do no more.
Interviewing Agents bluntly told [   ] that he had not been
truthful and his continued lack of candor was the reason he
remained where he was [   ] steadfastly insisted that there
was nothing he has hidden from investigators the entire time he
has been in custody

(U) (S/NF) Interviewing Agents spent some time reminding
[   ] of his transparent and frequent contact with [   ]
[   ] Furthermore,
Interviewing Agents logically laid out the facts of his
associations with Usama Bin Laden (UBL) and how that led to
interaction with [   ] Interviewing
Agents also interjected with comments made by [   ] which
showed [   ] overall complicity

(U) (S/NF) After a lengthy time, [   ] finally admitted
that he knew all along that when he was dealing with [   ]
[   ] that they were associated with Al Qaeda (AQ).
However, [   ] continued to deny that he knew [   ] was
associated with AQ   The interview was concluded

(U) (S/NF) By design, the mood throughout the [   ]
interview was hostile   Interviewing Agents refused to allow
[   ] to misdirect or deny known facts   Interviewing Agents
also maintained an aggressive attitude toward [   ] throughout
the course of the interview   Furthermore, Interviewing Agents
advised [   ] they felt his simple denials were childlike and
that it was shameful [   ]
[   ] Interviewing Agents believe that [   ] is egotistical
and enjoys playing the role of mentor. With [   ] being told
that Interviewers saw him so negatively, future statement by
[   ] might be influenced so he could avoid this negative
perception   Interviewing Agents believe [   ] feels that to
state he knew [   ] was AQ would be tantamount to signing a
confession   However, even if [   ] never provides truthful
statements on the topic of [   ] his fear of being viewed as an
intellectual or ethical inferior may drive him to be more careful
about making untruthful statements in other areas.

(U) (S/NF) On [   ] was reinterviewed
Interviewing Agents wanted to see how Paracha's attitude had
changed after the hostile nature of the last interview. [   ]
was greeted and asked how he had been feeling [   ] stated
that he had been experiencing dizzy spells and shortness of

b6 -3,4
b7C -3,4
b7D -1
b7F -1

1684

To   Counterterrorism From   Counterterrorism
Re: (U) ~~(S)~~ 315N-NY-285984, 05/02/2004

b6 -3,4
b7C -3,4
b7D -1
b7F -1

breath   Interviewing Agents spent a few minutes discussing
further[   ]health

   (U) ~~(S/NF)~~[   ]was then asked to talk about his
attitude toward the Taliban[   ]stated that throughout
history Pakistan and Afghanistan were so closely linked that they
could not be separated[   ]advised that the Taliban was the
only group that has been able to bring stability to Afghanistan.
[   ]believed that the Taliban maintained law and order and
successfully controlled the drug trade within Afghanistan

b6 -3,4
b7C -3,4
b7D -1
b7F -1

   (U) ~~(S/NF)~~[   ]stated that Islam is a flexible religion
and the Taliban's only problem was that it was not flexible.
[   ]explained that Afghanistan was not an educated society so
the only means to properly control the population was through
religion which the Taliban did do successfully

b6 -3,4
b7C -3,4
b7D -1
b7F -1

   (U) ~~(S/NF)~~[   ]then broadened the topic and discussed
Islam in relation to other religions of the Book (Christianity
and Judaism).[   ]stated that Islam forces no person to
change his religion and that actually Muslims have a
responsibility to protect non Muslims.

b6 -3,4
b7C -3,4
b7D -1
b7F -1

   (U) ~~(S/NF)~~[   ]was asked to discuss his views on
personal jihad versus group jihad[   ]stated that his view
of a personal jihad was for one to maintain self control and
contribute what one can to society Group jihad was in the
defense of the Islamic State. In a sovereign state with an army
there is no need for group jihad by the civilians. Furthermore,
[   ]stated that group jihad is authorized against the
government which poses the threat but not against the innocent or
civilians. Jihad in defense can be in the form of physical power
(action), tongue (verbal), or simply condemnation within one's
heart.

b6 -3,4
b7C -3,4
b7D -1
b7F -1

   (U) ~~(S/NF)~~[   ]was then asked that based on his believe
in the Islamic State ruling peacefully with persons of other
religions and the belief of group jihad only in defense against
an attacking government, what did he think of actions carried out
by UBL and AQ.[   ]stated that UBL had no authority under
Islamic Law to proclaim jihad. Interviewing Agents continued and
advised that though UBL did not have such authority he was in
league with others that did have the authority and supported
UBL's jihad proclamation Interviewing Agents asked[   ]if
he wished to see Christians hating Muslim's because of the
violent actions of a few[   ]reiterated that he wished

b6 -3,4
b7C -3,4
b7D -1
b7F -1

3

DETAINEES-1999

1685

1231

To   Counterterrorism   From   Counterterrorism
Re   (U) ⊠ 315N-NY-285984, 05/02/2004

Muslim and non Muslim could live peacefully [____] was told   b6 -3,4
that if this were truly his wish he could not logically support   b7C -3,4
UBL or AQ [____] remained quiet during much of this discourse   b7D -1
but finally agreed that what UBL did was harmful to the Islamic   b7F -1
cause.

        (U) (S/NF) At his point the interview was concluded.
Interviewing Agents did not notice any harmful effects as a
result of the adversarial nature of the previous interview
[____] spoke freely to Interviewing Agents and did not mention   b6 -3,4
the previous interview [____] has been in isolation for   b7C -3,4
several months and it is apparent [____] needs and enjoys the   b7D -1
interaction these interviews bring. Interviewing Agents feel   b7F -1
[____] can be pushed fairly far and it will not cause him to
cease speaking with Interviewing Agents

        (U) (S/NF) In general, Interviewing Agents believe [____]
relies on the fact that Interviewers do not have the knowledge to
refute many statements he makes [____] is free to make   b6 -3,4
comments on various topics in an authoritative manner and has   b7C -3,4
thus far not been challenged on his interpretation of the facts   b7D -1
When [____] is challenged on the statements he makes and those   b7F -1
challenges are backed with other evidence, [____] loses the
control he feels during the interview Interviewing Agents
believe asking [____] questions in which the Interviewers have
solid evidence to refute any possible lies and constantly
challenging [____] is the best approach to use at this stage
with him.

LEAD(s)

Set Lead 1:

4

DETAINEES-2000

1686

1232

To   Counterterrorism From   Counterterrorism
Re (U) ☒   315N-HQ-1406946-E, 07/28/2004

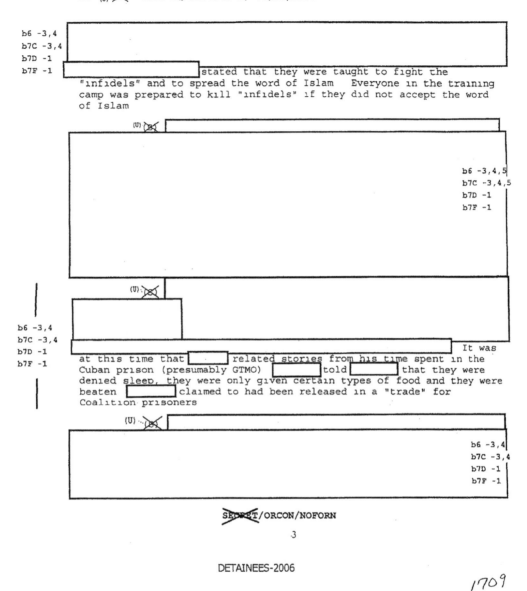

b6 -3,4
b7C -3,4
b7D -1
b7F -1

stated that they were taught to fight the
"infidels" and to spread the word of Islam   Everyone in the training
camp was prepared to kill "infidels" if they did not accept the word
of Islam

(U) ☒

b6 -3,4,5
b7C -3,4,5
b7D -1
b7F -1

(U) ☒

b6 -3,4
b7C -3,4
b7D -1
b7F -1

It was
at this time that [   ] related stories from his time spent in the
Cuban prison (presumably GTMO) [   ] told [   ] that they were
denied sleep, they were only given certain types of food and they were
beaten [   ] claimed to had been released in a "trade" for
Coalition prisoners

(U) ☒

b6 -3,4
b7C -3,4
b7D -1
b7F -1

DETAINEES-2006

1709

1233

UNITED STATES DISTRICT COURT
DISTRICT OF THE DISTRICT OF COLUMBIA
---X

SHAFIQ RASUL, *et al.*,

                      Petitioners,

          DAVID M. HICKS,

                      Petitioner,

         -against-

GEORGE W. BUSH, *et al.*,

                    Respondents.

---X

Civil Action No. 02-299 (CKK)

SUBMITTED UNDER SEAL

**AFFIDAVIT IN SUPPORT
OF AMENDED COMPLAINT
AND APPLICATIONS
FOR INJUNCTIVE RELIEF**

DAVID M. HICKS, being duly sworn, deposes and says:

1. I am David M. Hicks, a Petitioner in the above-captioned action, and I make this Affidavit, submitted under seal,[1] in support of my Amended Complaint, and my applications for injunctive relief.

2. I am a native and citizen of Australia, born in Adelaide August 7, 1975. I have completed the 9th Grade in the Australian school system.

3. This Affidavit provides an outline of the abuse and mistreatment I have received, witnessed, and/or heard about since I have been detained by the United States in Afghanistan, aboard U.S. Naval vessels and U.S. military aircraft, and at the U.S. Naval Base at Guantanamo Bay, Cuba (hereinafter "Guantanamo Bay"). I have been detained by the United States Armed

---

[1] This Affidavit is submitted under seal due to restrictions on information dissemination placed by U.S. military authorities on my attorneys and me. I have no objection to the unsealing of this Affidavit the Court determines it is appropriate to do so.

1

Forces from December 2001 until present. I arrived in Guantanamo Bay in January 2002. It does not detail all of the abuse I have received, or witnessed, or heard about, but merely sketches some of it. I have been careful to specify what happened to me, what I saw happen to others, and what I have heard about. During the course of my interrogations, I have repeatedly asked for a lawyer and why I am not being treated as a Prisoner of War.

4. Since I do not have access to either a typewriter or computer, this Affidavit has been prepared by my attorneys based on information I have provided to them. I have reviewed the Affidavit carefully, and verify that it is completely accurate.

5. I have been beaten before, after, and during interrogations.

6. I have been menaced and threatened, directly and indirectly, with firearms and other weapons before and during interrogations.

7. I have heard beatings of other detainees occurring during interrogation, and observed detainees' injuries that were received during interrogations.

8. I have been beaten while blindfolded and handcuffed.

9. I have been in the company of other detainees who were beaten while blindfolded and handcuffed. At one point, a group of detainees, including myself, were subjected to being randomly hit over a eight hour session while handcuffed and blindfolded.

10. I have been struck with hands, fists, and other objects (including rifle butts). I have also been kicked. I have been hit in the face, head, feet, and torso.

11. I have had my head rammed into asphalt several times (while blindfolded).

12. I have had handcuffs placed on me so tightly, and for so long (as much as 14-15 hours) that my hands were numb for a considerable period thereafter.

2

13. I have had medication – the identity of which was unknown to me, despite my requests for information – forced upon me against my will. I have been struck while under the influence of sedatives that were forced upon me by injection.

14. I have been forced to run in leg shackles that regularly ripped the skin off my ankles. Many other detainees experienced the same.

15. I have been deprived of sleep as a matter of policy.

16. I have witnessed the activities of the Internal Reaction Force (hereinafter "IRF"), which consists of a squad of soldiers that enter a detainee's cell and brutalize him with the aid of an attack dog. The IRF invasions were so common that the term to be "IRF'ed" became part of the language of the detainees. I have seen detainees suffer serious injuries as a result of being IRF'ed. I have seen detainees IRF'ed while they were praying, or for refusing medication.

17. I was told repeatedly that if I cooperated during the course of interrogations, I would be sent home to Australia after the interrogations were concluded. I was told there was an "easy way" and a "hard way" to respond to interrogation.

18. Interrogators once offered me the services of a prostitute for fifteen minutes if I would spy on other detainees. I refused.

19. Failure to cooperate meant the loss of the ordinary necessities of living, such as showers, sufficient food, relief from the prospect of IRF'ing and other regular abuse visited upon non-cooperative detainees, access to reading material, and social contact (including receiving mail).

20. During Ramadan, food was withheld from detainees after the break of the daily fast in order to coerce cooperation with interrogators. Detainees who refused to cooperate were

3

punished regularly, and denied the ordinary necessities of living.

21. I have been told that strobe lights and extreme cold were also used to disorient detainees in order to soften them up for interrogation. I have also heard that religious detainees were exposed to pornography, and were dragged around naked in order to break their will.

22. Detainees were not allowed to know the date, day, year, or time. We were deprived of any and all information and news from the world. Detainees were permitted very little exercise.

23. At one point during 2003 alone, my weight dropped by 30 pounds (and I was not overweight to start).

24. Other detainees also informed me that interrogators attempted to turn them against me by spreading rumors about me. In any event, due to the way interrogations were conducted, and the physical layout of the camps, it was obvious to all of the detainees who was being interrogated, for how long, and whether that detainee emerged abused or not (with the latter signifying cooperation). Thus, any detainee would know who was cooperating with the interrogators.

25. The interrogation process ruled the detention camps and the lives of detainees. Cooperation with interrogators offered the only means of relief from the miserable treatment and abuse the detainees suffered. Those who failed to comply suffered abuse until they gave in.

26. My conditions changed after I was moved to Camp Echo (as did the treatment afforded me by the military personnel on duty there) July 9, 2003, and then again after the visits from my attorneys began. However, at Camp Echo, I have been held in a solitary cell and have been so since arriving at Camp Echo. I was not allowed outside of my cell in Camp Echo for

4

exercise in the sunlight, from July 2003 until March 10, 2004.

27. As noted earlier, the above catalogue of abuse and mistreatment is not complete. It is but a summary of some of the abuse I suffered, witnessed, and/or heard about since my detention began. I would be able to provide further information and detail if the Court so desires, but a complete account would require a substantially longer document. In fact, at my request and due to the persistence of my lawyers, I have recently met with U.S. military investigators conducting the probe into detainee abuse in Afghanistan. Also, this is not the first time I protested my mistreatment, since on several occasions -- in Afghanistan, and later at Guantanamo Bay -- I informed representatives of the International Red Cross of the abuse.

WHEREFORE, it is respectfully requested that the Court grant the relief sought in my Amended Complaint, and for any such other relief that the Court deems proper.

DHicks
DAVID M. HICKS

Sworn to before me this
5th day of August, 2004

M. D. MORI
Major
United States Marine Corps
Judge Advocate

Appendix A

Approved by SECDEF In Dec 2002:

Category I
- Incentive
- Yelling at Detainee
- Deception
- Multiple Interrogator techniques
- Interrogator identity

Category II
- Stress positions for a maximum of four hours (e.g., standing)
- Use of falsified documents or reports
- Isolation up to 30 days (requires notice)
- Interrogation outside of the standard interrogation booth
- Deprivation of light and auditory stimuli
- Hooding during transport & interrogation
- Use of 20-hour interrogations
- Removal of all comfort items
- Switching detainee from hot meal to MRE
- Removal of clothing
- Forced grooming (e.g., shaving)
- Inducing stress by use of detainee's fears (e.g., dogs)

Category III
- Use of mild, non-injurious physical contact

Used Dec 2002 through 15 Jan 2003:

Category I
- Yelling (Not directly into ear)
- Deception (Introducing of confederate detainee)
- Role-playing interrogator in next cell

Category II
- Removal from social support at Camp Delta
- Segregation in Navy Brig
- Isolation in Camp X-Ray
- Interrogating the detainee in an environment other than standard interrogation room at Camp Delta (i.e., Camp X-Ray)
- Deprivation of light (use of red light)
- Inducing stress (use of female interrogator)
- Up to 20-hour interrogations
- Removal of all comfort items, including religious items
- Serving MRE instead of hot rations
- Forced grooming (to include shaving facial hair and head – also served hygienic purposes)
- Use of false documents or reports

Appendix B

RECOMMENDED READINGS

- Association of the Bar of the City of New York & Center for Human Rights and Global Justice, *Torture by Proxy: International and Domestic Law Applicable to "Extraordinary Renditions"* (New York: ABCNY & NYU School of Law, 2004).

- Bowden, Mark, "The Dark Art of Interrogation," *The Atlantic Monthly,* July/August 2004.

- Danner, Mark, *Torture and Truth: America, Abu Ghraib, and the War on Terror,* The New York Review of Books, October 2004.

- Fisk, Robert and Richard H. Curtiss, "Has America Adopted Israel's Legacy of Torture and Abuse?," *The Washington Report on Middle East Affairs,* July/August 2004.

- Goldsmith, James, "Text of Attorney General Lord Goldsmith's Speech on the Issue of Terrorism and Justice," 25 June 2004. <http://news.bbc.co.uk/2/hi/uk_news/politics/3839153.stm>

- Gillers, Stephen, "Tortured Reasoning," *The American Lawyer,* September 2004.

- Gonzales, Alberto R., "The Rule of Law and the Rules of War," *The New York Times,* 15 May 2004.

- Gonzales, Alberto R., "Martial Justice, Full and Fair," *The New York Times,* 30 November 2001.

- Hersh, Seymour M., *Chain of Command: The Road from 9/11 to Abu Ghraib,* Harper Collins, September 2004.

- Lewis, Anthony, "Making Torture Legal," *The New York Review of Books,* 15 July 2004.

- Levinson, Sanford, Ed., *Torture: A Collection,* Oxford University Press, 2004.

- Massimino, Elisa, "Leading by Example? U.S. Interrogation of Prisoners in the War on Terror," *Criminal Justice Ethics,* Winter 2004.

- Milam, Michael C., "Torture and the American Character," *The Humanist,* July/August 2004.

- Miles, Steven H., "Abu Ghraib: Its Legacy for Military Medicine," *The Lancet,* August 21–27, 2004.

- Niman, Michael I., "Strange Fruit in Abu Ghraib: The Privatization of Torture," *The Humanist,* July/August 2004.

- Priest, Dana, "CIA Puts Harsh Tactics on Hold; Memo on Methods of Interrogation Had Wide Review," *The Washington Post,* 27 June 2004.

- Priest, Dana and Bradley Graham, "U.S. Struggled Over How Far to Push Tactics; Documents Show Back-and-Forth on Interrogation Policy," *The Washington Post,* 24 June 2004.

- Ratner, Michael and Ellen Ray, *Guantánamo: What the World Should Know,* Carlton North, 2004.

- Tindale, Christopher W., "The Logic of Torture: A Critical Examination," *Social Theory and Practice,* Fall 1996.

Appendix C

TORTURE RELATED LAWS AND CONVENTIONS

- **Geneva Convention Relative to the Protection of Civilian Persons in Time of War** – Adopted on 12 August 1949 by the Diplomatic Conference for the Establishment of International Conventions for the Protection of Victims of War, held in Geneva from 21 April to 12 August, 1949. *Entry into force* 21 October 1950. Text available at: http://www.unhchr.ch/html/menu3/b/92.htm

- **Geneva Convention Relative to the Treatment of Prisoners of War** – Adopted on 12 August 1949 by the Diplomatic Conference for the Establishment of International Conventions for the Protection of Victims of War, held in Geneva from 21 April to 12 August, 1949. *Entry into force* 21 October 1950. Text available at: http://www.unhchr.ch/html/menu3/b/91.htm

- **The Convention Against Torture and Other Cruel, Inhumane or Degrading Treatment or Punishment** – ratified November 1994. US took a reservation to Article 16 (the definition of torture) by deferring to the 8th Amendment's prohibition on cruel and unusual punishment. Thus, the US is limited to no more than existing Constitutional restrictions. Text available at: http://www.unhchr.ch/html/menu3/b/h_cat39.htm

- **The International Covenant on Civil and Political Rights** – ratified by the US in 1992. The US took reservations so that the treaty is not self-executing in the US and so that the US is bound no further than the 8th Amendment. Text available at: http://www.unhchr.ch/html/menu3/b/a_ccpr.htm

- **The American Convention on Human Rights** – signed by the US in June 1977 but never ratified. Text available at: http://www.oas.org/juridico/english/Treaties/b-32.htm

- **The Rome Statute establishing the International Criminal Court** – the US signed this statute, but failed to ratify it and later withdrew from it. Text available at: http://www.un.org/law/icc/

- **The UN Universal Declaration of Human Rights** – UN declarations are not binding but may be evidence of customary international law. Text available at: http://www.un.org/Overview/rights.html

- **Eighth Amendment of the US Constitution** – prohibits cruel and unusual punishment. For its application to confinement, see *Hudson v. McMillian*, 503 U.S. 1 (1992); *Whitley v. Albers*. 475 U.S. 312 (1986); *Ingraham v. Wright*, 430 U.S. 651 (1977). For its application to sleep deprivations, see *Ferguson v. Cape Girardeau County*, 88 F.3d 647 (8th Cir. 1996); *Green v. CSO Strack*. 1995 U.S. App. LEXIS 1445; *Singh v. Holcomb*, 1992 U.S. App. LEXIS 24790. Text available at: http://caselaw.lp.findlaw.com/data/constitution/amendment08/

- **US Torture Statute** – 18 U.S.C. § 2340 is the US codification of the Convention against Torture and Other Cruel, Inhumane or Degrading Treatment or Punishment. It defines torture and establishes it as a federal crime, but does not create any private rights enforceable by any party in any civil proceeding. Text Available at: http://www4.law.Cornell.edu/uscode/18/pIch113C.html

- **United States Code of Military Justice (UCMJ)** – All US Military personnel are subject to the UCMJ. The UCMJ criminalizes things such as cruelty and mistreatment (Article 93), murder (Article 118), maiming (Article 124), and assault (Article 128). If an interrogation rose to the level of torture, it is virtually certain that some articles of the UCMJ would also be violated. Text available at: http://usmilitary.about.com/library/milinfo/mcm/blmcm.htm

Appendix D

CASES RELEVANT TO THE INCIDENCES OF TORTURE

- *Brown v. Mississippi*, 297 U.S. 278 (1936)
- *Watts v. Indiana*, 338 U.S. 49 (1949)
- *Youngstown Sheet & Tube Co. v. Sawyer*, 343 U.S. 579 (1952)
- *Spano v. New York*, 360 U.S. 315 (1959)
- *Wright v. McMann*, 387 F.2d 519 (2nd Cir. 1967)
- *Knecht v. Gillman*, 488 F.2d 1136 (8th Cir. 1973)
- *O'Brien v. Moriarity*, 489 F.2d 941 (1st Cir. 1974)
- *Estelle v. Gamble*, 429 U.S. 97(1976)
- *Eason v. Thaler*, 14 F.3d 8 (5th Cir. 1994)
- *Gherebi v. Bush*, 352 F.3d 1278 (9th Cir. 2003)
- *U.S. v. Brennan*, 58 M.J. 351 (C.A.A.F. 2003)
- *Hamdi v. Rumsfeld*, __ U.S., __ 124 S. Ct. 2633 (2004)
- *Rasul v. Bush*, __ U.S., __ 124 S. Ct. 2686 (2004)
- *Khouzam v. Ashcroft*, 361 F.3d 161 (2d Cir. 2004)
- *United States v. Toscanino*, 500 F.2d 267 (2d Cir. 1974), *rehn'g denied*, 504 F.2d 1380 (2d Cir. 1974)
- *Sosa v. Alvarez-Machain*, __ U.S., __ 124 S. Ct. 2739 (2004)
- *United States v. Usama bin Laden*, 132 F. Supp.2d 198 (S.D.N.Y. 2001)
- *United States v. Usama bin Laden*, 132 F. Supp.2d 168 (S.D.N.Y. 2001)

Also, as an Appendix to the August 1, 2002, memo from Jay S. Bybee, running from pages 47–50, is a list of cases in United States courts in which, according to Mr. Bybee, "courts have concluded the defendant tortured the plaintiff[.]"

Index